Michael Kammen

MYSTIC CHORDS
OF MEMORY

Michael Kammen is the Newton C. Farr Professor of
American History and Culture at Cornell University,
where he has taught since 1965. His recent books
include *A Machine That Would Go of Itself: The
Constitution in American Culture* (1987), which won
the Francis Parkman and Henry Adams prizes;
*Spheres of Liberty: Changing Perceptions of Liberty in
American Culture* (1986); and *A Season of Youth: The
American Revolution and the Historical Imagination*
(1978). He was awarded the 1973 Pulitzer Prize in
History for his *People of Paradox: An Inquiry Concerning the Origins of American Civilization.*

MYSTIC CHORDS
OF MEMORY

ALSO BY MICHAEL KAMMEN

*Sovereignty and Liberty: Constitutional Discourse
in American Culture* (1988)
Selvages and Biases: The Fabric of History in American Culture (1987)
*A Machine That Would Go of Itself: The Constitution
in American Culture* (1986)
*Spheres of Liberty: Changing Perceptions of Liberty
in American Culture* (1986)
*A Season of Youth: The American Revolution and
the Historical Imagination* (1978)
Colonial New York: A History (1975)
*People of Paradox: An Inquiry Concerning the Origins
of American Civilization* (1972)
*Empire and Interest: The American Colonies and
the Politics of Mercantilism* (1970)
*Deputyes & Libertyes: The Origins of Representative Government
in Colonial America* (1969)
*A Rope of Sand: The Colonial Agents, British Politics, and
the American Revolution* (1968)

EDITOR

The Origins of the American Constitution: A Documentary History (1986)
The Past Before Us: Contemporary Historical Writing in the United States
(1980)
*"What Is the Good of History?" Selected Letters of Carl L. Becker,
1900–1945* (1973)
The History of the Province of New-York, by William Smith, Jr. (1972)
*The Contrapuntal Civilization: Essays toward a New Understanding
of the American Experience* (1971)
Politics and Society in Colonial America: Democracy or Deference? (1967)

MYSTIC CHORDS
OF MEMORY

The Transformation of Tradition
in American Culture

MICHAEL KAMMEN

Vintage Books
A Division of Random House, Inc.
New York

First Vintage Books Edition, February 1993

Copyright © 1991 by Michael Kammen

All rights reserved under International and Pan-American Copyright Conventions.
Published in the United States by Vintage Books, a division of Random House, Inc.,
New York, and simultaneously in Canada by Random House of Canada Limited, Toronto.
Originally published in hardcover by Alfred A. Knopf, Inc., New York, in 1991.

Owing to limitations of space, all acknowledgments of permission to reprint
previously published material will be found following the index.

Library of Congress Cataloging-in-Publication Data
Kammen, Michael G.
The mystic chords of memory: the transformation of tradition in
American culture / Michael Kammen.
p.   cm.
Originally published: New York: Knopf, 1991.
Includes bibliographical references and index.
ISBN 0-679-74177-1 (pbk.)
1. United States—Civilization.   2. Patriotism—United States.
3. Memory—Social aspects—United States.   I. Title
[E169.1.K294   1992]
973—dc20   92-50069
CIP

Manufactured in the United States of America

10   9   8   7   6   5   4   3   2   1

For

JOHN HIGHAM

DAVID BRION DAVIS

and to the memory of

WALTER MUIR WHITEHILL

with Affection and Esteem

Contents

Introduction | 3

PART ONE: THE PROBLEM POSED
AND THE PERIOD BEFORE 1870

1. The Problem of Tradition and Myth in a Democratic
Culture | 17

2. "The Present Is Burdened Too Much with the Past" | 40

3. Motifs of Morality, Myth, and Memory in Antebellum
Culture | 62

PART TWO: CIRCA 1870 TO 1915

Prolegomenon: The Enhancement of Retrospective Vision | 93

4. The Civil War Remembered—but Unreconciled | 101

5. Ambiguities of Tradition: Celebrating the Past by Praising
the Present | 132

6. Mismatched Memories and Perplexed Patriotism: An Elitist
Preference for Old World Traditions | 163

7. "Memory Is What We Now Have in Place of Religion" | 194

8. "Millions of Newcomers Alien to Our Traditions" | 228

9. The Power of Place, Patronesses of the Past, and Varied
Sources of Transition in the Progressive Era | 254

Coda: Degrees of Distinctiveness: Comparisons | 283

PART THREE: CIRCA 1915 TO 1945

Prolegomenon: "The Emotional Discovery of America" | 299

10. In Quest of an American Aesthetic: Collecting Americana and
Seeing America First | 310

11. Authentic Museums to Educate the People about the History
of Progress | 342

12. Regional Rivalry, Local Pride, and the Contestation
of Memory | 375

13. Competing Conceptions of Cultural Identity: National
Versus Folk | 407

14. Memory in Politics: The Changing Role of Government | 444

15. The Changing Imperatives of Myth, Memory, and
Americanism | 481

Coda: Degrees of Distinctiveness: Comparisons | 515

PART FOUR: CIRCA 1945 TO 1990

Prolegomenon: Nostalgia, Heritage, and the Anomalies of
Historical Amnesia | 531

16. The Heritage Imperative: Popularizing, Collecting, and
Preserving | 537

17. The Public Sector and the Politics of Tradition in Cold
War America | 571

18. Nostalgia, New Museums, the Roots Phenomenon, and Reborn
Patriotism: Idiosyncrasies of Selective Memory | 618

19. Disremembering the Past While Historicizing the Present | 655

Coda: Degrees of Distinctiveness: Comparisons | 689

Acknowledgments | 705

Notes | 709

Index | 827

MYSTIC CHORDS
OF MEMORY

Though passion may have strained, it must not break our bonds of affection. The mystic chords of memory, stretching from every battle-field, and patriot grave, to every living heart and hearthstone, all over this broad land, will yet swell the chorus of the Union, when again touched, as surely they will be, by the better angels of our nature.

ABRAHAM LINCOLN (1861)

Tradition is as inalienable as blood inheritance. In short, we shall resemble our past as a son his father, but we shall be so different that our past would scarcely recognize us and would probably disown us.

RALPH BARTON PERRY (1924)

That which we remember is, more often than not, that which we would like to have been; or that which we hope to be. Thus our memory and our identity are ever at odds; our history ever a tall tale told by inattentive idealists.

RALPH ELLISON (1964)

FOR MORE THAN a decade now, the connection between collective memory and national identity has been a matter of intense and widespread interest. The phenomenon formally began in 1980 when the French, British, and Brazilian governments independently dedicated a year to the celebration or commemoration of *patrimoine,* national heritage, and *patrimonio.* In Israel, meanwhile, a veritable "memory industry" has developed: at least ten public institutions, such as museums and research centers, are specifically devoted to the Holocaust. During the mid-1980s, the country then called West Germany witnessed acrimonious public disputes concerning the most accurate understanding of National Socialism under Hitler; the proper mode of presenting German history in two new national museums (planned for Bonn and Berlin); and the psychological impact of popular television programs devoted to aspects of twentieth-century German history. In the Eastern bloc, Poland undertook a reconsideration of anti-Semitic activity in its past. In the Soviet Union, historians are busily engaged, at the government's behest, in rehabilitating the reputations of leaders once purged by Stalin, and they are rewriting modern Russian history in general. The Austrian government designated 1988 as a Year of Reflection, which means, more particularly, a year devoted to remembering German annexation in March 1938 and Austria's subsequent service as Germany's ally during World War II, a role that involved complicity in genocide.[1]

In response to this trans-national phenomenon, critics adhering to diverse ideological persuasions have suggested that societies in fact reconstruct their pasts rather than faithfully record them, and that they do so with the needs of contemporary culture clearly in mind—manipulating the past in order to mold the present. In France, for example, the designation of 1980 as *l'année du patrimoine* has been scornfully criticized as an attempt by the ministry of culture to legitimize some sort of mainstream cultural consensus. Similarly, Marcel Ophuls's film *The Sorrow and the Pity* uses cinematographic techniques in order to discredit popular memory as fundamentally self-justifying.[2]

Although most observers share the view that this filtering of selective memory is a familiar attribute of the human condition, they disagree whether its contemporary mode represents "business as usual" or something significantly new and different. The actress Simone Signoret took a position when she titled her charming autobiography *Nostalgia Isn't What It Used to Be*. Consistent with that sardonic outlook is the perception that *patrimoine* as a civic concept is of only recent vintage. Customarily its meaning was familial or personal, pecuniary and material. Its new visibility as a cohesive cultural and social notion, with wide application, occurred so swiftly during the 1970s that it nearly became trivialized overnight.[3] The same can be said of "heritage" in the Anglo-American experience, although its provenance and pervasive use antedate *patrimoine* by about ten or fifteen years.[4]

Others have insisted, however, that the manipulation of collective memory and the invention of tradition are markedly cultural manifestations that date from the later eighteenth century and have flourished ever since the second quarter of the nineteenth.[5] My own view is that the copious preservation of source materials and the impulses of historical writing in "modern" times (i.e., during the past two centuries), augmented by the relatively recent alliance between social criticism and historical understanding, should facilitate in our minds an informal differentiation of what is remembered into three categories. First, those memories, legends, and traditions that are truly venerable we tend, at the very least, to tolerate as socially or spiritually useful—as time-sanctioned myths.[6] Second, those memories, legends, and traditions whose origins are sufficiently recent to be accessible and therefore exposed by iconoclastic historians we tend to regard more suspiciously as self-serving rationalizations that sustain the political or economic superiority of one group or the value system of another.[7] And third, those memories and traditions so new in origin that the banality of their invocation is manifest we dismiss as mere nostalgia, as the exploitation of heritage, or as the utilization of utterly contrived myths.[8]

We have available positive as well as negative assessments of the cultural role of tradition. From an affirmative point of view, a surge of tradition can supply the basis for social cohesion, especially in a nation so heterogeneous as the United States. Where religious, ethnic, and regional diversity are such centripetal forces, a sense of nationality and of its symptomatic "official culture" can be useful. As Edward Everett of Massachusetts declared in 1824: "Divisions may spring up, ill blood may burn, parties be formed, and interests may seem to clash; but the great bonds of the nation are linked to what is past."[9]

From a critical perspective, on the other hand, traditions are commonly relied upon by those who possess the power to achieve an illusion of social consensus. Such people invoke the legitimacy of an artificially constructed past in order to buttress presentist assumptions and the authority of a regime.[10]

Significantly, however, there are essential attributes of memory and the social functions of tradition about which the left and the right agree (if I may use such simplistic ideological labels as a convenient form of shorthand). First of all, there is a shared perspective that the past is vital rather than dead. Two representative British Marxists remark that "memory is, by definition, a term which directs our attention not to the past but to the past-present relation. It is because 'the past' has this living active existence in the present that it matters so much politically." They thereby echo a famous essay by T. S. Eliot, "Tradition and the Individual Talent" (1917): "the historical sense involves a perception, not only of the pastness of the past, but of its presence. . . ."[11] The common ground beneath those two assertions sustains one of the underlying assumptions of this book.

A second attribute of tradition about which agreement exists is that it is, inevitably, a political phenomenon. Meyer Fortes, a British anthropologist, expressed the connection less ideologically than Everett and others: "the political and social structure, including the principal political values of a people, directly shapes the notions of time and of history that prevail among them."[12] We should add, however, that values are commonly contested, and consequently that attributes of time and history have also been contested. When such conflicts occur, we find ourselves tracing the politics of culture. That, too, will be a fundamental characteristic of this book.[13]

An inquiry concerning collective memory and the role of tradition in national context cannot ignore the history of American patriotism, a curiously neglected subject. The best (and almost the only) book to explore it in a sustained manner barely reaches the 1920s;[14] yet some of the most interesting phases of that phenomenon involve people who loved their country but rejected a particular cause: America First isolationists in the later 1930s; non-Communists who nonetheless detested the Cold War paranoia personified by the House Committee on Un-American Activities and Senator Joseph McCarthy; opponents of U.S. intervention in Southeast Asia during the 1960s; and so forth.[15]

Although one can speak of a tradition of American patriotism, it has in fact been a spasmodic tradition characterized by ups and downs. We assume that loyal opposition is not merely tolerated but valued in this country. Yet the precarious situation of Copperheads during the Civil War, of German- or Irish-Americans during World War I, and of conscientious objectors during the Vietnam years raises interesting questions about the limits of opposition in American political culture and the selective nature of memory where patriotism and nationalism are presumed to coincide with Americanism.[16] This work is inescapably concerned with such problematic connections.

The prominence of ambiguities and dualisms in American values will also pervade the book. For much of our history we have been present-minded; yet a usable past has been needed to give shape and substance to national identity. For much of our history we have shared a passionate commitment to progress; yet we've usually been most comfortable with the status quo. For much of our history we have professed a dedication to democracy; yet many of our leaders (political and intellectual) have feared an excess of democracy. For much of our history modernism has looked like an attractive goal, ranging from architecture to principles of education; yet the colonial revival and "back to basics" are more often "in" than "out." Consequently this book traces a long-standing dialogue, of sorts, between traditionalists and modernists: A dialogue "of sorts" because so often they spoke past one another.

Defining American traditions with anything approximating precision is difficult but not impossible. It can be difficult because traditions are, indeed, susceptible to change or demise. Henry Nash Smith's classic work, *Virgin Land,* is fundamentally a cultural history of the rise and fall of an American tradition: the agrarian tradition of the yeoman farmer that was idealized most eloquently by Thomas Jefferson.[17] Whereas Smith explains just what Jefferson meant, however, and then what weakened and subsequently destroyed the tradition, Christopher Lasch supplies an example at the opposite extreme. In the first five pages of *The New Radicalism in America,* Lasch alludes to the liberal tradition, the New England tradition, "a common tradition of patriarchal authority," the genteel tradition, and the reform tradition. None of these is ever defined or clarified; and Lasch simply assumes that the reader will understand in each instance what is meant.[18]

Considering the diverse ways in which notions of tradition have been invoked and used in American discourse, it may be helpful to provide some succinct working definitions that are external to that discourse itself. The most familiar, perhaps, is Edmund Burke's broad description of tradition and culture: "the peculiar circumstances, occasions, tempers, dispositions, and moral, civil, and social habitudes of the people, which disclose themselves only in a long space of time."[19]

Moses Finley, a historian of the ancient world, reformulated Burke's description with an added dash of social realism:

> There is the tradition which shapes a large part of our lives, perpetuating customs, habits of behaviour, rites, ethical norms and beliefs. There is nothing mysterious about tradition in this sense; it is transmitted from one generation to the next, partly by the ordinary process of living in society, without any conscious effort on anyone's part, partly by men whose function it is to do so: priests, schoolmasters, parents, judges, party leaders, censors, neighbours. There is also nothing reliable about this sort of tradition; that is to say, its explanations and narrations are, as anyone

can judge by a minimum of observation, rarely quite accurate, and sometimes altogether false. Reliability is, of course, irrelevant; so long as the tradition is accepted, it works, and it must work if the society is not to fall apart.[20]

Sociologists who are less skeptical and more theoretical call traditions "a consensus through time . . . beliefs with a sequential social structure. They are beliefs which are believed by a succession of persons who might have been in interaction with each other in succession or at least in a unilateral . . . chain of communication."[21]

An exploration of traditions in a particular cultural context may help us to determine the underlying basis of a community's or a nation's sense of identity. It can also clarify the acceptable grounds of social change. To be successful, for example, a reformer ordinarily must propose modes of change that seem consistent with a society's values. Non-traditional change is likely to be regarded with suspicion as threatening or even revolutionary.

It is a cliché, moreover, that traditions die hard. The more provocative problems—ones that are central to this book—concern the ways in which traditions are born, nurtured, and grow. At the American Museum of Immigration, located in the base of the Statue of Liberty in New York Harbor, we learn that Swedish immigrants to the United States concocted a word-concept for their new home. They called it *framtidslandet,* the land of the future. That has been a widely shared expectation, and its provenance is not hard to understand. *The basic question that this book asks is when and how did the United States become a land of the past, a culture with a discernible memory (or with a configuration of recognized pasts)?*

Such issues inevitably lead us to a cluster of closely related ones, most of them comparative in nature. Have Americans been more or less inclined than others to invent traditions? What are the political implications and cultural consequences of inventing traditions? What do we learn when we dig beneath the creation of Thanksgiving, Memorial Day, and Veterans Day? Why did Independence Day become an immediate festival in 1777, whereas Constitution Day has scarcely touched the American imagination?[22]

Twenty years ago historian J. G. A. Pocock emphasized the diverse ways "in which political societies generate concepts of their existence in time, and encounter problems which necessitate increases in historical awareness and critical ability, as a result of their efforts to legitimise and understand their existence as continuous political structures."[23] Although this book will necessarily be comparative therefore, I must acknowledge at the outset that contrasts seem to me ultimately more striking than similarities. I profoundly disagree with social psychologists and anthropologists who believe that the foundations of nationalism and patriotism are "more or less universal."[24] I find such writers inattentive to the particularities of history as highly significant variables. In the United States, for example, the creation of a viable political structure preceded a clearly articulated sense of history and national identity by nearly two generations. In nineteenth-century Wales, on the other hand, a cultural awakening long preceded its political counterpart.[25]

Some historians of patriotism and nationalism in Europe have been most impressed by the basic continuities of those phenomena. As J. H. Huizinga put it in 1940, "they have remained what they always were: primitive instincts in human society."[26] The nature of American patriotism in 1812 or in 1940 was qualitatively different from its character in, let us say, 1848 or 1898. The two former versions seem somewhat less sanctimonious yet more self-interested in terms of national security. The latter manifestations look more aggressively moralistic because they resonated with national myths and notions of racial superiority that had developed over time.[27]

Varied dimensions of American pluralism help to explain why the dynamics of tradition have worked in a distinctive manner here. And I shall contend that particularistic traditions have frequently co-existed in tension with unifying national ones. Timothy L. Smith, for instance, has rejected the melting pot as a helpful metaphor for comprehending historical reality. He insists, instead, that ethnic allegiance was "determined largely by the immigrant's identification with a particular religious tradition. The appeal of common language, national feeling, and belief in a common descent was sufficient in only a few minor cases to outweigh the attraction of religious affiliation as an organizing impulse."[28]

Similarly, Herbert G. Gutman and others interested in working-class social history have demonstrated the resistance of many immigrants to new modes of labor required by industrial capitalism. First-generation workers clung to their traditional notions of time and social relations. Daniel T. Rodgers acknowledges the "pull of the past" for these people, and he adds that because they came from very different pasts and entered an economy that was far from being uniform, the encounter with industrialization was multiform and complex, especially in terms of values and the variable transformation of Old World traditions.[29]

Discrepancies between diverse ideals and the grim underlying realities supply yet another leitmotif of this work. During the later nineteenth century, for example, Americans of all sorts had to confront a new economic order with a stock of assumptions deeply rooted in preindustrial society. If we turn to the realm of foreign relations, broadly conceived, their self-image was polarized between innocence and power. Americans wanted both images to be valid, somehow, and were reluctant to acknowledge that a problem of compatibility existed.[30]

Hence our sense of history plays tricks upon us. Or perhaps we only delude ourselves. Take as an illustration the American myth of success and our reputed reverence for success. It has, paradoxically perhaps, helped to shape what surely is a national tradition in which selected cases of failure or defeat not only are made honorable, but in many instances become more memorable than conventional victories. Although Sam Houston won a stunning triumph at San Jacinto (1836), which was a far more important battle than the massacre at the Alamo (also in 1836), San Jacinto has never captured the public imagination as the Alamo has. Consider also Robert E. Lee's defeat in 1865, and Custer's Last Stand in 1876.[31]

We arouse and arrange our memories to suit our psychic needs. Historians on the left are surely correct in referring to "the social production of memory," and in positing the existence of dominant memories (or a mainstream collective consciousness) along with alternative (usually subordinate) memories. Such historians are equally sensible to differentiate between official and more spontaneous or populistic memories.[32]

We should be very cautious, however, about taking for granted the cohesion, clarity, and retentiveness of either civic or popular memory. Abundant evidence demonstrates that both can be sorely truncated or blurred. How often have we been exhorted to recall some public catastrophe, often a humiliation, precisely because amnesia seemed ominous. "Remember the Alamo!" "Remember the *Maine*!" "Remember Pearl Harbor!" In a cartoon by Rowland B. Wilson that appeared in *Esquire* (March 1965), Mexican troops are storming the Alamo. Two soldiers carry a ladder together. The confident one says to his gloomy chum: "Oh, stop worrying—the public has a short memory!"[33]

The truth of that quip is trans-national, so much so that critics seem to vie with one another in deploring its distinctive validity in their own culture. Geoffrey Elton goes to excess in condemning Great Britain: "There is no country in which memories are notoriously shorter; nowhere else are actions—political, social, even personal—less influenced by earlier events or decisions; nowhere else does the present regard itself as less committed by what happened in history." In the United Kingdom, truly? But now listen to Meg Greenfield, the widely read American editorial writer: "We have no collective memory, none. If it happened more than six hours ago it is gone. . . . What this says to me is that we just don't know how to think about the past—and so we try not to. . . . There is neither memory nor history nor whole people nor even any sense of time."[34]

Hyperbole? Perhaps a bit. But such slings and arrows may serve to warn us that the more we read about memory, the more we also are reminded of amnesia. They are co-ordinate concepts because they remain constant realities. And unlike some recent enthusiasts for "popular memory" (embracing oral cultures, working-class and community history), Greenfield differentiates between memory and history. All of history cannot be remembered; and collective memory must be used with discrimination by the historian. What history and memory share in common is that both merit our mistrust, yet both must nevertheless be nourished.[35]

If collective memory (usually a code phrase for what is remembered by the dominant civic culture) and popular memory (usually referring to ordinary folks) are both abstractions that have to be handled with care, what (if anything) can we assert with assurance?

That public interest in the past pulses; it comes and goes.

That we have highly selective memories of what we have been taught about the past.

That the past may be mobilized to serve partisan purposes.

That the past is commercialized for the sake of tourism and related enterprises.

That invocations of the past (as tradition) may occur as a means of resisting change *or* of achieving innovations.

That history is an essential ingredient in defining national, group, and personal identity.

That the past and its sustaining evidence may give pleasure for purely aesthetic and non-utilitarian reasons.

And finally, that individuals and small groups who are strongly tradition-oriented commonly seek to stimulate a shared sense of the past within their region (William Sumner Appleton of New England), their social class (Henry Francis du Pont of Winterthur), their ethnic group (Carter G. Woodson, who established Negro History Week), their denomination (John Gilmary Shea and the Catholic Historical Society), or even their entire nation (George Bancroft).

They also seem to succeed in varying degrees, and for diverse lengths of time. Being a custodian of the past is primarily its own reward. Such custodians may exude a missionary impulse because they commonly regard people without tradition or a sense of the past as barbarians. Quite literally. That was true of Jacob Burckhardt of Basel, the nineteenth-century progenitor of cultural history; and it was equally true of Wallace Nutting, the remarkably influential American antiquarian who declared in his autobiography: "We are yet mostly barbarous."[36]

Indeed, custodians of tradition have been prone to fits of despair whenever the morale of memory lagged. Hence this passage in a private letter from historian William Roscoe Thayer to Henry Cabot Lodge in 1921, at the time of the Pilgrim Tercentenary:

> Our acceleration in adaptability to change, makes the new and unexpected quickly appear familiar and habitual. So we soon forget the past—an ominous fact at this time, when a thousand crazy novelties press for adoption and the steadying tradition of the past restrains nobody.[37]

It invariably vexes custodians of tradition that acts of memory never manage to keep pace with the new and unexpected—especially in a democracy where, for most of our history, the private sector was presumed to bear primary responsibility for matters requiring commemoration. We have customarily been slow in getting our act together. The Washington Monument, started in 1848, was finally completed in 1885. In January 1840 Andrew Jackson visited the battlefield near New Orleans to celebrate the British surrender on that site twenty-four years earlier. The Chalmette Battle Monument was not begun there, however, until 1850; and work continued sporadically until it was completed in 1908.[38] The American Museum of Immigration, conceived in 1952, actually opened in 1972. A Korean War Veterans Memorial on the Mall in Washington will not be completed until the mid-1990s.

The Vietnam Veterans Memorial in Washington, honoring those who gave their lives in our most controversial foreign war, is truly unusual because it required just three and one-half years from the start of fund-raising until actual completion. That commemorative monument also demonstrates the inadequacy of any sharp dichotomy between official and popular memory. Although located in a place of honor on the Mall, it was built with private contributions, and its dedication was avowedly not an official event of the United States government. It is apparent that people of many ideological persuasions, and also of none, are deeply affected by it.[39]

When and how a sense of tradition can have ideological consequences and help to define a culture or a subculture, especially in the United States, is one of the central themes of this book. Fanatical apologetics for the Confederacy and, even more, for the Lost Cause, provide one example.[40] Attempts to define and defend New England's Puritan legacy provide yet another.[41]

Robert Penn Warren has written that "to be an American is not . . . a matter of blood; it is a matter of an idea—and history is the image of that idea." If Warren is right, and I believe that he is, then newcomers (the ceaseless flow of immigrants and their children) can have an imaginative and meaningful relationship to the determinative aspects of American history.[42] Warren's vision makes it possible for newcomers to claim, as Fortinbras did to Horatio in *Hamlet*: "I have some rights of memory in this kingdom / Which now to claim my vantage doth invite me." [V, ii, 378–79]

A FEW WORDS may be in order about the organization of this book. Part One, which concentrates on contextual matters and on the generations prior to 1870, will address the problem of establishing a culture appropriate to a visionary polity, and describes the dialectic between those who wished to anchor culture in collective memory and those who strenuously repudiated the "burden of the past."[43] Part Two traces a major shift in sensibility during the four and a half decades following 1870. The Party of Memory gained ascendancy then, at least in defining cultural norms. Americans slowly improved their skills at celebrating all manner of things, past and present. History in general became the core of civil religion during the spiritual crisis of the Gilded Age. And national history in particular became the means used to transform un-American identities into those of compliant citizens with shared values.

In Part Three, which spans an era from the eve of World War I to the close of its sequel, the Party of Memory confronted and contested with forces of modernism. Museums and collectors defined an American aesthetic. Regional chauvinism (and conflicts) then built upon national pride. The democratization of tradition proceeded hesitantly as a great debate heated up between cultural populists and cultural elitists. Critics of a myth-making society acknowledged that its memory had been highly selective; and the epoch ended with what one writer called "another era of pseudo-patriotic flatulence."

In Part Four, which covers the decades since World War II, Americans respond with nostalgia to future shock and heightened anxieties. Interest in tradition gives way to an obsession with "heritage"—an elastic phenomenon that is both profitable and costly. It is so expensive, in fact, that for the first time government becomes quite a prominent custodian of tradition. The democratization *and* decentralization of tradition proceed apace, leading us to a highly embarrassing cultural anomaly: amnesia and historical ignorance in an age of great apparent enthusiasm for the past at every level of society and all modes of articulation, from high culture (so-called) to mass and popular culture.

These four phases, however, cannot be regarded as chronologically compartmentalized. History is never neat, and there has always been considerable overlap. I find it noteworthy that major changes and transitions occurred *within* my schematized periods as much as it did between them. The collecting of Americana was not so strong in the 1870s but rose rapidly at the turn of the century. Patriotism reached an all-time low during the later 1960s and early 1970s; yet it began to surge swiftly even before Ronald Reagan's election to the presidency in 1980. A revival of patriotism may very well have been more cause than effect in Reagan's case. Folk art, not yet trendy in 1960, sold for astounding prices by the mid-1980s.

Hayden White has written that "an especial interest in the history of thought and expression is, of course, characteristic of transitional ages in the lives of cultures; it arises when received traditions in thought and mythic endowments appear to have lost their relevance to current social problems or their presumed coherency."[44] We shall see shifts from a sense of the past achieved almost by inadvertence (prior to 1870) to an age of memory and ancestor worship by design and by desire (1870 to 1915); then to history for pleasure and profit, when tradition became a by-word yet remained contested (1915 to 1945); to an age of consensus and heritage by compulsion that seems in our own time to satisfy an array of psychic needs, commercial enterprises, and political opportunities.

Conflict and complexity are products of pluralism—of diverse groups responding in assorted ways to the exigencies of change. There is, nevertheless, a coherent story which I have sought to formulate and relate. Because the book explores many themes and lines of interpretation, it may be helpful to itemize the most important ones here. If the old proverb is valid that a picture is worth ten thousand words, perhaps a dozen or so signposts can help to make several hundred thousand words more comprehensible as we proceed. Therefore . . .

The role of tradition in American culture has undergone a series of major transformations in the generations since 1870. The most significant of these involved the Americanization of tradition after the turn of the century, followed by its imperfect democratization.

Public memory, which contains a slowly shifting configuration of traditions, is ideologically important because it shapes a nation's ethos and sense of identity. That explains, at least in part, why memory is always selective and is so often contested.

Although there have been a great many political conflicts concerning American traditions, ultimately there is a powerful tendency in the United States to depoliticize traditions for the sake of "reconciliation." Consequently the politics of culture in this country has everything to do with the process of contestation *and* with the subsequent quest for reconciliation.

Memory is more likely to be activated by contestation, and amnesia is more likely to be induced by the desire for reconciliation.[45]

It has been a dominant assumption for most of American history that the private sector rather than government ought to be the primary custodian of tradition—a tendency that becomes more obvious when we compare the United States with other societies, such as France or the Soviet Union.

Interacting considerations of class, ethnicity, race, regionalism, and a desire for social stability have been highly consequential in determining which traditions are dominant and which subordinate.

Wars have played a fundamental role in stimulating, defining, justifying, periodizing, and eventually filtering American memories and traditions.

The history of national memory is hard to separate from the history of patriotism, and therefore this work traces some major strands of that history in the United States.

Ever since the 1920s and '30s the history of American traditions and "heritage" has been increasingly intertwined with entrepreneurial opportunities in general and tourism in particular—most of all from the 1950s onward.

There has also been a relentlessly dialogical relationship between the values of tradition and progress (or modernism) in American culture. Although those values are commonly found in tension, hundreds of local histories frequently extol a "tradition of progress" that seems absolutely central to the community's evolution. By collective inference, that tradition of progress is then ascribed to the nation as a whole.

Regional rivalries and variations in the sectional sense of history are extremely significant. National traditions, moreover, are not merely an amalgam of local ones. Rather, communities may partially appropriate the form but not necessarily the content of national historical rituals.

Although there are many similarities between the roles of tradition and memory in the United States and in other societies, ultimately the differences seem more interesting and revealing. The differences have less to do with *what* is remembered, or *how* traditions are transmitted, and more to do with the politics of culture, with the American quest for consensus and stability, and with broad acceptance of the notion that government's role as a custodian of memory ought to be comparatively modest.

That in turn has meant that the process of transmission in the United States tends to be decentralized, ad hoc, diffuse, and relatively non-coercive—so long as ritualized observances, national symbols, and local customs are not flagrantly violated. If and when that point is reached, public opinion becomes more volatile and potentially coercive than government.

IF, DESPITE the size of this volume, certain segments of the story seem to be missing, that is because the book is not designed to stand alone. It follows and complements three others that I have written which are closely connected: *A Season of Youth: The American Revolution and the Historical Imagination* (1978), *A Machine That Would Go of Itself: The Constitution in American Culture* (1986), and *Selvages and Biases: The Fabric of History in American Culture* (1987). While those works and this one were conceived as a series, *Mystic Chords of Memory* has required the most difficult labor. Perhaps that is due to its broader scope, and to the fact that (unlike the others) it has no single point of departure: a pivotal event, a formative governmental charter, or a historiographical tradition. We might, therefore, recall a few lines from T. S. Eliot's "East Coker" in his *Four Quartets*.

> *And so each venture*
> *Is a new beginning, a raid on the inarticulate*
> *With shabby equipment always deteriorating*
> *In the general mess of imprecision of feeling.*

Part One

THE PROBLEM POSED
AND THE
PERIOD BEFORE 1870

Chapter 1

THE PROBLEM OF TRADITION
AND MYTH IN A
DEMOCRATIC CULTURE

I BEGIN WITH a contextual discussion of the problematic relationships between myth and memory, tradition and history, in a
culture that for most of two centuries has professed its commitment
to a democratic ethos. I am fascinated by the phenomenon of a society
becoming its own historian—for better and for worse.[1] Because these
relationships will pervade the entire book, this chapter has a different
texture and aim from all the rest. This one sacrifices chronological
specificity for the sake of comprehensive scope. On account of its concern with the question of continuities and discontinuities in American
culture, it examines evidence (and also notes its absence) from the
nineteenth as well as the twentieth century. Because I ultimately argue
for a rather distinctive configuration in American culture, the chapter
concludes with some systematic comparisons.

Bronislaw Malinowski, a pioneering anthropologist, once described
myth as a story about the past which has the function of justifying the
present and thereby contributing to social stability. That point of view
continues to be commonly invoked. Claude Lévi-Strauss, however, the
most influential anthropologist of the generation that followed Malinowski's, refined the analysis of myth and thereby raised it to a more
subtle level. He acknowledged that myths may be activated or reactivated in order to legitimize a version of history that is useful or attractive. He conceded that this kind of mythic history, purged and socially
purposeful, may be mobilized to bolster a traditional order on the basis
of a distant past. But it may also use a purged past as the foundation for
a future that is just beginning to take shape.[2] In short, we now recognize
that myth presented in the guise of history, or tradition as collective
memory, can serve conservative ends, or innovative ones, or even be
apolitical in the service of goals that are primarily aesthetic or spiritual.

The first section of this chapter explores the question of compatibility
between civic respect for tradition and democratic values. Section II

looks at the diversity of views concerning the social uses of myth and collective memory, takes note of the American obsession with authenticity, and reflects upon the past and future prospect of history serving as a corrective to misguided myths. Section III initiates the process of making comparisons—diachronic as well as synchronic—in order to open the issue of American "exceptionalism" as it pertains to the changing patterns of tradition that we will observe throughout the book.

I

WILLIAM EMPSON, the late English literary critic, once made a shrewd observation that contains broad implications still unexplored for understanding the evolution of culture in the United States. "One would expect," he wrote, "the democratic spirit of America to have produced a proletarian literature some time ago, but so far as I know the central theme is always a conflict in the author's mind between democracy and something else."[3] Although that contention—and the tensions it connotes—has been glossed in various ways for literature,[4] it has attracted less attention than it deserves for other aspects of American society, such as religion, manners, and leisure. At the turn of the century, for example, when Coney Island flourished, it precipitated symptomatic debate over the role and significance of popular amusement in a democracy.[5]

James Fenimore Cooper and Henry Adams, prominent figures in public affairs and in literature during the first and second halves respectively of the nineteenth century, each grappled with the problematic nature and implications of democracy. Herman Melville wavered between despair and faith in democracy. Subsequently, in a widely noticed essay titled "Democracy versus the Melting Pot" (1915), philosopher Horace Kallen, who had been a student of William James, advocated cultural pluralism rather than assimilation, and he pleaded for a non-coercive federation of nationalities that would retain their discrete identities.[6]

Considering this extensive array of connective concerns—almost everything except the problem of democracy and the duck-billed platypus—it is somewhat surprising that we do not yet have a work titled along the lines of "Democracy and Memory: Reflections on the Accommodation That Gradually Evolved in the United States Between Historical Concern and Democratic Values." Tocqueville noted the problem and warned about it more than once in the second volume of his *Democracy in America* (1840). "Among a democratic people," he wrote, "poetry will not feed on legends or on traditions and memories of old days."[7]

Intermittent discussions in the public press during the 1830s dealt with the need for balance in a republican polity between proper respect for the founders and "adulation or worship" which would be inappropriate. Some editorials made a particular point that in America an elite could (and in fact did) supply democratic leadership: "such men as Jefferson and Madison, who were born to Virginia's most prestigious and affluent families, also became devoted democrats."[8]

Adherence to republican values produced a palpable tension between democracy and tradition as customarily understood. John Quincy Adams caught the essence of it quite pithily: "Democracy has no monuments. It strikes no medals. It bears the head of no man on a coin." Consequently, memorials that elevated heroes above the folk seemed antithetical to popular sovereignty. Four nineteenth-century obelisks, for example, share a common characteristic. At Bunker Hill (built 1825–43), at Fort Griswold in Groton, Connecticut (1826–30), at the Chalmette Battlefield near New Orleans (1850–1908), and at the Bennington battle site in Vermont (1887–91), the markers are all unornamented. The absence of allusions to individual bravery and the anonymity of the soldiers buried there are deliberately democratic gestures.[9]

During the middle third of the nineteenth century there was not much room for maneuver on these matters. Nathaniel Hawthorne's enigmatic story "Earth's Holocaust" (1844) offered a meditation on the way that democratic reforms seemed to be antithetical to the preservation of culture and tradition—just the opposite of John Henry Newman's belief in Britain that tradition was democratic because it somehow filtered up from the faithful.[10] To most Americans, however, the issue appeared uncomplicated. Here are three instances:

- According to a contemporary, when Andrew Jackson lay dying at the Hermitage in 1845, he received a letter from a naval commodore named Eliot, who had just returned from a Mediterranean cruise with the sarcophagus of a Roman emperor. Eliot suggested that Jackson might want his remains placed therein; but the former President, derisively called King Andrew by his enemies, wrote back to Eliot: "I do not think the sarcophagus of a Roman Emperor a fit receptacle for the remains of an American Democrat."[11]

- John Russell Bartlett's *Dictionary of Americanisms,* first published in 1847, underwent a series of revisions during subsequent decades that enriched the tradition of native lexicography. Bartlett's interest in colloquialisms had an important democratic component because colloquial language seemed the repository of ordinary ideas and discourse—the essential spirit of the common man.[12]

- When the architect Richard Morris Hunt submitted designs in 1865 for gateways to the projected Central Park in New York City, critics repudiated his French-influenced drawings on grounds that

1.1 Edward Eggleston, a photo engraving that appeared in *Harper's* in 1886.
Courtesy of the Massachusetts Historical Society.

the very purpose of Central Park was to "translate Democratic
ideas into trees and dirt."[13]

During the final decades of the century, however, that perspective
became one minority point of view along a widely spread spectrum of
opinions concerning national memory and democracy. Edward Eggleston (see fig. 1.1) wished to write a social history of ordinary folk. As he
explained to his brother in 1880: "not a history of the United States,
bear in mind, but a history of life there, the life of the people, the
sources of their ideas and habits." Herbert Baxter Adams urged his
graduate students in history at Johns Hopkins to trace the evolution of
democratic institutions; and despite his admiration for German scholarship, Adams concluded that historical writing in a democracy could not
follow an aristocratic pattern more appropriate to the imperial Second
Reich.[14]

Even a rather stodgy, nativistic, ancestor-loving anthropologist like
George Brown Goode of the Smithsonian acknowledged that institutions devoted to social memory would have to be populistic. When he
presented a lecture at the Brooklyn Institute titled "Museums of the
Future," he advocated a new notion: "The people's museum should be
much more than a house full of specimens in glass cases." That same
year, 1889, saw the publication of a ten-volume compilation called *A
Library of American Literature: From the Earliest Settlements to the
Present Time*. One reviewer recognized that it was "questionable
whether all of the entries in the volumes can be considered 'literature,'
as the title suggests," and then commented upon the absence of critical
criteria as a basis for selection. Lest that appear to be a complaint,

however, this ideological rationale followed: "It is particularly congenial to American laws of society and politics that no one with such a task before him should assume such a position, but content himself with widening as far as practicable his schedules and leave the reader to exercise his own judgment."[15] In a democracy, Everyman's editorial judgment ought to be just as good as every other's.

At the opposite end of the spectrum, however, there were tradition-oriented groups and individuals deeply mistrustful of democracy, especially mass democracy. John Bach McMaster's *History of the People of the United States,* which appeared in eight volumes between 1883 and 1913, was decidedly not a populistic work. The author admired Alexander Hamilton and determined to "show up" Thomas Jefferson by exposing him as a man "saturated with democracy in its rankest form" who "remained to the last day of his life a servile worshipper of the people." McMaster's last words? An attack upon the popular election of U.S. senators. Bernard Berenson, another elitist who preferred the European past, exclaimed to a friend in 1898: "Instinctively I hate Demos."[16] An antiquarian dealer who made many sales to J. P. Morgan, the most voracious collector of his generation, recalled that "with all his patriotic belief in American institutions, and despite the largess of his public benefactions, he was undemocratic, and there is thus the interest of paradox in the fact that the American he seemed most to admire, and certainly whose manuscripts he was most ardent in collecting, was Abraham Lincoln."[17]

Ranged across the center of the spectrum at that time were the ambivalent, the inconsistent, and even the insincere. Exemplifying the first of those attributes, in 1893 a blue-ribbon committee headed by Harvard's President Charles W. Eliot recommended a standardized high school curriculum that emphasized history. When critics attacked the academic (meaning learned and elitist) emphasis of this proposed reform, Eliot answered that democracy would be enhanced by a single curriculum that ignored class lines and levels of student preparation. Edward Eggleston, whose egalitarianism was genuine, always reacted *against* the claims of labor when a major dispute occurred.[18]

What about inconsistency? Sons of the American Revolution whose commitment to indigenous political institutions and traditions was absolutely sincere wrote paeans of praise for democratic government followed by candid effusions for hegemonic imperialism: "I have never cared so much to see our territory increased as to see republican institutions possess the world." For insincerity verging upon hypocrisy, one only needs to read the accounts of Tammany Hall speeches on the Fourth of July.[19]

It is tempting and might be ever so tidy to see a clear transition to a new phase in which tradition and democracy were reconciled. That would, in fact, become the overall trend in the generations following the two world wars (as we shall see in Parts Three and Four below);

but the process did not occur easily and it encountered considerable resistance, especially during the interwar decades. Between 1915 and 1930 such critics as Irving Babbitt, the author of· *Democracy and Leadership* (1924), and Paul Elmer More, who wrote *Aristocracy and Justice* (1915), unashamedly declared that the humanist tradition was necessarily elitist and therefore incompatible with democracy. The two men were arch-defenders of what Harry Levin has labeled the tradition of tradition.[20]

Widely read writers like H. L. Mencken spouted anti-democratic utterances that seemed amusing to many in the 1920s, even as he continued to work with nationalistic fervor on his multi-volume histori-cal study of the American language. He loved the language and de-tested liberals. Joseph Hergesheimer, an extremely popular novelist in the years after World War I, collected American antiques, lived proudly in a colonial house, and probed the past in his fiction. In his autobiogra-phy (1925), Hergesheimer explained how he had discovered his true ideological identity as a neo-Federalist:

> The Federalists believed in strong leadership, in the superiority of one mind to the minds of the mass, of the people. . . . The majority managed their private affairs so badly, they were so wasteful and indolent, that I couldn't believe it was proper, in addition, to trust a country to them.[21]

Most of the so-called Southern Agrarians, or "Fugitives," who burst upon the scene with their manifesto at the end of the 1920s joined a strong attachment to tradition with a deep distrust of democracy, and doubted whether the two could be made compatible.

Reading the personal correspondence of prominent historians during these years may or may not be honorable; but it certainly is not edifying. The sentiments of James Ford Rhodes and (to a lesser degree) Albert Bushnell Hart might not surprise us, except perhaps for the blatancy of their bias. Rhodes acknowledged to Barrett Wendell, a literary historian at Harvard, that "I do not want the negroes to vote any more than you do. . . . I am working in a quiet way on the principle do not enforce the XVIII [Amendment] and we shall not insist upon the enforcement of the XV and the second section of the XIV."[22]

James Truslow Adams, perhaps the most widely read historian of the United States during the interwar years, lived for much of that time in London because, as he told many correspondents, "I loved the old America but I am getting most horribly sick of the new." More to the point are his complaints that democracy undermined the quality of leadership. "The wildest democrat cannot claim," he wrote in 1929, "that the mob is as high in civilization as the rare individual, but the attraction . . . of the mob is becoming, under modern conditions colossal, its drag, its pull. And it is felt more in America than anywhere." Adams, author of a best-selling two-volume text titled *The March of Democracy* (1932–33), feared a genuine "danger to the whole of civilization if so-called privilege disappears."[23] Although such sentiments were not meant for public consumption, they are highly symptomatic of a malaise that one scholar has called the crisis of democratic theory.[24]

The theme that recurs continuously and links the Late Victorians to their successor generation is a somewhat grudging sense that because democracy is inevitable we will have to make the best of it—for better or for worse. Expressions of that belief formed a monotonous litany from the lips of serious devotees of American culture.

- William Dean Howells (1897): "We may, some of us, not quite like the common man, and his rights and needs may bore us, but we cannot escape their presence . . . we soberly confront the new century, after a cycle of the supposition that they had been fully provided for by the Declaration of Independence and the Constitution of the United States."[25]

- Brooks Adams (1916): "You take your social and political creed as a matter of faith and not of reason. You believe in 'democracy' or as you say in 'the people,' exactly as a thirteenth century monk believed in the efficacy of the Virgin. . . . As long as our best intelligence worships 'the people' as the believers worshiped the cross, we are in imminent danger."[26]

- J. Franklin Jameson (1932): "My present mind, right or not, agrees with yours in mornful [sic] doubts as to the wisdom of the representatives of democracy in Congress assembled. For a good number of years my feeling respecting democracy has been that the best we can say is that other systems seem to work even worse."[27]

Positive as well as negative factors appeared following World War I to shape the democratization of public discourse. On the "pull" side, a rhetoric of self-determination surfaced from the Paris Peace Conference in 1919. On the "push" side we have a candid explanation that Bernard Baruch wrote (to Winston Churchill) for replacing Baruch's huge estate in South Carolina, called the Hobcaw Barony, with a modest retreat for vacations and entertaining: "the people are being taught that it is anti-social to enjoy such things."[28]

If some Americans levelled down for the sake of appearances, however, many others—especially those who wished to legitimize American literary traditions—did so in response to deeply felt ideological commitments. Stuart Pratt Sherman, who emerged in the 1920s as a pre-eminent literary critic, often wrote of the need for experiments in democracy and forced himself to reassess his intellectual obligations to Babbitt and More by asking: "What does democracy mean to me?" He resisted offers from prestigious, private Eastern schools and remained at the University of Illinois because of his devotion to populistic state education in the American heartland. Sherman determined to use American history and literature to develop a core of indigenous cultural traditions that could support his liberal vision of America. "When we grow dull and inadventurous," he wrote, "it is because we have ceased to feel the formative spirit of our own traditions."[29]

From the mid-1920s onward, frequent calls could be heard for literary and cultural histories of the American people. Vernon L. Parrington's widely read response, *Main Currents in American Thought* (1927–30), overtly contended that the nation's cultural heritage was compatible with its democratic ethos. In retrospect this three-volume work appears flawed precisely because it reductively delineates American devotion to democracy as a continuous tradition.[30] Constance Rourke firmly believed that a knowledge of popular traditions was vital to a democratic society, and in 1931 she published her classic book *American Humor: A Study in the National Character*. Two years later, following a leisurely dinner with Archibald MacLeish, Hervey Allen, and others, Stephen Vincent Benét noted in his diary that the group had discussed "really doing something about what we believe in both as regards literature and democracy." In 1940, when a Council for Democracy came into being, funded by Henry Luce, Benét began a stint as its propaganda person. The Fourth of July broadcast that he wrote in 1941, "Listen to the People," enjoyed extraordinary popular success.[31]

The same sort of emphasis also emerged in relation to American material culture, architecture, and the arts—even where elitist assumptions or associations had been customary. When Francis P. Garvan gave his magnificent "educational collection" of early Americana (especially furniture and silver) to Yale University in 1930, he envisioned a museum setting because "all these good things are the gift of God, intended for all, not for a few." When a controversy over the design of Thomas Jefferson's memorial in Washington heated up in 1937, the press reminded readers of his strong commitment to "the principles and potential genius of American democracy." In 1939, when Marian Anderson sang at the Lincoln Memorial because the D.A.R. had denied permission for an African-American to sing in Constitution Hall, Secretary of the Interior Harold Ickes, who introduced her, pointed to the Washington Monument and the Lincoln Memorial while lamenting that "in our time too many pay mere lip service to these twin planets in our democratic heaven."[32]

Although egalitarian values surged with special strength between 1935 and 1945, as we shall see in Part Three, after World War II a great many working-class Americans still shared the long-standing assumption that traditionalism and tradition-orientation served as impediments to a truly democratic society.[33] How that mind-set changed during the 1960s, 1970s, and 1980s will provide a major concern of Part Four.

II

BECAUSE "tradition" and "myth" used as word-concepts are going to recur throughout this book, it may be helpful to ask: What is the difference between the two? Although there is significant overlap, the words are not interchangeable. My Random House dictionary defines tradition as "the handing down of statements, beliefs, legends, customs, etc., from generation to generation, esp. by word of mouth or by practice." The big beige book defines myth as "a traditional or legendary story, usually concerning some superhuman being or some alleged person or event, with or without a determinable basis of fact or a natural explanation." A myth, then, is more likely to be fabulous than true (and less true than a tradition), more likely to involve some sort of story, and quite likely to concern deities, demigods, or heroes in order to explain aspects of a society's cosmology or sense of identity. By contrast, an essential aspect of a tradition is that it be transmitted. When the process of transmission is broken, a tradition is very much at risk.

Nevertheless, we find highly intelligent and reputable writers using "myth" and "tradition" in casual, virtually interchangeable ways. Hugh Trevor-Roper, for instance, has argued that history (our best-informed knowledge of the past) is vastly preferable to myth. Trevor-Roper refers pejoratively to "a hardened tradition, a national or partisan myth. We have seen enough historical myths in our time to realize how stunting— even, at times, how disastrous—they can be." I intend to be less casual in employing tradition and myth. But far more noteworthy at this juncture is the contrast between Trevor-Roper's scornful view of national myths and the upbeat outlook of an equally distinguished historian, William McNeill. After acknowledging that "most historians disdain myths," McNeill actually asserts that truth "resides in myth— generalizing myths that direct attention to what is common amid diversity by neglecting trivial differences of detail. Such myths make subsequent experience intelligible and can be acted on. . . . The simple fact is that communities live by myths, of necessity. For only by acting *as if* the world made sense can society persist and individuals survive."[34]

Now it is not only possible but likely that these two historians—each one possessed of remarkable range over time and space—mean something rather different by myth. For McNeill, it is a helpful explanation of why things are as they are, and it is subject to change when new knowledge dictates. For McNeill, humankind ought to be in control of its myths, whereas Trevor-Roper's myths are much less tractable and more monstrous. We are likely to be their captives. These contrasting views are instructive because we encounter both of them throughout our cultural history, a matter that we will explore with particular care in chapter fifteen.

The critical point here, however, is that American culture contains a dualistic tension where myths are concerned. We can be iconoclastic; but we are much more likely to be permissive and self-indulgent about myth. In his old age, for example, Daniel Boone denounced the anti-social legend that had been spread about him starting with John Filson's *The Discovery, Settlement, and Present State of Kentucke* (1784); but it made not a bit of difference. Myth turned out to be more attractive than truth. Similarly, Kit Carson repudiated spurious legends about himself before he died; but that didn't matter either.[35] Elliott Coues, a remarkable naturalist and frontier historian (1842–1899), made the following observation in 1897:

> It would surprise most persons to realize how quickly a neglected core of fact gathers the mold of myth. Take the Lewis and Clark Expedition, for example. Never, perhaps, was a true story more minutely and completely told; to know all about it, we have only to read what the explorers themselves had to say, less than one hundred years ago. But the take-it-for-granters, the forsoothers, the forgetters, the prevaricators, the misquoters, the unreaders— the whole tribe of quidnunc impressionists—have meanwhile found out more things that never happened in this case than they ever learned about what did happen.[36]

Myths and legends flourish despite the accessible bodies of factual information that contradict them. This seems to have been particularly true during the later nineteenth century, when large numbers of immigrants arrived in the United States with preconceived notions about the Land of Promise and had extravagant expectations as a consequence. They lived and died with hopes that had been shaped by a configuration of cultural myths.[37]

Anthropologists and social theorists have offered us a varied menu of theory and generalization about the nature of myth. Although this is not the place to sample that full menu, some of the most pertinent items can be assessed using American ingredients as a means of exploring the so-called problem of American exceptionalism. I have previously responded to Mircea Eliade's perception of myths of national origin in *A Season of Youth* and *A Machine That Would Go of Itself*; and I will do so in yet another way in chapter three below.

Claude Lévi-Strauss has insisted that among preliterate peoples "myths have no Author; from the moment when they are perceived as myths, and despite their real origin, they exist only as they are incarcerated in a tradition."[38] First, we should note in passing the near-conflation of myth and tradition. Second, and more to the point, I must insist that, with respect to American culture, Lévi-Strauss is sometimes illuminating but often irrelevant. What is called the "Country Boy" myth can be located in time with some precision. It burned brightly from about 1870 until 1910; it became a powerful fuel for American imaginations, and Horatio Alger exploited it to very good advantage in his popular tales for adolescents. The myth did evolve into a tradition, a kind of "urban pastoral"; and it does not have a particular author of origin. The same might be said of John Henry, the legendary steel-driving man who battled the machine. We can link the genesis of that ballad-cum-cultural myth to the Big Bend Tunnel built in West Virginia in the early 1870s. But despite the most meticulous research, scholars have abandoned hope of demystification. John Henry's saga scores a point for Lévi-Strauss.[39]

There are many other American myths, however, whose authors and origins are clearly recognized. Parson Weems's fables of George Washington, man and boy, supply an obvious example. James Fenimore Cooper was the first major American writer to create a complex, enduring myth of white–Indian relations and of life under frontier conditions. "Buffalo Bill" Cody is such an important figure in American culture because his career exemplified just how stereotypes of the Wild West came into being. Hence one scholar has offered a generalization, based upon a lifetime of study, that seems persuasive even though it is difficult to demonstrate conclusively: "In our short history we have probably created more 'heroes' by means of publicity and manufactured myth than have any of our older sister nations during their long histories."[40]

Describing and explaining how that penchant came about is one of the central themes of this book. But something can be said here concerning the key ingredients and dynamics of the process. Leaders of the American Revolution worried about the mythicization or distortion of what they had done. So much so, in fact, that they counselled extreme caution and patience in writing the history of the Revolutionary era. John Adams did so explicitly in 1784, for instance, and James Madison once again in 1823.[41]

Even though every nation needs a mythic explanation of its own creation, that process was paradoxically elaborated by the reluctance of Revolutionary statesmen to have their story told prematurely. Consequently the sectional crises of antebellum times caused the founders of the Union to receive an unusual degree of adulation—unusual when you consider that they were distant neither in documentation nor in memory. The authors of nineteenth-century schoolbooks accentuated the phenomenon by indulging in what has been called "indoctrination in national traditions."[42]

By the end of the nineteenth century a close student of the Revolution who had ancestral roots in it could write this indictment of myth-making in his native land. Notice, once again, that he does so comparatively, and reaches the conclusion that the genesis and role of myth in American culture have somehow been distinctive.

It is curious that American myth-making is so unlike the ancient myth-making which as time went on made its gods and goddesses more and more human with mortal loves and passions. Our process is just the reverse. Out of a man who actually lived among us and of whose life we have many truthful details we make an impossible abstraction of idealized virtues.[43]

The particular person referred to in that passage happened to be Benjamin Franklin; but it might just as easily have been George Washington, Robert E. Lee, Thomas A. Edison, Davy Crockett, Charles Lindbergh, or Babe Ruth. We prefer plasticized apotheosis to historicized memory developed in judicious doses.[44]

Nevertheless—or perhaps precisely in response to this tendency—writers of popular biography in the United States have professed their obsession with undercutting myth and achieving truth. When Henry Cabot Lodge published his laudatory *George Washington* in 1891, he insisted that he hoped to bypass "the statuesque myth and the priggish myth and the dull and solemn myth."[45] It is noteworthy that the words "true," "truth," and "truthful" appear with such frequency in the titles and prefaces of so many histories and biographies written (or called for) between 1870 and 1930. During the very period most prolific in the production of American myths, prominent as well as ordinary citizens issued pleas for the unvarnished truth.[46] As Henry Ford drove home from his notorious trial for libel in 1916—the one that prompted him to say that "History is more or less bunk. It's tradition. We don't want tradition"—he informed his secretary of his new resolve: "I'm going to start up a museum and give people a true picture of the development of the country."[47]

Ford's preoccupation with accuracy in matters of historical detail calls to our attention the irony that a nation of myth makers has been ceaselessly obsessed with authenticity. Even Parson Weems, our first fabulist, invoked his reliance upon "authentic documents"; and Edward Eggleston, who declared that the authenticity of his stories derived from Sioux or Chippewa mythology, insisted that historical novels "be the truest of books" in order to have "value as a contribution to the history of civilization in America." Eggleston's contemporary Frederic Remington felt that historical authenticity ought to be just as important as aesthetic qualities in art depicting Indians and life in the American West.[48]

John D. Rockefeller, Jr., and those associated with him in the restoration of Colonial Williamsburg, worried endlessly about authenticity in the tiniest details. Nothing pleased them more than unsolicited letters from tourists who expressed their delight in the "scholarly authenticity of the restoration" or their "amazement at the authenticity of the buildings." When commercial replicas of colonial furniture began to be marketed in the 1930s, they were invariably advertised as "authentic reproductions." The word "authentic" had long since achieved a perverse yet powerful resonance in American cultural discourse.[49]

More than once, however, the quest for authenticity required a hasty retreat that led straight to irony. In 1936 Selznick International Pictures purchased the film rights to *Tom Sawyer* and sent a contingent to study little old Hannibal, Missouri, as the film site. Even though Mark Twain's town was generally decayed and old-fashioned, it transpired that the film could not be made there because a few technological impediments, such as telephone poles and lines, spoiled its appearance as a period piece of the 1840s. Time had left the town behind, but it had also left traces that made Hannibal "too modern to authentically replicate its own past!"[50]

Nevertheless, the story of historic preservation in the United States, along with many other anomalies that will be encountered in the chapters that follow, leaves room for some skepticism about the American commitment to authenticity. Or else suggests that twentieth-century crusaders for truth in tradition needed to compensate for the lackadaisical attitude of the nineteenth. When the Betsy Ross House was "saved" from the wrecking ball in 1892, and subsequently opened to the public in 1898 as a museum, a few honest folks properly feared that it might not really have been Mrs. Ross's home. By 1949 the state of Pennsylvania was cautiously describing the house as the "traditional birthplace of the American flag. Although there is no proof that Betsy Ross lived here, the house is an interesting example of the homes of the period." Similarly, in 1897 an evangelist, the inventor of the "quick lunch," exhibited at the Tennessee Centennial celebration in Nashville a log cabin that was supposedly the birthplace of Abraham Lincoln. When a reporter interviewing the evangelist tried to learn some particulars about this humble structure, he received this reply: "Lincoln was born in a log cabin, weren't he? Well, one cabin is as good as another."[51] American authenticity has not always been true-blue.

Writers of imaginative literature rooted in historical materials have affected the role of myth and tradition in our culture in quite a different way. An antebellum novelist like William Gilmore Simms, composing relatively close in time to episodes involving white–Indian relations and the American Revolution, felt he ought to be faithful to historical facts but that he might take liberties with mythology. Esther Forbes, on the other hand, working a century later, reacted quite critically to what she regarded as an American obsession with authenticity in historical fiction, and admired Hawthorne especially because she believed that he, too, recognized the discrete qualities of history and fiction-writing while respecting both. Robert Penn Warren provided a third perspective when he prefaced his poignant prose poem about slavery with an assertion that myth was actually the common denominator for all historical writing, imaginative as well as fact-based narrative: "Historical sense and poetic sense should not, in the end, be contradictory, for if poetry is the little myth we make, history is the big myth we live, and in our living, constantly remake."[52]

I cannot say with assurance whether Warren consistently held to that

1.2   Henry Adams at Beverly Farms, Massachusetts, in 1883. Courtesy of the
Massachusetts Historical Society.

eloquent yet somewhat facile formulation. He wrote for more than six
decades and worked through various phases. But the formulation brings
us back, now at a different level, to the problem of history, myth, and
national identity. Ernst Cassirer, writing just when Warren did at midcentury, was more concerned with causal priority. "In the relation
between myth and history," Cassirer remarked, "myth proves to be the
primary, history the secondary and derived factor. It is not by its history
that the mythology of a nation is determined but, conversely, its history
is determined by its mythology—or rather, the mythology of a people
does not *determine* but *is* its fate, its destiny as decreed from the very
beginning."[53]

At first glance, that judgment appears to enjoy validity and broad
applicability. James Truslow Adams, as we have seen, distrusted democracy as a functional system and became increasingly disillusioned as the
decade of the 1930s progressed. Nevertheless, in 1932–33 he titled his
two-volume history of the United States *The March of Democracy,* with
the clear implication that this progressive development was attractive
as well as inevitable. A democratic ethos deserved a democratic narrative. Mythology had, indeed, determined history, even though the historian, in his heart of hearts, hoped that it might have been otherwise.
We shall encounter many other examples.

However provocative (and perhaps disillusioning) Cassirer's formulation may appear to us, it must be elaborated if we are to strengthen our
grasp of the connections between mythology, tradition, and history.
Marc Bloch, a distinguished practitioner of the historian's craft, once
offered a less vexing explanation of why cultural traditions tend to
diverge from the accepted record of what really happened. "By a curi-

1.3   Charles Francis Adams, Jr., in 1913. Courtesy of the Massachusetts Historical Society.

ous paradox," Bloch noticed, "through the very fact of their respect for the past, people came to reconstruct it as they considered it ought to have been."[54] Although the truth of that insight places a heavy responsibility for cultural demystification upon historians, it also reveals several brighter sides. First, it means that we need not be overly cynical about societies that "invent" traditions. Sometimes that occurs in order to perpetuate power relationships or to foist a mystique of false consciousness; but sometimes it actually occurs for benign reasons.[55]

There is no inexorable correlation between socio-political conservatism and some fatal attraction to myth or tradition. A fairly substantial group of American antiquarians who were active for several decades before and after 1900 were conservative in diverse ways and to varying degrees; but they could also be fiercely contemptuous of journalists or popularizers who perpetuated old legends and myths when they should have known better (and sometimes did). I have in mind a cluster of men, some of them still well known, others largely forgotten, who passionately wished to set straight some record that had been knocked askew: Henry Adams and his brother, Charles Francis, Jr. (figs. 1.2 and 1.3); Albert Matthews; Worthington C. Ford; Alexander S. Salley; and J. Franklin Jameson convey just a few examples.

C. Vann Woodward once called to our attention that "the twilight zone that lies between living memory and written history is one of the favorite breeding places of mythology." He had particularly in mind distortions and public misunderstanding pertaining to the genesis of Jim Crow laws during the 1890s.[56] But given the comparative brevity of recorded history in the United States and the casual nature of cultural memory here, Woodward's statement applies equally well to other traditions, fundamentally rooted in legend, that managed to form in just such a twilight zone. I have in mind, for example, myths pertaining to the Pilgrims, the Puritans, and the amusing matter of who first lived in log cabins and when. The genesis of the so-called log cabin myth, which incorrectly has the earliest settlers in the Chesapeake and New England building log cabins, has been traced to the period 1840–1910, when excessively imaginative magazine illustrators were even more mislead- ing than writers or ill-informed historians.[57]

It has been a commonplace to note, by the way, that widespread use of the camera during the later nineteenth century may have helped to make memories more precise and retrievable, an observation equally true of public figures and events as well as private lives. It is not com- monly noticed, however, that a series of technological innovations dur- ing the same period brought a profuse number of illustrations to the popular press, including weeklies, monthlies, and books. That visual material carried quite a potential for myth-making, or else for the renunciation of one myth as being false to the advantage of a rival myth. New technologies *could* serve as *aides-mémoire*; but they had an equal capacity to sensationalize, sentimentalize, or distort. Memory is always selective. Machinery is usually systematic. But when influential images are used selectively by editors, publishers, and authors, then a new element of deliberate caprice is added to public memory. That hap- pened in the United States during the later nineteenth and early years of the twentieth century.[58]

III

A FULL ARRAY of sustained comparisons must wait until we have examined a major phase of American history and memory in a substantive way. But we can begin with some broad and basic compari- sons. We know, for example, that the art of memory has been cultivated among early and "primitive" societies in order to perpetuate a public sense of chronology, values, and legitimacy. The Aztecs preserved their knowledge of events, despite the absence of literacy, by training desig- nated individuals to remember important historical speeches. They also used pictographic signs carved in stone in order to assist memory. In the Mande heartland of West Africa, at the culturally significant settlement of Kangaba, the bards of Mande gather every seven years to chant the narrative of their land.[59]

Despite ingenious studies that have been made of the extraordinary care with which public memory could be cultivated in pre-modern societies, we know that room for improvisation and revision existed and was permitted under certain political or social circumstances.[60] The same may be said of civic sermons in colonial New England, of historical orations in Revolutionary America, and of commemorative rhetoric in the United States prior to 1870, which was a great age of public oratory.[61] Statesmen used celebratory and ceremonial moments to invoke "the mystic chords of memory," as Abraham Lincoln did so poignantly in 1861 on the occasion of his first inauguration. And millions of American schoolchildren were required to memorize lengthy passages from the historical speeches of Daniel Webster, Edward Everett, and others.

Although no orator ever confessed that he filtered the past or invented national, sectional, or local traditions, in candid moments a speaker might acknowledge that the opportunity certainly existed. On December 21, 1870, for example, one of the most popular orators for historical occasions, Representative Robert C. Winthrop, spoke at Plymouth to commemorate the 250th anniversary of the landing there by the Pilgrims. "It is an old story, it is true," he conceded, "but there are some old stories which are almost forgotten into newness. There are some old stories which are actually new to every rising generation." And so he retold it, but not with the same narrative or emphases that Daniel Webster had used fifty years before, or in 1843.[62] Discourse concerning legends is malleable.

In his perceptive discussion of myth, memory, and history in ancient Greek culture, the late Moses Finley, commenting upon the oral transmission of mythical and semi-mythical pasts, observed that " 'tradition' did not merely transmit the past, it created it."[63] That too has been true, on occasion, in American culture; but as I hope to show in the chapters that follow, it occurred more commonly prior to 1920, and particularly before 1870. In the seven decades since 1920 we have frequently been disposed to forget, or to remember selectively, or even incorrectly. But when the age of oratory ended, when literacy became the norm, and when custodians of the past appeared in various professional guises, it became increasingly problematic to create the past. Re-create, yes. Create *de novo*? More difficult.

Another general characteristic that is commonly shared by tradition-oriented cultures, including the United States after 1870, is the use of monuments, architecture, and other works of art as a means of demonstrating a sense of continuity or allegiance to the past. Following the restoration of the monarchy in Britain, the tradition of May Day got revived and 6,325 maypoles were erected between 1660 and 1665. An atmosphere congenial to nostalgia for Merrie England also meant the exuberant revival of popular sports, such as horse racing and cockfighting.[64]

Erecting public monuments to celebrate events, ideas, or heroes began on a broad scale late in the eighteenth century when nationalism and political ideology started to supplant, at least partially, a role that religion had customarily fulfilled in civic culture. Public monuments honoring sundry military heroes for their successes in war had essentially been unknown before the French Revolution. Napoleon found that such statues could be a potent way to impress the public and promote devotion among his generals all at the same time.[65]

Historical art and architecture that appear banal or foolishly sentimental to us flourished in Western Europe during the nineteenth century. Although national chauvinism clearly served as the strongest stimulus, we also know that many artists employed history as a means of conveying attitudes they felt about their own time. The presence of a Gothic revival in Great Britain from the 1830s to the 1860s has long been visible, along with a strong interest in historic preservation. Only recently, however, have we been informed that the Victorians looked to the past in the realm of architecture for assistance in solving contemporary problems. A feeling existed, for instance, that viewing historic buildings would "elevate and enlarge the judgment of the people."[66] Some comparable phenomena and motives will be encountered in the United States, albeit less common, less successful in execution, and less well understood by the public.

Jules Michelet (1798–1874) and George Bancroft (1800–1891) played remarkably similar roles as the most popular and prolific historians of their respective countries. Michelet's six-volume history of France had appeared by 1846, whereupon he turned his attention to a four-volume work on the French Revolution, an event that he regarded as inevitable. George Bancroft's multi-volume *History of the United States* culminated with the American Revolution; and in 1882 he added a *History of the Formation of the Constitution of the United States* in two volumes. He, too, believed that his country's Revolution had been foreordained by a benign Providence. If Bancroft lacked Michelet's mystical belief in the proletariat, he certainly compensated as a Jacksonian Democrat with ardent partisanship and patronage that was more egalitarian than elitist.

ALTHOUGH we shall encounter still other parallels and similarities, I must now call attention to some equally striking contrasts. A sense of the past in general, and particular readings of national history, informed the practice of politics in Western Europe with an intensity not to be found in the United States during the nineteenth century. A careful study of England that is quite sensitive to variations by class concludes that at all levels of society "ideas of English history in one form or another figured as universal providers of political ideals or prudential wisdom, a warning or a guide, a weapon or an inspiration." Members of the upper classes simply assumed that knowledge of the past would reveal laws governing the proper conduct of human affairs, and this assumption "allowed their promiscuous use of historical argument in everyday political debate." Throughout the Crimean War historical polemics of various sorts supplied the framework for discussions of wartime economic issues, and strongly affected the government's fiscal and commercial policies as well.[67]

Among the petite bourgeoisie and labor leaders—readers of *Household Words* and the *Morning Advertiser* (the most widely read popular daily)—notions of history were equally important though different. Instead of emphasizing political and military history since the Glorious Revolution of 1688, they took a long view and complained of national deterioration and loss rather than accomplishments and progress. In the radical's reading of history, English liberties had been eroding ever since 1688. Their great ideals, local self-government and ministerial accountability, had been dangerously diminished by ambitious usurpers of the people's privileges. For the radicals, as Olive Anderson has written, "vague historical rhetoric powerfully strengthened the appeal of a movement which drew heavily upon many ancient strands of anti-government feeling."[68]

To put it simply, nothing comparable occurred in nineteenth-century American public discourse. Some history books were written, published, even purchased, to be sure. But public policy was infrequently discussed within any sort of historical context. Americans were much more likely to allude to the *burden* of the past than to possible *uses* of the past. The contrast in this regard between France and the United States is at least equally striking. The French Revolution of 1789 continued to be as controversial as its American counterpart of 1776 remained uncontested and a firm ground for national consensus. Our Loyalists had left, whereas their Royalists remained and, at times, became extremely vocal.[69]

Two significant sentences from Alexis de Tocqueville's other great book, *The Ancien Régime in France,* supply us with a point of departure for noticing additional similarities and contrasts:

> The French people made, in 1789, the greatest effort which was ever attempted by any nation to cut, so to speak, their destiny in halves, and to separate by an abyss that which they had heretofore been from that which they sought to become hereafter. For this purpose they took all sorts of precautions to carry nothing of their past with them into their new condition.[70]

At first glance, and anticipating the chapter that follows this one, similarities between the impacts of the French and American revolutions seem to be striking. During the decades, let us say, 1790–1850, a great many Americans wished to carry little or nothing of the past with them. But on closer inspection the contrasts are even more remarkable. The American patriots, 1765–'76, had rejected British rule rather than their own past. In fact, they repudiated British violations of Anglo-American political traditions that dated back generations and in some instances for centuries. Whig ideology invoked a political formula whose ingredients included large amounts of history and custom.[71] As Louis Hartz observed more than a generation ago, America had no *ancien régime* to reject.

Tocqueville, moreover, tossed in an important perception a few pages following the one just quoted. "The French Revolution," he noted, "has had two totally distinct phases: the first, during which the French seemed eager to abolish everything in the past; the second, when they sought to resume a portion of what they had relinquished." The net effect in France, then, was not a clean sweep of national memory. Napoleon, in fact, commissioned the production of a history that would integrate the *ancien régime,* the Revolution, and the re-establishment of order by himself into a single narrative framework. Its purpose was to provide a perspective on French identity that could command allegiance and be shared by all of the rival factions in France. After the work's publication in 1814, it became an immediate sensation. The intense interest in history that emerged after that date developed because each ideological interest group wanted to enlist history on its side.[72]

Nothing comparable took place in the United States, and Americans who visited nineteenth-century France often found themselves bemused by cultural contrasts. Following a look at the Louvre in 1858, Nathaniel Hawthorne noted that "the French seem to like to keep memorials of whatever they do, and whatever their forefathers have done, even if it be ever so little to their credit; and perhaps they do not take matters sufficiently to heart to detest anything that has ever happened."[73] While Hawthorne regretted that American memory was then so woefully underdeveloped, he believed that social memory must be discriminating to be meaningful.

A generation earlier, just when the young Hawthorne was searching for his own regional voice and personal medium as an American writer, France during the 1830s underwent the initial phase of an important transformation in which "the variety of local, traditional, popular cultures inherited from the past gave way before an official . . . national culture." Comparable developments had been gradually under way in Spain since the reign of Philip II, when the significant level of legend and oral history in village life very slowly began to be supplanted by nationalization, bureaucratization, and the recorded traditions of a larger, contextual culture. Even so, a historical anthropologist contends that in Spanish villages, "customs were not committed to paper until the sixteenth century, and often not until much later. The reign of memory had a longer life in the villages [than in metropolitan areas], and it was never superseded even after their customs were set down in writing."[74]

During the 1830s and '40s, however, local charters had to be recopied and got altered in the process. Village ordinances were created from and replaced "the flux of customs." Termination of the traditional practice of burying parishioners in the sanctuary of their church caused the meaning of a family tombstone in such settings to diminish—at first gradually and then more dramatically in modern times. Communities that had long existed as autonomous "mini-states," making and enforcing their own rules by custom and character, responded to pressures for national cohesion and homogeneity by seeking to maintain remembered customs under changed conditions. Sometimes that meant inventing or reinventing traditions; but above all, despite a marked growth of literacy since the 1830s, history has really not become a corrective to memory. The two remain intertwined. Local legends, as one scholar has written, show "how present the past is and how, at the same time, the past is reworked to shed light on the origin of things."[75]

We could pursue various points of similarity as well as difference between Europe and the United States that emerge from the trends I have just described. The most interesting, however, in my view, is this. Scholars have noticed the same process of centralization and nationalization that started in Europe around the 1830s and 1840s taking place in the United States half a century later. And the responsive reinvigoration of local traditions and memories also took place subsequently by half a century in the New World, during the 1930s.[76]

The pertinent lesson seems fairly clear. In the realm of social and cultural change there was a time lag of about two generations during the eighteenth and nineteenth centuries that helps to explain some—though by no means all—of the apparent cultural contrasts between the New World and the Old. American authors such as Cooper, Hawthorne, and their contemporaries made such a self-serving fuss about the difficulties confronted by would-be writers because no profession of letters existed in the United States. Literary historians have echoed that lament endlessly without ever asking when writing became a socially acceptable and profitable profession in Europe. The answer, we have learned, is about two full generations earlier, in the mid-eighteenth century.[77] It may well be that aspiring literati in the United States didn't know that; but now that we do it obliges us to add a category, called "time needed for catching up," to our customary ones of like and unlike.

When Marc Bloch investigated feudal society in eleventh- and twelfth-century Europe, he took care not to treat medieval culture as a monolith. Rather, he shrewdly recognized the variable age of "national" traditions (measured by epics, songs, and poems) in different polities: not very old in France; much more venerable in the Germanic areas; quite recent in Castile; and essentially none in Italy, where Latin chronicles filled the function of native epics elsewhere.[78] A similar sensitivity to time variations in the evolution of American traditions is imperative, and will receive special attention in chapters four, five, twelve, and fifteen below. For many groups, national memories have been less compelling or determinative than the feel for New England, Southern, Midwestern, Great Plains, or intermountain traditions.[79]

In recent years various sorts of historical issues have given rise to volatile public controversies in cultures around the world. They help to remind us that social heterogeneity is not the sole or necessarily the primary provocation for conflicting visions of "valid" customs. As the historian James Sheehan has observed, "it may be time to give up the idea that all of those living in a nation possess only one past and to accept the fact that nations, like every other sort of complex group, contain many different histories which often converge, overlap, or intersect, but which sometimes move in quite different directions."[80]

It has also been demonstrated that communities of various sizes, even small villages, possess multiple pasts comprised of diverse traditions. Sometimes that is due to ethnic or religious sectarianism within the community. Sometimes it results from conflict between local boosters, on the one side, who seek a highly positive image that can be legitimized by reference to a past that narrates a glorious or harmonious civic culture, and candid dissenters on the other side who take perverse pride in telling "it" like it really was: nasty, brutish, and persistent despite attempts to conceal conflict. Communities that contain conflicting memories are fascinating. Communities that have sought to conceal their conflicting memories confront the historian with an absorbing challenge.[81]

We acknowledge the conscious replacement of myth with "real" history as one of the principal achievements of Renaissance humanists. But in the twentieth century, with the professionalization of historical scholarship, we harbor a naive assumption that illusory legends and social myths will be molted like so many dead or useless skins. We encourage the expectation that truth will triumph. Ironically, however, professionalized history is much more remote from the lay public than popular histories by Bancroft and Parkman, Motley and Macaulay, were in the nineteenth century. They influenced public opinion to such a remarkable degree, at least in part, precisely because they committed the "Whig fallacy" of reading the past by the light of the present.

Moreover, recent studies have given us reason to doubt whether the professionalization of history has brought even the ordained custodians of memory as close to objectivity and truth as they would like to believe.[82] Responsible history—history that is sensibly pursued, carefully researched, and written with integrity—is supposed to serve as an antidote to socially pernicious myths and traditions. Responsible history can undoubtedly help. It sometimes has the same potent impact as the sun's ultraviolet rays upon vivid colors: exposing, bleaching, and diminishing.

Nevertheless, myths and traditions have their own resilience, not completely controllable. True history can never be totally disengaged from social memory, or serve as an exquisite corrective for its flaws. Not enough people pay attention to scholarly history. They never have, and I don't believe they ever will. Historians, for their part, are not infallible, even when they "merely" function in their capacities as custodians of the past. Historians are participating members of society regardless of whether they are unloving critics or uncritical lovers of their culture.

What people believe to be true about their past is usually more important in determining their behavior and responses than truth itself. Back in the early eighteenth century, Giovanni Vico proposed that proper understanding of the past would be achieved through "the popular traditions which must have had public grounds of truth." Half a century later, Johann Herder offered his own variations on that theme.[83] In twentieth-century America, as we shall see in Part Three below, Constance Rourke and many of her contemporaries would elaborate their own, home-grown, grass-roots variations. When that happened, tradition and democracy commenced an enduring reconciliation.

Chapter 2

· "THE PRESENT IS BURDENED TOO MUCH WITH THE PAST"

I N   T H E   Y E A R   1811 a hypercritical and cranky yet astute ex-President, John Adams, begged his confidant Benjamin Rush to write a treatise on "the causes of the corruption of tradition and consequently of the corruption of history. For myself I do believe that both tradition and history are already corrupted in America as much as they ever were in the four or five first centuries of Christianity, and as much as they ever were in any age or country in the whole history of mankind." What could have prompted such an apprehensive outburst? It was Adams's frustration with the emergence of warped perceptions of the American Revolution and its leaders' reputations less than one generation after the fact. Rush agreed wholeheartedly. "I have no hesitation," he responded, "in expressing a general want of belief not only in tradition but in recorded history and biography. The events of the American Revolution opened my eyes upon these subjects."[1] Such sentiments set the tone for American culture early in the nineteenth century. It may intensify the irony if we bear in mind that those two men had read and appreciated much more history than most Americans.

Nearly half a century later, which thereby helps to frame the chronological concentration of this chapter, Nathaniel Hawthorne viewed the frieze of the Parthenon, the Elgin Marbles, and some Egyptian sarcophagi at the British Museum. He then recorded two sentences in his private journal that may seem contrary to our conventional image of Hawthorne's mind-set. He must have meant what he said, however, and these ruminations are surely representative of the dominant view concerning tradition in the United States during the first half of the nineteenth century. "The present is burdened too much with the past," he wrote. "We have not time . . . to appreciate what is warm with life, and immediately around us."[2]

Hawthorne's ruminations, writ large, epitomize the central concern of this chapter. After recognizing that repudiations of the past formed a legacy from the colonial era and a dominant motif in the antebellum mind, we then notice the viability of Nature and Progress as surrogates for tradition—with a few mixed feelings about the blessings of Progress appearing by the third quarter of the nineteenth century. In section III we attempt to understand the most basic reasons for American ignorance of and indifference to the past: particularly pluralism (a diverse society that shared a future but not a common history); physical and social mobility; and the pervasive belief that government ought to bear little responsibility for the maintenance of collective memories. We then turn to foreign observers and find that they confirmed and reinforced the view of Americans as a present-minded people. Finally, by way of transition to chapter three, we conclude with the views of those who agreed with the preceding analysis but bemoaned the shallow condition of a culture that ranged from carelessness about its past to outright repudiation.

I

COLONISTS who rejected the Old World in favor of the New did not constitute a neat cross section of the societies from which they came. They were driven to leave by economic or religious distress, or else they were simply more adventurous than other folks. Either way, they might well have quoted Shakespeare's Richard II: "Throw away respect, / Tradition, form, and ceremonious duty." Challenges faced during the early phases of colonization, irrespective of region, tended to deflect settlers away from traditional ways of thinking and behaving. Even had they wanted to live customary lives, it simply was not possible. Often, however, a gradual recovery of tradition, or at least the appearance of it, occurred; but fresh waves of newcomers and unexpected crises or challenges shattered the illusion that custom or convention had been transplanted. From the very outset of American history, then, vacillation between experimentalism and traditionalism came to be established as an enduring pattern.[3]

For more than two centuries, however, experimentalism would dominate. During the 1630s a large migration of Puritans brought to New England John Calvin's notion of a "new order" necessary to an independent society; and a secularized version of that outlook recurred in the period of the young republic, 1783–1820, when a self-aware "new order of the ages" came into being. Historians of American sects and denominations noticed long ago that the founders of such groups seem to have been markedly unfettered by a sense of tradition. Sometimes that freedom simply occurred as a function of distance and historical ignorance. In other situations, though, it resulted from social and theological impulses. In 1754, for example, when the colonial Baptists called for a "new reformation," their leading spokesman, the Reverend Isaac

Backus, beseeched his brethren with this exhortation: "Be intreated no longer to take Things by Tradition."[4]

That attitude would be articulated even more frequently during the Revolutionary era by secular voices as well as clerical ones.[5] In 1776 Tom Paine determined to tear "the veil of sanctity from tradition" and expose the absurdities of orthodox political thought. When he wrote *The Rights of Man* in 1791, he elaborated his repudiation of the tyrannical past: "We have no occasion to roam for information into the obscure world of antiquity. The real volume, not of history but of facts, is directly before us, unmutilated by the errors of tradition."[6] Thomas Jefferson echoed those sentiments on several occasions, as when he told John Adams that "I like the dreams of the future better than the history of the past."[7]

During the distinctive period that we refer to as the early republic, moderates and conservatives found themselves awkwardly situated because the dominant value system, verging upon an ideology, made it unacceptable or unattractive to acknowledge either the past or the Old World as repositories of applicable wisdom. Timothy Dwight, a staunch New England Federalist, was obliged to concede that custom loomed as a burden impeding the path to cultural independence. And James Madison of Virginia, more of a moderate than his maverick friend Jefferson, nonetheless wrote these familiar phrases in *Federalist* number 14:

> Is it not the glory of the people of America, that whilst they have paid a decent regard to the opinions of former times and other nations, they have not suffered a blind veneration for antiquity, for custom, or for names, to overrule the suggestions of their own good sense, the knowledge of their own situation, and the lessons of their own experience?[8]

In many societies the force of tradition has served as a source of authority. But for much of American history the inhabitants of this continent clearly indicated that they did not want power to reside in pastness. They preferred, instead, the sovereignty of morality or perhaps natural law in tandem with their colonial charters; and following Independence, written constitutions implemented by statutes. The vehemence with which the past was rejected, even in the sixth and seventh decades after Independence, is astonishing. "We have outgrown tradition," boasted Orestes A. Brownson in 1836. "Probably no other civilised nation has at any period," proclaimed the *Democratic Review* in 1842, "so completely thrown off its allegiance to the past as the American." One year later George Perkins Marsh clarified in a sentence the cultural "law" that governed the situation: "It belongs to the character of youthful and vigorous nations to concern themselves with the present and the future rather than with the past. . . ."[9]

For Ralph Waldo Emerson that theme, voiced with variations, became a relentless refrain over a span of three decades, beginning with his essay "Nature" in 1836. In the well-known Divinity School Address (1838), Emerson saw memory and the soul in conflict, and opted for the latter. In "Self-Reliance" (1840) he postured rhetorically: "What have I to do with the sacredness of tradition?" And in "Memory" (1857) he mellowed just a bit by conceding that we "cannot overstate our debt to the past, but has the present no claim? This past memory is the baggage, but where is the troop? The divine gift is not the old but the new." Ultimately Emerson pleaded that Americans should "live by principles instead of traditions."[10]

His disciple, Henry David Thoreau, evoked similar views in discourse designed to be pithy. "Time hides no treasures," he insisted in 1849; "we want not its *then,* but its *now.*" Like Emerson, Thoreau rephrased that sentiment on numerous occasions; and his wail in the last chapter of *Walden* (1854) about the deep "ruts of tradition and conformity" would be explicitly echoed by such influential contemporaries as Catharine Beecher.[11] Walt Whitman likewise celebrated America in preference to Europe and the present at the expense of the past. "All the past we leave behind,"/ he sang in "Pioneers! O Pioneers!" (1865), "We debouch upon a newer, mightier world, varied world."

From the poetry of William Cullen Bryant to the prose of Herman Melville, the past appeared to be stifling, a force to be resisted.[12] Bryant began his poem "The Past" (1828) with these lines:

> *Thou unrelenting Past!*
> *Strong are the barriers round thy dark domain,*
> *And fetters, sure and fast,*
> *Hold all that enter thy unbreathing reign.*

Fiddle the past. As Emerson announced in his essay "The Young American" (1844), "America is the country of the Future." Touring the lyceum circuit, Emerson and his contemporaries made the word "new" a national buzzword.[13] Abraham Lincoln once mocked the Young America movement because of what he called its "great passion—a perfect rage—for the '*new.*'" But that was in 1859. Three years later, making an appeal to Congress for gradual and compensated emancipation of the slaves, even Lincoln succumbed, and his language has remained memorable ever since: "The dogmas of the quiet past, are inadequate to the stormy present. . . . As our case is new, so we must think anew, and act anew."[14] At Gettysburg the next year, Lincoln foresaw a new birth of freedom. The newness of America could be contagious.

Sidney Smith, that acerbic British critic, won no popularity contests in the young United States; but he got it right. "Others appeal to history," he snorted. "An American appeals to prophecy."[15] Obviously, prophecy must have appealed to them.

I I

THIS OBSESSION with newness, eventually manifest in all those characters named "Newman" in American novels, meant that the antebellum value system had more points to its compass than merely republicanism and the "burden of the past." The other two principal points were Progress and Nature. Identification with the latter has been much discussed and requires little in the way of commentary here except to note that proud boosters of "Nature's Nation" often found in the landscape, and especially in natural wonders, a meaningful surrogate for tradition. William Cullen Bryant referred to venerable trees as "God's first temples." A passage from *A Tour on the Prairies* by Washington Irving (1835) epitomizes a recurrent motif in nineteenth-century American travel literature. At one point on his tour Irving found himself

> overshadowed by lofty trees, with straight, smooth trunks, like stately columns; and as the glancing rays of the sun shone through the transparent leaves, tinted with the many-colored hues of autumn, I was reminded of the effect of sunshine among the stained windows and clustering columns of a Gothic cathedral. Indeed there is a grandeur and solemnity in our spacious forests of the West, that awaken in me the same feeling I have experienced in those vast and venerable piles, and the sound of the wind sweeping through them supplies occasionally the deep breathings of the organ.[16]

Native authors repeatedly insisted that natural wonders and antiquities in the United States were superior to their man-made counterparts in the Old World. In his own mind Thomas Cole saw painted landscapes of appropriate sites as the American counterpart of conventional historical paintings. He composed this passage in the same year that Irving wrote the one just quoted:

> He who stands on Mont Albano and looks down on ancient Rome, has his mind peopled with the gigantic associations of the storied past; but he who stands on the mounds of the West, the most venerable remains of American antiquity, *may* experience the emotion of the sublime, but it is the sublimity of a shoreless ocean un-islanded by the recorded deeds of man.[17]

For many, Nature's Nation meant no more than American romanticism. For some, however, it meant either a surrogate for tradition or, as we have seen, even something superior to it. Sometimes Emerson's compensatory chauvinism seems facile and simply transparent—with or without his enigmatic eyeball. An example occurs when he claims that we deserve the prize for both newness and oldness: a new culture in a natural setting so old that Europe cannot possibly compete with it.

> Let us live in America, too thankful for our want of feudal institutions. Our houses and towns are like mosses and lichens, so slight and new; but youth is a fault of which we shall daily mend. This land too is as old as the Flood, and wants no ornament or privilege which nature could bestow. Here stars, here woods, here hills, here animals, here man abound, and the vast tendencies concur of a new order.[18]

Comparable assertions, equally chauvinistic though suitably less complex, speckled the pages of nineteenth-century American schoolbooks.[19] Those passages tell us that Irving, Cole, and Emerson were not merely members of an elite who spoke only to one another. They had personal outreach, but also popularizers who made their views widely accessible. Moreover, this penchant for finding antiquities in nature turned out to be more than an aberration of antebellum culture. A renewal of that penchant late in the nineteenth and early in the twentieth centuries led to the creation of a national park system—one that would eventually include historic sites as well as natural wonders.[20]

CLOSE CONNECTIONS existed between Nature and Progress in the antebellum value system. The two were not viewed as antithetical. Asher B. Durand's handsome painting called *Progress* (fig. 2.1), also known as *The Advance of Civilization,* was one of seven works shown at the National Academy of Design in 1853. A reviewer for the *Knickerbocker* described it as being "purely American. It tells an American story out of American facts, portrayed with true American feeling by a devoted and earnest student of Nature."

Hyperbole aside, this is indeed a grand American icon that is extremely informative. Although it is obviously a landscape, and superficially a serene one, an immense amount of activity is actually taking place. In the lower right-hand foreground, livestock are being driven to market along a road that also bears a wagon heavily laden with supplies. Just beyond the road there is a lock-canal very much in use. Across the cove we see a steam locomotive hauling at least five cars. Two promontories beyond that there is a bustling town. We recognize the bustle by all of its belching smokestacks. Large mills and small workshops are busily productive. Steaming ships lie adjacent to the shore and fired-up factories are visible beyond the town.

Presumably a viewer of European descent would then have found Nature and Progress entirely compatible. Man has made "improvements" (a favorite keyword of the mid-nineteenth century); everyone

2.1   Asher B. Durand, *Progress* (1853), oil on canvas. Courtesy of The Warner Collection of Gulf States Paper Corporation, Tuscaloosa, Alabama.

is content and everything seems to be absolutely edenic. Lurking behind the dark and blasted trees in the left foreground, however, are several Indians. They surely view the whole scene as less than serene, and cannot be sanguine about what they see: namely, their world not merely transformed, but no longer even theirs. Progress for the white people means oblivion for them. It seems safe to say that Durand knew that and made his allegorical statement with the sense of inevitability that Roy Harvey Pearce has ascribed to most antebellum Americans: a lesser civilization must give way to a more "advanced" one.[21] That, in large part, is what progress is all about.

Durand's picture enjoyed popular success because it so resonated with the optimistic outlook of Nature's Nation—at least in the Northern states. An engraving of it, called "Advance of Civilization," appeared in *Ballou's Pictorial Drawing Room Companion* in 1855. Distribution of the engraving prompted local artists to paint amateurish copies on which we find fantastic or bizarre titles, such as *California.*[22] Success can be measured by its cheap imitations.

During the second half of the nineteenth century other artists shared Durand's vision that technological progress and manufacturing would not blemish Nature's Nation. In *Poughkeepsie Iron Works* (*Bech's Furnace*) (1850), Johann H. Carmiencke confines industry to the immediate foreground. Two goats graze on a pastoral hillside adjacent to the ironworks; and all the rest of the scene is a tranquil Hudson River landscape.

In Julian Alden Weir's *Factory Village* (1899), the factory is located beside water at the lower right and a telephone pole obtrudes in the center from the full-crowned trees of midsummer. Basically all, or nearly all, is lush and green. Three or four church steeples are visible, so once again progress appears to be non-threatening and minimally disruptive of the rural idyll.[23]

Some important works that celebrated progress got painted at the initiative of persons other than the artist. In 1857 Jordan L. Mott commissioned Christian Schussele to create a group portrait of eighteen living American inventors, including himself, who had "altered the course of contemporary civilization." Schussele then travelled to the home of each inventor in order to make sketches from life, and the picture appeared to be complete in 1861. Just before delivery was scheduled, John Ericsson's ironclad man-of-war, the *Monitor,* won a spectacular victory over the *Merrimac*; so Ericsson was hastily included in 1862 as an afterthought. That genre of heroic figures whose enterprise had transformed and improved the quality of life (or the possibility of violent death) was perpetuated in 1895 by Daniel Huntington's *The Atlantic Cable Projectors,* featuring Cyrus W. Field.[24]

The centrality of progress in nineteenth-century American social thought has been fairly well chronicled.[25] Less clearly understood, however, is the emergence of ambivalence about progress, privately and publicly stated, starting in the 1850s to '60s and accelerating thereafter. This ambiguity is important because it provided a nascent basis for nostalgia and tradition-orientation during the final third of the nineteenth century. Harriet Beecher Stowe stressed this sentence in her Preface to *Oldtown Folks:* "I would endeavor to show you New England in its seed-bed, before the hot suns of modern progress had developed its sprouting germs into the great trees of today." Henry T. Tuckerman, the noted travel writer, art critic, and commentator on American culture, observed in 1864 that "the geniality and dignity of the past are often lost in gregarious progress and prosperity."[26]

Cultural dialogues concerning progress as a mixed blessing occurred for diverse reasons in all sections of the country during the later nineteenth century.[27] In our own time we tend to overlook or scant those bypassed pockets of discontent where outright disillusionment has replaced ambivalence. One elderly man responded poignantly to the destruction of Joanna, Missouri, as a consequence of creating the Clarence Cannon (flood control) Dam: "This so called progress is nothing but destruction."[28]

The unsought side effects of technological innovation and industrialization have elicited elements of nostalgia and resistance to change ever since the second quarter of the nineteenth century. The Jeffersonian ideal of agrarianism persisted despite the prosperous appearance of manufacturing.[29] Then skilled artisans and craftsmen came to resent the menace that machines offered to traditional modes of life and work.

Hostility to progress eventually enhanced the status of traditional life-styles and values.[30]

The cultural history of railroads in the United States supplies an instructive lesson in the sequential metamorphoses of a single technological and industrial phenomenon. During a span of roughly a century and a half the railroad shifted from being a symbol of dramatic and unimagined progress (1830s and '40s) to representing abusive and regressive economic power (1880s and '90s) to becoming the object of wistful nostalgia on the part of tradition-oriented train buffs.[31] Tourists now thrill to the whistle of an olde-tyme steam train; we have museums entirely devoted to railroad history; and huge locomotive and diesel engines provide some of the most awesome exhibits in the Henry Ford Museum and the National Museum of American History at the Smithsonian Institution in Washington. We have passenger stations that have been abandoned by their lines and now serve as atmospheric restaurants. Retired railroad cars situated on adjacent tracks commonly serve as cocktail lounges. From dangerous cinder sparks to embers of sentiment: the railroad really exemplified Hawthorne's notion that progress is circular rather than linear. Here we have an instance of transformation: from innovation to tradition, via memory, in about five generations.

III

LET US RETURN to the post-Revolutionary generation, however, and look at the array of laments about historical ignorance and indifference to tradition. Jeremy Belknap, a New Englander and founder of the first state historical society (that of Massachusetts), sent this heartfelt complaint in 1784:

> If he [Dr. Samuel Johnson] had to write the History of a country, and to search for his materials wheresoever they were likely or *not likely* to be found; if he was to find that the "treasures" contained in "records" are to be explained by private papers, and that these are to be sought in the garrets and ratholes of old houses, when not one in a hundred that he was obliged to handle and decipher would repay him for the trouble; that "tradition," whatever it might "pour down," is always to be suspected and examined; and that the means of examination are not always to be obtained,—in short, if he had to go through the drudgery which you and I are pretty tolerably acquainted with . . . he would be fully sensible that to write an History as it should be is not so easy a work.[32]

A varied assortment of people who cared about the past—perpetuating the surviving sources and recording them accurately—added their voices. Thomas Jefferson found it unfortunate that so few public officeholders kept contemporary notes concerning their activities and work because without faithful personal records "history becomes fable instead of fact." When Peter Force decided in 1836 to gather primary materials pertaining to the American Revolution, George Bancroft urged him to commence his collecting in the South where the records were "in the least elaborate condition." (A tactful way of saying poor condition.) And some observers recognized that historically important speeches so often seemed ephemeral and consequently were lost altogether or else imprecisely remembered after the fact: a problem of "desultory association which identifies all spoken history and criticism with temporary occasions."[33]

Was the past poorly preserved and inadequately transmitted because of public indifference, or did the latter result from the former? I believe that the causal connections worked both ways; but John Adams placed blame upon the people. "There appears to me," he wrote in 1809, "to be a very extraordinary and unaccountable Inattention in our Countrymen to the History of their own Country. While every kind of Trifle from Europe is printed and scattered profusely, in America our own original Historians are very much neglected." Three months later he penned a plaintive follow-up: "The History of our Country is getting full of Falshoods and it is high time for some of them to be corrected."[34]

Surviving evidence suggests that citizens' knowledge and appreciation of European history wasn't very acute either. More to the point, however, is the comment by contemporaries that Americans had a limited attention span for history, even the history of their own heroes. In 1839 a newspaper notice complained that Jared Sparks's life of George Washington filled ten volumes. "Why will our literary men forget that readers in this country have no time to spend a life over a few volumes of history?"[35]

Moreover, despite some stereotypical images that we may have of patriotic enthusiasm in the antebellum United States, Americans at that time do not seem to have been very consistent about the observance of historic anniversaries. In 1837, for example, which was the fiftieth anniversary of the Constitutional Convention that had met in Philadelphia, the press remarked upon the absence of public celebrations in Baltimore and Alexandria, Virginia, on the Fourth of July. Apart from a military parade and an oration, the holiday even passed rather quietly in Washington, D.C. According to a local newspaper report that was reprinted in other cities, some residents took a steamer to the Potomac Pavilion at Piney Point in order to go swimming. Political history, quite clearly, was not the message of the moment. Perhaps the most notable aspect of Independence Day in our early history was *not* that it became an occasion for consensus, but rather that for a while memory frequently fell victim to fierce factional disputes. Partisanship and mutual recrimination became the order of the nation's natal day, rather than reciprocal congratulations based upon shared legends.[36]

Beyond indifference where there surely ought to have been hosannas, deliberate amnesia also occurred. Important episodes in the history of white–Indian relations were simply repressed—sometimes deliberately and sometimes by apparent inadvertence. Many aspects of the Loyalist experience during the War for Independence were conveniently forgotten. And the story of Texan independence and annexation during the 1830s and '40s remained two-dimensional until quite recently. As the most penetrating study of the subject observes, there is "no memory" of annexation as a major historical event. "What happened to the annexed Mexicans?" David Montejano starts his important book by noting "the fragile historical sense most people have of the American Southwest. The vestiges of a Mexican past are still evident. In the old cities of the region, the missions and governors' palaces, the 'old Mexicos,' the annual fiestas, and the like remind one that there is a history here, but it seems remote and irrelevant."[37]

If so, then why? The explanation has several facets and they involve more than just embarrassment, guilt, or the perpetuation of political dominance. We must begin, I believe, with pluralism. One of the most important psychological dynamics in the colonization of British North America arose from the fact that a mixture of peoples with diverse traditions had to learn how to co-exist, and after 1783 to create a common culture. As Sidney E. Mead once put it: "What they shared that bound them together was not a past, but the present and a future."[38]

By the first half of the nineteenth century obstacles to achieving a viable, coherent sense of national tradition were numerous: distinctive sections as well as value systems with conflicting self-images of one another and of themselves. Diverse political factions and parties. Even embryonic literary traditions that potentially led in disparate directions.[39] A careful study of educational content that examines the evangelical experience as well as public schools finds diversity rather than homogeneity to have been predominant: "members of an American neighborhood shared many hopes, but few memories."[40]

Some of the most striking and strident tendencies in American culture during the antebellum period—millennialism, utopianism, comeouterism, perfectionism, and especially evangelicalism—were not compatible with customary modes of religious and social organization. Adherents of these movements were far more interested in destiny than in history. They felt an affinity for prospective systems of belief that offered hope and gave meaning to the bewildering changes they underwent as a consequence of industrialization, commercialization, and secularization. They strongly preferred to think about time in theological and millennial terms rather than in historical or chronological terms. Ralph Waldo Emerson warned ministers to "beware of tradition"; and evangelical preachers envisaged the second coming of Christ as vastly more important than the remembrance of things past.[41] Although Christianity has been and can be a potent source and force for tradition, in eighteenth-century America it was not, except perhaps for the Anglican Church, which lacked vigor and became weakest in the two generations that followed the break with Britain.

The early republic was notably an era when the usual institutional bulwarks of tradition—law, education, and social structure, in addition to religion—did not function very well in that capacity. Look at the realm of law. James Wilson of Pennsylvania, one of the finest legal minds in the country, insisted that law should be grounded in moral obligation rather than custom or tradition. In 1836 a wistful Chancellor Kent of New York looked around at the erosion of traditional values and decried "the ardent thirst for pleasure and amusement; the diminishing reverence for the wisdom of the past; the disregard of the lessons of experience, the authority of magistrates, and the venerable institutions of ancestral policy."[42]

For most of the nineteenth century formal education gave short shrift to the past. American history remained very much a minor subject in the schools—rarely a required part of the curriculum. Extra-mural training was understandably present-minded.[43] A clearly delineated social structure, which had helped to serve as a bulwark of tradition in the Old World, simply did not exist in the New. The privileges of birth meant so much less here; fortunes were swiftly won but just as easily lost; the presumption of mobility became a cultural norm. And finally, the conventional wisdom about civilization developing through a tidy sequence of stages *over time* became meaningless in a country where an energetic traveller could experience all the phases in the course of a single journey. William Darby, for instance, recorded in his *Emigrant's Guide* (1818) that a trip from New Orleans westward to the Sabine River "showed man in every stage of his progress, from the most civilized to the most savage." Where the simultaneity of human development seemed to supplant the norms of evolutionary experience, the past diminished in significance.[44]

Relentless and recurrent patterns of mobility, especially westward migration, meant that the experience of newness became a familiar norm whereas the portents of pastness were irrelevant. E. L. Godkin, an acutely perceptive journalist of Irish origin, may have tended toward hyperbole, but his judgments invariably built upon a large kernel of truth.

New communities are springing up at the West every month, on whom the past has but little hold. They have no history, and no traditions. The great memories of the Revolution are far less potent swells in Iowa and Illinois than in Massachusetts. The West, in short, has inherited nothing, and so far from regretting this, it glories in it. One of the most marked results of that great sense of power by which it is pervaded, is its strong tendency to live in the future, to neglect the past. It proposes to make history, instead of reading it.[45]

To a newcomer who had not yet become an insider, like Godkin at that time, the absence of tradition presumably meant the existence of a vacuum. An uncertain present could give way to an unstable future. To observers with an emotional stake in the situation, however, like the editor of *Harper's,* it did not seem so hopeless. He figuratively foresaw a mental melting pot, a composite American mind: "The Celt, the German, the Englishman, the Italian," he mused, "can exist here only by parting with his national individuality; for he is placed in a current of influences which inevitably melts him down into the mass of American life." Despite differences with Godkin, despite his assurance that a "comprehensive national mind, harmoniously combining characteristics caught from all nations" would emerge, the editor of *Harper's* and Godkin shared a very basic assumption: they both looked to the future. A highly complex process had only begun. If Godkin's communities tended to populate the future, *Harper's* editor admitted that "it is not so much in the present as in the future that we have the grandest vision of the American mind."[46]

As with Asher B. Durand's panoramic vista, progress had happened, and it was happening; but the best remained ahead.

I V

WHAT, THEN, were the most pertinent consequences of such simplistic present-mindedness and future-orientation? First of all, and most generally, a superficial sort of self-knowledge. Wallace Stevens said it succinctly some years later:

> *The American will is easily satisfied*
> *in its efforts to realize itself in knowing itself.*[47]

Groups and individuals, by and large, were indifferent to their own histories. Identity was more commonly assumed or invented than inherited; and when it was knowingly inherited the process occurred mindlessly, without critical inquiry, without curiosity, without qualms. As one man of the cloth declared at Andover Theological Seminary in 1833: "We are forming a state of things, in this Republic, very much as if we had not the memorials of past ages."[48]

In consequence of this "state of things," the small number of people who did care about the past were perceived, at best, as being quaint; but for the most part they simply met with indifference. In 1824 John Fanning Watson of Philadelphia, an ardent antiquarian (in the richest sense of the word), submitted an essay entitled "Recollections of Ancient Philadelphia" to a daily paper with the expectation of awakening the public "to the utility of bringing out their traditions and ancient family records." It had scant impact. Three years later he proposed joining with others to purchase the Rising Sun Inn (the so-called Letitia Penn House). Watson hoped that the recently formed Historical Society of Pennsylvania might be willing to travel along "the steps of time" and take up quarters in the lower level. The idea won little support. In 1834–35 he pleaded that the venerable inn would make a "perfect museum where many of our citizens could be brought to deposit of their old relics." When Watson aroused no interest, he abandoned the project.[49]

A closely related consequence involved the widespread indifference to historic sites, which often resulted in neglect or actual damage. Philadelphians permitted Benjamin Franklin's home to be destroyed in 1812, and George Washington's presidential mansion in 1832. John Trumbull visited Independence Hall in 1819, three years after the original ornamentation had been stripped from the room where the Constitutional Convention met. "The spirit of innovation laid unhallowed hands upon it," he mourned, "and violated its venerable walls by modern improvement, as it is called."[50]

In 1837 an elderly man wrote a public letter complaining that the Old Court House on Second Street was, shamefully, going to be torn down in the name of progress. He speculated that Independence Hall might very well be next. The *Public Ledger* responded with a long editorial that represented the mainstream of opinion at that time: if society wishes to improve, the new must replace the old. Moreover, the *Ledger* declared, by European standards "our *antiquities* are too *modern* to excite veneration." As for Independence Hall, the *Ledger* had a suggestion, apparently quite serious: "let it come down, and be replaced by a marble building that shall be an ornament to the country; and let an apartment of it, directly on the site . . . be appropriated to the statues and portraits of the signers."[51] A tiny tableau of memories as tokenism. Obviously, authenticity had not yet become a by-word.

Consider a related paradox of American preservation history: namely, that there is often little or no correlation between a cultural legend and the physical remains connected to it—at least, little or no correlation in chronological terms. Take the case of the Alamo, for example. Although an Alamo myth managed to emerge within days of the Texans' defeat in 1836, the actual site in San Antonio did not begin to be regarded as sacrosanct until the very end of the nineteenth century.[52]

In Mark Twain's first major book, *The Innocents Abroad* (1869), he poked fun at sentimental rhapsodizing over historic ruins. I am persuaded that Twain's sarcasm—prompted by the great vogue enjoyed in Europe by Volney's tract titled *The Ruins* (1791) and by the popularity of classical ruins painted on large canvases by Hubert Robert, Francesco Guardi, and Giovanni Paolo—conveyed the dominant indifference to ruins that persisted for most of the nineteenth century in the United States. The reason, at least in part, can be found in an allegorical linkage

2.2   William Trost Richards, *Mount Vernon* (1855), oil on canvas. Courtesy of
the Newark Museum, Newark, New Jersey.

that was meaningless to Americans. In Europe, depicting ruined structures provided an iconological representation of civilizations that had
fallen. A homily was offered by the past to the present: Take heed. But
most Americans had such complete faith in their own destiny as a rising
nation—westward the course of empire takes its way—that lessons left
by ruined civilizations were largely lost upon them.*

Every so often during the middle decades of the nineteenth century
someone would visit Mount Vernon and then write a heart-rending
letter: "It is now in a very dilapidated condition" (1849); or, "I was
painfully depressed at the ruin and desolation of the home of Washington" (1852). In William Trost Richards's 1855 painting, dark shadows
create an aura that conveys more melancholy than romance (fig. 2.2).
By the 1870s, visitors to Monticello invoked the very same phrases:
"desolation and ruin"; "evidences of desolation"; and so forth.[53] Yet in
each instance a long and arduous campaign had to be mounted in order
to save the structure and site as "shrines" for posterity. In the case of
Mount Vernon it took decades. Monticello, more typically, required
several generations. The reasons why ruins suffered such neglect in the
United States, and why fund raising on their behalf proved to be so
difficult, are highly instructive.

A powerful presumption lingered on (far longer in the United States

---

*For the principal exception to this generalization, a privileged group of American artists
and travellers in Italy, see William L. Vance, *America's Rome*, I, *Classical Rome* (New
Haven, 1989), esp. 71–81.

than in Europe) that government bore virtually no responsibility for matters of collective memory, not even for the nation's political memory. That assumption, clearly rooted in the democratic ethos of a people's republic, stood for more than a century as a major impediment to the sustained role of tradition in American culture. If people wished to commemorate an anniversary, celebrate a battle, or save a historic site, they would have to take the initiative. The time, energy, and above all the money must come from them. Some unusual exceptions, decidedly not the norm, did occur: when Congress chose in 1838 to purchase the papers of James Madison, or subsequently to support the Smithsonian Institution (following a generous bequest by a British individual); or when the federal government commissioned a monument in 1881 to observe the centennial of victory at Yorktown, Virginia.[54]

A letter written to the Philadelphia *Public Ledger* in 1837 responded vigorously and negatively to the question: Should surplus "state" money be applied to the proposed monument honoring George Washington? A consensus did not exist, however, and this correspondent found a representative middle ground.

> We are opposed to the least expenditure of public money for the mere purpose of honoring individuals, however distinguished, and therefore say that all such things should be done by private munificence. We venerate as highly the character, and feel as grateful for the services of Washington, as any republican, or as is consistent with that self respect, without which no one can be a republican.[55]

The author did favor using public money for the Bunker Hill Monument, which had been under construction at a creeping pace since 1825. Monuments at the battle sites of Brandywine and Trenton were also acceptable because "such things are intended to honor the country, and patriotism is a republican sentiment." Events could be honored, or anonymous people in groups, rather than individuals.

Throughout the nineteenth century indifference on the part of government officials and the cavalier attitude of private individuals toward public records as a primary source of national memory frequently bordered on the bizarre. Some passages from the memoirs of a New York physician are fascinating yet horrendous by halves:

> Shortly after the beginning of the Civil War one of my patients, already mentioned, and wife of one of the assistant secretaries in Washington, returned home on a visit. When she came back to me she showed me a dozen or more letters, written by Washington, Franklin, and several other well-known officers, written chiefly from the winter-quarters at Valley Forge. I expressed my surprise that she should have them, as they all related to the public service and belonged in the Government archives. She told me that on

her way to the Capitol a few days before she had to pass between a dozen or more tobacco hogsheads filled with papers so that they hung over the sides. Seeing the name of Washington on a letter, she asked the foreman of some work going on if she could have it. She was told yes, and that she might take as many as she wished as it was a lot of rubbish which was to be destroyed. I immediately wrote to her husband and learned from him that in making room in the basement of the Capitol for a bakery, to bake bread for the Army in the neighborhood, these hogsheads of papers had been removed and, on the report that the papers were of no importance, they were all one night dumped into the Potomac River. On further investigation it was found that these were the Government archives which Mr. Madison, as President, had hastily packed in these hogsheads when the English were advancing on Washington during the War of 1812, and were sent into the country for their preservation. After the English had burned the city and had been driven off, these papers were brought back to Washington, and when the Capitol had been rebuilt they had been temporarily stored in one of the basement rooms and had been forgotten![56]

Is it any wonder, then, that the absence of a sense of tradition became a genuine worry to such men as Hawthorne and Rufus Choate at mid-century? Referring retrospectively to the 1850s, Henry Adams conjured up "a future America which showed no fancy for the past."[57]

V

FOREIGN OBSERVERS of the American scene were of several minds and had mixed feelings about the situation. Armchair travellers who only read or heard about the United States tended to be severely critical in general and invariably singled out the lack of either memory or any thirst for tradition. Many who managed to endure the rigors of New World wandering had few gracious words to offer.[58] This English view might be multiplied many times over: the Americans "have no *past*. The present is theirs, with its daily cares and pleasures; but they have so little to look back upon that they naturally glance a-head to what is to come."[59]

Those who moved about extensively or stayed a while usually made similar observations but compounded them with more complex comparisons. Michel Chevalier, for instance, who came between 1833 and 1835 on an engineering mission for the French government, could utter predictable prejudices—"In a society which has no Past, the Past counts for nothing"—but also be realistic about cultural conditions at home. "Our old European societies," he wrote, "have a heavy burden to bear; it is that of the Past. Each age is responsible for those that have gone before it and imposes a similar responsibility on those which follow it."[60]

Frederick von Raumer, a Prussian civil servant and historian, rendered a verdict in 1845 with which most residents of the United States would have happily agreed:

> America has no monuments, it is true; but she has a nature which joins all the venerableness of age to the elastic vigor of youth. . . . The poetry of the Americans lies not in the past but in the future. We Europeans go back in sentiment through the twilight of ages, that lose themselves in night; the Americans go forward through the morning dawn to day! Their great, undoubted, historical past lies near them; their *fathers* did great things, not their *great-great-grandfathers*![61]

Goethe and Hegel, surprisingly enough, had expressed similar sentiments two decades earlier. And the writings of Alexander von Humboldt, the prominent German geographer, would reinforce the inclination of such Americans as Thomas Hart Benton and William Gilpin to reject the influence of history and tradition.[62]

SHIFTING FROM European perceptions of the United States to actual comparisons, we must proceed cautiously and judiciously. There are genuine contrasts to be noticed as well as false or misleading ones. Starting with the former, it is true that Sir Walter Scott's enthusiasm for Anglo-Scottish border traditions and folklore, and his strong interest in history as a matter of process, of change over time, were vastly influential (even in the United States, though not to anything like the same degree as in Britain). After 1836 the proper care of public records became a matter of genuine national concern in England, a full century before anything remotely similar happened in the United States.[63]

Comparable tendencies were noticeable in France even earlier. François Guizot (1787–1874) was perhaps the most seminal figure there (fig. 2.3). He participated in a movement that founded the Ecole des Chartes (an academy for the professional training of archivists and historical editors) in 1821, and that began the publication of a vast *Collection de documents inédits sur l'histoire de France*. The Société de l'histoire de France got started in 1833, and soon launched its own series of publications. Two years later Guizot made an extraordinary recommendation to King Louis Philippe: "In my opinion," Guizot explained, "it is the government alone which can accomplish the great work of a general publication of all the important unpublished materials on the history of our fatherland. The gov-

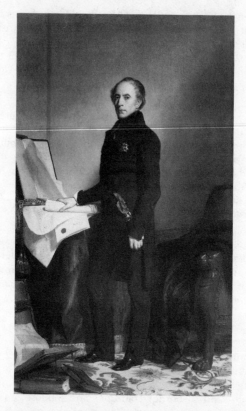

2.3   George P. A. Healy, *François Guizot* (1841), oil on canvas. Courtesy of the National Museum of American Art, Smithsonian Institution. Transfer from the National Institute.

ernment alone possesses the resources which such a large enterprise demands."[64] Comparable appeals were not made to the American government until the 1950s and '60s!

Moreover, the French state did become involved, remarkably early, in gathering national traditions. In 1852, for example, Napoleon III ordered primary school inspectors to start collecting all sorts of "traditional" materials: legends, ballads, historical narratives, martial and festival songs, stories, and so forth. Nothing along those lines occurred in the United States until the great WPA projects of the later 1930s.[65]

In 1882 Henry James not only made a kind of art tour of France; he also inquired about the remarkable network of municipal and local museums. To his fascination, and ours, he found that each year the national government purchased a certain amount of French art "culled from the annual Salons" for presentation to various museums.

Wherever the traveller goes, in France, he is reminded of this very honourable practice—the purchase by the Government of a certain number of "pictures of the year," which are presently distributed in the provinces. Governments succeed each other and bid for success by different devices; but the "patronage of art" is a plank, as we should say here, in every platform.[66]

And yet, in describing French culture during the later nineteenth century, Eugen Weber reminds us repeatedly that traditions seem to be immemorial simply because memory is short. "There is every indication that traditions are subject to change like everything else, and, of course, subject to outside influences."[67] Close inspection of the historical record reveals that we exaggerate, all too easily, contrasts between New World newness and Old World oldness, between the absence of traditions in one place and their perdurability in another. Jacques Bonhomme, for instance, a legendary peasant rebel of fourteenth-century France, was in fact created by Augustin Thierry, who wanted the French people to cherish their ancestors and national symbols. Thus Jacques Bonhomme appeared upon the nineteenth-century scene only about a decade before his American counterpart, Brother Jonathan, the youthful forebear of Uncle Sam. Similarly, Joan of Arc did not become a treasured heroic figure in France until the later nineteenth century, and did not achieve sainthood until the early twentieth. From the 1570s until the 1870s her story remained a pious legend to the devout, a scandal to skeptics, and an embarrassment to orthodox historians.[68]

There has been an unfortunate tendency to exaggerate the natural and indigenous qualities of popular culture in Europe and contrast them with the contrived or artificial nature of popular culture in America. Just as Mona Ozouf has shown the fertility of France in nourishing new national and regional myths after 1870, Carl Schorske has indicated that the Viennese bourgeoisie, at the same time, sought to schematize a past that really was not authentically their own.[69] A comparable point can be made for Great Britain, as we shall see at the close of Part Two. C. P. Snow's old don does not exaggerate very much when he declares that "nine English traditions out of ten date from the latter half of the nineteenth century."[70]

What ultimately matters most, however, is not the comparative newness of most so-called traditions, irrespective of place, but the uses to which those traditions are put, and by whom. We shall find that in the United States, more often than not, memory has served as a bulwark for social and political stability—a means of valorizing resistance to change. Such a pattern, however, is neither inevitable nor universal. In Great Britain, for example, from the 1780s to the 1860s radicals relied upon the rhetoric of patriotism as a "means of possessing the past" and consequently as a weapon in their arsenal of opposition. Folklore enthusiasts in France from about 1850 until 1890 wished to demonstrate that popular traditions had not only been a source of continuity and stability in the past, but also a vehicle for change and a means of enriching the cultural life of the people as well as the nation.[71] It is the *perceptions* of tradition and the *uses* of memory, not their mere existence, that ultimately matter.

V I

IN 1812 Goethe wrote seven lines whose intent is not entirely clear.

> *America, you are more fortunate*
> *Than our old continent*
> *You have no ruined castles*
> *And no primordial stones*
> *Your soul, your inner life*
> *Remain untroubled by*
> *Useless memory. . . .*[72]

Although he may genuinely have meant to convey a compliment, a patronizing cloud casts a shadow upon the sentiment; and one suspects that many European readers must have received the proposition with more derision than enthusiasm. We need only note in passing the irony of Henry James's negative (and notorious) litany of "lacks," published in his *Hawthorne* (1879).

The fact remains that a small yet vocal group of antebellum Americans felt deeply troubled by the irrelevance of memory to their contemporaries. In brief, they agreed that the cultural conditions described in this chapter predominated, yet they yearned for a richer alternative. In 1819 Washington Irving expressed a desire to "lose myself among the shadowy grandeurs of the past." Such contemporaries as James Fenimore Cooper and William Cullen Bryant joined Irving in the belief that Americans were genuinely handicapped by an absence of "the associations of tradition."[73]

In consequence, when Progress became the omnipresent ideal by midcentury, a few men, socially and politically prominent, raised their voices in protest. Speaking at Boston on "American Nationality" in 1858, Rufus Choate acknowledged the "one image of progress which is our history," but went on to condemn the fallacious philosophy "which boasts emptily of progress, renounces traditions, denies God and worships itself."[74]

The shrewdest and most poignant observers of the American scene in that era felt a sense of futility when it came to finding a positive place for the past in their art. They could do so; but it would warp and deny the social reality that they knew so well. Consequently Cooper, in *The*

Bravo (1830–31), acknowledged his contemporaries' belief that "the enjoyment of the past is like the pleasure of the fool who dreams of the wine he drank yesterday." And George Henry Boughton's illustration for *The Scarlet Letter,* called "Hester and the Clergyman," used as a caption Hawthorne's rhetorical *cri de coeur*: "The past is gone! Wherefore should we linger upon it now?" These were not the personal sentiments of Irving, Cooper, and Hawthorne. They were manifestations of cultural criticism.[75]

How then can we explain those traces of the past and selective enthusiasms for tradition that do come to mind when we think about the United States between Independence and the Civil War? The answer lies in the word "selective," and more particularly as well as precisely in an assertion made by Henry T. Tuckerman in 1864: "Except for the purpose of literary art and historical study . . . the past is rarely appreciated and little known."[76]

Chapter 3

MOTIFS OF MORALITY, MYTH, AND MEMORY IN ANTEBELLUM CULTURE

DURING THE FIRST half of the nineteenth century there were, to be sure, diverse objects and manifestations of memory along with the emergence of some self-appointed "custodians" and institutions that took an interest in tradition. We cannot overlook them because quite a few survived the dramatic cultural transformation caused by the Civil War, and they either planted seeds that flowered later or else played a direct role in the growth of American memory that followed the war. We must not, moreover, ignore the function of history in the quest for national identity during the antebellum decades, particularly the fuss that was occasionally made over "Founders"—whether they be Pilgrim, Puritan, or Revolutionary founders. Nor can we neglect the emergence of a Southern military tradition, which also left an enduring legacy.[1]

What seems most significant about American memory during this era, however, is its highly problematic nature: What part might it play in shaping notions of national identity? Whether historic sites and source materials would survive at all, and if so, with whose sponsorship? How to reconcile the history and traditions of Native Americans, if at all, with conventional notions of national memory? And what the relative impact would be of written history, which tended to moralize about the past, and of commemorative orations, which commonly mythicized the past. If the development of American memory has provided fertile ground for dualistic tendencies, the roots and tendrils of those double foliations are surely to be found embedded in the generations between the 1790s and the 1850s.

In order to appreciate the complexities of this period, it is useful to bear in mind that an orientation toward tradition in private lives antedated the appearance of any general or societal enthusiasm for myth and memory in the public culture. People who lived in small agrarian settlements during the eighteenth century—and a preponderant majority of American colonists did—cherished the ideal of family continuity within a fixed community. They resisted disruptions or changes in that pattern, just as (we now know) Americans active during the first third of the nineteenth century frequently felt reluctant to accept the shift to participatory politics so commonly regarded as an essential attribute of the Jacksonian era. Traditional folkways remained a potent force in private lives as well as in the civic culture of communities.[2]

Similarly, American uncertainty about the appropriate balance between Nature and the Progress of Civilization supplies a critical issue for anyone who hopes to understand the transformation of values that occurred during the middle decades of the nineteenth century. In matters of popular taste, for example, people loved prints made from landscape paintings that emphasized nature in its pristine form; yet the growing vogue of dime novels by the later 1850s repetitiously featured the American Revolution, restless movement into Daniel Boone's Kentucke, and then, with growing frequency, annexation of the West. It somehow seems fitting, therefore, that Daniel Webster liked to retreat to the solitude of nature when he needed to prepare his well-known addresses that commemorated key moments in American history. He mentally composed most of his 1825 Bunker Hill oration, for example, while wading in a trout stream as the compleat American angler.[3]

In contrast to the themes emphasized in chapter two, this one acknowledges that certain commemorative occasions did occur, that myths and some attendant rituals did emerge, that works of history (fiction, epic poetry, and non-fiction) achieved popularity even though their thrust was as much moral as memorial. A modest number of interesting antiquarians and tradition-oriented organizations appeared during the antebellum decades; and editors, preachers, artists, entertainers, and textbook writers tried to package the past in palatable ways. Whereas Americans conceded the existence of Native American traditions, they expressed profound ambiguity about them while essentially ignoring the existence of African-American culture. The chapter concludes with a brief look at the transformational role of the Civil War era in terms of its impact upon the function of change, feelings of loss, and pastness in American culture.

I

THOUGHTFUL OBSERVERS have noticed that in a new society some satisfactory explanation (or even myth) of origins can be a vital ingredient in the formation of national identity. We should not be surprised to find, therefore, that during the last decades of the eighteenth century and early years of the nineteenth the landing of the Pilgrim Fathers (the presence of mothers was taken for granted) became a powerful legend for New Englanders, commemorated annually on Forefathers' Day (December 21). What may startle us, however, is the fictive history and ideological manipulation of the Mayflower Compact. It had been almost entirely ignored by orators until 1802, when John Quincy Adams initiated a tradition that lasted about a generation in which the Compact was viewed as part of the repudiation of English domination and as the inauguration of indigenous American government, derived of necessity from a state-of-nature situation.[4]

During the 1830s and '40s, however, spokesmen for the Whig Party eulogized the Pilgrim Fathers as prototypical anti-Jacksonians, and the Mayflower Compact as a milestone in the growth of social order and cohesion. It represented, moreover, the transmission of English liberty rather than a rejection of ecclesiastical tyranny. As Charles Wentworth Upham insisted on Forefathers' Day in 1846: Plymouth Rock should be recognized as "the point from which the ever-advancing and ever-expanding wave of Anglo-Saxon liberty and light began to flow over America." The ebb and flow of ideological currents around Plymouth Rock have exposed, for more than two centuries, shifts in the nation's value system.[5]

The Pilgrims' story was so plastic and susceptible to manipulation for two reasons: first, unlike the Puritans, they did not leave behind an abundant "paper trail" of sermons, journals, correspondence, and records. Legends take hold more easily in the absence of countervailing information. Second, also unlike the Puritans, the Pilgrims were comparatively non-ideological; and once they had transplanted themselves, not especially dogmatic or theologically innovative. Whereas the Puritans have become controversial in American culture over the past century, the Pilgrims have not. The explanation for that distinction transcends our fondness for the holiday of Thanksgiving.

Despite significant historical differences between the Puritans and Pilgrims, however, there has long been a tendency—it dates back to the Plymouth Bicentennial in 1820, at the very least—to blend the two groups, to subsume William Bradford's small band of Separatists within John Winthrop's Great Migration of non-separating Congregationalists. And then, having blurred meaningful differences, Daniel Webster and the orators who were his contemporaries as well as their successors simply declared that Puritanism somehow was America's oldest tradition.[6] For more than half a century, that proved to be a popular tune. After the 1880s it began to strike a discordant note, however, as we shall see in sections II and III below.

Surpassing Humpty Dumpty, however, Calvinist eggheads fell from grace not once but twice. Puritanism as a tradition cracked toward the close of the nineteenth century because social change and new values altered the vision that many Americans had of what their culture ideally ought to be. Earlier in the nineteenth century Puritanism as a pious memory slipped rather than fell—it slipped into a secondary role behind the American Revolutionary experience because the latter was more recent and could explain a new civic culture and its institutional

3.1 Anon., *Parson Mason Locke Weems* (182–?), oil on canvas. Courtesy of the National Portrait Gallery, Smithsonian Institution.

3.2 Charles Willson Peale, *William Wirt* (n.d.: 1772–1834), oil on canvas. Courtesy of the Denver Art Museum.

arrangements; because Puritanism was a regional phenomenon whereas the Revolution was not only national but a unifying event; and because the military heroes of the Revolution basked in a plausible glory that made remote Calvinists pale by comparison.[7]

Besides, in a heterogeneous society that was becoming appreciably more expansive, the biographies of brave soldiers seemed preferable to the hagiography of saints. Cotton Mather's *Magnalia Christi Americana* was no match for Parson Weems and William Wirt as American Plutarchs (figs. 3.1 and 3.2). The nimbuses above numerous saints cast less of a glow than luminous figures of an indigenous Enlightenment: Franklin, Jefferson, Adams, Rittenhouse, Rush, Jay, Hamilton, and Madison, among others.

A persuasive case has been made that two generations of Americans who matured between 1790 and the 1830s connected their sense of freedom with a commitment to liberation from institutional constraints. That salubrious liberation, however, precipitated a crisis of identity because repudiation of the past left Americans of the young republic without a firm foundation on which to base a shared sense of their social selves.[8] In response to that crisis of cultural identity and legitimacy, the post-Revolutionary generation created a mythos of the American Revolution: a mythos that manifested itself in biography and history, art and fiction, poetry and oratory. Such a two-dimensional mythos, a *trompe l'oeil* of the historical imagination, served as a surrogate for history, and somehow fulfilled the nation's not-yet-so-compelling need for a sense of tradition.

Fourth of July festivities did manage to evoke, more often than not, an expected degree of patriotic fervor along with a less predictable yet pronounced frequency of paeans to memory (figs. 3.3 and 3.4). They were genuinely joyous occasions, and they anticipated the broadened base of concern for memory that would transform the cultural scene following the 1870s. At a dinner held in Richmond, Virginia, on July 4, 1837, toasts were offered to "the Memory of Washington" and to "the Patriots of the Revolution. When the festal cup is brimm'd, let memory twine the rosy wreath with the cypress that shades their graves." At another, sponsored by the Light Infantry Blues, glasses were raised to the memories of Washington, John Marshall (a native son of Richmond), and to "the memory of the Heroes and Patriots who fell in the last struggle with Great Britain," a reference to the War of 1812. At Beech Creek Academy in Hanover County, Virginia, remembrance made a gesture of intersectional respect with toasts to "the heroes and soldiers of the Revolution" and to "the memory of Jefferson, Adams and Monroe."[9]

This determination to honor heroes of the Revolution may have had a sectional emphasis, but it was genuinely a national gesture. Virginians willingly drank to John Adams. The gesture might also be non-partisan by that time. In 1837 and 1838 people drank to the memories of Federalists Washington and Marshall, to Democratic-Republicans Jefferson and Madison, to politicians now above party like James Monroe (who had actually opposed the Constitution half a century earlier in 1788), and to foreigners like Lafayette. Memory could sometimes cast a non-partisan net because it had been mythicized.[10]

In a new and busy land that largely lacked moments explicitly devoted to remembering the past, the Fourth of July served several purposes and in turn became memorable itself. Judges commonly sentenced convicted felons to be incarcerated until the next July Fourth.[11] Liberty's day of yesteryear thereby remained vital. It was inevitably a day of notable births as well as immortal deaths. Stephen C. Foster, for example, was born on July 4, 1826. When the news arrived several days later that John Adams and Thomas Jefferson had both died that very same day, friends of the family proposed that the baby be named Jefferson Adams Foster. Happily, he had already been designated Stephen Collins, in honor of a family friend; and the parents put friendship above patriotism.[12]

It seemed an omen of some sort when Nathaniel Hawthorne entered the world on July 4, 1804, in Salem; and Henry David Thoreau deliberately took up his austere abode in the woods by Walden Pond forty-one years later, on July 4, 1845. By the 1820s and '30s, the Fourth of July and the rituals associated with it had explicitly become central to civil religion in America. The editor of Lexington, Virginia's, *Gazette* asserted that the Fourth "ought to be regarded as our political Sabbath," a day unmarked by political rancor. On July 4, 1838, the highlight of the day in Albemarle County, Virginia, occurred when a resident "read

3.3   John Lewis Krimmel, *Fourth of July in Center Square* (1812), oil on canvas. The Pennsylvania Academy of the Fine Arts, Philadelphia. Pennsylvania Academy Purchase (from the Estate of Paul Beck, Jr.).

3.4   William P. Chappel, *Tammany Society Celebrating the Fourth of July, 1812* (1869), oil on canvas. Courtesy of the New-York Historical Society, New York City.

from the original draft of the Declaration, in the hand-writing of Mr. Jefferson himself. . . . This sacred relic of 'the times that tried men's souls,' was exhibited to the audience."[13]

A century earlier Montesquieu had devoted an essay to the religious politics of statesmen in ancient Rome. "They made a religion for the state," he wrote, "while others had made the state for religion."[14] Just as Montesquieu's famous dictum concerning the viability of republican government only in compact geo-political units had to be revised by James Madison in defending the new Constitution, so the judgment quoted above needs to be adjusted in order to understand civil religion in antebellum America. Residents of the young republic consecrated the state's origin and made a fetish of the Union that resulted. In 1825 Jefferson recalled "the sacred attachments of our fellow citizens to the event of which the paper of July 4, 1776, was but the Declaration, the genuine effusion of the soul of our country at that time. Small things may, perhaps, like the relics of saints, help to nourish our devotion to this holy bond of our Union, and keep it longer alive and warm in our affections."[15]

Civil religion sparked fireworks, by the way, when sabbatarianism came into conflict with the punctual observance of patriotic occasions. If the anniversary of a momentous event happened to fall on a Sunday, harsh diatribes were heard over the issue of postponing the actual celebration until Monday. When a parade, military display, and fireworks were held in New Orleans on Sunday, January 8, 1837, to honor Andrew Jackson's great victory there in 1815, a writer insisted that his countrymen should not, "in the midst of our patriotic exultation, forget our obligations to the religion of our own land . . . for no patriotism can flow from pure fountains, which overwhelms such considerations." The exposition is a bit muddled, but the sentiment is clear.[16]

Homemade fireworks and whiskey were not the sole sources of injury to body and soul on such festal occasions (fig. 3.5). Punishing heat, overzealous patriotism, and poor judgment killed Zachary Taylor. On July 4, 1850, he gave an oration at a ceremony associated with erecting the Washington Monument in the nation's capital. Because of the blazing heat, President Taylor drank an excess of ice water, then ate cherries, and followed with iced milk. That evening he suffered an attack of "cholera morbus" (probably acute gastroenteritis) and ran a very high fever from which he died four days later. Imprudent behavior on commemorative occasions could be lethal.

John Jay, a grandson of the first Chief Justice and U.S. minister to Austria during the 1860s, behaved more sensibly when he attended the Independence Day celebration held at Paris in 1866. (Presumably the heat was less suffocating than it had been in 1850 at Washington.) Jay suggested to a group of Americans gathered on that occasion that "it was time for the American people to lay the foundation of a National Institution and Gallery of Art." Such an idea had been in the air for

3.5 Susan Merritt, *Picnic Scene* [Fourth of July] (c. 1853), watercolor and collage on paper. Courtesy of the Art Institute of Chicago. Gift of Elizabeth R. Vaughan, 1950.

several decades.[17] Although it would not finally achieve fruition until the twentieth century, this sort of sentiment on behalf of institutions that might embody and promote national culture warrants our attention because the apparent achievement of such a goal would eventually provide a genuine stimulus to national pride.

I I

THE TITLE of a long-forgotten volume published in 1856 is fairly representative of manifestations of interest in memory—such as they were—to be found at that time. This oversized book, which included steel engravings of art works like Thomas Cole's *Dream of Arcadia,* is what we today would call a coffee table object. It nevertheless enjoyed a certain vogue and it *was* perused. The front cover flashed its name: *Ornaments of Memory, or the Beauty of History, Romance, and Poetry.* "Ornaments of memory" seems a very suitable way to describe written history, commemorative orations, and the growing desire for public monuments during the middle decades of the nineteenth century. Let us consider those three categories in sequence.

A fair amount of history was written, purchased, and even read at the time. That much is scarcely a secret. A distinction not ordinarily made, however, concerns the goal of this body of historical literature. Its purpose was not primarily memory, but morality. George Bancroft viewed history as an appropriate surrogate for religion because he believed in the centrality of moral progress over time. William Hickling Prescott assumed that he should keep a moral theme before his readers. John Lothrop Motley and Francis Parkman articulated variations on such themes. Although Parkman regarded the early Jesuit missionaries to North America as heroic martyrs, he also observed that their "equivocal morality . . . [was] built on the doctrine that all means are permissible for saving souls from perdition, and that sin itself is no sin when its object is 'the greater glory of God.' "[18]

If we hear much about morality and little of memory from the famous "romantic" historians, the same is true at the level of popular and mass culture among their contemporaries. The primary message of history in antebellum schoolbooks was also morality. In the case of Samuel G. Goodrich (better known by his pen name, Peter Parley), for example, moral instruction was the chief aim of his histories that appeared relentlessly for half a century starting in 1822. That applies equally to Emma Willard, a pioneer in education for women whose *History of the United States* first appeared in 1847. She repeatedly stressed the "youthful simplicity" and "maiden purity" of America. Our history was more instructive, and hence superior, because of its high moral quotient.[19]

While those who wrote history moralized about the past, those who gave orations perpetrated the casual mythicization of memory. On occasion, though not often, a contemporary would explicitly deplore this drift. In 1858, for instance, a speaker in Boston lamented "the irreverent tendency of the time—our careless indifference to the associations and memory of the past."[20]

Rather than heed that admonition, however, thousands heard (and millions eventually memorized) Daniel Webster's magisterial evocations of an inspiring golden age that was, in its tense as well as intent, the past perfect: "The First Settlement of New England" (given at Plymouth, December 22, 1820); "The Bunker Hill Monument" (at Charlestown, Massachusetts, June 17, 1825); "The Character of Washington" (Washington, D.C., February 22, 1832); "Remarks at Lexington, Massachusetts" (April 20, 1835); "Convention at Valley Forge" (October 3, 1844); "Remarks at the Revere House" (Boston, November 4, 1850); "Pilgrim Festival at New York in 1850" (December 22, 1850); and many others.[21]

Webster seems to have been in all the best places at all the right moments. If his rhetoric made them live in memory, his omissions and distortions helped to make them mythical. There is more irony than hypocrisy in the title that he chose for an address delivered eight months prior to his death: "The Dignity and Importance of History" (New York, February 23, 1852). We cannot stain him with the charge of cynicism because he genuinely believed the myths he declaimed; and so did most of his auditors.[22]

Quite a few of Webster's orations were occasioned by the beginning or the completion of a monument: there he stood at Bunker Hill when that marker was started in 1825, and once again eighteen years later for its dedication. In that very year, 1843, the Chief Justice of Rhode Island declared in an address: "O! let us build monuments to the past."[23] The spirit may have been willing, but public and private purses were inadequate. As we saw in chapter two, a curious combination of republican patience and human indifference tended to prevail until the mood of Reconstruction following the Civil War brought obelisks to village greens in memory of each community's casualties. During the first six decades of the nineteenth century, the justice's plea seems to have been largely ignored.[24]

In 1857, Henry T. Tuckerman proposed in the name of "remembrance" that Washington's birthday be made a national holiday. His motive was more political (in a constructive sense) than purely patriotic or worshipful. Sensitive to heightened sectional tensions, Tuckerman hoped that such a day might induce "a unanimity of feeling and of rites, which shall fuse and mold into one pervasive emotion the divided hearts of the country. . . ." He then suggested that tourism and heroic symbolism could somehow combine to calm troubled waters: "The fanaticism of party strife has awakened the wise and loyal to a consciousness of the inestimable value of that great example and canonized name [Washington], as a bond of union, a conciliating memory, and a glorious watchword."[25] American history, sanctified as memory and moralized in the person of George Washington, appeared to *some* people to possess adhesive value.

I I I

ANDREW HASWELL GREEN and Henry T. Tuckerman were practical men of affairs, but also genteel antiquarians in a sense that had no pejorative connotations at the time. To be a self-appointed custodian of the past did not seem contemptible, yet it tended to mark a man as being quaint if not quirky. One might indulge the whim of becoming an antiquarian or collector if one had independent means. Even when impelled by local or patriotic pride, however, it was extremely hard to make a livelihood from memories or memorializing.

The handful who succeeded had their ups and downs; but a collective profile gives us some hint of "remembrancing" as a vocation in mid-nineteenth-century America. John Warner Barber (1798–1885), engraver and regional historian, came from East Windsor, Connecticut, an old river valley town. He relied upon images to promote religion and history. It is symptomatic that in evangelical America he enjoyed considerably more success with *The Bible Looking-Glass* (1866), which preached the Gospel by means of pictures, than with *The History and Antiquities of New England, New York, and New Jersey* (1841), or *Incidents in American History* (1847), or *Connecticut Historical Collections* (1836). Henry Howe (1816–1893), a pea from the same pod, produced *Historical Collections of Virginia* (1845) and *Historical Collections of Ohio* (1847), popular pictorial works that telescoped past into present by means of travel through time as well as space.

Ephraim G. Squier (1821–1888), a journalist, diplomat, and self-taught archaeologist, moved to Chillicothe, Ohio, in 1844 and published the *Scioto Gazette*. In collaboration with Edwin H. Davis he studied the remains of the Mound Builders' civilization. The Smithsonian Institution published their findings in 1847, and four years later brought out another work by Squier, *Aboriginal Monuments in the State of New York*, that long remained authoritative. In 1860 he moved to New York City and became chief editor at Frank Leslie's publishing house. Under Squier's direction, *Frank Leslie's Pictorial History of the American Civil War* appeared in two volumes (1861–62).[26] His contemporary Joel Munsell (1808–1880) also combined the crafts of public-spirited printer, editor, and antiquarian through a roller-coaster career that took him from Greenfield, Massachusetts, over the Berkshires to Albany. He ought to be remembered, yet remains long forgotten, for his *Every Day Book of History and Chronology* (1858) and *The Annals of Albany* (1850–60) in ten volumes.

The career of John Fanning Watson (1779–1860) is especially indicative of the good faith efforts and failures of an antebellum antiquarian. In 1821 he published an open letter in *Poulson's American Daily Advertiser* in which he suggested that elderly Philadelphians should relate whatever they could recall of customs and manners in eighteenth-century Philadelphia. Despite the indifference that he encountered, Watson devised in 1822–23 a series of questions for "aged" persons in the area. In 1823 he admonished Richard Peters, an elderly lawyer, judge, and Revolutionary patriot, to "try to tell all the traditions you have ever heard." A year later he sought, once again, to awaken the public "to the utility of bringing out their traditions and ancient family records."[27]

Early in November 1824, Watson helped to launch the Society for the Commemoration of the Landing of William Penn (on the occasion of the 142nd anniversary of that event). Although the group decided to limit their activities to annual dinners, some members envisioned a more vigorous society that would preserve antiquities and even promote research. On December 2, 1824, the Historical Society of Pennsylvania was born of that aspiration. It moved slowly, however, and in 1830 Watson published his *Annals of Philadelphia*. One paper praised it as a "mass of traditionary lore, which but for him, must soon have passed into oblivion."[28]

3.6   Ben: Perley Poore at Indian Hill Farm, West Newbury, Massachusetts.
Courtesy of the Essex Institute, Salem, Massachusetts.

The career of Watson's Massachusetts contemporary Francis Calley
Gray (1790–1856) is instructive because it illustrates the ambivalence of
a nationalist who sought to compete with Europeans on their own
terms. Gray became the first serious collector of European prints on this
continent. His biographer finds his predilection consistent with a "personality dedicated for half a century to the advancement of American
culture in competition with that of Europe. Yet unlike the nativist
school, Gray based his hopes for the intellectual triumph of the New
World on the accomplishment of the Old."[29] Gray's remarkable collection has long been part of the Fogg Art Museum at Harvard University.

It is instructive to contrast Gray's taste and propensities as a collector
with those of another Massachusetts man born thirty years later, Ben:
Perley Poore (1820–1887), of Indian Hill in West Newbury (fig. 3.6).
Although he became a politically engaged journalist in Washington, and
eventually conducted historical research and edited documents for the
government, Poore developed a passion for the past quite early. From
1845 until 1847 he made investigations in Europe concerning the colonial history of Massachusetts. At midcentury he started to collect ceramics, metalware, furniture, and architectural elements. Much of this
material came to be displayed in period room settings at his home called
Indian Hill. He sought, in particular, objects that had historic associations: pieces of china and furniture that had been used in the White
House by every president from Madison to Lincoln; and a set of chairs
that once belonged to George Washington. For connections closer to
home he had a plain wooden chair which accompanied Newbury's first

settlers from England during the 1630s and a desk which had been owned by John Quincy Adams.[30] If Ben: Perley Poore is important as one of the earliest and most comprehensive seekers of Americana, he is also notable precisely because he was so unusual. His contemporaries liked and admired him; but they did not emulate him.

A comparable pattern appears when we look at tradition-oriented organizations that arose to promote the remembrance of national and local roots in a physically mobile society. Region-related associations seem to have thrived and enjoyed greater longevity than national ones—partially, perhaps, because of the psychological impact of all that mobility, but partially because nationwide organizations established prior to 1860 were not destined for permanence. An American Historical Society existed in the 1830s and '40s, but did not survive.[31] The Cape Cod Association was chartered in May 1851 by a group of prosperous Bostonians who shared Cape Cod ancestry. (A historian named Frederick Freeman brazenly promoted sales of his two-volume history of Cape Cod [1859, 1862] by dedicating it to the officers of the Cape Cod Association!)

As the out-migration of New Englanders persisted during the first half of the nineteenth century, New England societies sprang up and flourished in various locations. The New England Society of New York (the city) came first. Despite the preponderance of men from Connecticut among its founders, its initial dinner was held on December 21, 1805, and gave priority to the Pilgrims of Plymouth Plantation. Glasses were raised in response to four toasts: "The City of Leyden" and "John Carver," followed by "John Winthrop" and "The Memory of Washington."[32] The Father of His Country had been dead for only six years, so he needed no given name. Memories of Carver and Winthrop seemed much more remote. In the dim shade of memory, their full names were deemed necessary.

When the Society met on December 23, 1839 (to avoid a Sunday), the occasion seemed noteworthy both for the oration given at the Broadway Tabernacle by the principal speaker and because of the hostile press coverage. As for the latter, a reporter declared that Congressman Robert C. Winthrop of Boston spoke well but for too long. Following the dinner, however, "the speeches were nearly all stupid."[33] Could this denunciation have been prompted by a Yorker's gut response to Yankee arrogance? Perhaps. But just as likely it represented the puzzled reaction of a present-minded generation to what H. L. Mencken once called "bloviations" about the past. The Yorkers' day had not yet come, never mind their dinner.

Winthrop conjured up the spirits of greatness past, though not in any sort of coherent historical sequence: Queen Elizabeth, Miles Standish and the Pilgrims, Columbus, various other explorers, and then the settlement of early Virginia, which Winthrop praised. His ecumenical sectionalism reached its limit, however. Winthrop caused an audible stir when he criticized Southern slavery. After that he insisted upon John Adams's parity with Thomas Jefferson. "Though Virginia produced the hand that framed the Declaration of Independence, New England produced the eloquent tongue that first advocated its principles."[34]

If inter-regional rivalry reduced the impact of tradition-oriented associations, government at both the national and state levels scarcely considered itself a custodian of tradition at all, or even a sponsor of memory. The Rotunda of the United States Capitol was designed to accommodate eight majestic paintings on historical subjects. John Trumbull received the first commission in 1817; yet the full project was not finished until 1855. Partisan conflict and controversy plagued it throughout. After Trumbull completed his four renderings of Revolutionary events in 1824, thirteen years elapsed before agreement could be reached concerning the subjects and artists for three more panels. The eighth commission would not be issued until 1847; and perhaps it is no accident that the last turned out to be the least effective. *Discovery of the Mississippi by DeSoto, A.D. 1541*, by William H. Powell, simply isn't a very good painting. The other three latecomers at least had the virtue of geographical diversity: John Vanderlyn's *Landing of Columbus;* John G. Chapman's *Baptism of Pocahontas at Jamestown;* and Robert W. Weir's *Embarkation of the Pilgrims at Delft Haven, Holland.*[35]

During the 1790s the Department of State received official recognition as permanent repository of the nation's important documents, such as the Declaration of Independence, the Constitution, and papers of the Continental Congress. It is clear that most secretaries of state did not want to be bothered, and so they understandably relegated this archival responsibility to petty functionaries. In Robert C. Winthrop's Centennial Oration on July 4, 1876, he remarked that he had casually examined the original draft of the Declaration on several occasions. In 1884, when Mellen Chamberlain, a New England antiquarian, needed information about the Declaration, he corresponded with the Chief of the Bureau of Rolls in the State Department library.[36] Not until 1922 did the Department shed responsibility for all these sacred texts and shift them to the Library of Congress. So much for its passive function as keeper of the nation's documentary past.

Only one Secretary of State took an active role; and, perhaps predictably, that would be John Quincy Adams, who embodied a strong respect for history and tradition. In 1821 his appearance at the celebration of July 4 in Washington did much to make the day a distinguished occasion. He read passages from the original Declaration (there is no record that he held it with white cotton gloves) and gave an address that emphasized the Declaration as a harbinger of popular sovereignty. Two years later Adams authorized an exact facsimile to be engraved on copperplate and two hundred copies printed on parchment. As a result,

high-quality replicas could be seen throughout the United States. Finally, in the winter of 1823–24 the State Department took a most
unusual initiative. It authorized and distributed an engraving of John
Trumbull's exhaustively researched Rotunda painting of the Declaration being solemnly signed in Independence Hall.[37]

The capricious character of archival politics is best illustrated by the
career of Peter Force (1790–1868), a Washington printer and editor
with a passion for properly documenting the nation's genesis. Gathering and printing a truly comprehensive collection required approval by
the Secretary of State and significant appropriations by Congress. Secretary Edward Livingston received Force's first proposal in 1831. His
successor, Louis McLane, had little interest in the project; but Democratic Secretary John Forsyth (1834–41) became its advocate. The enterprise suffered a series of ups and downs during the subsequent
decade and finally, when William L. Marcy became Secretary in 1853,
he successfully sabotaged Force's dedicated effort. When Lewis Cass
replaced Marcy in 1857 there seemed to be a flicker of hope; but Cass
chose not to support Force, and that terminated a most remarkable yet
incomplete multi-volume work that scholars still use today. There are
two separate series, reflecting the rhythms of partisanship where none
should ever have appeared: *Tracts and Other Papers Relating to the
Origin, Settlement, and Progress of the Colonies in North America,
from the Discovery of the Country to the Year 1776* (1836–46 in four
volumes) and *American Archives* (1837–53 in nine volumes).[38]

The challenge of finding, preserving, and publishing essential sources
pertaining to the nation's history remained highly problematic for more
than a century. In 1858, the year after Force's hopes were finally
dashed, a few unusual individuals were just beginning to acknowledge
the magnitude and cultural significance of the problem. As James Parton, known as the father of American biography (fig. 3.7), wrote to a
historian, Henry B. Dawson: "I have long thought that the best way to
make the American people acquainted with the history of their country
is to render accessible to them the *sources* of that history—the raw
material as well as the woven narrative."[39]

During the first half of the nineteenth century, only a few Americans
had given any thought to the need, not only to preserve historic documents, but to transform chimerical wisps of memory into enduring
form and then to convert records into memoirs at the very least and
historical narratives at best. Not once but twice in 1805 John Adams
chided his old friend Benjamin Rush for irresponsible behavior: "I am
extremely sorry you relinquished your design of writing memoirs of the
American Revolution. The burning of your documents was, let me tell
you, a very rash action, and by no means justifiable upon good principles." Following another scolding three months later, Adams added:
"From the memoirs of individuals the true springs of events and the
real motives of actions are to be made known to posterity."[40]

More than six months after that, however, Adams had his own confes-

3.7   Oliver Lay, *James Parton* (1868), oil on canvas. Courtesy of the National Portrait Gallery, Smithsonian Institution.

sion to make. His sins of omission and commission nearly matched Rush's rash act of arson. As usual, Adams's *mea culpa* calls our attention to his sense of self-importance: "Of all men who have acted a part in the great affairs of the world, I am afraid I have been the most careless and negligent in preserving papers. I must write too many things from memory, and oftentimes facts to which there is no other witness left alive. The task, besides, is so extensive that I have not time left to execute it."[41]

Although Adams's despair may have been distinctive, the scenario he described must have been commonplace. And with the passage of time and proliferation of public events, the recognition that had prompted Adams's anguish became more pervasive, even among those much less prominent and self-conscious than he. Half a century later one old pioneer wrote to another about their experiences in opening the Ohio Valley to westward expansion: "You are wish[ed] to rescue from oblivion all the particulars you can; for how soon such events die out of the memory of the living—events which if committed to writing would invest history with ever growing freshness and interest."[42]

For another eighty years, however, the safekeeping of public documents—and hence of American historical memory—would remain largely a matter of private initiative and institutions. In 1867 Congress accepted a report that Peter Force's library and manuscripts constituted a national resource. The members appropriated $100,000 to purchase Force's collection, and it was loaded on wagons which lumbered to the U.S. Capitol. (A national archive would not exist until the 1930s, and a proper home for the Library of Congress not until the late 1890s.)[43]

For the government to acquire such a collection, however, was decid-

3.8   Thomas Sully, *Jared Sparks* (1831), oil on canvas. Courtesy of Reynolda House Museum of American Art, Winston-Salem, North Carolina.

edly not the norm and did not set a precedent—not for many years at least. In 1866 William Gilmore Simms's extraordinary collection (more than thirty years in the making) of documents from the Revolutionary era was sold to the Long Island Historical Society in Brooklyn, New York, a bizarre location for the Carolinian's treasures; and the superb library of Jared Sparks, one of the most eminent historians and the best-known documentary editor of his day (fig. 3.8), was purchased by the brand-new Cornell University, which had not yet opened its doors to students and still lacked a structure to house the Sparks collection. It was Cornell's distinction to buy rare books before it had a place to put them.[44]

The government simply was not ready to expand its role as custodian of the national past. In retrospect we can appreciate that purchasing the Force Papers was highly unusual rather than normative. Instead, in 1870 Secretary of State Hamilton Fish reorganized the State Department, along with its archives and library. Reducing the staff and accomplishing some budget cuts became an alternative to developing an acquisitions policy. The United States government had scant interest in national memory, and did not connect such interest as it did have to a documentary support system.[45]

From the vantage point of the late twentieth century we readily lose sight of the perspective of those who lived in the mid-nineteenth, when everything still seemed so new and when nearly everyone knew someone who had known participants in the Revolutionary generation. James Russell Lowell, writing in 1888, remembered quite well the mood at midcentury: "The hues of our dawn had scarcely faded from the sky. Men were still living who had seen the face and heard the voice

3.9   Richard Caton Woodville, *Old '76 and Young '48* (1849), oil on fabric. Courtesy of the Walters Art Gallery, Baltimore, Maryland.

of the most august personage in our history, and of others scarce less august than he. The traditions of our founders were fresh."[46]

That sense of intergenerational connectedness, bonded by intimacy, appears in such sermons as Lyman Beecher's *The Memory of Our Fathers* (1828) and in such paintings as *Old '76 and Young '48* (1849), in which a young officer recounts his experiences in the Mexican War of 1847–48 to a veteran of the War for Independence (fig. 3.9). A portrait of a Revolutionary hero hangs on the wall. Three African-American servants listen from the doorway. And, above all, representatives of three generations are present. The fact that members of the artist's family served as models for the scene simply personalizes the symbolic and realizes the myth while formalizing personal relations into a public statement.

I V

HOW CAN WE be sure that a sermon by Lyman Beecher or a genre painting by Richard Caton Woodville is culturally representative? The social theorist S. N. Eisenstadt has observed that lesser (and sometimes even spurious) intellectuals frequently enjoy particular importance in the construction of social and cultural traditions. The types of actors he has in mind may be teachers or clergymen, minor government officials or artists, or even individuals involved in popular entertainment. "It has become more and more apparent," Eisenstadt argues, "that secondary intellectuals may indeed play a central role in the broad process of construction and transmission of tradition. It may well be that it is they . . . who serve as channels of institutionalization, and even as possible creators of new types of symbols of cultural orientations, of traditions, and of collective and cultural identity."[47] For the period we have under consideration, that description is persuasively applicable to such diverse individuals as Mason Locke Weems and William Holmes McGuffey, Edward Everett and Robert C. Winthrop, Henry T. Tuckerman and Henry B. Dawson. In the era that we shall consider next, circa 1870–1915, it characterizes such influential figures as Edward Eggleston and S. Weir Mitchell, Martha J. Lamb and Alice Morse Earle, Paul Leicester Ford and Everett T. Tomlinson.

Timothy Flint (1780–1840), a Protestant missionary and writer from Massachusetts (Harvard College's class of 1800), provides for the antebellum era a veritable model of the "secondary intellectual" who channels myths and traditions. His novel *Shoshonee Valley* (1830) was the first to appear about the mountain men of the new and romantic trans-Mississippi frontier. A year later Flint edited the first widely read account of a trapper-hero's adventures, James Ohio Pattie's *Personal Narrative.* We cannot tell just how much of this swashbuckling tale is authentic and how much came straight from Flint's fertile imagination. In his Preface Flint included the customary declaration that he had not embellished the facts. But he offered the same disclaimer in his biography of Daniel Boone (1833), and we do know that it added or compounded more legends concerning Boone than any other single narrative. Flint's *Boone* enjoyed the popularity indicated by fourteen editions.[48]

Interestingly enough, whereas writers like Flint took extraordinary liberties with history yet insisted that they were faithful chroniclers, major novelists who were their contemporaries explicitly distinguished between traditions and true history; acknowledged that the former fed from the latter; and invariably invoked the writer's imperative of imagination in dealing with the local, regional, or national past. Washington Irving explained in the 1848 "Apology" to Knickerbocker's *History of New York* (1809) that his purpose "was to embody the traditions of our city in an amusing form" by means of "imaginative and whimsical associations so seldom met with in our new country." Therefore he satirized contemporary New York by preserving in amber bemused memories of its Golden Age. William Gilmore Simms's historical novel *The Yemassee* (1835) is set in South Carolina during the early eighteenth century. With the final chapter "our tale becomes history," that is, it emerges from the cloudy depths of time and verges upon the recorded past. "Where history dare not go," Simms explains, "it is then for poetry, borrowing a wild gleam from the blear eye of tradition, to couple with her own the wings of imagination, and overleap the boundaries of the defined and certain."[49]

By 1850, when Nathaniel Hawthorne wrote *The House of the Seven Gables,* he could turn to these and other forebears to build upon. He had also been thinking hard for almost a quarter century about the peculiar problem of writing romances in the United States. Although his lamentation about the lack of texture and tradition in American culture is commonly quoted from *The Marble Faun* (1860)—"a country where there is no . . . antiquity, no mystery, no picturesque and gloomy wrong, nor anything but a commonplace prosperity, in a broad and simple daylight"—his more complex and subtle comments on the relationship between history and tradition appear in *The House of the Seven Gables.* That relationship intrigued Hawthorne. He acknowledged that on occasion legends might transmit verities that strict history had somehow overlooked; yet he ultimately expressed a judicious mistrust of myths and legends, the popular manifestations of tradition. He phrased it this way in the very first chapter of *Seven Gables*: "Tradition,—which sometimes brings down truth that history has let slip, but is oftener the wild babble of the time, such as was formerly spoken at the fireside and now congeals in newspapers,—tradition is responsible for all contrary averments."[50]

As the novel proceeds, however, Hawthorne's predilection (most of the time) for history rather than tradition becomes much less important than his interest in the relationship between what people perceive as tradition and what he called "the transmitted vices of society." He noted both positive and negative attributes of collective memory with clear-headed sensitivity. The cultural role and viability of local legends obviously fascinated him, and he even wrote supportively of "chimney-corner tradition, which often preserves traits of character with marvelous fidelity." He nevertheless acknowledged the oppressiveness of "family traditions, which lingered, like cobwebs and incrustations of smoke, about the rooms and chimney corners of the House of the Seven Gables."[51]

Hawthorne recognized, however, to a greater degree than any of his contemporaries in the American Renaissance, that the past was not merely prologue to the present, but prophetic of it. From that perspective one ignored the past, meaning tradition as well as history, at one's peril. The old house served Hawthorne as a convenient symbol of the past precisely because of the villagers' tendency to ignore it—indeed, be oblivious to it. "It seemed as if the house stood in a desert, or, by some spell, was made invisible to those who dwelt around, or passed beside it; so that any mode of misfortune, miserable accident, or crime might happen in it without the possibility of aid."[52] Although we must not be

3.10   George P. A. Healy, *Henry Wadsworth Longfellow* (1862), oil on canvas. Courtesy of the Virginia Museum of Fine Arts, Richmond.

prisoners of the past, like Clifford and Hepzibah Pyncheon, neither should we impoverish our lives, our judgment, and our culture by neglecting its legacies.

Hawthorne's Bowdoin College classmate (1825) Henry Wadsworth Longfellow was more of an activist in terms of contemporary concerns, such as anti-slavery, yet he affirmed the cultural salience of tradition and myth less tentatively than Hawthorne. He did so self-consciously and confidently (fig. 3.10). Prior to the 1870s, only Parson Weems and possibly James Fenimore Cooper worked more effectively with quasi-historical materials to propagate American myths and popularize national legends. Longfellow took inchoate traditions and transformed them into memorable poetic narratives that millions mistook for history: *Evangeline* (1847), about the Acadians' tragic forced migration to Louisiana; *Hiawatha* (1855), his Indian edda; *The Courtship of Miles Standish* (1858), a Pilgrim pastoral that sold more than 15,000 copies on the first day of publication in Boston and London; and *The Tales of a Wayside Inn* (1863), which included "Paul Revere's Ride."

Longfellow not only achieved fabulous popularity with *Hiawatha,* his 150-page epic, but boldly carried off two rhetorical flourishes in his Introduction: the question, how do I know what I am about to relate? and then an explanation of why I have chosen to relate it. The Introduction starts with these two lines:

> *Should you ask me, whence these stories?*
> *Whence these legends and traditions. . . .*

After a few lyrical lines devoted to nature and geography, he supplies an answer: From the land of the Ojibways and the Dacotahs. Then more particularly:

> *I repeat them as I heard them*
> *From the lips of Nawadaha,*
> *The musician, the sweet singer.*[53]

The explanation gradually becomes more complicated and mystical. But with such categorical assertions, who could possibly doubt that Longfellow had a direct line to the Dacotahs? All that he had done was translate their hypnotic chant into English so that "Americans" could make a Native American myth of origins their very own.

Then the Introduction moves toward closure by seductively appealing to the reader to listen. If this is a rhythmic chant to be read, it is also a poem to be heard. The ear and the eye must co-operate in responding to *Hiawatha*, and they do so in such an effective way that the reader-auditor forgets to ask what nation? whose people? In the process, an act of cultural co-optation takes place.

> *Ye who love a nation's legends,*
> *Love the ballads of a people,*
> *That like voices from afar off*
> *Call us to pause and listen.*[54]

What Longfellow actually undertook is well established and does not need to be retold at length. Starting with virtually no knowledge of Native Americans, he read several works by the pioneering ethnographer of the Mississippi Valley, Henry Rowe Schoolcraft, and looked at the three hundred engravings in George Catlin's *Manners and Customs of the North American Indians* (1841). He examined a few other authorities, such as John Heckewelder, a Moravian missionary who wrote extensively about the Indians of the Susquehanna region in Pennsylvania.[55] Having absorbed a modicum of Indian folklore, tales, legends, and myths, he chose to weave together those that suited his purpose into the saga of a great culture hero: a George Washington of the primeval woods as it were, at one with nature and a devoted archetype of his people.

As the locale for his saga Longfellow chose Minnehaha Falls, which is actually quite close to Minneapolis, and around Lake Superior in general. He had not been there. He never even considered visiting there. And for an aesthetic form appropriate to an epic poem he turned to the "foreign" model most familiar to educated New Englanders, the Finnish *Kalevala*. Near the end, Longfellow could not resist the same troublesome temptation that Simms had succumbed to in *The Yemassee*: he jumped from primordial time to historical time, from some timeless age of Indian culture heroes to the seventeenth-century arrival of French missionaries. Longfellow later regretted this decision; but it really didn't matter. The poem swiftly became an immense international success.[56]

- In 1857 Senator Charles Sumner wrote to Longfellow from Scotland. Sumner reported seeing a handsome herd of cattle with a famous bull named Hiawatha and a cow called Minnehaha.[57]

- Augustus Saint-Gaudens, the American sculptor of French and Irish descent, loved *Hiawatha* as a schoolboy. When he reached Rome late in 1871 the very first project that he undertook was a statue of Hiawatha as a sadly pensive brave.[58]

The Tales of a Wayside Inn caught on with comparable speed. In 1864, less than a year after publication, Currier and Ives produced a colored lithograph, designed by Fanny Palmer, titled "The Wayside Inn." In 1870 James Madison Alden, a Yankee artist who provided some of the loveliest early sketches of the Pacific Northwest, produced a watercolor, "The Wayside Inn, Sudbury, Mass."[59]

Longfellow's afterlife, so to speak, supplies us with a hint of complexities yet to come. His work retained its remarkable appeal in middle-brow and in popular culture. In 1888, six years after his death, the Longfellow Statue Association of Portland, Maine, unveiled a statue of the poet and presented it to the city of his birth. An address delivered by the Association's president contrasted the rich trove of national memories now present with the vacuum that had existed earlier in the century. He therefore praised Longfellow for being able to write so creatively in an America that was culturally barren and devoid of literary traditions.[60]

Among an educated social elite, however, we find a few souls actively seeking to disentangle what really happened from fraudulent but beloved myths. In 1909, for example, Charles Francis Adams, Jr., fulminated against Longfellow for his foolishness and against fellow Brahmin Thomas Wentworth Higginson for perpetuating that foolishness. "The immense vitality of an historical myth," Adams wrote, "is proverbial; and every historical investigator has had good occasion to realize how impossible it is to 'exorcise,' so to speak, a popularly accepted legend." Adams explained that he had attempted such an exorcism "in the matter of Mr. Longfellow, and the strange perversion he has given to hard historical facts as respects Paul Revere and his famous ride, as well as other more remote, but not less interesting New England and Acadian legends."[61]

Adams added that he had been particularly appalled by a letter from Higginson that appeared in the *Boston Evening Transcript*. He could not at first determine whether Higginson "really believed in this tradition, as an historical fact; or whether he used it simply to make a good literary point, assuming that everyone knew how completely it was now discredited, and how long ago it had been thoroughly exploded." Adams then launched a tirade against Higginson for accepting the myth that Thomas Jefferson rode on horseback to the Capitol for his inauguration (rather than going by carriage) and hitched his own horse to a paling.[62] Adams preferred truth to fairy tales, especially if the tales were intended to exemplify an egalitarian ethos. Truth is particularly preferable to fiction when the fiction sustains a value system that one finds unwarranted.

V

I AM PERSUADED that *Hiawatha*'s popularity resulted, at least in part, from the solace it provided in assuaging the American conscience. It offered an acceptable resolution of an early "American dilemma": namely, what to do about Native American traditions. Longfellow took collections of ethnographic material and converted them into imaginative literature that exhibited a proud yet primitive people finally giving way to a more accomplished society foredestined to supplant them. *Hiawatha* salvaged the memories of a race fated to vanish from this land. Consequently, reading the epic and regarding it as part of *American* tradition seemed the next best thing to saving the Indian. Knowing and loving *Hiawatha* meant knowing the noble savage and perpetuating his traditions. Embarrassment (even shame) could be supplanted by vicarious pride via epic enchantment set in a remote and unknown place.

Anticipations of this psychological process began to appear several decades prior to the publication of *Hiawatha.* Newspapers routinely published accounts of prehistoric Indian sites and ruins that had been found. They were non-threatening, somewhat mysterious (how old? what purpose?), and intriguing precisely because they were so enigmatic. "The 'far West' abounds in antiquities" was a typical leader from the *St. Louis Commercial Bulletin* for a story about Indian graves and earthenware that had been found near Fenton along the Meramac River.[63]

In 1837 several Eastern newspapers lavished praise upon E. G. Biddle's *Indian History and Biography*: "As a work that may most truly be considered *National,* we feel particular solicitude that it should be universally known to the United States, and that all our citizens should possess themselves of a copy." The book narrated a highly selective account of North American Indians and included 120 portraits from the War Department's "Indian Gallery." Even the King of England requested a copy![64] At a time when Indian removal to the West was in process and decades of Indian war remained imminent, the book's warm reception seems in retrospect an insensitive example of cultural appropriation.

Curiosity and legends about Pocahontas, for example, ranged from the serious to the frivolous. Queries about her and about possible extant portraits appeared in the press on occasion when someone undertook "a work on aboriginal history." Her appeal has never waned—perhaps because history tells us that she saved the life of one white hero and married another. She also appears to us as a non-threatening Indian. Whatever the explanation, a Pocahontas Memorial Association existed during the early decades of the twentieth century;[65] and Howard Chandler Christy's oil-on-canvas *Pocahontas* (1926) shows a lovely, poignant, and nubile young woman, along with the legs (only the legs) of Captain John Smith to remind us of her great service to the spread of European civilization.[66]

I must acknowledge, once again, the genuine concern to preserve Native American traditions expressed by Catlin and Schoolcraft, already mentioned, as well as by William Leete Stone, the Albany journalist and biographer of Joseph Brant, and by Lewis Henry Morgan of Aurora, New York, the authority on Iroquois culture and, in many respects, the founder of American ethnography. In 1844, Morgan wrote to Stone informing him that he had been elected to the Grand Order of the Iroquois. Almost all of its members were Cayuga, Seneca, Tuscarora, Onondaga, and Oneida Indians. "We now hope to enlist the interest and aid of those literary Gentlemen of our Republic who have distinguished themselves in the field of Indian History and literature."[67]

Morgan then went on to add a plaintive appeal that he would repeat on many future occasions, public as well as private: "We need somewhere in our Republic an Indian Order, which should aim to become the vast repository of all that remains to us of the Indians—their antiquities—their customs—eloquence—history—literature, indeed every thing pertaining to them which can be rescued from the oblivion to which it is rapidly hastening." He concluded, however, on a strange note that sounded more like the nostalgic white Indian than the serious ethnographer: "Distant generations must look back to the Indian age for the fables, the antiquities, and the romance of America."[68] Hiawatha was on his way.

Contradictory and ambivalent perceptions of the Native American are revealed most vividly in antebellum public art. A work of sculpture by Horatio Greenough, *The Rescue Group* (1837–51), was placed outside the U.S. Capitol in 1853. A massive frontiersman overwhelms from behind a nearly naked savage intent upon massacring the white man's cowering wife and child. (Significantly, perhaps, that statue has been in storage at the Capitol Power Plant since 1958.)[69]

By contrast, some of the carved reliefs within the Capitol Rotunda tell a different story: *Landing of the Pilgrims*, in which a more decorously clothed Algonquian Indian offers an ear of corn to a Pilgrim who has one boot on shore and the other still in a skiff—his spouse and son looking ludicrously pious behind his protective cloak; and *William Penn's Treaty with the Indians*, in which a scroll-bearing Friend ("Treaty 1682") shakes hands with an Olympic-looking athlete who holds a huge peace pipe prominently in his left hand. Pocahontas preserves John Smith (all of him) in a third; but in the fourth relief, *Conflict of Daniel*

Boone and the Indians, grim and mortal combat is occurring, and a fallen brave lies beneath the combatants' feet. These four reliefs, located above the doors leading into the Rotunda, were executed between 1825 and 1827.[70] Perhaps it is significant that the three harmonious vignettes drew upon episodes in seventeenth-century history, whereas white–Indian conflict on the frontier was very much a reality in 1826–27 when Enrico Causici carved Boone battling the ferocious, hook-nosed red man.

From the 1840s onward, however, the dominant motif for Eastern artists who wished to make a statement about Native Americans in national tradition would involve neither conflict nor corny welcoming scenes. Rather, it would be the "Last of the Mohicans" motif, a poignant scene in which no white person is present to witness the tragic but inevitable demise of a doomed people. We see it in Alvan T. Fisher's painting *Remnant of the Tribe Leaving the Hunting Ground of Their Fathers* (c. 1845),[71] and in the marble sculpture by Hiram Powers titled *The Last of the Tribe* (fig. 3.11). Although she is nude from the waist up and wears a squaw's skirt, her face seems very much that of a European Caucasian. The "true" last of her tribe was obviously not available to model in Powers's studio.

A few whites, then, at least considered the Indian's tragic part in the American past and present, even though they responded inconsistently to such issues as friend or foe? victim or villain? By contrast, the African-American appears silently and unobtrusively in some historical art concerning the War for Independence.[72] But any claims that might appear on behalf of black participation in national history would have to be made by blacks themselves and could expect to be largely ignored.[73] William C. Nell, who was born in Boston and worked with William Lloyd Garrison, subsequently helped Frederick Douglass publish the *North Star* in Rochester. In 1855 Nell published his *Colored Patriots of the American Revolution.* When the Massachusetts legislative body rejected his petition to appropriate funds for a public memorial to Crispus Attucks, Nell took the initiative and in 1858 successfully revived the annual celebration of March 5 as Crispus Attucks Day.[74]

Except for publication of *The Negro in the Rebellion* by William Wells Brown in 1866, the role of African-Americans in national memory remained nominal; and the dominant culture inclined to amnesia on the subject. Within the subculture, needless to say, all sorts of traditions persisted, were perpetuated, and after Emancipation were created anew.[75]

V I

PRIOR TO the Civil War such orators as Daniel Webster and Rufus Choate could expound upon sacred aspects of the American past,

3.11   Hiram Powers, *The Last of the Tribe* (1867–72), marble. Courtesy of the
National Museum of American Art, Smithsonian Institution. Museum Purchase in Memory of Ralph Cross Johnson.

but their voices did not fully resonate with the future-oriented mainstream and its values, which emphasized new institutions and manners
as a model for the changing world that would someday catch up.[76]

Because we customarily connect the 1860s with sectionalism, there
is a tendency to forget how important the Civil War was as a stimulus
to nationalism, both North *and* South. The phenomenon occurred at
two levels. Most simply, and pervasively, new imperatives for loyalty
induced a growing reverence for familiar traditions that made loyalty
meaningful and hence explicable. What seems especially fascinating is
that each section did not draw exclusively upon its own legends. Not at
all. Confederate independence, according to a Methodist tract that
quoted John Winthrop of Massachusetts Bay, was meant to enable the
South, " 'like a city set upon a hill' [to] fulfill her God given mission to
exalt in civilization and christianity the nations of the earth."[77]

3.12   Winslow Homer, *The Veteran in a New Field* (1865), oil on canvas. The Metropolitan Museum of Art. Bequest of Miss Adelaide Milton De Groot (1876–1967), 1967.

At a more psychological level, war strengthened a Northern trend that had already begun to appear in recent decades: namely, the tendency to minimize genuinely revolutionary aspects of the American Revolution.[78] It also induced the desire for and growth of a conservative, organic view of society. In 1864, for instance, college students were likely to encounter a new kind of rationale for national chauvinism: "The organism of a nation! It enfolds and blesses races; it perpetuates traditions, ideas, examples, principles."[79]

Although the war wrought vast changes in American life, the full nature and extent of that transformation did not really become apparent until the twentieth century. That is not just because hindsight is twenty-twenty, as the cliché goes, but because shortsightedness occurred deliberately in the years following 1865. The dreadful, disruptive experience of war caused people to carry on, as they had to, by returning to familiar places, familiar routines, and resuming family responsibilities. Winslow Homer captured the enormous irony of that situation and that moment in a shrewd canvas that he chose to call *The Veteran in a New Field* (fig. 3.12). It may be a new (i.e., different) field of toil; but it is not an unfamiliar field of work. The soldier has returned home just in time for the harvest. No chance even to change his clothes! His jacket, canteen, and rifle lie on the ground. The veteran has stripped for action, and he remembers how to swing a scythe. Presumably his mind is mingling two disparate sets of recollections as he labors: agrarian routines and military memories. Both will remain with him even if, and when, he leaves the farm for city life and work. Ultimately, the point is that memories will become increasingly important in the years ahead.[80]

If the soldier has come home, he has also returned to his past. He has turned his back to us, who represent the future. Nevertheless, the life he has just lived, the battles he has been through, will soon become the stuff of legends and of history. It will be no easier to disentangle the two after 1865 than it was before. Yet the nature and function of tradition in American culture would change profoundly after 1870. Writing *The Innocents Abroad* late in the 1860s, Mark Twain was on target in more ways than one when he described the time then past as a period "before History was born—before Tradition had being."

Part Two

CIRCA 1870 TO 1915

THE ENHANCEMENT OF
RETROSPECTIVE VISION

T HROUGHOUT *The Education of Henry Adams* (first printed privately in 1907), the self-aware author frequently refers to "the generation of 1870." His sense of that singular year as a critical juncture in American culture and society is striking. "The generation that lived from 1840 to 1870," Adams mused, "could do very well with the old forms of education; that which had its work to do between 1870 and 1900 needed something quite new."[1] If his feel for phase seems persuasive in terms of an age of agrarianism and evangelical faith giving way to industrial innovations and religious skepticism, it is equally applicable in terms of collective memory and tradition beginning to play a more prominent role than ever before in American history.

Adams's perception of change coincides with my own; and various sorts of signposts assist in setting that era apart. In 1869, for instance, the Corcoran collection of art opened as a gallery in Washington, D.C., for "the encouragement of American genius"; and an essay titled "Americanism in Literature" appeared in January with this assertion: "It is better that a man should have eyes in the back of his head than that he should be taught to sneer at even a retrospective vision."[2] Looking back in 1910, the last year of his life, William James ruminated about the Civil War and the intervening decades with words that summed up some of the central moods of his mature lifetime: "Those ancestors, those efforts, those memories and legends."[3]

The importance of ancestors, memories, and legends will predominate in the chapters that follow, just as they did in American art of the period. In 1886, for example, Daniel Chester French began to sketch his superb statue titled *Memory,* a work that he did not complete until the eve of World War I (fig. P2.1). French's notes inform us that the mirror this allegorical figure is holding is so angled as to give her a retrospective view of the past. That device dates back to Elizabethan times, at least, when Richard Grafton's *Chronicle at Large* (1569) of-

P2.1   Daniel Chester French, *Memory* (1886–1914), marble. Courtesy of the
Metropolitan Museum of Art, New York. Gift of Henry Walters, 1919. (19.47)

fered "a glass to see things past, whereby to judge justly of things
present and wisely of things to come."[4]

In 1890 Claude Raguet Hirst painted a still-life, characteristic of the
era, called *Remember This.*[5] A year later Enoch Wood Perry produced
Memories, depicting an older woman and (perhaps) her granddaughter
who look up from a hand-held mirror in which they see themselves to
a painting of a predecessor, presumably the lady's own mother or
grandmother (fig. P2.2). It is not merely the continuity of generations
that is called to our attention by the artist, but the keen awareness of
that continuity which seems to have pervaded this period. When Barrett Wendell, who taught literature at Harvard, learned that an aunt
had died, he consoled her sister and companion with these words:
"There must be endless, constant comfort in the memory of your wonderfully unbroken and devoted lives together—lives which have had,
I think, a singular beauty, in their quiet maintenance of all that is best,
and simplest, and sweetest in the old traditions of New England."[6]

Anyone who probes historical sources for this period will be figuratively assaulted by the nation's arsenal of memory devices and by the
astonishing diversity of its stockpile. Personalized recollections of public affairs were provided by the artist Frederic Remington, by the activ-

P2.2   Enoch Wood Perry, *Memories* (1891), oil on canvas. Courtesy of the Artemis Gallery, North Salem, New York.

ist clergyman Moncure D. Conway, and by Henry Adams.[7] Ceremonial occasions and dedication events, such as the one held at George Washington's Valley Forge headquarters in 1879, brought on a burst of memories.[8] And some people even lauded the faculty of memory in general while others explored its physiology. Victorian cognitive science sparked curiosity about the actual process that enables the human brain to remember.[9]

The societal implications of personal memory for collective consciousness received sustained attention. A sermon preached at the famous Plymouth Church in Brooklyn on the final day of the nineteenth century asserted that "the past is valuable alike to the individual and to the race. . . . Man begins his career an infant, but memory gathers up the experiences, the observations, and the reflections of the yesterdays and carries them forward unto today."[10]

Published works of reminiscence were well received by the press as well as by the public at that time. When an English field marshal sent Henry James a volume of memoirs, the writer responded with more envy than gratitude: "I would give all I have . . . for an hour of your retrospective consciousness, one of your more crowded memories." Part of the appeal of James Ford Rhodes's multi-volume *History of the*

United States, spanning 1850 to 1877 (published 1892–1906 and reprinted as a uniform set in 1910), derived from the recent, tragic, and momentous nature of the period he covered. Contemporaries felt that he "awakened nostalgic memories of the past." A great many letters to Rhodes from enthusiastic readers attest to that impact.[11]

The public's new hunger for history, however, along with its blithe confidence in the veracity of whatever appeared in print under reputable auspices, began to elicit expressions of concern around the turn of the century from serious scholars and antiquarians. Apprehensions surfaced at an 1896 meeting of the nation's oldest historical society. Members wondered just how reliable oral tradition was—particularly recollections by elderly persons offered decades, even half a century, after the event in question.[12]

When Alfred Thayer Mahan began to prepare his naval autobiography in 1905, he wrote to old service acquaintances in search of reminiscences and anecdotes. He acknowledged in his letters, however, that "memory sometimes plays tricks after forty years." Be that as it may, *Harper's Magazine* published monthly selections from his memoirs; and *From Sail to Steam* appeared as a book in 1907. Three years later Charles Francis Adams, Jr., expressed sentiments that echo his great-grandfather's correspondence with Jefferson and Rush a century before: "It is perfectly amazing of what little value anything dependent on human memory is, long after the event. It is not worth the paper it is written on."[13]

Paradoxically, perhaps, less than a generation earlier technology had begun to develop in ways that could assist memory and in some cases verify or contradict it. The introduction of dry-plate photography in 1873, of rolled film in 1884, and of George Eastman's Kodak No. 1 four years later democratized the use of visual "record keeping" and popularized the belief that a camera could be "truthful" in ways that a painter might not, or at least not consistently so.[14]

Despite technology and the professionalization of history, however, memory continued to be mistrusted even as its vogue began to increase in American iconography. "Observe, now," Mark Twain wrote in 1883, "how history becomes defiled, through lapse of time and the help of the bad memories of men."[15] Following centuries of blithe confidence, attitudes toward the meaning and uses of memory had clearly become more complex. By "blithe confidence" I mean the willingness to legitimize social practices and institutions on the basis of custom. For a very long time members of traditional societies had relied upon custom and comfortably assumed that genuine customs were inscribed in "the memory of man."[16]

As the nineteenth century waned, however, that assurance faded. Three paintings of the period indicate the deep ambivalence of a culture torn between two pairs of possible inclinations. Eastman Johnson's *The Nantucket School of Philosophy* (fig. P2.3) emphasizes the will to believe: a predilection for reliving the past and a preference for the

P2.3   Eastman Johnson, *The Nantucket School of Philosophy* (1887), oil on canvas. Courtesy of the Walters Art Gallery, Baltimore, Maryland.

affirmation of folk memory rather than skepticism toward it. On Nantucket, where Johnson spent summers during the 1880s, the pleasure of the past prevails over a future that has grown dim, like the light in the old whalers' room.[17]

Thirteen years later, as the curtain closed on the nineteenth century, Kenyon Cox painted *Hope and Memory* (fig. P2.4). Here the issue is neither the pleasure nor the veracity of memory but the relationship between time and culture that Henry Adams also agonized about in the closing chapters of his autobiographical *Education.* In "The Dynamo and the Virgin (1900)" he explains that, having satisfied himself that the "sequence of their society could lead no further, while the mere sequence of time was artificial, and the sequence of thought was chaos, he turned at last to the sequence of force." Unfortunately, force was best represented by a brand new thing called an automobile—unfortunately "because this was the form of force which Adams* most abominated." And yet, as he acknowledged a page later, "if the automobile had one *vitesse* more useful than another, it was that of a century a minute; that of passing from one century to another without break. The centuries dropped like autumn leaves in one's road, and one was not fined for running over them too fast."[18]

Like Henry Adams, Kenyon Cox was a traditionalist. Whereas Adams

*Adams here refers to himself in the third person.

P2.4   Kenyon Cox, *Hope and Memory* (1900), oil on canvas. The Dixon Gallery and Gardens, Memphis, Tennessee. Gift of Mrs. Lyle Bentzen.

studied future prospects quite seriously before retreating to the past, Cox closed his mind to modernity, never mind the future. A stubborn critic of cultural innovation, Cox repeatedly declared in reviews of new exhibitions his preference for traditional aesthetic standards. By the time he painted his formal declaration of allegiance to the past in 1916, and titled it *Tradition* (fig. P2.5), he had become a prominent anachronism in American art.[19]

Kenyon Cox brings to mind a character created by Henry James in *The Portrait of a Lady* (1881). At one point James describes Gilbert Osmond, an American dilettante and widower in Florence: "He had an immense esteem for tradition; he had told her [the American Isabel Archer] once that the best thing in the world was to have it, but that if one was so unfortunate as not to have it one must immediately proceed to make it."[20]

P2.5   Kenyon Cox, *Tradition* (1916), oil on canvas. Courtesy of the Cleveland Museum of Art. Gift of J. D. Cox.

Although those are words written by a novelist, they represent neither a *reductio ad absurdum* nor even a caricature. In 1892, for example, when the University of Chicago was brand-new, a series of organizational meetings took place to plan dormitory life. At one of these, when graduate students and young instructors met to discuss a Graduate House, "the suggestion was made that any person desiring to establish a tradition should present the same in writing, and, after lying on the table for two weeks, it could be established by a two thirds vote—so hungry were we for traditions in those days."[21]

The idea of instant traditions seemed neither an oxymoron nor absurd. A hunger for tradition developed in Victorian America. The artist John La Farge and his contemporaries used such words as "tradition," "history," and "memory" frequently and interchangeably because "the present time of individual and nation was not fully intelligible without a consciousness of the past." When La Farge lectured to a gathering of young artists at New York's Metropolitan Museum in 1893, he spoke of art as being "composed of memories and affected by them."[22]

In recent years we have come to understand that instant and invented traditions fulfill needs that may be social, political, cultural, ideological, or any combination thereof. We have also been shown that "some traditions are more than dead memories; they are memories relived."[23] Abraham Lincoln's plea to the nation in his first inaugural address—one of the most moving in our history—relied heavily upon an appeal to relive meaningful memories. Halfway through he begged for prudence by raising this rhetorical question: "Before entering upon so grave a matter as the destruction of our national fabric, with all its benefits, its memories, and its hopes, would it not be wise to ascertain precisely why we do it?"[24] Notice that unlike Kenyon Cox, Lincoln did not regard memory and hope as alternatives, as an either/or proposition. The United States historically had both, and presumably still could because meaningful hope was contingent upon cherished memories.

The sentiment of Lincoln's final paragraph was suggested by Secretary of State William H. Seward; but the wording would be Lincoln's, particularly the invocation of national memory in his closing sentence:

> Though passion may have strained, it must not break our bonds of affection. The mystic chords of memory, stretching from every battle-field, and patriot grave, to every living heart and hearthstone, all over this broad land, will yet swell the chorus of the Union, when again touched, as surely they will be, by the better angels of our nature.[25]

Lincoln may well have been one of the closest students of American political discourse, for he echoed not one but two passages written by "Publius" (James Madison) in the winter of 1787–88:

> ▪ Hearken not to the unnatural voice which tells you that the people of America, knit together as they are by so many chords of affection, can no longer live together as members of the same family . . . can no longer be fellow citizens of one great respectable and flourishing empire.[26]

> ▪ What is government itself but the greatest of all reflections on human nature? If men were angels, no government would be necessary.[27]

Abraham Lincoln had a marvelous capacity for the well-turned phrase, but he also had a capacious memory for notable texts in the American tradition. Lincoln's own language would, in its turn, become canonical; so that "mystic chords of memory" could be struck once again, though in a different key, when Henry James pondered a "chord of remembrance" in *The American Scene* (1907). Between 1861 and 1907, American memory began to take form as a self-conscious phenomenon.

Chapter 4

THE CIVIL WAR REMEMBERED—
BUT UNRECONCILED

ABRAHAM LINCOLN'S motive in appealing to those mystic chords of memory was simultaneously simple yet daunting. He wanted to remind the intemperate partisans of regional rectitude that they also shared national responsibilities and allegiances. Somehow the centripetal tendencies that had become so powerful during the 1850s needed to be countered by unifying forces. Unfortunately, what Lincoln could achieve so skillfully with words would not prevail because passions and commitments to customary social relations made his eloquent rhetoric irrelevant. Might made right, eventually, or at least made a hesitant beginning in that direction. Yet the contrasting memories of this nation's most bitter domestic conflict persisted and remained more problematic than mystic, more discordant than harmoniously chordlike.

Although the American Civil War ultimately spawned diverse traditions, they really started as a series of unresolved tensions springing from oppositional possibilities: the imperative of remembering versus the comforting convenience of amnesia; reconciliation versus intransigence; the virtues of a New South versus the romance of a Lost Cause; and conflicting perceptions of patriotism versus treason. Equally problematic was the legitimacy of African-American commemorative occasions, especially when inconsistencies or variations resulted from diverse local and oral traditions; and finally, the need to depoliticize the past without making it vacuous, meaningless, or so homogeneous that no locality could take pride in a distinctive history and identity.

It was entirely predictable that Civil War "artifacts" would wind up in museums, monuments, imaginative literature, history books, and commemorative occasions. How the Civil War would affect the nation's memory and political culture was less predictable. The interplay of such human factors as inertia and indifference, pride and vindictiveness, honor and shame are peculiarly difficult to anticipate.

I

ACCORDING to an editorial that appeared in 1889, "events of the Civil war are now so far in the past that their anniversaries come and go without recognition save in exceptional cases."[1] Even as a generalization about collective memory, that was not altogether valid; and it had little meaning at all when applied to individuals, both prominent and obscure. The father of artist Frederic Remington, for example, S. Pierre Remington, served as a major in the first U.S. Volunteer Cavalry and was in charge when engagements or skirmishes took place. In 1895, fifteen years after the major's death, survivors of his command met for a reunion. One contribution prepared for that occasion was a poem titled "Retrospective," written by one of his men upon receiving a photograph of the beloved officer.

> *Backward, turn backward, oh, time in your flight,*
> *Make me a soldier boy just for tonight.*
> *Major, come back from the echoless shore,*
> *And take command again just as of yore.*[2]

That deeply felt and highly personal poem had not been written for publication. Though it may have been a romanticized effusion of nostalgia and affection, it surely represented the sentiments of many survivors.

Nevertheless, the 1889 editorial contained a hard kernel of truth. More than two years earlier, for example, a statue of the late President James Garfield had been erected on Capitol Hill in Washington by his old comrades in the Society of the Army of the Cumberland, regarded by many as the most successful Union force of the war. A newspaper report that appeared on May 13, 1887, made the unveiling sound like a very impressive occasion. Quite a few former Civil War generals attended, plus members of Congress as well as the Supreme Court. President Grover Cleveland gave an address about Garfield. Two days later, however, a less prominent article acknowledged that if Cleveland had not attended, the ceremony would have been "a dismal and utter failure." Interest on the part of Washingtonians was minimal, and even among survivors of the Army of the Cumberland it was nominal. Only President Cleveland's presence drew the rather modest crowd that did gather.[3] Those mystic chords of memory failed to play consistently.

A desire to honor the memory of those who lost their lives during the war, and the cause for which they fought, surfaced swiftly and spontaneously right after the war in 1866 and '67.[4] Several communities claim credit for the idea; but a small upstate town, Waterloo, New York, may indeed deserve pride of place. In any case the idea caught on immediately. The Grand Army of the Republic began to sponsor Memorial Day observances in 1868. Within a year thirty-one states had mandated the holiday.[5] It truly became an instant national tradition. In 1870 Elihu Vedder painted a seascape titled *Memory* in which an ethereal face appears against a background of waves gently lapping along a shoreline.[6] In imagery and tone, that picture explicitly seemed to anticipate the lines from "Retrospective" quoted above: "Major, come back from the echoless shore."

Within two decades Memorial Day had become, in a goodly number of communities, the occasion for multi-purpose festivities. Many people called it Decoration Day because a principal activity remained the decoration of graves. For the Grand Army of the Republic's huge parade along Fifth Avenue, however, Decoration Day might also have referred to all of the ribbons and medals proudly worn by those marching veterans. In 1887, moreover, some shrewd entrepreneur arranged for Barnum's Circus Day and the old Dutch colonial holiday of Pinkster to coincide with Memorial Day. By 1888 the day's pace had been clearly established: solemn memorial services and grave decorating followed by peppy parades, yachting, and athletic events. New York City's parade had the nationally desired note of reconciliation because the Confederate Richmond Grays marched amidst the Federal Blue. But in another respect New York's parade was atypical: the Sons of Veterans, consisting of "white and colored," marched together.[7]

Memorial Day originated for the South at Columbus, Georgia, under the auspices of a group of ladies in 1866. Their efforts seemed to stimulate the spread of Southern memorial associations; and in many places the same emphasis upon reconciliation recurred.[8] In 1887 the orator in Danville, Virginia, a former congressman, paid tribute to the Union dead buried in a nearby cemetery; and Union graves were maintained almost as carefully as those of Confederates. In 1889 the G.A.R. participated in Decoration Day ceremonies at Greenwood, Louisiana. Many of those occasions were at least bilateral, even if they could not be altogether bipartisan. By the turn of the century, meetings of the United Daughters of the Confederacy began with invocations to "the memory of the saints" and a prideful declaration of purpose: "To do homage unto the memory of our gallant Confederate soldiers." By 1916, moreover, ten Southern states had designated June 3, Jefferson Davis's birthday, as their Memorial Day.[9]

An essay about the various veterans' groups that appeared in a widely circulated magazine carefully described their structure, leadership, and organizational patterns. It also stressed that the purpose of the Loyal Legion, for example, was "to cherish the memories and associations of the war waged in defense of the unity and indivisibility of the republic."[10] Their functions and activities were, in fact, very broad: social, militaristic, political, historical, and above all patriotic. The historical dimension mainly took the form of re-enactments and of occasional activities on behalf of civics education in the schools—usually seen as a means of inculcating patriotism. Be that as it may, periodic reports indicate that Grand Army of the Republic leaders were "agitating this subject" of improved civics instruction.[11]

During the final decades of the nineteenth century, G.A.R. chapters enjoyed particular success in organizing ceremonial occasions at public halls, churches, and academies of music. These gatherings invariably sang patriotic songs, such as "My Country, 'Tis of Thee," "Vive l'Amérique," and "The Flag of the Free." Sometimes a chaplain or historian would speak about the writing of "The Star-Spangled Banner"; and while it was sung the shield of the United States and the G.A.R. badge were "alternately shown by stereopticon illustrations." Eventually it became possible for representatives of urban school systems to reassure leaders of the G.A.R. that "every pupil was familiar with all the national airs through having sung them daily."[12]

Reports of diverse G.A.R. celebrations reveal a range of possible, improbable, and unacceptable patterns of behavior and expression in the North at that time. An example of the possible but increasingly improbable category occurred at Woodstock, Connecticut, on July 4, 1887. A clergyman came from New York to discuss the significance of the Civil War in "The Second Birth of the Republic," and the president of Howard University talked about the unjust treatment of Negroes. An example of the impossible came on the same day from Terre Haute, Indiana, where festivities planned for Independence Day collapsed because the committee on arrangements invited (at the last minute) a socialist from Milwaukee to deliver the oration. The G.A.R. and other patriotic groups decided to boycott. Socialism was not merely un-American, but apparently antithetical to the principles for which battles on behalf of the Union had been fought.[13]

It is important to acknowledge that the Grand Army of the Republic, devoted as it was to mystic chords of memory, and large as its membership may have been, had no monopoly on patriotism or the ceremonial recollection of national history. Consider, for instance, New York's Fourth of July in 1888. Churches, ships in the harbor, and most homes were proudly decorated with bunting and flags. Civil War veterans who had just returned from their twenty-fifth reunion at Gettysburg held formal exercises at Battery Park. The venerable veterans of the War of 1812 met at Military Hall in the morning and then gathered for their annual dinner at noon. The New York State Society of the Cincinnati held an elegant repast at Delmonico's Restaurant, sparing no expense. The Cooper Union sponsored patriotic orations, a reading of the Declaration, and singing of "The Star-Spangled Banner." In Harlem the Veteran Zouaves, the Judson Kilpatrick Post of the G.A.R., and the Sons of Veterans all paraded. Thousands of people visited Grant's burial site. All in all, the day had become a mélange of memories, which perhaps helped to render the chords more mystic. On the other hand, enthusiastic reports of regattas and special athletic competitions suggest that memory was obliged to compete with physical fitness as a manifestation of muscular nationalism.[14]

At the close of that year General Joseph Wheeler introduced a bill in the U.S. House of Representatives to incorporate an organization called the Military Order of America. Its mini-history is symptomatic and therefore instructive in various ways. Most of its forty-three sponsors lived in the District of Columbia. Thirty-eight of them had fought for the Union and thirty-five belonged to the G.A.R. Five had fought for the Confederacy, however. Most were officers, but eleven of the group mustered in and out as privates. Their primary purpose is indicative of the ways in which Civil War memories were stretched to coincide with a larger network of national pride, militarism, and remembrance.

The group wanted to erect a "memorial building at the national capital that shall be a suitable monument to the valor, patriotism, and fidelity of the American soldier and sailor since the days of George Washington and the establishment therein of a war museum and library." Notice that the group asked for a legitimizing charter from Congress (but not funds), plus permission to build the monument. The order would be open to all American veterans (color was not mentioned as a basis for either inclusion or exclusion), sons of veterans who had reached the age of twenty-one, and other unspecified "patriotic citizens." Money to erect the monument would be raised from admission fees and dues.[15]

Although that particular order remained stillborn, its aspirations were characteristic of the time; and others proliferated, such as the National Association of Ex-Union Prisoners of War.[16] In 1887 the Boston post of the G.A.R. hosted a visit by members of the Robert E. Lee Camp of Confederate Veterans, who came from Richmond and enjoyed sightseeing in and around Boston. In September of that year the Farragut Post of the G.A.R. hosted in Evansville, Indiana (southern Indiana not far from the banks of the Wabash), the first North-South reunion sponsored by a G.A.R. post.[17]

When the widely read *Scribner's Magazine* ran an editorial in 1897 about a Confederate reunion being held in Nashville as part of Tennessee's centennial as a state, it pointed out that "a spirit of especial friendliness" prevailed at these reunions. *Scribner's* noted the initial presumption that forming the Grand Army of the Republic and the United Confederate Veterans "would tend to perpetuate bitter memories that were best forgotten. . . . But the result seems to have been strikingly at variance with such predictions."[18] Some memories may, in fact, have been pleasant or bittersweet; but a great many, as we shall see, were just plain bitter.

The influence of previous patriotic societies and veterans' organizations had been comparatively modest in the United States prior to 1870. After that date, however, their political and cultural impact became considerable. Four factors were primarily responsible. First, because the Civil War produced unprecedented numbers of potential members. Second, because sustained economic growth produced a level of prosperity that facilitated associational activity on a broad scale. Third, because the rapid growth of cities helped to make possible numerically strong local chapters. And fourth, because rapid expansion of a national rail network made it convenient for veterans and their families to attend regular encampments and meetings.[19] The role of railroads in the later nineteenth century marked the first in a series of transformations in American transportation extremely conducive to curiosity about tradition and the national heritage.

II

A SPIRIT of sectional reconciliation, and the remarkable speed with which it developed, has been chronicled in considerable detail.[20] From our perspective that process may say more about the capacity for amnesia than for forgiving; but at the time participants believed that they were dutifully, even joyfully, engaged in respectful acts of remembrance and rediscovered brotherhood. Reports, often bearing such headlines as THE BLUE AND THE GRAY, frequently appeared in the press of former Union and Confederate soldiers standing together at battlefields, by gravesites and monuments "in harmony," and that "love for the Union" had now been instilled in everyone.[21]

Regular reunions and anniversary banquets became the most formal and carefully planned opportunities for such sentiments, and the ones most accessible to the press. A representative episode occurred in September 1887, when the Seventh Connecticut Regiment held a reunion at which the honored guest was Confederate Colonel Charles H. Olmsted of Savannah, who had been captured by the regiment during the war. General Hawley (head of the regiment) and Colonel Olmsted each praised reconciliation and observed that Northerners as well as Southerners were equally patriotic Americans. According to Olmsted the brave deeds performed by both sides "will be cherished in the memories of the entire people." To celebrate George Washington's Birthday in 1888 an association bearing an improbable name, the Solid Southerners of New-York, held a banquet in honor of Washington, the South, "and the reunited Union." Colonel John C. Calhoun presided, appropriately; but Mayor Abram Hewitt gave a "rousing" speech in praise of the South, and Edward Atkinson of Boston talked about "Southern Industries."[22] Textiles could truly provide a tie that would bind.

By 1889 so-called Blue-Gray reunions, requiring extensive intersectional travel, had become festive affairs. When New York's Hawkins Zouaves arrived at the Fort Valley railroad station in Georgia, they were greeted by survivors of the Third Georgia Regiment and two thousand locals who turned out to witness the curious encounter. On September 20, 1889, a meeting in Chattanooga of the Society of the Army of the Cumberland culminated in a huge Blue-Gray reunion. Some 25,000 people attended a barbecue held at Crawfish Springs near the Chickamauga Battlefield. A Chickamauga Memorial Association was formally established, with directors drawn from both sides. The governor of Georgia and General W. S. Rosecrans gave the principal speeches, which predictably stressed reconciliation.[23]

The theme of turning swords into ploughshares—albeit popular—was less prominent, perhaps, than that of returning swords to their rightful owners. The press seized upon these human interest stories and deemed them eminently newsworthy. Thus in 1887 Captain James A. Marrow of Clarksville, Virginia, returned the sword of Lieutenant A. G. Case of Simsbury, Connecticut—a sword that had been captured by Confederates at Plymouth, North Carolina, in 1864. When Marrow learned that the sword's owner still lived, he wrote to Case: "I am a true American and have no desire to retain any relic as a triumph of Americans over Americans."[24] Reports of such chivalrous conduct restored American faith that a code of honor continued to exist in their culture even though it had been broken on occasion. Such tales reminded the reader that "relics" of the war still survived in private hands, which helped to sustain faith in a civil religion that continued to have crusading aspects and domestic dimensions.

It also became customary for special occasions that were utterly unrelated to the Civil War to be used as overt (or sometimes subtle) opportunities to trumpet the theme of reconciliation. That is just what President McKinley did in 1901 when he visited San Antonio and the Alamo. His perfunctory speech to a large audience at Travis Square (which did include veterans of both the Blue and the Gray) announced that "here are centuries of heroic memories," praised the brave people of Texas, and stressed sectional harmony.[25]

Similarly, on August 1, 1889, a new monument to the Pilgrims was dedicated at Plymouth. The memorial sought to tell the story of "the principles on which the famous old colony was founded." Figures surrounding the granite pedestal represented Faith, Freedom, Education, Morality, and Law. Although a goodly number of *Mayflower* descendants gathered for this occasion, the press concluded that "perhaps the most suggestive feature of the ceremonies is that the orator of the day is the Kentuckian W. C. P. Breckinridge and that John Boyle O'Reilly is the poet."[26] Presumably those who organized the affair wanted it to be national and inclusive rather than regional and elitist. Journalists clearly got the message and added their gentle touches of irony in response to the complexities of collective memory when 270 years of social change could no longer be ignored.

One of the most important cultural consequences of this quest for

4.1   Thomas Nast, *The Lost Cause: Lee Waiting for Grant* (n.d.), oil on canvas.
Courtesy of the Chicago Historical Society.

reconciliation and national harmony, however, was a blurring of specific historical memories into mythical sagas that were at least partially spurious. In April 1888 a great amount of grandstanding
preceded an elaborate banquet in honor of Ulysses S. Grant's birthday. Two weeks prior to the affair the press published a letter from
General William T. Sherman to prominent Confederate generals, officially inviting them to attend the gala event. Who knows how the
ex-Confederates reacted when Sherman informed them that "time
has developed the affectionate regard which the people of all sections entertain for the virtues of this illustrious man." At the banquet
itself Sherman presided and gave a self-serving speech. Chauncey M.
Depew then followed with a very long address in which he praised
Grant for being so conciliatory once the fighting had stopped. General William Mahone, a member of Robert E. Lee's staff during the
war, was received by this predominantly Yankee audience with great
enthusiasm. Mahone responded by emphasizing how courteous Grant
had been to Lee at Appomattox (but see fig. 4.1).[27]
After the turn of the century some Southerners surely must have

wondered whether there were any limits to this (not entirely sincere?) lovefest. In 1902 some Confederate veterans in Virginia started a fund to erect a monument to Grant in Richmond. The fund fizzled at sixteen dollars. Six months later a man in Morristown, New Jersey, proposed a more plausible project: paired statues of Grant and Lee in order to promote friendship between North and South. The unsuccessful appeal for funds from survivors of the war and their children praised the two generals and then added a touch of class, so to speak, by referring to "Grant, a worthy son of the plebeian element, and Lee, the son of a patrician family. . . ."[28] It is not possible to enumerate all of the sentimental and strange, sensible and foolish proposals put forward (and ignored) by well-meaning people.

Evidence of reconciliation—as an accomplishment and as an ongoing ideal—nevertheless accumulated during the first decade of the twentieth century. Yankees would be invited to address the annual dinner of the New York Southern Society, an organization with about one thousand members that usually gathered at the Waldorf-Astoria on George Washington's Birthday. Old Southern institutions like the College of William and Mary invited Northerners to deliver commencement addresses and conferred honorary degrees upon them. In 1906, for example, that College selected George C. Batcheller, a sometime officer of the New York Society of the Order of Founders and Patriots of America.

In 1907, the centennial of Robert E. Lee's birth, Washington and Lee invited Charles Francis Adams, Jr., of Boston and South Lincoln, Massachusetts, to address the College in Lee's Memorial Chapel at Lexington, Virginia. Because Adams admired Lee very much—a swiftly spreading trend in the North at that time—the anniversary occasion was a huge success. Adams proclaimed Lee "a great man,—great in defeat, a noble, moral character. The nearer I get to him, the more I admire him." On January 21, two days after Lee's birthday, Adams left Lexington by train. The entire student body came to the station to see him off and he departed "amid an ovation."[29]

The centennial of Abraham Lincoln's birth, February 12, 1909, turned out to be an elaborate patriotic occasion throughout much of the United States. Prominent men made pilgrimages to various Lincoln shrines: Theodore Roosevelt visited Lincoln's hoked-up birthplace at Hodgenville, Kentucky, and William Jennings Bryan spoke at Springfield, Illinois. Not only did Democrats join with Republicans in honoring the man who had preserved the Union, but some Southerners played a surprisingly conspicuous role and thousands of them paid public tribute to Lincoln's memory in 1909.[30]

So MUCH FOR mystic chords of memory and the wonderful rate of reconciliation. If we stopped here, however, we would be telling only half the tale, which has actually been the case more often than not.

Bitterness, vindictiveness, and resentment lay just beneath the surface and were vented in various ways. Those Southerners who joined in lauding Lincoln were usually willing to forgive or forget or both. Those with seared memories were unwilling to do either.

In 1908 a New Yorker wrote to Lyon G. Tyler, president of William and Mary, son of former President John Tyler, and a veritable switchboard for historical networks in the South, proposing that a memorial be erected to Lincoln in Richmond! The logic underlying this proposal seemed straightforward enough. Lincoln at heart was a "true friend" of the South and the region lost dearly by his assassination because his Reconstruction policy would have been much more benign than Andrew Johnson's. Tyler's response (see pp. 126–127 below) was fiercely negative, however, just as it would be to all such proposals for phony sectional harmony throughout his long life (1853–1935). Tyler represents the unreconstructed rebel, and he is important because his historical essays enjoyed such wide circulation throughout the South.[31]

We shall encounter Tyler and his impact once again in chapter twelve, because the most significant phase of his career occurred between 1910 and the early 1930s. Here it is appropriate—essential, in fact—to take note of his recalcitrant predecessors. Doing so enables us to see just how bitterly divided Southern society actually was during the final decades of the nineteenth century. The case of Paul Hamilton Hayne, a South Carolina man of letters, is instructive. The Northern apotheosis of Lincoln following his assassination enraged Hayne because he believed that Lincoln's martyrdom had led to a gross perversion of history in the popular mind. Poetry written in praise of Lincoln elicited this reaction from Hayne:

> Those "Homeric" *lines* on *Lincoln* (for instance), *may* be good, but I see continually between each stanza, a gaudy, coarse, not over cleanly, whiskey drinking, and whiskey smelling Blackguard, elevated by a grotesque *Chance,* (nearly allied to *Satan*), to the position for which of all others, he was most *unfit;*—and where memory has been *idealised* by Yankee fancy, & Yankee arrogance, in a way, that *would* be ludicrous, were it not *disgusting,* & calculated, finally, to belie the facts of History, and hand down to future times as Hero & Martyr, as commonplace a *Vulgarian* as ever patronized bad Tobacco, and mistook *blasphemy* for *wit!*[32]

Although his anti-Northern vituperation never diminished, in Hayne's later years he turned with almost equal venom upon younger Southerners who espoused New South doctrines of forward-looking modernization. "All the most-sacred memories & associations of the *Past* come over me," he wrote in 1885. *"How can* we,—you & I—and all persons of the *old regime* fail to regard with contempt the flippancy and irreverence of too many of our 'younger South' *brethren*?"[33]

Hayne spoke more eloquently than most (or more pathetically, depending upon your point of view); but his intensity of feeling had many counterparts. General Jubal A. Early, a tireless defender of the Confederacy and its cause, gave $1,000 toward the erection of a monument to Lee in Richmond. When he learned that Maine granite would be used for the pedestal, however, rather than Virginia granite, he terminated his fund-raising activities in New Orleans and vowed never to contribute another penny.[34]

Jubal Early served as first president of the Southern Historical Society, an organization founded at New Orleans in 1869, but relocated to Richmond in 1873 when it clearly appeared to be floundering. Its founders intended the parent society to have affiliated units in all of the Confederate states plus the District of Columbia; but these groups got off the ground even more slowly than the S.H.S. Its primary purpose was to set the record straight for posterity. A journal called *The Southern Magazine* would publish "valuable contributions to the history of the Confederate War." A broadsheet notice that resulted from the 1873 reorganization closed with a self-exhortation that also gently admonished others: "Let us, who are soon to be in that past to which we properly belong, see there are no gaps in the record. Thus shall we discharge a duty to the fathers, whose principles we inherit, to the children, who will then know whether to honor or to dishonor the squires that begot them."[35]

That seems quite a sobering burden of moral responsibility; but memory and the honorable perpetuation of tradition were taken seriously in the Old South during the 1870s. Hundreds of memorial meetings were held following the death of Robert E. Lee on October 12, 1870; and in many instances the loss of various little-known individuals received dutiful attention vicariously through services that honored and personified Lee.[36] Although the South lacked funds and adequate communications as yet, the decade of the 1870s was notable for attempts to honor Confederate generals in particular and the more abstract notion of Southern memory in general. One of the largest postwar gatherings of Confederate veterans took place in Richmond on October 26, 1875, in order to dedicate the first Southern statue to Stonewall Jackson. A loyal Virginian who acknowledged the social uses of history and memory also noted the need to "cast a halo of remembrance and of honour above those indefatigable pioneers, who have exerted themselves to rescue from oblivion such precious memories of the past."[37] Where tradition seemed to matter so much, memorialists might also receive warm appreciation.

It became the challenge of the 1880s to move forward from individual hero worship to more comprehensive control of the past by its most passionate partisans. The extent of personal isolation and inadequate communication is obvious in retrospect. Scattered but unco-ordinated individuals had similar goals in view. In 1888 a professor of history at

Georgetown College in Kentucky thanked Albert Bushnell Hart of Harvard for sending a copy of his new pamphlet, *History in High and Preparatory Schools.* "I hope its wise suggestions may excite much attention here in the South," he wrote, "where the study of History has not even begun to be properly cared for."[38] Little more than a year later, however, Henry E. Chambers published *A Higher* [more advanced? loftier?] *History of the United States.* Explicitly designed for "youth of the South," it declared that "the old civilization can never be forgotten. As long as the sons of the South bear its earlier traditions, its later memories, to heart, just so long will there be a source . . . of patriotism."[39]

During the 1890s, despite all of the attention focused then and since on Henry Grady's vision of a New South, a Confederate revival swept the region, especially visible in its larger cities. Genealogy became a particularly prominent obsession, and professional genealogists and antiquarians like Robert Alonzo Brock (1839–1914) of Richmond charged fancy prices for family information derived from their "Registers."[40] The romantic historical novels of Mary Johnston brought her adoring fan mail. The Chaplain General of the United Confederate Veterans wrote to her in 1899 expressing his admiration. "Let me suggest that when you have finished Colonial Virginia," he remarked, "you take up the home life of old Virginia in ante-bellum days, and that you then write on the many incidents of confederate days that form fit subjects for poetry and romance."[41]

Although various Southern writers in this period became preoccupied with the past, there is a genuine danger in lumping them all together and losing sight of the diversity in attitude, atmosphere created, and messages conveyed to their readers. Mary Johnston (1870–1936) and Ellen Glasgow (1874–1945) were both Virginians and virtual contemporaries. Each one was intrigued by the past, moreover, as a basis for imaginative literature. But there the resemblance ceases, as their novels and their autobiographies make plain. Johnston recalled that she "was born in an impoverished state of battle-grounds and impassioned memories." Her historical romances, which enjoyed great popularity, were composed with careful attention to factual accuracy. Yet her characters are as artificial as her story-lines are ceaselessly nostalgic. Mary Johnston's creative gifts did not grow, and her sense of the past remained static. In 1932 she wrote a short piece, "The Character of Lee," that in tone and substance might have been composed half a century earlier: "In the etheric stuff of which memory is made. . . ."[42]

By contrast, Ellen Glasgow chronicled but also gently chided Virginia history—before, during, and since the Civil War—asking at times, with genuine wonder: "What is memory . . . that it should outlast emotion?" In the best of her novels, in fact, such as *The Sheltered Life* (set in the period 1910–17), Glasgow carefully distinguishes among memory, myth, and history. Like John Adams she is keenly sensitive to the mendacity of memory. She uses General David Archbald, an aging veteran of the war who is deeply tradition-oriented, to demystify memory. At one point the general plunges "downward through a dim vista of time, where scattered scenes from the past flickered and died and flickered again. At eighty-three, the past was always like this. Never the whole of it. Fragments, and then more fragments. No single part, not even an episode, complete as it had happened."[43]

We encounter a comparable contrast between Thomas Nelson Page (1853–1922) and Joel Chandler Harris (1848–1908). Page did as much as any author to sentimentalize the myth of the Lost Cause and white heroism in the South. Between 1880 and 1910, as the pre-eminent literary spokesman for his region, Page shaped an image of the antebellum South as a golden age, and portrayed in print the plantation tradition that subsequently achieved mass popularity on the silver screen.[44]

Whereas Page celebrated a genteel planter aristocracy, Harris favored the middle-class, white independent farmer, though he depicted all segments of society, including blacks, with sympathy. Harris's re-creation of antebellum history had an entirely different social cast from Page's, one that anticipates some of the most important insights of modern social historians.[45]

To complicate matters, moreover, George Washington Cable (1844–1925) wrote about nineteenth-century Louisiana in *The Grandissimes* (1880), and in novels set during the Civil War and Reconstruction that infuriated apologists for the Old South by calling attention to miscegenation and dealing forthrightly with the social condition of Creoles and persons of color as well. Cable, who had served loyally in the Confederate Army, is customarily portrayed as feeling dismayed by the rage that his historical candor provoked. No writer responds happily to severe criticism, especially when it comes from those close to home. But Cable differed considerably from Page and by degree from Harris in his concern for social reform and his willingness to confront the determinative bond between past and present.[46]

Historians of the South have been preoccupied for a generation now by the issue of continuity versus change in the post–Civil War era; and the most recent scholarship seems to be more impressed by the persistence of tradition in the period 1870–1900.[47] Although I am too, I find it misleading to look at this period in terms of either/or. At first, sheer impoverishment and slow economic recovery caused some Southerners to call for far-reaching changes during the 1870s and '80s. After a quarter of a century, however, and the gradual return of prosperity, or at least its prospect, most Southerners peered at the future with hope but also turned to the past with pride. A visitor to the historic Tidewater section of the James River summarized this Janus-like outlook very well in 1891. He found the region "teeming with the traditions of past wealth and a romantic social history." Naturally, he added,

> it has taken a long time for the people to recover from the shock consequent upon the result of the war, and many have not yet

done so. . . . Though still most tenderly cherishing the past as a precious legacy, they realize and act according to the demands of the present, with the reasonable hope of reaping in the future a generous harvest.[48]

If feelings of continuity persisted despite the reality of change, it can also be said that change was accompanied by displays of history and tradition as signposts of continuity. In the spring of 1902, for example, an exposition opened in Charleston, South Carolina, a city of only 23,000 inhabitants and therefore much smaller than the sites of major expositions during the preceding decade. Historic documents, such as the original Ordinance of Secession "done" at Charleston on December 20, 1860, could be viewed amidst the benchmarks of progress. But the exposition's director of fine arts conveyed a striking sense of chauvinism when he explained to a national audience that this event had "brought to the surface in Charleston what remains of an early culture and civilization which has scarcely had its parallel in the United States."[49]

Three recollections by individuals from different parts of the South epitomize the diversity of Southern experience with tradition and memory, change and continuity, conflict and reconciliation. Woodrow Wilson, a Georgian with ties to Virginia, wrote in 1909 upon returning to the South after a prolonged absence that he discovered "a country full of reminiscences which connect me with my parents, and with all the old memories; I know again the region to which I naturally belong."[50]

William E. Dodd, the historian and diplomat, progressed from provincialism to a more liberal cosmopolitanism. As a student in Virginia during the 1890s he felt the fascination of a "great Southern past" and its rich trove of traditions. Starting in 1897 as a doctoral student in Germany, he discovered the "shadowy grandeurs" of a broader, deeper, and more complex past. Although he never lost his interest in Southern history, he would often write critically of the region's cultural shortcomings.[51]

The artist Thomas Hart Benton, born in 1899 on the edge of the Ozarks in Neosho, Missouri, recalled in his autobiography that "the town was addicted to celebrations. Confederate and Union gatherings occurred every year and the square would be full of veterans." On a daily basis during the 1890s old Civil War soldiers just sat around stores and livery stables and chatted. Such places served as "important centers of reminiscence and debate."[52]

If many Southerners became more misty-eyed and tradition-oriented with the passage of time, those tendencies made them all the more chauvinistic about their region. If such chauvinism served as an obstacle to reconciliation, however, so did spasmodic outbursts of Northern aggressiveness. Every so often, on some well-attended ceremonial occasion, a Northern band could not resist the temptation to play "Marching

Through Georgia," initially whenever General William T. Sherman was present; but the practice continued long after his death.[53] Reports of such incidents offended Southern sensibilities. So, too, did an episode in 1887, when President Cleveland (pressured heavily by the G.A.R.) refused to allow the return of captured Confederate battle flags to their states of origin—a decision that provoked a major brouhaha, but one that the Northern press and aging Union officers largely approved.[54]

Even through the 1890s and into the new century, reconciliation continued to encounter its potent nemesis: spiteful vindictiveness. In 1891 Senator Henry Cabot Lodge infuriated Southerners by publishing an essay in *The Century* titled "The Distribution of Ability in the United States." He deployed nine charts in order to "demonstrate" the overwhelming influence of Northeasterners (and especially New Englanders) on the development of American government, society, institutions, and morals. Lodge disparaged the South explicitly, and the hostile reverberations persisted for years. In a speech given by William Cabell Bruce at the University of Virginia in 1893, for example, he proclaimed that Lodge had lauded far too many New England nonentities, and that many men born in the South who subsequently moved west were not credited to the South in Lodge's unscientific survey.[55] The War between the States was thereby refought on grounds of achievement. It got very nasty.

I I I

IN 1903 Virginia and Pennsylvania jointly sponsored a proposal to erect a monument to Robert E. Lee on the battlefield at Gettysburg—an objective that would not actually be achieved until 1917. Early in the century Virginia also sought to honor Lee in Statuary Hall at the U.S. Capitol. The Grand Army of the Republic flexed every political muscle it could in order to prevent such a horrible desecration on behalf of a treasonous "conspirator."[56]

Despite those particular contretemps, however, the decades between 1870 and 1910 comprised the most notable period in all of American history for erecting monuments in honor of mighty warriors, groups of unsung heroes, and great deeds. The movement carried with it a kind of "contagion" that spilled from Civil War saints to battles and martyrs of other wars. Plaques were placed on buildings where famous people had performed historic acts, and other sorts of *aides-mémoire* emerged as standard fare on the menu of American culture.[57]

Most of this activity seems to have occurred free from controversy, although in 1903 the *New York Times* looked at three bills before Congress that would have provided public statues to Longfellow, L'Enfant, and John Paul Jones in Washington, D.C., and lamented "the hopelessly haphazard and random way in which we go about to commemorate our famous men." The *Times* noted that the Secretary of War served on twenty artistic commissions; found it absurd that he should have any sort of role as an arbiter of taste; and urged that all aesthetic decisions in the District be handled by a prudent commission.[58]

In most cases, however, the construction of memorials in the North was comparatively non-controversial and took two forms. First, there was the general monument honoring a group or category of persons, such as the Seventh Regiment Memorial designed by Richard M. Hunt in 1868–69 and completed four years later. Located on the west side of Central Park near 69th Street, it displayed a generic Union soldier with the motto *Pro Patria et Gloria.* The Soldiers and Sailors' Monument in Brooklyn's Prospect Park, begun with great fanfare in 1889, became the largest Civil War memorial in the nation. The granite arch stood seventy-one feet high, cost more than $250,000 to erect, and contained "relic rooms designed for memorial halls."[59]

The other type of monument honored particular people, and they were numerous. The ones to Abraham Lincoln alone included his mausoleum near Springfield (begun in 1869 and completed five years later) and Augustus Saint-Gaudens's standing figure (in front of a chair) which was unveiled in Chicago's Lincoln Park on October 22, 1887, to warm praise.[60] The case of Ulysses S. Grant turned out to be more complicated because of the considerable cost of his tomb on Manhattan's West Side and because his popularity stimulated competitive projects. Within two weeks of his death in July 1885, a Missouri Monumental Grant Association had been organized to raise money in St. Louis, and yet another at Fort Leavenworth, Kansas. The latter group moved with remarkable dispatch and unveiled its statue in record time on September 14, 1889. Coverage in the *Kansas City Times,* reprinted nationally, pursued the theme of regional reconciliation: "Those who sympathized with the South are not less glad to view a perpetuation of the memory of a brave Northern soldier than those who followed him."[61]

Meanwhile, in 1887 the G.A.R.'s commander-in-chief formed a Grant Memorial Committee to plan and raise funds for a monument in Washington, D.C. Two years later the executive officer responsible for completing Grant's Tomb in New York acknowledged "expressions of impatience over what may have seemed inexcusable delays on the part of the association." He called attention, however, to the causes then competing for major donations: $60,000 had just been raised for a statue honoring John Hancock; $30,000 for George McClellan; $500,000 to aid victims of the catastrophic Johnstown flood in Pennsylvania; and $150,000 for the Irish parliamentary fund. A plan was devised to raise $1,000 each from the 638 G.A.R. posts in New York State; but funds for Grant flowed sluggishly. In October 1889 General Charles H. T. Collins assumed responsibility for completing the job and issued a screed designed to energize the lethargic:

A sacred pledge made to the family of one of the most illustrious of Americans has been violated; a promise to those who loved him and revere his memory has been treated with indifference. . . . Statues of Liberty, memorial arches, and world's fairs all thrive, but the body of the Great American who made all of these glorifications possible lies neglected on a heath, a shame and a disgrace.[62]

Grant's Tomb was not completed and opened to the public until 1897. In 1938–39 nearly $300,000 was spent to refurbish the tomb, a project jointly sponsored by the Grant Monument Association, the New York City Parks Department, and the federal WPA. Basically, the tomb was sandblasted and cleaned, the park around it widened, and busts of five other Civil War generals, prepared by WPA artists, were executed for previously unfilled niches in the tomb. After many years of disharmony as well as halfwit humor ("Who is buried in Grant's Tomb?"), the mystic chords of General and Mrs. Grant's memory were played to completion.[63]

At first glance the saga of Southern monuments would appear to be less complex. The dedication in 1883 of Edward Valentine's recumbent statue of Robert E. Lee in the Lee Memorial Chapel at Washington and Lee University (fig. 4.2) was a wistful affair organized by the Lee Memorial Association and attended by some eight thousand people, including the widows of Generals Pickett, Stuart, and Stonewall Jackson. The dedication of a monument to Lee at Richmond in 1890 sparked immense interest across the South; and a memorial to John C. Calhoun erected at Charleston in 1885 also achieved plaudits.[64]

When we turn from the great heroes and prominent historical sites to ordinary communities, however, we find controversy, lethargy, and changes of heart. Southerners commonly divided over where to locate their local monuments: in a cemetery or, for example, "downtown" in some public place, such as the front of a courthouse. According to one common argument, memorials placed in cemeteries would not be widely noticed. Some advocates eventually began to urge that monument funds be directed to battlefield sites. It was not a simple issue, obviously, and it was not unusual for people who had built early obelisks in cemeteries subsequently to construct a second monument at the courthouse or village green. That happened at Fayetteville, North Carolina, for example, in 1868 and 1902: first a marker to the community's dead at Cross Creek Cemetery and then a statue at St. James Square in the center of town.[65]

Because of the widespread poverty afflicting the South for many years after 1865, the greatest surge in raising Confederate memorials actually occurred during the first decade of the twentieth century. Even then, most of the monuments erected were bronze rather than marble and were manufactured by Northern firms. The Monumental

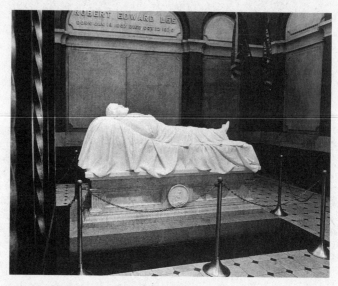

4.2   Edward Valentine, *Recumbent Statue of Robert E. Lee* (1883), marble. Courtesy of the Lee Memorial Chapel, Washington and Lee University, Lexington, Virginia.

Bronze Company of Bridgeport, Connecticut, for example, specialized in casting memorials to Union valor, but received a fair number of commissions from Southern cities and towns as well. When the president of the Southern Memorial Association of Fayetteville, Arkansas, was asked why anyone should build Confederate monuments, his answer contained irony and sincerity in equal measure: "We are correcting history."[66]

From our perspective, some of the most pathetic reminders of that tragic war are the markers placed by the graves of those, on both sides, who died very far from home, such as captured prisoners swept away by disease at distances too great for safe relocation and burial. At a small Confederate graveyard in Madison, Wisconsin, for example, the United Daughters of the Confederacy placed this marker in 1908: "To the Soldiers of the Southern Confederacy Who Died to Repel Unconstitutional Invasion, to Protect the Rights Reserved to the People, to Perpetuate the Sovereignty of the States."

IN ADDITION to graveyards, monuments, chapels, and statues, other sorts of physical objects and sites served to remind Americans of the human sacrifices and honors won in the struggle for worthy causes. There were temporary exhibits of war relics, such as the one at Boston in 1875, and then the gradual emergence of more permanent displays or museums. The Military Service Institution of the United States, formed in 1878, set up a war museum on Governor's Island in New York Harbor. It contained "treasures" from the War for Independence and the Mexican War as well as the Civil War: old battle flags, guns, cannons, coins, medals, and currency. Among its most cherished possessions were General Phil Sheridan's Winchester rifle and the card table on which George Washington wrote his farewell speech to his troops.[67]

The South needed a little longer; but taking its economic hardships into consideration, not all that much. In 1889 a Georgian proposed that the old capitol building in Atlanta be made into a Confederate museum. The state would lease the building at a modest rate to a small group of men who in turn would promise to spend at least $5,000 each year to create a Confederate library, picture gallery, and museum. After twenty years the property would be donated to the state and become a public trust.[68] Although that scheme did not succeed, plans for the establishment of a museum in Richmond were launched in 1890 with the formation of a Confederate Memorial Literary Society to preserve the wartime home of Jefferson Davis as a repository for Confederate memorabilia of all sorts. The museum finally opened in 1896 and attracted nearly ten thousand visitors per year from the outset.[69]

The press described "the popular Lenten amusement" of 1887 in which groups of women visited the Merrimac and Monitor Panorama on Madison Avenue in New York. Schoolchildren also came and often brought their history books. (The Panorama must have been thin on descriptive material.) After five weeks this "amusement" seemed to be so successful that its management decided to facilitate visits by veterans. Exhibits like the Panorama could travel, of course, and even more elaborate ones went on tour. In 1889, for example, a man from Kansas City purchased "John Brown's Fort" at Harper's Ferry. He intended to take the small fort apart and reconstruct it in various cities where people could find John Brown "relics" inside.[70] The Freedom Train of 1947 would not be the first occasion when historic objects were carried to the populace. In an age of memory, an entrepreneurial slogan might well have been: "Have relics, will travel." (See fig. 4.3.)

Yet another associational trend got under way in 1889. The reunion of the Society of the Army of the Cumberland met in Chattanooga on the anniversary of the bloody Battle of Chickamauga, at which 27,000 men were wounded or killed. During the reunion an association was formed in order to have Chickamauga declared "a national memorial field." It would be to the "West," they said, what Gettysburg is to the East. A former governor of Tennessee, speaking on behalf of Confederates, explained that Southerners strongly supported the idea of Congress purchasing the battlefield lands and creating a national park.[71]

Although it did not happen immediately, that sort of proposal surfaced increasingly during the 1890s and more frequently after the turn of the century. Nearly one hundred years later, in 1988, Congress would

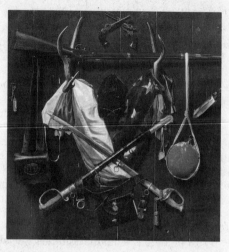

4.3   Alexander Pope, *Emblems of the Civil War* (1888), oil on canvas. Dick S. Ramsay Fund, Governing Committee of The Brooklyn Museum, and Anonymous Donors.

take action to protect the Manassas and Antietam battlefields in Virginia and Maryland from commercial development. A complete transformation had occurred. The rites of heritage now (selectively, at least) surpassed rights in property.[72]

I V

BECAUSE BATTLES rarely failed to fascinate the reading public, publishers found it commercially advantageous to refight the Civil War from time to time. Thus *The Century* magazine, whose circulation exceeded 200,000, ran a two-year series titled "Battles and Leaders of the Civil War" (1884–86). Then, between 1885 and 1910, the publisher G. P. Putnam undertook an ambitious program of producing the collected writings of American statesmen. In 1906 George W. Jacobs of Philadelphia brought out a series for younger readers called "The American Crisis Biographies." They were devoted to the "great American sectional struggle," and a descriptive flyer explained that the series would be "impartial, Southern writers having been assigned to Southern subjects, and Northern writers to Northern subjects."[73]

Perhaps that pattern of assignment reveals a curious notion of impartiality; but I believe it is fair to say that the American psyche was severely riven at the time between a genuine desire for fairness and a fierce impulse toward partisanship.[74] To illustrate the former, notice that in 1896 the National Encampment of the G.A.R. established a

Committee on School Histories because members felt that the Civil War was inadequately covered in most history texts. The surprising suggestion emerged that a joint North-South commission seek to develop a history that would be satisfactory to both regions. That did not come to fruition; but it is symptomatic of positive intentions and goodwill that did exist.[75]

Charles Dudley Warner, a Connecticut writer who reached a very broad public, visited the South in 1885 and again in 1887. Two years later, when Warner published his *Studies in the South and West,* he expressed a sentiment that may sound naive to us but which he genuinely believed: "for the past ten years there has been growing in this country a stronger feeling of nationality, a distinct American historic consciousness, and nowhere else has it developed so rapidly of late as in the South."[76]

Less attractive than such generosity, albeit understandable, was the tendency to re-enact the Civil War verbally by means of sectional chauvinism in textbooks and in the classroom. Moreover, chauvinism did not merely mean applauding the merits of one's own section; it meant deriding the others, and especially the former enemy. As Herbert Baxter Adams wrote of a Ph.D. candidate in history at Baltimore's Johns Hopkins: "[may he] be duly enrolled in that noble army of doctors who are now instructing and converting New England."[77]

It is commonplace to say that the Civil War resulted from both a fatal flaw and the incapacity of American politics to cope with the consequences of that flaw. We must recognize, however, that a willingness to permit the war's memory to be politicized also had damaging effects. It provided diversions that allowed people to ignore the legacies of that moral flaw: obligations to assist the freedmen. In addition it prolonged the process of healing and made it all the more difficult, thereby diverting attention from urgent social and economic problems. Politicization of the war's history may have been inevitable, but it was unproductive rather than prudent.[78] It assisted in shaping the identities of two powerful political parties; but, as Lord Bryce observed in 1888, those parties had replaced principles or tenets with traditions born of misguided memories and partial amnesia.[79]

SELECTIVE MEMORY helped eventually to facilitate reconciliation.[80] It also kept African-Americans outside the mainstream of retrospective consciousness, however, both national and regional. Therefore blacks perpetuated their own distinctive traditions and memories (see fig. 4.4). Frederick Douglass strove valiantly to remind all of his countrymen what the war had actually been about. "It is not well to forget the past," he declared in 1884. "Memory was given to man for some wise purpose. The past is . . . the mirror in which we may discern the dim outlines of the future." With the passage of time, and

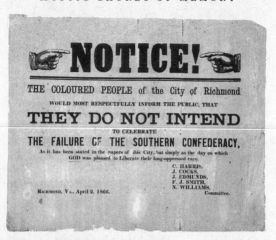

4.4 Broadside printed and posted by a committee of the Coloured People of the City of Richmond, 1866. Courtesy of the Virginia Historical Society, Richmond.

the rise of socially sanctioned racist barriers, Douglass's tone grew more strident and his substantive message more pointed. Speaking at Washington, D.C., in 1888 on the twenty-sixth anniversary of abolition there, he thundered like an Old Testament prophet: "Well the nation may forget, it may shut its eyes to the past, and frown upon any who may do otherwise, but the colored people of this country are bound to keep the past in lively memory till justice shall be done them."[81]

It became perfectly clear during the 1880s that a genuinely integrated collective consciousness was unacceptable to whites. In 1888, when the black community of Boston surmounted obstacles and after a long struggle unveiled a monument to Crispus Attucks, members of the Massachusetts Historical Society, the nation's oldest, indicated strong disapproval. In their view, "the famous mulatto was a rowdyish person, killed while engaged in a defiance of law [at the Boston Massacre of 1770]." From the perspective of Boston's Brahmin elite, Attucks was "not a fit candidate for monumental honors."[82] From the mid-1880s onward, therefore, African-Americans largely celebrated their heroes and pursued their own historic occasions alone. They did have positive things to say about Robert Gould Shaw of Boston,[83] Ulysses S. Grant, and especially Abraham Lincoln (fig. 4.5).

The blacks' collective memory of slavery remained vivid, as historians Eric Foner and Leon Litwack have shown.[84] But what they chose to emphasize by means of traditional activities each year was the memory of gaining freedom. Consequently in African-American communities, especially in the South, a day of prayer, preaching, and festivities usually known as "Juneteenth" came to be observed (fig. 4.6). The particu-

4.5   After Harry Roseland, *Old Couple Looking at a Portrait of Lincoln* (n.d.), oil on canvas. Courtesy of the National Museum of American Art, Smithsonian Institution. Transfer from the National Museum of African Art.

lar day chosen in the calendar year varied by locality: January 1 in New York City, Boston, and most of the deep South because the Emancipation Proclamation became effective at that time in 1863; June 19 because on that day in 1865 General Gordon Granger landed in Galveston, Texas, and read a governmental order that freed all of the slaves in East Texas; and various other dates in early February, August, and September because many communities celebrated either the anniversary of the day that they first learned of emancipation or the date of ratification of the Thirteenth Amendment, which made slavery illegal anywhere in the United States (fig. 4.7).[85]

The specific subject matter for orations on these occasions varied,

though there were common themes and shared aspirations: the broad
history of Africans in North America; assessments of current policies
affecting the civil rights or condition of blacks; and hortatory appeals
concerning "the duty of keeping in memory the great deeds of the past,
and of transmitting the same from generation to generation" (a speech
given by Frederick Douglass on Emancipation Day in 1883).[86]

Despite limited financial resources, constraints upon public activity,
and the threat of violence in many locations, black traditions began to
be marked with increasing visibility in the later 1880s. During the third
week of November 1887, for example, the African Methodist Episcopal
Church celebrated its one-hundredth anniversary with special services
in a number of cities. The denomination had been organized in Philadelphia by Richard Allen and Absalom Jones because they felt strongly
that blacks encountered a "want of Christian feeling" from white Methodists. By 1887 the A.M.E. Church had nearly half a million communi-
cants, three thousand churches, a publishing department, and a
quarterly magazine.[87]

In 1891 Edward A. Johnson wrote *A School History of the Negro Race
in America, from 1619 to 1890,* the first textbook in black history; and
in the years that followed correspondence took place between black
teachers, writers, and others seeking new information or "a list of au-

4.6 Winslow Homer, *Dressing for the Carnival* (1877), oil on canvas. The
Metropolitan Museum of Art, Lazarus Fund, 1922. (22.220) The scene depicts
a family preparing for Jonkonnu (or Jonkeroo), an Afro-Caribbean Christmas
masquerade tradition which continued after the Civil War as a celebration of
Emancipation and Independence. The older boy at the right holds a small
American flag. The little girl at the left holds a firecracker.

4.7   A store on East Main Street in Richmond, Virginia, decorated for Emancipation Day in the 1880s. Courtesy of The Valentine Museum, Richmond, Virginia.

thorities on the Ancient History of the Negro."[88] The American Negro Historical Society, organized at Philadelphia in 1892, remained primarily a local organization. The Negro Society for Historical Research, founded at New York in 1911 by John E. Bruce, Arthur A. Schomburg, and others, led eventually to the establishment of a unique research collection that became part of New York's public library system in Harlem.[89]

V

PROMINENT INDIVIDUALS who survived well beyond the Civil War received variable treatment, ranging from worshipful celebrity in the North for William Tecumseh Sherman, to courteous interviews with Robert Toombs at his home in Georgia, to dogged controversy concerning Jefferson Davis, who has been appropriately described as a "leader without legend."[90] Davis lived until 1889 and received substantial criticism in the South, where many tried to make him a scapegoat for the Confederacy's failure. In the North he would long be vilified as a latter-day Benedict Arnold, a traitor to his nation—all the more heinous because centennial events of the American Revolution provided several occasions during the later 1870s to recall Arnold's treachery.[91]

Davis spoke in New Orleans at the 1887 unveiling of an equestrian statue of Confederate General Albert Sidney Johnston on the twenty-fifth anniversary of the Battle of Shiloh, where Johnston died. General P. G. T. Beauregard, an old antagonist of Davis, felt that his own performance at Shiloh had been criticized in this speech; so the two engaged in a duel with words and memories that started in the *New Orleans Picayune* and then spilled over into the national press. Less than three months later Davis wrote a letter to the *Baltimore Sun*, rebuking President Cleveland for failing to return those captured Confederate battle flags. The *Sun* then ran an editorial correcting Davis's inaccurate version of the circumstances that had caused the flags to remain in Richmond when Confederate troops fled in 1865.[92]

A proposal in 1902 to erect a memorial arch to Davis in Richmond created a stir that bitterly split the Daughters of the Confederacy, a national organization with chapters in the North and West as well as the South. Ever so gradually, however, antagonisms began to heal and Davis's reputation was rehabilitated. His daughter Winnie, who came to be known as "the daughter of the Confederacy," spoke hither and yon about her father and the Lost Cause, and attracted very positive attention, often verging upon adulation.[93] In 1907 the Jefferson Davis Monument was dedicated in Richmond before 200,000 spectators, the largest crowd that had ever assembled to honor any aspect of the Confederate cause. That same year a Jefferson Davis Memorial Association became active in New Orleans (where he had died in 1889) in order to plan a testimonial monument for which the cornerstone would be placed on June 3, 1908, the one-hundredth anniversary of his birth.[94]

The year of Davis's centennial, sandwiched as it was between Lee's and Lincoln's, did not bring beatification; but it did mark a clear turning point in his posthumous reputation. The *New York Times* ran a full-page, though inconclusive, assessment of his role in American history. How would posterity regard him? Not so negatively as those who scorned him, said the *Times*, nor so positively as his loyal supporters would have liked.[95]

In the South, however, memorial tributes occurred in many locations. The College of William and Mary planned to place a portrait of Davis in its new library. In 1910 the University of Florida fired a teacher for saying that Lincoln had been a greater statesman than Davis! Within a few years public schools throughout the deep South began to close on June 3 in honor of his birthday; and Mildred Lewis Rutherford, Historian General of the U.D.C., consecrated her career to achieving vindication for Davis. Her biographical study of him appeared in 1916, followed in 1923 by *The South Must Have Her Rightful Place in History*, a pervasive sentiment throughout that region during the interwar decades.[96]

In 1908, when President Lyon G. Tyler of William and Mary (fig. 4.8) received a proposal from New York that a statue of Lincoln be erected in the South, he responded with a long letter that emphasized the need

4.8   Mary Travis Burwell, *Lyon G. Tyler* (1920s), oil on canvas. Courtesy of the Joseph and Margaret Muscarelle Museum of Art, College of William and Mary in Virginia.

for a realistic view of human nature and the inevitable residue of acrid memories. A statue of Lincoln, Tyler declared, "would simply revive memories that are now no longer bitter [he first wrote "prevalent" and then replaced it with "bitter"] in Southern circles. Mr. Davis and Mr. Lincoln represent two sections in 1861, which closed in a bloody encounter. It is folly to expect that either of them can be ever popular in the opposite sections. In spite of the fierce assaults to which Mr. Davis has been subjected, no one has ever been able to prove a thing against his private character, while his loyalty to his convictions [was] quite as strong and pure as Mr. Lincoln's."[97]

Five paragraphs later the feisty Tyler got around to his principal point, which a great many residents of his region undoubtedly shared:

> To ask the South to put up a monument to Lincoln, who represents Northern invasion of the homes and firesides of the South, would be as absurd as if I were to ask the North to put up a monument to Jefferson Davis. . . . I do not care to force [Davis's] memory upon a people with whom he is not identified. In the same way, I am sure that the South can never be brought to regard Mr. Lincoln in any other political light than that in which Mr. Davis is regarded by the North—as the champion of a section.[98]

So early as the 1880s, an occasional Southern voice spoke a kind word on Lincoln's behalf. But the overall "progression" of Lincoln's image in the South has been carefully traced by Michael Davis: from fool or buffoon to monster, to the incarnation of fundamental Yankee vices, to a gradual recognition that even this formidable antagonist had some redeeming human qualities.[99]

David Donald once shrewdly observed that in folklore, which is less politically partisan than "ordinary" public opinion, there were nevertheless two contrary notions of Lincoln: a Northeastern version in which he is pious, dignified, almost a demigod; and a Midwestern version that emphasizes the practical joker, the earthy raconteur, and a legendary frontier populist. Toward the turn of the century, Donald suggests, the two conceptions began to converge; and by the time of his centennial in 1909 the result was a "composite American ideal" with very strong appeal because "so many dear traditions" were joined in this one larger-than-life figure. Donald makes a provocative case that "the Lincoln of folklore is more significant than the Lincoln of actuality" because it is the folkloric Lincoln who "has become the central symbol in American democratic thought; he embodies what ordinary, inarticulate Americans have cherished as ideals."[100]

Collecting Lincoln legends, relics, and mementos emerged as a veritable cottage industry in the United States; and because his life ended with assassination and instant martyrdom, the process began early.[101] I am most intrigued by those individuals who explicitly articulated either the *obligations* of memory or else expressed reservations about the *mythicization* of history. In the former category we have examples ranging from Theodore Roosevelt to obscure Americans. One of them wrote to a friend in 1872, when former foes still slandered Lincoln: "Do not you and I owe it to the memory of the dead to vindicate [Lincoln] of these charges?"[102]

No one experienced greater anguish at the maudlin idealization of Lincoln than Walt Whitman, whose admiration for Lincoln verged upon love. Whitman blamed the biographers and historians, above all others, for their apparent inability to resist hyperbole. "This sort of thing does throw a doubt upon all history," Whitman wrote, and "eats away at its foundations. . . . My experience with life makes me afraid of the historian: the historian, if not a liar himself, is largely at the mercy of liars." Whitman complained that if someone so much as casually told a Lincoln story, a day or two later it would appear in a newspaper—"foisted on Lincoln"—and become part of the canonical "facts" forevermore.[103] As an interesting example of the process at work, of history being fictionalized while the fiction is regarded in turn as authentic history, one can read the positive reviews of Edward Eggleston's novel *The Graysons* (1888), in which Lincoln appears as a young country lawyer.[104]

Fundamentally, we find the full politicization of Lincoln's memory by

1887, when the Republican Party began holding annual rallies on his birthday. The historical man had become a potent symbol. We can also take the measure of his immense appeal in 1905, when a publisher indicated that demand for a multi-volume set of Lincoln's writings exceeded interest in the works of any other national leader. And we witness his emerging stature as a national hero in 1907 when Mark Twain pleaded that Lincoln's birthplace in Hodgenville, Kentucky, be saved. Twain noted that Kentucky had raised regiments for both the Blue and the Gray. Consequently, why not make the birthplace a "national park of patriotism"?[105] Local entrepreneurs may have had a stake in the questionable legitimacy of that humble Kentucky cabin; but the Lincoln Farm Association had its offices at 71 Broadway in New York City. The classic gap between country and city had in this instance been considerably narrowed.

Perhaps immortalization must inevitably be accompanied by distortion, although I sometimes wonder at the public's willingness to accept mythical history that is patently unreal and verges upon the bizarre. In the case of Abraham Lincoln I have in mind his pairing with George Washington, a tendency toward twinning that makes sense in associational terms—why not link the Father of His Country with its Saviour?—but not to the point of anachronism or a casual process of fading out one figure and supplanting him with the other.

The connective nexus in American iconography began immediately in 1865, as Marcus Cunliffe has carefully shown.[106] But the decade of the 1880s capped it off. In about 1881 the irrepressible Erastus Salisbury Field painted his whimsically serious sextet, *Lincoln with Washington and His Generals* (fig. 4.9). Washington's left hand clasps Lincoln's, and his right hand is clapped firmly upon Lincoln's shoulder. The generals, of course, are Lincoln's rather than Washington's: Ambrose E. Burnside, Ulysses S. Grant, Rutherford B. Hayes, and Chester A. Arthur. It's an idiosyncratic selection of generals, except that five of the six also happened to serve as President. All but Washington and Grant, it might even be argued, became President by a fluke.[107]

In February 1887, after Governor Joseph B. Foraker of Ohio gave a Lincoln's Birthday banquet speech to the very large Republican Club of New York, the *Cleveland Plain Dealer* did a bit of investigative journalism and discovered that he had given virtually the same speech three years earlier at a celebration of George Washington's Birthday. Does an all-purpose speech imply interchangeable statesmen? A year later 2,500 people came to the Chicago Union League Club's observance of Washington's Birthday at the Central Music Hall. Chauncey M. Depew, one of the most popular speakers of that era, chose as his theme "the political mission of the United States." Although he mentioned Jefferson, Hamilton, Webster, and especially Lincoln quite often, he barely referred to George Washington at all.[108]

Had Lincoln and Washington been made the Tweedledum and

4.9   Erastus Salisbury Field, *Lincoln with Washington and His Generals* (c. 1881), oil on canvas. Courtesy of the Morgan Wesson Memorial Collection, Museum of Fine Arts, Springfield, Massachusetts.

Tweedledee of American politics? Not quite. An extraordinary resurgence of respect for Washington actually took place during the final quarter of the nineteenth century.[109] And Washington's appeal cut across sectional lines in a way that Lincoln's clearly did not. To arouse an aura of national cohesion, one invoked the founder, not the rail-splitter, whom some people continued to perceive as a nation-splitter. In 1907, when the director of the Jamestown [Tercentenary] Exposition contemplated "having one day devoted to an historical celebration," he recommended October 19, the anniversary of the Battle of Yorktown in 1781. "It would be a day of National importance," he wrote, "honoring Washington, reviving the memories of Yorktown and dwelling on the country as a whole."[110] If you really needed mystic chords of memory, George Washington remained your man.

   Let us return, however, to the problematic reality in people's minds of an unreal past. In May 1907, at that Jamestown Exposition, Governor Claude Swanson of Virginia addressed members of the Association for the Preservation of Virginia Antiquities. "Our national story," he informed them, "reads more like a romance than a history."[111] Their memories, we might add, tended to remember more romantically than historically.

Four years earlier, by contrast, Ambrose Bierce recalled some ordinary men who had been killed in an obscure place and were buried in forgotten graves: "They did not live through the period of honorable strife into the period of vilification—did not pass . . . from the era of the sword to that of the tongue and pen." Perhaps it is no coincidence that a decade later Bierce himself disappeared without a trace, like those victims of the Civil War he so bleakly mourned in "A Bivouac of the Dead."[112] Bierce did not believe that romantic stories made a proper history. But then, he was not a representative American.*

*The notable political cartoonist Thomas Nast (1840–1902) was nearly as unrepresentative because of his harsh critique of public affairs and tawdry attitudes in Gilded Age America. His cartoons illustrate, anticipate, and validate many of the central themes of this chapter. See the fascinating work by Morton Keller, *The Art and Politics of Thomas Nast* (New York, 1968). More particularly, for Nast's sardonic treatment of "reconciliation," see fig. 14 in that book; for the pairing of Washington and Lincoln, see fig. 4; for the theme of treason and betrayal, see figs. 18 and 22; for the villainous Jefferson Davis in 1870, see fig. 23; for Tammany hypocrisy in the service of its political objectives, see fig. 31; for the cruel neglect of African-Americans, see figs. 56, 57, and 61; and for the politicization of memory, see fig. 217.

Chapter 5

AMBIGUITIES OF TRADITION:
CELEBRATING THE PAST
BY PRAISING THE PRESENT

ALTHOUGH THE CIVIL WAR cast a very long shadow, Americans had manifold anniversaries to celebrate during the final quarter of the nineteenth century. Consequently interest in the past began to flourish despite the presence of conflicting views of tradition and residual ambivalence about the social uses of memory. The big expositions that occurred with rhythmic regularity between 1876 and 1915 revealed an on-going obsession with progress that swiftly became, in the minds of many, a Tradition of Progress.

After discussing those impulses and ambiguities in the first two sections, and observing the process by which Americans learned how to commemorate, we turn in section III of this chapter to the idiosyncratic colonial revival, particularly the role played in it by architects, artists, and antiquarians in the broadest sense of the word—people who did much to publicize and popularize traces of the nation's past.

With section IV we look at nationalism in the arts by noticing the emergence of museums of history and art, patrons, collectors, and the tradition-oriented organizations to which they belonged. Among the varied motifs that recur—such as the centrality of the private sector or the tension between nature and culture—none seems more striking than the discrepancy between rhetoric and reality. While people still paid lip service to democracy by stressing the educational role that institutions of memory should play, elitism rather than egalitarianism characterized most of those institutions. Although the masses were discussed, their presence was attractive only at the turnstiles of expositions. Otherwise collective memory tended to be exclusive, which meant that it was less than truly collective.

I

GENERALIZATIONS about American feelings toward native traditions during the later nineteenth century are hazardous because the evidence drifts in contradictory directions. If we read only what prominent and prolific New Englanders had to say, for example, we might come away with the feeling that little had changed since Emerson's heyday. Some intellectuals may have become prospective members of the party of memory; yet they despaired of finding any sustaining uplift in the culture at large. Charles Eliot Norton, for example, Harvard's prominent aestheticist, seemed utterly unaware that local traditions existed in vernacular architecture and the decorative arts. Writing in 1889, moreover, political scientist A. Lawrence Lowell noted "how little respect the American has for the past, and how ready he is to try experiments."[1]

Four years earlier, however, Brooks Adams had declared that "modern America is ruled like England, by means of a mass of custom and tradition which silently shapes itself to the changing wants of the people." Was Adams being naïvely populistic and myopic? Perhaps a bit; but in 1875, on the eve of the nation's Centennial celebration, the reliably judicious James Russell Lowell put lines in a poem that generalized from knowledge of his native land: "Nations are long results," he wrote, and "from a doughty people grow, the heirs / Of wise traditions widening cautious rings."[2]

The contrasting visions competing for validation at that time are clearly illustrated by Mark Twain and Edith Wharton, each an astute observer yet neither without prejudice. Twain, the Midwesterner who moved to New England early in the 1870s, took a position that may seem apologetic or insecure but was in fact intended to be culturally assertive. "The world and the books are so accustomed to use, and over use, the word 'new' in connection with our country, that we early get and permanently retain the impression that there is nothing old about it." Twain is tricky, however, because as Bernard DeVoto observed, young Samuel Clemens "had guffawed at reverend traditions. . . . He had laid hands of violation on literary and artistic traditions toward which these people had yearned from childhood."[3]

Wharton's outlook and priorities were just the opposite. She cherished the past and therefore chose to emphasize in her prose its connectedness to the present. Although she approved of innovation in imaginative writing, it need not occur at the expense of all that appeared most attractive in the heritage of Western culture. Compared to Europe, however, the United States seemed shallow; and so she regretted the reality of newness that Twain believed had been so exaggerated. "The American landscape has no foreground," Wharton wrote to a friend, "and the American mind no background." In 1911 she sold The Mount, her handsome home at Lenox in the Berkshires, and made her permanent home in France. By her own choice, Wharton ceased to have any sort of physical tie to the United States.[4]

Obviously, there existed contradictory perceptions of the relative presence or absence of tradition in Victorian America. In part the explanation for such a discrepancy lay in varied attitudes people held toward Europe, because the presence or absence of palpable pastness is a relative matter of attitudes. The discrepancy may also be understood, however, in terms of divergent definitions of tradition, and of the sources of tradition with which people resonated. To Henry Adams, for instance, the writing of his *History of the United States* was a dutiful but tedious performance. It did not provide the same sort of personal pleasure as did *Mont-Saint-Michel and Chartres.* Such a sequence—multivolume labors succeeded by a discursive act of love—reminds one of the obligation imposed on Jacob in the Old Testament, to marry the homely Leah first in order eventually to gain her attractive sibling, Rachel. In sharp contrast to Adams, however, we have Alice French, a Massachusetts woman who moved to Arkansas and then Iowa where she wrote "local color" novels under a pseudonym, Octave Thanet. A year after Adams finished his nationalistic and literate *History* (1891), Thanet could offer this comment based upon a very different sense of American culture: "Everywhere [in the South] not only ideas and plots are repeated, but the very words often are the same; one gets a new vision of the power of oral tradition." Thanet's America was more geographically specific and yet more self-replicating than Adams's. Also less refined. She consequently employed a more socially inclusive meaning of tradition than anything envisioned by Adams.[5]

Variability in the acuteness of American retrospective vision tended to be accentuated rather than rectified by foreigners, who often inscribed epigrammatic views in highly visible publications. Oscar Wilde, whose American tour in 1882 had been a *succès de scandale,* has a character quip in 1893 that "the youth of America is their oldest tradition. It has been going on now for three hundred years." Not long after that, however, a Frenchman whose penchant was more sociological than rhetorical would write of the United States: "where everything is of yesterday, they hunger and thirst for the long ago." In 1898, however, Beatrice Webb's keen eye and candid pen noted a certain stubborn pride in America's freedom from tradition and (compared to England) suffocating conventions.[6]

I I

THE YEAR 1876 marked the Centennial of American Independence, the effective end of Reconstruction, and the resumption of a nominally reunited nation. George Bancroft finished his monumental *History of the United States* in that year. And, long forgotten but highly symptomatic, President Grant's eighth and last annual message to Congress apologized for the "errors of judgment" that had occurred during his two administrations. Grant's ploy of claiming political inexperience and blaming subordinates may have been an old one; but he also took an unprecedented tack—an appeal to history as the ultimate judge of virtue, based upon the assumption that rectitude is relative rather than absolute: "Mistakes have been made, as all can see and I admit. . . . History shows that no Administration from the time of Washington to the present has been free from these mistakes. But I leave comparisons to history. . . . Failures have been errors of judgment, not of intent."[7]

Actually, historical comparisons became popular and commonplace in American culture during the 1870s, though with no consistent pattern or outcome. We must at least acknowledge that not everyone who offered paeans of praise to progress did so unequivocally. Spokesmen for the various Protestant denominations tended to laud the progress of civilization in general and that of the United States in particular; but many of them also revealed a certain ambivalence, or at least concern, by perceiving progress as a dialectical rather than a unilinear process. When William Maxwell Evarts, prominent attorney and Republican voice for American civic culture in the 1870s and '80s, gave a Centennial oration on July 4, 1876, his observations on the nation's material development had an anachronistic quality. The "power" that he ascribed to the United States was rooted in agriculture rather than industry or technology. Perhaps Evarts had such a subtle sense of progress that he preferred to emphasize pastoral continuity rather than the visibly startling dynamics of change.[8]

The dominant outlook of the 1870s, however, was less ambiguous and more resoundingly upbeat. In 1870, for instance, James Parton, the popular biographer, launched his career as a public lecturer. He presented his standard spiel, "One Hundred Years Ago," on the lyceum circuit, in country churches and schoolhouses as well as large halls in Eastern cities. Parton described the nation's economic growth and political maturation, the people's struggle against adversity and their eventual development into a great industrial nation. That blend was so well received that after a year Parton added to his repertoire several lively and presumably timely topics: "The Pilgrim Fathers as Men of Business," "The Fun of Our Forefathers," "Jefferson and Hamilton," and "The Friendship Between Thomas Jefferson and James Madison." (Parton had an affinity for scrutinizing personal relationships. His wife, Fanny Fern, a popular writer herself, passed away in 1872; four years later Parton married her daughter, his own stepdaughter.)[9]

Though the rationale for the great Centennial Exposition held at Philadelphia in 1876 was historical, the exhibits, orations, and publications put out for the occasion tended to celebrate the present at the expense of the past. One printed tour guide managed to muddle up the Minute Men of the Revolution with the Pilgrims, and crowed that Peregrine White's little cradle "remains a mute witness of the wonderful story of American progress with which all tongues are busy now."[10] The great exposition, which remained open to an enthusiastic public for six months, contained remarkably few historical displays; and their invariable message was to glorify the present rather than to explain the past, never mind understand it on its own terms. As one journalistic guidebook declared: the "New-England Ivy Cottage" was consistently crowded with tourists eager to view the "ancient costumes of the inmates," namely, young women in olde-tyme outfits who explained the uses of peculiar cooking utensils "whose very simplicity made them incomprehensible to the victim of modern improvements."[11]

This mood of self-congratulation had been building for several years. Late in 1874 *Harper's* launched a two-part series subtitled "Our Colonial Progress." The first installment, straightforwardly political, emphasized the novelty of popular sovereignty as a creative doctrine in the 1770s. Part Two, however, "Mechanical Progress," highlighted such developments as new agricultural implements along with the steam engine and its application.[12] Americans looked to the past in order to enhance their appreciation of the present. In 1876 Charles W. Eliot, Harvard's young president, articulated a lament to which few were willing to listen: "I think we Americans particularly need to cultivate our historical sense, lest we lose the lessons of the past in this incessant whirl of the present."[13]

Although the substantive historical content of commemorative exhibitions did increase incrementally between 1876 and 1915, Eliot's words turned out to be neither heeded nor prophetic. Rather, a highly representative feature story appeared in the *New York Times Magazine* in 1909. In the 120 years since 1790, it asserted, progress had been continuous and could be discerned in five clear phases: 1790 to 1816, 1816 to 1842, 1837 to 1858, then the tumultuous epoch from the presidency of Lincoln through that of Chester A. Arthur, and finally "the wonderful quarter century" from 1885 until 1908. If not day by day, then certainly decade by decade, in every way, we got better and better. Curiously enough the periods were identified by the presidents who governed during them, almost like the reigns of sovereigns; yet the achievements listed for each era are technological and material, especially involving transportation innovation and the utilization of natural resources. The essay included a considerable amount of statistical detail on aspects of economic and other forms of growth. It concluded with a prophecy: New York City would some day become the financial capital of the world.[14]

Thereafter the fascination with progress persisted, though it became a bit less brazen and abrasive. When Newburyport, Massachusetts, celebrated its tercentenary in 1930, "community progress" was emphasized; and when Herbert Hoover spoke a year later at the sesquicentennial of the Battle of Yorktown, he lauded "this vast pageant of progress." For the remainder of the 1930s, however, Americans heard rather less of progress; and more than a handful may have contemplated a world of infinite regress.[15]

BACK IN 1876, when that rhetorical panorama of Progress began to unroll in American discourse, the reality of relentless improvement seemed beyond dispute. What lay ahead would be the responsibility of remembrance. Orators speculated optimistically about the manner and content of American memory. When Robert C. Winthrop addressed the citizens of Boston on July 4, 1876, for example, he acknowledged that the century just concluded had brought wonderful changes throughout the world.

> I would not disparage or depreciate the interest and importance of the great events and great reforms which have been witnessed during their progress, and especially near their end, in almost every country of the Old World. Nor would I presume to claim too confidently for the closing Century, that when the records of mankind are made up, in some far-distant future, it will be remembered and designated, peculiarly and preëminently, as The American Age.[16]

Outside of Boston, however, optimism might at least be modified by a mixture of self-congratulation and the recognition that room for improvement in *some* respects was conceivable. On July 15, 1876, the *New York Herald* offered a remarkably apropos admission: "Americans like ourselves, are better at doing things than commemorating them."[17] Although that condition began to improve in 1876, we must be careful not to confuse commemoration with genuine remembrance. Americans celebrated more than they remembered or learned. Those responsible for the Centennial Exposition in Philadelphia declared that their primary objective was to educate the nation. The fine print noted, however, that education might equally serve the purposes of "profit" and "national duty." The need for national harmony was not overlooked either; and many speakers, printed materials, and events undertook an explicit "mission of reconciliation."[18]

Another major and related theme that received prominent attention was peace—peace in general. On that score, however, the exposition was more ironic than irenic. The United States Government Building, the only structure representing the nation as a whole, presented a formidable display of guns, cannon, ammunition, military and naval equipment. Some foreign visitors openly objected to the massive American arsenal and wondered whether it was only coincidental that a model hospital was located nearby. Nevertheless, it bemused a few and troubled some people that promotional literature could insist the exhibit had been conceived with "the single view of erecting here a monument dedicated to the fruits of Peace."[19]

The longer we focus upon the Centennial, the more ironies seem to compound one another. Although the exposition celebrated technology and its implications for industrial power, for example, little attention was paid to three inventions that all made their debut in 1876: the telephone, the electric light, and the primitive typewriter. All three would revolutionize American social and economic life. But visitors to Philadelphia may have been too preoccupied with their glorious present to contemplate the future in a truly imaginative way. To compound irony with tragedy, the Native American was largely ignored at Philadelphia. The Smithsonian Institution had one exhibit on Indian life; and a lacrosse match took place—so that, although news of Custer's "last stand" on June 25 took a few days to reach Philadelphia, white rage found little on which to vent itself in Fairmount Park.

The year 1876 also happened to be the third year of a severe national depression, a year of whiskey frauds, shady railroad subsidy deals, diverse political scandals, and Boss Tweed's arrest in New York City. Politically active feminists even disrupted proceedings at the exposition. For many, therefore, it was a good year either to contemplate a more serene and distant past, a golden age of fantasy, or else to focus on the wonders of innovative mechanized power, which could not be directly tainted by the stench of corruption.[20]

Its substantive historical content does not qualify 1876 as a remarkable year for American memory. Mount Vernon managed to get a little more notice than usual, as did the onset of Revolution in 1776. The likes of *Harper's Weekly* declared in an editorial that there were Americans "to whom the memory of the men who established our independence is so precious." But William Dean Howells directed his skepticism toward history as artifice. After visiting the exposition and finding mainly false traces of the American past, he winced and warned that "one's passion for historic wardrobes mounts." A quarter century later Howells remained unpersuaded that costume romances could achieve much as either history or literature. He spoke for tough-minded critics, however, and not for the masses, who loved the stuff throughout the 1890s.[21]

A year after the dust of closure settled upon the Centennial, one contemporary asked hopefully: "Have we not discovered that we too have a past worthy of study?"[22] The correct answer could be measured as a matter of proportion. Interest in history most certainly increased in the quarter century that followed, and opportunities to display that interest were provided by various anniversaries of battles, the farewells of flawless leaders from their faithful men, and critical moments in nation-building, mostly from the Revolutionary era.[23]

Such opportunities were also supplied by the various expositions that served to celebrate some pivotal moment in the past along with a particular city's capacity to generate enough capital, civic pride, and energy to mount an expensive yet ephemeral extravaganza. We now know a great deal about these events, especially the World's Columbian Exposition held at Chicago in 1893, the Trans-Mississippi Exposition at Omaha five years later, the Pan-American Exposition at Buffalo in 1901, the Louisiana Purchase Exposition at St. Louis in 1904, Portland's Lewis and Clark Centennial and American Pacific Exposition and Oriental Fair of 1905, Seattle's Alaska-Yukon-Pacific Exposition of 1909, and the expositions held at San Francisco and San Diego in 1915 and 1916.[24]

Each one of these turned out to be notable for reasons that were predictable as well as entirely unforeseen: the assassination of President William McKinley while he attended a public reception at Buffalo; the significance of three great innovations that could be celebrated at St. Louis (the motorcar, aeronautics, and wireless telegraphy); and the opening of the Panama Canal in time for San Francisco's splash, an opening that meant an immense reduction in the distance that separated our Pacific rim from Europe.

Less frequently noticed yet highly significant are two trends that accompanied these familiar phenomena. First, although progress remained very much in the forefront of everyone's consciousness, organizers and visitors alike, memories of various kinds and history in diverse modes steadily achieved greater prominence. The sheer quantity of historical exhibits increased quite markedly, even though their quality could never satisfy an austere soul with such high standards as Henry Adams. He devoted an entire chapter of *The Education* to Chicago in 1893, and experienced mixed emotions: "For the historian alone the Exposition made a serious effort. Historical exhibits were common, but they never went far enough; none were thoroughly worked out."[25]

At least Adams yearned for quality. He may have played the outsider's role, yet he remained a Yankee chauvinist. Genuine outsiders could be quite acerbic in their assessments, and they make Adams appear positively sympathetic. "Touchstone" evaluated for England's *Saturday Review* the 1889 centennial of George Washington's inauguration as president. Recalling the hoopla of 1876, "Touchstone" said that "certainly no nation ever celebrated itself so assiduously before, but then no nation ever had such a chance. It has not been given to any other big people that we ever heard of to exist for 100 years under the most favorable circumstances." So, much of the credit was due to good fortune rather than good judgment or awesome talent. Then the ungracious visitor gave his British readers the sort of snideness that many must have craved. The Americans, "Touchstone" proclaimed, "possess the merit of making the most of what history they have. . . . It is not, perhaps, proportionate in variety and general interest to the size of the Union or the amount of cotton, corn, and pigs their territory can grow, but, such as it is, it is their own."[26]

Some complaints about the public visage of American memory, however, revealed a convergence of British and American vexations. Visitors to Washington, D.C., for instance, often lamented the lack of inscriptions on statues of historical figures. At the turn of the century, Americans also expressed their irritation at being unable to tell one hero from another. Whereupon a visiting Briton published an open letter in which he lamented that "foreigners were apparently expected to be familiar with the features of Gen. [Winfield Scott] Hancock, or else to waste time asking questions, and that if they did the latter, they would probably find that they were talking to Americans who were no more familiar with Hancock's face than they were." Congress responded to this outburst by appropriating $100 in order to place inscriptions on the monuments to Hancock and Lafayette.[27]

Be that as it may, more painters and sculptors did turn their hands to historical subjects during the last two decades of the nineteenth century, and we know of some who had been especially energized by one or another centennial exposition. A typical example of a second-rank artist so inspired is provided by Alfred Wordsworth Thompson (1840–1896), who gained recognition for his patriotic scenes of early American history, such as *Old Bruton Church, Williamsburg, Virginia, in the Time of Lord Dunmore* (1893).[28]

A number of creative individuals received their historical stimuli by serendipity. In 1879 Walt Whitman went a long way west in order to attend a celebration of the twenty-fifth anniversary of the settlement of Kansas. Why? Because Colonel John W. Forney and the Old Settlers of Kansas Committee invited Whitman to read his poetry at the celebration held in Lawrence, Kansas, on September 15 and 16, 1879. There were various individuals like Forney, largely invisible to us today, whose tireless initiative facilitated observances for which the general public had not exactly been longing. Colonel R. E. Peyton of Virginia, just such a person, was described in 1888 as a man "who takes great interest in the celebration of anniversaries of great events in American history." He organized, raised funds, galvanized, and when necessary shamed people into an appreciation of national memory.[29]

The word "national" is critical in this context, because a second trend in the period under scrutiny that really has not been noticed previously involved the tension between national memory (often mentioned though not easily achieved) and local allegiance, which generated enthusiastic responses much more readily. In 1904 yet another booster of American memory offered this exhortation in a widely circulated magazine:

> If education has taught us aught, it has shown us that it is worthwhile to celebrate our significant anniversaries. Under favorable circumstances the commemorations may be made an incentive to fresh endeavor, a stimulus to appreciation of natural advantages, a tie to bind the people of widely scattered sections, and a power

to form and develop the national sense in the fact that our past history is not the heritage of one place, but of the nation.[30]

It remains an unchallenged perception of American culture in those days that nationalism presumably caused every chest to swell with patriotic pride. It is also a textbook cliché that nationalism translated swiftly into jingoism. Nevertheless, *local* pride was much more likely to energize the observances that really engaged people; so place-specific activities served as the strongest impulse to memory in a dual sense: the celebrations not only evoked remembrances of things past, as they were supposed to do, but local events tended to linger in the community's memory, to serve as moments of self-definition and often as models for groups and communities elsewhere.

Some of these events have been little noticed because they seem sectarian, even though they are very much part of an important larger pattern. In 1880, for instance, Mormons celebrated the jubilee of their founding as a denomination, and on July 24, 1897, the fiftieth anniversary of the Saints' arrival in the valley of the Great Salt Lake. Ever since then July 24 has been observed in Utah, with considerable exuberance, as Pioneer Day. In 1901 the Daughters of Utah Pioneers began meeting annually for a noon luncheon on the 24th at the Hotel Utah in Salt Lake City. Elsewhere, in August 1887 the village of Lititz, in Lancaster County, Pennsylvania, celebrated its one-hundredth birthday. The observances made much of Moravian history, acknowledged with pride that no non-Moravians had been permitted to settle in the town until 1855, that the Church owned or controlled most enterprises in Lititz, and that the town had never had either a policeman or a single arrest.[31] Saints, East and West, derived great satisfaction from their jubilees and centennials.

Anniversaries of discovery, exploration, and pioneer settlement also became popular favorites. St. Augustine, Florida, could praise Ponce de León's initial arrival in America and his subsequent "discoveries." Early in 1888 the Associated Pioneers of the Territorial Days of California dined at a restaurant on New York's Fifth Avenue to celebrate the fortieth anniversary of the discovery of gold at Sutter's Mill. This exclusively male gathering mainly reminisced about the gold rush days. On April 7, 1888, the Ohio Society held an elegant banquet at Delmonico's in honor of the initial settlement of the Ohio Valley a century before. In Marietta, on the banks of the Ohio River, the old community was not only peopled to the bursting point, but so decorated with bunting and flags that it resembled a toy town.[32]

That local enthusiasm, in turn, led to observances of the centennial of the Northwest Territory and of Cincinnati, which supplied an occasion for editorials to appeal for national as well as local sentiment. *Everyone* should take pride in the toughness of Ohio's pioneers because they braved the elements and Indian attacks. Moreover, the original states' "great act of patriotism" in giving up their ancient claims to pieces of the Northwest Territory had made possible the remarkable Ordinance of 1787 and the subsequent creation of numerous states that expanded the Union. At Cincinnati in 1888 the big buzzwords were "Progress" and "private donations" in order to erect a huge centennial building next to the Music Hall. In a truly bizarre arrangement, when it turned out that President and Mrs. Cleveland could not be present on July 4, the widow of former President Polk "opened" the Cincinnati Grand Centennial exhibition by turning a key in her Nashville home that somehow activated machinery in the Queen City.[33]

The next year turned out to be a gala one for festivities in Connecticut. First came the 250th anniversary of John Davenport and others founding the New Haven Colony. That meant parades and banquets in addition to solemn exercises held in churches. There followed a remarkable series of 250th anniversaries: of Connecticut's 1639 colonial charter; of Milford, Guilford, Stratford, and Madison; of Guilford's venerable Whitfield stone house, started in 1639 and still standing to this day; of various Congregational churches. The variety of activities was simply extraordinary: historical orations ad infinitum, some by luminaries who travelled long distances; exhibits of "numerous valuable relics"; a seven-hour service on Sunday, August 25, in Milford's First Congregational Church; athletic games, literary exercises, concerts, fireworks, and the dedication of new bridges. Tiny Milford also managed to do the very thing that W. Lloyd Warner would notably analyze for Newburyport, Massachusetts, in 1930: a historical parade in which people wore costumes and carried artifacts derived from the seventeenth, the eighteenth, and the first half of the nineteenth centuries.[34]

Many communities customarily managed to make some contemporary necessity coincide with the celebratory occasion. The Allegheny County Centennial Exhibition, generously supported by the citizens of Pittsburgh through popular subscription, used the first of its three days to dedicate a brand new courthouse. Annapolis observed its bicentennial in 1889 with an "industrial display," which seems strangely inappropriate for a small and venerable seaport. Perhaps the town fathers wished to make a prophetic statement.[35]

During the week of September 9, 1889, Baltimore launched a six-day celebration of Fort McHenry and the "battle of the Star-Spangled banner." Although these particular festivities have long since been forgotten, they received elaborate press coverage at the time. The *New York Times* declared that the events being remembered "were of national importance"; and descriptions of the affair certainly make it clear that people with clout agreed. President Benjamin Harrison came to Baltimore and reviewed a four-hour parade that included fifteen thousand men and one thousand floats, some of which were actually historical in nature. At the conclusion of a re-enactment of the Battle of North Point, "The Star-Spangled Banner" was performed by a 415-person band and chorus of 500. If long is good and big is best, then Baltimore had it all for the seventy-fifth anniversary of its self-defense and the inspiration for what eventually was named (in 1931) our national anthem.[36]

Anniversary season in 1889 seems to have become a coastal contagion. Six weeks later Boston remembered that George Washington had visited there for six days one hundred years earlier. So, not to be left completely in the wake of Philadelphia, New York, Washington, and Baltimore, Bostonians conducted a sedate meeting at Old South Church and listened to a chorus sing spiritual and patriotic songs. The turn-of-the-century mood seemed especially conducive to singing the praises of major American cities. An article that appeared in *Munsey's* in 1902 lavished affection on Boston and made "tradition" sound like the grandest attribute imaginable. As the visitor climbed Boston's "tortuous, cobblestoned streets every step emphasizes the fact that this is the birthplace of a nation. . . . That tradition is the inspirational force of all New England. It is a tradition of liberty fiercely fought for."[37]

Midwestern cities wanted a piece of the publicity also, and some genuine historical sentiment existed; but not enough, alas, to bring Detroit's dream of a bicentennial memorial monument to fruition in 1901, and not enough to prevent academic and journalistic condescension when Chicago planned a centennial for 1903. In the case of Detroit, nothing seemed to develop as desired. In 1898, when a big bicentennial exposition was proposed for 1901, the organizers discovered that they were too late. Buffalo had pre-empted their year. A great Doric column, "the highest in the world," had to be abandoned because no funds could come from government or taxes and voluntary contributions fell vastly short of the necessary goal. The romantic history of the Old Northwest would surely furnish many suitable subjects for the "groups of statues suggested as accessories to the memorial": Cadillac, La Salle, St. Clair, Joliet and Marquette, George Rogers Clark, and perhaps even Pontiac and Tecumseh. No Doric column meant no heroic statues, which in turn meant not much of a civic history lesson for Detroit. The press talked it all up, however, and any native who bothered to read the fine print could swell with a strong sense of tradition: "Detroit is senior among the Western cities, and if we consider her record as a fur-trading post in 1610, she antedates Philadelphia and Baltimore." Ah, yes. But longevity is not enough. Old money was needed to make tradition manifest in Doric monuments and statues of historic heroes. The spirit seemed to be willing, but not the provincial purse.[38]

Newer states suffered from some of the same difficulties, as Tennesseans noted when they observed their centennial in 1897 at Nashville. One chauvinist put it this way when the affair got into gear: "Vermont and Kentucky entered the Union in 1791, but allowed their hundredth anniversaries to slip by without celebration; Tennessee has set the example for younger States, and upon a scale that will hardly be surpassed." The road to Nashville's successful commemoration had not been an easy one, however, and three statements that clarify the route that was followed, and its rationale, are remarkably representative of the circumstances of remembrance in America at that time—save in one respect pertaining to race.

- When the state and national governments refused to contribute a penny, "there ensued a generous rivalry of private contributions, which thoroughly demonstrated the patriotic character of the enterprise." Two million dollars were raised when shareholders invested five dollars apiece.

- "Of paramount significance is a noble structure fronting the Parthenon, devoted to the first exhibition by the negro race in America, contributed by organizations created for the purpose in the principal cities of the Union. Herein are displayed the records of a century's progress from barbarism to civilization, a presentation doubtless without parallel in the history of mankind."

- "The pride of Tennessee in its past suggested a History Building, which, although it came somewhat as an afterthought, is in admirable accord with the original plans, which it perfects and dignifies. . . . The interior consists of five compartments, devoted respectively to history and antiquities, the Confederate Veterans, the Grand Army of the Republic, the Colonial Dames and the Daughters of the Revolution, and miscellanies."[39]

I cannot say how noble that "noble structure" actually was; nor is it clear just how "civilized" the Negro would be made to appear in 1897.

By the mid-1890s some people along the Western coast of North America had begun to clamor for their proper place in national as well as regional memory. Boosters of the Vancouver Centenary asserted in 1894 that Columbus, his successors as well as his Norse predecessors, had all received homage. Consequently "the local pride of Pacific America now demands the honors due the discoverers of the western shores of the New World." One publicist described the fact that George Vancouver sighted Cape Mendocino in 1792, made worthy explorations of the California coast in 1793 and 1794, but then added in all seriousness: "It is no longer questioned that some Chinese Leif Ericsson touched upon the Pacific coast centuries before Sir Francis rode in the shadow of Tamalpais."[40]

During the fifteen years that followed, a marvelous mélange of places seized some historical pretext for celebrations that would bring people and publicity to their communities. In 1902 Wilkes-Barre, Pennsylvania, reminded the nation that coal had first been burned in the United States right there on February 11, 1802. Moreover, the grate in which that coal was fired still existed because it had been carefully preserved in the very house where it initially contained coal. At San

Antonio, where the anniversary of Sam Houston's victory in the Battle of San Jacinto (April 21, 1836) had been observed since 1896, the whole affair was upgraded to a week-long "Battle of Flowers" featuring a pageant, starting in 1904. Early New England, New York, and New Jersey towns continued to whoop it up when their 250th birthdays rolled around.[41]

The centenaries of Ralph Waldo Emerson and Nathaniel Hawthorne in 1903 and 1904, respectively, received their due also. In fact, Salem, where Hawthorne was born, and Bowdoin College, his alma mater, vied in an unseemly rivalry to have the more prominent speaker, and the like. Whereas the festivities honoring Emerson stretched over a "fortnight," Hawthorne's took the form of literary fêtes at several locations, including Concord, Massachusetts, where Julia Ward Howe, Charles Francis Adams, Jr., Thomas Wentworth Higginson, and Moncure D. Conway gathered on July 4, 1904.[42]

The tercentenary of settlement at Jamestown, Virginia, provided the occasion for a seven-month exposition to be held in Norfolk (since the site of Jamestown itself remained a mosquito-infested swamp); and one of the state exhibition catalogues at Norfolk summarized very well the outlook that had been dominant for decades:

> The Past of a locality, presented in a history, acts as an incentive to the Present and Determines the Future. It shows what has been done by heroic characters, or rather, what great things were accomplished by those, possibly simple-living folk, who did their full duty, and the people of the present age, imbued with the spirit of progress invariably desire to surpass the efforts of those who went before.[43]

The past perceived as being determinative. The past as a benchmark to be surpassed. A fortuitous mix of unmatchable heroes and humble folk way back then. The spirit of progress in our own time. Such suppositions were essential ingredients for a heady elixir that many drank happily at the turn of the century.[44]

Sentiments in the West deviated very little from that formula; but acts of remembrance occurred more slowly, in stages, just as they had in the East for much of the nineteenth century. In 1897, for example, the fiftieth anniversary of the massacre of missionaries Marcus and Narcissa Whitman occasioned ceremonies in Walla Walla, Washington, and at the mission site, as well as the creation of a memorial park. Subsequently the Whitman Memorial Association raised a permanent monument in the form of a granite cenotaph. A memorial chapel was erected in 1908; and at the centenary of establishing the Whitmans' mission, August 13–16, 1936, the monument would be reconsecrated as a "national" shrine.[45]

III

IN 1897, when the Whitmans were honored in Walla Walla, a middlebrow writer back East by the name of Anne Hollingsworth Wharton published two books that serve usefully as gauges of the contemporary climate of opinion. One was a biography, *Martha Washington,* and the other bore the title *Heirlooms in Miniature.* They followed the success of her earlier work, *Through Colonial Doorways,* which had appeared in 1893. The appeal of such books reminds us that a colonial revival was well begun by the time the century wound down. Although the revival's relationship to American nationalism has been clearly demonstrated, the ambiguity of its role as a litmus of American antiquarianism is less apparent.[46] As a manifestation of American memory it managed to be simultaneously symptomatic yet highly idiosyncratic.

Vincent Scully has written quite persuasively of the period beginning in the 1870s that "this was a self-conscious generation, tormented, as the men of the mid-century had seldom been, by a sense of history, of memory, and of cultural loss." Scully then went on to show, however, that "colonial" came to be an amazingly elastic rubric. To some architects and their clients it implied structures as well as detail work that were fundamentally Georgian, or perhaps more particularly Palladian. To others, however, colonial meant something closer to late medieval: the sorts of homes constructed in seventeenth-century New England. As the movement gained momentum, moreover, colonial might also refer to a prettified "Dutch colonial" that displayed little that was either Dutch or genuinely colonial. And finally, as the revival reached its ultimate phase, just about anything remotely traditional could qualify, including Greek Revival facades on bastardized, nondescript boxes that casually carried the label "colonial."[47]

Architects who made important contributions to this movement did not function as a cohesive group sharing a coherent philosophy. For quite a number of its most influential participants, the movement was in fact a passing fancy. Arthur Little visited nineteen early American homes in 1877 and made a great many sketches. A year later he published the widely noticed *Early New England Interiors,* and then moved on to other aspects of design that attracted him even more. Like so many of his contemporaries in the movement, Little had interests that were more aesthetic than historical; and his career also demonstrates the absence of a monolithic movement. He had scant contact with other architects who shared his fascination even during that brief phase in the later 1870s.[48]

To complicate matters, moreover, some of the most dedicated antiquarians denied that so-called colonial revival structures had authentic connections with truly American architectural traditions. Samuel

Adams Drake, a New England preservationist, argued in 1894 that the fad for pseudo-colonial structures amounted to "a vicarious atonement for our sins against the substance," meaning genuine landmarks that had been mindlessly torn down.[49] In Drake's critique we find epitomized the controversy between purist preservationists and tradition-oriented aesthetic eclecticists.

We have tended too blithely to assume that if the colonial revival had its origins in the later 1870s, which it did, then it must have become culturally dominant during the 1880s. When we look broadly at the various forms of popular literature produced then, along with declarations of doubt privately expressed, we come away with quite a different picture.

A sequence of three essays that appeared in *The Century* from 1881 until 1883, for instance, suggests how gradually this trend took hold of the American imagination. The first essay, a highly nostalgic piece about the Ephrata Cloister in Lancaster County, Pennsylvania, started with these two sentences: "Antiquarian hankerings do not find much material to feast upon in America. . . . We have no lumber-rooms of history, no remains of architecture illustrative of the march of civilization." Nine months later a story about the quaint but by-passed town of Castine, Maine, lauded it for being "overlaid with traditions" yet lamented that "a tranquil sleepiness has come over the old port in these later years." The tone of this piece conveyed a profound sense of discontinuity with a way of life both neglected and nearly forgotten. The third essay, "Old New York and Its Houses," expressed outright enthusiasm for quaint doorways, mantels, newells, and miscellaneous "colonial fragments," thereby fulfilling, at last, our stereotype of the prevailing mood in the 1880s.[50]

The pattern among writers and intellectuals whom we have long presumed to be partisans of early America also appears less than clear cut. Edward Eggleston, the popular novelist and social historian, wrote *A History of Life in the Thirteen Colonies*, which was initially serialized, chapter by chapter, in *The Century* between 1882 and 1885. Although Eggleston certainly did not romanticize American origins, his affection for the period was clear and contagious.[51] Woodrow Wilson, on the other hand, began his doctoral studies at The Johns Hopkins University in 1883 and promptly informed his fiancée that he would resist the faculty's enthusiasm for digging into the "dusty records of old settlements and colonial cities, [and] rehabilitating in authentic form the stories, now almost mythical, of the struggles, the ups and downs, of the first colonists here there and everywhere. . . ." Henry Cabot Lodge, who also felt a strong attachment to early America, made a valiant effort to differentiate the deleterious aspects of colonial "mental dependence" from enduring virtues that had developed in that phase of our history.[52]

Moreover, despite what *Harper's Weekly* called "the rage for old furniture," despite the appeal of re-created colonial kitchens (as well as pictures of them), and despite an enthusiasm for "relics of colonial days," warnings did appear in the press that some pieces currently being purchased by antique collectors were fraudulent—reproductions being made to look old in New York "reproduction" factories.[53]

The rage for "relics" covered quite a gamut, ranging from excitement about an early seventeenth-century cradle to objects related to railroading. "Relics of Old Railroads" ran the headline for a story about a proposed museum at Grand Central Station that was envisioned "as a means of showing the progress in railway appliances and for the preservation of relics of the old railroad days." Venerable houses chock full of historic furniture, documents, and ancient imprints could generate attention, as did "Revolutionary relics" (letters and journals, snuff boxes and powder horns, Bibles and swords) displayed in the historical rooms of the Wadsworth Atheneum in Hartford, Connecticut.[54]

An unabashed and pervasive craze for colonial furniture, silver, various other artifacts, and entire homes did not really begin until the early 1890s; but then it became an absorbing passion of American society, the upper crust as well as segments of the middle class, for more than a decade.[55] In 1906 Boston's Museum of Fine Arts mounted the first major exhibition of American-made silver ever held in the United States. The catalogue from that show, *American Silver,* remains a landmark publication in the history of American artisanship; and the appearance in 1913 of *American Church Silver,* written by E. Alfred Jones and sponsored by the National Society of Colonial Dames, represented a new level of achievement in research on the decorative arts in the United States.[56]

The key individual in this entire surge, however, was unquestionably Alice Morse Earle (1851–1911), who became the most frequently consulted authority on American antiques. Born in Worcester, Massachusetts, she grew up in a family that had strong antiquarian instincts. Her childhood home was called a "veritable museum." From 1874 until her death, Earle lived in Brooklyn Heights, New York, and wrote seventeen books about the lives, manners, and customs of colonial America. *The Sabbath in Puritan New England* (1891) enjoyed great success and went through twelve editions. That may seem improbable to some of us today; but if so, it is a measure of stark cultural change over the past century. Books like *China Collecting in America* (1892), *Home Life in Colonial Days* (1907), *Child Life in Colonial Days* (1899), and *Stage-Coach and Tavern Days* (1900) passed through countless printings and did much to make the colonial revival a genuinely popular phenomenon during the last years of the nineteenth and first decade of the twentieth centuries.

The varied manifestations of this phenomenon and its impact were manifold. First, designers, architects, and manufacturers paid it the compliment of imitation. To be derivative did not matter. Commercial success did. Colonial revival armchairs and side chairs, sofas, desks, and other furniture were produced in abundance during the generation that followed 1876. Even an innovative designer like Gustav Stickley started out during the 1890s by emulating early American models at his chair factory. Edward Bok, the editor and publisher, promoted a "Colonial Home" by architect Ralph Adams Cram that could be built in 1896 for $5,000. By 1910 any number of rather ordinary firms began to distribute catalogues for their reproductions of colonial furniture; and in 1915 a company based in Chicago claimed that it specialized in the adjustment of "the Colonial style to articles of furniture not in use in Colonial times."[57]

Second, even though Wallace Nutting later helped to legitimize such doings by proclaiming that he "would much prefer a fine reproduction to a cheap antique," in reality early American art objects were not very expensive, certainly not by comparison with European counterparts; and those who owned American objects were eager to legitimize their collections by lending them for special shows. In 1909 the Metropolitan Museum of Art in New York held the first major loan exhibition ever of early American furniture, metalwork, ceramics, and portraits (fig. 5.1). The public response was extremely enthusiastic and the exhibition came to be considered "epoch-making."[58]

Third, although this activity largely took place at the level of high (or elite) culture, it had more than a modicum of "trickle-down" impact. We know that by 1904 interest in American music had become evident and a modest revival of American folk art was under way.[59] Curiosity about colonial artists had been visible back in the early 1880s, a trend that Oscar Wilde not only noticed during his American tour, but

5.1   The Hudson-Fulton Loan Exhibition of Americana at the Metropolitan Museum of Art, 1909. Courtesy of the Metropolitan Museum of Art.

devoted a serious lecture to in 1883 after he returned to England.[60]

During the three decades from about 1885 until 1915 some native artists found themselves attracted to early American subjects. A representative example would be Francis Davis Millet (1846–1912), whose studio in East Bridgewater, Connecticut, contained not merely early American objects, but even an early American kitchen that had been reconstructed with considerable devotion to authenticity. In 1886 Millet painted *At the Inn,* a homey, colonial scene in which a gentleman sits alone at a round gateleg table and a serving girl holding a pitcher seems to await his command.[61]

Although Edward Lamson Henry (1841–1919) was undoubtedly the artist most devoted to nostalgic scenes from an older America,[62] two others deserve special mention because their styles and social roles were so different: Howard Pyle (1853–1911), whose approach was influenced by his vocation as a book illustrator; and Childe Hassam (1859–1935), one of the leading American Impressionists, who painted largely to please himself but, like Pyle, held passionate views about the attractiveness of colonial America.

Pyle's earliest New World ancestor on his father's side arrived in 1682 with William Penn; and despite Pyle's numerous battle pictures, he identified with his Quaker heritage. He had an extraordinary knowledge of American history, especially of the colonial and Revolutionary periods, and he could be fanatical about the accuracy of detail in his historical illustrations. When Woodrow Wilson wrote a series of essays on George Washington for *Harper's Monthly* in 1895, he insisted that Pyle be enlisted as the illustrator. These pictures also appeared in the book version (1896), and were so widely praised that a group of patriots purchased the originals for donation to the Boston Public Library. Pyle also prepared the pictures for Henry Cabot Lodge's *Story of the Revolution* (1898); for *Hugh Wynne: Free Quaker* (1897), the best-selling novel by S. Weir Mitchell (see fig. 5.2); and for Margaret Deland's *Old Chester Tales* (1899). He achieved considerable renown as well for his large scenes of struggle in the cause of Independence, such as *The Attack Upon the Chew House* (1898), from the Battle of Germantown in 1777, and *The Battle of Nashville* (1906), a mural in the State Capitol of Minnesota.[63]

Childe Hassam's roots were Puritan rather than Quaker. He had known and admired colonial church architecture during his youth in Dorchester, Massachusetts, and as a young man he frequently visited the rustic fishing village at Gloucester. He would eventually immortalize the old Congregational church there in 1918; but in 1903 and again three years later he captured the essence of that handsome early American church at Old Lyme, Connecticut, near Long Island Sound. The neo-Palladian style of these churches symbolized for Hassam traditional American aesthetic achievements and social values. He expressed his feelings about such structures, especially his boyhood memories of them, with intense sentimentalism.[64]

5.2   John Singer Sargent, *S. Weir Mitchell* (1903), oil on canvas. Courtesy of The Mutual Assurance Company, Philadelphia, Pennsylvania.

Not far from Old Lyme, in Greenwich, Connecticut, Wallace Nutting began in 1904 to produce his "Colonial pictures," which achieved enormous vogue among the American middle class over the next quarter century. More than any other individual, Nutting epitomized the commercial rewards to be reaped from the nostalgic appeal of the colonial revival (fig. 5.3). Late in the nineteenth century he began to buy early American houses as well as furniture of all sorts. His purpose, as explained in his autobiography, was very clear: "with a series of old dwellings of progressive dates from 1640 to the decline of taste, to have a background appropriate to every American period. . . . It was a vast program for a private person, but, once undertaken, it was never abandoned till all the phases of early America had been depicted."[65]

Although Nutting's autobiography is immodest and sanctimonious, it is undoubtedly accurate in explaining his own point of view, as well as the wide appeal of his pictures set in their slice-of-period-life still shots:

> The old-fashioned interior [is] so absolutely appropriate as a visual reminder of the good taste of the past, and so full of sentiment and historical suggestion. It is possible that the wide diffusion of these prints may have fostered the taste for antiques. At any rate the vogue for antiques, however it was stimulated, became so strong a trend that every family of any pretension to have a proper home, began to collect in a large or small way.[66]

5.3   William C. Loring, *Wallace Nutting* (1925), oil on canvas. Wadsworth Atheneum, Hartford, Connecticut. Gift of Wallace Nutting.

The peak of popularity for Nutting's photographs occurred in the decade following 1905. (Notice the titles of two typically broad-appeal books that appeared in 1916: *The Colonial House* and *The Quest of the Quaint.* [67]) Then came his reproductions of seventeenth-century furniture, followed by the sale of entire houses filled with originals, and eventually the purchase of his finest treasures by the younger Pierpont Morgan for donation to the Wadsworth Atheneum in 1926.

Nutting also recognized rather shrewdly that urbanization and industrialization made many Americans nostalgic for a more rural and pastoral era, when the pace of life seemed slower and the passage of time was measured in a cyclical fashion by the four seasons rather than in a relentlessly linear manner. His hand-colored photographs of fruit trees in blossom beside country lanes did extremely well. Here, once again, we encounter a strikingly curious if not paradoxical attitude in a man who personified the colonial revival in America as much as any single person. With a picture, he observed, "it is an incident not a history that interests." [68]

In 1895, just when Nutting's career was getting under way, *The*

Century published a piece about "American Rural Festivals." At first glance it seems more comprehensive than incisive. It meanders geographically from Salt Water Day on the Jersey shore to the Ice Glen Procession at Stockbridge in the Berkshires, then to the Canoe Club's public parade at Bar Harbor, Maine (a pageant of the sea), and on to the flower parade in Cazenovia, New York, the Grass Parade (a harvest festival) held at Onteora in the Catskills, the parade of new watering-carts at East Hampton, Long Island, and the Tub Parade in Lenox, Massachusetts, a showcase for two-wheeled pony carts. What cohesive theme could possibly tie together these disparate local happenings? Two points, basically: that we Americans remain very much in touch with nature, and that all Americans, regardless of wealth or social status, can enjoy such traditional aspects of yesteryear. The author stressed the importance of broad participation in rural festivals: "the supreme recommendation of uniting all classes of the summer population. Nowhere in America is anything heartily enjoyed wherein the rich and leisurely pass by on wheels to be gazed upon by their less prosperous countrymen afoot." If social stratification was a dirty little reality, rural festivals might not eradicate it but could very well make everyone feel more sanguine about it.[69]

I V

ONE INTRIGUING aspect of this back-to-nature movement during the 1890s is that it altered the way artists schematized history in the American landscape—or, one might say, it altered their sense of fit between nature and culture, between residues of tradition and their environmental context. Back in the mid-1850s, for example, Jasper F. Cropsey painted *Washington's Headquarters on the Hudson* (fig. 5.4). Perhaps the place is Newburgh; but it is impossible to tell because the scene is so dark, desolate, wild, unmilitary, and highly romantic. We can discern a ruin, and perhaps shadows of a small village. The very humble headquarters seems virtually deserted despite the fact that a few years earlier, in 1850, that structure had become the first historical site so designated in the United States (by New York State). (See fig. 5.5.)

Many years later, in 1892, an aging Cropsey titled a very different sort of landscape *Old Redoubt, Washington's Headquarters* (fig. 5.6). This time the vista is clear and unobstructed. Nature is now under control, and it suitably frames the historic site. All is in accordance with Frederick Law Olmsted's criteria for an idealized landscape: broad and serene views of an under-inhabited land—an overall vision of noble simplicity and controlled grandeur.[70] Historical memories are now exquisitely framed by natural amenities, and the site has been transformed from desolation to preservation.

5.4   Jasper F. Cropsey, *Washington's Headquarters on the Hudson* (1855?), oil on canvas. In the collection of the Corcoran Gallery of Art, Gift of William Wilson Corcoran.

ALTHOUGH NOT MANY patrons and collectors were as yet interested in American art—never mind art with historical themes—a few ardent nationalists began not only to reorient their own collections, but to push public institutions in that direction. Soon after the turn of the century a lumberman named Benjamin Ferguson left his entire estate of $1 million to the Chicago Art Institute, the interest to be expended on the "erection and maintenance of enduring statuary and monuments in the parks, along the boulevards or in other public places within the City of Chicago, commemorating worthy men or women of America, or important events of American history." In 1905 a citizen of Boston, Charles Hayden, bequeathed $100,000 to the Museum of Fine Arts there for the purchase of paintings by "modern" American artists. The Art Institute of Indianapolis had recently become the beneficiary of a public-spirited association whose announced policy was "a steady recognition of American art."[71]

One of the most important trends in American cultural life ever since the 1870s had involved the founding of museums followed by hesitant attempts to define their mission and clientele, and then the growth of their role as municipal institutions that could be a source of pride yet needed support.[72] As we shall see in chapters seven and

5.5   Edmund C. Coates, *Hasbrouck House* [or *Washington's Headquarters at Newburgh*] (1871), oil on canvas. New York State Historical Association, Cooperstown.

5.6   Jasper F. Cropsey, *Old Redoubt, Washington's Headquarters* (1892), oil on canvas. Courtesy of the Cropsey Foundation, Hastings-on-Hudson, New York.

eleven, the proper scope of their inventory, and more particularly the Americanness of those collections, required more than a generation to clarify.

It is significant that most of these institutions began, at least in theory, with a remarkably egalitarian rationale: to serve the public, and primarily in educational ways. Nevertheless, as repositories of unique documents and works of art, rare books and objects of decorative or historic value, the trustees of these places found it prudent to be rather more exclusive than their benefactors had intended. When Walter L. Newberry died in 1868, his will provided for the establishment of a library that would be free and open to the public in Chicago. He envisioned a "magnificent public charity." The initial trustees decided to make it a "library of reference," however, more of a scholarly refuge and "gentleman's library." Although the Newberry Library was in theory open to the public, the rareness and value of its collections made it virtually impossible for a mass audience to use, appreciate, or even see most of its treasures. The media seemed very much in favor of that outcome. As the *Chicago Times* declared when the Newberry opened in 1887: "a library exclusively for reference is a select affair; it bars out the mob, and limits its use to the better and cleaner classes."[73]

Despite their elitism, these were years of remarkable growth and activity for learned societies, independent research libraries, and well-endowed foundations like the Carnegie Institution in Washington, D.C., that sponsored historical and archaeological investigations.[74] The inaugural meeting of the Bibliographical Society of America took place in 1904 at the Inside Inn in St. Louis. Within a few years more specialized organizations were being planned, such as the National Naval Historical Society; and contextual discussions voiced points of view one simply did not hear twenty-five or thirty years earlier, the sort of statement made by Otis Mason, for example, when he addressed the American Folk-Lore Society in 1891 as its president. He quaintly spoke about the present in the past tense: "In the last decade of the nineteenth century, when the world was looking forward, it was a relief to vary this mental attitude by occasionally glancing backward, and considering the past as it appeared by its survival in the present."[75]

On June 9, 1898, the Massachusetts Historical Society voted to appoint a committee on historical manuscripts. Its charge was to seek out privately owned collections that related to the history of Massachusetts or the nation; to receive on deposit collections that might be "endangered"; and to calendar papers already possessed by the Society but languishing in storage.[76] This timely action is revealing because all sorts of treasures from the American past seemed to be changing hands during the quarter century that followed 1885, and many were indeed unappreciated or at risk. At a public sale in 1887, George Washington's message to Congress in 1793, a rare imprint, sold for thirty cents. The

"Massachusetts Indian Psalter," printed in 1709 in the Algonquian language, went for four dollars. The autographs of prominent Americans, ranging from John Adams to Charles Sumner, sold for capricious prices, mostly quite low. When art objects with historic associations were auctioned, attendance was often meager. The situation seemed particularly serious in the South, where funds for non-essentials remained scarce. Two great paintings by Asher B. Durand, *Morning* and *Evening,* sold at a New Orleans auction in 1889 for $130 each.[77]

George S. Hellman, one of the most influential dealers trading in Americana around the turn of the century, obtained from the heirs of Hawthorne, Thoreau, and John Fiske the manuscripts of those men and other significant authors as well. Fiske's widow wished to dispose of his papers, she said, because she so feared loss by fire. Stephen H. Wakeman, a wealthy and cultured New Yorker, spent years quietly gathering a private trove of manuscripts by major American writers. He owned, for example, the originals of Hawthorne's *Blithedale Romance,* Poe's *Tamerlane,* important essays by Emerson, poems by Whittier, and Thoreau's journals. Eventually, when Wakeman decided to dispose of his collection, he determined that he would sell it only to J. P. Morgan; but Wakeman then sought a price higher than any single purchase of manuscripts that Morgan had ever made.[78] The transaction remained precarious for a while because Morgan much preferred European antiquities to American ones. Even so, by 1883 Morgan had acquired an Eliot Indian Bible, a complete set of autographs of signers of the Declaration of Independence, and an autograph letter by George Washington. Morgan subsequently favored Lincolniana, though in 1909 he added a very considerable purchase of general Americana from Wakeman.[79]

We have long associated overtly acquisitive instincts with Gilded Age America, so it is scarcely surprising that men (and a few women) who acquired railroads and steamships, mines and manufacturing enterprises, would eventually turn their hands (and their bankrolls) to the acquisition of objects that simultaneously could show them to be cultured, patriotic, and, in the most literal sense, patronizing: that is, patrons of their nation, class, interest group, and perhaps even community. Names like Morgan, Frick, Vanderbilt, Carnegie, and Huntington are now identified with great libraries, museums, universities, and, most broadly, with incredible collections of civilization's treasures. Once upon a time those men were mainly known as malefactors of great wealth. To the extent that they are now known as benefactors, their money bought respectability.

In a curiously unexpected way, people who today care about heritage and who feel some need or attraction to the presence of the past owe obligations roughly equal in size to the malefactors who collected for the sake of status or prestige and those genteel Americans who felt repelled by their *arriviste* contemporaries and retreated into a cocoon that the historian Jackson Lears has labeled anti-modernism.[80] The

motives and aspirations of these people were complex and highly conflicted, however, as we shall see in the next two chapters. It is not
sufficient to say that because of their critique of post–Civil War America, men like Herman Melville, Henry James, and Henry Adams "each
tended to identify himself with the past, with some older period or
tradition." Adams, after all, who became both an astute historian and
a nostalgic antiquarian, said that he wished to resist being "dragged"
into "American antiquarianism, which of all antiquarianism he held the
most foolish."[81]

Very few, however, could view themselves, their vocations, or their
society with the same detachment that Adams managed to achieve.
Archaeologists, anthropologists, and folklorists unself-consciously undertook an array of antiquarian projects by the later 1880s. Such people
no longer seemed so quaint and consequently were not so easily ignored as they had been for three quarters of a century.[82]

Throughout the last two decades of the nineteenth century John
Fiske crisscrossed the country giving well-attended lectures on aspects
of United States history: the discovery of America, the struggle between
France and England for possession of the New World, the thirteen
colonies and their effect upon the mother country, Las Casas, and Benedict Arnold were among his most popular presentations—from Portland, Maine, to Portland, Oregon. If his boastful letters to his wife can
be believed, he went from one triumph to the next.[83] American history
seemed to occupy a fairly substantial place in the niche reserved for
aural public culture in late Victorian America.

Those who achieved acclaim on the lecture circuit usually enjoyed
exceedingly widespread sales of their books as well. Fiske is only the
most obvious example; his works are still abundant on the shelves of
second-hand bookstores throughout the country. In 1868 the Boston
publisher Ticknor & Fields urged James Parton to prepare a series of
historical episodes for publication in *Our Young Folks.* His first installment, an introduction for children to the history of the United States,
appeared early in 1869 as "The Mariner's Compass." It was well received and Parton continued to contribute to *Our Young Folks*
throughout the magazine's existence. During the 1880s book publishers
began to undertake ambitious multi-volume series that sold well. The
most popular tended to be biographies of American statesmen, most
notably an extensive collection under the supervision of Boston's John
T. Morse.[84]

Houghton Mifflin also commissioned an "American Commonwealth
Series" of state histories; and the earliest anthologies of American imaginative writing began to appear at this time. In 1889 Thomas Y. Crowell
published *A Century of American Literature, Benjamin Franklin to
James Russell Lowell: Selections from a Hundred Authors.* The com-
piler seems to have been a bit defensive about the scissors-and-paste
character of his work, but explained that he intended it to serve as a

companion volume to genuine histories of American literature that would undoubtedly appear soon. Even some newspaper editors hungered for historical tidbits that they could run—presumably because such snippets were believed to enjoy popularity, though it is possible that they also served usefully as space fillers. In either case, the managing editor of the *Boston Evening Transcript* told the director of the Massachusetts Historical Society that "anything in the line of fresh products of historic research would be particularly in our line."[85]

More serious and extended enterprises proved to be possible though problematic in this period, particularly if they required any sort of public support. The Ford brothers of Brooklyn, for example, raised in a wealthy family that valued history, books, and tradition, made enduring contributions: Worthington C. Ford as an editor, scholarly librarian, and sensitive nerve center for colleagues in the historical community; and Paul Leicester Ford, the energetic collector, bibliophile, historical novelist, and editor of documentary series that are still in use, who was tragically murdered by a deranged brother, Malcolm Webster Ford (who took his own life with the same revolver). Paul spent the afternoon before his death at the Lenox Library looking for information germane to an annotated edition of Weems's *Life of Washington.*[86]

In response to a resolution passed by the 53rd Congress, James D. Richardson began the preparation in 1893 of a massive compilation, *The Messages and Papers of the Presidents.* Six years later he completed the work in ten volumes that were published by the U.S. government. The set remains invaluable to this day. On the minus side, prominent historians and some sympathetic advocates talked intermittently between 1901 and 1909 about the need for a multi-volume dictionary of American biography on the model of Britain's highly successful *D.N.B.* The Carnegie Historical Fund wouldn't support it, and the young American Historical Association (founded in 1884–85) couldn't.[87]

J. Franklin Jameson of the A.H.A. provided an interesting defense of why the time did not yet seem ripe for such an ambitious undertaking. His explanation hinged upon the relative shallowness of historical activity and awareness in nineteenth-century America. An adequate infrastructure of books and biographies existed for the colonial and Revolutionary periods, but not for the nineteenth century. "Our nation has during that period not cared for biography to anything like the extent that the English have. Yet the success of a biographical dictionary," he wrote, "depends upon the presence of a multitude of works of that kind." Jameson singled out the absence of biographies concerning "that very important body of men who have made the economic and industrial history of the country. I suspect that we should also find, as a consequence of this same national indifference to a good biography, that we have not a sufficient supply of trained biographers to generate such a dictionary at a proper rate." Jameson urged, instead, giving immediate precedence to preparing a "scientific" atlas of American historical geography.[88]

Whereas the long-discussed *Dictionary of American Biography* got under way during the 1920s, and appeared in twenty volumes between 1928 and 1937, Charles O. Paullin's *Atlas of the Historical Geography of the United States* was not published until 1932.

Nevertheless, the first decade of the twentieth century did witness the emergence of landmark publications that would long be used and that served as harbingers of work to come in the years following World War I. Between 1904 and 1907 the twenty-seven-volume series edited by Albert Bushnell Hart of Harvard appeared, *The American Nation: A History*. Heavily dependent upon a burst of historical scholarship that emerged between 1885 and 1905, this massive undertaking became the first broad-gauge synthesis of historical knowledge about the United States, prepared in a manner suitable for the college student and general reader alike. Swift completion of that project seemed nothing less than breathtaking.

And in 1908–09 a comparable sense of excitement greeted the appearance of major editorial projects that rendered classic texts available in reliable form, such as William Bradford's *History of Plymouth Plantation, 1606–1646* (1908), edited by William T. Davis, and *John Winthrop's Journal*, or "History of New England" from 1630 until 1649, edited by James K. Hosmer (1908). As one enthusiast commented (still smarting from the *D.A.B.* debacle): "It is upon those new editions [that] I count. I there hope to see a standard established, and a line of work initiated, which, so far as I know, have as yet no examples in America. We will establish a precedent, and open a field of usefulness."[89]

This proud determination not merely to make traces of the past accessible, but to pioneer in doing so, grew slowly yet steadily in the four decades following 1870. In 1871, for example, Christopher C. Langdell introduced the case method to legal study at Harvard. His approach rested on the assumption that close study of past judicial decisions would reveal the basic principles and rules of law that had led to those decisions. History could be utilitarian in the quest for socially functional knowledge. The case method caught on and soon became dominant.[90]

As nationalism achieved greater intensity, however, even antiquarianism might seem socially functional. People who formed societies for historic preservation justified their activities in terms of an obligation to the nation and to posterity. George Francis Dow (fig. 5.7), chief curator from 1898 until 1918 at the Essex Institute in Salem, the nation's oldest local historical society (founded in 1821), declared in 1900 that "We are the builders and the preservers for those who are to come after us." In 1907 he pioneered the use of period rooms in the Institute's renovated museum, an innovation that spread rapidly during the next two decades (fig. 5.8). In 1910 he moved the seventeenth-century John

5.7   George Francis Dow (1868–1936). Courtesy of the Essex Institute, Salem, Massachusetts.

Ward House to the grounds of the Essex Institute, thereby making it more accessible to tourists. Dow also decided to use costumed guides as yet another attraction for tourists.[91]

And in 1912 a woman who had recently visited the new outdoor museums in Scandinavia utilized a national forum to plead for similar places of memory in the United States. Her pitch must have seemed beyond cavil. We ought to have innovative museums because change is occurring so rapidly that older ways of life are disappearing. "Change is the very breath of our nostrils," she noted; so "why not an American folk-museum to preserve the memory of vanishing phases of the national life?"[92]

WHEN PEOPLE IN THE United States had spoken pejoratively of the burden of the past, they felt no compelling need for either historical length or depth. If such occasions as the Fourth of July obliged them to think about the past at all, they could casually start their memory span with the 1760s, and largely ignore what had preceded that decade except for a few discoverers and explorers. The history that followed 1789 presented two problems: it was potentially divisive, both morally and politically; and it verged upon the present, mere current events.

As collective historical consciousness grew, however, and as Americans became more tradition-oriented, they needed to make some adjustments in the apportionment of significance. The importance of 1776 and 1787 had to be seen against the perspective of colonization, settlement, expansion, and the growth of democratic institutions. Conse-

5.8   Period room, a parlor, constructed and arranged by George Francis Dow in 1907. Courtesy of the Essex Institute, Salem, Massachusetts.

quently the diverse celebrations that took place between 1876 and 1915 had the effect of levelling the landscape of American memory. As retrospective vision improved, the society looked at a limitless horizon: limitless not only in terms of future prospects, but in terms of a past that stretched from sea to shining sea. In 1888 the press noted wistfully that Evacuation Day in New York—the anniversary of the British troops' departure in 1783—had lapsed into neglect, even though it had once been celebrated like Patriots' Day in Boston or Defenders' Day in Baltimore. Six months later, when "Veterans' Day" approached in May, the press observed that Memorial Day, "as the occasion for military and civic display, has usurped the place formerly held by the Fourth of July."[93]

The landscape of the past changed its appearance as the meaning of the past altered; and so the uses of memory altered accordingly. Memories were value-laden, and therefore underwent adjustment when a transformation occurred in the dominant system of cultural values.

Chapter 6

MISMATCHED MEMORIES AND
PERPLEXED PATRIOTISM:
AN ELITIST PREFERENCE FOR
OLD WORLD TRADITIONS

I

BETWEEN 1870 AND 1915 many Americans developed or acquired enthusiasms for tradition which took diverse forms. Manifestations appeared in architecture and the arts, in monuments and literature, in expressions of national patriotism and local pride, in antiquities from Europe and Asia as well as from colonial America. Despite the conceivable coherence of this pattern, a cluster of issues accompanied the phenomenon that could not be readily resolved. The most problematic issue involved choices between the relative merits of Old World and New World traditions, between nationalism defined primarily by people from the Northeast and local chauvinism arising in other parts of the land, and between the unattractive spectre of anti-democratic sentiments widely shared by many custodians of memory versus an inherited egalitarian ideology.

A number of these tensions are epitomized by the careers and attitudes of two individuals who were deeply interested in the past and its meaning for the present. Let us look first at the example of Jared Clark Markham of Jersey City, New Jersey, who not only designed the monument for Saratoga Battlefield along the upper Hudson River (1877–82), but also published a pamphlet about the monument in 1886 and included a brief but fascinating essay titled "National Monumental Art." It made explicit a number of the major questions just mentioned; and the representative nature of his concerns makes it worthwhile to quote him at length.

> Monuments erected by the Republic should have a broader character and a far deeper interest than those of a monarchy. Being truly the work of the people, they should so record the traditions of the people as to build up a true national art, a high tone and spirit, a pride of nationality, and a pure and lofty patriotism. Hence it will be seen that we have no precedents to

guide us in our monuments; that like our constitutions and our
laws, they must grow out of the character and requirements of
the people. . . . Now it is that we are to either assert and maintain our intellectual and spiritual independence, and express it
in our art, or we are to abandon our own character, our own
history, our own life, our own art, and adopt those of another.
Our students of art return from abroad . . . thoroughly convinced that all the fit subjects of art are in foreign lands. . . .
That we have no traditions to illustrate; no character to express;
no history to record; no scenery to portray.[1]

Bernard Berenson, Boston's brilliant émigré from Lithuania, also
loved history and tradition; but as a Harvard student during the mid-
1880s he found himself attracted to the European rather than the
American past. Not *all* of the European past, however, only the
more refined portions. When Berenson's mother expressed a desire
to visit her old home in Russia, Berenson was aghast—he felt certain
that "the medieval barbarism of life" there would disgust her. In
1900 he candidly remarked that the "life of dignified luxury" suited
him very well. In 1903–04, when Berenson and his British wife,
Mary, made a six-month return visit to the United States, they felt
like cultural missionaries. Americans seemed naive, immature, less
than fully civilized. The Berensons' visits to homes of rich and famous people in New York, Boston, Newport, Philadelphia, Baltimore,
Buffalo, Pittsburgh, Cleveland, Detroit, and Chicago pleased them in
one respect, however: their hosts collected Italian and Egyptian objects, along with French Barbizon paintings. The aesthetic situation
did not seem altogether hopeless.[2]

In reality there were, at the very least, four rather different positions
being voiced simultaneously. The most subtle (yet simplistic) was articulated in 1904 by one of Berenson's former teachers, the Harvard
philosopher George Santayana. "This country," he wrote, "has had the
privilege of beginning with all the advantages of [European] tradition
and with none of its trammels." Popular dime novels of the 1870s and
1880s, on the other hand, revealed a greater degree of chauvinism and
less ambiguity concerning indigenous possibilities. "We, also, have our
traditions," one of them declared, "different in kind, but of wild and
marvellous interest."[3]

A third position, which I believe to have been dominant during these
decades, insisted that traditions were not simply lying around waiting
to be socially useful or aesthetically attractive. They needed to be
sought out, noticed, and applied. Moreover, implicitly or explicitly,
traditions were by their very nature European. That was certainly true
for Richard Morris Hunt, the most prestigious American architect during the final quarter of the nineteenth century. He not only preferred
to "apply ideas taken from traditions of the past to the construction
problems at hand," but insisted that "eminence in our profession can

alone be gained by a thorough study of the works of the past." We know from Hunt's numerous commissions that for him the preferred past was not early American but French Renaissance. Kenyon Cox, the prominent artist who was Hunt's contemporary, offered identical advice when he lectured at the Art Institute of Chicago. The path he advocated, repeatedly and passionately, was "to steep one's self in tradition; and then to set one's self to invent new forms which shall be guided by the principles and contained within the boundaries of the old—that is the only way to study design."[4] The extent to which Cox experimented with "new forms," however, is manifest in his painting titled *Tradition* (see the Prolegomenon, fig. P2.5), which is traditional in message, form, and content.

A fourth option was not so much a position as it was a commonplace mode of relating to the past: an eclecticism that gave pride of place to American nationalism yet did not preclude non-American traditions, heroes, and events that seemed in some sense to form a prologue to our present and future. In 1893 two ordinary and highly patriotic individuals who shared compelling interests in the past concocted the idea of having a Columbian Liberty Bell that would henceforth be rung on the anniversaries of major events in world history. The dominant criteria for determining major events? They must in some manner mark the world's progress toward its present condition of liberty.[5]

The unresolved dualism that yoked a desire for genuine antiquity with mawkish stirrings of American nationalism becomes most clearly manifest at the climactic moment in *The Innocents Abroad,* Mark Twain's first book. It is a work imbued with Twain's persistent scorn for Old World pretensions and for Americans' unwarranted admiration for pasts other than their own. When, however, Twain encountered an Egyptian sphinx, the experience overwhelmed him and silenced his sassy contempt for the perdurable past. The pyramid of Cheops, he wrote,

> was looking over and beyond everything of the present and far into the past. It was gazing out over the ocean of Time—over lines of century waves which, further and further receding, closed nearer and nearer together, and blended at last into one unbroken tide, away toward the horizon of remote antiquity. . . . It was the type of an attribute of man—of a faculty of his heart and brain. It was MEMORY—RETROSPECTION—wrought into visible, tangible form. All who know what pathos there is in memories of days that are accomplished and faces that have vanished . . . will have some appreciation of the pathos that dwells in these grave eyes that look so steadfastly back upon the things they knew before History was born—before Tradition had being. . . .[6]

So even Mark Twain could succumb to the power of a man-made enigma that had endured for millennia. Twain published that book in

1869. A year later the Metropolitan Museum of Art and the Museum of Fine Arts were founded in New York and Boston. Egyptian treasures would be prominently displayed in areas adjacent to Greco-Roman casts. Other new museums soon came into being, with comparable collections. The New York State Museum emerged in 1870 as well. Therefore we can say with assurance that a newly institutionalized respect for the past was clearly launched around 1870.

Less clear then, however, and for decades to come, were the proportionate emphases to be given Old World artifacts and New World traditions. Each had its advocates, and some people supported both but for different reasons. It took more than four decades to resolve this contest over priorities. That surely meant that it must have been a fascinating epoch of shifts in people's taste, allegiances, and cultural values. William T. Walters of Baltimore, who left that city a splendid collection of diverse art, had some interest in American works; yet his son Henry did not. Louisine Havemeyer collected Old Masters and French Impressionist paintings with considerable enthusiasm. When her daughter, Electra Havemeyer Webb, decided to collect Americana, especially folk art, her haughty mother chided her: "How can *you*, Electra, you who have been brought up with Rembrandts and Manets, live with such American trash?"[7]

More than thirty years ago the historian Henry F. May sensibly suggested that "something called tradition plays a very large part in the way people deal either with daily routine or with catastrophe. . . . Tradition centers in assumptions of value, however inarticulate, which have been inherited from the past." The evidence that I have seen, however, indicates a more gradual and slightly later transition than May envisioned when he asserted that, as of 1912, "Americans for a long time had wanted to construct their own tradition, yet the European and English past was the only past that was available."[8] The Americanization of memory involves a more complicated and wrenching story than we have hitherto recognized.

I I

AS THE PRESENT century emerged on January 1, 1901, the *New York Times* published a feature whose ostensible focus was a celebration of the United States, past and present. It paid predominant attention to Europe, however, and the accompanying editorial offered a weak acknowledgment but not an explanation: "We have devoted what may seem to be a disproportionately large part of this review to European affairs."[9] The mere fact that an acknowledgment seemed called for marked a turning point, because for thirty years past Europe had been the cynosure of cultural attention and measurement. This was generally true in the arts, and particularly so in painting, as a casual glance at American impressionism reveals. William Merritt Chase put the matter succinctly in 1872: "My God, I would rather go to Europe than to Heaven." Partiality for European music may have been even stronger though less pithily expressed. It certainly was manifest in concert programs.[10]

One might reasonably expect a stronger emphasis upon Americanness in the Western part of the nation; but the creation of culture and concern for tradition during those years remained very much the purview of migratory Easterners, whose memories were inclined in that direction and whose criteria of taste still came largely from trans-Atlantic images and impressions. Resorts in the Rocky Mountains were defined in terms of Swiss or Austrian alpine analogies. Resort architecture in California followed Mediterranean models. The most lavish California seashore community, built in 1904–05, was predictably named Venice. Visitors to the Grand Canyon commonly tried to describe it in terms of roughly comparable European sites; and they drew parallels between Pueblo villages of the Southwest and sites (as imagined) in ancient Egypt and Nubia, Nineveh and Babylon. In 1880 Lew Wallace, then serving as territorial governor of New Mexico (1878–81), published *Ben-Hur*, which sold more than 2 million copies. This Indiana man of letters and Civil War general sat down at his desk in the ancient governor's palace at Santa Fe and constructed a gripping narrative about the rise of Christianity amidst the late Roman Empire.[11]

Neither the subject nor the success of *Ben-Hur* should be perceived as some isolated or freakish episode.* From 1904 until 1915 Pasadena's Tournament of Roses, which began in 1889, featured Roman chariot races complete with drivers dressed in togas. A Venetian water carnival appeared at Santa Cruz in 1895, and a Greek temple was erected at San Francisco that same year. As late as 1909, when the most influential figure in theatrical extravaganzas wrote about "American Pageants," he did not seem to notice the anomaly in his presentation. After mentioning a pageant of Canterbury pilgrims held at Gloucester, Massachusetts, a neo-classical masque mounted by Augustus Saint-Gaudens at Cornish, New Hampshire, and a Redwood Festival called "The Hamadryads" put on by the Bohemian Club north of San Francisco, Percy MacKaye declared that "pageantry is poetry for the masses" and therefore relates directly to "the vital question of the function of art in the democracy."[12] The ideology may have been American, but the preferred medium apparently need not have been. If the anomaly bothered anyone, comments went unrecorded.

The popularity of pseudo-historical pageants was, perhaps predictably, accompanied by enthusiasm for historical games. The develop-

---

*In 1889 a monument to the soldiers of the Confederacy, planned for Richmond, was designed to stand above a column modelled after Pompey's Pillar in Alexandria, Egypt. (See *NYT*, Sept. 28 and Nov. 23, 1889, pp. 4 and 1.).

ment of educational playing cards shows a symptomatic pattern. "The Game of Kings," a card game, made its initial appearance in 1845; "Sovereigns of England" in 1880; and finally a derivative entertainment, "Presidents in the White House," became available in 1896. A year earlier the Educational Game Company of America, located in Brooklyn, New York, brought out "A Trip Through Europe" followed fairly promptly by "A Trip Through the United States."[13] Perfect parity had not quite been achieved as yet; but popular culture seems to have been moving in that direction by the turn of the century.

A similar pattern prevailed among those who collected antiques. Until the turn of the century, "collecting antiques" normatively meant European and Oriental objects. In a few categories, such as items directly associated with a very famous personage, pieces of Americana were competitive in value. By 1908–09, a rapid increase in the cost of Old World antiques drove some purchasers to look seriously at native items, and that in turn persuaded dealers who have since become famous as purveyors of Americana to reorient their diversified inventories more in the direction of American craftsmanship.[14]

A comparable tendency occurred among those who acquired American art. There had been some collectors during the 1830s, '40s, and '50s, primarily in the New York City area because "new money" had begun to accumulate there. Most of them acquired European paintings as well, and their portraits are revealing because they invariably present these people with an Old World or Far Eastern art object prominently in view. After the Civil War it became absolutely unfashionable to obtain American art. Isabella Stewart Gardner of Boston, J. Pierpont Morgan, and Arbella Huntington of Pasadena and New York (who married her own nephew, Henry, after bearing him a son), are among the most prominent late nineteenth-century Americans who lusted after Old Masters.[15]

In 1887 a special sale of American art was arranged in New York City "for the purpose of testing the market for American art" (according to the press). Although no major collectors appeared, a modest but "appreciative" audience bought about half of the works offered. Another account described the auction as "spiritless" because there was little competition. As late as 1910, in fact, at a typical sale collectors would pay $20,000 for a painting by Bouguereau but only $260 for one by Albert Pinkham Ryder. Not until 1892 would there be a single dealer in New York (William MacBeth) who specialized in American paintings.[16]

Given the temper of the times, comparatively few artists felt much incentive to paint American scenes that were historical or even genre works. One thinks instead of *The Parthenon* (1871) by Frederic E. Church, or *Ruins of the Parthenon* (1880) by Sanford Robinson Gifford, or *Stonehenge* (c. 1882) by William Trost Richards.[17] European-born artists who emigrated to the United States had a double excuse, so to speak. When Domenico Tojetti, an Italian who settled in San Francisco, painted *The Progress of America* in 1875, he could not have produced a more baroque and Italianate allegorical picture: a woman riding in a chariot drawn by two white steeds, with ethereal cherubs wafting hither and yon.[18] Grateful immigrants gladly celebrated their adopted homeland, but with familiar devices and mannerisms.

Still other newcomers, however grateful, retained not merely Old World techniques, but memories as well. Hans Heinrich Bebie emigrated from Zürich soon after 1840 and became a popular Baltimore artist. His affection for the homeland was nevertheless entirely compatible with American taste in the postwar era, exemplified by his *Reminiscence of Europe,* a charming oil on canvas executed in 1876. It combines a festive street scene, genre painting, and clever perspective skills that are utterly "un-American" notwithstanding all the chauvinism of that Centennial year.[19]

The Pennsylvania Academy of the Fine Arts, the nation's oldest, did not exhibit very much in the way of historical art; and when it chose to do so acted on the presumption that European historical events and personages would have considerably more appeal. That seems to have been an accurate assumption. In 1883, for example, the Academy made a special effort to encourage American historical art by sponsoring a competition restricted to that field alone. But only four artists submitted entries and the affair was a fiasco.[20]

(Precisely because premonitions of genuine change are not commonplace, those that do appear deserve notice. When the American artist Edwin White [1817–1877] painted *The Antiquary* in 1855, he depicted a sixteenth-century Florentine collector examining an old coin. In 1870 Edward Lamson Henry [1841–1919], who loved to paint scenes that sighed heavily with nostalgia for early America, wrote this sentence to Southern sculptor Edward Valentine: "I never thought to write you before that . . . my stock in trade is that of an antiquary."[21] Given Henry's relentless attraction to colonial and Revolutionary times, he clearly meant an *American* antiquary. In 1870 such a species was neither abundant nor notably self-aware. Henry's awakening seems to have been an omen.)

The situation in architecture was predictably similar to that in painting. The colonial revival could scarcely keep pace with at least three European styles that offered stiff competition. I call them medieval, modified Renaissance, and just plain eclectic. Sydney George Fisher, a Philadelphia gentleman lawyer, conveyed part of the immense irony in 1897. The Centennial Exposition of 1876, he observed, "aroused an unfortunate interest in European forms of building. Our people, having suddenly awakened to the thought that they had no architecture beyond the proportions of a dry-goods box, ran riot, and, under the name of Romanesque, disfigured the country with all manner of grotesqueness and individual conceit. . . ." Although Fisher acknowledged that the colonial revival subsequently came into its own, that trend certainly did not meet with universal approval. In 1891 one critic argued that the very notion of an indigenous American architecture seemed "an illustration of the same delusion which animated people in the Middle Ages concerning the philosopher's stone."[22]

Among the three non-American traditions that vied for favor and support, the eclectic might very well be designated as the tradition of tradition. An extended editorial published in 1897 proclaimed that the "trouble with modern architecture is that the traditions are broken." It concluded with equal clarity: "Since the world began no man has ever designed a good building independently of tradition."[23] Nothing wishy-washy about that anonymous critic.

Cass Gilbert, the dominant figure in American architecture following Richard Morris Hunt, certainly agreed. The State Capitol that he designed for Minnesota early in the twentieth century provided a kind of neo-classical pastiche. John La Farge, who got a commission for major murals in it (they became quite controversial), decided to draw upon four different civilizations by depicting Moses, Socrates, Confucius, and a medieval mélange. As La Farge wrote to the state commissioners when pleading for payment: "In these four subjects I have to study the architecture, the landscape, the costumes, and the general habits of four different nationalities, widely removed from each other by time, by race and by different civilization."[24] There we have tradition for its own sake, and rather at random: nothing American, nothing even neo-Scandinavian for Minnesota, not even that elusive chimaera called Western Civilization. Instead, an unmeltable pot of traditions.

A number of prominent American firms, like McKim, Mead, & White, succeeded in persuading their clients that the United States had (or perhaps ought to have) some sort of special relationship to "the Renaissance," however vaguely defined. This trend started during the 1870s, achieved a kind of apotheosis in the Boston Public Library (1887–95), flourished in bastardized forms at the 1893 Columbian Exposition in Chicago, in sundry urban railroad stations, in several major museums (such as the Art Institute of Chicago and the Corcoran in Washington, D.C.), and in countless French Renaissance châteaux that Richard Morris Hunt raised for the rich and infamous along Fifth Avenue and other fashionable locations. Once again, tradition for the sake of continuity and cultural legitimacy enjoyed a peculiar currency. Charles McKim wrote to an artist friend: "As Rome went to Greece, and later France, Spain and other countries had gone to Rome, for their own reactions to the splendid standards of Classic and Renaissance Art, so must we become students, and delve, bring back and adapt to conditions here, a groundwork on which to build."[25]

The medieval revival had its architectural exponent in Ralph Adams Cram and a spiritual standard-bearer in Henry Adams.[26] Bizarre structures turned up in unlikely places, such as the medieval castle built at Leadville, Colorado, in 1895–96. But this movement managed to transcend architecture and included enthusiasm for medieval literature and legends, the decorative arts, and even political institutions. Herbert Baxter Adams successfully transmitted to a generation of Johns Hopkins graduate students (mainly during the 1880s) the notion that American governmental arrangements, in all their democratic glory, somehow originated in the German "tun" and got transmitted to the New England town by way of the olde English witenagemot.[27]

As for the decorative arts, one need only look at Howard Pyle's illustrations for such popular works as *Otto of the Silver Hand* (1888), "The Pilgrimage of Truth" (1900), "North Folk Legends of the Sea" (1902), and *The Story of King Arthur and His Knights* (1902–03), to see just how deeply Pyle must have empathized with realms of imagination evoked by Robin Hood, Sir Tristram, the Lady of Shalott, Morgana, and Abbot Otto of St. Michaelsburg.[28]

Mark Twain may very well have been the most vocal nay-sayer in reacting against the medieval revival. It is impossible to gauge whether his scorn had any impact upon those, like Pyle, who were so prone to romanticize the Middle Ages. But the ferocity of Twain's attacks does serve to remind us that he surely was more representative of a society that preferred progress to regress. "I do not live backwards," he declared. In *Huckleberry Finn* (1884), Twain ridiculed Tom Sawyer's impractical desire to do everything according to books he had read about medieval times. Twain's real target, of course, was not the Tom of his own fabrication but the pernicious influence of Sir Walter Scott, Victor Hugo, Alexandre Dumas, and others who fantasized about the simplicity, nobility, and bravery of a purer folk whose like had not been seen for many centuries.

A Connecticut Yankee in King Arthur's Court (1889), a novel concerning the "transposition of epochs," finds the Middle Ages unattractive and compares them unfavorably with the later nineteenth century. Although Twain acknowledged the sheer tensile strength and persistence of tradition, he ended chapter 18 by minimizing the significance of "traditions [that] went but little way"; and in chapter 9, "The Tournament," he revenged himself upon Sir Dinadan, teller of time-encrusted jokes. "Who can hope to know," Twain's narrator asks rhetorically, "what my feelings were, to hear this armor-plated ass start in on it again, in the murky twilight of tradition, before the dawn of history. . . ."[29]

Mark Twain deserves our praise for differentiating so thoughtfully between tradition and history. Although he found most traditions foolish, he took history seriously, reflected upon its meaning in a variety of ways, and speculated more engagingly than most American writers about the problematic cultural consequences of romanticizing or misperceiving the past.[30]

We shall explore some sustained comparisons at the close of these chapters, yet it is essential to notice here in passing that the medieval revival in the United States had its counterparts (actually precursors) in Western Europe. Not only did the Gothic revival in Great Britain antedate our own, but Viollet-le-Duc had begun his overzealous restoration of medieval Carcassonne more than a generation before significant historic preservation got under way in America. Most important, quite a few critics of uncontrolled change in Victorian Britain and France shared a covetous vision (or call it fantasy perhaps) of medieval society as a marvelous social order.[31] In that respect, at least, writers like Thomas Carlyle make Henry Adams look derivative rather than, as we usually tend to see him, *sui generis*.

ADAMS WOULD NOT have thrilled to being described as "derivative," but it cannot be denied that he as well as many of his American contemporaries were Francophiles. The impact of Second Empire French culture, especially in the arts, between the mid-1850s and the 1870s was quite striking. The response to that vogue, however, was hardly monolithic. In 1871 Paul Hamilton Hayne wrote with contempt of "the friends you mention who have become so captivated with France, that they can't abide this 'rude' land." James Parton, on the other hand, descended from Huguenot stock, began to work on his *Life of Voltaire* as early as 1866, and devoted himself intensively to completing the project between 1876 and 1881, when the book appeared.[32]

Acts of cultural Francophilia continued to be diverse and intense, but they took place primarily at the level of high culture. In 1879, when Jules Bastien-Lepage completed his handsome and powerful painting, *Joan of Arc Listening to the Voices* (fig. 6.1), it was promptly purchased in Paris by an American collector and taken to Boston, where the picture received lavish praise. All through the 1880s, Richard Morris Hunt continued to design French Renaissance mansions for his wealthy patrons.[33] And in 1882 Henry James toured the Loire Valley, where the Château de Chambord in Blois, built by King François I early in the sixteenth century, touched him deeply. "I enjoyed my visit to this extraordinary structure," he wrote, "as much as if I had been a legitimist; and indeed there is something interesting in any monument of a great [social? political?] system, any bold presentation of a tradition."[34]

Cultural Anglophilia developed a little more slowly because of the hard feelings resulting from virtually every American war between 1776 and 1865. In many locations, cultural Anglophilia somehow coexisted with political Anglophobia. For those in arts and letters, however, unmitigated admiration and affection were swiftly consummated. Edwin Austin Abbey (1852–1911), a Philadelphian, prepared illustrations for *Harper's Weekly,* and then for *Scribner's,* specializing in historical subjects. In 1878 he settled permanently in London and produced a very substantial body of art devoted to English life in the seventeenth and eighteenth centuries.[35]

6.1 Jules Bastien-Lepage, *Joan of Arc Listening to the Voices* (1879), oil on canvas. Courtesy of the Metropolitan Museum of Art.

The appearance of James Bryce's *American Commonwealth* in 1889 elicited from Edward Eggleston a long and laudatory review that seems, in retrospect, remarkably deferential though rather acute in several of its responses. Ultimately, Eggleston acknowledged, a few Americans may be familiar with some of their history; but even the most esteemed historians here lacked powers of explanation and the analytical skills of their British counterparts.

> We hardly deserve the compliment [Bryce] pays us in saying that Americans know their own history better than Englishmen do that of their country. This may be true respecting the diffusion of historical knowledge in America, and it may be true of the work of students upon certain periods of our history, such as the crisis of the Revolution. But the action of cause and effect and the continuity of institutions and usages have been little understood, because some of our most patient and learned historians have been men tolerably incapable of penetration into that history which underlies history.[36]

In 1896, when Eggleston published his discourse on early America, he dedicated the book to Bryce in a manner that seems fulsome even by late Victorian standards. Its unabashed Anglophilia, moreover, may not have been entirely welcome in portions of Eggleston's native Middle West. "In giving an account of the origins of the United States," he explained, "I have told a story of English achievement. It is fitting that I should inscribe it to you, who of all the Englishmen of this generation have rendered the most eminent service to the United States."

The growth of rapprochement between 1892 and 1910 led to a reconsideration of the once despised Loyalists, though largely among certain elite circles and scholars. Barrett Wendell, who taught literature at Harvard, became intrigued by Thomas Hutchinson, the last colonial governor of Massachusetts, and acknowledged to a biographer of Hutchinson his feeling that "we of posterity owed him and his fellow loyalists" a "debt of justice." Non-partisan sympathies developed quite slowly, however, and in 1910 Charles Francis Adams, Jr., still lamented the fact that "patriotic American historians have passed very lightly over the character of the Revolutionary loyalists, and the treatment meted out to them."[37]

Affirmations of fairness and forgiveness had a way of stimulating reciprocity. In 1900 the popular historian John Fiske received an invitation from the Secretaries for the Memorial of Alfred the Great, based in London, to deliver an address at "the millennial" of the death of Alfred, to be celebrated at Winchester, his capital and burial place, in September 1901. Fiske and his hosts looked forward to "an occasion which holds a profound meaning for all inheritors of the great struggle of the people for liberty and self-government and education and religious freedom."[38] Although such effusions contained a heady mix of myth and hyperbole, they resonated very well at that time on both sides of the Atlantic.

Another prominent historian, James Ford Rhodes, loved Oxford because it seemed so richly steeped in traditions. Rhodes wryly proposed a swap to an unamused don: "You might trade us Oxford and its architecture for a few of our Steel Works. We would work up the tradition if we could get the buildings." Rhodes knew perfectly well that traditions really cannot be "worked up," at least not authentic traditions, though even as he wrote all sorts of relatively recent "traditions" were being blessed. In yet another public expression of Anglophilia, a featured exhibit at the Louisiana Purchase Exposition in 1904 included historical photographs taken by Sir Benjamin Stone—an exhibition arranged by a recent U.S. consul in Birmingham.[39]

The growing sense of a unified Anglo-American civilization was reflected in the collecting policies of such men as Henry Clay Folger, Henry E. Huntington, William Andrews Clark, and William L. Clements, each of whom ultimately endowed a great research institution.[40] Their outlook was well represented by Brander Matthews, a professor of English and American literature at Columbia, who reacted vehemently in 1908 when an organization appeared, called the American Language Legion, "formed to urge upon us the right and the duty of declaring that we will no longer speak English, but American."[41]

Matthews concluded his brief but meandering essay with an appeal for the proper recognition of American literature as a branch still deeply embedded in the trunk of its British parent. "Here is the mistake of those who like to set American literature up over against English literature—by so doing they seem to deprive us Americans of our inheritance in Chaucer and Shakespeare and Dryden. American literature, properly considered, is only one of the subdivisions of English literature in the past hundred years."[42]

Seven years later yet another Anglophile, Senator Henry Cabot Lodge, would confront the same issue but somehow manage to sound anti-British, all the while insisting that the United States derived its culture from a shared Anglo-American heritage. Lodge "one-upped" the British by declaring that his countrymen had retained original patterns of usage long since lost in the mother country. His hymn of praise to the English language in an older, unadulterated form, "with its history and traditions, with its literature and its unequalled richness," signified a moment of transition from cultural bilateralism to a strident national chauvinism that would almost become abrasive in the years following World War I.[43]

III

IF WE PAUSE for an overview of the period 1870–1915, what we notice repeatedly is a pattern of transformation in which, at first, Old World traditions are deemed preferable whereas those of the New range from despicable to being barely acceptable; then American thought and culture is subsequently found worthy of recognition, at least; and third, as the era closes, indigenous customs begin to enjoy, in the eyes of some prominent spokesmen, preferential status. There were exceptions to this rhythm, to be sure, because history is never neat or symmetrical. As early as 1875, for example, Paul Hamilton Hayne, who had once (like Longfellow) written a poem derived from Scandinavian models, complained to Sidney Lanier that the Maryland poet appeared "to think it is an artistic mistake to choose any of the old world legends."[44]

All Americans did not see eye to eye, even sympathetic ones devoted to the mores of a single section of the country. Nevertheless a general configuration took shape that recurred in literature, history, the arts and antiquities. The next four sections of this chapter will delineate that configuration, notice the nascent nationalism that ultimately affected it, look at the attendant reorientation of collectors, patrons, and cultural institutions, and close with attention to some implications for perceiving chronology, geography, and early inhabitants: the "discovery" of pre-Columbian history and the birth of enthusiasm for traces of the Indians' past, primarily in the American Southwest.

Between 1872 and 1880, when Edith Wharton was an adolescent

with a ravenous appetite for books, very few works by American authors resided in her father's elegant library. Although related to Herman Melville, she was not permitted to read his books because her judgmental parents regarded him as too bohemian. She would discover the classic American writers much later, and on her own. Instead she developed, during the 1870s, an enthusiasm for ancient history that subsequently was supplanted by serious investigations in Italian history. In 1898 she began to keep a list of her favorite books. None written by an American author appeared until 1909: *The Portrait of a Lady* by Henry James.[45] Wharton's pattern may have been a little extreme; but I consider it a caricature of the norm that may actually have been closer to the norm than to caricature.

The path followed by James himself was in significant respects well established by then. Certain key moments are very instructive nonetheless. In 1867, at the age of twenty-four, he wrote to a friend in Paris:

> We young Americans are (without cant) men of the future. I feel that my only chance for success as a critic is to let all the breezes of the west blow through me at their will. We are Americans born. . . . I look upon it as a great blessing; and I think that to be an American is an excellent preparation for culture. We have exquisite qualities as a race, and it seems to me that we are ahead of the European races in the fact that more than either of them we can deal freely with forms of civilization not our own, can pick and choose and assimilate and in short (aesthetically &c) claim our property wherever we find it. To have no national stamp has hitherto been a regret and a drawback, but I think it not unlikely that American writers may yet indicate that a vast intellectual fusion and synthesis of the various National tendencies of the world is the condition of more important achievements than any we have seen. We must of course have something of our own—something distinctive and homogeneous—and I take it that we shall find it in our moral consciousness, our unprecedented spiritual lightness and vigour. In this sense at least we shall have a national *cachet.*[46]

That outlook was literally encapsulated in "A Passionate Pilgrim," an early story by James about a sickly American who visits Paris and utters these words before expiring: "There's a certain grandeur in the lack of decorations, a certain heroic strain in that young imagination of ours which finds nothing made to its hands, which has to invent its own traditions and raise high into our morning air . . . the castles in which we dwell."[47]

By 1879 the arch and more familiar James published his constantly quoted study of Hawthorne, in which he enumerated all that America lacked in terms of traces of tradition and concluded that "it takes a great deal of history to produce a little literature." Twenty-five years later he revisited the United States and summed up his experience with a more generalized and gloomy critique called *The American Scene* (1907), a book about "the lights and shades of remembrance." What he encountered in Boston, as he perceived it, "was a perpetual repudiation of the past, so far as there had been a past to repudiate." Scorn compounded his dismay. While visiting Harvard he saw "in the distance a distinguished friend, all alone . . . but to go to him I should have had to cross the bridge that spans the gulf of time, and, with a suspicion of weak places, I was nervous about its bearing me."[48] Surely that is one of the cleverest images ever devised to describe the precarious relationships of past and present, of friendship and the haunting fear that change and multiple passages create impassable distances.

He responded to New York City by expanding upon his long litany of lacks ("no . . .") in *Hawthorne*. The 1907 list is not often cited, perhaps because of its comparative brevity, perhaps because James expanded his lament from the stuff of literature in particular to the stuff of civilization in general. In America, he scowled, "by the failure of concurrent and competitive presences, the failure of any others looming at all on the same scale save that of Business, those in particular of a visible Church, a visible State, a visible Society, a visible Past; those of the many visibilities, in short, that warmly cumber the ground in older countries." James compared the "tabernacle of Grant's ashes" with Napoleon's tomb at the Invalides, "a great national property," as a means of deprecating the fragile quality of American heroic traditions compared with their powerful counterparts overseas. In this book, above all others, James sought "things to play on the chords of memory and association." He found the United States pitifully deficient.[49]

The problem with citing Henry James, of course, is that, however pithy, he is unrepresentative. During his first decade abroad as a mature writer gradual changes occurred in the United States, changes that we can uncover retrospectively which would not have been visible to him. In the mid-1880s, when a literary revival took place at Harvard, American authors were barely discussed and the editors of *Harvard Monthly*, a new magazine, asserted that artistic development "is all but impossible in this country." That literary journal had virtually fizzled by 1910. Meanwhile, expectations that a genuinely American literature would emerge, one worthy of the name, began to appear by 1888.[50] Less than three years later hosannas greeted the completion of an eleven-volume series edited by Edmund Clarence Stedman and Ellen M. Hutchinson, *A Library of American Literature* (1888–90). The editors felt that their "National gallery" presented a "rare conspectus of American life—yes, of American history, in all departments of imagination, action, and opinion." In extending congratulations to the editors, *The Century* magazine expressed pride in having been "so closely connected with the remarkable development of our native literature during the past two decades." Stedman and Hutchinson had "done American literature, American history, and American patriotism a great and lasting service."[51]

The transformation of sentiment concerning American historical literature took place less systematically. Voices talked with varied timbres, even after the turn of the century. Alfred Thayer Mahan's vastly influential book, *The Influence of Sea Power Upon History,* appeared in May 1890 and enjoyed a broad readership despite its intense concentration upon English, Dutch, French, and Spanish struggles for empire in the period 1660 to 1783. Americans enjoyed reading European history, especially if they believed that it contained utilitarian lessons for them.* In 1903 a prominent popularizer took up the issue in terms of deriving pleasure from the past. "The truth is," he wrote, "that in many respects—in the atmosphere, in the variety of incidents and characters— the story which the Old World Historian has to tell is a better story to tell than ours is." William Garrott Brown perpetuated an argument that had been commonplace two generations earlier, as we saw in Part One:

> Writing in a land where nothing is so rare as ruins, for a people whose faces are set toward the future . . . the American historian has not so good an opportunity for many of the effects which have been as common in history as in other forms of literature. The range of motives is not so wide.[52]

His was no longer a representative voice, however, or one sensitive to change. Six years earlier Sydney George Fisher, the genteel Philadelphian, correctly called attention to the resuscitation of public interest in the nation's past, particularly the colonial period. As early as 1885, in fact, *The Century* had heaped praise on Edward Eggleston's innovative history of the colonies and did so using criteria that seem amazingly modern:

> It has been the custom to write colonial history by narrating the public events, such as the appointment of a new governor, or a quarrel between a governor and an assembly. . . . While the public events are mostly trivial, the social history is of the greatest consequence. . . . To trace the gradual change to modern American forms; and to tell the strange story of white and black slavery in the plantations, are among the important and neglected portions of American history that are being set forth comprehensively in this work.[53]

Early in the 1870s young John Fiske had been appointed an instructor in history at Harvard. He taught the colonial period because those in

---

*Late in the 1870s, when John T. Morse of Boston proposed a series of American biographies to Henry Holt, the publisher replied sharply: "Who ever wants to read American history?" Morse reflected years later that "I had to admit, as I surveyed the American plain, that it spread a barren prospect before us." (John T. Morse, "Incidents Connected with the American Statesmen Series," MHS *Proceedings,* 64 [1932], 371, 372.)

charge asked him to do so, and to please his patron, Mary Hemenway. But, as he explained to a friend in 1879, "it is not the colonial history that I thirst after . . . it is the medieval history & the study of early institutions which comes exactly within my own special line of studies. . . . If I were worth $1,000,000 I should spend the rest of my life in studying early institutions & the growth of European society."[54]

During the next two decades, needless to say, Fiske performed an amazing about-face. Perhaps he felt a fresh breeze of inspiration when he received a letter from Lewis Henry Morgan, the venerable founder of American anthropology, later in 1879. "Much of the historical and scientific work of the English speaking race must be done over; and Americans must do it. [Henry Cabot Lodge struck just the same chord a quarter century after that.] We are freer in our minds, socially, morally and politically, than an Englishman." Morgan ended with an unabashed confession: "I admit myself intensely American."[55]

In 1896 an essayist reported in *The Century* that for about a decade the emphasis upon U.S. history had steadily grown in colleges and secondary schools. Just at that time Carl Becker was studying with Frederick Jackson Turner at Wisconsin; and years later Becker reflected that if Turner "knew that Europe was infinitely richer than the United States in historic remains and traditions, I never heard him mention the fact, at least not with the appropriate air of regret for missed opportunities."[56] That statement stands in strong contrast to the anguish conveyed by William Garrott Brown above. Americana was becoming acceptable.

I V

ASSORTED FACTORS helped to assure that turnabout, as we shall see in the next two chapters, but none seems to have been more potent than the renaissance of patriotism that began to be manifest late in the 1880s and absolutely surged during the following decade.[57] If we ask what prompted the patriotism, a simplistic line to take would be jingoism, sensationalism on the part of the penny dailies, Spanish-American War fervor, and so forth. Although those developments surely contributed, I believe that too little attention has been devoted to *fin-de-siècle* introspection. When William Dean Howells weighed the "Modern American Mood" in 1897, he noticed "a self-scrutiny much more unsparing than we once used" and commented in passing on the "present thoughtful mood."[58] I do not believe that such remarks can be dismissed as rhetorical because Howells tended, if anything, toward being a rather caustic critic of American society.

His assessment is noteworthy and prescient because it welcomed an augmented democracy in terms of broadened opportunities for all, economic as well as political; because it found the mood of critical self-analysis healthy; and above all because he believed that the criteria of judgment had been beneficially transformed. "The national attitude is self-critical, and if the standards by which we try ourselves are not those of Europe, but are largely derived from within ourselves, they are none the less severe and none the less just." Howells then referred with admiration to "the quiet of our patriotism"; and he proceeded to define his meaning with a diachronic comparison to the shallow patriotism born of insecurity and anxiety that characterized earlier decades. "We have really more faith in the republic than they had, for we have found that it works, and they could merely believe that it would work."[59]

More than any other individual, perhaps, Howells seemed to set the tone and establish an agenda for serious discussion. In 1901, when *Scribner's* devoted a long editorial to the subject of national tempera- ment, it began by agreeing with a recent essay by Howells that the "best material for great poetry . . . is that yielded by a half-mythical, heroic past." Although the essay offered no answers, it did not hesitate to pose impossibly large questions. "What produces temperament in a people?" it asked. "Is it that half-mythical, heroic past which feeds the imagina- tion? Must a people have had a long past, and a great deal of varied history, to possess temperament?"[60] The third of these questions, espe- cially, seems highly symptomatic of the reflexive tone among thought- ful people in the United States as the twentieth century started.

Connections between national style ("temperament") and national symbols (of a mythical and heroic past) had seemingly been nagging the American psyche for more than a decade. In 1888 James Russell Lowell expressed the hope that meaningful patriotism consisted of more than "equal parts of lifelong association, hereditary tradition, and parochial prejudice." The following year anxious tremors surfaced because the United States lacked a national hymn. The *New York Times* went to town on that one. It had snide comments about each and every candi- date, *viz*: "the Star-Spangled Banner has the poetical merit of a Bowery melodrama set to music that is as cheap and tawdry as the verse." The *Times* then observed, however, that a peculiarly American type of ballad had in fact developed. "The distinguishing feature of the Ameri- can song is the fact that its theme is always death." A considerable amount of pseudo-scientific evidence followed: "A statistician has re- cently ascertained that 94 percent of all songs written in the United States are, as he calls them, mortuary songs. They refer either to the death of one or more beloved objects, or to cemeteries, tombstones, coffins and like cheerful matters." Several long and rather hilarious paragraphs later, the editorial concluded that perhaps it would be best to wait until "we have outgrown the fondness for graveyard ballads before trying to produce a new national hymn."[61] Although the *Times* may have kept tongue firmly in cheek, those who had agitated the issue were perfectly serious.

In 1900 Professor Moses Coit Tyler of Cornell came to Chautauqua,

New York, and delivered a lecture, "The Problem of a National Name," that was elaborately covered by the press—virtually verbatim in fact. Tyler (who was, incidentally, constantly obsessed with the prospect of his own death)[62] provided a perfectly amazing performance by discussing every name that had ever been contemplated for the U.S.A., and why each one failed: Columbia back in the days of Timothy Dwight and Joseph Hopkinson; the United States of Allegheny, proposed by Washington Irving and supported by the New-York Historical Society in 1845; William Gilmore Simms's preference for Appalachia over Alleghenia; the Republic of Washington; Fredonia; and even Cabot (with its citizens, consequently, being Cabotians); and so forth. This lecture effectively addressed American traditions that once were, or that might have been, or else had become futile and forgotten. He touched upon lapses of American memory, aspects of national mythology gone awry, and above all the contemporary concern—patriotic to its core—with the shell if not the substance of social identity.[63]

Ultimately Tyler believed that too much time had passed. Therefore we were stuck, for better or for worse, with the United States of America. He concluded by explaining the entire process (or failure of process) in terms of a law governing the growth and strength of traditions. All artificial attempts to replace America with a new name were doomed to failure

> because they were in violation of this obvious historic law, that whenever the name of a country or of a people has become a matter of general usage among men, that name has thereby passed beyond the reach of alteration under mere criticism, whether on the score of original injustice or of original indefiniteness or lack of euphony, or what not.[64]

Somehow we seemed to have these deficiencies that urgently needed to be supplied, like a national hymn; yet it also appeared to be too late to innovate, to invent traditions, because as Tyler pointed out, the cake of custom mysteriously managed to remain very firm. Even so, that did not prevent people from trying; so the years between 1890 and 1910, particularly, twinkled with proposals for the establishment of assorted traditions, such as making Columbus Day a national holiday, or establishing Flag Day (1893), or for "tracing certain trails and roads of the United States, mapping out places of historical interest, Indian villages and things of that sort."[65] (See fig. 6.2.)

A sense of place translated into enthusiasm for historical geography, and that, in turn, took the form of regionalism and local pride. A man like Charles Lummis, Harvard College '81, developed a passion for the Southwest in general and for Los Angeles in particular (to which he left an idiosyncratic but important museum collection). I'm not sure which angered Lummis more: Americans devoid of interest in history, or

6.2 Edward Penfield, *Legal Holiday, Washington's Birthday, February 22nd. No Business Transacted* (New York, 189–?). Library of Congress Poster Collection, Division of Prints and Photographs.

Americans obsessed with European history and culture (fig. 6.3). In 1891 he published *Some Strange Corners of Our Country,* a book that vividly described the Grand Canyon, the Petrified Forest, cliff dwellings, Cañon de Chelly, Montezuma's Well, the Penitentes, the Moqui Snake Dance, and various archaeological sites as well as Indian legends. He began *Strange Corners* with a sermonic judgment:

> This book is meant to call your attention to the Southwest, which is the most remarkable area in the United States and the most neglected—though by no means the only one worth learning about and seeing. The whole West is full of wonders, and we need not run to other lands to gratify our longing for the curious and the wonderful. The trip abroad may at least be postponed until we are ready to tell those in foreign lands something of the wonders of our own.[66]

Today Lummis is little known outside the Los Angeles area; but his legacies include a load of exuberant books and magazines, the Southwest Museum, and the Lummis Memorial Association. He also served as a major stimulus for enthusiasm concerning art depicting the West, but above all works executed by Western artists. A Society of Western Artists, formed in 1896, mobilized a travelling show each year and became quite an effective organization by 1910. In that same year the Architectural League of the Pacific Coast mounted an exhibition of designs and etchings by architects from the Pacific rim. The display proudly made a circuit from San Francisco to Los Angeles to Portland and Seattle.[67]

6.3   Charles F. Lummis at his home, El Alisal, in 1902. Courtesy of the South-west Museum, Los Angeles. Photo #24381.

Interest in the old California missions also began to grow among the general public at this time, which helped to spark the genesis of concern for preservation and restoration. The author of one popular book that appeared in 1905 explained in his Preface that "I am but one of the great mass of laymen who love the Old Missions for their own sake, for their history. . . . For nearly twenty-five years I have venerated them; I have made pilgrimages to them; and several times sent both artists and photographers to bring me their impressions of them."[68]

That kind of antiquarian enthusiasm, based upon a blend of national loyalty and strong allegiance to a particular region or locality, developed rapidly during the first decade of the twentieth century. The Burton Library in Detroit, Michigan, founded by Clarence M. Burton, a Detroit lawyer and the owner of an abstract and title company, provides a prime example. Burton spent a large amount of his own money "having the archives in Paris thoroughly ransacked for materials pertaining to Detroit and Michigan, commencing at as early a date as anything could be found, and extending to the end of [the] French regime." He then had all of these papers transcribed and translated at considerable expense—they filled twenty-four volumes—for publication by the state historical society. Burton also raised funds for the transcription of another twenty-four volumes of records from archives in Montreal, still more from the major collection gathered by the Canadian archivist in Ottawa, plus church records, cemetery inscriptions, and newspaper clippings.[69]

One of the intriguing, though not altogether unique, aspects of the Burton Library involved its reliance upon both private and public funds. Burton purchased original materials with his own resources, and he paid for those countless pages of transcriptions. But he also persuaded the state historical society to undertake publication of the records, and to provide a place for the Burton collection in the State Library, as well as exhibition space in the State Capitol. Finally, the state of Michigan even supplied a modest subvention of $4,000 each year. Staff members of the Burton Library all worked as volunteers. The public and private funds that could be obtained were used entirely for "printing and collecting historical matters, and collecting a museum of Michigan Pioneer relics."[70] This sort of arrangement became increasingly characteristic in areas beyond the Eastern seaboard, with the proportion of public money increasing as one moved across the Mississippi.

V

BACK IN THE 1850s one William Pidgeon, an Indian trader who knew the trans-Mississippi West quite well, published *Traditions of De-coodah and Antiquarian Researches.* "It yet remains for America to awake her story from sleep," he began, "to tell the tale of her antiquities, as seen in the relics of nations, coeval, perhaps, with the oldest works of man." After noticing how much interest had recently been stirred in Old World ruins, he deplored the pitiful ignorance and neglect of the "equally ancient relics of this broad country."[71]

A meaningful response required more than twenty-five years; and even then the results turned out to be considerably less than Pidgeon and successors like Charles Lummis had hoped for. The two biggest barriers of resistance, apart from distance and inaccessibility, turned out to be money and the magnetic attraction of Old World History. After its founding in 1879, for example, the Archaeological Institute of America became far more concerned about classical archaeology than indigenous sites. For several decades classical archaeology received considerably more financial support from institutions and individuals.[72]

In 1882 the Historical and Genealogical Society of New England lobbied Congress for the first time on behalf of legislation to protect American antiquities located on federal land. Senator George Frisbie Hoar of Massachusetts presented the bill with vigorous references to "magnificent ruins" and "decaying antiquities"; but Senator Preston B. Plumb of Kansas spoke for the overwhelming majority when he insisted that private associations should assume more responsibility because there were so many ruins. How could the government possibly afford or manage to protect them all? The proposal died in Plumb's committee; and a subsequent one (for a single site) did not appear until 1889. A report titled "What the United States Government Has Done for History," published in 1895, opened with this signal of distress: "It was not till about 1875 that the Government and people of the United States seemed to realize that our country has a history."[73]

Even 1875 seems, in retrospect, a premature date. Participation by Native Americans at the Centennial Exposition held at Philadelphia had to be cancelled because Congress refused to supply funds. Such resistance was not simply the result of anti-Indian hostility. Rather, many legislators sincerely wondered about the constitutionality of subsidizing any portion of an anniversary celebration. The records make clear, however, that the notable absence of Native American history and culture at Philadelphia owed much to an incapacity on the part of Euro-American society to see any enduring value in Indian traditions.[74]

Mark Twain was not flailing unfairly in *Innocents Abroad* (1869) when he castigated "that poor, useless, innocent, mildewed old fossil the Smithsonian Institute." Marked improvements and activity began to occur there during the 1880s, however. It is symptomatic that the Smithsonian's Bureau of Ethnology was renamed the Bureau of American Ethnology in 1894.[75] The Peabody Museum had been founded at Harvard in 1866, and started by collecting Indian artifacts from the Merrimac Valley of Massachusetts, then objects from Northern Europe, and eventually even extensive treasures from the famous Stone Age caves in France. By 1877, when its own building was finally erected, the Peabody's inventory had become extremely eclectic and included items from the trans-Appalachian Indian mounds and from the western United States, which would eventually become the source of its greatest strength.[76]

During the 1880s popular curiosity about Indian lore began to appear; and, droll though it may seem, no one's curiosity was piqued more than Mark Twain's. In *Life on the Mississippi,* his discussion of the river's northern stretches is salted with frequent reminders that the region being traversed "is rich in Indian history and traditions" or "blanketed with Indian tales and traditions."[77] (One might fairly wonder whether the tales were by or about Indians.) The discovery of modest but ancient Indian stone relics in New England seemed to be newsworthy; and so was an exhibition of Zuñi artifacts that began in New Orleans and finished its tour in Washington, D.C.[78] In 1889 a single event precipitated formation of the Association for the Preservation of Virginia Antiquities: the collapse of an old Indian ruin known as Powhatan's Chimney. By 1901 some bibliophiles specialized in books pertaining to Native Americans.[79]

In those parts of the nation where Native Americans were no longer a menacing presence, preserving their artifacts became an act of showcase piety. In those areas where tension or actual conflict persisted, the Indian in art seemed tamer than in reality, and therefore could serve diverse symbolic purposes as well. Frederic Remington's success and meteoric rise in 1885–86 occurred because he had just visited Geronimo's territory and made sketches there at a time when the populace was utterly fascinated by the fierce Apache leader. In 1886 Cassily Adams painted his gigantic version of *Custer's Last Fight* (9½ by 16½ feet). The Anheuser-Busch Brewing Company managed to acquire it in litigation involving a claims settlement, had it touched up and lithographed in 1895, and a year later began issuing copies as a promotion for Budweiser beer. *Custer's Last Fight* became the most famous (or notorious) saloon painting in all of American barroom history! Thomas Hart Benton, who possessed some sensitivity to the role of art in American myth-making, painted a parody in 1946 that he called *Custer's Last Stand: A Bar-Room Picture in the St. Louis Mode.*[80]

In the realm of sculpture we encounter some ironic inversions. Daniel Chester French, who is best known for the Minute Man at Concord and Abraham Lincoln in Washington, received the commission for a Francis Parkman memorial and decided to model a solemn and majestic Indian warrior for placement in Jamaica Plain, Boston (1897–1906). "The Indian does not represent any particular Chief," French wrote in 1908, "but only one of the five nations (in the costume of the Iroquois) about which Parkman wrote so much."[81]

Cyrus E. Dallin, on the other hand, the most distinguished sculptor of Plains Indians, launched his career at the age of twenty-two with a prize-winning design for an equestrian statue of Paul Revere in Boston. (He was actually permitted to complete it fifty-six years later, in 1940.) In the meantime Dallin, who was born in Springville, Utah, in 1861, achieved renown for *The Signal of Peace,* a life-sized equestrian Indian statue that earned a first-class medal at the World's Columbian Exposition in 1893. A wealthy judge promptly purchased the bronze for the city of Chicago and it was formally dedicated in Lincoln Park a year later. Dallin completed *The Medicine Man* in time for the Paris Salon of 1899, where it was a great favorite. The Fairmount Park Association of Philadelphia bought it.[82]

For the Louisiana Purchase Exposition in 1904 Dallin executed *The Protest,* a large mounted warrior wearing a war bonnet, his head thrust forward boldly, his right arm and fist raised in a gesture of clear defiance. It brought Dallin yet another gold medal. At the Paris Salon of 1909 he won again, this time for the last work in what he now conceived to be a four-part series that symbolized the tragic saga of white–Indian relations. Dallin named it *The Appeal to the Great Spirit,* in which a despondent Indian whose cause on earth has failed calls upon Powers of the Spirit for deliverance and ultimate sanctuary. It stands on a pedestal in front of Boston's Museum of Fine Arts. He also designed the Pilgrim Tercentenary half dollar in 1920 and a muscular, massive (twice life-size) statue of Massasoit which stands imposingly on Coles Hill in Plymouth, Massachusetts, overlooking the site of Plymouth Rock.[83]

Real Indians had largely disappeared by then from the mainstream view; so their legends could be approvingly used for aesthetic and symbolic motifs, as Dallin did, and to promote tourism. As *The Independent* remarked with open cynicism in 1903: "Good Indian legends can be grown in almost any locality with a little care and attention." During the 1890s ethnographers and anthropologists issued more frequent appeals that Indian myths and traditions be collected.[84]

This convergence of serious and questionable motives meant that after the turn of the century various sorts of efforts would be intensified in order to collect, preserve, record, and even romanticize the earliest inhabitants of North America. In 1902 a new journal, *Records of the Past,* began publication in Washington, D.C. Although it took an interest in assorted antiquities, its special focus was well summarized in the opening of its introductory essay: "The most perplexing problem confronting the historian of the human race is the presence of prehistoric man in the Western Hemisphere as the builder of great temples, palaces, mounds and pyramids." Two paragraphs later the editor asserted that "special attention should be called to American antiquities. . . . Many Americans are more familiar with the antiquities of Europe, Asia and Africa than those of the West."[85] The history of Native Americans only became useful when cultural resistance to Europe began to be important.

This hortatory piece observed that American ruins "rival in interest those of the Old World, with the added mystery that we have no tangible clue" to the Mound Builders of the Ohio and Mississippi valleys, the cliff dwellings and pueblos of the Southwest. It included a prophetic appeal that a general law for the preservation of antiquities be passed, with the details of its application left to the Department of the Interior, and ended with an expression of humiliation "over the failure of this Government to protect the ruins within its territorial limits,—ruins that bear witness to a race of great builders, long since vanished."[86]

That very year, as it happened, Representative John F. Lacey of Iowa, accompanied by Edgar Lee Hewitt, a young archaeologist from the West, visited some of those pueblos and cliff dwellings—a tour that marked a dramatic turning point and had significant political impact. Nearly four years of hard politicking lay ahead, but in 1906 Congress finally passed the first major Antiquities Act in our history. The narrative of that political battle has been ably told.[87] Key components of the Act provided penalties for anyone who undertook unauthorized excavations on federal lands, or harmed any historic or prehistoric ruin; it empowered the President to declare historic landmarks and public monuments, or set aside public lands in order to protect such sites; and facilitated the awarding of permits to examine and excavate ruins, provided that the work was undertaken by reputable institutions and "that the gatherings shall be made for permanent preservation in public museums."[88]

Additional legislation along these lines would not come for a full generation; but a beginning had been made, and the federal government at last accepted some responsibility for the nation's physical heritage out of doors. Every phase that followed would be equally hard fought, however.

V I

EARLY IN 1902 the *New York Times* published a remarkable letter from someone identified only as CRITIC. An extract illuminates several important points:

> Why is it when some historic spot is likely to pass away Congress or a State Government is generally called upon to save it? Why is it we are not more interested in the preservation of links with the past? If I am not mistaken, women are more inspired with this spirit than men: in fact, we are indebted to their noble work for most of what has been accomplished. And yet we have plenty of men of leisure, cultivated taste, and generosity, desirous of using their means to the best possible advantage, not simply for themselves, but the welfare of others yet to come.[89]

The particular role played by women as custodians of tradition in the United States has in fact been neglected; and as it happens, their enthusiasm for Native American antiquities played an especially noteworthy part in the developments that we have just been following. In 1885, for example, Miss Alice Cunningham Fletcher of Boston and New York became the primary patron of excavation and preservation at the Serpent Mound in Ohio. A year later Mary Hemenway of Boston, an extremely wealthy widow, commissioned and subsidized a major Southwestern Archaeological Expedition that led directly to Frank Cushing and others spending seven years with the Zuñi and Hopi tribes; and, equally important, she funded the publication of a five-volume report of the expedition's "findings." Finally, just at the turn of the century a group of energetic women formed the Colorado Cliff-Dwellings Association and launched a vigorous effort to establish Mesa Verde as a national park.[90] (See fig. 9.1.)

We shall look more closely at the notable impact of women when we consider historic preservation in chapter nine. The proper note on which to close this chapter, however, involves Americanization of the chords of memory as the first decade of the twentieth century drew to a close. An obvious example with which to begin is the deeply influential loan exhibition of Americana held in 1909 at the Metropolitan Museum of Art (see fig. 5.1). Enthusiasm ran so high, and the desire to locate an institutional home for the nearly nine hundred items loaned by Eugene Bolles and others was so great, that Mrs. Russell Sage, yet another rich widow, was persuaded to purchase the Bolles Collection and make a gift of it to the Metropolitan Museum. She did just that, and eventually it became the core of the Met's American Wing when it opened fourteen years later.[91]

Looking back forty years after the fact, one of the people who had pushed for that famous Hudson-Fulton loan exhibition in 1909 explained his motives: "It seemed to me [that] a museum which showed Greek, Roman, Egyptian, Chinese, and other Eastern things surely ought to show to its public the things America had accomplished."[92] Nevertheless, despite this extravaganza, the Metropolitan remained one of the slowest and last of the major museums to take American art seriously. In 1899 the trustees talked about devoting a special gallery to American painting (which had recently been done at the Art Institute in Chicago), but they took no action. In 1905 the very same discussion occurred, followed the next year by a gift from a major donor to acquire works by living American artists—an important step, though hardly tradition-oriented. By 1911, however, Kenyon Cox, a conservative arbiter of artistic taste, proclaimed that the Met had achieved an "admirable nucleus of a collection of contemporary American art, formed almost entirely within the last five years."[93]

Acceleration elsewhere occurred a little more rapidly, though not by very much. As early as 1889 an exhibition of pictures by Americans had been held in Washington, D.C., under the auspices of the Lady Managers of the Garfield Hospital. Until 1907, however, the so-called national collection in the capital consisted almost entirely of European art. (For purposes of comparison, in 1900 the National Gallery in London possessed twenty-three paintings by Englishmen of scenes from English history, which suggests a somewhat stronger sense of national tradition.) In 1907, however, William T. Evans gave the United States a fine collection of American art, though it consisted mainly of works by post–Civil War painters. These were placed on temporary display at the Corcoran, while Evans and others urged the federal government to erect a suitable building as a national gallery—an event that eventually transpired more than thirty years later.[94]

Evans is highly representative because he began by collecting European art but switched when his wife gave him a copy of George W. Sheldon's book *American Painters* (1879). Evans was deeply involved in organizing "The Comparative Exhibition of Native and Foreign Art," sponsored in 1904 by the Society of Art Collectors, a show that principally ranged American tonalist landscapes against French Barbizon painting. Between 1907 and 1916 Evans gave one hundred fifty American works to the Smithsonian Institution and fifty-four to the Montclair Art Museum, in Montclair, New Jersey, where he lived for a period in the former home of George Inness.[95]

When public appreciation of American artists increased in the years

1904 to 1906, several of the major museums acquiesced in the establishment of "picture funds," usually by public subscription, to facilitate the acquisition of works by American artists. This was precisely the case at the Detroit Institute of Art, for example, where the original collection (opened in 1885) consisted entirely of European Old Masters, ethnographic, archaeological, and Oriental objects. Once again, however, American art tended to mean recent: not too new, and not very old, but just right! Only in 1930 did Detroit's trustee and major benefactor, Robert H. Tannahill, organize a loan exhibition of American colonial and early Federal period art. By 1908 wealthy businessmen of various sorts had initiated a pattern of making comprehensive bequests to museums for the acquisition of American paintings. This occurred in Boston, Philadelphia, Worcester, Pittsburgh, Cincinnati, Indianapolis, Chicago, and St. Louis.[96]

In 1910 a society in Chicago known as the Friends of American Art was organized. It had 142 members who supplied a five-year subscription to purchase works by Americans for the Art Institute. The next development, perhaps inevitably, would involve closer inspection of what had been acquired, exploration of systematic comparisons, and the self-scrutinizing question: "Is Our Art Distinctively American?" Initially, in this early phase, the process of groping produced only vague answers: "Perhaps one of the best evidences of the progress we are making toward the producing of a distinctively American art is our great advance in public taste." The author made no attempt to define either the causal connection that he had in mind or the meaning and implications of "public taste."[97]

The transformation of public taste had its predictable counterpart in the private sphere. Needless to say, the two overlap considerably; but, if anything, changes in the objectives of private collectors tended to anticipate and directly affect the policies of museums and comparable institutions. Throughout the post–Civil War era, affluent Americans pillaged the European past and brought back every conceivable sort of antiquity. The voracious appetites of J. Pierpont Morgan and the Vanderbilts are merely the best-known.* What could be more apropos than Morgan's decision to hang in the East Room of his library a sixteenth-century tapestry (woven in Brussels) titled "The Triumph of Avarice"? His appetite for art treasures seems to have been bottomless as well as geographically relentless. "I have done with Greek antiquities," he once announced, "I am at the Egyptian."[98] Significantly enough, one of the few personal photographs that he permitted shows him standing before the Antinous at the Villa Albani in Rome during April 1907 (fig. 6.4).

A modest shift had already begun to occur, however, and it should be

---

*The Pabst Mansion in Milwaukee, Wisconsin, was completed in 1893 as a magnificent Flemish Renaissance home for an American beer baron.

6.4   J. Pierpont Morgan at the Villa Albani in Rome, April 1907. Courtesy of
the Archives of The Pierpont Morgan Library, New York.

no surprise that an interest in Indians initiated it. During the winter of
1905–06, Edward S. Curtis, whose passion it was to photograph Native
Americans in serene and noble poses, returned to the East from a
preliminary expedition. Theodore Roosevelt supplied him with a letter
of introduction to Morgan, and the two got along very well. They
schematized a twenty-volume set of pictures accompanied by texts, to
be published in a limited edition of five hundred sets. Morgan agreed
to provide $75,000 to help defray Curtis's field expenses, to be paid in
$15,000 installments over a five-year period. When that sum proved
insufficient, Morgan added more in 1909; and after his death in 1913 his
son chose to continue supporting Curtis.[99] The outcome was a magisterial American classic, Curtis's twenty-volume opus, *The North American Indian* (1908–30).

   In 1909 Stephen H. Wakeman, a veteran collector of literary
Americana, sold Morgan a yellow pine box containing thirty-eight
manuscript notebooks, or journals, kept by Henry David Thoreau
(who undoubtedly constructed the box himself).[100] It is difficult to
imagine a more bizarre juxtaposition than the literary remains of our
austere naturalist reposing in the lavish Gotham book-tomb of our
most notorious capitalist.

   Isaac Newton Phelps Stokes, the affluent New York architect and socialite, collected European and Oriental art objects from 1885 until 1909, when his enthusiasm changed course sharply to early Americana. We know that Franklin Delano Roosevelt was gathering Americana as early as 1908. In that same year *The Century* ran a feature story about the historical collection of china and silver that had gradually been reassembled at the White House since 1901. During the 1890s some insiders noticed that little of the presidential china or silver that had been used ever since 1789 still remained in the White House; but one of the difficulties Theodore Roosevelt's wife encountered when she took up this challenge was the "meagerness of detail in many of the official records." Prior to the twentieth century a very scant sense of tradition got transmitted from one first family to the next. The inspiration between 1901 and 1909 was above all patriotic.[101]

Nevertheless, that inspiration left several important issues unresolved for years to come. Would prominent political families and rich entrepreneurs permanently serve as prominent arbiters of American culture? A grateful chauvinist could write in 1908 that "the wealthy business man, usually stronger in patriotism than in careful connoisseurship, wisely acquired [in the late nineteenth century] the habit of leaving to our various institutions special funds for the purchase of American paintings."[102] The administrative power of museum trustees remained very strong, however, with important consequences for policy, for decisions affecting American taste, memory, and a sense of the past—or perhaps we should say, of various pasts in conjunction with one another.*

Yet another issue that lingered, and had been more than latent throughout the post–Civil War era, concerned the complex nexus between patriotism, the past, and civil religion. One more extract from that letter written by CRITIC in 1902 is apropos.

> [Old landmarks] appeal to us, they renew old reminiscences, and when party animosities are forever buried future generations will be thankful for their preservation, and also proud to recognize that men and women of this wonderful present, with all its splendid energy, pride, and ambition, were not unmindful of sacred memorials of the seventeenth century.[103]

---

*See, for example, the public career of George Clinton Batcheller, an extremely wealthy manufacturer whose Puritan ancestors reached New England in 1636. A charter member of the Order of Founders and Patriots of America, and of the Sons of the American Revolution, "it was owing to his generosity that the Betsy Ross Flag House Association purchased the property in Philadelphia, known as the old flag house, which insures its permanent preservation as the historic 'birthplace of Old Glory.' " (*National Press Bureau* Advance Service, Jan. 2, 1908, p. 1, copy in the Lyon G. Tyler Papers, group 2, box 15, SLWM.) We now know that the Ross House, if not the myth of Ross herself, is utterly without foundation—see Richard Shenkman, *Legends, Lies, and Cherished Myths of American History* (New York, 1988), 147–48.

Sacred memorials, shrines, temples, relics, pilgrimages, and venerated ancestors: such word-concepts carried a great deal of meaning in American culture during the later nineteenth and early twentieth centuries. The relationship of that meaning to myth, memory, and history receives more intensive exploration in the next chapter.

Chapter 7

"MEMORY IS WHAT
WE NOW HAVE IN PLACE
OF RELIGION"

A S THE NINETEENTH CENTURY moved along, the moral values that had been central to early American theology passed from that ethereal sphere to the realm of conscience; and then, with the first major flowering of native literature, to the realm of imagination as well. Conscience and imagination did not disappear in the decades following 1870; but it does seem fair to say that their social significance diminished, that moral concepts came to be secularized even more into polite or genteel culture. Protestant Christianity remained a bulwark of tradition, and vice versa; but the pervasive force of religion declined and a spiritual crisis occurred that was aptly summarized by the title of Elihu Vedder's 1887 painting, *The Sorrowing Soul Between Doubt and Faith.*[1]

The implications of Darwinism and the impact of science in general meant that tensions between doubt and faith would increasingly be resolved in favor of the former, with important consequences for the role of history and tradition in American culture. They began to enjoy a primacy hitherto unknown. Thus Henry Adams, looking back from the early years of the twentieth century, remarked that "the great word Evolution had not yet, in 1860, made a new religion of history."[2] That is what gradually happened, however, with consequences not only for historical consciousness, but for enduring perceptions of Puritanism, for the practice of filiopiety, for the power of tradition-oriented organizations, and for notions of intergenerational relations.

Although tradition and faith remained compatible in many regions, and could even reinforce one another, particularly in the South, tradition often tended to become a surrogate for faith or revealed religion. In ways both subtle as well as overt, history turned out to be a vital component in American civil religion. Thomas Jefferson anticipated this tendency in November 1825 when he gave to his grandson, Joseph Coolidge, Jr., the portable desk on which he had written a draft of the

Declaration of Independence. Jefferson provided the following affidavit to accompany that small mahogany piece inlaid with a narrow band of satinwood: "Politics as well as Religion has it's superstitions. These, gaining strength with time; may one day, give imaginary value to this relic, for it's association with the birth of the Great Charter of our Independence."[3] Indeed it would, when more than half a century later the superstitions of some became the cherished myths of their progeny.

I

T. S. ELIOT once asserted in an influential essay that "no culture has appeared or developed except together with a religion."[4] That dictum has a certain sweeping applicability for the first 250 years of American history; and it does not entirely cease to be relevant after 1870. Religion often remains a vital cultural force long after its theological substance has been diluted. Consider Puritanism in nineteenth-century New England, or Hispanic Catholicism in the twentieth-century Southwest, or millennial Protestantism in the South. Consequently I do not wish to suggest that orthodox Christianity and cultural traditions terminated their compatibility in the later nineteenth century. For Cynthia Coleman, a principal organizer in 1889 of the Association for the Preservation of Virginia Antiquities, an abiding affection for the past certainly did not supplant revealed religion; and the same applies to Lora Ellyson, another early president. William Wirt Henry surely spoke for many in the South when he declared in 1893 that "in listening to the voice of history we well recognize the voice of God."[5]

Other sources spoke in less sanguine tones, however. Abundant evidence suggests that postwar Southern faith in the Lost Cause served many as a surrogate for conventional belief. Paul Hamilton Hayne, the unreconstructed South Carolinian, managed to maintain both of his faiths. He never doubted the morality of slavery or the correctness of secession; but in 1883, writing a poem called "The Decline of Faith" for *The Century,* he acknowledged the presence of a serious spiritual malaise: "Creeds fall, shrines perish; still the Soul lives."[6] Perhaps for Hayne and his dear friends Charles Gayarré of Louisiana and Sidney Lanier of Maryland, Christianity remained a comfort as undeviating loyalty to the Old South credo started to crumble.[7]

The generation that succeeded them, however, seemed to love religion less and history more; and correlations between the two were neither accidental nor casual. We know that Mary Johnston (1870–1936), Virginian author of twenty-two popular romances, including *To Have and to Hold* (1900), moved steadily "away from dogma in religion" and that history satisfied a large emotional hunger for her. Thomas Dixon (1864–1946), a North Carolinian, became a Baptist minister in 1887 but resigned his ministry twelve years later to become a lecturer and novelist. He enjoyed immense success with *The Leopard's Spots* (1902), *The Clansman* (1905), and *The Traitor* (1907), historical tales that take place during Reconstruction, romanticize Ku Klux Klan activity, and are aggressively Negrophobic. An immensely influential film, D. W. Griffith's *Birth of a Nation* (1915), was based upon *The Clansman* and contributed to critical American notions of Reconstruction, in the North as well as in the South, for years afterward.[8]

Those who remained content to romanticize the past and perpetuate faith in that fantasy world were able to maintain a reasonably coherent vision of how the present had evolved and why certain values, such as racial supremacy and separation, should be maintained. For those who placed their faith in historical memory, however, major controversies such as the on-going issue involving the veracity of the Mecklenburg (North Carolina) Declaration of Independence raised doubts about the reliability of history as an adequate underpinning for certitude. As one participant in that particular embroilment declared in 1875: "We should review history and see the foundations on which our faith in it may rest."[9]

During the 1880s and '90s, when increasing numbers of people turned to history as a source of inspirational value as well as specific knowledge, they urgently needed to believe that such information could be verifiable and reliable. Hence the appeal of what we call scientific history, as well as the concerns for collective memory discussed in the two preceding chapters. Whereas American historical writing had originated as a form of social criticism from the poignant perspectives of such as William Bradford and Cotton Mather, it came to be transformed and professionalized several centuries later, not as a form of social criticism (that would be the purview of the Progressive generation), but rather as part of a quest for moral truths that could be known with assurance and that would thereby provide a firm foundation for national identity and patriotism.[10]

In 1865, for example, when Charles Francis Adams, Jr., read John Stuart Mill's essay on Auguste Comte, the French founder of sociology, it turned out to be a transforming experience. Adams recalled half a century later in his autobiography that Mill's essay "revolutionized in a single morning my whole mental attitude. I emerged from the theological stage, in which I had been nurtured, and passed into the scientific." Adams became a skeptic, rarely attended church services, and cherished American history as an alternative value system.[11]

Brooks Adams reported his brother Henry's "regret at the loss of religious faith"; but Henry compensated with an extraordinary combination of rationalism, aestheticism, and above all a commitment to writing history as an act of critical allegiance and in order to provide a standard of measure for change over time. Those are the connecting links between his nine-volume *History of the United States (1800–*

1817), his *Albert Gallatin,* and his *Mont-Saint-Michel and Chartres.* Faith provides more consolation than doubt, however. Consequently, late in life Adams told a friend that he needed "badly to find one man in history to admire. I am in near peril of turning Christian, and rolling in the mud in an agony of human mortification."[12]

Neither the Adams brothers nor other Americans were at all unique or even unusual in their anguish and the alternatives to faith that attracted them. In England such figures as James Anthony Froude and Arthur Hugh Clough underwent and wrote about comparable crises several decades earlier. Thomas Babington Macaulay rejected his parents' intense evangelicalism while he was a student at Cambridge in the 1820s. Jacob Burckhardt, who had chosen history as his vocation by 1842, considered himself an unbeliever and mocked conventional piety.[13]

According to Erich Heller, however, whose explication is shrewd and subtle, Burckhardt remained "firmly rooted in the Christian tradition of Europe. He continued to eat the bread and drink the wine, and called them by the names of culture and tradition. Religious crisis he regarded as only one more historical variation and change embedded in the spiritual *continuum* without which history would have meant nothing to him." In discussing Italian humanists of the fifteenth and sixteenth centuries, moreover, Burckhardt supplies ample evidence that we are not imposing upon him an interpretation that suits our own perspective. "After they became familiar with antiquity," he wrote of the humanists, "they substituted for holiness—the Christian ideal of life—the cultus of historical greatness."[14]

Those insights, Heller's and Burckhardt's as well, are remarkably applicable, with appropriate variations, to a significant number of Americans during the second half of the nineteenth century. Shifting from theology to history as a vocation was hardly without precedent: Jared Sparks, George Bancroft, John Gorham Palfrey, and Charles W. Upham had all begun as Unitarian clergymen before turning to national, regional, or local history, editing documentary texts, or teaching.[15] The five examples that follow, however, underwent transformations quite comparable to Burckhardt's.

■ James Parton (1822–1891), who achieved immense popularity as an historical biographer, was raised in a strict pietistic family, found himself deeply beset by religious doubt, revolted against Calvinism, became effectively an agnostic in 1868 (though T. H. Huxley did not "invent" that word-concept until 1870), and by 1871 found himself powerfully attracted to Voltaire and Jefferson, two freethinkers, as subjects for extended biographies.[16]

■ Edward Eggleston (1837–1902), the most influential American social historian of his time, suffered intense personal conflict between the ages of thirteen and thirty because he felt torn between the intellectual life stimulated by his father and several other relatives and the evangelical Methodism of his stepfather. In 1856–57 he became a circuit-riding Methodist preacher, yet confided to his journal that he wavered between zealous faith and doubt. Even when the appeal of circuit-riding died for him, he resolved to pray for three hours daily; and he continued to attend the annual Methodist Conference until 1865. The next year he turned his hand to journalism and fiction, which he pursued for more than a decade. In 1875 he published a critique of Methodism and became the pastor of a Congregational church in Brooklyn after insisting that its members waive adherence to any formal creed. By the later 1870s his enthusiasm for American history had taken hold, and for the next twenty-three years it became his obsession. In 1882, when President Jacob Gould Schurman of Cornell invited him to preach there, Eggleston declined twice and never preached again. He had become too much of a skeptic. In September 1884 he went to Saratoga, New York, in order to participate in the organizational meeting of the American Historical Association, and served a term as its president fifteen years later.[17]

- James K. Hosmer (1834–1927) was an eighth-generation American and the first of his line born outside of Concord, Massachusetts. He was the son of a Unitarian minister in Northfield, and the grandson of the senior pastor at Plymouth's First Church, which, as Hosmer wrote in his autobiography, "came by unbroken tradition from the Pilgrims." The word "memory" recurs throughout that autobiography; and it is clear that in early manhood Hosmer felt torn between the customary vocation of his lineage and history as a calling. Although ordained as a Unitarian clergyman in 1860, he soon abandoned the ministry as a career, became a prolific historian, antiquarian, and librarian, and confessed in his manuscript autobiography that it became "expedient to keep out of sight the fact that he had once been a minister."[18]

- Hosmer's close friend John Fiske (1842–1901) wrote a much briefer autobiography in which he relates that he "experienced religion" at the age of fourteen and joined the orthodox Congregational Church. By the age of seventeen, he continues, he had decided to devote his life "to the study of the origin & progress of the human race. Three subjects thus came uppermost,—Christianity, Evolution, and the general study of history. I drifted rapidly away from the orthodox theology." Mary Hemenway, that wealthy Boston widow, became his patron, which permitted him to devote extensive time to the study of history. In 1878 Fiske was invited to present a series of six public lectures concerning the history of the United States at the Old South Meeting House in Boston, a historic structure that Mrs. Hemenway had done so much to preserve a few years earlier. As a result of that series, Fiske explained, he devoted himself "exclusively to American history." During the two decades that followed he gave lectures throughout the country, and most of them eventually appeared in book form. In 1883, for example, he launched a "course" of thirteen public lectures at Old South concerning the American Revolution.[19]

■ Albert Jay Nock (1873–1945), son of an Episcopal clergyman and grandson of a Methodist preacher, was himself ordained to the Episcopalian ministry in 1897 and for twelve years he served a series of churches in Titusville, Pennsylvania, Blacksburg, Virginia, and Detroit, Michigan. In 1909 he left the active ministry in order to join the staff of the *American Magazine.* Thereafter he refused even to acknowledge his clerical past; and in 1924, following his mother's death, Nock renounced his holy orders. He had become a skeptic and a strong traditionalist for whom Jeffersonian values served as a surrogate for Christianity. His best-known books, *Jefferson* (1926), *Our Enemy, the State* (1935), and *Memoirs of a Superfluous Man* (1943), along with a large corpus of serious yet uncollected essays, reveal the strength of his conservatism, patriotism, and nostalgia.[20]

The list of influential historians of the United States, as well as collectors and purveyors of Americana who were ordained or attended divinity school, is quite substantial. It includes Moses Coit Tyler, Wallace Nutting, and David S. Muzzey, whose history textbook enjoyed phenomenal success for sixty years. Each one suffered from either periodic crises or a permanent crisis of faith.[21] We can also point to a pantheon of historians who came from extremely pious family backgrounds, who were subjected to strong pressures to select the ministry as a career but resisted on grounds of conscience and turned to history as a source of values if not an actual creed. Prominent examples include John R. Commons, Walter Prescott Webb, Carl L. Becker, and William L. Langer.[22]

Although these men, each in quite a different way, explained the past to other professional historians, to the public, and even to policymakers, taken together they supplemented rather than supplanted the active role of those who did choose to be clergymen. The recruitment of value-expounding "reinforcements," as it were, expanded the cadre of tradition-oriented spokesmen in American society; and that expansion helps to differentiate the post-1870 era from the generations (even centuries) that preceded it. Writing of the Middle Ages, Marc Bloch once noted that a lack of education among the laity explained the power of clerics both as interpreters of the ideas of great men and as transmitters of cultural traditions. What happened after 1870 is that secular leadership was *added* to the clergy's normal roles in fulfilling those functions.[23]

During the second half of the nineteenth century it was not at all unusual for sermons to convey historical content. In fact, when evangelicalism diminished following the 1850s, the pulpit came to be used increasingly as a place for the discussion of traditional culture.[24] Beginning in the 1890s such men as the Reverend W. Herbert Burk of Valley Forge and the Reverend W. A. R. Goodwin of Williamsburg, both Episcopalians, took a dynamic role in transforming those sites into historic "shrines." As Goodwin proudly explained to John D. Rockefeller III in 1934, after Colonial Williamsburg opened to the public, they could and would "reproduce the symbols and sacraments of the past."[25]

When Reverend Burk spoke about building the George Washington Memorial Chapel and gathering a collection of Revolutionary "relics" for the museum at Valley Forge, he consistently described historical objects and events in the language of religion. That pattern had steadily increased ever since 1875–76, when furniture for patriotic purposes had been made from an old maple tree cut down in Philadelphia's Independence Square; from the old Cambridge elm under which George Washington took command of the Continental forces in 1775; and from Connecticut's Charter Oak, in which the colony's legitimizing charter had been hidden from royalist agents back in the seventeenth century. Certain cherished pieces of furniture were deemed sacred on account of their historic roots (rather than because of termites, blights, or burrowing beetles).[26]

Similarly, in June 1888 the Washington Association held a reception at the Morristown, New Jersey, mansion that the Commander-in-Chief had used as his headquarters during the severe winter there in 1779 (see fig. 14.10). The featured attraction prior to the reception: an opportunity for guests to view Washington-related "relics" in the mansion. Creative re-use of decorative art objects with religious as well as historical associations became especially appealing at the turn of the century. An elevator installed in the White House in 1902 (used there until 1946) had oak panelling taken from the Old South Church in Boston. In 1989 that elevator was permanently installed in the National Museum of American History, part of the Smithsonian Institution in Washington, D.C. Its panelling had gone from ecclesiastical-historical to secular-functional and finally, almost a century after being assembled, to the status of being a ritual-historical quaint curiosity.[27]

In discussing the cultural role of sacred symbols, anthropologist Clifford Geertz has sensibly observed that they function in order to "synthesize a people's ethos—the tone, character, and quality of their life, its moral and aesthetic style and mood—and their world view . . . their most comprehensive ideas of order."[28] Such symbols also convey messages and guidelines about the society's origins, its most cherished values, and the allegiances that it requires of its members. Hence the significance of certain historic sites, structures, objects associated with heroic figures, flags, and holidays.

The 1937 proposal to tear down a church that had been built at

Oyster Bay, Long Island, back in 1724 elicited an angry letter that is very symptomatic of dim future prospects as viewed by those piously disposed to make "backward glances." This angry individual was equally apprehensive at the possibility of the church being razed, or that Henry Ford might "carry it off for his collection" of historic buildings at Greenfield Village in Dearborn, Michigan. "Put a fence around it," pleaded the letter writer; "treasure it as part of a life when men lived earnestly and believed in a God."[29]

During the period that we have under consideration, attention actually was paid, more often than not, to the anniversaries of churches as congregations as well as physical structures. This tended to be one point where piety and cultural memory coincided. Hence the centennial observances in 1888 for the Friends Meeting House in Plainfield, New Jersey (the oldest building in Plainfield); the centennial of (Northern) Presbyterianism held in New York City in that same year; the centennial of the Methodists in Connecticut a year later; a huge commemoration in 1889 for the "Log College" in Neshaminy, Pennsylvania, the first institution devoted to training Presbyterian ministers in the colonies;[30] and a series of Roman Catholic centennials that started at Baltimore in 1889, shifted to New York City a few weeks later under the aggressive auspices of the United States Catholic Historical Society, then to Monroe, Michigan, to honor Catholicism in the Old Northwest, and finally to Boston in 1900 for the organization of the New England Catholic Historical Society. It set an agenda that included as one of its primary projects a systematic effort "to have an historical record of every parish in New England."[31]

Starting early in the 1890s people found themselves encouraged by newly formed preservation associations and educational foundations to make "pilgrimages" to historical sites, such as Jamestown and Mount Vernon in Virginia, or Independence Hall in Philadelphia. In 1894, for example, the American Society for the Extension of University Teaching, associated with the University of Pennsylvania, planned a ten-day "historical pilgrimage" along George Washington's "itinerary to historic spots in the North" one hundred years earlier. One of the most creative features of this centennial safari, according to its organizer, "will be an address at each place for the purpose of showing the contribution of that place to American history. . . . At the close of the pilgrimage we shall publish a souvenir volume on historic towns, which will include the addresses." He added a postscript that called attention to his recent essay in the *Review of Reviews* on the "Revival of the Historical Pilgrimage."[32]

Southerners seem to have been more inclined than others to invoke sacred spots (Thomas Nelson Page on Jamestown in 1890), holy ground, hallowed ground, the need for reverence, altars of our past, and so forth. When the United Confederate Veterans held their reunion at Charleston, South Carolina, in 1899, a reporter described the onetime warriors as being devout as any pilgrim going to "the tomb of a prophet, or a Christian knight to the walls of Jerusalem." Within fifteen years most Civil War battlefields in the South had been informally designated as pilgrimage sites with holy shrines to be visited.[33]

It is essential to note, once again, that neither the language nor this behavior was uniquely American during that generation. In 1877, for instance, William Morris wrote of the "sacred monuments" of Britain's growth and hope; and by the turn of the century pilgrimages had also become popular there, though English nostalgia tended to be somewhat more literary and cultural in its orientation, and perhaps less political or military than it was in the United States.[34] In any case, the phenomenon was Anglo-American in scope because Americans who visited Great Britain not only trekked to sites associated with the ancestors of Washington, Franklin, the Pilgrims, and others, they also worshipped (especially in the 1860s and 1870s) at places unrelated to the American past. Moses Coit Tyler made what he called a "deliberate pilgrimage to Coleridge's grave," somehow touched the poet's coffin, and referred to Coleridge's remains as "that sacred dust."[35]

Americans were likely to be less restrained and more maudlin than the English in seeking permission "to worship at this shrine of our independence" (Monticello) or to visit a "shrine of national patriotism" (Mount Vernon).[36] It is clear that by 1909 they even acquired a strong sense of the cultural transformation that had taken place over a span of two full generations. The author of an essay about "Famous American Shrines" that appeared in *Munsey's* in 1909 made this accurate observation:

> In the middle of the nineteenth century Americans had not become inspired with a sentiment of reverence for the landmarks of their national history. . . . We have learned to travel, to move about, and to make pilgrimages to places which are growing richer and mellower with suggestion every year.[37]

The article traced a route from Concord to Bunker Hill, Boston and Plymouth Rock, Independence Hall, the homes of Washington, Jefferson, and Robert E. Lee, various sites in Richmond, the Alamo, Gettysburg, New York City for Fraunces Tavern and Grant's Tomb, and concluded with "memorials" associated with Abraham Lincoln, ranging from Washington, D.C., to Hodgenville, Kentucky. It was a sentimental if slightly chaotic tour de force—not historically accurate in every particular, yet a remarkable litmus of the spirit of the times in both high as well as popular culture. "Concord itself is full of memories"—that sort of meaningless, pseudo-spiritual mist.[38]

As one might expect from pp. 129–130 (in chapter four), George Washington and Abraham Lincoln remained the most sacred among a heavenly host of saints: the Peter and Paul of American patriotism. Not

7.1   Burial site of Mary Ball Washington, Fredericksburg, Virginia.

surprisingly, given the Victorian crisis of belief, one could honor the two immortals either as angelic or as merely heroic in a secular sense. *The True George Washington* by Paul Leicester Ford (1896) openly questioned his subject's spiritual commitment. Woodrow Wilson's biography (1896) made no mention of Washington's religious beliefs.[39]

In the mid- and later 1880s, on the other hand, completion of the Washington Monument reinforced the idealization that had begun with Parson Weems. John Ward Dunsmore (1856–1945), a painter obsessed with Mount Vernon and its master, depicted the place in dozens of versions.[40] Benson Lossing and others made a self-conscious pilgrimage to the nation's capital just to see General Washington's clothing displayed in the great model hall at the Patent Office. For decades Mary Ball Washington, the President's mother, was referred to in certain circles as "Mary, the Mother of Washington" (fig. 7.1). (Did she, too, have a huge retinue of artists present to paint her Annunciation?) And in 1901 the Most Worshipful Grand Master of Massachusetts Masons presented his members with a lock of (Mason) George Washington's hair ensconced in an urn of solid gold: "It appears before you a priceless relic," he proclaimed, "worshipped by the [Masonic] followers as coming from that noble head which a more imaginative people would have beatified with the halo of a saint."[41]

When the Washington Memorial Chapel was designed for Valley

Forge at the start of the century, the sanctuary received two matched narrative series of thirty-six stained-glass windows. One set depicts scenes from the life of Christ while the other side of the chapel has scenes from the life of George Washington. Comparable individuals, after all. Because Abraham Lincoln had been assassinated in 1865 on Good Friday, and various other coincidences swiftly ensued, they elicited all sorts of analogies between Jesus and the martyred President; and an elaborate religious mythology developed during the following decades. Visitors to Lincoln's tomb near Springfield were shown a room filled with Lincoln relics, after which a group leader would typically declare that "our visit to this sacred monument is not a mere individual tribute, but a significant pilgrimage. . . ." The party would then troop off to see Lincoln's hallowed home in Springfield.[42]

These manifestations of civil religion related directly to the surge of patriotism. Consequently phrases like "patriotic hymns and anthems" appear in contemporary news coverage of commemorative gatherings. The press featured essays on "PATRIOTISM" based, for example, on new books bearing such titles as *American Patriotism: An Essay* (1887), which contended that sufficient national spirit could solve many of the country's social and political problems.[43] The G.A.R. made a practice of acquiring and presenting American flags to public schools and colleges, based on the assumption that a sacred mission might be accomplished now that "the national colors adorned the desk of every principal of every public school in the city and that every pupil was familiar with all the national airs through having sung them daily."[44] Incidents that indicated any sort of dishonor to the American flag, or simply insufficient enthusiasm for the Stars and Stripes (such as a weak response to a call for cheers), seemed to be worth a story, and sometimes an extended one. Flag worship was a prevalent phenomenon between 1885 and 1915.[45]

It is vital to acknowledge, once again, that various manifestations of nationalism became either a complement to or an alternative for both orthodox religion and the sense of stability that comes with continuity tied to rootedness. This has been suggested in a general way for Victorian Britain, and it has been applied to the substantive content of what was taught in French classrooms under the Third Republic. In analyzing the quarter century following 1880, Pierre Vilar might just as well be describing the United States at the same time. Vilar emphasizes "la corrélation entre l'abandon de la pratique religieuse et la constitution d'un ensemble de pratiques républicano-patriotiques."[46]

Moreover, it was a matter of necessity rather than convenience for those who challenged the established order (and its values) by offering not merely an alternative vision of society but an attractive though ersatz set of loyalties, goals, and procedures for achieving it. Thus, as one historian has observed, Spanish anarchists drew upon Roman Catholic rituals during the final quarter of the nineteenth century in order to promote their program. People accustomed to ritual do not respond well to those who would deprive them entirely of meaningful ceremonies. Spanish radicals recognized that reality, and they systematically developed secular procedures comparable to familiar religious rites as a means of enticing people ideologically. This phenomenon did not necessarily occur only from the top down, moreover. Civil religion could be a spontaneous emanation from the masses. As a Russian peasant wrote in 1925: "We ask that a book be published, fully comprehensible to peasants, about the life and work of dear Comrade Lenin and his legacy, so that this book could be our replacement for the Gospel."[47]

In the United States, patriotism and hero worship enjoyed a very broad appeal that cut across class lines. Certain holidays that had historical origins or associations, such as the Fourth of July and Thanksgiving, did so too. During the later nineteenth century, it remained customary to attend religious services on Thanksgiving morning. By the 1920s that practice had largely ceased, though an editorial in the *New York Times* pronounced Thanksgiving to be still the most religious holiday of the year (presumably excluding Christmas and Easter because they were specifically Christian in origin), and the *Times* crowed that this "is exclusively an American day."[48]

Many of the pageants and anniversary celebrations that took place prior to 1910 had religious overtones (or undertones) in varying degrees, even if they occurred simply at the level of tradition and remembrance being invoked in terms of secularized piety. Yet here, too, national and local observances, as well as the anniversaries of organizations and institutions, like churches, tended to blur class lines, even though distinctions between leaders and participants might be obvious to almost everyone concerned.[49]

Other modes of engagement with the past, however, tended to be more elitist or were either confined primarily to the affluent or to those belonging to older American families irrespective of their wealth. Attendance at the better museums and art galleries, at the public lectures of Edward Eggleston and John Fiske concerning aspects of American history, was primarily by the "better sort." How many others would have been comfortable listening to Fiske discourse on "The English Race and Its Manifest Destiny," one of his set pieces for an 1880 circuit that took him from Boston to the Midwest; or viewing the Copp Collection of Colonial Costumes at Washington, D.C., in 1898; or hearing the humanities, from Plato to Emerson, discussed as a substitute for the historically tainted scriptures? Victorian cultural institutions provided many people with places and circumstances where encounters with tradition fulfilled a need once served by spiritual zeal. For Constance Rourke, who became a literal "seeker" of Americana and a leader in the new American renaissance of the 1920s and '30s, her childhood upbringing in the 1890s included diverse artistic interests but no religion whatsoever.[50]

The American Scenic and Historic Preservation Society, founded in

1895, issued a descriptive pamphlet early in its career that claimed it to be "the first society in this country to merge Art and Historical culture in one organization, thereby imparting an aesthetic interest to Historical work and making History, in turn, the handmaiden of Art." In addition to being true, that formulation calls to our attention a very broad transformation, begun half a century earlier, when for many people the preferred mode of reckoning the ancient past shifted from the use of biblical time to that of geological time, a tendency reinforced by the great surveys in topography and natural history that took place during the third quarter of the nineteenth century.[51]

Even as the erosion of millennialism caused people to contemplate the nation's past and future in terms of historical change and hence historical time, the proliferation of historical tales and anecdotes made mythical time—that is, heavy reliance upon sacred stories related to such moments as 1492, 1607, 1620, 1630, 1776, etc.—a genuine competitor with historical time and a complex source of false historical consciousness. Americans *believed* that they knew much more about the past than they actually did. Not only was the very basis of belief undergoing change, however; so was the place of belief itself in the nation's sense of its own traditions.[52]

I I

DURING 1886–87 a connected series of episodes in publishing, art, and politics revealed that the role of Puritanism and of traditions associated with it in American culture had reached a critical turning point. As if to herald this shift and the uncertainties that accompanied it, essays appeared in middlebrow journals of opinion bearing such titles as "Does the Puritan Survive?" and, more prescient still, "From Puritanism—Whither?"[53] An answer that lauded the founders' contribution appeared on Thanksgiving Day 1887 when an imposing nine-foot bronze statue titled *The Puritan* was unveiled in the community of Springfield, Massachusetts (fig. 7.2). Augustus Saint-Gaudens, who had worked on it since the early 1880s, began with a particular personality, Deacon Samuel Chapin, who had left Roxbury, Massachusetts, in 1642 to minister to this new community in the Connecticut River Valley; but ended by distilling the embodiment of a social type and rendering a powerful iconic figure.[54]

The year 1887 also marked an important turning point in the history of New England town politics and its social basis because in that year the Irish bloc gained control of Quincy's town meeting, an act that left members of the Adams family aghast. It is no coincidence that Brooks Adams published a controversial reassessment of his ancestors' legacy that same year, in a serious historical work that was perceived as being anti-clerical, anti-Puritan, and perhaps even an attack upon religion in

7.2   Augustus Saint-Gaudens, *The Puritan* (1899), bronze replica of the larger-than-life statue (1887) in Springfield, Massachusetts. Courtesy of the Herbert F. Johnson Museum of Art, Cornell University.

general. Most of the reviews were not merely critical but hostile; and what matters most from the broader perspective of American cultural change is not that someone like Brooks Adams bashed the Puritan reputation for piety and integrity, but that his doing so unleashed a debate that persisted for decades.[55]

Before we proceed to that conflict, it is worth noticing once again (in an exploration of memory and amnesia) how commonly the Puritans and Pilgrims came to be confused, even in the words and works of art created by well-educated people. The Pilgrims, who started a colony at Plymouth in 1620, differed in theology, politics, and temperament from the Puritans, who founded Massachusetts Bay ten years later. Even though the latter swallowed up the former governmentally in 1691, a sense of separate traditions rooted in distinct histories persisted until the post–Civil War era. After that artists were more likely to become casual about the differences. In 1870 *Harper's Weekly* published its initial drawing by Edward Austin Abbey, called "The Puritans' First Thanksgiving." In 1903 the New England Society of Pennsylvania commissioned Saint-Gaudens to cast a full-sized replica of *The Puritan* for placement in Philadelphia. Saint-Gaudens, however, could not bear to send a "mere" replica to such an important city, so he made a few changes and called it *The Pilgrim* so that Philadelphians could feel that they too owned an original work by Saint-Gaudens.[56]

Early in June of 1885 a huge crowd gathered at 72nd Street in Central Park in New York for the unveiling and presentation to the city of a Pilgrim statue designed by John Quincy Adams Ward. General Stewart L. Woodford, president of the New England Society of New York, opened the festivities by proclaiming (unhistorically) that "the work and influence of the Puritans had done more than all else for the great city in which we reside." George William Curtis, the journalist, novelist, and editor of *Harper's,* then gave an overly long, historically confused, yet rather representative address in which he described the impact of Puritan principles upon sequential epochs of American history. His half-apologetic tone was as characteristic of the age as his sense of intergenerational continuity. "We must not think of Puritanism as mere acrid defiance and sanctimonious sectarianism," he warned, "nor of the Puritans as a band of ignorant and half crazy zealots." Then, without missing a beat but muddling some historical realities: "We raise the statue of the pilgrim, that in this changeless form the long procession of the generations which shall follow us may see what manner of man he was to the outward eye, whom history and tradition have so often flouted and traduced."[57]

In describing the statue itself, the *New York Times* even added to the blend of predictable criticism and grudging admiration. The Pilgrim had an "air of truculence," and from a distance a "somewhat peaked and sour visage." Upon closer inspection, however, Ward's statue seemed less gloomy—all of which had symbolic meaning because truculent and sour were just how Bostonians appeared to most urbane Knickerbockers.[58]

The observance of Forefathers' Day (December 21, when the Pilgrims landed at Plymouth Rock in 1620) throughout much of the Northeast created part of the problem because at some point in time, impossible to pin down with precision, "forefathers" became a generic term. Thus in 1887 the Pilgrim Church in Harlem celebrated it with a dinner of New England dishes, such as baked beans and pumpkin pie. The waitresses, we learn, wore "Puritan costumes."[59]

Among those who did appreciate (and insist upon) the difference, the most visible were men devoted to keeping the Pilgrims' memory alive and meaningful, such as Albert Matthews and Arthur Lord. The latter served at various times as head of the Pilgrim Society at Plymouth, as head of the Bunker Hill Monument Association, and as principal organizer of the very elaborate tercentennial held at Plymouth in 1920.[60] Called "the caretaker of the Pilgrim tradition," Lord wrote *Plymouth and the Pilgrims* for that occasion; and he loved to deliver an address (which he never published, so that it would always be at hand for oral presentation) titled "The Value of Tradition." This was not the pietistic exhortation that one might expect. It quite seriously explored, for example, passage of a law by Massachusetts in 1898 declaring that in court-room proceedings no statement once made by a person now deceased "shall be excluded as evidence on the ground of its being hearsay, if it appears to the satisfaction of the judge to have been made in good faith before the beginning of the suit, and upon the personal knowledge of the declarant." In brief, Lord regarded hearsay evidence as a valuable form of traditional lore that deserved serious consideration at law as well as in society at large.[61]

He then moved on to an intricate discussion of the reliability of oral traditions in validating familiar aspects of the Pilgrim narrative—"certain historical incidents," he called them. Lord acknowledged that the "permanence of a tradition depends necessarily upon the retentiveness of human memory," and, not surprisingly, he had considerable faith in that faculty. Having "established certain rules" for the verification of oral tradition, he proceeded to discuss the Mayflower Compact, the Pilgrims' Patent to settle in North America, Plymouth Rock as their actual landing place, the "myth of Mary Chilton" as being the first person to step upon the Rock, and even the courtship of Miles Standish. In every instance Lord relied upon verbal gymnastics that followed some variation of this formula: in assorted situations men of "position and standing" had relied upon these traditions and "adopted a course of conduct, which it is inconceivable would have been adopted by them if they had doubt upon the genuineness of the tradition; and the fact that the tradition was stated and accepted as evidence long before any controversy arose as to the genuineness of the tradition, would seem to justify its admissibility as evidence, and uncontrolled by other tradition or uncontradicted by any other tradition . . . may well be accepted under the general rule."

Lord conceded that reputable antiquarians of the past generation had called attention to the "untrustworthiness of personal recollection." Following a fair amount of flim-flam in dealing with that problem, he concluded with an uncritical assertion of his satisfaction with the veracity of history passed along by word of mouth in a comparatively closed community:

> The delight of the hearers in the cottage, in the village inn or the more stately hall, was the romance, story, ballad and tradition of the past. The frequent repetition of the story tended to ensure its verbal accuracy. Men who had heard the tale insisted it should be accurately retold. If a variant from the tale appeared, however, it did not impair the body of the tradition.[62]

I rather imagine that members of those groups most likely to invite Arthur Lord to address them would be readily inclined to agree with him. As with revealed religion, some people are prepared to accept oral tradition, variations and all, as an act of faith.

Among those who understood the distinction between Pilgrims and Puritans there was a tendency to compare the latter unfavorably to the former because the Pilgrims could not be accused of religious intolerance or intellectual arrogance. They had been persecuted rather than persecutors.[63] They lived austere, proto-Yankee lives, co-existed harmoniously with the Indians, and gave us the first Thanksgiving. They could even be depicted as early democrats: "They brought no titles or ranks, priestly hierarchy, no ecclesiastical ranks and orders, no complicated system of fees," declared Congressman William C. P. Breckinridge of Kentucky on August 1, 1889, at the national dedication of the Pilgrim Monument at Plymouth.[64]

The hoopla caused by this dedication aroused the ire of New York newspapers, which had been much kinder four years earlier when Ward's Pilgrim statue, holding the Bible with a sword between its pages, had been unveiled. The 1885 donors as well as the sculptor were Yorkers, after all, even if their ancestors had (uncontrollably) been Yankees. A *New York Times* editorial in 1889, on the other hand, seemed to confuse the Pilgrims with the Puritans by contending that anti-Pilgrim sentiment had increased, even in New England, partially because romanticism had given way to realism. Moreover, since the New England temper had been dour and artistically stifled for more than two centuries, many "worthy and noble souls" had chosen to "escape from the sad shores about Cape Cod"; and they found in New York "quite as much real godliness and far more liberality than in Plymouth and Boston."[65]

The code word "liberality" conveyed a number of nuances: criticism of the austere Calvinist observance of the traditional sabbath; the presumption that they were customarily dreary, "tart of tongue, and disdainful of the amenities of life"; or, as John Dewey declared in 1902, recreation is a neglected ethical force, but "our whole Puritan tradition tends to make us slight this side of life, or even condemn it."[66]

Then there were endless charges of intolerance, not only pertaining to the seventeenth century, but bitterly made by Irish immigrants who had worked for and with latter-day Puritans ever since the 1840s. John Muir, the great naturalist, regarded the Puritans as "pious destroyers" of the landscape (just how they were worse in this respect than settlers elsewhere is not clear); and Mr. Dooley, Finley Peter Dunne, laid guilt upon them for Indian atrocities in his droll praise of Thanksgiving (which, of course, confused the Puritans with the Pilgrims once again): " 'Twas founded be th' Puritans to give thanks f'r bein' presarved fr'm th' Indyans, an' . . . we keep it to give thanks we are presarved fr'm the Puritans."[67]

Those who lived beyond New England's boundaries and visited the region during the 1890s regarded it as lacking in "intellectual energy," religious commitment, and cultural vitality. A once sturdy set of regional values seemed to be in decline. Some people found a certain comfort in the belief that Puritan progeny no longer defined the nation's cultural agenda and interpreted its past from such a partisan point of view. After Edward Eggleston published *The Beginners of a Nation* in 1896, Brander Matthews of Columbia wrote him an affectionate note in a tone of mock derision: "What kind of a history do you call that book of yours? It violates all the traditions of American literature—first in not being written by a New Englander."[68]

The word "Puritan" had appeared as an epithet in the South as early as 1826. More than a generation later, in the 1860s and '70s, some Southerners created a deliberate caricature of what Puritanism had been and meant historically. By the 1880s the harshest recriminations against New England's customary cultural hegemony occurred in the former Confederate states. On Washington's Birthday in 1889, for example, the Society of the Army and Navy of the Confederate States held its annual reunion. At the banquet a belligerent ex-general declared that a "Southern gentleman can whip a Puritanical Yankee every time." Finally, as a double illustration of regional rivalry, a *New York Times* editorial criticized Congressman Breckinridge of Kentucky for speaking too piously at the Pilgrim Monument dedication in August 1889. The *Times* opined that the Pilgrims *and* the Puritans had been intolerant and closed-minded, their ideas "narrow and distorted," and a "highly-civilized modern man would have found himself much more at home in other colonies." It surely sounded as though all the other regions were ganging up on poor old New England.[69]

IF WE DO not weigh the evidence judiciously, however, these intersectional antagonisms will sound indistinguishable from those of the following generation, which were considerably more acrimonious. For many Americans of the later nineteenth century, Puritanism and its legacy were recognized as the mixed blessing that they in fact were: a despotic theology counterbalanced by political impulses that offered liberal possibilities. When Senator Henry Cabot Lodge addressed the New-England Society of Brooklyn, he struck a remarkably balanced note. (He also observed that "Forefathers' Day were two words that opened the book of memory.") When the Reverend Richard S. Storrs of Brooklyn, the most prominent pulpit orator of his time, spoke on "The Puritan Spirit" at Boston's Tremont Temple in 1889, he too was positive yet candid. And this fair-minded detachment showed up in private correspondence as well as public discourse. In 1907 President Theodore Roosevelt wrote the following to Charles F. Lummis in Los Angeles: "We Americans of today are wise in developing the joy of living which the Puritan lacked, and the toleration he no less lacked; but let us see to it that we do not lose his iron sense of duty, his unbending, unflinching will to do the right."[70]

Moving from the center of the spectrum to the end, there remained a considerable number of vocal and perfectly sensible individuals who between 1880 and 1910 not only retained an extremely positive view of the Puritans, but felt nostalgia for the qualities of intense faith, imagination, and courage that seemed to be in short supply in late Victorian America. John Greenleaf Whittier exemplifies this perspective among poets, and John William De Forest does among novelists. When the Society of Colonial Wars in the State of Minnesota held its annual dinner at St. Paul in 1898, the obligatory series of toasts included one to "The Puritan Character." In writing about the contribution of New Englanders to the West, Albert Bushnell Hart of Harvard commented that the single most notable gift had been "the Puritan strength of character," and more particularly the ideal of an educated ministry. "The Puritans have been," he declared in 1907, "the little leaven that leavened the whole lump."[71]

At times the rhetoric indulged by some of these speakers and writers strikes us as being somewhere between naive and mindless. Yes, they were capable of attributing religious liberty, political equality, and even the genesis of democracy to the Puritans.[72] Nevertheless, in their shrewder moments they ascribed to Puritanism certain political assumptions that moderate and conservative Victorians cherished and that are, in fact, even recognizable to modern students of seventeenth-century America. "This is the Puritan principle," proclaimed George William Curtis in 1876: "Those men stood for liberty *under the law.*" A speaker at an anniversary dinner in 1887 candidly directed his focus to this theme: "The idea of Puritanism and Conservatism allied, of Puritanism and Anarchism opposed."[73]

Although Senator George Frisbie Hoar of Massachusetts did not write as much or as well about American history as his junior colleague, Henry Cabot Lodge, no other senator has ever identified so passionately with the Puritans. Hoar was a Unitarian by affiliation, yet he really remained a Congregational Calvinist by persuasion. His ancestors had been Calvinists and Hoar took second place to no one in his admiration for ancestors. He also made a kind of mystical link between Calvinism and correct ideas about government: "They governed themselves, and they believed that a free people should govern itself, by a law higher than their own desire. Duty and not self-indulgence, and future good in this world and the other, and not a present and immediate good, were the motives upon which they acted."[74]

Despite Hoar's immense pride in his New England ancestral stock, he could be ecumenical if not catholic in his public addresses on commemorative occasions. The subjects of his orations predictably include John Winthrop, Samuel Adams, and Daniel Webster, but also Thomas Jefferson and that classic topic "The Character of Washington" as well. When a statue was dedicated at Worcester to Hoar's memory in 1908, the speakers called him a great patriot, a man of principle, and the "Last Puritan."[75]

Looking back a generation from the perspective of the early twentieth century, Henry Adams made the wry observation that America seemed to be "becoming more and more indifferent to the Puritan except as a slightly rococo ornament." That quip was prompted, however, by Adams's reaction to the most monkish of New England antiquarians, such as John Gorham Palfrey.[76] When the Puritan (or aspects of Puritanism) were depicted in American art, they were rendered, more often than not, with strength and sympathy. Examples range from Thomas P. Rossiter, *Puritan's Daughter* (1859), to Edwin Austin Abbey, *The Trial of Mrs. Hutchinson* (c. 1875), to Abbey's *Stony Ground* (1884), in which a Puritan family discusses biblical texts at home, to Daniel Chester French's fine statue of John Harvard (1883–84) in the College Yard, to John Rogers's model of John Eliot, the Indian missionary (with a chief and a squaw humbly at his feet), to Frederick Burr Opper's mildly irreverent cartoons of Puritans and Pilgrims, drawn in the 1890s,* to Howard Chandler Christy's four illustrations for *Puritans* (1905), which were executed with a deft and delicate touch (fig. 7.3).[77]

One of the few artistic interpretations compatible with the doom and gloom emphasis ordinarily ascribed to that period is *The Puritan* by Frank E. Schoonover (fig. 7.4), a disciple of Howard Pyle in the Brandywine School.[78]

The Pilgrims have less commonly provided inspiration for artists. During the first half of the nineteenth century a few were attracted to the *Landing of the Pilgrims at Plymouth,* such as Samuel F. B. Morse in 1810–11 and Felix Michel Corné at the time of the bicentennial in 1820. These are basically descriptive seascapes that blend the historical with a touch of genre art. They lack the emphasis upon intense faith, courage, and the continuation of a quest that characterize Robert W. Weir's huge work in the Rotunda of the U.S. Capitol, *Embarkation of the Pilgrims at Delft Haven, Holland, July 22nd, 1620* (1837–47), or *The Pilgrim* (1929), a figure carved in walnut by Enrico Glicenstein and subsequently cast in bronze.[79]

Puritans as well as Pilgrims have figured to a greater degree in American literature, although the latter have been more likely to appear in folklore or poetry than in serious imaginative literature. During the 1870s passionate assertions seem to have been more common than insightful discussions of literary achievements or social realities. Thomas Wentworth Higginson made an ardent case on behalf of the Puritan origins of a genuine national culture in the United States; and at the end of that decade a less prominent author insisted in the *Atlan-*

---

*"Please do not take the Pilgrim Fathers as a joke," wrote Waldo G. Leland to Worthington C. Ford on August 7, 1908. "They would never understand such an attitude toward them and I fear that their descendants . . . would not understand it either. Besides if you take them as a joke they point no moral, whereas if you regard them as a horrible example you get lots of moral, and why write history if there is no moral to it?" (Ford Papers, box 5, NYPL Annex.)

7.3 Howard Chandler Christy, Four Illustrations for *Puritans* (1905), pen and ink on board. © 1989 Indianapolis Museum of Art, purchased from the Sarah F. Banning Fund.

tic that the United States had "no past, no national tradition, no history" to which the creative spirit might appeal other than Puritanism.[80]

For several decades following the 1870s the reputation of American Puritanism was really in a state of disputed disarray: staunchly defended by some apologists within New England, yet criticized by others who had been born to the old Brahmin elite. It was also the subject of snide remarks in the middle states, and openly resented in the South because of what seemed to be a long tradition of cultural dominance over the nation as a whole. Although the South did not lack piety, the section detested the holier-than-thou posture of New England moral-

7.4   Frank E. Schoonover, *The Puritan* (1898), oil on canvas. Courtesy of the
Brandywine River Museum.

ism. Meanwhile, some bold antiquarians in the Northeast began to
collect Pilgrim period furniture;[81] and a few persons defiantly called for
an end to apologetics. Humble pride, they insisted, was more seemly
than blithe provincialism. "Is not the foolish sensitiveness about our
forefathers a mark of the provincialism of our intellectual life? All of our
local historians are engaged in defending somebody."[82]

I I I

DURING THE CENTURY that immediately followed comple-
tion of the Revolution, the cultural role of ancestors was not particularly
prominent. Some clergymen took the position that if the newly independent Americans failed to fulfill their destiny as a chosen people, they
would disgrace "the ancestors from whose loins we spring." Half a

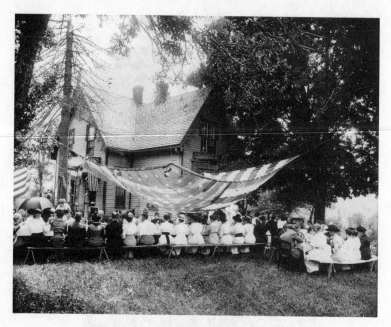

7.5 Carr-Todd family reunion, Toddsville, New York, 1914. Courtesy of the
New York State Historical Association, Cooperstown.

century later Daniel Webster and other prominent orators would echo
that admonition.[83] Ralph Waldo Emerson, on the other hand, also spoke
for many when he said that "reverence for the deeds of our ancestors
is a treacherous sentiment. . . . Give me insight into today, and you may
have the antique and future worlds." Alexis de Tocqueville viewed such
present-mindedness more in terms of the sociological implications of
American individualism. "Not only does democracy make men forget
their ancestors," he wrote, "but also clouds their view of their descendants and isolates them from their contemporaries."[84]

When we scrutinize evidence available for the three decades following 1885, however, we are obliged to conclude either that Tocqueville
was not a good prophet on this issue, or else that a remarkable transformation in social values had occurred. People still wished to be worthy
of their progenitors, and many of them expressed just the eagerness for
continuity that Tocqueville had found wanting. As Oliver Wendell
Holmes, Sr., put it, he preferred "the man who inherits family traditions
and the cumulative humanities of at least four or five generations."
National reunions became commonplace for large extended families
that were not particularly prominent but had been around for a long
time (fig. 7.5). And by 1910 it was customary for family associations to
place memorial markers at the gravesites of early American forebears.[85]

Exhortations to filiopiety appeared frequently in the more "tasteful" magazines. An 1894 editorial in *Scribner's* observed that in "these days, when there is so much talk of heredity, we ought to recognize . . . our obligations to the decent men and women from whom we have the good fortune to be derived." It concluded that people should feel grateful for their "good blood." Several years earlier, in 1887, Henry Cabot Lodge had also pleaded that filiopiety ought to be indulged in order to do justice to the genuine contributions of the Puritans, who had not received proper appreciation. "The religious form of ancestor worship has departed long since from our race," he asserted, "but the sentiment remains." Then came a curious message that, I have no doubt, Lodge genuinely meant:

> The people of the Western world turn their ancestors to better account, by using them as an argument in favor of benefits to be conferred upon themselves. To us in this country, where all hereditary distinctions have been from the outset wisely abolished, ancestors are chiefly useful as furnishing pleasant opportunities of this kind for mental and moral improvement. To the New Englander they have an especial value, because his retiring and modest nature makes him unwilling to assert himself or sing his own praises.[86]

It is undeniable that ancestor worship enhanced a person's feeling of rootedness, both in general ways and in a more specific sense. We have already encountered such organizations as the New England Society of New York and the New York Southern Society, both of which flourished at that time. We know that Lodge referred to Nahant, Massachusetts, as his "ancestral acres"; that he was fascinated by the exploits of his forebears, wrote a biography of his great-grandfather George Cabot, and criticized his Harvard student Edward Channing for "debunking" their common ancestor, Francis Higginson.[87] Senator George F. Hoar shared Lodge's love of the old Massachusetts Bay Colony, insisted upon the importance of family traditions at Concord in particular (with which many contemporaries agreed), and made the ill-informed contention in 1902 that Americans were more interested in family descent than the British, who were able to take their lineage for granted.[88] Hoar could not have been more wrong about the British, though he was at least correct in the sense that Americans were more apprehensive about their genealogies and about particularly being able to "prove" them.[89]

For white Southerners the anxiety level rose a little higher because non-Caucasian genes infused many of their most distinguished bloodlines. Be that as it may, a plausible argument has been made that the religion of the Lost Cause in the post–Civil War era was in significant part a cult of the dead that found a measure of compensation in filiopiety. When a Norwegian visitor toured the South in the winter of 1908–09, he carefully noted the obsession with ancestors in Charleston and New Orleans. It remains difficult to peruse any set of Southern family papers without encountering numerous references to "family traditions."[90]

Sheer nostalgia partially underlay the phenomenon; and it was not unusual at the banquets of organizations like the St. Nicholas Society of New York to hear such toasts as: "St. Nicholas, bring back to us tonight the sweet fancies of the past." The desire to improve or advertise one's social status got to be an even more important factor. A professor at the University of Vermont observed in 1886 that the "American of the present day . . . would rather know who was his grandfather in the year 1600, than to know who will be the next president." In consequence those who managed major research libraries wasted a lot of time and energy (from their point of view) responding to impossible genealogical queries. "We are still being bothered by ancestor hunters and aspirants for the D.A.R. and Sons," wrote the chief of the Manuscripts Division at the Library of Congress.[91]

Although the Sons of the American Revolution emerged gradually as an organization between 1876 and 1889, and the Society of the Cincinnati had originated directly following the Revolution, most of the familiar (and exotic) societies based upon lineage appeared during the 1890s, notably the D.A.R., the Colonial Dames of America, the Society of Colonial Wars, the Society of Mayflower Descendants, and the Colonial Order of the Acorn. Others were formed soon after the turn of the century, including the Order of the Founders and Patriots of America, the Descendants of the Signers of the Declaration of Independence, and the Order of First Families of Virginia, 1607–20.[92] A volume simply titled *Ancestry,* published at Philadelphia in 1895, listed forty-seven patriotic societies already in existence!

We know a great deal about the personality conflicts among their leaders, which commonly caused splits and the creation of splinter and rival organizations. We know that those who could not meet the elitist criteria for membership that most of these groups established were likely to organize ones of their own that had similar titles, like the Patriotic Societies of America, but with more permissive standards for admission. And we should note the concerns of some insiders who felt that an imbalance existed between self-satisfied filiopiety on the one hand and the inculcation of informed nationalism based upon historical knowledge on the other.[93]

National symbols derived from history became increasingly noticeable, ranging from the name given to the presidential yacht, called the *Mayflower,* to the formation of organizations, like the Mary Washington Association of America, that undertook the placement of markers and other historical activities, to even greater attention being devoted to sites (and kinship ties) associated with heroic individuals, particularly Washington, Jefferson, Paul Revere, and Abraham Lincoln.[94]

Theodore Roosevelt is an especially engaging figure to watch because he embodied such a closely knotted cluster of germane emotions. Fascinated by and proud of his lineage, he had the motto from his family crest carved over one entry door at his home, Sagamore Hill, on Long Island: *Qui plantavit curabit* (He who has planted will be preserved). He nevertheless embraced and called attention to the diversity of American origins, with highly nationalistic consequences. When the American-Irish Historical Society invited T.R. to attend their opening meeting in 1897, he wrote to express his regrets, though hardly in a perfunctory manner.

> All these associations do good. We are a new people, derived from many race strains, and different from any one of them, and it is a good thing to have brought before us our diversity in race origin. Like most New Yorkers, whose American ancestry goes back for more than two centuries, I have an ancestral right to belong to several societies of this kind, and I enjoy equally the dinners of the Hollander, the Scotchman, and the Irishman. It seems to me the one lesson to be remembered always by those who belong to these associations is that in time their descendants will most surely have the right to belong to many other similar associations; for in time the different strains of blood will all be blended together. . . . When that time comes . . . the chief thing for all of us to keep in mind is that we must be good Americans, purely as such, no matter what be our creed or our ancestry in Europe.[95]

The late nineteenth-century creation of diverse organizations devoted to the history of hyphenated Americans has received much less attention than activities by the more visible and (in recent generations) commonly derided groups, such as the D.A.R. and the S.A.R. But Huguenots met during the 1880s to evoke "solemn memories" of the "sufferings of our ancestors." A national congress of local Scots-Irish societies met each year between 1889 and 1903 to exchange information and sing the praises of their forebears. A Pennsylvania German Historical Society was founded in 1891 at Lebanon, Pennsylvania, though the leaders subsequently relocated its headquarters to Philadelphia. Their constitution stated these objectives: "To perpetuate the memory and foster the principles and virtues of the German ancestors of its members."[96]

Associational activity also occurred at this time in the trans-Appalachian region, and even in the trans-Mississippi West. Formation of the Montana Society of Pioneers in 1884, for example, led to the writing of numerous memoirs that we might otherwise not have. Many of these people, moreover, internalized a cyclical sense of the historical process, and those notions gave meaning to their lives and a fascinating form to their narratives. In Harriet Sanders's memoir, for example, she compared the arrival of her overland party at Bannock, Montana, in 1863 to the landing of the Pilgrims in 1620. The analogy clearly implied that her cohort of pioneers had comparable significance for Montana history. The Society initially declared that an individual needed to have arrived by May 26, 1864, prior to the legal creation of Montana Territory. By 1901 the date had been extended to December 31, 1868, in order to ensure an adequate membership.* The critical point, however, is that when the early pioneers reached the gold camps during the 1860s, they had no sense of shared identity. That had to be created over time, and needed to be reinforced by exchanging memories of similar experiences.[97]

For groups like the Montana Society of Pioneers, pride of place became more meaningful than particular bloodlines, just as many organizations back East venerated those who had been participants at place-specific events, such as the Indian massacre that took place at Wyoming, Pennsylvania, during the American Revolution, or the Valley Forge encampment. According to a fund-raising circular issued in 1899 by the D.A.R., the fact that "our ancestors were among those brave men who there suffered and there endured will imbue many of us with deeper interest and a more earnest effort to further the project. But Valley Forge belongs to us all. Its memories, its associations. We are all Daughters of the Revolution. . . ."[98]

Well, sort of. Despite that final flourish, the fact remains that organizations like the D.A.R. were quite deliberately designed to be exclusive rather than inclusive. In *Dusk of Dawn* (1940), W. E. B. Du Bois described his application for membership in the S.A.R., his acceptance by the Massachusetts branch, and then his rejection by the national headquarters in Washington, D.C., on expressly racist grounds. One result of his rejection was the establishment (based in New York City) of the more inclusive Descendants of the American Revolution.[99]

American-style ancestor worship was more comprehensively racist than merely Negrophobic, however. A strident belief in Anglo-Saxon supremacy had provided a potent theme ever since the 1840s, but reached its apogee during these very years, 1885–1915. Owen Wister described the American cowboy as a lineal descendant of "fighting Saxon ancestors," praising him in the context of chivalric ancestor worship; and Frederic Remington even supplied an utterly implausible illustration of the cowboy set against a shadowy background of armored knights, plumed gentry, and bearded mountain men.[100]

The passion for genealogy that became so intense during the later nineteenth century did not simply develop from social climbing and the desire to affirm as well as demonstrate high status. Many of these people really did believe in the biological implications of bloodlines. Nathaniel Southgate Shaler, the eminent Harvard geologist, meant it literally in 1888 when he stated that "a man is what his ancestral experience has

*Membership in the Society of California Pioneers remains limited to direct male descendants of male or female pioneers who arrived in California prior to January 1, 1850.

made him." Hence the perceptions of a direct link between ancestry and achievement. Heredity truly mattered. Thence the imperative of presenting authentic documentary evidence when seeking membership in the snootier organizations that staked their claims in the seventeenth and eighteenth centuries. As one authority put it: "The science of genealogy, like that of history, has in these days become more exact and more exacting. Reputable genealogists now scan their authorities with suspicious care, give scant credence to family traditions, and rely on documents and affidavits."[101]

If you believed in good bloodlines, of course, then you were equally disposed to believe in bad bloodlines. Hence the turn-of-the-century fascination with sordid families like the Jukes and the Kallikaks, with imbecility transmitted from generation to generation. The relative isolation of those who lived in Appalachia made them a curiosity to more socially "advanced" Americans. For quite a while the belief persisted that characteristics of frontier folk remained unchanged. Consequently they were known, with a wondrous absence of irony, as "our contemporary ancestors."[102]

Equally without irony, members of American society who felt so strongly about bloodlines as destiny also believed in self-help, that man could be the master of his own fate. They loved to read about heroes, heroines, and prominent families of high achievers. The Hall of Fame, an elected pantheon of great national figures, was started at New York University late in the 1890s; and people exchanged private letters in which they ranked the most eminent candidates for a hypothetical "Temple of Fame." In 1903 an article about Statuary Hall in the U.S. Capitol Building called it the American Westminster Abbey.[103]

William E. Dodd belonged to a small but vocal minority who opposed the excessive filiopiety characteristic of those three decades that followed 1885. "We deny infallibility to the popes of Rome," he remarked in 1913, "and claim it for our ancestors." Prior to 1885 the occurrence of such quips was rare yet memorable. Abraham Lincoln is supposed to have said that "a man who boasts only of his ancestors confesses that he belongs to a family that is better dead than alive." And Mark Twain gave Huck Finn the great one-line finesse: "I don't take no stock in dead people."[104] That sort of iconoclasm did not appear often after 1885, and then it tended to be either subtle or else relatively private, as when Charles Francis Adams, Jr., of impeccable lineage himself, recorded in his diary for March 1893 that he had delivered a "screed on ancestor-worship in history" to some utterly astonished members of the Thomas Shepard Society in Cambridge, Massachusetts.[105]

When Johan Huizinga, the versatile Dutch historian with his own affection for both local history and antiquarianism, visited the United States during the 1920s, he noticed what he called "an ancestral romanticism"; and he saw in it "an element of the strong and naive ancestor worship which in its more banal forms is also characteristic of America."[106] From a comparative perspective, however, Huizinga's pejorative observation contained a touch of unfairness. We now know that practices and motives similar to those in the United States developed simultaneously among the socially pretentious *haute bourgeoisie* of Western Europe.[107]

We also know, however, that in medieval, Renaissance, and early modern Europe ancestor worship had been a sincere and serious matter. In medieval times a cult of the dead led to the quest for genealogical knowledge—highly useful information because prohibitions against incest made it imperative for people to be well informed about kindred relations. In lower Brittany, where a tradition-oriented society has long existed, the occasion of marriage is accompanied by a ritual known as *recueillement sur les tombes,* a respectful visit to the tombs of deceased members of both families, the bride's and the groom's.[108]

As Claude Lévi-Strauss has observed, in traditional societies that emphasize cyclical persistence and continuity rather than change, a close identification between the living and the dead matters a great deal and leads to some form of veneration for ancestors. Prior to Christianization, the pagan Norsemen practiced ancestor worship. The Catholic Church actually took action to prohibit that, and offered as a surrogate the countermyth of Christian martyrs and saints. In such situations, where Christian tradition displaced ancestor worship, we see an inversion of what happened in the United States at the close of the nineteenth century.[109]

Contrasts with Asian, Melanesian, and African cultures are even more striking than comparisons with Europe. The anthropologist Meyer Fortes once offered a fundamental distinction that serves us well. Where ancestors are genuinely worshipped, and not just commemorated or taken into account for cultural or social purposes, the "medium of relationship with them takes the form of ritual." Actual prayers, libations, sacrifices, and similar activities are different in their qualities and implications from "analogous and homologous nonritual secular activities. It is this that justifies us in speaking of ancestor worship, rather than of institutionalized reverence for or piety towards ancestors."[110]

To put the crux of comparison most crudely, Americans used "ancestor worship" primarily to enhance the prestige of the living more than to honor the dead, and they pursued aspects of ancestor worship in order to marginalize or exclude less "desirable" inhabitants. In places like Japan and Melanesia, especially Papua New Guinea, ancestors really are revered and become sources of inspiration for the most significant works of art produced by the society (figs. 7.6 and 7.7).[111]

Finally, anthropologists also make us aware of one other fundamental difference. In the most venerable forms of ancestor worship, an important aspect involves the "generalization of ancestry," that is, what matters most are the social origins of the tribe as a *whole,* rather than

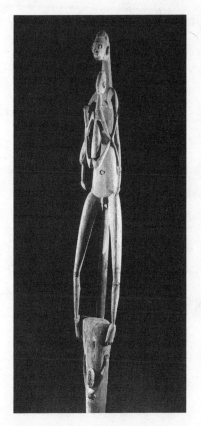

7.6 Ancestor pole, Asmat People of
New Guinea (c. 1900), wood. Courtesy of the St. Louis Art Museum.

7.7 Ancestor tablet, Papuan Gulf,
Wapo-Era Rivers (c. 1900), wood and
shell with red and white paint. Courtesy of the St. Louis Art Museum.

personal aggrandizement or that of one's particular ancestors. Among
certain tribal groups in Africa, prohibitions against the use of genealogical practices within the "chapel" or place of worship serve to minimize
the "individualization of the ancestral cult."[112] Among such groups the
goal of ancestor worship is homogeneity and cohesion, rather than
defining degrees of belonging in response to the presence of "outsiders," who may be regarded with contempt, awe, or respect (fig. 7.8), as
we shall see more fully in the following chapter.[113]

7.8 Urhobo ancestor spirit figure, Nigeria (c. 1890–1910), carved wood covered with kaoline and blue and black paint. Courtesy of the Los Angeles County Museum of Art. Gift of Dr. and Mrs. Richard N. Baum.

IV

DESPITE the critical comparisons and inferences that I have drawn, there remains an attractive aspect to the American concern for intergenerational continuity that emerged late in the nineteenth century. It may well have occurred as a poignant response to the realities of change that appeared so swiftly as consequences of industrialization and urbanization. As the novelist Mary Johnston wrote in her autobiographical notes: "I have the sense of continuity—ancestral life is nothing more nor less than the love of the whole." Musing in 1901, William Dean Howells was less sanguine and more complex, but equally interested in the dynamic implications of unforeseen and unplanned change. "All the good in the world did not perish with our fathers who had such admirable sons," said Howells; "and have we been so wasteful of our patrimony as to have none of it left to hand down to the next generation?"[114]

The fundamental focus of this concern involved the broad issue of cultural transmission; and its most vivid, immediate expressions have been left to us by artists who, despite their diverse social origins, seem to have been resonating in unison to a common concern. An early example is the lush green landscape by Thomas Anshutz titled *Farmer and His Son Harvesting* (1879), an emphasis upon intergenerational co-operation that became a ubiquitous theme in American photography at the turn of the century.[115]

Subsequent and virtually simultaneous illustrations include *Three Generations* (1897), in which Charles M. Russell depicted Native Americans in a natural setting (fig. 7.9), and Charles Grafly's *Generation to Generation* (1897–98), a work in bronze (fig. 7.10) that offers a variation on a piece titled *Aeneas and Anchises* that he modelled in 1893 but did not cast until sometime after 1906. The motif was taken from that familiar passage in Virgil's *Aeneid* when the Trojan hero staggers from the burning city carrying his aged father on his back and leading his own son, Ascanius, by the hand.[116]

A complex blend of wistful nostalgia, ardent patriotism, and more than a touch of anxiety about what lay ahead in the new century undergirded this expressive outburst on behalf of familial continuity. As the colonial revival reached its apogee in the 1890s, references to "the generation of our grandmothers" became commonplace. A book titled *Historic Houses of New England* referred with reverent tones to "ancestral homes that have descended from generation to generation." And Wallace Nutting's book *Massachusetts Beautiful* waxed enthusias-

7.9   Charles M. Russell, *Three Generations* (1897), oil on canvas. Courtesy of the Sid Richardson Collection of Western Art, Fort Worth, Texas.

7.10   Charles Grafly, *Generation to Generation* (1897–98), bronze. Courtesy of the Pennsylvania Academy of the Fine Arts, Philadelphia. Gift of Dr. Charles H. Drummond. The boy is meant to be twelve years old and the bearded man over sixty.

tic about "the completest chain of heredity known to human beings."[117]

Meanwhile, on a spring morning in 1904, the final year of his life, Senator Hoar summoned members of his family (including two young granddaughters) to his bedside in Worcester and, propped up by three horsehair bolsters, declaimed to his personal assembly:

> Ladies, this is the 19th of April. One hundred and twenty-nine years ago, today, your Grandfathers, to wit, my Grandfather Samuel Hoar, my Great-grandfather John Hoar, my Great-grandfather Abijah Peirce, with our Great-uncle Leonard Hoar, and our Great-uncle Samuel Farrar, and a few others, went to the Bridge at Concord and drove the British Army back to Boston. Three Cheers!![118]

Within little more than a decade, however, palpable signs of change appeared. One indication is a painting by Henry F. Taylor titled *From*

7.11   Henry F. Taylor, *From Generation Unto Generation* (1915), oil on canvas. Courtesy of the Cincinnati Art Museum; The Edwin and Virginia Irwin Memorial.

Generation Unto Generation (1915) that utilizes cubistic techniques in such a way that it is unclear whether continuities are being transmitted or broken (fig. 7.11). Taken simply as a work of art, irrespective of its symbolic content, the picture was more than a harbinger of modernism. Two years later Joseph Hergesheimer published his long historical novel *The Three Black Pennys,* concerning three very different generations and the changes that they revealed in an old Pennsylvania family (involved in the iron industry) and its socio-economic values. Hergesheimer's emphasis concerned discontinuity and the absence of meaningful retrospective relationships, or even sensitivity to family traditions. That work appeared in 1917, and it was very widely read.[119]

Chapter 8

"MILLIONS OF NEWCOMERS

ALIEN TO OUR TRADITIONS"

D URING THE LATE 1880s, James Russell Lowell described a recent experience that disturbed him deeply. He believed, moreover, that the episode conveyed a profoundly
important message about the implications of social change in the
United States. While strolling through Boston's Public Garden he noticed two Irishmen looking at an equestrian statue of George Washington and "wondering who was the personage thus commemorated. I had
been brought up among the still living traditions of Lexington, Concord, Bunker's Hill, and the siege of Boston. To these men Ireland was
still their country, and America a place to get their daily bread."[1]

Not only did Lowell feel perplexed by social change, he also wondered whether equality, which for so long had been a sustaining American principle, might not "indeed prove dangerous when interpreted
and applied politically by millions of newcomers alien to our traditions."[2] We turn next, therefore, to interconnections between ethnicity
and class; and more specifically to several sorts of response to the great
waves of immigration that began in the later nineteenth century: empa-
thetic or at least tolerant reactions that eventually enhanced the teaching of American history in public schools; ugly xenophobic responses
that sought undemocratic solutions in the name of preserving an older
notion of democracy; and constructive behavior that provided a creative though undeniably manipulative rationale for historical museums
and preservation activities.

First, however, we must begin with the newcomers themselves, not
merely because they stimulated these responses, but because they too
felt torn by ambivalence between older traditions of their own and
potential new allegiances, and in so many instances they suffered from
divided loyalties and bifurcated identities (fig. 8.1). They found themselves subjected to powerful pressures that came not only from old
stock Yankees, but from the first members of their own ethnic groups

8.1 William James Glackens, *Italo-American Celebration, Washington Square* (c. 1912), oil on canvas. Courtesy, Museum of Fine Arts, Boston. Emily L. Ainsley Fund.

to "make it" in American society. It has become commonplace today to question whether the melting-pot ideal was ever really a viable one. Less commonly considered is the historical question: what proportion of the new immigrants had much enthusiasm for (or even comprehension of) the melting pot, either as a desirable goal or as a meaningful metaphor?

I

FOR VERY LARGE numbers of newcomers, irrespective of country or region of origin, their behavior was basically guided by Moses' admonition to the Israelites just before they entered the Promised Land: "Remember the days of old, consider the years of many generations" (Deuteronomy, 32:7). Organizations of English immigrants and their progeny formed a federation in 1875 known as the North American St. George's Union and held annual conventions on a regular basis until 1905. Use of the Welsh language in Welsh-American communities did not die out until after the first decade of the twentieth century. Members of the Gaelic Society kept visions of Ireland vivid in

New York City, particularly memories of Irish heroes like Tom Moore, whose statue in Central Park they faithfully decorated on Memorial Day.[3]

Some groups, like the Bohemians, were sufficiently well established in Iowa, Chicago, and New York by 1885 to pay a sentimental visit to relatives and friends in their native land (now Czechoslovakia). In June 1885 a mass meeting of Hungarians resident in New York City (there were about 17,000, and the number increased rapidly each year) met to form a Hungarian mutual aid society. Some of the newest arrivals had been harshly mistreated by their own countrymen, who routed them, for example, to the mining area of Pennsylvania—to do work for which these agricultural laborers were not temperamentally suited.[4]

Substantial numbers of Jewish immigrants from tiny villages in Eastern Europe and Russia who settled along the Lower East Side of Manhattan, in Brooklyn, and later in Queens formed fraternal organizations called *landsmanshaftn* in order to assist one another, minimize the need even to deal with "outsiders," and join together in reproducing their familiar ways of life and rituals of death. One newcomer eventually mastered English so well (not customary) that he left an eloquent testimony to their dilemma: "The alien who comes here from Europe brings with him a deep-rooted tradition, a system of culture and tastes and habits—a point of view which is as ancient as his national experience. . . . And it is this thing—this entire Old World soul of history that comes in conflict with America as soon as he has landed."[5]

Immigrants pursued many modes of resistance to these pressures, some of them comparatively passive in the realm of cultural preservation, others quite active in terms of political responses to powerful changes that were reshaping Europe. In terms of the former, evening discussion groups met at Hull House in Chicago to talk about their respective ethnic traditions. They even established a labor museum so that parents could demonstrate to their children the craft skills they had once practiced.[6]

When the international crisis created by World War I deepened, and U.S. involvement became ever more likely, numerous ethnic groups that supported the Allied cause sought to enhance their own prestige and aid their countrymen in Europe by supporting Liberty Bond drives, military recruitment efforts, and special flag-raising ceremonies. Prominent Slovaks, Italians, Poles, and Ruthenians in the Pittsburgh area did so, to cite just one community.[7]

This situation offered the national government a marvelous opportunity to connect American policy goals with ethnic causes, and the Wilson administration seized it. Woodrow Wilson dedicated July 4, 1918, to immigrant Americans. The President and Mrs. Wilson personally hosted representatives of thirty-three groups (including Albanians, Armenians, Swiss, Syrians, and Ukrainians) on a pilgrimage to Mount Vernon by means of the presidential yacht, the *Mayflower*. Wilson used this occasion to energize support for his policy objectives of self-determination and the formation of a League of Nations after the war. Loyalty to Old World ethnic ties did not inevitably conflict with either red-blooded Americanism or enthusiastic support of U.S. foreign policy.[8]

It had not always been so easy to keep multiple allegiances co-ordinated; and even during the Wilson years, to look at only one phase, hyphenated Americans did not receive consistent signals from administration spokesmen. Although the federal government assumed full responsibility in 1890 for processing immigrants, cultural policies (such as they were) vacillated in unpredictable ways. On May 10, 1915, when Wilson addressed a group of newly nationalized citizens in Philadelphia, his message was not only inconsistent with what it would become three years later, it was not even internally coherent. "You have just taken an oath of allegiance to the United States," he reminded them. "Of allegiance to whom? Of allegiance to no one unless it be to God." But then: "You have taken an oath of allegiance to a great ideal, to a great body of principles, to a great hope of the human race." He continued by adding a piece of urgent advice, namely, that as American citizens they were "not only . . . to think first of America, but always, also, to think first of humanity."[9]

The prudent aspect of Wilson's appeal was that partisanship rooted in old-country issues not be permitted to affect American politics. But if one of the major ideals of civilization in the United States is that people should be free to express their diverse interests, then, as political scientist Mona Harrington has written, "the open expression of dual loyalties inevitably raises problems of conflicting loyalties with the potential for causing trouble both within the United States and between the United States and other countries."[10]

Although each and every individual, family, and immigrant community had to face this dilemma on its own terms and in its own way, and although there existed a dramatic spectrum that ranged from eager assimilationists to self-imposed ghettoists, there also emerged, gradually yet inexorably, two patterns that affected large numbers of hyphenated Americans—and both patterns pertain directly to the transmission of memory and tradition.[11]

The first of these patterns involved the creation of societies quite different from self-secluding organizations like the Jewish *landsman-shaftn*. Rather, these would be historically self-aware associations that managed to walk a tightrope between the perpetuation of ethnic pride and full identification with the American dream. Such associations met much less often than the *landsmanshaftn* and did so largely for social and ceremonial observances, rather than for the management of day-to-day existence. In 1888, for example, a big celebration took place in Minneapolis (along with lesser ones elsewhere) to commemorate the 250th anniversary of the Swedes first settling at Fort Christina on the Delaware River.[12]

The following year anniversaries and activities of this sort became commonplace. Americans from Bohemia began a movement to erect a monument at the gravesite of Augustine Herman, a Bohemian who had settled in Maryland during the later seventeenth century and left a handsome estate known as Bohemia Manor. A German-language daily published in Milwaukee, along with dozens of other German newspapers, urged the establishment of a national German-American holiday.[13] And in November the centennial of the first Catholic diocese created in the United States was celebrated in Baltimore at the first Roman Catholic cathedral built in this country. Receptions, speeches, and torchlight parades preceded the dedication of a new Catholic University of America in Washington, D.C.; and all the while a Catholic lay congress met in Baltimore for the presentation and discussion of papers.[14]

The second pattern, which has received considerable attention from various sorts of social scientists as well as thoughtful journalists, is fairly predictable yet quite important to the spasmodic rhythms of memory in American culture—and we continue to see and live with its consequences today. Crudely simplified, the pattern looks roughly like this: the initial immigrant generation strives to perpetuate the language, customs, relationships, and sense of identification with the old country. Their children regard such manifestations of tradition as embarrassing obstacles to being accepted as full-fledged Americans; so they seem to undergo deliberate cases of amnesia and deny their own heritage. Their children, in turn, undergo a fascinating reversion, which Marcus Lee Hansen, a founder of immigration history, designated as a virtual "law": the predictable pattern of third-generation interest in their ethnic group's origin and development in the United States. "Whenever any immigrant group reaches the third generation stage in its development," he wrote, a spontaneous impulse occurs which moves various members of that group, coming from "different positions in life and different points of view to interest themselves in that one factor which they have in common: heritage—the heritage of blood."[15]

The social dynamics of third-generation Americans jump considerably ahead of our story, however, and we will catch up with them in Parts Three and Four of this book. In terms of the retention of Old World ways by the first generation, however, several different sorts of pressures worked against them. The first, and most obvious, is that sheer survival, primarily in economic terms, required concessions to American working conditions; and that, in turn, meant concessions to a culture of industrialization and its customs. Such adaptation did not inevitably mean blotting out older memories and mores entirely; but it definitely weakened or altered them. The imperative of adaptation and the process of acculturation did not produce a uniform "product," however, for as one historian has shrewdly noted, precisely because the workers "came from widely different pasts into a far from uniform economy, the encounter with industrialization could not but be complex and multiform."[16]

The second type of pressure, which we will explore much more fully in the next section of this chapter, came from spokesmen of moral stature whose public discourse demanded assimilation. Early in 1888, for example, the Reverend Charles H. Parkhurst of the Madison Square Presbyterian Church in New York declared that foreigners, such as the Irish and the Germans, would only be welcome if they abandoned their native customs and traditions in order to live as "real" Americans did. Because the ethnic minorities were presumed to have played no role in fighting for or preserving the United States, they had no right to request that their languages be taught in the schools, or to express their views concerning temperance, sabbatarianism, and similar issues.[17]

A third source of pressure, perhaps the least familiar and also the most difficult to handle, came from early arrivals among the immigrants themselves. A guidebook prepared for immigrant Jews during the 1890s, for example, offered this advice for success in the New World: "Hold fast, this is most necessary in America. Forget your past, your customs, and your ideals. . . . A bit of advice to you: do not take a moment's rest. Run, do, work, and keep your own good in mind."[18] It is not the emphasis upon the pursuit of self-interest that seems startling. It is, rather, the assumption that inherited traditions were inevitably and absolutely obstacles to the achievement of self-interest.

Even within any single ethnic group, however, it is difficult to describe a particular response and consider it normative for that group. At one extreme among the Jews were the *landsmanshaftn* that accepted isolation from the mainstream as the prudent price of achieving a safe haven. At the other extreme there was the ruthless determination to Americanize and be successful regardless of the emotional or psychological cost—a pattern so poignantly illustrated in Abraham Cahan's novel *The Rise of David Levinsky* (1917) and in real life by Hollywood mogul Samuel Goldwyn, who started life in Poland as Schmuel Gelbfisz, and walked westward across Europe in 1895.[19]

Sprawled across the center of the spectrum was the dominant majority: those who did not need or wish to shed their identity of origin, yet found much to admire and aspire to in American society and its values. Such people founded the American Jewish Historical Society in 1892 in order to preserve memories of their distinctive experience but *also* to demonstrate the patriotic contributions they had made to their adopted country. In 1914, when the curator of the Society's collections issued an appeal for an appropriate museum and repository, he offered a statement representative of many other groups as well:

> Surely the Jewish people of America should have sufficient pride of race and take sufficient interest in the achievements of their forebears on American soil, to provide, if not pretentious, at least a modest and substantial, home for such collections as we have accumulated. Many of the historic objects in our possession are of a character to arouse patriotic pride, and when exhibited will

serve . . . to remind the world that the Jew in America has been
a pioneer and a co-worker in the upbuilding of the American
States and of the Nation.[20]

A quest for balance characterized the activities of many such organizations. In 1889 when the First Hungarian Social and Benevolent Society held its annual reception and ball, the members dedicated two new
flags, one American and the other Hungarian. A U.S. soldier held the
former while a hussar held the latter. They then draped the two flags
together. After that a tableau was presented, entitled "Columbia's
Greeting to Hungaria." Finally, Julius Pataky delivered an oration in
which he urged those assembled to "love the red, white, and blue, as
he knew they revered and loved the red, white, and green."[21]

The intensity of feeling that many immigrants expressed for traditional American ideals usually gratified those of older stock but, under
certain highly charged circumstances, could easily serve as an extreme
irritant. In 1918, for example, Judge Henry DeLamar Clayton, Jr., presided over the immensely controversial case of five Russian-Jewish immigrant anarchists accused of distributing two leaflets protesting
American intervention in the Russian Revolution. This became the
landmark free speech case known as *Abrams* v. *United States.* Judge
Clayton, a Southern conservative who had rather strong prejudices,
became utterly outraged when Jacob Abrams, one of the defendants,
referred to the founders of the American republic as "my forefathers."[22] Although hyphenated Americans frequently identified with
whatever they found most admirable in the values and history of the
United States, bigots who felt a proprietary relationship to that history
often regarded such patterns of affiliation as presumptuous.

The most germane point to be made about the melting-pot concept is that it remained more controversial among spokesmen for the
immigrant groups than it did among old stock Americans. Israel
Zangwill introduced the notion with his very successful play *The
Melting-Pot,* which opened a long run in 1909. Zangwill's drama describes an idealistic and young Jewish immigrant to the United States
who feels strongly that Old World ethnicity or national identity
ought to be ignored or forgotten in the United States so that all the
diverse fragment-groups might fuse together in creating a new and
superior American nationality.[23]

Such an accommodating and non-threatening notion sounded immensely attractive to true believers already devoted to American traditions; and as early as 1906–07 we find a burst of similar sentiments
appearing in middlebrow as well as high culture journals of opinion.
Brander Matthews of Columbia University observed in 1907 that the
process of assimilation and Americanization had been going on for
generations, "with no violent modification of American ideals." He
appeared sanguine in projecting continuity in American values and

culture despite major changes in the composition of American society.[24]

A journalist who wrote the final installment (called "The Americans in America") in a thirteen-part series (1906–07) about the "leading races that have contributed" to the making of the United States, essentially agreed.* He believed that an American character had developed, even though it remained "unfinished"; and he declared that it resulted primarily from two sources: political liberty and the blending of many peoples. Although he reiterated most of the meaningless clichés about equality and liberty in the United States, and accepted without question the European belief that Americans lacked reverence for the past, he gallantly defied the powerful recent fad of ancestor worship:

> Judging from the individuals who are oftenest marked out as typical of this country, Americanism appears not to be a matter of birth so much as of quality. On the one hand, we have a Levi P. Morton, whose ancestors arrived in the Mayflower days, and on the other, a J. J. Hill, who was almost old enough to be a voter before he set foot in the United States. The late Governor Pingree, of Michigan, whose ancestors had been in America for eight generations, was a man of the people, but not more so than the late Mayor Jones, of Toledo, who was rocked in a Welsh cradle, or Carl Schurz, who had become an American in sentiment years before he became one geographically.[25]

When Henry Charles Lea, the great medievalist, died in 1909, much was made of the fact that his father's ancestry derived from people who had accompanied William Penn to his colony in 1682, while his mother was the daughter of the Irish patriot and publicist Mathew Carey, thereby providing young Lea with that "emancipating mixture of blood and of tradition which has seemed the explanation of so much genius."[26]

It is reasonably clear, in retrospect, that social status and wealth were key determinants of ethnic pride and interest in the transmission of ethnic or national identity. Henry Lea could comfortably be proud of his part-Irish lineage; and Horace Kallen remains justifiably famous as

---

*The essays in *Munsey's Magazine* included the Jews, Scots, Germans, Irish, English, French, Canadians, Scandinavians, Welsh, Italians, Dutch, and Spanish. Africans and Asians were notably omitted. In 1913–14 *The Century* ran a similar twelve-part series (vols. 87–88) by the prominent sociologist Edward A. Ross. The topics and their manner of presentation were a little more sophisticated though fundamentally exclusionist: (1) economic consequences of immigration; (2) American and immigrant blood; (3) immigrants in politics; (4) racial consequences of immigration; (5) origins of the American people; (6) the Celtic tide; (7) the Germans in America; (8) the Scandinavians in America; (9) the Italians in America; (10) the Slavs in America; (11) the Hebrews of Eastern Europe; and (12) the lesser immigrant groups in Europe. It promptly appeared as a book, *The Old World in the New: The Significance of Past and Present Immigration to the American People* (New York, 1914).

an advocate of cultural pluralism. Kallen opposed assimilation and insisted that it was undemocratic to expect ethnic groups to submerge themselves into some broadly nondescript "American" nationality. There may once have existed a genuinely unified type of nationality in the United States, Kallen argued in 1915, but that had been atomized by sequential waves of immigration. Consequently the United States did not and could not have a distinctive nationality. Rather, it comprised a political state within which people of diverse nationalities lived.[27]

Curiously enough, Kallen's widely noticed 1915 essay, "Democracy versus the Melting Pot: A Study of American Nationality," made frequent mention of the respect that is owed to ancestors: the ancestors of diverse immigrants! Referring to ethnicity and the newer American, Kallen commented that "behind him in time and tremendously in him in quality, are his ancestors; around him in space are his relatives and kin, carrying in common with him the inherited organic set from a remoter common ancestry."[28] So immigrants also had bloodlines, and also should be respectful of their forebears. Madison Grant, the Anglo-Saxon supremacist, may have been a far cry from Horace Kallen; but their basic presuppositions in the realm of cultural biology were not so very far apart.

We are just beginning to appreciate the embarrassment of alien nationality, the repression of ethnic memory, and the trauma as well as the delight of discovered identities on the part of third- and fourth-generation hyphenated Americans. These are the descendants of obscure immigrants and working-class folk in the period 1885 to 1915 who were too fearful, ashamed, and in some instances, perhaps, too realistic to aspire to assimilation. Their goal was to be left alone, to avoid notoriety, to remain anonymous—even, in vital respects, to their own children and grandchildren. One major consequence of this deliberate repression of memory is that the early history of labor union activity, and the subtleties of class-consciousness in the United States, have too long been, and may yet remain, two-dimensional and incomplete.[29]

I I

IT IS TOO EASY to assume that most Americans of older stock turned xenophobic, either vocally or else quietly in their heart of hearts. Those who did so eventually had a profound impact upon American politics, society, and culture, and we must pay close attention to them. But for a properly balanced picture we should also notice those who maintained perspective. In 1892, when Edward Eggleston received a bizarre letter from one Henry Baldwin, a super-patriot (about whom more in a moment), the novelist and social historian gave Baldwin a polite brush-off: "I do not quite sympathize with you in regard to the influence of foreign emigrants upon the institutions of this country. . . . Our ancestors were as much frightened, a hundred and fifty years ago, at the coming of foreigners as we are now."[30]

More affluent Americans who enjoyed the means to travel abroad and write about their experiences could be condescending, but nevertheless offered a prudent perspective that, unfortunately, was not heeded even by all members of their class. Following a trip to the Near East during the mid-1890s, for example, Constance Fenimore Woolson reminded her readers that "it is impossible to comprehend any nation not our own unless one has lived a long time among its people, and made one's self familiar with their traditions, their temperament, their history."[31]

In 1903 a gentleman disheartened by the chest-thumping "patriotic discourses" of relative newcomers, and by incessant and predictable allusions to the great deeds of "our forefathers," wrote a convoluted but iconoclastic letter which the *New York Times* published. Here is the most puncturing paragraph:

> When we consider the fact that, at the time when "our forefathers" were performing their meritorious deeds, and for many years thereafter, the ancestors of the vast majority of the present inhabitants of the United States, including those of our patriotic orators themselves, were peasants and laborers in Ireland, or Germany, or Austria, or Italy, and were profoundly indifferent to, if not in absolute ignorance of, the existence of America, this phrase "our forefathers" seems a trifle inaccurate, to say the least.[32]

Although the anxiety level of American nativists is well known, the variety of stimuli to which they responded has not always been appreciated in its full complexity. Let us look at them in ascending order of importance. First, their fierce concern about the perils of communism and socialism, so often cited at patriotic gatherings. Perhaps they were needlessly naive, and certainly they cherished the status quo.[33] But the first Communist International had flourished from 1864 until 1869, and subsequently moved its headquarters to the United States early in the 1870s. (It was disbanded, however, at a Philadelphia conference in July 1876.) One assertive line in the *Internationale* cannot be ignored: the proclamation that "No more tradition's chains shall bind us!" Fearful Americans consequently dug in their heels on behalf of familiar customs that offered the reassurance of stability and order.

Second, so many of the nativists genuinely believed in a fixed and immutable domestic past. Dramatic social change could be difficult to contemplate; and the apparent decline of social cohesion at home just plain frightened them. As Frederic Remington said to his good friend Owen Wister in 1893: "This continent does not hold a nation any longer." Many commemorations of American history during the later nineteenth century took the form of nostalgic affirmations of an idealized and serene version of the past. Hence the unintended irony of the name given to a pervasive New England phenomenon: village improvement societies. Hence, more apropos perhaps, at the turn of the century some one hundred New Hampshire towns joined in celebrating Old Home Week.[34]

Third, even for those fervent patriots who took pride in territorial expansion, the consequences of colonialism could be worrisome. Some remained mindlessly sanguine, to be sure. As one author began his nationalistic book: "From beginning to end there is little to regret and much to admire in the story of American expansion." Some nativists mixed curious combinations of populism and cultural imperialism. An American chauvinist from Chicago, a man of middle-class origins and not from the social elite, wrote to an organizational fanatic in Newark, New Jersey, that "the principles enunciated in the Declaration of Independence of the U.S.A. are to go around the world and in time control all governments and command the support of all peoples. . . ."[35]

Despite such confidence in the universality of American values, we know that many felt genuine concern if not revulsion against bringing under the flag of the United States millions of men, women, and children who had "neither language nor traditions nor habits nor political institutions nor morals in common with us." That is why an extremely tradition-oriented American like R. T. H. Halsey (1865–1942), who played such a critical role in developing collections of Americana for the Metropolitan Museum of Art, so passionately wished to preserve those elements that seemed to him unique in the early American character.[36]

Older citizens like James Russell Lowell, who had been notably egalitarian four or five decades earlier, wondered out loud whether the principle of equality might not prove dangerous: "We have great and thus far well-warranted faith in the digestive and assimilative powers of our system; but may not these be overtaxed?"[37]

The transformation of their attitudes occurred in phase with the escalation of their apprehensions. During the 1860s, members of the old elite could regard immigrant neighborhoods as calm and deferential subcultures, appropriately tradition-oriented in their own way. "Whole communities now are nationally representative," one writer observed. "Each people finds its church, its *fêtes*, its newspaper, costume, and habits organized in America." By 1884, however, in an essay devoted to the theme of democracy and its future hopes amidst the sharply altered composition of society, Lowell contrasted the darkening prospects of a contemporary polyglot culture with the stabilizing customs of "tradition and habit" that had characterized the founders.[38]

When a new book called *America Heraldica* appeared in 1887, concerning the crests, arms, and mottoes of families that had settled in the United States prior to 1800, one reviewer welcomed it with a reminder that a century earlier signs of nobility seemed both dangerous and inappropriate; but now that a stable democracy had developed, people with distinguished lineage should feel proud to explore their personal heritage. In fact, noble aristocrats of an American sort could serve the nation as a moral core and thereby demonstrate that dishonesty was really not socially pervasive.[39]

A deceptive litany in praise of democracy appeared with considerable panache during the later 1880s, including such widely noticed books as *Triumphant Democracy* by Andrew Carnegie in 1886 and *The Working of the American Democracy* by President Charles W. Eliot of Harvard in 1888. That mood turned sour, however, as the growing stench of immigrants seemed steadily more noxious. Even political reformers like the Mugwumps were mostly social elitists who shared grave reservations about the actual practice of democracy.[40] Members of the Brahmin class slid into a mood of bathetic nostalgia. In 1891 Phillips Brooks, an erstwhile patrician reformer, joined the Sons of the American Revolution because it seemed appropriate to "go in for the assertion that our dear land at least used to be American." When Henry James returned in 1904 after twenty-some years away, it horrified him that an Italian immigrant living in Salem had never heard of the House of the Seven Gables and could not direct James to it.[41]

The sad yet predictable consequence turned out to be virulent xenophobia. John Fiske, that philosophically cosmopolitan historian, had a strong partiality for life in small New England towns like Petersham, Massachusetts, "where neither Irishman nor Negro ever sets foot." In 1894 Fiske accepted the presidency of the Immigration Restriction League.[42] In 1888 a huge hullabaloo occurred in New York City when Mayor Abram Hewitt rejected a request from the aldermen that on St. Patrick's Day the national, state, municipal, and Irish flags be displayed at City Hall. "I am in favor of raising the American flag . . . under any pretext," Hewitt declared, "but foreign flags under no pretext." Hewitt even wrote a lengthy public letter to indicate that he previously had denied requests to fly British, French, German, and Italian flags. He conceded that Americans had roots in many other nations; but insisted that citizens of the United States now lived under a single flag that stood as a "symbol of sovereignty." Allegiance of any sort to other nations, even if it was merely sentimental, could be divisive.[43]

Hewitt himself may well have been more politic than xenophobic. But his actions and utterances gave substantial encouragement to others who harbored uglier emotions. A big rally held at the Cooper Institute to show support for Hewitt's policy set a tone of "America for the Americans." An editorial in the *New York Times* insisted that participants in the rally had been "animated only by disinterested patriotism," and accused the aldermen of pandering to the large number of foreign-born voters in the city. Politicians ought to ensure that there is only an "American vote," preached the *Times*; and concluded that displaying the American flag exclusively "is an object lesson which the most ignorant foreigners cannot fail to understand."[44]

There may be a tendency to assume that the immense wave of immigrants who came from Central and Southern Europe at the close of the nineteenth century helped to diminish anti-Irish and anti-German feeling because more menacing threats now supplanted them. Not exactly. Xenophobia tended to be comprehensive rather than clearly focused; and prejudices against the earlier immigrants not only had a long time to fester, but Yankees were more likely to make contact with the earlier arrivals and their children than with the newest of the new, who tended to "disappear" into ghettoes or else move along to remarkably homogeneous proletarian "communities" in northern New Jersey or urban Wisconsin.[45]

While the anti-alien sentiment and snobbery that flared up in this period are well known, less clearly understood is the contest for recognition that occurred—recognition of ethnic contributions to American history. The Irish somehow managed to lose more of these struggles than they won—concerning, for example, how many Irish troops had fought with the Whig side in the American Revolution, or the fact that Cushing, Maine, had once been called St. George because its initial settlers were Irish.[46] German-Americans achieved only marginally greater success. The press in 1889, for example, tells us that Germans in New York City passed a resolution expressing their hot "indignation" that a German coat of arms had been omitted from the City Hall centennial decorations. This seemed a sufficiently clear signal that municipal leaders held the German-Americans in "contempt."[47]

Meanwhile, a fiercely contested struggle took place in San Antonio, Texas, for control of the local chapter of an organization called the Daughters of the Republic of Texas. It had been formed in 1891 for three benign purposes: to perpetuate the Texas heritage, to preserve historic landmarks and documents, and to encourage the study of Texas history. All of that may seem blandly non-controversial; but the stakes were high in San Antonio for two reasons: first, because the Alamo had been allowed to deteriorate and had been commercially exploited as a wholesale-retail liquor emporium. The winner of this struggle would be positioned to not only "save" the Alamo but control the interpretation of its history. That, in turn, leads to the second reason. For many years the "Anglo" community in Texas had acted as though no one but Anglos had been present and martyred at the Alamo, when in fact a significant number of Tejanos (Texans of Mexican descent) had fought bravely and also lost their lives at the Alamo. For their children and grandchildren, the issue of who ran the Daughters would determine whether or not they would ever receive credit in the historical record.[48]

This conflict, which came to be known as the Second Battle of the Alamo, involved two formidable women: Miss Adina de Zavala and Miss Clara Driscoll. The former was the granddaughter of a Mexican-born

Texas patriot, Lorenzo de Zavala, first vice president of the republic of Texas. She had established San Antonio's founding chapter of the Daughters of the Republic of Texas. She also represented a school of thought absolutely certain that a particular commercial structure was actually the former convent and main building of the old mission—the very spot where Davy Crockett, Jim Bowie, and William Travis had made their last stand. In 1908 a new song, "Remember the Alamo," was dedicated to her, and she was called by some "The Heroine of the Alamo."[49]

Clara Driscoll, born in Refugio County to wealthy second-generation parents of Irish descent, was educated in New York and then in Paris. When she returned to Texas in 1901 it horrified her to see that the Alamo was deteriorating badly, that the city of San Antonio had condemned a part of the arcade on two sides, and that her native state might actually lose its most historic "shrine," only to have it replaced by a hotel. She promptly undertook a fund-raising appeal to the people of Texas, but achieved negligible returns. So she decided to use her own inheritance to buy the Alamo from the Hugo & Schmeltzer Company, which wanted $75,000. If the state of Texas repaid her someday, that would be fine. But this tough-minded twenty-three-year-old, who had learned in Europe to revere historic sites and structures, recognized her civic duty and determined to act accordingly.* Although the deed was written in her name in 1904, Driscoll had a clause inserted to the effect that she had bought it on behalf of the Daughters of the Republic, who were to maintain it as a shrine with an appropriate garden.[50]

Eventually the state of Texas was shamed into reimbursing her and formally turned responsibility for the property over to the Daughters. Years later, however, in 1934, when the state's appropriation proved inadequate to buy land around the Alamo in order to create a park, she personally purchased the shacks facing Alamo Plaza for $65,000 and presented that property to the state, thereby making possible the gardens that beautify the site today. It certainly helped that her father had owned a large ranch, served as the president and largest stockholder in the Corpus Christi National Bank (the biggest financial institution in that part of the state), and worked actively to make Corpus Christi the second-largest port in Texas.[51]

Her fund-raising letters rang all the chimes of civil religion. She called the Alamo a shrine and a sacred ruin; described it at night "when the moon throws a white halo over the plaza"; evoked the "martyrdom of the brave spirits" who died there; and, when her fame rocketed across the land in 1904–05, she became known as the Saviour of the Alamo.

*On January 14, 1901, she wrote the following to the *San Antonio Express:* "To live for any length of time in the Old World spoils one for things and places which savor of newness. . . . Their monuments, that speak to them of the valor of their forefathers, are held as things sacred."

Adina de Zavala, meanwhile, who was not a wealthy woman, tended to be ignored just as swiftly as Clara Driscoll became the toast of all Texas. The two women and their followers fought bitterly over how best to preserve the site. De Zavala wanted to emphasize its background as a Spanish Catholic mission and restore the main building (the convent) to its original appearance. The Driscoll faction wished to concentrate on the Texan Revolution of 1836, and therefore regarded the chapel as the most significant structure. They believed that the chapel would be appreciated more, in fact, if the convent were actually removed! This emotional struggle persisted intermittently from 1911 until after the Texas Centennial in 1936. Although Driscoll's vision of the Alamo triumphed, one stunning irony must be noted. Most of the physical labor required to realize Driscoll's desires was supplied by workers from the Tejano community.[52]

"ANGLOS" who lived in the Northeast, which primarily means persons whose ancestors came from Great Britain and northwestern Europe, had problems of their own with non–"Anglo-Saxon" persons and their historical traditions. Because of the hostility directed at Italian immigrants, for example, strong resistance arose (starting in 1892) to making Columbus Day a legal holiday. As one newspaper editorial put it in 1903, "nobody needs a 'day off' every year to think about COLUMBUS and the discovery of America. . . . Nobody but our engaging friends of the Mafia would need all day in which to celebrate the feat of their compatriot."[53]

Starting in the later 1870s and continuing for almost half a century, old-stock New Englanders developed quite an enthusiasm for old Norse history and literature in general, but especially for the notion that Norse explorers had landed on the North American continent long before Columbus. One consequence was the formation of a Scandinavian Memorial Association. Another was a decade of agitation for a statue of Leif Eriksson in Boston. The unveiling took place in 1887,* accompanied by a lengthy oration.[54] In 1926 a fraudulent Norse inscription was found on a boulder located on No Man's Land, three miles south of Martha's Vineyard. The rock actually bore the name of Leif Eriksson in runic letters, along with the date MI. It is possible that the person who carved it simply wanted to honor Eriksson. In any case, it cannot be authentic for numerous reasons: some of the runic characters used did not exist in the year 1100; Eriksson could not have undertaken his earliest voyage until 1103; and climatic conditions surely would have eroded much of the inscription had it actually been there since 1100.[55]

The intensity of feeling generated by these ethnic rivalries is respon-

---

*In October 1949 a statue of Leif Eriksson was erected in front of the Minnesota State Capitol in St. Paul on the occasion of its territorial centennial. The Minnesota Leif Eriksson Monument Association, Inc., raised the necessary funds by popular subscription.

sible for some of the most controversial hoaxes in all of American history, such as the Kensington Rune Stone, which apparently got planted on a Minnesota farm during the 1880s by Scandinavian-Americans determined to undercut in 1892 the four-hundredth anniversary of Columbus's "discovery." The so-called Vinland Map, which surfaced in New Haven in 1965, but may have been forged early in the 1920s by an anti-Italian professor of ecclesiastical law in Yugoslavia, provides yet another, more recent example.[56]

Although the controversies involving Columbus and Leif Eriksson were generated by ethnic tensions, they had an interesting "spillover" effect: namely, a growing fascination with the political and cultural geography of American origins.* Whether or not the very name "America" derived from Amerigo Vespucci became a source of international debate for more than fifteen years after 1875. During the later 1880s a theory surfaced that a group of Christian abbots may have reached the shores of North America eight hundred years before Columbus. (It was based on idiosyncratic readings of a sixth-century Latin manuscript written by St. Brendan, who was born in Ireland in 484 and supposedly led an expedition to the New World in 515.) The myth of a Welsh prince named Madoc, a fabulous navigator, also enjoyed currency for a while.[57]

This curious trend even caused affluent collectors of the period to focus their interests in particular ways. During the 1890s, for instance, Henry E. Huntington became intensely interested in various books that opted for divergent ethnic claims concerning the discovery of America: Italian, Norwegian, Icelandic, Welsh, and even Chinese. For advocates of the United States as the finest exemplar of social pluralism, the politics of culture became less important than a kind of proto–melting pot lesson. When the Reverend Richard Storrs sought to explain the "distinctive American Spirit," he insisted that it was not "the creature of one school of theology. It had no narrow insular origin. . . . Holland and France, as well as England, had contributed to it."[58]

It is important to note that the apparent tolerance in Storrs's perspective was confined to respectable nations of Western Europe. With the addition of Northern Europe, meaning most of Scandinavia, the limits of a pluralistic vision, at least for Yankees, was largely set for more than a generation. On Memorial Day in 1939 the *New York Times* ran an editorial that would have been inconceivable three or four decades earlier: no single race or ethnic group built America alone; those who fought in all of our wars, including the Revolution, came from many different countries, practiced different faiths, and had various skin colors. "There has been a change, no doubt, in what is called the American type, but not so great a change as might be supposed."[59]

---

*Not until 1964 did Congress pass two separate laws making both Columbus Day and Leif Eriksson Day "perpetual" commemorative days (i.e., the laws did not need to be re-enacted annually).

I I I

BACK IN 1907, however, when Brander Matthews speculated about "The American of the Future," he seemed to be responding to those apprehensive "full-blooded" contemporaries who wondered whether they were witnessing the end of American civilization as they and their forebears had known it. Matthews's positive point of view, which certainly was not representative of his class, derived from his upbeat reading of American social history and its dynamics over time. "The American of to-day," he wrote, "whatever his descent, has most of the characteristics of the American of yesterday. Ideals endure, and [traditional] aspirations have not been blunted by time or turned aside by alien influences." He insisted that the process of assimilation, which had worked so well for generations, would continue to do so in response to the latest wave of newcomers, despite their strange appearance; and that cherished national values would remain unchanged:

> In some mysterious fashion we Americans have imposed our ideals on the Irish and on the Germans, as we are now imposing them on the Italians and on the Russian Jews. The children and the grandchildren of these ignorant immigrants learn to revere Washington and Lincoln, and they take swift pride in being Americans. They thrill in response to the same patriotic appeals which move us of the older stocks.

He even went so far, albeit cautiously, as to assert that the "commingling of stocks" had been beneficial—or at least that "its results are acceptable to us at present."[60]

For those who shared Matthews's optimism, the vital component in the whole Americanization process had been (and would continue to be) education, with the history and traditions of the United States as its most essential ingredient. As a consequence, from the mid-1880s until World War I, every conceivable mode of education was viewed as a potential contribution to solving the nation's pressing social problem of extreme heterogeneity. Some serendipitous achievements occurred as a result in the realm of historic preservation, curriculum changes, the more diversified content of commemorative occasions, and the perceived value of historical materials in museums. In 1875–76, when the campaign to save Old South Church in Boston was launched, sponsors called attention to its indispensable role as a "classroom" for the enhanced appreciation of American history. Decades later the D.A.R., the Colonial Dames, and Henry Ford would explain that such sites as the Paul Revere House and the Wayside Inn ought to be restored and opened to the public because of their indispensable potential for transmitting American memories and values to immigrants.[61]

In the realm of extra-mural education, an early example is supplied by the Massachusetts Society for Promoting Good Citizenship, formed in 1889, which produced books and pamphlets on the history of American institutions and sponsored public lectures on various civic issues. In New York City that same year Colonel George T. Balch began to proselytize among teachers on behalf of a General Plan for the Patriotic Education of the Youth of America. His particular pitch? Patriotism incarnate as the manner in which American history must be taught in all schools, parochial as well as public, and in those run by the Children's Aid Society too. The children of paupers would surely carry home to their parents the lessons of American patriotism. Many clergymen also augmented the historical content of their sermons. Older, more established members of the craft unions believed that new immigrants could only be recruited as members after they had been properly Americanized in these ways.[62]

Although many of the concerned participants in this movement for Americanization believed in "siphoning up" to the adult immigrants by means of their children, still others subscribed to the probable success of information and proper sentiments "trickling down" because of both class stratification and intergenerational instruction. Some people even recognized that a fair number of the old-line Americans were either historically ignorant or else indifferent; consequently a multi-purpose outreach program could enlighten several segments of the populace sequentially if not simultaneously.[63] Thus in 1900 the Architectural League of New York met to propose that a Temple of Liberty be erected at Madison Square in Manhattan. Its members felt the need for a "rallying place" where the "masses of humanity" could be imbued with the true meaning of liberty. The temple would be "a veritable historical monument and contain the pictures of every great event of our history, and portraits and statues of every great man our country has produced."[64]

Attention to history in general entered the American high school curriculum more swiftly than it did at the elementary level. Between the 1860s and the close of the century, history came to be reasonably well established as an available option. By 1900 a few states, such as Massachusetts, New York, and Illinois, made U.S. history a required subject. But it was not until the period 1900–15 that such a pattern became widespread, partially in response to recommendations made by a series of prestigious academic commissions that appeared between 1892 and 1908.[65] This trend received reinforcement, however, from the social and ideological impulses that we have just examined. In 1883, for instance, Edwin Mead inaugurated a program for immigrant children in Boston's North End. Although Irish and Italian youngsters learned about Bunker Hill, Copp's Hill, Old North Church, and the Mathers' tomb, the net outcome was considered disappointing.[66]

Six years later more than three hundred educators met in conference at New York's College for the Training of Teachers to discuss a program for the upgrading of instruction in American history. The single most important reason cited was the immense influx of newcomers who knew nothing about the United States. Nicholas Murray Butler of Columbia, who presided at the gathering, appointed a committee to create a program that would implement the consensus achieved at that conference. A public letter written in the mid-1890s by a faculty member at Teachers' College of Columbia University made crystal-clear just how political and conservative the new presentation of American history would be. It is, he explained approvingly, "the history of a people developing in a way never known before; not, as in Europe, from non-liberty to greater freedom and democracy, but from liberty to greater and greater limitations on that liberty."[67]

The response of a small, sensible minority was represented by a man like Edward Eggleston, who did prepare a reader in United States history for children,* but subsequently confessed to a colleague that he did not "care for historical study for the sake of American citizenship." That approach and rationale, Eggleston felt, had "made half a nation of irrational jingoes."[68] The feelings of a much larger yet far less rational minority were clearly revealed by this extract from a letter to the *New York Times*: "The public school system of this country is a great factory, where the raw material from foreign lands is manufactured into patriotic American citizens, with the language, the sentiments, the patriotism, the manners, the customs, and the National aspirations of Americans."[69]

Twenty years earlier, in 1883, *Harper's* had mocked the ignorance of New York's immigrants concerning the historical origins and objectives of patriotic parades. Six years later the Grand Marshal of the Washington Inauguration Centennial Civic and Industrial Parade presented a banner to eight organizations of the German-American butcher industry because of their enthusiastic participation in the parade. The Columbian Exposition held at Chicago in 1893 aimed quite openly at Americanizing the newcomers with nuanced versions of patriotic history.[70] These impulses would eventually culminate in the explicit rationale that underlay the Hudson-Fulton double celebration held in New York during 1909. Edward Hagaman Hall, its principal organizer, made this revealing statement in his Introduction to the huge two-volume "report" that appeared one year after the extravaganza:

> The people of every nationality were invited to take part in the parades and festivals, and an effort was made to make them feel that the Celebration belonged to them as much as to the older

*"Think of writing a book," he quipped to his daughter as he neared completion (1894), "with the long words di-vi-ded in-to syl-la-bles. . . . When I'm dead & gone some men and women will remember that I picked the pebbles out of the way for their baby feet."

inhabitants; that by adopting our citizenship they adopted our traditions and institutions; and that their pride and loyalty should be as great as those of the descendants of the pioneer settlers. It requires but little reflection to perceive the great value of acquainting our adopted citizens with the fact that we *have* a body of worthy traditions and attaching them to those traditions. The power of tradition has been one of the most fundamental and conservative forces of all peoples of all times.[71]

Museums of Americana were also deeply affected by these assumptions, and at the very same time. In 1908 some staff members at the Children's Museum in Kingston Park, Brooklyn, became alarmed when they found that many of their young visitors were "as innocent of all knowledge of Plymouth Rock or Gettysburg as they were of Greek. On the other hand, practically all of the small people were well versed in the Socialistic doctrines of Europe and could talk quite learnedly of Bebel or Marx." A reader three generations later cannot help suspecting an overreaction based upon anxiety. Be that as it may, the curatorial staff perceived that history as it was being taught in the lower grades of the public schools failed to make an impression on many of the foreign-born children; so they innovated various techniques designed to be more vivid than the classroom, ranging from living history tableaux to live puppet shows that would illustrate instructive episodes from the American past.[72]

The Essex Institute in Salem, Massachusetts, the oldest local historical society in the United States, underwent a remarkable transformation during the first decade of the twentieth century. The development of period rooms, creative exhibition cases, an emphasis upon ordinary objects used in domestic life, many of them archaic and utterly unfamiliar to "modern" men and women, and the use of well-informed guides wearing colonial costumes—all of these devices flourished while George Francis Dow served as director and curator from 1898 until 1918 (see figs. 5.7 and 5.8). The story of his tenure has recently been well told. Pertinent to our context here, however, is the stimulus for and response to Dow's creative efforts. When the Institute's new museum opened in 1907, enthusiastic comments from the Salem press are quite revealing though scarcely surprising at this point. One writer expressed the hope that signs advocating membership in the Institute would appear in shops and factories throughout Beverly, Peabody, and Salem—all Essex County towns.

> Of course I know there are some who would decry such a suggestion and intimate that the shops are full of Greeks, French and "all kinds of foreigners." The reply to such an observation should be "all the more reason why somebody should take a hand and try to Americanize the best of this material." They are here, they already hold the balance of power in city politics, and if they are

not given the hand of fellowship and assimilated and inspired with respect for American ideals and American institutions, they will get absorbed and go to swell the columns of socialism, militant laborism, and other worse isms.[73]

It is clear, by the way, that with a few exceptions like Edward Eggles-ton, Charles A. Beard, James Harvey Robinson, and William E. Dodd, teachers, writers, and academic scholars were not immune to these sentiments. A great many of them tended to glorify the national past, to praise the conservative forces of ordered liberty, and to omit those problematic aspects of American history involving Native Americans, African-Americans, and dissenters.[74] Thus in 1910 the Anglo-American Authors Association, Inc., housed on Manhattan's Fifth Avenue, began to publish "A Grandfather's Historical Stories of Our Country" in ten profusely illustrated volumes for juveniles. They would inculcate all of the "correct" values, particularly among those overly large groups most in need of indoctrination.

Scholars, writers, and administrators responded deliberately to the imperatives of social change. The American Historical Association's Committee of Seven on the Study of History in Schools did a bold and unusual thing in 1897. It decided to seek permission from the British, French, and German governments to visit some of their secondary schools in order to learn more about their methods of teaching history. So Charles Homer Haskins went to France, Lucy M. Salmon to Ger-many, H. Morse Stephens and George L. Fox to England. Tenement-house reformers in New York City did just the same sort of thing at that time;[75] and the Pittsburgh Survey of 1909 marked the first attempt to gather together diverse experts in order to compile a comprehensive summary of social and economic conditions in an American city. During the next two decades the American city became both an artifact and a laboratory for close study—quite a different way in which Americana came to be "discovered" after 1909. By 1928 there were 2,700 such compilations of data concerning American urban centers.[76]

I V

WHEN WE LOOK more closely at the passion for tradition on the part of most nativists during the later nineteenth century, we dis-cover a deep-seated resistance to (often resulting from a genuine fear of) change. That much is now well established and has been described in quite some detail as an aspect of anti-modernism. Less familiar is the fact that nativism as well as anti-modernism were not sentiments con-fined to the upper class. They were widespread among the "middling" classes and also appeared among working-class Americans, usually on account of their resentment of low-paid foreign labor.[77]

I shall turn to these latter groups momentarily. First, however, we must recall just how obsessed people of this generation really were with genealogy. Even *Harper's Bazaar* and daily newspapers made fun of a Cape Cod man who boasted in court in 1887 that "they ain't a drop of foreign blood" in him because all of his ancestors had arrived on the *Mayflower*. More serious because far more typical was the attitude of George Brown Goode, a naturalist and museum administrator at the Smithsonian Institution in Washington. He believed in heredity as a matter of science as well as religion, and observed that "one of the elements of satisfaction in genealogical study legitimately arises from the success of our attempts to establish personal relations with past ages and to be able to people our minds with the images of our forefathers."[78]

Goode had been among the organizing members of the Sons of the American Revolution in Washington, D.C.; and like many such enthusiasts, he eventually belonged to several patriotic and historical societies. That pervasive commitment provides a partial explanation for the incredible proliferation of these organizations beginning in the 1890s. Equally important in understanding that proliferation, as noted in chapter seven, was the proclivity among founders and members to quarrel, with one faction establishing either a still more exclusive splinter group or else a more accessible one; or, in some situations, simply one that they could control. Because so many of the genteel ladies who belonged were also aware of a small but very vocal group of feminists known as the New Women, they formed their own socially conservative coalition known as Wimodaughsis, a word made up of the first syllables of wife, mother, daughter, and sister—all of which they felt quite proud to be.[79]

The craze may have achieved its drollest moment when, as a hoax, someone proposed a Society of Descendants of Non-Combatants, for the offspring of Quakers and others who had not fought for reasons of conscience. The most bizarre extreme surely was realized in the Order of the White Crane, organized in Pima, Arizona, and named for White Crane, the Hereditary Chief of the Ancient Tribe of Ojibway Indians. This group admitted only the royal descendants of Aztec or Toltec kings, or else of colonial settlers who had arrived prior to 1783. Potential members without royal Indian blood had to be of "Aryan" stock.[80]

It may be helpful to pause for a moment of comparative perspective. Although this phenomenon was not uniquely American, neither was it universal or inevitable. If anything, the use of genealogy for *inclusive* purposes is probably more common around the world than this trend toward exclusiveness. Among the Tiv of northern Nigeria, for instance, genealogies are not regarded as historical accounts of kinship in the past so much as they constitute a summary of extant social relationships. When those relationships change, the genealogies are changed accordingly. As the historical anthropologist Keith Thomas has acknowledged, this pattern of malleability works well enough for cultures dependent upon oral tradition. Once genealogies have been recorded, however, it becomes far more difficult to change them deliberately, for whatever purpose.[81]

IN 1904 a lengthy editorial that appeared in *Scribner's* argued that the United States really needed a "republican aristocracy" because patriotism was more important than the "development of exclusiveness." Lest this sound too oxymoronic to be credible, it must be kept in mind that it did not seem at all self-contradictory at the time because so many Americans did believe in democracy as an ideal, but also felt that if the latest immigrants were not to dominate eventually, a political coalition of respectable Caucasians, irrespective of class, would be essential.[82]

That imperative conveys at least an implicit acknowledgment that social stratification and ethnic diversity existed. It should also be noticed that tradition-oriented groups sponsored philanthropic programs and activities that benefited the less fortunate. The press gave full coverage in 1876, for example, to the Martha Washington Reception and Centennial Tea Party in Aid of St. John's Guild.[83] One of the finest antiques fairs held anywhere in the United States still takes place annually under the auspices of East Side House, a "social settlement" formed in 1891. The proceeds from ticket sales (to see and buy high-quality antiques) are transformed into social services for the poor in metropolitan New York.

The complexities of class emerged with greatest fascination in the ceaseless activities and correspondence of William O. McDowell of Chicago and Henry Baldwin of New Haven: both of them ardent nationalists (but also internationalists in their own quirky ways), both members of patriotic societies, and both nativists who were paranoid about potential conspiracies. To judge by the syntax and spelling of their letters, along with letters written to them by others, they were not well-educated people.* There is a genuineness about their passion, however, and a sense of urgency as well, that cause them to come alive from the pages they wrote in a way that most cold-fish patricians do not. As Baldwin informed a correspondent in San Francisco, he sought support to achieve the "Americanisation" of America, and the world beyond as well.[84]

Beginning in 1889, Baldwin put together a circular letter and sent it to many organizations and individuals. He called for all of the patriotic societies in the United States to convene a national council at Chicago. He especially hoped for Southern participation because, in his view,

---

*Many of the organizations were associations of mechanics, and one group that corresponded with Baldwin was the Columbian College of Citizenship in Columbus, Ohio, "A School of Citizenship for the Masses."

"the South is practically more American than the North" (presumably because the South had fewer immigrants). Although the annual meetings did not attract many people, they did lead to the creation of a National Council of Patriotic Organizations, and bestowed upon Baldwin a title: the Custodian of American History. "This office has been created," according to Baldwin's wordy letterhead, "in order to gather for reference facts of all kinds respecting America," and also a "Library Americana" which would eventually be deposited in a national headquarters to be established in Washington, D.C. If a national university was ever established, as Baldwin fervently hoped, one of its most important schools would be devoted to Americana. Baldwin elaborated his concerns for George Brown Goode of the Smithsonian. The teaching of civics had been sadly deficient in American schools; and when it had occurred, it had been

> for the aid of the ruler, while it ought to be for the instruction of the voter *first*. . . . American history is but little known. The Schools learn [i.e., teach] something of English History and the English Constitution, but practically, American History and American Constitutional laws are known by few who have made these studies a specialty.[85]

For more than a decade this indefatigable character pestered all sorts of individuals and offices, especially in Washington, D.C., along with organizations throughout the United States. He did at least locate some soulmates who shared his obsession with secrecy in the face of conspiracies. A leader of the American Patriotic League wrote to him from San Francisco to say, first, that his own association was too busy to join in the National League for the Defense of American Institutions; and second, that when the American Party had been "Sold out," most participants abandoned it but a hardy remnant formed a secret society of "native Americans." Unfortunately, he confessed, "we had it so Secret that a person could not speak to an outsider but he was liable to breake his Obligation in some way. Consequently we made but little progress."[86]

McDowell, meanwhile, an aggressive, flamboyant, litigious, and unstable fellow, had written in 1889 to the president of every republic in the world, apparently because he hoped to create internationally connected societies composed of the descendants of men who had established independence in their respective countries. In 1892 he pleaded with Baldwin to change his "line" from pan-Americanism (purely geographical) to pan-republicanism, which concerned the birth, growth, and progress of democratic institutions. McDowell also harangued Baldwin because "the body that elected you [to be the Custodian of American History] was not incorporated and has no legal existence." McDowell then urged Baldwin to will his Library Americana to the

Sons of the American Revolution, a properly incorporated organization. Within a decade Baldwin's letters to McDowell had become pathetic accounts of his inability to bring any of his projects to fruition. By 1893 McDowell had managed to alienate leaders in most of the major societies; but he now served as chairman of the Columbian Liberty Bell Committee, chairman of the Human Freedom League, and chairman of the General Committee for a National Flag Pole at the Highlands of the Navesink in New Jersey.[87]

McDowell's enthusiasm for republican values must have had some impact, because in 1901 Baldwin explained his goals in this manner: "Our purpose is not a Library, it is rather a design to strengthen the government, and the defeat of foreign and domestic conspirators who are persistantly planning for the overturning of Republican institutions." The most menacing conspirators seem to have been based in Austria, especially among Jewish bankers in Vienna. Semites merely constituted new weapons in the hands of an old enemy, however, going back at least to the establishment of a St. Leopold Foundation at Vienna in 1829. By 1902 Baldwin had broken with McDowell, and held him responsible for mismanagement of organizational funds. By then Baldwin was also seventy and worn out. He wrote endless, semi-literate letters, and his name appeared on all sorts of odd letterheads, such as the Cuban-American League, and Chairman of the Board of Trustees, Department of History, "University of United States." These were mostly fantasies of unclear purpose and vainglory that never achieved fruition.[88]

In May of 1901, not long before the rupture with McDowell, Henry Baldwin prepared a seven-page, semi-autobiographical memorandum which he mailed from New Haven to McDowell in New York City. The reason for writing this document is not entirely clear; it seems to have been put together for the benefit of the first meeting of the trustees of his beloved Library Americana—a rather long-winded explanation of how "the institution," as he called it, had come about.[89]

Baldwin supplied a discursive history of nativist responses to threats from newcomers, starting with the United Sons of America in 1844, and then various other societies whose purpose was the preservation and perpetuation of American institutions. He waxed especially enthusiastic about the founding in 1889 of the Sons of the American Revolution: "and with it came that which should have come all along with the movements that went before—An American Spirit." He then reviewed his own intensive activities ever since 1889 on behalf of that Spirit. He disclaimed any serious knowledge of history because his formal education had been cut short in 1846 when, at the age of fourteen, he began to work in the law office of his father, Simeon Baldwin.

What emerges most clearly is an obsession with conspiracies that threatened his beloved land, especially from anarchists, Italians, Jews, and bankers; the urgency of his commitment to immigration restriction in order to protect native-born wage workers;[90] his partially democratic impulses in the populistic sense that we ascribe to the 1880s and '90s; his desire to collect and commemorate the important texts and events of American history; and finally his fantasy—which it truly was—that somehow all of the zealous, sparring, spiteful patriotic societies could set aside their petty personal feuds and form a grand coalition or network that would effectively shield American liberty—"which liberty we as Patriot Sons of our Patriot Fathers ought to maintain in its fullness. Where are the men for the work???"

Henry Baldwin felt unworthy of his wise and courageous forebears, yet he had internalized that powerful sense of intergenerational continuity that was so pervasive among men and women of older stock at the turn of the century. Although he loved the past and revered tradition, he lived in the present because a mighty struggle had to be fought if the republic that he and his father cherished was going to endure. Baldwin is a forgotten man. I suspect that he must have been a prig, a nag, and a nuisance to know. But he and his broad network of contacts reveal to us a mind-set that cannot be ignored if we wish to understand Yankee anxiety over the prospect of massive immigration in late nineteenth-century America.

Chapter 9

THE POWER OF PLACE,
PATRONESSES OF THE PAST,
AND VARIED SOURCES
OF TRANSITION IN THE
PROGRESSIVE ERA

T HE PHASING of this book depends upon a schematiza-
tion of certain pivotal periods of change that took place after the
Civil War, in the wake of World War I, and following World
War II. There is an alternative (perhaps I should say additional) way of
thinking about the cultural *longue durée,* however, that deserves mention. If we consider the two centuries since the close of the American
Revolution, myths have persisted and historical awareness has existed,
with varying degrees of intensity, throughout. But in terms of a dominant feeling for continuity or discontinuity, the centuries split fairly
clearly into two segments of roughly equal length. Writing in 1888,
James Russell Lowell conveyed a strong sense of transition occurring in
his mature years. Up until the third quarter of the nineteenth century,
he noticed, "the traditions of our founders were fresh. . . . This was what
may be called the Fourth of July period of our history."[1]

Lowell perceived shifts, however, that historians interested in American collective consciousness during and since the Progressive era have
confirmed. As one of them commented a few years ago, "public historical imagery" in the twentieth century primarily emphasizes "the dis-
junctions, rather than the continuities, between what it depicts as local
communities of the past and mass society of the present."[2] Many factors
contributed to the transformation. First, the sheer passage of time permitted a transition from myths sustained by memory, however flawed,
to illusions of memory perpetuated by allusions to comfortable myths.
Second, transformations in technology, particularly photography and
half-tone illustrations in popular publications, produced an abundance
of *aides-mémoire* that surely enhanced a sense of the past, all the while
highlighting contrasts between what we were becoming and what we
had been, once upon a time.[3]

Third, and apropos of that reference to the Fourth of July period in our history, secularization along with increased social complexity brought changes of mood and style in the annual days of observance— changes that many contemporaries recognized. We must acknowledge, once again, the persistence and continuity of some genuine traditions. In 1910 the Bunker Hill Monument Association still held its annual meeting on June 17, and listened to three speeches on historical or political topics.[4] Exemplars of change are more striking, however. On May 30, 1888, when Memorial Day ceremonies were held in New York at the Metropolitan Opera House, Chauncey Depew, who presided, declared that Memorial Day should no longer be a day of mourning and sorrow but a day of celebration. Because men had sacrificed their lives in the Civil War, Americans were now able to live in a strong and united democracy. In 1900, when May Day became the occasion for music, merrymaking, and popular entertainments, an editorial acknowledged that the Pilgrims and Puritans would have considered such activity as "heathenish," which was absolutely true.[5]

While this chapter highlights the transitional decade from about 1905 until 1915, its primary themes concern the strong sense of discontinuity felt at the start of the century, the nostalgia induced by swift change, and the extent to which history and myth became all the more inter- twined despite some calls for differentiation. Following a brief look at the Fourth of July as an exemplar of changing traditions, we turn in section II to early attempts at historic preservation; in section III to the special role of women as patrons of the past; in section IV to the com- plex responses that Progressives felt toward tradition in American life; in section V to the on-going significance of localism and regionalism in a nation that remained diverse and decentralized, with an attendant pride of place; and finally, in section VI, to the rise of civic pageantry in comparative perspective.

I

ALTERATIONS in the mode of observance deemed appropri- ate to the Fourth of July had been occurring ever since the 1840s; but they became more pronounced toward the end of the nineteenth cen- tury, though allowance must be made for regional variations and, even more important, differences between rural communities and major urban areas. In 1889 New York City was comparatively quiet on the Fourth. Trinity Church played its chimes, veterans raised the American flag at Mount Morris Park, and two surviving veterans of the War of 1812 met with friends for lunch and discussed old times. A gathering at the Cooper Institute sang "The Star-Spangled Banner" and listened to a reading of the entire Declaration of Independence. Special gather- ings took place sponsored by Council No. 1 of the Benevolent Order of

Veteran Firemen and the Harlem Democratic Club; the Washington Heights Century Club (a patriotic organization) heard speeches; so did the Eight-Hour League, the Turn Verein Bloomingdale, the German Odd Fellows, the 69th Regiment, etc. All in all, however, people "could not remember a quieter Fourth of July."[6]

By contrast, on July 4, 1891, the town of Muncie, Indiana, was absolutely packed for a festive celebration. On July 4, 1925, however, the inhabitants of Muncie took advantage of the new auto-mobility and turned to the road. The town was nearly deserted on the Fourth. In Southport, Connecticut, people simply ignored a law prohibiting firecrackers. Anonymous enthusiasts set them off for four consecutive days and nights.[7] In New York City, though, an editorial noticed the comparative success of a twenty-five-year campaign for a safe and sane Fourth. By 1910 it had come to be known as "Tetanus Day." In the mid-1930s observers suggested that perhaps people had "outgrown the thunderous, rough-house Fourth." It was by then more nearly a day of leisure than of exuberance, with the noise level only "an echo" of what it once had been. Some inhabitants still attended traditional patriotic programs; but to most people the day meant an opportunity for sports, recreation, rest, or travel rather than speeches, parades, and pageantry. Times had changed.[8]

As the Thanksgiving holiday approached in 1911, *Munsey's Magazine* took advantage of the seasonal mood to make a general assessment, for which the publisher commissioned rather elaborate albeit solemn illustrations. Early on came an embarrassing admission. Nearly 140 years after Independence, "this nation still has no national holiday." In a legal and technical sense that may have been true, but not in terms of custom; so the essay proceeded to review those six that had been memorialized in one way or another, resulting in "a nation more closely welded together by this inheritance of great memories, as a living people made stronger with the strength of the dead." By calendar sequence that meant the birthdays of Washington and Lincoln, Memorial Day, July 4, Labor Day, and Thanksgiving.[9]

The most predictable aspect of the article appeared in its emphasis upon national cohesion. Despite the diversity of these holidays in origin and character, each one reflected some interconnected aspect of American culture: "always one nation, always the same nation." Not exactly true, but understandable as wishful thinking. Next came a prophetic part, surprising for its realism and unwillingness to insist upon a never-changing past. "Measured by the distances of history," it acknowledged, "this nation has only entered upon its life."

> If a long future should await it, other great Americans will be born whose birthdays will force their way in to the calendar. There will be other state documents perhaps as vital as its first Declaration of Independence; there will be other wars; there will be other

dead. Thus our boundaries of national gratitude are not finally set.[10]

To cap it all off, the reader encounters some surprises. They should not really be so startling if we recall the general desire for sectional reconciliation. Could anyone believe that a thousand years hence Americans "would still be concerning themselves with memories of the Civil War?" Then came the assertion, quite valid in certain respects, that Thanksgiving was the least distinctively American holiday because it is the most "human," that is, universal in its aspirations and appeal. Labor Day would perhaps be the most enduring because it was the least historical and because of the centrality of labor to society. "Labor never gets old, never comes to an end. . . . All things else in the nation can never combine against labor. It would be the pillars of the temple combining against the foundation."[11]

Perhaps in the fullness of time that will turn out to be true. It is not easy to predict (never mind explain) the politics of national memory. Although most Americans hold the U.S. Constitution in very high regard, Constitution Day enjoyed only a brief and superficial history, and the Bill of Rights has scarcely been honored at all.[12] The massacre at Fort Phil Kearny—when Captain Fetterman led eighty men to their deaths—shocked the country in 1866; but it did not become a legend or a myth because Fetterman lacked the notoriety and flamboyance of George A. Custer.[13] The centennial of the Emancipation Proclamation started few ripples in 1962 because the South refused to be officially reminded of its peculiar institution.

Although the moods of memory can obviously be capricious, a glance at the decade from about 1906 until 1915 not only conveys strong hints of transition in American feelings about tradition, but a growing awareness on the part of some contemporaries, at least, that a transformation had already begun. Listen to John Dos Passos's reminiscence of his fairly old-fashioned adolescence, around 1906–08, when one little pal said, "Let's play Washington at Valley Forge," and roles were assigned, including Washington, of course, Lafayette, Benedict Arnold, and the Green Mountain Boys. Their enthusiasm outstripped their historical veracity.[14]

Then look at the steadily rising stock of American history and literature. Writing *The Wine of the Puritans* in 1908, Van Wyck Brooks wailed that "American history is so unlovable." In less than two decades he reversed himself by 180 degrees. When John Macy first published *The Spirit of American Literature* in 1908, the very choice of his title seemed perverse because he could not have been more condescending and pejorative. "The American spirit in literature is a myth," he wrote, because it lacked distinctively American qualities: it had "too little savour of the soil." In 1915, however, when Fred Lewis Pattee of Penn State (who held the first chair in American literature at any American

university) brought out *A History of American Literature Since 1870,*
he prophetically titled chapter one "the second discovery of America,"
he emphasized the impact of the Civil War on national literature, and
he stressed distinctively American qualities overall.[15]

In 1910 the Drama League of America was founded at Evanston,
Illinois. In 1910 conductor Walter Damrosch and the New York Philhar-
monic tried to play (at a rehearsal) Charles Ives's first symphony; although they gave up after a struggle, it represented a new initiative. In
1910 John A. Lomax began to publish cowboy songs, a major turning
point in the history of American folklore.[16] In 1910 a group of gentlemen in the Northeast who shared an enthusiasm for collecting Americana formed the exclusive Walpole Society. Soon after that Francis P.
Garvan began to collect antiques. He started with English objects but
swiftly shifted to American ones. And in 1912, at the age of seventy-one,
James Ford Rhodes wrote from Florence, Italy, that nothing appealed
to him "so much as American history and politics. It does not show
culture to say so, but the Middle Ages and the Renaissance and their
glorious products pale with me in comparison."[17]

By 1911 Wallace Nutting was ready to sell his "staged" photographs
of quaint New England scenes, mostly made with seventeenth-century
settings—the "Pilgrim Century," it came to be called. Nutting's first
full-scale catalogue appeared in 1912: enthusiasts could now achieve
instant quaintness. By 1912 George Francis Dow had completely restored the old Ward House in Salem, so it was accessible to tourists as
an adjunct of the Essex Institute. History and tradition, myth and memory were becoming intertwined (rather than differentiated) in just the
manner that a few concerned individuals had hoped might be avoided.
Noticing this rush of enthusiasm for Americana in notions as well as
artifacts, one prominent historian took an upbeat but unrealistic tone.
"The large ideas which we have loved all along," wrote William E.
Dodd, "will become the more sacred by reason of the removal of the
myths and shams upon which a so-called patriotic affection has been
wasted."[18]

Myths and shams were clearly not being shed, however. If anything
they proved extraordinarily tenacious, even among professional historians, most of whom felt quite comfortable with the status quo and did
not want to be bothered with revisionism and the recognition of new
realities. In 1910, when Appleton and Company, the publishers of a
widely used U.S. history textbook for high schools, asked Andrew C.
McLaughlin and Claude H. Van Tyne to give "a little more space" to
Native Americans, the authors dragged their feet. Van Tyne reassured
McLaughlin that their sense of proportion was just right. They had told
of the "effect of the Indians wherever their existence changes the forward movement of the white man"; but they refused to "use them
merely to amuse the boys." The editor at Appleton's Educational Department had calculated that McLaughlin and Van Tyne gave the Indi-

ans a grand total of 170 words. The exceedingly vexed authors remained adamant.[19]

The same sort of resistance to change actually provided a powerful impetus for the preservation movement during this same period of time—although, as we have seen, fascination with prehistoric Indian civilizations had helped bring about passage of the Antiquities Act in 1906.

I I

THE SLOW and hesitant emergence of historic preservation activities in the United States involves a story that has now been narrated in considerable detail from its stop-and-start genesis during the third quarter of the nineteenth century through the later 1940s.[20] It may be useful, nonetheless, to indicate some of the chronological correlations between that movement and the contextual developments of which it has been an important part. In 1909 the American Historical Association proposed the creation of a Historical Sites Commission because "in no state has the work of ascertaining and marking sites been consistently done." A decade later author Edith Wharton declared that America had begun to reveal an "eagerness to beautify her towns, and to preserve her few pre-Revolutionary buildings—that small fragment of her mighty European heritage."[21]

Prior to the final decades of the nineteenth century, most historic sites in the United States had been sadly neglected, physically altered, or just plain demolished. In 1816 the state legislature of Pennsylvania, eager to raise money to erect a new capitol in Harrisburg, hoped to sell Independence Square and all of its buildings, including Independence Hall, for $150,000. Subsequently the Philadelphia home in which James Madison had lived became a ragpicker's headquarters; a municipal dog pound was located in the basement of Independence Hall until 1851; and the house where Thomas Jefferson wrote his first draft of the Declaration of Independence found functional use as a hot dog emporium on the street level with shabby apartments above.[22]

All of that could happen despite the fact that Independence Hall was frequently referred to during the 1840s and '50s as a possible shrine, and Edward Everett urged in numerous speeches during the 1850s that people make pilgrimages to it. As late as 1870 the legislature ordered that all structures in the square except Independence Hall be destroyed—an order that was not repealed until 1895. In 1871 a proposal appeared—though it failed to progress—that the square and all of its structures be made a permanent memorial. Significant restoration was not undertaken by the D.A.R. until 1896–98. The legislature did not appropriate funds for a thorough restoration of Independence Hall until 1910, and the work was finally completed by 1913. Proponents of preservation raised their voices from time to time, but they could muster comparatively little in the way of either political or grass-roots support.[23]

The saga of the Wayside Inn near Sudbury, Massachusetts, is less familiar yet remarkably similar. The family of the original proprietors had actually closed the inn before October 31, 1862, when Longfellow rode out from Cambridge in quest of historical inspiration. The inn simply stood abandoned until an antiques enthusiast purchased it in 1897. It then became a popular resort for cycling and sleighing parties; and Universalist ministers also held regional retreats there until 1919, when the owner's widow closed the place down. Three years later Henry Ford bought the inn, restored it, protected it from commercial incursions, and even got the Commonwealth to accept Ford's relocation of a modern highway that ran much too close to the historic site.[24]

The sole name with sufficient national appeal to make historic preservation relatively easy during the second half of the nineteenth century was, predictably, that of George Washington. Not only did a ladies' association led by Ann Pamela Cunningham raise enough money to "save" Mount Vernon during the 1860s and '70s, but during the 1880s interest arose in erecting a "simple memorial hall" at the site of Washington's birthplace. In 1892 schoolchildren accumulated funds to restore the interior of a spinning house at Mount Vernon; and between 1890 and 1896 the brand new Association for the Preservation of Virginia Antiquities saved the home of Mary Ball Washington, George's mother.[25]

The A.P.V.A., as it has long been known, was organized in January 1889 by a group of genteel women and a few men located largely in the Tidewater area of Virginia. They were distressed by the dilapidated condition of historic places and structures in the vicinity of Williamsburg, Jamestown, Richmond, Fredericksburg, and Cape Henry. Within the first eight years of the Association's existence its members acquired, most notably, the Powder Magazine and the site of the colonial capitol in Williamsburg; plus twenty-two acres at Jamestown where the church tower and tombstones were repaired and a sea wall was begun in order to protect the ancient island from further erosion by storms and tides along the James River.[26]

Like most early preservation organizations, the A.P.V.A. devoted its energies primarily to placing memorials, tablets, and making repairs at places with particular historical connections. Patriotism and commemoration vastly outweighed aesthetic value as motivating factors—a ratio that would be reversed with the emergence of an American aesthetic a generation later in the 1920s. When the Powder Magazine at Williamsburg was acquired and converted into a colonial museum, for example, the initial expenditure went for the installation of two stained-glass windows honoring Governor Alexander Spotswood and rebel leader Nathaniel Bacon. Architectural restoration as we understand it simply was not a matter of interest or concern.

Although its counterpart, the Society for the Preservation of New England Antiquities, was not born until 1910, the later organization actually had a thirty-five-year gestation period. The crusade to save Boston's Old South Meeting House in 1876 attracted considerable attention and succeeded. Then, during the summer of 1877, three young partners in an architectural firm that subsequently became eminent as McKim, Mead, & White made a tour of New England in order to study and sketch early American buildings—a tour that would be almost as important for the genesis of the colonial revival as it would for the preservation movement in New England. Out in the foothills of the Berkshires, the Pocumtuck Valley Memorial Association received a charter in 1870 and dedicated its Memorial Hall (originally built in 1797–98) as a museum ten years later. Although its initial mission concentrated upon the "collecting and preserving of such memorials, books, papers, and relics as would illustrate and perpetuate the history of the early settlers, and of the race which vanished before them," interest in the architectural legacy of the Deerfield-Greenfield area was stimulated and ultimately led to the restoration of many significant structures in that region, especially at Deerfield during the 1950s.[27]

In 1888 the Haverhill Whittier Club expressed its determination to preserve the home of John Greenleaf Whittier, the beloved Quaker poet, as a "perpetual memorial." The retired merchant who owned the house promised to maintain it well and even make it accessible to visitors. Throughout 1889 the state of Connecticut celebrated all manner of 250th anniversaries, quite a few of them associated with venerable structures in places like New London, Guilford, and Milford that were "still in a remarkable state of preservation." Within a decade the town of Litchfield in northwestern Connecticut began a long-term and amazingly concerted effort to restore its colonial ambience, and did so with such relentless thoroughness that one wag later quipped: "The village looked more colonial in 1930 than it *ever* did in the colonial era."[28]

Beyond being a beneficiary of the colonial revival, the preservation movement also received reinforcement from the snob appeal associated with homes that were old and elegant and had some sort of historic association. For about two decades beginning in 1885, the public seemed to thrive on essays concerning early American houses. Gardiner's Island, located in Long Island Sound, was particularly intriguing because a single family had owned it ever since Charles II bestowed it upon Lion Gardiner back in the seventeenth century. More than two hundred years later it remained "a sea island quite unspoiled by time or pseudo-progress, yet the seat of a luxurious and independent home."[29]

At the turn of the century a cascade of sentimental books, pamphlets, and essays appeared—some of them quite maudlin in fact—that lauded old landmarks because of their "power to reproduce the moods of the past and increase the vividness of reminiscence." The mystique of preservation was evoked through nostalgic lamentations over the price of progress and the disappearance of familiar landmarks. One essayist captured the *fin-de-siècle* ambivalence this way: "However much one may rejoice in the progress, the development of industries, conveniences and advantages and the whole inspiring energy of the twentieth century, there is still something akin to sadness in the removal of old landmarks which have come to be seen through an atmosphere of fond associations."[30]

Lamentations began to be heard outside of New England as well. Andrew Haswell Green, founder in 1895 of the American Scenic and Historic Preservation Society (incorporated by the state of New York), offered this complaint: "Other than the City Hall, where in New York is there left a public building or monument of historic value?" When Henry James visited in 1904, he noted "the law of the increasing invisibility of [New York] churches." Positive responses to these poignant wails did occur, however. During the 1890s, for instance, Theodore Roosevelt played an influential role in saving the small cottage where Edgar Allan Poe once lived in the village of Fordham. In 1883 the city had refused to accept it as a gift. In 1896 T.R. declared in the *Review of Reviews* that "Poe was perhaps the most brilliant genius America has ever developed . . . and we have too few historic sites to preserve to afford to waste this one." Less than a month later the mayor of New York approved a bill that authorized preservation and removal of the cottage to Poe Park.[31]

As we have already seen (chapter eight, pp. 240–242), a movement to regain the mission chapel at the Alamo was launched in 1883, and the culmination of Clara Driscoll's struggle to rescue that site came in 1905 when the governor of Texas conveyed the property to the Daughters of the Republic of Texas.[32]

In the Southwest, especially New Mexico, the discovery of ancient settlements started to pique popular interest as early as 1885; but not until 1907 did the Archaeological Institute of America create the School of American Archaeology as a sub-unit to study and preserve the mysterious prehistoric ruins there. In 1909 the government of New Mexico granted the school space in the Palace of the Governors at Santa Fe, with the understanding that as a part of its program the school would establish and develop a Museum of New Mexico. During the first three decades of its existence, field crews from the school took part in digs and preservation work at numerous sites throughout the Southwest.[33]

Back in 1862 Abraham Lincoln returned California's old Spanish missions, many of which had fallen into private hands, to the Catholic Church. Their condition continued to deteriorate, however, and by the mid-1880s Charles F. Lummis and George Wharton James, civic leaders in Los Angeles, launched a campaign to restore the missions. They lectured all over the state; and in 1888, along with their friend Adam Clark Vroman, organized the Association for the Preservation of the

Missions. Vroman, a superb photographer, devoted the decade following 1895 to compiling an exhaustive pictorial record of the missions. By
1900 newspaper publisher Randolph Hearst had sensed the existence
of popular enthusiasm for saving the missions and threw the influence
of his *San Francisco Examiner* behind the movement.[34]

In 1895, meanwhile, Lummis broadened his concerns beyond the
missions and wrote editorials urging that artifacts which had originated
in the Southwest not be sold off to enhance Eastern or European collections. In 1895 Lummis also organized the California Landmarks Club
in order to save and restore historic structures generally, not just the
missions. Lummis gained support from members of the Sierra Club and
other wilderness conservation groups; their achievements included the
preservation of old Spanish structures in San Diego.[35]

By the end of the 1880s, meanwhile, the press reported widespread
sentiment throughout California for the restoration of Sutter's Fort,
where gold had first been discovered in 1848–49. According to the
Sacramento *Record Union,* a feeling was spreading that the "old relic"
should not be allowed "to disappear"; and that a "memorial hall" (like
George Sheldon's in the Pocumtuck Valley of Massachusetts) ought to
be erected near the fort to house "relics of the pioneer era." By the
close of 1889 the man who owned Sutter's Fort succumbed to public
pressure, agreed to sell it, and even pledged a contribution to assist in
preserving "the historic old site."[36]

All of these activities only signify scattered beginnings that met with
sporadic success. In Great Britain, by contrast, a Society for the Protection of Ancient Buildings, the first preservationist pressure group there,
was launched in 1877. The movement was explicitly linked to "patriotic
reverence" by 1884; and eleven years later a group of private citizens
formed the English National Trust in order to preserve and exhibit
historic sites and scenic places. In 1901 a man named C. R. Ashbee tried
to create an American National Trust but did not succeed. The formation of such an organization lay almost half a century in the future.[37]

In the interest of fairness, it must be noted that for more than a
generation the English National Trust grew quite gradually. By 1942 it
had six thousand members and owned six historic houses that were
open to the public. By 1974, though, it had 480,000 members and
owned 230 accessible historic structures.[38] Such rapid postwar growth
certainly exceeded in quantitative terms what happened throughout
the United States (by 1989 the National Trust for Historic Preservation
had 220,000 members); yet the overall rates of expanding enthusiasm
were comparable.

From 1870 until 1915 the United States government basically refused
(with a few exceptions) to assist in historic preservation activities. Between 1880 (when Senator Justin Morrill of Vermont proposed a bill
pertaining to Revolutionary battlefields) and 1886, eight relevant bills
were introduced but none was enacted. During the 1890s Congress

9.1   The south half of Cliff Palace, the largest cliff dwelling at Mesa Verde National Park. Courtesy of the National Archives Trust Fund Board.

authorized the establishment of five major Civil War battlefields as national military parks: Chickamauga, Antietam, Shiloh, Gettysburg, and Vicksburg. A few battle sites from the Revolutionary War were added, and by 1906, as we have seen, limited protection became available for Indian pueblos and cliff dwellings. Hence the early emergence of Mesa Verde National Park (fig. 9.1).[39]

It has to be conceded that governmental stinginess was reinforced by strong ideological predilections among some of the leading preservationists themselves. William Sumner Appleton, the most stalwart missionary on behalf of the Society for the Preservation of New England Antiquities, fervently believed that the private sector should bear the full burden of responsibility, ranging from manual labor to financial accountability. Most New Englanders who shared his commitment to saving historic structures also shared his fear that government money might mean government control of presentation, use, and interpretation for the public. They believed that nothing could conceivably be worse for the sanctity of American traditions than for the government to become their custodian.[40] In 1912, when the campaign to "save" Monticello was heating up, Appleton wrote the following to one of the most avid would-be rescuers of Jefferson's architectural masterpiece:

I am a tremendous believer in buying Jefferson's home for preservation, but as luck will have it I am also an ardent Jeffersonian in my principles, and can't help feeling that Jefferson would turn in his grave at the mere suggestion that the Federal Government should buy his home by right of eminent domain.[41]

An unusual situation existed in Tennessee because the state owned the Hermitage, Andrew Jackson's home near Nashville, and proudly claimed to be the only one in the Union "to purchase and preserve for public use the manor of a distinguished son." During the later 1880s, however, when it became apparent that the state was not doing a satisfactory job of maintenance, the legislature decided to turn the home, its grounds, and Jackson's tomb over to the Ladies' Hermitage Association, a patriotic group of Nashville women who hoped to preserve Jackson's estate by raising money in a nationwide campaign. They eventually succeeded and obtained enough funding to purchase hundreds of Jackson relics still privately owned.[42]

Some states at least made a start toward saving their heritage of natural wonders and scenic beauty. In 1864, for example, Yosemite Valley was ceded to California for protection as a state park; and in 1885 New York State created a Niagara Falls Reservation as well as the Adirondack Forest Preserve. The federal government at first moved cautiously along such lines, in part because commercial interests were politically opposed to removing land from potential exploitation. Yellowstone National Park, the first, was created in 1872. Eighteen years later Congress established a national park surrounding Yosemite gorge, along with Sequoia and General Grant national parks. Following a nine-year moratorium, a decade of highly significant "set asides" occurred: Mount Rainier (1899), Crater Lake (1902), Devil's Tower in Wyoming, proclaimed as the first national monument (1906), Mesa Verde in Colorado and Petrified Forest in eastern Arizona (1906), the Grand Canyon as a national monument, proclaimed by Theodore Roosevelt in 1908, Mount Olympus in Washington (1909), and Glacier National Park in Montana (1910).

Three analytical emphases have been offered to explain the most basic impulse underlying this surge of concern. According to the oldest, credit is really due to middle-class professionals, such as engineers and scientific managers who effectively became active during the 1890s as a precursor of the Progressive movement. The second line of interpretation, quite different, credits tradition-oriented sportsmen drawn primarily from the social elite, who pleaded for a national conservation policy in order to protect their favorite "playgrounds" from spoliation by economic interests. A third mode of explanation joins the second in believing that the impact of environmentalists like John Muir and the Sierra Club has been overrated, but asserts instead, rather vaguely, that "America's incentive for the national park idea lay in the persistence of a painfully felt desire for time-honored traditions in the United States."[43]

I do not regard these divergent emphases as being mutually exclusive, however, and I would add to them the particular power of pastoral nostalgia on the part of urban Americans, middle class and elite alike, as still another factor to be considered.[44] The role of environmental conservationists should not be minimized, though, because they, to a greater degree than engineers or sportsmen, were imbued with both a sense of the past and a feeling of obligation to posterity—the interconnectedness of generations as a matter of social integrity and personal honor.

I I I

REFERENCES to the Mount Vernon Ladies' Association (1856) and the Ladies' Hermitage Association (1889) serve as a timely reminder that from the outset, socially respectable women played a prominent role—not only in historic preservation but in other tradition-related activities as well. We have already encountered Mary Hemenway, the wealthy Boston widow who in 1876 contributed half of the $200,000 needed in order to save Old South Meeting House from destruction. She also proposed that the restored building be used as a "study institute" to promote popular interest in American history. She subsidized John Fiske during the initial stage of his career as an unaffiliated writer and lecturer; assisted James K. Hosmer as his patron also; underwrote the cost of several series of historical lectures at Old South; and starting in 1884 she paid for the publication of hundreds of Old South Leaflets, each one an essay on some aspect of American history—usually colonial and with a focus upon New England. Beginning in 1881 she also sponsored high school essay contests on assigned topics in American history.[45]

It has been asserted, with particular reference to material culture and the colonial revival, that during the late nineteenth century, "women were the primary custodians of the American heritage in its tangible manifestations, the keepers of the flame that burned upon the ancient hearth of the colonial past."[46] That may overstate the case a bit, but it contains a genuine kernel of truth. It would not have surprised Washington Irving, who regarded "excellent old ladies" as natural guardians of tradition, or Benjamin Franklin, perhaps, who observed that Indian women farmed, prepared food, raised children, "and preserve and hand down to Posterity the Memory of public transactions."[47]

Although such a formula would be far too simplistic for the stewardship of memory in late nineteenth-century America, the opportunities and roles that were gender-specific require notice. To begin with, "memory" was a key word in the vocabulary of an intelligent and sensitive person like Alice James. Travel writers such as Anna Bowman Dodd commonly declared that "Memory had been startled into a curious, retrospective journey." And the author of an autobiography in 1909 wrote that a woman should "borrow from the fires of the heroic past to kindle the fires of the future; to preserve to that end the memory of the deeds of those whose lives have set them apart in the history of our country."[48]

Women took particular pride in demonstrating their patriotism, as we have seen. A group of them who could not qualify for the organizations with strict ancestral requirements formed their own in 1894 and called it the Patriotic League of the Revolution. Their primary purpose? To "create and promote interest in all matters pertaining to American history, to collect and preserve relics of the period of the American Revolution, and to foster patriotism."[49]

The (relatively) egalitarian encroachment of such groups only caused the snobs to aspire to more exquisite snobberies. Maryland's Special Executive Historian, appointed by the governor to prepare an exhibit for the Jamestown Tercentennial at Norfolk in 1907, concocted proposals which the senior historian at the Carnegie Institution in Washington managed to squelch:

> To illustrate the educational status of our early settlers, masses of their original signatures—hundreds of them. To demonstrate their social status, the heraldic seals attached to their signatures on legal documents. The original signatures of great numbers of Colonial women to show that women could write and were educated in those days.[50]

The feminist impulse had made an occasional appearance ever since the 1880s. When Marietta, Ohio, observed its centennial in 1888, Mrs. Mary A. Livermore gave an address on "Woman's Place in the Early History of the Country." When the Woman Suffrage Association of Massachusetts sponsored a historical pageant at Boston, its tableaux depicted colonial times, the Revolution, the Civil War, and the development of the women's suffrage movement. When New York City announced its plan to host a world's fair in 1892, Susan B. Anthony sent the mayor a request asking whether one of the permanent buildings could be dedicated to women. It would be called the Isabella Temple, "and in it should be shown the work of woman as a helpmeet worthy of man." Charlotte Smith, president of the Women's National Industrial League, echoed that proposal and requested that Congress erect a statue to Queen Isabella in Washington, D.C. Either a Spanish or an American sculptress would have been acceptable.[51]

The American social elite probably knew more about Isabella Stewart Gardner (1840–1924) than it did about the patron of Columbus. Mrs. Gardner had become prominent as an art collector, enigmatic *grande dame,* resident of a Venetian palace on the Fenway in Boston, and, beginning in 1887, patron of Bernard Berenson, the brilliant young art historian and subsequent arbiter of taste.[52]

Whereas Mrs. Gardner and her protégé reflected the preference that many felt for Old Masters and the European past, Mrs. Thomas Jefferson Coolidge, Jr., sponsored Fiske Kimball's career as an architectural historian starting in 1914. (The shift in taste that accompanied the time lag, 1887 to 1914, is highly symptomatic.) Kimball began his intensive work on Benjamin Latrobe in 1916. Three years later the Metropolitan Museum of Art invited Kimball to present a series of five lectures on early American houses. He did so in 1920 and they were published as *Domestic Architecture of the American Colonies and of the Early Republic* in 1922.[53]

Women served as patrons of tradition and Americana in diverse ways. Abby Aldrich Rockefeller collected early American folk art. When she initially displayed the collection at Williamsburg in 1935, the public response was so enthusiastic that she allowed the exhibit to remain on loan; and five years later she donated her collection to Colonial Williamsburg, where it now is housed in a museum of its own. Elsie Clews Parsons was well educated and did scholarly work in sociology, history, anthropology, but especially folklore. She used her wealth to collect and assist others in collecting folklore during the early years of the twentieth century. She became a kind of financial "angel" to the American Folklore Society and financed field trips by younger scholars. She was also a feminist, a pacifist, a serious researcher into Native American lore, and a translator of their tales.[54]

A disproportionate number of these women had roots in Boston, New York, or Philadelphia, along with ties to the exclusive crowd that summered at Newport, Rhode Island. Martha J. Lamb, historian and editor, began working on her history of New York City at the end of the 1860s. The first volume, which covered the colonial period to 1775, appeared in 1877. The second volume, which spanned more than a century, 1775 to 1880, was published a year later in 1881. She fully subscribed to the Whig belief in progress that characterized the optimists of her era. As she wrote in her journal on June 14, 1885: "History shows us that we are better than the people who preceded us; and I am ready to believe that a wiser generation will come after us."[55]

Alice Foster Perkins Hooper (Mrs. William), a New Englander who became a very close friend of Frederick Jackson Turner, had an insatiable enthusiasm for American history and ardently supported educational reform that would enhance its study in the schools. She pleaded with anyone influential—at historical societies, schools, and among state boards—that history ought to be made the core of a sound curriculum.[56]

Women artists could also be supportive of tradition in general and of Americana in particular. Violet Oakley, for instance, who painted the U.S. history murals in the Pennsylvania State Capitol at Harrisburg

(1902–27), also received commissions to decorate private homes of the rich and respectable. She favored English neo-Renaissance (or Elizabethan) settings, and labelled a typical lunette "The Child and Tradition." Gertrude Vanderbilt Whitney, despite being associated with modern American art, had very eclectic tastes, cared about American aesthetic traditions, admired Buffalo Bill so much that she modelled an equestrian statue of him, and served a vital function as the sponsor of aspiring young artists in New York City.[57]

Many of the women we have mentioned were also collectors. Considering the broad diversity of their interests, Wallace Nutting's gender-typed generalization seems more absurd with every passing year: "Men," he wrote, "because they seek prettiness less than solidity, are better collectors than women."[58] Abby Aldrich Rockefeller, Gertrude Vanderbilt Whitney, Electra Havemeyer Webb, and Ima Hogg differed as much from one another in their tastes as they did from Henry Francis du Pont, Francis M. Garvan, James Ten Eyck (who specialized in china and gave his collection to the Albany Institute of History and Art), Judge Alphonso Clearwater of Kingston, New York, who in 1919 donated to the Metropolitan Museum of Art his superb 550-piece collection of American silver, and R. T. H. Halsey, a remarkable patron of the American Wing at the Met. Stereotyping by gender is a very precarious business, particularly when it pertains to obsessions with Americana.[59]

I V

A NUMBER of conventional assumptions about the so-called Progressives that have been widely accepted do less than full justice to the diversity, complexity, and sometimes strained ambivalence of their thinking: an older view that they were ardent social and political reformers; a revisionist view that in their heart of hearts they were deeply conservative and only advocated moderate reform as a means of forestalling much more radical change; and a perception of them as people basically committed to the status quo but with allowance for changes that might improve the quality of life in America for members of their own social stratum—the upper middle class—and their posterity.

Several works published during the 1980s, however, have offered a more subtle and sensitive reading of their nostalgic mood, their conflicted relationship to modernism, and the rationale for progress that was acceptable or meaningful to them. First, we now realize that each of the major theorists of Progressivism had a deeper concern for history and the lessons of the past than we formerly realized.[60] Second, we are especially well informed about the commitment to change, mindful of the past, that characterized most prominent public leaders of the Progressive movement. As Woodrow Wilson declared in a 1912 campaign speech (titled "What is Progress?") that defined the point of departure for his New Freedom doctrine: "I believe that the ancient traditions of a people are its ballast." And then, muddling his metaphors,

> You must knit the new into the old. You cannot put a new patch on an old garment without ruining it; it must be not a patch, but something woven into the old fabric, of practically the same pattern, of the same texture and intention. If I did not believe that to be progressive was to preserve the essentials of our institutions, I for one could not be a progressive.[61]

Third, we are beginning to acknowledge that social theorists and critics during the Progressive era scrutinized the generation that followed 1875 and wondered whether the United States had "badly wrenched its traditions of social cohesion in its spectacular leap from village to city." The historian Daniel T. Rodgers has suggested that many of the Progressives felt strong twinges of nostalgia for an earlier, simpler, less corrupt, and less corrupting past.[62]

The problem posed by even these nuanced generalizations is that American culture was so swiftly becoming more heterogeneous. It is true that during the later nineteenth century various newspapers that reflected a wide span of public opinion looked to the past as a means of measuring progress. When William Dean Howells made an optimistic assessment of the "Modern American Mood" in 1897, he expressed the hope that Americans would remain true "to the ideals of the past." An ardent conservationist like John Muir nonetheless admired technological wizardry and progress in general, nor did he oppose the coming of big business to the West. There are even connections between Progressivism and the historic preservation movement.[63] We seem to forget, for instance, how much Herbert Croly cared about the history of American architecture, and that six years before he published *The Promise of American Life* he brought out *Stately Homes in America from Colonial Times to the Present Day* (1903).

Other voices, however, sang quite different tunes. To take just one prominent example, when Walter Lippmann wrote *Drift and Mastery* in 1914, he hammered hard in order to persuade readers that "tradition will not work in the complexity of modern life."

> For if you ask Americans to remain true to the traditions of all their Fathers, there would be a pretty confusion if they followed your advice. There is great confusion, as it is, due in large measure to the persistency [with] which men follow tradition in a world unsuited to it.[64]

A critic of regional parochialism, particularly in New England, observed caustically in 1908 that "a settled and fixed society tends to develop a spirit of caste, a narrow outlook, a distaste for travel, and a slavish adherence to old traditions and customs which may be, and often are, exceedingly foolish."[65]

One perceptive and provocative attempt to make sense of these divergent tendencies has emphasized the Progressive era as a unique and transitional generation, one characterized by "innovative nostalgia." That concept, devised by the historian Robert Crunden, recognizes that the very same people could be enthusiasts for change without repudiating the past entirely or remaining ignorant of it. The concept enables us to understand how such creative people as Charles Ives, Frank Lloyd Wright, and Robert Henri were genuinely spiritual contemporaries who differed in temper from those who preceded and those who followed them. It is certainly a more satisfactory way of dealing with the transformation of American culture than looking at a controversial event like the Armory Show of 1913 and baldly declaring that at that moment the republic of taste in America split into two camps: modern and traditional.[66]

An either/or approach based upon the assumption of inevitable cultural cleavage is surely less reflective of human realities than the notion of innovative nostalgia. John T. Morse, an aging yet active New England biographer and antiquarian, wrote a wonderfully indicative sentence to his friend Henry Cabot Lodge in 1921. "It's a queer condition," he concluded; "I find that I live only in the past, and yet am more than ever interested in the future; the present is rather a matter of indifference."[67]

The major difficulty with Professor Crunden's mode of interpretation, however, is that it is especially geared to explaining what became of Protestant moralism and the New England heritage: What secular options were available to those who sought creative careers in which they could express their Calvinist conscience? Although those are important and worthy issues, they tend to scant the growing significance of regionalism and localism in American culture generally during the generation that began to come of age in the 1890s. Because nationalism as an ideology did not abate, students of the period have found it relatively easy to make assertions about the nation as a whole. The sum of its parts, though, was somehow not the very same thing as the whole. John Dewey put it pithily in 1920: "Take all the localities of the United States and extract their greatest common divisor, and the result is of necessity a crackling surface."[68]

V

DEWEY did not believe that very much could be considered genuinely "nation-wide" anyway: perhaps the high cost of living, Prohibition, and "devotion to localisms." Whereas national phenomena seemed bland to him, local news at least had "flavour"; so Dewey dismissed the pejorative notion of people and things being "provincial." Rather, they were "just local, just human, just at home, just where they live." Not surprisingly he deplored the uniformity implied by pressures for "Americanization."[69]

John Dewey must have assumed that he struck an outrageously icono-clastic stance in proclaiming that "locality is the only universal." In point of fact, however, that sentiment had found devotees ever since the 1870s, most particularly among tradition-oriented Americans. Dur-ing the spring of 1876, when the Centennial of Independence started warming up, President Grant urged Americans to write (and then pre-sumably to read) the histories of their towns, counties, and states. An extraordinary number of people heeded his call, and the final quarter of the nineteenth century became a fertile time for the production of local history. In 1894 one typical enthusiast wrote to Henry Baldwin (the Custodian of American History) to explain that "my purpose and wish is to put on record, and to instruct our people in matters of their own local history, to which, though full of interest and of praiseworthy incident, they evince far too much indifference."[70]

In one of his earliest medieval romances, Sir Walter Scott remarked that "tradition depends upon locality," and then proceeded to elabo-rate upon the assertion.[71] Scott's work enjoyed considerable popularity in the United States, and we hear frequent echoes of those four words in the period under consideration. They occur in various settings, rang-ing from enthusiasts for the newly popular local color literature to architects who shared the same spirit. "Our antiquity," shouted an 1877 editorial, "should be considered a precious inheritance, and, if rightly used, can scarcely fail to be of service to architectural design, in aiding to confer upon it that sentiment of locality which, for obvious reasons, should be encouraged and cherished."[72]

New Englanders had shared that sentiment for quite some time and continued to do so even when critics, many hostile but some friendly, complained of their "narrowness."[73] St. Augustine, Florida, the oldest settlement in North America, began to receive protective scrutiny dur-ing the later 1880s when new hotels and other structures related to tourism threatened the integrity of that early Hispanic community. During the 1890s the United Confederate Veterans began a deter-mined effort to improve the quality of history books available in South-ern schools—which meant telling the tale of controversial local and regional events with a secessionist spin.[74] It is no coincidence, I believe, that in *Absalom, Absalom!* Faulkner sets the burning of the Sutpen house in the year 1910—the violent and deliberate destruction of a plantation house that is so symbolic of morbid regional memories. Writ-ing in 1935, Faulkner used the year 1910 to mark the closing of an era laden with myth as well as elusive history—the two inextricably inter-twined.

As local and regional pride heightened the importance of historical consciousness, state and local historical societies became increasingly significant. Quite often, once again, domination of these institutions could mean controlling the identity of an area as well as matters involving family pre-eminence. Professor Lucy M. Salmon, who taught history at Vassar College for many years, pleaded with the American Historical Association to be involved with local historical societies and to help them interconnect.[75] In 1906 a nasty conflict exploded between the State Historical Society of Missouri, which was state-supported and based in Columbia, and the Missouri Historical Society of St. Louis, which had been privately established in 1866 immediately after the war. In the trans-Appalachian region generally, where financial support from the state legislature mattered a great deal, officers of the societies solicited letters from eminent outsiders quite candidly to impress the public in general and the "members of our legislature in particular with the estimate that is placed on the work of the Society."[76]

Regional organizations recognized the political necessity for decentralization, so the Ohio Valley Historical Association, which held its inaugural meeting at Cincinnati in 1907, moved along in subsequent years to Marietta, Frankfort, Kentucky, and Indianapolis. In newer and less populated areas where historical celebrations were a comparatively recent phenomenon, however, co-operation was more likely to occur than conflict. Beginning in 1901, for instance, the Oregon Historical Society and the Oregon Pioneer Association jointly dedicated the Champoeg Monument on the fifty-eighth anniversary of the first settlers' organizational meeting at the Willamette River. Thereafter Champoeg Day festivities were held annually, collaboratively, and enjoyed considerable popularity.[77]

Historical awareness and a concern for tradition developed with somewhat different dynamics in the trans-Mississippi and intermountain West. Initially, during the territorial phase, a sense of the past was weak because the recorded past had been extremely brief and problems of economic and physical survival predominated. New communities were understandably more concerned about whether they would have a future than whether their past was interesting or just how it had shaped their lives. Many towns that felt so eager for "progress" in any way, shape, or form regarded retrospective glances as myopic. *Overland Monthly,* a regional magazine founded by Bret Harte in 1868, was characteristically "devoted to the development of the country." In 1902, when the issue of preserving traces of Spanish settlement arose in Los Angeles, the local Chamber of Commerce lauded "the sea of modern American progress."[78]

Where leisure facilitated the formation of cultural organizations, their top priority was customarily to promote a sense of serving civilized ladies and gentlemen rather than rustic rubes. Surviving programs and minutes of the Cosmos Club of Missoula, Montana, a cultural association formed in 1896, provide a useful litmus. Selected programs concerning historical and artistic themes include "A Forgotten Chapter of New France" (1896), "American Painting" and "Montana Life in the

Early Seventies" (1897), "American Traits in American Art" (1910), "Amateur Plays and Pageants" (1914), and "The Making of Montana" (1915).[79]

Idaho provides us with a representative sense of the pace and manner in which interest in the past emerged. The Idaho Historical Society originated early in 1881, almost a decade before statehood, as the Historical Society of Idaho Pioneers. W. A. Goulder, a miner and journalist, served as secretary and as the first salaried historian. E. A. Stevenson, another miner and territorial governor, became president of the Society in 1885. The Sons and Daughters of Idaho Pioneers remains an obscure organization that confirms historian Robert G. Athearn's belief that for several generations in the early West, ancestor worship (in the form of idealization of the pioneers) was the dominant mode of local historiography. In 1907 John Hailey, a stageline operator, miner, sheep rancher, meat-packer, and congressman, established Idaho's first state museum. (The present museum, located in Boise, opened in 1950 and receives about 200,000 visitors each year.) In 1910 the Idaho Pioneer Association decided to commemorate the fiftieth anniversary of Franklin, the first permanent settlement in Idaho. Governor James H. Brady proclaimed June 15 as Pioneer Day, a state holiday; but the annual program has tended ever since to highlight athletic events and dances more than history.

The first decade of the twentieth century certainly brought a general quickening of interest in local and regional traditions. As cemeteries grew larger, for example, they often were regarded as shrines where local history that remained a part of living memory might be reflected upon. In 1903 Charles Lummis founded the Southwest Society of the American Institute of Archaeology; and in 1907 it became the Southwest Museum of Art, History and Science, located on the outskirts of Los Angeles.[80]

Just when these activities started to perk up, some partisans began to complain about Eastern ignorance and condescension toward Western history. Having criticized a "slavish adherence to old traditions and customs which may be, and often are, exceedingly foolish," one writer/critic acknowledged that the sheer passage of time had given the Eastern seaboard certain cultural advantages. "Yet there are counterbalancing disadvantages," he commented, "while the advantages are only temporary."

> The West, too, is growing old, and with its age is acquiring a quietness and poise, an elegance and culture, a delightful society, a refined wealth, and a real love of the beautiful and elevated. Never without traditions—and of the most inspiring kind—it is being more and more influenced by them. The great historic background, which has always existed, is more and more coloring our life. . . . We are gradually opening our eyes to the splendor of

our heritage. The names of Western heroes are on every tongue. Books describing their exploits are widely read. When the people of Indiana reflect that the territory which they inhabit has owed allegiance to three flags they realize that they and their civilization are not of yesterday. The influence of the past is being felt here as in New England, and we are all growing old together.[81]

The author concluded, however, with an appeal, like John Dewey's, for a sense of nationalism undergirded by diversity. "It is not well that the Yankee should be like the Southerner, or the Southerner like the Westerner. The levelling and assimilating forces may spoil our whole national life."[82]

Ironically, it would be genuine Eastern ignorance of the inauthentic yet romantic West that prompted patterns of fascination and identification which have endured to the present. Buffalo Bill Cody launched his first Wild West act in 1872, and by 1888 his elaborately staged extravaganza had literally become a circus. Cody understood quite early that most Easterners had no idea what Indian civilization or cowboy life was like, or what existence on the Great Plains really entailed. After eleven years as an actor who played cowboy parts, a new season was arranged for Cody and company in 1883. His Wild West show performed at fairs and at racetracks. Three years later his troupe put on its first "great spectacle": a re-enactment of Custer's massacre at the Little Big Horn. A new chapter thereby opened in the history of American popular and mass culture, one that would take the Wild West show from Los Angeles to London and beyond.[83]

Nostalgia can be so contagious. (As late as the Civil War it was still diagnosed on hospital charts as a physical ailment, not merely a morose state of mind.) Between the 1880s and 1915, men and women who had known the "Old West" at first hand felt twinges of loss at its disappearance. Not long after the myth of the Lost Cause came to dominate the South, writers like Theodore Roosevelt, Owen Wister, Emerson Hough, Bret Harte, and others molded an equally powerful and enduring myth of a West-that-might-have-been for many but certainly not for most. Wister's Anglo-Saxonism had the effect of locating Wyoming, at least culturally, somewhere between East Anglia and Mount Vernon. "This little, coherent, self-respecting place," he wrote of Wyoming, "was also full of life; retaining its native identity, its English-thinking, English-feeling, English-believing authenticity holding on tight to George Washington and the true American tradition."[84]

A few tough-minded newspapermen recognized that mythicization had begun to betray the changing realities of their region. In 1902 an editor of the *Denver Republican* tried to explain why real Westerners didn't read westerns: "The writers of to-day are laying on false colors and make no allowance for the changes that have taken place in the actual conditions of the West." The wild-eyed Texas steer had been supplanted by the gentle and bulky short-horn. Cowboys and round-ups had given way to fencing and ranches. The cowboy still existed, but his lifestyle no longer resembled that of Genghis Khan and his gang of men so attached to their horses that they could scarcely walk a straight line on terra firma.[85]

In September 1910 Pendleton, Oregon, sponsored the first of its now famous round-ups, a reverent if rowdy act of remembrance; and in that same year Frederick MacMonnies unveiled his statue of Kit Carson, the crowning figure on the sculptor's memorial to the pioneers in Denver. *The Century* magazine explained that the primary motif of the Pioneer Monument "seeks to express the expansive character of the West and its people [and] to reconcile sculpturesque quality and decorative style with the portrayal of types of character, without the loss of local definition." Three years later Teddy Roosevelt's autobiography expressed unabashed nostalgia for the loss of an Old West that he had loved, now mostly gone, reduced to "dead memories."[86]

In 1907 Charles Lummis chose a motto for his museum in Los Angeles: "Tomorrow is the flower of our yesterdays." Back in the 1890s Lummis had begun appealing to his countrymen to See America First; and by 1911 and 1912 associations bearing that name were established in Baltimore and Chicago. The Great Northern Railroad promptly made See America First its motto. In 1911 legislation was introduced in Congress that envisaged no fewer than seven national highways, including a transcontinental one. In 1912 the Yellowstone Trail emerged, and a year later the Lincoln Highway.[87]

With amazing promptness, roadside historical signs as well as markers on buildings began to appear by 1913–14. Articles in popular magazines were devoted to historic roads, "discovering" hidden places, and stirring tales of travel in the United States."[88] Hotels and other accommodations for tourists started to spring up, usually with an architectural style appropriate to the locality, such as mission-style inns in the Southwest.*

In 1922 Willa Cather made her first trip to the Southwest and was thrilled by the ruins of the cliff dwellers. Whereas Henry Adams had earlier found tradition in medieval France, and Edith Wharton had more recently done the same, Cather was a prescient precursor of those with an urge to find authentic American traditions. In Nebraska she wove the ways of recent immigrant pioneers into the stuff of imaginative literature. In the Southwest she found ancient civilizations and tales of early Europeans who made contacts, both friendly and hostile, Christian and craven, with Native Americans.[89]

---

*Commercial entrepreneurs predictably tried to use history as a gimmick. Automobile dealers pleaded with the California legislature to improve El Camino Real because of its historical importance—even though one pioneer (writing in 1905) insisted that the road was utterly phony. There had been no roads between the missions when he visited them during the 1850s, never mind a *Camino Real*.

Particularity of place, which had exerted a very powerful grip ever since the 1870s, would do so even more in the three decades that followed 1910. According to the conventional wisdom, American nationalism grew during the later nineteenth century as a parallel response to the contentious expansion of European imperialism. Perhaps in part; but American nationalism may also have been a compensatory response to the powerful pulls of regionalism and localism. Pride of place played a critical role as a stimulus for the most particular manifestations of memory and tradition. The prospect of excessive fragmentation helped to make ardent nationalists of many.

V I

DISPARATE or diffuse though they may seem, local pride and regionalism, the early thrust of historic preservation (exemplified by the A.P.V.A. and the S.P.N.E.A.), even the way that many Progressives directed their energies (such as neighborhood settlement houses), all touched a common chord that Henry James played upon in describing his return visit in 1904. "We like the sense of age to come," he surmised, "locally, when it comes with the right accompaniments, with the preservation of character and the continuity of tradition." That insight may also help to explain the special appeal of civic pageantry, particularly during the years from about 1905 until 1917. Pageants, like historic preservation, provided visible manifestations of the past. As one writer put it in 1914, the pageant was "a drama of which the place is the hero and its history is the plot."[90] Because you could see them, celebrate them, even participate in them, pageants provided immense appeal. They are inextricably a part of Progressive era culture, and a nostalgic one at that. For a few innovative individuals they became vehicles for creative nostalgia. More on them in a moment.

Although the community pageant movement has not been neglected by historians, they have tended to concentrate upon its heyday in the early twentieth century, and to a lesser extent its British roots, thereby neglecting its American origins along with a culturally prominent legacy that continued to have extraordinary impact during the 1920s and '30s (see chapter thirteen below).[91] Scholars have largely overlooked the popular role of historical floats included in the huge parade held at New York City on May 1, 1889, to honor the centennial of George Washington's first inauguration. A commercial firm in Philadelphia constructed most of them; and prominent themes included the Discovery of the Hudson River, the First Continental Congress, Signing of the Declaration of Independence, General Washington and His Generals Mounted, Washington Crossing the Delaware, Washington at Valley Forge, and, predictably, the Inauguration of Washington. Ethnicity also had its day. German-American floats included one that honored German opera and Wagner in particular, and another devoted to fairy stories and the Brothers Grimm.[92]

The press, moreover, designated the immense military parade on April 30 as a "Military Pageant." The naval display held on the 29th, the date of Washington's arrival at New York City by water, was referred to as "the pageant on the water" even though one purpose in the minds of those who organized it was to demonstrate grave weaknesses in the modern Navy and Merchant Marine.[93]

The mass appeal of these theatrical presentations gave them a certain vogue. Late in September that same year, when Hartford observed its 250th anniversary, a so-called National Pageant included historical tableaux with scenes of Columbus at Queen Isabella's court, the landing of the Pilgrims, the banishment of Anne Hutchinson, the concealment of Connecticut's charter, a reception given by Martha Washington, the Boston Tea Party, and the Battle of Bunker Hill. A group of high society people from Boston and New York put on a series of comparable tableaux late in November 1889, with the same thematic emphases, ranging from Columbus through the Pilgrims to Revolutionary episodes. For the dedication of Grant's Tomb in 1897, moreover, an extensive historical pageant was added to the predictable march of military units.[94]

All of these were, it is true, more nearly parades with historical components than genuine pageants in which thousands of people participated as well as observed. The subject matter of Progressive era pageants was more likely to be local or regional rather than national; but they did build upon the touch of ethnicity already noticeable in 1889 by explicitly including a float or scene for each ethnic group of any numerical consequence in the community. At New York's Hudson-Fulton celebration in 1909, the German-Americans were prominent once again; and in 1912 W. E. B. Du Bois wrote a Pageant of Negro History (called "The Star of Ethiopia") for the NAACP. It had its premiere at New York City in 1913, followed by productions in Washington, D.C., in 1914, Philadelphia in 1915, and Los Angeles in 1925. The occasion for its premiere was the fiftieth anniversary of the Emancipation Proclamation. Du Bois recalled almost twenty years later that every night when the pageant was presented, "it simply jammed the armory where we were, and received considerable notice."[95]

Another new emphasis that emerged after 1900 involved instruction to the populace, as it were, on the uses of leisure and the desirability of developing a "sense of play." Whereas the first decade of pageantry (1889–99) was motivated primarily by patriotism, nationalism, a desire to commemorate heroes, and a love of pomp, spokesmen during the second decade spoke of the civic value of "public play," the importance of "variety in form and color," and, a touch of Progressive ideology, "our belief . . . in the popular form of government."[96]

Within a decade American pageantry had become explicitly linked, despite its clear nostalgia for earlier, more harmonious, and less heterogeneous times, to an ethos of democracy and the desire for a "Drama of Democracy" that would be inclusively participatory. Percy MacKaye emerged as the most prominent "philosopher" of the new civic pageantry—what he liked to call the "New Fourth of July." His major statement of principle, which appeared in 1910, was representative both in its declared purposes and in its ambiguities. He stressed the need to highlight democratic values, to acknowledge American pluralism and draw upon ethnic folk cultures, to "make much of the tradition of your own locality" by finding regional folklore, to "use only American material," and to "adopt the theme of liberty."[97]

The element of ambiguity involved that old, still unresolved issue of the relationship between past and present. How to show their organic connection? How to glorify progress without minimizing the past? How to celebrate tradition without neglecting the wonders of the present? Happily for MacKaye, he and a colleague were invited to plan a two-year pageant that would celebrate the Fourth of July at Pittsburgh in an innovative way. If MacKaye's solution was logical and symmetrical, it also, at least implicitly, reflected the strong sense of historical discontinuity that developed early in the twentieth century. In the first year at Pittsburgh, MacKaye explained, it would "emphasize chiefly the pageant material of the past in symbols of national and local history, folk-lore, and tradition. In the second, it will emphasize the pageant material of the present in symbols of the colossal industry, science, and labor of today, and the world-promise of those vast forces for the morrow."[98]

There is an ironic element in MacKaye's staunch Americanism because he had nothing but praise for the theme chosen by Gloucester, Massachusetts, for its pageant held in August 1909: the Canterbury Pilgrims. MacKaye felt no sense of contradiction, however, because he believed that the "folk-pageant symbolizes the fusion of many nationalities in the American nation." In 1908, after an especially colorful and popular historical pageant took place in Philadelphia as the climax of Founders' Week there, Ellis Paxson Oberholtzer, director of that pageant, felt so inspired that he went to Europe for more than a year to study techniques of pageantry that had been successful. His report to the nation, which appeared in 1910, ranged from the sublime to the ridiculous, and then on to the kind of awakened chauvinism which anticipated the pride in America's past that would roar like cannon fire following World War I.[99]

■ Sublime: "Of all the pageant-fields that I have seen, however, that found in Quebec, in 1908, was the most to be admired. On the Plains of Abraham, with the St. Lawrence's silver surfaces beyond, and the green, fir-clad hills of Canada piled high above the stream, in the fading lights of the far Northern summer evening, the scene was incomparably beautiful."

- Awakened chauvinism: "It may be thought that America holds in its past little that is old or various enough to lend itself well to such representations. Its history begins only at a point where the period covered by the pageant in England is usually brought to an end. This is a superficial judgment. Many American neighborhoods can boast of episodes in their history which may be impressively set forth in a pageant, and it will be surprising if such plays and processions are not seen in increasing numbers in this country."

Devotees of the new civic pageants, like Oberholtzer, believed that they marked a step upward in terms of elegance, an improvement upon the "old American street procession of cheaply decorated wagons and 'floats' on civic holidays." And some organizers, like Roger N. Baldwin of the St. Louis Civic League, who planned the highly successful 1913 extravaganza for that city, made at least a token effort to connect history with urban goals. Underlying his "greatest civic drama ever projected," he explained, lay "the idea of building on a spectacle of the past a new city unity for the future."[100]

Amidst the plethora of places putting on pageants, the most striking change that occurred during the decade prior to 1913 (when the American Pageant Association got organized) involved the growing notion that spectacles of the past ought to be place-specific. One only needs to compare the St. Louis narcissism of 1913, which was devoted to the history of that city and its origins, with Cincinnati's Venetian pageant in 1903, highlighting San Marco Cathedral, a doge's palace, canals, and Marco Polo. One constant element retained its importance throughout these years, however: holding a pageant in honor of a pivotal event or individual in the community's history. In the summer of 1908 the Rufus Putnam Memorial Association of Rutland, Massachusetts, celebrated Putnam's departure in 1788 to establish Marietta, Ohio. (They featured a procession of covered wagons.) In 1915 the citizens of Lincoln, Nebraska, swept across their pageant field dressed up as grasshoppers in order to re-enact the horrendous invasion of those devastating eaters during the 1870s. In 1918 the Old Salem Lincoln League honored the young lawyer who began his career in that tiny Illinois town.[101]

More often than not, these civic pageants presented a skewed view of history, and did so in several different respects. First, because they devoted far more attention to early events, rather less to intermediate ones, and not much at all to the recent past. The clear implications? Early history is more significant than later developments, and the inference that the past is discontinuous with the present. Second, they tended to create a misleading, if not a false sense of solidarity and harmony. No one watching a local history pageant would suspect that class conflict had ever occurred in the community.[102]

On the positive side, however, such spectacles were designed to advance the cause of democracy; and even though the contributions of all groups did not receive equal representation, most members of the community could be participants. These outdoor festivals required casts of thousands, and for many people just being a part of the "cast" enhanced their sense of civic pride. The pageants did, as a rule, acknowledge ethnic diversity, an inescapable reality that received growing recognition between 1892 and 1918.[103]

Pageants were also, undeniably, inspirational. The historian William Langer long remembered a grand parade he watched as a child in Boston, during the early years of this century, that managed to celebrate Evacuation Day (General Howe sailed from Boston for Halifax, Nova Scotia, on March 17, 1776) simultaneously with St. Patrick's Day. Yankees and immigrant Irish turned out in force, though in response to different stimuli. Similarly, Johan Huizinga tells us in an autobiographical essay that his interest in history was first aroused at the age of seven by a pageant in which university students, resplendent in medieval costumes, celebrated the liberation of Groningen, Holland, in 1506.[104]

Although much is known about the political and cultural role of pageantry in medieval and early modern Europe, and though some of these festivals have persisted into our own time, we must be careful to compare what is genuinely comparable, that is, American and European pageants whose origins date back no more than a century.[105] We should not be surprised to learn that similarities are about equally striking as differences. Pageants in late Victorian and Edwardian Britain did not commonly depict or celebrate events that occurred later than the sixteenth century because the pageants tended to serve as protests against modernity rather than provide some sort of symbolic framework that might describe successive stages of social, political, and technological evolution leading the spectator to understand how the present had unfolded. In that respect, civic pageantry in American culture came a little closer to fulfilling the quest for a usable past, rather than serving as a pure nostalgia trip.[106]

A different contrast emerges when we include Latin American cultures, particularly the pageantry associated with carnival, because where pageantry is not directly associated with civic culture and the state, it is more likely to be disorderly.[107] In the United States, by contrast, civic pageants and parades were and are, as a rule, extremely well organized and orderly, as the state and society, working in concert, would like them to be.[108]

On July 4, 1889, President Benjamin Harrison chose as the subject for his oration "Our Nation's Growth as Compared with Other Nations." We necessarily turn to sustained comparisons in the next chapter. We may conclude this one by noting a pertinent parallel and an acute perception of difference. Those who have studied late nineteenth-century culture on both sides of the Atlantic agree that a powerful, shared impulse caused men and women to look to the past for guidance and comfort because they felt ill at ease with the transitional character of their own time. Moving from an outworn past into an unknown future, they wished to believe that understanding the past would enable (or at least assist) them in locating, and perhaps even in preserving, their proper place along the continuum of time.[109]

An American who had spent almost twenty-five years in England, however, with extensive travel on the Continent as well, could not resist declaring in 1907 what some of his countrymen had long been feeling: "It takes an endless amount of history to make even a little tradition."[110]

Coda

DEGREES OF DISTINCTIVENESS:
COMPARISONS

I

ALTHOUGH THE CRISPER perspective that comparisons can provide is instructive and therefore essential, several caveats ought to be kept in mind. First, there is a natural tendency to turn for aphoristic comments to writers and critics who crossed cultural boundaries and served up pithy trans-national epigrams. The dilemma presented by such people—however intriguing they may be as individuals—is that they were invariably idiosyncratic, and more often quotable than typical. They cannot be placed entirely off limits, however, without genuine loss. I mistrust the caustic observations of a Matthew Arnold or an Oscar Wilde, yet I very much value those by Edward A. Freeman, James Fullarton Muirhead, and Paul Bourget.[1]

A second caveat concerning random or singular statements, especially ones drawn from a transitional era, is that so frequently they fail to reflect changes in the individual observer's outlook. Take Edith Wharton as a case in point. In a travel book about France published in 1908 she expressed disdain for the paucity of tradition in her native land and made invidious comparisons. Visiting the medieval cathedral at Amiens, for instance, inspired Wharton with reverence for "the long rich heritage of human experience." She felt somewhat embarrassed by "the cathedral's word to the traveller from a land which has undertaken to get on without the past, or to regard it only as a 'feature' of aesthetic interest, a sight to which one travels rather than a light by which one lives." That's a heavy trip, to use the slang of more recent times. Yet ten years later, when Wharton wrote another book about French culture, her tone changed considerably.

> America, because of her origin, tends to irreverence, impatience, to all sorts of rash and contemptuous short-cuts; France, for the same reason, to routine, precedent, tradition, the beaten path. . . . The first thing to do is to try to find out why a people, so free

and active of thought as the French, are so subject to traditions that have lost their meaning.[2]

Although the writings of Henry James must be used with caution for other reasons, his travel books are nonetheless rich with intriguing insights. When he made his own tour of France in 1884, for example, he recognized that bad taste from an earlier era somehow seems less offensive than contemporary vulgarity, and that unattractive traditions camouflaged with quaintness could disguise many follies. After acknowledging some crassly self-indulgent bas-reliefs at a Renaissance mansion in Bourges, James candidly asked why they seemed inoffensive. "To-day we should question the taste of such allusions, even in plastic form, in the house of a 'merchant prince' (say in the Fifth Avenue). Why is it, therefore, that these quaint little panels at Bourges do not displease us? It is perhaps because things very ancient never, for some mysterious reason, appear vulgar."[3]

Finally, there is always the temptation to take at face value the casual judgments of wise people we respect for other writings and reasons, even though they never so much as set foot in the United States. Jacob Burckhardt, the great Swiss scholar who is regarded by many as the "founder" of cultural history, revered "the past as a spiritual *continuum* which forms part of our supreme spiritual heritage." Primitive peoples, he declared, "are barbarians because they have no history." Next, almost in the same breath, he announced that there were people like Americans who

> renounce history; people, that is, of unhistorical cultures who cannot quite shake off the old world. It clings to them parasitically in the shape of such things as the crests of the New York plutocracy, the most absurd forms of Calvinism; spiritualism, etc., and finally in the formation of a neo-American physical type (from a motley immigration) of uncertain character and durability.[4]

It is not that Burckhardt lacked a kernel of truth—as far as he went. It is the ill-informed absolutism of his judgmental partisanship that makes it unreliable. If only he had approached American civilization with a fraction of the subtlety and complexity that he brought to bear upon Renaissance Italy. His sentences concerning America seem like cheap shots by comparison.[5]

THE GREAT IRONY, perhaps, is that unbeknownst to Burckhardt, even as he lectured in his beloved Basel, virtually every society in Europe, and some in the Far East, such as Japan, was passing through a roughly comparable phase of obsession with national memory and its underlying myths. As we have already seen in the case of the United States, a powerful tendency was at work, worldwide, to appreciate cultural identity in historical terms.[6] Particular motives and manifestations varied from one country to the next, as we shall see; but the degree of synchronization in time is rather extraordinary, and the fundamental similarities are nearly equal to the contrasts (which I will attend to later in this Coda).

In his synoptic view of Europe at the close of the nineteenth century (actually 1889 to 1914), the Dutch historian Jan Romein perceived a pervasive crisis of values and offered the insight that frequently a cultural crisis may encourage nostalgic enthusiasm for the past. The Renaissance had done just that, he wrote, "but far from denying reality it had tried to refurbish old norms." Eugen Weber has added the suggestion that French culture during the 1880s and '90s exhibited a startling "discrepancy between material progress and spiritual dejection."[7] I only wonder why Professor Weber finds this startling, because similar discrepancies appeared in several neighboring nations as well as in the United States.

The causes of that widespread crisis of values are manifold, and some of them have already been touched upon. The social and economic impact of industrialization, accompanied by the development of technologies that facilitated the growth of mass culture, provide one obvious source. Anxieties about the dramatic expansion of the electorate, especially in Great Britain but also in France, aroused concern about the politics of culture appropriate to polities more democratic in potential than they ever had been.[8] Tradition and the illusion of continuity may also have seemed especially attractive in a period notable for international tension and the apparent decline of political stability. Finally, when biblical scholars in Germany and France applied historical criticism to Scripture, and showed how religious orthodoxy had changed over time, it created immense agitation both within the churches and among society at large—an unrest that Darwinism only compounded.[9]

The establishment in 1876 of universal manhood suffrage in France led to a series of educational reforms under the Third Republic, most notably the Primary Education Law of 1882, which made education from the ages of six to thirteen free, obligatory, and "neutral" (meaning a ban on all forms of religious instruction in schools). By removing religion from public education, the republicans eliminated a traditional source of moral and patriotic indoctrination. Needing a surrogate, the ministry pumped in large doses of nationalistic history and hero worship, which meant that figures as diverse as Napoleon and Joan of Arc enjoyed cult status during the later nineteenth and early years of the twentieth centuries (see fig. 6.1).[10]

It was not coincidental that people made pilgrimages to the provincial cottage of the Maid of Lorraine at Domrémy, because pastoral nostalgia became an especially powerful spiritual force. The reason lay, partially, in the gradual transformation of rural France. It had been traditional, for example, to visit the home of a neighbor to borrow a few embers in order to re-start the fire on the hearth. By 1890, once matches became commonplace even in the remotest parts of France, such visits ceased to be necessary. An occasion for sociability was lost in the process. The decline of the village mill and smithy had the same effect, a phenomenon with its counterpart at the same time in the United States when the introduction of rural free delivery caused the decline of the local post office as a socially significant gathering place.[11]

Historians of England have noticed a sentimentalization of rural life beginning in the 1880s that can be linked directly to the growth of strains in urban society. The result, especially in the Edwardian years prior to World War I, was a popular movement "back to the outdoors" as the countryside became an accessible and popular site of leisure activities for the upper middle class, the gentry and nobility. A "rural vision" emerged in consequence: the belief that country and village life must be cleaner, healthier, and generally superior.[12]

That same vision not only appeared as a dominant motif in American art, but provided an Anglo-American pastoral rationale for the sale of Wallace Nutting's photographs. As he wrote in his autobiography, "The true life of any nation is found in its small towns. There the flavor of local customs is most pronounced. There the homely national characteristics appear as in Constable's paintings." Forty pages later Nutting added a touch that perhaps seemed less patronizing two generations ago than it does to us today: "The city man needs to get into the country though he need not dwell there, and the country man may need to go into the city though we hope he will not dwell there."[13]

Similarly, the colonial revival in the United States was anticipated more than a decade earlier in England by a comparable phenomenon sometimes known as the Queen Anne movement and sometimes called Old English. In terms of material culture and the decorative arts it blended several periods and types, all post-medieval but pre-Georgian. The most commonly heard buzzword was "quaint." The British and the French virtually seemed to vie with one another in producing historical art, art that illustrated episodes from the nations' pasts, their literature, and especially their most patriotic and enigmatic myths (fig. C2.1). In Italy, meanwhile, a fresh recognition of the culture's artistic heritage appeared with the appointment of a fine arts commission charged with making an inventory of national art treasures in order to protect them from being plundered by foreign purchasers.[14]

Whereas collecting had long been the domain of aristocrats and wealthy individuals who achieved status from serving as patrons of artists and the arts, by the later nineteenth century museums began to flourish in Europe: large and small, public and private, national and provincial, some dedicated to the fine arts but others devoted to local history, or ethnography, or even (starting in Amsterdam in 1893) what were called museums of security, that is, educational museums designed to demonstrate new safety measures in an age of rapid industrialization and changing technology.[15]

C2.1 Pierre Puvis de Chavannes, *Ludus pro Patria* (1880–81), oil on canvas.
Courtesy of the Metropolitan Museum of Art. Gift of Mrs. Harry Payne Bingham, 1958.

Collecting various forms of folklore developed during the course of
the nineteenth century, especially the final third, as an activity that
strengthened nationalism in established countries, sustained it in newly
independent ones like Greece, and became a matter of local pride in
those where national identity already seemed secure. Folklore began to
emerge in the United States as a credible discipline and a favored
activity for amateurs after 1888.[16]

Various sorts of cultural revivals, folkloric and historical, became immensely important in terms of ethnic, racial, and national identity during the late nineteenth century. King David Kalakaua of the Sandwich
Islands (Hawaii) was elected to the throne there in 1874 and made a trip
around the world in 1881. Despite his cosmopolitanism—or perhaps
because of it—he undertook an official revival of Hawaiian traditions.
He fostered the revitalization of native crafts and culture; and he rein-
stated public performances of the hula dance, which had been sup-
pressed by Calvinist missionaries from New England during the 1830s
despite on-going protests from native islanders and some foreigners.
This final attempt to maintain customs that were several centuries old
ended with Kalakaua's death in 1891.[17]

F. A. Munch, a Norwegian professor of history, helped to "create"
Norway by giving scholarly credibility to the notion of Norway as a
great center of medieval civilization. Frédéric Mistral played a comparable role for Provence in southeastern France and for the revival of
Provençal language, literature, and folklore. Whereas historical hoaxes
that served cultural and political purposes had been commonplace from
medieval to early modern times—one recalls the Donation of Constan-
tine, the Chronicles of St. Denis, the forgery of Annius in 1498, and
Macpherson's phony Gaelic epic, *Ossian* (1760–63)—the later nineteenth century unabashedly resuscitated or even "invented" traditions
and made no bones about doing so.[18]

Although the perception of invented traditions can provide sound
cultural history as well as a valid form of social criticism, we do run the
risk of excessive cynicism by failing to discriminate between spurious

traditions, genuine ones that got revived for social or psychological reasons, and cultural politics in which real traditions are manipulated in order to legitimize power or the dominance of a particular social group. We must acknowledge that the decades from about 1875 until 1915 did indeed constitute a fertile period for the creation of new myths, symbols, and traditions. In France, for example, the year 1880 marked an extraordinary convergence of related events, ones that can be dated with precision. On February 24 in that year the first monumental statue was erected to the French Republic; and subsequently the Communards of 1871 received amnesty in order to reintegrate them into the Republic; "La Marseillaise" was designated as the national hymn; and July 14 became a national fête now known as Bastille Day, inaugurated with a ceremony at the anti-German statue representing the city of Strasbourg.[19]

In England the process occurred a bit more subtly. We notice the sequential launching of *The New English Dictionary* in 1884 and the *Dictionary of National Biography* a year later. As one student of the period has commented, cultural activities rooted in the past received formal recognition and codification as "contributions to the evolution of the English national culture which had produced the present. Nowhere was this more evident than through the establishment of a national literary tradition within the emergent discipline of English literature."[20]

Matters get more complicated, however, when we examine the activities of Lord Curzon as Viceroy of British India from 1898 until 1905. When he became fascinated by the deserted imperial city of Fatehpur Sikri, built in the sixteenth century by the Mughal Emperor Akbar, Curzon decided that the government of India had a serious responsibility to preserve "the striking or beautiful or historic fabrics of a bygone age." After he visited the famous caves at Ajanta, and the magnificent Mughal structures at Agra, he successfully persuaded the home government to appoint a Director General of Archaeology in India. When Curzon visited Mandalay, he was appalled to learn that palaces and other historic buildings were being used as clubs and offices; so he ordered that a series of these venerable structures be restored to their original condition, both as a "model of the civil and ceremonial architecture of the Burmese kings" and as a "compliment to the sentiments of the Burman race." Lord Curzon may very well have been an arrogant man, but it is difficult to doubt the genuineness of his desire to restore and preserve indigenous traditions that ranged from architecture to ritual.[21]

The same holds true of the Gaelic revival that occurred in Ireland between 1890 and the early 1920s, a movement intended to permeate all aspects of Irish life and eventually rebuild a modern Gaelic civilization from within. Although founding the Gaelic League as a countrywide educational effort marks the revival as a major feature of cultural nationalism, its manifest political dimensions had profound implications for the making of an Irish national state. We therefore must appreciate that national myths and legends may be used as a revolutionary force, and not inevitably as a conservative one. During the 1890s the Daughters of Ireland were actually radical nationalists who taught Irish sagas at night classes to laborers who subsequently fought in the Rising of 1916.[22]

The authenticity and venerable quality of Russian traditions has also been demonstrated, along with careful attention to the natural demise of certain legends, such as the myth of the czar late in the nineteenth century, when they ceased to be meaningful or appropriate.[23] Two generalizations emerge from this mélange of instances. First, that it simply will not do to make the cynical assumption that all modern traditions are specious or else are of relatively recent vintage, and that all myths are malleable means of perpetuating subordination or manipulation by elites. Second, it may be useful to notice the distinction that Karl Mannheim made between *traditionalism*—the emotional and relatively inarticulate tendency to cling to established values and inherited patterns of living—and *conservatism,* which he viewed as "conscious and reflective from the first, since it arises as a counter-movement in conscious opposition to the highly organized, coherent and systematic 'progressive' movement."[24]

Just as the Irish example reminds us that tradition is not inevitably a conservative force, so too the seventeenth-century Battle of the White Mountain, which became a major myth in Czech history, supplied a focus for modern Czech nationalism by explaining why the Habsburgs and the Roman Catholic Church seemed to be enemies of an autonomous Czech state. Finally, and most familiar, French ministers during the Third Republic invoked all sorts of national traditions to support the Revolutionary legacy of Liberty, Equality, and Fraternity. Between 1875 and 1912 Ernest Lavisse produced an extraordinary series of history texts for the primary schools and lycées. He managed to bridge the worlds of popular and scholarly writing, and constantly stressed the potential value of history as an instrument of patriotic instruction if not indoctrination. "My children," he declared in a speech given in 1905, "our Fatherland is not merely a territory, it is a human structure, begun centuries ago, which we are continuing, which you will continue. . . . A natural instinct binds us to our ancestors with a sort of sacredness. . . . It gives us a feeling of continuity."[25]

Ultimately, however, it really is not satisfactory to label the uses of tradition in late nineteenth-century France as either progressive or liberal. The historian Eugen Weber has shown the growth of popular interest in French national history between 1876 and 1893, just when it surged in the United States. But he also demonstrates that patriotic sensibilities at the national (as distinct from the regional) level had to be inculcated and learned.[26] That process required the politicization of culture, as it did in the United States, though not with the same intensity or degree of controversy here as in France.

I I

SEVERAL DECADES prior to the French Revolution, one of its intellectual and spiritual progenitors, Jean-Jacques Rousseau, recommended to the Polish regime a means of instilling a sense of national tradition and pride in the Polish people: hold a patriotic festival, he urged, around a monument inscribed with the names of stirring events from Poland's history. That formula came to be so ubiquitously realized in practice that one hundred years later we find a common theme recurring in major European novels: a group (or groups) of people gather together to celebrate a ritual or observe a festival. Then hostile forces abruptly disrupt the occasion, and a symbolic battle is waged. This pattern in imaginative literature reminds us that culture became politicized precisely because culture could be such a potent weapon in public affairs.[27]

Texts that were used in the teaching of history provide a prime illustration. Nowhere was their content neutral; everywhere in nineteenth-century Europe they were subject to control. In England they were intended to "educate the rising generations to uphold the tradition of society rather than to reform it." History in Britain remained a discipline devoted to demonstrating the traditions of civil and religious liberty, but also the obligations of citizenship. Textbooks remained consistently conservative in the social values they conveyed; and their authors clearly excised, as far as possible, controversial material. During the Second Empire in France the Minister of Public Instruction (1863–69) hoped to improve the quality of historical study throughout the educational system in order to bolster the privileged position of the propertied classes and, as Duruy explained to Napoleon III in 1863, "in order to create a legitimate counterweight to that democracy that is overflowing everywhere." Proper control of pedagogy in Czarist Russia was also a matter of considerable importance.[28]

By contrast, history books for the schools in nineteenth- and early twentieth-century America were patriotic and tradition-oriented, to be sure; but control was not centralized, the market dictated what was written and used rather than some ministry of education, and a greater degree of idiosyncratic randomness characterized the contents and interpretive tone of national history texts.[29]

Because Americans of "older stock" began to despair that genuine cultural homogeneity could ever be achieved, and because they believed they had a reasonably well-defined political nation by the end of the 1870s, they sought social order and political allegiance based upon

a rudimentary knowledge of the national culture and its most fundamental myths. They said, in effect: You newcomers cannot possibly
share the feel of our memories; but you can be loyal and deferential to
our judgment of how we ought to do things based upon the social and
political system that we have inherited.

Elsewhere, especially in Europe, national myths and traditions could
assist in controlling either subject peoples or else the lower strata in
society. Historical traditions could also, however, supply grounds on
which trampled nationalities might seek cultural recognition or even
political autonomy. Either way there was a realistic recognition of the
dynamics of cultural politics. As one French historian wrote as early as
1818: "Our century is singular in that it apprehends by memories, as it
makes politics with memories."[30]

In the United States, by contrast, there often seems to have been a
certain naïveté about such processes and their consequences. Moreover, national traditions elsewhere appeared to their elites as potential
weapons for managing the newly unleashed mass culture. In America
popular culture may have looked vulgar to the upper class, yet less
politically threatening than the mass culture associated with recently
enfranchised proletariats of Great Britain, France, and Germany
seemed to those who held the reins of power there.[31]

The situation in Germany was more complicated than in the United
States. First, because social stratification was more complex in the Ger-
manies of Bismarck and Kaiser Wilhelm II. Whereas *national* traditions—such as the proliferation of Bismarck towers after 1898—were
largely invented by the bourgeoisie, *dynastic* rituals were important
and attractive to the nobility. And, as the historian George Mosse has
shown, popular culture and mass culture could both be potent factors
in public life. Second, although much enthusiasm for ritual and tradition
existed at the beginning of Wilhelm's imperial reign (1888–1918), boredom had bred considerable opposition by the close of it.[32]

Although many people believed that the issue of German identity
had been resolved with unification and creation of an empire in 1871,
others remained apprehensive about the persistent tension between
cohesion, fragmentation, and Prussian dominance. The fact that the
kaiser held two titles, as Emperor of Germany and as the King of
Prussia, troubled many Germans living south of Prussia. These regional
tensions and their resulting anxieties had counterparts in post–Civil
War America, as did the great passion in both countries for erecting
public monuments to cultural and political heroes. A key difference
should be noted, however. Although ancestor worship became quite
important in German culture between about 1894 and 1913, those
being esteemed were viewed as ancestors of the entire German nation
rather than particular families or individuals.[33]

A comparison that is commonly (yet erroneously) made emphasizes
similarities between the traditions of the American and French revolu-

tions in their respective cultures. The American Revolution remained uncontroversial, and to repudiate it was simply unthinkable; whereas the French Revolution never ceased to have its partisans, such as the historian Albert Sorel, and its harsh critics, such as Hippolyte Taine. The latter, shocked by the excesses of the Commune in 1871, decided to write a history of France since 1789. He believed that the Revolution had resulted from teachings of impractical dreamers whose influence upon doctrinaire demagogues was responsible for a rebellion lacking a genuine cause. Ultimately Taine decided that democracy had been a great evil and a continuous source of trouble in French history. Taine's work, which began to appear in 1875, enjoyed considerable popularity throughout the Third Republic and he was idolized by royalists and conservatives who yearned for a sense of continuity with the pre-1789 *ancien régime.*[34]

Augustin Cochin embellished Taine's anti-democratic and pro-Catholic views. A strongly tradition-oriented individual, he felt certain that tradition and democracy were absolutely incompatible. By 1904 Cochin had decided that the outbreak of the French Revolution had been due to a national conspiracy on the part of a secret enclave of traitors. His views had immense appeal for the right-wing Action Française movement and provided a point of departure for reactionary histories written during the 1920s that blamed the French Revolution on Masons and Jews. The Action Française, which remained influential for half a century starting in 1890, wished to minimize the importance of the French Revolution as a pivotal event in the nation's history, along with other libertarian activities during the nineteenth century, and determined to find a golden age of order and stability in medieval times and during the *ancien régime.*[35]

A more appropriate comparison, actually, would involve the cultural impact of the French Revolution and the American Civil War—both events deeply divisive in enduring ways, both events continuing to be invoked in domestic politics for generations, and both events having profound cultural consequences—creative as well as destructive. The French, like the Americans, continued to be obsessed with defining national character—their own as well as others'—and looked to such momentous events as these for evidence that would resolve the enigmatic mysteries of national character.[36] In 1899 a French woman was eager to translate John Fiske's *History of the United States for Schools* because "we should have only a very imperfect idea of your national character and of your genius, if we were to continue ignorant of those long combats against the blind force of Nature, and the not less blind oppression of tyrants."[37]

I I I

AS WE HAVE SEEN, basic similarities concerning the cultural role of tradition may even have outnumbered differences between the United States and Europe, although the contrasts are certainly significant and should not be minimized. When we turn to China and Japan for comparisons, the differences are much more striking but for divergent reasons: in the case of China because it had not yet undergone either industrialization or "modernization" as political sociologists understand that concept; and in the case of Japan because both of those phenomena were following in the wake of dramatic political change that required legitimization—the Meiji Restoration of 1868 that ended (at least formally) centuries of feudal rule.

In China the principles of Confucianism, ingrained for so many centuries, required "submissiveness to the mores and the norms," reverence for the past and respect for history, love of traditional learning, "courage and sense of responsibility for a great tradition." Subtle studies of "medieval" and early modern China have shown that "change within tradition" was possible but required both favorable social conditions and considerable resourcefulness on the part of would-be innovators. The culture had powerfully established mechanisms for resisting pressures upon the status quo, and this was particularly true of responses by the ruling elite.[38]

In Japan, on the other hand, the last three decades of the nineteenth century witnessed a radical process of creating traditions wholesale, doing so from the top down (literally by imperial edict), and succeeding (more often than not) with remarkable effectiveness. In 1876, for example, less than eight years after the Meiji restoration, a German doctor asked a Japanese what he perceived as some of the problems inherent in the mythical and historical explanations that had been offered on behalf of the new Meiji state. The Japanese responded very simply that "We have no history. Our history begins today."[39]

Candor, understatement, and realism can be wonderfully refreshing. As part of the restoration in 1868–69 the new government had attempted to establish National Shinto as a state religion. When that failed, patriotism replaced National Shinto at the government's behest. Superficially, then, there seems to be a basic similarity between the United States and Japan from the 1870s onward: patriotism became a form of civil religion. The critical difference, however, is that in the United States this occurred as a matter of individual acts of ardor and conscience, following personal crises of faith, whereas in Japan the initiative came from on high, which proved to be determinative even when it provoked private "moments" of soul-searching. As the anthropologist Robert J. Smith has written, an Imperial

Rescript on education in 1890 became the "basic sacred text of the new religion of patriotism."[40]

And yet, even an emperor who is revered as a god cannot alter social relationships overnight, or assumptions about those relationships that have persisted for many centuries. Consequently some fundamental customs persisted that set Japanese values in stark contrast with contemporary American ones. The Japanese people shared, for example, a "feeling of unconditional connectedness," which meant that they not only had a common cultural heritage, but were ultimately blood relatives. The United States, on the other hand, was in Robert H. Wiebe's insightful phrase, a "segmented society" that not only lacked a feeling of connectedness but became more heterogeneous and fragmented with every passing year.[41]

The mobilization (even the fabrication) of national myths for political purposes occurred in Japan and Germany during the close of the nineteenth century to a degree unknown in the United States; and subsequently the Union of South Africa—with government and the ruling social elite working in tandem—did just the same sort of thing to rationalize its policy of racial apartheid.[42]

Compared with government's heavy hand in the manipulation of tradition in Germany, France, Japan, and the Soviet Union as early as the 1920s, the government of the United States at least remained relatively consistent in its hands-off policy.[43] Not until Wilson's official propaganda efforts of 1917–18 on behalf of the Allies, and later Franklin D. Roosevelt's literal theft of Abraham Lincoln as a political symbol from the Republican Party during the 1930s, do we have egregious examples that are remotely comparable to what occurred earlier in Berlin, Paris, and Tokyo.[44]

The social dynamics of political mythology are strikingly similar in the United States and in South Africa, not simply because myths of racial supremacy were and remain central to both, but because government policy followed rather than led: in each instance it ratified traditions that had evolved informally from "below" over several generations. The two nations may be very different, indeed, in the overall configurations of their cultures; but the politics of race, racial memory, and myth share a common pattern in which one casts a longer and even darker shadow than the other.[45]

I V

THE MOST widely shared common denominator (at that time) in the societies we have been examining was nostalgia—in the warped modern sense rather than its original meaning, *viz*: yearning for a golden age in less complex, more harmonious times.[46] Nostalgia as we have now used the concept for about a century tends to deny the notion that progress or change is very likely to have fortuitous consequences. Nostalgia is especially likely to occur in response to dramatic or unanticipated alterations, like a revolution or a civil war, a stunning transformation of the sort that rapid industrialization brings, or the crumbling of a venerated value system, like revealed religion. All of those phenomena, and their predictably attendant concerns, were present during the years from 1860 until 1917. Hence an atmosphere so extraordinarily conducive to the newer meaning of nostalgia. People seemed to thrive upon the backward glance, not so much for purposes of escapism, though that inclination certainly existed, but because the creative consequences of nostalgia helped them to legitimize new political orders, rationalize the adjustment and perpetuation of old social hierarchies, and construct acceptable new systems of thought and values.[47]

It is precisely because so much that genuinely mattered was new that people needed notions of the past that would help to define their national identities in positive ways, and required secure traditions to serve as strong psychological anchors. Otherwise, as one momentous century ended and the prospect of a new and uncertain one loomed, they faced the future as culturally displaced persons. Nostalgia meant more to them than consolation. It provided identity, integrity, and perhaps even a sense of security—however false.

Our enduring legacies of that nostalgic surge take several forms. The most visible are great public monuments of various sorts: statues, memorials, obelisks, fountains, cemeteries, and other structures, as well as battlefields that were "saved" and set aside under private or public auspices. Sometimes conditions changed so rapidly that monuments had to be redefined or even abandoned. In 1849, for example, immediately after the heady days of republican revolution in France, a statue was dedicated to the new constitution. It had barely been started, however, when the constitution was violated. Upon its completion in 1854, under a different regime, the statue received the designation "Law."[48] It may be a lesser irony of that era that the word "monument" is derived from the Latin root *monere,* meaning a reminder. Many people seemed desperately to need such reminders; and as we have seen from James Russell Lowell's stroll past the equestrian statue of Washington in Boston's Public Garden, numerous newcomers could not be reminded of what they had never known.[49]

A less visible legacy, though vastly more important, consists of the myths that were actually made back then, the extant legends that got refurbished and perpetuated, the traditions and their symbolism that still abide with us—some of which we take for granted until a threat to national security, or a so-called malaise, or a particular political campaign, causes them to be resuscitated. We have already encountered some of these. Many others lie ahead.[50]

Finally, and most elusively, a third sort of legacy emerged at that time, although it was not commonly acknowledged as such and is reluctantly recognized even in our own time—wherever it occurs in the world. I have in mind the existence of conflicting or contradictory traditions in the same locale—one of them dominant, perhaps, and the other one dissenting, or even repressed from time to time. The dynamics of incompatible traditions have been known to ignite combustible situations.[51] They present a powerful and particular challenge to the historian of memory, along with the prospect of cultural pyrotechnics.

Eugen Weber has hit upon a felicitous phrase in writing of lore that was transmitted by peasants in rural France. He calls the memories of old people the "archives of the poor."[52] Unfortunately, we know from the testimony of individuals ranging from Thomas Jefferson to Ronald Reagan just how fallible the memories of the *affluent* can be. The archives of the poor must be approached with equally appropriate caution. Nevertheless, they too must be used if memory is to prevail over amnesia, knowledge over agnosticism, and wisdom over a warped or wasted past.[53]

CIRCA 1915 TO 1945

"THE EMOTIONAL DISCOVERY

OF AMERICA"

T HE INTRUSIVE THRUST of modernism during the interwar decades—as a mode of thought and as a way of life—is more familiar than the simultaneous revival of traditionalism. If pressed to connect the two, we might bring to mind "debunking" as a topical 1920s trend: puncturing the past in order to bring it down to non-heroic yet human proportions. Whether we contemplate art, architecture, techniques of design, or imaginative literature, we associate modernism with men and women who probed the realms of instinct and the irrational: individuals like Freud, Proust, Joyce, Gertrude Stein, and Faulkner who plunged into inquiries concerning the self—to some degree self and society, but ultimately self—and who embarked upon a *voyage intérieur* that went far toward defining what modernism would be about.

Because of all the attention that modernism (and even futurism) has received from analysts, we lose sight of the extraordinary resilience and rich social texture of tradition orientation during the 1920s and '30s: the creation of a historically based public culture for the nation as a whole and for most of its regional and ethnic components as well. Traditionalists were attracted to meaningful, purposive myths that could explain and justify how their "world" had come to be the way it was. They still wanted histories that were "true" and historical objects that were "authentic," key words that recurred with amazing pervasiveness. Ideas such as instinct, impulse, the subconscious, and the irrational made them apprehensive because such notions conveyed the potential for disorder. Most tradition-oriented people did not like disorder, whether it be personal, political, or social. What has not been appreciated, however, is that being traditional did not necessarily mean being derivative. As we shall see, a combination of willfulness and necessity often made for creative modes of traditionalism.[1]

Unlike the self-styled modernists, however, traditionalists did not possess much sense of irony. When a "first settler" reappeared in the finale of the Pageant of Schenectady (1912) to view the twentieth-century city, he voiced strong approval of "Mr. Modern" and the radiant "Spirits of Light" provided by the General Electric Company. We needed Alfred Kazin to write of the so-called lost generation that "their detachment from the native traditions now became their own first tradition." Amidst all of the curiosity aroused when Henry Ford "saved" the Wayside Inn in 1923–24, another patron of culture and tradition, Grace Coolidge, at least had the wit to remark that once upon a time even the Wayside Inn had been brand new.[2]

The crucial point is that the interwar decades were permeated by both modernism *and* nostalgia in a manner that may best be described as perversely symbiotic. That is, each one flourished, in part, as a critical response to the other. Most of the time, however, there was little if any recognition that an oxymoronic condition persisted: nostalgic modernism. In 1926, for example, advertisements by C. W. Post, the breakfast cereal magnate, declared that "modern conditions of living and working have banished the Early American breakfast, probably forever!" Nevertheless, as the historian Harvey Green has commented, ads conveyed the impression that one still could eat Post Toasties or Kellogg's All-Bran with a neo-colonial spoon in a colonial-style kitchen (otherwise complete with the latest modern equipment), "thereby feeling a unity with both the colonial and the modern world."*[3]

Although much that was said and done in the name of nostalgic modernism seems amusing, banal, or lacking in self-awareness, one *apparent* oxymoron, democratic traditionalism, really was not. Despite encountering resistance in some quarters and generating uncertainty in others, the determination to democratize tradition gradually emerged as one of the most interesting and important features of the interwar years. The genesis of that determination, however, has roots at the start of the twentieth century. In 1904, for example, citizens of Minneapolis gave a public dinner to honor the retirement of James K. Hosmer, the Pilgrim descendant, as beloved head of the municipal public library. One speaker paid tribute to Hosmer's embodiment of cultural heritage and public service by validating the imperative of well-informed and articulate decision making. "In a democracy," he said, "every man is expected to form an opinion. But that opinion floating around somewhere in the dark recesses of our subconscious being, generates no motion, no force, leaves no record. Opinion to be effective must have voice."[4] A successful democracy requires educated leadership.

---

*The J. Walter Thompson advertising agency, very much preoccupied with modernity and with changing people's taste, had a colonial-style private dining room at its Manhattan office suite. When the agency moved to the Graybar Building in 1927, the familiar colonial dining room was disassembled and installed in new quarters.

Less than a decade later the historian William E. Dodd, democrat and traditionalist, applied this message in a more particular way to excesses of patriotism hyped by historical ignorance—a combination that he deplored. Speaking on George Washington's Birthday at Trinity College in North Carolina (which later became Duke University), Dodd complained that "we have erected a huge fabric of tradition, error, and sometimes actual falsehood." He appealed for serious and dispassionate study of the past, and invoked the tragedy of Civil War as an object lesson in how things can go haywire when rigid adherence to regional tradition displaces informed understanding of how a situation evolved. "Men had suffered themselves to be blinded by a false patriotism," he declared. "North as well as South men refused to read history and recognize the truth." He concluded by sounding a note that would become increasingly familiar in the quarter century that lay ahead: "There are many men who have never been willing to allow that the United States is or ought to be a democracy; to them it is patriotism to dress up and romanticise the facts of our national development."[5]

By the early 1920s an impulse not merely to reconcile, but to accommodate tradition to the democratic ethos was voiced by opinion makers and creative people in many areas of American life. John Dewey declared that "we can retain and transmit our own heritage only by constant remaking of our own [social] environment." James Truslow Adams surveyed the mindless attacks upon "unpatriotic" (meaning pro-British) history textbooks made by several state legislatures in 1922–23 and concluded with a tone less hopeful than apprehensive:

> If democracy rejects the truth, will it slowly retire again, as in the Middle Ages, to the quiet cell of its cloistered votary? . . . The influence of democracy in the long run upon intellectual life has yet to be determined, and there rests upon the more cultured elements among the public a very genuine and solemn obligation.

Referring to a sensible citizenry of informed individuals, Adams expressed the concern that "if it should come to prefer flattering local legend to critical analysis, if it should demand passionate propaganda in place of reasoned statement . . . then the outlook for the writing of history which should be both popular and truthful would indeed be dark."[6]

For most of the 1920s Thomas Hart Benton worked on a massive, uncommissioned set of murals—a narrative series organized by "chapters" that he called "The American Historical Epic." In his autobiography Benton explained that the regionalist movement, in which he played a central role, had its roots in "that general and country-wide revival of Americanism which followed the defeat of Woodrow Wilson's universal idealism" at the close of World War I. Overall, Benton believed, "it was a period of improvement in democratic idealism."[7]

Students of American literature, likewise fascinated by the "awakening national consciousness," attempted in the early 1920s to reassess canonical authors and works according to criteria appropriate to the role of "literature in a democracy." One consequence was the appearance of judgments that seem quirky to us today but are highly symptomatic of the mood seventy years ago. The reader was urged to heed, for instance, that Hawthorne's "warnings are for a new world that has broken with tradition," and that Mark Twain described a "new world on the Mississippi where tradition, in the fresh, crude light, showed its seam of decay."[8]

At exactly the same time, the early 1920s, Stuart Pratt Sherman swiftly rose to prominence as the foremost literary historian and critic in the United States. One complex theme stands out in high relief as the most prominent in his essays: a need to explore and expound upon American tradition in general and the Puritan contribution to American culture in particular—all the while insisting that writers were "ignoble" if they did not concern themselves with democracy. As he indicated to a friend on New Year's Day in 1923: "There is no question at the present time requiring more thinking, calling for a more definite stand, and demanding more *explicit* expression from the man of letters than precisely the question: What does democracy mean to me?"[9]

Late in 1920 Sherman engaged the critic and cultural historian Ludwig Lewisohn in a dialogue concerning the relative merits of tradition and freedom (or modernism). Sherman even made explicit why he emphasized tradition so strenuously: "Through tradition we get our standards. By keeping our tradition alive we preserve our standards. By making our tradition vital, bringing it to bear upon current work, we may hope to produce something equivalent to the 'thoroughbred' in literature."[10]

We owe a particular debt to Sherman for succinctly summarizing an important aspect of the climate of opinion that persisted throughout the twenties and thirties—one that will supply the focus of the six chapters that follow. Sherman did so in a lecture that he presented late in 1924 to the American Academy of Arts and Letters and published the following spring. He titled it "The Emotional Discovery of America," and began with a descriptive statement that is also a perceptive value judgment: "As an emotional fact [America] doesn't 'stay put': she is constantly being discovered and lost again; and our history is the enemy of all our thin and dwindled traditions about her." Toward the end he offered a peroration that came from the heart yet also happens to have been historically true:

> The age in which we now live appears to me to be a great and fascinating period in the emotional and literary discovery of America, because the woods are full of lighted torches, are full of men and women bent on exploring and reporting the truth as

they see it, and nothing but the truth, and great areas of repressed truth about their own lives and about the lives of the American people.[11]

It is difficult to render an accurate account of the frequency with which that ubiquitous word "discovery" recurred during these two decades. Waldo Frank (1889–1967), the novelist and cultural critic, had written *Our America* in 1919 and then serialized *The Re-discovery of America: An Introduction to a Philosophy* in the *New Republic* (1927–28) before pulling the essays together in book form a year later in 1929. A few of the chapter titles tell a great deal about Frank's orientation: The Last Days of Europe, The Grave of Europe, Our Women, Our Folk, Mystic America, Capturable America, and The Symphonic Nation. Although it is a quasi-mystical book, often opaque, Frank made clear his preference for a tradition of idealism (associated with Columbus and Roger Williams) rather than the pragmatic American tradition (associated with George Washington and Benjamin Franklin). Frank's most vigorous point, however, was that "a tradition lives only when each succeeding generation recreates it."[12] Nostalgic modernism.

For intellectuals like Frank, Sherman, and the journalist Ernest Boyd, the process of exploring America could be comparable to looking closely in a mirror and discovering deformities, such as unprincipled materialism, the dour features of Puritanism, and so glaring a gap between dreams and realities "that the American observer loses his bearings." Boyd believed that "it is the duty of an American to have a long memory, and once again he is caught in the neglect of his duty."[13] Their readers tended to overlook the shadows, however, saw only the bright side, and responded more positively. After James Boyd published *Drums* (1925), a historical novel about the American Revolution, he received this sort of fan mail from a woman in Brooklyn, New York: "I have to thank you for a clearer vision of my country in embryo. . . . DRUMS has made me proud of my nationality, consciously so."[14]

Creative contemporaries could also be upbeat but varied in their degrees of optimism. During the early 1920s William Carlos Williams gladly crusaded for American writers and artists to choose indigenous subjects and use native modes of expression. Constance Rourke, the innovative folklorist and historian of American culture, acknowledged that "we sometimes seem to be hunting for a tradition . . . but traditions are often hard to discover, requiring a long and equable scrutiny; they are hard to build, consuming an expanse of time which may pass beyond a few generations."[15]

Although many Americans had long believed that they shared a manifest destiny, and aspired to the achievement of a distinctively American character, the emotional discovery that took place during the 1920s produced a vulgate of American exceptionalism never before known. The phrase "strictly American" popped up boastfully throughout the country, though most commonly perhaps in conjunction with vernacular architecture or various forms of folk art and manifestations of material culture. An essay in *Scribner's* announced that "remodelled farmhouses in New England are strictly early American"; signs that advertised White Taverns, a large chain of luncheonettes, proclaimed that they were strictly American; and when Henry Ford's new museum opened in 1933 at Dearborn, Michigan, he proudly told a reporter that "we have no Egyptian mummies here, nor any relics of the battle of Waterloo nor do we have any curios from Pompeii, for everything we have is strictly American."[16]

Beneath these declarations of cultural independence there lay a tortured love-hate relationship with Great Britain in particular and a larger context of cultural isolationism in general. During the years 1917–18, when America had been Britain's ally in the war, pro-British propaganda poured forth and a patriotic association known as The American's Creed was formed in Baltimore and Washington, D.C., that included Hamlin Garland, Ellen Glasgow, Booth Tarkington, and many other prominent figures on its letterhead. Despite its name, the group's Anglophilia was reflected in a pamphlet it published under the title *A Heritage of Freedom.*[17]

After the war a literary nationalist like Brander Matthews made no attempt to disguise his admiration for British culture, and even published an essay designed to convey forgiveness for the persistence of British condescension during the course of the nineteenth century. James Truslow Adams, who became the best-known writer of American history during the interwar years, lived and wrote for much of the 1920s in London, where he felt more comfortable. Not a member of the lost generation at all, he simply disliked swift social change and what he considered the vulgarity of contemporary American life. "I loved the old America," he told a friend in 1930, "but I am getting most horribly sick of the new." And then to accentuate Adams's sense of disillusioned contrast: "If a man wants to study mass production let him go to America. If he wants to study humanity, let him come here. If he wants the common man plus a Ford let him go to the U.S.A."[18]

In retrospect that last sentence seems not merely ironic but prescient as well. Henry Ford democratized travel in the United States by making automobiles affordable for the middle class. In the process he also made a great many out-of-the way natural wonders and historic sites accessible. Nothing would have pleased him more than receiving credit for bringing the common man to American history and vice versa (fig. P3.1). A revolution in automobile travel occurred between 1912 and 1928 in the United States, a revolution that enhanced tourism in ways that were essential to the story that follows in this section. As Sherwood Anderson and Stuart Pratt Sherman both noted in 1924, Americans began to "wander about" as never before. In 1925 Corra Harris, a popular writer for the *Saturday Evening Post,* found herself bored and

P3.1   Henry Ford in 1933. From the collections of Henry Ford Museum &
Greenfield Village, Dearborn, Michigan.

restless. When she told George Lorimer, the *Post*'s editor, that she had
a trip around the world in mind, he urged her to stay at home: "Look
over our beloved country first."[19]

By 1927–29 historic markers began to appear along the shoulders of
American highways, most of them placed by the states, but some by
patriotic societies. For motels, eateries, and service stations that sprang
up during the 1920s and '30s, the preferred style, predictably, was
colonial revival. Travel may have meant progress, yet it fostered tradition. Once Colonial Williamsburg formally opened to the public, no
group met there more faithfully than the travel industry's trade association; and Kenneth Chorley, the president of C.W., Inc., never failed to
give them a warm early American welcome.[20]

In the absence of visitor surveys and transcribed interviews, we cannot say just how discriminating the tradition-oriented tourist turned out
to be during the 1930s. Which seemed more authentic: reconstructed
colonial buildings at Williamsburg or the brand new Colonial Village
built for Chicago's Century of Progress Exposition in 1933, which included reproductions of the Paul Revere House from Boston and the
House of the Seven Gables from Salem? How much more "authentic"
are reproductions located on their original foundations than reproductions situated a thousand miles from home? Did more than a very few
visitors care, or consider it an issue worthy of contemplation?[21]

Paul Fussell has written engagingly about British travel and tourism
between the wars. He finds in this fascinating body of literature "an
implicit rejection of industrialism" and a nostalgic celebration of a
Golden Age that Fussell believes can be located in the mid-nineteenth
century. Affluent people travelled in order to experience the past, he

observes, and so "travel is thus an adventure in time as well as distance."[22] Although an American elite experienced many of the same emotions at the time, they did not have such easy access to travel in exotic places; they did not have a "class" of Oxbridge writers geared to create or contribute to such a genre of travel literature; and the United States scarcely had much of an audience ready to receive such a genre. Consequently Americans tended to substitute historic sites and museums for the luxuries of extended travel in distance and time.

During the 1920s and '30s—an extraordinary era of transformation for older American museums, and of genesis for new ones—there was too much diversity to permit a singular philosophy or ideology concerning museum policy. Nevertheless, a few common threads connected them, primarily the belief that a museum ought to serve as an educational institution and that Americana deserved pride of place. Beyond a considerable degree of consensus on those two points, divergence was illustrated by an essay that appeared in 1922, written by an Associate in Industrial Art at the Metropolitan Museum of Art in New York. After playing the two reflexive chords just mentioned, Richard F. Bach urged that distinctions between high art and the art of design be abolished, that distinctions between hand-made and machine-made objects be minimized, that the commercialization of culture would enhance the uplifting of taste (and vice versa), that museums ought to co-operate with the producers of American industrial art, that the manufacturer ought to regard the museum as "an addition to his own facilities of production," and that a redefinition of progress (as compared to 1850 or 1876) was needed: namely, that "the new thing is better because it is based upon study of the old."[23]

Bach's nationalism was manifest in his closing sentence, that only "the best design is good enough for America and that the best resources must receive constant use to achieve that end." At a time when modernism and traditionalism ordinarily represented conflicting points of view, Bach was somewhat unusual in his desire to reconcile the two, a desire at least partially reflected in his definition of progress. Ever since 1918–19 and the patriotism engendered by war, however, such figures as Van Wyck Brooks and William Carlos Williams had begun to assert that a nation's culture must inevitably be derived from its history—a point of view that William Faulkner, Robert Penn Warren, and John Dos Passos would articulate over the next few decades.[24]

Some American artists also reflected this point of view, though in very diverse ways, during these years. Charles Demuth would juxtapose a pristine colonial cupola against a cityscape that reflected the ungainly forms and colors of industrialization (fig. P3.2). Flattened cubism worked extremely well in conveying the feel of urban crowding, and managed to ask, implicitly yet urgently: Whither the traditions of American design? Five years later Stuart Davis would apply modernist techniques to traditional subjects: an older house with a wharf and barn

P3.2   Charles Demuth, *Lancaster* (1920), tempera and pencil on paper. Courtesy of the Philadelphia Museum of Art. The Louise and Walter Arensberg Collection.

and a two-masted sailing ship that may be going nowhere. There is an enigmatic element in *Early American Landscape* (fig. P3.3); and trees that at first appear to be dead in fact have sprouted a whimsical crown of fresh leaves. Although form and color must have been more important than content to Davis, the selection of his subject matter could not have been more appropriate in 1925, and the co-ordination of nature and structures in this picture may very well be meant to indicate that Davis, too, shared the view that culture is rooted in the past even though it must continually devise new modes of expression.

The chapters that follow in this section will describe and explain the emergence of an American aesthetic, centering upon simplicity, and a passion for Americana that swept the nation during the 1920s; the partisanship promoted by regionalism and a resulting intensification of allegiance to regional memories and observances; a fascinating debate over the most meaningful fulfillment of tradition orientation (a national high culture or the recovery and proper recognition of American folk culture?); protests against excessive romanticization of the American past giving way after 1939 to an affirmation of the profound social value of myth in times of national and international crisis; and the transformation of patriotism from an unfashionable phenomenon (in certain cerebral circles) during the 1920s and early 1930s to a reassertion of its dominant role in American values by the close of the thirties.

Careful attention to chronology is particularly important for this period because all groups and influential individuals were not in phase with one another, which makes generalizations especially hazardous. One careful scholar has noted condemnations of American culture by Lewis Mumford as well as others during the later 1920s; hence she concludes that the resuscitation of national culture and the ardent invocation of American traditions did not really occur until the 1930s.[25] I am persuaded, however, that the genesis of this shift in sentiment was already under way by the second decade of the twentieth century, and flourished throughout the 1920s.[26]

For a symptomatic innovation in the national vocabulary, notice the repetitive use of the word "rise" in books and essays about American history and culture: *The Rise of American Civilization* by Charles and Mary Beard (1927); *The Rise of the Common Man* by Carl R. Fish (1927); *The Rise of the City, 1878–1898* by Arthur M. Schlesinger (1933); and James Truslow Adams's essay for the *New York Times* (1939), titled "1789–1939: A Nation Rises."[27] Obviously, those must have been yeasty years, a time when memory leavened.

The most intriguing index of the transformation we are about to

P3.3   Stuart Davis, *Early American Landscape* (1925), oil on canvas. Courtesy of the Whitney Museum of American Art, New York.

witness can be found in the changing attitudes of assorted individuals. In 1918, for example, when Carl Sandburg was forty years of age, he wrote in "Cornhuskers," a poem, "The past, I tell you, is a bucket of ashes." Just eight years later, when he published *Abraham Lincoln: The Prairie Years,* Sandburg made this suggestive assertion in his Preface: "Perhaps poetry, art, human behavior in this country, which has need to build on its own traditions, would be served by a life of Lincoln." Sandburg subsequently completed four more volumes, which enjoyed enormous popularity, collected American folk songs, and wrote poetry that utterly reversed the position he had aggressively staked in 1918.

Similarly, Van Wyck Brooks complained in 1918 that in the United States old things were uninteresting because they failed to convey the feel of tradition, that he could not find a sense of continuity, that America lacked "sympathetic soil" that could nourish the growth of cultural traditions. In 1921, however, he moved to the old town of Westport, Connecticut, which he liked because of its location in a "long settled region" where he could find "at least a rill of tradition." Following his deep depression and breakdown during 1926–27, Brooks gradually emerged as a cultural super-patriot who is best known for his five-volume series called *Makers and Finders: A History of the Writer in America* (1936–52). Long before those volumes began to appear, however, it is possible to trace his transformation in successive editions of *The Ordeal of Mark Twain,* which first appeared in 1920 and was so strikingly revised by 1933.[28]

Memory, we well know, can be selective and capricious. On one occasion Aaron Copland looked back to the 1920s and recalled that "Tradition was nothing; innovation everything." History and life are more complicated and convoluted than that, though, because elsewhere Copland tells us that by 1921 he had "discovered" Walt Whitman's *I Hear America Singing,* and that he subsequently stressed "the need for a specifically American speech in our serious music." The modernist might or might not also be a traditionalist; but he clearly felt the need to take native traditions into account.[29]

Ellen Glasgow, the novelist born in Richmond to an aristocratic Southern family, rejected the sentimental style in her region's fiction without repudiating the importance of a historical sensibility or the inescapable role of memory for class and gender, region, and race. In one of her finest novels, *The Sheltered Life* (1932), Glasgow conveyed in a single sentence so much of the ambivalence as well as the nuanced motives that profoundly affected the Americans who are described in this section. "People who have tradition are oppressed by tradition," she observed, "and people who are without it are oppressed by the lack of it—or by whatever else they have put in its place."[30]

Chapter 10

IN QUEST OF AN
AMERICAN AESTHETIC:
COLLECTING AMERICANA AND
SEEING AMERICA FIRST

TWO BRIEF ESSAYS that appeared in 1922 and 1925 set the tone and clearly indicate several dominant tendencies in the transformation of collective memory in the United States between the wars. The first essay, written by a curator at the Cleveland Museum of Art, suggested that "the multiplication of young art museums is creating in the country a great educational power." In addition to reiterating the civic benefits of art museums, which by then was a well-worn theme, the author also appealed for a democratization of these institutions. In the past, he acknowledged, collections "tended to express the [curatorial] interests of scholars and the enthusiasms of donors, resulting in a certain aloofness from common interests and common needs." He did not believe that responsiveness to community interests inevitably meant any dilution of standards. "In cultivating public taste," he explained, "it is not necessary to begin with the poor and progress toward the excellent. One can begin with the easily comprehended and progress toward the more difficult—more complex and subtle, always on a high plane."[1] Level up, in other words.

The author also subscribed fully to American exceptionalism, felt committed to a more flexible notion of what qualified for exhibition in a museum (objects designed with an industrial purpose, for example), and believed that art museums should reach out to city schools more than they had; but ultimately he kept a conservative social goal in view. Precisely because industrialization had caused a decline in the quality of life, museums were essential to occupy leisure time with diverting interests. The day had gone when laborers derived pleasure from their work: "The factory town has the greatest need of the museum of art to supplement its schools, not primarily as a factor in vocational training, but as a stabilizing influence among the laborers."[2]

Although every curator at each American museum did not share all of those sentiments, they were highly representative, nonetheless, and suggestive of motifs that will emerge in this chapter and dominate the next one. Individuals are even more interesting than institutions, however; and in the circumstances we are about to examine, many institutions emerged as the immortalized shadow of an individual. Hence the fortuitous timing of a new monthly magazine, popular in purpose, that began to appear in 1925, less than a year after the opening of the American Wing at the Metropolitan Museum of Art in New York, and a year before John D. Rockefeller, Jr., became fascinated by the notion of restoring Colonial Williamsburg—which entailed, among other things, gathering a great amount of early Americana.

The new monthly, called *The Americana Collector,* printed a full-page declaration of faith in its first issue. The pious tone and intensity of the true believer are even more striking than the substance. "Americana is not a hobby," it began, "it is a creed." The publisher acknowledged that it was perfectly legitimate to collect anything from anywhere; yet to him "it seems that only the Americana collector has reached the heights of supreme contentment. . . . Americana is something that if it grips you once, will change your habits, temperament and view of life. Pity the one that never came under its spell."[3] An amazing number did, however, and they represented the middle class as well as the elite. They collected eclectically, ranging from art and rare books to the decorative arts (both high and folk) and pre-industrial farm tools. They collected everything under the sun, they loved to travel in search of potential treasures—cruising for relics, one might say—and although they could be fiercely competitive in their quests, they shaped informal networks as well as long-lived organizations. They felt patriotic, possessive, proud, and in touch with the past—in various combinations and with different degrees of intensity. Their cultural influence turned out to be incalculable.

I

IT MUST BE acknowledged at the outset that European objects and ideas did not utterly vanish from the American consciousness when World War I ended. A serious two-volume work such as Henry Osborn Taylor's *The Medieval Mind: A History of the Development of Thought and Emotion in the Middle Ages,* published in 1911, had an enduring impact upon Theodore Roosevelt, Edith Wharton, and other figures half a generation younger. Although we most readily associate John D. Rockefeller, Jr., with Williamsburg and several other early American restorations in the lower Hudson Valley, it should be kept in mind that he also subsidized the Cloisters between 1929 and 1938, *pari passu* Colonial Williamsburg, and that he loved the medieval mystique of the Cloisters, located at the northern tip of Manhattan, at least as much as he did the Tidewater sites in which he took such a strong patriotic and aesthetic interest.[4]

Other collectors retained their Anglophile predilections despite touches of enthusiasm for Americana. Wilmarth S. Lewis, for example, collected eighteenth- and nineteenth-century English literature—manuscripts as well as books—and eventually became obsessed with the works of Horace Walpole. Rarely in the history of collecting, in fact, have a patron and the person he "patronized" become so closely identified. Lewis did not go so far as to build a reproduction of Walpole's neo-Gothic estate, Strawberry Hill; instead he kept his collection in an ever-growing colonial farmhouse located in Farmington, Connecticut.[5]

Owen D. Young, chairman of the board of General Electric, also collected rare books, especially first editions of English and American authors. Although he started as early as 1898, Young did not become a serious collector for a quarter of a century. From 1923 until 1930 he pursued his avocation with intensity—gathering first editions in fine condition of Shakespeare, Keats, Thackeray, the Lambs, Dickens, Lewis Carroll, and Trollope. Although he initially concentrated on English authors, he eventually bought works by Poe, Emerson, Hawthorne, Cooper, Whitman, and Twain. Even so, the collection remained predominantly British; and in 1941 he sold part and gave the rest to the New York Public Library—the largest and most important individual cache given to that institution up to that time.[6]

Owing to the economic difficulties that deeply affected Europe in the years following World War I, Old World antiques were abundant and inexpensive. A fair number flowed into the United States as a result, along with bizarre reports of unusual collections in Europe, such as N. C. Rothschild's flea collection which he kept at his home in Tring, England. Every flea was kept "in a little vial of spirits, each marked with the place and the host . . . on whom they were found."[7]

Quite a few of the most notable American collectors, whose hoards have long since become the foundations for important museums, began briefly as Europeanists. The Wells family of Southbridge, Massachusetts, started before the war with a taste for English and French antiques; but shifted to rustic Americana during the mid-1920s, and by 1926 decided to specialize in New England country furniture and decorative arts. Within a year the Wells brothers had added a two-storey ell to the family house and also converted two huge barns in order to display the collection. In November 1936 the Wells Historical Museum opened to the public in Southbridge, proclaiming that its mission was educational and that its focus would be the period prior to industrialization. Ten years later, on June 8, 1946, it reopened in expanded form, but with the same mission and emphasis, as Old Sturbridge Village.[8]

Miss Ima Hogg of Houston, Texas, whose father had been a Populist governor of that state during the 1890s, began buying antique English furniture in 1917, got her first American piece in 1920, and emerged as an active enthusiast for Americana in 1922–23. By the end of that decade her primary interests had shifted to a variety of civic causes; but in 1946 colonial furniture attracted her attention once again, and within a decade eighteenth-century paintings as well, particularly ones by John Singleton Copley. In 1954, with Henry Francis du Pont's Winterthur as an inspiration, she began to envision her mansion, Bayou Bend, as a house museum. It opened to the public in 1966 (figs. 10.1 and 10.2). Meanwhile, like Henry Ford, she got interested in the restoration of historically intriguing structures. During the 1950s Miss Hogg restored Varner, a Greek Revival plantation home built around 1834 in West Columbia, Texas. (Her father had bought it in 1901.) Early in the 1960s she purchased the Stagecoach Inn at Winedale in Fayette County, Texas: a site that reflected the culture of early German immigration to Texas. It was dedicated in 1967 amid the exuberant strains of a German-American polka band.[9]

The emergence of this passionate preference for Americana occurred swiftly and with remarkably little hesitation between about 1913 and 1923. In 1913, for instance, Isaac Newton Phelps Stokes, a New York City socialite and architect who had been trained at the Ecole des Beaux-Arts in Paris, rejected an opportunity to acquire early European lithographs because "they fall outside of my field of collecting, as I am interested only in Americana." Another ardent Francophile, James H. Hyde, concerted a plan late in 1917 to build for American students in Paris a residence "in the American style of the end of the XVIIIth century."[10] Other committed Americanists felt no anomaly in going to Europe in order to compose an intensely American work. Stephen Vincent Benét wrote *John Brown's Body* in Paris during 1926–27 because the cost of living was so much lower there. "Living abroad," he informed a friend in 1928, "has intensified my Americanism." Similarly Constance Rourke went to England with her mother in 1929–30 to work on *American Humor: A Study of the National Character.* In Rourke's case there is no clear explanation; but she was not the first and by no means the last to do so.[11]

When the Museum of Modern Art was being organized in 1929, some people felt apprehensive that inadequate attention to American artists would be offensive to some. An editorial in the *New York Times* speculated that "it must occasion a little surprise, not to say regret, that the first exhibition is to be French. American artists will feel that they might well have been given the earliest chance in an American museum of contemporary art to show what they can do." A few were undoubtedly displeased; but by the close of the twenties people managing institutions of art and memory wished to utilize exhibition emphases and techniques that might be distinctively viable for them.[12] Many also felt perfectly comfortable with combinations that seem strange only in retrospect because of stereotypes that we have ascribed to them. Although we think of Joseph Hirshhorn as an exuberant collector of modern and contemporary art, he started by collecting first editions of books, and by 1933 his domestic taste turned to eighteenth-century American furniture. He had such special affection for a Simon Willard

10.1   Miss Ima Hogg in the drawing room at Bayou Bend, Houston, Texas, 1948. Courtesy of The Museum of Fine Arts, Houston.

10.2   Queen Anne bedroom, The Bayou Bend Collection, The Museum of Fine Arts, Houston. Gift of Miss Ima Hogg.

10.3   Clara and Henry Ford walking in Greenfield Village on their fiftieth wedding anniversary in 1941. From the collections of Henry Ford Museum & Greenfield Village.

tall clock that each time he went through a divorce settlement he hid the clock in a dealer's warehouse.[13]

Collecting, then, was generally *not* the sort of rational, orderly, and prudent activity that we tend to assume it always must have been. Collecting cannot be explained exclusively in terms of class, gender, region, or motive, all of which varied considerably. Some of the great collectors were men and women whose spouses ranged from supportive to indifferent. (Some men appear to have become collectors in order to get away from their wives.) Some married couples shared the love of collecting but specialized in different areas of expertise (Arbella and Henry Huntington, or Abby Aldrich and John D. Rockefeller, Jr.), while still others had enthusiasms that converged and made countless decisions as a team (Clara and Henry Ford [fig. 10.3]). Sometimes a parent and child collaborated as collectors (the J. P. Morgans or Henry and Edsel Ford); but more commonly the focus of collecting involved intergenerational rebellion or else a quest for personal identity (Louisine Havemeyer and Electra Havemeyer Webb).[14]

Consequently we must ask *what* they collected, and then the more complicated question *why* (complicated because the answers are so diverse and combined in various patterns), and finally inquire about the cultural consequences and legacies of their activities and criteria as collectors: consequences for museums and other institutions, for the dominant configuration of social values, and for human relationships. It is more than mere irony that many of these people who took such pleasure in the past came to cherish a way of life that they personally or else their parents had made passé or irrelevant. Industrialists like the Rockefellers, inventors like Henry Ford who changed forever the way millions of Americans lived, and innovative manufacturers like the du Ponts acquired vast fortunes that facilitated collecting; but their nostalgia was just as genuine as that of humbler folk who cannot be accused of compensating for guilt or re-creating in a figurative "dollhouse" a mode of life that they had done much to destroy. It is also endlessly intriguing that a number of fundamentally anti-intellectual individuals, like Henry Ford, ceaselessly stressed the importance of popular or mass education in explaining the transformation of their collections as museums, villages, or as major gifts to institutions already in existence, such as universities or libraries.[15]

I I

IN SEVERAL respects books were among the easiest objects to collect because of their compact size (compared with antique furniture, paintings, and sculpture) and because a discerning eye was less essential. The early major collectors in the United States tended to be interested in Americana, though by no means exclusively so. William K. Bixby of St. Louis retired in 1905 at the age of forty-eight and began to seek rare books of all sorts. He slacked off for a period and then bought books and manuscripts at quite a clip from 1920 until 1929. His Americana included the original manuscripts of Thoreau's *Walden,* Major André's journal, and Aaron Burr's journal. Henry E. Huntington also started to collect books early in the century, and retired from business in 1910 in order to devote himself full time to the pursuit of Anglo-Americana, especially from the early modern period. Between 1911 and 1917 he spent $6 million on his library. After 1920, when it was moved to San Marino, California, his emphasis upon Americana deepened. He acquired the Stevens collection of eighteenth-century pamphlets bearing upon the American Revolution, for instance; and in 1922 his range of interest enlarged to include the whole area of the Great Plains, the Rockies, and the old Spanish Southwest. By 1927 Huntington's collection had been made accessible to researchers, and Max Farrand arrived to serve as first director of the fledgling institution.[16]

Although the great collections of Anglo-American books, maps, and manuscripts, such as William L. Clements's (an engineer who headed the Industrial Works of Bay City, Michigan), originated early in the twentieth century, they served as exemplars for subsequent accumulations of rare books and related materials that also landed, eventually, at the library of some major university. Tracy W. McGregor of Washington, D.C., for instance, relied heavily upon Randolph G. Adams, director of the Clements Library, for advice during the early 1930s; and he left his rare Americana to the University of Virginia at his death in 1938 because "not one of the great libraries of American history was then located in the South." Decentralization of resources played a significant part in the democratization of tradition in the United States during the 1930s and '40s.[17]

James Ford Bell, who built the huge milling empire known as General Mills, began like so many other affluent but amateurish bibliophiles with Shakespeare first folios, the poems of Robert Burns, some Caxton imprints, and various editions of *Poor Richard's Almanack*. During the 1930s and '40s, however, his focus sharpened and he concentrated upon the history of exploration, geographical knowledge, and the economic expansion of the Western world. Bell called book collecting "an invaluable aid to man's memory of events past and present." He gave that collection to his alma mater, the University of Minnesota, in 1953, and from then until his death in 1961 worked closely with the collection's curator to expand and enhance it.[18]

The most momentous phase in the collecting of Western Americana occurred during the second quarter of the twentieth century. For several decades late in the nineteenth century, however, Hubert Howe Bancroft had been the pioneer in this area, gathering more than sixty thousand books and pamphlets plus an immense number of manuscripts—a collection that was eventually acquired by the University of California and housed in a separate library on the Berkeley campus. Subsequently Henry Raup Wagner, a mining engineer, not only obtained works voraciously but performed an invaluable service by publishing thematic bibliographies from time to time. Yale University acquired his first "harvest" in 1916. Subsequent ones ended up at the Huntington Library.[19]

William R. Coe's interest was piqued when he acquired a cattle ranch in Wyoming; but over a period of forty years his enthusiasm widened to include the entire area of the Louisiana Purchase and the Pacific Northwest (including Alaska and the Canadian Northwest). He gave his treasures to Yale late in the 1940s. Everett D. Graff, a contemporary of Coe, embraced the entire trans-Mississippi West and read books as well as buying them. His have ended up at the Newberry Library in Chicago.[20]

Thomas W. Streeter, who began as a Boston lawyer but became a banker and financier in New York, retired from most of his business activities in 1939 to devote himself fully to his collection of Americana, which he started in 1920 at the age of twenty-seven: books, broadsides, pamphlets, and maps that ranged from the discovery of America to the origins of American aviation, and from the earliest settlements along the Atlantic coast to the last frontier in Alaska. The sale of his collection by Parke-Bernet at auction occurred over a three-year period (1966–69) following his death in 1965. It became the single greatest landmark in the purchase history of American books, both because of the sheer number and rarity of what he owned and the extraordinary purchase prices. It is a useful litmus of change to compare the spectacular prices achieved at the Streeter sales with the generally modest prices that were realized at Americana book sales during the mid- and later 1930s.[21]

Collecting American decorative arts, especially those objects that we associate with "high culture," tended to be dominated prior to the 1920s by men of old Yankee families, especially in Connecticut, though not necessarily men of phenomenal wealth.[22] Richard Townley Haines Halsey, known to his friends as R.T., was born in Elizabeth, New Jersey, to an affluent and conservative family with New England roots that sank back to 1630. Although his father bought him a seat on the New York Stock Exchange, Halsey's great love remained American history and art. Between 1899 and 1936 he produced a series of meticulous books and catalogues designed to accompany exhibits that drew heavily from his own extensive and eclectic collections: views of early New York on dark blue Staffordshire pottery (1899), colonial silver used in New York, New Jersey, and the South (1911), depictions of Franklin and his circle (1936), and English cartoons pertaining to the American Revolution (1939). He loaned important pieces of furniture and silver to the Hudson-Fulton show at the Metropolitan Museum of Art in 1909, and eleven years later he loaned about one third of the items for the Duncan Phyfe exhibition at the Met, which created a rage for Phyfe furniture that really has not diminished since. In 1914, when Halsey was elected a trustee of the Metropolitan, he promptly became chairman of its Committee on Decorative Arts, thereby solidifying a very intimate institutional relationship that continued until his death in 1942.[23]

In 1914, however, that committee scarcely qualified as a significant one in the Met's overall scheme of things. As recently as 1909 the museum did not own a single piece of American furniture, and the director believed that "the American arts and crafts were not worthy of exhibition," a view widely shared by top museum administrators in the United States at that time. Within a decade Halsey envisioned a special section of the museum devoted exclusively to American decorative art. In 1918 he explained to the chairman of the board how colonial plans and views might be used most effectively. He indulged in a bit of nativism quite characteristic of the day: "They would have intense interest to all Americans as well as to many of our people of foreign ancestry who are attempting to become good Americans." When the new Wing opened late in 1924, the consummation of Halsey's vision for the Met, he gave an address that was reprinted as the Introduction to *Homes of Our Ancestors.* One extract typifies a set of connections taken absolutely to heart by members of the American patriciate who wished to believe that a usable past inhered in material culture:

10.4   White pine New England "dresser" (c. 1740–70). Courtesy, The Henry Francis du Pont Winterthur Museum. Gift of the Webb family to the Museum.

Traditions are one of the integral assets of a country. Much of the America of today has lost sight of its traditions. . . . Many of our people are not cognizant of our traditions and the principles for which our fathers struggled and died. . . . A journey through this new American wing can not fail to revive those memories and bring with it a spirit of thankfulness that our great city at last has a setting for the traditions so dear to us and invaluable in the Americanization of many of our people to whom much of our history has been hidden in a fog of unenlightenment.[24]

Henry Francis du Pont of Delaware (1880–1969) is well known for having developed the most comprehensive single collection of early American furniture as well as related decorative arts, and for tastefully arranging them into rooms that were time- and place-specific. What few people recognize is the representative evolution of his interests as a collector. For at least five or six years after 1917 he collected English and Continental antique furnishings for his apartment in New York City. In 1923, however, he and his wife visited the summer home of Mr. and Mrs. J. Watson Webb at Shelburne, Vermont, and a few days after that the house of Henry Davis Sleeper at Gloucester, Massachusetts. A white pine country "dresser" made in New England during the mid-eighteenth century (fig. 10.4) that du Pont saw at the Webbs' so intrigued him that he promptly decided to acquire only Americana thereafter.[25]

He stocked what became his magnificent museum with pieces for which he paid record prices at auctions, but also by snagging bargains from private individuals on automobile forays into the countryside, especially in the mid-Atlantic region from the lower Hudson River Valley to Baltimore. A home that the du Ponts were planning to build at Southampton, Long Island, became a kind of "experiment station," with Sleeper acting as an adviser, in creating comfortable rooms where early Americana fit handsomely in rooms panelled with woodwork removed from colonial houses that were destined for destruction. Although these period rooms were designed to be eminently livable, du Pont and his lawyers created a Winterthur Corporation as early as 1930 whose purpose, eventually, would be to maintain the place in perpetuity as a museum. Du Pont's notions of both education and the public were highly elitist, but his sense of educational mission was entirely characteristic of his generation.[26]

Electra Havemeyer Webb, whose collection of early American country pieces so inspired du Pont, was his chronological contemporary. She too came from a family of great wealth (the Havemeyer sugar fortune), and there are uncanny parallels in the eventual institutionalization of their avocations. Although the concept of creating a museum for her Americana occurred in 1929, she did not act on the idea until 1947, when she and her husband began to purchase and move early Vermont structures, for which he had particular affection, to Shelburne (fig. 10.5). The museum opened in 1952: twenty-nine buildings situated on twenty acres.* She differed from du Pont in her special fondness for folk art, especially large pieces of folk sculpture, such as trade signs and weathervanes. She also felt perfectly comfortable ranging well into the nineteenth century, and even into objects that were not entirely handcrafted (a restriction that remained a principle of orthodoxy for du Pont).[27]

The matter of timing here is noteworthy. Although Electra Webb actually started acquiring Americana as early as 1907 at the age of eighteen, she did not emerge as an aggressively active collector until the 1930s when she became a client of Edith Halpert, one of the pioneering dealers in American folk art. That, in turn, reflects the relatively late "blooming" status of Webb's specialty. Not until the later 1920s did so-called primitives even begin to be regarded as worthy antiques, and consequently they remained relatively inexpensive until well after World War II. Another notable figure, Elie Nadelman, the innovative and modernistic sculptor, married Mrs. Joseph A. Flannery in 1919. Between 1923 and 1938 they acquired a charming personal collection of American folk art; and they made their New York home accessible as a private museum as early as 1926. Four years later Holger

---

*By 1987 the Shelburne Museum owned 180,000 objects and artifacts housed in thirty-six structures.

10.5 Electra Havemeyer Webb at the Champlain Valley Fair, September
1947. Courtesy of J. Watson Webb, Jr., and the Shelburne Museum, Inc.,
Shelburne, Vermont.

Cahill organized an influential folk art exhibition at the Newark Museum, for which he drew heavily upon the personal collections of the
Nadelmans and Hamilton Easter Field. Simultaneously Abby Aldrich
Rockefeller commenced her superb collection of "naive" art, mostly
paintings, but some prints, needlework, trade signs, and weathervanes
as well.[28]

How folksy could you possibly get? The answer is "very" if you were
sufficiently wealthy and willing to be regarded as not merely eccentric
but an absolute oddball. Henry Chapman Mercer of Doylestown, Pennsylvania, had several antiquarian passions, including ceramic tiles and
pottery. Deeply influenced by the Victorian arts and crafts movement,
Mercer envisioned in 1898 the construction of a tile works that could
supply hand-designed decorative tiles for homes and institutions all
over the world. Meanwhile he also had a passion for local history and
archaeology, became a principal patron of the Bucks County Historical
Society, and gathered a phenomenal collection of pre-industrial tools
and implements that reflected the gradual transformation of agriculture and artisanal crafts in the nineteenth-century United States. In
1916 he built in Doylestown a six-storey reinforced-concrete museum
to accommodate his large and ungainly harvest of thirty thousand objects that ranged from tiny tools and toys to huge wagons and sleighs.*
It would be almost half a century before outdoor villages and museums

*There is a similar museum, except for its "un-American" focus, built at Gloucester,
Massachusetts, in 1926–29. John Hays Hammond, Jr., a prolific inventor, designed a
medieval-style castle and museum overlooking the Atlantic Ocean to house himself as

began to catch up with his vision of the importance of man the tool-maker and user, man the source of production and nourishment. The history of everyday life became trendy during the 1980s; but Mercer was well "into it" almost a century earlier.[29]

If we ask why these people collected, the answers are even more diverse than what they sought to possess. Begin with the most obvious reason, sheer love of country: old-fashioned patriotism that often verged upon chest-thumping chauvinism. We find it, for example, in a fascinating "open letter" to John D. Rockefeller, Jr., written by the editor of *The Americana Collector*. It is an unabashed appeal for the creation of a Rockefeller Foundation of Bibliographical and Historical Research because "such an institution would become one of our richest assets for a patriotic people. Our heritage from the heroic past must be preserved as continued guidance and inspiration to ourselves and to all mankind." The same spirit animated one of Stephen Vincent Benét's most striking ballads, written in 1927, "American Names." It opens with the line "I have fallen in love with American names," and the fourth stanza contains both the geographical range desired and the nemesis being rejected:

> *I will fall in love with a Salem tree*
> *And a rawhide quirt from Santa Cruz,*
> *I will get me a bottle of Boston sea*
> *And a blue-gum nigger to sing me blues.*
> *I am tired of loving a foreign muse.*[30]

Second, some devotees expressed overt sentiments of anti-modernism and of nostalgia for a simpler way of life that seemed all but lost. When Joseph Hergesheimer, the prominent novelist, wrote "Of Ultimate Antiques" in 1928, he evoked a "gentle voice, the voice of a tradition"; he spoke of "a palpable tradition of human dignity"; and he explained that he wished to create, "in a house eminently suitable for it, the spirit and appearance of an America definitely lost in reality."[31]

Third, there was the sheer pleasure that certain people, commonly called "junk snuppers," derived from the quest itself: poking around in musty shops looking for surprises, knocking on the doors of total strangers who lived in venerable farmhouses along rural roads, making outrageously low offers for possessions that the owners simply took for granted. They weren't antiques; just "our stuff—been in the family forever." Some snuppers were city people who had recently bought an old country house themselves and wanted to furnish it inexpensively with appropriate pieces from the area. Some loved the thrill of finding bargains at a country auction. One anonymous writer, obsessed with

---

well as his collection of four hundred–plus Roman, medieval, and Renaissance artifacts: tombstones, wrought-iron beds, delicately carved chests, macabre paintings, Gothic tapestries, sheet music, etc. (NYT, Oct. 9, 1988, p. A58.)

early American mantels and hardware in particular, salivated over the "solid, simple, dignified and lovingly wrought craftsmanship of a hundred years ago"; and he or she then acknowledged a compulsion to be authentic: "the selfish desire to keep my house in period, to have genuine details instead of imitations."[32]

Fourth, although the quest for early American objects—an activity popularly dubbed "antiqueering" in 1924—could stimulate stiff competition and even bitter rivalry, it could also be conducive to camaraderie: comparing notes and triumphs, exchanging tips, and generally having fun with friends who shared an enthusiasm in common. George Horace Lorimer, editor of the *Saturday Evening Post,* was just such an enthusiast. He loved early American silver and furniture, glass and flasks, carved eagles, and Navajo rugs. He eventually gave the best of his Americana to the Philadelphia Museum of Art, and the remainder sold at auction for more than $1 million. What Lorimer liked best about "antiqueering," however, was friendship. Along with Joseph Hergesheimer and Kenneth Roberts, he loved to scour the countryside by car, especially the area around Lancaster, Pennsylvania. Like a fishing expedition when the fish just wouldn't bite, the trio always had a grand time together anyway, and reminisced about their many jaunts as junk snuppers. Roberts even wrote a satirical spoof that made their "antiquamania" sound zanier than it actually was.[33] The surname of specious Professor Kilgallen referred to spirits they consumed despite Prohibition, as well as the high spirits of the chase.

Some of these collegial connections resulted in organizations that have endured to this day. In 1884 nine men met in New York to form a club that would have as its object the "literary study and promotion of the arts entering into the production of books." The Grolier Club grew from those origins, and it has had an important influence upon book collecting, bibliography, and American libraries.[34]

Henry Watson Kent was a Bostonian with deep ties to Norwich, Connecticut, and for thirty-five years an administrator at the Metropolitan Museum of Art devoted to American decorative arts. In 1910 Kent, who personally knew most of the prominent collectors, proposed the creation of a small society of reputable collectors (no junk snuppers) to be called the Walpole Society.* Most of the original members, though not all, were New Englanders. They liked to call themselves "students of the early years of Colonial history," and what they did several times annually was visit restored houses, carefully scrutinize collections and their provenance, dine and drink well, and congratulate one another on their superb taste. Members included George Francis Dow, Henry Francis du Pont, R. T. H. Halsey, Norman Morrison Isham, Henry Wat-

---

*More specialized groups came a generation later. The Pewter Collectors Club of America, for instance, founded in 1934, sponsored major exhibits at Boston's Museum of Fine Arts in 1935 and at the Metropolitan Museum in 1940.

son Kent, Thomas Winthrop Streeter, and Thomas Tileston Waterman, the historian of early American architecture who made himself indispensable as a consultant to Henry Francis du Pont.[35]

A fifth stimulus, scarcely surprising, was commercial. During the mid-1920s Americans had money to invest. They did so in diverse ways—some wise and many foolish. But by 1924 the word had spread widely: "Antiques, you know, are an investment first, a money outlay second. . . . You can always resell at a profit—big profit," according to the *Saturday Evening Post,* with its circulation then at more than two and one-quarter million readers. Even Joseph Hergesheimer, whose motives were primarily sentimental and patriotic, acknowledged publicly that "I began, of necessity, actually to consider antiques in the light of an investment."[36]

During the mid- and later 1920s the spurt of popular writing concerned with collecting American antiques was so pervasive that one could virtually experience the phenomenon vicariously. It is difficult to say with assurance, but many essays written for mass circulation magazines seemed to touch all possible bases—appreciation, cynicism, flippancy, reverence, humor at the expense of dealers and pretentious collectors, but ultimately patriotism. No matter how one felt about a fad that was "fast becoming a national pastime," the reader could eventually find a congenial point of view.[37]

Ultimately, however, the cultural significance of this craze is that it demonstrates the emergence by 1923–28 of an American aesthetic. The meaning of that transformation appears with striking clarity when we compare the basic motives behind enthusiasm for Americana during the 1880s and '90s with those that dominated the next generation. As late as 1908, when George Sheldon wrote his "Note to Visitors" as a preface to the *Catalogue* for Memorial Hall in the Pocumtuck Valley, he explained with pride that "not a single article is here preserved on account of its artistic qualities. The collection is founded on purely historical lines and is the direct memorial of the inhabitants of this valley, both Indian and Puritan." Tables on which important people had written their works or signed momentous documents seem to have been especially prized: the cherry table used by Noah Webster when he compiled his dictionary was cherished by the New Haven Colony Historical Society even more than the two-hundred-year-old writing table used by President Timothy Dwight of Yale. In 1887 it was deemed newsworthy that a man in Reimersburg, Pennsylvania, owned a table and four chairs that had once belonged to William Penn. Eleven years later the table on which General Grant wrote the terms of surrender in 1865 elicited even more interest.[38]

It generated considerable curiosity in 1887 when a man who owned the stovepipe hat worn by Abraham Lincoln en route from Springfield to his first inauguration refused to sell it even though many believed that it properly belonged in the National Museum in Washington, D.C.

The exhibits of historical "relics" at the Columbian Exposition held at Chicago in 1893 highlighted their connections with historic figures rather than their aesthetic qualities. The same was true of bidders' interests a decade later at an auction held in Baltimore of Americana owned by Dr. William H. Crim.[39]

Within little more than another decade, however, Wallace Nutting began to preach a gospel far more concerned with stylistic simplicity and "fine lines" than with social and political history as the primary rationale for possessing Americana. Late in 1924, just after the American Wing of the Met opened, a major collector named Louis Guerineau Myers wrote lovingly of the interest and importance of local clues in ascribing origins. Before launching into a lengthy statement of particulars, he explained that "in the course of time a sense of structural as well as other values is developed in one who lives with such things that no amount of academic research could impart. In this way I feel that these things were made in our native workshops."[40]

One anonymous writer in the *Saturday Evening Post* (surely Hergesheimer or Roberts) called attention to "the solid, simple, dignified and lovingly wrought craftsmanship" of early Americana; and a few months later a frequent contributor on the subject of colonial objects made several widely shared observations in writing about the "collecting vision": first, that museums placed their treasures more prominently "when the wood has set the stamp of Colonial rather than Dutch or English make"; and second, praising the "present desire for the Pilgrim era, the early American, the simple," because it had the effect of "putting a quietus on overrestoration by putting a premium on original condition, simple finishes, bare wood."[41] All of these attributes contributed to the new American aesthetic of the 1920s.

Its manifestations appeared, moreover, in areas well beyond antique collecting. In 1921 the *New York Times* praised Monticello as a work of art, and three years later Fiske Kimball published an influential essay concerning the artistic significance of Monticello. Also in 1924, John Tasker Howard published *Our American Music: Three Hundred Years of It.* And four years after that Kimball (by then director of the Philadelphia Museum of Art) published a history, *American Architecture*, and Thomas Eddy Tallmadge brought out *The Story of Architecture in America.* * The rationale articulated on behalf of historic preservation increasingly referred to "colonial beauty," or "history and beauty."[42]

In the realm of outdoor sites, the private sector tended to be several decades ahead of government in responding to this impulse. An empha-

---

*At the Columbian Exposition held at Chicago in 1893, twenty-one of the thirty-nine state buildings erected were in some sense early American in style. By the close of World War I, even the design of U.S. steamships had been affected. Passenger areas were likely to have colonial revival design. The smoking room of the S.S. *Hawkeye State*, for example, had a mantelpiece that replicated one at Mount Vernon.

sis upon the "picturesque" appeared frequently in the early twentieth century in publications of the American Scenic and Historic Preservation Society, or in the restoration of Fruitlands (1915–30), a short-lived utopian community from the 1840s that lingered on a lovely pastoral slope outside of Harvard, Massachusetts. Outdoor historical museums had their American genesis in 1925 at Decorah, Iowa, when an association of Norwegian-Americans assembled a group of settlers' cabins and opened the "village" to the public. By contrast, the National Park Service continued well into the 1930s to make its restoration decisions on traditional grounds: a building could qualify only if it had been associated with some important historic individual or event. Aesthetic criteria were appreciated but could not alone provide legitimacy.[43]

A comparable phenomenon occurred among painters, art critics, those who ran art galleries, and those who collected art—despite the inevitable internationalism of all four endeavors after 1913. An artist and critic as conservative as Kenyon Cox, who had customarily looked to Europe for criteria of judgment, began in 1911 to praise "the American school" (referring to such artists as Childe Hassam and J. Alden Weir) precisely because they were "singularly old-fashioned." Even though they had studied in Europe, they developed distinctive styles of their own. In 1932 an artist with values very different from Cox's gave an address to the Federation of Arts in which aspects of an American aesthetic were advocated with more fervent national chauvinism. "No American art can come to those who do not live an American life," Thomas Hart Benton declared, "who do not have an American psychology, and who cannot find in America justification of their lives."[44]

Duncan Phillips, an elegant collector, primarily though not exclusively of modern art, opened his Washington, D.C., home to the public as a museum in October 1921. Although he was immensely fond of various European artists, he declared in 1922 that his cardinal principle would be "to make the gallery as American as possible." He became an early and bold patron of Milton Avery, Arthur Dove, John Graham, and various other contemporaries. From 1905 until 1917 Alfred Stieglitz ran a gallery known as 291 in Manhattan. In 1925 he opened the Intimate Gallery; but five years later, significantly, he started An American Place gallery, and it retained that distinctive name until his death in 1946.[45]

Sellers of American antiques and those responsible for certain sorts of art galleries not only internalized this American aesthetic themselves, but did much to spread it. Israel Sack, who by 1930 had become the pre-eminent dealer in colonial furniture, used to say of an unusually fine piece of early American craftsmanship: "It speaks to me." Edith Halpert and Holger Cahill, two influential figures in the world of Americana during the 1920s and '30s who helped to shape some of the most significant collections, valued the aesthetic qualities of an object far above any documentary or historical signifi-

cance that it might have. Halpert's Downtown Gallery began mod-
estly in Greenwich Village in 1926, and for many years it remained
one of the few completely dedicated to Americana, American artists,
and the best in modern American art.[46]

I I I

H A L P E R T and one of the artists she "handled," Charles
Sheeler, are especially interesting because they exemplify so forcefully
that traditionalism and modernism were not mutually exclusive. Halpert and Sheeler not only valued both impulses, but successfully connected the two and used each one to reinforce the other. Both of them
believed that early American handicrafts and folk art anticipated trends
in contemporary design; and in 1931, when Halpert wrote a press
release to introduce her new American Folk Art Gallery, she observed
that "it is this relationship and continuity which is being stressed" by
both of her galleries.* Halpert became a major source of folk art for
Abby Aldrich Rockefeller, and in 1935 Halpert supervised the installation of Mrs. Rockefeller's collection at the Ludwell-Paradise House in
Colonial Williamsburg. Holger Cahill wrote the manual for hostess-
guides to that exhibit. Connections were closely knit.[47]

Halpert also arranged for Sheeler to go to Williamsburg for three
months during the winter of 1935–36 to "document" for the Rockefellers, particularly with photographs, what was being done there.
Sheeler's efforts to combine avant-garde developments in the international art world with indigenous artistic traditions, however, dated back
almost a quarter of a century. Sheeler had known Henry Chapman
Mercer ever since 1910, when he rented a farm cottage from him in
Doylestown. Sheeler loved early American furniture and handicrafts,
and had owned various examples of both. His friends, Mr. and Mrs.
Walter Arensberg, owned an intriguing mixture of modern art and
colonial furniture (like Edith Halpert, Elie Nadelman, and later Joseph
Hirshhorn); and in August 1917 Sheeler wrote to Arensberg urging him
and his wife to spend a summer weekend in Doylestown. "We might
inquire of Mr. Mercer if he can tell us where any early American
furniture is to be found. Now will you come?"[48]

At first glance Sheeler's temperament seems to abound with
strange contradictions. Although he was genuinely devoted to early
American subjects and traditions for his work, the new technology

---

*These views were also shared by Duncan Phillips in forming his eclectic collection in
Washington, D.C., between 1918 and 1966. His testamentary statement included this
sentence: "It has always been the policy of The Collection to stress the continuities of art,
the evolution of tradition by experience and the necessity to test the innovations of the
present hour by reference to the sources in the past which have stood the test of time."
(Marjorie Phillips, *Duncan Phillips and His Collection* [Boston, 1970], 305.)

and industrialization also fascinated him. He admired Cézanne and
Picasso above other artists, and made caustic comments about such
American predecessors as Bingham, Homer, and Eakins. As an artist
he is best remembered for exploring with great precision the form of
factories, cranes, oil refineries, and locomotives. Yet Sheeler's interiors (painted and photographed) are filled with handmade objects:
country and Shaker pieces, Windsor chairs, pottery, early fabrics and
woven things. He once said of Shaker handicrafts: "I don't like things
because they are old, but in spite of it." The implication was that
form mattered above all, yet other evidence suggests that history as
well as the aesthetic values of an older America had a powerful hold
upon him. Hence his several paintings of the Ephrata Cloister in
Pennsylvania and various Shaker buildings, mostly done around 1934,
and a series of works made at Williamsburg in 1936: oils of the Governor's Palace and Bassett Hall (a mid-eighteenth-century house
where the Rockefellers stayed), along with careful drawings done in
Conté crayon of early American kitchens.[49]

Sheeler comfortably combined his interests in cubism and American
vernacular structures. Fundamentally, forms and objects from the past
could serve contemporary artistic endeavors. He shared, along with his
good friend William Carlos Williams, a vision of "living American history." By contrast, Childe Hassam (who was twenty-four years older
than Sheeler) found early American homes, barns, churches, and quilts
so appealing because he felt a preference for the values and social
conditions of colonial times. (Hassam's father, incidentally, had been a
collector of Americana.)[50]

Several other American artists shared this enthusiasm for an American
aesthetic, but their motives may have been less diverse and run less deep
than Sheeler's and Hassam's. N. C. Wyeth and Norman Rockwell were
skillful illustrators who responded to commissions that in turn derived
from popular culture and what some publisher or editor believed would
help to sell books and magazines. Hence Wyeth's *Thanksgiving Day*
(1921) or Rockwell's "The Kiss," a sweet cover illustration for the *Saturday Evening Post* in which a young man (with a clarinet under his arm),
circa 1775, bestows a kiss upon a willing colonial maiden.[51]

As a young man, Howard Chandler Christy illustrated lush editions of
Longfellow's *The Courtship of Miles Standish* (1903) and *Evangeline*
(1905). Between 1908 and 1915 Christy returned to his boyhood home in
Ohio, installed a cannon, played reveille, raised the American flag every
morning, and generally felt considerable nostalgia for the ceremonies as
well as the routine of military life. During the mid-1920s he hoped to
paint a series of twelve pictures to be used in a new monthly publication
of the American Legion—the originals to be hung at the Legion's national headquarters in Indianapolis.* "There will be romance in all of

*The intended subjects included a Puritan girl; a Puritan boy who has just killed an Indian;
Pocahontas saving Captain John Smith at Jamestown; "colonial days"; Captain John C.

them," Christy said. "I'm always seeing the romance in all that stuff and that is what I like to paint." Early in August 1945, at the age of seventy-two, he happily returned to Columbus, Ohio, for the unveiling of *The Signing of the Treaty at Greenville* in the statehouse on the occasion of the sesquicentennial of that important event in his state's history.[52]

I shall have much more to say about Gutzon Borglum and Mount Rushmore in chapter fifteen. In this context, however, it is necessary to note that the Danish-American sculptor was a chronological contemporary of the artists we have been discussing, and shared their nationalism, their love of American history, and their determination to use art to enhance patriotism. In 1937, after twelve years of intermittent personality conflicts and controversies, Borglum declared: "If America wants a product of art, if America wants an interpretation of Washington's character, of Jefferson's intelligence, of Lincoln's vision and soul, of Theodore Roosevelt's force and modernness—then she must trust to the judgment, insight and understanding of an artist." Despite his appeals for complete control of the project, he did not succeed in getting a great hall placed within a man-made cave in the Black Hills. Borglum never conceived of anything on a modest scale; but in this instance his notion had a certain attractive logic. He believed that art with a historical theme should be related by cultural information to the civilization that produced it. That was what he wanted to display in his great hall.[53]

Commemorative sculpture somehow managed to be controversial more often than historical art—perhaps because of the subject matter, but also because it usually had been commissioned as a public monument of some sort, frequently involving citizens' dollars. Borglum never completed his bas-relief memorial to the Confederacy at Stone Mountain, near Atlanta, Georgia, because of his long absences from the site, his temperamental nature, and his demands for money above and beyond what the contract specified.[54]

Another wild contretemps, unrelated to Borglum, occurred from 1920 until 1924 when the president and trustees of Washington and Lee University decided to enlarge (really replace) the Lee Memorial Chapel in Lexington, Virginia, because it no longer could accommodate the growing student body of the college where Lee himself had been president from 1865 until 1870. Lee was buried in a crypt of that chapel, and the sculpture of him in mortal repose above the crypt by Edward Valentine had been deemed a sacred shrine ever since its dedication in 1883 (fig. 10.6). Mrs. Maurice Moore of Lynchburg, Virginia, a member of the Mayflower Society and several other patriotic and Confederate organizations such as the United Daughters of the Confederacy, did an extraordinary job of political mobilization in order to keep the chapel unchanged. Mr. and Mrs. Woodrow Wilson took Mrs. Moore's side; and

---

Frémont's expedition into Oregon and California; California days of 1849; Lewis and Clark at the Columbia River canyon.

10.6 The Lee Memorial Chapel, Washington and Lee University, early in the twentieth century. Courtesy of Washington and Lee University, Lexington, Virginia. The Miley Collection.

she received a letter from the secretary to President Coolidge that declared: "In a sense this shrine belongs not alone to the South but to the Nation at large." Congressman S. O. Bland of Virginia told Mrs. Moore that he had last visited the chapel in 1922. "When I entered the building," he wrote, "I felt that I was on holy ground. I believe everyone else going there feels the same way." Still another correspondent referred to the chapel as "the South's most sacred shrine."[55]

Those who appreciated that the university needed a larger auditorium for convocations were generally sympathetic but unpersuaded. Frances Parkinson Keyes insisted that "the demands for the present and the future should not, and I believe need not, conflict with the cherishing of the past." Perhaps the most intriguing response, however, came from Philip A. Bruce, a prominent historian of Virginia, a vigorous conservative, and one who cared deeply about the Confederate cause. Bruce wondered whether a new and vastly enlarged mausoleum might not be

> more in harmony with the character and fame of General Lee than the present very homely structure. Lee did not consent to the design of the present building because he considered it to be peculiarly appropriate, but because the poverty of the hour permitted of nothing better. If all the visitors who will flock to this shrine in the future were to be restricted to Southerners who understood the impoverishment of those times, the retention of the present structure would be most advisable, but as time goes on, and convenient public highways to the North are constructed, a thousand tourists will go to Lexington from that quarter to the

five hundred who will come from the South. The impression of the great world at large of General Lee in death would not be deepened by the sight of the present plain—I might almost say humble—building. It would simply arouse a sense of *pity* in the foreign mind, which would be lacking essentially in sympathy. My own idea was that the chapel should be taken down and reconstructed elsewhere on the grounds as the most sacred souvenir of a very sad period, but that, in its old place, the admirers of the hero should be permitted to erect a noble building more commensurate with the greatness of his achievements, and the estimation in which his memory is held by the people of the world.[56]

With the support of the Association for the Preservation of Virginia Antiquities, and despite the opposition of the General Convention of the U.D.C., officially adopted at three consecutive annual meetings (1920–22), Mrs. Moore and the Virginia U.D.C. prevailed. Early in 1924 the trustees of Washington and Lee withdrew their plan for an elaborate new memorial chapel honoring Robert E. Lee. As a Lynchburg attorney told Mary Moore: "A champion of tradition you are and I do honor to the Conqueror!!"[57]

By contrast, doing honor to Abraham Lincoln proceeded without controversy. Early in 1911 Congress passed an act providing for the construction of a monument to Lincoln in Washington, D.C., and created a commission to determine a suitable location and design. Twenty months later that commission submitted its report. Meanwhile, in 1912, a bronze statue of Lincoln standing, done by Daniel Chester French, was dedicated at Lincoln, Nebraska. It was a highly successful work, with the Gettysburg Address inscribed on granite as a backdrop; and its appeal made it virtually inevitable that French would be commissioned to model a seated Lincoln for the Memorial in Washington. (French also happened to be a close friend of Henry Bacon, the architect who designed the Memorial.)

Late in 1914 French received the commission. In order to avoid any conflict of interest he resigned as chairman of the Commission of Fine Arts, whose ultimate approval would be required. He completed a small model of the seated Lincoln during the summer of 1915. French used a life mask that had been made by Leonard Volk, and completed a seven-foot model by October 1916. All sorts of problems arose because the electric lights within the Memorial created bizarre effects on Lincoln's face. Although these problems were not fully resolved until 1927, the Memorial was dedicated on May 30, 1922, just when the fracas concerning the Lee Chapel was heating up.* The seated Lincoln enjoyed immediate approval, and French explained that what he had

---

*In 1930 a Lincoln Memorial Commission rejected a proposal to construct a "symbolic building" in Springfield in memory of Lincoln, and favored instead the restoration of all buildings in Illinois that were associated with the life of Lincoln.

sought "to convey was the mental and physical strength of the great President and his confidence in his ability to carry the thing through to a successful finish."[58]

ALTHOUGH we cannot say what the silent, brooding Lincoln ponders, we do know that during these years conservative political leaders, irrespective of party allegiance, invoked American traditions in support of their policies and appeals. That had indeed been the point of Lincoln's play upon mystic chords of memory in his first inaugural address: to conserve the Union. In 1912, after Henry Cabot Lodge offered a major speech opposing the heated issue of initiative, referendum, and recall of judges, Barrett Wendell told him that that speech and another one Lodge had given recently at Raleigh would "last as long as our traditions last." The man whom Lodge helped make President in 1920, Warren G. Harding, asserted: "I like the dependableness of tradition." During the 1920s the uses of Americana could be utterly banal as well as occasionally inspirational.[59]

These were also years when history- and hero-oriented organizations appeared and disappeared, or more commonly, redefined their missions and underwent transformations. The Abraham Lincoln Association, for example, known originally as the Lincoln Centennial Association and based in Springfield, had been organized in 1909 to promote the centennial of Lincoln's birth. From then until 1924 its principal function was the annual observance of Lincoln's Birthday. In 1924 its leaders reorganized the association to undertake activities that would be broader in nature: "to preserve and make more readily accessible the landmarks associated with his life; and actively to encourage, promote and aid the collection and dissemination of authentic information regarding all phases of his life and career."[60]

The National Association of State War History Organizations first met in 1920 and within a year had representation from twelve states plus the participation of Eben Putnam, Historian of the American Legion. In 1921 a Patriotic Societies Conference was held at St. Louis for the informal exchange of information and ideas. After a decade of highly visible activity, however, a number of these patriotic and ancestral organizations suffered from declining membership, a crisis of purposeful identity, or both (fig. 10.7). Several of them, like the D.A.R., became the butts of hostile or satirical humor. In 1932, just when the D.A.R. got involved in a brouhaha with Grant Wood because of his droll painting *Daughters of Revolution,* the Colonial Dames of America in Virginia rededicated itself to new programs, an action inspired in part by the restoration of Colonial Williamsburg. A year later, on George Washington's Birthday, the Virginia Society, Sons of the Revolution, and its rival, the Virginia Society, Sons of the American Revolution, recognized the folly of rivalry at a time of declining membership and resources; so they held a joint celebration at the John Marshall Hotel in Richmond.

10.7   Daughters of the American Colonists, Pocahontas Chapter of Virginia (1920s). Courtesy of the Virginia Historical Society.

Stringfellow Barr gave the principal address, titled "George Washington, Conservative Revolutionary."[61]

Patriotism was not on the wane, in fact, but it did undergo reorientation (and hence reorganization) in several key respects. Writers of various sorts—essayists, social critics, biographers, popular as well as scholarly historians, and journalists—all played an essential role in this process.

I V

FROM the appearance of its very first issue in January 1924 until October 1941, H. L. Mencken's monthly, *The American Mercury,* included a section called "Americana." It really served as a kind of miscellany of charming trivia that were more often irreverent than patriotic. Here is an example that Mencken labelled "Début of a new crime in the land of Blue Laws, as reported by the Waterbury *Republican*":

> Amelia Moses, eighteen, was arrested yesterday by Lieutenants Timothy Hickey and Milton MacMullen of the Detective Bureau, charged with being in danger of falling into vice.

That suggests just one end of the spectrum, and perhaps the less representative one. Constance Rourke, on the other hand, published an essay in *The Nation,* called "Traditions for Young People," in which she professed her faith that young people "can be permitted to share in the current movement toward a discovery of the American past, particularly in its concern with our cultural traditions." Such sentiments may have been more widely shared in the heartland of America than along the more jaded Eastern seaboard.[62]

During the years from 1919 until about 1936, some Americans became increasingly self-conscious about the words they used and wondered just how distinctive they were. Once again, a trans-generational contrast is apparent, and it demonstrates in yet another way the emergence of an American aesthetic. Back in 1887 the president of the American Association of Writers told that organization's third annual convention (forty people meeting at Indianapolis) that the increasing use of dialect in American literature was an unfortunate development. He insisted that the use of folk idiom revealed "a total lack of patriotism in our literary life" and urged authors to achieve a "nobler strain of art" in describing the United States.[63]

H. L. Mencken's truly remarkable compilation, *The American Language: An Inquiry into the Development of English in the United States,* first appeared in 1919, went through four editions by 1936, and volumes of the *Supplement* started to emerge in 1945. As Edmund Wilson observed in a shrewd essay prompted by the fourth edition, "the work has been brought to maturity." Wilson also declared that the first edition in 1919 had served as a herald of a new phase in the development of American cultural studies. Meanwhile a journal called *American Speech* was started in 1925; and that same year Sir William Craigie, one of the compilers of the *Oxford English Dictionary,* sailed for the United States to begin work on a dictionary of "American."[64]

The appearance of an American aesthetic in imaginative literature at this time has by now received careful attention from others. Willa Cather did not care for change and felt strong sympathies for those, like herself, who were tradition-oriented. She wrote her own spare and unsentimental sort of elegy to the passing of the pioneer, and evoked moods of remembrance in her novels *The Professor's House* (1925) and *My Mortal Enemy* (1926). Stephen Vincent Benét's first venture into Americana was called "The Ballad of William Sycamore, 1790–1871" (1922), a poem that revealed his affinity with robust national origins and his belief that the values of that formative era had not dissolved. One assessment found in it "the incarnation of the pioneer spirit set to perfect American transposition of the old ballad music." Benét published *Spanish Bayonet* early in 1926, a well-received historical novel, and later that year he began *John Brown's Body,* which was destined to become the most popular American epic poem since Longfellow's *Hiawatha* and *Evangeline.* In 1930 John Dos Passos published *The 42nd Parallel,* the first novel in his *U.S.A.* trilogy, collected as such in 1938, which also included *1919* (1932) and *The Big Money* (1936).

10.8 John R. Dos Passos (c. 1935), gelatin silver print. Courtesy of the National Portrait Gallery, Smithsonian Institution, Washington, D.C.

Taken together they offer a panoramic view of social change and commercialization in the United States during the first three decades of the twentieth century (fig. 10.8). Although harsher and more critical than Benét, Dos Passos shared his contemporary's belief that American history and traditions not only could but should be the stuff of indigenous literature.[65]

Academic respectability for native writing was a gradual achievement but, not coincidentally, occurred exactly in phase with all of the other rhythms that we have noted. The first course in American literature given at an American university was taught at Princeton in 1872; but that signifies very little. During the half century that followed 1876, only four Ph.D. dissertations prepared in the United States dealt in any way with North American literature. Meanwhile, *The Cambridge History of American Literature* appeared in four volumes between 1917 and 1921. F. O. Matthiessen, who shared Edith Wharton's experience of growing up utterly ignorant of American literature, began to read American authors for the first time while doing graduate study at Oxford in 1923. For the rest of the decade he would be influenced by the critical essays of Van Wyck Brooks, and we can trace a trajectory across a full generation that is truly symptomatic. Brooks had observed in 1920—responding to Stuart Pratt Sherman's rhetorical essay "Is There Anything to Be Said for Literary Tradition?"—that Ralph Waldo Emerson had proclaimed the only genuine American tradition: trampling on tradition. Within a decade Brooks had changed his tune; and well before his suicide in 1950 Matthiessen would write that "we can take no tradition for granted, we must keep repossessing the past for ourselves if we are not to lose it altogether."[66]

Meanwhile Vernon L. Parrington published his huge multi-volume work, *Main Currents in American Thought,* between 1927 and 1930. Two new journals appeared: *The New England Quarterly* in 1928 and *American Literature* in 1929. During the early 1930s Lewis Mumford shifted his stance from "our past still lies ahead of us" to vigorous paeans concerning the value of our "heritage"; and Constance Rourke reiterated in several formats that "'Tradition, even in new literatures, has always formed a basic soil; ours is rich enough if it can only be fully seen."[67] Carl Van Doren, who taught American literature at Columbia from 1911 until 1934, thereafter rounded out the remaining sixteen years of his life with a striking series of popular works in American cultural and political history, including his prize-winning *Benjamin Franklin* (1938), *The Secret History of the American Revolution* (1941), *Mutiny in January* (1943), and *The Great Rehearsal* (1948), concerned with writing and ratifying the United States Constitution.

Books about American history enjoyed considerable vogue during the second quarter of the twentieth century. In some instances the bestsellers were iconoclastic and did not fear offending some small portion of the population with differing ideological commitments. Claude Bowers, for example, a skillful journalist, did well with *Jefferson and Hamilton* (1925) and *The Tragic Era* (1929), concerning Reconstruction after the Civil War, because he took highly polemical positions: pro-Jefferson and anti-Republican. When James Truslow Adams published *The Living Jefferson* in 1936, he received warm fan mail. William Allen White, himself an opinionated newspaperman from Kansas, called the book "a gorgeous job," and told Adams that he was performing "a great service to your country by illuminating our past. We cannot understand the present—much less plan for the future, unless we comprehend with some degree of intelligence the actual meaning of the past."[68]

For others the appeal of American history hinged more upon the desire to reverse, or at least challenge, long-standing stereotypes concerning our cultural inferiority or disadvantages in comparison with Europe. They did so in diverse, often contradictory ways, however. Writing in 1927, for example, Carl Becker made a virtue of our supposed shallowness. "We have not the racial and religious antagonisms of Europe," he wrote (Al Smith had not yet been nominated for the presidency, and there was no civil rights movement at that time!). "We lie less uneasy under the heavy weight of tradition." Matthew Josephson returned from Europe at the very same time, determined to find out for himself whether American civilization was utterly devoid of texture.

I was full of enthusiasm for my mission. Our historic expatriates, Nathaniel Hawthorne and Henry James, had long contended that it was impossible to create a good literature in the United States because there was no aristocracy here; there were no quaint folk customs and no picturesque ruins. Well, I would see the purple slabs of Chicago for myself, and the mechanical monuments Henry Ford had built at River Rouge.[69]

A particular enthusiasm for American biography developed with growing intensity during the years after 1912, but especially during the 1920s. William Cabell Bruce (1860–1946), who came from an old Tidewater family and served in the U.S. Senate (1923–29), was decidedly not a "debunker." He dealt equitably with Benjamin Franklin in two different books and with John Randolph of Roanoke in two volumes (1923). Bruce hailed from an area with a rich sense of tradition; and that is what he liked to stress, especially when he gave occasional speeches on biographical subjects. Gamaliel Bradford (1863–1932) came from an equally venerable Massachusetts family: he happened to be a direct descendant of Governor William Bradford of the Plymouth Colony. Bradford enjoyed considerable commercial success with *Lee the American* (1912) because Southerners viewed it as a long-awaited sign of Northern understanding and respect. He followed swiftly with *Confederate Portraits* (1912), *Union Portraits* (1916), *Portraits of American Women* (1917), *American Portraits, 1875–1900* (1922), which was so well received that it went through six editions, and *Damaged Souls* (1923), which examined a very odd and somewhat motley assortment of personalities who could not collectively qualify for any pantheon of heroes owing to rather diverse reasons: Benedict Arnold, P. T. Barnum, John Brown, Aaron Burr, Ben Butler, Tom Paine, and John Randolph.

Contemporaries who wrote about this vogue ran through various (and sometimes contradictory) reasons for praising the trend. First and most predictably, national chauvinism. "When the books are biographies of Americans," one man boasted in 1929, "something even more sacred than mass approval attaches to them; they are part of the great American system, one more reason for patriotic enthusiasm." The author vacillated, however, between finding in all of these books evidence of cultural cohesion (the existence of an American type) and recognition of the diversity among Americans—which in theory, at least, was a good thing. An assessment of no less than seventy recent biographies tried to play it both ways: "In America I generally have a keener sense of locality than of nationality"; nevertheless, all of these books "have some things in common which transcend regional boundaries." In the final analysis, however, this job lot of verbal portraits "revealed many interesting varieties of American character."[70]

V

THE CLEVER yet coy title of this multi-profile assessment, "Seeing Americans First," deliberately extended to the realm of reading a pervasive motif that made the national landscape itself the central feature of an American aesthetic. That same year, 1929, Booth Tarkington, the popular novelist, produced an essay whose thrust, not altogether clear, was designated "America and Culture." He dealt primarily with European stereotypes of American barbarism, and warned those who wished to travel abroad that they would encounter "a great deal of nonsense concerning American manners, customs and lack of culture." He made a virtue of our social insecurity and simultaneously blasted Old World smugness by noting that American culture at least had "the vigor and generosity that will save it from self-worship; for self-worship means stagnation." Unlike Europeans, we were not decadent. He ended by noting that even our proudest nationalists were not parochial: "our patriots and railroads and hotel keepers have raised the cry . . . 'See America First'; and even they do not entreat us to see America only."[71]

The "travel industry," broadly defined, unquestionably had a major stake in urging Americans to see their own country; and in this area, at least, the government had for many years been a willing collaborator. In August 1883, for example, the Northern Pacific Railroad Company completed its main line connecting Minneapolis–St. Paul with the Puget Sound area, a distance of 2,168 miles. A gala celebration held in September was attended by all sorts of VIP's, including officials of the federal government which had done so much to make it possible.[72]

The National Highways Association, formed in 1912, received a major boost in 1927 when the New York State legislature made an appropriation to erect road markers that would observe the 150th anniversary of the War of Independence. Virginia soon followed this example and called its system "history written in iron." According to a lengthy essay in the *New York Times,* proponents of historical markers believed that they would "everywhere awaken local pride and so encourage individual efforts to preserve and beautify historical monuments [i.e., sites and structures]. Not only visitors but permanent residents as well are learning, and seeing, local history through the agency of roadside markers."[73]

Some roads were constructed or proposed for the exclusive purpose of facilitating nationalism and tourism. As early as 1902, for example, the Jefferson Memorial Road Association was organized to promote construction of a three-mile avenue that would connect Monticello with the University of Virginia, "in that way contributing to the diffusion of a larger degree of patriotism throughout the land." During the

1930s a suggestion surfaced that the road on Long Island known as the "Circumferential Highway" or Belt Road be renamed the Whitman Highway in honor of the greatest American who "hailed from" Long Island. Even more important, however, was the completion in 1936–37 of long-span bridges that bonded the United States as never before and made historic sites as well as ordinary travel vastly more accessible and convenient: the Mark Twain Bridge across the Mississippi River at Hannibal, Missouri, which President Roosevelt dedicated in 1936; the San Francisco Bay Bridge, which opened in November 1936; and the Golden Gate Bridge, which was completed the following summer.[74]

Tourism accelerated at a rapid rate between the later 1920s and the mid-1930s, hard times to the contrary notwithstanding. During the summer of 1929 the *Saturday Evening Post* printed a droll caricature on its cover: an overweight and overdressed urban male (the *Brooklyn Times* sticks out of his jacket pocket) sits uncomfortably astride a donkey and makes his descent into the Grand Canyon. He pays little attention to the stunning scenery because he is too busy reading a book titled *See America First.* In an equally typical activity (almost as vulnerable to caricature), 1,500 delegates to the triennial meeting of the General Federation of Women's Clubs, held in Detroit, made a pilgrimage to Dearborn in order to visit the Henry Ford Museum and Greenfield Village.[75]

Tourism aside, however, we must not underestimate the importance of "seeing America" to those who hoped to interpret American civilization by writing about it or painting it. After retiring in 1904 as head librarian in the Twin Cities, James K. Hosmer decided that he wanted to write the story of the American Civil War, but that in order to do so properly he would have to visit all the scenes of battle and the major campaigns. By 1911 Stephen Vincent Benét, whose home base was considerably closer in Carlisle, Pennsylvania, had already visited a great many important Civil War sites more than once. Thomas Hart Benton tells us in his autobiography that during the early 1920s he "began exploring the back countries of America by foot, bus, and train, searching out American subject matter." Constance Rourke and Zora Neale Hurston did the same in search of folk art and folklore; and in 1937–38 Edward Weston used a Guggenheim Fellowship to record the regional diversity of the Western states with his camera. In 1939 Grant Wood wrote to John Dos Passos, whose work he had just been reading, "You must travel about the country a good deal. Do you ever get out to Iowa? If so, why don't you stop with me for a visit?"[76]

D. H. Lawrence had a penchant for the perverse, and derived special pleasure from defying conventional wisdom. In 1927, having travelled in Mexico and the American Southwest, he provocatively inverted the traditional verities by referring to Mediterranean cultures as "so eternally young, the very symbol of youth! And Italy, so reputedly old, yet for ever so child-like and naïve! Never, never for a moment able to comprehend the wonderful, hoary age of America, the continent of the afterwards."[77]

THE GROWING ease of travel made cultural institutions generally more accessible to Americans during the interwar years, and more particularly those out-of-the-way places that had played a prominent part in their history. Travel contributed to the democratization of tradition during the 1920s and '30s, and thereby helped to blur some of the distinctions between high culture and popular culture that had become fairly rigid in the half century that followed 1870. As early as 1922 we find essays by museum professionals advocating both Americanization of content and democratization of the museum as a public institution.[78]

That objective swiftly became, at least on paper, the stated goal of every conceivable kind of tradition-oriented cultural institution, ranging from Colonial Williamsburg and the Henry Ford Museum (as we shall see in the next chapter) to the Metropolitan Museum of Art and the Phillips Collection in Washington, D.C. Public education became the pervasive by-word. Duncan Phillips began his testamentary statement by referring to the gallery "which I founded as an educational institution in 1918." Wallace Nutting observed in his autobiography that "the collector is always getting an education"; and he advertised that four of the historic house museums that he had assembled could be reached along a sixty-five-mile automobile circuit starting from Boston. Then came the touch of promotional altruism (which he undoubtedly believed): "the roads are to be our most hopeful educators. They are the common school of the world awheel."[79]

After World War II, when museums, historic sites, and restored villages achieved such enhanced prominence in the American landscape, this educational mystique became ubiquitous, even within the most elitist circles. In 1954 the board of trustees of Sleepy Hollow Restorations, located in the lower Hudson River Valley (Rockefeller-supported projects that then primarily meant Philipsburg Manor and Sunnyside, the home of Washington Irving), decided that "the educational potential of the restorations" warranted augmentation of the exhibits and an "expanded on-going educational program." Two prominent staff members who opposed this policy change were eased out and Harold Dean Cater became the new executive director. He took office in October 1955 after spending six months surveying other museums and historic restorations in the East and Middle West. Dana S. Creel, chairman of the board, made very explicit its new orientation:

> The Board is anxious to enliven both restorations to make them more interesting and valuable as educational projects. Whatever is done in this way will be carrying out the Board's fundamental objective of increasing the educational merit and the signifi-

cance of these restorations while carrying forward their established traditions.[80]

Blurring the lines between high culture and popular culture sometimes occurred by serendipity, sometimes by careful planning, but most
often simply because new fads or an altered climate of opinion made
it inevitable. Picture, if you will, the elegant, arrogant dealer in rare
books and manuscripts, A. S. W. Rosenbach of Philadelphia, sitting on
his bed in 1926 wearing a nightshirt and scratching himself, drinking
a bottle of whiskey each day, while Miss Avery Strakosch teased information and anecdotes from him about clients, collectors, and rivals in
the trade. She served as the ghostwriter for his essays that enjoyed
immense popularity when they appeared regularly in the *Saturday
Evening Post* during 1927. Rosenbach received three hundred letters
per day in response to "Talking of Old Books" and its sequels. The
collected pieces then appeared as a volume called *Books and Bidders*
at the end of 1927. One of the great snobs in the world of collectors had
"written" (or at least scratched and talked) a bestseller.[81]

Stephen Vincent Benét feared that his epic poem *John Brown's Body*
would be his least successful work because it was too long and scholarly.
It became a smash hit instantaneously in the fall of 1928, led the bestseller list month after month, and obliterated any meaningful distinction between serious and commercially popular literature. Similarly,
though much less surprising, when Benét completed his poem "Listen
to the People," he read it over the radio on July 4, 1941, and *Life*
magazine printed it. It too enjoyed enormous success. Later that year
the film version of Benét's folk tale "The Devil and Daniel Webster"
appeared. Few imaginative writers in the United States have done so
much in so short a time to bring the American past to the people as a
vibrant, inspiring, moralizing force.[82]

CALVIN COOLIDGE took a genuine interest in American history and historical places. A book of aphorisms attributed to him and
published the year after he became President included these ten words
of wisdom: "No people can look forward who do not look backward."[83]
A decade later an iron sign appeared on the greensward where visitors
approach the Henry Ford Museum. "The farther you look back," it
reads, "the farther you can look ahead." Did Ford plagiarize Coolidge?
Or did the aphorism simply stick in Ford's mind when he first heard or
read it in 1923–24? I do not know; but by 1923–24 Henry Ford had
become hooked as a collector of Americana, as a man with an educational mission to grass-roots America, and he would increasingly be
recognized as the genuine Janus of American culture. Henry Ford was
indeed filled with nostalgia; but he most certainly looked to the future
as well.

Chapter 11

AUTHENTIC MUSEUMS TO
EDUCATE THE PEOPLE ABOUT
THE HISTORY OF PROGRESS

D URING THE 1920s AND '30s—more specifically the
decade that spanned 1924 to 1934—a few very rich collectors
and a small group of prestigious museums fundamentally transformed the presentation of Americana to the people of the United
States. They created precedents and set standards that still affect the
nature of collective memory in this country, even for those who have
chosen to break with such precedents and wish to transform the standards. In addition to figures already discussed, such as Electra
Havemeyer Webb, Henry Francis du Pont, and R. T. H. Halsey, we now
have primarily in view Henry Ford, John D. Rockefeller, Jr., Robert
Weeks de Forest, and a few latecomers who appeared on the scene in
the mid-1930s, like Maxim Karolik in Boston.

During these years great private collections emerged from protected
cocoons into, or else were directly created to be, major national museums. Affluent collectors collaborated closely with existing museums in
order to help expand their presentations of Americana. Some extant
institutions became boldly innovative and transformed themselves—
invariably in the *name* of education and "authenticity" even if not
consistently in their spirit. Because Henry Ford had an obsession with
authenticating the origin of "Mary Had a Little Lamb," for instance, he
"saved" the Redstone schoolhouse (renamed the Wayside School) and
published a forty-page booklet about the genesis of the poem.[1] A considerable amount of invaluable historic preservation occurred—along with
some questionable reconstructions, a fair number of transplanted structures, and a few phony ones with flimsy historical pedigrees.

Whereas the decade of the twenties was more notable for the creation or transformation of great national caches of memory, the decade
of the thirties would be somewhat more important for the emergence
of regional or local repositories. If competition occurred among individuals and institutions, so did co-operation. If authenticity appeared

as a by-word, commercialization of the past became a by-product of this general attraction to the candle of the quaint. And commercialization of tradition could be fraught with folly. Wallace Nutting, for example, disliked anything made later than the early eighteenth century. By 1930, however, he was manufacturing seventeenth-century versions of an oak radiator cover, a stenographer's swivel chair, and an oak chest adapted for typewriters.[2]

Ultimately, by the later 1940s, cultural institutions that one generation earlier had been poised between a commitment to and a suspicion of the coming of modernity willingly participated in the commercialization of tradition and the modernization of national memory. In the worst possible situations, the trivialization of tradition occurred. In the best, we got the democratization of tradition. As so often happens, the interwar years gave Americans splendid memories and star-spangled amnesia. The consequences are still with us.

I

IN DIVERSE yet connected patterns, the major collections began making their way into institutions during the later 1920s. In 1926, for example, J. P. Morgan, Jr., purchased from Wallace Nutting a substantial hoard of early American furniture and decorative arts and donated it to the Wadsworth Atheneum in Hartford, Connecticut, where the Morgan family roots ran deep. In that same year, Arthur A. Schomburg sold his unique collection of African-American books, printed materials, and engravings to the New York Public Library. Four years later Isaac Newton Phelps Stokes gave his invaluable accumulation of American iconography, maps, and views to the same institution; and in 1930 Henry Francis du Pont, who had been collecting Americana for less than a decade, made arrangements for Winterthur eventually to become "a museum and arboretum for the education and enjoyment of the public."[3]

Meanwhile Francis P. Garvan, who started to gather Americana around 1912, gave his collection (numbering some 100,000 pieces in all) to Yale University in 1930. In doing so he referred to it as a "comprehensive educational collection," and in this instance that really meant something. Two years later the curator of Garvan's collection, John M. Phillips, offered the first university course emphasizing material culture and the decorative arts in United States history (affectionately called "Pots and Pans" by the students).[4] Early in 1932 Louis Hertle gave Gunston Hall, the eighteenth-century home of George Mason, to the Commonwealth of Virginia (subject to life use by the grantor). It would be administered by the National Society of the Colonial Dames of America and by a board of regents. The enabling act passed by Virginia's legislature used characteristic language: "said estate to be forever held by the Commonwealth sacred to the memory of George Mason."

Collectors like Schomburg and Garvan continued to work very closely with and act on behalf of the institutions that received their treasures. Edward Drummond Libbey, the successful glass manufacturer, gave the city of Toledo, Ohio, its art museum in 1901. Following his death in 1925 his widow, Florence Scott Libbey, continued to be a generous benefactor; and when she died in 1938 her will included an endowment to the museum for the acquisition of American painting and decorative arts.

The most unusual example of a person collecting for and closely with a museum, however, is provided by Maxim Karolik, an extraordinary patron of Boston's Museum of Fine Arts. He came to the United States in 1922 as an émigré opera singer from Russia, and gave public concerts in the Northeast as well as singing privately at soirées attended by socialites. At one of these he met Martha Codman, a multi-millionaire spinster descended from very old Boston and Salem families. When they married in 1928 she was nearly seventy, almost twice Karolik's age. He had enormous energy and enthusiasm for the art and artifacts of his adopted country. Between 1935 and 1938 the Karoliks developed an arrangement with the Museum of Fine Arts whereby they would accumulate a collection of early American furniture, portraits, and silver with the curatorial advice of museum staff—the collection destined as a gift for the museum. The sole criterion for selection would be artistic quality rather than association with historic persons or events— yet another example of the emergence of an American aesthetic.[5]

All of the purchases for this superb harvest were made during the years 1935 to 1941, and they greatly enhanced the fine pieces that Martha Codman had already inherited from several segments of her family. She kept these heirlooms at her lavish home in Newport, Rhode Island, where she died in 1949. On December 2, 1941, the Museum of Fine Arts proudly unveiled the Martha and Maxim Karolik Collection of Eighteenth-Century American Arts (c. 1720–1820). Maxim Karolik had been the aggressive partner in this arrangement, and his taste, eye, and philosophy determined most of the acquisition decisions. He wanted it to be a national rather than a provincial collection; he preferred high-style pieces to folk art, but he insisted (with a democratic flourish) that the Karoliks were presenting it "to the people, through the museum." Maxim Karolik's populism might be suspect, but not his passionate patriotism. "The beauty of this collection," he wrote, "springs from the roots of this nation. . . . It contains its own national characteristics. . . . It expresses its own idiom, which is definitely American."[6]

By the later 1930s Karolik had already started to form a second and quite separate collection of American paintings from the period 1815– 65: in part because the Museum of Fine Art's holdings were so weak for that era, but also because it was still viewed as a "barren period" in the history of American art. William G. Constable, who came to the Museum as Curator of Painting in 1938 and worked closely with Karolik as a consultant, loved the Old Masters and would not have chosen to emphasize the acquisition of nineteenth-century American pictures on his own initiative.* Because the half century that followed 1815 was decidedly not in vogue, prices remained low, which delighted the man who referred to himself as Maxim Karolik of the Minimum Prices. He pursued neglected painters like Martin Johnson Heade, Fitz Hugh Lane, and John Quidor, as well as a significant group of "native" artists. Few of his pictures ran more than $1,000, and many of them cost less than $500. During his most intensive period of acquisition, 1942–45, Karolik bought 234 paintings, and the completed collection cost less than a quarter of a million dollars! In retrospect, he got quite a bargain.[7]

In 1942, while Karolik was assembling this collection, he published an essay in the *Atlantic* that conveys with heartfelt sincerity his feelings about treasure hunts, the materials obtained from them, the society they represented, and its values. If he revealed contradictory tendencies, that should not be surprising in a Russian refugee who had married a Brahmin of great wealth yet expressed "deep faith in the common man" and explained that he admired Newport for its colonial atmosphere "with a settled tradition behind it." He praised the "beautiful simplicity of eighteenth-century American homes," idealized the social elite of that era, and insisted that democracy existed (and had been aspired to) in the age of the American Revolution![8]

Karolik's statement predictably reflected the anxious patriotism of wartime as well as the exuberance of a nation emerging from a decade-long depression. He voiced the hope that the skill, quality, and beauty of early American objects would "symbolize not only the return of prosperity and comfort; it will also symbolize our return to 18th-century principles." He predicted a "stampede to refurnish homes with the things or in the style of the past," a stampede that in fact had already begun; and having enjoyed the use of Miss Codman's fortune for almost fifteen years, he rather ingenuously hoped that the rage for colonial things would not mean "reproductions made by machines or by mediocre craftsmen.† The 'trend toward the past' I interpret as the return to creative craftsmanship." Karolik, too, had been infected by the contagion of "authenticity." His prediction that a pervasive revival of the "style of the past" would occur turned out to be accurate: and not so much the uncomfortable Pilgrim century furniture that Wallace Nut-

---

*When the Metropolitan Museum of Art in New York mounted a major "Life in America" exhibition in 1939, it was the first comprehensive assemblage of nineteenth-century American landscape, genre, history, and portrait paintings staged in the twentieth century.

†Colonial Williamsburg began to manufacture reproductions of its furniture in 1937; Old Sturbridge Village first did so in 1948, two years after it opened to the public.

ting had favored, but the more elegant, refined, and comfortable styles of the eighteenth century.[9]

Karolik felt by 1949 that his harvest of nineteenth-century paintings seemed complete, but the Museum of Fine Arts did not have new galleries ready to display it until 1951. In the meanwhile this gregarious, generous, and engagingly complex man insisted upon democratizing what it meant to be a patron: "We are not 'Patrons of art' or 'Public Benefactors.' We refuse to accept these banal labels. We accept with pleasure only one label: 'useful citizen.' " Nor did his energy and enthusiasm cease with the grand opening in 1951, his second at the Museum of Fine Arts. He then created a private collection (1950–55) of 150 additional American paintings that had Boston as its home court but was basically intended to travel. In 1956–57, for example, it made the rounds of twelve major museums. Finally, in 1962, the year of his death, the Museum published the *M. and M. Karolik Collection of American Water Colors and Drawings, 1800–1875*. This third and final phase of his remarkable enterprise actually included works of sculpture, as well, especially "primitive" pieces.[10]

Although there is no instance of closer or more creative collaboration between donors and an established museum, several prominent institutions of tradition independently began to find new ways to exhibit and interpret their Americana, especially during the 1920s. So early as 1907, as we noted in the preceding section, Salem's Essex Institute became the first American museum to install so-called period rooms in an effort to provide an integrated presentation of contemporary objects, artistic as well as functional. By 1910 George Francis Dow, the Institute's director, had moved the John Ward House, one of Salem's oldest (c. 1685), to a spot behind the Institute where Dow adapted the Skansen notion of an open-air museum and supplied guides wearing colonial costumes. It was symptomatic of the times, however, that Dow's purpose was not so much aesthetic as the appearance of historical reality. Consequently, the use of reproductions was acceptable to him, though it would not have been to the likes of Karolik thirty years later.[11]

In 1914 Luke Vincent Lockwood, a pioneering collector, member of the Walpole Society, and prolific writer on colonial furniture, joined the board of governors of the Brooklyn Museum. It was no coincidence that almost simultaneously the Museum established a Department of Colonial and Early American Furniture. One year later the Museum acquired woodwork and all of the trim for its first period room; and in 1929, fourteen years later, it opened to the public a group of twelve such rooms. Several of these had for centuries been part of the ground floor of the seventeenth-century Nicholas Schenk farmhouse in Brooklyn. In 1953 that same museum became the first to introduce a series of nineteenth-century rooms, two of them dating from Saratoga Springs in 1854. In 1971 the Brooklyn Museum installed an Art Deco library that had been designed for a Park Avenue apartment in 1928. This, surely, was the first twentieth-century period room placed in any American institution.[12]

The Metropolitan Museum of Art followed the trend in 1924, as we shall see momentarily, and the concept then caught on with extraordinary speed: Philadelphia and Boston in 1927–28, Baltimore in 1930, St. Louis and Minneapolis in 1930–31. Henry Francis du Pont installed no fewer than twenty-three period rooms at Winterthur between 1929 and 1931. The concept then simply took over the whole of his accordion-expanded home between 1933 and 1951. Boston's Museum of Fine Arts purchased a treasure in 1923: Oak Hill, the residence built in 1801 at Danvers by a daughter of Elias Hasket Derby, the Salem shipping impresario. The interior woodwork of those rooms had been designed and executed by Samuel McIntire, master carver of Salem. His signature touches—sheaves of wheat, baskets of fruit, and garlands of flowers—became crucial design motifs of the neo-classical style. The other superb rooms installed by the Museum of Fine Arts in 1928 came from a Georgian mansion built in Portsmouth, New Hampshire, by the Jaffrey family in 1740.[13]

Despite the fact that the Jaffrey House had fallen into serious neglect by 1920 and truly needed to be dismantled in order to be "saved," the quest by museums and collectors for early American panelling in order to create period rooms seemed to some purists a very serious threat to *in situ* historic preservation, and brought about sharp conflicts among small but opinionated groups who all wanted to love the material past but in different ways and at different locations. William Sumner Appleton, devoted leader of the Society for the Preservation of New England Antiquities, became a highly visible opponent of period rooms "ripped" from their contextual wombs; and he served on the board of the Committee on Colonial and National Art of the Archaeological Institute of America, which flourished during the 1920s under the leadership of Fiske Kimball, an architectural historian at the University of Virginia who subsequently became director of the Philadelphia Museum of Art. Few directors, by the way, worried as much about authenticity as Kimball did—which meant not only having correct things, but knowing precisely how they ought to be arranged.[14]

ONE OTHER individual whose collection gave rise to an institution ought to be mentioned in this setting because the trajectory of his career illuminates both similarities and differences among the patterns we have been tracing. Thomas Gilcrease, who made his money in Oklahoma oil, took a trip around the world in 1925–26. He observed in Europe that knowledge of civilizations is reconstructed from things that they leave behind. Because the state of Oklahoma had no museum or major library, no organization that represented the civilizations that had been there prior to the white man, and none that told the story of native tribes since the seventeenth century, he dedicated himself to filling that void. Gilcrease began to buy rare books and documents, then Indian art and artifacts of the region. The outbreak of World War II in 1939 made him even more cognizant that objects outlast people, and that the surviving remains of past cultures must be cherished. Consequently he decided to devote his full attention to acquisitions, and like Maxim Karolik he remained extremely active during the war years. Curiously enough, Gilcrease located a considerable amount of Native American material in England.[15]

In 1942 he formed the Thomas Gilcrease Foundation, with a portion of its funds permanently allocated for the education of Native Americans. The cream of his collection went on public view in temporary quarters until 1949, when the Gilcrease Museum of History and Art opened in Tulsa. Initially, history tended to overwhelm art in the Gilcrease because he ambitiously sought to tell the story of America from prehistoric times to the present, with special emphasis upon the Indian and the development of the Southwest. Aesthetic quality mattered less to Gilcrease than documentary value and historical interest. In 1953–54, when he encountered serious financial setbacks, the citizens of Tulsa voted to float a bond issue in order to pay Gilcrease's creditors. He then gave his collection to the city. Subsequently (1954–57) he became deeply interested in early American archaeology, and eventually was more engaged by American art generally, though his focus continued to be historical art and art that depicted life in the Southwest.[16]

In 1987 the redesigned and expanded Gilcrease Institute reopened following a spectacular facelift. Today it imparts historical information effectively, but its predominant impact is aesthetic—an American regional aesthetic in a museum of national importance. It thereby demonstrates, yet again, how decentralization contributes to the democratization of tradition and culture in the United States.

I I

ROBERT WEEKS DE FOREST, scion of an old Connecticut family, was serving as secretary to the board of trustees at the Metropolitan Museum of Art (an influential position) in 1909 when the Hudson-Fulton celebration became the occasion for that unprecedented exhibition of early American furniture and decorative arts (see pp. 188–189 above). Looking back, he felt that that display had been planned in order to "test out the question whether American domestic art was worthy of a place in an art museum." The substantive issue, in fact, was whether such artifacts ought to be categorized as ethnography or as art. The sheer success of the show in terms of attendance, and the prompt purchase of two thirds of its nine hundred objects by Mrs. Russell Sage as a gift to the Museum in 1910, set in motion a sequence of concerns and events that reached a grand climax in November 1924: the opening of the Met's American Wing, with the Sage bequest as its foundation.[17]

The sequence followed these lines: support from Mrs. Sage, who just happened to be a legal client of de Forest's; the very active role that R. T. H. Halsey started to play at the Met in 1914; de Forest's becoming president of the Met in 1913, and being succeeded as secretary by Henry Watson Kent, an ardent lover of early Americana and a founder of the Walpole Society; Halsey's leadership in locating superb architectural interiors all along the Eastern seaboard that could be installed in the Museum as backdrops for the furnishings; and finally, the ability of Halsey and Kent to infuse the generous de Forests with their own passion for Americana. By 1920 the plan for an American Wing had been formulated and the de Forests had decided to foot the bill and make the Wing their major gift to the Met.[18]

At the grand opening in November 1924 Halsey waxed eloquent about the Americanizing role of traditions ingrained in material culture. Somehow, all of that wonderfully glistening mahogany and all of those ball-and-claw feet would make new immigrants into more sober citizens.

- Said Halsey: "Traditions are one of the integral assets of a country. . . . Many of our people are not cognizant of our traditions and the principles for which our fathers struggled and died."

- Said de Forest: "We are honoring our fathers and our mothers, our grandfathers and our grandmothers, that their art may live long in the land which the Lord hath given us."

- Said Elihu Root (first vice president of the Museum): Halsey, de Forest, Kent, and all the rest who had made the Wing a reality "formed an old-fashioned American community, and in their spirit was born again that atmosphere that produced whatever was fine and warming and delightful in old American life."[19]

The immediate reactions of journalists to the new Wing were almost as enthusiastic as the "popular" response, though the former ranged from banal ("those ancestors of ours had taste equally if not surpassing ours!" to astonishment ("AMERICAN ART REALLY EXISTS") to genuine perplexity on the part of a young but astute critic of taste like Lewis Mumford. After calling it superb, and not merely an exhibition of art but "a pageant of American history," he began to speculate about its potential impact in terms of that old matter of the delicate balance between tradition and innovation: "One's enthusiasm for this achievement is tainted by the feeling that the lessons people will take away from these rooms are not precisely the lessons one would wish them to have learned. Where could I buy something like *this*? How could I copy *that*?"[20] Mumford feared that features of poor taste in early American decorative arts would make a comeback "with the august stamp of tradition." He strongly preferred seventeenth-century functionalism to eighteenth-century precious elegance. And the Federal period made him uncomfortable because it connected too readily with mindless spreadeagle nationalism. He offered a combination of queries and exhortations that seem shrewd in retrospect but were hardly representative at the time.

> What is to keep us from harnessing machine-production to a sickly desire to counterfeit the past? I know of no other purge or preventive than understanding. So let us wander through these rooms and find out for ourselves what there is in American tradition that we can build upon; what there is which genuinely unites us with our past and promises a legitimate offspring in fresh art. How can we turn this spinsterly desire for ancestors into a virile effort to beget a new issue?[21]

The impact of the American Wing rippled out in a pool of predictable ways. The Met itself felt encouraged to follow up with an influential series of more specialized temporary exhibitions: architectural details of exteriors of early American homes (1927); early New York silver (1931); American japanned furniture (1933); New York State furniture (1934); prints that George Washington lived with (1935); Franklin and his circle (1936); American pewter (1939); watercolors of early American houses (1940); the China trade and its influences (1941); the Greek Revival in the United States (1943); and so forth. Joseph Downs, its devoted curator for several decades, looked back in 1946 and reaffirmed the Wing's unabashed elitism:

> The American Wing presents an aspect that is disappointing to certain visitors who believe that the everyday life of the average early American should be represented. . . . We can rightly judge a cultural period by its greatest achievement rather than its mean average. The American Wing is not ethnographical, concerned with the habits and customs of man, but is the esthetic expression of artisans even before painting, sculpture, and other graphic arts found a foothold.[22]

Certain interesting exceptions to his high-style preference pushed their way in, however, and provided a modest touch of ethnicity in what otherwise was predominantly an Anglo-Dutch colonial display. In 1933 Mrs. Robert W. de Forest donated her collection of the domestic arts of Pennsylvania Germans who had emigrated in the eighteenth century; so the next year two new galleries were installed to accommodate her generous gift of "colorful peasant art": a paneled room from Lancaster County, and a room plastered in plain white to set off the richly decorated dower chests, sgraffito and slipware pottery, fraktur drawings, and metalwork.[23] Similar rooms subsequently appeared at du Pont's Winterthur. Somehow, Pennsylvania "Dutch" stuff was not tainted by ethnography. Its appeal must have been purely aesthetic. Exceptions are funny that way.

The ripple-out effect inevitably reached other museums, which also installed permanent exhibits (though on a more modest scale), and encouraged special shows. In 1926, for example, the Colonial Dames of Minnesota held an exhibition of "Colonial Articles" belonging to members of that society. In 1927 the *D.A.R. Magazine* urged patriotic Americans to reproduce in their homes the furniture and decorative arts to be found in the American Wing. Collectors of early Americana began to abound, and dealers proliferated to fill their needs and make a profit. Every major city started to have an annual antiques fair—triple-threat events that usually managed to be socially prestigious, highly entrepreneurial, and often philanthropic as well.[24]

The Metropolitan Museum's charter, granted by the city in 1870, contained a passage that is interesting for its implications, the frequency with which it was borrowed or adapted (as we shall see), and the Museum's persistent failure to honor it. The charter had been awarded for the purpose "of encouraging and developing the study of fine arts, and the application of the arts to manufacture and practical life, of advancing the general knowledge of kindred subjects, and, to that end, of furnishing popular instruction and recreation."[25] The American Wing was from its inception, and remains to this day, a glorious achievement; but for much of the Museum's distinguished history its custodians have averted their gaze when "popular instruction and recreation" have raised their vulgar heads.[26] (In 1908 the trustees in fact deleted "and recreation" from the charter.) What they believed they *had* achieved, however, and proudly touted, was "authenticity."

I I I

IRONICALLY, Henry Ford sought deliberately to fulfill in his own institutions of memory and patriotism that intermittently neglected aspect of the Met's mission (fig. 11.1). In 1930, after John D. Rockefeller, Jr., had visited the Wayside Inn in Massachusetts, he wrote Ford to express pleasure and surprise that Ford was "carrying on [such an] extensive educational enterprise." In 1936, when the Ford Museum and Greenfield Village had been open for three years, a journalist asked Ford why such a practical man had devoted so much time and effort to collecting early American furniture. "How is it that you find so much to admire in Duncan Phyfe's designs?" Ford shot back a revealing response:

> Who said I liked Duncan Phyfe's furniture? This museum has been organized for the purpose of teaching. In it we show the develop-

11.1   Henry Ford, c. 1935–39, in the Ford homestead at Greenfield Village. From the collections of Henry Ford Museum & Greenfield Village.

ment of many things we use today. . . . Whatever is produced today has something in it of everything that has gone before. Even a present-day chair embodies all previous chairs, and if we can show the development of the chair in tangible form we shall teach better than we can by books.*[27]

Although the catchphrase "a man of contrasts" has surely been overused, it is unavoidable in the case of Henry Ford. Consider two of the most famous quotations associated with him. In 1916, when his contretemps with the *Chicago Tribune* began, he indicated to a reporter his contempt for history. "It means nothing to me," Ford exclaimed. "History is more or less bunk. It's tradition. We don't want tradition. We want to live in the present and the only history that is worth a tinker's dam is the history we make today." In 1929, however, Ford declared his purpose in establishing the Edison Institute, a precursor to and (after 1933) a part of his Museum and Greenfield Village: "When we are through, we shall have reproduced American life as

---

*This theme became distinctively Ford's: "I am collecting the history of our people as written into things their hands made and used . . . a piece of machinery or anything that is made is like a book, if you can read it."

lived; and that, I think, is the best way of preserving at least a part of our history and tradition."[28]

At first glance, the explanation for this anomaly must seem simple: Henry Ford clearly underwent a profound transformation between 1916 and 1929. That is not the answer, however, despite the fact that he did change in some respects. Ever since the early years of the twentieth century he had been intrigued by the complex relationship between past and present. Although he did have sentimental feelings about his own youth and education, his "problem" was really quite simple: he needed to establish a means of relating to the past, for himself as well as others, that did not depend upon books.

Ford was not a reader, but objects and their evolution fascinated him. Consequently he accumulated an overwhelming collection that is just the opposite of the American Wing at the Met: far more evolutionary than aesthetic, far more functional than elegant, far more ethnographic and egalitarian than elitist. Henry Ford identified with the common man. From the perspective of someone who did not know him, Ford quite understandably seemed to be a man of contradictions. That same journalist who interviewed him in 1936 called Ford a man of opposites: "A visionary and a dreamer, he is intensely practical." Walking through Greenfield Village with Ford seemed utterly bizarre. "It was a strange sensation to pass old wagons while walking with one who had rendered them obsolete." The newspaperman recognized that Ford wished to communicate the history of progress, and that such an ambition clarified some of the apparent dualisms: "The creator of mass production, he turns in admiration to the handiwork of the lonely craftsman. While collecting relics of the past he is constantly looking toward the future."[29]

Because Ford regarded Thomas A. Edison as the greatest man alive, he started collecting Edison memorabilia as early as 1905. Because Ford was a moralist, he began to gather McGuffey Readers in 1914. He wanted to restore moral principles to education because, in Ford's view (himself indoctrinated by McGuffey Readers): "We learn from the past not only what to do but also what not to do." In 1919 Ford decided to restore his boyhood home as a memorial to his parents. When local dealers in antiques learned of the project, they began combing the countryside and rummaging in attics. Ford was soon besieged by junk snuppers. Most of that restoration was completed by 1926.[30]

Ford took to collecting Americana in a somewhat random fashion in 1920. Within three years his acquisitions had achieved amazing proportions both in terms of quantity and their actual size. He had become the most comprehensive collector of Americana—ever. In 1923 he bought and repaired the little red schoolhouse that he had attended in Dearborn Township's Scotch Settlement district. He actually ran it for several years as an experimental school where three- to six-year-olds learned both from new pedagogical techniques and from McGuffey's first Reader. A year later he acquired the 1836 Botsford Tavern, located a few miles west of Detroit. It served as an informal museum until 1934, when Ford opened it for public dining. Ford often behaved more like a magpie (in the name of authenticity) than a discriminating collector. In restoring the Botsford Tavern a dead cat was found which had fallen behind a partition and either suffocated or else died of hunger. Ford insisted that the cat be placed in a small case with a glass top in the Ford Museum. It remained on display for several years.[31]

Meanwhile, on June 20, 1923, Ford and three cronies drove from Boston to South Sudbury to look over the venerable Red Horse Tavern, known since 1863 (when Longfellow published his *Tales*) as the Wayside Inn. Local enthusiasts described the tavern as the oldest in the United States, and Ford had decided to buy it. He moved, characteristically, with remarkable speed. Within two weeks he had purchased more than a dozen neighboring homes and farms in order to isolate and cleanse the inn of modern anachronisms and potential encroachment.* Eventually, with its affiliated old-time schools and farms, the Wayside Inn property spread over 2,667 acres on eighty-eight parcels of land in the towns of Sudbury, Framingham, and Marlborough. By 1928 Ford had deeded eighteen acres to the Commonwealth of Massachusetts and received permission to move the existing "highway" away from the inn (eighteenth-century tavern owners must have spun in their graves at the idea of such anti-entrepreneurial lunacy) at a cost to Ford of $330,831.[32]

Ford had not yet developed a master plan for the comprehensive collection of objects and buildings that he envisioned for Dearborn, Michigan. So the Wayside Inn and its satellite structures became a kind of laboratory where he could experiment with a totally new concept in the educational presentation of Americana. On this site Ford set out to display not simply a single famous structure but an entire functioning community of homes, farms, schools, craft shops, a chapel, and a tavern. The purpose, as Ford put it, was "to show how our forefathers lived and to bring to mind what kind of people they were." In a book published in 1926, Ford elaborated upon his personal rationale for historic preservation. He conceded that "we are a new country and nothing is very old," but insisted that the American public ought to know "as nearly as possible" the "exact conditions" under which their forebears had lived. "We have both lost and gained in the movement of modern industry. Our gains are many times greater than our losses; we can keep all of the gains and repair some of the losses."[33]

---

*Ford turned the responsibility (and opportunity) of furnishing the inn over to Israel Sack, a dealer in American antiques who was then still located in Boston. Sack apparently obtained all of the necessary furniture within two weeks. Despite Ford's notorious anti-Semitism, he and Sack enjoyed a congenial professional relationship for several decades. (Sack and Wilk, *American Treasure Hunt,* 69–70, 72.)

Although Ford remained proud of what he accomplished with the Wayside Inn "community," he began to lose interest in it by 1927 because of the intensity of his collecting and planning at Dearborn. In 1944 Ford transferred ownership of the inn to a Massachusetts charitable corporation. When fire destroyed the original tavern in 1955, along with nearly every object that Ford had put into it, the *Christian Science Monitor* launched an immediate campaign to rebuild it, the Ford Foundation kicked in more than half a million dollars, children from Hawaii to Chile contributed coins, and the Wayside Inn rose once again like a phoenix from the ashes.[34]

When Ford first contemplated a major museum in 1919–20, he had "industrial history" in mind. That component was never lost; and in September 1928 the revered Edison himself arrived to place the cornerstone for the Edison Institute of Technology and Greenfield Village. Most of Menlo Park, Edison's 1876–85 laboratories in New Jersey, was transported to Dearborn piece by piece and reassembled there.* But gathering all of the seventeenth-, eighteenth-, and nineteenth-century antiques and curios for the Wayside Inn and Botsford Tavern vastly expanded Ford's vision as well as his appetite. When he realized that a huge structure would be needed for his museum, Ford tried to purchase Independence Hall in Philadelphia, with the idea of transplanting it to Dearborn. After he learned to his frustration that it was not for sale at any price, he built a larger than scale combination of Independence Hall, Congress Hall, and the old City Hall of Philadelphia. Like Ford's collection, the museum meant to contain it would be an architectural mélange.[35]

A "street" of early American shops began to take shape within that structure in 1931—the first installation on such an ambitious scale in any American museum. It remained incomplete and subject to change throughout the 1930s. Greenfield Village, immediately adjacent to the Museum, consisting of structures brought from hither and yon (Noah Webster's house, a courthouse where young Abe Lincoln defended clients, the Wright brothers' bicycle shop, etc.), began to take form in 1927 and was largely complete by 1944, one year before Ford suffered a stroke.[36]

Unlike some collectors who are single-minded, and others who are enigmatic, Ford was voluble, quotable, and proudly eclectic. "We want to have something of everything," he said in the twenties. He felt acutely sensitive to the accelerating pace of social change. "Danger to our country is to be apprehended," he observed, "not so much from the influence of new things as from our forgetting the values of old

---

*As of May 1988, the Henry Ford Museum still displayed prominently a test tube containing "Edison's Last Breath." It is said that Ford asked Edison's son, Charles, to collect an exhaled breath from his expiring hero and friend of many decades. That test tube, along with Edison's hat and shoes, was found at the Fords' Fair Lane mansion following Clara Ford's death in 1950.

things."[37] Although Ford insisted that progress and nostalgia, the industrial present and the agrarian past, were entirely compatible, he swung back and forth between them with the regularity of a metronome. He liked nothing so much as a stroll through the village at twilight with his wife (see fig. 10.3), "enjoying the comfortable atmosphere of the past." Yet he also felt it imperative to remind the American public "how far and how fast we have come in technical progress in the last century or so. . . . Is it likely that we shall stop now?"[38] Not likely at all.

The public began to be officially admitted to the Museum on June 22, 1933. Within three years the crowds exceeded anyone's expectations. (The whole enterprise engaged Ford so deeply and personally that Museum and Village operations went into limbo from the time of his stroke in 1945 until his death in 1947.)[39] The appeal had several sources. Unlike the Georgian elegance of the American Wing, which seemed intimidating and just too perfect for many visitors, the greatest strengths of Ford's collection were drawn from the nineteenth century, especially the second half; and they ranged from amusing small toys to huge machines. Although the Museum itself may not have been on a human scale, its eclecticism (and foibles) made it seem far more accessible to visitors.

Henry Ford's anti-intellectual obsession with education by means of objects rather than books was effectively communicated to the masses. Even his patriotism—which Halsey, de Forest, Kent, and other prominent Wingers certainly shared—somehow seemed more inclusive and egalitarian. "It is to be an institution of learning," Ford wrote, "for young fellows and old fellows, for everybody who wants to know the greatness of our country and what has made it great." Journalists who wrote about Ford were not consistently friendly; but more often than not they acknowledged his public generosity and his common touch. One writer observed that Ford had accumulated his phenomenal array of objects "to save them for America." His collection "is a free gift, to be enjoyed by the nation now and for all time."[40]

The same author also gave specificity to Ford's impact in democratizing the role of museums in American culture: "These hand-turned, rush-bottomed chairs are the middle-class cousins of Duncan Phyfe tables, Savery highboys, Sheraton desks, Chippendale cabinets stored elsewhere in protective wrappings. . . . [Ford's] aim is to show how the man of ordinary means furnished his house and maintained it."[41]

The ultimate compliment, however, may have come from a man very different in temperament yet embarked at the same time upon a similarly fabulous enterprise: John D. Rockefeller, Jr. After the Rockefellers visited Dearborn in the autumn of 1929 for the Edison Institute's dedication, Rockefeller sent a heartfelt note of appreciation: "I fancy no one was more interested in your old village, through which you showed me personally . . . than I was, because of what we are doing at Williamsburg. You have already wrought wonders, and all with the high purpose of stimulating youth to noble endeavor."[42]

Less than seven months later Rockefeller could not resist stopping to see the Wayside Inn en route to his summer home on Mount Desert in Maine. He dropped in unpretentiously for lunch, and was overwhelmed by the hospitality of an extremely attentive staff. Once again he sent Ford the most genuine appreciation and praise: "Please accept my congratulations on what you have accomplished and on the influence, educational, historical and from a patriotic point of view, that the Inn is having daily on untold numbers of people."[43]

Frank Campsall, who ran the inn for Ford, zipped off an enthusiastic report of Rockefeller's visit to Edsel Ford in Dearborn, who by then was deeply involved in his father's operations—both at the factory and at museum sites (fig. 11.2).

> At noon time a short dark gentleman arrived and inquired if he might have lunch. When the young lady at the desk asked his name, he said very modestly, "Mr. Rockefeller," John D. Rockefeller, Jr. We had been expecting him, but hardly expected that he would arrive, unannounced, in such an unpretentious way! But he came alone and primarily to learn something of the management of the Inn—that he might incorporate some of the workings of this Inn into his own, recently acquired Raleigh Tavern at Williamsburg, Virginia.[44]

Despite the fact that Ford and Rockefeller had fundamentally private temperaments, and that their interests as collectors overlapped, they decided as early as 1929 to co-operate rather than compete, and their

11.2 Henry and Edsel Ford in the Plympton House, 1941, at Greenfield Village. From the collections of Henry Ford Museum & Greenfield Village.

relationships concerning Americana, philanthropic interests, and even vacations at Seal Harbor, Maine, remained congenial throughout their lives. The Reverend W. A. R. Goodwin, whose determination led to the restoration of Williamsburg, wrote to Ford's aide for restorations explaining how many letters Rockefeller received offering quality objects for sale. Goodwin volunteered to forward many of these to Ford if he was interested. "Mr. Ford is creating a museum. We are only interested in furnishing houses and have no definite museum plan in mind," Goodwin explained.[45]

The Rockefellers made occasional visits to Detroit and Dearborn in the autumn, and the Fords came to Williamsburg several times in late April, when the flowers were most lovely and the heat not yet a problem. When Rockefeller wrestled with logistical arrangements in planning the Williamsburg Inn, Ford supplied precise information that ranged from salary scales and tipping regulations to levels of staff and menus. In 1935 when Kenneth Chorley, the president of Colonial Williamsburg, Inc., wanted to put several eighteenth-century coaches and perhaps even sleighs into active service, he sent senior staff members to Greenfield Village to observe how all the details of routes and maintenance were handled there. Henry and his son Edsel could not have been more obliging.[46]

From time to time each man tried to interest the other in some pet project—as in 1929, when Rockefeller inquired of Ford about possibly supporting the preservation of Friendship Hill, Albert Gallatin's historic home in western Pennsylvania. The Fords indicated quite candidly that they were utterly preoccupied at that time in Dearborn; and Rockefeller graciously backed off, declaring that he had no personal interest in Gallatin's home "other than a general interest in the preservation of important historical monuments."[47]

I V

WILLIAMSBURG, Virginia, did have a life prior to its restoration during the decade that followed 1928. It had been a very lively place in the eighteenth century when it served as the colony's capital. Even half a century after Richmond supplanted it in political prominence, the Fourth of July could be quite a gala occasion. In 1837, for example, on the Golden Jubilee of the Constitution, the Williamsburg Light Infantry Guards paraded along with the Norfolk Light Artillery Blues (did they somehow manage to perform in Norfolk on the very same day?). Solemn exercises were held at the College of William and Mary, founded in 1693, and celebratory dinners took place.[48]

Following the Civil War Williamsburg fell under a dark cloud for more than half a century: impoverished, the College struggling for its very life, with shabby touches of old elegance here and there. Genteel ways compensated somewhat for the general seediness. A visitor from Baltimore in 1887 who wrote an account commented upon the carriage that met her: it had a large hole in the floor through which the driver "warned me not to precipitate myself." At the only hotel in "the village" she found "nice airy rooms with very clean muslin curtains and pillow covers," a parlor with Chippendale chairs, old family portraits, "and various other signs of better days."[49]

A time would come, however, when many of the locals would look back with nostalgia to those somnolent days before the Rockefeller blitz. In June 1928, when the residents finally realized what was about to hit them, they convened a public meeting. A minority view, expressed with intense feeling nonetheless, asked two rhetorical questions: "We will reap dollars, but will we own our town? Will you not be in the position of a butterfly pinned to a card in a glass cabinet, or like a mummy unearthed in the tomb of Tutankhamen?"[50] Prior to the Rockefeller restoration the College had about 150 students, and the total population did not exceed 2,000 souls, including several hundred at the state insane asylum, easily the most prominent institution in town. One inmate, who clearly had not lost his wits entirely, described Williamsburg as a place where "one thousand lazy live off five hundred crazy."[51]

THE REVEREND W. A. R. GOODWIN (fig. 11.3) first became the Episcopal rector at Bruton Parish Church in 1903, was transferred to St. Paul's at Rochester, New York, in 1909, and then returned to Williamsburg in 1923 as head of the Department of Biblical Literature and Religious Education and director of the endowment campaign at William and Mary. He began his second rectorship at Bruton Parish in July 1926. Restoration of that historic church had occurred in 1907 at the time of the Jamestown Tercentenary, a big year for visitors if not for modern tourism in the Tidewater region. Goodwin's presence at the parish in 1907 helped to provide the stimulus, and in 1924 he sent a most unusual letter to Edsel Ford, whom he did not know. "Seriously," Goodwin began, "I want your father to buy Williamsburg, the old Colonial capital of Virginia at a time when Virginia included the land on which the Ford factory is now located [Michigan], as in those days the western boundary of Virginia was the Pacific ocean." Following three paragraphs in which he lovingly described the town, Goodwin boldly told Ford that "It would be the most unique and spectacular gift to American history and to the preservation of American traditions that could be made by any American." Then came the one-two punch:

Other men have bought rare books and preserved historic houses. No man yet has had the vision and the courage to buy and to preserve a Colonial village, and Williamsburg is the one remain-

11.3   The Reverend W.A.R. Goodwin and his dog Alaska (date unknown). Courtesy of Colonial Williamsburg Foundation.

ing Colonial village which any man could buy. . . . Unfortunately you and your father are at present the chief contributors to the destruction of this city. With the new concrete roads leading from Newport News to Richmond and with the road to nearby James-town passing through the city, garages and gas tanks are fast spoiling the whole appearance of the old streets and the old city, and most of the cars which stop at the garages and gas tanks are Ford Cars!

Unfortunately Ford's brother, William, leaked copies of this letter and accompanying photographs to the press, and newspapers re-sponded by running extracts or accounts of Goodwin's gutsy proposi-tion even though they wondered about some of the possible consequences. The *Baltimore Sun,* for example, worried that "a sense of unreality, of artificiality would attach to Dr. Goodwin's dream city. Would he people the House of Burgesses with wax figures?"[52] And so forth.

In any event, the Fords did not seem to be interested, although in April 1926, right after John D. Rockefeller had been Goodwin's guest at Williamsburg, Goodwin continued to woo Ford via the manager of

11.4   The Reverend W. A. R. Goodwin and John D. Rockefeller, Jr., October 4, 1928. Courtesy of Colonial Williamsburg Foundation.

the Ford dealership in nearby Norfolk. That effort came to nought, as had a 1923 approach to J. P. Morgan, Jr.[53] But not all affluent juniors are alike. John D. Rockefeller, Jr., was quite smitten by the tour he received (fig. 11.4), and within half a year decided to embark upon the most extraordinary restoration project in all of American history. Because that story has now been told quite fully from several points of view, I will concentrate upon selected aspects most germane to the focus of this book.[54]

Although Rockefeller was a self-effacing and cautious man (fig. 11.5), his enthusiasm was such that he too moved with prudent speed. Following a second visit in November 1926, he sent Goodwin a lengthy and explicitly unofficial letter of understanding. Although thousands of details and hundreds of major decisions remained to be made—how to purchase properties covertly so that real estate prices would not skyrocket? whether to reconstruct major buildings where nothing at all remained to restore?—the letter is remarkable for its vision, clarity, and overall grasp of the potential and implications of this enterprise. Rockefeller requested particular information concerning the historical importance of various properties, and their present financial situations (pertaining to mortgages, etc.); reaffirmed their joint decision to concentrate at first on two points—where the House of Burgesses stood and the "district in the vicinity of Bruton Church, Wythe House and the Common" (fronting the area where the Governor's Palace would be rebuilt); and, quite remarkably, he reiterated that "this proposition would not interest me unless some complete thing could be done and so tied up with the University and its historical department as to insure

11.5 John D. Rockefeller, Jr. (date unknown). Prints and Photographs Division, Library of Congress.

not only its permanent maintenance but its permanent use as a centre for the study of American history."[55]

During 1927–28 Rockefeller maneuvered covertly and anonymously to acquire as much of the crucial real estate as possible. On June 12, 1928, it was revealed that the mysterious "Mr. David" who was swiftly gobbling up choice parts of the town was, in fact, Rockefeller. A Boston architectural firm, Perry, Shaw & Hepburn, was retained in an active (not just a consulting) capacity, and "restoration" (meaning archaeology, serious research into old records, relocating and rehabilitating structures) got under way. A barebones chronology can provide a sense of pace: in October 1932 the first conference of an Advisory Historians' Committee was held in Williamsburg; in 1933 the Raleigh Tavern was rebuilt and the Wren Building restored at the College; in 1934, the most momentous single year, the Governor's Palace and the Capitol were completed, the first Garden Week occurred, with hostesses in colonial costumes as an experiment, and on October 20, President Roosevelt dedicated Duke of Gloucester Street as "the most historic avenue in all America" (fig. 11.6); in 1936 the Public Gaol was finished; in January 1937 *Landscape Architecture* magazine devoted an entire issue to Colonial Williamsburg, *National Geographic* featured it in April, and the Craft House opened in October; in 1939 a Board of Advisory Historians was created for the Research Department, Goodwin died, and Mrs. Rockefeller donated her folk art collection to C.W.; in 1940 the George Wythe House was completed; in 1949 the Powder Magazine; and in 1951 the Brush-Everard House.

During the critical half-dozen years from 1928 until 1934, Goodwin

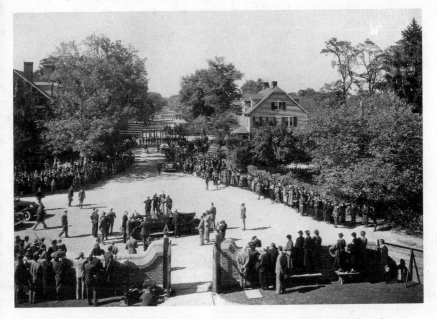

11.6 President Franklin Delano Roosevelt at the opening of Duke of Gloucester Street in Colonial Williamsburg, October 20, 1934. (Photo taken from the Capitol.) Courtesy of Colonial Williamsburg Foundation.

played a variety of essential roles, from handling real estate to soothing local ruffled feathers to providing general counsel involving problems of policy and history. In October 1930, for instance, he prepared a lengthy memorandum, a kind of "think piece," that touched upon diverse matters. He predicted that purists would come for purposes of study and in order to copy details.

> Others will come to see the creation as a whole. They will see it not so much through pure intellect and reason as they will in the light of a stimulated imagination. To them the Restoration will open vistas that will beckon fancy and inspire dreams. To these the touch of the theatrical will be an inspiration.
> . . . Then there will be the multitude. To them the Restoration may be the beginning of an interest. For them there should be some measure of appeal that might approach the spectacular in order to attract attention, provoke inquiry, and inspire further interest.

Goodwin proposed that Duke of Gloucester Street be closed to cars so that "theatrical" scenes could be facilitated:

A cart driven by an old negro; an ox-cart standing by a water
trough; a stage-coach with coachman, footman, and driver, standing in front of the Tavern and used when desired to drive tourists
around. . . . Such scenes would show ancient modes of life and
costume and would appeal to many who will not understand the
fine points of architecture.[56]

Goodwin may or may not have been a social snob, a racist, or an
entrepreneur; but various visitor surveys conducted over the years
demonstrate that he was surely a realist in acknowledging the diverse
interests and cultural backgrounds that tourists would bring to Williamsburg.[57]

Finally Goodwin acknowledged that top staff members and early
advisers to C.W. did not agree on the criteria for acquiring antiques to
furnish all of the public buildings and private residences at the restoration. Would pieces made in England be acceptable? Historically there
would have been quite a few; but some consultants felt strongly that
Williamsburg ought to showcase only the finest traditions of American
craftsmanship, design, and materials. What about pieces made in the
Northern colonies? There certainly were many Philadelphia pieces
crafted for clients outside Pennsylvania. Goodwin exposed the basis of
the dispute:

Both Mr. Perry [a historical architect from Boston] and Mr. Myers
[a prominent collector from New York], while appreciating the
great value of procuring Virginia-made furniture or American-
made furniture used in Virginia during the Colonial period, seem
not disposed to purchase such furniture unless it is perfect of its
kind in workmanship and design. They are also disposed, if I
understand correctly their position, to not approve the purchase
of English-made furniture, of the period of our work. . . .

Goodwin indicated his sensitivity to regional pride by urging that a
Virginia-based architect be added to the staff in order to "remove the
criticism . . . often heard, that the Restoration is entirely a reflection of
the New England mind."[58]

Goodwin's remarkably comprehensive "memorandum" calls several
important points to our attention. First, that Rockefeller and his salaried staff managed to garner advice and input from the finest experts
in the United States, such as R. T. H. Halsey, Louis Guerineau Myers,
and Henry Francis du Pont.[59]

Second, there was a grave and persistent problem with local and
sectional sentiments—both being very strong and sensitive to slights. As
Goodwin candidly said (privately) in 1929: "The Restoration is being
done . . . not primarily for the present and certainly not for the present
inhabitants of Williamsburg, but as a witness to the future of the glories
of the hallowed past." The mostly Northern personnel who trooped in

and took over in order to "save" Williamsburg were outsiders; and the locals never lost sight of that as a social reality. The proud Pulaski Club of Williamsburg, which had been established in 1779, did not invite John D. Rockefeller, Jr., to become a member until 1950.[60] When Kenneth Chorley, president of C.W., Inc., spoke to the Rotary Club of Williamsburg in October 1934, he regarded it as a major diplomatic mission and exuded every ounce of charm and tact that he could muster. "We have not attempted to transform Williamsburg into a museum," he explained. "We have done something which makes a number of our buildings resemble museums, but after all the city is a living community."[61]

That politesse was smashed to smithereens in 1935, however, when a two-year struggle arose over the question: Should C.W. exhibition buildings be open to the public on Sunday mornings prior to one o'clock? Many devoutly Christian locals, and some visitors, felt deeply offended. Other visitors were equally annoyed, obviously, when they could not complete their appointed rounds expeditiously. Many of the hostesses, though, simply refused to "play history" instead of being pious or relaxing with their families. Chorley clearly wanted to stay open; and it was the Reverend Goodwin of Bruton Parish who actually proposed Sunday morning opening as an experiment during the summer of 1935. Rockefeller "checked" with Goodwin a year later to see how the experiment had gone, and was "glad to find that your Church has been so little affected by what seems to be public demand which the Restoration has not felt it could ignore."[62]

John D. Rockefeller, Jr., was a conscientious Baptist, a sound businessman, and a gracious soul who did not like to offend anyone. Since he could not be assured of Divine guidance directly in this matter, he did the next best thing: he consulted Harry Emerson Fosdick, his minister at the Riverside Church in Manhattan, who, by chance, had spent ten days in Williamsburg enjoying Rockefeller hospitality in November 1935. Fosdick did an absolutely masterful job of discreet investigation. On the one hand, people come long distances, most commonly on a weekend, and "are grievously disappointed if they discover the public buildings closed." On the other hand, "it is against the Virginia tradition and would be against the colonial tradition to open public buildings for a fixed charge on a Sunday morning . . . [moreover] opening them for a charge is the one place in the program at Williamsburg where captious minds might suspect some element of commercialism." Fortunately, Fosdick happened to attend a luncheon where all the ministers of the community were present; he took their pulse and concluded that "with one exception I do not think any of them felt very strongly about it."[63]

Given Harry Emerson Fosdick's considered blessing to continue the policy that he preferred, Rockefeller sent off a judicious reply and rationale to the original complainant.

We continue unqualifiedly to share, as we always have, the feeling of those who would preserve, if possible, the ancient quiet and peace of the Sabbath Day in Williamsburg, giving the fullest opportunity for church attendance to those who desire it. However, the consensus of opinion seems but to confirm the position which we have already taken, namely, that to follow that policy would work a real hardship to the many from outside who can only visit Williamsburg on Sunday, and who, generally speaking, would not be in church if they were not there.[64]

When spiritual values and local custom came into direct conflict with patriotic values and touristic traditions, the latter mustered clerical as well as secular support. Predictably, it prevailed.

During the early 1930s Goodwin and Chorley kept sectional cordiality uppermost in their minds. Goodwin told the committee on antiques in 1931 that he would not oppose "the purchase of a few more Northern objects, if they can be purchased reasonably on the understanding that they might later be sold if not needed." The next year, when Chorley addressed the Colonial Dames of America in the State of Virginia, he sounded more unctuous than chivalrous:

That any citizen of New York should be permitted to address a Virginia audience—particularly an audience of Virginia Colonial Dames, on the subject of Southern Colonial history, architecture and gardens is the most astounding instance of Southern hospitality I have ever heard of.

He then informed the Dames that their organization and his, fortuitously, shared a common purpose: "The collection of manuscripts, traditions, relics and mementoes of bygone days for preservation, to commemorate the history and success of the American Revolution . . . to diffuse healthful and intelligent information in regard to American history and tending to create popular interest therein," and so forth.[65] Healthful, like an autumn tonic?

Two years later Chorley expressed satisfaction in seeing "so many evidences of a true national interest in Williamsburg." Just before Christmas he told the assembled hostesses and candidates for the guide service at C.W. to beware of sectional chauvinism. "There is no battle between Jamestown and Plymouth," he declared; "there ARE bitter skirmishes between ignorant human beings. . . . There is no war between Colonial Williamsburg and Colonial Boston, the war was with Great Britain." By 1935 Virginia journalists were calling Kenneth Chorley the "Virginia Yankee." A higher form of hyphenated Americanism, perhaps. Later that same year a woman reported from Cape Cod that a lecture on the Williamsburg restoration given at Harwich Port had been a huge success. C.W. had, indeed, become a national rather than a regional success, and had done so virtually overnight.[66]

Neither Rockefeller nor his staff anticipated such success. One of his oldest employees, the grand vizier of his New York office, acknowledged in 1932 having "grave doubts as to whether Williamsburg will be the mecca for enough people to really make it worth while. The town is too far away from large centers." During the late summer of 1933 Rockefeller told Chorley, rather apprehensively, that "we have not yet had time to decide how to operate the reconstructed town."[67]

During the first week of April 1934, however, Williamsburg simply bulged with visitors. Chorley said that he didn't know why, "except that we have had an extraordinarily good week of weather, people seem to be traveling again, and perhaps it is due to the publicity which we got in connection with the opening of the Capitol." Whatever the cause, official attendance figures for C.W.'s first decade are truly impressive:

1932	4,047
1933	13,248
1934	31,457
1935	62,172
1936	95,497
1937	151,036
1938	170,872
1939	153,206
1940	185,726
1941	210,824

In 1942, because of the war, attendance plummeted to 48,271 and it did not surpass the 1941 high until 1950, when the Cold War made Williamsburg a very special American icon, as we shall see in chapter seventeen.[68]

The unanticipated surge of popularity during the mid- and later thirties brought diverse consequences—mostly positive but a few of them negative or even regrettable. A blistering conceptual critique in 1938 from Frank Lloyd Wright had little impact. One of Mr. Rockefeller's staff architects wrote a rebuttal and that was the end of it. Wright would have been *persona non grata* in Williamsburg. Although Rockefeller spent winters during his final decade (the 1950s) in Arizona, not so far from Taliesin West, I doubt whether he ever bothered to look in on Wright.

Some critical voices complained that Rockefeller spent untold millions on dead structures and their precious contents while so many living Americans went hungry and homeless during the Great Depression. C.W.'s unofficial response was unintentionally amusing: Tell the world how *un*extravagant the whole enterprise was. According to one story that floated in 1930, authentic antiques were actually cheaper than reproductions because the latter were sturdier and less soiled or damaged. According to another, no antiques had been purchased from speculators or pricey dealers; and many had come as donations from people eager to be associated with the restoration. Chorley instructed the hostesses to be very careful in responding to inevitable questions about cost, and not to emphasize luxury, especially in the decorative arts.[69]

The most tragic aspect of the whole enterprise, however, is that it resulted in the destruction or relocation of homes and community institutions of blacks, and it strained relationships between blacks and whites. What makes this especially ironic, of course, is that the Rockefeller family, starting with the generation of John, Jr., has for a long time made African-American education and social justice a major object of their philanthropy. A visit to the Hampton Institute in April 1926 helped to bring JDR, Jr., within Goodwin's grasp—a neglected fact. Rockefeller may have been comfortable with a hierarchical status quo, but he was not a Negrophobe. He did not feel satisfied with the quality of red bricks being made for the reconstructions and restorations until his staff found, by serendipity, Babe Sowers, a black man who still molded bricks by hand on a farm near Winston-Salem, North Carolina, just as his great-great-grandfather and everyone in between had done. Babe Sowers became a hero to the Rockefeller purists. He could mold twelve bricks a minute, or four thousand per day. John Henry, move over and make way for Babe Sowers, a man whose legendary efforts were witnessed and documented.[70]

By the early 1940s, however, Rockefeller had acquiesced in the argument that white tourists would be comfortable only if African-Americans were visible in eighteenth-century livery as deferential servants but invisible as twentieth-century free persons. A separate dormitory was constructed for "male colored help"; relocated housing for blacks was carefully kept beyond the view of tourists at C.W.; and the Williamsburg Inn and other dining and guest facilities remained strictly segregated. In 1943 Rockefeller drafted for Chorley's use a "statement to be made to any colored person applying for accommodations at any of our hostelries": "The management has not thus far found it practicable to provide for both colored and white guests. I (or we are) [sic] am sorry we cannot accommodate you (or cannot take care of you; or cannot offer you hospitality)."[71]

The media, needless to say, which lavished much attention on Williamsburg—all of it upbeat—never mentioned racial matters: over and over again the press doted on costume balls, the revival of handicraft industries, all the Washington dignitaries who attended the grand opening of the inn, and exquisite gardens that bloomed in the spring.[72]

The staff, meanwhile, kept busy trying to cope, among other things, with success. What to do about people who made professional tours (for fees) in which they lectured elsewhere about Colonial Williamsburg, showing lantern slides that they had privately made right after touring C.W.? Chorley conceded that they could do little or nothing. What to

do about people, some of them socially prominent or politically influential, who desperately wanted to borrow or buy architectural plans of
"some of the smaller houses" in Williamsburg? Kenneth Chorley gave
a polite no to that one. "The main reason why we have set this policy,"
he told Edward R. Stettinius, "is that we do not feel that it conforms
with the ethics of the architectural profession. In addition, there are
usually so many alterations which are necessary to adapt one of the
buildings to another site that it has not proved to be a practicable
procedure."[73]

Despite the impression one might all too readily receive that Chorley
was little more than a public relations manager and a mouthpiece for
Mr. Rockefeller, as president of the restoration and then of Colonial
Williamsburg, Inc., during the 1940s Chorley wrestled with some very
tough policy decisions, quite often wisely, and he was a master of the
five- to six-page memorandum in which he would lay out for Rockefeller possible policies, their rationales, and their long-term implications.
In 1940, to supply just one example, a major question arose: what to do
about original manuscripts, documents, maps, and books? Chorley's
lengthy memorandum is a model of careful deliberation (if, of course,
one assumes that the only people who mattered ate with china and
silver and owned unique documents of diverse sorts). It is an elitist
perspective, to be sure, but it was also formulated more than half a
century ago.

> Now if we are going to carry out our policy of trying to *recreate
> Williamsburg* as it was in the eighteenth century, in so far as it
> is humanly possible to do so, then must we not agree that books,
> manuscripts, maps, and documents were just as much a part of the
> life of the people in the eighteenth century as were the beds they
> slept in, the china they ate from, and the silver they used at their
> meals. As a matter of fact, from another point of view, these
> documents are more valuable than the furniture and furnishings
> the people lived with because they constitute the only written—
> and therefore the only fully reliable—record of life in the eigh-
> teenth century.[74]

Predictably, perhaps, Chorley became the point man, a kind of missionary who proselytized on behalf of historic preservation with Colonial Williamsburg as the model. Early in December of 1941, for
example, he spoke at Raleigh to the North Carolina Society for the
Preservation of Antiquities. The title of his talk? "The Significance of
the Preservation of Historic Sites, with Especial Reference to Tryon's
Palace." His two basic themes: the pursuit of authenticity and the patriotic, social, and economic importance of tourism. After the war Chorley
worked out a formulaic speech that delighted audiences from Newport,
Rhode Island, to Charleston, South Carolina: talk about the saga of

Williamsburg for a while, and then lavish praise upon the treasures and the historical significance of the place he was visiting. His ubiquitous and multi-purpose message was summed up in a single sentence at Newport. "A few hundred years from now," he told the crowd, "the present shabby evidences of our early beginnings will be among the most priceless treasures in our nation's heritage." The past was surely a sound investment. Heritage had hurtled off on its career as a contemporary by-word in American culture. And Williamsburg would be the grand-daddy of them all.[75]

Fundamentally, in this instance, Chorley spoke prophetically. In addition to Charleston and Newport, the profound influence of C.W., Inc., would be seen in large ways as well as small in Bath and New Bern, North Carolina; at New Castle, Delaware; at East Hampton, Long Island; at Plimoth Plantation on the south shore of Massachusetts Bay; at Grace Episcopal Church and at the Moore ("Surrender") house in Yorktown, Virginia; at New Orleans, at Fort Ticonderoga, and at Charles Town, West Virginia. If Williamsburg isn't the grand-daddy, then it has certainly been the mother lode, especially in training historical architects. That specialized and highly skilled profession simply did not exist prior to 1930. It has flourished since 1945 under the supervision of men (mostly) who cut their professional teeth at Williamsburg.

V

THERE is a tendency, then, for obvious reasons, to attribute all good things (and a few not so good) in the realm of historic preservation and collecting Americana to the benign impact of Henry Ford and John D. Rockefeller, Jr. That is an unhistorical perspective, however, because institutions of memory, and specifically American ones, did not begin *de novo* in 1932–33 at Williamsburg and Dearborn, and we therefore do an injustice to their predecessors if we subscribe to such a partial perspective. The Daughters of the American Revolution, for instance, began to own collectibles as an organization around the turn of the century and opened a "museum of revolutionary relics" in 1909; their holdings have increased quite steadily ever since. The D.A.R. Museum, located a few blocks from the White House in Washington, cannot begin to exhibit at any one time all of its silver, needlework, furniture, eighteenth-century ceramics, and paintings. Most of its decorative arts collection (50,000 items) is American; but some of the choicest pieces are objects made in Europe that influenced, or were emulated by, American craftsmen. The D.A.R. Museum owns, for instance, a silver cup made in 1789 by the Parisian silversmith Denis Colombier which provided a model for eight cups produced by Paul Revere in 1795.[76]

Moreover, even the Rockefeller interest in natural history and historic preservation antedated Williamsburg. JDR, Jr., made modest contributions toward the preservation of George Washington's head-quarters at White Plains in the years after 1917. Because most visitors to national parks know so little about the scenery that they see, the National Park Service decided early in the 1920s to enhance its interpretive programs. For the 1924 season a Rockefeller grant of $70,500 made possible a specially designed museum at Yosemite Park that explained the geology, flora, fauna, and history of that distinctive area. In 1927 a smaller Rockefeller grant facilitated a similar museum at Grand Canyon. Early in the 1930s, when the Wakefield National Memorial Association became obsessed with re-creating George Washington's birthplace, John D. Rockefeller, Jr., purchased the site for $115,000, and also donated bricks manufactured at Williamsburg for the reconstruction of a house about which nothing was known.[77]

Because the principal Rockefeller home was situated at Pocantico Hills in North Tarrytown, it is not surprising that John D. Rockefeller, Jr., eventually took an interest in historical aspects of the lower Hudson Valley.[78] During the early 1940s he assisted the Historical Society of the Tarrytowns in preserving a 1683 Dutch manor house called Philipse Castle; in restoring Washington Irving's home, Sunnyside (during 1945–47); and subsequently in purchasing Van Cortlandt Manor in 1953, restoring it, and then turning it over to Sleepy Hollow Restorations to manage. Staff members came up from Williamsburg to assist in these activities, especially involving architecture and landscaping. Rockefeller's input aroused enthusiasm and activity on the part of a newly formed Hudson River Conservation Society.[79]

In 1943 a ranking member of Rockefeller's staff politely but firmly chided the Historical Society of the Tarrytowns' director for making extravagant claims in an article on behalf of Williamsburg. Referring to the "mutually beneficial relationship Colonial Williamsburg enjoys with organizations," many of which had undertaken restoration and preservation work, the C.W. official stressed that "our policy has always been to lean over backwards to make no statements that could in any way be construed as belittling their efforts or comparing their work with ours."[80] That was not only a politic policy, it had a firm basis in terms of chronology and causation. Something was clearly in the air during the mid- and later 1920s, of which Williamsburg was very much a part. In 1924 the *Saturday Evening Post* ran an article about the restoration of fine colonial architecture and praised the work of early American craftsmen.[81]

Soon after World War I, William Sumner Appleton, lifeblood leader of the SPNEA, spoke of the need for an outdoor museum in New England that would preserve buildings that might otherwise be lost. During a rainy weekend in 1926, ten years before the Wells brothers purchased a 167-acre farm that subsequently became the site of Old Sturbridge Village, Albert B. Wells went "antiqueering" with a friend in Vermont and promptly developed an intense personal interest in the furniture, tools, and material culture of early, rural New England. Within a few years his collection had swiftly outgrown his home, various additions, and barns. Old Sturbridge existed in embryo before the Wells brothers had ever heard of C.W. Similarly, Mystic Seaport Museum was founded in 1929 by three residents of Mystic, Connecticut, who believed that relics of the colonial maritime past were being rapidly lost or destroyed. The village museum opened its doors to the public in 1930 with one building and one boat, the sandbagger *Annie*. Those three founders also knew nothing of Williamsburg. They perceived their own challenge and defined their own mission. By 1980 their successors had assembled sixty buildings, three major ships, and more than two hundred small craft.[82]

Two vital distinctions ought to be kept clearly in mind. First, the decades from about 1908 until 1928 were notable for efforts devoted to the preservation of individual historic structures, usually churches or else the homes of famous people, like Alexander Hamilton and Nathan Hale, or small utopian communities like Bronson Alcott's Fruitlands, located in Harvard, Massachusetts.[83] Such activities by no means ceased in 1928; but the next few decades were more notable for the creation or preservation of historic villages, of historic urban districts (starting at Charleston, South Carolina, in 1931), of more complex sites to administer and exhibit, such as manors, gristmills, and entire Spanish mission complexes, or old colonial towns like Annapolis, Maryland, and Bath, North Carolina.[84] As available funding and popular enthusiasm grew, the whole scale of preservation activity increased.

The second distinction to be borne in mind involves the contrast between those major national projects that were initiated during the 1920s—national in interest, recognition, and the financial support they received—and the proliferation of more modest local museums during the 1930s. Sometimes their modesty was the result of scarce resources; but the phenomenon arose from an explosion of local pride and appeal based upon the "discovery" of neglected local resources.* Salem's Pioneer Village emerged in 1930 as part of the celebration of Massachusetts Bay's tercentenary. The first annual exhibit of Sandwich glass took place in that old Cape Cod community in 1931; a significant local glass museum soon followed—all resulting from an initiative taken by the local historical society in 1925 to celebrate the centennial of the Sandwich glass factory. The Museum of the City of New York opened early in March 1936 with exhibits designed like stage sets: 1673, the opening of New York-to-Boston mail; 1830, a ship semaphore on Staten Island, the "wireless of the day"; 1858,

---

*The Transylvanians, an association founded in October 1929, had nothing to do with Dracula. Its members wanted to learn more about, and to commemorate, the settlement of an area around Henderson, Kentucky, once known as Transylvania.

Samuel F. B. Morse and the first Atlantic cable; 1867, the first stock ticker; 1888, Wall Street during the Great Blizzard; and so forth. In September 1937 an affluent couple bought the 161-year-old Squire Enoch Perley House in South Bridgeton, Maine, and moved it to land along Highland Lake, where it would be restored and serve as a local museum.[85] These activities were highly representative of tradition-orientation as a local impulse during the 1930s.

The two by-words that bubble up constantly, no matter which historic site we look at, great or small, are "authentic" and "education."* The man who in 1927 moved Mitchie Tavern, located near Monticello in Virginia—where so many patriots had talked politics and swapped local gossip—in order to preserve it as a local museum, insisted that he had "taken every care to retain an authentic colonial atmosphere." When Edward M. Riley, for many years the director of research at Colonial Williamsburg, was asked what constrained the quest for authenticity in re-creating an eighteenth-century community, he mentioned two considerations: public health and law![86]

Educational service to a republican citizenry had been among the stated goals of Jeremy Belknap in 1791 when he formed the Massachusetts Historical Society, the first of its kind in the nation. Although the Society did sponsor lecture series and similar events from time to time, the goal of public education was honored more often in theory than in practice by institutions of memory in the nineteenth-century United States. When Clara Endicott Sears opened her Indian Museum at Fruitlands in 1929, however, she insisted upon its educational purpose. When Old Sturbridge Village was still in gestation in 1938, its founders emphasized that it would be "for the educational benefit of the public"; and Ward Melville proposed just the same thing when dedicating the Carriage Museum at Stony Brook on Long Island.[87]

We have already heard from Rockefeller and Ford concerning their similar sense of mission, particularly for young people. Edward M. Riley, who had academic training, said that what he loved most about his work at Williamsburg was the opportunity to teach, "not in a classroom of 25 but of millions."[88] When Kenneth Chorley addressed the hostesses and guide candidates at Williamsburg in 1934, he posed a series of rhetorical questions to them. "What is it that we are to teach? It is HISTORY in its real and broader sense. And what is history? Briefly, it is the truth about the past." He then followed with an anti-academic diatribe that, despite its obviously defensive tone, was and remained representative of the outlook of those who administered such institu-

---

*Kenneth Chorley wrote the following in 1941: "When Mr. John D. Rockefeller, Jr., undertook this project, he did so on one condition—that the work should be done accurately. In consequence, authenticity has been virtually the religion of our institution, and sacrifices have been offered before its altar. Personal preferences, architectural design, time, expense, and, at times, even the demands of beauty have given way to the exacting requirements of authenticity."

tions of memory for the next two generations. To the narrow and "bigoted historian," Chorley chanted,

> he who seeks to gain the experience of the ages through man's written record alone, through dates and duly recorded and authenticated statements, to him Williamsburg is apt to be a none too familiar name and its present state that of a theatrical and popular sideshow for the amusement rather than the education of man. . . . Yet, the real, the broad historian will make haste to claim these various phases we have mentioned—architecture, decoration, gardens, and the like—as great extensions of the annals and archives of history. . . .[89]

Then came Chorley's grand finale, which he gradually made formulaic and repeated on dozens if not hundreds of occasions during the next quarter century. He genuinely meant it, however, because we also encounter these sentiments in private memoranda intended solely for John D. Rockefeller, Jr., who was already a convert. "Why do we wish to teach history?" Chorley asked. "The answer is simple and plain. Cicero said 'To be ignorant of what happened before you were born is to be forever a child. For what is man's lifetime unless the memory of past events is woven with those of earlier times.' "[90] That message, voiced in various modes, has been the dominant motif at most institutions of American memory ever since.

Chapter 12

REGIONAL RIVALRY, LOCAL PRIDE, AND THE CONTESTATION OF MEMORY

DURING THE 1920s, despite the centrifugal power of nationalism, various sorts of local and regional historical observances occurred even though they did not attract widespread notice. Examples might include Deerfield, Massachusetts, celebrating its 250th anniversary of settlement in August 1923; the sesquicentennial in 1929 of General Sullivan's march through central New York in order to "pacify" potentially hostile Indians; and observance that same year by the Lincoln-Douglas Society of Freeport, Illinois, of the seventy-first anniversary of those historic debates—an opportunity to unveil a new bronze statue of Lincoln.

During the subsequent decade such observances enjoyed increased popularity, especially when they involved local celebrations of events of national or regional significance: the Yorktown victory sesquicentennial in 1931; the bicentennial less than a year later of George Washington's birth; creation of the George Rogers Clark Memorial Sesquicentennial Commission in 1933, an affair of special importance in Illinois and Indiana; the tercentenary in 1936 of Long Island's settlement; the sesquicentennial in 1938 of the Northwest Territory, marked by the remembrance of June 15, 1788, when civil government had first been established at Marietta, Ohio, and followed on July 8, 1938, with a memorial to the "Start Westward of the Nation." In that same year Stephen Vincent Benét was invited to write a Tercentenary Ode to honor the initial meeting of the General Court of the Colony at New Haven, Connecticut.[1]

In 1928 a gentleman in Indiana correctly declared that "interest in American history with special emphasis on local history is spreading." He might very well have said local, state, and regional. In April 1933 the newly formed Pennsylvania Historical Association held its start-up meeting at Bethlehem, Pennsylvania, and adopted a constitution. The following year it launched a quarterly journal. On June 27, 1934, the

12.1   George R. Boynton, *Dixon Ryan Fox* (c. 1933), oil on canvas. Courtesy of the New York State Historical Association, Cooperstown.

Women's Club of Lancaster County, Virginia, sponsored Lancaster County Historical Day and called attention to the need for proper preservation and restoration of local records.[2] During the early 1930s John Crowe Ransom, Allen Tate, and others developed what they called an "aesthetic of regionalism" in literature. Meanwhile Grant Wood, John Steuart Curry, and Thomas Hart Benton sought a similar emphasis in painting; and quite a cluster of prominent historians became fascinated with regionalism as a means of testing the famous contentions about the frontier and sectionalism put forward by Frederick Jackson Turner.[3]

A highly representative figure in this movement was Dixon Ryan Fox (fig. 12.1), who served as the president of Union College in Schenectady from 1934 until his death in 1945, but more crucially, served as an energizing force while president of the New York State Historical Association from 1929 until 1945. His papers show him to have been a tireless source of encouragement to local historians throughout the state. Typical is this sentence from a letter that he wrote in 1937 to Mrs. Walter A. Hendricks of Penn Yan: "I continue to be deeply gratified at your success in preserving the Seneca history and tradition, particularly that you have induced Jesse Cornplanter to write down your old legends."[4]

Just beneath the surface of this apparently benign but bland surge of enthusiasm for local traditions and history, however, stormed a roiling sea of inter-regional rivalries and resentments, a yearning for cultural respect or recognition, and *occasional* cordiality. Sometimes the cordiality seems to have been genuine, but at other times a very thin veneer that barely concealed not decades but generations and even centuries of seething hostility. Here are three choice cuts from an expansive side of flesh that remained raw and festering during the interwar years.

- 1922: "I have read with great interest the little pamphlet, 'Virginia First,' which you were kind enough to send me. You make a very strong case. . . . [But] there is room enough and glory enough in this great America for Virginia and Massachusetts both and above all there is need enough for all of us [to] do our very best to sustain and illustrate the splendid traditions of our ancestors."[5]

- 1923: "I have had a distinct sense of disappointment in reading your article on John Randolph in Harper's Magazine. . . . I think it unfortunate that you depend so much upon Henry Adams, a man who shows his inveterate prejudice against everything Virginian throughout all his writings. . . . Adams in his biography speaks a good deal about gouging and fighting in Virginia. He might have used his talents to better advantage on the 'bundling' and 'tarrying' which was so common in New England. Doubtless Virginia was not a country of perfect manners or morals—I do not claim it was—, but there is plenty evidence that New England was no better."[6]

- 1924: "I sympathize with you in your attempt to make southern history vital, but I think you go too far when you speak of the ignorance of the North in southern history. There is just as great ignorance in the South on northern history, and both sections have been guilty of emphasizing their provincial spirit at the expense of balance. . . . Heaven knows there has been distortion on both sides to such an extent as to make it necessary to rewrite a good part of our history. . . . I am a New Englander by descent, but I had the good fortune to be born in New York and was bred there, so that on my return to New England I can feel the provincial atmosphere and laugh at the self-centered satisfaction of the descendants of the old settlers. That does not make me, however, any the less sensitive to the provincial in the South, which is based upon a deeper ignorance of the past than the smug attitude of the New Englander."[7]

I

THE CENTRAL problem, however, was that New England smugness had been around long enough and had achieved sufficient notoriety to offend people in other parts of the country. During the

1920s, when "Puritan-bashing" became a popular national pastime, Yankee insensitivity persisted even in public utterances and intersectional correspondence. As late as 1927 the well-known biographer Gamaliel Bradford (New England to his knobby kneecaps) could write the following to a prominent Southerner who edited a journal and had an extensive network of correspondents: "What chiefly impresses me, as I have recently been engaged in writing a study of Calhoun and in emphasizing the importance of State Rights, is that it is only some dozen of the States that can have any such sense of historical tradition. Through the great body of the West, state feeling is merely geographical, hardly even political, much less historical."[8]

Reactions within New England to that sort of arrogance varied. Insiders who originated elsewhere, such as Arthur M. Schlesinger, a professor of history at Harvard who had been reared in Ohio and initially taught there as well as Iowa, found New England provincialism amusing (in an irksome way). "I have passed on to [Samuel Eliot] Morison the corrections you noted," he told Allan Nevins in 1928, "but not the accompanying suggestion that he and my elder colleague [Edward Channing, who retired in 1929] should spend five years in that remote region, the West. Why should they be interested in that far-flung dependency of New England?" Another insider with a detached perspective, Worthington C. Ford, "editor" at the Massachusetts Historical Society, found it refreshing when James Truslow Adams needled New Englanders in 1923 with the publication of his irreverent and best-selling book, *Revolutionary New England, 1691–1776.*[9]

One dynamic very much in evidence throughout these tensions and conflicts has to gladden the heart of a practicing historian. Contemporaries seemed to recognize that writing history and biography from a particular point of view profoundly affected the sense of identity and self-image of people at most levels of society and in all parts of the country. Abraham Lincoln's most important early biographer, Josiah G. Holland, was a moralizer reared in the New England tradition. Because his book appeared in 1866, it established a frame of reference against which subsequent biographers would chip away for generations. Whether or not Lincoln really did like to tell earthy stories (Lyon G. Tyler of William and Mary called him "a vulgar dirty talker") and whether it mattered that he "used fine language in his public communications" became hotly contested during the 1920s.* William E. Dodd, a Southerner who taught American history at the University of Chicago,

---

*A number of ardent Confederate supporters tried to warn Tyler that after a while his printed attacks proved counterproductive. "I don't say they are not justified in truth, but they are just quoted per se without comment . . . in the Northern press. . . . It makes people angry and even more vicious than they were before. My contention is that if you fight for principles consistently, personalities will take care of themselves." (Matthew Page Andrews to Tyler, June 24, 1932, Tyler Papers, group 1 [Family], box 20, SLWM. See also Robert M. Hughes, a Norfolk lawyer, to Tyler, June 19, 1928, ibid.)

tried to no avail to persuade Tyler that Lincoln's language rose "to a high level."[10]

Tyler, the son of former President John Tyler's virile old age, served for many years as president of William and Mary. What he and Dodd and so many other educators recognized was the dominance exercised by New Englanders over textbook writing and the teaching of American history everywhere for more than a century. John Bach McMaster, whose vantage point was the middle states and the West, expressed his frustration with that hegemony in 1894.[11]

This reaction against New England's cultural hegemony had begun to brew more than thirty years prior to 1915. During the subsequent three decades, however, it developed into deep resentments openly expressed. David Potter, a courtly and judicious Southerner, remarked much later in an interview that Frederick Jackson Turner was "a Wisconsin boy reacting against the New England monopoly on learning. . . . His treatment of the frontier reflects the denial of the unique importance of New England."[12]* Because New England architects played such a crucial part in the restoration of Colonial Williamsburg, Virginians frequently grumbled that the project seemed "entirely a reflection of the New England mind."

The second American civil war, if I may call this phenomenon by that name, had as its principal stakes matters of self-respect and cultural autonomy. It was fought and refought during the interwar years by educators, by serious journalists, by the popular press, and by demagogic politicians. At the level of educators we encounter Southerners as well as Northerners constantly trying to persuade latter-day fire-eaters to cool it.

- A Negrophobic woman in Athens, Georgia, who detested Henry Cabot Lodge's *Short History of the English Colonies in America,* wrote to Albert Bushnell Hart of Harvard: "Of course you have gotten your authority from New England and that is in largest measure absolutely unjust to the South. We cant blame those writers for we have not done our duty [in writing history texts from a Southern perspective]. . . . Now, Dr. Hart, too many of our Southern boys are going to you to be educated. You must get straight on Southern history."[13]

- In 1928 Hart chided long-time correspondent Lyon G. Tyler for his recently published verbal assassination of Abraham Lincoln: "We in the North are richer than you in the South because

---

*Turner did write, however, that "there is too much reviling of the Puritans in these days, as there was undue praise and over-emphasis of their work—not to say misconception of their purposes earlier. . . . Still, though I am of Puritan ancestry, Puritan marriage, and of a Puritan University(?) [Harvard, 1910–24], I am also rather contented that I didn't live in the Boston of the seventeenth century, and am convinced that their rum needed some water!" (Turner to Dixon Ryan Fox, April 7, 1922, Fox Papers, box 8, NYSHA.)

we are perfectly willing to include among our great countrymen, Robert E. Lee. . . . We are that much richer, and you obstinate and prejudiced Virginians refuse to share in the greatness of Abraham Lincoln, a man of your own strain! . . . You must be in the habit of reading the lucubrations of the Historian General of the Daughters of the Confederacy, who is one of the worst malignants of our time."[14]*

■ The president of Storer College in Harpers Ferry, West Virginia, acknowledged receiving from Tyler a monograph titled *Secession, Insurrection of the Negroes, and Northern Incendiarism.* "I have read it very carefully and with much interest. In this year of grace, is it worthwhile to revamp provincial hatred? Is it worthwhile to warp history to suit a disagreeable and long since past contention?"[15]

Anti-Lincoln scorn by Southern die-hards persisted throughout the 1920s and into the 1930s. I do not for a moment doubt the intensity and sincerity of their beliefs. Perfectly respectable Southern scholars speculated in print about the fact that Lincoln's paternity had been ascribed to so many men (hence there *must* be something problematic about it); and a prominent journalist could write privately that "Lincoln was pretty much like a 'yaller nigger,' in that he was as secretive as any human ever was. . . . And then, too, he could on occasion tell as big untruths as any politician in history."[16] It is clear, however, that all of this vituperation made very good copy; and a number of magazine publishers sought just the right (meaning credible) author for slashing journalism that might increase circulation. As the editor of *Plain Talk* explained in 1928: "An attack on Lincoln would have greater strategical value coming from a Northerner than it would from a Southerner. In the latter case everyone would yell, 'Bias.' "[17]

To unregenerate Confederates, the greatest blasphemy of all—attempts to link Lee with Lincoln, in spirit as well as in blood—occurred late in the 1920s. First there was a proposal in 1927 to name a new institution in Kansas City the Lincoln and Lee University. The United Daughters of the Confederacy fought that one with all the fury they could muster, and they won. Then came the publication in *Good Housekeeping* for January 1929 of an essay by Parson William A. Barton, a conciliator, that traced the Hanks genealogy all the way back through ancestral mists in order to demonstrate that Lincoln and Lee were ultimately kin. That predictably provoked a refutation from Lyon G. Tyler (on the grounds that Joseph Hanks of Hampshire County could

*Actually, Tyler received much support from the Sons of Confederate Veterans. As Arthur H. Jennings, chairman of the S.C.V. History Committee in Lynchburg, Virginia, told him: "We suffer in this country from our publicists, editors and preachers, and TEACHERS (ye Gods) all of whom with rarest exception are sunk deep into the Lincoln bog of myth and silly lies." (See Jennings to Tyler, Jan. 10, 1928, and Jan. 5 [?], in Tyler Papers, group 5, boxes 5 and 8, SLWM.)

not conceivably have been the essential link, Joseph Hanks of Richmond County), and earned for Tyler the eternal love of Lee devotees
who experienced unbearable anxiety at the mere title of the piece:
"Lincoln Was a Lee." Tyler also received a modest amount of mail from
Northerners, like the man in New Castle, Pennsylvania, who wrote: "I
sincerely trust that you have successfully spiked this lie, as I would feel
greatly humiliated if it was proven, in any manner whatsoever, that the
immortal Lincoln was related to a dirty rebel."[18]

The *Confederate Veteran,* a magazine founded in 1883, remained
especially vigilant in printing rebuttals to perceived slights and Northern nonsense. It officially represented no fewer than four organizations:
the Confederated Southern Memorial Association, the United Confederate Veterans, the United Daughters of the Confederacy, and United
Sons of Confederate Veterans. If the U.D.C. was not the most shrill
among the quartet, it surely became the most aggressive during the
1920s and 1930s. As one journalist reported, members felt missionary
zeal about preventing "sanctified relics" of the Confederacy from "falling into irreverent northern hands." They also managed to erect more
monuments, plaques, and memorials to Jefferson Davis than had been
put up to honor any president of the United States except Washington
and Lincoln. They ensured that more than one highway would be
named in honor of Davis. In 1929 the U.D.C. pleaded that New Orleans
mothers keep their children away from Lincoln's Birthday celebrations.
Some little tykes had not only participated the year before, but they had
actually recited the Gettysburg Address.[19] Oh, treacherous woe!

Various other allies fought (or refought) what they believed to be a
just war. The Confederate Memorial Literary Society, and the Confederate Museum in Richmond both played significant roles. The museum's curator reported that visitors often wept when looking at the
coat and sword worn by Lee when he surrendered at Appomattox
(*"these are northern people,"* she remarked). "One day I was telling a
young couple from Philadelphia about our soldiers, their sufferings,
their bravery etc, and I looked, and the tears were rolling down their
faces—I felt dreadfully as I did'nt [sic] realize that they would be so
overcome." Miss Harrison, the curator, must have been a marvelous
thespian.[20]

Woodrow Wilson, yet another Virginian, took considerable pride in
his ancestors, and commented in London during 1918 that the "stern
Covenanter tradition that is behind me sends many an echo down the
years." Wilson also developed a romantic affection for the South of story
and legend. His *Robert E. Lee: An Interpretation* (1909) reveals pride
that his section had taken up arms in 1861 along with a realistic attitude
toward the fate of the "Lost Cause." It is ironic, therefore, that Tom
Watson, the Georgia demagogue, vilified Wilson in 1912 for being pro-
Northern and anti-Southern. It simply wasn't so, and Watson's tactic did
not work.[21]

No single individual did nearly so much as Lyon G. Tyler to keep the

Confederate torch alight (see fig. 4.7). He moved to Williamsburg in 1888, helped to re-open the College of William and Mary, served as its president until 1919, and founded the *William and Mary Quarterly* as a "private venture" in 1892. Prolific as a historian, editor, and polemicist, Tyler became most feisty during the years from 1920 until his death in 1935. In 1929, for example, he produced a pamphlet for true believers called *The Confederate Catechism*. He distributed initial copies to persons on his extensive mailing list; but within a few months many of those recipients, ranging from Florida to Ohio and from South Carolina to California,* had ordered copies by the hundreds to sell or distribute—as one correspondent wrote from Columbus, Ohio, "in a section of the country where the besotted ignorance and prejudice of the generality of the denizens respecting the War between the States, Lincoln and the South are appalling." Compliments poured in and the demand continued for years.[22]

No one remained more fanatical as a hawker and wholesaler of the *Catechism* than Mary D. Carter of Upperville, Virginia, who would not miss an "opportunity to do some missionary work among the heathen." Her intensity elicited not only a polite yet unpersuaded reply from the Henry B. Joy Historical Research Library in Detroit, but a private communication to Tyler from the chairman of the Text Book Committee of the Sons of Confederate Veterans in Baltimore: "I can't tell you how much damage Miss Carter's monomania or megalomania has done to the cause throughout the South. It has caused a reaction against us in the North where people were inclined to begin to view us with more kindly feelings. . . . What we want to do is to appeal to the reason with as little reference to personalities as possible, and yet with profound respect for principles."[23] Some of the Southern die-hards had subtlety, but a substantial number did not.

Tyler led one last crusade, starting in 1931, when he entered his seventy-ninth year. For at least three decades he and many other Southerners had bemoaned their condition of "educational slavery": the lack of good history texts written for secondary schools from "their" point of view, with the lamentable consequence that books by Northern writers had been adopted in the old Confederacy.[24] By 1931 the basic text preferred throughout the entire United States, in fact, was *A History of the American People* by David S. Muzzey, a New Englander who loved the Union and did not like the peculiar institution of chattel slavery. Advocates of the Old South implored Tyler to produce, once again, one of his marvelous antidote pamphlets; and it did not require very much special pleading because Muzzey had unkind words for feisty John Tyler, the tenth president.[25]

---

*The historian for the California Division of the U.D.C. wrote from San Diego to request fifty copies at five cents apiece. "I have been rather appalled," she explained, "at some of the ignorance of Southern history, which I find out here." (Miss Mary Vivian Conway to Tyler, March 31, 1930, Tyler Papers, group 1, box 20, SLWM.)

Lyon G. Tyler's counterblast ran 106 pages, was ready by the summer of 1932, and was warmly welcomed by predictable people in predictable places. A gentleman in Petersburg, Virginia, wrote appreciatively and urged the formation of some sort of organization "that would help to preserve Southern History and Traditions in their CORRECTNESS." A U.D.C. historian in Pine Bluff, Arkansas, complained that "use of such books in public schools, south, shows that propaganda and commercial methods, of questionable nature, has fastened on the schools thru the purchasing agencies and the boards." An officer of the U.D.C. who lived in Chicago (she was the national chairman of Southern Literature for Home and Foreign Libraries) sent copies to the History Department at Yale. When true believers get to "networking," they can be bold indeed.[26]

Thomas Perkins Abernethy, an irascible historian of the Southern frontier who taught for decades at the University of Virginia, wrote to express his full agreement with Tyler's critique. He blasted those in Richmond who selected textbooks as being "largely politicians and victims of the Northern gospel of efficiency and they are helping the South to forget its past." He then acknowledged, however, that "the weakest point in our case is that the South has taken so little interest in historical scholarship. We have sentimentalized too much and taken little care of our documents." Abernethy was generally correct, though not entirely so. Dunbar Rowland (1864–1937), for example, served for years as director of the Mississippi Department of Archives and History, as secretary of the Mississippi Historical Society, and as Historian General of the United Confederate Veterans. In those capacities he devoted fifteen years to collecting and publishing the letters, papers, and speeches of Jefferson Davis. When the editors of the new *Dictionary of American Biography* failed to invite Dunbar to prepare the sketch of Davis, he launched a rocket-like treatise at them.[27]

Richard N. Current has made the intriguing suggestion that "Southerners, while more taken with tradition, have been less interested in history than New Englanders or Midwesterners have been."[28] If Current is correct,* there could also be a kernel of truth in the obverse: that outside the South a preoccupation with progress and innovation (c. 1876–1939) caused history to be treated with respect as an educational discipline but tradition per se to be regarded somewhat warily as a potential impediment to progress.

---

*The evidence seems inconclusive. In 1903 the governor of North Carolina asked, in a speech at Jacksonville, Florida: "Are we to forget the memories of the past; to break away from our traditions?" Five years later a Norwegian historian toured the South and reported (many years afterward, in an autobiography) that "Everywhere they faithfully guarded their past. In every single state, the government had established a department of history, not equally well equipped in every case, but in every instance testimony to the honor in which their historical recollections were held."

I I

THUS FAR we have seen sectional pride in general and Civil War scars, more particularly, as causes of inter-regional resentment and tension. Other factors also contributed, however, in ways that were complex because they remained both dynamic and divided: dynamic in the sense that shifts in outlook by the very same group or individual occurred, and divided in the sense that each section exhibited devoted chauvinists as well as critical loyalists. No one chastised New England for its historic intolerance more harshly than Brooks Adams. No one loved and defended the early history of New England more ardently than Senator Henry Cabot Lodge; yet they always remained the best of friends.[29]

Bernard DeVoto blasted New England's arrogance to his friends *there,* but boasted to the nation at large of the region's cultural depth and durability. "Almost alone in America," DeVoto declared, New England "has tradition, continuity."

> Not a tradition that everyone can admire, not a continuity of perfection, but something fixed and permanent in the flux of change and drift. It is the first American section to be finished, to achieve stability in the conditions of its life. It is the first old civilization, the first permanent civilization in America.[30]

In part it was this snide business of "firstness," of pride in priority, that so infuriated Southerners who knew that Jamestown had preceded Plymouth by thirteen years, and that the Virginia colony received a legitimizing charter from the Crown which Plimoth Plantation never had—merely possessing a precarious patent.[31]

Celebration of the Pilgrim Tercentenary (almost a year late, in August 1921) turned out to be a major and on-going provocation. The United States Congress not only appropriated $400,000 to support the event, an action that was unprecedented, but the Federal Plymouth Tercentenary Commission (an organization almost without precedent also) met in the autumn of 1920 and essentially ratified planning presented by the State Tercentenary Commission in collaboration with local committees from Plymouth and Provincetown. Senator Lodge of Massachusetts, chairman of the federal commission, managed to finesse everything handsomely; and the speakers at Plymouth included President Harding, the governor of Massachusetts, and the Dutch and British ambassadors. What they said seems to have been less memorable than the traffic jam—the worst ever in southeastern Massachusetts; but Lodge printed and distributed his own speech widely, which self-consciously evoked memories of Daniel Webster's famous oration at the Pilgrim Bicentennial in 1820.[32]

The tercentenary produced a fair amount of nonsense but at least a small porringer of prudence as well. A shrewd essay that appeared in *The Century* warned against the danger of anachronism—in this instance, assuming that the Pilgrims admired the same virtues that we do. The author perceived that the Pilgrims' "essential ideals and purposes are in danger of being obscured by the mists of ancestor worship." He correctly declared that if we casually "Americanize" those who came during the colonial period (by viewing them as ourselves in costume), two results could occur: "One is to minimize the significance of the American Revolution, and the other is to devitalize the history of the period which preceded it." He acknowledged that the Puritans as well as the Pilgrims "had opinions which they held with great tenacity and had purposes which gave unity to their lives. They were good haters, and they hated some things which we tolerate."[33]

Animosity hung in the atmosphere like heavy humidity that summer, and the onset of local tercentenary tensions simply served to provoke Southerners who had been seething for decades.[34]* Philip A. Bruce, a distinguished Virginian obsessed (ever since 1906) with vindicating the Old South, visited Provincetown in August 1920 for its local celebration of the tercentenary and sent Lyon G. Tyler a copy of the printed program along with a covering letter characteristic of hundreds that he wrote until his death in 1933.

> Provincetown is claiming everything. I was under the impression that Plymouth was the *Holy of Holies,* but it seems that the people of this little town are denying this as strenuously as we are doing [?] at old Jamestown. . . . The world is now perfectly convinced that the birthplace of the nation was really on the shores of Cape Cod, and this belief is due entirely to the vociferous propaganda that has been going on ever since the fall of the Confederacy. Bancroft, who wrote before the war, took no such position, nor did any of the early historians. We were conquered, and one of the penalties was the stealing of our history along with a good many other robberies.[35]

Tyler took up the challenge by writing a barrage of pamphlets bearing such titles as *Propaganda in History* (1920) and *Virginia First* (1922?), intended for classroom use in the South and asserting the primacy of Jamestown over Plymouth, Patrick Henry over James Otis as the first Revolutionary patriot, and Lee over Lincoln as a man of honor. Tyler even told Bruce not to "emphasize aristocracy" in writing the history of colonial Virginia: "it's just what the Yankees wish you to do. . . . My idea is that Virginia had a splendid and spectacular aristocracy

---

*In Henry Grady's influential speech "The New South," given at Delmonico's Restaurant in New York City on December 22, 1886 (Forefathers' Day), the Georgia journalist did criticize Northerners for failing to mention the Cavalier along with the Puritan in schoolbooks concerned with the genesis of American history.

but it was nothing like as powerful as the aristocracy of New England, in other words, that there was less of democracy in those countries than there was in Virginia."[36]

Although Bruce applauded the products of Tyler's pen, he recognized that time, talent, and sheer industry had left the South in the position of playing catch-up for many years to come: "The Pilgrims have beaten the Jamestown settlers in history, because, from the start, they had a talent for the use of the pen; and that talent has only grown more active with the progress of the years." Ultimately, however, he blamed the South's disadvantage upon its defeat in 1865 and agreed with Tyler that "this is the penalty which the conquered always have to pay for their failure." Bruce regarded it as all but inevitable that "a triumphant North would rob the defeated South of its history by systematic reconstruction and suppression of facts." He also detested the histories written by many "reconstructed" Southerners ("this writer, with the snarl of a hyena, and the pitiless ferocity of a ghoul. . . ."), and feared that the New South would distort his beloved section's history even more than Northern writers had done. "The materialistic bee has begun to buzz in the Southern Ear."[37]

Beyond the legacy of defeat, people like Bruce, Tyler, and their considerable network blamed the poor quality of Southerners serving in Congress ("a shoddy lot"), the unwillingness of wealthy Southerners to "establish publishing houses to preserve the truths of Southern Civilization," and the harsh reality that "northern historians are so warped by the myths and traditions of the conqueror that they, as a rule," cannot tell the truth "no matter how kindly they may feel."[38] While wallowing in all of this self-pity, however, these men persisted in their pursuit of primacy for the South. They investigated, for example, whether James Rumsey of Baltimore (and later Berkeley Springs, [West] Virginia), had not invented the steamboat earlier in 1787 than John Fitch, a Connecticut Yankee, so that the earliest American steamboat had perhaps made its debut on the Potomac rather than on the Delaware.[39]

On one matter where boasting rights counted mightily, Tyler struck gold. For decades the press, as well as private persons, had been making such statements as: "Each year Thanksgiving becomes more and more a national and less a New-England holiday." Nevertheless, credit for originating this important American custom continued to belong to the Pilgrims.[40] In 1931, however, Tyler found in a collection of papers pertaining to early Virginia located at the New York Public Library a document indicating that the first Thanksgiving observance had occurred in 1619 at Berkeley Hundred, a plantation near the falls of the James River. Glory hallelujah! Primacy right smack in the center of the Pilgrims' pride.[41] In 1958 the Virginia Thanksgiving Festival was founded as a delayed consequence—largely a touristic enterprise.

Within just a few years of Tyler's find, however, new vitality seemed to give Southern history a fresh glow, and its advocates a shot of adrenalin. Natchez, Vicksburg, and Mobile began to hold spring festivals intended to portray just how romantic life had been in the Old South. Garden clubs abounded and antebellum mansions, open to the public, reappeared with the bloom of youth. Southerners wrote aggressive letters to Northern editors criticizing (citing chapter and verse) "a tendency to lean too far to New England and the Puritans as founders of our country." The *New York Times* ran a feature on venerable Southern homes situated from Maryland to Florida, gave Colonial Williamsburg lots of press coverage, and in 1937, when Richmond celebrated its bicentennial, the *Times* cheerfully called the former Confederate capital "fortunate in having sons and daughters more competent than any outsiders to sing her bicentennial praises." A little bit patronizing, perhaps; but *Gone With the Wind* had been a national bestseller since 1936, and so was Douglas Southall Freeman's four-volume biography of Robert E. Lee (1934–35). Freeman told Ellen Glasgow in 1938 that "we Southerners had one consolation: If our fathers lost the war, you and Margaret Mitchell . . . have won the peace."[42]

FOR A VARIETY of reasons, New England and its transplanted progeny never entirely lost faith in their heritage, and people of Puritan stock scattered all across the land retained at least a vague sense of allegiance to ancestors who had been God-fearing, self-governing pioneers. When Oliver Wendell Holmes, Jr., spoke in 1902 at the unveiling of memorial tablets in Ipswich, he said of his Puritan forebears that "I love every brick and shingle of the old Massachusetts towns where once they worked and prayed, and I think it a noble and pious thing to do . . . to keep our memories, our reverence and our love alive and to hand them on to new generations all too ready to forget."[43]

Eleven years later the poet Vachel Lindsay suggested that the United States become a new New England of "ninety million souls." In that same year, 1913, Litchfield, Connecticut, became the first town in America to remodel its historic architecture and landscape comprehensively in the colonial style. By 1930, with the Congregational Church reconstructed and Tapping Reeve's old law school (the very first in America) restored, Litchfield had quietly become New England's Williamsburg—sans admission fees, sans hostesses in costume, sans p.r.[44]

The Pilgrim Tercentenary did not prove to be quite so ephemeral as many other such observances. Joseph Dillaway Sawyer (1849–1933) developed a kind of cottage industry for Pilgrim books with which people who owned Wallace Nutting's Pilgrim Century furniture could stock their shelves. In 1921 it was *"The Pilgrim Spirit," shown in the Pilgrim Pageant staged at Plymouth, Mass., July and August, 1921.* The following year he brought out a *History of the Pilgrims and Puritans, Their Ancestry and Descendants* in three volumes; and three years later an update with no fewer than 1,700 engravings, *The Romantic and Fascinating Story of the Pilgrims and Puritans,* also in three volumes. This must have been a profitable venture for the Century History Company or else the big revised edition would never have seen the light of day. A rather mysterious and exclusive association known as the Pilgrims of the United States was formed, and Nicholas Murray Butler of Columbia University served for a while as its president.

Although a few scholarly types like Victor Hugo Paltsits of the New York Public Library and Samuel Eliot Morison of Harvard could explain the precise distinctions between a Pilgrim and a Puritan, most people could not and didn't care. Calvin Coolidge seemed to embody all of the qualities, good and bad, of both: dour, taciturn, ethical, frugal, a countryman when he needed to be and an advocate of sobriety and social control when those virtues were called for. David Starr Jordan, the distinguished naturalist and former president of Stanford University, worked positive statements about the Pilgrims *and* the Puritans into an essay for *Nature Magazine* in 1928 (which predictably set Lyon G. Tyler off like a Fourth of July firecracker).[45]

A plainspoken but well-informed gent from Limerick, Maine, determined to defend Jordan and thwacked Tyler as good as he had given, which meant three very blunt (single-spaced) pages of Down East piss and vinegar. "I have actually found an apparent disposition," he wrote, "to charge with falsehood any writer who is even of New England ancestry. I don't think any such vicious sectional assault has been made in our history, against any group of States, as seems to be under way just now against New England." He spoke the truth. That same year, 1928, a South Carolinian toured the Northeast. He kept his eyes open but his mind closed. He liked Portsmouth, New Hampshire, because it reminded him of Charleston, but he complained that everything had "shrunk." It seemed to him that he "could smell puritanism and ship carpentry about even the best of it—a sort of shop keeping small farmer respectability about the worst and a figurehead carvers ship cabin idea of scale and ornament about the rest."[46]

That Puritan-bashing became trendy during the 1920s is well established and well documented.[47] A few important aspects of the phenomenon are less clear, however. First of all, some of those who initiated and perpetuated the trend themselves had very deep familial roots in New England's stony soil. Brooks Adams and his older brother, Charles Francis, Jr., are obvious examples. More interesting and complex because of his apparent ambivalence is the case of popular writer Arthur Train. In 1929 he published an essay in the *Saturday Evening Post,* titled "Puritan's Progress," in which he expressed skepticism about the vaunted virtues of progress and ended with a nostalgic reaffirmation of the old Puritan verities, a validation of tradition on spiritual and metaphysical grounds. This, mind you, in a mass media piece. One year later, however, he offered a personal recollection of his Boston boyhood, where he was born in 1875. As he conceded: "That Puritanism encouraged and accentuated a consciousness of sin in the young is one of the worst indictments against it." Train acknowledged that he gradually discovered "there were other worlds possessed of other standards where, by some curious paradox, people were not damned for doing the very same things that would have damned them in Boston." In retrospect, Puritanism seemed a dim mist of "encircling gloom."[48]

A second group who assaulted the Saints and their heirs were highly cultured Yorkers who had undergone some form of personal conflict or professional slight. Judge Alphonso T. Clearwater of Kingston on the Hudson, who left his superb collection of early American silver to the Met, wrote in 1932: "If you had had my experience with the Puritans and Pilgrims of Boston, you would have learned that they regard themselves as among the Lord's anointed, and they feel that it is an act of treason to send a piece of old New England silver to any place but the [Boston] Museum of Fine Arts." When the distinguished anthropologist Ruth F. Benedict found the Dobu Indian culture repressed and hostile to one another, she compared their temperament to that of the early Puritans. When James Truslow Adams, the popular historian from eastern Long Island (an area actually settled by Puritans who had crossed the Sound), published his critical two-volume history of colonial New England, Samuel Eliot Morison sought to correct him in a confrontational way:

> Our ideas of puritanism in this generation are apt to be derived either from some prim old great-aunt, or from an anti-saloon league person, both of whom represent a degenerate and negative type of puritanism. I feel when reading your books and articles that you are continually putting up this latter type as a sort of straw man in place of the veritable positive puritan of the seventeenth century.[49]

Third, young Van Wyck Brooks of Plainfield, New Jersey, educated at Harvard College, did more than any member of his generation to excoriate the Puritans and "that old New England culture." He followed his first book, *The Wine of the Puritans* (1908), with various essays repudiating his own heritage, mainly in the name of the rebellious élan that seemed to spark so many members of his cohort. After he matured, however, Brooks somersaulted himself into an old Connecticut town where he wrote immensely popular, middlebrow bestsellers like *The Flowering of New England* (1936). Malcolm Cowley praised this book in a review titled "The Puritan Legacy," a review in which Cowley seemed grateful that Americans were now "turning back to the great past in order to see the real nature of the traditions that we are trying to save." Several decades had brought an extraordinary cultural flip-flop.[50]

One other highly influential critic, H. L. Mencken, published "Puritanism as a Literary Force" in *A Book of Prefaces* in 1917. His essential message, which he voiced with amusing variations for many years: Puritanism is the root of all that's unattractive about American culture, compounded over time by evangelism, moralism from political demagogues, and relentless money-grubbing.[51] Stuart Pratt Sherman, the respected literary critic, found Mencken's acerbic perspective pernicious and offered an alternative view in 1921 that very gradually, over a quarter century, gained increasing numbers of adherents. Sherman began with certain basic assumptions: that "we are not exceptionally rich in spiritual traditions"; that a genuinely meaningful literature and culture had to be concerned with truth and morals; and that the most "fundamental American tradition" had been Puritanism.[52] Sherman's next step strained credulity at the time, but became the new conventional wisdom by 1944 when Ralph Barton Perry published *Puritanism and Democracy,* a 641-page missal that managed to combine diverse historical value systems into a single mega-creed.*

Sherman found in Emerson and Whitman "the religion of a Puritan democracy" and then insisted that a "Puritan democracy is the only kind that we have reason to suppose will endure." He believed that one of the primary purposes of scholarship was to

> connect us with the great traditions and to inspire us with the confidence and power which result from such a connection. Puritanism, rightly understood, is one of the vital, progressive, and enriching human traditions. It is a tradition peculiarly necessary to the health and stability and the safe forward movement of a democratic society.

The meaning that Sherman ascribed to Puritanism may have worked for him because it was so expansive, flexible, and fairly unhistorical.[53]

Some of his most thoughtful allies, however, such as V. F. Calverton, a socialist critic, were less optimistic than Sherman precisely because they paid more attention to major forces of historical change. Calverton declared in 1931 that Puritanism had been misunderstood and served as a "philosophic scapegoat for a whole generation of writers." He argued that contemporary woes in American culture could not be blamed on the Puritan tradition because it had, in fact, disappeared long ago and "been superseded by that of the manufacturing, capitalist class." The contrast gave Calverton pause, and in his view, it should have provided the United States with an agenda for self-correction:

> With the Puritan the stress had been upon character; with the capitalist class the emphasis was upon reputation. It was not what

---

*Although the connection has not been noticed, Perry was influenced by a philosophical historian of British culture, A. S. P. Woodhouse, who published *Puritanism and Liberty* (London, 1938), with the perspective that Puritanism helped to beget both democracy and liberty.

a man was that counted any longer, but what he was reputed to be. . . .

It was this capitalistic class, this industrial bourgeoisie, with its emphasis on respectability, that stamped out all genuineness from literature—and life. The role of the Puritan, despite the severity of his ideals, was far less vicious.[54]

The initial resurrection of Puritan ideals was confined largely to New England and the Northeast. A National Society of Puritan Descendants appeared early in the thirties with its headquarters appropriately located on Beacon Street in Boston. The deepening economic depression served clergymen, politicians, and orators as a springboard for urging a return to time-honored values. A feature story stimulated by Alf Landon's presidential candidacy in 1936 managed to have it both ways. Kansans subscribed to the old "Puritan ideals of order, thrift, piety and respect for law." Nevertheless, this author announced, Kansas Puritanism had not been dour: "If the Kansan never conceded that enjoyment is the main end of existence, he never objected to it as a by-product."[55]

At the celebration of the centennial of Mark Hopkins, a renowned educator who from 1836 until 1872 served as the most influential president of Williams College, a distinguished Harvard philosopher insisted that the Puritan value system stimulated "an intense concern for the welfare of others; and that it was less prone, in fact, to develop gloom than to develop dignity." That same year, 1936, another educator turned Calverton's argument around with the contention that "the American family in the business class is of the Puritan type": that is, concerned with thrift and accumulation, the exaltation of manual labor, the importance of housekeeping as an end in itself, esteem for trade and profit not merely for purposes of "acquisition" but (rather mysteriously) for their own sake.[56] The rehabilitation of Puritanism could be every bit as specious as its devastation had been two decades earlier!

The changing reputation of Puritanism was appropriately reflected in the arts and related areas of cultural creativity. Whereas Edward Hopper's painting *Two Puritans* (1945) features two plain, white early American homes,[57] Paul Sample's complex vision of a New England *Church Supper* (fig. 12.2) contrasts the small, idealized village of yesteryear in the historical background with the emotionally drained gloom, gossip, hypocrisy, and retrospection of a rural gathering in 1933. In front of the white-gloved lady who exposes her knee to the leering old men, a young girl takes her first bite from an apple. Perhaps she is a pre-pubescent Eve about to acquire secular knowledge and understanding. Perhaps the day will come when she will expose more than a shapely leg, and thereby tarnish even more this Yankee town that seems unworthy of its past.*

---

*In 1934 Howard Hanson completed his opera *Merry Mount*, about a group of rebels that flouted community mores. Frank Lloyd's *Maid of Salem*, a movie about the Salem witch trials, opened in March 1937.

12.2   Paul Sample, *Church Supper* (1933), oil on canvas. Museum of Fine Arts, Springfield, Massachusetts. The James Philip Gray Collection.

Nostalgic memoirs of old New England towns appeared in the popular press throughout these years, invariably recalling "mossy traditions" or "the New England tradition of neatness and cleanliness," or attending the Friday evening prayer meeting at which "two elderly rustics engaged in their favorite pastime of praying at one another." The first issue of *Yankee Magazine* appeared in 1935 with an essay titled "What Is a Yankee?" The answer confirmed certain stereotypes, but with affection rather than malice: a Yankee was a native of rural New England recognizable "often by physical characteristics. He is usually thin and wiry, rather tall and angular, with high cheek bones and pointed chin." In fact, he looked like Calvin Coolidge. And he was "automatically a conservative, distrustful of innovations and suspicious of strangers."[58] *Yankee Magazine* continues to thrive, and so does that perception of a Yankee.

III

WE HAVE PAID close attention to critics of the Puritan legacy, to some apologists for the Puritan tradition, and especially to Southern resentment of New Englanders because those attitudes were highly visible when they were not overtly virulent. What about the West: how Westerners regarded their own region, and how the older sections viewed the West? We can conveniently begin with New England feelings about trans-Mississippi America, and then shift to the Western sense of its own past and distinctive contributions to the nation.

It is problematic to generalize about Yankee attitudes toward the American West because there is no singular pattern. Some people like Alice Foster Perkins Hooper, who had been raised in Burlington, Iowa, cared passionately about Western history and felt betrayed when President A. Lawrence Lowell allowed Harvard's collection of trans-Mississippi Americana to languish even before Turner retired in 1924.[59]

During the summers of 1925 and '26, when the Great Northern Railroad sponsored historical expeditions across the Great Plains to Montana and then to Astoria on the Pacific coast of Oregon, Samuel Eliot Morison, Harvard's Brahmin historian, accompanied the unprecedented ventures and praised them lavishly in a published report that followed the second expedition in 1926. "They mark a new chapter in historical education," he wrote: "an historical synthesis in which the actual sites, and often actual participants, give unique vitality to our past." Ralph Budd, the Great Northern's enterprising president, regarded his primary objective as being educational, and made the dedication of historical monuments and markers a particular purpose of both expeditions. Morison reported that Budd "hopes to promote local patriotism and regional culture; not as a counterbalance but as an enrichment to national patriotism and American culture."[60]

Over the course of a century New Englanders had apparently developed a more expansive vision. At the time of the Oregon Trail Centennial in 1930, some people derived ironic pleasure from a Senate speech once given by Daniel Webster, that quintessential New Englander: "What can we ever hope to do with the Western coast—a coast of three thousand miles, rock-bound, cheerless, and uninviting, and with not a harbor on it? What use have we for such a country? Mr. President, I will never vote one cent from the public treasury to place the Pacific Coast one inch nearer to Boston than it is now." What a marked contrast to the speeches and ceremonies held on December 1, 1937, at Ipswich, Massachusetts, to mark the 150th anniversary of the covered wagon trek, "America's departure to the other sea."[61]

Assorted residents of the East could be very cranky critics; and it did not seem to matter whether they had actually seen the West or not. A

Philadelphian who wrote a travel piece for the *Atlantic* in 1932 lavished praise upon the Williamsburg restoration; yet the upper Great
Plains and mountain West did not interest him. "These miserable Western states have nothing, and they are a drain upon the entire country."
He clearly had a problem with trans-Appalachian egalitarianism. "What
is our chief contribution to the world?" he asked. *"Democracy,* that
horrid farce which thoughtful men fear." A North Carolina couple who
had been in Los Angeles for all of eight months told friends back home
that "it is all too damned nigger rich. Somehow life here is a gaudy
filling station, and the land is not sanctified. It has to be coddled and
watered to grow anything." After complaining that the film community
lacked enough imagination to make a Civil War movie that would be
sympathetic to the South, one unreconstructed rebel wrote his regionalist *cri de coeur*: "I've in mind [writing] an apology for the Confederate
individualist, who wanted none of your hog and hominy democracy
from Iowa, none of the austere town-meeting of New-England."[62]

Actually, despite all of the canards about Californians living only in
the present and for the future, interest in the past and in local traditions
there began to perk up, selectively, around the turn of the century. A
Landmarks Club appeared in 1895 at Los Angeles; and in 1899 its
president, Charles F. Lummis, announced that efforts were under way
to preserve the ruins of the San Diego Mission: contributions would be
cheerfully received. Later that year Lummis used the magazine he
published to plead for funds to restore the missions at San Juan Capis-
trano and San Fernando. In 1906 E. W. Scripps built more than one
hundred miles of roads at his own expense so that he could visit historic
and scenic places in San Diego County.[63]

By 1915, as the appointed time for the Panama-California Exposition
approached, restoration work at the San Diego Mission intensified and
a local journalist wrote with pride of the Latin legacy that North American conquerors should appreciate: "with the passing of the weaker
[Hispanic civilization] they left a legacy of their art and culture, which
the survivor [the Anglo-Saxon] has gladly possessed to beautify and
decorate his own. They left us their tradition, their romance, and their
musical nomenclature." One man who visited San Diego in 1915 and
again the following January explained that the exposition had a "distinct
character which is due to the happy combination of a distinct type of
architecture, reviving the resplendence of the Spanish-Mexican baroque and the more simple form of the Mission style of New Mexico and
California, both associated with the romantic events of the early history
of America."[64]

Many of the structures erected at Balboa Park in 1915 were utilized
once again twenty years later when another "international" exposition
was launched in order to tout four centuries of progress and achievement. According to one press release, San Diego "is considered the
logical site for such an exposition because it claims to be the birthplace

of civilization in the West." The explorer Cabrillo first touched the mainland there in 1542, and Spanish priests established an early mission in 1769. The transportation section of the 1935 fair included a special area "devoted to the historical phases of travel. Many relics which played an important part in the development of travel in the United States are being assembled. These include such colorful objects as the horse trappings of the early Spanish Dons, the ox-carts of the first settlers, covered wagons, stage coaches and other crude vehicles." There were also roads intended to suggest historic highways of the Pacific rim: the Gold Road of Panama, an ancient Inca road in Peru, the old Spanish highway in Mexico, the Santa Fe and Oregon trails, and Alaska's Fairbanks Highway. The Screen Actors Guild of Hollywood supplied a display of its treasures: some of Mary Pickford's curls, Charlie Chaplin's shoes, and George Arliss's monocle, among others.[65]

A comparable combination of local pride and economic desperation energized planning for the Texas Centennial held in 1936.* Those involved acknowledged the need to display Texas's economic resources to the nation. In 1934 advocates of Dallas as the principal exhibition site insisted that the centennial theme ought to be a century of progress made possible by the patriotic sacrifices of the state's founders. A candid dual theme of "patriotism and commercialism" emerged amongst the planners by the early 1930s; but Texan chauvinism and ambivalence about outsiders soon became manifest: "Please remember," wrote one commission member from Mission, Texas, "they don't possess the love of our traditions like the people who live here."[66]

In 1937 a state commission in Utah selected Mahonri M. Young, a grandson of Brigham Young, to design the "This Is the Place Monument" to commemorate the latter's famous words proclaimed in the foothills of Emigration Canyon. Ten years later, in 1947, more than fifty thousand people were present when the monument was dedicated during Utah's centennial celebration. In terms of observing Mormon traditions, however, that event marked more of a culmination than a beginning. Mormon Pioneer Day had been observed in Salt Lake City on July 24 ever since 1889, at least, and the Mormon sculptor Cyrus Dallin (see pp. 186–187 above) had prepared the bronze-gilded angel Moroni for the spire of Mormon Temple during the 1890s. His Memorial to the Pioneer Mother of Springville, Utah, was unveiled in his hometown on Utah Pioneer Day, July 24, 1932.

Historical art inspired by nostalgia for the Old West dated to the early 1890s, when Harper's publishing house released publicity material designed to enhance the popularity of Frederic Remington's illustrations.

---

*Texas and Indiana both dedicated war memorials in 1936. The one at Gonzalez, Texas, commemorated the spot where the first shot had been fired in the struggle for Texas Independence. The Indiana War Memorial, national headquarters for the American Legion, was erected in Indianapolis with an allotment of $195,000 from WPA funds.

"The building up of the West," it ran, "formed an era that is past; but the scenes have left [Remington] upon the stage, with an enthusiastic memory filled like a storehouse with accurate notes." By 1894 Remington himself felt that "the West is all played out," and his art self-consciously emphasized either the settlement of the West as a historical phenomenon or else the "disappearing West." In 1907 his close friend Teddy Roosevelt emphasized from his bully pulpit the view that Remington's pictures portrayed a vanishing way of life in the United States.[67]

By the second decade of the twentieth century, art depicting Western history, especially white–Indian relations—both friendship and conflict—became so popular that private individuals commissioned paintings and murals for their homes. In 1922, when the novelist and essayist Emerson Hough was looking for an artist to illustrate his "Old Trails" stories for the *Saturday Evening Post*, W. H. D. Koerner had established himself as the romantic yet realistic successor to Remington and Charles Russell. Koerner completed twenty-four illustrations for *The Covered Wagon*, a novel by Hough that appeared in eight installments, one of the longest series the *Post* had ever carried. Between 1919 and Hough's death in April 1923, he and Koerner collaborated on a series of projects that achieved astounding popularity. Standard themes in Koerner's work were The Rustlers, Sioux Circle, Wagon Master, Romance on the Overland Trail, Trail Herd to Wyoming, and This Gun Says Quit. The public loved it, and several of their collaborative projects provided the basis for successful films.[68]

In 1922 a new museum opened in Santa Fe that was devoted to presenting the art and culture of the Southwest. Its principal benefactor, Frank Springer, had originated in Iowa, like Emerson Hough, but developed a passion for the history and architecture of New Mexico. Prior to World War I he developed a vision of a fine arts museum that would do justice to his adopted region. When he offered to put up $30,000, the state of New Mexico decided to match it; and when he doubled his offer, the state increased its contribution accordingly. Six separate Franciscan mission churches of the seventeenth century were incorporated into the museum's facade design, along with elements of Pueblo Indian architecture. Furniture was designed especially for the museum on the basis of old Spanish prototypes found in remote areas of New Mexico. One result was a wave of imitation in Santa Fe and then elsewhere in the Southwest, in public as well as private buildings. This gallery of native arts and crafts had the same sort of impact upon its region as the American Wing of the Met had two years later, though mainly in the eastern United States.[69]

Similarly in 1923 W. Parker Lyon, a millionaire businessman and former mayor of Fresno, California, decided to devote his personal fortune to preserving the "romance and tradition of the two-gun, two-fisted gold-rush days" of California. In less than a decade he had accumulated more than forty thousand items, ranging from twelve thousand Indian arrowheads (the largest collection in the world) to stage-coaches that once crossed the rough roads from Sacramento to Mexico. Lyon built an old adobe structure, called the Pony Express Museum, in Kewen Canyon, San Marino, near the southern boundary of the old Rancho San Pasqual and not far from the San Gabriel Mission.* He somehow managed to acquire wonderfully diverse objects rich in anecdotal and historical associations: the travel trunk once used by Father Junípero Serra, founder of the California mission system; the .44-caliber Colt revolver taken from the dead body of Billy the Kid after he had been shot by Sheriff Pat Garrett; a bar taken from an old gold rush saloon in Mariposa (patronized by Frémont, U. S. Grant, Bret Harte, Mark Twain, and many others). It was an amazing collection for one man to have compiled and it promptly became accessible to the public.[70]

More than a decade earlier an intrepid man launched a series of incredible exploits from his home in the state of Washington. Ezra Meeker had left Indiana for Iowa in 1851. He crossed the plains to Oregon in 1852, stayed there briefly, and then settled along Puget Sound and in Puyallup, where he built the first pioneer's cabin and remained as a farmer and hops grower. Long fascinated by the Pacific Northwest, and deeply impressed by the history of America's great westward migration at midcentury, he resolved in 1905, at the age of seventy-five, to devote the remainder of his life to commemorative marking of the Oregon Trail. In 1906–07 he recrossed that "trail" from west to east, stopping frequently to paint inscriptions on landmarks and urging residents of assorted settlements to establish suitable monuments and inscribed stones. From the end of the Trail in St. Louis he continued all the way to Washington, D.C., by way of Ohio and New York, in his prairie schooner. Understandably he received amazing amounts of publicity; and in 1907 President Roosevelt even advocated government support to help mark the Trail properly.[71]

When Meeker made speeches and gave interviews to reporters, two words recurred, almost obsessively: "memory" and "patriotism." He urgently hoped to "perpetuate the memory of the old Oregon Trail," he was determined to kindle "a flame of patriotic sentiment" in the rising generation, and he wished to "keep alive the memories of the past." His ultimate tangible goal? A national highway, known as Pioneer Way, that would run from the Missouri River to the Pacific. In 1907 he went back to Portland, Oregon, where he had lived in 1852–53, and joined two thousand Oregon Trail pioneers who were enjoying a reun-

---

*In 1935 a group observed the seventy-fifth anniversary of the Pony Express by following one of the original trails by airplane. A ten-passenger aircraft left St. Joseph, Missouri, stopping in Omaha, Cheyenne, and other sites en route to its final destination in Sacramento. (NYT, Mar. 31, 1935, sec. 11, p. 17.)

ion. In 1910 he repeated the trek east. Six years later he covered most of the Trail, but this time by car. In 1924, at the age of ninety-three, he followed 1,300 miles of the Trail in a light aircraft.* Two years after that he founded the Oregon Trail Memorial Association, with headquarters situated in New York City. In 1928 he tried to follow his beloved route once more by automobile, became ill in Detroit, and died at the age of ninety-eight.[72]

Meeker was a man of less than medium height and slender build; he had a luxuriant shock of snow-white hair and an unforgettably bushy beard (fig. 12.3). From 1906 until 1928 he established himself as the American pioneer incarnate: an author, lecturer, and essential ornament to any celebration of pioneering. He could be careless about particular dates and incidents, but he conveyed authenticity and integrity in ways that touched Americans of all strata. His desire to mark each of the old trails in the West and to organize lecture tours for himself and others made considerable contact with popular culture. His hope that motion pictures would be created about the trans-Mississippi West made contact with mass culture. His wish that appropriate museums and libraries would be built connected popular with high culture.[73]

On July 27, 1921, Meeker gave a characteristic speech at the site of Old Fort Hall (located near Pocatello, Idaho). The occasion: the eighty-seventh anniversary of the first sermon preached west of the crest of the Rocky Mountains. He told the assembled throng that they had a duty to themselves and to future generations: "to the record of true history. . . . A people that fails to record its history falls short of fulfilling a destiny of highest civilization." And he offered the traditionalist's most dire warning to those indifferent to his plea: "We are soon to see this landmark inundated by the inexorable march of progress." Seven years later, when Meeker died, officers of the Oregon Trail Memorial Association made a commitment that the movement should maintain an emphasis upon educational activities and be kept free of commercialism.[74]

Even though the great trans-continental migration by wagon had been a phenomenon of the mid-1840s through the 1860s, Meeker mobilized so much momentum that the period from April 10 until December 29, 1930, was designated as the Covered-Wagon Centennial year.† Journalists got so excited in Lancaster, Pennsylvania, where covered wagons were first built, that they muddled their metaphors: "What a mine of romance, tragedy, and tradition is woven through the history of the covered wagon." The Boy Scouts of America participated fully.

---

*In 1932 a collateral descendant of George Washington flew, in a single day, over all the routes that Washington had covered in his entire lifetime. The plane made brief stops to refuel.

†On April 10, 1930, a replica wagon train departed from St. Louis for the Idaho-Oregon border. On October 10, designated by educators as Oregon Trail Day in Idaho, the train began its return trip to St. Louis.

12.3   *Ezra Meeker* (1921). Courtesy of the Division of Prints and Photographs, Library of Congress.

Boise, Idaho, sort of jumped the gun and held Boise Basin Days on June 12, 13, and 14. The American Legion and the Business Men of Boise jointly issued a souvenir program, *Pioneers, O Pioneers!* The Capitol Boulevard Memorial Bridge in Boise was dedicated to the Pioneers of the Old Oregon Trail. Japanese-Americans in Idaho whose ancestors could not have had the slightest connection to the Oregon Trail paid homage to its importance while wearing traditional Japanese outfits (fig. 12.4). As July 4, 1930, neared, large crowds headed for Independence Rock, Wyoming, where a three-day celebration took place. Eagle Scouts from New York City arrived in the "oxmobile" now owned by Henry Ford but originally built for Ezra Meeker.[75]

On December 29 communities all across the United States honored the pioneers as well as the centennial of Ezra Meeker's birth. Speeches and popular music of the covered-wagon era were broadcast on the radio. The president of the Oregon Trail Association took the occasion of his after-dinner speech to beat the drum for equity in regional traditions. The children of America, he insisted, were "not getting a square deal" because the history of the East received disproportionate attention in schools "and the history of the West less than was due it." Ray Lyman Wilbur, Secretary of the Interior, spoke at the American Women's Association clubhouse in New York City and used the opportunity to transmit a homily. Pioneer days were not yet past, he declared,

12.4 Japanese-Americans celebrate the Oregon Trail Centennial in Idaho (1930). Photograph courtesy of Professor Robert C. Sims, Boise, Idaho.

because the depression necessitated a revived pioneering spirit. "New pioneering is required to adapt our established governmental machinery so that it can play its part in maintaining a uniform distribution of opportunity and a fair distribution of the benefits brought to us by science." The historical meaning of his message may have been vague, but his sense of urgency seemed genuine.[76]

INEVITABLY, perhaps, all of this commemorative trans-continental trekking called attention to the need for improved highways. J. N. ("Ding") Darling, a nationally beloved cartoonist based in Des Moines, Iowa, recognized the impact of those historical hegiras begun by Ezra Meeker in 1906–07.* Darling proposed a "scenic avenue across America" and became involved in the designation and protection of campsites along the Lewis and Clark Trail. Equally predictable, conservationists started to complain that the Good Roads movement would ruin remaining "patches" of Western wilderness. Easterners, especially, despite their enthusiasm for progress in general, did not want the West to change. They hoped that somehow it could remain an "over-sized museum" for nature lovers and historically minded individuals. By the 1920s, however, many people from all sections began to feel a sense of loss and nostalgia for the Old West. Owen Wister published *When West Was West* in 1928, a collection of wistful tales that looked

---

*Darling's most famous drawing (January 11, 1917), which marked the death of native Iowan Buffalo Bill Cody, was called "Gone to Join the Mysterious Caravan."

back fondly to simpler days. The dude ranch reached the peak of its popularity during the interwar years. A democratization of its clientele (compared with three or four decades earlier) began to occur. Shrewd Western entrepreneurs recognized commercial potential in a waning-of-the-West syndrome. Consequently the 1920s marked a pivotal moment in the self-aware marketing of regional traditions: rodeos, mock cowboy fights, roped-off business districts, and so on. The West began to promote the Wild West when it recognized that the real thing was just about gone.[77]

The heyday of the rodeo in the intermountain West has been dated very precisely to the period from 1914 until 1939. A transformation took place during that quarter century in which riding and roping went from being *primarily* utilitarian to becoming an important form of entertainment. Rodeos got to be especially attractive as a featured event on the Fourth of July. In Grangeville, Idaho, Border Days meant a parade of Indians, drill teams, saddle horses, a bathing beauty contest, and a rodeo. In Idaho Falls the Fourth of July meant a fifty-mile pony express race, a sheriff's posse, and a rodeo. In St. Anthony the celebration of Pioneer Days came during the fourth week of July—Mormon style. Cheyenne had its Frontier Days; rodeos came to the Cow Palace in San Francisco and to New York's Madison Square Garden. But above all, Pendleton, Oregon, revived and (by 1935) romanticized its old round-up: a "Westward Ho!" parade with two thousand Indians, Buffalo Bill, Lewis and Clark, George A. Custer, stagecoaches and covered wagons once "actually used on the Oregon Trail" were hauled out of museums and mobilized. "The Old West Lives Again in the [Pendleton] Round-up."[78]

In 1915 a Portland artist named Theodore Gegoux read an account of the organizational meeting of early settlers at Champoeg in 1843 and became fascinated by the whole episode and its historical significance. Consequently in 1918 he moved into the state's newly constructed Pioneer Memorial Building in order to produce a grand historical painting. He completed *The Birth of Oregon* in 1924; it measured seven by eleven feet. It was still unsold when Gegoux died in 1929, but the state finally acquired it in 1968. A statue called *The Pioneer* (inspired by Saint-Gaudens's *The Puritan*, 1887) was unveiled at Eugene in 1919. And *The Circuit Rider*, sculpted by A. P. Proctor, was completed in 1923 and located on the west grounds of the old Oregon Statehouse in Salem.[79]

In 1920 the D.A.R. began actively placing historical markers and statues in Idaho: at Lemhi Pass, for example, where Lewis and Clark crossed into the state back in 1805; a marble figure of Sacajawea in the city park at Lewiston; at the Lapwai Mission site established in 1836; near the bridge crossing the Clearwater River, a site designated in 1923 because it had the first home, school, church, orchard, and mill, and was the birthplace of the first white children born in Idaho. Farther south, on the bridge crossing the Snake River at Homedale, a tablet was placed which reads: "Oregon Trail 1842–1865. Erected by Idaho Pocahontas Chapter D.A.R. 1920."[80] Why Pocahontas rather than Sacajawea in Idaho? Ask the Idaho D.A.R.

The Sons of Idaho organized themselves as a voluntary association at Boise on May 20, 1925. Their purposes included stimulating public interest in Idaho history, finding and marking its historic places, honoring the names and recalling the deeds of Idaho's white pioneers, and holding an annual picnic on Pioneer Day, designated as June 15 because records seemed to show a long tradition of reliable weather occurring on that date! In 1933 the Sons and Daughters of Idaho Pioneers, assisted by the *Idaho Statesman,* a newspaper, acquired two log cabins built in 1863, the year that Boise began. The structures were moved to Julia Davis Park, where a "Pioneer Village" was established. Early in the 1970s the Idaho Historical Society took responsibility for preserving the cabins, moved them to a spot adjacent to the State Museum, and added other historic Idaho structures.

The chronological rhythms of historic preservation in Montana seem to be quite similar. In the case of Fort Owen, for instance, a judge had commented in 1876 that it was crumbling; but nothing was done for more than half a century. In 1920 the property was given to the Society of Montana Pioneers. Seven years later that group, along with the Daughters of Montana, met in Missoula and made plans to restore the fort. Those plans never materialized because of insufficient funds. Another good-faith effort in 1930, involving the Stevensville Service Club and the Missoula Chamber of Commerce, came to nought for financial reasons also. In 1937 Fort Owen was purchased by a small group of tradition-oriented citizens determined to establish a state-recognized historic site. This group restored the east barracks. In 1956 the property was given to the state, and a year later the University of Montana and the Bitterroot Historical Society made an arrangement with the Parks Division of the Montana Highway Commission to excavate and reconstruct the fort. Excavation extended over a period of five years, but no restorations took place because of inadequate funds. In 1968 administration of the fort passed to the Montana Fish and Game Department. In 1970 Fort Owen was designated as a National Historic Site, and four years later the Stevensville Historical Society took responsibility for continuing the project.[81]

IN 1946 Bernard DeVoto, the Utah-bred, lapsed half-Mormon long since relocated in Cambridge, Massachusetts, and New York City, issued one of those intermittent blasts at his beloved West's seeming incapacity to develop a clear-headed and authentic sense of its own identity. He singled out the widely observed festival "whose generic name might be Frontier Week." Usually generated by the chamber of commerce, "it is aimed at the tourist trade and retail sales." DeVoto found it phony and objectionable. He then launched into a characteristically merciless tirade that was unpleasant but mostly true: "There is no harm in celebrating the past if the celebration involves some knowledge of what it was or some respect for it, but Frontier Week seldom involves either. It is conducted without reference to history, it is empty of idea and emotion, its data are anachronistic and preposterous." DeVoto summarized the quality and accomplishments of tradition-related activity since 1920:

> In twenty-five years the celebration of the Western past has grown enormously. It has grown, however, chiefly in business sagacity and in noise; little increase in knowledge or understanding is visible. The West has found its history a valuable asset but remains widely uninterested in doing anything about it beyond hoking it up for tourists.* Western antiquarians, local historians, collectors, and annalists are as enthusiastic and expert as those anywhere else, but they are few and forlorn; the historical societies (several of them very distinguished), societies for the preservation of antiquities, and similar groups, are small, handicapped by poverty, and under some public derision. Apart from advertising or at most ancestor worship, public feeling for the past is lethargic.[82]

If DeVoto sounds about as patronizing as some of those New England snobs quoted at the beginning of this section, there are several crucial differences: DeVoto loved the intermountain West, defended it against the mindless ignorance of Eastern provincials, and wrote equally ferocious screeds directed at New England smugness. "Bennie" DeVoto developed a tart tongue at an early age and never played favorites. He criticized everyone, at all possible points of the compass.

I V

ALLEN TATE, like DeVoto, harbored deeply ambivalent feelings about his own native section, the South, and eventually Tate also moved far from his origins, to the University of Minnesota (1951–68). Like DeVoto, Tate experienced peculiar circumstances in his family background and Kentucky childhood that left him with a lifelong interest in personal roots and regional history. As a young man he tried to capture key aspects of the Southern past as the stuff of imaginative literature. Hence his "Ode to the Confederate Dead" (1926) and his biographies of Stonewall Jackson in 1928 and Jefferson Davis a year later. He then contracted with a publisher to write a biography of Lee, but abandoned the project in 1931 because he found Lee not to his

*In 1935 Greyhound began its "Western Wonder Tours," with six passengers.

liking. The ambivalence of a tortured soul had begun to emerge; and late that same year, writing for a Yankee magazine, Tate made the somewhat enigmatic yet prescient observation that "Sectionalism, or politics, is public tradition, and tradition is private, or unconscious sectionalism."[83]

Tate's widely read essay for the collection called *I'll Take My Stand: The South and the Agrarian Tradition* (1930) closed with yet another enigmatic and controversial utterance that was symptomatic of profound ambivalence about his ancestral section. "We are very near an answer to our question," he wrote: "How may the Southerner take hold of his tradition? The answer is by violence." Exactly what he meant by violence has always been unclear; but in 1930 he explained to a friend that the Agrarians' (or Fugitives') "entire program is based on the assumed fact that the tradition is there to work on; otherwise we are only American liberals offering a new panacea and pretending to a concrete background that doesn't exist." He seems to have felt disquiet because the South failed to present him with a clearly usable past.* After 1933 Tate largely set the South aside as a prime focus for his writing, and became much less preoccupied than he had been with "southernism."[84]

By the early 1930s even Donald Davidson, also a Fugitive and one of the organizers of *I'll Take My Stand,* began to reconcile his strident Southern sectionalism with a broader Americanism, and the appeal of tradition with the imperative of democracy, both manifest in his 1932 book, *The Attack on Democracy.* In that same year the aging Lyon G. Tyler received a letter from William Browne, an antiquarian and register of deeds from the Berkshires who had maintained a friendly correspondence with Tyler concerning historical matters for several years. Browne gently chided Tyler for the excessive claims made in his pamphlets, and seems to have used good humor as a successful salve. "Virginia and Massachusetts," he declared: "They should stand as the twin sisters of our Union of indivisible states. Up here we have many a girl named Virginia. But it would be too much to expect any Virginia lass to be named . . . Massachusetts."[85]

Diverse expressions of a desire for sectional reconciliation, private as well as public, had been heard increasingly since the later 1870s, and with growing intensity after the turn of the century. In 1912 a man from New Orleans told a Pilgrim descendant living in the North that "the South is as glad that the Union was preserved and that they are in the United States instead of a separate confederation as anybody in the United States. The majority of intelligent people discuss the war very

---

*Lewis P. Simpson has made the plausible argument that Tate was troubled by his perception that the Old South had been "overrun" early on by a divisive and fragmentary Protestantism. Consequently it lacked a common core in terms of shared allegiance to a unifying traditional religion, and therefore lacked a prime requirement of traditional society. (*The Dispossessed Garden: Pastoral and History in Southern Literature* [Athens, Ga., 1975], 80.)

freely. . . . Lincoln and Grant stand as high in the South as they do in the North."[86]

The healing process occurred more swiftly after 1927. An article in *The Century* that emphasized the role of change in explaining culture insisted that Puritans and Cavaliers had been equally steeped in tradition: "both converted their past into new accomplishments." When the Virginia Division, Sons of Confederate Veterans, concluded its thirty-third annual convention on June 21, 1928, it adopted a resolution to "adjourn in the memory and honor of Abraham Lincoln . . . whose death was a distinct blow to the South, resulting in a national calamity." Conversely, the campaign to save Stratford Hall in Virginia (Robert E. Lee's birthplace) was initiated jointly in 1928 by a U.D.C. chapter in Greenwich, Connecticut, and one in Washington, D.C.* One year later a Robert E. Lee Memorial Foundation was incorporated in New York. While the administrative nerve center remained in Greenwich, architectural aspects of the restoration were handled from Knoxville, Tennessee.[87]

Periodically during the 1920s Worthington C. Ford of the Massachusetts Historical Society tried to persuade Lyon G. Tyler to visit that venerable organization and present a learned paper. The American Antiquarian Society, which is based in Worcester, pulled off the coup on April 16, 1930, in Boston, when Tyler gave a paper titled "New England's Contributions to Virginia" and Albert Bushnell Hart offered one called "Washington as a New England Man." The antiquarian warriors and geezers were getting *gemütlich*. Eighteen months later a man from Greenville, South Carolina, complained to Tyler that "people here generally admire Mr. Lincoln. . . . They pay many dollars for northern humbug, and very little for Confederate Catechism, or anything else favorable to the South." In 1933, when Tyler sent James Truslow Adams one of his screeds, Adams reminded the Williamsburg die-hard that he (Adams) was "half Northern and half Southern in descent. . . . My mother was a New Yorker and I myself have been about the United States so much and spent so much of my time in Europe that I am not conscious of any sectional bias at home."[88]

When James Boyd, the popular North Carolina writer, completed his Revolutionary War novel *Drums,* he wanted to title it *These United Colonies.* Maxwell Perkins, his editor at Scribner's, read the manuscript and loved Boyd's emphasis upon the creation of a nation: "The latter part of the book where the realization of the Americans that they are an entity, that they are all the same people, however different . . . is extremely moving." Boyd cared very much about the old American verities and ardently believed that the Tar Heel tradition epitomized

---

*In October 1889 the City Council in Fredericksburg, Virginia, passed a resolution thanking the Old South Church [Boston] Monument Association for undertaking a project to complete the monument to Mary Ball Washington there. (NYT, Nov. 1, 1889, p. 4.)

them. He wrote in 1925 that "this state contains, I think, more of the elements which have gone to make America than does any other." He mentioned the coastal grandees and the Appalachian mountaineers, the Scots Highlanders and the Moravian community at Salem, the English in the East and Scots-Irish in the Piedmont. Boyd successfully demonstrated to his many readers that national, regional, and local pride might all go hand in hand.[89]

By the later 1930s this phenomenon could be seen at every cultural level.* Hollywood released an utterly anachronistic film, *Maid of Salem*, in which Fred MacMurray, a fugitive from Virginia, dashes up on horseback to save Claudette Colbert, the Puritan maiden condemned to die as a witch. As his horse halts breathlessly at the gallows, MacMurray utters the eternally romantic rhetorical question: "You know I love ya, doncha?" A few months later Worthington C. Ford told James Truslow Adams: "how anyone, North or South, at this day can harbor so much as a trace of sectional feeling is beyond my comprehension." In 1941, as this era came to a close, Van Wyck Brooks revealed to Adams his dilemma in completing *New England Indian Summer, 1865–1915*: how to "retain the *regional* note at a time when New England was merging in the nation."[90]

A large measure of reconciliation did indeed occur; but all the while a new and different debate heated up. Sometimes it took the form of vigorous dialogue, and at other times people literally spoke past one another. The question of how best to seek and define American culture—as a national culture (meaning high culture as well as nationally integrated), or in terms of folk culture—would be the most hotly contested and interesting issue of the fifteen years that followed 1925.

---

*William E. Dodd told Lyon G. Tyler that his lectures on Southern history at the University of Chicago were extremely well attended. "If I were to say that the northerners are more southern in the large sense than southerners themselves, you possibly would not agree. . . . There has been almost a complete revolution in the basic thought of this part of the country during the last twenty years, and that revolution is due to the fact that northern society has become more conservative and more stratified socially and leaders are everywhere, in private conversation if not public speech, disposed to regret the way the civil war worked out. This somewhat snobbish social attitude is not altogether consoling to me." (Dodd to Tyler, Jan. 15, 1932, Tyler Papers, group 5, box 7, SLWM.)

Chapter 13

COMPETING CONCEPTIONS
OF CULTURAL IDENTITY:
NATIONAL VERSUS FOLK

In Europe throughout the nineteenth century a strong, widespread interest in both national and folk culture became apparent, without any special sense of tension between the two as rivals for social allegiance. Quite the contrary, the revival or rediscovery of folk culture was regarded more often than not as a reinforcement or boost to nationalism. Thus Edward A. Freeman, the eminent Victorian historian, wrote in the 1870s: "If there is anything truly national in the world, it is the old heroic songs of the English folk."[1]

Such matters did not receive extensive discussion in the United States at that time. But American attitudes on the affinities between the two cultural realms underwent periodic oscillations. Around midcentury a view similar to the European one prevailed. Thus, in 1857, the same year that Longfellow published *Hiawatha*, Francis Child, an eminent Harvard professor who wished to teach "the great themes of modern literature," also published his influential work *English and Scottish Popular Ballads*. Within a few decades, however, the notion took hold that high culture and popular culture ran along separate tracks—one of them elevated—and really could not be interactive, never mind mutually supportive;[2] and this remained the dominant outlook until well into the next century.

It was around the mid-1920s that this view began to be challenged; and for quite a number of interesting and ultimately influential people, it became a major priority to combine elite and popular culture or else to give laurels to the latter at the "expense" of the former. The implications of their efforts for American notions of tradition, and the degree to which they succeeded or failed, have never been described or explained. For a period of about fifteen years the struggle between supporters of a national culture and advocates of folk culture even surpassed in volubility the long-standing conflict between tradition and a democratic ethos.[3]

Before proceeding any further, it may be useful to offer two very approximate sets of definitions. Advocates of a national culture did not issue a cohesive manifesto (except for Ezra Pound) or agree upon a precise agenda, but collectively they had the following objectives or qualities in mind: first, a culture that would not be parochial or sectional in emphasis; second, a culture that would be different from any other, especially in terms of its literature; third, one that would compensate for the excesses of American heterogeneity and provide some basis for cultural unification; fourth, one that would signify social maturity, a national coming-of-age; fifth, one that reflected the belief that, by definition, a nation could not achieve greatness without manifestations of a national culture. Finally, many of the spokesmen for this camp had little faith in the "common man" and tended to be anti-democratic. Henry L. Mencken, Frank Lloyd Wright, and Alfred Stieglitz supply some choice examples.

Although the advocates of folk culture occasionally referred to themselves as a "coterie," they did not speak with a single voice. In general, however, they tended to be populistic, to believe that truly indigenous traditions must come from the "folk," and that achieving a culture worthy of the name was altogether compatible with both democracy and tradition. Second, they valued particularity of place, especially in terms of regionalism in art and literature. (They frequently referred to "local art expression.") Third, they emphasized the importance of folklore, myth, and legend. Fourth, they cherished ethnic diversity, ranging from the ballads of Appalachian whites to earthy black blues and the cultural contribution of "the Negro farthest down" (Zora Neale Hurston's phrase). Fifth, they pleaded for attention to non-literary sources of cultural understanding, such as the decorative arts, tools, and especially memory (once labelled the "archives of the poor").

They shared at least one fundamental premise with those who sought a national culture, however: namely, the belief that genuine folk cultures differ from one another and achieve distinctive national configurations. The key to understanding national character—a widely shared objective—lay in discerning those distinctive configurations.[4]

I

FROM the later 1920s until the mid-1930s an elusive topic became commonplace in the popular press: essays concerned with defining the notion of culture in general and the nature of American culture in particular—invariably with special reference to the implications of accelerating social change for indigenous traditions. The essayists tended to approve of the Western and Northern European sources of American values, and to view infusions from the rest of the world as being problematic at the very least. They called attention to the homogenization of American culture as a mixed blessing, but usually did not regard it as a suffocating phenomenon. "We recognize clearly a distinct American type of culture as having evolved," one remarked. "Yet no less certainly are regional forms of that culture taking shape before our eyes, types growing out of the special restrictions and opportunities offered by the different sections of the country."[5]

Some of these pieces took a Pollyanna position. "Once you define culture as an interplay of life and ideas," for example, "you can accept with equanimity the changing form which culture wears." On that basis both the Puritan and the Cavalier turned out to be cultured people, each one in a manner appropriate to his region, "yet they both converted their past into new accomplishments, and neither was altogether like his phase of English life from which he came." Other writers, however, were much more defensive in response to foreign slights, or to the alien perception that America lacked culture. Booth Tarkington supplies such an example in 1929. His essay concluded by praising American culture—remaining rather vague about its substantive qualities—for avoiding self-worship, for being neither rigid nor decadent, and explained that it was unfinished, still very much in the process of formation. Others were confused and confusing in their lame efforts to explain whether America could achieve a distinctive culture. A few pleaded for autonomy to the point where they verged upon cultural isolationism; and several simply made outrageous claims, such as: "American civilization . . . actually leads the world."[6]

Some of the popularizers who pursued such a line gave it an explicitly political twist. The principal sources of trouble, they argued, were radical social critics, radical historians, and the radical press. These conservative popularizers were invariably xenophobic, and they expressed open anger at the calls of people like Horace Kallen for cultural pluralism. "To hear some of these protesting gentlemen," a vituperative patriot declaimed, "one would think that America had no history, no traditions, no coherent fabric of civilization, but that all of us had been dumped down together at Ellis Island a few short years ago."* He added a sentence that combined historical truth with conservative fantasy: "America is not a wilderness plastic to the latest touch; it is a settled country with traditions extending back three centuries and with a resident population deeply attached to those traditions and determined to develop them along traditional lines."[7]

This ideological insistence upon a richly textured national past complemented the yearning for a "usable past" so forcefully articulated by

---

*This essay was illustrated with a symptomatic "cartoon." In front of a large mural depicting the Pilgrims, Valley Forge, diverse pioneers, Gettysburg, and the little red schoolhouse, a wild-eyed radical (holding a sheet labelled "Americanski Propaganda") shouts: "America has no background—no history—no atmosphere—no national character—no traditions—NO SOUL."

the young Van Wyck Brooks and other members of his alienated circle. Between them, despite the diversity of their motives and cultural concerns, they set a certain tone for the 1920s. By 1930–31, once the Great Depression settled upon the nation like a vast cloud of gloom, sheer nostalgia emerged as yet another force that made the society's vision remarkably retrospective. In 1930, when James Boyd published *Long Heat,* a historical novel, Thomas Wolfe scribbled a meandering but appreciative letter to his fellow Carolinian:

> The book has a great deal of the magnificence, the savagery, the power and the beauty that the early history of this country has. . . . Some hundreds of my kinsmen and forefathers are buried in the earth of this country: Many of them I know were hunters and pioneers with Crockett's blood in them. The other day I went down for the first time to the Pennsylvania Dutch country—my father came from there.[8]

Publication in 1931 of James Truslow Adams's *The Epic of America* brought spectacular commercial success because it made the same sort of statement collectively rather than autobiographically. By the mid-1930s, even the American left had joined this tradition-oriented bandwagon, albeit for its own political reasons. As Michael Gold wrote in the *Daily Worker* in 1935: "The chief battleground in the defense of culture against fascist barbarism is in this question of the national tradition." Some years later Esther Forbes, the New England novelist and folklorist, would look back and observe that during the depression the United States became "very curious about her own past. . . . It was then the word 'Americana' moved from the library shelf to the cocktail lounge."[9]

Forbes's interests and career serve as a useful warning before we plunge into a division of the dramatis personae in this story as being either advocates of a national culture or else devotees of folk culture. For a full appreciation of many creative figures that dichotomy is simplistic, and Forbes provides a prime example (fig. 13.1). Best known as the author of *Johnny Tremain* (1943) and *Paul Revere and the World He Lived In* (1942), her love of folk culture is reflected in *A Mirror for Witches* (1928), set in seventeenth-century New England, and especially *Rainbow on the Road* (1954), which gets directly to the folk with its tale of an itinerant limner during the early nineteenth century.

Other instances of influential individuals who invoked American memories as nationalists as well as regionalists, and who did so for purposes of both "high" and popular culture, would have to include Edward Eggleston, the novelist and social historian; Hamlin Garland, the Midwestern fiction writer; Percy MacKaye, author of pageants and producer of theatricals; Stephen Vincent Benét, the poet, balladeer, and unabashed writer of historically enriched war propaganda; Thomas

13.1   Esther Forbes with Sir Tristram at her home in Worcester, Massachusetts (February 1937). Courtesy, American Antiquarian Society.

Hart Benton, the aggressively nationalistic regionalist painter; and the composer Aaron Copland, who commented that "after *El Salón,* I occasionally had the strange sensation of being divided in half—the austere intellectual modernist on one side; the accessible, popular composer on the other."[10] In 1922 Deems Taylor, a serious and widely respected music critic, called for more attention to American folk songs. And the rise of collectors' clubs as a cultural phenomenon of the 1930s simply defies reductive categorization. The collectors came together in specialized groups to swap, sell, and discuss American pewter and glass, lamps and clocks, china and buttons, dolls and pre-industrial tools.[11]

Having acknowledged the somewhat (or sometimes) arbitrary nature of my categories, however, I must insist upon the dynamic of an ongoing dialogue—a hotly contested debate at times—best exemplified by the differences that separated two devoted friends: Van Wyck Brooks and Constance Rourke (figs. 13.2 and 13.3). She rejected his early and oft-repeated dichotomy between highbrow and lowbrow in America. She also rejected his belief that the primary (almost the exclusive) sources for the study of culture were materials of literary merit. Rourke insisted upon placing folklore alongside more traditional "literature" and in similar terms. That also suited her determination to seek unity in American culture, to bridge or connect the so-called strata. Consequently she rejected any singular emphasis upon proletarian literature because doing so would remove one very central strand of the national tradition from its larger context.[12]

13.2 Van Wyck Brooks (c. 1950), gelatin silver print by Clara E. Sipprell. Courtesy of the National Portrait Gallery, Smithsonian Institution, Washington, D.C.

13.3 Constance Rourke (1928). Courtesy of the Yale Collection of American Literature, Beinecke Rare Book and Manuscript Library, Yale University.

There is a real risk of overemphasizing the differences between Brooks and Rourke. Each one—although in different ways—became a chauvinist for American culture, wished to democratize it, believed that previous studies of it had been excessively narrow because they were too genteel or elitist, and that literature as well as analyses of it should be more closely in touch with the lifeblood of society. Following Rourke's premature death in 1941, Brooks gathered a collection of important yet disparate essays by her, had them published as *The Roots of American Culture* (1942), and wrote a sympathetic introduction to the volume. Rourke often used Brooks's terminology, though with different emphases, and she was very much aware that her assertions were presented within a frame of reference or set of criteria established earlier by him. She wrote to Brooks in 1939, near the end of her life, thanking him for his warm words about a recent article that she had published: "It represents a kind of research, hardly at all in books [i.e., not derived from books as sources], almost wholly among people, which has always interested me greatly."[13]

The fact remains that her commitment to democracy and to the accomplishments of the "folk" was considerably stronger and more focused than his. She searched for indigenous, grass-roots materials in order to offset his middlebrow emphases, and she never lost faith that populistic traditions not only existed but mattered more than others. Unlike Brooks, she was profoundly interested in and influenced by Johann Herder's notions concerning the nature of culture. In his most important work (1784–91), Herder had insisted that historical writing ought to portray the varied layers of a people's culture rather than the highest peaks of achievement alone. He believed that the basic folk cultures differed from one another and became concentrated in distinctive national patterns. Building upon Herder, Rourke asserted in her best-known book, *American Humor,* that "traditions cannot be improvised in the slow minds of whole peoples" and that "it is only when traditions are deeply established that a whole literature can be created."[14]

Rourke liked to say of those who cared deeply about America's cultural heritage that "we make a coterie." Nevertheless, the differences among Rourke, Brooks, Lewis Mumford, Bernard DeVoto, Constance Lindsay Skinner, F. O. Matthiessen, and many others are significant as well as revealing. There were, in fact, several coteries that scarcely overlapped, as we have seen and shall see in the pages ahead. But even within what Rourke perceived as *her* coterie, the variations in motive, approach, and emphasis are very striking.[15]

In 1931, for example, the same year that Rourke published *American Humor,* a work that makes the comic folk tradition absolutely central to a proper appreciation of American culture, Mumford published *The Brown Decades: A Study of the Arts in America, 1865–1895,* a volume that originated as a series of lectures presented at Dartmouth College late in 1929. Mumford's book concentrates upon architecture, engineering, landscape design, and painting. It ignores folk art and has little to say about vernacular art and architecture. It also perceives the three decades following 1865 as being absolutely formative for modern American culture, whereas Rourke regarded the antebellum generation (1830–60) as far more determinative. Even so, just to complicate matters, she refers in *American Humor* to the "short and broken cycle of American life; traditions are even now only beginning to take a coherent shape."[16]

Similarly, Bernard DeVoto and Carl Sandburg affirmed the primacy of American folk culture while Ezra Pound (who originated in the intermountain West, like DeVoto) and F. O. Matthiessen (whose geographical roots were disparate) preferred high culture in the form of work produced by serious writers and found American folk culture either inadequate (Pound) or else uninteresting (Matthiessen). To highlight the fact that this dichotomy was a "vertical" one that had little to do with either class, regional origin, or race, one need only look at participants in the Harlem Renaissance of the 1920s and early 1930s, who split on both sides of the debate and thereby embodied it in microcosm, especially at the

13.4   Zora Neale Hurston by Carl Van Vechten (April 3, 1935). Reproduced by permission of the Carl Van Vechten Papers, Collection of American Literature, Beinecke Rare Book and Manuscript Library, Yale University.

peak of its definitional phase during the later 1920s. Wallace Thurman, Zora Neale Hurston, Arthur Huff Fauset, Richard Bruce Nugent, and Claude McKay stressed the distinctiveness of black ethnicity, particularly among the working classes. They loved the earthy, hedonistic, and bohemian aspects of folk culture. By contrast Walter White, James Weldon Johnson, Mary White Ovington, Benjamin Brawley, Jessie Fauset, and Alain Locke were far more assimilationist, more likely to speak for and write about the black middle class, and wanted African-American culture to be viewed as an integral and highly significant part of American national culture.[17]

Once again, these categories and distinctions cannot be made too neat and tidy. Langston Hughes, Arna Bontemps, and Countee Cullen all had one foot quite comfortably planted in each camp. Those who felt enthusiastic about *Fire!!*, a radical new quarterly that appeared in 1926, disliked *Green Pastures* (1930), a "folk-type" play that the more elegant African-Americans admired, while the latter, including W. E. B. Du Bois, despised *Fire!!* or else found it an embarrassment.[18]

It is a matter of some consequence that Zora Neale Hurston, the novelist, collaborator with Langston Hughes, and collector of African-American folklore (fig. 13.4), had been a graduate student in anthropology at Columbia under the guidance of Franz Boas (and to a lesser degree Ruth Benedict). Constance Rourke was also influenced by the

Boasian approach to cultural studies, as were many of her contemporaries. That pattern enables us to delineate what amounts to a "paradigm shift" that took place between two generations.[19] Edith Wharton and her contemporaries had been very deeply fascinated by *The Golden Bough,* a massive work by Sir James Frazer, the Scottish anthropologist, which first appeared in 1890 and was then revised and expanded in twelve large volumes between 1911 and 1915. *The Golden Bough* was a vast compendium concerning primitive cults, rituals, beliefs, magical practices, taboos, myths, and festivals drawn from a very wide range of sources. Although it sacrificed depth for breadth, Frazer's work gave Wharton, T. S. Eliot, and many other tradition-oriented writers a functional definition and rationalization of cultural memory and the social role of myth.[20] When Boas displaced Frazer as the most influential anthropologist, it marked a gradual shift in orientation and emphasis among intellectuals from myths to more tangible cultural survivals and the need for careful, precise descriptions of them. Or, to put it differently, from an evocative anthropology of tribal memory to a more analytical ethnography of folk cultures.

Robert Redfield, a distinguished anthropologist of the generation that followed Boas's, differentiated between Great Traditions (roughly comparable to high culture) and Little Traditions (roughly comparable to folk culture).[21] The most essential point, of course, is that both exist; therefore the critical question concerns our understanding of their relationship and the flow of influence between them. As I have already attempted to indicate, these cleavages and polarities are not and cannot be exquisitely symmetrical. But the dialogue that took place for two decades starting in the 1920s is fairly epitomized by a pair of sentences. There is Van Wyck Brooks (just a quid out of character, perhaps) saying that "it is the minor books and writers that bring forth a culture, creating the living chain that we call tradition." And then there is Joseph Downs, curator of the American Wing at the Met, declaring that "we can rightly judge a cultural period by its greatest achievement rather than its mean average."[22]

I I

AS WE HAVE SEEN in several previous chapters, diverse manifestations of the desire for a national culture had appeared with rhythmic regularity for more than a century prior to 1920. In 1889 a general lamentation concerning the absence of a national song caused John Philip Sousa to say that the composition of such a song must be "the outcome of some national event." Louis Sullivan and Frank Lloyd Wright argued the case for a "national style" of architecture, one that would help to provide the unified civilization that seemed so lacking in the United States.[23]

Those who pleaded for a national culture during the interwar years, however, were largely prompted by two quite different sorts of stimuli: first, a desire for the ultimate healing of national wounds that dated back to the period 1861–65; and second, a largely belletristic concern for imaginative works that would demonstrate the existence of something distinctive that could be called an "American civilization." A loosely cohesive group of intellectuals who hankered after such a thing included Randolph Bourne, Stuart Pratt Sherman, Waldo Frank, Van Wyck Brooks, Lewis Mumford, Thomas Craven (seeking Americanism in art), and Harold Stearns.[24]

The Golden Jubilee years of the Civil War, 1911–15, helped to stimulate a new national synthesis concerning that pivotal event and its meaning: first, that secession had been wrong and preserving the Union right; second, that terminating slavery had been a good thing, especially for white people in all sections; and third, that Northern leaders had been misguided in their policies of Reconstruction because premature attempts to provide complete rights for former slaves had resulted in grave injustices being perpetrated against Southern whites. That message emerged with amazing consistency in historical fiction, popular films, and a substantial body of serious writing.[25]

The Virginia Monument dedicated at Gettysburg in 1917, surmounted by an equestrian statue of Robert E. Lee, was the first such monument funded there by a former Confederate state. The Gettysburg Battlefield Memorial Association had actively discouraged Southern memorials for decades. When Mary Johnston, the Virginia author of best-selling novels, spoke at White Sulphur Springs in 1932 on "The Character of Lee," she scarcely mentioned the war, its causes, or its consequences. She observed instead that Lee, like Lincoln, was truly a national hero. "Both these men are now and will remain not sectional, but American, but universal." She remembered Lee as a conciliator rather than as a rebel: "Sorrow he knew, but not bitterness. He moves about in the old vast rooms, he walks the old, forever-stretching verandahs of the old hotel that so many of us here hold in memory. . . . In the etheric stuff of which memory is made that hotel yet rises within this great hotel."[26]

Meanwhile, the process of making a national icon of Lincoln began to accelerate. A painting by Childe Hassam titled *Lincoln's Birthday* (1918) found its way to the Huntington Museum of Art in West Virginia. Lincoln Road in Miami Beach, Florida, was laid out to be the Fifth Avenue of the South, an incongruous avenue of luxury shops catering to the whims of the wealthy. In 1920 Herbert Croly, hitherto known as an admirer of Alexander Hamilton, published an essay which insisted that Lincoln's complexity had never been adequately appreciated, and expressed the hope that someday Americans would aspire to the model that Lincoln offered them. "The memory of Bismarck belongs chiefly to the German national imperialists," he wrote. "The memory of Gladstone belongs chiefly to laissez-faire liberalism; even the memory of

Washington belongs more than anything else to the successors of the Federalists. But the memory of Lincoln belongs to all his fellow-countrymen who can guess what magnanimity is."[27] Croly's powerful treatise *The Promise of American Life* (1909) had been, among other things, an exploration of the potential for achieving a national culture.

In 1935 a proposed joint reunion at Washington of federal and Confederate veterans almost collapsed because the G.A.R. could not abide the thought of latter-day rebels displaying the detested Confederate flag. Virginius Dabney, a respected journalist from Richmond, pleaded for concessions from both sides and reminded them that Lee had advised his former troops and the Southern people as a whole "to abandon all these local animosities and make your sons Americans." In 1937 the same issue loomed like a dark cloud that threatened to wash out the seventy-fifth anniversary joint reunion to be held at Gettysburg in July of 1938. Some G.A.R. chapters threatened to boycott if the U.C.V. truly intended to unfurl the treasonous Stars and Bars. Those same Northern chapters also condemned the Pennsylvania State Commission that was planning the affair (in order to promote tourism?) because it used the phrase "war between the states" rather than "Civil War."[28]

Ultimately the 1938 Blue-Gray encampment was notable because seven states, including Virginia and Tennessee, erected the Eternal Light Peace Memorial, which differed from all of the other memorials at Gettysburg because it emphasized peace rather than war.[29]

Meanwhile, on May 22, 1937, at a Blue-Gray reunion held in Vicksburg, Colonel U. S. Grant III and J. C. Pemberton joined hands at the "Surrender Monument" where their grandfathers had led the opposing forces seventy-four years before. Two years later, in 1939, a society was formed, known as the Descendants of Participants in the Campaign, Siege and Defense of Vicksburg, which planned to meet in May on what was termed "the world's most perfectly preserved battlefield." Hostility had given way to harmony among the few remaining survivors, and to proper preservation of the historic site.[30]

The quest for memory seemed to quench any thirst for animosity. On September 17, 1937, President Roosevelt visited Antietam Battlefield to commemorate the seventy-fifth anniversary of the bloodiest day of battle ever fought on United States soil. FDR emphasized that the country was whole once again, blamed Reconstruction for promoting sectional hatreds, and then clasped his hands on the joined arms of a ninety-four-year-old Union veteran and a ninety-eight-year-old Confederate veteran.[31] They all lived happily ever after, though not for very long.

IF ABRAHAM LINCOLN increasingly became the foremost American folk hero, immortalized above all by Carl Sandburg in six boxed volumes (1926–39), George Washington remained the national symbol incarnate, and the bicentennial of his birth in 1932 turned out

to be a treacly year in which Americans literally oozed through hero
worship. When Congressman Sol Bloom, director of this patriotic extravaganza, invited Edwin Markham (author of *The Man with the Hoe*)
to write a poem for the occasion, he first replied that "I love Washington, and I wish to pay him the noblest homage that lies in the power
of my pen." Three and a half months later Markham still hadn't delivered and complained that "it is no easy task to compress a heroic career
into sixty-four lines."[32]

Edgar Lee Masters, a Midwestern poet who achieved instantaneous
fame in 1915 with the publication of *Spoon River Anthology*, also
turned his hand to historical and biographical subjects during the 1930s,
such as "George Rogers Clark" and "The Rock of Acoma"; but looking
back he bemoaned the precarious character of such materials as stuff
for the writer's craft. When he read *The World of Washington Irving*
by Van Wyck Brooks in 1944, he sent the author a line that seemed to
project forward to Masters's own time a familiar feeling that he ascribed
to the problem of literary nationalism in the young republic: "Somehow
all those men seem thin and bloodless to me, as if they had nothing to
work with or on—and maybe that was the case."[33]

Brooks himself is an extremely complex subject to "get right" on this
issue, and for several reasons: first, because his own views shifted very
strikingly over time; and second because he was sensitive to contextual
changes that occurred during his own mature lifetime—particularly
when they pertained to the prospect of achieving a national culture. He
addressed the topic head-on in 1917 with an essay titled "Toward a
National Culture." He felt an awakening of national awareness but
wondered what would come of it. At least Brooks concluded his wistful
speculation with a fairly clear sense of what he wanted to be able to
affirm, and why:

> Americans, north, south, east, and west, have ceased to be "simply
> folks"; they have ceased to be merely Texans and Kentuckians and
> Californians and New Englanders, satisfied, so far as the art of
> writing is concerned, with the dialect and local color of a "Ken-
> tucky literature," or what not. They have become, to our imagina-
> tion, human beings, and human beings faintly flushed with that
> desire for a higher life that implies a life in common. . . . If this
> leads into the idea of a "national culture" to come it is only in
> order that America may be able in the future to give something
> to the rest of the world that is better than what the rest of the
> world at present calls "Americanism."[34]

In *The Ordeal of Mark Twain* Brooks supplied a very clear clue
concerning his inability to share Rourke's enthusiasm for the centrality
of folk culture in antebellum America. Referring to the times in which
Twain came of age, the 1840s and '50s, Brooks may even have aimed

this sentence at Miss Rourke's determined gaze. It was a nation, Brooks insisted, "that had no folk-music, no folk-art, no folk-poetry, or next to none, to express it, to console it."[35]

A bizarre mix of writers for middlebrow magazines continued to echo Brooks well into the 1930s—"We are a nation without legend or folk-lore"—and academic patriots started calling in the mid-1920s for a body of literature that would be genuinely national in scope rather than regional or parochial, because "our American literature is something different from anything else in the world."[36]

Ezra Pound's contribution to this on-going discussion was characteristically eccentric, cryptic yet shrewd, insistent yet inconsistent. Exhibit A has to be his lavish praise for the Jefferson–Adams correspondence (1937) in which he declaimed that "if we are a nation, we must have a national mind"; and subsequently, with challenging swagger, "How you expect to have a nation with no national culture beats me." The following year he swung into high gear and produced Exhibit B, "National Culture: A Manifesto." He began with a historical vision that ran exactly contrary to the conventional wisdom: "A national American culture existed from 1770 till at least 1861." Edgar Lee Masters must have gagged on that one; and Van Wyck Brooks's hair would have stood straight up had he not been wearing a brush cut already.[37]

Then, almost halfway into the essay, Pound let the reader know precisely where he stood regarding this decade-long debate. A sequence of three sentences increased slightly in length as Pound proceeded: "A national culture has a minimum of components. If the production be simply unconscious we are in a state of folk culture only. Any more developed phase must of necessity include criteria which are, as criteria, capable of comparison with the best alien criteria." He wrapped the piece up with queries and challenges. Did even a few hundred Americans value a national culture "sufficiently to conserve it"? Was anyone really ready to make a decision "as to the bases" of an American national culture? So let's take stock of what we've got, and after doing so let's publish and distribute what's worthwhile. Having said all of that, and having dismissed folk culture, the fact remains that from the later 1930s onward Pound exulted in American slang and colloquialisms![38]

However paradoxical Ezra Pound may have been, he was in tune in one respect at least: the 1930s as a decade was notable for the presumption that high culture and popular culture really could be bridged, and perhaps even, with sufficient extension, mass culture as well. Organizations so diverse as the Yale University Press and the conservative National Security League turned to nationwide radio in order to disseminate as widely as possible the contents of books about American history and "suitable speeches" on all of the "patriotic days of the year," such as George Washington's Birthday. In 1934 the editor of the *Journal of the National Education Association* and chairman of the National

Committee on Education by Radio pleaded for the desirability of a national culture.[39]

Professional historians in search of a fresh synthesis of new knowledge about the American past looked increasingly to social history, "the evolution of the self-consciousness of a keenly self-conscious people," which meant casting a far more populistic net than most scholars had in the past. And people like Hallie Flanagan, a theater director who played the most pivotal role in vitalizing WPA dramatic productions all across the land, promoted a movement that would create a "national culture by and for the working class of America."[40] The democratization of culture in general, but of national memory and tradition especially, made a great leap forward during these years.*

III

IF HENRY FORD had democratized American transportation by 1916 with annual reductions in the cost of his Model T automobile, Bennett Cerf similarly helped to democratize accessibility to books (and consequently to culture) by founding Random House and the Modern Library series in 1925–27. The style and substance of American writing began to be more egalitarian as well. Writers like Willa Cather and Ernest Hemingway quite deliberately chose prose styles that would make them accessible. When James Boyd wrote a historical novel about the Civil War, *Marching On* (1927), he decided to focus on James Fraser, the son of a poor white North Carolina farmer, and on the feudal Southern economic system. His editor at Scribner's, Maxwell Perkins, warned that "If you put in the leaders, it would become like the old time historical novel, where the hero encountered everybody of importance in an altogether impossible way"; and after Perkins had read some of the manuscript he added that he liked the fact that James was not an officer, "because to do that would have been to follow the old historical romance."[41]

As the depression deepened and the 1930s progressed, innovative modes of imaginative literature became steadily more populistic. Carl Sandburg's *The People, Yes* (1936) offered a panoramic depiction in verse of the American spirit as expressed in folklore and folk history— an affirmation of his faith in the common man. In 1937, when playwright Paul Green pioneered his symphonic historical dramas with *The Lost Colony* at Roanoke, he designated his personal creation as "the people's theater." Thornton Wilder's *Our Town* (1938) dealt entirely with unassuming, everyday people in simple settings, and as Aaron Copland put it, "looked back at an America of simple, homespun values

---

*Constance Rourke asserted in *American Humor* (1931) that humor served as the solvent that melted distinctions between highbrows and lowbrows in the United States.

that seemed to have been lost."[42] Wilder succeeded so well that a film version enjoyed its Hollywood premiere in May 1940.

An almost missionary sense of urgency prompted diverse efforts to preserve evidence of American pasts that were rapidly disappearing from view. Hence Henry Chapman Mercer's rationale for his quirky yet comprehensive collection of pre-industrial tools in Doylestown. In 1925 he declared his prime motive: "Veneration for the past." Many of the documentary photographers so active during the 1930s felt a responsibility, expressed by Walker Evans, to record things that were "passing out of history." John Collier, Jr. (1884–1968), sought to capture the heterogeneity of American communities and their unrecorded traditions. His camera immortalized Amish farmers in Pennsylvania, Portuguese fishermen in Rhode Island and New Bedford, Massachusetts, and Acadian farmers in Maine. Jack Delano felt driven to make a historical record of festival customs observed by ordinary Americans. Consequently he photographed in lavish detail the ritual feast of a family in Ledyard, Connecticut, on Thanksgiving Day.[43]

Similar impulses motivated local and state historians, and they often became very vocal about their egalitarian views and objectives. Systematic and non-selective reading of early newspapers, one declared, gave access to "the daily life of the people"; and by the 1930s historians in the upper Middle West claimed that "the idea of studying American history from the bottom up rather than from the top down" had originated in their region.[44]

Genealogical pursuits also became democratized during the 1930s. Interest in family history spread swiftly, and the emergence of family associations meant the appearance of many weighty tomes, usually published at each family's expense. In April 1930 representatives of more than thirty family associations met near Boston and established the Federation of American Family Associations. Within a year it began to publish *The Genealogical Directory*, which initially listed more than five hundred family associations. Handbooks and guides to genealogy proliferated, bearing such titles as *Genealogy as Pastime and Profession* (1930), *The Art of Ancestor Hunting* (1936), and *Searching for Your Ancestors* (1937). Every major city suddenly had at least one reputable genealogical bureau; and a representative ad in one prospectus raised this rhetorical question: "What triumph of the rod and reel ever gave the thrill of ecstasy with which we land an elusive ancestor in the genealogical net?" An essay that appeared in 1938 indicated just how much the personal pursuit of tradition had been transformed since those exclusive ancestral associations came into being during the 1890s. "Truly one of the blessings of American democracy," it declared without irony, "is that it has brought genealogy and pedigrees and an escutcheon within the reach of the common man. . . . It is only in America where the butcher, the baker and the bookstore-dealer may aspire to genealogical distinction."[45]

War and battle monuments became democratized when generic figures like Johnny Reb or an anonymous World War I non-commissioned
soldier rather than a heroic general or some prominent politician appeared in bronze. In 1935 New York's Mayor Fiorello La Guardia gave
a talk in which he insisted that culture belonged to the common man
as much as it did to *Mayflower* descendants. He asserted that art was
more widely appreciated in the United States than anywhere else in the
world because our egalitarian educational system had awakened a latent hunger for beauty. In 1936 and 1937 the centennials of the first two
McGuffey Readers were observed. McGuffey received special praise as
the first American to prepare textbooks designed for public rather than
private schools.[46]

Perhaps this enthusiasm for democratic development via education
achieved its *reductio ad absurdum* in 1936 when Teachers College at
Columbia University created a Laboratory in Readability whose mission
was to translate "hard" books and texts into easy reading. Accessibility
to the common man became the be-all and end-all of culture. Let's level
down rather than up. Naturally they began with an egalitarian document, the Declaration of Independence, so two staff members translated that sacred text into accessible English. No one had ever accused
Thomas Jefferson of writing inaccessible English; but apparently it
seemed just too highfalutin for Everyman and Everywoman. The new,
streamlined version started this way:

> When for a long time two countries have been a part of the same
> government, and when one of these countries decides to break
> away and take its rightful place in the world as a separate nation,
> men and women everywhere will want to know why this has been
> done.[47]

It seems just a bit flat; but fortunately it flopped and hasn't been heard
from since.

A VERITABLE PASSION for historical pageants persisted
through the interwar years, and it is tempting to tack that phenomenon
onto our history of levelled traditions. In 1921, for instance, the president of the Virginia Historical Pageant Association patiently explained
that his group had "departed from the time worn method of raising
funds by subscription from business and moneyed interests, an unique
method having been adopted which gives everyone an equal share in
assuring the success of the Pageant."[48]

Be that as it may, the most interesting and important new emphases
impelling pageantry during these decades have less to do with democratization than with other concerns. A greater degree of community
inclusiveness had, after all, been a major objective of the great "wave"

of pageants that occurred between 1909 and 1917.[49] There are demonstrable signs of continuity despite evidence that during the 1920s some authors gently spoofed the more ludicrous aspects of community historical pageants, and some scholars lamented that "all the emphasis seems to be on pageants, publicity and the work with the schools."[50]

Whereas most pageantry in the Progressive era had primarily been prompted by municipal pride and the desire to demonstrate community cohesion in the face of increasing social pluralism, the "new" pageantry of the interwar decades added half a dozen fresh concerns. First, there were numerous pageants connected more closely than ever before to the commemoration of specific historical anniversaries and associated memories: the fiftieth anniversary in 1926 of Custer's Last Stand (when Calvin Coolidge of Vermont wore a ten-gallon hat) and the fifty-first in 1927 (when Coolidge wore a full headdress and was officially adopted as a Sioux); a pageant held in 1925 at Charlotte, North Carolina, to celebrate the spurious Mecklenburg Declaration of Independence; a Tercentenary Masque organized ten years later in honor of the creation of Boston Common in 1635; a historic pageant at East Lyme in 1935 to honor Connecticut's tercentenary; a historical pageant the following year at Fort Ticonderoga to observe the 161st anniversary of its capture from the British by the Green Mountain Boys; a pageant held at Annapolis, Maryland, in 1937 to honor the 200th birthday of Charles Carroll, who had signed the Declaration of Independence; and another the same year when New York City paid homage to the sesquicentennial of the signing of the U.S. Constitution—a pageant in which members of the Federal Theatre Project dressed as Washington, Hamilton, Madison, Franklin, and Roger Sherman.[51]

Second, pageants were created in order to commemorate particular historical events or "firsts" that mattered to a state or region, such as Idaho's "magnificent pageant of progress" held in June 1930 with such hoopla as Boise Baisin Days; or Covered-Wagon Days, a commemorative pageant presented annually in Salt Lake City starting in 1930; or the Pioneer Day celebration—three days of pageantry—held in Bismarck, South Dakota, in 1936 to note the seventy-fifth anniversary of its creation as a territory; or the extensive pioneer caravan pageant held in August 1938 as a vivid part of the Northwest Territory Sesquicentennial.[52]

Third, pageants were now even more likely to be created for commercial and promotional purposes, though usually they received some more or less transparent cover of altruism. The expeditions to the northern Rockies and to the Pacific Northwest, sponsored in 1925–26 by the Great Northern Railroad, fit into this category; and the pageant created in July 1926 at Longview, Washington, on the Columbia River, was quite typical. So was the Oregon Trail pageant held at Meacham, Oregon, in 1923; and the popular Spanish Mission pageants put on in California in 1923, 1934, 1937, and 1940. So were the rodeo festivities that attracted numerous tourists from the late 1920s onward, and the Deadwood Days of '76 Show in South Dakota.[53]

The Chicago World's Fair of 1933, known as the Century of Progress International Exhibition, included historical pageantry, and so did the World's Fair held at New York City in 1939. The costumes designed for the sesquicentennial of George Washington's first inauguration, reenacted on April 30 of that year, offered quite a spectacle. The press did observe, however, that when George Washington (impersonated by cartoonist Denys Wortman) entered the fairgrounds in his 160-year-old coach, it seemed a bit incongruous in the "World of Tomorrow."[54]

Fourth, a fresh concern for theatricality as a means of making American memories appealing emerged during the 1930s. Historic sites might be magnetic or inert, depending upon their promoters' vision and thoughtfulness in making what W. A. R. Goodwin called "an appeal to the creative imagination." In 1934 Goodwin drafted a six-page, single-spaced memorandum, "The Theatrical Appeal to the Imagination," for John D. Rockefeller III. Goodwin explained that he and others contemplated

> stimulating the imagination through theatrical effects, and we considered, without seeking to reach any definite determination, the possible use of Pageantry, and agreed that, in so far as this method was used, it would be most important to have meticulous care given to the proper designing of costumes. . . . We even considered the thought of encouraging the citizens of Williamsburg and the people in the stores to wear Colonial costumes during the week of Pageantry.[55]

They did, too, and revels in early American get-ups became all the rage in Williamsburg after 1935. We have already noted Paul Green's innovative work with theatrical history during the thirties and forties; and by 1941 such distinguished writers as Sherwood Anderson had acquired enthusiasm for writing the likes of a "Night in Old San Antonio" pageant.[56]

A fifth stimulus blended political and social motives, sometimes with unexpected—even bizarre—twists. When a President's Birthday Ball was planned in January 1935, its chief feature would be a Pageant of America, and more particularly original costumes symbolic of the chief natural resources of the United States were to be worn. In September 1937 a farcical re-enactment of the Boston Tea Party took place—sponsored by people who claimed to be descended from royalty. They dressed in colorful aristocratic costumes, not like Indians. The quartet of co-operating organizations were called the Society of Americans of Royal Descent, the Society of Descendants of Knights of the Most Noble Order of the Garter, the Colonial Order of the Crown, and the Plantagenet Society. (I don't believe that any of them has been heard from since.) And then, humdrum by comparison, the Washington Headquarters Association, consisting of D.A.R. members, held a costume party every May at the Jumel Mansion (George Washington's temporary base in northern Manhattan after he retreated from Long Island in 1776).[57]

Finally, we must recognize the growing utility of multi-purpose pageants, that is, ones that not only combined several of the features already mentioned, but celebrated more than one historical event or tradition. The designation of Pioneer Day in June 1936 was meant to be "an occasion for the rubbing of Aladdin's lamp to bring back the glories of the past and the men who played the leading roles in the drama of Dakota." At Fort Lincoln State Park, three miles southwest of Bismarck, people re-enacted the day that General Custer led his cavalry forth to catastrophe; and they paid homage to Lewis and Clark, to the French explorer Sieur de La Vérendrye, to the Sioux, and to the Scottish Highlanders who arrived in the nineteenth century. Similarly, 100,000 people came to Maryland in 1937 to watch a re-enactment of the Battle of Antietam on the occasion of its seventy-fifth anniversary. That re-enactment, however, capped "the historical pageant and exposition called 'On Wings of Time,' " which included the 200th anniversary of the creation of Washington County and the 175th anniversary of the founding of Hagerstown, Maryland.[58]

African-Americans were not notably visible in about 98 percent of these pageants, though that began to change after 1925. At Philadelphia's Sesquicentennial of Independence in 1926, a fiasco that dragged on for months, numerous pageants with patriotic themes took place, including two organized by and fully participated in by African-Americans. When Richmond, Virginia, observed its bicentennial in 1937, some locals found it rather bold that a black man was permitted to lead an ox in the "Cavalcade of the Cavaliers Fête."[59]

Although I cannot claim that W. E. B. Du Bois directly triggered this very slow "rise," it just so happens that in 1925 he published a charming story about the planning of a pageant (concerning contributions to American civilization) to be held in a "middle" Indiana town. The tale (as narrated by a white committee member) satirizes the lily-whiteness of pageants held in the United States up until that time, and in a relatively short space managed to cover numerous Negro contributions to American culture as well as white resistance to recognizing them.

> Well, we took up education next and before we got through, in popped Booker T. Washington. And then came democracy and it looked like everybody had had a hand in that, even the Germans and Italians. The chairman also said that two hundred thousand Negroes had fought for their own liberty in the Civil War and in the war to make the world safe for democracy. But that didn't impress Mrs. Lee or any of the rest of us and we concluded to leave the Negro out of democracy.[60]

Du Bois not only chose quite deliberately to emphasize the importance of folk culture in this story, at one point he even quoted (non-pedantically, without citation) from H. E. Krehbiel's *Afro-American Folk-Songs* (1913). By 1925 a folk movement was very much under way and gave fresh vitality to discussions of tradition and memory in the United States.

I V

OBVIOUSLY, some interest in folklore and folk culture could be found in the United States prior to the interwar years. It emerged as an academic enthusiasm late in the 1880s, when not one but two professional associations were formed. Scholarly essays soon began to appear, journals were established, and even some state-based organizations such as the Virginia Folk-Lore Society, founded in 1913.[61] Its stated purpose was "to collect and thus to preserve the words and music of the English and Scottish ballads that drifted across with our first settlers and that have been transmitted from century to century by oral tradition." It should come as no surprise that the angle of vision of these early folklorists was basically elitist. Figures like George Francis Dow, who did such innovative work for the Essex Institute in Salem at the turn of the century and published books like *Every Day Life in the Massachusetts Bay Colony* (1935), had nonetheless a rather romantic and exclusionary vision of the early folk in English America.[62]

The seeds of a more egalitarian emphasis were sown by disparate members of the next generation. Young Constance Rourke, for instance, spent 1908–09 in Europe examining European folktales. After she returned to the United States Rourke devoted more than a decade to extensive travel in quest of comparable American materials. In 1920 her efforts began to bear fruit: an essay on Paul Bunyan that appeared in the *New Republic.* As one obituary correctly observed in 1941, her work, "sometimes called 'living research,' obliged her to visit all parts of the United States, to mingle with and get to know well all types of people."[63]

From the mid-1920s into the '30s her obsession spread swiftly. In 1923 Carl Sandburg visited with Walter Prescott Webb in Chicago to discuss their mutual interest in collecting folklore. In 1927 and again the next winter, Zora Neale Hurston (sponsored by Franz Boas and Columbia) made trips to small black communities in the South, especially rural Florida, to collect African-American folklore. Jan and Cora Gordon travelled through the Southeast collecting folksongs in 1927.[64] In 1935 Holger Cahill, a museum man who sought folk art for Abby Aldrich Rockefeller's fledgling collection, wrote to his client:

> I have completed the first "leg" of my trip through the South, combing the principal towns of the Atlantic seaboard from Vir-

ginia to Florida. The trip has convinced me that the south, equally with the north, is filled with folk art and that as people become more interested in it more and more of it will be revealed.

During the later 1930s WPA programs of the New Deal were devoted to the nationwide search for folk materials of all sorts.[65]

In 1930 Ruth Suckow, a novelist from Iowa, published in *Scribner's* an essay entitled "The Folk Idea in American Life." Its emphases, ambiguities, and confusions are symptomatic of an idea whose time had, perhaps, *almost* come but had not quite crystallized or achieved consensus among its diverse body of adherents. She correctly noted that for several years there had been a "fairly determined search for the folk principle in American life." She recognized a kind of exotic quest for "the primitive" by outsiders among African-Americans, Indians, hillbillies, cowboys, and outlaws. She then registered a series of complaints: that little of the folk material uncovered thus far meant much to the ordinary American; that a basic homogeneity underlay the appearance of diversity in American culture; that strangely enough, "those who have been hottest on the scent of a 'folk arts,' a foundation, a tradition, a beginning, are the same rebellious children who have totally, explicitly revolted from the 'folk' practices of their own communities." After directing hostility toward the "intelligentsia" and toward aesthetes, she concluded (not altogether coherently) that "the folk spirit is the basic, unifying element of that intellectual and aesthetic confusion—that bewilderment of variety—of which we are hearing so much just now."[66]

Between 1927 and 1937 Stephen Vincent Benét and Constance Rourke, both independent writers, epitomized as well as any of their contemporaries the hot pursuit of and passion to communicate American folk culture. In 1927, as Benét neared completion of his epic poem *John Brown's Body,* he made oblique reference to the young American expatriates by proclaiming that "We also have a heritage—and not all of it wooden money." Getting more specific in a subsequent letter: "We have our own folk-gods and giants and figures of earth in this country. I wanted to write something about them."[67] Ten years later, in a speech before the American Library Association, Rourke offered similar observations. After noting that young people ought to be "permitted to share in the current movement toward a discovery of the American past, particularly in its concern with our cultural traditions," she specified:

> We are beginning to suspect that folk music has taken a distinct course in this country. . . . Our education has been and still is almost exclusively literary. We still have a long way to go if the balance is to be redressed, if the many arts which have been intertwined in our culture are to be evoked, and if we are to regard these as essentials in themselves and not merely as "background." . . . Obviously the arts grow from tradition, slowly, yet

we seem to forget that fact in many of our plans for education and in much of our contemporary [cultural] criticism.[68]

In addition to the music mentioned by Rourke, we must also notice those who led the way in vitalizing American folk art, crafts, and folklore—recognizing all the while that there were persons, organizations, museums, festivals, and foundations under whose auspices some overlap occurred. These were not mutually exclusive categories. We must also recognize the role of regionalism in this phenomenon, and the fact that not all sections or regions played equally important parts. Appalachia, for example, had special significance. In 1917 a British folk song collector named Cecil J. Sharp came to Knoxville, Tennessee, performed some traditional Scots-Irish and Celtic songs, pleaded that the integrity of Appalachian folk culture be respected (in the face of philanthropic do-gooders who wanted backward Appalachia to "catch up" with the rest of the nation), and asserted the "supreme cultural value of an inherited tradition." Within a year, curiously enough, *The Century* magazine (very much upper "middlebrow") published an essay titled "The Mountaineers: Our Own Lost Tribes." And within a decade assorted individuals, many of them not professional writers or artists, felt an imperative to preserve this threatened subculture. As a lawyer put it to Paul Green: "typical mountain life will soon be a thing of the past and by the time another generation comes along with the effects of good-roads, the Smoky Mountain Park, and the wide expanse of commercial development which is now well under way, the isolated life of the mountaineer will only be a memory."[69]

Similarly, between 1921 and 1923 fellow Texans Frank Dobie and Walter Prescott Webb resolved to preserve the historic traditions and folkways of the Great Plains, an enthusiasm that swiftly infected others in Austin and elsewhere. When Bernard DeVoto published *Mark Twain's America* in 1932 he was prompted, in part, by his rage at the ignorance of folk culture on the American frontier exhibited by Van Wyck Brooks, Waldo Frank, and Lewis Mumford. As DeVoto insisted in his Preface, "such things as negro witchcraft and the idiom of frontier humor have proved to be of absolute importance for the object of this book." Frank Owsley had comparable ends in view when he worked on *Plain Folk of the Old South* (1949).[70]

Women played a notably prominent role in the pursuit and presentation of folklore. In addition to Rourke, already cited in several contexts, young Esther Forbes published essays in the *Boston Transcript* in 1924–25 that revealed her enthusiasm for early New England folklore. Zora Neale Hurston cared about class as well as race: hence her decision to write about "the Negro farthest down." In the course of a 1934 newspaper interview she commented that "It would be a tremendous loss to the Negro race and to America if we should lose the folklore and folk music, for the unlettered Negro has given the Negro's best contribution to America's culture." Her *Mules and Men* (1935), the first popular book about Afro-American folklore ever written by a black person, presented samples of an oral tradition that exemplified a distinctive system of behavior and belief.[71]

By the early 1930s such books had begun to proliferate for diverse sections and subcultures of the United States: Marion Nicholl Rawson, *From Here to Yender* (1932), rich with proverbs and sayings from peddlers and travellers in New England and upper New York; Florence Bennett Anderson, *Through the Hawse-Hole* (1932), based upon the family traditions of a Nantucket whaling captain; and Vance Randolph, *Ozark Mountain Folks* (1932), a book about witches and witch-riders, "literaries" and singing schools, the folk beliefs and customs of a neglected American region.

As early as 1926 Edmund Wilson remarked that "there appears to be a steadily increasing interest in the study of American folk-songs." The following year Carl Sandburg published his *American Songbag,* the first commercially successful anthology of its kind. In 1928 the Library of Congress established the Archive of American Folksong.* Then books like *Devil's Ditties* by Jean Thomas began to appear (1932), in this instance a compilation of songs and notes about the Kentucky singers who first made them known to the author; and in 1934 John Lomax published *American Songs and Ballads,* the single most influential compendium of American folk songs.[72]

In the meanwhile John Powell of Richmond, Virginia, had emerged as an energetic collector, entrepreneur, and information "switchboard" for those who shared his passion for American folk music. College presidents sent him long letters seeking advice about means of reviving folk traditions in music; Powell's own work, such as a Fantasy on American Fiddler Tunes, was performed by the Chautauqua choral group; the Yorktown Sesquicentennial Commission wanted him to participate in a special program in October 1931; composers wrote to offer their works for performance at his highly successful annual festival held at White Top in southwestern Virginia beginning early in the summer of 1931.[73] By that time G. Schirmer had published a piece by Powell called "From a Loved Past" and he had completed an opera based upon Longfellow's "Evangeline."†

In 1933 Eleanor Roosevelt was persuaded to attend the White Top Folk Festival as guest of honor, which enhanced its prestige and pro-

---

*For half a century it remained part of the Library of Congress Music Division; but in 1981, as a consequence of the American Folklife Preservation Act (1976), it became the Archive of Folk Culture, a unit of the American Folklife Center.

†Among Powell's papers there is a proposal that someone sent to him from Montana for an elaborate "State Festival of Art, Music" which included a 1,000-voice chorus, a "pageant depicting distinctive Montana experiences and a barn dance in which Montana pioneers will participate," and "a drama definitely Montanan in origin, character and presentation."

vided Powell with an influential "patron." Her presence also called the festival to the attention of NBC, which promptly invited Powell to organize a series of Southern Folk-Music Programs for radio broadcast. Powell proceeded to do so, and to besiege Mrs. Roosevelt with unctuous letters asking her to open the first broadcast with a few words of introduction. He inundated her with incantations about the importance of tradition and the American musical heritage. He closed by enumerating three irresistible reasons why the series was worthy of her support:

> First, historically, for it is decidedly a link with the pioneer life and teems with qualities which we all keenly feel the need of bringing into activity and prominence once more. Secondly, aesthetically, for in the great body of our folk-music is the basis of a fresh and lovely art music, with almost infinite variety and truly our own. It offers to our native composers a treasury of material and a musical language for their creative work in which they will be at home. In addition it has for literary workers a world of suggestion. And, finally, sociologically; we have already found that in many cases the recognition of their music's value has brought a revival of self-respect and re-awakened joy in living to the bearers of the tradition, who have been burdened with the economic difficulties of an unrelenting struggle and who have been psychologically depressed by the weight of prevailing standards of taste in which they had no part and with which they could have no sympathy.[74]

Mrs. Roosevelt consented and spoke from the White House on February 21, 1934, initiating the series. Powell's national visibility now skyrocketed, he became more obsequious than ever and felt emboldened to approach the President's wife about an entire folk program that would emanate from the White House. He called to Mrs. Roosevelt's attention the fact that at Virginia's State Choral Festival in 1932 the opening speaker

> set forth the basic importance of folk-culture in the art and life of a nation. He stressed Dvorak's love of America and how he had labored to make us realize the beauty and importance of our folk-music and had shown us how to use this material in the higher art forms through his New World String quartette and his New World Symphony.[75]

Although Powell did not succeed with this particular mission, his projects and career continued to flourish.[76]

So did the development and recognition of vernacular music in American culture. By 1934 the National Federation of Music Clubs had become an enthusiastic sponsor of the White Top Festival. In 1930 the Festival of American Music got under way as an annual showcase for new works by young composers. Aaron Copland, who had incorporated jazz into his compositions during the 1920s, turned to folk materials in the following decade for *Billy the Kid* (1938), a cowboy ballet; for *John Henry* (1939) by utilizing folk tunes that Alan Lomax had assembled; for the movie score used to accompany *Our Town*; for his *Lincoln Portrait* and *Rodeo* (both 1942); and for *Appalachian Spring* (1944), in which he immortalized an exquisite and simple Shaker air. The year 1939 marked some sort of apogee, surely, because in that year Elliott Carter provided the music for *Pocahontas* and Earl Robinson collaborated with John Latouche in composing *Ballad for Americans*, a powerful work first broadcast on CBS in November 1939 and recorded for release the following year. It included, for example, the same section of the Gettysburg Address that Copland would use in his *Lincoln Portrait*.[77]

Aficionados of folk crafts also began to appear during these years. Richardson Wright, for instance, the editor of *House & Garden*, undertook a study of itinerant tradesmen in America from the mid-eighteenth century until the eve of the Civil War: nomadic carpenters, pewterers, weavers, teachers, limners, and others with wares. By the mid-1930s exhibitions of singular categories of objects, such as weathervanes, started to occur; and in 1936 the Newark Museum sponsored a pioneering show of American folk crafts called "Old and New Paths in American Design—1720–1936." Assisted by the Federal Art Project of the New Deal's WPA, the museum included a broad array of traditions, ranging from Shaker furniture to Native American crafts from New Mexico to Pacific coast pottery.[78]

The prime movers in collecting, selling, and displaying American folk art at this time were relatively few and concentrated in the vicinity of metropolitan New York; but their impact turned out to be quite striking. Hamilton Easter Field (1873–1922), a wealthy Quaker artist from Brooklyn Heights, established two small art colonies in Maine where he infected quite a number of young artists with his enthusiasm for early Americana in general and collecting folk pieces in particular. Elie Nadelman (1882–1946), the modernist sculptor, and his wife collected both European and early American folk art and in 1926 established in their home at Riverdale, north of Manhattan, an informal museum of folk art. In 1935 it became a genuinely public museum (rather than a semi-private assemblage) open on a limited basis.[79]

While Holger Cahill served on the staff of the Newark Museum (1922–31) he organized in 1930 the first major exhibition of American folk painting and followed that success a year later with a show featuring folk sculpture.[80] Meanwhile, in 1926 Edith Halpert opened the Downtown Gallery in Greenwich Village. Initially attracted to contemporary American art, she "discovered" folk art as a result of spending summers in New England during the later twenties. Consequently she opened the American Folk Gallery in 1929 as an adjunct to the Downtown, swiftly acquired Mrs. Rockefeller as a client, and assembled the nucleus of a collection for her.[81] Halpert also helped Electra Havemeyer Webb to make acquisitions that became part of the Shelburne; and it seems fair to say that Mrs. Rockefeller and Mrs. Webb shared a point of view expressed on more than one occasion by the latter: "I try to find the art in folk art."[82] What differentiated them from people like Constance Rourke, perhaps, was Rourke's determination to find the *folk* in folk art.

Abby Aldrich Rockefeller began to collect in 1930—just when she was also deeply engaged in establishing the Museum of Modern Art— because Edith Halpert made the tantalizing comment that contemporary artists needed ancestors. One thing led quickly to another. Rockefeller's folk art collection first went on public view in 1935 at the Ludwell-Paradise House in Williamsburg. In 1939 she presented the collection of about four hundred objects to Williamsburg and three years later ceased acquiring American "primitives."[83]

WHILE PEOPLE like Halpert and Cahill served as mentors to the millionaire acquisitors, mere academic mortals gradually began to introduce college students to American folk culture—despite strenuous resistance from more orthodox faculty members who referred to such courses as "singin' and stompin.'" After 1931 Harold W. Thompson, who then taught at Albany State Teachers College, turned his attention increasingly from English and Scottish literature to American literature and folklore (fig. 13.5). He started to offer a course on the latter in 1934, most likely the first comprehensive survey taught to undergraduates at any American institution. That course, which evolved as Thompson explored the field, became the model for many others that subsequently appeared at scattered universities. Soon after Thompson published his delightful magnum opus *Body, Boots, & Britches* (1939), he joined the English faculty at Cornell, where he taught folklore to about five hundred students each semester. Meanwhile he was constantly in demand as a speaker and gave as many as fifty talks per year to audiences at Cornell and across the country.[84]

The appeal of Thompson's teaching, lecturing, and writing was notable. Numerous folklore societies were established between the later 1920s and the mid-1940s. The Folklore Institute of America began at Indiana University in 1942; and *The Magazine Antiques,* a high-style and prestigious journal of the decorative arts ever since its founding in 1922, devoted a special issue to folk art in May 1950.[85] By 1935, meanwhile, folk festivals had begun to proliferate—egalitarian events at which professionals and amateurs, collectors and dealers, scholars and raconteurs gathered to learn, have a good time, and just "be."[86]

One response to this burst of enthusiasm was organizational: the creation of formal networks to facilitate communication and the support of worthy projects. As the chairman of a newly formed Interna-

13.5   Harold Thompson by Christian Midjo (c. 1940), oil on canvas. Courtesy of the New York State Historical Association, Cooperstown.

tional Commission on Folk Arts (based in Manhattan) wrote in 1932: "there has been no established authority for the whole field of the folk arts of this country. Now that the need for this has come, it has to be created by drawing together various essential elements which, combined, will constitute such authority." A few years later Holger Cahill organized the Index of American Design, a thorough iconographic survey of early American folk and graphic arts. And by 1945 some states, such as Minnesota, had established a Folk Arts Foundation which sponsored broad programs of public education and research (the quest for folk ballads, tales, dances, games, proverbs, place names, cuisine, textiles, and household wares).[87]

One of the most intriguing and frequently poignant aspects of this entire episode involved the return of young writers who had been expatriates during the 1920s but took an active part in the folk and regionalist movements by the mid- and later 1930s. As early as 1934, in fact, Malcolm Cowley commented that many of the "exiles" had begun to realize that the United States "possessed a folklore, and traditions, and the songs that embodied them." Erskine Caldwell, for example, came back from Europe and Asia and undertook editorial responsibility for the "American Folkways" series of regional books that appeared between 1941 and 1955. Caldwell collaborated with his wife,

Margaret Bourke-White, in producing volumes that combined her photographs and his texts, such as *Have You Seen Their Faces?* (1937) and *Say! Is This the U.S.A.?* (1941).[88] Other major publication projects started at the same time, such as the "Rivers of America" series that Constance Lindsay Skinner launched in 1937 and Carl Carmer took over with Hervey Allen following her death two years later.

SOME INDIVIDUALS obviously went beyond collecting, compiling, exhibiting, performing, and selling the "artifacts" of folk culture. They used it as the basis for their own creative and sometimes highly innovative efforts. In 1932, for example, while Stephen Vincent Benét began writing a notable series of American folktales, he told a friend that "the thing, of course, is to make the people come alive. They do, if you can dig them out of the dust." In "The Devil and Daniel Webster" Benét managed to revitalize a somewhat staid, tarnished, and remote historical figure into a fantasized folk hero. The *Saturday Evening Post* first published the story in October 1936; it enjoyed immediate popular success and has ever since. In 1939 it was made into a one-act folk opera, for which Benét wrote the libretto; and two years later a film version of the tale appeared.[89]

Meanwhile Percy MacKaye wrote folk plays that celebrated what he regarded as the primordial Anglo-Saxon and Celtic folk heritage of New England and rural Appalachia.[90] Paul Green's outdoor drama, *The Lost Colony,* opened on Roanoke Island, North Carolina, during the summer of 1937 as part of the 350th anniversary observance of "the birth of English civilization in the New World." (English voyages in 1587 that did not result in permanent settlement were recognized as an auspicious start.) Thereafter Green was deluged with fan mail, letters from people in other parts of the country attempting to write similar historical dramas accompanied by music, promoters who wanted him to write a folk play for their locale, and aspiring writers who pleaded with Green to read and assist them in getting their work performed.[91]

The artistic movement known as regionalism, most prominently represented by Thomas Hart Benton, Grant Wood, and John Steuart Curry, eagerly put the folk and popular culture prominently in its work. When Benton received a commission in 1936 to paint large scenes inside the Missouri State Capitol in Jefferson City (he used oil and egg tempera on linen mounted on panel), he depicted Indians and fur traders, pioneers and covered wagons, black slaves at work and being whipped. This was unusually populistic and iconoclastic for a public structure at a time when myths and legends of affirmation still predominated over realism or social criticism.[92]

The fact that Benton's historical murals frequently caused controversy serves as a reminder that the egalitarian (often pro-proletarian) passion to give folk traditions a dominant place in national culture evoked criticism from varied voices and sometimes caused damaging storms. Although Stanley Edgar Hyman, the respected literary critic, admired and praised the work of Constance Rourke, he believed that she romanticized folk traditions, he found her concept of folklore thin and underdeveloped, and he remained unpersuaded that American folk traditions had sufficient homogeneity to supply the underpinnings for a genuinely cohesive national culture.[93]

Quite a different angle of critical vision came from the folk themselves. In 1941 James Agee and Walker Evans published *Let Us Now Praise Famous Men,* following almost five years of travel and interviewing among hardscrabble farm laborers in the Deep South. Although Agee found indigenous traditions among the folk, he also felt the need to improve their lot by changing the socio-economic system that oppressed them. Consequently *Famous Men* is a book in which concerns for tradition and democracy are compatible, and in which "memories of the past were juxtaposed with conversations in the present."* It should be noted, however, that after the book appeared, some of Agee's humble folk felt exposed, exploited, and humiliated. Their resentment of his "honest" portrait of their hard lives burned with intensity, a pattern that has been repeated in similar circumstances several times since then.[94]

Be that as it may, the cultural critic Hilton Kramer has eloquently epitomized the idealism and the very genuine achievement of those whose 1930s crusade we have been describing:

> This attempt to come to terms with the problems of the present prompted, at the same time, a remarkable effort to take possession of the American past—the hidden, unofficial past, the past that lay buried in the folklore and folk art and local legend which, until this new consciousness was turned upon it, was rarely given its due in the formal histories of the nation.[95]

V

IN RUTH SUCKOW'S 1930 discourse, "The Folk Idea in American Life," she called attention to foreign folklore that immigrants brought with them to the United States. Eight years later Benjamin A. Botkin, a prominent folklorist, urged that a folk festival soon to be held at Raleigh, North Carolina, in May 1938 offer an opportunity for members

---

*The quotation is from historian Richard H. Pells, who shrewdly observed that John Ford's film *How Green Was My Valley* (also 1941) struck a similar note. It presented a faithful depiction of class stratification among Welsh workers; yet its central purpose was not merely to demonstrate the woes of humble miners, but to commend the virtues of family solidarity and social tradition. (See Pells, *Radical Visions and American Dreams,* 246–47, 251, 280.)

of ethnic minorities to present the particular backgrounds and problems of their groups, "social and economic and cultural, in the matter of increasing participation in American diversity." Even a few Yankees of older stock felt appalled at the homogenization of American culture and indicated a certain sympathy for more adequate attention to the sources of American diversity. As Worthington C. Ford exclaimed to James Truslow Adams in 1938: "To meet the same manner, the same speeches, the same smiles from Bangor to Los Angeles! Heavens, is that what our ancestors fought for?"[96]

Numerous obstacles barred the way, however, to hyphenated Americans who might have wanted to display or celebrate their ethnic traditions. As we have already seen in chapter eight, from the 1870s until the years following World War I they were expected to be the passive (and grateful) recipients of older American memories and customs that had been established long ago in the seventeenth and eighteenth centuries. During the two decades that followed 1919, xenophobia may have diminished somewhat but it certainly remained a visible social force directly linked to the felt need for broad acceptance of a unified national tradition. Edith Wharton spoke for many when she bemoaned the "heterogeneous hundred millions of American citizens . . . without uniformity of tradition."[97]

Quite commonly the residents of older stock simply refused to recognize that newcomers either possessed meaningful traditions of their own or, if they did, that those traditions could conceivably make any sort of contribution to American culture. Unfortunately, as Willa Cather commented in 1924, "their American neighbors were seldom open-minded enough to understand the [immigrants], or to profit by their older traditions. Our settlers from New England, cautious and convinced of their own superiority, kept themselves isolated as much as possible from foreign influences."[98]

More generous Americans recognized that patriotism run amok created ugly social prejudices, declared that "we are all hyphenated," and appealed for sympathy toward recently arrived groups, especially those who try "to rise above the contradictions of a double loyalty."[99] So many of the newcomers themselves, of course, brought with them not merely traditions but also high expectations and gratitude for the comparative freedom of their new circumstances. A very significant number either wanted to shed their "outmoded" cultural baggage or else preferred to utilize or display its contents only within the intimacy of family or other members of their subculture. In terms of the comfort provided by self-awareness, very few had any way of knowing that breaking with "outmoded" traditions had long since become an American tradition itself.[100]

Two groups enjoyed comparatively smooth paths in terms of a comfortable reconciliation (or co-ordination) of hyphenated Americanism and "100% Americanism": the Scandinavians and the French. Coincidentally, the moment of awakening, activity, and acceptance for both groups occurred around 1925. A Swedish Colonial Society had existed for some years prior to that date, but it remained small, exclusive, and inconspicuous. In 1925, however, the New Sweden Memorial Commission launched its plans for a park on the Delaware River to commemorate the three hundredth anniversary of the founding of New Sweden. Five years later the Augustana Historical Society was created in order to perpetuate the later and much larger migration of Swedes to the upper Middle West. In 1937–38 a great deal of well-organized and visible activity heralded observances of the three hundredth anniversary of Swedish settlement in the Delaware Valley, most notably an exhibition of Swedish crafts and paintings that opened at Rockefeller Center and then travelled across the country.[101]

The Norse-American Centennial celebration, held at Decorah, Iowa, during the summer of 1925 became the genuine moment of genesis for a Norwegian-American historical organization that would be national in scope. The notion of such a society had been discussed as early as 1907 and again in 1913, but without success. It finally came to fruition at St. Olaf College in Northfield, Minnesota, in October 1925. Within eighteen months the Norwegian-American Historical Association had made arrangements to employ an agent in Oslo who would search for materials of special interest to the Association, especially newspaper items pertaining to emigration from Norway. Soon October 9 came to be designated as Leif Eriksson Day—the timing quite deliberately selected to enable Scandinavian-Americans to pre-empt Columbus Day by seventy-two hours! In the early 1930s an American-Scandinavian Foundation was providing fellowships to young people prepared to undertake research in the history and culture of their several civilizations.[102]

The chronology of French-American commemoration turns out to have been remarkably comparable. In 1882, as Mark Twain duly noted, New Orleans intended to celebrate the bicentennial of LaSalle's trip down the Mississippi which brought him to the site of New Orleans. When the critical moment came, alas, flooding occurred and local energies as well as surplus funds "were required in other directions." So nothing happened. Late in 1925, however, the Illinois Society of the National Society of the Colonial Dames of America held exercises at the Chicago Historical Society in honor of the early explorers Joliet, Marquette, LaSalle, and Tonti, the first white men known to have passed along and charted the Chicago River. The two historical expeditions sponsored by the Great Northern Railroad in 1925 and 1926 placed markers to such early explorers of the upper Great Plains as Vérendrye; and the second expedition even included five French high school students as invited guests. In March 1926 the Huguenot Society of South Carolina unveiled a monument on Parris Island to celebrate the first Protestant settlement on the North American continent: by Jean Ribaut for Admiral Coligny and the Huguenots in 1562.[103]

In 1926 John D. Rockefeller, Jr., gave $450,000 for a five-year project to transcribe European documents pertaining to American history. The focus of this enterprise became 340 volumes of manuscript material transcribed in Paris and deposited at the Library of Congress after the first year (1927). The subsequent yield turned out to be 317,000 pages of French documents. In 1935 a cottage built in 1776 near Green Bay, Wisconsin, by Joseph Roi, a French voyageur and fur trader, became an unusual museum (and was proclaimed the oldest surviving house in the Old Northwest). On July 8, 1938, René de Saint Quentin, French ambassador to the United States, gave a featured address as part of the Northwest Territory celebration.[104]

The situation for German-Americans, who remain to this day the most numerous group of hyphenated Americans, was understandably less smooth. In 1915 the National German-American alliance erected a statue of Baron Von Steuben overlooking the Grand Parade at Valley Forge. Public pressure soon demanded that it be removed from view and it was not replaced on its original site until 1978. A so-called National Historical Society was formed in 1927 in order to improve American attitudes toward persons, customs, and things of Germanic origin. German-American businessmen supported it, and a scholarly research staff was employed to prepare articles and disseminate their findings to history teachers in the public schools. At Memorial Day exercises held in 1939 at the Carl Schurz statue on Riverside Drive, members of the German-American and Austrian-American societies pledged their loyalty to the United States and criticized those who "have fallen under the influence of foreign leaders."[105] Despite the very substantial impact of German-Americans upon the culture of this nation, their public image and attitudes toward their traditions have involved a veritable roller-coaster ride.

Although tradition-oriented Jewish-Americans have pursued varied "routes" and preferences, a common denominator for them has been their ardent patriotism. Lee Max Friedman (1871–1957), the son of a Union Army officer, was born in Memphis, Tennessee, but became a lifelong resident of Boston and successful lawyer with a strong interest in American-Jewish history. In 1905 he served as chairman of the Boston celebration of the 250th anniversary of the settlement of Jews in the United States. Fifty years later he was the primary speaker at Symphony Hall in Boston for the tercentenary. He remained active in the American Jewish Historical Society from 1903 until his death, served as its president (1948–53), obtained transcripts and translations of European records relating to American-Jewish history, acquired a remarkable personal collection of Judaica, gave many manuscripts and rare imprints to the A.J.H.S., and subsidized a lot of its documentary publications.[106]

Sol Feinstone (1888–1980) followed quite a different path. He emigrated alone to the United States from Lithuania in 1902 with a penny in his pocket and absolutely no English. He started working in the sweatshops of Manhattan's Lower East Side but eventually amassed both a fine education and a fortune in real estate investments and construction. He began collecting American historical documents during the mid-1920s, and in 1960 created the David Library of the American Revolution on his 200-acre farm located at Washington Crossing on the Delaware River in Pennsylvania, all of which he gave to the state of Pennsylvania. He also donated the historical library of the Freedoms Foundation in Valley Forge, Pennsylvania; endowed lecture series on the subject of freedom at a number of universities; and subsidized an annual awards program for plays concerning freedom written by college students. In 1976 President Gerald R. Ford invited Feinstone to the White House to thank him for these patriotic endeavors, including the gift of 126 George Washington letters to the Mount Vernon Ladies Association (for which Feinstone had paid $250,000 at auction).[107]

In October 1936 more than five thousand people of all faiths assembled at a statue of Roger Williams (erected by Jewish-Americans sixty years earlier) in Philadelphia's Fairmount Park to observe the three hundredth anniversary of Williams's banishment from the Massachusetts Bay Colony. On Memorial Day in 1937 the New York Council of Jewish War Veterans met at the New Bowery Cemetery (the earliest extant Jewish burying ground in the United States, dedicated in 1683) to honor Jews who had fought in the American Revolution. (Lieutenant Colonel Samuel Adams Cohen served as chairman of the planning committee for that occasion.) Two years later, at a similar service, the president of the Union of Orthodox Jewish Congregations of America, which sponsored the ceremony, read a letter condemning bigotry written by George Washington. Rabbi David da Sola Pool of the Spanish and Portuguese Synagogue stated that fourteen recognizable graves of Jewish men who died in the War for Independence still existed.[108]

Otherwise the later 1930s produced a miscellany of (sometimes contradictory) testimony concerning various ethnic heroes. A Scandinavian explorer of the Arctic claimed that North America had been discovered by the Irish nearly seven centuries before Columbus. Others contended that Columbus never set foot on North America at all; and Italian-Americans responded with understandable outrage to this "historic lie." In 1935 Hawaii's 140,000 Japanese residents observed the fiftieth anniversary of the initial forced migration of Japanese laborers to Hawaii, while others of European descent celebrated the centenary of the sailing of the first Protestant missionary ever sent to China by a religious organization.[109]

Hispanics had cause for historic pride at the close of the decade. In 1937 the restoration of St. Augustine, Florida, a project sponsored by the Carnegie Institution, got considerable attention and the scale of this enterprise received favorable mention alongside Colonial Williamsburg. Two years later, when Arizona celebrated the four hundredth anniversary of its discovery by Father Marcos de Niza, a monument was dedicated to that priest, a pageant was held in Tucson, and an increase in tourism was anticipated. In 1940 New Mexico had occasion to observe the four hundredth anniversary of the coming of Coronado; and ceremonies held at Gallup conveniently coincided with the annual Indian Ceremonial Exhibition held there.[110]

ALTHOUGH the history of African-American self-awareness has been richly chronicled by others, its relationship to our narrative cannot be ignored. Various voices made important contributions prior to 1925. In 1882–83 George Washington Williams published his pioneering *History of the Negro Race in America from 1619 to 1880: Negroes as Slaves, as Soldiers, and as Citizens.* More than a quarter of a century later Charles Victor Roman repeatedly delivered an address titled "A Knowledge of History Conducive to Racial Solidarity," a speech that influenced young Carter G. Woodson—so much so that he would include it in his *Negro Orators and Their Orations* (1925). John R. Lynch worked diligently to set the record straight concerning Reconstruction with revisionist attacks upon widely read works by James Ford Rhodes and Claude Bowers; but he was utterly ignored in the historical profession and largely unread by members of his own race.[111]

The turning point occurred swiftly on several fronts during the mid-1920s. In 1924 W. E. B. Du Bois received a plan for creating a Department of Negro History, Literature and Art at the 135th Street Branch of the New York Public Library, along with some sort of society or foundation to support such a collection. It was suggested that classes or clubs be formed for the study of Negro history and culture, and that the collection might provide essential materials needed for instruction.[112] Publication the very next year of *The New Negro,* edited by Alain Locke, was a cultural event for several reasons; and it included an essay by Arthur A. Schomburg, the extraordinary collector of books and rare materials pertaining to African-American history and literature. That essay opened with these two unequivocal sentences: "The American Negro must remake his past in order to make his future. Though it is orthodox to think of America as the one country where it is unnecessary to have a past, what is a luxury for the nation as a whole becomes a prime social necessity for the Negro."[113]

In 1926 the Carnegie Corporation (at the request of the National Urban League) purchased Schomburg's collection for $10,000 and presented it to the New York Public Library, which deposited it at the main branch in Harlem. Although Schomburg continued to work there as curator of the Division of Negro Literature, History and Prints until his death in 1938 and added extensively to the collection, it has not received adequate care, staff, or financial support from the city in the decades since. Schomburg's impact as a collector, as co-founder of the Negro Society for Historical Research, and as president of the American Negro Academy made him an incalculable force for the promotion of

13.6   Carter G. Woodson. Courtesy of the Moorland-Spingarn Research Center, Howard University, Washington, D.C.

interest in black culture. Because of his origins in Puerto Rico, moreover, his purview included Afro-American civilization in the New World generally.[114]

The most energizing figure of all, however, was Carter G. Woodson (1875–1950), a man who pursued his mission relentlessly for almost four decades (fig. 13.6). After studying at the Sorbonne in 1906–07 and receiving his Ph.D. in U.S. history at Harvard in 1912, he moved swiftly into the difficult roles of organizer, mobilizer of others, and fund raiser. In 1915 he established the Association for the Study of Negro Life and History. Less than a year later he founded the *Journal of Negro History* and served for many years as its editor. In 1926 he launched Negro History Week and selected February as the most suitable month because of the birthdays of Abraham Lincoln and Frederick Douglass. That observance enjoyed immediate success, became an annual event, and has since been expanded from a week to a month. In 1937 he inaugurated the *Negro History Bulletin,* richly illustrated in order to reach a more general audience than the *J.N.H.,* especially high school students.[115]

Following Woodson's death in 1950, one of his closest associates wrote (privately) an absolutely candid characterization of this complex man who never married and whose work was his life: "Dr. Woodson was a bundle of contradictions. He was vindictive and mean and a Silas Marner. On the other hand, he was kind and generous and would go out of his way to support causes other than his own."[116] Be that as it may, his single-mindedness and consistency are exemplified by two extracts from his writing. The first is from a speech that he gave in 1921 at the Hampton Institute (now University). Negroes, he asserted, "have traditions . . . of which you can boast and upon which you can base a claim for a right to a share in the blessings of democracy." The second is from an essay that he wrote five years later for the inauguration of Negro History Week: "If a race has no history, if it has no worth-while tradition, it becomes a negligible factor in the thought of the world, and it stands in danger of being exterminated. The American Indian left no continuous record.* He did not appreciate the value of tradition; and where is he today?"[117]

Langston Hughes emerged in the mid-1920s as an advocate of the black masses, of folk culture, and of the blues. He expressed this aspiration in 1929: "To create a Negro culture in America—a real, solid, sane racial something growing out of the folk life, not copied from another, even though surrounding race." Arna Bontemps soon followed with novels derived from African-American history as well as folklore, and with essays whose point of view is epitomized by this sentence: "there is no surer mark of maturity than the ability to see oneself in time." In 1937 Representative Arthur W. Mitchell of Chicago, the only Negro member of Congress then, indicated his determination "to establish a national shrine for the Negro race at the birthplace of Booker T. Washington in Franklin County, Virginia."[118]

One other salutary development must be noticed in this connection: the genesis of white interest in black history and traditions. Carl Van Vechten's role as a catalyst in the Harlem Renaissance is well known. He genuinely believed in the "power of the folk tradition." George Gershwin called *Porgy and Bess* a folk opera because he regarded it as a folk tale in which the characters sing folk music. He explained in 1935 that he hoped "to have developed something in American music that would appeal to the many rather than to the cultured few."[119]

Much less familiar are the efforts of men like Howard W. Odum and Guy Benton Johnson to study race relations and black folkways during the 1920s and '30s in North Carolina, where the atmosphere was considerably less congenial than it was in New York City. The legend of John Henry racing the steam drill came in for intensive historical investigation at this time, for example. And by 1942 African-American culture had begun to receive at least a niche in the mainstream museum of memory. In that year Henry Ford, who greatly admired George Washington Carver, restored his plantation birthplace and moved it to

---

*It seems appropriate to note the response made by Chief Seattle in 1852 when the U.S. government inquired about the purchase of tribal lands. "Every part of this earth is sacred to my people," he said. "All are holy in the memory and experience of my people." Therefore, he pleaded, if we sell you our land, "Care for it as we have cared for it. Hold in your mind the memory of the land as it is when you receive it." (Joseph Campbell, *The Power of Myth* [New York, 1988], 34–35.) On May 13, 1939, the five-hundredth anniversary of the establishment of the League of Iroquois Nations ("the first American democracy") was commemorated at the Tonawanda Reservation in western New York with the dedication of an Iroquois "longhouse." Members of the Seneca Nation put on a pageant written by Chief Nicodemus Bailey. (NYT, May 14, 1939, sec. 3, p. 5.)

Greenfield Village in Dearborn. Also in 1942, Constance Rourke's last book, *The Roots of American Culture,* included an essay titled "Traditions for a Negro Literature."[120] Change was in the air.

AN EXTRAORDINARY dialogue accompanied by substantive developments took place between the mid-1920s and the eve of World War II. The basic stimulus was an egalitarian and populist impulse. The outcome, despite some vigorous resistance, was a highly significant democratization of diverse American traditions; a levelling of local and regional legends; and a far more inclusive social repository for American memories. The process as a whole was propelled by intellectuals of various sorts, as we have just observed. But it also received major assistance from the federal government, as we shall see in the next chapter.

Chapter 14

MEMORY IN POLITICS:
THE CHANGING ROLE
OF GOVERNMENT

A CONSIDERABLE AMOUNT has now been written about the active role of New Deal agencies in discovering, celebrating, interpreting, painting scenes, and dramatizing episodes from American history. It is also fair to infer that this fresh degree of federal concern for cultural resources and local traditions established an important precedent for the decades subsequent to World War II, when government assumed responsibility for American memory to a degree and in ways hitherto unanticipated. There is a very real sense in which Americans broke with an ingrained habit of mind (let the private sector do it) in order to rescue and restore to prominence a range of particular traditions. Needless to say, impoverished yet creative people were also salvaged in the process. That was the principal objective, in fact. The circumstances were such that assisting Americans helped to save Americana.

The narrative is more complex than those elementary observations might suggest, however, and for several reasons. On the one hand, a noticeable growth in governmental engagement with the past actually antedated the first term of Franklin Delano Roosevelt starting in March 1933. Therefore, some attention must also be given to the Coolidge and Hoover years. On the other hand, as late as 1939–41 we still encounter a strong residual and principled antipathy, especially in the Congress, toward governmental action on behalf of either the substance or the symbols of American culture. Moreover, the augmented role of government turned out to be less effective than it might have been—not only because resources tended to be spread quite thin, but because of bureaucratic turf wars and consequent conflicts.

Finally, some interesting and unexpected examples of co-operation or mutual support between the public and private sectors made the politics of memory during the 1930s less predictable and more pluralistic than one might expect. There was a greater degree of continuity in terms of pattern and process than we have hitherto recognized. Nevertheless, the 1930s was, undeniably, a distinctively transitional decade in terms of perpetuating and presenting the meaning of America. Never again would that manifest responsibility remain primarily (indeed, almost entirely) in the hands of private individuals and organizations.

I

A GLANCE back to the last fifteen years of the nineteenth century serves to remind us that Congress remained reluctant to spend money on historical monuments, commemorative occasions, or the preservation and utilization of either documents or other traces of the past, such as structures, sites, and important memorabilia. The centennial observance of the U.S. Constitution held at Philadelphia in 1887 had not received a penny from Congress and only modest support from the state of Pennsylvania. The centennial of national government getting under way, glorified at New York City late in April 1889, depended heavily upon private donors and the sale of parade tickets. In 1889–90, when New Yorkers optimistically expected that the city would host a great Columbian Exposition in 1892, they simply assumed that between $10 and $15 million would have to be raised by private subscription. The advocates of a rival extravaganza to be held in Chicago sent letters to congressmen in order to mobilize support, but wisely established a major stock company in order to provide for adequate funding. Congress had almost no sense of responsibility for the four hundredth anniversary of American origins.[1]

The prospect of potential museums and government-supported research in American history fared little better at the turn of the century. A national museum of agriculture, for example, discussed intermittently from the 1840s until the end of the century, never got beyond the stage of dull exhibits in Washington, D.C., housed in a few wooden structures that were demolished in 1905. The notion of a national "Economic Museum of Agriculture" quickly became little more than a faint memory. Moreover, historians at that time regarded the Smithsonian Institution as being strangely indifferent to history. It is quite symptomatic that proposals made early in the century to establish a School of American Historical Studies in Washington turned out to be abortive—in 1901–02, then again in 1916, and once more in 1923. It was conceived by its sponsors as a "clearing-house for many kinds of historical work in this country, especially such as have relation to the history of the federal government," and its opponents agonized about possible questions of conflict and problems of co-operation between private sector historians and government agencies.[2]

As for the systematic maintenance of written records, an essential element in the perpetuation of reliable public memory, almost no one in a position of responsibility seemed to care. At the close of the nine-teenth century a White House secretary explained that until recently "hardly a scrap of paper was kept here to show what a President did or why he did it." Less than a decade later, not long before Charles A. Beard began his research at the Treasury Department concerning the financial investments of the founders, a custodial attendant at the Trea-sury sold at least one cartload of historical records to a local junk dealer. The records that survived were stored in a manner that made them barely accessible.[3]

The State Department had responsibility for many of the nation's most important records; but a small staff and an utterly inadequate system of achieving access to the records meant that aspiring research-ers needed to obtain a permit from the Secretary of State. Such permits tended to be awarded on capricious grounds and, most often, on the basis of personal connections. Although the State Department main-tained a modest historical library and a Bureau of Rolls, they were notably under-used. Some people believed, with cause, that it was easier to do research pertaining to American history in European repositories than it was in the United States.[4]

Although President Rutherford B. Hayes had recommended to Con-gress the creation of a national archive in his annual messages of 1879 and 1880, such a project did not actually gain approval and go forward for more than fifty years. During the later nineteenth century no con-sensus emerged as to whether the nation's documents would be better managed by the government or by a private organization such as the American Historical Association. During the first decade of the twen-tieth century it became clear that for logistical as well as financial reasons, only the government *could* manage such an undertaking. De-spite the strong advocacy of Theodore Roosevelt, however, the project made no progress, and failed to gain sufficient support in Congress during the subsequent two decades. By that time every major nation in Europe had established a repository for its public records.[5]

Just as the United States government had an unimpressive record during the nineteenth century of occasionally (and unenthusiastically) purchasing major collections of historical manuscripts (the Force library in 1867 in addition to the Madison, Jefferson, Washington, and Franklin papers), it had an equally poor record in the realm of documentary publications.* The State Department produced occasional volumes of early records pertaining to the post–Revolutionary era; but they were neither well edited nor sensibly arranged. An independent report pre-pared in 1908 by a Committee on the Documentary Historical Publica-tions of the United States Government revealed bizarre and perplexing

---

*The major exception being the U.S. War Department's seventy-volume *War of the Rebellion . . . Official Records of the Union and Confederate Armies* (1880–1901), on which the government spent some $3 million.

practices, like authorizing different people to undertake similar projects, such as editing the texts of early American charters and constitutions. Historians and archivists wondered how they might use the report to prod Congress into some sort of action; but they met with no success. In 1912 one deeply concerned director of a state historical society grieved because "our government has been so backward in historical publications."[6]

The subsequent decade brought rather inconclusive signs of change in basic assumptions, but no clear pattern. In 1920, for example, Congress appropriated $400,000 to support the Pilgrim Tercentenary Commission acting in co-operation with the town of Plymouth, Massachusetts—an uncharacteristically generous sum that helped to make the festivities of 1920 and 1921 unusually elaborate and well publicized. As a consequence, perhaps, Congress at least took notice of the sesquicentennial of Independence in 1926, the bicentennial in 1932 of George Washington's birth and in 1943 of Thomas Jefferson's. With the exception of Washington's year-long festivity, however, these events were not very well funded.[7]

At the level of state government, expectations were even more murky during the 1920s. When Ezra Meeker exhorted an Idaho audience in 1921 to erect an obelisk in honor of the Oregon Trail pioneers, his uncertainty about the matter of responsibility was characteristic of that transitional time: "Whether such a monument should be erected and maintained by the city of Pocatello, or whether it should be by the state or by the nation is a matter of detail not affecting the desirability of the movement or the duty of the present generation. It is certain not to be accomplished without a special organization for the purpose." In 1927, however, Virginia undertook the first large-scale attempt to identify historic sites for motorists; and other states followed its example within the next three years.[8]

Although U.S. participation in World War I brought about an increase in centralized power for the national government, and a flurry of activity by historians and others hired by government, the short-term legacy of that experience was ambiguous. Considerable hostility toward government authority became manifest throughout the 1920s, with the result that very few individuals viewed Wilson's use of history and historians as a positive precedent.[9] Although people were accustomed to presidents invoking the past in order to legitimize a policy or lay claim to some segment of the electorate, few were prepared to accept the notion of government as a prominent custodian of American traditions.[10]

I I

AMERICANS have been inclined to depoliticize their past, as we have seen and will see with even greater specificity in successive chapters, yet their leaders have invoked and utilized mythic pasts in diverse ways—notably powerful in Abraham Lincoln's discourse and then perhaps culminating in F.D.R.'s appropriation of Lincoln as a political symbol during the mid- and later 1930s. A few of our presidents, most prominently Theodore Roosevelt and Woodrow Wilson, wrote a great deal of history long before they achieved the nation's highest office. Both of these men had a broad vision of American development that shaped their values and policies. On one occasion, prior to his White House years, Wilson remarked to a dinner companion how unfortunate it was that Americans "did not much dwell on their historic past; [and] did not make use of it."[11]

To learn that Wilson expressed such sentiments does not come as a surprise; but his successor as President, Warren G. Harding, conveyed very similar views in a considerably more elaborate statement. We shall never know how much of the passage that follows may have been written by Harding's private secretary; we only know that Harding approved and signed this letter in response to an invitation to attend the opening of an Institute of Modern History at Bowdoin College in Maine.

> In our own country it seems to me there is altogether too little knowledge of our national story, too little interest in and serious study of it. One has many times seen the high school student who had completed his studies in an intermediate text book on American History promptly close the volume with the announcement that "he knew about history." I fear that cheerful attitude is not by any means confined to students of high school age.[12]

Whereas Harding seems to have kept his commitment to history rather well concealed from the public, Calvin Coolidge dourly offered historical homilies on appropriate public anniversaries. In 1925, for example, his speech on the occasion of the Norse-American Centennial drew lavish praise from correspondents. One such letter, written by reform Democrat, lawyer, and diplomat Oscar S. Straus, seems not to have been sent tongue-in-cheek even though it verged upon being maudlin:

> You so properly emphasize the value of the knowledge of our historical development for the future well being of our country. The danger is that from lack of information, many of our people take a narrow view of our foundations, and an authoritative state-

14.1   Men working on the face of George Washington at Mount Rushmore. Note the "sculpting" of granite being assisted by dynamite. Courtesy of the National Archives Trust Fund Board.

ment so scholarly presented, has a value far beyond the present. I wonder how you find the time for the accurate researches of which your addresses give such remarkable evidences.[13]

The inception of "sculpting" and related work at Mount Rushmore in August 1927 provided Coolidge with yet another opportunity to laud the lessons of history (fig. 14.1). Because Coolidge had chosen to locate his summer White House in the Black Hills of South Dakota, he did not have to go very far in order to offer one of his pithy observations about the value and meaning of Gutzon Borglum's proposed memorial. "The people of the future," Coolidge declared, "will see history and art combined to portray the spirit of patriotism."[14] The President then turned and handed Borglum a set of drills.

By pure coincidence, just when Borglum made the decision to include Theodore Roosevelt among his four monumental busts, the Roosevelt Memorial Association failed in its highly political effort to have a Roosevelt Memorial located at the Tidal Basin area in Washington, D.C. Despite widespread admiration for T.R., government officials recognized that he could not be honored above Thomas Jefferson; so a committee of the House of Representatives decided to reserve the

14.2 Governor Franklin D. Roosevelt dedicating a bust of Lord Cornwallis
at York Hall, the home of Thomas Nelson (wartime governor of Virginia), used
as Cornwallis's headquarters near Yorktown, Virginia. The dedication opened
the sesquicentennial of the American victory at Yorktown, October 16, 1931.
Courtesy of the Franklin D. Roosevelt Library, Hyde Park, New York.

coveted Tidal Basin site for Jefferson.[15] That episode is significant not
merely as a declaration of historical pre-eminence, but because Congress refused to capitulate to pressure from a prestigious coalition of
private individuals. On this occasion, government decided to take deci-
sive action in a controversial matter involving relative merits and the
memories of two national heroes.

Franklin Roosevelt, even more than his cousin Theodore and far
more than his immediate predecessor, Herbert Hoover, had an astute
sense of the potential role of myth and tradition as formidable political
weapons. Whereas Hoover's ventures into history were comparatively
non-political and bland—such as his 1930 Proclamation setting aside
Jamestown, the Yorktown Battlefield, and peripheral parts of Williamsburg as a Colonial National Monument, to be administered by the
National Park Service*—F.D.R.'s uses of the past were shrewd and
self-serving (fig. 14.2). In 1932, when the country's mood made flexibil-

---

*Near the close of the Proclamation the following paragraph appeared: "Nothing herein
shall affect the property or other rights of individuals, partnerships, associations, corporations, or others, within the areas hereby designated as the Colonial National Monument."
Hoover took care not to violate a sacred American tradition in the process of establishing
a new one.

14.3 Washing the Andrew Jackson memorial statue in Lafayette Square, opposite the White House. Courtesy of the National Archives Trust Fund Board.

ity and change especially attractive, Roosevelt seized a symbolic opportunity to demonstrate that, unlike Hoover, he was not paralyzed by custom or inertia. Upon receiving the Democratic nomination, F.D.R. flew to Chicago in order to give the first acceptance speech ever made to a party convention. "I am here to thank you for the honor," he informed the delegates. "Let it . . . be symbolic that in so doing I broke traditions."[16]

It was Roosevelt the iconoclast who admonished a frosty D.A.R. convention in 1937 to "Remember, remember always, that all of us and you and I especially, are descended from immigrants and revolutionists." A year later he began a persuasive policy speech with four words that had particular potency at that time and in that context: "Let me talk history." He also liked to quote a four-word maxim of Justice Oliver Wendell Holmes: "We live by symbols." F.D.R. urged that Holmes's generous financial bequest to the United States be used to perpetuate "the deepest tradition" that Holmes embodied. According to Roosevelt, "that tradition was a faith in the creative possibilities of the law."[17] Part of F.D.R.'s success in projecting an appealing image lay in his distinctive capacity to connect innovation with tradition.

Above all, Roosevelt had an uncanny instinct for political pedigrees and the casuistry of party affiliation. He insisted that in 1904 he had voted for T.R. because his cousin had been more of a Democrat than the actual Democratic nominee, Alton B. Parker. Following F.D.R.'s victory in 1936 he requested that the inaugural grandstand in front of the White House reproduce the facade of Andrew Jackson's mansion, the Hermitage. The uses of political symbolism rarely escaped him (fig. 14.3).[18]

His enduring pursuit of the Lincoln image (and thereby of Lincoln's legitimizing mantle) persisted for more than a decade. As early as 1929, when F.D.R. began his tenure as governor of New York, he mentioned to journalist Claude Bowers the need for "us Democrats to claim Lincoln as one of our own." During his first presidential administration Roosevelt mentioned Lincoln often, quoted him in support of policy initiatives, and on Lincoln's Birthday in 1935 made a public display of meeting with the only surviving man who had guarded Lincoln's body when it lay in state back in April 1865.[19] In mid-June of 1936, while returning from visits to the state centennial celebrations in Arkansas and Texas, F.D.R. even made a well-publicized pilgrimage to the Kentucky log cabin in which Lincoln was supposed to have been born. Roosevelt's remarks on that occasion were briefer than the Gettysburg Address—and much less memorable. Nevertheless, he had by then managed to depoliticize American party history, because a fair number of his countrymen simply assumed that Roosevelt and Lincoln surely shared a party affiliation and represented a prominent line of continuity in American leadership. During the five years that followed, Roosevelt's speechwriters and other close associates never missed an opportunity to somehow connect the squire of Hyde Park, a patrician Democrat, with the Midwestern rail-splitter from Springfield, a Republican with the common touch.[20]

Just as presidents do not alter or adjust a nation's values in a vacuum, neither can they reorient a society's sense of the past without considerable assistance—not to mention the society's willingness or even desire for reorientation. We must recognize the increasing number of people in public life at this time who felt a genuine enthusiasm for American history and traditions and believed that the government and prominent officials should actively participate in rituals of commemoration. R. Walton Moore, for example, who had been a member of Congress from Virginia, became an assistant secretary of state under F.D.R. and frequently served as a conduit between tradition-minded groups and the President. Although Moore's love of Americana was genuine, he recognized the political uses of the past at a time when partisan symbols tended to have historical elements. Early in 1936, for instance, when a Virginia congressman pleaded with Moore to persuade F.D.R. to make an address at Monticello on Jefferson's Birthday (April 13), Moore explained to the President that he had fended off the appeal but that later in the year, "while the campaign is getting under way," a stop at Jefferson's home might be highly productive in terms of public relations (fig. 14.4).[21]

Representative Sol Bloom of New York, who served in Congress from 1923 until his death in 1949, became an extremely visible history buff and figuratively wrapped himself in the flag of patriotism. He served as director of the George Washington Bicentennial Commission, director general of the U.S. Constitution Sesquicentennial Commission (1935–

39), chairman of the committee responsible for celebrating the 150th anniversary of the U.S. Supreme Court (1939–40), director and a U.S. commissioner of the 1939 World's Fair. Bloom became a tireless promoter of the nation's political past; and his speeches convey a clear sense of the assumptions that directed his energies. In 1932 when he spoke at Edenton, North Carolina, Bloom essentially responded to the rhetorical question: What's so significant about this bicentennial? He asserted that reviewing a long and honorable history gave Americans "a new feeling of stability. . . . It enables us to feel that we are no longer a 'young' or 'new' nation, but now stand as a fixture among the firmest and strongest nations of human history." During the Constitution's sesquicentennial his formulaic presentation was called "The Heritage of Americanism."[22]

William Williamson, a lawyer and judge who represented South Dakota in Congress from 1920 until 1932, wrote the original legislation that made Mount Rushmore possible and remained closely associated with the project from its inception in 1924 until its completion in 1939 (fig. 14.5). Although a chauvinist on behalf of his state, he was also a nationalist whose Americanism had roots in a highly personalized past. The entire project, he informed Congress in 1928 when appealing for

14.4   President Franklin D. Roosevelt at Mount Rushmore, South Dakota, dedicating the bust of Thomas Jefferson by sculptor Gutzon Borglum, August 30, 1936. Courtesy of the Franklin D. Roosevelt Library, Hyde Park, New York.

14.5 Mount Rushmore National Monument, Keystone, South Dakota. Courtesy of the National Archives Trust Fund Board.

an appropriation, was "symbolical and allegorical. Washington symbolizes the founding of our country and the stability of our institutions; Jefferson our idealism, expansion, and love of liberty; Lincoln our altruism and sense of inseparable unity; while Roosevelt typifies the soul of America—its restless energy, rugged morality, and progressive spirit. The memorial, as a whole, will idealize all that is best in our national traditions, principles, and form of government."[23]

Louis C. Cramton also exemplifies the growing enthusiasm for history and a genuine commitment to its support. As a Progressive Republican in Congress (representing Michigan, 1913–31), Cramton felt particular admiration for Stephen Mather of the National Park Service, for the biographer Douglas Southall Freeman, and for John D. Rockefeller, Jr., because of his notable contribution to historic preservation. For several years following his defeat in 1930 Cramton worked as a special assistant at the Interior Department, primarily doing research and writing for the National Park Service, an agency just beginning its ascent in terms of administrative clout and a broad range of responsibility for historic sites.

Members of Franklin Roosevelt's cabinet were often asked to present addresses at dedications and commemorations that the President could not attend. Given the size and skills of their staff support, they usually presented accurate accounts; but when they did not it became a matter of note. In 1937, for example, Postmaster General James Farley dedicated a new post office in Arlington, Virginia, and managed to place Sir

Walter Raleigh in the wrong place at the wrong time and also to locate Roanoke Island in Virginia rather than North Carolina. These lapses received front-page coverage (presumably because of heightened historical awareness and state pride rather than an obsessive public interest in James Farley's command of historical facts). While gently chiding Farley, a *New York Times* editorial explained that his errors were entirely understandable. "As we remember our school books," it observed, "everything from the vicinity of Florida up to Canada was 'Virginia' in the vague and spacious time of Elizabeth. Indeed, if Mr. Farley will look at a map of Virginia in those days it will remind him tremendously of a map of the Roosevelt States last November."[24]

I I I

ONE PROMINENT transitional feature of the 1930s involved the gradual growth of co-operation between governmental agencies at several levels and the private sector when occasions arose for commemorative events or ritual observances. The Massachusetts Tercentenary of 1930 derived financial support from the state but also from individuals and communities. It enjoyed what is known in convenient jargon as "vertically integrated support." It also enjoyed a considerable degree of success as measured by community participation, popular enjoyment, and educational impact. In addition it supplied a legacy in the form of re-created historic sites (managed by private groups): Pioneer Village in Salem, Fort Massachusetts in North Adams, and the Aptucxet Trading Post in Bourne at the entrance to Cape Cod.[25]

The Yorktown Sesquicentennial Association, Inc. [1781–1931], also depended upon an interesting and representative pattern of collaboration. The Reverend W. A. R. Goodwin of Colonial Williamsburg, Inc., served as president along with Senator Harry F. Byrd of Virginia as vice president. The Association raised more than $42,600 by public subscription; the state allocated $62,500; and the federal government contributed $43,000 by means of budgetary sleight of hand. Although Herbert Hoover served as honorary president of the Association, separate U.S. and Virginia commissions emerged—especially appropriate, perhaps, in a region where the states' rights tradition remained quite strong.[26]

The 1932 bicentennial of George Washington's birth also aroused multi-level support, and it enjoyed a considerable amount of popular appeal—as much as any celebration of its kind in U.S. history. It certainly mattered that Congress provided for a planning committee as early as 1925. Mark Sullivan, the influential journalist, observed that the activities recalling diverse aspects of Washington's career "happened to come at a time when refreshment of the American public at the springs of their traditions was peculiarly needed." Others, especially older Americans, welcomed the bicentennial because they feared that the "memory of Washington was becoming a little dim with the lapse of years and the change in the character of public sentiments, for it is no longer as easy as it once was for our people, especially our young people, to appreciate a dignified eighteenth-century gentleman, a Virginia squire and magnate."[27] After Sol Bloom's commission had placed 750,000 copies of Gilbert Stuart's *Washington* in as many American schoolrooms, the Father of His Country had become ubiquitous even where he was not overwhelmingly appreciated.

In 1934 the New York Southern Society decided to honor the 150th anniversary of the birth of President Zachary Taylor, who had been born in Orange County, Virginia, in 1784. If that seems to mark a swing from the sublime to the ridiculous, perhaps its lesson is that the 1930s was a magnanimous decade. Governor Pollard of Virginia appointed a commission to plan and publicize the event. President Roosevelt agreed to serve as honorary chairman and explained to R. Walton Moore his understanding that "the function of this Commission is educational." Moore gave a speech honoring the hero of the Mexican War on July 4, 1934, at the University of Virginia; but the major festivity occurred on Taylor's birthday, November 24, when the Southern Society sponsored a gala dinner at the Waldorf-Astoria Hotel in Manhattan. Its press release explained that the event was part of the Society's program of "keeping alive the history and traditions of the South [and] to demonstrate the great Presidential tradition of exalted purpose, regardless of section or party." Once again, private initiative had garnered the co-operation and support of prominent officials in state and federal government.[28]

Civil War anniversaries remained especially popular during the 1930s, despite the cost of travel and re-enactments during hard times. In May 1935 the Fredericksburg Battlefield Park Association and the National Park Service co-sponsored a re-enactment of the Battle of Chancellorsville (on its 72nd anniversary) in which U.S. Marines and cavalry participated along with cadets from the Virginia Military Institute.[29]

Two years later the Park Service took the initiative in mobilizing an assortment of private individuals and associations in a collaborative effort to erect a monument to Stonewall Jackson, who had died at Chancellorsville. The superintendent of the four National Battlefield Areas in that vicinity described the commemorative occasion as being "somewhat in the nature of a pilgrimage" at which the new Park Headquarters-Museum Building in Fredericksburg would be officially opened. The culmination of a carefully planned day involved formal presentation to the Secretary of the Interior of the deed "conveying ownership of the Jackson Shrine," the house in which he died.[30] This transaction may be less significant for its quasi-religious tone than for its pattern of government assumption of responsibility for property that had previously been privately owned.

Even so, the trend developed slowly and tentatively. In September 1937 a two-week observance known as the National Antietam Commemoration was held at Hagerstown and at the Antietam Battlefield in Washington County, Maryland. No federal appropriation was forthcoming to assist this seventy-fifth anniversary observance; and the same was true a year later of the Blue-Gray reunion at Gettysburg. An explanation *may* be found in the substantial financial support given in 1937–38 by Congress to the sesquicentennial of the U.S. Constitution. The faucet could not open up a limitless flow at that time.[31]

Congress also supported in a modest way the sesquicentennial celebration of the Northwest Ordinance and Territory in 1937–38—an interesting observance because of the logistical complexities that it faced, the co-operation that it managed to achieve among six states, a great many local communities, and some federal agencies. Its difficulties and failures are also instructive.

Advance planning for this year-long event began in 1935 and received co-operation and input from numerous volunteers. Beyond that, however, the customary pattern of private sector dominance did not occur, which marks this commemoration as a notable turning point. Although the Northwest Territory Celebration Commission (a mix of public officials and private individuals appointed by President Roosevelt) made a strenuous effort to involve church groups, it received a lackadaisical response from churches, which came as a baffling surprise.[32] Perhaps some of the major denominations had become so engaged in preparations for the Swedish-American Tercentenary in 1938 that they had little left in terms of time or money for the less ethnic and more secular territorial celebration.

Whatever the reason, the Northwest Territory Commission functioned in ways that one might have expected from an anniversary organization during the second term of the New Deal. In producing a much-needed history of the region for primary and secondary schools, the Commission enjoyed co-operation from the Federal Writers' Project, especially in the final production stages. Other printed materials, such as maps and historical brochures concerning the Northwest Territory, were prepared by the FWP of the Works Progress Administration in Ohio.[33] Recognizing that pageants and related physical set-ups would require the hiring of a substantial work force, the Commission resolved early on that "so far as practical, men from relief rolls or other able men needing work are to be employed." President Roosevelt came to Marietta, Ohio, on July 8, 1938, to give an address and unveil a national memorial to the Start Westward of the Nation. State governors and their staffs co-operated, as did the state tourist bureaus.[34]

One of the few "untoward" aspects of this observance involved interregional resentment, though it seems in retrospect both predictable and significant. Because the earliest white settlers in Ohio had come from Massachusetts, a caravan left Ipswich in December 1937 and followed the original route of the initial settlers to Marietta, a journey of many months. By way of response, however, the instructions emanating from Ohio for those who performed historical pageants in the six states of the Old Northwest included some arrestingly didactic and chauvinistic lines:

> A hundred and fifty years ago, the text books were written by men in the settled· communities along the Atlantic seaboard from whom the old northwest territory which later became the present states of Ohio, Indiana, Michigan, Illinois, Wisconsin and a part of Minnesota was farther away to them than Siberia is to us today.
> The men and women who carried the nation toward the western ocean were *makers* of history rather than *writers* of it. They knew more of the long rifle and the woodsman's axe than of quill and parchment; and their days were too full of action for writing or recording.[35]

Apart from the mildly anti-intellectual tone, this boosterish admonition reflected the strident regionalism so characteristic of the 1930s. Regionalists were not averse to receiving national support, however, so yet another typical pattern emerged in 1937 when a museum honoring John James Audubon was built in Audubon Memorial Park near Henderson, Kentucky. The $73,000 museum received joint funding from the federal government and from private Audubon societies around the country. Men from the Works Progress Administration and from the Civilian Conservation Corps provided much of the labor force to erect the museum.[36]

At just about the same time Congress appropriated $5 million for the federal government's participation in the 1939 World's Fair, to be held at New York. After all, an editorial observed, the Fair "is to be essentially a national commemoration." That was not altogether accurate, because the city of New York had so much at stake in terms of prestige and enterprise. Nonetheless, by 1937 Congress had begun to recognize just how much it could assist economic recovery by making monetary infusions in carefully selected locations. It has been said before in other contexts, yet remains so true, that the key to understanding the growth of governmental support and responsibility for American traditions during the New Deal era is the simple fact that Franklin Roosevelt's policy sought to spend the country out of the depression. Had there not been a Great Depression during the 1930s, it might have taken considerably longer for government at any level to concern itself with American history, myths, and museums.[37]

I V

BEFORE we examine the various ways in which American culture received support from Roosevelt's fiscal policies, we should note the upsurge of patriotism that occurred throughout the decade and had a significant impact upon sentiment for various sorts of American traditions. Here again we find that the phenomenon had its roots during the Hoover years, although not from anything that President Hoover himself said or did. A general enthusiasm for Americana, regardless of one's ideological perspective, grew steadily during the later 1920s.[38]

In 1931 Congress finally made "The Star-Spangled Banner" our official national anthem, a status that it had informally enjoyed for several decades. The U.S. Navy adopted it as early as 1889, and the Army soon followed. Nevertheless, thirty-five bills introduced in Congress between 1910 and 1930 failed, and the range of objections seems in retrospect both long and ludicrous: first, the fact that its melody had originated as a drinking song; second, that it expressed feelings hostile to Great Britain; third, that its lyrics glorified martial rather than peaceful sentiments; fourth, that its melodic range, especially the high notes, made it difficult to sing; and finally a general sense that the song seemed antiquated or out of date.[39]

Although Woodrow Wilson had upgraded its status in 1917, when the martial spirit gained new adherents in the United States, opposition remained vigorous even though very few people rejected it for all of the reasons enumerated above. Some individualists who disliked Prohibition because it was a *national* directive did not care to have any national anthem for the very same reason: officials in Washington, D.C., should not tell the entire country how to behave. Herbert Hoover, by the way, took no interest in the proposal, and thereby missed a chance to ride a wave of patriotic enthusiasm that started to crest late in the 1920s. A coalition of congressmen and super-patriotic private citizens led by Mrs. Reuben Ross Holloway of Baltimore lobbied with great energy, collected a petition with 5 million names, and simply wore down their inert opponents.

When the bill passed in 1931, it received little national publicity. Only the Baltimore area really took note of the new official status; and not until World War II came along did many Americans discover that, at last, they had a national song (fig. 14.6).[40]

Franklin Roosevelt seems to have been quite simply shrewder than Hoover in utilizing patriotism as a basis for mobilizing support and defusing opposition. At times Roosevelt's rhetoric could be hollow even though unassailable; and at other times he invoked nationalistic language in a manner that more recently has come to be recognized as the imposition of cultural hegemony. In 1935, for instance, when F.D.R.

14.6 Fort McHenry National Monument and Historic Shrine, Baltimore, Maryland. A replica of the fifteen-star "spangled banner" flies from a restored flagstaff located in the parade ground on the very spot where the original flagstaff stood in September 1814. Courtesy of the National Archives Trust Fund Board.

urged Congress to approve the entirely laudable Historic Sites bill, he insisted that it would serve as a much-needed stimulus to patriotism. "The preservation of historic sites for the public benefit, together with their proper interpretation," he declared, "tends to enhance the respect and love of the citizen for the institutions of his country, as well as strengthen his resolution to defend unselfishly the hallowed traditions and high ideals of America."[41]

During the early to mid-1930s, a period that straddled the Hoover and Roosevelt presidencies, American society increasingly needed and sought a meaningful sense of its heritage in crisis times. By 1935–36 a great many observers believed that a new and vital cultural nationalism had in fact arrived. Hallie Flanagan, who directed the Federal Theatre Project, urged directors to search for and mount plays that probed the American past.[42] Similarly, in 1937 the Federal Writers' Project put together *American Stuff*, an anthology of Americana—short stories, poems, and folklore primarily, though it also included some notable social criticism, such as Richard Wright's "The Ethics of Living Jim Crow." The main objective of those responsible was to gather documentary evidence of an "exact American idiom" as opposed to traditional literary English. Hence their enthusiasm for folk sayings, convict songs, market cries, and square dance calls. Although *American Stuff* did not enjoy broad success in its own right, its outlook and contents turned out to be influential.[43]

Just as writers wove American words into anthologies, so collectors of indigenous art, artifacts, and the decorative arts found that prices became affordable because of the depression. Many affluent collectors put their treasures up for sale, and frequently the beneficiaries of these sad separations were museums, historical societies, and other sorts of public institutions. Consequently the 1930s witnessed a major movement of important pieces of Americana from private hoards to accessible repositories. In some instances interesting or important collections were simply donated to the United States: in 1937 Secretary of the Interior Harold L. Ickes formally accepted an assemblage of unique firearms presented to the nation by the Society of the War of 1812. Sometimes the gifts made up in charm what they lacked in historical significance, as when the Lancaster County (Pennsylvania) Historical Society was given an Easter egg that had been decorated in 1776.[44]

The steadily growing appeal of Americana meant that early American architecture would be, by far, the most popular building style of the 1930s. In 1938, when the *Architectural Forum* published its Five Star Questionnaire, 60 percent of those polled preferred the colonial style; and of those some 30 percent indicated a fondness for the Dutch colonial. Closer examination reveals, however, that particular labels were not very meaningful because they were so casually used. The Cape Cod cottage, categorized as colonial, began its phenomenal rise to the top of the "list" in 1932—perhaps because it was small and affordable, but also because it evoked nostalgia for earlier and simpler times. Ironies abound in this craze for the colonial. Early Pennsylvania farmhouses enjoyed such a vogue that they emerged far from context, as in Beverly Hills, California. A colonial image provided the architectural backdrop for almost every Hollywood film set amidst a contemporary urban environment.[45]

If we correctly associate the 1930s with regionalism, the colonial revival adapted to that phenomenon also. As David Gebhard has observed, one difference between the colonial revival in the 1930s and its predecessors involved "its ability to establish a series of repeated national images found coast to coast but at the same time to encourage the development of regional types. In each instance the unspoken desire was to develop an image that would be tied to the national colonial tradition but at the same time would be responded to as specific to the locale."[46]

The revival had a remarkably homogenizing effect upon architecture in public places. Service structures on newly completed parkways and roads were invariably neo-colonial. Newly built restaurants and funeral homes favored the early American image. And it soon became clear that the federal government preferred the colonial style. Few new post offices turned out to be anything but red brick neo-Georgian. Franklin Delano Roosevelt had long been enthusiastic about early American architecture, and on several occasions he personally intervened to ensure that federal post offices in the area near Hyde Park would be built in the colonial style. Predictably, perhaps, the Century of Progress Exposition held at Chicago in 1933 featured a Colonial Village.[47]

Inside those neo-Georgian post offices the newly painted murals sponsored by the Treasury Department Section of Fine Arts were most often historical in emphasis, with special attention being given to community origins or to events of regional or national significance that had occurred in the area. Karal Ann Marling has made a persuasive case that historical tableaux supplied the most popular mode and theme in federal and other public facilities because the past was comparatively non-controversial. Since Americans disagreed about numerous policy issues during the 1930s, history seemed a kind of neutral ground. (Not that some post office murals did not turn out to be controversial. They did, but usually for reasons unrelated to history per se.)[48]

The same held true for the Federal Writers' Project in general (1935–41) and its best-known achievement, the state guidebooks, in particular. Alfred Kazin correctly called those WPA guides a repository and a symbol of the "reawakened American sense of its own history." A revival of interest in national values and traditions unquestionably suffused American thought during the 1930s; and beyond the sincere manifestations of patriotism that prompted such enthusiasm, it is clear that the past was potentially less divisive than the present. If policy makers and New Deal agencies turned to American history as a source of stability, the sources suggest that the populace at large found such solutions satisfactory and frequently pleasing.[49]

Although political issues, values, and traditions were commonly discussed during the 1930s, they often tended to be depoliticized and historicized in a consensus-building way. People with quite different ideological perspectives somehow managed to agree upon the meaning of Roosevelt's victory in 1932: "A mandate from the people to return to the old faith"—the old faith remaining unspecified, presumably because it meant different things to latter-day Jeffersonians and Federalists.[50] Thomas Jefferson himself finally achieved the non-partisan status accorded to a statesman, rather than being viewed as a party leader, and Americans of all persuasions accorded him respect as a founding patriot (fig. 14.7). Pockets of neo-Hamiltonians ceased to be very visible or vocal, a condition that they could quietly enjoy as they observed F.D.R. and Treasury Secretary Henry Morgenthau pursue Hamiltonian economic policies designed to strengthen the federal government's

14.7   The unfinished statue of Thomas Jefferson, prepared by Rudulph Evans for the Jefferson Memorial in Washington, D.C. The figures in the foreground are Rudulph Evans and the playwright Sidney Kingsley, author of *The Patriots* (1943). (Taken at the sculptor's studio.) Courtesy of Sidney Kingsley.

grip upon an economy that was nationally integrated in ways that Alexander Hamilton could hardly have envisioned.[51]

It has become a commonplace observation that the Communist Party of the United States strove throughout the later 1930s to Americanize its image—by lavishing praise upon the founding fathers, for example. Writers on the left, irrespective of party affiliation, insisted that an American Revolutionary tradition did indeed exist, and that its genesis would be found in the Declaration of Independence and events surrounding 1776—a creative political moment *unlike* the French and Russian revolutions. As V. F. Calverton phrased it, the great challenge in 1934 was "not that of debunking our past but of revaluating it in terms of our revolutionary tradition. In a word, we must learn not to scoff at our revolutionary past but to build upon it and advance it." The tendency to "scoff and sneer at American traditions" angered Calverton, and he accused other radicals of customarily dismissing the past as being irrelevant to present needs and future programs. He pursued what seemed a realistic and well-informed recognition that "the American masses are neither as radical as the revolutionaries have made them out to be, nor as unchangeably individualistic as the reactionaries think they are."[52]

It surely is one of the most notable aspects of American political discourse during the 1930s that almost everyone, ranging from radicals to reactionaries, rooted his policies in vaguely formulated "American traditions" and explained his positions accordingly. It is also worthy of notice that if radicals sought to Americanize and soften their image, conservatives (with some highly vocal exceptions) felt compelled to move toward the center and, like the Communist Party after 1934, embrace various nationalistic symbols and ceremonials. In 1932, for example, James M. Beck, a conservative congressman from Pennsylvania, published caustic criticism of the methods and expenditures of the George Washington Bicentennial Commission. He viewed the enterprise as a "needless waste of the public monies." Two years later, however, Beck reversed himself and offered extravagant praise for Sol Bloom, the Commission's chairman. Two years after that, in 1936, William Randolph Hearst compared Franklin D. Roosevelt to Andrew Jackson because of Roosevelt's democratic principles and policies.[53]

If American traditions provided common ground for both the political left and right, distinctions between elite and popular culture tended to be similarly blurred. Serious professional writers worked alongside amateurs under the auspices of the Federal Writers' Project, and critic Harold Rosenberg urged elimination of the arbitrary distinction between fine art and folk art. As government supplanted private sources as the major patron for the arts, recognition that government in a democracy ought to be egalitarian brought the belief that cultural activities sustained by the government ought to be democratized. Hence the murals that were painted for courthouses, post offices, and other public structures emphasized native themes and ordinary people. The various art projects were intended to bring visual pleasure to the people and employed large numbers of artists who varied greatly in the range of their skills.[54]

SURELY one of the most striking developments of the 1930s, one that cannot be emphasized too vigorously, is that patriotism and populism came to be joined—a combination that had not consistently occurred before because populists more often than not voiced major grievances against the regime. When Lewis Mumford wrote that the state-by-state guides prepared by the Writers' Project—so rich in history, folklore, and a sense of place—were his generation's "finest contribution to American patriotism," he described a phenomenon that really was unprecedented in the cultural history of the United States.[55]

V

THE NATIONAL PARK SERVICE had begun to democratize its efforts during the 1920s because Stephen T. Mather, its first director, became more concerned with middle-class interests than with those of the patrician elite that had dominated conservationist affairs in the United States ever since the 1880s. That impulse to broaden its clientele intensified during the 1930s when the Park Service, like so many New Deal cultural projects, connected patriotism with populism as its guiding spirit. Verne Chatelain, the chief historian working for the Park Service, explained its interpretive mission in 1935 in these words: "to recreate for the average citizen something of the color, the pageantry, and the dignity of our national past." By 1937 Park Service field historians began to extend their outreach by participating in interpretive radio broadcasts in the vicinity of their parks.[56]

The process that brought the National Park Service from conserving natural wonders and sites to being an agency of historical transmission occurred very swiftly during the Hoover presidency. The initial National Park Service Act passed by Congress in August 1916 carried a mandate to preserve resources for the use and pleasure of the people, yet leave their potential unimpaired for future generations. During the thirteen years of Mather's directorship, the environment and its wonders were perceived as a grand open-air panorama. Mather's director of public relations explained in 1923 that "our national parks system is a national museum."[57]

During the 1920s and continuing into the thirties, however, the Park Service certainly was not oblivious to entrepreneurial opportunities—as a means of enhancing its political role and clout as well as of mustering allies in the private sector (fig. 14.8). Those in charge of the Service hoped to attract tourists and their dollars, and consequently decided to develop facilities within the parks in order to make them "natural resorts." Commercial campaigns by townspeople living near the parks and monuments were encouraged because they led to striking increases in visitation figures. At Carlsbad Caverns in New Mexico an almost symbiotic relationship between the Park Service and the local chamber of commerce resulted in dramatic improvement in the site's accessibility and popularity. In 1928–29 the Cavern Supply Company, already present as a seasonal concessionaire within the monument, was permitted to build a stone, pueblo-style structure at which it sold lunches and souvenirs. This became the first permanent concession structure at any national monument. In 1929 the company started to serve lunches inside the cave, 750 feet beneath the earth's surface. While Stephen Mather's administration wished to prevent exploitation of the parks and monuments, increasing the volume of tourism became

14.8   President Warren G. Harding, Secretary of the Interior Hubert Work, National Park Service Director Stephen Mather, and Superintendent Horace M. Albright at the grand canyon in Yellowstone National Park, July 2, 1923. Courtesy of the National Archives Trust Fund Board.

a top priority during the latter half of the 1920s. Compromises inevitably had to be made.[58]

Although the earliest National Park museums and interpretive programs did appear during the 1920s, a series of extraordinary changes occurred between 1929 and 1933, when Horace Albright succeeded Mather as director. Albright introduced a Division of Education in order to augment his agency's interpretive role and, quite candidly, to enhance the status of the Park Service within the Interior Department and within the federal government in general. History education became an explicit priority of the Park Service at the very same time that John D. Rockefeller, Jr., and Henry Ford stressed exactly that imperative as a major objective of their respective private undertakings. Educating the American people could be done by means of architecture, artifacts, and historic sites. Hence the Park Service decision to reconstruct earthworks and eighteenth-century buildings brought Jamestown and Yorktown, Virginia, within the orbit of its educational program early in the 1930s.[59]

In 1931 Verne E. Chatelain of Peru State Teachers College in Peru, Nebraska, accepted an appointment that placed him in charge of historical research and interpretation for the Park Service. As he explained to a friend: "The government is hoping to make each park the center of far reaching activities in local history, that is, the park or monument is to function very nearly as a local historical society—collecting, editing and popularizing." This marked a striking new departure for the Service in particular and for the federal government in general.[60] A pivotal prelude occurred in 1930 when Congress passed an act—as a result of extraordinary pressure from super-patriots in the private sector—that placed the George Washington Birthplace National Monument located in Wakefield, Virginia, under Park Service management. Albright and his staff had the unenviable task of interpreting a highly controversial house that had been reconstructed on the wrong location and on the basis of no reliable documentation as to the appearance of the eighteenth-century original. This sentimental fantasy became one of the most difficult burdens the Park Service has ever borne; but the responsibility swiftly signified that preservation and protection of "historic" buildings and locations had become a basic part of the agency's work.[61]

The most crucial opportunity during Albright's tenure at the Park Service occurred in April 1933, when he received an invitation from the White House to accompany the President on a Sunday outing intended to visit a typical CCC Camp in the Blue Ridge Mountains of Virginia. On the return trip along Skyline Drive, Albright sat with Roosevelt for four hours and used this unique period of access to persuade F.D.R. that preservation of historic sites, especially battlefields, had been inadequately handled by the War Department and consequently really ought to be turned over to the Park Service. Their touring car passed within close proximity of several famous sites of Civil War conflict. Roosevelt thought of the Revolutionary War battlefield at Saratoga, New York, which for years he had wanted to have set aside as a park.[62]

The outcome of Albright's remarkable salesmanship occurred within just a few months. That summer the President signed an executive order transferring all national military parks, battlefields, and national monuments from the Agriculture and War Departments to Interior, and more particularly to supervision by the Park Service. How convenient that between 1926 and 1933 the War Department had in fact completed a nationwide survey of American battlefields! During Albright's years as Mather's subordinate he had chafed at his chief's inadequate interest in historic places. Albright had much more enthusiasm than Mather for preservation and found the prospect of Park Service responsibility for public interpretation of the American past very attractive indeed. He had achieved a personal triumph and thereby effectively transformed the scope and profile of Park Service activities.[63]

Albright's administrative legacy (he left Interior for the United States Potash Company late in the summer of 1933) included such icons as the Gettysburg Battlefield, Fort McHenry near Baltimore, the Castillo de San Marcos in St. Augustine (fig. 14.9), and the Statue of Liberty. In March 1933 Jockey Hollow near Morristown, New Jersey, where George Washington and the Continental Army had wintered in 1779–80, became the first of many national historical parks (fig. 14.10). Thereafter the customary distinction between national parks and monuments grew less consequential; and the states began to follow suit by setting aside parks and developing comparable programs of historical interpretation. The Park Service promptly created the Historic American Buildings Survey later in 1933; and in 1935 when Congress passed the Historic Sites Act, it explicitly confirmed that a central role for the Park Service in historic preservation should be fostered by the federal government. A poster designed for the Park Service in 1934 by Dorothy Waugh carried a legend that managed to encapsulate both the customary and the newly expanded roles of the Park Service: "The Adventures of Today Are the Memories of Tomorrow."[64]

14.9   Castillo di San Marcos: the bridge leading into the fort at St. Augustine, Florida (October 20, 1946). Courtesy of the National Archives Trust Fund Board.

14.10   The Ford Mansion at Morristown National Historical Park, George Washington's winter headquarters in 1779–80 (shown on Nov. 10, 1939). Courtesy of the National Archives Trust Fund Board.

The quadrupling of historical areas administered by the National Park system as a result of the 1933 reorganization put the Park Service at the very forefront of the fledgling preservation movement. Congressional appropriations to support the Service increased dramatically and the agency established its own Branch of Historic Sites and Buildings responsible for the preservation, development, and interpretation of significant cultural resources throughout the land. New Deal programs that were run under other auspices co-operated by helping to train Park Service personnel in historic preservation techniques and policies as well as connections between popular education and historical interpretation. Public awareness of the need for historic preservation increased markedly as a consequence.[65]

By 1936–37 the range of Park Service responsibilities included twenty-three national scenic areas of major importance, such as Yosemite and Yellowstone; close to fifty national monuments; around forty national military parks, battlefield sites, and memorials; plus assorted other areas that brought the total above one hundred sixty. It operated three national surveys, including the Historic Sites Survey of the Branch of Historic Sites and Buildings. It also conducted a nationwide program involving state co-operation in park development that shaped basic recreation and conservation policies in numerous states. In order to achieve such an ambitious program it employed some 14,000 people and operated 600 CCC camps at which 120,000 young men worked.[66]

The dramatic expansion and considerable success of the Park Service during the 1930s must be attributed to numerous and diverse factors:

14.11   Ronald F. Lee (1905–1972), energetic Chief Historian of the National Park Service, 1938–1951. Lee entered the Park Service in 1933 and wrote extensively about its military and historical sites. Courtesy of the National Archives Trust Fund Board.

the commitment and personal aggressiveness of Horace Albright; bureaucratic opportunism; a genuine recognition of the imperatives and realities of both federalism and regionalism; and more than a touch of ideological populism combined with a tough-minded recognition that the restoration of historic sites could assist the process of economic recovery while policies designed to foster recovery could also bestow great benefits upon the nation's built heritage (fig. 14.11). It should come as no surprise that in the process of expansion and transformation the Park Service began to develop a sense of its own traditions and potential. To a greater degree than most, it became a federal agency with an almost strident sense of purpose and memory.[67]

IN AUGUST 1935 Congress passed an act "to provide for the preservation of historic American sites, buildings, objects, and antiquities of national significance." The bill began with an unprecedented declaration that it would now become a "national policy" to protect such places for public use—a much different and broader scope than the Antiquities Act of 1906, which was still in effect and remained useful on occasion. Much of the new law was devoted to a lengthy list of expanded spheres of authority given the Secretary of the Interior: to make surveys, investigations, and collect data; to acquire historic properties in the name of the United States; to enter into agreements designed to protect and preserve property; to erect markers to

14.12 The Custom House, a historic structure at Salem Maritime National Historic Site, Salem, Massachusetts. Courtesy of the National Archives Trust Fund Board.

commemorate historic places; and to "develop an educational program and service for the purpose of making available to the public facts and information pertaining to American historic and archaeological sites, buildings, and properties of national significance." It also called for an Advisory Board on National Parks, Historic Sites, Buildings, and Monuments; provided for co-operation among various levels of government in order to achieve the objectives of the Act; and facilitated the creation of technical advisory committees.[68]

The press responded with enthusiasm and loved to suggest lists of places and locations that should now be "saved" or restored: Spanish missions in the Southwest; the Santa Fe Trail and the Natchez Trace; Derby Wharf and a host of buildings in Salem, Massachusetts (fig. 14.12); antebellum plantation homes; the route of the Pony Express; the overland stage and places along the Oregon Trail. Some people saw in the Act proof positive that a new and much-needed cultural nationalism had truly arrived. Because organizations and private individuals could nominate potential historic places, the process of creating new sites and symbols seemed at first to have been dramatically democratized. In practice, however, because the Park Service became inundated with requests, it had to establish nominating procedures that regularized the process but may also have stifled proposals from regional, minority, and relatively uninfluential groups that found it hard to fulfill lofty criteria for "national significance."[69]

That such a problem arose and could not be readily resolved serves

14.13   The Plunkett-Meeker House and the Pattison-Hix Tavern at Appomattox, Virginia. Courtesy of the National Archives Trust Fund Board.

to remind us that despite the government's rapidly growing role as a
custodian of tradition during the 1930s and beyond, co-operation between the public and private sectors remained essential, and prominent groups or persons were more likely to achieve their goals than
humble ones. Those who ran Colonial Williamsburg worked closely
with the National Park Service during the 1930s, as did the Society of
Colonial Wars. For some years after Horace Albright actually left the
Park Service for the private sector, in fact, he continued to maintain a
cordial correspondence with John D. Rockefeller, Jr., about matters
pertaining to preservation and the administration of historic sites. Park
Service officials often capitulated to pressure from local elites even
when their wishes ran counter to agency policies or guidelines. That
occurred at Wakefield (George Washington's birthplace) in 1930–31, at
Gettysburg in 1933, and again after 1945 when the McLean House
(where Lee surrendered to Grant) and a dozen other structures were
reconstructed at Appomattox (fig. 14.13).[70]

By the end of the decade procedures for conducting relatively congenial negotiations between government and non-profit associations had
been worked out. Early in 1940, for example, the Federal Hall Memorial Associates, Inc., made an agreement with the Secretary of the
Interior to develop a long-range historical program for the Federal Hall
Memorial Historical Site in New York City. They essentially concurred
on a plan to operate a national museum commemorating the founding
of the federal government and related historical events. Similarly, in

September 1940 the Association for the Preservation of Virginia Antiquities negotiated an arrangement with the Park Service to develop a co-operative, unified program of development and administration for the entire Jamestown Island area, including the planning and location of parkways, causeways, a National Park Service Museum with galleries assigned to the A.P.V.A., "and with archeological trenching and investigations of the historic end of the Island, belonging to the A.P.V.A., to be carried out by the archeologist of the Park Service."[71]

Both sides seemed extremely pleased by the arrangement; but an acknowledgment that appeared near the end of the press release anticipated the needs and aspirations of many private organizations in the decades that lay ahead: "The Contract protects the [A.P.V.A.] in many important particulars where it would be at a disadvantage without the contract. The paper also provides for investigation on our property which promises to produce results of great historic value, which could not be hoped for if the Association were called upon to bear the expense, and stipulates that no steps can be taken in this connection without the approval of the Association for the Preservation of Virginia Antiquities."[72]

In quite a different area, albeit one exemplifying the same sort of pattern, Luther Evans (who ran the WPA Historical Records Survey) worked collaboratively with the D.A.R. and the United Daughters of the Confederacy, especially on records of genealogical interest.[73] Program chiefs who worked for the various New Deal cultural agencies had almost as much motivation for entering into such co-operative relationships as the private organizations did. The reason was quite simple. Many members of Congress, regardless of their party affiliation, still did not believe that the U.S. government should fund cultural or artistic programs and institutions. Late in 1935, when the House of Representatives debated yet another appropriation for Mount Rushmore, Congressman Marion A. Zioncheck of Washington terminated discussion of the bill with these words: "The whole thing would not be so bad if George Washington knew that these hills [in South Dakota] existed before he died."[74]

By 1939 Congress had in fact disbanded four of the New Deal relief projects that promoted the arts and American culture. A great many voters and their elected officials did not regard artistic innovation and cultural improvement as a public responsibility. The concept of cultural democracy, much discussed during the mid-1930s, never became a universally accepted and clearly established public policy. Whereas the National Park Service proved to be enduring, most of the cultural relief programs did not. Their legacy does indeed remain, but almost all of the programs had been terminated by 1942.[75]

VI

IT IS SURELY intriguing that the most celebrated and best remembered contributions of the New Deal to American culture, taken
as a cluster, turned out in the short run to be ephemeral as a precedent.
In many instances the products themselves do survive—guidebooks,
murals in public buildings, ex-slave narratives, archives of documents
and of American design, collections of folklore and folk music—but the
concept of sustained governmental support for national, regional, and
local traditions was too new and too curious by conventional American
criteria to outlive the depression and the onset of World War II. Only
gradually in the postwar era would those precedents be recalled and
invoked, though never fully replicated. Although major pieces of supportive legislation have appeared since the mid-1960s, the flurry of
government-managed cultural creativity and stocktaking that occurred
between 1935 and 1941 remains unique in United States history.

The impressive litany of programs has become reasonably familiar
by now. In 1933 the Civilian Conservation Corps began (among its
many other projects) to restore places of historical interest and to improve public access to them. In that same year a National Park Service architect proposed to Secretary of the Interior Harold Ickes that
unemployed architects could be given the job of surveying and recording the features of historic structures throughout the United
States. Within weeks the Historic American Buildings Survey hired
some 1,200 architects. By 1938 they had produced 24,000 measured
drawings and 26,000 photographs of 6,389 older structures. This
five-year effort was particularly notable, as Michael Wallace has observed, because so many of the buildings surveyed had "no connection whatever to famous men; their historical importance was rooted
in local memories and traditions."[76]

The Works Progress Administration put creative writers and historians to work in the Federal Writers' Project. The state guidebooks,
compilations of local lore, and collections of contemporary literature
that they produced varied greatly in quality; but the best of them had
permanent value, and many "alumni" of the program became prominent figures in American letters during the subsequent generation.
While the substance of their work emphasized traditional Americana—
rediscovering a land and its heritage—their attitude and focus were
populistic, highlighting the works and days of ordinary people. The
WPA had an explicit position that American folklore was public rather
than private property and that folklore research ought to be a shared
and public endeavor. In 1938 the WPA inaugurated a Joint Committee
on Folk Arts.[77] The net result was an astounding multiplication of the
sort of work that Constance Rourke and a few others had done privately
on 'heir own initiative during the 1920s and early '30s.

Henry G. Alsberg, director of the Federal Writers' Project, did a remarkable job of co-ordinating resources and standards of purpose and format for state programs that ranged from headstrong and enthusiastic to hesitant or inert. As the head of a federal program he had to walk a precarious tightrope in order to justify his funding and the worth of what his numerous writer-researchers were doing. Early in 1936 the *New York Times* gave Alsberg an opportunity to explain the "American Guide" series to a sympathetic public as well as to skeptics who viewed the whole thing as "make work." Two sentences from his essay suggest that Alsberg was a pragmatist with more than a few political bones in his body.

> It is our aim to make the work not only of value to historians, scientists, teachers and their students but to business men and those interested in the vast industrial resources and machinery of the United States. As well as a cultural worth, the guide will have a distinct commercial use for those who wish to employ it for their business and professional purposes.[78]

To those who admire what the Project ultimately achieved, including a "Life in America" series, a life-history program produced by the Southern regional office, and the collection of autobiographical narratives from former slaves (in collaboration with Fisk University), Alsberg and his staff deserved enthusiastic accolades. They had hastened the vital process of native self-discovery. From the perspective of state-based directors and their writers, however, Alsberg seemed excessively bureaucratic, driven by political considerations, and heavy-handed at times in terms of censorship. Late in 1937, for example, Alsberg actually set up a formal censorship mechanism for the FWP under the direction of Mrs. Louise Lazell, who devoted herself to searching for actual or potential Communist propaganda, especially in the state guides. Needless to say, many of the state programs deeply resented such surveillance.[79]

Ultimately the completed product seems to have mattered more in American memory than the troubled process. In November 1941, when the last of the state guide volumes appeared in print, President Roosevelt proclaimed "American Guide Week." It had taken six years to produce fifty-one volumes (for the forty-eight states plus Washington, D.C., Alaska, and Puerto Rico). The total output was actually much larger (some 276 volumes and 701 pamphlets) because there were also guides to a great many cities and smaller communities as well as thematic and regional volumes such as *The Oregon Trail* or *The Ocean Highway* (from New Jersey to northern Florida). Robert Cantwell prized the guides to counties and small towns above all the rest because they constituted the first attempt *ever* to compose a social history of the United States in terms of its communities. "It is one kind of experience to read, in Beard or Turner, about the opening of the West," he wrote, "but it is another kind of experience to read about the rise and fall of Chillicothe in relation to the railroads, or of Galena in relation to the world of lead."[80]

Artists presented a comparable panorama of American life, past and present, in more than 2,500 murals created by the Federal Art Project. A majority of them depicted historical episodes or narratives that were invariably informative though occasionally controversial. Historical subjects enjoyed high priority precisely because they seemed less likely to provoke conflict.[81]

Holger Cahill (1893–1960) played an especially important catalytic role because of his organizational work both for museums and later for the federal government. Although he wrote art history as well as fiction throughout his life, Cahill is best remembered for his impact as a populist in the arts. As a staff member at the Newark Museum (1922–31) he organized at Newark the first major American exhibition of folk art in 1930, followed a year later by a display of native folk sculpture. He also helped to develop the private collection of Abby Aldrich Rockefeller, as we noted in chapter thirteen. As director of the WPA's Federal Art Project he initiated the *Index of American Design,* a comprehensive inventory of enduring value that he published in book format and that has been expanded steadily ever since. It emphasizes the decorative arts, folk motifs, and antiques of all sorts. He drew attention to so-called primitive painters, many of them anonymous; and was equally dynamic in working with museums, private collectors, and eventually for a New Deal program. He persevered in establishing numerous community art centers and served as chairman of the American Handicraft Council's board.[82]

During World War II Cahill organized at the Metropolitan Museum of Art a display titled "Emblems of Unity and Freedom," using objects drawn from the *Index of American Design* and even some from his own remarkable collection, such as a superb copper weathervane of the Statue of Liberty and another one of Miss Liberty (or perhaps Columbia) supporting an American flag. Cahill's essay introducing these varied sorts of patriotic symbols insisted that "it is a responsibility of the artists and writers who are placing their skills at the service of the national war effort to familiarize themselves with this traditional material."[83]

The WPA's Federal Theatre Project encouraged innovation in modes of presentation, but the material itself was derived from American history and folk culture. Although the programs were uneven in quality, they enjoyed considerable success and provoked lively contretemps as well. In 1937, for example, when the Dock Street Theatre in Charleston, South Carolina, underwent reconstruction courtesy of WPA auspices, claims emanated from Carolina that this had been the very first American theatre. The Research Department at Colonial Williamsburg promptly countered with its claim that the first theatre in the colonies had actually been erected as early as 1716 in Williamsburg.[84] Several of the WPA cultural projects had the unintended effect of kindling regional rivalries involving primacy with respect to national traditions.

A very different sort of controversy is exemplified by *Frankie and Johnny*, a ballet created in 1938 by Ruth Page and Bentley Stone for the Federal Theatre's Chicago Dance Project. A work that has subsequently become a classic part of the American repertoire received scorn at the time from haughty critics, journalists, and citizens who felt appalled by the idea of a publicly financed ballet about pimps and prostitutes. Those who approved of it admired the ballet's "folk spirit or folk-myth" qualities, whereas the opposition emphasized its sensuality, earthiness, and "lowlife" aspects. Even Carl Sandburg, an advocate, termed the substance of the story "America's classical gutter song." To universalize (or at least to Americanize) messages about jealousy, passion, and spontaneous rage, the authors shifted the scene of action from its original 1890s St. Louis setting to an Everywhere, contemporary urban street scene. We may casually regard *Frankie and Johnny* as one of the finest American character ballets. In 1938, however, it outraged many and raised serious doubts about the propriety of directing federal funds to "profane" cultural endeavors.[85]

WITH THE HAZE of more than half a century intervening, it is tempting to look back myopically and assume that creating a National Archives in Washington was achieved with consensus and without much resistance, whereas "lowlife" dances or murals by progressive artists that called attention to racial injustice inevitably aroused storms of protest.[86] In reality resistance was offered by *someone* (and frequently by coalitions) to almost any form of federal spending to preserve American culture. A national public archive system had been opposed for more than three decades prior to its implementation in 1934, whereas the WPA- and Treasury-sponsored cultural projects did not come under heavy fire until particular endeavors appeared that offended certain self-appointed arbiters of public taste. Then, late in the 1930s, sentiment slowly began swinging back toward the private sector as the most suitable savior of American traditions.

In contrasting the apparent success and permanence of such entities as the National Archives and Park Service with the transitory existence of various WPA and Treasury arts projects, two characteristics of government must be kept in mind: resistance to change in tandem with bureaucratic resilience. It is extremely difficult to get Congress to pass a law, whether its purpose is to designate a national anthem or to provide perpetual care for the country's documentary records. Once the Congress has taken such an action, however, that body is more likely to provide on-going support than to reverse itself. By contrast, it is much easier for the executive branch to bring a new program into being, especially in crisis times; but it is difficult to perpetuate essential funding for such programs if the mood of Congress or the public becomes in any way critical or skeptical. Executive branch initiatives that are born in response to one crisis may very well die in consequence of another. The coming of World War II provided just such an opportunity for congressional opponents to curtail WPA programs that had engendered hostility since 1938–39.[87]

Precisely because pacifism was quite strong during the 1930s, well-placed individuals wondered what might happen to emblems of tradition in the event of war. Consequently all twenty-one members of the Pan-American Union signed a treaty in 1935 that provided for the protection of cultural institutions in time of war and stipulated that each nation should furnish a list of designated cultural institutions within its boundaries.[88]

As threats to international peace and stability grew stronger during the later 1930s, so did the domestic peace movement within the United States. Its impact was reflected in various cultural activities and artifacts. Sponsors of the Northwest Territory celebration in 1937–38, for example, specified that the great Ordinance of 1787 had been an achievement of peace rather than war. The American Military Institute was established in 1937 by peace-loving soldiers and scholars with a strong interest in military history. The following year Hervey Allen enjoyed popular success with an anti-war historical novel, *Action at Aquila*, that takes place in Virginia during the Civil War. His message seemed quite clear: War has never really resolved anything. Only businessmen and crooks benefit from war. What had the Civil War brought about but the "complete fracture of the past in its own familiar surroundings"? Human bonds ought to be stronger than sectional hatreds, and the precious continuity of past and present must not be broken.[89]

The proper observance of Memorial Day in 1939 became a perplexing affair; and looking at the nation as a whole it was quite clearly an ambivalent one. Rallies for peace were held in many locations, and the tenor of public remarks at those places seemed to echo Hervey Allen's tone in *Action at Aquila*. Elsewhere, however, speakers acknowledged that although everyone desired peace, sometimes war could not be avoided. In Washington, D.C., Memorial Day was marked by a major parade along Constitution Avenue and special exercises in the House of Representatives. The primary focus of attention, however, became Arlington National Cemetery, where a service held at noon was attended by numerous patriotic and veterans groups. Senator Robert A. Taft of Ohio spoke of the need to stay out of the European war, yet he then acknowledged that Americans must not "take our heritage for granted" and should always "fight aggressively for the retention of American ideals and the American way of life." Taft not only talked in clichés, he seemed to support both sides of the issue. His ambivalence appears to have been highly symptomatic.[90]

Although the nation felt suffused by patriotism between 1939 and 1941, it was not always evident from newspaper editorials and films just what sort of message the publishers and producers intended to convey. I am uncertain whether many of them really knew themselves. In *Mr. Smith Goes to Washington,* the second most popular film of 1939 (after *Gone With the Wind*), Jefferson Smith, a wide-eyed, newly appointed senator, took a bus tour upon arriving in the nation's capital. For several minutes Frank Capra's camera scans nearly every important monument, statue, and document associated with American patriotism, including the flag, the Declaration of Independence, and the Lincoln Memorial. Isolationists and internationalists could each feel reassured that *their* sense of the American heritage must be the correct one, although the audience that attended the premiere at the D.A.R.'s Constitution Hall in Washington apparently did not feel entirely sanguine about the sincerity or depth of Capra's patriotism.[91]

The coming of war in 1941 was accompanied by a curious irony. The government invoked and utilized American traditions on behalf of the war effort—scarcely a surprise. Outspoken ideologues did the same. John Dos Passos published *The Ground We Stand On* in 1941 because he believed that Americans "as a people notably lack a sense of history." Calling his initial chapter "The Use of the Past," he declared that a "sense of continuity with generations gone before can stretch like a lifeline across the scary present." He hoped to remind his fellow countrymen that "in spite of hell and high water men in the past managed to live for and establish some few liberties."[92]

If it appears predestined that writers and government officials alike would mobilize the past in attempting to cope with the "scary present," it may seem odd that Franklin D. Roosevelt responded with mixed signals to the potential significance of recording history in the making. Early in the war a group of prominent historians approached the President to request immediate access for historians to the materials that would be needed to write a comprehensive history of the war. On March 4, 1942, F.D.R. honored their request, at least in part, by asking executive agencies to arrange for the preservation of records and for subsequently relating their administrative experiences during the war. On the other hand, he also refused to permit any historian to be assigned to the White House during the conflict.[93]

By 1942 virtually all of the WPA projects established to recover or perpetuate pieces of the American heritage had been closed down. In 1943 the tactical practice of using the Antiquities Act of 1906 as the authority for establishing new units in the National Park system came to an abrupt halt. Roosevelt proclaimed Jackson Hole a National Monument that year, but thereafter no more were added until 1961.[94]

All in all, the decade following 1932 witnessed a dramatic breakthrough in the government's sense of responsibility for America's historic and physical inheritance. Then came an abrupt halt and a period of retrenchment. A gradual resumption of responsibility developed slowly during the 1950s, and swiftly in the decade that followed. We shall return to that aspect of the story in chapter seventeen; but before doing so we must turn our attention to the self-aware use of mythic pasts in American thought and culture during the interwar years.

Chapter 15

THE CHANGING IMPERATIVES
OF MYTH, MEMORY,
AND AMERICANISM

ALTHOUGH A substantial amount has now been written about the social functions of myth, a basic distinction may be helpful in understanding the relationships between myth, collective memory, and cultural criticism during the interwar years in the United States. On the one hand there is a proof-seeking and critical view of myth as inaccurate or even distorted history. On the other there is an approving notion of socially cohesive legends or stories rich in symbolic meaning, comprised of incidents and characters who are larger than life, regardless of whether they are heroes or villains.[1]

Both perceptions will be found in American thought from the 1920s through the 1940s, and they occurred in a relationship that was not only dialogical but symptomatic of an underlying uneasiness concerning the power of myth. Despite our stereotypes about the popularity of "debunking" during the 1920s and the romantic or parochial appeal of Americana in the 1930s, the dominant dynamic seems to have been more nearly the reverse: namely, that various manifestations of myth enjoyed a pervasive and notably uncritical currency during the twenties, but then for about a decade (1929–38) some serious doubters and doubts came to the surface. The menace of totalitarian regimes thereafter made myths look politically and socially useful as never before, however, and a virtual consensus to that effect curtailed criticism and meant that national myths would be viewed in favorable terms throughout the 1940s.

Having described such a crisp pattern, however, I must swiftly acknowledge its reductiveness and the need for qualifications. There was vocal cynicism during the 1920s and countless commemorations took place during the thirties. At any given moment patriotism might appear fashionable with members of a social elite and with veterans' organizations but utterly *infra dig* among intellectuals and assorted professionals. Any assertion that myths rob us of our real history might be countered with the declamation that myths give meaning to a culture and express its values. Pleas for demythologizing met with stiff resistance, yet the perpetuation of myths in mass and popular culture also met with scorn in certain quarters.

In sum, every tendency seemed to elicit a countertrend, and representatives of certain social groups frequently made unexpected observations at the "wrong" time, that is, out of phase. Early in the 1930s, when Van Wyck Brooks launched his up-beat five-volume "Makers and Finders" series on American culture, he turned 180 degrees from his persistently critical posture over a twenty-five-year period. When *The Flowering of New England, 1815–1865* launched that series in 1936, even the literati responded in a mixed manner that seemed to typify the uncertainties of the era. John Dos Passos did not like it, but Edmund Wilson did; and Malcolm Cowley believed the volume served a useful purpose by "turning back to the great past in order to see the real nature of the traditions that we are trying to save, and in order to gain new strength for the struggles ahead."[2]

From the turn of the century until the coming of World War II, moreover, many Americans who seemed quite comfortable with what they knew to be national myths and patriotic symbols nevertheless insisted upon their desire for historical accuracy, realism, and authenticity in museums, restoration projects, pageants, and related phenomena. They wanted their collective memories to be at the same time sanguine and supportive but somehow unwarped and true. As one D.A.R. member said when her organization started to collect Americana: "To gather up these relics and to examine and perpetuate traditions as authentic as accepted chronicles, and often much more authentic, are among the duties of our Society."[3] The United States experience with mythic memories became a delight for Pollyanna and Cassandra alike because it simultaneously confirmed the hopes of one and the apprehensions of the other. The tension that emerged as a consequence has permeated American culture ever since.

This chapter is particularly characterized by contrapuntal impulses because in the period under discussion critical cynicism vied with intense patriotism as responses to the prevalence (and high awareness) of mythic memories. Section I tries to indicate the extraordinary range of attitudes, positive as well as negative, concerning the role of myth in American culture. It pays special attention to controversies involving history textbooks and to the popularity of historical shrines and pilgrimages as prominent features of civil religion in the United States. It also recognizes the complex relationship of myth and regionalism by looking at the Mount Rushmore story, at persistent feelings about sectionalism and the Civil War, and at Western myths.

Section II concentrates upon patriotism during the 1920s, with special attention given to anniversary observances, the affirmation of myths and legends, hero worship, and the reasons why patriotic myths persisted despite a spate of unpatriotic, anti-heroic skepticism, and the gradual waning of ancestor worship as a cultural phenomenon.

Section III emphasizes the democratization of tradition during the 1930s, speculates about the anomaly of memory lapses in a society increasingly preoccupied with retrospection and recovering the past. It notes the expanding importance of travel in exposing greater numbers of Americans to national, regional, and local traditions. Section IV looks more closely at the pivotal years 1939–41 in terms of the institutions and processes that transmit traditions, in terms of the heartfelt resurgence of patriotism, and the reasons why Americans briefly deviated from their normative pattern of seeking to depoliticize the past, usually by fabricating a history of consensus.

I

PRIOR to World War I, some members of American society had been notably self-aware about the political and cultural complexities of native myths. According to the most familiar complaints, we did not have enough of them to sustain our creative imaginations—a woe that began with Washington Irving and continued to be voiced several generations later by Henry James. When Joel Chandler Harris of Georgia tapped a rich lode of Negro folk humor and oral traditions, he simply seemed to enrich the local-color school and American literature in general. Few people thought critically about such arcane matters as ethnic borrowing, cultural appropriation, and the implications for legends that underwent contextual transplantation. Similarly, listen to these unself-conscious words spoken at St. Paul in 1899 by the Governor of the Society of Colonial Wars in the State of Minnesota. He wanted to explain why the group so valued genealogy.

> We have found out something in regard to our ancestors which interests us, deeds of heroism, or it may be merely a humble part taken in the laying of the foundations of this Republic, half told, half hinted romances, occasionally a spicy little scandal or quarrel, but more often life histories of Christian fortitude, love, and unselfishness. These are the historic lore that genealogy furnishes, besides stimulating our interest in the notable events of that period of our country's history.[4]

At the same time Theodore Roosevelt and Woodrow Wilson both read widely but wrote divergent interpretations of the frontier and its historical as well as mythical meaning for Americans. Whereas T.R. revealed his nostalgia for the old frontier as a lost way of life, gone forever, Wilson projected an optimistic determination to have the progressive possibilities and legacies of frontier life carry forward into the twentieth century. The point is not merely that T.R. and Wilson developed different interpretations of the frontier experience, but rather that they presented to the public, without a shred of self-consciousness, divergent myths and explanations of the relationship between past experience and future prospects in the United States.[5]

In 1915 and 1916, however, a shift was manifest in essays by two contrasting individuals. Henry Cabot Lodge expressed his strong concern about myths "which masquerade as history." He made a series of concerned observations that flowed naturally from his point of departure: historical myths develop quietly and then commonly remain unchallenged for centuries; historical myths can be mischievous by distorting "important facts on which history turns and by which judgments are made." And then his most crucial point, a candidly new turn in public discourse: "The myth, or tradition, as it is sometimes called, has necessarily a touch of imagination, and imagination is almost always more fascinating than truth. The historical myth, indeed, would not exist at all if it did not profess to tell something which people, for one reason or another, like to believe." Lodge pointed out that with the passage of time it became increasingly difficult to set the record straight. The fables of Parson Weems, for example, had been "shattered again and again, but they live on in the popular mind, and nothing can extirpate them."[6]

Just a year later James Harvey Robinson, the revisionist historian at Columbia University, attacked the mythic basis for nationalistic patriotism. In retrospect his policy inferences seem logically sound, though not the historical foundation on which he based them. In a capsule history of nationalism he declared that patriotism "is a recent thing," which may seem absurd to us; yet he persuasively contended that "the chief quarrel with patriotism is its innate tendency to precipitate war with other groups upon the most trivial pretenses." It is difficult to dissent on that point.[7]

Within a few years Henry Seidel Canby expanded the laments of Lodge and Robinson into a much broader critical indictment: namely, that American education, while purportedly liberal, "looked prevailingly backward for inspiration. . . . We were linked to tradition; we were made profoundly and sincerely liberal, at least in our theories of life; but we were implored to stand pat." Canby sounded a chord that others would replay in various keys over the decades ahead. In that endless discord between tradition and progress, Canby believed that tradition had basically prevailed in the realm of American education.[8]

Between 1921 and 1927 Canby's rather sweeping complaint became particularized and politicized by charges that new U.S. history textbooks conveyed a pro-British bias and contained anti-American propaganda. Although the United States and Britain were allies in 1917–18, charges began to circulate that Americans had been lured into a needless war and that Britain was responsible for postwar economic problems.[9] The upshot was a surge of anglophobia, nationwide attempts to purge schoolbooks of any positive content regarding Great Britain, and the circulation of a pamphlet titled *Treason to American Tradition* (distributed from Boston to Los Angeles) that took a darkly conspiratorial view of the entire business. Patriotic societies distributed it and belabored school boards to scrutinize potential texts more carefully. Historians and other writers, meanwhile, bitterly resented interference by ignorant laymen and politicians who saw some possible advantage in giving John Bull a bloody nose.[10]

James Truslow Adams produced a manifesto in which he called attention to the conflict between the past as Everyman prefers it (i.e., encouraging or sustaining popular myths) and the need for accurate and professional historical writing. To Adams, a diligent historian who enjoyed a broad audience (and just happened to be an anglophile), the nature of the problem and identity of the villains seemed quite evident:

> On all sides the American historian meets organizations devoted to the glorification of the past, societies formed to celebrate the deeds of ancestors, racial groups bent on magnifying the share of certain elements in the formation of our country, "patriotic" groups bent on distorting the glorious story of human America into an allegory of the conflict between the powers of darkness and the powers of light.

Adams urged a realistic recognition that "legends have crumbled under critical examination"; but he feared that a combination of meddling politicos and Canby's tradition-oriented "democracy" would plunge the nation into intellectual confusion.[11]

Actually these kinds of contretemps were not entirely new in the 1920s; only their virulence, intensity, and nationwide configuration. Boston had a flare-up in 1888 because of complaints by the Irish there that teachers and a standard textbook were both overtly anti-Catholic. Charges that texts were "soft" on Britain had arisen from time to time; and Southerners pressured publishers to excise ugly words like "rebellion" when describing the Civil War. In every instance vested interests made a concerted effort to protect their good name and to perpetuate visions of the past that felt comfortable or comforting.[12]

In 1927 Chicago's new mayor, William Hale Thompson, launched a major offensive against pro-British history books being used in the schools. Although he made some authors very uncomfortable, including David Muzzey and Arthur M. Schlesinger, he mainly succeeded in making himself the butt of numerous jokes. The cartoon most widely reprinted used Prohibition as its point of reference. A policeman stops a suspicious-looking truck and asks the driver what he has. "Only booze," the man answers. "Drive on, brother," says the cop. "I thought it was history books." Schlesinger and others were deluged with requests from the media for interviews and for editorials "on the difficulties of a historian, if he must guide his pen to meet the requirements of 100% American school committee politicians."[13]

In addition to pro-British textbooks, anglophobes like "Big Bill" Thompson did have one other "type" of evidence that aroused their suspicions. Ever since the early twentieth century, enthusiasm had steadily emerged for the preservation and visitation of American "shrines" in England. Primarily that meant the ancestral homes (or home-places) of men like John Adams, Franklin, and Lincoln, but above all George Washington.[14]

In 1914 Washington's ancestral home, the Sulgrave Manor House, had actually been purchased by the British Peace Centenary Committee. The creation of a Sulgrave Institution with large lists of highly prominent names on its letterhead was meant to foster Anglo-American friendship. Late in 1918, moreover, the chairman of its board of governors proudly explained that "School books have been rewritten upon the basis of truth, which are about to be issued by the five leading publishers of America." The Institution also intended to support an international observance of the tercentenary of the landing of the Pilgrims, along with "the approximate anniversary of the second settlement of Virginia, which events marked the beginning of the founding of American institutions."[15]

Several of the documents that describe most fully the Sulgrave Institution's purpose specify "having presented [the Manor] to the American people as a shrine and place of pilgrimage," or, according to the president of the Colonial Dames in 1924, refer to the Washington family home "as a shrine of common pilgrimage for English and American travelers."[16] That kind of language, suggesting what has been termed civil religion, retains a certain nineteenth-century quality; and we do indeed have, for example, envelopes from the Civil War era on which Miss Liberty appears holding an American flag. Above them is the pious legend: "For Our Altars and Our Firesides."[17]

Although it has not been remarked upon, such religious language appeared throughout the interwar years, used especially (but by no means exclusively) in connection with George Washington. At the unveiling of Washington's bust at Mount Rushmore on July 4, 1930, the presiding officer referred to the site as "America's Shrine for Political Democracy"; and many people hoped that Rushmore would eventually come to be called simply "The Shrine of Democracy" (fig. 15.1). Each year when Washington's Birthday drew near, the press announced that pilgrims would be attracted to shrines associated with his life. On June 1, 1939, the Sons of the American Revolution dedicated Washington Hall at the World's Fair in New York as a "patriotic shrine for patriotic societies from all parts of the United States."[18]

Sites like Valley Forge, Jamestown, and Monticello were increasingly referred to as shrines, as were Stratford Hall, the Virginia birthplace of

15.1 Mount Rushmore with Washington and Jefferson completed. Work on the bust of Lincoln is in progress at the right (mid-1930s). Courtesy of the National Archives Trust Fund Board.

Robert E. Lee, and a five-acre plot in Indiana where Wilbur Wright began his life. Schools and academies wished to have chapels that would honor American heroes (alongside Christ) in stained glass.[19] In 1924 the Constitution and Declaration of Independence went on public display at the Library of Congress in a specially constructed marble "shrine."[20]

Four years later John D. Rockefeller, Jr., informed Reverend Goodwin that he looked forward "with keen anticipation to the day when Williamsburg shall be a national historic shrine." It had, in fact, been Goodwin's practice since at least 1926 to invoke that notion constantly and casually. In 1929 he told Henry Ford of the need for "further acquisition and preservation of memorials which witness to our historic past," and asserted that their great legacy to the future lay in "creating shrines and providing means by which ideals of our glorious past can be presented and perpetuated."[21]

Despite economic hardships and impediments to travel, undertaking pilgrimages to historic shrines seems to have achieved maximum popularity during the 1930s. Some of them became annual events, such as the Fiesta San Jacinto pilgrimage to the Alamo each April 22, or the historic home and garden pilgrimage that took place each spring in Natchez, Tennessee. Some were essentially unique events on account of the cost and logistical problems involved. That was the case in August 1936 when sixty-three members of the Louisiana Association of Acadians made a "sentimental journey" to Grand Pré, Nova Scotia, where their ancestors had been exiled by the British in 1755. Six men and fifty-seven women representing every parish in Louisiana visited Halifax, Montreal, and Toronto along their itinerary; they re-entered the United States at Niagara Falls and continued to Chicago, Dallas (to attend the Texas Centennial celebration), Houston, and finally back to Lafayette, Louisiana, their point of departure.[22]

Needless to say, a striking proportion of these pilgrimages was directed to the homesites of great men. Adult groups as well as Boy Scouts made annual trips to Theodore Roosevelt's estate at Oyster Bay on Long Island. Abraham Lincoln's tomb near Springfield, Illinois, supplied yet another magnet. And pilgrimages to Mount Vernon or else retracing Washington's 1789 trip from there to New York City became popular, especially in 1932 and 1939.[23]

Although the decade following 1922 is customarily recalled as a time when "debunking" was in vogue, most Americans actually resisted demythologizing, and the canonization of statesmen into demigods proceeded at a brisk pace. In 1923–24 a group passionately dedicated to the memory of Robert E. Lee, and determined to "memorialize" him, waged a successful public campaign to have the Lee Chapel at Washington and Lee University remain unexpanded and unaltered as a permanent shrine. In the words of the energetic Daughter of the Confederacy who led this crusade, it should be regarded as " 'a temple not made with hands,' since its builder was one who walked not after the flesh, but after the spirit."[24] Between 1923 and 1925 the Thomas Jefferson Memorial Foundation mounted its successful campaign to purchase Monticello from private owners and make it, too, a shrine.[25]

Leaders of the Sulgrave Institution began planning as early as 1924 for the bicentennial of George Washington's birth to be held in 1932. Its board of governors explained in a five-page printed resolution both the magnitude of the anniversary and their reasons for getting under way so early:

> WHEREAS, past experience has taught that it takes from five to ten years to complete fitting and adequate plans for the commemoration of outstanding historic events; and
> WHEREAS, heretofore, the celebration of epochal events has always been marred by the incompletion of preparations, monuments, etc., etc., necessitating delays in the inauguration of commemorations. . . .[26]

Between 1931 and 1933 a series of memorial busts was installed and unveiled at the old House of Delegates in the Virginia State Capitol: Thomas Jefferson, James Madison, and James Monroe in 1931; Matthew

15.2 Gutzon Borglum in 1934. Courtesy of the National Park Service.

Fontaine Maury in 1932; and Cyrus H. McCormick the following year.
The American Friends of Lafayette, an organization founded in 1932,
promptly began to make plans for the observance in 1934 of the centenary of his death. Legends about the lives of George A. Custer and Davy
Crockett continued to flourish as well.[27] By contrast, when Edgar Lee
Masters had the temerity to publish a biography critical of Abraham
Lincoln, he was not only attacked vituperatively in the press: a bill was
actually introduced in Congress that would have barred the book from
the U.S. mail! And in 1935 when Daniel Boone's role in the founding
of Kentucky was minimized at a public commemoration of the creation
of that state's legislature, the ensuing spat shattered the proceedings as
Boone devotees trotted off the stage in tears.[28]

GUTZON BORGLUM, an American-born sculptor of Danish
extraction, felt deep admiration for Abraham Lincoln and for the democratic ideals and institutions of the United States. The westward sweep
of American civilization inspired his imagination (fig. 15.2). He first
visited the Black Hills of South Dakota in September 1924, a spectacular time of year to be there, and within a year he had decided to
enshrine Washington, Jefferson, Lincoln, and Roosevelt in the massive
granite outcroppings. In October 1925 he arranged for a pageant to be
held that would symbolize the successive owners of the site. He included a Sioux warrior dressed in full regalia and various others who
impersonated French, Spanish, and English explorers. A sense of the
theatrical was literally second nature to Borglum, and he had long
contended, vociferously, that "the greatest stories of the world, the
stories of America, go unrecorded in our public parks and galleries."

Intensely patriotic (and equally egocentric), he determined to give American heroes maximum visibility and artistic permanence. Upon completing his initial visit to Harney Peak in 1924 he proclaimed that "American history shall march along that skyline."[29]

Borglum also believed that sculpture should be related to the civilization that produced it—particularly by historical and cultural information. His grand scheme for the mountain envisioned a great hall filled with exhibits composed of such data. Although he did not achieve that dream, an interesting issue arose in 1930 that caused the press to focus national attention on the project. President Coolidge had promised in 1927 that he would write an inscription to be carved for posterity: a summation of American history that would appear in gilded letters cut 5 inches deep on an entablature 80 by 120 feet in size. Borglum believed that the inscription would be visible from a distance of three miles. Neither Borglum nor the commission had specified a word limit; but when journalists began referring to the project as a 500-word history of the United States, Americans became fascinated by the problematic challenge of such terseness.[30]

Always a publicity hound, Borglum hired a public relations agency in Chicago to promote the whole affair, and its efforts succeeded in quantitative terms. Just during January of 1930 stories appeared in 317 newspapers (located in 36 states) with a total circulation in excess of 13 million. The *Chicago Tribune* decided to sponsor its own contest and offered a $1,000 prize for the best 500-word history of the United States. (A professor of American religious history at the University of Chicago won.) Cartoonists and editorial writers had a field day with the episode. The *Brooklyn Eagle* ran a cartoon showing Coolidge, dressed as a cook, stirring a huge volume of history in a pot of hot water. The caption read: "Boiling It Down." In London the *Daily Telegraph* offered only scorn: "Quite jolly must be the nation which can write its history in 500 words." Borglum, undaunted, observed that the author of Genesis had told the entire story of creation in fewer than eight hundred words. When Coolidge finally produced a partial text, emphasizing the Declaration of Independence and the Constitution, Borglum didn't like it, tactlessly insisted upon "improving" it with a heavy hand, and the altered text was published without Coolidge's approval.[31]

Predictably, this aspect of the project came utterly unravelled, no narrative got carved on Mount Rushmore, and Coolidge's capacity as a historian became a national joke. His reputation for taciturnity was enhanced, however. Asked to write the historical meaning of America ever so briefly, he wound up with a few words and no permanent inscription. Following Coolidge's death in 1933 Borglum pursued the notion of a mini-history for several more years, and managed to generate a nationwide essay contest sponsored by the Hearst newspaper syndicate. Borglum rejected the winning entry, and that apparently put an end to the matter. In 1975, however, the National Park Service erected a bronze plaque bearing the prize-winning essay from that 1935 Entablature Contest.[32]

From 1916 until 1925 Borglum had done battle with assorted and obdurate foes over his commission to carve a monument to the Confederacy and to the "tragedy of a nation" at Stone Mountain, Georgia, not far from Atlanta. The coming of World War I interrupted progress; the Stone Mountain Association, with which Borglum went through endless quarrels, needed to be reorganized in 1922, and then three years later it decided to fire Borglum. He left a completed bas-relief of Robert E. Lee (always intended as the artistic centerpiece), an unfinished relief of Stonewall Jackson, and a roughed-out rendering of Jefferson Davis. Although many Southerners expressed enthusiasm, public opinion was largely indifferent; and outside of the South people felt that it was improper to glorify traitors to the Union. Some patriotic societies in the North and West condemned the enterprise as a "memorial to disunion." According to one journalist writing in 1926, however, the monument "proclaims that the Confederate chiefs are entitled to remembrance because they possessed courage, faith, and honor." Failure to complete Stone Mountain revealed the limits of sectional reconciliation as late as the mid-1920s. The hesitant response by Congress to Borglum's plea for support was also a sign of the times.[33]

Most Southerners remained sufficiently custom bound that public sculpture and other sorts of historic memorials had to be fairly conventional in order to win their favor. In 1939, for example, when the Virginia State Art Commission selected a "modernistic and impressionistic" model for an equestrian statue of Stonewall Jackson to be erected on the battlefield at Manassas, it aroused a furor. Members of the U.D.C. and the Sons of Confederate Veterans complained that the horse was too stocky and the rider looked more like U. S. Grant than Jackson. Similar episodes occurred at regular intervals.[34]

Memories of the Confederacy, real and contrived, remained warm and ardent during the interwar years. As late as 1924 the caretaker at Monticello flew a Confederate flag above his home. Those who wrote about the experience of Johnny Reb in historical fiction most often asserted that he had fought to maintain a chivalric code against the rising dominance of materialistic values. "Not the fortunes of war, not the moral order of the universe," wrote Ellen Glasgow realistically, "but economic necessity doomed the South to defeat. In the coming industrial conquest, the aristocratic tradition could survive only as an archaic memorial." The myth of the Lost Cause lived on, however; and there is evidence that it even did so in hearts and homes north of the Mason-Dixon line.[35]

It is noteworthy that the Williamsburg restoration made such a swift transition from being initially perceived as inappropriately disruptive to becoming the saviour of a venerable Southern past. Early in 1932, for example, when the Williamsburg chapter of the U.D.C. complied with wishes of the Rockefeller organization in moving the local Confederate monument (a marble shaft) from the Palace Green to the town cemetery, a brouhaha occurred because conservative natives felt ardently that Confederate memorials should not be casually moved. Letters appeared in local papers saying that the shaft had actually been illegal, or that sufficient time had not been allowed for voices of protest to be heard. Most dramatically, on January 21, 1932, at the very spot where the monument had been located, a six-foot cross appeared. It was draped in mourning cloth and bore a placard that read: "Crucified on a cross of treachery." By 1935, however, Williamsburg had become a place for "reverent contemplation of the storied past." Some Southern myths withered but would not die. Still others actually took on new life.[36]

ALTHOUGH the American West during these same decades also perpetuated myths, they were much less likely to become a *cause célèbre,* in part because they enjoyed such appeal throughout the rest of the nation and in part because most Westerners wanted some basis for believing that certain episodes and a distinctive way of life set them apart from all others. Legends and stereotypes sprang up swiftly and they customarily went unchallenged. As one poet put it in 1934:

> *So I ask myself if I can still remember*
> *How a myth began this morning and how the people*
> *Seemed hardly to know that something was starting over.*[37]

A few iconoclasts (who published almost exclusively in Eastern journals of opinion) lamented the self-delusion that seemed to pervade their region. Carey McWilliams distributed the blame among popular fiction writers like Emerson Hough, scholars like Frederick Jackson Turner and his disciples, and the producers of romantic films. McWilliams argued that as the last American region to be settled, the West,

coming into self-consciousness, found that it had a difficult problem to solve. How was it to dispose of the outlandish Myth about its origins, attributes, and identity? It was necessary, obviously, either to accept the legend or to repudiate it harshly and irrevocably. With childlike ingenuousness, the West not only accepted the legend, but naïvely built it out to epic proportions. To the mythological figures of the presettlement period, it added the Cowboy, the Miner, the Engineer, the Homesteader, and the Tramp. It avidly seized upon the last vestiges of its romantic origins for profitable preservation and established traditions which flourish in the Pendleton and Cheyenne Rodeos, and the California Fiestas of today.[38]

For several decades Bernard DeVoto bewailed the relentless process of distortion. "We see ourselves not as we are," he wrote, "but as the myths have made us out to be." One fantasy that especially vexed DeVoto concerned the West as "the last great stand of American individualism—the place where a man dares to be himself against the world." From his perspective, that myth simply violated historical realities; but his hot temper may very well have caused him to overreact. "The West has never been individualistic and is not now," he insisted. "In the nature of things, no horde of individualists could have existed in the desert to which the pioneers came. Only a completely cooperative group, who shared the rigors of the land and banded together to resist them, could have survived."[39]

When DeVoto returned to this general theme in 1934 he challenged the enduring myths of the Western frontier as a place that has "meant escape, relief, freedom, sanctuary." After carefully explaining the realities that lay behind these distortions, however, DeVoto then turned the tables in order to indicate that myth-making worked in perverse ways. "Looted, betrayed, sold out," he snarled, "the Westerner is a man whose history has been just a series of large-scale jokes. That comicality has helped to form the image which the dominant East has chosen to recognize." On balance this may very well have been DeVoto's most affectionate, almost sentimental statement about the role of his native region in national culture: "The West is the loveliest and most enduring of our myths, the only one that has been universally accepted." By 1946 he had returned to his earlier emphasis: the Western propensity for self-delusion by believing all the fantastic qualities ascribed to frontier America by ignorant outsiders.[40]

I I

COMING to terms with American culture in the 1920s and 1930s can be problematic because generalizations are hazardous and ambiguities abound. In 1932 Albert Jay Nock called it "another era of pseudo-patriotic flatulence," and so it was. Social critics enjoyed a field day at the expense of super-patriots; ancestor worship began to wane, gradually became less fashionable, and less pretentious even where it clearly persisted; and the democratization of tradition continued to be manifest in a variety of ways. Before turning to the "new realism," however, we must take into account the varied phenomena that provoked Nock's scorn.[41]

Although the Pilgrim Tercentenary in 1920–21 aroused genuine interest and enthusiasm, we now know that it created considerable resentment among Southerners who felt put upon by perennial New England claims of primacy. We also know that a fair amount of sham lay behind the facade of authenticity and remembrance. In 1820 Daniel

Webster had predicted that a century hence "the voice of acclamation and gratitude, commencing on the Rock of Plymouth, shall be transmitted through millions of the sons of the Pilgrims, till it lose itself in the murmurs of the Pacific seas." For the tercentenary celebration, therefore, Governor Coolidge of Massachusetts put through a telephone call to Governor Stephens of California, while thousands in Plymouth listened—to Coolidge only. Stephens had in fact gone hunting that day, and not-so-silent Cal actually spoke to Stephens's secretary; but the throng assembled at Plymouth never knew that they were observing a fraud rather than Webster's prophecy being truly realized. Sometimes authenticity must defer to public relations.[42]

Genuine as well as contrived anniversaries continued to be observed during the decades that followed. If success and failure are measured in terms of attendance, sales, and enthusiasm, then there seems to have been no clear-cut pattern. The Sesquicentennial of Independence held at Philadelphia in 1926 turned out to be a fiasco. Despite extensive exhibits, events, and fanfare, only 10 percent of the 50 million visitors who were anticipated actually showed up. Poor planning and wretched weather did not help; but public interest seems to have been muted in any case.[43] The low degree of interest is all the more puzzling because nationalistic enthusiasm for historical Americana, as we saw in chapters ten and eleven, could not have been more in vogue during 1926.

By the end of the twenties proud provincialism seemed to generate greater esprit than leaving one's community to celebrate some national anniversary in a distant location. Local commemorations thrived for a decade. In 1930 the Pavonia Tercentenary aroused interest in the early Dutch settlements of northern New Jersey: Bayonne, Hoboken, Weehawken, North Bergen, and Secaucus. The bicentennial of Patrick Henry's birth had its locus in Hanover County, Virginia, in July 1936. In addition to concerts, colonial balls, historical tours, and exhibits, the high point involved a "great historical pageant" depicting the life and times of Henry and involving a cast of more than one thousand people. It was a sign of the times that Congress appropriated $10,000 to defray expenses. William C. Bullitt, a lineal descendant of Patrick Henry and American ambassador at that time to the Soviet Union, represented President Roosevelt on the big day at the county courthouse.[44]

In May 1937 a proud Committee for the Celebration of the Tenth Anniversary of the First New York–Paris Flight sponsored tributes to Charles Lindbergh at places ranging from the Waldorf-Astoria to Little Falls, Minnesota. Two years later Oklahomans sought to "recapture a romantic past" by observing the half century that had passed since the opening of Oklahoma Territory to white men and women. These kinds of local festivities became prominent features on the field of memory during the 1930s.[45]

Ancestor worship, which had been such a prominent craze at the turn of the century, had become less intense as a generalized phenomenon by the 1920s, yet it clearly remained a social force that motivated high-minded people to participate on diverse commemorative occasions.[46] As with the growing appeal of local observances, however, acts of historic preservation or tradition-oriented piety increasingly occurred on account of a personal sense of devotion to forebears. Thus a descendant of Alexander Hamilton played a prominent part in saving his New York country home, the Grange, in 1924; and two years later Philip A. Bruce wrote a characteristic notice concerning a judge who loved Virginia passionately, not only because he had passed his life there but because "his ancestors had passed their lives there." Judge Watson might easily have been a character in one of Ellen Glasgow's novels.[47]

Beginning as early as the mid-1920s, however, iconoclastic statements started to appear that indicated a trend away from ancestor worship in some quarters. Chauncey Brewster Tinker produced an essay, "On the Importance of Being Indifferent to One's Ancestors," in which he acknowledged that his lineage went back a long way in New England history through undistinguished Connecticut farmers. A decade later Constance Rourke made the same point in a more generalized way.[48] William Faulkner, meanwhile, published *Absalom, Absalom!* (1936), in which he punctured Southern myths of pure bloodlines. Charles Bon, the illegitimate son of Thomas Sutpen, has Negro blood; and Thomas's legitimate son, Henry, has an illegitimate half-Negro sister, Clytemnestra Sutpen.

Robert Gwathmey made exactly the same point in a striking picture titled *Ancestor Worship* (fig. 15.3). Gwathmey (1903–1988), who came of an old Virginia family, decided to make a deliberate statement and wrote of his painting:

The broken-down aristocrat stands in front of his Georgian wall, assuming the gesture of his forebear's portrait on that wall. Looking beyond are two women preoccupied with grave stones. The past, if you will.

Then there are three little boys, alike in every way, except that there is gradation in complexion. Miscegenation if you will. The last figures I fell upon estimated that 70% of southern blacks had a degree of white blood.[49]

Although ancestor worship gradually became less fashionable, other modes of patriotism and piety persisted. In 1922 Representative Benjamin L. Fairchild introduced a bill making any form of disrespect for the United States flag a crime; and in 1930 calls were heard for the formulation of an official flag etiquette. Between 1924 and 1930 the United States Flag Association became quite active and devoted inordinate amounts of time and energy to the collection of materials for a "manual of patriotism" prepared for the "boys and girls of America" and a Flag

15.3 Robert Gwathmey, *Ancestor Worship* (1945), oil on canvas. Courtesy of
Anne Katherine Gwathmey.

Temple designed to display a "Patriotic Panorama." Its leaders, who
included Charles Evans Hughes, Governor Al Smith of New York, and
Samuel Gompers, sought the advice of professional historians in selecting twenty-one potentially canonical incidents that illustrated national
development in terms of "American ideals, traditions, principles, and
institutions."[50]

Reproductions or modified imitations of Independence Hall had appeared at regular intervals following the first one at the 1893 Columbian Exposition in Chicago, a structure that served there as the
Pennsylvania State Building. Other replicas appeared subsequently at
the Jamestown Exposition in 1907, the Panama-Pacific Exposition at
San Francisco in 1915 (complete with the actual Liberty Bell displayed
inside), and on various university campuses: Johns Hopkins in 1915,
Dartmouth in 1926–28, four others in 1930 alone, the Henry Ford
Museum in Dearborn, and then during the 1930s diversification into
prisons and savings banks as well as additional academic administration

buildings. Because of the depression they were sometimes referred to as "stripped colonial"; but they indicated an on-going fondness for Independence Hall as an institutional motif (as well as resistance to architectural innovation).[51]

During the mid-1920s American journals of opinion that sought to please the self-satisfied middle and upper classes ran diverse essays explicitly in praise of national myths. Some of these pieces seemed a bit defensive at their point of departure, as though well aware that "debunking" enjoyed current appeal in certain circles. One piece in *Scribner's,* for example, started out this way:

> A nation without myths would be impoverished in a most impor-
> tant element of culture, but it does not thereby follow that a
> nation may not have too many. . . . We treat them with more
> respect than we used to, calling them more often than not a
> legitimate part of a nation's history.

The author insisted that it would be altogether American for myths to "flourish among us," and boasted that for such a young society "we are doing pretty well in the matter of myths." Legends pertaining to national origins were vital, and "good hero myths" seemed well suited "to tell the young of the tribe around the campfire. The myths of a people have ever been a potent force."[52]

The *Saturday Evening Post* ran a steady stream of essays in defense of American character as exemplified by native myths. Popular journalists like John Erskine took up the cudgels against "debunkers" and insisted that we must revere our heroes. He suggested that antipathy to myth was a "strange obsession; nothing is more deeply rooted in our nature than the myth-making faculty, and perhaps nothing is more wholesome." If we have appropriate affection for native heroes, he suggested, "we then improve their memory by seeing in them deeper and deeper virtues, and by mercifully forgetting those weaknesses of theirs which were their handicaps in life, and which seem irrelevant to their fame." Erskine excoriated those who wished to substitute new traditions for tried and true ones, and insisted that "our instinct is correct that all books which revise downward an ideal memory have in them the principle of defect and poverty." He concluded by asserting that historical myths fulfilled an instinctive need: "To think of all myths as a deception which nature plays upon us is to set up a fundamental antagonism between us and our minds."[53]

WHAT MAKES this era so interesting, however, is that romantic patriots and apologists were responding quite vehemently to cynics, highbrow critics, and academic skeptics. The dialogue really began to heat up in 1920–21 when H. L. Mencken and George Jean Nathan mocked the mythologizing of American history that had been perpetrated by George Creel's wartime propaganda committee in 1917–1919. By 1923 James Truslow Adams heralded his unhappiness with the patriotic organizations then so active in promoting myths and "false legends" concerning glorious moments and heroes in the nation's past. One year later an important essay in *The Century* insisted that a country could not simply command loyalty: it had to attract and deserve it. "Patriotism is a result rather than a cause of a sound national life," Glenn Frank explained. "The professional patriots put the cart before the horse." Fred Lewis Pattee, a pioneer in the field of American literary criticism, lamented in 1924 that in all the available histories of U.S. literature there is "always the repetition of a standard series of well-worn myths."[54]

No fewer than three quite separate yet simultaneous tendencies can be discerned in the fifteen years that followed. The least provocative though probably the most pervasive involved a repudiation of the "debunkers," a strenuous affirmation that national heroes and myths made social cohesion more meaningful, followed by the perpetuation or even the creation of community myths in many of the post office and other public murals painted by New Deal–supported artists.[55]

The second trend involved an expansion of the negative judgment already noted, a point of view increasingly shared by cultural critics like Lewis Mumford, poets like William Carlos Williams, historians like Charles A. Beard (fig. 15.4), civil servants active in historic preservation like Leicester B. Holland, and influential journalists like Bernard DeVoto, who informed a friend that American history "is the most romantic of all histories. It began in myth and has developed through three centuries of fairy stories."[56] Variants of that view gained increasing numbers of articulate adherents, such as Carl Sandburg, who insisted that "the reality is better than the myth"; and Talbot Hamlin, a distinguished architectural historian, who told John Dos Passos that "American History as usually taught is extraordinarily full of pure myth, unfounded conventions, and artificial categories."[57]

A third trend—certainly the most complex—involved men and women of discernment who somehow managed to take *both* sides on this issue, sometimes by changing their position over time but more often by coming down on one side or the other depending upon the writer or situation to which they were responding. That was true of artist Grant Wood, who produced a series of droll paintings that effectively demythicized American history (such as *Paul Revere's Ride* [1931], *Daughters of Revolution* [1932], and *Parson Weems' Fable* [1939]), yet accepted the functional importance of myths to a democracy.[58]

Stephen Vincent Benét, the poet and storyteller, supplies a similar example (fig. 15.5). Although he loved American history and traditions, he wanted to bring them down to earth but also make them attractive

15.4   Charles A. Beard (n.d., c. 1915). Courtesy of the Division of Prints and Photographs, Library of Congress.

and meaningful to the populace at large. "It is worthy to assemble facts," he asserted in 1939, "to put truth in the face of legend, to investigate impartially, to throw new light on an old problem." The international conflict that swiftly became manifest brought Benét to believe that national myths must be taken seriously and be deployed by those who could do so constructively.[59]

Finally there is the case of Constance Rourke, vexed because Van Wyck Brooks frequently declared that the United States had no myths and hence no cultural texture.* Rourke believed that Americans had created a great store of myths, which she found revealing and felt determined to record. Although she located the rise of this tendency in the antebellum period, Rourke never developed a genuinely historical explanation of the phenomenon. It seemed to satisfy her that establishing the creation and perpetuation of myths by the folk was vital in order to get at the true meaning of tradition in the United States.[60] Nevertheless, James Truslow Adams's popularization of the notion of an "American dream" annoyed Rourke because it seemed to her a contrived

---

*"We have no myths," he had written, "there is nothing childlike in our past, and when we look to our ancestors to help us we find them almost as grown up and self-conscious as ourselves." Brooks, *The Wine of the Puritans* (1908). Between 1926 and 1934, however, Brooks made almost a complete turnabout.

15.5   Soss Melik, *Stephen Vincent Benét* (1939), charcoal on paper. Courtesy of the National Portrait Gallery, Smithsonian Institution, Washington, D.C.

rather than an authentic myth. Other writers and scholars, meanwhile, lavished praise upon Adams for what seemed to them a most felicitous and uplifting notion.[61]

Within each region, and at any given time, one cannot help being impressed by the absence of consensus on these matters. A Southern novelist with an abiding affection for history, Ellen Glasgow, might observe disparagingly that a particular fictional character, just like her native Virginia and the entire region, was blithely "unaware of the changes about them, clinging, with passionate fidelity, to the ceremonial forms of tradition." Meanwhile Stark Young, another prolific Southern writer, heaped scorn on Henry Ford as an exemplar of the nostalgia of false consciousness—an oblique way for Young to say that, unlike the industrialized North, genuine vestiges of the Old South were worth preserving.[62]

Some myths persisted because a cohesive group, like the Mormons, shared some purposeful need that the legends and traditions fulfilled. Similarly, Zora Neale Hurston did not mince words when she proposed to W. E. B. Du Bois the creation of a cemetery for the "illustrious Negro dead." Don't bother with a chapel, she wrote. "Let there be a hall of meeting, and let the Negro sculptors and painters decorate it with scenes from our own literature and life. Mythology and all."[63]

Some fables, like that of the Kensington Rune Stone in Minnesota, persisted because of ethnic pride and the inability of scholarly iconoclasts to affect more than a few like-minded souls. Still other fables, such as the spurious location and architectural style of Wakefield (George Washington's birthplace), persisted because National Park Service personnel were so embarrassed by their collusion in the foolish enterprise that they would not inform the public just how phony the site really was.[64]

During the winter of 1936–37, when the Betsy Ross House got refurbished in Philadelphia and was placed on a canonical list of historical shrines, a few critics threw fits over the "perpetuation of the traditional and mythical." People called attention to the lack of any evidence that Ross had hand-made the first Stars and Stripes. But to no avail. The author of one representative rebuttal asked why there was "anything wrong with perpetuating the traditional and mythical? It seems to me that we in the United States have too few traditions and myths, as it is, to go about destroying them." That appears to have been the dominant sentiment in the realm of popular culture; yet a fair number of educated patricians supported it as well.[65]

So too, in diverse ways, did writers of fiction who hoped to reach the broadest possible public. A romantic author like Hervey Allen adhered closely to mythic formulas. A realist like James T. Farrell believed that the sense of historical mission was fading in the United States. And correspondence among writers of fiction as well as folklore Americana contained dialogues concerning the proper tone for children's books "centered about this set-up of a real American mythology."[66]

Richard H. Pells has provided an insightful explanation for the limits of myth criticism during the Great Depression, despite the recognition by so many that Americans had long been a self-deceiving nation of myth-makers: "What began as an effort to reconcile the individual to society ended with an indiscriminate celebration of the family, the group, the region, and the nation. In the process, the intellectual's desire to participate in the affairs of his country drove him to treat ideas not as tools of inquiry and analysis but as weapons or myths in the contest for popular approval."[67] The altered nature of myth in relation to American memory and culture was even more complex than that, however, as we shall see in the section that follows.

III

ALONGSIDE the simultaneity of contradictory tendencies during these two decades, some irreversible shifts can also be discerned. The cerebral cynicism of the 1920s that fostered the production of iconoclastic history and biography declined after 1929, partially in response to vociferous condemnation of books or essays that affected such a tone. At just about the same time, many of the so-called expatriates of the lost generation decided to return home. Matthew Josephson recalled in retrospect that "a great eagerness to visit Juggernaut in his native habitat seized me." Two sentences from Josephson's memoir provide a clearer if more prosaic explanation: "Although I had traveled about Europe a good deal I had really not seen enough of my own country, and was now resolved to do something about it. We talked much in those days of 'rediscovering America' or 'accepting her' as if one had much choice. . . . Many voices, native and foreign, clashed in intermittent debate over the country's destiny."[68]

It is important to note that these trends began prior to the crash in October 1929. Economic downturns do affect culture and commemorations, but indirectly and broadly rather than immediately or palpably. Simply to observe the Centennial Exposition of 1876 or the Columbian White City in 1893 or the enthusiastic bicentennial of George Washington in 1932, one would scarcely realize that one major depression was fitfully ending (1876), another just starting (1893), and a third nearly hitting rock bottom (1932).

Observers who cared about American culture, however, did comment upon the steady and irreversible transformation of the landscape—human, built, and natural—and the implications of those changes for the spiritual character of American life. One writer remarked in 1930 that the "bleak little churches are gone from all but a few rural waysides. . . . But they have expanded into the big community churches . . . that attempt, in the old spirit, to centre in themselves the social activities of the community." (See Paul Sample's *Church Supper*, fig. 12.2.) And people responded to these transformations in diverse ways. In 1929 Robert Weeks de Forest called the American Wing of the Met "an aesthetic shrine." A character in Ellen Glasgow's *A Sheltered Life* observed that "it does seem funny . . . that the less religion people have, the more they seem to desire it in their ancestors."[69]

President Roosevelt explicitly gave voice to such sentiments on several occasions. In June 1936, for instance, when he attended a religious service in Rockport, Arkansas, he offered a succinct homily on the religious tradition in American frontier settlements and westward expansion. He combined certainty about what once had been with the hope that some element of that legendary faith might endure into the future.

> I always remember that in the earliest days of the white settlement of North America, in the days of the landing at Plymouth, the colonization of Jamestown and the founding of New Amsterdam, the first thing that the earliest colonists did when they set foot on shore was to hold a religious service. It seemed to be in our American blood. And so, as the Nation developed and as men moved across the Alleghenies and across the Mississippi, religion went hand in hand with them.[70]

Roosevelt's frequent exhortations that Americans should cherish their customs and collective memories typify a persistent theme throughout this period. Willa Cather, Edgar Lee Masters, and Wallace Stevens made it a motif of their prose and poetry.[71] Eugene V. Debs and other public figures drew upon memories of an earlier, more pastoral America.[72] Walter Lippmann wanted to "preserve the rich texture of memory," and Carl Becker explained that "the chief value of history is that it is an extension of the personal memory, and an extension which masses of people can share, so that it becomes, or would ideally become the memory of a nation, or of humanity."[73]

What actually took place seems to have been persistently disappointing, however, and it surfaces in the form of a frequently repeated lament during the interwar years. "It is the duty of an American to have a long memory," declared the biographer and essayist Ernest Boyd in 1926, "and once again he is caught in the neglect of his duty." The Oregon Trail Centennial in 1930 prompted the *Saturday Evening Post* to criticize "a public that always takes its past for granted," a theme that various writers who hoped to reach a broad readership voiced on numerous occasions.[74]

This phenomenon was markedly acute in relation to the economic depression of the 1930s. Life histories recorded by the Federal Writers' Project reveal the extent to which activist women were omitted from both personal and public memories of the labor union movement. Studs Terkel has documented with poignant detail the tendency for working-class as well as middle-class people to repress or even genuinely forget particulars of the prolonged and problematic period they had lived through. In some instances they did so deliberately in order to "protect" their children. In many other cases their purpose seems to have been self-protection: an effort to insulate themselves against painful or shameful recollections. "It wasn't as if it was a memory," said one person Terkel interviewed, "but an open wound."[75]

Carl Sandburg surely had just these impulses in mind when he wrote "I Am the People, the Mob":

> *When I, the People, learn to remember, when I, the*
> *People, use the lessons of yesterday and no*
> *longer forget who robbed me last year, who*
> *played me for a fool—. . . .*[76]

In one sense, the efforts by Sandburg and others to politicize memory were an aberration from American custom (except in crisis times), as we shall see in the next section; yet in another sense his exhortation to avoid amnesia recurred across class lines. In speeches to many different groups, Kenneth Chorley, the president of Colonial Williamsburg, asked rhetorically whether the patriots of Revolutionary times were dead or asleep. "Do they live in history? Some so live—but wander aimlessly through its pages . . . exiles in a land of fleeting memory." Van Wyck Brooks employed similar language from the 1930s onward, and Sol Bloom's speeches on commemorative occasions sought to cajole his audiences as "patriotic Americans conversant with the rich treasure of history, tradition and memory that has come down to us with the years."[77]

The annual observance of Memorial Day late each May elicited endless and predictable incantations concerning the imperatives of memory and remembrance. Every so often, however, a speaker used the occasion to reiterate or reinforce the kinds of sentiments that we have been noticing. In 1937, for example, a preacher at New York's Cathedral of St. John the Divine warned a large crowd that "one of the weaknesses of our day is the neglect of memorials. The present bulks too large. It is fashionable today to forget the past. There are many foolish people who feel that they must date everything from the present and that there is nothing to be learned from the past."[78]

However platitudinous those words may sound, they were indicative of a steady swing of opinion in a politically moderate and tradition-oriented direction during the mid- and later 1930s. People who had been radicals not long before now felt a strong need to protect democracy against attacks from the extreme left as well as from the right. Cultural populism for patriotic purposes was in vogue by 1937. While Constance Rourke highlighted the "people's past," Archibald MacLeish wrote about "The Tradition of the People."[79]

The democratization of tradition, a transformation that began earlier, as we have seen, accelerated its pace during the decade following 1929 and we encounter diverse manifestations of it. First, historic figures whose stock had not previously been particularly high—such as Tom Paine, Roger Williams, and Paul Revere—achieved a prominence that had been denied them when they seemed excessively fanatical or merely middling in social status. As Esther Forbes wrote to her editor while working on the prize-winning biography of Paul Revere: "He represents a typical and important type of man about which very little is written. I mean the simple artizan. . . . [Revere] worked with his hands all his life."[80]

Second, genealogy became even more accessible as a result of new organizations and publications designed to broaden interest and prospective clientele. Quite obviously the Institute of American Genealogy, the *Journal of American Genealogy,* and the *Handbook of American Genealogy* were commercial ventures; but they made the process less exclusive and less closely tied to membership in archly patriotic societies. The American Historical Society, Inc., Publishers, declared on its letterhead in 1934: "Genealogical Service with Cited Authority." The enterprise published works of history, biography, genealogy, and heraldry. It shared a building on Eighth Avenue in New York with the National Americana Society, Inc., which specialized in publishing records pertaining to seventeenth- and eighteenth-century families, a service that helped to facilitate the work of genealogists.[81]

Third, fresh expressions of interest in ordinary folk, family lore, and everyday life became manifest. Photographic essays that appeared in popular magazines featured the contents of an attic in an old home, a nineteenth-century spinning wheel, a device for skeining yarn, and a child's rocker. New history books designed for children appeared. Short and unpretentious histories of small communities were written and circulated within the community, often in a format other than formal printing, typed or mimeographed.[82]

Fourth, there was less emphasis upon heroic individualism and more on the collective efforts of groups. In 1936 the Northwest Territory Celebration Commission arranged for Gutzon Borglum to prepare a memorial or monument in which "the grouping should represent, that is convey the impression of a *number*, a section of a body of people. The *Northwest* was a mass movement, not two or three adventurers." A stone monument already stood in Marietta, Ohio, honoring General Arthur St. Clair, the territory's first governor. But most citizens of the community did not even know that it existed; and "many other governors have been inaugurated and have gone into the limbo of forgotten things." The time had come for homage to the many thousands of anonymous pioneers.[83]

When public sculpture enjoyed its greatest vogue, from the 1880s to the 1920s, historical heroes and symbolic figures like Victory or Civic Virtue had predominated. The commissions that resulted from the Ferguson Monument Fund, established in Chicago by a lumberman in 1906, are instructive: Fountain of the Great Lakes (1913), Statue of the Republic (1918), Alexander Hamilton (1918), Illinois Centennial Statue (1918), Eugene Field (1922), Fountain of Time (1922), George Washington (1925), and Père Marquette (1926). Then a subtle yet discernible shift began. Bridge Houses (1928) honored the early settlers of Chicago. The Bowman and the Spearman (1928) honored Native Americans. And Triton Fountain (1931) commemorated John Ericsson and the coming of Swedish-Americans as a group.[84]

It became increasingly apparent after World War I that successful public sculpture needed to be civic in a non-partisan way, but above all it had to be non-controversial. Starting in 1930, "public sculpture" in the broadest conceivable sense became less allegorical and more functional. Its purpose was not so much to perpetuate myths as it was to inspire or assist the process of remembrance while directly facilitating people's needs. Hence the building of new bridges and highways, often with memorial and historical markers, became a kind of surrogate for conventional public sculpture. By 1930 it was possible to reach Mount Rushmore by automobile; and by 1937 there were three main roads leading to it, each of them hard-surfaced.[85]

In 1933 the George Rogers Clark Sesquicentennial Commission of the United States and its counterpart organization for the state of Indiana invited numerous guests to come to Vincennes for exercises in commemoration of the 150th anniversary of the Peace of Paris terminating the War for Independence. The highlight of this occasion involved dedicating a new interstate bridge "with its monumental approach in the memorial grounds," and sealing the cornerstone of a building commemorating the acquisition of the Old Northwest.[86]

Early in 1935 Congress approved the possible construction of a memorial boulevard linking the three national shrines of Mount Vernon, the Lincoln Memorial, and the Gettysburg Battlefield (an odd project meant to be seventy-five miles long and costing nearly $7 million). By October 1935, however, improved highways (like Route 90) that ran along the Gulf coast connected St. Augustine all the way west to San Diego, thereby making the Old Spanish Trail much more accessible to tourists. When Texas celebrated its centennial in 1936, special note was taken of this extensive and historic link-up across the southern United States. The previous year Wisconsin observed the centennial of its Old Military Road, which had really been the crucial mode of facilitating settlement in the interior of that territory.[87]

If the coming of the automobile permanently altered the face of pastoral and pre-industrial America, the automobile and its attendant modes of access, highways and bridges, made it possible for vastly increased numbers of Americans to see historic sites and national monuments. Back in 1916 George Francis Dow of Salem had worried that the advent of tourism would result in superficial visitation patterns, hasty impressions, and consequent distortions of history and memory. In several respects he may have been correct; but within a quarter of a century sheer access to the American past and topographical wonders had undeniably been democratized.[88]

The symbolic culmination of this connection between tradition and travel occurred in mid-April 1939 when a sizable group, including actors in eighteenth-century costumes, put on a "re-enactment pageant" to commemorate George Washington's historic journey from Mount Vernon to Manhattan in order to be inaugurated and establish the new national government. The group travelled in a period coach, followed the first President's route as closely as possible, and stopped in each city along the way to achieve maximum visibility and be received by patriotic groups and government officials. The venture was jointly sponsored by the New York World's Fair Corporation, the U.S. Constitution Sesquicentennial Commission, the D.A.R., the S.A.R., and other societies. When the entourage left Mount Vernon, the cartoonist portraying Washington spoke to the nation over NBC Radio, and cameras recorded the colorful scene.[89]

Although the public response was generally positive, some people protested the prolonged ceremonial stop in Washington, D.C., because that city had not existed in 1789. Others who lived between Baltimore and Wilmington felt cheated because the actors covered their stretch by bus rather than horse-drawn coach in order to remain on schedule (fig. 15.6). At Princeton University some students shouted "rude" comments at George Washington, and rumors circulated about a plot to

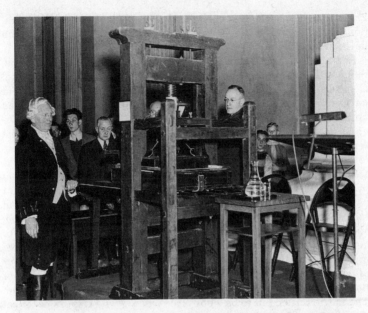

15.6   The George Washington inaugural entourage visiting the Franklin Institute in Philadelphia, April 1939. From the Century of Progress-World Fair Collection, Yale University Library, Manuscripts and Archives.

steal his coach. By April 24, however, when Washington and his party enjoyed a ticker-tape parade up Fifth Avenue, some 3 million people had viewed this mini-pageant, almost as many as had lived in the entire United States in 1789. On May 6 a five-year-old named Robert E. Lee Williamson, representing the National Society of Children of the American Revolution, presented the first historical collection to the museum of Washington relics housed in Washington Hall at the World's Fair. That brought three consecutive weeks of neo-Federal quaintness to a close.[90]

Editorial comments noted similarities between 1939 and 1789, "a period of doubt and depression [when] Washington himself was filled with forebodings." They remarked most extensively, however, on the dramatic transformations that had occurred in technology. Whereas the re-enactment pageant had taken eight days, for example, the trip could have been made by airplane in two and a half hours.[91] Ever since the 1880s, when use of the camera began to be commonplace, technology had started to enhance the potential of memory—both personal and public. The number of people who brought cameras to the Centennial at New York in late April 1889 was absolutely unprecedented, and the police were extremely solicitous in assisting individuals with cameras to get through crowds in order to have unobstructed views. The *New York*

Times stated that "the photographic records of the three days' celebration will be as ample as the written." That marked a major transition in the recording of American history.[92]

By the 1920s various sorts of groups began to contemplate the preparation of historical films for use in the schools. In 1942 the Library of Congress initially considered radio programs and films as means of enhancing its capacity to distribute information; and that same year an Eastman film called *Eighteenth Century Life in Williamsburg, Virginia,* set in 1757, was made and first shown at Rockefeller Center. Its reception was extremely favorable. As the *New York Sun* put it, "moving pictures can make ordinarily dry museum material come alive."[93]

No other medium could approach the impact of film in conveying images of the American past to a mass audience. Although a fair amount has now been written on the subject, several points cannot be stressed too strongly. First, for every phenomenal success, such as *Gone With the Wind,* many other films were swiftly forgotten, and some turned out to be absolute disasters. A producer like Charles Ray hoped to achieve great appeal with costume dramas. In order to make *The Courtship of Miles Standish* in 1923, for example, he built a full-size reconstruction of the *Mayflower* at an expense of $65,000, very extravagant for that time. The movie turned out to be a box-office fiasco. Frank Capra's historical and patriotic films did far better during the 1930s because he always arranged for upbeat endings—correctly assuming that that would please the populace. When John Ford converted historical novels into films, he arranged the content to suit his own conservative and chauvinistic predilections. However romanticized and non-credible *Gone With the Wind* may seem to us, such Southerners as the president-general of the U.D.C. felt that it was "wonderfully faithful to the traditions of the South." Americans in other regions do not seem to have disputed that belief.[94]

It is all too easy to overlook the likelihood that in many situations the democratization of tradition could have retrospective rather than radical implications. When John Steinbeck wrote *The Grapes of Wrath* (1939), his sympathies were clearly with the Okies. Among the statements that that widely read novel sought to make were two which are related: even poor people have histories, and in their own way they understand that perfectly well. When the migrants are loading their jalopies for the rugged trek to California, they are told they have no space for such mementoes of the past as letters, old hats, china dolls, and photos. That reality brings a sense of despair, because they "knew the past would cry to them in coming days. . . . 'How can we live without our lives? How will we know it's us without our past?' "[95]

15.7   Jo Davidson, *Carl Sandburg* (1939), bronze. Courtesy of the National
Portrait Gallery, Smithsonian Institution, Washington, D.C.

I V

IN RETROSPECT, 1939 seems to have marked a clear turning
point in the history of American culture as well as international affairs,
and their transformations were quite clearly connected. First, note just
a few of the landmarks. Carl Sandburg published all four volumes of
Abraham Lincoln: The War Years in 1939 (fig. 15.7). Gutzon Borglum
essentially brought his work on Mount Rushmore to completion. Earl
Robinson introduced his "Ballad for Americans," a cantata for baritone
solo and mixed chorus, on the radio. E. P. Conkle's *Prologue to Glory,*
a hit play about Abraham Lincoln and Ann Rutledge that was fostered
by the Federal Theatre Project and enjoyed considerable success in
1938, moved on to Broadway and then to the World's Fair in May 1939.
Abe Lincoln had unquestionably emerged as the populist hero of the
depression era.[96]

Simultaneously, colleges and universities began to offer courses in
American Studies in which young people would find out about "American traditions and problems." The dean of one college explained that
"we ought to learn and formulate very carefully the nature of Americanism, or the American way of living which we are saying we wish to
defend and preserve." In 1939 the Metropolitan Museum of Art in New
York City mounted an immensely popular exhibit titled "Life in America." It marked the first time that genre paintings had ever been used
to provide a kind of visual historical narrative. And Francis H. Taylor,
about to become that Museum's dynamic director, called for the democratization of American museums generally. The time had come, he
declared, for museums to fulfill their educational responsibilities.[97]

For just about a decade notions of patriotism, tradition, and national character had been very much in the air, but alongside assorted competing notions. Suddenly the former group became far more prominent in public discourse, along with "Americanism," because of a rapidly intensified sense that democracy was being threatened both at home and abroad.[98] Even as the World's Fair in New York glorified democracy, both as a government and as a way of life, sophisticated writers who had until recently felt jaded in a suitably fashionable way began sending one another the most extraordinary, earnest, and apprehensive letters. In 1939 Dorothy Thompson told James Truslow Adams that she and several others had suddenly decided that "a document should be formulated which would be an acceptance of the challenge to freedom and democracy, a sort of credo, as clear and precise as the Communist Manifesto. We took the Declaration of Independence and attempted to re-phrase it to the present situation." Thompson and her friends set to work gathering signatories to their manifesto.[99]

Within a year the frenetic pace of concern intensified, and such people as Helen Keller were collecting money, rather than signatures, to be used on behalf of the American Rescue Ship Mission. Keller's letters were redolent with the language of American heritage and history, of Lexington and Concord.[100] James T. Flexner sent Esther Forbes a letter that was representative yet remarkable:

> In these days when European civilization is tearing itself apart much of the torch of culture is being handed to us, but we cannot carry it on adequately merely on the basis of the European tradition which has developed such cancers. We must explore our own past to find other, stronger roots based on a continental federation, on a peaceful mingling of races, on a hardy and unsophisticated democracy that grew naturally from a hardy and rough environment. Of course it is possible to overstress the idiginous [sic] parts of our tradition, but certainly it is permissable to dwell on them now since they have for so long been neglected. What we need, I feel, is an intelligent patriotism, based not on fear or the desire to hear the eagle scream, but on a factual re-evaluation of our civilization.[101]

In the autumn of 1940 James Boyd, the engaging historical novelist and essayist from North Carolina, recruited an outstanding cast of writers to prepare a series of radio scripts concerned with the roots and development of an American citizen's fundamental rights. Unsponsored and unpaid, this group called itself the Free Company and took as its essential mission a dramatic presentation of the Bill of Rights. "Our only purpose," Boyd explained, "is to remind people, in this hour of danger, how precious the American way of life is." The writers felt determined to reach the broadest possible audience and by May 1941 there were, indeed, more than 5 million faithful listeners. Despite the self-evident "Americanism" of the scripts, however, more conservative listeners and the Hearst papers disliked the internationalism and liberal tone of the programs. The Guardians of American Education, for instance, informed Attorney General Francis Biddle that the Free Company seemed anti-American! Needless to say, civil liberties groups loved the broadcasts; and William Saroyan stated that the group's purpose "is to help every kind of American to re-awaken to the privilege of dwelling in America, and of being an American."[102]

Boyd's "team" included Saroyan, Archibald MacLeish, Stephen Vincent Benét, Robert Sherwood, Orson Welles, Maxwell Anderson, Sherwood Anderson, Paul Green, and Walter Van Tilburg Clark. Their eleven programs were heard on CBS and enjoyed extensive rebroadcasts despite the flak that came from isolationists, Negrophobes, and others who harbored conspiratorial anxieties. More than seven thousand copies of the scripts were sold and the Free Company received more than ten thousand fan letters. The project essentially helped to set the tone for a series of similar undertakings that followed during the war years, such as Sidney Kingsley's play *The Patriots* (1943), which takes place early in the presidencies of Washington and Jefferson, and the writings of Esther Forbes. In 1944 Forbes explained why she had written the durably appealing *Johnny Tremain* for adolescents and young adults (fig. 15.8). She intended to show, as she phrased it, "that these earlier boys were conscious of what they were fighting for and believed it worth dying for, and that many of the same issues are at stake in this war as in the earlier one. We are still fighting for simple things, 'that a man may stand up.' "[103]

BY POLITICIZING the American past, what Forbes, Kingsley, Boyd, and many others did between 1940 and 1945 basically stands as an aberration, a relatively brief deviation from the norm in a liberal society based upon consensus intended to assure stability. For a long time prior to 1940, and once again from the 1950s onward, the dominant tendency was to depoliticize or "center" American traditions and myths. Thomas Jefferson and Abraham Lincoln became broadly acceptable in a non-partisan way precisely when they ceased to be politically controversial. Repositories of a shared past such as Henry Ford's Greenfield Village or Old Sturbridge Village were quite carefully depoliticized. The most popular historical art of the 1930s was appealing precisely because it, too, had been neutered. Even quondam traitors or persons of questionable virtue, like Aaron Burr and Benedict Arnold, enjoyed unprecedented acceptance and interest during the interwar years because they were presented in comparatively non-partisan contexts emphasizing human interest.[104]

Contemplating the past in non-crisis times seemed to call for balance—contrapuntal qualities and emphases came to the fore. The Santa

15.8   Bernard Perlin, *Americans Will Always Fight for Liberty, 1778–1943* (Office of War Information Poster No. 26). Library of Congress Poster Collection, Division of Prints and Photographs.

Fe Fiesta, for example, was a major cultural event that took place there annually in September on the anniversary of a 1680 rebellion in which fifty-two Spanish friars were killed by Indians. Each year the fiesta featured on a designated Sunday a procession to the Cross of the Martyrs, which marked the spot of the killings. The next day a re-enactment of the entry into the city of Spanish deliverance from the heathens was counterbalanced by a "hysterical pageant" intended to offset the intense historical pageant. Artists and writers concentrated their efforts on the hysterical pageant, which thereby helped to depoliticize the serious legacy of inter-ethnic conflict from the later seventeenth century. That kind of anesthetic tended to minimize potential tensions inherent in American memory.[105]

Antiseptic history was well suited to prevail under ordinary circumstances, when phenomena such as "hysterical pageants" made the past pleasant and amusing if not actually a source of comfort. "In times of crisis," however, as Alfred Kazin observed in 1942, "people prefer to take their history straight, and on the run."[106] So they did, in a sense, although history deployed as wartime propaganda is not exactly

...we here highly resolve that these dead
shall not have died in vain...

REMEMBER DEC. 7th!

15.9   Allen Russell Saalburg, *Remember December 7th!* (Office of War Information, 1942). The legend reads: " . . . we here highly resolve that these dead shall not have died in vain." (In 1944 General Motors published a poster with the same legend.) Library of Congress Poster Collection, Division of Prints and Photographs.

"straight." Its warp is simply different from the woof of "normal" times (fig. 15.9).

Kazin made another, equally important point in that same remarkable first book, *On Native Grounds*—an observation that reminds us of the profound, underlying ambiguities of American culture throughout the half century following the 1890s. He noted "the greatest single fact about our modern American writing—our writers' absorption in every last detail of their American world together with their deep and subtle alienation from it. There is a terrible estrangement in this writing, a nameless yearning for a world no one ever really possessed."[107]

Add to such a dualism one other that has persisted even longer in American culture, the one involving those antipodal possibilities of tradition and progress. The New York World's Fair of 1939 epitomized a crucial ambivalence between the two. Because it was occasioned by the sesquicentennial of George Washington's inauguration and the nation's genesis, it began with costume drama and wallowed in mock nostalgia. Its real *raison d'être,* however, was the celebration of contemporary technology and an expectant wish to peer at the future.[108] That peculiar concatenation of tradition and progress had been a prominent feature of American culture during the mid-nineteenth century; it reappeared forcefully in most of the great expositions (including 1939); and then emerged in diverse modes after World War II, when old myths would turn up in new bottles.

When and if Americans bothered to recognize that other societies also perpetuated myths for political purposes, they infrequently specified any clear criteria that might differentiate our "good" myths from "bad" ones elsewhere. Paradoxically, when tradition and memory were perceived in the form of myth, they seemed to be more contestable and a greater source of tension in domestic as well as international relations.

Coda

DEGREES OF DISTINCTIVENESS:
COMPARISONS

I

I N 1930 Lewis Mumford called attention to the newness of American traditions and asserted his belief that "our past still lies ahead of us." He then offered a kind of bad news–good news formula in order to find virtue amid vacuousness. "In America all things flow," he wrote, "and the least reliable way of gauging our future is by examining the contents of our past. Our very lack of tradition, which has prevented us from building upon our successes, also keeps us from stewing so long in our errors."[1]

One of the critical components in Mumford's assessment was distinctiveness. Many spokesmen for his generation believed in American exceptionalism, especially in the realms of tradition, myth, and memory. In Mumford's view the present-mindedness of his countrymen was entirely compatible with appreciation for the past. In fact, each enhanced the other. "A genuine tradition," he noted, "does not stifle but reinforces our interest in the present, and makes it easier to assimilate what is fresh and original."[2]

Similarly, V. F. Calverton concluded that the revolutionary tradition in the United States was indigenous and unlike Europe's; that it could and should be made attractive to the masses; that the American Workers' Party properly belonged here whereas the American Communist Party did not. History, in Calverton's view, had made the United States different.[3] After reading Ruth Benedict on the imperatives of cultural relativism and particularism, Constance Rourke concluded that American mythology was unique in its character and configurations. W. H. Auden went overboard, perhaps, when he declared in all sincerity that "the invention of mythologies is an American specialty."[4]

The appeal of American exceptionalism did not remain constant in form and content, however. For longer than the first quarter of the twentieth century a majority of those in the mainstream simply assumed that immigrants ought to adapt by adopting American traditions, customs, and ceremonials, and by shedding their "alien" memories like so much dead skin. In 1917, on the other hand, James Harvey Robinson lavished praise upon an essay written by a Romanian immigrant "who tries to rise above the contradictions of a double loyalty." Robinson mocked those narrow-minded patriots whose conventional perspectives did not permit them to perceive the textured richness of the Romanian's background.[5]

During the interwar period many older immigrants remained fiercely loyal to their time-honored ways and rituals. In New York's Little Italy, for example, one week was set aside each year so that members of the community could "refresh themselves, reestablish their memories, and relocate their stability by returning to their hometowns in religious spirit." Parents strove diligently to inculcate in their children the customary Catholic beliefs and rituals that had been brought from southern Italy and especially Sicily. Looking back from 1930, Lewis Mumford expressed a minority view that became the dominant perspective in little more than a decade:

> How deliberately we impoverished ourselves by the doctrine of the melting-pot, which robbed the newcomer of his own individuality without giving him a fresh culture in anything but the externals of manners. Now, however, that our regional cultures are beginning to emerge through the dull whitewash of political and industrial uniformity, it will be possible to encourage the existence of older cultural traditions, thus permitting their integration in a new America, instead of hastening their disuse and annihilation.[6]

If the response to newcomers by old-stock Americans was grudging or ambivalent at best, the assessments offered by those who went abroad were likely to be more clear cut. Because so many of those who travelled were intellectuals of one sort or another, their reactions tended to be more progressive and positive than those of people who remained at home, apprehensive about racial purity and the perpetuation of 100 percent Americanism. During the 1920s, for example, John Dewey became intrigued by the Soviet Union. "Freed from the load of subjection to the past," he observed, "it seems charged with the ardor of creating a new world." William E. Dodd, a distinguished historian, served as U.S. ambassador to Germany during the 1930s. His letters to friends at home from Berlin reveal his mounting concern at the politicization of German culture and especially the use of educational institutions to inculcate new myths and spurious traditions.[7]

Even a casual look at the social dynamics of myth and the uses of tradition in Europe suggests that adherence to American exceptionalism was neither wrongheaded nor naive. It has been shown that the pervasive attachment to "Holy Russia" in that country was not only a deeply felt myth of the people but that it was anti-statist as well. Nothing truly similar evolved in the United States, although the Jeffersonian hostility to government and glorification of the independent yeoman bears a superficial resemblance.[8]

In Germany the capacity to conflate past and present and the willingness to straddle cultural strata occurred much more readily than in the United States. During the later nineteenth century, for example, the spontaneity of successful festivals held in honor of recent military triumphs conveniently managed to incorporate memories of distant events. Elements of tradition and of the "old" were commonly used to create and legitimize new traditions that had political value for Bismarck and his successors. Turning ahead more than a generation, we find that Hitler had dualistic predilections because he combined without any sense of disjunction selected aspects of high culture and of folk. He admired the ornate architecture of late-nineteenth-century Vienna, yet remained obsessed with a bizarre notion of the Volk, a concept that connected contemporary Germans with ancient Greeks as well as sturdy Teuton forebears of the sort immortalized in Wagner's portrayal of Germanic myths.[9]

Observers have commented that whereas historic site museums in the United States invariably present guides dressed in period costumes, this practice is not commonly found in Europe. It has been noticed, in fact, that European visitors to American museums seem to find costumed guides and craft demonstrations somewhat embarrassing. The causes of this contrast, however, are not at all clear. Do American museum-goers have underdeveloped imaginations that need to be stimulated? Do they regard museums and visits to historic sites as a form of popular entertainment in a way that European tourists do not? We cannot say with assurance, but these are genuine possibilities.[10]

In Japan, where the socio-political uses of statist myth and underclass memory have received careful recent study, we learn that the heroic deeds of peasant martyrs in the early modern era have helped to provide energizing focus for a sense of collective identity among powerless social groups. We have scant evidence of anything comparable in the United States prior to the late nineteenth century, when the Haymarket anarchists in Chicago provided one of the first in a series of American working-class instances of martyrdom that have been discontinuous and readily blocked from the memories of that disparate class.[11]

Carol Gluck, meanwhile, has demonstrated the enduring and stabilizing success of political myth-making in late Meiji Japan. The concept of *kokutai*, a form of national character, became pervasive and popular by the late 1880s. The ancestral tradition of the imperial family—utterly spurious in terms of genuine continuity and the antiquity of various rituals—became virtually synonymous with Japan as a nation and provided a past that seemed ageless and secure in its venerable practices. By 1908 the attributes of *kokutai* had become immutable, whereas writers in the United States, such as Mumford as late as 1930, continued to insist that "we are through with pioneering, the period of preparation; and we are entering upon a period of fulfillment." Elsewhere national character seemed finally fixed if not predetermined. Here most commentators still found it to be in flux and susceptible to new influences.[12]

Consequently the American preoccupation with defining national identity that persisted through the 1930s and beyond was not simply a response to ravaging economic crisis or an anxious attempt to make sense of the country's unplanned cultural diversity, even though both stimuli were unquestionably present. Attempts to define national identity had been going on for much more than a century. To some outsiders it seemed a disturbing collective trait, itself a part of the national character. But to numerous insiders it became apparent that such an inquiry must be a permanent condition precisely because American civilization was so pluralistic and protean.[13]

That aspect of the quest most clearly prompted by the crisis of the 1930s, however, called for national regeneration, and in the process of democratization prompted a romanticization of the people as an abstract ideal: the folk. Figures like Rourke and John Powell looked back fondly to earlier times when "the folk" implied a shared culture in an age of greater national and ethnic unity. Incantations of folkish nationalism and insistence upon the morale-building attributes of myth had the effect—consciously desired or not—of blurring the harsh social realities from which everyone sought relief, if not through outright improvement of them, then by means of selective memory and indiscriminate amnesia.[14]

If the belief in American exceptionalism seems in retrospect to have been parochial and perhaps naive, it should be kept in mind that non-American critics and observers reinforced the notion of a distinctive civilization in the United States—sometimes for better, sometimes for worse. It seemed to make no difference whether the critic had actually seen the U.S.A. or not. Knowing it vicariously was sufficient to feel certain that it was different. Perhaps it was a mutant or regressive "throwback," perhaps an uncanny anticipation of the future; but in any case, it surely was different.[15]

I I

SO MUCH for the history of self-perception and the reinforcing views of "significant others." Even a casually panoramic look at European cultures during the half century prior to 1940 shows numerous parallels. Many of the trends that we have noticed were, in varying degrees, international ones. The strongest appearance of distinctiveness will be found in the particular configuration of trends in any given nation. A swift sweep across Europe, from west to east, will illustrate the point.

During the earliest decades of the twentieth century a sentimental rediscovery of rural England occurred, prompted in large part by the century-long psychological impact of industrialization and urbanization. A comparable pattern of Arcadian nostalgia took place in the United States, where the advent of both phenomena was more recent and took place with more jarring speed.[16] During that same period the teaching of national history received a major upgrading in both countries. In Great Britain, in fact, history became a compulsory subject in secondary schools in 1900, a trend that very soon had its counterpart in the United States. As a direct response, also in both cultures, the writing of history texts shifted from enthusiastic upper-middle-class amateurs to schoolteachers themselves in tandem with university scholars. Unabashed nationalism and a determined drive for stable homogeneity underlay these parallel developments within the Anglo-American world.[17]

Between 1914 and 1930 many of the same contradictory impulses that we have been noticing in American culture also appeared in Britain, though frequently a decade or so earlier. Mainstream figures in popular culture as well as among the elite made an emphasis upon national "heritage" a standard aspect of public discourse. Nevertheless, the sort of irreverent history and biography known as "debunking" during the American 1920s also enjoyed a very considerable vogue in England. Lytton Strachey's *Eminent Victorians* (1918) is merely the best-remembered illustration of the genre. Strachey, like Leonard Woolf, felt that "we were part of a negative movement of destruction against the past."[18]

During the later 1920s and early 1930s the American "Agrarians"— or Fugitives, as they were also known—centered in Nashville, Tennessee, and led by Donald Davidson, defended a traditional, pre-industrial way of life justified by Jeffersonian values. In England, Edmund Blunden passionately defended the English countryside against commercial despoilers. For Blunden and a like-minded group, agrarian England seemed every bit as precious as the celebrated heritage of British literature, and considerably more vulnerable. We do not know whether the American Fugitives influenced Blunden, or vice versa; but the two groups were clearly transmitting on the same wavelength.[19]

In 1937 Gertrude Stein left the pleasures of Paris to visit England, where she found that custom and tradition exerted a far stronger hold than they did in France. Stein encountered what she regarded as a "healthy preoccupation with tradition. Tradition was everywhere in England."[20]

In France, particularly during the interwar years, many different stimuli for patriotism existed: the government and its bureaucracy, the educational system, the military, the churches, the press, radio and

cinema, and private societies with their panoply of symbols and ceremonies. Despite that range of sources, however, the most strident custodians of national tradition tended to be politically on the right. An
ideological program begun by the Action Française in the 1890s was
perpetuated by Jacques Bainville and a cluster of royalists who enjoyed
considerable success in popularizing an avowedly monarchist interpretation of French history. The writings of Bainville and his circle during
the 1920s and 1930s were suffused with nostalgia because the republican present seemed barely tolerable to them and the future looked
extremely ominous.[21] In 1940 Maréchal Pétain yearned for the miracu-
lous appearance of another Joan of Arc. The royalists' faith in the restor-
ative power of national traditions gave way to a despair so deep that
memory overwhelmed both courage and hope.[22]

Also during the interwar years France, like the United States, witnessed on-going contention and debate over the proper definition of
national culture. Although Vichy (pro-Nazi) traditionalists expressed
enthusiasm about native folklore because they felt that it emerged
authentically from natural sources, Constance Rourke had vigorous
populist counterparts in France. The most notable was Georges-Henri
Rivière, first director of the museum of French popular arts, who was
a Socialist working within the Popular Front framework. Rivière and his
colleagues were eager to give the workers back their "heritage" and
recapture the popular imagination. Most interesting, perhaps, Rivière
valued cultural tolerance and had an inclusive vision of French society
that embraced both modernism and traditionalism.[23]

Turning to the influence of memory and its application in quite a
different sphere, we have the remarkable saga of Edmond de Rothschild of Paris pouring large amounts of his personal fortune into Palestine in an effort to restore the ancient Jewish homeland. The history of
the Holy Land had the sort of obligation and ideological meaning for
Rothschild that Colonial Williamsburg did for John D. Rockefeller, Jr.
It is not inconsequential that people made pilgrimages to both places
as a result of the two philanthropists' benevolence.[24]

The German National Museum established at Nuremberg in 1852
expanded steadily in the generations that followed. Its remarkable collections expressed "romantischer Historismus," the history of our romantic past. Such a museum had no true counterpart in the United
States for many years, least of all the Smithsonian Institution, which
sponsored research and displayed exhibits that aspired to be scientific
rather than romantic. The emotional impact of that museum in Nuremberg began to have American analogues in the early 1930s, however,
when places like the Henry Ford Museum and Colonial Williamsburg
opened to enthusiastic visitors whose patriotic pulse quickened as a
consequence of coming to see Americana on display.[25]

Finally, Stalin's manipulative use of Lenin's memory and the creation
of a Lenin cult during the 1930s was surely more devious and heavy-

handed than Franklin D. Roosevelt's maneuvering of Lincoln's memory; yet the exploitation of a historic leader for personal and partisan advantage seems more similar than not. Each man rather presumptuously wrapped himself in the legitimizing mantle of a much-admired predecessor. Moreover, the centennial of Lenin's birth on April 22, 1970, was celebrated in the Soviet Union in a manner that was strikingly reminiscent of the 1932 bicentennial of George Washington's birth. All manner of Lenin artifacts and trinkets appeared for sale in 1970. The commercial exploitation of founding fathers seems to occur irrespective of economic or political systems.[26]

S O M E of the most striking analogies to the workings and role of tradition in American culture are to be found—perhaps predictably—in the histories of three other nations that once were British colonies: Australia, Canada, and South Africa. In Australia, for example, national identity had long been associated with and derived from Great Britain. After 1870, however, native-born Australians (of European descent) became more influential in shaping and articulating national legends. The Australian Natives' Association, founded at Victoria in 1871, achieved rapid popularity. As a consequence the characteristics deemed "typically" Australian came to be less those found among London clubmen, and instead a fascination with the rugged life of the frontiersman developed a powerful hold. Practicality, companionship, generosity, and versatility became part of the litany of virtues ascribed to bush-men, those tough yet tender characters who sang to their cattle while camped for the night so that the livestock would not stampede. For various reasons the bush-men developed a large repertoire of ballads, and those songs supply some of the richest historical evidence for the values and traditions associated with the bush-men. Similar to the situation in the United States involving the economic decline of the cowboy, myths and memories of the bush-men became prevalent soon after the physical and psychological isolation of bush life began to wane.[27]

When we turn to the establishment of historic sites and memorials in Canada, similarities to the pattern that emerged in the United States significantly outweigh differences. The creation of national historic parks in Canada occurred in 1914, two years earlier than the emergence of the U.S. National Park Service. Although Canada's Historic Sites and Monuments Board was formed in 1919, thirty years prior to the National Trust for Historic Preservation in the United States, its initial focus concerned the selection and interpretation of sites from a national perspective, an approach that corresponded very well with American developments during the 1920s. The Canadian Board also had to confront problems that arose from attempting to interpret the history of a heterogeneous country from a homogeneous national perspective. In yet another similarity the Board came into being because of successful lobbying efforts by groups who cared about "heritage" issues, but more particularly about military sites. The Department of Militia and Defence had been disposing of forts that were legacies from the old British regime, but many local groups wanted them preserved as monuments to a heroic past.[28]

Contrasts are noteworthy but less numerous. The Canadian government became an active participant in the historic preservation movement a bit more than a decade earlier than its southern neighbor. The Historic Sites and Monuments Board was formally created to advise the Canadian government about sites that deserved official recognition. In a striking reversal of the American pattern, however, the Board was dominated by Easterners from Quebec, Ontario, and the Maritimes, with the consequence that central and western Canada were severely under-represented in the selection of historic sites. Not until 1938, for instance, were there any members who represented Saskatchewan and Manitoba. Critics still complained after World War II that the Canadian West was woefully neglected in both the number and the kinds of sites designated.[29] By contrast, the U.S. National Park system, including historic sites and their interpretation, had a very strong orientation toward the trans-Mississippi West until well after World War II.

Ultimately, however, two related parallels seem especially noteworthy. First, that a "heritage movement" developed in Canada during the second and third decades of the twentieth century, which certainly had its counterpart (moving a few steps behind, perhaps) in the United States. Second, the 1908 tercentenary of the founding of Quebec City by Samuel de Champlain served as a major stimulus to that heritage movement, especially in terms of battlefield sites, architecture, and material culture—a role fulfilled analogously in the United States by the Hudson-Fulton commemoration of 1909 in New York. By the 1930s in both countries local observances had become more effective than national ones. In 1933, for example, the placement of a memorial at Gaspé, Prince Edward Island, and commemoration of the 150th anniversary of the founding of New Brunswick as a province were quite comparable to various state commemorations taking place in the United States.[30]

Other spheres of legend and memory, however, call our attention to contrasts. Canadians have no idealized national figure comparable to Miss Liberty or Uncle Sam. They do not have prominent or revered heroes comparable to Washington, Jefferson, Lincoln, and others in the "lower 48." As one observer has written: "Canadians showed an attraction for group or collective heroes, since their environment was to be mastered more by organization men—the Hudson's Bay Company trapper, factor, or trader; the Royal Canadian Mounted Policeman; the Saskatchewan graingrowers' associations; or, earlier, the servants of New France—than by individuals."[31]

C3.1   George Lois and Carl Fischer, *Don't Burn Your Flag—Wash it!* (1972).
Library of Congress Poster Collection, Division of Prints and Photographs.

National holidays have never enjoyed the prominence in Canada that they have in its southern neighbor, and such appeal as they do possess only dates from the later nineteenth century. There are virtually no national holidays that honor heroic individuals (like Washington, Lincoln, and Martin Luther King, Jr.), and only three of any kind that are observed in all the provinces: Victoria Day (May 24, formerly Empire Day), Canada Day (July 1, formerly Dominion Day), and Remembrance Day (formerly Armistice Day). Some celebrations, moreover, such as St. Jean Baptiste Day (June 24) and Orange Day (July 12) are more likely to aggravate sectionalism than to foster Canadian cohesion. Similarly, even though the maple leaf was proposed as a national symbol as far back as 1806, the process of discussing and reaching agreement upon the appropriate design for a sovereign flag turned out to be long, acrimonious, and surprisingly recent (1921–64). Public opinion divided bitterly over various possibilities, and the formal decision finally reached in 1964 did little to heal the wounds that had been opened. Needless to say, nothing remotely comparable to the American flag fetish has ever appeared in Canada (fig. C3.1).[32]

With the exception of Quebec City and Montreal, public monuments have not been common in Canada and they attract little notice. Nor are there counterparts to such mythic or sentimental sites as Plymouth Rock, Independence Hall and the Liberty Bell, or Gettysburg Battlefield. The most ubiquitous public monuments pertain to World War I. Although Canadians made genuine contributions and sacrifices for that cause, it was not a distinctively Canadian phenomenon. The fragmented nature of Canadian identity is exposed by the issue of whether "God Save the Queen," "The Maple Leaf Forever," or "O Canada" ought to be the national anthem. Canadian schools have not been used to promote *national* consciousness and assimilation to anything like the same degree as in the United States. As one observer remarked: "The teaching of a national history creates national myths which facilitate nationalism—but there are ten versions of Canadian history taught in the schools." In 1897 the Canadian Education Association was unable to persuade the provinces to adopt a single standard text for the teaching of Canadian history. That established a pattern of fragmentation for the twentieth century. Fragmentation is not inherently bad; nor is standardization necessarily good. My point is simply that striking contrasts exist in the transmission of collective memory in two societies that seem, superficially at least, to be more like each other than either one resembles cultures outside of North America.[33]

Canada has, of course, a dualistic Anglo-French heritage, with tensions arising from dominance by the historically English majority. The United States also has an imbalanced dualistic heritage, Anglo-Spanish, although the Hispanic sense of collective memory, and a consequent emphasis upon Hispanic-American traditions, has only come to the fore in recent decades. Needless to say, the United States has still another imbalanced dualism involving the partial repression of African-American traditions by a continuum of white majorities. The most interesting comparison in that regard is with South Africa, where the Afrikaners followed the British in mistreating native populations but carried the process a step further after achieving political dominance in 1948. The policy of apartheid evolved historically with a veneer of legitimacy derived from traditional Calvinist theology sustaining the Boers' sense of special destiny as a chosen people.[34]

The Afrikaners depended heavily upon a cluster of historical myths in order to rationalize their repressive hegemony and policy of racial separation. The vital elements within that cluster involve a Great Trek to the interior made by Boers in 1838 in order to achieve autonomy from the British in their own promised land. That trek led to the Battle of Blood River and a sacred covenant that was allegedly made in the wake of a Boer victory achieved despite a vast numerical (but not military) disadvantage. It took more than a full generation for any consensus to develop concerning the mythic aspects of those events.[35]

By 1938, however, the centenary of the Great Trek and Battle of Blood River enjoyed very broad appeal among Boer descendants. Approximately one-tenth of the entire Afrikaner people attended the ceremonial placement of the Voortrekker Monument near Pretoria. A 1938 re-enactment of the Great Trek featured eight oxwagons and a good many participants. Its symbolic and ideological purposes highlighted Afrikaner unity and their insistence upon strict cleavage of the races. Events planned in conjunction with the Oregon Trail Centennial in 1930 were much more subtle in their racism. Memories of conflict between whites and hostile Indians were occasionally invoked; but the primary emphasis in public relations was placed upon a remembrance of national and ethnic unity in the United States.[36]

I I I

IN THE FINAL analysis, the validity of comparisons remains very much in the eye of the beholder. The persuasiveness of comparisons is variable because so much of their meaning depends upon time, circumstance, and how relatively political or apolitical the beholder is. Johan Huizinga, for example, was an astute historian with a keen comparative eye whose understanding of Dutch culture penetrated with considerable depth. Looking at the Netherlands, past and present, he was struck by his countrymen's "relative insensibility to myth and rhetoric. It may be a handicap to our imagination and enthusiasm," he conceded in 1935, "but as a political quality, this deficiency must undoubtedly be counted a positive and salutary factor."[37]

A year later, however, as Hitler and Mussolini cast ever more menacing shadows across Europe, Huizinga's gloom brought to the surface his innate elitism and caused him to issue a book-length manifesto representative of many other conservative intellectuals during the later 1930s. "For the shallow, semi-educated person the beneficial restraints of respect for tradition, form and cult are gradually falling away." Observing the highly successful mobilization of the masses in Italy and Germany had caused Huizinga, along with so many others, to become deeply cynical about mass and popular culture alike. Such phenomena not only encouraged deception and manipulation, but caused a disintegration of collective memory as a benign and positive force in political culture.[38]

The coming of World War II had a remarkable impact among the anti-Fascist nations and their spokesmen in restoring faith in the utility of tradition and collective memory as bulwarks of democracy. One consequence, however, was that some writers truly believed they could square the circle. That is, given the ideological imperatives of the day, and the desire to sanctify democracy itself as an enduring tradition with deep roots, advocates of the Allied cause made spurious connections that sounded grand but lacked any genuine historical grounding. In 1943, for example, Jacques Maritain wrote *Christianity and Democracy*, in which he condemned the "bigoted dread of the Gospel which

[has] spiritually disarmed the democracies and ruined from within their authentic vital principle." Maritain looked hopefully to a future that would "open up the path to a new civilization and a new democracy whose Christian inspiration will call forth . . . the living traditions of Christ's religion."[39]

At just the same time Ralph Barton Perry, a Harvard philosopher, produced a huge book called *Puritanism and Democracy,* in which he attempted to synthesize in the service of American patriotism two virtually antithetical traditions. It is difficult to imagine how many readers, even serious ones, made it through all 641 pages of Perry's text. But those who did were treated to intellectual gymnastics of this sort:

> Puritanism and democracy are in a measure coincident and allied. . . . They both affirm the same Occidental Christian code of justice, compassion, and personal dignity. . . . But if puritanism and democracy reinforce one another's truths and aggravate one another's errors, they also serve to correct and complement one another's limitations. . . . As puritanism stresses the sinfulness of Adam after the fall, so democracy stressed his innocence before. Puritanism supplies the pessimistic realization of man's present predicament, democracy the optimistic affirmation of his hopes and possibilities.[40]

Then came Perry's peroration: part exhortation and partially an act of intellectual amalgamation that would have left Thomas Jefferson and John Winthrop equally astounded. Perry proposed that Americans "take puritanism and democracy as symbols of piety . . . looking for their constituents of truth in order that we may reaffirm them; reaffirming them in order thereby to maintain our moral identity and the stream of the national life."[41] Perry's earnestness matched that of Maritain. In times of international crisis, platitudes may sound like plausible formulations, and the will to believe goes a very long way toward veiling improbable combinations.

If the exigencies of war could apparently justify a syncretism of sacred and secular values, it also facilitated a soothing reconciliation of tradition and progress. Folklore might be used, for instance, to tell the people that democracy and progress would succeed precisely because Americans had good values, were virtuous people, and had attractive traditions sustaining them. In 1941 a scriptwriter explained to James Boyd just how an allegorical treatment of the Paul Bunyan legend could be presented to a radio audience of the Free Theatre. Why Paul Bunyan? Because in native folklore he was "the greatest American—the big feller—the man who cleared the forests faster than the others, who led the way across the plains, who threw up factories and led progress in America. He is the concentration of the spirit and action of democracy."[42]

Although the penchant for taking those kinds of cultural liberties intensified during wartime, their precedents can be found in historical films made in diverse Western nations prior to 1939. Following the war, however, film, radio, and eventually television played increasingly important roles in yoking ideology with tradition and pseudo-memory.[43] The result would be a homogenization of collective consciousness never before known, and an emphasis upon memory that seemed only to result in ever more frequent episodes of collective amnesia.

Part Four

CIRCA 1945 TO 1990

NOSTALGIA, HERITAGE, AND THE ANOMALIES OF HISTORICAL AMNESIA

W HEN THE UNITED STATES entered World War II, composer Aaron Copland eagerly wished to contribute to the cause in some way. André Kostelanetz suggested to Copland that he compose a patriotic work in the form of "a musical portrait of a great American." Although Copland felt particularly attracted to Walt Whitman, he eventually selected Abraham Lincoln and by mid-April of 1942 completed his "Lincoln Portrait," a thirteen-minute work for full orchestra and a speaker. Its opening line, "Fellow Citizens! We cannot escape history," would be echoed by many other creative Americans during the three years that followed.[1]

On a surface level, at least, war stimulated interest in the American past throughout the populace at large, not merely among the well educated. One close observer commented in 1943 that "campaigns for the more energetic teaching of American and British history in the schools are being carried on. Various national organizations have taken up the cause of better historical education." Seventeen months later Charles Beard informed a friend—accurately, I believe—that "Americans are interested as never before in their history." The ever popular James Truslow Adams received a remarkable amount of fan mail. "By your writing," one man stated, "you maintain the American historical traditions."[2]

As we have already noted, the international threat of totalitarianism intensified public commitment to democratic institutions, especially their connection to enhanced understanding of American national identity. Journals of opinion were inundated with essays concerning democracy and national character; and numerous books stressing the latter, especially, also appeared. Ultimately, however, the cultural relativism of the 1930s that had been disseminated beyond academe by writers like Ruth Benedict and Carl Becker had to be reconsidered because the war caused Americans and their Allies to think in terms of moral absolutes.[3] The recently held view that one political philosophy was as valid as another, so long as it worked for its adherents, seemed intellectually bankrupt in the face of fascism. If cultural relativism implied moral relativism, both would have to be discarded in favor of a traditionally defined idealism.

It should come as no surprise that the wartime frame of mind helped to enhance an almost reverential regard for the history of the United States. When Justice Felix Frankfurter spoke on Jefferson's birthday in 1943, he declared that "we come to patriotic shrines not to vaunt new ideas but to draw strength from the past. . . . Faith is not self-generated. It is moral energy stored up from the past." Less sanctimonious observers noted the heightened interest in history and predicted that it would be "stimulated still more by the problems and tastes of post-war days."[4] That proved to be notably true, in fact, because the nation emerged from war with its myths not merely intact but fairly sanctified.

One mode of postwar anti-Americanism abroad, however, took the form of utter scorn for the absence of a symbolically viable past in the United States. At the coronation of Elizabeth II in 1953, for example, British chauvinist Richard Dimbleby remarked that Americans were so "lacking in tradition" that "they must wait a thousand years before they show the world anything so significant or so lovely" as the pomp and pageantry of that ceremony.[5] The United States did not lack its own forms of non-monarchical pageantry, in fact, whether it be the colorful Washington-Rochambeau Celebration held on July 8, 1955, at Newport, Rhode Island (the pageant depicted George Washington's fateful meeting with Rochambeau in 1780), or various pageants inspired by the founding of Jamestown, Virginia (1607–1957), and then the Civil War Centennial during the early 1960s.[6]

In 1949 a Polish foreign service officer made his first visit to Washington, D.C., and received an inspiration there to reflect upon the legendary origins of great cities in general, though perhaps of Warsaw in particular. Czeslaw Milosz, later a Nobel laureate in literature, recalled how "The enemy debased memory, ascribing to himself / both ancient and future glory." He concluded by musing that "a country without a past is nothing." Amid the ruins of Warsaw he recalled seeing

> The ashes of centuries mixed with fresh blood.
> Pride then left us and we rendered homage
> To men and women who once lived and ever since
> We have had our home founded in history.[7]

Milosz's moving poem sets the tone, in so many ways, for the internationalization of nostalgia and preoccupation with aspects of "heritage" (as a pervasive cultural phenomenon) during the postwar era. What took place in the United States was not unique even though it had its own distinctive manifestations: a growing concern with collective memory on the part of some individuals in response to apparent social amnesia on the part of many; a fitful desire that waxed and waned to recover vernacular culture along with a gradually growing interest in the history of ordinary folk and everyday life; and a proprietary view of national patrimony despite the fact that pluralistic diversity made it increasingly illogical to conceive of heritage as some sort of singular phenomenon or monolith.[8]

The year 1945, surely one of the most fateful in modern history, brought a pronounced sense of discontinuity between past and present, and that in turn would have major implications for the anxious mood of the 1950s, and more particularly for the wistful nostalgia of the seventies and eighties. Charles Beard had written during wartime that "a sense of history in a people is, in my opinion, necessary for continuity in institutional life and for adaptation to changes bound to come."[9] Lacking an authentic or meaningful sense of continuity, many Americans managed to create one by dramatically increasing their attendance at museums, historic sites, and villages, and by participating in activities that ranged from battle re-enactments to historic preservation at the local level.

Nostalgia per se was not an utterly new or unprecedented social phenomenon. Its occurrence had been commonplace among soldiers who served in the Revolution and the Civil War—although their nostalgia primarily manifested the original meaning of that concept: a yearning for one's distant home rather than for some earlier time sentimentalized as a golden age.[10]

The widespread wish for a return to "normalcy" that pervaded during the early 1920s may very well have marked the genesis of nostalgia as we understand that mood in contemporary times. During the 1930s we find it in public culture as well as in the arts. Arshile Gorky, the émigré artist, for example, painted an extensive series of studies in 1931–32 titled *Nighttime, Enigma, and Nostalgia*; and more than one artist who created murals for federally funded New Deal projects defined his or her intent as the creation of a nostalgic scene.[11] In 1939, at the time of New York's World's Fair and the San Francisco Exhibition, there was abundant evidence of nostalgia for the so-called Gay Nineties in general and for Chicago's Columbian Exposition of 1893 in particular. A *New York Times* editorial acknowledged that "we are rather looking back from a world hag-ridden with ideologies and the threat of Armageddons to a simpler world in which life was easier to live and to understand."[12]

Following World War II, nostalgia emerged as a pan-Atlantic phenomenon, although in Western Europe it tended to have a greater degree of historical specificity, being concentrated upon the decades just prior to 1914.[13] During the 1960s the American psychohistorian Robert Jay Lifton introduced his provocative notion of "protean man," a new and different sort of personality in terms of psychological orientation, character, and identity. According to Lifton, protean man was the product of "historical dislocation," a person profoundly affected by an unsettled feeling of change owing to a "break in the sense of connection which men have long felt with the vital and nourishing symbols of their cultural tradition."[14] If Lifton is correct, and I find considerable validity in his insight, it helps to explain the rising popular appeal of tradition and history, however superficial that interest may seem to us in retrospect (or even as contemporaries who have witnessed the occurrence as a phase of popular culture). An unself-conscious mode of compensation has been at work in which the apparent presence of the past thinly veils a disturbing reality—our genuine distance from the past in time as well as knowledge and understanding.[15]

All of these themes will be prominent in the concluding chapters that follow, along with the cultural and psychological consequences of bewilderingly swift social change. The superficial sense of the past in recent decades is also rooted, at least in part, in a set of circumstances described by one prominent sociologist early in the 1960s. "In our own time," observed Maurice Stein, "the development of historical consciousness has become even more difficult. . . . Contemporary society changes so rapidly in its external features that the relevance of the recent past hardly has time to sink in before the physical evidence for its existence disappears."[16]

As for the 1960s considered as a deviant cultural "episode," that decade clearly has a different tone and texture that sets it apart from the rest of the period since 1945. Even so, the consequences of the sixties in terms of tradition and collective consciousness are highly congruent with what we have been examining. When Kenneth Keniston, a sympathetic social psychologist, looked closely at the culture of rebellion in the 1960s he found a great many people who were emotionally "stranded in the present." These were people, mainly in their teens and twenties, who could not relate to the past because they rejected it wholesale.[17] Their doing so caused an overcompensation manifested as nostalgia by some of their older contemporaries and by much of the populace as a whole during the seventies and eighties.

Although some segments of American society were certainly inclined to take the past seriously, and continue to do so, in mass and popular culture national history became a diversified form of entertainment: commercialized tourism; entrepreneurial urban restorations that brought back the past as an atmospheric boutiqueish habitat for a relatively young and prosperous upper middle class; films and docudramas of a historical nature made for television; and of course, the influential but highly selective presentation of the national past at places like Disneyland, Disney World, and especially (with fabulous technology) at EPCOT Center.

For the irony of apparent continuity amidst the reality of discontinuity, it should be noted, first, that Walt Disney visited Henry Ford's

P4.1   Samuel Johnson Woolf, *Walter Elias Disney* (1938), charcoal on paper.
Courtesy of the National Portrait Gallery, Smithsonian Institution, Washington, D.C.

Greenfield Village in Dearborn during the early 1940s and made mental notes of what he witnessed and its impact upon visitors (fig. P4.1).
It should also be noted that the historical section of Disneyland not only
has a Liberty Square where nostalgia is sanctified, but the "organization
of procession," in Philip Johnson's felicitous phrase, makes the past
orderly, sanitized, seemingly innocent, and, of course, fabulously unreal.[18] That is also what makes it so palatable, profitable, and apparently
persuasive.

An entrepreneurial mode of selective memory has achieved amazing
commercial success, though the price of selective memory has been
indiscriminate amnesia. That will be our dominant concern in the final
section of this book. Chapter sixteen describes the origins of a "heritage
phenomenon" as a response to postwar anxiety and the sense of sharp
discontinuity, emphasizing such trends as the historic preservation
movement, collecting memorabilia, and the new presentation of historic sites and museums. Chapter seventeen takes the Cold War as its
point of departure and looks at the government's emergence as a major
custodian of tradition, a new and not entirely comfortable role. Chapters eighteen and nineteen correspond, very roughly, to the 1970s and
1980s, even though some chronological distinctions and emphases are
inevitably arbitrary. The pervasiveness of nostalgic yearnings, the pecu-
liarity of disremembering amidst pride in the past, an expanded role for

the media in presenting "memories," and the commercialization of tradition supply some of the central themes that have characterized our own time with its strangely superficial sense of history as heritage—a commodity to be packaged in hundreds of ways ranging from docu-dramas to "collectibles" at flea markets.

Chapter 16

THE HERITAGE IMPERATIVE: POPULARIZING, COLLECTING, AND PRESERVING

T HIS CHAPTER concentrates upon shifting American responses to tradition in an age of anxiety: a time when concerns about national security, swift social change, and a profound sense of historical discontinuity troubled people deeply. Vague though genuinely felt threats to "freedom" caused people to think wistfully about individualism, self-reliance, and other verities associated with the colonial period and the early republic. A quest for timelessness that would counterbalance the perplexities of change provided comfort to some. Popularizing the past in various ways made it more socially inclusive; and commercializing the past, especially in terms of tourism, made it profitable for many. The net effect meant that traditionalism kept pace with modernism, at least in the realm of national taste and the uses of leisure.

In section I we look at the genesis of the "heritage syndrome," a climate of opinion or mood that has steadily intensified over the past four decades. Special attention is given to various attempts at popularizing history, along with efforts by hyphenated Americans to pay considerably more attention to their backgrounds, which has greatly enlarged the sphere of tradition-oriented Americans. In the realm of artisanship, older and individualized crafts looked attractive in an age of standardization. The calm of rustic museum villages looked desirable in an age of intense bustle; but artists and intellectuals caused some significant intergenerational disputes involving how best to present and explain American traditions.

Section II turns to patriotism in general, but more particularly as it was inspired by historic sites, museums, and restoration projects. Visitor responses available in the archives of places like Williamsburg are very revealing about national pride, the uses of history in civil religion, and notions of a "living past" voiced by people at various social levels. Section III examines a wide range of touristic sites, from Shaker communities in the Northeast to Disneyland and Knott's Berry Farm in Southern California. The common denominators in postwar statements of mission stressed their educational objectives and their desire to preserve oases of the pastoral, pre-industrial past at a time of startling technological and urban change.

Section IV focuses on the National Trust for Historic Preservation, alongside private and state restoration projects that were fostered or encouraged by it. Connections between the preservation movement and economic imperatives are noted, as well as governmental impact upon the movement by means of court decisions and other measures.

The fifth and final section speculates about the ingredients most responsible for success and failure in tradition-oriented enterprises: why, for example, the personal interests and obsessions of individuals tend to be more influential and enduring than grandiose schemes guided by lofty abstractions. The quest for personal immortality has had a powerful impact upon American museums. The growing enthusiasm for folk art, which emerges as a phenomenon that cuts across lines of wealth and social status, turns out to be a big boost for both nationalism and democracy—a harnessed pair not always compatible prior to 1945, but increasingly so thereafter.

Ultimately, however, the most vital stimuli for national memory and its varied manifestations in this period were worries about security, freedom, swift social change, and a sense of radical discontinuity with the world as it had hitherto been known.

I

ALTHOUGH allusions to "heritage" began to appear in public discourse during the 1930s, particularly in conjunction with historic preservation efforts, the word emerged as a virtual cliché in the years following World War II. A typical pamphlet explained in 1945 that "only by education and more education can we persuade Richmond to save the unique heritage of its past." Late in 1947, when the Pennsylvania National Shrines Park Commission submitted a report to Congress, it referred to the "core of our spiritual heritage." *American Heritage* magazine made its initial appearance in 1947; scholars and writers used the phrase casually in their correspondence; events frequently carried such labels as the Virginia Heritage Dinner (held on February 1, 1957, in Richmond); and the Civil War Centennial also helped to bring the word into common parlance during the later fifties and early sixties.[1]

After making visits to Colonial Williamsburg, a remarkable number of ordinary Americans spontaneously wrote to John D. Rockefeller, Jr., to express their deep and genuine enthusiasm at "seeing so many young people—studying & becoming aware of the heritage and traditions of our wonderful country" (1952). A connection to patriotic inspiration occurred frequently: "You made it possible for us to enjoy our heritage and store our memories with its strong faith in freedom." More often than not these were family affairs shaped by a zealous sense of mission: "Last fall my husband, our two teen age daughters and I visited Williamsburg for three days. They were three of the most wonderful and exciting days we have ever spent in the pursuit of our heritage."[2]

In 1954, soon after *American Heritage* changed ownership and format, its new management promised potential subscribers "a good deal of nostalgia," thereby revealing their shrewd sense of the contemporary mood. Throughout the 1950s those impromptu letters of appreciation received by the Rockefellers revealed more than an undercurrent of yearning for earlier times. In 1958 one man explained, following a repeat visit with his family, that "in this age of mediocrity in standards of production, public behavior and patriotism, it was a most refreshing and heartening experience to spend a couple of days in your island of craftsmanship, courtesy and finest tradition." Such words as "dignity," "charm," "calm," and above all "tradition" recurred constantly.[3]

At a time when discontinuity seemed so perplexing, a sense of permanence and timelessness carried enormous appeal. Kenneth Chorley, the president of Colonial Williamsburg, made this a recurrent theme in speeches that he gave to diverse audiences all over the United States. "The most striking feature of America today is change," he asserted. "In a highly mobile, rapidly shifting society, we are in danger of losing our perspective, and of losing a refreshing contact with the well-springs of the American tradition." Once again, candid visitor responses to C.W. indicate a deeply rooted ambivalence concerning the price of progress. One woman followed her expression of gratitude for the opportunity to relive the past with this sentiment: "I just wish we could bring back the colonial people to see the progress we of the future have made." A month later another individual thanked Rockefeller for "creating a spot in this world where ugliness is absent. There are so few places where commercialism, industry and other works of man do not mar the landscape."[4] Throughout the 1950s one of the few on-going complaints involved the presence of automobiles in the restored area. "As an ardent photographer," lamented a man from San Francisco, "I had a distressing time in Williamsburg because of automobiles interfering with otherwise fine photographs of historic buildings." One major innovation in technology had the capacity to spoil the aesthetic application of another.[5]

The irony of all that anti-automobile sentiment, of course, lies in the intimate connection between cars and widespread access to meaningful places from the American past. In the year 1895 there had been twenty historic houses and four registered automobiles in the United States. By 1955 about 1,000 historic restorations existed along with some 61,301,000 cars. In 1954 approximately 48 million people visited historic sites and buildings in the United States. Two years later the MISSION 66 program began to transform national parks and monuments with arrangements for food and housing, visitors' centers, and carefully planned trails. Seeing the national heritage became vastly easier and more comfortable. Tradition had been made readily available to the mobile middle class.[6]

Innovations in the technology of printing accompanied by bold and clever marketing techniques made *American Heritage* a swift commercial success by 1955 and a conspicuously prominent one between 1960, when subscriptions reached 309,000, and 1968, when they peaked at almost 336,000.* Because a lavishly illustrated hard-cover magazine of history had never before been published in the United States, it enjoyed an element of novelty and became (in the words of one editor) "an ideal coffee table item." In addition, public enthusiasm for the Civil War Centennial coincided with Bruce Catton's early and visible association with the magazine. Those who managed it felt that they maximized subscriptions by giving away Catton's *Illustrated History of the Civil War* as a generous premium for joining.[7]

Attempts at accomplishing that sort of success dated all the way back to 1907, in fact, when the first *Journal of American History* appeared. Edited by Francis Trevelyan Miller, it was produced in New Haven, Connecticut, by the Associated Publishers of American Records. Although it anticipated *American Heritage* in a stylistic sense, we can discern one litmus of twentieth-century change in the more elite clientele that subscribed back in 1907. As a member of the editorial board explained: "This is the first time that an elaborately illustrated and illuminated journal of this character has been undertaken in this country. The cordial reception it is receiving in houses of culture is very gratifying . . . but it needs the loyalty of all discriminating and patriotic Americans."[8] It disappeared from view within three years.

During the 1920s many popular journals of opinion ran occasional articles about aspects of American history, as we have seen; and polemical pamphlets of the sort that Lyon G. Tyler produced, usually anti-Northern diatribes, achieved fairly wide circulation. Some mysterious and extremely ephemeral organizations that appeared briefly, like the National Historical Society (based in Washington, D.C.) and the United States History Association (based in Boston), produced such items as *Uncle Sam's History of the United States Written by His Own People*. But unlike *American Heritage* a generation later, these received contempt rather than cooperation from serious historians capable of writing for a non-academic audience.[9]

For almost a decade, starting in 1938, Allan Nevins, Henry Pringle, Marquis James, Henry Steele Commager, and Condé Nast co-operated

---

*By the early 1980s the circulation level had dropped to around 130,000, though the renewal rate remained extremely high, at about 80 percent.

diligently in an effort to bring into being a "popular historical monthly." Their objective, as Pringle phrased it in 1941, was to "excite popular enthusiasm and appreciation for American history and world history as it touches American." When the American Historical Association backed away from a project that seemed suspect because it would not be scholarly, Nevins and his friends formed the Society of American Historians in 1939, selecting Douglas Southall Freeman to be its first president and Carl L. Becker of Cornell as vice president. The popular magazine that they envisioned was initially to have been called *History*; and a widely distributed announcement explained that "readability, interest and accuracy are, in equal importance, the standards by which contributions to *History* should be judged."[10]

The war caused this project to be placed on hold; but in 1947, before a trial balloon version of *American Heritage* was released, Nevins explained the persistent impulse to a colleague. "One of my passions," he wrote, "is the idea that historical writing ought to be kept fresh, simple, literary, and unpedantic. We academic people are always in danger of cultivating a sterile scholasticism, which is one of the reasons why the best historical writing is done by non-academic folk like Douglas Freeman, Carl Sandburg, Claude Bowers, and Truslow Adams." For a few years John D. Rockefeller III supported the cost of getting *American Heritage* started; but when it went commercial and hard cover in the mid-1950s he felt that his backing was no longer essential. Its phenomenal success proved him to be correct. At about the same time, in response to similar stimuli, some of the state historical societies located in the Middle West transformed their quarterly historical journals from dry, scholarly, and unattractive formats to well-illustrated magazines, printed on glossy paper, designed to appeal to the "average individual who wants to see somewhat livelier material and more drawings and pictures."[11]

The success of *American Heritage* became apparent in its influence, which took diverse forms. *Tradition, the Monthly Magazine of America's Picturesque Past*, published by the American Tradition Corporation in Detroit, lasted for only five volumes from 1958 until 1962. It was too modest in size, quality, and subscription-getting strategies to survive. Its demise indicated that "more" (more permanent in format and more expensive) was more likely to succeed. *American History Illustrated* was established by the National Historical Society based in Gettysburg during the mid-1960s and has always shown particular partiality for Civil War politics and battles. The Pioneer American Society, with headquarters in Baton Rouge, came into existence in 1967 and publishes a modest journal, *Echoes of History*, devoted to precise descriptions of the American landscape and its earlier buildings. The organization's motto is: "For those who enjoy old things."

The impact of *American Heritage* could also be seen in the mass circulation weeklies and monthlies. In 1955–56, for example, *Life* magazine devoted a major series to "America's Arts and Skills: The Traditions That Shaped U.S. Taste." When *Life* collected the photographic essays in book form, it reached an audience estimated at 25 million people. *Life*'s editors emphasized "the great traditions of American design and taste" and called attention to the way "colonial artists created useful and beautiful objects." The very titles chosen for each section read like a litany (if not a caricature) of cherished American values: The Look of Liberty in Craftsmanship; The Sturdy Age of Homespun; The Fabulous Frontier; all with a ubiquitous leitmotif—that self-reliance shaped the rustic arts in America.

An abiding affection for early Americana persisted in the postwar years. Supreme Court Justice William O. Douglas lived in a colonial revival home in suburban Maryland and owned a cocker spaniel named Colonial. Artists like Molly Luce (1896–1986) were attracted to American historical scenes that highlighted patriotism and continuity, such as her 1945 painting called *Four Generations*. Within a few years prosperous corporations like J. Walter Thompson and Armand Hammer's installed authentic historical rooms in their New York City headquarters because doing so seemed to provide the right sort of dignified atmosphere. During the summer of 1947 people from Dun & Bradstreet went to Williamsburg in order to collect ideas and information "for the development of a 'theme' for the design of an office building" planned for lower Manhattan—with the hope of "incorporating certain features of early American design," more particularly "certain of the rooms in Federal Hall" where George Washington had been inaugurated in 1789.[12]

Because many people believed that our participation in World War II had, at least partially, been directed at saving European civilization, the celebration of certain hyphenated American traditions also enjoyed special legitimacy in the postwar years. The Minnesota Finnish-American Historical Society was founded at St. Paul in 1943 and remained active with this objective: "to encourage and try to keep alive some of the worthwhile customs and traditions peculiar to the Finns." The Swedish Pioneer Centennial was celebrated in several parts of the country in 1948 (an arbitrarily chosen date). And for American Heritage Day in 1957, the 350th anniversary of permanent settlement at Jamestown, the College of William and Mary mounted an "Old World Heritage" exhibit.[13]

Beyond books and printed materials prepared for a general lay audience, some of the most memorable ways of popularizing American history had commonly been developed in conjunction with the big anniversary exhibitions. In 1914, for example, New Orleans planned to welcome the opening of the Panama Canal with a Southern States Pan-American Exposition at which, among other extravaganzas, the organizers intended to erect a facsimile of eighteenth-century New Orleans: "The buildings will be absolute reproductions of famous historic dwellings." In 1936–37 the U.S. Constitution Sesquicentennial Commission devised an elaborate marionette show "which would present a history lesson of our Country to the children." Its scenarios ran a predictable gamut ranging from the "discovery of America" by Columbus, then "going into the Indian inhabitants," and highlighting the events of 1776, 1787, and 1789.[14]

Development of new technologies, however, would have the greatest impact upon the commercial popularization of U.S. history; and the seeds for such developments began to germinate during the early 1920s, when a few imaginative people devoted a lot of effort to converting a fifty-volume collection called *The Chronicles of America* into a "series of Picture Chronicles . . . all calculated to make American History attractive to the young people"; plus films based upon as many of the volumes as possible. As one enterprising fellow observed in 1921: "The motion picture as a medium of communication is here to stay, and the sooner we can find a practicable means of conveying history to the people through this medium, the more effective will be our work and the greater our success." Within a year that concept was being considered by several groups: scholars, public school educators, publishers, and film makers.[15]

Because the technology and distribution networks were not yet ready, however, visual materials for educational purposes did not become effectively available until the later 1940s (when Williamsburg began to make films) and the 1950s when the Henry Ford Museum inaugurated its own television show, "Window to the Past," using Detroit's educational TV station, which had just commenced operation. In 1954 Allan Nevins provided playwright Paul Green with materials so that he could prepare scripts about John and Abigail Adams for the widely watched Omnibus television series. Within a quarter of a century programs like "The Adams Chronicles," "Collision Course: Truman and MacArthur," "Roots," and "I Will Fight No More Forever," ranged from the founders to slavery to mistreatment of Native Americans, and reached vast audiences that would have been simply inconceivable a few decades earlier.[16]

Because we now take this sort of programming for granted, it is all too easy to forget that presentations about the past made on the radio, during the thirties and forties especially, paved the way in terms of dramatic design and techniques of selectivity in response to time constraints. One series that was highly symptomatic of these now forgotten efforts, and of the success that they enjoyed, emerged in upstate New York as a response to the late 1930s enthusiasm for local history. Titled "History Was Made Where You Live," the program had so much appeal that its producers prepared a one-volume version of the entire series in printed form. When these projects were effective they had a way of appearing, eventually, in multiple formats, each one enhancing the visibility of the others.[17]

Presentations of the past by means of the media did not initially *supplant* the written word. Instead, book publishers became the beneficiaries of intensified interest in national, regional, and local history. The extensive series of volumes on the rivers of America, edited by Carl Carmer and Hervey Allen during the 1940s and 1950s, for example, sold extremely well; and in a typical undertaking, the University of Chicago Press decided in 1961 to prepare "a treasury of the living documents of the American tradition." Its statement of scope and purpose explained that "Americans have been able to multiply their newspapers, magazines, and books, but not their sacred documents. In a democratic society, such documents must make their way, not only among an elite, but among the millions." If the democratization of tradition had been under way for more than a generation, perhaps something approaching the proletarianization of tradition was now coming into view.[18]

In a closely related development, the Fund for the Republic established an American Traditions Project in 1957 in order to "dramatize incidents illustrating how the good sense of Americans has prevailed in their daily lives, particularly in conflicts or disputes which may never have reached the headlines." The project, called Democracy in Action, was launched on George Washington's Birthday in 1957 with a dinner held at the Mayflower Hotel in Washington, D.C., at which Bruce Catton was the featured speaker. The enterprise undertook educational projects that emphasized application of the Bill of Rights to various hypothetical situations; it sponsored an American Traditions essay contest in 1957; it presented awards to figures who seemed exemplary in the preservation of American traditions; and it produced a volume of essays entitled *The American Tradition*. The project ran out of steam (and funds) in 1959, however; and its anti-Communist tone marked it very clearly as a liberal phenomenon especially responsive to the Cold War mood of the mid- and later 1950s.[19]

DURING the postwar decade writers and artists tended to divide along generational lines: those ready to affirm traditional American values (primarily those over the age of fifty) and those less enthusiastic about the past, per se, whose mood was more forward-looking. Edmund Wilson confessed to John Dos Passos in 1951 that he found "memory" problematic and derived little pleasure from re-entering the past. Archibald MacLeish responded graciously but with candor to Dos Passos's deeply felt conservatism. "I don't understand your politics these days," the poet confessed, "but I do understand what you say of the institutions of the Republic and bless you for it. They do indeed have to be saved from those who would save them to destroy them." A year later Richard Chase urged American intellectuals to maintain "the tradition of critical non-conformism going back to Thoreau and Melville." Why? Because from Chase's ambivalent perspective, "this is, fundamentally, our *only* useful 'tradition,' if by 'critical non-conformism' one means a sustained dissent from and commitment to America."[20]

The younger literary and cultural critics tended to be more concerned about contemporary issues and the recent past, whereas those who had come of age between 1910 and 1930 were much more likely to feel affirmative rather than alienated or critical. In 1950 when Mark Van Doren, an elder statesman of American letters, read (in manuscript) Irving Howe's new book on Sherwood Anderson, he directed a harsh blast to Lionel Trilling, his junior colleague at Columbia: "I hadn't quite realized how completely sick his generation is with what it calls history, and with what I would call peeping at the recent past as if that were the all-in-all." Trilling responded tactfully but with undisguised sympathy for Howe: "Don't you think that there are times when a strong interest in the recent past is natural and legitimate? It arises when social and cultural change seems especially rapid and momentous." Trilling felt that Howe had in fact been "generous" because "he has the contrary of the impulse to belittle the past."[21]

Clear-cut patterns are hard to find in the postwar scene. Despite widespread expressions of interest in American folklore, for example, Carl Sandburg's literary populism of the 1920s and 1930s ceased to be in vogue, and the immense prestige that he had so recently enjoyed was supplanted by scorn and neglect during the later 1940s. Robert Penn Warren, on the other hand, who also drew upon historical and folk materials for much of his free verse, enjoyed considerable appeal. Esther Forbes, whose last years as an active writer were devoted to New England folklore, voiced the new mood—so different from the documentary 1930s—that elevated myth and personal beliefs above historical realities. As she explained to a friend while working on her last book, "what one believes happened is more enduring, in a way more 'true,' than reality."[22]

A similar absence of consensus occurred in the arts. While chauvinistic Americanism seemed to satisfy the mainstream, younger dissenting painters like Robert Gwathmey insisted upon calling attention to racial injustice and the hidden barriers of class and social stratification in the United States. Others among his contemporaries retreated into abstract expressionism, however, which gave the appearance of political neutrality or indifference. A skillful choreographer like Erick Hawkins, whose *Parson Weems and the Cherry Tree* has become a classic of modern dance, used mythic materials in a droll and playful manner, much as Grant Wood had done, so that audiences really could not tell whether Hawkins's appropriation of national legends was affectionate and affirming or iconoclastic and critical. Performed to early American folk tunes reworked by Virgil Thompson, *Parson Weems* has been aptly described as "a mostly funny meeting of American naïveté with commedia dell'arte." In a 1980 interview, however, Hawkins tipped his

16.1   Andrew Wyeth, *Memorial Day: Mother Archie's Church Near Chadd's Ford, Pennsylvania* (watercolor), 1946. Charles Henry Hayden Fund and Abraham Shuman Fund. Courtesy of the Museum of Fine Arts, Boston.

hand, at least partially: "No matter how beautiful the tradition of the past," he said, "you can't rely on anybody else's authority. You have to dig it out yourself."[23]

I I

THE DIFFICULTY for an artist or writer who hoped to achieve any degree of success seemed very simple: patriotism was basically "in" and cynicism was "out" for more than fifteen years following the end of the war. The symbolic tone was appropriately set in 1946, when Andrew Wyeth (then age twenty-nine) painted *Memorial Day: Mother Archie's Church Near Chadd's Ford, Pennsylvania,* which includes a man sitting reflectively on a pew, and an American flag in the upper corner (fig. 16.1). The flag, prayer, mother, and father: no doubt the notion came straight from Wyeth's heart. Victory had given way to visions of just causes and righteous memories.

Following World War II, speakers at the Alamo in Texas were usually military heroes who reaffirmed our divine destiny and regarded communism as a moral challenge to the spiritual resources of America. Observances at the Alamo provided true patriots with an ideal opportunity to "examine the American spirit." Simultaneously, between 1951 and 1957 aerial re-enactments that simulated World War II battles originated in Texas, spread swiftly across the South, and enjoyed considerable appeal. What began as annual fighter aircraft shows in Harlingen, Texas, somehow led to re-enactments of the bombing of Japan—the only feature of these curious postwar rituals that became controversial in any way. In 1957 a new and bizarre connection developed between such aerial battles and the Confederacy. People gathered and participated in rituals that glorified the culture of the Old South as much as they commemorated events from World War II. Two very different episodes in American history became blended, and viewers came away with an illusion that the Confederacy must have won a century earlier, and was still winning.[24]

Visitors to sites like Colonial Williamsburg commented constantly throughout the 1950s that going there instilled or else enhanced very powerful feelings of national pride and patriotism. A high percentage of those who sent heartfelt letters to John D. Rockefeller, Jr., informed him that they were newcomers or else the children of immigrants: "To me the beginnings of freedom," one wrote, "are like hallowed ground."[25]

Predictably, perhaps, such places continued to be venerated as "shrines" by large numbers of people from all strata of society. Some tourists at Williamsburg referred to "these sacred stones"; and a very typical pilgrim thanked Rockefeller for "the refreshing and inspiring shrine of patriotism and culture you have made available to us all."[26] Many other sites, ranging from the Alamo to Sunnyside (Washington Irving's gabled house in Tarrytown, New York) to the home of George Washington's mother in Fredericksburg, Virginia, were frequently referred to as "sacred shrines"[27] (figs. 16.2 and 16.3).

The pilgrimage metaphor also persisted throughout the 1950s, though it is clear, once again from self-generated letters, that to most of those who used the word it meant more than a metaphor.

- "If it were possible for every youngster to make a 'pilgrimage' to Williamsburg, we would probably never be in danger of losing our freedom."

- From a man who spent a week at Williamsburg in 1959: "The patriotic pilgrimage has been a source of constant inspiration."

- From a Pittsburgh woman who went for four days in 1959: "I just want to thank you with all my heart, for being such a wonderful partner of Our Heavenly Father in re-establishing this wonderful place to help us Americans understand our wonderful heritage."[28]

16.2 Home of Mary Ball Washington, Fredericksburg, Virginia.

16.3 Hugh Mercer Apothecary
Shop, Fredericksburg, Virginia.

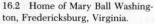

By 1947 members of the Holland Society were making pilgrimages to
the early Dutch sites located in the lower Hudson River Valley; and
within two years the Westchester County Historical Society had begun
to arrange for an Annual Fall Pilgrimage to Sunnyside and the nearby
Sleepy Hollow Restorations.[29]

CONSIDERING the widely shared language of civil religion
that transcended sectional boundaries, and the growing ease of travel
that truly nationalized tourism, one might come away with the superficial impression that regional chauvinism had ceased to be meaningful.
Although the sharp rivalries and resentments we noted during the half
century prior to 1940 diminished somewhat, they certainly did not
disappear. An organization like the Mayflower Society flourished between 1947 and 1955 in order to preserve "the best in Pilgrim traditions." After Esther Forbes published *Rainbow on the Road* in 1953,
she received a characteristic fan letter from John P. Marquand. "Somehow you have caught the whole spirit of New England," he wrote,
"which I used to recognize when I talked to very old people during my
childhood." Forbes responded with delight. "It was the old N.E. that I,
too, remember the elderly droning on about that I tried to get."[30]

Following World War II a fair number of Westerners professed that
their region was more Western than it had ever been before. Some of

that hyperbole, however, was clearly aimed at tourists, who came to figure ever more prominently in the section's economy. The immense popularity of A. B. Guthrie's fiction helped to sustain some claims on behalf of Western individualism, hardihood, and a strange sense of timelessness despite the striking changes that had occurred over the span of a century. In *The Big Sky* (1947), Guthrie's absorbing novel about the mountain men during the 1830s and 1840s, Boone Caudill ruminates on the passage of time while living in contentment with Teal Eye among her people, the Piegan Indians.

> Life went along one day after another . . . and the days went together and lost themselves in one another. Looking back, it was as if time ran into itself and flowed over, running forward from past times and running back from now so that yesterday and today were the same. Or maybe time didn't flow at all but just stood still while a body moved around in it.[31]

Dick Summers, one of the last mountain men, connects *The Big Sky* with Guthrie's absorbing sequel, *The Way West* (1950), the narrative of an overland caravan that struggles from Missouri to Oregon in 1846. When Summers anticipates the annual trappers' "rendezvous" in 1837, his mind reaches back to earlier, simpler times in a way that mirrors the postwar mood of wistfulness. "Half the pleasure was in the remembering mind," Guthrie reflects; and the reader feels powerfully a poignant sense of time that has passed irrevocably. The very nature of memory is made manifestly bittersweet.[32]

The nature of memory in the West was not one-dimensional, however. An acknowledgment of ethnic diversity in the region that emerged during the 1930s became a significant cultural force by 1950 when Montanans initiated a Festival of Nations attended by more than twenty groups, but especially Finns, Italians, Slovenes, and Croatians. Hour-long "nationality programs" were presented to capacity crowds in a civic center that was transformed into a museum. Despite all of the attention to ethnic foods, costumes, and heritage in general, however, this on-going festival at Red Lodge always featured an exhibit devoted to the Old West—the pre-ethnic, pre–melting pot, American West.[33]

The Jamestown Festival of 1957 brought to fulfillment those Southern hopes and dreams that had been shared a generation earlier by Lyon G. Tyler, Philip A. Bruce, and David Rankin Barbee. This eight-month celebration was extremely well publicized. Many different groups within Southern society participated, and the Episcopal Church used its network and hierarchy to help make the 350th anniversary of permanent settlement in British North America a national event. Above all, however, for Southern chauvinists it became a year to savor because Virginia's priority in the genesis of U.S. history finally escaped from New England hegemony and won widespread recognition.[34]

The swift success and favorable publicity achieved by Colonial Williamsburg proved to be influential as well as infectious. As early as 1939 the Tarrytown Historical Society approached John D. Rockefeller, Jr., with a request for funds to transform the Philipse home into a "historic shrine." The Society's president acknowledged publicly that plans to restore St. Augustine, Florida, would do for the early phase of Hispanic colonization what Williamsburg had achieved for the eighteenth-century South. "Yet the Tarrytowns, with the story of the North, are just as rich in lore, and, in my opinion, have a richer historic background than either of the other communities—and no Northern restoration has been attempted."[35]

Rockefeller's estate, located at Pocantico Hills in North Tarrytown, was close by; and as his interest in the various projects grew, so did his financial support. In fact, the concept of Historical Monuments, Inc., was developed by 1944 so that Rockefeller might undertake for historic buildings in New York State something comparable to his efforts in Virginia. Although the corporation never came into being, Rockefeller lobbied discreetly and effectively with Governor Thomas E. Dewey in 1944 on behalf of a bill in the New York Assembly that would permit historical societies and structures to charge admission. Rockefeller's prestige in the field of historic preservation enabled him to mobilize the interest of Stephen C. Clark and Dixon Ryan Fox, the chief patron and president, respectively, of the New York State Historical Association based in Cooperstown.[36]

Despite the same concern for authenticity and substantial attention to public relations, Sleepy Hollow Restorations did not achieve the immediate success that Williamsburg had enjoyed ever since 1933. A special visiting committee came for four days in 1952; and Harold Dean Cater, director of the Minnesota Historical Society, was brought in 1955 to professionalize and run the cluster of Tarrytown sites. Soon thereafter a variety of special programs at Philipse Castle and Sunnyside began to attract more visitors, and special attempts were made to "reach" Dutch as well as Dutch-American tourists. Amateur archaeologists were even permitted to "dig" under controlled circumstances, a practice not allowed elsewhere and one that administrators at Colonial Williamsburg regarded as a highly problematic precedent.[37]

By 1959 attendance had improved, though not as much as the Sleepy Hollow administrators had hoped; so they commissioned a visitor survey using a questionnaire carefully designed by a Madison Avenue public relations firm. Close to one thousand responses were returned and the complaints formed a fairly clear pattern. First, admission prices seemed too high for those in the "lower salary bracket." Second, some found the tours too "regimented" and occasionally rushed at Sunnyside. Third, people resented not being allowed to take photographs inside the buildings. Fourth, those who encountered school tours of small children were not happy. And finally, reactions to the souvenir shop called attention to problematic prices and insufficient variety. Significantly, Colonial Williamsburg provided the most frequent basis for comparison.[38]

Positive responses also followed a pattern: children enhanced their understanding of colonial America; the guides were well informed and the costumed "hostesses" added warmth and charm; the contrast between "then" and "now" seemed especially fascinating (note the emphasis upon historical discontinuity). A few representative extracts convey the flavor of these candid responses.

- From a woman in Toledo, Ohio: "I love to see the beauty and artistry of Colonial homes of the wealthier American. It's wonderful to keep all such shrines preserved for posterity."

- From a man in Eastport, Long Island: "The women who spoke with me about Sunnyside and Philipsburg Manor were well informed, neat in appearance, and above average in class. Keep them that way!"

- From a man in Preakness, New Jersey: "I feel that it is a very important function to show how the early Dutch families lived as New York was started out by the Dutchman [sic]. It had a culture particularly interesting in pattern, with such a sharp contrast with today's living."

Despite the concern felt by those responsible for Sleepy Hollow, their visitation figures in 1957 increased 39.5 percent over the previous year. The director of development at Williamsburg gathered statistics from sister institutions and tried to keep close track of how historic sites were faring. His compilation for 1957 suggests that tourism oriented to the past had begun to surge in the later 1950s. All of his sources showed some sort of increase:[39]

Mount Vernon	4.5%
Monticello	2.6%
Mystic Seaport	17.00%
Old Sturbridge Village	17.06%
Corning Glass (free)	25.00%
Greenfield Village	30.00%
Mariners Museum (free)	6.9%
Cooperstown	20–30%

Colonial Williamsburg has always kept careful count of its own attendance figures. Although they are higher in absolute numbers than those at similar places, the rates of change and proportions are symptomatic. They leaped from nearly 94,000 in 1945 to more than 166,000 the following year. A decade later (1956), they rose above 341,000; by 1966 to more than double that, at 722,000; and then the record peak in the year of the American Revolution Bicentennial (1976), at 1,289,302. There has been a gradual decline since that time, as we shall see in chapter eighteen.

During the 1950s, especially, Williamsburg's staff were attentive to visitor responses, both qualitative and in the aggregate. When a friend of John D. Rockefeller III wrote an insightful twenty-four-page confidential analysis of public reactions to C.W. in 1954, the reaction at the top was swift. Administrative officers were informed that after January 1, 1955, "we will no longer talk in our presentation program about 'things' but we will talk about 'people.' " On the more "scientific" side, in 1960 C.W. hired the firm of Child & Waters to devise a Visitor Analysis Study; and the instrument that firm designed can only be described as exhaustive. It ranged from an evaluation of hotels and motels to the quality of the introductory film, *The Story of a Patriot,* to assessments of the craft shops, to comparisons of the exhibits requiring tickets of admission with those that did not.[40]

Some of the observations and recommendations made in 1954 are revealing both for their substance and because it took more than two decades for many changes to occur. Quite a number of visitors, for example, refused to believe that the Brush-Everard House had been built as a middle-class artisan's home. "They want to see how really poor people lived, and slaves, and indentured servants. The absence of any evidence of lower-class life gives some visitors a feeling that either Williamsburg is ashamed of this aspect of colonial life . . . or simply negligent in giving the whole picture." After the writer of this report, aptly named Arthur Goodfriend, had summarized or quoted the views of numerous tourists, he diffidently offered a few friendly yet critical suggestions of his own. Two of them are particularly penetrating:

> Williamsburg's appeal seems directed more to the eye than to the spirit. Its emphasis is more on material things, and less on men and ideas. . . . If Williamsburg's message is not as visible as its beauty, little wonder. To build and furnish a fine house is a hard and challenging task. But to install memories and meanings . . . is a task transcending in difficulty all others.[41]

Some additional problems that arose during the postwar years seem less metaphysical and had more to do with social relations. Overt discrimination against Jews who tried to make reservations at the elegant Inn provoked ire and bitter letters of protest. When an occasional Jew served on the board or staff at C.W., it appears to have been regarded as something of an anomaly.[42] Racism remained a more serious and a more visible problem. During the fifteen years following 1945, African-American residents of the community, as well as tourists, suffered from various forms of discrimination, most of them the humiliating result of demeaning conditions of work and segregated public facilities. They could not buy a meal in the restored area or anywhere near it. Restrooms were marked "Ladies" and "Gentlemen" for whites but "Men" and "Women" for blacks. They were not even permitted to *enter* the famous Inn. A lengthy report written in 1951 by Winthrop Rockefeller's black chauffeur enumerated the grievances felt by local residents: loss of desirable property locations as a result of the restoration; no place to go for leisure after work except for two dilapidated "beer rooms"; only one place to see movies, the black high school (when it was in session); and the demoralization of leaders within the black community.[43]

John D. Rockefeller, Jr., did not wish to flout Southern customs, nor did he want affluent whites to be uncomfortable or, worse, feel discouraged from coming to Williamsburg. In 1948 he discussed with the manager of the Arizona Inn in Tucson how that exclusive place kept undesirables away. The answer, in brief, JDR conveyed to Kenneth Chorley: "They never make any bookings by letter unless they, personally, know the person or until they have thoroughly looked him up." The various ways of accomplishing that objective would do credit to the FBI. When Rockefeller received the black chauffeur's report, he sent Chorley a long response whose tone was clear from the outset: "it would appear that the colored people of Williamsburg do not recall what the Restoration has done for them, both directly as well as indirectly." The African-Americans knew perfectly well what JDR could not comprehend: separate meant considerably less than equal. As early as 1950, however, his son John III acknowledged "how little we have to offer [Negroes] in the community."[44]

White visitors were largely oblivious to racial tensions at Williamsburg. One woman wrote on luxuriant stationery from Palm Beach following her visit: "From the negro maids in the kitchens to the very charming ladies in the Governor's Palace—we found a tremendous amount of civic pride." Another woman who had spent two weeks there in 1959 sent her note of appreciation from Menlo Park, California: "The atmosphere generated by two colors of employees expressing the best in friendliness, personalized service and unfailing good manners to continuous thousands is phenomenal."[45]

Insensitive letters were less common than effusive or banal ones. The history master at Mercersburg Academy in Pennsylvania explained that he brought his students every year because Williamsburg stood out as "one of the great cradles of American culture and tradition." An anonymous person wrote to JDR from Lynn, Massachusetts, that he or she "found antiquity, beauty, peace and tranquility. . . . I hope when the time comes, you will go straight to heaven." An individual in Sacramento followed his visit with just the sort of letter that Rockefeller, Ford, and others who had undertaken similar enterprises loved to receive: "In this atomic age of struggling for future survival, most of us overlook the lessons that can be learned of the past. . . . No detail was

left undone [at Williamsburg] to give to living America a most important phase of our proud heritage."[46] Two phrases recur constantly in
Rockefeller's fan mail and in response to visitor surveys: "authentic"
and "living past."

One other category of correspondence should be noted: requests for
information about particular artifacts and for advice about the administration of such a place. Even more important, however, was the sheer
inspiration that Williamsburg provided to people like those in Winston-
Salem who decided in 1950 to restore Old Salem, a Moravian settlement that developed during the third quarter of the eighteenth
century.[47]

In the later years of his presidency, when a well-trained staff could
be relied upon to mind the shop at home, Kenneth Chorley became a
kind of evangelist and cheerleader for historic restorations. He spoke
in July 1957 to the Preservation Society of Newport County in Rhode
Island, an organization established ten years earlier. Chorley's host
explained to him that "local people do not yet appreciate the advantages which would accrue to them from an expanding program of
historic preservation in Newport." In one place after another Chorley
stressed the economic benefits of museum villages, restorations, and
historic preservation. In May 1957, when he spoke in Burlington, Vermont, at a luncheon to honor the Webbs on the tenth anniversary of the
Shelburne Museum, Chorley devoted a substantial section of his address
to "The Economic Impact of Shelburne Museum" in which he calculated that over the course of a decade it had brought more than $1.8
million into the local economy. He offered the same sort of emphasis in
July 1965 when he spoke at Wentworth-by-the-Sea in Portsmouth, New
Hampshire. Chorley lavished praise upon the Strawbery Banke project
that was just then getting under way. "I wonder if you realize what a
bargain Strawbery Banke has," he asked. "It paid $28,646 for 9½ acres
of land in Portsmouth and 27 eighteenth-century buildings. Frankly, I
never in my life heard of such a purchase." His major admonition to his
audience: Don't be derivative, don't imitate any other restoration project, and above all, be authentic.[48]

If I have devoted what may seem disproportionate space to Colonial
Williamsburg, it is not merely on account of its primacy in time or the
comprehensiveness of its archival records. It is fundamentally because
of C.W.'s immense impact upon subsequent projects that have been
diverse in nature and geographically distributed; its powerful image
among the elite as well as the middle class; and, as we shall see in the
following chapter, its co-operative role with government as an active
participant in the Cold War's politics of culture.

As a final example of C.W.'s curious capacity to attract all sorts of
people and to elicit mixed reactions, it should be noticed that James
Agee, best known because of his fascination with poor white sharecrop-
pers in the Deep South, paid a visit to Williamsburg early in 1955 in

order to explore the prospect of making a short film about the American Revolution. He never did, although his imaginative plans for such a movie are intriguing. Agee's reaction to Williamsburg is interesting because it encapsulates the overall ambivalence that we find when we tally up the balance sheet of raves and criticisms written during the postwar years. "I was about equally impressed and depressed by the Restoration," he wrote, "as too Churchy, museum-like and dead—and was encouraged that when I spoke frankly of this, every member of the staff agreed with me."[49]

I I I

I N 1 9 4 4 , even before the war ended, Kenneth Chorley wrote to his counterpart at the Henry Ford Museum and Greenfield Village because both were beginning to contemplate "post-war plans" for their respective projects. Chorley and some of his staff made a visit to Dearborn that year in order to "look over some of the things which Mr. Ford has done."[50] Very soon after this visit, however, Ford suffered a stroke and remained incapacitated until his death in 1947. Within a few years the Museum and Village in Dearborn not only began to increase their holdings and exhibits, but notably expanded their educational efforts, which ranged from popular radio and television programs related to American history by way of the collections, to a more "high-tone" annual lecture series concerning antiques that has brought leading authorities on American decorative arts and culture to Dearborn every year since 1952. A decade later the Robert H. Tannahill Research Library was created in the Education Building, thereby consolidating for the first time in forty-one years all of the books, manuscripts, and photographic materials that were previously scattered in different areas of this extensive museum complex. Tannahill had been a lifelong supporter of cultural institutions in Detroit, a collector of art and antiques, and for many years prior to his death in 1969 a trustee of Greenfield Village and the Ford Museum. The library includes manuscripts, rare books, a special collection of American business archives and inventories, a large gathering of trade catalogues, another section devoted to prints, maps, sheet music, broadsides, and frakturs, yet another that concentrates on the history and development of photography, a special collection of early American paper currency and stamps, and a remarkable file of eighteenth- and nineteenth-century newspapers.[51]

By the 1980s administrators in Dearborn had clarified their focus— not easy to do given the extraordinary diversity of their collections— and it is characteristic of the era that the key word in their detailed thematic statement is "change": "This main theme of change has within it several sub-themes: How our life at home, at work, and in the community has changed. . . . How the way we make, sell, and buy things has changed. . . . How the way we spend our leisure time has changed."[52]

Meanwhile the earliest "living farm" museum and village in New England changed its name from Quinebaug Village to Old Sturbridge Village and opened to the public on June 8, 1946. Eighty-one curious visitors came that day, and another 5,100 by the close of the season in early October. The following year a craft reproductions shop was opened in the Wight House, and in 1948 the first Village development plan was prepared. Three years later automobiles were barred from the exhibition area and a horse-drawn Carry-all tour was inaugurated. A program for school groups also began on a limited basis in 1951. The following year a research department got started, one that has expanded steadily and impressively ever since. That same summer quite a few major structures were installed and dedicated, including the Isaiah Thomas Printing Office (c. 1783), moved from Worcester, Massachusetts; the Pliny Freeman Farm (1801); the John Fenno House (1704), from Canton, Massachusetts; and a covered bridge (1870), from Dummerston, Vermont. In 1953 an outdoor theatre went up and offered Benét's *The Devil and Daniel Webster* as its first production. In 1958 the Village hosted a preservation planning conference in conjunction with the Society for the Preservation of New England Antiquities.[53] All in all, the institution had followed a highly representative evolution during its developmental years—although it must be kept in mind that each one of these places had its own distinctive if not idiosyncratic history.[54]

The Shaker Museum located in the upper Hudson River Valley at Old Chatham, New York, developed from the compulsive collecting of John S. Williams. He started with an enthusiasm for antique farm equipment, but switched to Shaker tools and artifacts in 1936 when he came upon a "mine of material" nearby in New Lebanon, New York, where the Shakers founded the Mother House of the Order at the close of the eighteenth century. By the later 1940s Williams had accumulated so much material that he decided to make it accessible to the public in a museum. It opened in 1950 and has been augmented ever since. Williams's principal aim was to provide a broad picture of Shaker life and culture. Consequently, he explained, "great emphasis has been laid on those tools with which the Shakers worked, as well as many simple things with which they lived." The Museum's trustees and director refer to it as an educational institution that "memorializes the work and beliefs of a relatively small religious sect whose influence on the United States was completely out of proportion to its numerical size."[55]

It is inescapable that so many of these museums have resulted from the personal interests (and often, but not always, the wealth) of a single individual. In the case of Richmondtown Restoration, however, located on twenty acres in the wooded highlands of Staten Island, a man of modest means named Loring McMillan poured his singular energy and determination into a local history project that had its genesis in 1935 but did not really begin to grow, acquire properties and artifacts, until the years from 1945 until 1958, and formally opened in 1964. It aspires to be a "living museum of the 200-year history of a village," rather than a re-creation devoted to a particular period, like Williamsburg.[56]

Knott's Berry Farm in Southern California had its literal genesis in 1920 when Walter Knott, then thirty-one, rented ten acres in Orange County and planted berries. His wife became famous for her fruit pies, so they opened a restaurant during the 1930s. In 1940 they created Ghost Town with a cyclorama—a gigantic circular painting that depicted the early migration by Conestoga wagon of Knott's forebears into the West. One man's hobby and modest beginnings led to the re-creation of a complete frontier town, with everything from saloons to livery stables. In 1950 Knott bought and relocated from Colorado a narrow-gauge railroad. The route of the Denver and Rio Grande Western in its new Buena Park setting covered one mile. It opened to the public in January 1952—the only narrow-gauge passenger train in the United States operating on a year-round daily schedule.[57]

Knott subsequently added more acreage with Western trappings, and by 1955 completed Calico, the re-creation of a California desert community where the Knotts had once lived. The mining town at Buena Park offered tourists more attractions than they would ever have seen at any single historical mining town, and included a Wild West pageant. Tourists at the level of mass and popular culture enjoyed it, and in Orange County they also seemed to resonate to Knott's strident commitment to free enterprise. Notions of personal liberty and individualism that Knott associated with nineteenth-century frontier America inspired his ideological commitment.[58]

In 1955, just when Knott's version of the Wild West experience reached completion, Disneyland opened in Anaheim, not far away, featuring Main Street, U.S.A., a turn-of-the-century streetscape, scaled to three-quarter size, in which the daunting pace of twentieth-century social change was not permitted to intrude. History is not merely present owing to architectural style, but by virtue of such traditional landmarks as a memorial obelisk in the town square to Civil War dead. With the passage of several decades, however, the immense influence of Disneyland made it more and more difficult to distinguish between what really happened in times gone by and what is *supposed* to have happened. In 1974, for example, the town of Medina, Ohio, emulated Disneyland and created new "historic" structures that had never even existed in Medina. In the realm of actual historic preservation, efforts to revitalize Main Street in American communities during the later sixties and seventies owed much to Disney's fantasy creation of 1955.[59]

More historical and less commercial motives seemed to be emerging in central and Northern California. In 1957 a preservation activist in Carmel sought advice from Henry Flynt, who had been responsible for the attractive restoration of Old Deerfield, Massachusetts.[60] The man explained that he and others in the Monterey area wanted to benefit from the experience accumulated at places like Deerfield, Williamsburg, and Lincoln's New Salem in Illinois. Two years earlier the National Trust for Historic Preservation was bequeathed Casa Amesti, one of the fine adobe homes in Monterey, built early in the nineteenth century. Local activists faced a problem because with the old Mexican Custom House, the Robert Louis Stevenson House, and the Larkin House, it had an embarrassment of riches. They could not all be converted into museums, and needed to be used in diversified ways, public and private, just as the Flynts had done at Deerfield.[61] Eventually they were all "saved," and the National Trust played an important part in the process.

IV

FORTUNATELY, several volumes pertaining to the history of the National Trust have already been written and do not need to be recapitulated here. Nevertheless, some basic aspects of the narrative that are especially germane to our concerns must be acknowledged.[62] Otherwise the growing enthusiasm for many aspects of historic preservation during the past three decades would lack context and coherent meaning.

In 1947 a National Council for Historic Sites and Buildings emerged from an informal confederation of interested organizations. It received active support from prominent citizens and from the National Park Service. Members regarded themselves as an educational, policy-forming, public interest group. They looked to the British National Trust, which had been operative for half a century, as a model in key respects. Congress then passed an act establishing a National Trust for the United States, but did so with the understanding that no funds would have to be appropriated. Those who spearheaded the movement made a commitment to find support from non-governmental sources. The whole venture remained right in line with traditional American assumptions about the responsibility borne by the private sector for the perpetuation of culture. In that sense this organization, led by a coalition of patricians, scholars, and Park Service veterans, determined to be innovative in redeeming a rich heritage and chose to be self-consciously old-fashioned.[63]

By 1949, when the permanent Trust supplanted the temporary Council, the latter had already assisted in several local campaigns to save historic houses; it had supported the preservation of superfluous military property having historical significance, and the survey of archaeological remains located in river valleys likely to be flooded. It had also prepared criteria for the selection of historic sites and buildings, had begun to collect data about them and, in response to a request from the Secretary of the Interior, created a committee to study the need for a nationwide inventory and survey of historic landmarks.[64]

Between 1948 and 1956 individual memberships in the Trust grew slowly, from 165 to almost 1500; but organizational membership leaped from 35 to 182 societies, thereby including virtually all major organizations either directly or indirectly preoccupied with historic preservation. The Trust concerned itself with preservation legislation at every level, from national and state to local, which largely involved historic zoning. The Trust also developed, as a service, what its director called the "archive," an expanding information file about historic sites and buildings in the United States that became sufficiently well known and accessible that it could be used by journalists and activists as well as by the staff. Business organizations and chambers of commerce were impressed by the Trust's survey of travel to historic sites and buildings open to the public in 1954—a total of almost 50 million visits. Tourism had become a very important part of the U.S. economy, and the American past figured prominently in that picture.[65]

In dealing with the wide variety of projects that arose, the Trust's staff relied upon personal consultation, offered assorted materials to ad hoc groups and organizations, advice and encouragement based upon cumulative experience in the field, and efforts to influence or "arouse the local conscience." An extract from the director's 1956 summary report of the first seven years gives a sweeping sense of particulars:

> The projects were sometimes statewide in character, as in Texas, Tennessee, Rhode Island, and Pennsylvania; sometimes they were concerned with city-wide programs, as in Tombstone, Arizona; Galena, Illinois; New Harmony, Indiana; Annapolis, Maryland; and Bethlehem, Pennsylvania; perhaps most frequently they dealt with single projects like the Adam Thoroughgood House and St. Luke's Church in Virginia; or the Helen Keller Birthplace in Tuscumbia, Alabama; or Kingsbury Plantation on Fort George's Island, Florida; or the Juliette Gordon Lowe House in Savannah, Georgia; or the Old Gaol and Sheriff's House in Wiscassett, Maine.[66]

The Trust gradually began to acquire, on a highly selective basis, sites (usually given with endowment for their maintenance) that were historically significant and geographically dispersed, such as the home of Woodrow Wilson in Washington, D.C., and Casa Amesti in Monterey, California. It has continued to publish its directory of *Private, Nonprofit Preservation Organizations: State & Local Levels.* And in 1973 it launched Preservation Week, an annual observance supported ever since by the President of the United States, a majority of state governors, and a great many mayors, who issue proclamations and make symbolic appearances acknowledging not merely the significance of such a week but the importance of saving the nation's built environment from needless deterioration or destruction. Individual membership has grown steadily since the mid-1950s as increasing numbers of people have become involved in local causes and have come to understand that the National Trust is, in the broadest sense, an educational organization that receives little federal support. As prospective members are informed, it is a "national, non-governmental organization providing for the safeguarding of America's heritage of sites, buildings and objects significant in our history and culture."[67]

As a co-ordinating and energizing organization, the Trust takes pride in work done and battles won by others at every level—quite often with moral or managerial support from the Trust. At the state level there have been historical preservation commissions since the early 1950s. They sponsor conferences devoted to such issues as "adaptive re-use" of historic sites in which municipal officials, commercial developers, and ardent preservation buffs who are private citizens participate cheek by jowl. The Preservation League of New York State, for instance, has been particularly active since 1974 in co-ordinating 350 organizations across the state; and in 1986 it promulgated "Architectural Heritage Year," a celebration of three centuries of architectural development in the Empire State.[68]

Although the National Trust and its co-ordinate societies could and frequently did make potent allies in the fifties and sixties, some of the most interesting campaigns during the earlier years of preservation activity arose from the enthusiasms and place-specific commitments of wealthy individuals who acted independently. As early as 1938 Miriam Wilson purchased the old Slave Mart in Charleston, South Carolina, and restored it as a museum that made most of the white community extremely uncomfortable. When she died in 1959 Miss Wilson deeded the Slave Mart to the Charleston Museum, which declined the gift. A few years later two of her devoted friends bought it, and it remains a museum whose sordid history has now been meticulously authenticated.[69]

Benjamin Rufus Kittredge restored Cypress Gardens, an antebellum plantation near Charleston where he and his wife lived from 1947 until 1964, when he gave it to the city—a non-controversial gift. Mrs. Lammot du Pont Copeland had numerous pet projects but the restoration of Gunston Hall, George Mason's home not far from Mount Vernon, remained a particular favorite. In 1955 Kenneth Chorley and a small group of Williamsburg "angels" urged Governor Robert B. Meyner of New Jersey to rehabilitate and make creative use of Morven, an elegant mansion built in Princeton by the Stockton family early in the eighteenth century. It was used as the governor's residence in several administrations until 1982.[70]

By the early 1960s widespread concern about lost landmarks and about criteria for preservation selection, principles of restoration, and proper adaptive use brought about a well-noticed four-day international conference held at Colonial Williamsburg, which co-sponsored the conference along with the National Trust. Their collective motives arose from a growing concern about "America's disappearing cultural heritage as the country's growth and change threaten to eradicate the buildings of the past." Speakers included the Inspector General of the Historic Monuments of France, which was responsible at that time for cleaning landmarks in Paris, and Stanislaw Lorentz of Warsaw, the man in charge of Poland's postwar reconstruction of Nazi-damaged cities. His account of the reconstruction of old town centers that had been bombed fascinated the group. The principal issue underlying the conference, however, involved the relative merits of preservation versus reconstruction, a debate that has remained controversial in the United States since the early 1930s. It had long been the position of both the National Trust and the Park Service that "it is better to preserve than to repair, better to repair than to restore, better to restore than to reconstruct." Reconstruction had become so trendy in recent years that genuine old buildings were destroyed in order to replace them with modern fabrications of earlier structures that may once have existed on the same or perhaps on an adjacent site.[71]

Critics challenged such inauthentic sentimentalism for the pre-industrial past and condemned sins of destruction committed in the name of nostalgic national chauvinism. They argued that a genuine 1840 house is preferable to a phony 1740 one; and Osbert Lancaster, a prominent British authority, asserted that "much of our pleasure derives from the complete integration of past and present. I am on the whole against selective restoration." The major issue remained unresolved as the conference closed, and fundamentally those involved today are not much closer to achieving consensus.[72]

From the early sixties through the seventies a great many struggles occurred in various localities among preservation groups, private developers, and public agencies determined to achieve urban renewal. Landmark commissions were often caught between Scylla and Charybdis, but varied considerably in their actual authority or capacity to mobilize public opinion. Sometimes private citizens were delighted by new tax incentives that encouraged rehabilitation, but in many other situations the designation of "historic districts" by landmark preservation commissions frustrated individuals who found that they could not alter their homes in any way without obtaining permission and then undergoing close scrutiny. Churches commonly fought against the conferral of "landmark status" because of the fear that required maintenance costs would bankrupt the congregation. One outcome was simply to donate a historic church to the National Park Service, which happened in 1980 when St. Paul's Episcopal Church in Mount Vernon, New York—where John Peter Zenger had covered the election story that led to his famous freedom-of-the-press case—was on the verge of physical disintegration.[73]

For more than a decade following 1973, four noteworthy developments in American preservation took place *pari passu*, three of them positive and one quite depressing because it concerned a whole sequence of setbacks that arose from changing governmental priorities and policies. The last-mentioned trend marked a dramatic reversal from the upbeat mood that accompanied the widely publicized appearance in 1966 of a handsome volume titled *With Heritage So Rich: A Report of a Special Committee on Historic Preservation under the Auspices of the United States Conference of Mayors* (published by Random House in New York).

Starting with the negative side: Early in 1976 the administration of President Gerald R. Ford announced that it intended to reduce by one half federal spending on the preservation and restoration of historic landmarks. In the year of the Revolution Bicentennial Ford urged reduction of what had been a $20 million appropriation to $10 million. The National Park Service protested that $400 million per year would be needed for a decade just to take care of the identified backlog of preservation needs and projects. Although Congress resisted and various organizations compensated for some of the shortfall, the Reagan administration announced early in 1981 that for budgetary reasons it planned to reduce funding for the national preservation program almost to nothing. The Historic Preservation Fund has limped along ever since; and a cordial alliance between government and the National Trust that reached a peak in 1966 has become increasingly tenuous.[74]

On the positive side, however, the U.S. Supreme Court rendered a decision in 1978 that Grand Central Terminal in New York City could be declared a historic landmark, thereby limiting architectural alterations without violating the constitutional rights of owners or developers. (The Penn Central Transportation Co. had planned to lease the "air rights" above the Terminal to a builder who intended to place a fifty-five-storey office structure on top of the 1913 Beaux-Arts masterpiece station.) This particular case had been fought in various courts for a full decade, and it immediately established a national precedent that municipalities could create landmark designations in order to protect culturally significant properties from demolition or unreasonable alteration. Although the legacy of that case, *Penn Central Transportation Co. v. New York City*, seemed threatened by a case that came from California in 1986–87, it remains the law and has profound consequences for preservationists.[75]

By 1977 more than four thousand historic preservation organizations existed in the United States, some of them prestigious in their membership and programs, but most of them very much at the grass-roots level. They played an active and vital role in their communities, and scarcely a week passed when some new "save," adaptive re-use, or change of custody wasn't announced. They ranged from "Art's Auto" in Pawtucket, Rhode Island, to the entire town of Waterford, Virginia, to

Eleanor Roosevelt's home (Val-Kill) in Hyde Park, to the massive Lit Brothers' department store in Philadelphia.[76]

Yet another positive trend in this period took the form of a growing desire by private individuals to restore old homes. A publication started to appear in 1973 known as *The Old House Journal: Restoration and Maintenance Techniques for the Antique House*. Within five years an observer noted that new owners of old Federal-style homes in Newburyport, Massachusetts, were reconstructing the genealogies of their houses rather than their family histories! In 1978 the Historic House Association of America became active and immediately began to receive annual grants from the National Trust. By 1982 its membership of 1,600 included owners of country estates, urban row houses, and stone cottages. During the mid-1980s "This Old House" emerged as a highly popular television program, and the news media ran regular feature stories on unusual or innovative uses of older homes.[77]

In the four decades following 1949, historic preservation came a very long way. It had been transformed from an enthusiasm indulged by the well-to-do and well educated to a passion shared by large numbers of ordinary Americans. It had matured in terms of sophistication well beyond the construction of shopping malls with replicas of Independence Hall (1963–65), or the dedication of "Independence Hall" at Knott's Berry Farm on July 4, 1966. Walter Knott wanted his Liberty Bell to be authentically cracked rather than drilled. Consequently, he had the bell frozen in dry ice. Then a heli-arc torch could be applied to a built-in fracture line. The bell cracked perfectly![78]

The National Trust for Historic Preservation, by its very nature, has been concerned with "properties," both in the sense of real estate and with connotations of social qualities, such as values. A concern for collective identity rooted in history has persisted in a prominent way. The elegant report titled *With Heritage So Rich* (1965) asserted that "a nation can be a victim of amnesia. It can lose the memories of what it was." Seventeen years later, when National Trust President Michael L. Ainslie spoke at the Lincoln Memorial on the occasion of Lincoln's Birthday (February 12, 1982), he raised this question: "Without a national memory, what will there be to inspire future generations to proceed confidently?"[79]

By the close of 1985 the Trust had achieved a measure of tangible success that its founders could scarcely have envisioned. Its annual budget of $18 million is derived from private contributions, endowment funds, and dues paid by 165,000 members. Moreover, although the Reagan administration attempted every year, 1981–85, to curtail federal funds for the Trust, Congress overrode the administration each year and, in 1985, appropriated $4.41 million. Back in 1949 the founders had not sought or received a penny from the public trough. The Trust now administers seventeen historic properties, publishes a monthly newspaper and a bimonthly magazine, and has provided leadership in more than twenty-five cities to rehabilitate old and historic buildings as part of the urban revitalization process. It has not only helped to achieve cooperation between developers and preservationists, but during the mid- and later 1980s aspired to help shape urban policy. According to J. Jackson Walter, who became president in December 1984, "We are interested in developing a public, private partnership that uses historic preservation as an ongoing principle, rather than having government go it alone, cities go it alone, companies go it alone."[80]

As we shall see in the next chapter, that statement was not just Reagan-era rhetoric. It represented a mood, if not a formula, that had been in the air, at least with respect to American traditions, since the 1950s, and in a still broader sense ever since the 1930s.

V

WHEN we try to comprehend the whole panorama of historical enterprises during the second half of the twentieth century, we are immediately struck by the sheer number of success stories, like that of the National Trust. We hear and know far less about the failures, even though there have been some whoppers. The failures are highly instructive, in fact, and can help us not only make sense of the successes, but perhaps even discern a distinctively American pattern in them.

Let us examine the strange case of The Hall of Our History, Inc., a fiasco first envisioned in 1938 by an architect named Eric Gugler. Although the concept began to take shape in 1941, World War II blanketed it with obscurity. In 1946, however, a prominent group of citizens from Georgia contemplated it as a memorial to Franklin D. Roosevelt. Even though the Roosevelt family expressed interest and promised to donate a large farm in the Pine Mountain area not far from Warm Springs, the form of the memorial was never settled upon. In 1950 one of the Georgians, Henry J. Toombs (who had designed the Little White House at Warm Springs), suggested changing the nature of the project to a "national shrine depicting the historical basis of our American heritage." Such a project had long been envisioned by Eric Gugler, who specialized in public memorials. By 1953 Gugler had become chairman of the policy board of The Hall of Our History.[81]

The elaborate scheme for the project is simply astounding. A prestigious board of trustees numbering between ninety and one hundred persons was envisioned, with President Eisenhower serving as honorary chairman. Physically the structure was to take the form of a "vast court" that would present in "sculptured relief and carved inscription" the history of the United States from Columbus to World War I. "It will be the biggest history book in the world," located in an open granite structure (with ninety-foot walls) designed to surmount a prominent mesa-like knoll overlooking the Pine Mountain area and adjoining the Franklin D. Roosevelt State Park. The state of Georgia was supposedly prepared to donate 2,000 acres, and plans were discussed to obtain even more land in order to "protect the view from the site to the horizon." The estimated cost was $50 million over a ten-year period, with fund raising based upon a popular appeal similar to that used by the March of Dimes for polio. Start-up funds would be sought from charitable groups and foundations, both corporate and private. The financial campaign would be decentralized, headed on the state level by the director of each state historical society, and carried out by county and local groups responsive to him. Finally, perhaps the ultimate in naïveté, "one half of the proceeds of each popular financial appeal will be retained by the local state group to preserve and restore local historical shrines at the discretion of the local group."[82]

Although Judge Learned Hand, a New Englander sitting on the federal bench in New York, published a laudatory essay about the project in the *Atlanta Journal and Constitution Sunday magazine,* and thereby called national attention to the enterprise, its most striking feature, apart from elephantine proportions, was its emphasis upon decentralization. The planners seem to have been genuinely concerned about "matters of local historical interest," and they urged consideration of six proposals: publishing state, county, and local histories for use in the schools; establishing county museums and historical centers; preserving sites and properties of local historical interest; encouraging projects for junior historians; encouraging historical tourism and commemorations; funding radio and television programs concerning local history.[83]

NEEDLESS to say, the project never got going. Its sheer scale, cost, and location were all wildly unrealistic. At that very time, however, other multi-million-dollar history projects, some of them also set at remote sites, succeeded. Can any crucial differences be identified? With few exceptions the major presentations of Americana—restorations, museums, villages, whatever—began not as memorials to heroes or abstract idealizations of United States history. Rather, they originated as the passionate commitment of a compulsive collector or wealthy individual with a vision of some highly tangible configuration of physical artifacts that interested him or (more than occasionally) her.

American collectors have tended to be possessive, competitive, and eager for a certain sort of immortality. One man who devoted half a century to collecting American firearms told the founder of the Valley Forge Museum that "I want my collection to be kept together, for if it be sold it will be scattered, and no one will know that I had any interest except the making of money. Then, if it be sold my rivals will buy the arms they need to make their collections greater than mine."[84]

Most of the major museums developed as the lengthened shadow of someone's enthusiasm. Ford and Rockefeller are obvious examples that have already received sufficient attention. In 1947 Henry Francis du Pont recognized that his collection of early American furniture and decorative arts must eventually become a museum; Winterthur opened to the public in 1951. Electra Havemeyer Webb's museum of Americana, ranging from fine art to folk, began to be planned in 1947 and opened at Shelburne, Vermont, in 1952. The Thomas Gilcrease Museum of American History and Art opened at Tulsa, Oklahoma, in 1949.[85] Henry N. Flynt started collecting autographs and historical documents during the 1930s. In 1945 he and his wife, Helen Geier Flynt, purchased and restored the Deerfield Inn. Two years later they decided to restore the Jonathan Ashley House as a monument to Deerfield's intriguing colonial past. Five years and numerous restorations later they opened Historic Deerfield to the public, replete with fifteen thousand early American artifacts. In 1953 the James Ford Bell collection of books and maps pertaining to the age of discovery, colonization, and Americana became available as a special collection with its own curatorial staff at the University of Minnesota.[86]

In 1957 the Abby Aldrich Rockefeller Folk Art Museum opened at its new permanent home in Williamsburg; and four years after that Amon Carter's collection of Western American art was established as a museum in Fort Worth, Texas. In 1966 Bayou Bend, the Houston estate of Miss Ima Hogg, opened as a house museum of early American furniture and decorative arts. Miss Ima began collecting during the 1930s, was diverted to civic philanthropic interests for fifteen years, and then returned to Americana with great enthusiasm during the fifties and sixties. She became a prominent habitué of the popular Williamsburg Antiques Forum, which had been established in 1949 (fig. 16.4).[87]

During the 1950s a number of these affluent collectors gathered for congenial soirées, called house parties, at each other's home. The regulars were Electra Webb, Henry and Helen Flynt, Ima Hogg, Katharine Murphy, Maxim Karolik, and Lloyd Hyde, who specialized in manuscripts. Henry Francis du Pont joined them on occasion. Alice Winchester, for many years the editor of *Antiques,* attended a lot of these occasions held at Deerfield, Shelburne, Bayou Bend, Pokety, and spots in and around New York. Her recollection of them is instructive:

> They were social occasions where the collectors took delight in entertaining each other beautifully amid their collections, using and enjoying their precious antiques, serving luxurious meals on 18th-century porcelain and silver. We made tours of their respective museums, admiring the beauties and having a private view of the latest acquisitions. Of course much of the talk was about antiques, with constant interchange of information and gossip, and a certain amount of friendly competition.[88]

16.4   Mrs. Katharine Murphy, Miss Ima Hogg, and John Graham at the 1962 Williamsburg Antiques Forum. Graham, Director of Collections at C.W., became legendary because of his numerous purchasing coups for Colonial Williamsburg. Courtesy of the Colonial Williamsburg Foundation.

Bernice and Edgar Garbisch, who were also a part of that social circle, began to collect American "primitive" art in 1944; and filled Pokety, their summer home on the eastern shore of Maryland, with seventeenth- to nineteenth-century art. By 1969 they had assembled more than 2,600 works, now referred to as "naive" rather than primitive (which sounded pejorative to folk art enthusiasts); and a major loan exhibition held at the National Gallery of Art in Washington foreshadowed the permanent gift of much of their Americana to that Gallery and the nation in 1954 and 1957. Mrs. Garbisch was the daughter of Walter Chrysler, the automobile manufacturer; and her brother, Walter, Jr., became a prominent aficionado of European art, mostly Impressionists and their successors. His extraordinary collection went to the Norfolk Museum of Arts and Sciences, which was then renamed the Chrysler Museum.[89]

One is tempted to connect this relatively recent enthusiasm for folk art with a further democratization of tradition in American culture: a glorification of humble, often anonymous artists and artisans who lacked formal training and expressed the values and visual images of ordinary men and women. That would only be partially valid, however, because many of the trendsetters in this area were multi-millionaires who felt attracted to a neglected field of Americana—one that expressed national chauvinism in an innovative and sprightly manner and that seemed to present "tradition" in a suitably modern guise. Less affluent collectors and institutions were indeed attracted to folk art precisely because the vernacular culture seemed more appropriate to a gradually growing egalitarian ethos.[90]

At the opening of the Abby Aldrich Rockefeller Folk Art Museum in 1957, its first director, Mitch Wilder, asked rhetorically why a fresh surge of interest in "folk" art had occurred. After citing aesthetic and documentary considerations, he noted the existence of "sentimental attachments—bringing visual memories of our fathers and their forebears." Addressing an elite and elegant audience (present by invitation), he looked back to the movement's genesis during the 1930s and offered this democratic and nationalistic explanation. "Many people saw for the first time," he observed, "the inheritance which was theirs—without strings and without ideas borrowed from abroad. Moreover, this insight was comprehensible in American terms, for it spoke of a grass roots America which was a part of our common experience."[91]

Ward and Dorothy Melville were wealthy and philanthropic residents of a village named Old Field, located near Stony Brook, Long Island, when they became enthusiasts for all aspects of that area's history. They began to collect objects of historical and aesthetic interest with the ultimate goal of a museum in mind. Ward Melville first obtained a fair number of fine landscape and genre paintings by William Sidney Mount, who had lived in Stony Brook during the mid-nineteenth century. After making his museum intentions official in 1942, and hiring some curatorial staff in 1945, Melville gathered a representative assortment of excellent carriages. That enabled him to open his horse-drawn carriage museum to the public in 1951. Two other structures have been added since then, each one highlighting American material culture of the region in an eclectic way. The Melvilles also saved and restored a number of important historic buildings in the area, and developed special depth in costumes, toys and games, tools, and hunting decoys. They eventually enhanced the carriage museum by adding antique vehicles from Western Europe.[92] Once again, considerable resources and highly personal interests made a distinctive enterprise grow and succeed.

One other pertinent example is provided by Henry Hornblower II, a Boston stockbroker, history buff, and founder of the outdoor museum called Plimoth Plantation. The concept originated in his childhood when he spent summers at Plymouth during the 1920s. He subsequently persuaded his father, a third-generation member of the Hornblower family in the securities business, to give the Pilgrim Society $20,000 in order to acquire land and begin planning. In 1947 Plimoth Plantation was established as a non-profit corporation with Hornblower, age thirty, as its president. Their goal was to reconstruct the Pilgrim village as it had been in 1627. The project proceeded deliberately and carefully in the face of considerable skepticism. Houses and a fort-meetinghouse were completed by 1957 when a replica of the *Mayflower* arrived from England to considerable international fanfare.

Soon thereafter the Hornblowers gave a large piece of their family estate three miles south of Plymouth, at Eel River, where the 1627 village was eventually reconstructed during the 1960s. Prominent archaeologists, architects, naval historians, and graduate students from Harvard participated with zest and scholarly precision.[93] Visitors continue to be initially puzzled, amused, and then delighted when they discover that the costumed guides speak only seventeenth-century English. The use of modern vocabulary draws either a blank stare or else the query: "What does that mean?" No anachronisms allowed! The practice is very effective as a pedagogical device.

Needless to say, not every great historical collection, dream, or restoration has eventually become a discrete and autonomous institution. Some have been given in their entirety to an existing institution while retaining their integrity and provenance as a particular person's passion. That happened in 1930 when Francis P. Garvan gave his phenomenal collection of early American furniture to Yale, and in 1977 when the University of Connecticut acquired the rare books and imprints spanning 1783 to 1826 gathered by Pierce Welch Gaines. Frank C. Deering of Saco, Maine, left his fine collection of American books to the Newberry Library in Chicago. But as if to demonstrate that collectors do not care to be predictable, the most omnivorous American bibliophile of all, Thomas W. Streeter, permitted his amazing compilation of Americana to be sold following his death in 1951. The collection was so large that it required three separate auctions; the catalogues have remained invaluable works of reference ever since.[94]

More recently there have been occasions when great collections were auctioned and dispersed following the owners' deaths. A case in point would be the sale at Christie's in 1981 of American pewter that had belonged to George and Marian Jenckes (Pennsylvania textile manufacturers), a collection described as the finest of its kind offered at public auction since the 1930s. Increasingly common is the practice of major institutions arranging to place extraordinary private collections on exhibit as a means of wooing a highly desirable potential donor, who receives as recompense recognition, praise, and gratification. This was the case in 1986, for example, when the National Gallery of Art exhibited the early American furniture owned by George M. and Linda H. Kaufman, and in 1989 when the same institution displayed the American paintings of Richard Manoogian, a Detroit industrialist who has assembled a notable range of native treasures—an exhibit that subsequently moved to major museums in San Francisco, New York, and Detroit.[95]

Variations of these patterns become precedents in their own right. Joseph Hirshhorn, a self-made industrialist and financier, had collected and lived with eighteenth-century antiques for some fifteen years when he began buying modern sculpture avidly at the end of the 1940s. In 1954 he added an enthusiasm for more traditional American art, ranging from Eakins to Sloan, Prendergast, Henri, and Arthur Bowen Davies. Throughout the 1950s he assembled a spectacular collection of twentieth-century art; and late in 1964 the Secretary of the Smithsonian Institution, S. Dillon Ripley, approached Hirshhorn with the suggestion that he give his treasures to the United States under the aegis of the Smithsonian. President Lyndon B. Johnson intervened on behalf of this request and the highly unusual outcome is a museum named for the donor, built by the government at a choice location on the Mall in Washington.[96]

That agreement was formally achieved in 1966, the same year that Congress passed the National Museum Act and the National Historic Preservation Act. The latter established the National Register of Historic Places, among other things. For almost two decades the federal government had steadily been assuming greater responsibility as a primary sponsor, custodian, and co-ordinator of collective memory in the United States. How that happened, and with what consequences, is the subject of our next chapter.

Chapter 17

THE PUBLIC SECTOR AND
THE POLITICS OF TRADITION
IN COLD WAR AMERICA

ALTHOUGH THE MOBILIZATION of American resources mandated by World War II meant a drastic reduction of government spending on cultural programs, precedents had been established during the 1930s that would be expanded significantly during the decades following 1946. In some instances, obvious lines of interrupted continuity serve to remind us that government customarily proceeds at an agonizing crawl as a custodian of tradition. On December 31, 1935, for instance, Franklin D. Roosevelt designated the Jefferson National Expansion Memorial in St. Louis, Missouri. A "designation" does not provide for action, however; so the national historic site did not receive authorization until May 1954, and construction of the Memorial itself was not completed until the 1960s.[1] Public memory in a democracy makes haste slowly: *festina lente*. That had become a clearly established pattern during the nineteenth century: at Bunker Hill, the Washington Monument, and Grant's Tomb—to cite just a few of the most familiar examples.

Many of the "promises" made prior to 1945, moreover, remained forever unfulfilled. During the war, for example, President Roosevelt asked Congress for an immense appropriation in order to construct a vast new military headquarters: the Pentagon. When Congress balked because it could not imagine that Defense would need the world's largest office building once the war ended, F.D.R. pledged to use the massive facility as a national archive following the war. His offer may or may not have been sincere; but needless to say, the Pentagon has never become a cultural repository—not in the ordinary use of that concept, at any rate.[2]

Nevertheless, a public sense of the past became more evident than ever before in the decades following World War II. In 1948 Harry S. Truman shrewdly ran against the Republican ghost of Herbert Hoover rather than against the formidable dullness of Thomas E. Dewey. Similarly, the historian Ernest May has demonstrated persuasively that U.S. foreign policy during the Cold War era tended to be a reflection of backward glances to regretted events of the interwar years. And it became commonplace to say that we were inclined to prepare for the "next" war as though it would nearly replicate the last one. To a much greater extent than we usually acknowledge, then, memories and misperceptions of the past have played a crucial role in shaping both public opinion and governmental policies.[3]

Ironically this penchant was not always self-evident to contemporaries: foreign policy decisions tended to be shrouded by national security considerations, and domestic initiatives required politically palatable rationalizations. Only years after the fact, if at all, do we learn that policies were shaped either by inertia or by an individual's personal sense of custom, that is, an official's feeling that "this" is the way such-and-such had normally been done, or else the belief that a reading of history "taught" that thus-and-so seemed the prudent course of action to follow. Harry S. Truman may be the most notable exemplar of that attitude; but most presidents since Woodrow Wilson, in fact, have responded in such a manner to one degree or another.[4]

Although the government's role as a major custodian or sponsor of civic memories expanded steadily during the third quarter of the twentieth century—which provides the central concern of this chapter—it must be noted that many of the most significant "events," such as the Civil War Centennial (1961–65) and the Bicentennial of Independence (1975–76), were decentralized by design and enjoyed far more success in scattered localities than at the national level. Enthusiasm for regional and local history flourished at the very time when federal initiatives were most visible—yet frequently less than fully successful. As we shall see in the next two chapters, the "heritage phenomenon" and the nostalgic mood of the 1970s and '80s has meant, more often than not, that amnesia at the national level would occur concurrently with active and willful memories at the community level. For diverse reasons that should become clearer as this final section unfolds, the centralization of political power and economic largesse in the United States has been accompanied by a decentralization of memory-related activities and the uses of tradition.[5]

I

THE DYNAMICS of international relations and ideology during the Cold War era have become a familiar story by now. But if we contemplate the politics of culture at that time, a limited range of references comes to mind: the Hiss, Rosenberg, and Oppenheimer security cases as morality tales spawned by an age of anxiety; the dramatic appearance of Arthur Miller's play *The Crucible* in 1952; and the National Security Council's document (or report) Number 68, written early in 1950 by Paul Nitze—a paean of praise for American domestic values that presumed an American consensus concerning those values—a seminal document (accidentally declassified in 1974) that supplied a cultural supremacy rationale for U.S. foreign policy during the Cold War.[6]

The array of cultural responses was more diverse than that, however, yet cohesive and patterned like a carefully designed fabric. In the autumn of 1947 the Junior Museum of the Metropolitan Museum of Art opened a didactic exhibition called "The New Nation: 1783–1800." The Museum supervisor, who had worked closely with the American History and Citizenship Project of the American Wing in planning this *E Pluribus Unum* show, called attention in her press release to "a parallel between the free world's present struggle to unite and the American colonies' attempts at unity." The contents of the show—which started with the Great Seal of the United States, "what it means and how it was chosen"—were carefully co-ordinated with history and social studies programs in New York City schools. The exhibit remained in place for three years and offered an unabashed connection between capitalism and patriotism. The motif of room number 2 was "The Stars and Stripes in World Trade."[7]

Few levels or manifestations of cultural expression seem to have been untouched by this mentality. When *American Heritage* first appeared, its Cold War rhetoric was prominently displayed. Popular fiction, such as A. B. Guthrie's *The Way West* (1950), emphasized traits of national character that had graced the pioneers: leadership, integrity, courage, and above all a bold love of freedom. Scholars and intellectuals were scarcely immune. Writing shortly after the appearance of Guthrie's Pulitzer Prize–winner, Perry Miller viewed the American literary tradition as a weapon in the struggle against communism. "Through the American novel and play," he declared, we could "communicate with free men everywhere. Because this is a literature of criticism in the name of the fundamental man, it is a literature of freedom."[8]

The study of military history in civilian universities increased steadily in the years after 1945; and it is clear in retrospect that apprehensions of the postwar world generated among natural and social scientists a strong interest in national security studies. During the 1960s those elite fighting units known as the Green Berets came to be viewed as lineal heirs of Daniel Boone and an integral part of America's fierce frontier heritage—but with the added advantage of group discipline. Some people even spoke of the desirability of forgoing some degree of individualism and personal autonomy in order to achieve an enhanced objective of national mission and collective security.[9]

The most elaborate ideological undertaking of the early postwar years, however, managed to include and balance both aspects of that value system. Between 1947 and 1949 the Freedom Train visited 322

17.1   The Freedom Train. Courtesy of the National Archives Trust Fund Board.

cities in its 413-day tour, travelled some 37,000 miles through all 48 states, and received more than 3.5 million people who viewed (usually in haste, owing to the crowds) 127 documents displayed on board the train (figs. 17.1, 17.2, and 17.3).

The project had its genesis in April 1946 when William Coblenz, assistant director of the Public Information Division at the Department of Justice, decided to spend his lunch hour viewing exhibits at the National Archives, a nearby building on Pennsylvania Avenue. A display of German surrender documents along with Hitler's last will and testament especially fascinated Coblenz. Realizing that most Americans would never get to the Archives to see either the special German exhibit or the permanent display of state papers prominent in U.S. history, he went to see the archivist about the possibility of assembling a mobile museum. He had in mind a Bill of Rights exhibit contrasting texts from American history and the Nazi era in Germany. Following a show at the Department of Justice, it would tour the country in a single railroad car attached to a regular train.[10]

Attorney General Tom C. Clark took to the idea immediately. As he told a congressional committee several years later, he saw in it the "means of aiding the country in its internal war against subversive elements and as an effort to improve citizenship by reawakening in our people their profound faith in the American historical heritage." On April 20, 1946, Harry S. Truman told Clark that the concept had his "strongest endorsement," a statement that proved to be prophetic because less than eleven months later the President announced the Truman Doctrine, an early salvo in the fight against communism. After that the President devoted many months to campaigning with Congress for large-scale foreign aid initiatives aimed at conveying American "rights and privileges" to "freedom loving people throughout the world" (fig. 17.4).[11]

17.2   Thousands of people waiting in line outside Union Station in Washington, D.C., to board the Freedom Train. Courtesy of the National Archives Trust Fund Board.

17.3   Three elderly visitors tour the Freedom Train. Courtesy of the National Archives Trust Fund Board.

High-level staff from the National Archives and Justice Department undertook initial planning; but when it became clear that major funding would be required, Clark turned to friends in the private sector and received very enthusiastic responses from the president of Paramount Pictures and other movie executives. It also turned out, most serendipitously, that the Advertising Council, headed by Thomas D'Arcy Brophy, had similar interests. Their goal, like Attorney General Clark's, was to "re-sell Americanism to Americans." On December 10, 1946, Clark met with forty prominent leaders of the press, radio, motion picture industries, and the heads of several major governmental institutions, such as the Library of Congress and the Archives. He explained to them his desire to dramatize "the American way of life through the traveling exhibition of the most impressive collection of original American documents ever assembled." In conjunction with the exhibition there would be an educational and patriotic media campaign produced by the sorts of organizations and corporations present at that and subsequent meetings—all to be co-ordinated by the Department of Justice.*

At a meeting held in New York City early in January a series of major decisions was made: to include only American documents and to omit any Nazi or other contrasting statements; to underwrite the project with private funds; and to have an entire "Liberty Train" with its own special schedule rather than a single railroad car attached to a regular passenger train. On February 14, 1947, the American Heritage Foundation was incorporated under the leadership of Winthrop W. Aldrich, chairman of the Chase Manhattan Bank, Louis A. Nevins of Paramount Pictures, and with Brophy as president. It would be a non-profit, non-partisan, educational foundation, directed by private citizens and supported by the private sector. The name of the project was changed to Freedom Train; and in order to publicize its tour and its agenda a conference took place at the White House on May 22, 1947. The guest list glittered with political, social, financial, and media personalities. Abundant backing became available to the American Heritage Foundation. And it was announced that the Freedom Train's tour would begin at Philadelphia on September 17, the 160th anniversary of the signing of the U.S. Constitution.

The documents chosen for inclusion on the train were even more glittering than that guest list. Never before or since have so many cherished pieces of Americana been assembled in one "place": the Treaty of Paris (1783), the Northwest Ordinance, the Bill of Rights,

---

*Few if any of these people knew about a precedent, the Lenin Train of 1918. In mid-August that year a propaganda train entirely covered with frescoes of heroic workers and soldiers was sent from Moscow under the auspices of the Bolshevik All-Union Central Executive Committee. This turned out to be the first of several trains sent to the Soviet front lines laden with books, brochures, newspapers, posters, films, and trained agitators. On the roof of the train the painted slogan appeared in bold Cyrillic characters: "Workers of the World, Unite."[12]

the Emancipation Proclamation, and George Washington's annotated copy of the Constitution came from the National Archives. Historical societies, universities, private collectors, and government agencies contributed others, such as Jefferson's draft of the Declaration of Independence, the Mayflower Compact, Washington's Farewell Address, the original manuscript of "The Star-Spangled Banner," Lincoln's Gettysburg Address in his own hand, the United Nations Charter, and the log of the U.S.S. *Missouri* giving details of the Japanese surrender ending World War II.

Some critics expressed disappointment at documents that were not included, such as the Wagner Labor Relations Act of 1935; Executive Order 8802, which established the Fair Employment Practice Commission; the President's Committee on Civil Rights Report; and the Truman Doctrine. The Heritage Foundation explained in response that it would not include documents regarded as partisan, controversial in nature, or pertinent to current legislative consideration. Other critics called the Freedom Train a product of "Wall Street Imperialism," and regarded it as a conservative coup for the Republicans. Some members of the Republican-controlled Congress, on the other hand, feared that

17.4   President Harry S. Truman reaches for his fountain pen to sign the register at the Freedom Train in September 1947. Attorney General Tom C. Clark and Chief Justice Fred Vinson stand nearby. Courtesy of the National Archives Trust Fund Board.

17.5 Four visitors at the Freedom Train exhibit. Courtesy of the National Archives Trust Fund Board.

the real beneficiary of the tour would be Truman and his party. African-Americans expressed concern that segregation might be permitted in Southern cities. In September, however, the Foundation announced that it would not tolerate any form of segregation during the scheduled visits and asked area directors to determine the racial policies of all cities that wished to be included on the tour. All but two Southern cities, Memphis and Birmingham, indicated their willingness to comply; and the two recalcitrant cities were dropped from the tour (fig. 17.5).

The train was powered by a sleek 2,000-horsepower electric diesel, loaned to the Foundation by the American Locomotive Company and christened "The Spirit of 1776" with a bottle containing water from the Atlantic and Pacific oceans, the Great Lakes, the Gulf of Mexico, and the Mississippi and Potomac rivers. The completed train was painted white with a red and blue stripe along both sides of its entire length, some 800 feet. The words FREEDOM TRAIN appeared in gold letters on alternate cars, and the others displayed a golden eagle. On September 16, when the train arrived in Philadelphia, the Foundation launched its media blitz. Irving Berlin's specially commissioned song, "Freedom Train," already recorded on Decca Records by Bing Crosby and the Andrews Sisters, was introduced on NBC by Vic Damone. Radio and television stations, newspapers, and magazines sparkled with stories. By the time the nationwide tour officially ended on January 22, 1949, the Foundation had received from its clippings service more than 440,000 items. The print media helped in many other ways as well. *Reader's*

Digest, for instance, reprinted 3.5 million copies of an article about the Bill of Rights that was given to visitors on the train. *Look* magazine prepared more than 775,000 copies of an illustrated 32-page booklet, *Our American Heritage,* that supplied information about the major documents.

By and large the project seemed to be a fabulous success. Great numbers of people lined up to glimpse the precious cargo, gladly took a Freedom Pledge, and signed a Freedom Scroll. Attempting to promote a kind of grass-roots revival of patriotism, the Foundation arranged early in its planning that each community's scheduled stop would coincide with a Rededication Week in local communities. Approximately 50 million Americans participated in these events and activities. *Our American Heritage,* a film made for the Foundation by Dore Schary through the facilities of RKO Pictures, was released to theatres throughout the country and was very widely viewed.

Following an initial tour of the Northeast the Freedom Train had a Thanksgiving rendezvous in Washington, D.C., before starting its Southern swing. On November 27, 1947, Truman and Clark both issued statements in conjunction with the capital visit. They contrasted American freedom with conditions abroad and linked the train's meaning to the Cold War debate concerning anti-communist foreign aid. The small number of protesters, mainly leftist radicals and pacifists, were carefully tracked by the FBI. Director J. Edgar Hoover sent the Attorney General no fewer than nine reports on those who found the Freedom Train offensive.

The American Heritage Foundation had been disingenuous from the outset in announcing at the White House conference held in May 1947 that the entire undertaking resulted from a spontaneous "citizens movement." The vast majority of Americans did, indeed, respond positively (figs. 17.6 and 17.7); but the fact remains that initiative and execution resulted from very careful planning at the highest levels, public and private, and that media co-operation has never been more effusive in response to any such enterprise in all of American history. The Foundation was candid in asserting that domestic and international conditions at the time called for a response equal to that required "in time of war."

Even the local Rededication Weeks and Days largely followed a script mailed out by the Foundation as part of an elaborate Publicity Portfolio that also provided materials for local media along with an American Heritage Radio Kit which did the same for local stations. The kits consisted primarily of scripts concerning the Freedom Train. No objections were raised if communities had supplementary ideas of their own; but nothing was left to chance. Taped recordings of the "Freedom Pledge" were also made available to radio stations, read by fifteen prominent entertainers ranging from Gene Autry to Ronald Reagan.

In its emphasis upon advertising and effective communication, this

17.6   A family group viewing historic documents on the Freedom Train in Washington, D.C. A special contingent of twenty-seven U.S. Marine guards accompanied the train. Courtesy of the National Archives Trust Fund Board.

17.7   Young Americans look at the Bill of Rights on October 20, 1948. Courtesy of the National Archives Trust Fund Board.

whole episode anticipated one of the primary attributes of the Civil War Centennial Commission (1957–65) and the Statue of Liberty Centennial (1986). Brophy had been president of one of the largest advertising companies in the United States and was also the founder and director of the Advertising Council, which originated during the war as an entrepreneurial propaganda organization. On the other hand, unlike later commemorative events of the 1970s and '80s, the Freedom Train did not result in the promotion or endorsement of corporate sales. It promoted patriotism but not products. It made "Our American Heritage" a hackneyed phrase that appeared relentlessly from orations to upbeat cartoons—a legacy that has endured for more than four decades.

I I

ALTHOUGH John D. Rockefeller, Jr., did contribute to the fund-raising campaign for the Freedom Train, neither he nor his staff paid very much attention because their own institution underwent a major transition during the later 1940s, one equally responsive to the Cold War climate. As Kenneth Chorley wrote to John D. Rockefeller III in 1948, "with freedom and human liberty being challenged everywhere, there has probably been no time in our history when the things for which Williamsburg stands and the teachings of Williamsburg were needed as much as they are today."[13]

Throughout World War II, and even prior to formal American entry following the Japanese attack at Pearl Harbor, John D. Rockefeller, Jr., and his associates actively promoted the cause of patriotism.[14] The Publicity Department at C.W. announced late in 1941 that war had not made Colonial Williamsburg superfluous: "On the contrary we feel very strongly that it is a vital element in national defense." John D. Rockefeller III proposed to William S. Paley, the president of CBS, "a series of historical radio programs to try to awaken in the citizens of this country a consciousness of their own traditions." By May 1942 the restoration had converted to a "war basis." The commanding officer at Fort Eustis, Virginia, agreed to make Williamsburg a part of the "official training program." More than three hundred soldiers were brought to C.W. daily in order to tour the restoration, listen to lectures by staff members, and view films concerning the cradle of American liberty.[15]

Following the war, however, when JDR, Jr., began turning ultimate responsibility for Williamsburg over to his oldest son, the two found that they disagreed about its future mission and priorities. Whereas the father remained preoccupied with expanding and perfecting the physical restoration, John D. Rockefeller III felt that *his* contribution, and that of his generation, ought to involve the enhanced use of C.W. for educational programs and international relations. In 1949 the son reminded his father that C.W. had "tremendous potentials for public

service." Early the next year he created a Special Survey Committee
to determine how those "potentials" might best be achieved. The committee's charge took the form of two questions: "What was the significant contribution of Williamsburg in the eighteenth century? What can
be the relationship of that contribution to the contemporary scene?"[16]

During the summer of 1950 Rockefeller sent two members of the
committee to Europe on a kind of ideological "fact-finding" mission. An
in-house memorandum explicitly stated the threefold purpose of their
trip:

> (1) to search out the positive qualities of faith which are sustaining
> those who resist totalitarianism and to see how these qualities of
> faith can be used to inspire others; (2) to see at first hand the
> successes and failures of communism, and to evaluate the reasons
> which make for either success or failure; (3) to benefit Colonial
> Williamsburg's program with knowledge gained from the experi-
> ence of those abroad who share a common heritage of freedom
> with America.[17]

After visiting "those areas of greatest conflict between the ideals of
self-government and the ideology of communism," Kershaw Burbank
and John Goodbody held lengthy discussions with their boss, which they
then summarized in exhaustive detail in accordance with the Rockefeller practice of putting all communications permanently on paper. They
organized their analysis into sections: the basic concepts of communism
(Stalinism); the appeal of communism; key points at issue in the ideological war between communism and democracy; the common heritage
among free people; eighteenth-century American contributions to this
common heritage; changes necessary to strengthen democracy; and
key talking points (including "dignity of the individual compared with
slave state robot"; "right to belong to private citizens' groups by free
association as compared to obligatory, state organizations of communism"; "the rights of opposition, disagreement and compromise vs.
absolutism of Marxism"; "freedom of ideas vs. thought control"; "the
right of private ownership and of inheritance").[18]

Following their return these two staff members also conducted extensive conversations with members of the Russian Research Center at
Harvard, with distinguished historians of the United States at Harvard
and Yale, editors at *Time* and *Life*, State Department personnel, and
officials at the Carnegie Endowment for International Peace—all of
which they reported in minute detail to Rockefeller. As a result, by
March 1951 a series of projects had been developed that involved
co-operation between C.W. (with its educational resources) and the
Citizenship Education Project, the New York State Board of Regents,
the State Department, and the Department of Defense. As Rockefeller
explained to his friend John J. McCloy, U.S. High Commissioner for

Germany in 1950, "nearly half a million people visit Williamsburg each year, but we are anxious to make the Restoration also meaningful in the lives of the many millions in the country who will never be able to go there."[19]

The Special Survey Committee produced an eight-point agenda that appeared, on its face, mildly ideological in tone: for example, (1) "To help strengthen our democratic way of life in this country today" and (5) "To strengthen the educational and interpretive efforts of Colonial Williamsburg so that they will be directed toward the people of this country in relation to contemporary world problems." By March 1951, however, a series of programs were proposed and swiftly implemented that made C.W. the most vocal nongovernmental pulpit for patriotic discourse in the United States. The winners of a nationwide essay contest called Voice of Democracy were brought there for extensive panel discussions with distinguished guests. As Kenneth Chorley put it, "I do not know of anything which will make these young people think more about the problems of Democracy, how to improve it, how to maintain it, and what we can do about Communism, than these panel discussions."[20]

In 1950 John D. Rockefeller III urged the State Department to regularize a practice that had begun unofficially almost five years earlier: including C.W. on the itineraries of distinguished foreign visitors to the United States (fig. 17.8). Although Rockefeller's request might seem to us self-serving in an institutional sense, it was tendered without hypocrisy and explained in terms of properly comprehending the relationship between tradition and progress in the United States.

> Because of the emphasis we Americans so often attach to technology and progress, we are sometimes misjudged by visitors who would assume that our native traditions go no deeper than our automobiles and television sets. To those in search of a deeper understanding of our country Williamsburg offers tangible evidence that human freedom, self-government, and sovereignty of the individual have been the well-springs of our greatness. I believe that this nation can be better comprehended through a knowledge of its roots and traditions.[21]

The State Department responded positively to his proposal and implemented it regularly thereafter. In addition to the usual twenty-four-hour visits by individual heads of state, when Ronald Reagan hosted an economic summit meeting of the seven leading industrial powers he chose to have it meet in Williamsburg. The most memorable photo opportunity showed the seven conferring in the council chamber of the reconstructed eighteenth-century Capitol. After three decades of symbolic visits by anti-communist heads of state, however, the 1980s witnessed an ecumenical shift in January 1984 when Prime Minister Zhao

17.8   Sir Winston Churchill and General Dwight D. Eisenhower on Duke of
Gloucester Street at Colonial Williamsburg on March 18, 1946. Courtesy of the
Colonial Williamsburg Foundation.

Ziyang of China and his entourage received the usual treatment and
photo opportunities similar to the sort shown in figure 17.8.[22]

In 1951 an on-going series of Williamsburg Conferences on International Affairs began to take place. Many of them were genuinely educational, but some seem to have been arranged as much for their
ideological publicity value as for their substantive content and consequences. An illustration of the latter occurred in June 1952 when fifty
exiled "leaders" from Eastern Europe met at the colonial Capitol to
discuss and adopt a Williamsburg Declaration embodying a pledge to
restore the principles of liberty to people in oppressed countries
(fig. 17.9). In May 1954 Secretary of State John Foster Dulles appeared
as the featured speaker at an annual event called Prelude to Independence. C.W. spokesmen explained that "each year in order to remind
men of our basic American concepts of liberty and individual rights,"
the site would observe May 15 to July 4 as a Prelude to Independence
Period. The opening date commemorated the promulgation of Virginia's Declaration of Rights in 1776. Two years after Dulles launched
the ceremony, Dag Hammarskjold, Secretary-General of the United
Nations, appeared as the featured speaker and was joined by twenty-
four ambassadors to the United States from countries affiliated with the
U.N.[23]

In 1957 the annual Governors' Conference met at C.W. and President Eisenhower addressed the group. That same year Queen Elizabeth II and Prince Philip made an appearance in conjunction with the 350th anniversary of the founding of Jamestown. For a decade thereafter a veritable parade of international dignitaries passed through with flourishes, yet unruffled; but much of the lustre wore off in November 1967 when President and Mrs. Lyndon B. Johnson attended services at Bruton Parish Church on Duke of Gloucester Street and were startled, to say the least, when the Episcopal rector used the occasion of his homily to raise embarrassing questions about the war in Vietnam (fig. 17.10). Ceremonial and state visits did not cease thereafter, but their serenity could no longer be taken for granted. In a very real sense, the dialogue about democratic values that JDR III envisioned in 1950 had been transformed from a pro forma public ritual to a meaningful engagement with few holds barred.

Ironically, however, John D. Rockefeller III grew increasingly disenchanted with his role and accomplishments at C.W. and began a process of personal withdrawal in 1952 that culminated in his resignation the following year and its reluctant acceptance by the board in 1954. His motives are complex and had much to do with his abiding respect for his father. Whereas JDR, Jr., cared passionately about the physical restoration of the eighteenth-century town and had relatively little interest

17.9 Exiled leaders from Eastern Europe signing a Declaration of Freedom in the House of Burgesses of the eighteenth-century Capitol, Colonial Williamsburg, June 1952. Courtesy of the Colonial Williamsburg Foundation.

17.10   President and Mrs. Lyndon B. Johnson leaving Bruton Parish Church, Colonial Williamsburg, in November 1967 after the minister preached a sermon critical of the war in Vietnam. Courtesy of the Colonial Williamsburg Foundation.

in contemporary ideological conflict, his son's priorities were exactly the reverse and consequently he felt that he had fallen short in his fiduciary responsibilities. A surprisingly formal correspondence between father and son refers to "the tension of past conferences" between the two. Early in 1955 JDR III offered a very brief explanation to Kenneth Chorley: "One of my main concerns was that Williamsburg should be a significant and constructive force and factor in our world of today—not just an appealing and interesting reminder of the past."[24]

In accepting his resignation the board prepared a statement of appreciation that acknowledged his "constant emphasis" on Williamsburg's "broad mission," his concern for new educational techniques, publications, and the production of audio-visual materials intended for wide distribution. Its members also recognized his outreach to both governmental and non-governmental agencies in such fields as public service and education. John III had developed co-operative programs with the armed forces and the U.S. Information Agency, and had urged the enhancement of instruction and entertainment for visitors from abroad.[25]

Although it seems harsh, in retrospect, to label so sensitive and gentle a man as JDR III a "Cold Warrior," the reality remains that he was one. He saw a polarized world in which "democratic beliefs are in conflict with totalitarian ideology," and determined to use his influence and his father's beloved historical project in order to tip the balance in that conflict. It is essential to bear in mind, for the sake of perspective, that when JDR III embarked upon his plan for an ideologically didactic C.W., this sort of unsolicited letter was coming in by the hundreds if not thousands from visitors to the restoration: "It is entirely necessary," wrote a man in Hagerstown, Maryland, "that our historical institutions be preserved, developed and maintained in full vigor as a stimulus for the preservation of our National Security."[26]

Although John III left the helm, an experienced and self-confident Kenneth Chorley remained to manage and perpetuate most of the aspirations of both Rockefellers, father and son. The restoration flourished as a tourist attraction, to be sure, and co-operated with the New York State Regents' program to enhance the "teaching of American history and heritage . . . in the ideological war against communism." In 1955 the trustees of C.W. bestowed their first Williamsburg Award upon Sir Winston Churchill. That prominent anti-communist received $10,000 and a town crier's bell, selected as a symbol because in the eighteenth century "the town crier summoned the citizenry to play their part in developing a government by and for the people."[27]

The agenda at Colonial Williamsburg combined symbol and substance, history with contemporary concerns, patriotism with educational programs. Its activities were particularly characteristic of the age because C.W., a private corporation, worked closely and effectively with an extraordinary array of public sector "agencies," ranging from the State Department to national commissions and state boards.[28] The ease with which C.W. co-operated with government as joint "custodians" of national traditions was not so easily replicated by less prestigious and well connected groups. Nevertheless, that pattern of shared responsibility has persisted ever since 1950, and is one of the most indicative aspects of the role of tradition in recent American cultural history.* The politics of culture no longer requires a sharp delineation between public and private sectors. In fact, appeals for co-operation have now become the norm.

I I I

D U R I N G a period spanning well over three decades starting in 1955, the United States had occasion to commemorate most of the major events in its history along with the special birthdays of some celebrated heroes, such as Chief Justice John Marshall (1955), Woodrow

---

*Speaking at Portsmouth, New Hampshire, in July 1965, Chorley declared that "Strawbery Banke is a great idea for many reasons. It brought together the Federal Government, the State, the Municipality, and private sources all joined together in a united program. This to me is a great step forward in the development of our cultural activities in America, for it was only a short time ago that all governments—Federal, State and Municipal—took the position that culture was the responsibility of private citizens and not of Government."

Wilson (1956), Alexander Hamilton (1957), and Abraham Lincoln (1959). None of these turned out to be notably memorable occasions, however, despite the increasing availability of state and federal funds as well as support from private organizations. The Civil War Centennial and the bicentennials of Independence, the Constitution, and of the Bill of Rights proved to be problematic in their own ways, though each for its own reasons. A pattern can be discerned in the assumption shared by most organizers that the celebration of these anniversaries should be largely decentralized—a decision that eventually accounted for most of what seems positive in retrospect—and in the assumption that some degree of commercialization was either inevitable, desirable, or just plain essential.

We shall concentrate here primarily upon the Civil War Centennial as a case study: partially because its neglected records are in fact stowed at the National Archives in 101 boxes, whereas the records generated by programs in 1976, 1987, and 1989 are not;[29] and partially because the Civil War Centennial seems to have been so clearly symptomatic of broader issues and tensions in American culture at the time, such as sectionalism, racism, commercialism, and a penchant for recalling particulars (battle formations, for example) more effectively than causes, consequences, and the properly contextualized meaning of great events.

Inseparable from any assessment of national anniversaries, moreover, is the peculiar fever chart of American patriotism, 1955 to 1989, and with it the gradually diminished importance of hereditary and patriotic societies in the United States. However one may feel about them, those organizations had undeniably spurred American memory in manifold ways for half a century starting in 1890. Their declining impact in the subsequent half century may have contributed to the democratization of memory, but it has almost certainly diluted its intensity. Democratization and decentralization are unquestionably laudable, but they do seem to be accompanied by a certain sense of lassitude, of ceremonials and parades poorly attended, of speeches cynically heard, of flags that flutter only lightly in the breeze because the vigorous winds of strident nationalism are less fashionable than they were six or seven decades ago.

UNLIKE the two-hundredth birthdays of George Washington (1932) and Thomas Jefferson (1943), Alexander Hamilton's (January 11, 1957) aroused comparatively little public interest. Although no memorial was erected, a spate of biographies did appear, which may actually do more to immortalize an individual than granite obelisks or mini-temples made of marble. A national bicentennial commission, chaired by Senator Karl E. Mundt of South Dakota, sent thousands of letters to radio and television stations, to various sorts of writers and publications, to libraries, museums, and galleries—all to little effect. The American Bankers Association and the American Bar Association "pledged" their support, which seems appropriate; but so did the American Dental Association, the American Farm Bureau Federation, the American Pharmaceutical Association, the Loyal Order of the Moose, and Rotary International. The age of accessible organizational address lists had begun, and comprehensive mailings made possible the phenomenon of "me-tooism" without requiring commitment or meaningful content.

The membership lists of several historical and collector's organizations were used to request participation in the "Treasure Trove" search for Hamiltoniana and the sponsorship of local celebrities. One place that did so gladly was the decayed industrial town of Paterson, New Jersey, which Hamilton had founded. But the commission's hope to have at least one Hamilton article appear in every major magazine fell short. The fact that Hamilton had come to be perceived as a kind of generic founding father, rather than the highly idiosyncratic individual he actually was, is reflected in President Eisenhower's proclamation, dated September 17, 1956, which blandly called attention to Hamilton's "sincere efforts and inspiring leadership in the work of the men who laid the foundations, raised the structure, and built the sustaining traditions of the Government of the United States."[30]

The 150th anniversary of Abraham Lincoln's birth in 1809 aroused a greater degree of enthusiasm, complete with some highly predictable features as well as others that seem more surprising. The states of Illinois and Indiana along with the highly active Lincoln Group of the District of Columbia began to push hard in 1957 for legislation that would create a national Sesquicentennial Commission. That prompt mobilization proved to be important, and state commissions emerged a year later. Their press releases correctly anticipated a surge in visitation to such Lincoln "shrines" as his birthplace near Hodgenville, Kentucky, the Lincoln Memorial in Washington, as well as New Salem and Springfield, Illinois. The Boy Scouts of America planned a national Lincoln "pilgrimage" to Springfield and New Salem in April 1959; and the state of Illinois prepared a mobile museum that would tour the state starting in March. The Freedom Train as an educational technique had left at least one legacy.[31]

On February 12, 1959, Carl Sandburg delivered the Lincoln Day address before a joint meeting of Congress attended by the Supreme Court, the cabinet, and the diplomatic corps—a highly successful occasion. Somewhat less predictable was the speaker selected for the Sesquicentennial Dinner held that evening in Springfield, Illinois: Mayor Willy Brandt of West Berlin. The chairman of Illinois's commission, Newton C. Farr (a prominent Chicago real estate man and longtime Civil War buff), explained that the dinner would take as its theme the "world-wide significance of Lincoln." The occasion turned out to be a Cold War speech that has to be understood within the context of the frightening international crisis involving Berlin in 1958–59. Mayor Brandt explained that "this man does not belong to you alone, my friends; he belongs to all of us," and indicated early in the speech that his visit to the United States had strengthened his "conviction that Berlin can rely on its friends and that we shall march forward shoulder to shoulder, permitting nothing to come between us."[32]

Following lavish praise for the "truths which Lincoln spoke here in Springfield" in June 1858, Brandt insisted that they were "perhaps even more applicable to the present situation of the German people than to the one which he faced." Turning to the predicament of a divided Germany and a cruelly partitioned Berlin (analogous to a divided Union in 1861–65), he moved to the heart of his message: that Berlin had once more become the "target of Soviet probing and blackmail and which in the months to come will yet be the subject of much agitation, for the climax of the Soviet-provoked crisis has not yet been reached."

Brandt concluded with extracts from the Gettysburg Address and highlighted their international implications concerning the need for sacrifices in the name of freedom. He called attention to the fact that ever since the Berlin blockade of 1949 the Freedom Bell had hung in the town hall of West Berlin. "It came to us from your country with parchment scrolls bearing the signatures of 15 million American men and women. Each day at 12 noon we listen to the sound of this bell, which reminds us of what we have to preserve and what we yet have to achieve." Abraham Lincoln's mystic chords of memory had acquired a dramatically expanded meaning that even he might not have anticipated.

U N L I K E the bicentennial observances of Independence in 1976 and the Constitution in 1987, assorted private organizations and activities helped to prepare the way for the Civil War Centennial. In addition to the sesquicentennial of Lincoln's Birthday, annual Ulysses S. Grant Pilgrimages began to be sponsored in the mid-1950s by the U.S. Grant Council, Boy Scouts of America, in Illinois. These tributary treks to Grant's home in Galena apparently had a certain appeal, though there is reason to believe that the Scouts simply went along with what their scoutmasters told them had been planned. Besides, Grant himself supplied an exemplar of the adolescent urge to get away from home—even if it could only be for a few sober days in the case of well-behaved Boy Scouts.

Far more of a factor, discussion groups known as Civil War Round Tables had flourished ever since the later 1940s, starting in Chicago and New York City, spreading swiftly to other large and medium-sized cities—not to mention places like Big Creek Gap in Tennessee. Round Tables also achieved popularity at U.S. military installations around the world, such as the Air Force base in Wiesbaden, West Germany. Civil

War buffs appeared in many guises and expressed their enthusiasm in diverse ways. Philip D. Sang, a Chicago businessman and philanthropist, gathered a remarkable collection of Civil War documents and memorabilia, including Lincoln's personal presidential seal, which was made of brass with an ivory handle. Roger Sessions, the noted composer, became an ardent student of the Civil War and loved to visit battlefields. He wrote a cantata for soloists, chorus, and orchestra based upon Whitman's elegy for Lincoln, "When Lilacs Last in the Dooryard Bloom'd."

In the late 1950s a fair number of older organizations still existed with some sort of Civil War connection, even though their membership had been much reduced: the Sons of Union Veterans (organized in 1881), which continued to hold annual encampments, the Ladies of the Grand Army of the Republic, the U.D.C. and the Daughters of Union Veterans, the Sons of Confederate Veterans, the National Woman's Relief Corps (an auxiliary group to the G.A.R.), the Honorary Society of the Confederate States of America (with its headquarters in Upper Darby, Pennsylvania!), the Confederate High Command, and a representative local group affiliated with the Soldiers and Sailors Memorial Hall of Allegheny County, Pennsylvania, erected at Pittsburgh in 1910 to memorialize those from the county who served in the war and also to house relics from the events of 1861–65.[33]

Museums and historic sites continued to flourish, especially when they commemorated the best-known event in a community's history: the Warren Rifles Confederate Memorial Museum in Front Royal, Virginia; the Pennsylvania Rifle and Indian Museum located between Reading and Pottstown; the Fort Monroe (Virginia) Casemate Museum, founded in 1951 by a retired Army colonel; the Ordnance Museum at the Aberdeen Proving Ground in Maryland; the Mansfield Battle Park Museum in Mansfield, Louisiana, where a battle occurred on April 8, 1864; Bosworth Memorial Hall, a Civil War museum located in Portland, Maine, with organizational roots that dated to 1867; and Kennesaw Battle-Rama, the "World's Finest Civil War Diorama and Museum," in Kennesaw, Georgia. For all of these institutions, and for many others like them, the Civil War Centennial provided the perfect opportunity for a kind of renaissance of activity and even legitimacy.

Late in 1955 the Virginia Civil War Centennial, Inc., received a corporate charter from that Commonwealth in consequence of a resolution originated by the Richmond Civil War Round Table. According to its president, the organization was "designed first to capture and officially hold the title . . . against possible acquisition . . . by persons whose sole interest in securing such a title would be for commercial purposes. Second, the corporation was designed to promote, by historical, patriotic and civic associations throughout the state, such exercises, events and other commemorative activities as would appropriately pertain to the Centennial Years."[34]

Although the Centennial did not lack for stimuli, Cold War antipathies intensified the martial rhetoric if not the motives of some participants. In April 1958, seven months after Congress created a national Civil War Centennial Commission, John C. Pemberton (the grandson of a namesake who had surrendered to Grant at Vicksburg) presented the gold medal of the Washington, D.C., Civil War Round Table to another grandson, U. S. Grant III. Secretary of the Army Wilbur C. Brucker asserted on that occasion that Americans should heed the heroic example of both sides in the sectional conflict because they now faced "the most ominous challenge since the birth of the nation" from the "Communist conspiracy."[35]

The selection of General Grant to serve as chairman of the Commission turned out to be as unfortunate as it was perhaps inevitable. From 1926 until 1933 he had been director of Public Buildings and Parks in Washington, D.C. Following his retirement from the U.S. Army in 1946 Grant served for six years as a vice president of The George Washington University; as president of the Columbia Historical Society in Washington, D.C., from 1952 until his death in 1968; and in 1955 he became chairman of the National Committee of the American Museum of Immigration. His major responsibility there was to raise $5 million in order to construct a museum at the base of the Statue of Liberty where contributions to American civilization made by immigrants from all over the world would be displayed.[36]

As a venerable patriot with enthusiasm for tradition, and for sectional reconciliation, Grant surely must have seemed the ideal choice in 1957 when President Eisenhower asked him to serve. In addition to all of his public duties and history-related activities, he had been second in command to Representative Sol Bloom in running the George Washington Bicentennial back in the early 1930s. Few people recalled, perhaps, that in 1949 Grant had been attacked by columnist I. F. Stone for assisting the real estate interests of Washington, D.C., in perpetuating Jim Crow ordinances that kept African-Americans ghetto-ized in the nation's capital. That would be remembered in 1961, however, when several racist incidents involving the Commission essentially precipitated Grant's resignation as chairman.

In 1959, moreover, Grant permitted a 1940 article attributed to Father Charles Coughlin to be mailed to 2,500 members of the Military Order of the Loyal Legion of the United States, which Grant headed. Entitled "Abraham Lincoln and the Rothschilds," the essay suggested that the Civil War had been fought in order to gain financial control of the political entities that would survive. The Anti-Defamation League of B'nai Brith called upon Grant to repudiate the piece, and several U.S. senators pressed him hard for a retraction—which he eventually provided in a rather vague and halfhearted fashion.[37]

Fundamentally, Grant seems to have been a well-meaning yet insensitive and not very energetic traditionalist. In all fairness it should be

17.11   Karl S. Betts being sworn in as executive director of the Civil War
Centennial Commission on April 3, 1958, by Floyd E. Dotson, chief clerk at
the Department of the Interior. General U. S. Grant III stands between them.
Photo by Abbie Rowe, courtesy National Park Service.

noted that he was seventy-seven years old when his service as chairman
began, that his wife was extremely ill, and that he tried to run the
Commission by commuting from his retirement home in isolated Clinton, New York, to Washington and many other sites where meetings
and ceremonies took place. Those conditions did not suggest a likely
formula for success.

While sincerely committed to the notion of a depoliticized commemoration (he declined to write an introduction for a book dedicated to the
Union soldier), Grant bumbled his way into becoming a divisive figure.
Despite his personal belief that battle re-enactments were unwise, he
nonetheless advised local groups that such events supplied an effective
means of gaining the "interest and understanding of the young people
in their country's history." Although he strongly hoped to avoid crass
commercialism being connected with the Centennial, his staff and associates were almost entirely drawn from public relations and advertising backgrounds, which meant that tasteless incidents were likely to
occur, and they did.[38]

In the spring of 1958 Grant and the executive committee of his
twenty-five-member Commission chose Karl S. Betts, a Washington and
Baltimore businessman who was also a Civil War enthusiast, to serve in
the key position of executive director (fig. 17.11). The Commission
proudly informed the press that Betts "has had a long career in advertis-

ing and publicity work." Predictably Betts followed a Madison Avenue approach to his job, which meant making as many people feel good about the Civil War as possible by emphasizing sectional reconciliation and avoiding potential controversy. Unfortunately this also meant ignoring, almost entirely, racial issues in the Civil War era and a role for African-Americans in the Centennial.[39]

Late in 1957, while Betts served as chairman of the National Centennial Committee that was pushing for legislation that would create the Commission, he wrote a lengthy letter to the director of the National Park Service in which he sketched out the most urgent priorities as he saw them.

> I sincerely believe that the next six months should be devoted to selling the coming Centennial observance on a national scale. To do this, it would in my opinion be wise to develop contacts with the most important business groups in the United States likely to become interested in this program; namely, the Association of American Advertising Agencies, Association of American Railroads, American Automobile Association, National Association of Travel Organizations, American Society of Travel Agents, National Association of Radio and Television Broadcasters, and the United States Chamber of Commerce. There are many others. . . . Some attention of course may be given in the early stages to the promotion of special events during the four-year observance, but I cannot help but feel that this is a matter of secondary importance to the main job of securing the cooperation of the heads of the greatest enterprises in the country. If this can be done, this group will come up with many splendid, practical suggestions which will accomplish our common aim of cementing the unity of the American people, linked together with the high purpose of preserving the rich traditions left us by the Civil War.[40]

Kermit V. Sloan, who served as chairman of the Commission's Committee on Advertising, headed the Public Relations Department of the Curtis Publishing Company in Philadelphia. Betts loved Sloan's proposal that there be an award for the best advertising identified with the Centennial each year. Sloan, known to all of his friends as "Snuffy," was a past president of the Washington Civil War Round Table and a close friend of Betts. Jim Brown, manager of corporate public relations for Batten, Barton, Durstine & Osborne on Madison Avenue, served as a very active member of the Centennial Committee on Advertising. And George C. Whipple, public relations manager for the *Ladies' Home Journal,* worked as director of public relations for the Committee. All of those men with rich experience in p.r. clearly felt that their committee could not get along without a good p.r. man. Oddly enough, however, in 1962 Betts's successor expressed the view to Grant's successor that the Committee on Advertising had not been notably effective.

That committee did anticipate the numerous queries that came from corporations, smaller businesses, and especially from advertising specialists, and in April 1960 produced a detailed brochure, *Aids for Advertisers.* It observed that "the American people have always responded to advertising with a historical motif." Its list of "Suggested Tie-Ins" started with this one: "A *food* advertiser could compare today's nutritious, convenient food with the sorry fare of the military and civilians of 1861–65." *Printer's Ink,* the advertising trade journal, gave the brochure a warm endorsement and added that "Americans have always responded to advertising with a nostalgic appeal." The journal began its coverage with a not-so-gentle admonition:

> Mounting national interest in the Civil War Centennial now getting under way can mean dividends to advertisers who tie in with it intelligently and tastefully. The four-year commemoration is sure to generate additional advertising and promotion dollars. Many companies are already beginning programs focused on the Civil War, some based on years of planning. For example: New products are getting a special send-off. A new bourbon, Johnny Reb, is currently getting the full treatment from distributor, "21" Brands. The whiskey, aiming for national distribution by June, is now being introduced market by market, with sales promotion and advertising, as well as packaging, built around the Confederacy (introductory sales force wears Confederate uniforms). Toys, books and records are another major product field, with such items as Civil War games, toy weapons, uniforms and equipment getting a major ad push this Christmas.[41]

The only counterbalance came from the National Better Business Bureau on Park Avenue and took the form of a service bulletin that appealed for good taste in advertising. Some examples from its list of a dozen tips are revealing:

> Maintain a sense of appropriateness. Don't run an ad about General Lee on Lincoln's birthday, and vice versa.
> Don't make fun of antiquated habits and customs. They were not funny in their day. Remember, we will probably seem quaint to the people of a century hence.[42]

Not all displays were as low-key as the window exhibits at Gimbel Brothers department store in Philadelphia (fig. 17.12).

The public statements of purpose that General Grant and others made were significant because they reiterated them on so many occasions and because they tended to be paraphrased or plagiarized by state and local officials, by the media, and even by advertisers. In November 1959 Grant offered a typical speech to the 81st General Conference of the National Guard Association of the United States, meeting in San

17.12   Civil War Centennial display at Gimbel Brothers department store in Philadelphia (1962). This particular exhibit concerns the anti-slavery movement that helped to precipitate the war. Courtesy of the National Archives Trust Fund Board.

Antonio. He pleaded for a commemoration rather than a celebration, and hoped for a "deeper appreciation of the enduring contribution those men made to our country's heritage." He also emphasized the importance of decentralized initiatives and broadly based participation. The Commission's Advisory Council, he noted, consisted of six hundred men and women from every state. The work of state and local Centennial committees would be crucial, along with all sorts of private organizations and institutions. In suggesting that the "spectrum" of Centennial activities was "almost unlimited," Grant's manner of illustrating the general point was symptomatic: "All major segments of the travel industry are perfecting bold and elaborate measures to bring visitors to Civil War battlefields and other sites on a scale surpassing anything in the Nation's history of mass tourist travel. Map publishers and oil companies are preparing attractive maps that will both guide and inform this unprecedented number of visitors."[43]

Late in 1961, when historian Allan Nevins replaced Grant as chairman of the Commission, he issued a one-page statement that indicated what his priorities and emphases would be (fig. 17.13). Some were quite similar to his predecessor's: cohesion rather than conflict; learning the lessons of national tragedy and the need for mutual understanding. Others, however, were quite new: commemoration of civil as well as military events; the profuse publication of educational books, popular

17.13   Allan Nevins being sworn in as chairman of the Civil War Centennial Commission in November 1961 by Floyd E. Dotson. Edmund C. Gass, associate director of the Commission, stands between them. Courtesy of the National Archives Trust Fund Board.

as well as scholarly; the need to inspire poets, essayists, novelists, and composers with the moral meaning of American history; and above all, equality of recognition, specifically of racial recognition. "Southerners died for what they believed a just cause," Nevins declared. "A host of white northerners died for what they held a sacred duty; a host of Negroes died, many in the uniform of the United States, for the achievement of freedom and human equality. We must honor them all."[44]

Although sectional antagonisms arose in specific situations, usually involving racial attitudes, the theme of reconciliation that Grant and Nevins both stressed was remarkably pervasive. The letterheads of numerous organizations and committees were carefully printed in blue and gray. Memorial services honoring those who died for the Confederacy were held in Chicago and Boston. At the latter, organized by the local U.D.C. chapter, the pledge of allegiance was followed by a salute to the Confederate flag, "with affection, reverence and undying remembrance." The small city of Fitzgerald, Georgia, publicized itself because it had been settled by 2,700 Union veterans not far from the spot where Jefferson Davis was captured. The title of Fitzgerald's popular outdoor drama? *Our Friends, the Enemy.*[45]

Balance became virtually an obsession with the Commission. The Centennial's opening ceremony took place on January 8, 1961, simultaneously at two locations: Grant's Tomb in New York City, where U. S. Grant III spoke, and Lee's Tomb in Lexington, Virginia, where Congressman William M. Tuck, vice chairman of the Commission and former governor of Virginia, spoke. Wreaths were placed at both sites. The official opening of the Centennial in New Jersey on February 21, 1961, was marked by the presence of a colorful delegation from the North-

South Skirmish Association, a group of Civil War enthusiasts who reactivated venerable military units and appeared in full battle regalia.

Many cities anticipated the commemoration in 1958 and 1959 by offering gala fund raisers called Centennial Nights. These posh affairs were usually held at large hotels (or, in the case of St. Louis, at the country home of beer baron August A. Busch) and received regional attendance. Local newspapers reported the events in elaborate detail.[46] Whereas the wearing of "centennial dresses" and period accessories became fashionable for women who attended "memory banquets" in the North, fashion shows emerged as a commemorative feature in the former Confederacy. Manufacturers produced Civil War dresses, lingerie, and riding outfits. Author and historian Bruce Catton complained on a visit to Richmond that the Centennial "ought never to be regarded as a four-year costume ball."[47]

An important aspect of the balancing act concerned the meeting place of the Commission's annual National Assembly, composed of about 340 representatives from civic, patriotic, and historical organizations. (The Commission and its administrative staff usually met immediately prior to this two-day affair.) The sequence of locations ran as follows: Washington, D.C., in 1958 (when invitations reached historical societies barely a week prior to the Assembly); Richmond in 1959; St. Louis in 1960; Charleston, South Carolina, in 1961; Columbus, Ohio, in 1962; Boston in 1963 (a desperate effort to drum up some interest in aloof New England); Atlanta in 1964; and Springfield, Illinois, in May 1965 (only five commissioners attended—not a quorum—so the other twenty had to be polled by mail about the concluding decisions).

The Charleston Assembly in April 1961 precipitated the nastiest incident of the entire Centennial—one that lingered in memory and seriously tarnished the Commission. Betts had neglected to check the racial policies of the Charleston hotel that had been selected, and its management adamantly refused to accommodate a modest number of black delegates. The New Jersey contingent protested vehemently; the national media picked up on it. Betts and Grant grumbled and hesitated before consenting to relocate the assembly to the Charleston Naval Base, a federal facility. For five months thereafter the episode festered. Members of the Commission who had been unhappy with Betts's leadership on many counts, and with Grant for giving Betts his full support, forced a meeting of the Commission at Washington in August that turned out to be explosive.

The dissidents insisted upon having a stenographer present, and the fifty-page transcript crackles with sparks of acrimony. Professor Bell I. Wiley of Emory University in Atlanta declared that "our situation, in the eyes of the nation, has been deteriorating over a long period of time." Grant suggested that Congressman Fred Schwengel of Iowa was "not too friendly to the workings of the commission." When Grant tried to point to the Commission's accomplishments, Wiley responded that he did not "think it right for us to claim credit for what has been done down on the grass roots level." He then lamented that Betts "has never shown an aggressive and hearty interest in the work of the historical activities committee." When the Commission voted to fire Betts, Grant swiftly quit.[48]

Following Betts's face-saving resignation two weeks later, he was replaced as executive director by James I. Robertson, a tactful Virginian and a history professor who had written extensively about the war.[49] Grant submitted his resignation to President Kennedy immediately, and was temporarily replaced as acting chairman by Congressman Schwengel, who had declared at the stormy session that "there is an apparent lack of statesmanship in handling delicate and sensitive problems [which] makes it necessary to find new leadership." Allan Nevins joined the Commission as Grant's permanent successor on October 13, 1961. Although he suffered a heart attack in January 1963 (he was seventy-two) and became incapacitated for several months, Nevins led the Commission with intellectual vigor and prudence for the remainder of its existence.[50]

When sparks flew early in 1962 over whether and how to commemorate the centennial of the Emancipation Proclamation—many Southern delegates and state commissions dragged their feet and mobilized a separate Southern Conference of Centennial Commissions—Nevins repeatedly expressed his determination that all fifty states should "recognize the importance of the Proclamation." With co-operation from the National Capital Parks Commission he arranged for a dignified ceremony to be held at the Lincoln Memorial on September 22, 1962, asked Archibald MacLeish to write a special poem for the occasion, Ulysses Kay to compose a new piece of music, and Mahalia Jackson to sing, and got Governor Nelson Rockefeller of New York to appear and present an original draft of the Proclamation to the Library of Congress (fig. 17.14).[51]

From February until late August 1962, Nevins believed that he had a firm commitment from the White House that President Kennedy would give the principal address at the ceremony; but Kennedy, contemplating a re-election campaign in 1964, apparently decided that the honor was not worth offending white Southerners for, and he declined. Thereupon Nevins pleaded with Adlai Stevenson of Illinois, then ambassador to the United Nations, to serve as speaker, and he graciously consented. Although some white traditionalists did not care for Mahalia Jackson's gospel music, the media indicated that her powerful voice and sheer presence simply stole the show (fig. 17.15).[52]

MacLeish's poem, which has not been remembered, remains a moving contribution to the literature of American memory. He began by using the Potomac's movement as a metaphor for the nation's past: "We bring the past down with us as you bring your/sodden branches. . . . We bring the past down with us, the shame gathers/And the dream is lost."

17.14 The Centennial observance of the Emancipation Proclamation, September 22, 1962, at the Lincoln Memorial in Washington, D.C. Courtesy of the National Archives Trust Fund Board.

After lines about Lincoln's agony and determination to save the Union, MacLeish came to the war itself:

> *The guns begin, [he]*
> *Emancipates—but not the slaves,*
> *The Union—not from servitude but shame:*
> *Emancipates the Union from the monstrous name*
> *Whose infamy dishonored*
> *Even the great Founders in their graves . . .*
>
> *He saves the Union and the dream goes on.* [53]

Less than a year later Dr. Martin Luther King, Jr., stood at the same spot and demonstrated just how passionately the dream persisted.

Nevins's determination to avoid another fiasco like the one at Charleston in April 1961 basically prevailed. A major test would occur at the Vicksburg Centennial in July 1963, and Robertson's last-minute report to Nevins assured him that the blunders made by Betts and Grant would not recur:

17.15 Governor Nelson A. Rockefeller, Ambassador Adlai E. Stevenson, Circuit Judge Thurgood Marshall, and gospel singer Mahalia Jackson at the centennial observance of the Emancipation Proclamation, September 22, 1962, at the Lincoln Memorial in Washington, D.C. Photo by Abbie Rowe, courtesy National Park Service.

All of the commemorative programs will be held on National Park Service ground and will be therefore void of any discrimination; the two-day historical seminar in which I am a participant will likewise be held at the park and open to the public on a non-segregated basis; and I have been informed by NPS officials in Vicksburg that certain hotels and motels will *quietly*— and unknown to the public—accept Negroes who are members of state commissions or serving in some other official capacity. I think this last-named development is truly one of the miracles of our century.[54]

One wishes that the hotel integration had been less covert; but the event went smoothly, the people of Vicksburg gradually became aware that a milestone had been passed, and in a little more than two years considerable progress had certainly been achieved.

In 1966, when the time came for the Commission to issue its final report, Nevins adamantly insisted upon *full* disclosure of just exactly what had happened at Charleston in 1961, even if it meant embarrassing people still alive, plus the relatives of deceased participants, and even U. S. Grant III, whom Nevins described as being "dead above the neck." Nevins had the singular capacity to see and understand the Centennial in the broader context of social change. He insisted that the Commission's final reckoning must be candid and clear. It would have to include:

> (1) a statement that the beginnings of the commemoration coincided with a great national movement for the granting of equal rights to the Negro, which was resisted earnestly in some Southern quarters; and (2) that Southern leaders in the movement for commemoration formed an organization of their own, and made strenuous efforts to use it in bringing pressure upon the National Commission to take no stand on the question of equal rights. In doing this, they came into collision with the announced purpose of the national Government to see that all federal agencies complied with the explicit requirements of the Fourteenth Amendment, and to see that the Negro was not only given full equal rights, but was welcomed to them.[55]

With a very few exceptions, ranking officials of the national government contributed relatively little to the Centennial's success—such as it was. Most senators and congressmen who served on the Commission had poor attendance records at its meetings. Congress did appropriate $100,000 per year to support the Commission's activities between 1958 and 1965, of which 55 percent went for staff salaries. Grant and Betts had to lobby hard for the renewal of the appropriation each year, and Grant understood full well what sort of approach was most likely to succeed. He told Betts in 1961 to apprise the House Appropriations Committee that disseminating knowledge of the Civil War would be "an inspiration to better citizenship today and greater patriotism, which is certainly needed today in the face of subversive forces among us."* He also urged Betts to highlight the fact that "we are not paying with federal funds for any of the ceremonies, re-enactments or other events—that is being handled voluntarily by local committees and State Commissions."[56]

Grant and Betts believed in the virtues of decentralization for practical as well as policy reasons, and consequently they were committed to leaving local groups alone to "do their own thing"—except when the aggressive and active Virginia State Commission appeared to be excessively chauvinistic. In 1960 the national Commission became deeply

---

*Members of the Commission and its staff were required to swear and sign a full-page affidavit that read, in part, "I am not a Communist or Fascist. I do not advocate nor am I knowingly a member of any organization that advocates the overthrow of the constitutional form of the Government of the United States, or which seeks by force or violence to deny other persons their rights under the Constitution of the United States."

disturbed when it learned that a few months earlier the Virginians had issued a "boastful and even arrogant" news release stating, in Betts's words, that the "whole national commemoration was to be centered in Virginia, that the state had suffered more than anyone during the war, and [that] it deserved and intended to secure the recognition by everyone that it was to be the center of all Centennial activities." Betts added that he had received complaints from the commissions in many other states, and warned Virginians that the whole episode had done more "to hurt your tourist travel than anything that could have happened."[57]

Within the proud Old Dominion a highly successful grass-roots program of organizing commemorative events on the local level began in 1959 and remained both vigorous and visible during the years from 1961 to 1965. A monthly newsletter produced by the state commission kept communities apprised of what would be happening throughout the state. As the Centennial moved toward closure, however, Virginians once again became proprietary in their outlook, complained bitterly about an invitation that North Carolina had cheekily extended to President Johnson to speak there, and pleaded with the national Commission for concentration in 1965 on "one observance where we can give real voice to a positive program of tribute to the brave American soldiers of both north and south. . . . Naturally . . . this one program should be on the anniversary of Appomattox, the end of the war in people's minds throughout the world."[58]

On April 9, 1965, an elaborate program at Appomattox was, in fact, jointly sponsored by the Virginia Commission, the local county commission, and the National Park Service (fig. 17.16). The publicity and the program brochure emphasized the historic preservation efforts that had been accomplished, thereby "gradually turning the 'village time' back" to 1865; and the climax of the day, in fact, involved dedication of the recently reconstructed Appomattox County Court House. The actual surrender and demise of the Confederacy were not explicitly mentioned. Instead, what had occurred at Appomattox was deemed significant because "here a reunited nation [hardly!] began again to move in concert toward strength and world power." The Virginia Commission and the Park Service somehow managed to extract a mythic Confederate moral victory from the facts of defeat, with histrionics and warped history as minor costs.[59]

Elsewhere we find varied modes of local commemoration causing much less controversy and more in the way of education. Clio took to the road in many states. Wisconsin and Illinois had historymobiles, and the New Jersey National Guard set up a militiamobile. Civil War tours became popular, so travel agencies as well as the "hospitality industry" thrived. The state of Kentucky developed a systematic four-year program that set up county committees, mobilized the media, service clubs, and various sorts of existing organizations, sponsored essay contests and other educational programs, devoted attention to the more

17.16   Centennial Day at Appomattox Court House, April 9, 1965. Courtesy
of the National Archives Trust Fund Board.

than three hundred "skirmishes" fought in Kentucky, developed or
improved battlefields as tourist sites, searched for Civil War records and
relics, and so forth. A few states did more, but many did a good deal less.
Kentucky's program seems to have been fairly representative.[60]

Some communities showed considerable initiative and esprit in developing programs appropriate to the locality (fig. 17.17), while others
blandly wrote to the national or state commissions in search of ideas,
guidelines, suggestions, and, hopefully, an appearance by a prominent
speaker.[61] There tended to be a notable amount of apathy on the geographical fringes. After a visit to New England's conference of centennial commissions in 1960, Grant lamented that because "they have no
battlefields in their territory they cannot expect much benefit from the
Centennial. New England people are not prone to enthusiasm, except
when running for President." In California, on the other hand, the state
legislature directed its commission to commemorate the "successful
role performed by the United States Naval Squadron of the Pacific from
1861–1867." California planned activities for 1965–66 that would be
linked to the restoration of constitutional government in Mexico following the overthrow of Archduke Maximilian and the withdrawal of Napoleon III's forces from Mexico in 1867. Why? Because "the influence of
the United States and of California was brought to bear immediately

17.17 A family group singing popular Civil War songs at Wickham-Valentine House during the city of Richmond's *Vignettes of the Civil War.* Courtesy of the National Archives Trust Fund Board.

after the cessation of hostilities in April 1865 in the American Civil War."[62]

The most problematic and controversial sort of Centennial activity turned out to be battle re-enactments. Colorful organizations were devoted to them, and they unquestionably enjoyed popular appeal. Grant had been unwilling to encourage them, for a number of reasons: he did not believe that they could be "made true to history"; they were expensive; and they required "much training and preparation to make them successful dramatically." When Bruce Catton spoke in Richmond, he indicated his discomfort with the whole concept and wondered where the mania would end. "Is it proposed to re-enact the burning of cities, the march to the sea, the appalling bloodshed of this most sanguinary conflict?" Many in the general public agreed; but no other commemorative activity so aroused the excitement of children, and of childlike adults (fig. 17.18).[63]

Allan Nevins did not care for re-enactments and declared that "we [speaking *ex cathedra* for the Commission] are anxious not to give too much emphasis to battles, which get all the attention of State and local authorities anyhow." He insisted upon more attention being given to the home front during the war, and was delighted when Robertson reported that "the people at Antietam are perhaps in serious trouble where their re-enactment is concerned." The Department of Defense, it turned out, dragged its feet "in the matter of

17.18 Re-enactment of the First Battle of Manassas, July 29, 1961, at Manassas National Battlefield Park, Virginia. Some fifty thousand spectators attended. Courtesy of the National Archives Trust Fund.

securing Army troops, equipment, and machinery to take care of their cast of fighters." Looking back when the Centennial had ended, Acting Director Gass acknowledged that the press loved to publicize re-enactments because they were easily understood by the broadest possible audience. To his way of thinking, simulated battles were "duck soup for the righteous, the kneejerk liberals, and the literate snobs." Gass also complained that "think" magazines tended to criticize "gimmickry and commercialism."[64]

Aside from academic scholars, intellectuals and social observers had surprisingly little to say about the Centennial. Robert Penn Warren was one important exception. The extended essay that he published in 1961 combined extravagant claims for the war's centrality with penetrating insights concerning each section's capacity to disfigure or disremember the past. His eulogy for the South took the form of a shrewd phrase: "In the moment of death the Confederacy entered upon its immortality." Warren's comprehension of myth-making as a social process brought him to an acerbic judgment of the Northerner, who "tends to rewrite history to suit his own deep needs." He backed that up with substance: "When one is happy in forgetfulness, facts get forgotten. In the happy contemplation of the Treasury of Virtue it is forgotten that the Republican platform of 1860 pledged protection to the institution of slavery where it existed."[65]

Like Penn Warren, Edmund Wilson felt passionately that the Civil

War had been a great "pivot" in the nation's consciousness and culture. Hence Wilson's years of labor to produce the huge and judicious volume *Patriotic Gore: Studies in the Literature of the American Civil War* (1962). Hence his frustration with literati who ignored his book, and with students of American culture who had managed to sidestep the war for so long because it seemed inconsequential or vulgar. Wilson complained to John Dos Passos that Van Wyck Brooks's five-volume "Makers and Finders" series had "bypassed the Civil War by covering the period first in one of his New England volumes, then in one of the volumes dealing with other parts of the country—so you never get the crisis at all. He [Brooks] told me he thought it was a bore."[66]

Civil War novels have long been with us, but almost none of the memorable or most popular ones appeared during the Centennial era. Popular culture magazines trivialized and sometimes even scorned the Centennial. Because the *Saturday Evening Post* wanted to do something different in conjunction with the Centennial, it quite literally chose trivia as its "handle": in December 1960 it began to run a series of "little-known incidents of the war."[67] In July 1961 *Holiday* magazine, a popular travel journal, used a full-page editorial to call the Civil War Centennial a "shabby circus." The state of South Carolina promptly cancelled its advertising in *Holiday*.

Odd though it may seem, the television industry regarded the impending commemoration with nervous skepticism. William S. Paley of CBS responded cautiously to an inquiry from Betts. Programs would be forthcoming only if the event turned out to be one of "general interest to the country," which Paley doubted would be the case. A media insider explained to Betts why advertising agencies and potential sponsors seemed so "chilly." He believed that Madison Avenue people "not only are ignorant of national interest in the Centennial and the War—they are *afraid* of it. Their fears are primarily based on the reaction of the South to television programs about the period."[68] Folks below the Mason-Dixon line did not care to be exposed or condemned. Silence might not have been bliss, but it seemed preferable to moral condemnation.

Starting in 1963, however, some of the best television programming about the war years began to occur when scholars like Nevins and Henry Steele Commager were interviewed in lively discussions that sparked even livelier debates concerning such issues as the relative greatness of Lincoln and Lee.[69]

Nevins's largest concern was to make the Centennial genuinely educational, and his executive director, James I. Robertson, as well as Professor Bell I. Wiley of the Commission, shared that concern. Early in 1963 Robertson observed to Nevins that "since its birth in 1958 this Commission has done absolutely nothing for the benefit of younger generations"—despite thousands of informational requests that poured in from schoolchildren. By October, however, Robertson had prepared a *Student's Handbook on the Civil War* that proved both popular and effective. The response to it turned out to be one of the most positive elements in the Commission's history.[70]

Nevins's determination to make the Centennial an educational success at every social level prompted him to call attention to civil affairs and to the role of women. Lest that sound startlingly modern or "liberated" for the early 1960s, it should be kept in mind that some professional women and numerous women's organizations were actively concerned about patriotism, history in general, and the Civil War particularly. Adele Nathan of New York City, for example, had acquired a reputation for developing effective historical pageants. In 1952 she produced a TV show called "Mr. Lincoln Goes to Gettysburg," sponsored by the Western Maryland Railway; so, predictably, she was picked to plan events for the Gettysburg Centennial early in July 1963.[71]

Those on the Commission staff who were most concerned about developing effective programs for and about women quite candidly felt that they had to pre-empt females in the hereditary societies who would otherwise concoct unsound or silly activities for the distaff side. As Executive Director Robertson wrote to Congressman Schwengel late in 1962: "I feel it imperative that we initiate definite plans for our 1963 women's program as soon as possible. If we wait too long, the United Daughters of the Confederacy, the Daughters of Union Veterans, and other hen houses may embark on separate programs that will clash, be inadequate, and be unbalanced."[72]

The involvement of women and their organizations only partially accounted for the quasi-religious tone that Centennial activities and participants sometimes struck. In 1960 Senator Joseph C. O'Mahoney of Wyoming, an original member of the Commission, introduced a joint resolution (that ultimately did not succeed) establishing a "national shrine commission to select and procure a site and formulate plans for the construction of a permanent memorial building in memory of the veterans of the Civil War." The Stonewall Jackson Memorial, Inc., a private group, administered several "shrines," including Jackson's home in Lexington and his headquarters in Winchester, Virginia. An association known as Garden of the Patriots ran a pious program called "History Happened Here" that placed plaques at suitable sites in honor of neglected heroes.[73]

Visits to many of these sites, especially in the South, were invariably referred to as "pilgrimages." Mississippi seemed to specialize in arranging for such events—riverboat cruises at Vicksburg, tours to points of interest at Jackson, to historic sites at Columbus, and attendance at a Confederate Ball at Holly Springs—but the All-South Centennial Commission, based at the chamber of commerce in Montgomery, Alabama, arranged for pilgrimages to the "Cradle of the Confederacy" that would include the first White House of the Confederacy, the Capitol Building, old homes, and "other historically correct and significant structures." *A Guide for the Observance of the Centennial of the Civil War,* pro-

duced by the national Commission very early in its existence, encouraged "religious services to coincide with important national events of
the Civil War era."[74]

Southerners most passionately devoted to the Lost Cause did not
share a consensus about priorities and enthusiasms. Some of the more
cerebral and ideologically conservative complained about writers and
history buffs who timidly "concentrated on the non-controversial military aspects" rather than making a bold case *against* democracy, for
example. Members of an organization called the Confederate High
Command, however, sequentially based in St. Petersburg, Florida, and
Nashville, Tennessee, had a craving for military history, loved to stage
re-enactments, and by 1964 had established an extraordinary network
of branches not only in the South but in Canada, England, France, and
Germany. It also had correspondents living in Switzerland, Belgium,
and Burma. Some of its politically prominent members included Senator Harry F. Byrd of Virginia, Congressman William Cramer of Florida,
former Texas Governor Price Daniel, and the mayor of New Orleans.[75]

From 1958 onward the national Commission fostered local initiative.
It spurred the state commissions to encourage historical societies, patriotic and service organizations to sponsor programs. Nevertheless, it also
maintained a standing legislative committee that was responsible for
reviewing and reporting on "such measures as may be pending before
Congress that are of direct concern to the Commission." One member
of that committee, Conrad L. Wirth, happened to be director of the
National Park Service. When he addressed the National Assembly at
Richmond in April 1959, Wirth offered a degree of co-operation that
became extremely important to the Centennial during the next six
years.[76]

The Department of the Interior authorized Wirth and the Park Service to undertake as part of its long-term MISSION 66 enterprise an
extensive program of development at various Civil War sites "so that
fitting observances may be held at each as its centennial occurs." The
Park Service projected expenditures of some $25 million by 1965:
$18 million of that for physical improvements and more than $5 million
for the proposed acquisition of 13,000 acres of land. As Wirth explained
when he launched into the heart of his pitch to the Assembly:

> Once a battlefield in its original state is lost, no museum exhibit,
> no monument or marker can recapture it. And significant areas
> associated with great battles of the Civil War are fast disappearing
> beneath the bulldozers clearing the way for the onrush of modern
> urban development. If we are to obtain and preserve key portions
> of this historic land the action must come quickly, or it will be too
> late.

Wirth proceeded to sketch out some of the legal complexities involved, the bills recently introduced in Congress to permit the exten-

sion or acquisition of various sites, and pleaded for broadly based support in the on-going battle against the bulldozer. He closed on a note
of praise for the current administration's strong support for measures
"designed to combat the loss of historic values," and added that President Eisenhower had done much to "facilitate the accomplishment of
Civil War area conservation goals."

Curiously enough, however, despite his long military career, his
home at Gettysburg, and his *ex officio* status as honorary chairman of
the Civil War Centennial Commission, Dwight D. Eisenhower kept an
incredibly low profile throughout the entire Centennial. He lent neither his prestige nor his presence to one of the oddest, most prolonged,
and often strained commemorations in American memory.

I V

CONRAD WIRTH'S appeal for co-operation among the Park
Service, the Congress, and Centennial activists in order to salvage
pieces of the nation's physical heritage anticipated major issues and
developments of the next two decades. On the one hand, state and
federal funds aimed at urban renewal and massive highway construction threatened and, indeed, destroyed significant portions of that heritage—a story that has been told from various perspectives, most of them
critical.[77]

At the same time, all three branches of the federal government assumed considerably more responsibility for preserving and protecting
the nation's past: with legislation, with well-publicized (but politically
cautious) leadership from the Kennedy White House, with substantial
appropriations that those two branches agreed upon, with a notable
expansion in the scope of Park Service activity, and with some vital
decisions by the Supreme Court that bolstered the preservation movement immeasurably.[78] Between 1961 and 1979 the federal government
became a principal sponsor and custodian of national traditions, but
then began a process of fiscal and administrative retrenchment that has
continued ever since. Although we cannot look at every program and
initiative in detail, it is possible to glimpse an overview of the process
by which this extraordinary set of circumstances came about.

For purposes of continuity we can start with the Park Service. During
the later 1940s both the public and the Park Service began to regard
site development and interpretation as paramount, rather than remaining content with the protection of natural wonders or historic areas.
Combined with a marked growth in leisure, affluence, and transportation networks, the consequences turned out to be quite striking.
Whereas in 1950 the national parks reported 33 million visitors, by 1983
the figure had leaped to 327 million, one and one-half times the entire
population of the United States. The MISSION 66 program (1955–66),

17.19   Entrance to the Custer Battlefield National Cemetery, showing War Department buildings, October 25, 1935. National Park Service photograph by Roger W. Toll.

designed to coincide with the Golden Jubilee of the Park Service, meant a striking expansion in historical programs and in *types* of historical sites. Congress took notice and co-operated in terms of both augmented appropriations and legislation. If the Antiquities Act of 1906 had initiated the precedent of federal legislation to preserve cultural resources that lay (or should lie) in the public domain, the Archaeological Resources Protection Act of 1979 perhaps marked the culmination of the long shift from a comparatively passive role for government to a much more active one.[79]

Each historic site in the Park Service network had its own distinctive evolution, and we need a veritable typology in order to perceive the kaleidoscopic pattern. Older places underwent transformations. The Custer Battlefield in Montana, for example, which had been designated a national cemetery in 1879, became a National Monument in 1946 (fig. 17.19). In 1952 a modest museum was opened on the site, and by 1975 it received more than a quarter of a million tourists per year. Other locations, such as Independence Historical Park in Philadelphia, underwent elaborate development as a result of municipal initiative and a very extensive urban renewal program during the two decades following 1945.[80]

Still other sorts of sites involved elements of serendipity, family dispersion, and a sense of filial responsibility by patrician descendants. Hence the John and John Quincy Adams home in Braintree and the

Craigie House (Longfellow's home in Cambridge) came to be administered by the Park Service between 1946 and 1972. The first residence
of a famous American writer—Hawthorne's in Concord, Massachusetts—became part of the system in 1965 when the Minute Man National Historical Park was created. During the dozen years that
followed, Congress added four more authors' homes to the system: Carl
Sandburg's at Flat Rock, North Carolina, in 1968; Longfellow's in 1972;
Eugene O'Neill's in 1976; and Edgar Allan Poe's in 1978.[81]

Changing assumptions about American society and its components
eventually caused Ellis Island to be added to the Statue of Liberty as
a place significant in the history of American ethnic diversity. Recognition that the early history of industrialization and technological development deserved a place in the nation's memory brought Lowell
National Historical Park into the system in 1978. And private collectors
gradually began to consider national parks as appropriate repositories
for their cherished caches. In 1978, for example, Valley Forge National
Historic Park acquired for $640,000 one of the largest private collec-
tions of Revolutionary War weapons, including muskets, rifles, swords,
and cannons. This arsenal of 1,500 pieces and related items came from
George C. Neumann, a businessman in Durham, Connecticut, and one
of the founders of the Brigade of the American Revolution.[82]

A different kind of public-private institution, the presidential library,
has generated intermittent controversy ever since F.D.R. established
his at Hyde Park in 1939 (fig. 17.20) and Congress passed the Presidential Libraries Act in 1955. They have customarily been built with pri-

17.20 A panel in Franklin Delano Roosevelt's library in the South Wing at
Hyde Park, New York. (Note the three marine paintings at the top.) Courtesy
of the National Archives Trust Fund Board.

vate funds, usually at or near the hometown of a former president, but are subsequently operated and maintained by the federal government. Each one involved its own idiosyncratic arrangements. The Hoover Library opened at West Branch, Iowa, in 1962; Truman's at Independence, Missouri, in 1957; Eisenhower's at Abilene, Kansas, in 1966; Johnson's at Austin, Texas, in 1971; and Kennedy's at Boston in 1979. The vexed issues are numerous and remain largely unresolved: is their cost to the taxpayer justified ($9.5 million in 1980 and $25 million by the end of the decade), or would a single, centralized presidential archive be far more efficient? To what extent is it appropriate for them to be museum memorials as well as libraries? Does any portion of a president's papers (from his term or terms in office) remain private rather than public—a contested matter especially in the case of Richard M. Nixon.[83]

Although historians have been quite interested in particular presidents as well as the presidency as an institution, they have not paid very much attention to presidential traditions and to the variable role of American presidents as arbiters of tradition.[84] In John F. Kennedy's inaugural address he called for pride in "our ancient heritage," and with the active participation of his wife Kennedy followed up in specific ways. They wrote to prominent figures in American culture and solicited (from John Dos Passos, for example) "any suggestions you may have in the future about the possible contributions the national government might make to the arts in America." In 1962 presidential assistant Arthur M. Schlesinger, Jr., explained to a number of American historians and writers that "Mrs. Kennedy is deeply interested in realizing the full potentialities of the White House as an expression of American culture and the American experience. Her redecoration program* has included the Library on the ground floor; and it is her hope that this Library may contain the books which will best represent the history and culture of the United States." Scholars were invited to make recommendations, and Mrs. Kennedy also asked distinguished librarians and bibliophiles, such as C. Waller Barrett, to serve as an advisory committee.[85]

Subsequently the Congress passed in 1966 the National Museum Act and the National Historic Preservation Act, which provided immense financial and moral support for museums and preservation programs. Other legislation such as the Presidential Recordings and Materials Preservation Act and the Museum Services Act followed in the mid-1970s. These did not come easily, however, because fiscal conservatives who bitterly opposed the Preservation Act believed that such work was an "obligation of the local communities and states." As Representative

---

*The public expressed strong interest in this program. The first printing of *The White House: An Historic Guide,* published late in 1962, reportedly sold a million copies within a few months and the booklet subsequently went through numerous reprints.

Craig Hosmer of California put it: "Washington cannot do everything. Let us keep the hands of Washington, its resources and its politics, out of the arena of local historical interest. In short, if Jubilation T. Cornpone's birthplace is to be preserved, Dogpatch should do it!" Only the most persistent lobbying by influential insiders, like Gordon Gray of the National Trust for Historic Preservation, made possible the passage of such legislation.[86]

Its enactment did much to transform historic preservation from primarily a patrician concern to a broadly based nationwide movement that soon received reinforcement from a series of legislative and executive policies: the Environmental Protection Act of 1969, which strengthened the situation of preservationists; Executive Order 11593, signed by President Nixon in 1971, requiring federal officials in all departments to conduct inventories of historic properties within their jurisdictions and make every effort to protect them; the Housing and Community Act of 1974, which required communities to consider restoration rather than demolition in planning urban renewal; and tax provisions of legislation in the 1970s that awarded significant advantages to developers who renovated historic commercial structures. By 1980 more than $100 million in federal and state matching funds were being spent each year on preserving the nation's built environment.[87]

THE NATIONAL MUSEUM ACT of 1966 opened with the sort of affirmation that made Congress sound like an institution thoroughly committed to a custodial role for American memory: "WHEREAS national recognition is necessary to insure that museum resources for preserving and interpreting the Nation's heritage may be more fully utilized in the enrichment of public life in the individual community. . . ." And so forth. In reality, however, congressional action of this sort occurred in an ad hoc rather than a systematic or sustained manner, and most efforts along these lines encountered serious resistance. The number of members with a *genuine* commitment to improving the nation's capacity for memory was very modest: Senators John Sherman Cooper of Kentucky and Mike Mansfield of Montana, Representatives Richard Bolling of Missouri, Robert G. Stephens of Georgia, Fred Schwengel of Iowa, and a few others.[88]

It is a strangely straitened list, which may help to explain why governmental activism in support of tradition lasted less than two decades. In 1978 the Department of the Interior effectively eliminated a well-established program: the National Survey of Historic Sites and Buildings, initially authorized by Congress in 1935. Department Secretary Cecil Andrus did create a new bureau, the Heritage Conservation and Recreation Service; but he cared far more about land use than he did about historic heritage, and in any case James Watt, his successor, abolished the new bureau in 1981. That would set the tone for an extraordinary series of program cuts throughout the Reagan years.[89]

V

THE "PARTNERSHIP" between public and private sectors that became such a policy by-word of the 1980s was obviously not a new notion in the history of preserving the nation's patrimony. Numerous state and national parks came into being because of private and local initiatives. Many of the activities, souvenirs, and publications available at the parks are made possible by such private groups as the Custer Battlefield Historical and Museum Association. And the National Park Service has for some time had complex and mutually beneficial relationships with diverse non-federal and non-profit as well as commercial enterprises that serve visitor needs in various ways.[90]

Starting in the 1960s Clement E. Conger began to acquire distinctive examples of American Federal period furniture, painting, sculpture, china, and the decorative arts in order to create a stunning collection for the diplomatic reception rooms of the Department of State. (President Nixon subsequently asked Conger to assume that responsibility for the White House as well.) Obtaining these objects, many of them unique and rich in historical associations, has not cost the taxpayer a penny because Conger persuaded people to give them to the nation and raised millions of dollars from private donors in order to purchase what could not be begged or borrowed. At the same time, Conger's controversial but highly successful "hard sell" has placed the executive branch of the federal government in competition with private collectors, historical societies, and museums for desirable Americana available at auctions, galleries, and estate sales—thereby driving up prices that have recently become wildly inflated.[91] We have public-private competition as well as co-operation.

The National Historical Publications Commission was successfully launched in 1964 when the Ford Foundation made a $2 million grant to the National Archives Trust Fund Board in order to encourage the publication of documentary source materials pertaining mainly to the founders. The widely praised multi-volume project called Literary Classics of the United States, jointly funded by the Ford Foundation and the National Endowment for the Humanities, makes major works available in compact editions at popular prices. The diverse commemorative observances that took place between 1961 and 1987 all involved dispensations by national commissions to private enterprise in order to provide funds for programs by raising revenues for the private organizations.[92]

Prodding the nation's memory and developing suitable programs to perpetuate it continued to come from the private sector throughout those years. In 1965, for example, a director of the Land Use and Management Program of Resources for the Future, located in Washington, D.C., proposed a "system of living, operating historical farms, to portray some of the main elements of U.S. agricultural history." Such farms have, in fact, flourished ever since the mid-1970s, though in an ad hoc and individualized rather than a systematic manner. Similarly, little had been planned to honor the centennial of Franklin D. Roosevelt's birth in January 1982 until a twenty-nine-year-old private individual in Chicago swung into action and mobilized public institutions, private resources, and considerable publicity. (Although Congress passed a joint resolution in 1955 to establish a commission to formulate plans for a memorial to F.D.R., no major memorial yet exists though serious planning actually got under way early in 1990, thirty-five years after the initial resolution.)[93]

The federal government did, however, respond to a newly pervasive recognition of American populism and pluralism that arose during the later 1960s and early 1970s. It did so by approving legislation designed to enhance aspects of the American experience that had been ignored and repressed earlier in the twentieth century. Between 1968 and 1972, for example, a growing desire to claim affiliation with some ethnic group, however broadly defined, became manifest. The Republican Party even created a National Heritage Groups Council; and in 1972 the National Park Service opened the American Museum of Immigration at the Statue of Liberty.[94]

The Ethnic Heritage Studies Act of 1972 acknowledged that "in a multi-ethnic society a greater understanding of the contributors of one's own heritage and those of one's fellow citizens can contribute to a more harmonious, patriotic, and committed populace," and therefore provided assistance primarily aimed at enhanced educational programs in ethnic studies. It authorized the U.S. Commissioner of Education to make grants to, and contracts with, public and private non-profit organizations and institutions in order to assist them in "planning, developing, establishing, and operating ethnic heritage studies programs." By 1973–74 the results could be seen nationwide: courses in Italian-American, Polish-American, German-American, and Greek-American studies swiftly appeared, among others, at universities and high schools, alongside curriculum development for blacks, Hispanics, Chicanos, and Native Americans. Some of these programs have quietly disappeared, especially the so-called white ethnic studies; but many of them have expanded.[95]

Ever since the mid-1960s there has also been a broadening enthusiasm for folklife, or, as the specialists prefer to call it, "vernacular culture." The irony, of course, is that the growth of professionalism in this area has put those at the grass roots in an awkward situation; and even more critical, eagerness to recover vernacular culture has occurred at a time when the power of mass and popular culture has made it all the more difficult to do so. Such television programs as "The Beverly Hill Billies" have cast a shadow across our notions of what the "real thing" might have been like.[96]

Although a folklife bill was first introduced in Congress in 1969, the American Folklife Preservation Act that finally won approval in 1976 provided for much less than its advocates sought. The declaration of purpose with which it opened offers lofty and warming sentiments but closes with a statement of restraint:

> The diversity inherent in American folklife has contributed greatly to the cultural richness of the Nation and has fostered a sense of individuality and identity among the American people. . . . The encouragement and support of American folklife, while primarily a matter for private and local initiative, is also an appropriate matter of concern to the Federal Government.[97]

The Act principally established an American Folklife Center at the Library of Congress, appropriating budgets of $133,500 for its first year of operation, $295,000 for its second, and $349,000 for its third. Perhaps the most intriguing segment of the legislation, however, occurred in section two, where a definition was courageously supplied:

> The term "American folklife" means the traditional expressive culture shared within the various groups in the United States . . . expressive culture includes a wide range of creative and symbolic forms . . . these expressions are mainly learned orally, by imitation, or in performance, and are generally maintained without benefit of formal instruction or institutional direction.[98]

A little more than a year later, after President Jimmy Carter caused Secretary Cecil Andrus to convene a National Heritage Trust Force, that body defined the cultural heritage of the United States as "historic or cultural places, collections and objects, arts and skills, and folklife and contemporary cultures." For the federal government to provide criteria and guidelines, as the Congress did in 1976 and the executive branch did in 1977, meant that a shift had occurred in some basic assumptions that people made about the government's proper role in the nation's cultural life and values. Nevertheless, Congress would not pass the National Heritage Policy Act of 1979, which the Carter administration's task force had recommended. There is the absolutely anomalous legacy of the sixties and seventies: government took three steps forward and two steps backward.[99] The more things change, the more they remain the same, almost.

NOSTALGIA, NEW MUSEUMS, THE ROOTS PHENOMENON, AND REBORN PATRIOTISM: IDIOSYNCRASIES OF SELECTIVE MEMORY

A LTHOUGH SOME AMERICA-WATCHERS saw signs of nostalgia during the 1960s, that mood did not become truly pervasive until the subsequent decade. In 1971 *Time* magazine printed an essay, "The Meaning of Nostalgia," because the phenomenon suddenly seemed ubiquitous. The essay opened with a rhetorical query: "How much more nostalgia can America take?" The quotient, as it turned out, seems to have been virtually unlimited. In 1973 *Newsweek* devoted an extended feature titled "Exploring America's Past" to the connection between nostalgia and a swift rise in history-related tourism: "Americans seem to want to see and touch anything old—the genuine old, if possible, but even the hokey and plastic 'old' will do if nothing better is available." Two years later a prominent observer remarked that "looking backward has again become a major industry." That has basically remained the situation ever since, despite some peaks and valleys.[1]

The reasons why will become clearer in these next two chapters, but a few generalizations are needed at the outset. Nostalgia is most likely to increase or become prominent in times of transition, in periods of cultural anxiety, or when a society feels a strong sense of discontinuity with its past. All three of those tendencies became apparent in the sixties and then were absolutely manifest during the seventies. Nearly identical surveys made in 1959 and 1976 indicated a pronounced increase in the concern that people felt about their communities, their country, and their interpersonal lives. Various "liberation" movements made traditionalists uneasy, but also meant that the newly liberated themselves could not (or would not) rely upon conventional roles, relationships, and assumptions to steer them through stages of the life course—especially in relation to others in the community. Although many people derived pleasure and pride from liberation, prominent voices in the society as a whole expressed a sense of disquiet and disjuncture with the familiar past.[2] As Archibald MacLeish wrote to John Dos Passos in 1967: "The way I know I'm really old is the world—it's an old man's world to me—far worse than the one I knew forty years ago. (But what bothers me is that the young think so too: *no* one loves this world.)" And then in a subsequent letter: "God it's an odd thing—time. It really does move. And it moves us. Throws us all over hell."[3]

Symptoms and signs of mood swing have been abundant. Constant references to such concepts as post-industrial, post-modern, and post-structural convey the sense of being adrift because we must surely be living in a liminal phase between the present and the future, without meaningful linkages to the past. Not only do the epochs of the founders and of the Civil War seem remote, so does the New Deal. Even the 1960s have already been historicized. Radical pressures for social change swiftly proved unsettling for mainstream Americans who found their roots in the past to be rather shallow, perhaps even parched. Wallace Stegner put it this way in 1969: "Fearing the loss of what little tradition we have, we cling to it hard; we are hooked on history."[4]

The particular manifestations that being "hooked" actually took were at least partially based upon a rejection of the unattractive consequences caused by industrialization; yearnings for the pre-industrial era as a golden age of pristine simplicity; and a feeling of lost cohesion. Hence the appeal of hippie communes during the 1960s and after, but also of living-history farms: quaint museum villages like Old Bethpage located in central Long Island; historic towns that took care to compose and preserve themselves well, like U. S. Grant's Galena, Illinois; and, by the later seventies, even small mill towns in rural settings like Waterford, Virginia.[5]

Scholars have recently called to our attention, however, the complexity of multiple associations that encumber old buildings, especially for working-class people:

> The assumptions of social reformers and planners that the working-class past in these industrial settings must be eradicated because it symbolizes poverty, grimness, and exploitation, misses what the workers themselves feel about their world. They were willing, and at times eager, to recall the bitter times along with the good. Both were part of their entire life story and were deeply enmeshed with their sense of place. Memories of struggle with poverty, daily two-mile walks to the factory, unemployment and strikes, illness and death were all part of that story, and were intimately linked to the buildings. Beyond their individual experiences, buildings were so significant to people's memories because of their associations with other people, such as family members, friends, neighbors, and fellow workers, with whom they had shared these experiences.[6]

The nagging ambivalence of retrospection cuts across boundaries of class, ethnicity, and region. The ordinary vocabulary of nostalgia, however, cannot do justice to that ambivalence, and the clichés of the past quarter century seem to have been uttered, more often that not, with innocent assurance and clarity. When Miss Ima Hogg spoke at the dedication of Bayou Bend Museum at Houston in 1966, she expressed the hope that her home and collection of Americana would serve "to bring us closer to the heart of an American heritage which unites us." Four years later Lewis Mumford remarked that he and his generational cohort had been "fellow workers in the task of reclaiming our American literary heritage." Malcolm Forbes, the flamboyant publishing tycoon, was one of the most omnivorous collectors of his time and explained his compulsion with a succinct sentence in his autobiography: "For me usually nostalgia is the real culprit, the trigger." A few pages later he added that "what we buy has to fill my sons and/or me with some new—or old—emotion, a sense of recollection or nostalgia."[7]

At a time when social mobility, status, and personal security seemed especially elusive and consequently all the more desirable, a great many Americans turned to particular pasts—national, ethnic, and familial—in search of solace. Assorted memories converged, diverged, and then converged yet again like some unpredictable medley measured out by a synthesizer. Visitation figures at historical sites and museums waxed dramatically in the 1970s and then waned quite without warning during the eighties. Patriotism, hero worship, and their historical underpinnings rose and fell and then rose once more during the quarter century following 1960. It was, in fact, the best of times as well as the worst of times for American culture—with manifold implications for collective memory, amnesia, and national self-knowledge.

This chapter begins with an overview of the "heritage syndrome," primarily during the 1970s and 1980s. Section II notices the growing diversity of historic preservation activities that flourished during the seventies, particularly their vigor at the grass-roots level along with their consequences for the commercialization of American memories. The section concludes with attention to recent trends in collecting Americana, and recognizes that on-going democratization has been partially offset by a dizzying upward price spiral for quality collectibles.

Section III looks at newer museums and finds them increasingly specialized and topical but more generally educational than ever before. Attendance at many of these museums has become highly problematic, however, because of competition created by alternative stimuli that range from theme parks to television docudramas about historical events and personalities. Section IV examines the "Roots phenomenon," a dramatic expansion in the diversity of social groups concerned about their past. Section V recognizes the ups and downs of patriotism in the United States, and calls attention to strident advocates of American exceptionalism among creative writers and artists in recent decades. The chapter concludes with a note on comparability, thereby anticipating (and connecting with) the Coda to Part Four, which concludes the book.

I

FOR APPROXIMATELY a full generation, beginning in the mid-1950s, "heritage" has been one of the key words in American culture. The frequency of its usage has also increased markedly in Great Britain and the Commonwealth, to be sure, and in some of the same ways;[8] but the popularity and pervasiveness of this buzzword in the United States have become utterly astounding. Therefore the phenomenon requires our attention for various reasons but particularly because it can illuminate the complex (and often self-contradictory) transformation of historical consciousness among Americans derived from diverse backgrounds: diverse in terms of region, ethnicity, class, and levels of education. Notions of "heritage" in American popular culture are richly revealing for anyone interested in the status of history and historical understanding in contemporary society.

Before getting to the "how" and the "why" of this trend, however, we must start with the seemingly simple, basically descriptive "what." Ultimately we want to specify the implications of a cultural trend; but first we must describe it, exemplify it, and, precisely because it is so widespread, try to break it down into comprehensible categories.

At the loftiest level, for instance, one immediately thinks of the National Trust for Historic Preservation, established at the end of the 1940s. Its enticing brochure, which makes an attractive appeal for membership, has three carefully chosen words placed on the cover: "Guarding America's Heritage." A major report, co-sponsored by the National Trust and Colonial Williamsburg in 1965, carried the title *With Heritage So Rich.* One also thinks of the Museum of Our National Heritage, which opened in Lexington, Massachusetts, on April 20, 1975, under the auspices of the Scottish Rite Masonic organization.

At the state level we find that "heritage" has gradually broadened its meaning. In 1957, for example, five organizations jointly sponsored an elegant Virginia Heritage Dinner in order to celebrate "the 350th Anniversary of the Founding of Our Country." That really meant the first permanent English colony, established at Jamestown. The occasion also seemed to use heritage as a near synonym for history.

In 1974, after eight years of developmental planning, the Wisconsin Department of Natural Resources established an outdoor historical park on forty-three acres of land at the edge of Green Bay on the Fox River. It is called Heritage Hill State Park, and the cover of its big brochure defines its mission as "preserving our heritage through 'Living History.' " The four illustrative sections of that brochure are desig-

18.1   William F. (Woody) Vondracek, *Dade Heritage Days* (poster printed in Miami in 1987), silkscreen print commissioned by the Art Deco Society of Miami. Courtesy of the Library of Congress Poster Collection, Division of Prints and Photographs.

nated as Pioneer Heritage, Heritage of Growth, Military Heritage, and Religious and Small Town Heritage.

The increasingly ecumenical nature of "heritage" is exemplified by New York, which observed an Architectural Heritage Year in 1986 (promoted by the Preservation League of New York State), and had 1988 designated (by Governor Mario Cuomo) as Community Heritage Year. The latter was occasioned by the bicentennial of the 1788 Town Laws, which brought new towns into being and defined the responsibilities of all existing communities in the Empire State.[9]

At the local level "heritage" is most notably hooked up with historic preservation, although the chosen sites may vary considerably in character (fig. 18.1). In northeastern Massachusetts, for instance, Heritage Park in downtown Lowell, run by the National Park Service, is a nineteenth- and early twentieth-century industrial restoration. It offers a sharp contrast to rustic Historic Deerfield, Inc., located near the Berkshires and established in 1952 as Heritage Foundation by Mr. and Mrs. Henry Flynt in order "to promote the cause of education in and appreciation of the rich heritage of the early colonies."[10]

Architectural preservation is the primary mission of the Heritage Foundation of Oswego, New York; the Naperville Heritage Society in

Illinois, which received its impetus in 1968 when a venerable mansion was on the verge of destruction; the Athens-Clarke Heritage Foundation, which has maintained the Church-Waddel-Brumby House (1820) as a Welcome Center for Athens, Georgia, since 1971; and Texas Heritage, a private organization that is restoring the home built by a Fort Worth cattle baron back in 1912.

The Dallas County Heritage Society was formed in 1966 to prevent the destruction of Millermore, the largest surviving antebellum home in Dallas (built 1855–62). Most of the structures in Old City Park are Victorian, however, and the Society's leaflet makes the following claim: "Walking across their floors, peeking into their rooms, using their tools and toys and trivia. . . . [sic] People are history. How people have lived is the basis for how we see life."

Houston's counterpart is called the Harris County Heritage Society, a private, non-profit organization that also maintains a cluster of nineteenth-century buildings, "Where Houston Remembers." Members of the Society serve as docents in Sam Houston Park, "work in the Yesteryear Shop and Tea Room, organize and host lectures and workshops, and stage the annual Heritage Ball, Candlelight Tour and other special events."

Various structures located at Heritage Square in Los Angeles began to undergo restoration in 1968 owing to the joint auspices of the Cultural Heritage Foundation and the city's new Cultural Heritage Board. The endeavor proceeded at a snail's pace, however, because the city contributed no money to the project and volunteers came and went, but mostly went. As the *Los Angeles Times* remarked in 1976, this reflected "the sluggish historical consciousness for which the region is noted."[11]

Pasadena, on the other hand, which has a Cultural Heritage Commission, adopted a cultural heritage ordinance in 1976 that requires permission in order to demolish buildings that are more than fifty years old. The commission is then allowed thirty days to determine if the building in question has historical or cultural significance and whether it can be saved.[12]

Heritage is not invariably used as a codeword for the salvation of old structures. Sometimes it signifies the struggles for survival that various groups and subcultures have undergone. In 1982, for example, the Indiana Committee for the Humanities, the Indiana Historical Society Library, and the Muncie Public Library produced a striking photographic exhibit entitled "This Far by Faith: Black Hoosier Heritage."[13] The display was accompanied by a booklet with the same title, and a brochure that began: "Our heritage stares out at us from each photograph in this exhibit." It ended with Langston Hughes's short poem "History" (1934):

> *The past has been*
> *A mint of blood and sorrow—*

> *That must not be*
> *True of tomorrow.*

A long-neglected Georgian mansion (Belmont) in Philadelphia became the subject of considerable controversy in 1987–88 after the American Women's Heritage Society (a predominantly black organization) spent more than $50,000 on repairs, fitting out period rooms that range from early American to contemporary, and sponsoring frequent exhibits "that emphasize Black history and achievement." Several civic groups strenuously disapproved of what was done with Belmont (overlooking the Schuylkill River and Fairmount Park), however. A report prepared by a charitable foundation declared in 1987 that "this current use may not be the best use. This house may be a property of such consummate value to the city that it should be more open to the city, possibly as a reception center for dignitaries." Philadelphians have been fighting over the most appropriate use and presentation of their urban heritage.[14]

For certain groups, "heritage" has become an ideologically useful or meaningful label. The Heritage Foundation headquartered in Washington, D.C., serves as a conservative think tank and political action group. It also publishes a fair amount of literature to promote and explain its causes, which include a vigorous defense of the free enterprise system. Yet another Heritage Foundation, based in Trumbull, Connecticut, displays on its letterhead a screaming eagle perched upon an open Bible, below which a dozen words from Psalm 61 appear: "Thou hast given us the heritage of those that fear thy name." Nationalism and fundamentalism can comfortably complement one another.[15]

The heritage emphasis has also become valuable to entrepreneurs offering safe havens in a world that is commercial as well as secular, self-indulgent, and intensely concerned with social status. Heritage Hills of Westchester, New York, offers condominiums in a thousand-acre "country setting of beauty, woods, ponds and streams." Where is the heritage?

> The recreational opportunities are the best. Heritage Hills offers a private golf course and health club with gym, saunas and whirlpool. There are swimming pools, tennis courts and a jogging path. The homes are the best. Fine craftsmanship and quality are evident throughout these beautifully designed homes. . . . There's even a private shuttle service to the nearby commuter train station.

A much more lavish set of homes, located near Morristown, New Jersey, is offered by New Vernon Heritage at prices starting at $1.2 million. Where is the heritage? According to one advertisement, "the architecture, reflecting a return to the classic, will include English manors, French chateaus, and Irish country houses." A rather eclectic heritage, if you will, and if you are willing to live with mixed manors.

In the world of business, "heritage" seems to connote integrity, authenticity, venerability, and stability. Hence the Heritage Federal Bank in Franklin, Tennessee; Realty World-Heritage Realty for vacation sites in Maggie Valley, North Carolina, snuggled along the edge of the Great Smoky Mountains; the Heritage Building, a large office complex in downtown Dallas, Texas; and Heritage Hall Gallery in Lansdale, Pennsylvania, the home of the Heritage Collectors Society, which specializes in restoring, framing, and selling historic documents for "interior accent." A decorator's delight: cover your walls with "original documents signed by those who shaped our nation's destiny."

As for achievement recognition, in 1982 the National Endowment for the Arts created a program of National Heritage Fellowships, "the country's highest award for accomplishment in a traditional arts field." Three years later the recipients included a Hawaiian quiltmaker from Honolulu who hand-stitched more than one hundred quilts and designed more than four hundred quilt patterns; a Sioux from Grass Creek, South Dakota, who strove to preserve the Indian craft of porcupine quill decoration; and a working cowboy who "has told more tall tales and sung more cowboy songs than anyone in Mountain View, Arkansas, can count."[16]

These $5,000 fellowships are awarded on a one-time-only basis by the Folk Arts Program at the National Endowment. For our purposes they fill out the heritage spectrum, ranging from institutions to individuals, from the public sector to the private, from statements of purpose to advertisements, and from identity to destiny. The question yet remains, however, what does heritage actually have to do with history and social memory? Basically, I suppose, the essential answer must be "everything and nothing." In some situations, such as Heritage Hills condominiums, the word-concept bears absolutely no relationship to the past. It is simply a euphonious phrase that portends a sheltered if not sybaritic lifestyle.

In other situations heritage seems to be very nearly a euphemism for selective memory because it entails, in functional terms, what history has customarily meant in everyday practice: namely, that portion of the past perceived by a segment of society as significant at any given moment in time.[17]

In still other situations heritage is virtually intended as an antidote to historical actuality, or else it passes as sugar-coated history. But that really means more than mere palatability. It involves an explicit element of anti-intellectualism—the presumption, for example, that history experienced through sites and material culture must be more memorable than history presented on the printed page. An advertisement for New Jersey's *Heritage Guide* shows a winsome modern lass seated at a Chippendale game table from the Revolutionary era. Above her flaxen hair are two lines with a didactic imperative: "Let Your Children Experience American History Instead of Just Reading About It."[18]

Many of those who run outdoor museums and similar sites make strident claims about the authenticity of what they have to offer. They also tend to make pejorative statements about the perils of historical imagination—as though that were an undesirable quality to encourage in adolescents. And the promotional materials of such administrators are likely to claim that hands-on heritage-as-history guarantees enjoyment, unlike the deadly dull sort of history that is dispensed in the classroom, the library, and via the medium of print. Take, as one representative illustration, these exuberant assertions from the initial page of a booklet produced by Heritage Hill State Park in Green Bay, Wisconsin:

> You don't have to imagine how life was in northeast Wisconsin 100 years ago! When you leave Heritage Hill's Visitor Center, you will actually experience the past through living history.... The people who "live" in Heritage Hill's historical structures eat, work, dress and talk exactly as though they were living in bygone days. To them, modern conveniences and language patterns do not exist. ... Living history brings an added dimension to the historical museum which allows you to learn about your "roots" and enjoy it![19]

When we ask why the heritage rubric has sustained such remarkable appeal, we must return to nostalgia. The nation has been hankering after various imagined golden ages—for more innocent and carefree days—since the early 1970s. There is nothing necessarily wrong with nostalgia per se, but more often than not the phenomenon does involve a pattern of highly selective memory. Recall the good but repress the unpleasant. And that is just what has happened. The 1965 report published by the National Trust, *With Heritage So Rich*, articulated the problem succinctly: "A nation can be a victim of amnesia."[20]

The heritage syndrome, if I may call it that, almost seems to be a predictable but certainly a non-conspiratorial response—an impulse to remember what is attractive or flattering and to ignore all the rest. Heritage is comprised of those aspects of history that we cherish and affirm. As an alternative to history, heritage accentuates the positive but sifts away what is problematic. One consequence is that the very pervasiveness of heritage as a phenomenon produces a beguiling sense of serenity about the well-being of history—that is, a false consciousness that historical knowledge and understanding are alive and well in the United States.[21]

Although American knowledge and understanding of history are not altogether healthy, neither is the outlook quite so grim as it may sound. An upbeat emphasis upon heritage can serve as a stimulus to prudent public policy and to enhanced concern for a more meaningful relationship between past and present. As a *New York Times* editorial phrased the matter in 1975, referring to New York City's landmark legislation and the campaign to save Grand Central Terminal, repercussions of that legislation "are already being felt in other places where the problem of the preservation of a city's and a nation's heritage meet the problem of economic hardship and the rights of property."[22]

One of the most attractive aspects of this heritage surge involves the development of contacts, even enduring relationships, between popular and academic history. Scholars have been writing for *American Heritage* ever since it began to appear in its present guise during the mid-1950s. Energetic and creative teachers of history and social studies in our primary and secondary schools are now publishing essays with such titles as "Planning for Local Heritage Projects." Staff members at the Smithsonian Institution, assessing the forthcoming quincentennial of Columbus's arrival in the Western Hemisphere (1992), have observed that "historic anniversaries are even more important to us as a time to focus on our civic heritage and in the case of Columbus, on our world heritage."[23]

Precisely because the heritage phenomenon has become so strong, and because some of its features may seem superficial or self-serving for assorted groups or individuals, there is a genuine risk that critical observers may conclude that "real" history is 180 degrees removed from the tainted stuff that parades as heritage. What nonsense! Serious history has always contained elements of national mythology. It can be too easily overlooked that for generations scholarly students of American history have been motivated by a passion to describe and explain the national heritage. In 1953 Samuel Flagg Bemis wrote Van Wyck Brooks a paean of praise for "all of those high-minded things of our heritage and the goodly currents of our life which you have done so much to hold up before the American people."[24]

Moreover, high-minded creative writers and artists who were neither professional historians nor conservative white males like Bemis, and whose past supplied a saga of punishment rather than praise, nonetheless felt compelled to contemplate their heritage and communicate their apprehensions and ruminations. Hence Countee Cullen's long poem "Heritage," written in the 1920s.[25]

> *One three centuries removed*
> *From the Scenes his father loved,*
> *Spicy grove, cinnamon tree,*
> *What is Africa to me?*

Cullen's wistful lines, along with comparable works by members of many other ethnic groups and subcultures, urge us to acknowledge the presence of multiple heritages—surely no shock in a nation of immigrants. Cullen's poignant poem also reminds us that heritage need not be a mindless affirmation of congenial memories. It has become commonplace to say that one sound reason for studying history is to enrich the understanding of identity—one's own along with those of the several groups with which one identifies. That, too, is a legitimate preoccupation of those intrigued by heritage.[26]

There are, in addition, events and anniversaries that inevitably remind us that history as heritage has not been free from tension, conflicting value systems, or even violence. In 1983, for example, the Gettysburg National Military Park, Gettysburg Travel Council, Gettysburg College, and the Mason-Dixon Civil War Collectors Association began to sponsor Civil War Heritage Days—more than a week of living history encampments, a re-enactment of parts of the Battle of Gettysburg (July 1–3, 1863), and a Civil War Collector's show. In 1986 the fourth annual Civil War Heritage Days were attended by more than fifty thousand people.[27]

The unfortunate thing about this heritage boom is that it can lead, and has led, to commercialization, vulgarization, oversimplification, and tendentiously capricious memories—which means both warping and whitewashing a fenced-off past. Any or all of those processes provide a disservice to the groups affected.[28]

The redeeming virtue of heritage, however, is that it can also serve as a powerful stimulus to the popularization, and hence to the democratization, of history. Heritage that heightens human interest may *lead people to history* for purposes of informed citizenship, or the meaningful deepening of identity, or enhanced appreciation of the dynamic process of change over time. American responses to "progress," for instance, have frequently followed patterns of ambivalence or suspicious challenge rather than mindless approval[29]—a lesson that history can teach whereas "heritage" is less likely to do so.

I I

LATE IN 1981 a National Trust board member from Jacksonville, Oregon, offered a definition of cultural heritage that is noteworthy for its breadth as well as its rather vague closing emphasis. Cultural heritage, he explained at the second Tourism and Heritage Conservation Conference of the Pacific Area Travel Association, "is an accumulation of large traditions. Social, racial and religious, frequently built up from beyond time and memory." Four more paragraphs sketched out a vast array of components; but then Robertson E. Collins concluded that "all this and more describes the cultural heritage of a country. It is buildings and it is more than buildings."[30]

It is certainly true that from the 1970s onward historic preservation organizations and their activities became quite central to the American sense of "heritage." The National Trust expanded its programs, the number of properties that it administers, and its publications. Imitative magazines produced by commercial enterprises also began to appear, such as *American Preservation,* produced in Martinsville, New Jersey. Even more striking, however, historic preservation became a genuinely grass-roots activity. Fund-raising campaigns to restore structures linked in some way to intriguing figures, such as Peter Stuyvesant, became commonplace. Private individuals and entire families determined to have venerable yet little-known structures—such as Nottoway Mansion near Baton Rouge and Tudor Place in Georgetown (Washington, D.C.)—restored to period authenticity and made accessible to the public. Architectural styles that had long been neglected, such as French Second Empire or English Gothic Revival, came to be refurbished with tender loving care. And the designation of historic districts by landmark preservation commissions meant astounding triumphs over developers for those who cherished architectural treasures.[31]

During the 1970s it even became apparent that developers were not inevitably the enemies of tradition. James W. Rouse of Baltimore, "father" of Columbia, Maryland, inaugurated a whole new phase of urban development by creating the center-city "festival marketplace," first at Faneuil Hall in Boston (c. 1976) and then at "Harborplace" in Baltimore (c. 1980). A dynamic entrepreneur with a strong social conscience and a refreshing respect for the past, Rouse demonstrated that shrewd developers could even be the allies rather than the adversaries of preservationists.[32]

The Stevensville Historical Society, located twenty miles north of Missoula in Ravalli County, Montana, shows just how close to the grass roots this whole movement could get. Stevensville had been the site of the first permanent white settlement in Montana; and in 1974 residents of the Ravalli area undertook as a bicentennial project the restoration of Fort Owen, a trading post established nearby in 1850. Although it had been proclaimed a national historic site in 1971, the place stood in sad disrepair; so several local groups made a commitment "to reconstruct Fort Owen to represent an authentic, active trading post of the period." The Ravalli County Bicentennial Committee found "increasing interest in the past and increasing awareness of local history," and declared that restoration of the fort would "insure that this part of our western pioneer heritage will not be lost for future generations." The committee also awarded funds to the St. Mary's Mission Historical Foundation for restoration of the old mission at Stevensville, and to the Bitterroot Historical Society for work on a tepee museum in Hamilton, Montana. That sort of enthusiasm surged across the United States during the 1970s.[33]

Although past-oriented organizations remained active throughout these years, they varied greatly in their priorities and emphases. The Society of Mayflower Descendants in Idaho, for example, seemed strangely oblivious to local and regional history. Instead its members met to read aloud passages from the chronicles of the Pilgrim Fathers, especially Elder Brewster's speech, and to study or compare genealogies. When the organization decided to meet more often, it chose November 21 (Compact Day), April 2 (supposedly the occasion of the first election held in North America), and April 15 (the day the *Mayflower* sailed back to England). Lest all of this sound inappropriately elitist for pioneering Idaho, it should be acknowledged that one member informed the group that the Mayflower Compact had been the first such charter "ever to allow all classes to sign it." In the decades following World War II, even hereditary societies needed an egalitarian touch.[34]

The sheer diversity of historical organizations scarcely seems surprising for such a heterogeneous society; yet examples of their variety deserve mention because so many of them are not well known. The Brigade of the American Revolution, formed in 1962, is dedicated to "recreating through 'living history' the common soldier as he participated on both sides" of the Revolution. Some of the particulars are rather fascinating. According to its leader, the brigade

> is made up of individual groups (minimum 4 men) which take the identity of actual units in a specific year from 1775–1783 and, after considerable research, recreate the clothing, arms, and accouterments [sic]. Their authenticity extends to reproducing buttons and buckles from actual artifacts, as well as period shoes, eyeglasses, etc. Synthetic fabrics are prohibited.[35]

A Jefferson Davis Association was chartered in Texas in 1964, the same year that Memphis, Tennessee, unveiled a huge, long-planned bronze statue of Davis. In 1978 Congress finally passed a bill restoring Davis's citizenship; and when President Carter signed it into law, he observed that "our nation needs to clear away the guilts and enmities of recriminations of the past."[36]

The National Historical Society was established as an organization "designed to enrich the appreciation and understanding of American history." Its primary focus, however, was the Civil War and military history in general, an emphasis reflected in the contents of its magazine, *American History Illustrated.* Within less than two decades membership had reached 150,000. The Freedoms Foundation, with its headquarters located at Valley Forge, is also tradition-oriented; but its primary concern is not American history so much as promoting private enterprise and rewarding its advocates with lavish awards.

Still other sorts of associations and commemorative activities emerged as manifest signs of the times. The observance of Negro History Week, which began in 1926, was expanded to Black History Month in 1968. The American People's Historical Society, a populist organization based in Burlington, Vermont, was one of several that appeared in the 1970s as the Bicentennial of Independence drew near. It prepared films and recordings for TV, radio, and the classroom that emphasized American radicalism. The Women's Hall of Fame, Inc., located in Seneca Falls, New York, became active at the same time, as did the YIVO Institute's program of conferences concerning "culture and community among New York Jews."

Diverse organizations, commercial as well as scholarly, made their memory-related "products" available at a price. From 1973 until 1988 the American Heritage Society published a bi-monthly magazine titled *Americana,* a popular publication aimed at collectors. The American Antiques and Crafts Society was "formed by collectors for collectors in response to a growing need for information and expert guidance in distinguishing the good from the bad . . . the authentic from the bogus." A pictorial Hearst magazine called *Colonial Homes,* initially conceived in 1965, began to appear on a regular basis in 1976–77; and by 1980 its circulation had reached 510,000, a remarkable rate of growth. Its schedule shifted from twice yearly in 1976 to quarterly the next year and bi-monthly as demand increased at the close of the decade.

In 1978 the Mystic Seaport Museum Store produced a 48-page multicolored catalogue that ranged from scrimshaw reproduction bookends to marine paintings. In 1979–80 a serious press made available a two-volume *Handbook of American Popular Culture.* The University of Mid-America's Office of Marketing and Information, located in Lincoln, Nebraska, developed and disseminated a thirty-program radio series titled "Foundations of American Nationalism." And the Dunlap Society (a non-profit association "dedicated to making all aspects of America's art better known and appreciated") prepared for sale a comprehensive visual archive of American art.

ALTHOUGH various sorts of organizations proliferated, they appealed to individuals and were composed of individuals; consequently we must shift the spotlight to people as collectors, to their intense enthusiasms, and to the transformation that occurred in the collecting of Americana during the quarter century that followed the early 1960s. Rita Reif, a writer for the *New York Times* who covered the market for antiques, commented in 1978 that "we are, it seems, a nation of squirrels, acquiring and stowing away collectibles to enjoy at our leisure." Looking back six years later, Reif observed that an "antiques fever swept America in the 1970s, spawning hundreds of antiques fairs, a host of new categories of specialty auctions, scores of collecting societies, dozens of books and several magazines." By 1978, she noted, "Americans could go to an antiques show every day of the year except Christmas, New Year's and Good Friday."[37]

A magazine advertisement by the prominent auction house Sotheby Parke Bernet was symptomatic of the new mood as well as the growing commercialization of a trade hitherto too dignified to hustle customers.

"Collecting historical American books and manuscripts is a serious business . . . but it can be great fun as well." Two years after that ad first appeared, an essay in *The Magazine Antiques* echoed this cosmic declaration from the *New York Herald Tribune* in 1929: "America today is a nation of collectors more cosmopolitan than any the world has ever known. Yet in the midst of cosmopolitanism our collectors remain finely national. The most widespread love among them is for the relics of our ancestors."[38]

Raw statistics are interesting, but are not an entirely reliable measure of the phenomenal growth and transformation that took place during the 1970s. Subscriptions to *Antiques*, for example, grew from fewer than 34,000 at the end of 1951 to 46,000 in 1965 to a peak of more than 84,000 in 1975. The gradual decline thereafter reflected a sharp increase in subscription rates rather than diminished enthusiasm for American antiques. In the seven years following Sotheby Parke Bernet's introduction of "Americana" as a catalogue category in 1973, the number of subscribers quadrupled. At the end of 1979 *Time* devoted a cover story to the "Art and Antique Boom."[39]

A selection of sequential headlines from the *New York Times*'s unsystematic coverage of this whole phenomenon is highly symptomatic: "Record Prices: New Marks Are Posted at Auctions by 18th-Century American Furniture" (1972); "Stunning Prices for American Rarities" (1978); "Record-Setting Auction Stars of 1978" (1979); "$18.9 Million Art Sale Sets Record" (1980), referring to the Garbisch Collection of folk Americana; "A Boom Time in Americana" (1980); "The Prizes That Set a Record at Auction in 1980" (1981); "Big Year for Americana" (1981); "Sales of Americana Upstaged Those in All Other Categories" (1982); and so forth. The pattern could not be clearer.[40]

There is far more to the story, however, than record-setting sales can reveal. Predictably, for example, interest in Civil War memorabilia increased during the early 1960s; but long after the centennial had ended, dealers were pleasantly surprised to find that enthusiasm persisted. Moreover, the collecting of Americana became increasingly exotic and focused. A mortgage banker specialized in land grant documents and real estate–related autographs. Other clients concentrated on the letters of robber barons, or documents relating to church-state controversies, or to the ephemera of everyday life: railroad tickets, legal summonses, trade cards, handbills, and posters. The Ephemera Society, formed in 1975, proclaimed 1980 to be World Ephemera Year. Younger (and often less affluent) collectors tend to be intrigued by the commercial artifacts spawned by a consumer culture. And the 1980s brought intense competition among African-Americans for what they term Black Memorabilia, ranging from dolls to sambo statues to unusual posters rich with cultural associations. The National Black Memorabilia Collectors' Association is a rapidly growing organization.[41]

The democratization of collecting since the 1950s and 1960s conveys a dual meaning concerning the heterogeneity of who collects and the eclecticism of what they collect: inexpensive commemorative plates, chamberpot lids (yes, just the lids, because they can be readily displayed with brackets on walls), costumes, old tractor seats, multi-colored glass insulators from quondam telephone poles, souvenir spoons that are place-specific, and so on. One of the best documented working-class collections, and one of the most valuable, consists of the harvest of jubilee parish albums from hard-coal communities gathered by a Polish-American laborer, Edward Pinkowski, that has been relied upon to illuminate the lives and traditions of Poles who worked in the anthracite region of Pennsylvania.[42]

The democratization of collecting has also helped to clarify the somewhat murky distinction between collecting and possessing. It has been observed that people like J. P. Morgan, Henry Ford, and William Randolph Hearst were really possessors because they acquired on such a vast scale, lacked genuine clarity of focus in their holdings, relied upon agents and dealers to make selections for them, and kept large amounts of "stuff" still unpacked in storage. Others, like Henry Francis du Pont and Electra Webb, are properly considered collectors because they were so personally involved in the choice of individual acquisitions and had a much clearer rationale for their collections, which achieved cultural cohesion as a consequence.* Most middle-class and working-class collectors are, indeed, collectors rather than mere possessors because they seek and select their own acquisitions and have much more precisely defined areas of interest than the so-called "proud possessors."[43]

Starting with the Williamsburg Antiques Forum in 1949, and subsequently at similar annual conferences held at such places as the Henry Ford Museum and the Pennsbury Manor seminars (spring and fall at Morrisville, Pennsylvania), collectors of all kinds could gather to exchange information, listen to lectures by experts on Americana, and view exhibits specially prepared for the occasion. At each institution the period from 1972 until 1976 seems to have been golden, which suggests a double irony: first, the gasoline shortage supposedly made travel especially difficult at that time, and second, the decline in registrations after 1976 does not signal a real decline in the number of active collectors. It merely means that competing attractions and diversions have flourished since then, including the most elaborately organized antiques shows, such as Philadelphia's annual University Hospital Antiques Show or New York City's Winter Antiques Show, sponsored by the East Side House Settlement and the National Antique and Art Dealers Association.[44]

Although American folk art has enjoyed a considerable and steadily

---

*Friends who raised their eyebrows at Maxim Karolik's expenditures for Americana were informed that his Bostonian wife was delighted that he spent money only on inanimate objects.

growing vogue since the later 1960s, and though objects that postdate the age of handicrafts (1840 to the present) have become as acceptable (if not quite so respectable) as pre-industrial items, it would be unwise to assume that either trend is a clear litmus of democratization. Folk Americana of high quality has been fetching very fancy prices over the past fifteen years: cigar store Indians that sell for $125,000; wooden eagles carved by Wilhelm Schimmel that may easily top $30,000 at auction; and decorative weathervanes of patinated whales, horses, and figures of Miss Liberty that are almost as dear. Folk art began its dramatic ascent because of aesthetic qualities as well as novelty. Much the best of it is now far beyond the purse of "ordinary" collectors.[45]

Margaret Woodbury Strong of Rochester, New York, provides an interesting example of a relatively recent "possessor" whose diversified objects are drawn from the industrial era (largely 1830 to 1940) and are middle-class in content (lots of ordinary toys and household pieces) yet so comprehensive as to be extraordinary in their total scope and value. During the 1950s and 1960s she acquired 50 different categories of objects that ranged in depth from 86,000 bookplates to 27,000 dolls. At her death in 1969 this formidable woman, the largest private shareholder of Kodak stock, owned more than 300,000 items, including bells, bicycles, books, trade catalogues, cameras, canes, candlesticks, carousel figures, circus artifacts, dollhouses with miniature furniture and ceramics to fill them, doorstops, daguerreotypes, millstones, minerals, napkin rings, samplers, shells, ship models, and thimbles, to mention only a few. By 1968 she had applied for and received a provisional charter from the New York State Board of Regents to establish as an educational institution the Margaret Woodbury Strong Museum of Fascination. Because of the vastness of her possessions and the need to create an innovative institution in order to present them, her showcase did not open to the public until 1982.[46]

One of the most notable innovations at the Strong Museum is its presentation of densely clustered "study collections" in secondary spaces: a way of making the depth and variety of objects accessible to visitors who are themselves serious collectors. That arrangement calls to our attention the symbiotic relationship between museums and collectors. An unusual or creative exhibit, such as "Century of Revivals" at the Newark Museum in 1982, may spark new enthusiasms among collectors, just as changes in exhibition policies (such as uncluttering period rooms in the interest of historical authenticity) may enhance the educational quality of an institution's presentations. On the other hand, when a wonderful private collection is placed on semi-permanent loan, which happened in 1969 when Philip H. Hammerslough entrusted his cache of American silver to the Wadsworth Atheneum in Hartford, the museum and the general public benefit enormously. For all of these reasons, the recent history of American museums requires closer attention.[47]

I I I

THE ESSENTIAL story involves an astounding increase in the number of new institutions as well as the expansion of museums in general and historical museums in particular, accompanied by rising anxiety about the vicissitudes of visitation figures and the tough struggle for financial support. Some of the more recent museums are devoted to certain characteristics or features of a major event, like the American Revolution, as exemplified by the Drummer Boy Museum that opened in Brewster, Massachusetts, in 1961. Others concern particular aspects of national or regional commerce (such as the Museum of Tobacco Art and History located in Nashville) or else a specific vocation (like Fred Hunter's funeral museum in Hollywood, Florida, which displays old embalming tools, a 1917 Ford Model T hearse, intricately braided wreaths of human hair, and a 1,500-pound glass coffin). Some contain great treasures that are protected by state-of-the-art security devices, while others are "hands-on" facilities where visitors are encouraged to touch the objects (such as the Victorian-style Brennan Mansion in Louisville, Kentucky).⁴⁸

A number of the nation's more established museums have undergone major expansions and facelifts (the American Wing of the Metropolitan in 1979–80), or have added elegant new structures that make it possible to bring all sorts of long-hidden treasures out of storage (the DeWitt Wallace Decorative Arts Gallery at Colonial Williamsburg in 1985).⁴⁹

The Smithsonian Institution, which already includes as part of its system several of the most popular museums in the world (the National Air and Space Museum had more than 14 million visitors in 1984, the Museum of Natural History had more than 6 million, and the National Museum of American History nearly 5.5 million), continues to add more components—among them the National Building Museum, devoted to architectural history, and museums of African and Asian art located behind the landmark Smithsonian Castle on the Mall. A Holocaust Museum that is being erected on the Mall (unrelated to the Smithsonian) will contain a hexagonal memorial called the Hall of Remembrance and a brilliant plan for narrating as well as explaining the enormous human devastation it is designed to commemorate.⁵⁰

In a nation that numbered more than 8,200 museums by the end of 1988 (55 percent of them history-related), diversity seemed desirable as well as inevitable. A disproportionate number of them, often called living-history farms or villages, are devoted to the agrarian America beloved by Thomas Jefferson. Even these are heterogeneous, however, because the Claude Moore Colonial Farm at Turkey Run, near the Potomac River, and the Farmers' Museum in Cooperstown, New York, evoke the everyday lives of pre- and post-Revolutionary hardscrabble farmers, while the Queens County Farm Museum in the heart of one of New York City's densely populated boroughs provides a startling oasis and reminder of the pre-urban past. Conner Prairie Pioneer Settlement, nestled northeast of Indianapolis in Noblesville, Indiana, and the Genesee Country Museum in Mumford, New York (located in the heart of the Finger Lakes), suggest different stages of nineteenth-century settlement and small-town life. Waterloo Village in Stanhope, New Jersey, on the other hand, which opened in 1965, shows an ironworking community on the old Morris Canal and serves as a reminder that many industries developed in the countryside.[51]

The institutional history of industrialization in conjunction with immigration and urbanization has developed more slowly because of the assumption, only partially correct, that few people are likely to feel nostalgia for factories or sentimental about sweatshops. Baltimore has its Museum of Industry; and in 1983 the Paterson, New Jersey, home of Pietro Botto, an Italian silk weaver who died in 1945, opened as the American Labor Museum, devoted to the lives of blue-collar workers. Botto's house had been a rallying point for 24,000 workers during the extremely bitter Paterson silk strike of 1913. It is part of an innovative three-site exhibition that also includes the Paterson Museum, where the silk-manufacturing process is explained, and Lambert Castle, which delineates the lives of those who controlled the industry.[52]

The history of transportation has done somewhat better because old-time transport is more readily romanticized and can be fun for children. Hence in 1983–84 Scranton, Pennsylvania, provided an infusion of funds plus abandoned railroad yards in order to become the new home for Steamtown, U.S.A., designated as the "world's largest operating steam railroad museum," using one hundred pieces of rolling stock purchased from Bellows Falls, Vermont (the museum's home since 1966), in time for the 1984 tourist season. Folks back in Vermont, saddened at being bought out, persuaded the Scranton entrepreneurs to leave them a single steam engine and a few cars to be used for local excursions. "At least we will have a train," one man sighed. "We want to keep the memory of steam locomotives going."[53]

The romance of the sea provides an on-going magnet for the mariner's compass. In addition to Mystic Seaport in Connecticut and an array of whaling museums from eastern Long Island to New Bedford and Nantucket, Massachusetts, more recent innovations include the South Street Seaport in lower Manhattan (where Wall Street bustles cheek by jowl with the age of sail); the 43,000-ton aircraft carrier *Intrepid,* which has been refitted (1981–82) at a Hudson River pier as a floating museum of naval aviation; a Museum of Yachting located at the entrance to Newport Harbor in Rhode Island (1985); and plans for an Ocean Liner Museum where majestic and elegant vessels can be remembered, like the *Normandie,* which in 1935 broke the trans-Atlantic speed record for ships.[54]

By the 1980s a veritable array of such specialized museums, most of them semi-historical in character, began to appear—at least in the planning stages of what invariably is a long and complex process: the Technology Center of Silicon Valley in San Jose, California, with exhibits depicting the history and application of the scientific principles on which the electronics and biotechnical industries of that area are based; and the Computer Museum, the world's most complete collection of computers, many of them the so-called early dinosaur models, housed in a converted nineteenth-century warehouse adjacent to Boston's financial district. Near Lyndhurst, New Jersey, close to the Hackensack Meadowlands, where garbage has been dumped by the ton for half a century, there is now a museum devoted to trash. Visitors walk through a cross section of a dump, surrounded by a depressing accumulation of household junk: old telephones and milk containers, broken toys and rusted car fenders, bald tires, empty bottles, and discarded newspapers. Although the museum is meant to be educational, the project director concedes that keeping garbage interesting is not easy. Just a bit more attractive, perhaps, is the McDonald's Museum, dedicated at Des Plaines, Illinois, in 1985 at the site where Ray Kroc opened his first drive-in restaurant thirty years earlier.[55]

Regional and local museums continue to flourish, ranging from Pilgrim Hall, the Museum of Pilgrim Possessions in Plymouth (established in 1824 and now the oldest public museum in the United States in continuous service), to the Permian Basin Petroleum Museum and Library Hall of Fame, located in Midland, Texas, a facility that is well funded by various oil companies. Topical or thematic presentations began to enjoy a special vogue during the 1970s and have proliferated ever since. The Museum of Vintage Fashion opened in 1978 within a seventeen-room home at Oakland, California; the clothing extends from the early 1800s through the 1960s, and was collected over a thirty-year period. Ben Thacher's Old Sound Museum opened in 1976 at East Dennis on Cape Cod. His collectibles range from magic lanterns to talking dolls; but the heart of the exhibition consists of old phonograph records gathered from second-hand shops and flea markets. The Dog Museum of America, a creation of the American Kennel Club, opened on September 15, 1982, in Manhattan. A typical exhibit, "The Dog Observed," presented a history of the dog in photography. The salt museums in Syracuse and Watkins Glen, New York, relate the history of salt mining in the Finger Lakes region.[56]

Fortunately, history with a human face compares favorably with canines and salt. In 1985 an opulent Chicago hotel that once served as Al Capone's Prohibition era headquarters began the process of conversion to a museum honoring achievements by women throughout the world. The project, which aims for completion in 1992, is being developed by the Sunbow Foundation, which promotes the training and placement of women in the building trades. In 1983 the War Memorial Museum located in Newport News, Virginia, which had customarily devoted its displays to uniforms and weapons used by white males, decided to add extensive exhibits concerning the experience of women and African-Americans in the U.S. military. The National Afro-American Museum and Cultural Center, funded by the state of Ohio, opened at Wilber-force, Ohio, in April 1988. The Center intends to offer television and radio productions, travelling exhibits, and a degree program in museum studies. Later that same year Elmer and Joanne Martin opened in Baltimore the first wax museum devoted entirely to historic black persons. Referring to the need to interest young people in African-American history, Elmer Martin explained his rationale in this way: "Documents and books won't get their attention. But you put a wax figure way down at the end of a room, kids will gravitate toward that figure. Once we get their attention, we can teach."[57]

By the close of the 1980s an entire cluster of museums began to emerge whose focus is the disinherited peoples of the United States and their histories: the Smithsonian's new National Museum of the American Indian, planned for the 1990s, will draw upon its own rich holdings as well as the extraordinary collection gathered early in the twentieth century by George Gustav Heye—an array of artifacts ranging from Aztec to Zuñi that has never been adequately attended. If the Museum of Immigration inside the Statue of Liberty celebrates the process of arrival, the Lower East Side Tenement Museum (also scheduled to open in the mid-1990s) will describe what happened to the newcomers after they settled in. The National Civil Rights Museum planned for Memphis, Tennessee, intends to show artifacts pertaining to economic boycotts, lunch counter sit-ins, freedom rides, school desegregation, voter registration drives, the famous marches on Montgomery and Washington, and the histories of the Southern Christian Leadership Conference, SNCC, Core, and the NAACP.[58]

As the range of subjects deemed suitable for museum presentation expands, so does the potential scope for controversy in an area where the politics of culture can be highly combustible. Rival members of the same ethnic group may vie for control of an important collection because such control can easily mean dominance in explaining the group's history and identity. Sometimes a sympathetic outsider raises a ruckus over the government's mismanagement of a museum facility: that happened in 1980 when critics faulted the federal government because of "white bias" in its curatorial administration of the Museum of the Plains Indian located in Browning, Montana. Or conflict may arise when an entrepreneurial history buff wants to add a sound and light show, pretty guides in period costumes, and perhaps even a daily battle re-enactment at a site such as the Alamo, where the Daughters of the Republic of Texas remain determined to perpetuate the status quo at their shrine.[59]

Museums have become involved in court disputes with collaborative institutions, such as colleges, over legal title to various artifacts, sometimes numbering in the thousands or tens of thousands. Whether or not museums should pay property taxes has become a hot issue, especially as municipal revenues drop and museum sales of reproductions, subscriptions, magazines, and other profit-making ventures thrive.[60]

Scholars differ with museum directors and curators over policy issues that primarily concern insiders: How should objects be presented? Should the museum staff seek to level up or level down? Is collecting information just as important as collecting objects? Scholars on the left are especially critical of mass culture versions of American history (particularly in theme parks) that seek to sanitize the past and sidestep unsettling controversies. EPCOT's presentation of the "American Adventure" at Disney World in Florida (1982–), for example, has been frequently criticized as a hymn of praise to progress, with no acknowledgment whatsoever of the Vietnam War, ghetto revolts in the 1960s, feminist and ecological movements, or Watergate. Although "American Adventure" undeniably has its populist aspects, the visitor achieves no sense of continuity concerning the active role played by discontented people in shaping American history.[61]

It is no secret that presentations of the American past at Disneyland in Anaheim (1956–) and Disney World in Orlando (1971–) are shallow entertainments. The Hall of Presidents at Disneyland (designed in 1957–58) evokes a pantheon of heroic statesmen rather than imperfect politicians. The Carousel of Progress (1964) creates an implicit tension with the nostalgia evoked by Main Street, U.S.A. Much of Future World is actually devoted to the remembrance of things past—a tricky paradox that manages to be extraordinarily symptomatic—and EPCOT's "American Adventure" romps through nearly four centuries of history in twenty-nine minutes flat. Disney's "imagineers," masters of audio animatronic engineering, have mythologized and sanctified an untroubled narrative—bland precisely because it is so selectively soothing in line with the politics of nostalgia.[62]

ALTHOUGH theme parks that make any sort of historical presentation do compete with more traditional sites for visitors, it would be a serious mistake to assume that tourism has not been an on-going preoccupation of those who administer historic sites. Kenneth Chorley kept the Rockefellers faithfully apprised of C.W.'s attendance rates compared to previous years and to other, similar magnets such as Mount Vernon, major national parks, and even "tourist attractions in Europe."[63] Within less than four decades, as it happened, places of wonder and memory moved from marginal status to an absolutely central role in American tourism. In 1916 roughly one American in three hundred visited a national park; by 1954 the ratio had become one in three. Consequently those who administered historic sites could not afford to neglect touristic considerations—comforts, advertising, competition, the rising cost of admission, etc.—and "visitation" became an obsessive concern by the later 1970s, when circumstances conspired to reduce the absolute number of visitors or slowed the rate of growth that had zoomed upward between the mid-1950s and the mid-1970s.[64]

Attempting to discern a clear trend is difficult, and efforts to explain any sort of pattern are well-nigh impossible. Between 1975 and 1977, for example, attendance at all outdoor museums along the Eastern seaboard declined, on average, by about 22 percent. In the Middle West and elsewhere, however, attendance increased (e.g., by 16 percent in Wisconsin), particularly at national parks and historic sites. In part the explanation lay in what might be called Eastern overexposure during the peak years of the American Revolution Bicentennial, 1975–76. In part, too, there seems to have been the belief among potential visitors that the trans-Appalachian West was uncrowded and inexpensive whereas the East must be congested and costly. To some degree regional pride and self-discovery made a difference. And, in fact, rapidly rising costs aggravated by runaway inflation, plus declining income from investments and visitation, forced Eastern museums to boost admission rates after 1976 to levels that many found outrageous.[65]

Visitation figures at historical museums for the period 1978–90 show a sluggish rate of growth or actual decline at some institutions, but also substantial increases for many, including the Hagley Museum (of early technology) in Delaware; Historic Deerfield; the Shelburne Museum; the Preservation Society of Newport County; the Henry Ford Museum and Greenfield Village; and Conner Prairie in Indiana. Mount Vernon, Colonial Williamsburg, Plimoth Plantation, and Strawbery Banke have also done well—a credit to name recognition and willingness to invest in advertising. C.W., Inc., became the first history museum in the United States to install a toll-free number promotion and advertise on television. A person could dial 1-800-HISTORY, request information, and promptly receive a vacation planner and an attractive magazine-sized color booklet on Williamsburg, with detailed information about its facilities and rates.[66]

Statistics for the 1980s are unreliable in several respects. Figures reported by the American Association of Museums would seem to suggest a decline in the founding of new museums following 1967–76, the peak years. But responsibility for gathering the data passed into less reliable hands, with a clearly confirmed tendency toward underreporting. Moreover, the decade of the 1980s saw a marked pattern of diversification in which resources once earmarked for museums went instead to new centers for science and technology, for zoos and aquaria, for botanical gardens and arboreta. In addition there has been a marked increase in alternative modes of "history" and "historical entertainment." It is not easy for conventional museums to compete with robotic presidents who have authentic hairlines and the capacity to speak!

If declining rates of museum attendance require any additional explanation, one should also note the rise of a remarkable range of historical "docudramas" and other series on television, a fair number of them very good. In sum, for many years a person who wanted to learn about the past without turning a page or cracking a book went to a museum, a restored village, or a historic site. The operative definition of what passes for popular "history" has been considerably broadened over the last dozen years, however, sometimes in bizarre and unsettling ways. Further, it is no longer necessary to go very far from home or spend much money in order to acquire historical information and memories. Local historical societies, third-rate historical fiction, American history on records and tapes, and above all television dramatizations of events that mostly happened "only yesterday" keep large numbers of people satiated.

I V

DURING THE MID- AND LATER 1970S, collective memories of ethnic groups, multi-generational families, and even individuals achieved a visibility that they had not previously enjoyed. As a consequence, what might be called subnational and subsectional traditions have been noticed as never before. Although the most conspicuous event in this change was clearly Alex Haley's *Roots,* published as a book in 1976 and first viewed by many tens of millions on television early in 1977, the "Roots phenomenon" did not strike as a bolt from the blue. It had, in fact, roots of its own.[67]

When Van Wyck Brooks looked back to the 1920s from the perspective of 1951, he recalled an impulse among many acquaintances to seek identity and community in a particular sense of place. In many instances, Brooks wrote, "the artists and writers had grown up in a still raw West or had returned from Paris in search of 'roots,' that shy and impalpable quiddity the lack of which, they felt, had made them frequently shallow and generally restless. No word was more constantly on their lips. . . . No European could understand this constant American talk of roots."[68] Certain sects and denominations, such as the Mormons, have been preoccupied by genealogy for many decades because they believe that non-Mormon ancestors can receive redemption if they are properly traced and identified. During the 1960s, however, the Latter Day Saints professionalized their own records and created ultramodern archival facilities that have been a boon to large numbers of non-Mormons ever since.*

---

*Mormons have formed an organization known as Ancestry, Inc., based in Salt Lake City, whose purpose is the production of publications designed to facilitate genealogical research.

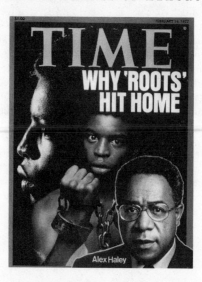

18.2 *Time* cover featuring Alex Haley, February 14, 1977. Copyright 1977. Time Inc. Reprinted by permission.

During the early and mid-1970s abundant evidence appeared to indicate that interest in family history was running high. When asked about the crowded reading tables at the New York Genealogical and Biographical Society in 1974, for example, the president of the National Genealogical Society noted a growing sense of rootlessness in American society. "The three-generation family scarcely exists any more," he observed. "Grandparents no longer take the youngsters on their knee and tell them about *their* grandparents. The sense of human continuity is lost, sad to say, and there is a growing realization that it's something precious."[69]

The social and cultural impact of Haley's *Roots* is virtually incalculable (fig. 18.2). Its twelve-hour adaptation televised in January 1977 broke all audience records in the medium, won nine Emmy awards, and, most important, was believed to have had a salutary impact upon race relations in the United States. A little more than a year later ABC offered "Roots: The Next Generations," a fourteen-hour sequel that also enjoyed considerable impact. The spillover effect was immediate: enthusiasm for African-American genealogy; diverse exhibitions pertaining to black family life; a new home in Harlem for the Schomburg Center for Research in Black Culture, prompted in part by an immense increase in the use of its facilities. The trend shows no sign of slackening.[70]

The popularity of Haley's *Roots: The Saga of an American Family* affected segments of the white population in various ways, ranging from serious debates over the nature of "faction" (the fictional presentation of a narrative based upon historical facts), to imitative books that attempted to do for obscure pioneers and working-class whites what Haley had achieved on behalf of his forebears.[71] For many who found themselves intrigued by this trend, the quest for family information was inseparable from the quickening of pride derived from an enhanced sense of place.[72]

Many African-Americans also had a precise albeit distant sense of place, feelings made increasingly complex by the mass migrations of blacks from the rural South to the urban North. As one woman declared at a meeting of the Afro-American Genealogical and Historical Society of Chicago: "When you say Mississippi, it's a magic word for black Chicagoans. It means memories, good and bad. It means home."[73]

No aspect of Haley's comet-like flash outpaced the new passion for genealogy. Virtually none of these record-obsessed researchers sought to write a literary bestseller along the lines of *Roots*. Few of them had the ability or the savvy to supply a rich historical context, as Haley had done. Almost all were seeking names that would fill in blanks, clarify relationships, and provide a sense of continuity in time if not in place. Hence the typical product would be a typescript or a mimeographed family record, almost as thick as a Sears catalogue, filled mostly with names, dates, and documentation based upon county records, wills, deeds, bonds, court minutes, as well as military, church, and cemetery records.

Early in 1979 the Gannett News Service syndicated nationally a series of three unusually long feature essays that carried symptomatic leaders: (1) "Many Americans were looking for 'roots' before Haley's book"; (2) "Roots hunters regard National Archives as a mecca"; and (3) "Want to trace your roots? Start at home." Similar pieces appeared in the national and local press throughout the later 1970s and on into the 1980s. They sparked widespread enthusiasm for amateur oral history with increased reliance upon tape recorders rather than interview notes or sheer memory; a search for old photographs and accompanying quests to identify anonymous faces; and form letters mailed to all members of the extended family asking for basic biographical information. With the compilation of data drawn from diverse sources, ranging from family Bibles to baptismal and marriage certificates obtained at churches to public records located in county courthouses and town halls, Everyman and Everywoman were well on their way to becoming their own historians.[74]

A swift spillover affected diverse ethnic minorities and hyphenated Americans. Early in 1980 Arthur Kurzweil published *From Generation to Generation: How to Trace Your Jewish Genealogy and Personal History*. Advertisements for the book began with boldface type: **Trace Your Jewish Roots.** In 1980 President Carter proclaimed April 21 to 28 as Jewish Heritage Week. During that week a stout touristic volume appeared, bearing the title *American Jewish Landmarks: A Travel Guide and History*. It listed 1,000 towns and cities that are home to 2,000 landmarks, 800 Jewish institutions, and 2,000 synagogues. By the mid-1980s sales of Judaica to collectors and museums were booming. Perhaps the ultimate sign of arrival appeared late in 1980, however, when the D.A.R. opened an exhibition of decorative arts in Washington, D.C., called "The Jewish Community in Early America, 1654–1830" in honor of Jews who had contributed to colonial and Revolutionary development.[75]

Yet another interesting spin-off from the "Roots phenomenon" meant that well-established American families ceased to feel much if any awkwardness about celebrating their lineage and permitting the observances to be publicized by the media.[76] In May 1980, for example, eighteen direct descendants of John Jay gathered at his homestead in Katonah, New York, for the first in what they hoped would become a regular series of Jay family reunions. The following year a large number of Livingstons met for their first reunion at Clermont, an elegant Federal period estate overlooking the Hudson River near Germantown. The Aaron Burr Association, formed in 1946, felt sufficiently comfortable about their devotion to his memory that the 1986 meeting held at Princeton, where Burr is buried, received extensive press coverage. Dorothy Peterson (whose great-grandmother was the great-granddaughter of Burr's older sister) put it this way to reporters: "So many things prove that Aaron was no worse and probably a lot better than Thomas Jefferson or Alexander Hamilton."[77]

It has been said that the family association, organizing large reunions at regular intervals (annually or once every three to five years), is a distinctively American social phenomenon—different in its emphasis and mode of organization from the Scottish clan. Although documented instances date back to the turn of the century (see fig. 7.4),[78] the phenomenon has proliferated among "ordinary" Americans since the 1970s. In 1983, when four generations of Risleys from all over the United States gathered in East Hartford, Connecticut, to celebrate the 350th anniversary of their initial ancestor's arrival in the colonies, the official family historian commented that "there may be great men around them somewhere, but they were mainly loyal supporters. They have tended to identify with the common man."[79]

By the mid- and later 1980s African-Americans had brought the concept of "family" identity and unity to a remarkably fresh and unusual level of definition. One group organized a massive reunion of 1,500 descendants of former slaves who had toiled at Somerset Place—once the second largest plantation in North Carolina and now a state park. This gathering in 1986 actually brought together the offspring of twenty-one interconnected slave families who worked on that vast rice and corn estate from 1786 through Emancipation. Governor James G. Martin even spoke at this event; but the most significant words came from Dorothy Spruill Redford, who organized it after spending five years of relentless research in an effort to figure out her lineage and that of many others in relation to the chattel at Somerset Place, once owned by planters named Collins. "From this day forward," Mrs. Redford declared, "there will always be a shared recognition. They'll think of the Josiah Collins family, but they'll think of my family too." The plantation is a "living monument to ordinary folks—to our toil, our lives, our lineage."[80]

Affirmations of African-American continuities have highlighted their pride in being American as well as in their African heritage. Although the ambivalence of national sentiment on the part of blacks is sometimes apparent, attention to that ambivalence should help us recognize the ambiguities of patriotic feeling for other segments of American society in recent decades as well.

V

PATRIOTISM in the United States has undergone a wild and perplexing roller-coaster ride ever since the early 1960s when civil rights activism and then opposition to the war in Vietnam caused a dramatic decline in conventional manifestations of patriotism. During the 1970s some thoughtful individuals sought to separate loyalty to one's country from the right—indeed the responsibility—to oppose unwise or unethical national policies. Meanwhile, some members of the counterculture sought to use or even appropriate national icons and historic sites for their own ends. That only served to intensify confusion about nationalism because the signs of one person's patriotism became the emblems of another person's iconoclasm. Even before the Reagan era, wistful yearning for national pride started to reappear. Although it persisted throughout the 1980s, many critics believed that national amnesia rather than true memory kept the quest alive. Civil religion resting upon a hollow sense of history seemed to become the last refuge of scoundrels posing as patriots—or so it appeared to cynics. What actually occurred is more complicated still.[81]

Once upon a time, during the four decades that followed 1917, the meaning of patriotism and its desirability had gone largely unchallenged in mainstream America. People certainly differed over matters of policy, foreign and domestic, but love of country seemed to be a pervasive sentiment. What began in 1918, for example, as the National Citizens' Creed Contest promoted by the Vigilantes, a "Non-Partisan Organization of Authors, Artists, and others for Patriotic Purposes," soon became The American's Creed, an impassioned group with headquarters in Washington and Baltimore. By 1923 the American Patriotic League had been established in Los Angeles "to advance American ideals and American principles through the medium of motion pictures."[82] Similarly, one cannot peruse the papers of anyone remotely engaged in public life between, say, 1939 and 1945 without finding the texts of assorted speeches bearing such titles as "The American Faith— Reaffirmation."[83]

During the fifteen years that followed World War II American nationalism remained ardent. That is the conventional wisdom in describing the Cold War at its peak; and on the surface, at least, it seems correct.[84] One finds, for instance, the existence of American Coalition: An Organization to Co-ordinate the Efforts of Patriotic, Civic and Fraternal Societies to Keep America American; and one finds a National Park Service historian asserting in 1958 that national parks should inculcate "true patriotism" in order to overcome "provincialism" and localism. At first glance, at least, all the vital signs of national sentiment seem to have been healthy (fig. 18.3).

Beneath the surface, however, not only do we find as much apathy as enthusiasm, but all was not well even among the most faithful keepers of the flame. Unpublished minutes of meetings held by the Sons of the American Revolution acknowledge that they had a problem getting members to attend during the 1950s.[85] Some of these organizations, moreover, seem to have placed elitist social considerations above cooperation with others—even where coalition building would have been beneficial to the cause of patriotism.

In 1956, for example, when Virginia patricians were planning an elaborate Jamestown Festival to commemorate the 350th anniversary

18.3   Independence Day parade, Philadelphia, Pennsylvania, July 3, 1951.
Courtesy of the National Archives Trust Fund Board.

of English colonization in the New World, commission members found it awkward to work with a staunchly patriotic group that was passionately eager to make a contribution: the Naturalized Citizens of America, Inc. Its leaders, with names like Bruni, Caravati, Haboush, and Spinella, wanted to undertake a nationwide campaign among naturalized Americans to raise funds in order to build reproductions of the three plucky ships that had arrived in 1607: the *Susan Constant,* the *Discovery,* and the *Goodspeed.* When the Virginia Commission asked the Naturalized Citizens to discontinue their fund drive, the latter, quite understandably, felt rebuffed. Dr. R. H. Bruni, their president, politely "expressed the opinion that full cooperation had not been extended to his organization by the Commission."[86]

If snobbery could take precedence over collaborative patriotism during the later 1950s, within a decade the situation had become still more complicated because conflict over cultural symbols, and consequently the politics of culture, now involved critical radicals, liberals, and conservatives rather than simply tensions among diverse super-patriots. Between 1965 and 1980, for instance, extremist protesters promised terrorist attacks against the Washington Monument and the Statue of Liberty. They threatened the establishment by menacing its symbols of memory. Similarly, during the later sixties and early seventies, anti-war groups staged prayer vigils, peace rallies, and demonstrations in front of the Alamo in San Antonio. In May 1982, on the other hand, the Ku Klux Klan gathered at the Alamo in order to stage a protest against communism.[87]

Turning to the world of film and popular culture, we find the same sort of conflict involving familiar symbols of American nationalism. In 1971 when Arthur Penn was interviewed about his film *Little Big Man,* which offered a satirical-critical view of General George A. Custer at Little Big Horn, Penn responded that he wanted to ask "Why?" of the American past. Penn had felt personally staggered by news of the My Lai massacre in Vietnam, and he felt strongly as a result that the nation should be reminded of the antecedents of such sordid episodes in its history if it wished to avoid their repetition in the future.[88]

Between 1977 and 1986, on the other hand, a patriotic/popular culture interpretation of what might have happened at the Alamo prevailed over a more skeptical/scholarly view. Those in the latter category who dared to suggest that Davy Crockett had honorably surrendered and was executed by the Mexicans received hate mail and were branded as Communists. Instead, the Daughters of the Republic of Texas decided that John Wayne's film version, *The Alamo* (1960), in which Crockett never gives up and dies a martyr, must be correct and declared that alternative explanations, however scholarly, were surely dead wrong. Myth tends to triumph over historical facts; and in this instance, at least, mass culture and learned culture went their separate ways.[89]

In 1973 John Schaar, a historian of political thought, published a long and shrewd essay called "The Case for Patriotism," in which he laid bare most of the strange complexities that had been unravelling for almost a decade. He insisted that nationalism and patriotism were separable even though related, and he contended that a "revived radicalism must be a patriotic radicalism." After acknowledging that the "nation exists only in repeated acts of remembrance and renewal of the covenant through changing circumstances," Schaar made a series of explicit historical connections between patriotism and social protest. A sense of patriotic duty, he declared, had inspired the civil rights activity of the 1960s. Similarly, the 1962 Port Huron Statement made by Students for a Democratic Society offered a "version of an active and cooperative citizenry who see the political system as *their* system, and who understand that if the system is to survive according to its own principles, it will survive only by their efforts."[90]

Schaar concluded with a series of observations that deserve reiteration on account of their acuity and because they have been lamentably ignored. "The task of the patriot today," he argued, "at least in the United States, is to work to weaken the principle of nationalism and to cut its connections with the state." He subsequently differentiated between the "modes of knowledge and ignorance characteristic" of nationalism and patriotism. "The knowledge of the patriot, especially of the natural patriot, is rich in memory or history. . . ." Schaar then called attention to an essential need—"a principle of political loyalty that can keep alive a noble tension between love for one's own place and respect for the places of others"—and closed with a summation. Patriotism, he argued, "is less a program and a set of forces than a way or style of being in the world. The patriot keeps his eye on the past, on places and things, on traditions."[91]

Although Schaar spoke for no one but himself, his views deserve attention for several reasons. First, because there is good reason to believe that a substantial minority of Americans, at least, shared his outlook even though very few of them could articulate it so eloquently. Second, because we find echoes of his perspective appearing subsequently in Great Britain and elsewhere.[92] And third, because Schaar helps to remind us that for several decades there had, in fact, been voices in the land that were "rich in memory or history," that evoked American knowledge which was "concrete and conservative" and did so in an emotional tone made up of nostalgia mixed with reverence *and* innovation. We find them in the 1950s and 1960s, for instance, when Thornton Wilder chose American characteristics as the subject for his Charles Eliot Norton Lectures at Harvard University. Hence these words, representative of his essential outlook, drawn from his presentation concerning the American language:

> The American space-sense, the American time-sense, the American sense of personal identity are not those of Europeans—and in

particular, not those of the English. The English language was moulded to express the English experience of life. The literature written in that language is one of the greatest glories of the entire human adventure. That achievement went hand in hand with the comparable achievement of forging the language which conveyed so accurately their senses of space, time, and identity. Those senses are not ours and the American people and American writers have long been engaged in reshaping the inherited language to express our modes of apprehension.[93]

We find a comparable view conveyed in the artist Tom Wesselmann's extended series of paintings called the *Great American Nude* (1957–65), and in Larry Rivers's deliberate linkage between the nude and the American flag. These artists were familiar with European aesthetic conventions and wished to differentiate their work. Hence their strident emphasis upon American distinctiveness: Wesselmann's nudes are available, wanton, and commercial. They also reflect the artist's internalization of the Kinsey Report, of Hugh Hefner's *Playboy* "philosophy," which was achieving swift notoriety (and popularity) at the time, and of then recent Supreme Court decisions that altered orthodox criteria of obscenity. Wesselmann's nudes assert both his and *their* First Amendment right to freedom of expression.[94]

His nudes convey a strong sense of national identity, of nostalgic patriotism that in John Schaar's sense is emancipated from aggressive nationalism. Wesselmann's *Great American Nude #4* (fig. 18.4) incorporates familiar icons—Gilbert Stuart's portrait of Washington, early American wallpaper, the flag and the pineapple (customary symbol of hospitality)—as a means of insisting upon the Americanness of this nude, shades of Matisse to the contrary notwithstanding. The nude is very pink and presents herself quite wantonly to George Washington's seemingly indifferent gaze.* His coolness oddly offsets her provocative eroticism, but the rationale involves more than mere balance.[95] The vulnerable woman, presented so explicitly as a sex object, dominates the foreground and therefore the present. George Washington and his early American accessories are all located in the background, and hence in the past. If the painting seeks to be American, it is also explicitly a statement about change over time and cultural discontinuity. Whereas the past is flatly two-dimensional (except for the American landscape that recedes into the distance), the present could not be more three-dimensional and threatens to sprawl into the viewer's lap.

It should come as no surprise that imaginative and artistic invocations of George Washington during the quarter century following 1961 coin-

---

*One is reminded of Nathaniel Hawthorne's rhetorical question: "Did anybody ever see Washington nude? It is inconceivable. He had no nakedness, but I imagine he was born with his clothes on, and his hair powdered, and made a stately bow on his first appearance in the world."

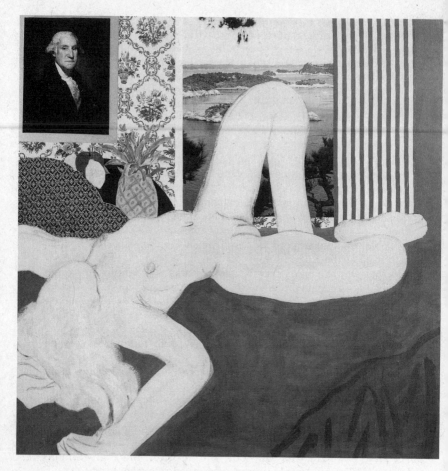

18.4 Tom Wesselmann, *The Great American Nude #4* (1961), oil and collage on fiberboard. Hirshhorn Museum and Sculpture Garden, Smithsonian Institution, Gift of Joseph H. Hirshhorn, 1966.

cide with the roller-coaster ride that American patriotism underwent during those years. In 1961, for example, Kenneth Koch wrote a play titled *George Washington Crossing the Delaware* in response to Larry Rivers's painting of the same name done a few years before. Although Koch's play is called a comic pageant, it is neither irreverent nor iconoclastic. Referring to Rivers's work, Koch explained that he "liked his mixture of romance, heroism and humor, the lightness about a historical event." Although the play was originally written to be performed by children, it has always been done by adults in its various revivals (fig. 18.5). Koch described the theatrical tradition in which he worked as

18.5   Alex Katz, stage set and props for Kenneth Koch's drama *Washington Crossing the Delaware* (1961), acrylic and oil on wood, and porcelain teapot. Courtesy of the National Museum of American Art; gift of Mr. and Mrs. David K. Anderson, Martha Jackson Memorial Collection.

18.6   Robert Arneson, *George and Mona in the Baths of Coloma* (1976), ceramic. Courtesy of the Stedelijk Museum in Amsterdam.

one best marked by such adjectives as "heroic, operatic, imaginative and poetic."[96]

By the 1970s George Washington's erotic indifference had given way to the lechery of folklore, but directed at Mona Lisa rather than Sally Fairfax, his neighbor in northern Virginia (fig. 18.6). Robert Arneson's droll spoof surely signals the disenchantment with cherished icons of nationalism that occurred in the wake of Watergate and Vietnam. By the 1980s, however, traditional iconography was back in vogue once again. Thus in 1986–87 the Fraunces Tavern Museum selected as the emblem for its exhibit "Capital City: New York After the Revolution," an engraving and etching titled *Sacred to Patriotism* that featured George Washington in full-dress uniform as Commander of the Continental Army.

It would be misleading to assume, however, that somehow patriotism had risen like a phoenix from the ashes. Traditional patriotism had passed through a slough of despond, to be sure, but it had never lapsed or collapsed, even during the depths of the Vietnam War. In November 1979, after the Ayatollah Khomeni authorized an assault on the United States Embassy in Teheran and the seizure of many American hostages, traditional patriotism made a swift comeback. Ordinary folks interviewed in modest restaurants and bars acknowledged "a lot of the waving-the-flag type of thing."[97] That impulse toward national chauvinism exploded with exuberance at the 1980 Winter Olympics when the U.S. hockey team defeated its Soviet archrival.

By the mid-1980s orthodox Americanism was very much in vogue once again, prompted by President Reagan's rhetoric, catastrophic setbacks for U.S. Marines in Beirut, splendid little wars in places like Grenada, and assorted other episodes foreign and domestic. The grass-roots upsurge of nationalistic feeling received reinforcement and legitimacy from conservative intellectuals like Morris Janowitz, a political sociologist, who produced in 1984 a controversial work of advocacy, *The Reconstruction of Patriotism: Education for Civic Consciousness.*[98]

Thereafter a diverse concatenation of events continued to rekindle strong sentiments of national patriotism: the centennial celebration of the Statue of Liberty in 1986 (which also annoyed a goodly number of Americans as well), George Bush's presidential campaign motifs in the autumn of 1988, the Supreme Court's five-to-four decisions in 1989 and 1990 upholding the right of protesters to burn the American flag (an action that provoked howls of rage), and the centennial late in 1989 of the founding of the Sons of the American Revolution. As the organization's president general told the media: "As descendants of the original Revolutionary War patriots, we feel that we have a special calling to keep freedom's fires burning."[99]

.   .   .

A S   W E   S H A L L   note in the Coda to this section, most of these trends and impulses were not uniquely American. European Architectural Heritage Year had been proclaimed in 1975. Five years later the British Parliament passed a National Heritage Act, and France declared 1980 *l'année du patrimoine.* Just as heritage and its synonyms seemed to become almost ubiquitous, so the "Roots phenomenon" became manifest in France and elsewhere. By the later 1970s a revival of enthusiasm in the U.S.S.R. for the Russian national past easily surpassed adherence to Marxism and Leninism as the dominant cultural mood. As George Gibian wrote in 1979: "The ruling passion is for old icons, old chests and other Russian antique furniture, and for the traditional hallmarks of the Russian countryside—onion-dome churches and birch trees."[100]

Gibian was also aware at the time, however, of important *differences* between the two situations—differences that had everything to do with the politics of culture. Nostalgia for the old Russia had its roots in anti-statist feelings, deep resentment of the dominant Communist Party and its official policy of hostility to religion. Hence an outpouring of Russian sentiment for matters involving religiosity in general and Orthodox Christianity in particular. In 1979–80, moreover, the political status quo in the U.S.S.R. seemed firmly fixed, the governing forces extremely stable; and many people felt that an oppressive bureaucracy and party apparatus had stifled all that was most beautiful and beloved about the "old" and truly Russian Russia. Americans in 1979–80, by contrast, had a much stronger sense of flux, of on-going discontinuity, and the likelihood of political and social change. Therefore their yearning for the past had somewhat different stimuli and expectations.[101]

Ultimately these differences seem to have been more significant than the superficial similarities involving symptoms and manifestations. In May 1972, when the famous old English train called the *Brighton Belle* made its final trip, one passenger offered an American journalist this intriguing comment:

> It's the end of a tradition. We shouldn't throw away our traditions like that. Soon we won't have any left. And where will it go? The trains will probably go to America. . . . I suppose they'll run her back and forth across London Bloody Bridge in Arizona. . . . You Yanks buy everything. Well, you need tradition over there, don't you?[102]

Well, yes and no. Nothing is quite so simple or so unidirectional as it may seem at a glance. The United Kingdom not only has its own peculiar heritage phenomenon, but ever since 1961 it has also had the American Museum located at Claverton Manor, a 125-acre estate near Bath. Established by a New York psychiatrist who retired to England and an English-born antiques collector who emigrated to the United

States, its purpose was to offset the "distorted, vulgar" view of America created by Hollywood and television. In addition to a considerable inventory of eighteenth- and nineteenth-century furnishings and decorative arts, the museum has some unique items with historical associations: a pedestal table that is believed to have belonged to Peregrine White, born in 1620 aboard the *Mayflower* near Cape Cod; the interior of a tavern from Pelham, Massachusetts, where Shays' Rebellion was plotted in 1786; a Greek Revival room with Duncan Phyfe furniture and Benjamin West paintings.[103]

Arizona may have gotten London Bridge, but Bath has sixteen remarkable period rooms that bulge with quality Americana. Perhaps it's the great heritage inversion. Perhaps each side has disposable goods and interchangeable tourist attractions. Perhaps objects and the subjects of another culture's nostalgia can somehow seem less banal than one's own.

Chapter 19

DISREMEMBERING THE PAST
WHILE HISTORICIZING THE
PRESENT

I N T H E T R E A T M E N T of recent times that ensues in this chapter, we consider what Americans at various political and social levels seem to recall and what they reject about the past. Following a close look at Ronald Reagan and public rituals of memory, we turn to evidence derived from tests and surveys that show an anomalous pattern of factual ignorance despite broader familiarity with subjective and contextual historical realities. Americans not only learn selectively, they also remember selectively, and there is an approximate pattern to be discerned.

Section III pays particular attention to the contemporary commercialization of memory, which is also a filtering process in its varied manifestations: the media, tourism, advertising, and seductive shopping at neo-colonial malls and fairs. History proved to be a profitable enterprise in the 1980s. Section IV observes that the democratization of tradition has reached a kind of apogee in recent years (compared with one or two generations ago, never mind a century), and that vernacular culture now enjoys an appeal that cuts across social strata. The development of pride within African-American culture is yet another important dimension of the democratization process.

Section V notices the concept of memory in imaginative literature and art during the past decade, and then concludes with reflections upon the complex yet intriguing relationship between history and collective memory in our own time and in the years ahead. History does not necessarily provide a sound basis for prophecy; but if this overview has taught anything, perhaps it has demonstrated that predicting the past is nearly as perplexing as forecasting the future. Surely the past is equally full of surprises, anomalies, and enduring mysteries. That is why history never ceases to fascinate us.

. . .

TWO AMERICAN novels written early in the 1980s are remarkably prescient about the nation's propensity throughout that decade to remember at a shallow level of material things while forgetting
at the deeper level of public affairs and personal experience. To begin
with the former, Larry McMurtry's *Cadillac Jack* concerns a restless
man in his early thirties who is a "scout": he buys miscellaneous antiques from oddly assorted people and then resells them to dealers and
collectors. His rootless meanderings hither and yon across the country
are significant because statistics do indicate that one in five Americans
moves each year. And Jack deals in objects from the past that once
belonged to someone else. The objects may be interesting or attractive,
but their provenance is obscure. They are pieces of the past unencum-
bered by memories.[1]

Souvenirs by W. D. Wetherell is more complicated. Its principal
characters are Elaine Collier, a baby boomer born in 1946 who restores
antiques ("I patch up the past"), and Mr. Powers, who wants to obliter-
ate and forget the 1960s because his son died in Vietnam. Whereas
Powers needs amnesia, Elaine and her mother dwell in the past because
Elaine "desperately needed new memories." She and her mother invent memories of a brother and son who never existed. Wetherell
remarks that "The wrong people remember. The wrong people forget." People with painful memories seek to shed them, whereas those
who live in a vacuum concoct memories. "There are a lot of ways to
shatter your past," we are told. Yet a victim of the Holocaust refuses to
deceive herself and remembers accurately. "The past had to be remembered totally or not at all." That turned out to be the problem of the
1980s (and the subject of this chapter): selective memory and soothing
amnesia.[2]

Between the mid-1970s and the end of the eighties a reasonably clear
pattern and response appeared. A 1975 *Guide to Trivia Collecting*
announced that "we are [currently] engulfed by a wave of homesick-
ness for the past." A few social critics advised against "misplaced and
dolled-up nostalgia"; but the beat went on and so did the buzzword
until about 1985, when warnings started to flash, like feature stories
bearing such titles as "Writers and the Nostalgic Fallacy."[3] Within a few
years serious critics were discussing "The Nostalgia Disease"; and in
1987–88 three men in their late twenties (from Los Angeles, Chicago,
and New York) organized the National Association for the Advancement of Time (NAFTAT). Calling the baby boomers "fifty million teen-
agers who never grew up" and cannot stop reliving the 1960s, the
presentist pleaded: "Let's make nostalgia a thing of the past." Their
other slogan is "Boycott the Past." Why? Because 1980s pop culture "is
so firmly entrenched in the '60s that kids who would otherwise be
discovering the world around them are wishing they had gone to Woodstock." The three young organizers of NAFTAT blame what they call
the "media nostalgia complex" for catering to the vast swell of baby
boomers, thereby crushing contemporary creativity.[4]

The irony, of course, is that so many of the people who set the tone for the 1960s were themselves present-minded and future-oriented. Consequently one critic in 1964 decried what he called "the attack upon memory," and summed up the crisis of his age in a single sentence: "Cultural life depends upon the remembrance of acknowledged values, and for this reason any sign of a prejudice against memory is a signal of danger." But how dangerous is prejudice directed against false memories of pseudo-events? As one of the organizers of NAFTAT explained in 1989: "they're celebrating the 25th anniversary of the '64 World's Fair, which in itself was the 25th anniversary of the '39 World's Fair. So it's the 50th anniversary of World of Tomorrow. . . . All we're doing is remembering the future as seen in the past, which is pretty weird."[5]

During the century that started with the 1870s, as previously large constituencies for orthodox religion and philosophy shrank, mythology (in various guises) gained importance. That meant, among other things, that popularized versions of the past became more prominent and culturally influential. Following World War II communism turned into the sort of ominous spectre that atheism had been a century before. Communism was feared for many reasons, but one of them had to do with its repudiation of and break with the past. Therefore "Americanism" came to connote a love of continuity and respect for the past, even though Americans are supposed to be wildly in love with progress!

When international communism weakened as a political force and as a governing ideology, when *glasnost* and *perestroika* became commonplace words in the United States, negative references that had once been useful in defining Americanism became much less so. The foundations for national myths of long standing started to crumble, and even serious intellectuals began to contemplate whether a culture could function without the stabilizing crutch of myth. William H. McNeill, a prominent historian, asked, "How can a viable balance between myth making and myth breaking be assured? How can a people know what to believe and how to act?" Many of McNeill's colleagues were disturbed by his call for the revitalization of "public myth," especially at a time when books, films, and media programs about Vietnam seemed to be creating a new mythology in which the U.S. government disappeared as a devastating force, the Vietnamese people ceased to be victims, and the principal focus of concern became psychic stress for those veterans who survived 'Nam and needed to reconstruct their lives.[6]

The 1980s appear in retrospect to have been a most anomalous decade, as we shall see in the following pages: a time of surging public interest in the past, but also a time, according to polls and tests, when ignorance of United States history proved to be astounding; a time when spurious traditions were concocted and commercialized, but also a time when vernacular arts and folk culture flourished as never before. If American myths really were on the wane, then the sources and

nature of Ronald Reagan's success become more difficult to comprehend. Had we developed a serious problem of amnesia, as many critics
claimed?[7] (See the 1980 assertion by Meg Greenfield quoted on page
9 of this volume.)

If indeed mythology became less potent, had memory done the
same? Or had memory never been so very viable? Did we suffer from
pervasive amnesia rather than possess a healthy concern for collective
memory? Did the difficulty lie in the politics of culture generally, or in
the personality and temperament of a few prominent politicians? The
problem is most easily associated with the latter, but it was generic to
much of the populace at large, aggravated by the media, by commerce,
and by corporate America. Nevertheless a few hopeful signs remained
as the decade closed. Realists recognized that social memory was a
highly flawed artifice that could flourish at the expense of authentic
historical knowledge.[8] Hence an exhibition at the New Museum of
Contemporary Art called "The Art of Memory/The Loss of History."
Realists also recognized that new technologies of audio and video recording enhanced the virtues of print media as *aides-mémoire.* That
realization gave new meaning to an ancient Chinese proverb: "The
strongest memory is weaker than the palest ink."

I

EARLY IN 1990, after Ronald Reagan agreed to give video-
taped testimony for use in the trial of Admiral John Poindexter, his
former National Security Adviser, Herblock produced for national syn-
dication a cartoon that showed the aging former President looking
puzzled, his brow furrowed and his index finger poised at his temple.
The label on this videocassette read "Ronald Reagan in the Iran-Contra
Story: The Amnesia Years." Off to the side were these words: "The
gripping story of a man and his obsession, his close associates, special
funds and a shaky memory bank"[9] (fig. 19.1).

Two points must be acknowledged at the outset. The first is that
political amnesia, historical ignorance, and manipulation did not origi-
nate with Reagan. We have learned, for instance, that the famous photograph of the flag raising on Iwo Jima in March 1945 actually combined
two distinct events that occurred on separate days. The more photo-
genic flag raising (choreographed to keep Marine morale high in the
face of great adversity) followed the somewhat less theatrical but more
heroic act that took place in the face of enemy fire. The second photo
opportunity was staged by Marine commanders working in conjunction
with the press at a time when the Marine Corps feared that it would
be absorbed into the U.S. Army soon after the war and thereby lose its
proud tradition as an independent fighting force. Although the Corps
had many opportunities in subsequent years to set the record straight,

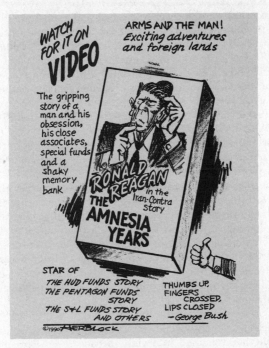

19.1 Herblock, "Ronald Reagan in the Iran-Contra Story: The Amnesia Years." Copyright 1990 by Herblock in *The Washington Post.*

it had participated in a manipulation of imagery too successful to be demystified.[10]

So it transpired that the less authentic Rosenthal photo (rather than the historically more correct Lowery photo) became the single best-known icon and collective memory of war after 1945. Nine years later the Iwo Jima Memorial, a bronze immortalization of the Rosenthal photo, was dedicated near Arlington National Cemetery. By the end of the 1950s souvenir models of the Marines' symbol of triumph over the Japanese at Iwo Jima had become big sellers; and no one seemed to mind that the models were clearly marked "Made in Japan."

Reconciliation proceeded with so much success that a joint Japanese-American ceremonial "reunion" took place on Iwo Jima in February 1985. It was a poignant occasion for many of the American veterans (we know much less about Japanese reactions) because capturing that island took the lives of 6,621 Americans and caused 19,217 casualties in addition. "Jesus, there are a lot of memories," said Joe Buck of Cherokee, Oklahoma, as he paced back and forth waiting for the service to start.[11]

A different kind of example: When Jacqueline Kennedy Onassis was redecorating the White House in 1961–62 in order to beautify it and make it more historical, she relied a great deal upon Harold Sack and his family, prominent dealers in early American antiques with a "shop" on 57th Street in New York. On one occasion the President's wife admired effusively a hand-colored engraving of the Battle of New Orleans in 1815. When Sack offered it to her with his compliments, Mrs. Kennedy accepted with pleasure and explained that she wanted to give it to her husband for his birthday. After examining the engraving a bit longer she asked Sack, "Just whom were we fighting then?" After he explained, she nodded and commented with a laugh: "We fought so many different people, I have never been able to keep track of them!"[12]

The second point that must be made, however, is that Ronald Reagan's lapse(s) of memory concerning the Iran-Contra affair was not an isolated aberration. It epitomized a pervasive pattern. He played fast and loose with the facts of American history because being the Great Communicator meant more to him than being a public educator. Early in 1981, for instance, Reagan asserted in a one-hour interview with Walter Cronkite that "Franklin Delano Roosevelt made a speech in Chicago at the dedication of a bridge over the Chicago River. In that speech he called on the free world to quarantine Nazi Germany." Actually F.D.R. gave that speech in 1937, rather than 1938 as Reagan declared a moment later, and F.D.R. never mentioned Hitler, Nazi Germany, or a plan for quarantine. His target was clearly imperial Japan, which had recently renewed its fierce attack on China.[13]

In yet another televised interview, broadcast on Christmas Day, 1981, Reagan insisted (as he had in 1980 during his first campaign) that "many of the New Dealers actually espoused what today has become an epithet—fascism—in that they spoke admiringly of how Mussolini had made the trains run on time." Numerous respondents called Reagan's remarks "a gross distortion of history." At a press conference held in 1982, Reagan replied to one question with a mini-history of United States involvement in Vietnam. Many of Reagan's statements were factually incorrect, confusing, and vulnerable to challenge on interpretive grounds. By the close of that year political scientist James David Barber could remark that "Ronald Reagan is the first modern President whose contempt for the facts is treated as a charming idiosyncrasy." After more of the same, one caustic critic referred to Reagan's "reign of error."[14]

Three decades ago Clinton Rossiter (and others) commented that "the Conservative's reverence for God is matched by his respect for history. . . . History is the creator of all the Conservative holds dear." That may have been true once upon a time, but it became inoperative from the moment Reagan's first administration began to make policy choices based upon budgetary priorities. In the spring of 1981 it proposed a reduction in the Historic Preservation Fund from $35 million to $5 million per year, a move to kill the national preservation program and totally eliminate aid to state preservation offices. So much for the

New Federalism! A year later Reagan's proposed budget for fiscal year 1983 aimed to cut off National Trust programs without a penny.[15]

Throughout 1982 the National Archives found its personnel being decimated by budget cuts. When the records declassification division had its staff slashed from one hundred to twenty-five workers, the flow of documents needed by scholars working on recent history was reduced to a trickle. The same cuts meant that thousands of hours of Richard M. Nixon's White House tapes would not be reviewed and released to serious students for many years. Meanwhile the White House announced a program designed to make it much easier for officials to stamp "Top Secret" on government documents. As one historian explained, the new initiative would also enable federal officials to keep classified many documents that were thirty years old or more—papers essential to investigative searches and public knowledge. Despite eloquent testimony by Barbara Tuchman, Alex Haley, and other prominent writers, the well-organized protest made little headway against Gerald P. Carmen, head of the General Services Administration, which had supervisory responsibility for the Archives. Mr. Carmen was a former tire dealer who became chief political adviser in Reagan's 1980 New Hampshire primary campaign.[16]

Given Mr. Reagan's unconcern for those who are custodians of the nation's memory, ironies abound. Halfway through his tenure the President gave full access to his papers and activities to Edmund Morris, the English-born biographer of Theodore Roosevelt who has been anointed to prepare the authorized biography of Ronald Reagan. To borrow a phrase from Garry Wills, the wistful Mr. Reagan seems to have a keen eye for "memories of the future."[17] An intensification of the irony appears in the closing paragraphs of Reagan's 1989 Farewell Address:

> We've got to teach history based not on what's in fashion but what's important: Why the Pilgrims came here, who Jimmy Doolittle was, and what those 30 seconds over Tokyo meant. . . . If we forget what we did, we won't know who we are. I am warning of an eradication of the American memory that could result, ultimately, in an erosion of the American spirit. Let's start with some basics—more attention to American history and a greater emphasis on civic ritual.[18]

If only his utterances and policies had reflected the substance of that perspective during the preceding eight years. In the harsh light of history, Ronald Reagan's peroration sounds very hollow indeed. At the Bitburg cemetery in West Germany he had declared: "I want to focus on the future. I want to put that history behind me." Watching Mr. Reagan address the American people brings to mind a painting by Christina Ramberg titled *Vertical Amnesia* (1980), which depicts a headless and hence a heedless torso.[19]

Outside observers reinforced what American sensibilities told us about the 1970s and especially the 1980s. In the spring of 1982, when *Orchids in the Moonlight,* a new play by Carlos Fuentes, had its American premiere, the playwright remarked in an interview that "it is a play about memory. . . . Our civilization is based on amnesia." When asked about the Reagan administration's Latin American policy, Fuentes called it a policy that ignored historical lessons and that "suffers from acute amnesia."[20]

Rarely have public policy and collective memory been reversed more dramatically than in the case of the Vietnam War. Late in April 1975, after the final U.S. military withdrawal, most Americans felt more than ready to follow President Ford's lead in deliberately disremembering the war. Journalist Fox Butterfield called it a "trance of collective amnesia." On Sunday, November 11, 1984, however, approximately 150,000 people attended ceremonies on the Mall in Washington at which President Reagan officially "accepted" the Vietnam Veterans Memorial on behalf of the nation. (It had been dedicated two years earlier—a very peculiar time lag.) Simultaneously the privately funded Parks and History Association, along with the National Park Service, published a four-color, thirty-page booklet, titled *Let Us Remember,* that documents the brief history of young Maya Ying Lin's controversial memorial. Its design is deliberately ambiguous in order to permit a wide variation in response. There is no doubt about the striking and sometimes unexpected expressions of patriotism that occur at the Vietnam Memorial, or that it accommodates and generates diverse rituals of remembrance.[21]

One of the most commonly overheard remarks at the Memorial is interesting, in part, because it is not true: "It [the war] is beyond politics now." Although the war, its memories and memorials, as well as the imaginative fiction, films, and artistic works inspired by it continue to be controversial, there seems to be an American penchant for depoliticizing the past in order to achieve at least the illusion of consensus.[22]

The Vietnam War is only the most obvious example. Another involves the way that Martin Luther King, Jr.'s, memory has been carefully filtered now that his birthday has become a national holiday and he enjoys heroic status. The non-violent Christian integrationist leader of 1956–64 is remembered rather than the more acerbic anti-poverty activist and strident opponent of the Vietnam War, 1965–68. The radical image of Martin Luther King, Jr., has been depoliticized so that he is a charismatic advocate of civil rights rather than a more broadly based critical conscience who sought social change for oppressed peoples at home and abroad.[23]

Other examples of the depoliticization of memory will be found in the editorial policies and contents of *American Heritage*; in the study guides prepared for teachers to accompany the classroom use of historical docudramas shown on TV; and in the vision of American development presented at Disneyland in Anaheim and at Disney's EPCOT Center in Orlando.* When Congress inaugurated a year-long centennial observance for Dwight D. Eisenhower late in March 1990, it did so in a genuinely bipartisan mood. Democrats as well as Republicans wore "I Like Ike" buttons.[24]

I I

IF PUBLIC FIGURES find it convenient to have highly selective memories, and if leaders as well as followers seem to feel more comfortable with a depoliticized form of consensus history, then what do ordinary Americans learn, know, and above all remember about their past? Some of our best answers derive from a series of surveys, queries, polls, and tests that date from the start of the twentieth century when Charles Francis Adams, Jr., a prominent gentleman historian, conducted his very own (printed) survey to check upon his impression that the "coming generation" no longer had the "patience to apply themselves to any considerable task, and that, accordingly, what might be called the continuous reading of [historical] authors has passed out of vogue."[25]

In 1922 the American Historical Association appointed a commission co-chaired by Henry J. Johnson of Columbia Teachers' College and Arthur M. Schlesinger (then at the University of Iowa) to examine the presentation of social studies in secondary schools. Its survey results turned out to be mixed, inconclusive, and ultimately inconsequential.[26] During the 1930s the Carnegie Corporation appointed a blue-ribbon commission, funded it fairly well, and then waited through several years of fierce conflict among committee members, especially the feisty Charles A. Beard. The Commission did sponsor publication of no fewer than seventeen volumes of reports and explorations of special topics; but once again the only agreement that emerged concerned an urgent need to improve the quality of instruction in history and the social studies. Substance and methods remained deeply divisive issues.[27]

By 1942–43 the development of "scientific" testing techniques had reached the point where it seemed possible to examine high school students along with the legendary "man in the street" in order to find out precisely what they knew (or recalled) about the American past. President Dixon Ryan Fox of Union College and his former colleague, Allan Nevins of Columbia, promoted the idea; the Carnegie Corporation sponsored its preparation, and the *New York Times* its implementa-

---

*In 1984 the guidelines of one textbook publisher included the admonition not to mention "political figures over whom controversy still exists: F.D.R., Nixon and Agnew, for example," or "living people who might possibly become infamous." (Quoted in Diane Ravitch, "Decline and Fall of Teaching History," NYT *Magazine,* Nov. 17, 1985, p. 56.)

tion. Fox called it a "uniform objective examination on the facts of American history such as any citizen ought to know."[28]

From the *Times*'s perspective the results were disappointing if not disastrous. Only 6 percent of those tested, for example, could name the thirteen original states. From the viewpoint of people involved in teaching social studies (a mix of civics, economics, sociology, and history), however, the exam appeared excessively fact-oriented and failed to ask about values. Why was it necessary for good citizenship to know who was President during the War of 1812 or the Mexican War? Who cared when the Homestead Act was passed, or what was the minimum price per acre of federal public land sold at auction before passage of that Act? (The answers were 1862 and $1.25.)[29]

That sort of controversy has been with us ever since. A survey taken in 1975 by the Gallup Poll revealed that 28 percent of the American public could not identify what pivotal event had occurred in 1776, and 19 percent did not know that Columbus undertook his first voyage to the New World in 1492.[30] A much more elaborate test, called the *New York Times* American History Knowledge and Attitude Survey, was given to college freshmen in 1976 with scandalous results. The four senior scholars who helped to supervise it were Professors C. Vann Woodward of Yale, Benjamin A. Quarles of Morgan State, Bernard Bailyn of Harvard, and William E. Leuchtenburg, then of Columbia (now at the University of North Carolina). The test was much less fact-oriented than its 1943 predecessor and presented questions concerning major trends, causal relationships, reasons for social or political protest, and the purposes of U.S. policies. It required judgment as well as basic knowledge, and most of those who took it performed poorly on both counts. One of the many immediate consequences was an indictment of high schools in the United States for lessening their commitment to the teaching of U.S. history.[31]

By the later 1970s many of the state commissioners or boards of education undertook their own investigations. They usually arrived at similar conclusions; and some of their recommendations were noteworthy (although, alas, largely ignored). North Carolina's Joint Committee on the Status of History in the Public Schools asserted that "History has an abiding respect for the stubborn persistence of tradition in shaping our lives. History studies our cultural roots, and it creates a sense of time and place that informs our perspective."[32]

Various people launched thorough investigations of history textbooks then in use. The most widely noticed of these inquiries, undertaken by Frances FitzGerald and published in *The New Yorker* and then as a book in 1979, offered a kind of good news–bad news scenario. The good news was that ever since the 1960s it had become commonplace to acknowledge that the United States had developed as a multi-racial and multi-cultural society. The bad news was more complex. First, U.S. history texts were notably deficient in economic analysis: they "never actually explained how the American economy worked, or how it had changed over time"; second, the texts were not only evasive about Vietnam but unable to present a coherent picture of U.S. foreign policy, which in turn seemed a clear "signal of their deep confusion about the place of the United States in the world"; and third, the era following World War II emerged as "the period of maximum ahistoricism—the presentation of American democracy as a Platonic form abstracted from history."[33]

By the early 1980s a pattern of dramatic informational disintegration and attendant confusion began to be apparent among students, teachers, and educational administrators alike. A 1981 survey conducted by the Council on Learning revealed astounding student ignorance of the world beyond their own national borders. The following year a twenty-four-page report found the level of geographical literacy in the United States to be "appallingly low" in comparison with knowledge levels in other industrialized nations. By 1983 the states seemed to be scrambling in all different directions: some going "back to basics" in the teaching of history while others (such as New York) proposed to replace courses that had been more or less chronological in organization, re-packaging the past under such new conceptual slogans as "power," "technology," "change," and "environment."[34]

Between 1985 and 1989 one grim assessment followed another. Diane Ravitch, a prominent historian of education and the author of several critiques, bemoaned the potential implications of historical illiteracy—once again in terms of the politics of culture. Professor Ravitch called attention to futuristic novels, such as Aldous Huxley's *Brave New World,* in which the regime successfully wages a "campaign against the past" by banning the teaching of history, shutting down museums, and destroying historical monuments. Even without such an explicit policy, the United States seemed to be suffering the functional consequences of indifference toward the past.[35]

MEANWHILE, outside of the classroom and beyond the abyss of bad textbooks, American memory among the people—especially working-class people, the offspring of immigrants, and those with a commitment to preserving their pasts—began ever so gradually to achieve a modicum of vitality. In 1980 the old industrial town of Lawrence, Massachusetts, relived one of the least known yet most important episodes in the history of American labor—a nine-week strike in 1912 by 25,000 woolen-mill workers who were enraged by the mill-owners' plans for a 20-cent-per-week wage cut. Although that successful strike became the first major union victory of the era, and led to widespread improvements in wages, hours, and conditions for hundreds of thousands of immigrants employed in factories, its basic story was not even familiar to residents of Lawrence. Ignatius R. J. Piscatello, president of the local historical society which helped to arrange a day of ceremonies, speeches, and skits in 1980, explained to the media that "people here are still afraid to talk about the events of those days, afraid to let their names be used, afraid of recriminations even after all these years."[36]

Obscure immigrants who had played representative roles in the history of American industrialization began to tell their stories, or else permit others to tell them. Children of those workers, victims of willful disremembering on the part of their parents, began to hear poignant sagas unearthed by investigative journalists and impassioned historians. In 1981 the American Federation of Labor and the Congress of Industrial Organizations designated its annual meeting as a centennial convention and declared that the labor movement was entering its "second century." The Federation, with its new-found sense of historical identity, traced its origins to a meeting held in Pittsburgh on November 15, 1881, when 107 union men formed the Federation of Trades and Labor Unions. Some historians demurred, however, and insisted that such festivities were misleading because the labor movement actually antedated 1881 by many decades.[37]

Amidst all of the controversy concerning how much Americans know or do not know about the past, and how easily they tend to forget, critics and commentators are likely to lose sight of a basic distinction between remembering facts and dates correctly, on the one hand, and remembering experiences or other "events" that are not necessarily time-specific. Americans remember prominent people even though they cannot supply the dates, let us say, of their tenure as president. They remember folk songs. They remember at least some of the rights vouchsafed to them by the Bill of Rights. The lay person's memory tends to be people-oriented, impressionistic, and imprecise. When those whose vocation it is to be custodians of memory go without presuppositions in search of information, they are often astounded by the historical as well as the personal knowledge that *can* be recovered: from an individual or a religious sect, an ethnic or a racial group. This has been notably true of African-Americans, European immigrants, and survivors of the Holocaust, for example.[38]

The people who administer those embarrassing history tests and surveys analyze the results they receive in terms of region, race, gender, and so forth; but there is one potentially interesting category of people not accounted for because, for various reasons, they are rarely among the "testees." If history buffs, earnestly committed amateurs, took those tests they would not score very well either, for the most part. Partially, perhaps, because they tend to focus upon a very particular sort of historical enthusiasm, such as Civil War battles, or tomahawk throwing. But once again, their sense of the past is linked to *types* of historical events, such as the annual fur-trappers' spring rendezvous that was an important time in the lives of mountain men in the Rockies and Bighorn Mountains during the middle third of the nineteenth century.[39]

History is not chronology for ordinary folk. It involves a sense of memorable individuals, of pivotal events that caused permanent alterations in a community, of the texture of human relationships where threads are broken and the fabric is subsequently restitched. Even measured in these terms, however, one major category of Americans may be the least historical in outlook: evangelical Christians, Pentecostals in particular. According to Joan Didion they lack a secular, or to them, profane, sense of tradition. History does not interest them because they are preoccupied with preparation for salvation and the world to come. As Didion puts it, "in the interior wilderness no one is bloodied by history."[40]

Any evaluation of the relative roles of memory and amnesia in American culture must ultimately acknowledge that we increasingly tend to measure how we are doing (in terms of collective knowledge) by how well we commemorate anniversaries. Those events get the greatest amount of media coverage by far: while they are being planned, when they become imminent, while they are happening, and then, inevitably, a retrospective assessment of how it all turned out. I have hundreds of newspaper clippings with leaders like "West Coast Monument Planned for Bicentennial"; "Yorktown Set to Relive Pivotal Battle" (the bicentennial of Cornwallis's surrender in 1781); "When We [Pennsylvanians] Turn 300: What Will, Won't Be Done"; "An Old Holiday Reborn" (Evacuation Day, when the Redcoats left New York City in 1783); and so on.[41]

We also measure the success of "public history" by the size of the crowds that turn out for parades and exhibits; by the authenticity of such annual re-enactments as George Washington crossing the Delaware River on Christmas Day in 1776 (for many years the part of Washington was played by Philadelphia City Councilman John B. Kelly, Jr., brother of the late Princess Grace of Monaco); by the amount of interest sparked as a result of some major celebration, such as the Bicentennial of Independence; and by the durability of historical dramas, such as Paul Green's "people's theater" held out of doors at night at historical sites throughout the South.[42] All of these may be valid indices of past-orientation in the United States; but they cannot and should not be the only ones, or even the principal ones.

III

IF ARTIFICIALITY has become increasingly irksome among a people who aspire to authenticity, it must also be noted that mediated history is an appropriate *double entendre* to describe a major trend that has taken place since the 1960s. For better and for worse, the media convey a fair amount of what passes for history and memory. In so doing they frequently mediate between people and historical events, sites, or situations. The press, radio, television, and film have assumed (or achieved) an ever larger responsibility for explaining America, as well as the meaning of America, to Americans and others. In so doing they have reduced the role of writers, of sermons and speeches, of live ceremonial and ritual occasions (because scheduling is often arranged to suit the networks' needs or convenience), of regional chautauquas and denominational "assemblies." Consequently they have diminished the felt need for full knowledge of American history as a basis for understanding national identity.

We should acknowledge straightaway that this is not a totally new issue, hitherto unnoticed. An interesting cohort of people who came of age early in the twentieth century felt apprehensive about the adverse (or potentially negative) impact of technology upon traditional aspects of American civilization. Stark Young (1881–1963), the Southern writer; J. Frank Dobie (1888–1964), the Texas folklorist; Thomas Hart Benton (1889–1975), the peripatetic Missouri artist; and Lewis Mumford (1895–1990), the New York culture critic and student of cities, all shared such anxieties even though each was very much a rebel and an innovator in his own way.[43] A concern for traditions, and for creative uses of the past, does not necessarily make one a conservative. Along with many others, these men worried about the price of progress precisely because they wished to harness progress for the improvement of culture.

No sensible person could condemn technology in a wholesale manner as the enemy of tradition. Radio and television have revolutionized the range of communication and the dissemination of knowledge about American life. A memory-oriented series like "Roots" had a positive impact that is simply incalculable. And quite a number of history museums are not only using technology to make their exhibits more interactive, and hence more interesting, but are devoting some of their most engaging shows to consequential features of the development of technology in America. The history of mass production and of streamlining as an appealing design technique provides only two from a plethora of positive examples.[44]

Undesirable aspects of the new (and now not-so-new) technology have been discussed ad infinitum elsewhere. In film and television dramas the plot so often concerns a wholesome and innocent society threatened from the outside by some overwhelming evil. In standard fare our problems are rarely of our own making, and our values are not ordinarily challenged or even questioned. The TV western arrived in 1955 with "Gunsmoke," "Cheyenne," and "Wyatt Earp"; it enjoyed stupendous popularity as mass culture, evoked nostalgia for simpler times, and supplied grotesque distortions of the realities of Western history. Film, especially, has wreaked equal havoc with the realities of Southern history—reinforcing stereotypes, romanticizing a world that never was, and distorting realities.[45]

Film director George Lucas presented Americans with a fantasy in *Star Wars* (1977) that has been aptly described as "a redreaming of

American memory that includes the Vietnam experience as a traumatic passage to a higher plane of understanding." If *Star Wars* offered a simple-minded reprise of certain American myths, *The Empire Strikes Back* (1980) and *Return of the Jedi* (1983) included celebrations of victory that drew in vague and misleading ways upon the American Revolution, World War II, and science fiction. In 1986 those films held three of the top five positions on the list of all-time box-office successes.[46]

A PATTERN that began to appear in the 1970s became a major problem and issue by the later 1980s, namely, the utilization of historical commemorations as televised special events that got grossly commercialized through hefty sales of exclusive advertising rights to big corporate sponsors. Particular brands of cola, wine, sausage, hotel chains, and other products or industries bought into and "brought you" the centennial of the Statue of Liberty in 1986, and less flagrantly the bicentennial of the U.S. Constitution a year later. The United States had begun moving toward the commercial management of public memory. This may have been an inevitable outcome of the Reagan era, but its implications are quite extraordinary. As the historian Susan G. Davis has remarked, in "corporately sponsored events, live or televised, the way we experience the past and present, the very experience we have to interpret is being rebuilt for us through marketing strategies."[47]

The most important figure in this whole phenomenon, for better and for worse, is the television and motion picture producer David Wolper, a man who has made more than five hundred films and has received two Oscars, forty Emmys, seven Golden Globes, and five Peabody awards (fig. 19.2). He is responsible for the justly acclaimed "Roots" series on television (1977), but also for the glitzy and vacuous "Liberty Weekend" (1986). Born in New York City in 1928, Wolper began his career as a travelling salesman for television films. In 1958 he learned about a remarkable collection of official Russian footage documenting the Soviet space program—one of the hottest news subjects at that time. Wolper took one look, purchased all 6,000 feet, and formed Wolper Productions in order to make films for TV. "The Race for Space" first aired in 1960 and won numerous awards. A selection of what followed includes "The Making of the President" in the 1960 and 1964 campaigns, based upon Theodore H. White's popular books; "The Rise and Fall of the Third Reich," based upon William L. Shirer's best-selling book; "They've Killed President Lincoln" (1971), which initiated a popular new type of entertainment, the docudrama; four shows about the Civil War made in conjunction with *American Heritage* (1973–74); and many biographical specials (fig. 19.3).[48]

Wolper's enthusiasm for American history is genuine if not deep. He collects historical autographs and specializes in Lincolniana. He ac-

19.2   David L. Wolper with Alex Haley (c. 1976). From the David L. Wolper Library.

19.3   David L. Wolper with a billboard promoting his documentary specials for television, including "D-Day," "The Legend of Marilyn Monroe," "Pro Football: Mayhem on a Sunday Afternoon," "A Thousand Days," and "The General," made between 1962 and 1965. From the David L. Wolper Library.

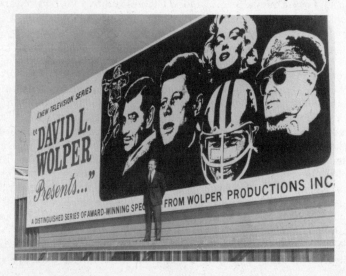

19.4   A consortium of American historians meeting with David L. Wolper in 1973 to plan the American Heritage television series. Included from the left are Barbara W. Tuchman, Wolper, James MacGregor Burns, Theodore Strauss, Bruce Catton, Walter Lord, Oliver O. Jensen, and John A. Garraty. C. Vann Woodward sits at the center right (wearing dark-rimmed glasses). From the David L. Wolper Library.

quired the television rights to Carl Sandburg's *Lincoln* and produced a six-hour mini-series starring Hal Holbrook (1974–75). Early in 1975 President Gerald Ford selected Wolper as the only person from the film industry to serve on the American Revolution Bicentennial Commission. Like so many others in this narrative, Wolper cares about authenticity and uses professional historians as consultants (fig. 19.4). He can be disarmingly candid about his attitude toward historians. In an interview recorded by the American Film Institute he said:

> Let me tell you how I do the docudrama. First, I get an historian who is going to be my expert on that docudrama. Historians disagree on things too. If you get three historians in a room, they'll give you three different versions. I get one historian and say, "This is my historian." To the historian I say, "This is my docudrama. This is what I am doing. You read the script and tell me what's wrong and what's right."[49]

Wolper's professional criteria are pragmatic and rather casual. In 1985–86 he produced a twenty-four-part series, "North and South," based on John Jakes's best-selling novels about the friendship between a Northern industrial family and a Southern plantation family prior to and throughout the Civil War. Jakes had a career in advertising before he turned his hand (with great success) to historical fiction early in the 1970s. Wolper has insisted of "North and South" that "We keep everything in an historical perspective. I have an historian working on the

piece, as well as the author, John Jakes, who's an historian himself."
Wolper concedes that wherever possible docudramas must have a
happy ending. The final installment of "Roots" ended just after the Civil
War, when Chicken George and his family had achieved freedom.
"That was important. We had to have an ending like that on American
television; if we had a negative ending, we would never get the show
on the air."[50] Perhaps, but the historical complexities indicated by the
broadside shown in figure 4.4 suggest that poignant frustrations and
ambiguities can be considerably more intriguing than reductive happy
endings.

Wolper acknowledges that a great deal of the programming on American television is poor; but he makes no apologies for seeking the broadest possible audience. After a reviewer for *Time* magazine wrote that
"Roots," as a program, was "middle class," Wolper acknowledged that
it was indeed. "I tried to make it a program that would appeal to the
largest audience. I didn't want to do a low-class program, and I didn't
want to do a program that would chase the audience away [because it
was too cerebral]." He also happens to believe, however, and this may
set him apart from most other TV producers in the United States, that
three ingredients are vital to the success of a television docudrama: a
best-selling book as the basis, a sociological problem, and a historical
dimension.[51]

Given Wolper's stupendous success through more than three
decades, it is difficult to deny the viability of his formula, which says a
great deal about the orientation of mass culture in our time: a curious
concatenation of celebrity, social issues, and what might pass for popular historicity. Judged by whatever criteria, highbrow or middlebrow,
Wolper's triumphs vastly outnumber his lapses, and that too is indicative of improvement in past-based television programs during the
1980s. The "down" side of history now receives more adequate attention than ever before in docudramas and documentaries. The availability of file tape makes the presentation of "instant history" possible when
a famous person dies or a significant event needs to be recalled. The
principal disadvantage, of course, is that file tape fosters a form of
presentism in which contemporary history is privileged in a curious
way. We have seen and heard Dr. Martin Luther King's marvelous "I
Have a Dream" speech so many times in various contexts that it remains quite vivid, whereas Lincoln's Second Inaugural and Washington's Farewell Address—which ought to be equally important texts in
the American memory—can barely be recalled at all.[52]

THE PROFIT motive has perhaps been even more important
than technology in reshaping the forces that affect (and warp) a collective sense of tradition in the United States. Reflecting upon uses of the
"Confederate heritage" earlier in the twentieth century, Richard Har-

well perceived that "the past was something to be remembered only by old women and college professors. Only when remembrance promised financial gain did the New South take it to its heart."[53]

During the 1950s and 1960s it began to be apparent that tourism promised considerable financial gain—so much so that in 1964 Jonathan Daniels declared that "History is a cash crop." A decade later, as places to go and things to see started to proliferate in a manner almost too promiscuous to keep pace with, Stephen Spender suggested that Americans seemed to be "treating history as though it were geography, themselves as though they could step out of the present into the past of their choice."[54]

By the 1980s that proclivity offered opportunities that the so-called hospitality industry found irresistible, and the Travel Industry Association of America inaugurated an ambitious five-year campaign called "Discover America." The president of T.I.A. explained that in 1985 Americans had spent $257 billion on domestic travel. The organizers of "Discover America" wanted to increase that figure to $300 billion by 1990. Since people did not require special encouragement to visit relatives, the focus of this campaign became scenic and historic places.[55]

Arthur Frommer, a well-known authority on travel, for example, suggested four "weekend getaways" with historic significance: Springfield, Illinois ("Land of Lincoln"); Boston, Massachusetts ("On the Freedom Trail"); Atlanta, Georgia ("The Crossroads of Dixie"); and Truckee, California ("Gateway to the Golden West"). *USA Today* ran a colorful special section to explain why each of these places promised to leave the visitor overwhelmed with historical knowledge and memories. In case you are wondering about Atlanta, by the way, it offered the double dip: a major Confederate supply center as well as a city associated with Martin Luther King, Jr., and the civil rights movement. From scenic Truckee the tourist could view Donner Lake, named in memory of the pioneers who perished in that treacherous pass during the winter of 1846–47. And then from Truckee it would be just a hop, skip, and a jump to such quaint towns of the gold rush country as Sierraville and Sierra City.[56]

The travel boom became an attractive magnet for non-profit organizations that find extra revenue a handy asset. The Smithsonian Institution, for one, published no less than a twelve-volume set titled *The Smithsonian Guide to Historic America* at $17.95 per book. A feature story about the project made access to the past sound painless and mindless in equal measure.

> A trip down memory lane usually is a do-it-yourself venture. You load the family in the car and go. But now there's a new tool: *The Smithsonian Guide to Historic America.* This 12-volume set spells out itineraries region by region, then pleasantly digresses on the history that flows by the car windows.[57]

Back in 1955, when Frederick L. Rath, Jr., served as director of the National Trust, he came up with a charming remark in one of his many upbeat speeches: "Not too many years ago travelers went to watering places. Today we can encourage them to come to remembering places." Thirty years later another of Rath's inspirations, the Eastern National Park & Monument Association, concocted a travel inducement called PASSPORT, a 104-page booklet "designed to serve as a constant companion to visitors to parks. It records visits through the insertion of ten annual stamps, one national and nine regional, and by cancellation stampings in all parks visited." PASSPORT became effective on May 18, 1986, the start of National Tourist Week.[58]

This flurry of interest and activity caused states to budget more for tourist advertising, though a much larger proportion of investment in historic tourism, by far, came from the private sector.[59] Whenever the private sector itself became a menace to historical legacies, however, coalitions of alarmed citizens, non-profit groups, and even the federal government got activated. That occurred in 1986–87, for instance, when real estate developers cast covetous eyes (and potential covenants) on land adjacent to the Manassas Battlefield in northern Virginia. A National Heritage Coalition came together, practiced the politics of historic preservation with great panache, and Congress (after hearing testimony from professional historians) passed an act that saved the land—an extraordinary legislative "taking" of property.[60]

A few enterprising companies have been savvy enough to collaborate with the National Trust rather than fight it, and the most engaging campaign has come from the Jack Daniel Distillery in Nashville, which prides itself on being the oldest *registered* distillery in the United States. Ever since the start of 1985 it has been engaged in a "Celebrating the Best of America" program connected to a contribution by the distillery to some local historic restoration or preservation project based upon Jack Daniel's sales in that market during the promotional month. The gift simply comes from current sales revenue. According to the company officer in charge, "our marketing group here (in Nashville) selects the markets to receive the program and we work with the National Trust for Historic Preservation in choosing the landmarks to be featured." The distillery puts on a "heavy publicity effort in both print and broadcast media." The historic preservation groups who have collaborated with Jack Daniel say that "this publicity plus the advertising is as valuable as the actual cash contribution."[61]

Over a five-year period (1985–89) the Jack Daniel promotion assisted the Scott Joplin home in St. Louis, the Washington Monument in Baltimore, the Joel Chandler Harris House in Atlanta, Faneuil Hall in Boston, the Frank Lloyd Wright home in Chicago, St. Charles Streetcar 919 in New Orleans, the Margaret Mitchell House in Atlanta, Jubilee Hall in Nashville (at Fisk University), and many others. It is a shrewd and interesting program that has been good for Jack Daniel's bourbon and for a great many historic sites as well.

Latching on to national traditions is not a new phenomenon in American advertising. Back in the 1930s, for instance, the United Brewers Industrial Foundation took full-page ads in the *Atlantic Monthly* featuring Uncle Sam (and no trace of beer) in order to urge people to take "the straight road ahead, which is the way of moderation and sobriety." The point, of course, turns out to be that beer is "*in fact* the bulwark of moderation . . . according to the verdict of history." And so on. A fairly soft sell.

During the 1980s, however, the litany of products invoking some specious linkage with "tradition" became utterly numbing, and never (well, hardly ever) seemed to need the faintest sort of justification or genuine connection: Thomson (clothing), "Tradition Like You've Never Seen It Before"; Van Heusen, "an American Tradition"; a Wallachs "Guide to Good Traditions"; Albany Amber beer, "Tradition, Bottled"; Ghurka, "a Lasting Tradition"; Aramis 900 Cologne for men, "Tradition with a dash of the unexpected"; Paul Stuart (clothing), "Building on Tradition"; London Fog, "the Tradition of Quality"; the Drake (hotel in Chicago), "Where tradition works wonders"; Lord & Taylor (department stores), "Welcoming American Traditions"; and, a touch of variation by Schumacher Fabrics, "Historicism makes a comeback—was it ever away?"

The list is virtually limitless; but there is also a special category—though I am not at all certain whether its distinctiveness lies more in its naïveté or in its presumptive appeal: "Start a family tradition with this Howard Miller clock"; "Begin a Tradition" with porcelain religious figures from Brielle Galleries; Pottery Barn, "a catalog of new traditions"; "A New Boston Tradition: The Meridien (Hotel) Weekend"; "New Traditions" (in men's clothing) from Graham & Gunn, Ltd.; "Revive an American Tradition," the Verdin Company's streetclocks, tower clocks, and clock-chiming systems; and the most relentless and lavish of all, "How a Tradition Begins," the Ralph Lauren Home Collection, and "How a Tradition Becomes," Polo Ralph Lauren.

DURING THE 1970S, decay in downtown areas of American cities grew aesthetically intolerable and economically disastrous, so chambers of commerce and business communities suddenly became interested in historic preservation and restoration because that held out the one remaining hope for survival. Meanwhile gigantic shopping centers with acres of parking began to appear in the suburbs and even in rural areas. At some of them the architectural design can only be described as Nondescript Banal; but in others, which almost resemble theme parks, the design was (and remains) Neo-colonial Banal. In Central Valley, New York, for example, near Harriman on the west side of the Hudson River, old-fashioned lampposts are adorned with American flags at an early American–motif village called Woodbury Common Factory Outlets that opened in 1986. It follows the pattern of Liberty

Village, also a center for factory outlets located in Flemington, New Jersey, since 1981. The landmarks at Woodbury Common are two eighty-foot colonial towers, each one with a triple cupola resting on a rustic fieldstone first level with Palladian windows.[62]

It is invitingly dismal and easy to dismiss these trends of the 1980s as no more than rampant corporate commercialism and what sociologist Dean MacCannell has designated as "staged authenticity." Such cynicism would be understandable but nonetheless simplistic. Although a clear pattern is undeniably discernible, nagging complexities appear to make the pattern somewhat less tidy. Places like Woodbury Common are not so very different in atmosphere, for example, from the neo-colonial pageants and fairs that steadily gained popularity between the 1960s and the 1980s. People offered things for sale at each, and customers came to both sorts of places in search of bargains amidst leisurely, pleasant, and traditional surroundings. Does it make such a colossal difference that the colonial fair at Chadds Ford, Pennsylvania (initiated in 1958; institutionalized in 1968), also features eighteenth-century craft demonstrations and that the raffle prize is an Amish quilt? Perhaps the difference is one of stylish degree rather than one of stark contrast.[63]

Similarly, in an age when so many people wear (and wear out) jeans with amazing gracelessness, the manufacturer Levi-Strauss cannot possibly be hurting; nor does it need to be preoccupied with public relations. Nevertheless it sponsored an important, costly, and remarkably self-aware conference, titled "Inventing the West," aimed at scholars and anyone else interested in myths of the American West (fig. 19.5). This highly successful event took place in August 1982 at Ketchum, Idaho, where Ernest Hemingway lived (near Sun Valley).

The parodic poster reminds us once again of the ceaseless problem of authenticity. What to do, for instance, when serious scientific research reveals that important public rooms at Mount Vernon, Monticello, and Colonial Williamsburg were actually painted colors that seem ghastly to our decorous eyes? Many people hate to see historic "shrines" change in any way; and a goodly number of these folks have actually painted rooms in their own homes the very colors that they once saw at those beloved eighteenth-century sites. What are they supposed to do now—repaint their rooms in garish colors; or else, Heaven forbid, be inauthentic?

Early in the 1980s a fierce brouhaha broke out in pristine Litchfield, Connecticut, where for so many decades every structure in town had been, by some invisible code, white with the darkest of green shutters. Then the Litchfield Historical Society, by definition an arbiter of knowledge and taste, decided to paint two of the town's most historic structures, the Tapping Reeve House and Law School (the first in America), peach and gray respectively. Townspeople thought the ultimate outrage had been committed until members of the United Methodist Church, following a fire, repainted their (hitherto white) late Gothic

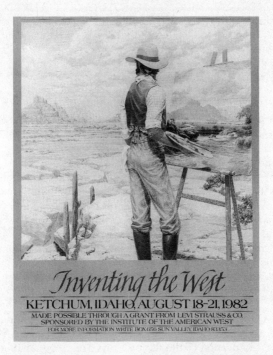

19.5   "Inventing the West," poster for a conference sponsored by the Levi-Strauss Company held at Ketchum, Idaho (where Ernest Hemingway lived, near Sun Valley), in August 1982.

Revival building light gold and dark gold with blue window sash trim. The roof became tricolored: gold and two shades of brown. "Horrible," declared one lifelong resident. "It's just a lousy shame." A member of the borough board of burgesses added: "I firmly believe the town should be all white." The traditionalists do not have history on their side, as it happens, because early American structures were not all white—far from it. The board member sputtered that "historical accuracy can be carried too far." When history and tradition are at odds, the level of unpleasantness is likely to intensify.[64]

After a while it became a bit unclear just who is responsible for creating or for perpetuating phony pasts and who is the truly justified purist. Authentic early American furniture began to fetch prices that outreached any scale anyone had ever imagined. In 1986 a Philadelphia pie crust tea table sold at Christie's for $1,045,000, the highest price ever paid anywhere for a piece of American furniture. By June 1989 that seemed a mere trifle because a New York dealer paid $12.1 million for an elaborately carved eighteenth-century tall desk from Newport, Rhode Island, the highest price ever paid at auction for an object other than a painting. Under the circumstances it should come as no surprise that the 1980s was also a decade that saw a booming business in the manufacture and sale of "authentic reproductions" of colonial furniture.[65] Some folks are forced into phony pasts by circumstances beyond their control, like inflated values.*

DESPITE all the complaints about the need for public austerity and economizing, the 1980s also seems to have been a fine time for facelifting and refurbishing icons of tradition. It required a year-long project and $654,000, for instance, to clean up the Maine Memorial at Columbus Circle in Manhattan. The seven-ton statue of Columbia triumphant had been erected in 1913 to commemorate the sinking of the battleship *Maine* early in 1898. Plymouth Rock, the boulder that marks the spot where the Pilgrims are supposed to have come ashore, has a major crack that is about two and one-half feet long. To avoid the embarrassment that would result if it split in half, a mason mixed a special mortar to match the color and consistency of repairs made during the nineteenth century. (There were also hairline cracks within the main fracture and in some other areas of the rock.)[66]

The San Jacinto battle flag, carried into the fray by a cadre of Kentucky men who volunteered to help Texas win independence from Mexico in 1836, has long been in shreds; in fact, only about 70 percent of the painted portion of the flag still survives. Early in 1990 a textile conservator in Sharpsburg, Maryland, located in the Appalachian foothills, began taking the flag apart and with the help of a microscope and techniques learned from years of study, will try to restore what remains of the precious banner. It has hung in the Texas House of Representatives since 1933. The flag conveys a certain Gallic quality because it shows a woman with one breast bared who is brandishing a sword with the banner "Liberty or Death," all painted on silk.[67]

Despite enduring veneration for such objects as Plymouth Rock and the battle flag of San Jacinto, indications began to emerge in the 1980s that the regard for sacred objects and places from the American past was ever so gradually being secularized. In and around Springfield, Illinois, for example, there have long been green signs that direct pilgrims to "Lincoln shrines." By 1988, however, all of the signs read "sites" instead of "shrines."[68]

---

*It had been a long-standing tradition for visitors to Monticello to toss a Jefferson nickel through the iron fence onto Jefferson's grave monument—and make a wish. During the 1970s, however, with inflation running out of control, people began throwing George Washington quarters instead of nickels. Five cents just didn't fetch what it used to.

I V

ALTHOUGH the so-called New or Neo-Conservatism flourished during the 1980s, the democratization of tradition that began fitfully in the 1930s and started to accelerate once again in the postwar years persisted and, if anything, intensified. When the inaugural issue of *American Heritage* appeared in December 1954, Bruce Catton declared in an eloquent statement of editorial policy that the magazine would be at least as interested in "the doings of wholly obscure people" as it would be in "great men." Catton then added, as a declaration of faith, "the belief that our heritage is best understood by a study of things that the ordinary folk of America have done and thought and dreamed since first they began to live here."

Although *American Heritage* never really fulfilled such an egalitarian aspiration, many other organizations and individuals have steadily moved in that direction. In the realm of historic restoration, for example, the mud-and-wicker hovels of early Jamestown were reconstructed during the 1950s. "Typical" slave quarters have been rebuilt at Gunston Hall, the Virginia plantation home of Revolutionary statesman George Mason. And a dozen miles away near the Potomac the National Park Service opened the Turkey Run Farm early in the 1970s in order to show the lifestyle of a poor white yeoman farmer and his family on the eve of the American Revolution. Within a decade more than fifty such "living history" programs had emerged across the United States under various auspices—state, local, and private. Their primary purpose has been the re-creation of everyday life as lived by ordinary folks, rather than exquisite architectural preservation, formal gardens, and manicured lawns.[69]

Collectors and the harvesting of Americana not only became democratized but well-nigh proletarianized in many areas. Flea markets, house sales, and local auctions of collectibles attracted an ever-widening public. In absolute numbers (rather than dollars), more people sought rare beer cans, old Coke bottles, and lengths of uniquely fashioned barbed wire than those in quest of Queen Anne side chairs made in Philadelphia or a mahogany bombé bureau from Massachusetts. One news item in March 1990 described a man in Trenton, New Jersey, employed by the state prison, who collects electric chair memorabilia.

Although the pursuit of American folk culture is part and parcel of this phenomenon, we must be careful to note that that pursuit has been multi-layered. It includes several discrete constituencies, each with its own objectives, motives, purses, and consequences. Taken together, it is true, they have given vernacular culture a visibility and importance that it never enjoyed previously, and in doing so they have added new dimensions to the democratization of memory in the United States. But the particular variations on a theme are even more revealing than the overall motif itself.

During the interwar years, men like J. Frank Dobie of Texas and John Jacob Niles of Kentucky pioneered in collecting stories, legends, and ballads of the people. Niles began in the 1920s with songs of southern Appalachia and ended in 1972 with the Niles-Merton Song Cycles, a musical accompaniment to the poems of Thomas Merton, the late Trappist monk and philosopher. In 1935–36 Dobie did battle with those planning the centennial celebration of Texan Independence because he wanted less emphasis upon the exaltation of political and military heroes and greater attention to the folk. He also expressed an almost unprecedented, populist concern for those who would attend the exposition: "If you wish human beings, whether young or old, to regard history, then touch their imaginations. Literal catalogues of fact and literal statues will not kindle their interest."[70]

During the 1940s and 1950s a modest number of intensely committed individuals nourished the gradual growth of exhibitions and publication outlets for folk art and folklore. Carl Carmer, a non-academic writer and editor, was one of the most important; and like others in this still small circle, he differentiated between genuine folklore and commercial gimmickry aimed at mass culture, such as the Davy Crockett craze of the 1950s. As he explained to a friend in 1962 while preparing an essay, he wished to emphasize that Abraham Lincoln was "mightily influenced by the folklore of his day; that both Robert Frost and Carl Sandburg have made effective use of American folklore in their poems; that some of our finest novels . . . have had a generous background of our folklore."[71]

By the later sixties and seventies folklore centers and archives began to be institutionalized at important locations where curators collected, organized, preserved, and also sponsored events that brought people with common interests together. Two of the most notable examples are the Southern Folklife Collection at Chapel Hill, North Carolina (1968), and the American Folklife Center at the Library of Congress in Washington, D.C. (1978).

Simultaneously, as we have seen from the stories of people like Abby Aldrich Rockefeller, Electra Havemeyer Webb, and Elie Nadelman, connoisseurship of "fine" American folk art (at first called "primitive," then "naive," and then "innocent") developed gradually during the 1930s and 1940s, primarily on aesthetic grounds and because those elitist collectors saw continuity between primitive art and modern art, which most of them also loved and some, like Nadelman, even created. It can be amusing (and somewhat mind-boggling) to trace the records of what Mrs. Rockefeller paid for her treasures during the 1930s, because the prices ranged from $100 and $200 per item up to top prices of $3,500 for a *Peaceable Kingdom* by Edward Hicks and $4,800 for a carved wooden eagle. In 1981, when the folk art gathered by Jean and

Howard Lipman over a forty-year period was sold to New York's Museum of American Folk Art for $1 million, that sale helped to establish certain types of folk art as an alternative form of high art. A Pennsylvania dower chest, dated 1816 and painted in shades of brown and yellow with red decoration embellishing a spread-winged eagle on the front panel, was now coveted every bit as much as fine Chippendale, Sheraton, or Heppelwhite.[72]

By the 1980s American folk art, ranging from weathervanes to decoys and from one-dimensional portraits to toys, often meant costly collectors' items and status symbols for which people competed fiercely. In 1987 the prestigious Hirschl & Adler Galleries, dealers in American art, opened Hirschl & Adler Folk across the street on Madison Avenue at 70th Street in New York. Stuart P. Feld, the sole owner of Hirschl & Adler after 1983, was a prime mover behind this influential expansion—influential because its exhibitions of portraits, jacquard coverlets, country furniture, and miscellaneous wood as well as metal animals exert a powerful effect upon collectors, museums, designers, and prices.[73]

Twenty years earlier, however, Feld (then an associate curator at the Metropolitan Museum of Art) had challenged those who ascribed to "primitive" art so much originality, spontaneity, and wondrous naïveté. Based upon his meticulous research, in fact, he persuasively demonstrated just how derivative and crudely executed many were. So many "great" works of the folk imagination, according to Feld, turned out to be poor copies of once popular but now obscure engravings. Nevertheless between 1963 and 1983 the stature of American folk art rose magically by many cubits.[74]

In contrast the triumph of vernacular culture at a truly grass-roots level is really quite a different and separate story, a story involving Eliot Wigginton and his Appalachian high school students in Rabun Gap, Georgia, rather than a Madison Avenue story. The first issue of *Foxfire*, which appeared in 1967, was financed by $400 that Wigginton's students raised from parents and local businesses. Much of the information about Appalachian mountain craft traditions—how to make a cornshuck hat, a flintlock rifle, a fiddle, or a friendship quilt—came from elderly members of the community. By 1980 more than five thousand regular subscribers to the quarterly magazine from all fifty states faithfully read the precise, step-by-step, illustrated instructions to these venerable skills; and ten times that number perused the carefully collected information reprinted in the sequence of ever more successful *Foxfire* books.[75]

Modest grants from the National Endowment for the Humanities in 1970–71 enabled Wigginton's students to acquire more sophisticated tape recorders for oral interviews. Battery-powered videotape equipment made it possible for them to go into the hills to preserve on film the way one man made wooden shingles with a mallet and froe, another one used the small bone of a turkey's wing as a turkey call, and still another told tales of mountain life. Gradually the *Foxfire* concept spread to neighboring communities, and eventually to others far away and quite different from Rabun Gap, such as the Pine Hill School of the Ramah Navajo Tribe in Ramah, New Mexico. Students there received credit in their English class for producing a quarterly journal of Navajo history, art, and poetry. The astounding success of Wigginton's program eventually led to creation of the Foxfire Fund, a non-profit organization that seeks support for such diverse projects as Foxfire Video, Foxfire Records, the Foxfire Press, Environmental Studies, and so forth. Wigginton epitomizes his persistent yet controlled ambition with these words: "I do care that the kids I teach have a deep-seated appreciation for all that was, and is, fine and honorable about the culture they represent."[76]

It would be premature to maintain that vernacular culture and traditions "triumphed" in the 1980s. But they unquestionably achieved their apogee thus far in terms of visibility and influence upon Americans' sense of who they are collectively and how they came to be that way. The weak and the meek may not yet have inherited the earth, but at least they found that they were on the map. Books pleading for protection of their way of life appeared. Legislation aimed at the preservation of their heritage was passed. And more than rustic nostalgia lay behind it all. Developers and organizations even brought historic preservation into dilapidated areas of older cities, such as Savannah, where the Victorian District is undergoing a transformation designed to save buildings but also to preserve the neighborhood's racial and economic mixture. Leopold Adler, a former stockbroker who runs the non-profit Savannah Landmark Rehabilitation Project, has demonstrated there that vernacular architecture and a sense of community can be economically viable for all.[77]

AFRICAN-AMERICANS comprise the predominant group living in Savannah's Victorian District, and their role, too, is symptomatic of changes that began in the sixties and seventies but blossomed during the 1980s. Black residents of the district have not simply been passive beneficiaries of white philanthropy. The NAACP and other African-American organizations worked closely with Adler's Landmark group to make things happen. It is that element of participation, and the willingness of all parties to co-operate, that seems to set the 1980s apart as a decade of achievement for black history in museums, in the classroom, in preservation and archaeology.

Glance back a generation for an instructive contrast. In 1956 W. E. B. Du Bois sent a challenging letter to the board of directors of the NAACP. It began with these lines:

> Gentlemen:
> I am venturing to write to remind you that the year 1957 will usher in a series of centenaries which deeply affect the history of the Negroes and of this country. May I point out a few:

1957: One hundredth anniversary of the Dred Scott decision.

1959: One hundredth anniversary of the death of John Brown.

1961–1965: One hundredth anniversary of the participation of American Negroes in the Civil War.

1963: One hundredth anniversary of the Emancipation Proclamation.

1968: One hundredth anniversary of the death of Thaddeus Stevens, of the enfranchisement of the freedmen, and of the Freedmen's Bureau.

1972: One hundredth anniversary of the birth of Paul Laurence Dunbar.

1976: One hundredth anniversary of the Bargain of 1876.

There are many other significant anniversaries which recall Negro history and the cultural tie of the black man with American history. If we neglect to mark this history, it may be distorted or forgotten.[78]

Little of that agenda was achieved, partially because the energies of NAACP staff at that time were so deeply engaged by legal battles arising from desegregation, and partially owing to resistance by whites of the sort encountered during the Civil War Centennial. In 1957, when Virginia observed the 350th anniversary of its founding at Jamestown, the organizing commission belatedly approved a request made by Elder Lightfoot Solomon Michaux for permission to hold ceremonies at the Court of Welcome on August 20, 1957, "marking the anniversary of the arrival of the first Negroes in America." The observance had to be a segregated event and it received no attention from the white press. For yet another decade, speeches and public events pertaining to black traditions did not achieve much visibility or have broad impact, even within the African-American community at large. It is an accurate barometer that the narrator of Ralph Ellison's *Invisible Man* (1952) recognizes only near the close of the book that he is defined by his past and that "I began to accept my past."[79]

The community museum created at Anacostia, a predominantly black section of Washington, D.C., took root in 1967, had a somewhat shaky start in terms of financial support, facilities (it began in an abandoned movie theatre), conventional types of exhibits, and the absence of professionally trained staff. The person appointed to plan and run the museum was a thirty-year-old youth worker. By 1980, however, the Anacostia Museum had become a model of what neighborhood museums might aspire to: a place that felt welcoming, that supported community activities, and that conveyed to young people a sense of pride in their heritage. The Black American West Museum, which occupies several crowded rooms in the basement of a city-owned building in Denver, Colorado, had similar origins but largely resulted from Paul Stewart's belief that there must have been black pioneers, cowboys, stagecoach drivers, saloon keepers, miners, and farmers. By 1983 his museum contained eight hundred tape-recorded interviews with African-American pioneers.[80]

The Valentine Museum in Richmond originally opened in 1898 in the handsome 1812 Wickham-Valentine House. For more than eight decades it remained a sterile, lily-white, patrician institution devoted to archaeology and historical artifacts from the area. In 1984 the Valentine acquired an energetic director who swiftly hired a staff imbued with the new social history. Together they redefined the museum's mission: to interpret Richmond life and local materials "in the context of American urban and social history." The staff did not simply abandon the white elite that built and developed Richmond; but it added innovative and candid exhibits concerning the working class and the sizable black community. Hence no fewer than five major exhibits that attracted national attention, including "In Bondage and Freedom: Antebellum Black Life in Richmond" (1988) and "Jim Crow: Racism and Reaction in the New South" (1989). The latter included signs for segregated restrooms, a coin bank in the exaggerated shape of a slave "mammy," a leather whip used on black chain-gang workers, and a white Ku Klux Klan robe complete with pointed hood.[81]

Comparable signs of change have been noticeable in archaeological digs and historic preservation activity during the 1980s. There, too, the vernacular has become racially more inclusive. Colonial Williamsburg's assistant director for African-American interpretation admits that Williamsburg was "never a place for [modern] blacks to come to," and that "we're going to have to show rebellion, violence and racism in a way we haven't done." Five miles away at a 1755 plantation called Carter's Grove that C.W. owns, three eighteenth-century dwellings on the "farm quarter" were completed early in 1989 so that visitors could have a more complete view of plantation life in the Tidewater region. A few rare slave cabins that survived the ravages of time have been used as prototypes. Similarly, archaeological work begun at Monticello in 1980 revealed many traces of black life along Mulberry Row, a 1,000-foot-long avenue once lined with seventeen slave structures mentioned in Thomas Jefferson's papers.[82]

At Middleburg Plantation near Charleston, South Carolina, anthropologists and archaeologists are uncovering clay-plaster walled structures that retain African features, such as smoke holes rather than chimneys. In 1981 the Virginia birthplace of Lott Cary, a former slave who became a prominent missionary in Liberia, was proposed as a national landmark for inclusion on the National Register of Historic Places. The Charles City County administrator announced that if the state and federal governments took no action to mark the site properly, then the county was prepared to do so. That was a very striking indication of change. And in 1988–89, when the Mississippi legislature established a Historic Properties Trust Fund, it specified that the 1841 William Johnson House in Natchez should be the first acquisition. This

simple Greek Revival home belonged to a free black who was a successful barber and businessman. He also happens to have kept a diary that
is regarded by many as the "most accurate account of day-to-day life"
in Natchez prior to the Civil War. (Restoration was made possible in
part by $7,000 raised by the Jack Daniel Foundation for Preserving
American Landmarks and Traditions.) Future plans for the Johnson
home include a museum of Natchez black history.[83]

The movement to include more information about minorities in history texts for secondary schools began to gain momentum in the mid-
1970s. Four surveys made between 1968 and 1974 of the most widely
used textbooks showed progress—from *no* volume treating minority
groups adequately in 1968 to nine out of eighteen that were examined
achieving designations ranging from good to excellent. Attention to
women and Hispanics was slower in coming; and the history of Native
Americans as autonomous subjects rather than victims during the contact period has been particularly difficult to correct. It presents a special
problem for those who are planning major programs in conjunction
with the 1992 quincentennial of Columbus's "discovery" of America.[84]

Progress has been made in other areas, however, concerning the
proper place for custody of a minority group's patrimony. In 1989, for
example, New York State agreed to return twelve wampum belts, some
of which had been in the state museum for almost a century, to the
Onondaga Nation. "These belts are our archives," said a spokesman for
the Onondaga; and a chief who represented the tribe at negotiations
with the state explained that the belts had been used to record the
history of the Iroquois Confederacy and were meant to be present at
all meetings held by its chiefs.[85]

Later in 1989 the Smithsonian Institution responded to protests by
consenting to return more than eighteen thousand ancestral remains to
American Indians, Eskimos, and Aleuts for burial. Those groups had
long sought the return of the remains for religious reasons. Similarly, in
1990 the Dickson Mounds Museum in Lewiston, Illinois, decided to
close an exhibit that featured the exposed graves of 234 prehistoric
Indians. Those graves had been the main feature of a state museum
near a community of three thousand people that attracted some eighty
thousand visitors each year. The remainder of the "museum," the actual mounds, will remain accessible. As the director explained, "there
is no question of moving the burials because they have been here for
1,000 years and they have never been moved."[86] Good sense and sensitivity can be quite compatible.

V

JUST AS "heritage" emerged as a national buzzword of some
ill-defined consequence in American culture during the third quarter

19.6   "Memories: Step Back in Time," an emporium on Route 17 in central New York.

of the twentieth century, so "memory" surfaced with almost equal force during the 1980s. Once again a glance backward for contrast can be instructive. A short story published in 1966 about a joint encampment that took place at Gettysburg in 1913 utilized dialogue to expose the persistent ambiguity of social responses to memory. The ex-Confederate grandma "remembered too much. Sometimes a good memory does you no service." But a younger member of the family poignantly asked Grandpa, the aging veteran, "How can you help re-membering?"[87]

By the 1980s that sort of ambiguity had virtually disappeared because memory had become a commercial as well as an imaginative impera-tive. Prominent novelists like James McConkey and Saul Bellow pub-lished *Court of Memory* (1983) and *The Bellarosa Connection* (1989). Art museums devoted exhibitions to a newly named subgenre, "mem-ory painting," meaning works primarily by artists without formal train-ing (like Grandma Moses) that seek to "recapture personal recollections on canvas." The Rhode Island Historical Society devoted an exhibition to the ways in which women of the Victorian era memorialized rites of passage in the female life cycle. The curators called the show "Forget Me Not: Ritual and Remembrance in the Lives of Rhode Island Women."[88]

On the commercial side one finds shops and emporia, like the one near Liberty on Route 17 in central New York, with names like "Memo-ries: Step Back in Time" (fig. 19.6). In 1988 a popular magazine began publication in Boulder, Colorado. Its title? *Memories: The Magazine of*

Then and Now. And in 1980 the Book-of-the-Month Club launched a new subscription series called The American Past consisting of elegantly reprinted and abundantly illustrated books "about the people who shaped America and the great events they inspired." The promotional brochure widely mailed by Edward E. Fitzgerald, president of the Club, noted a common theme of the books selected: "They describe the shrewd idealists who settled our country and the chances that our predecessors took to make America great." What an intriguing echo of the unifying theme chosen for the "American Adventure" pavilion at Disney World's EPCOT Center: "America is ultimately a nation of pioneers, of dreamers and doers, driven by the kind of venturesome and restless spirit that feeds on challenges, revels in milestones, thrives on innovations."[89]

For the protean middle class, apparently, the American experience has been memorable for its milestones, not for its grinding and sometimes grating millstones.* Turning from metaphors to reality, however, millstones grind and transform—one from above working abrasively against one below. That is apt because of the way that our customary sense of stratification among American places of memory is being levelled. Independence Hall, the Lincoln Memorial, and Mount Vernon are obviously different from Elvis Presley's Graceland, the Baseball Hall of Fame, and Disneyland. Yet all of them, and so many others, are places to which many of the same Americans make pilgrimages.[90] If anything, attendance at popular-culture shrines has taken up some of the slack noticed in declining visitation at "higher" (not necessarily high) culture places of memory. Indeed, the popular-culture shrines are partially responsible for that slack.

The blurring of distinctions occurs with increasing frequency in other areas as well, such as ethnic cuisine. Many eating places that have a national or ethnic identity may very well encroach upon the domain of others. A restaurant called the Irish Brigade, located downtown in touristic Fredericksburg, Virginia, for instance, predictably serves Irish stew, seafood chowder, and Irish soda bread. But it also offers Irish nachos, fried mozzarella, and Cajun fries—all to be enjoyed beneath green banners blazoned with golden Irish harps. From a different angle, the editors of the *Encyclopedia of Southern Culture* (1989) offer one reason why a core of Southern traditions will endure: "There are some Northerners who move down here and become more Southern than Southerners, and so the region's myths keep getting adapted."[91]

Historian Michael H. Frisch has argued that the relationship between history and memory is peculiarly fractured in contemporary American life.[92] He is partially correct because the social diversity of the United States really means that we have multiple memories rather than a

---

*On a corner store in McCall, Idaho, however, a bronze plaque declares: "On This Site in 1897 Nothing Happened."

monolithic collective memory. He is also partially correct because nostalgia and amnesia are natural antagonists of meaningful historical knowledge. Nevertheless, there are reasons why the obverse of Frisch's generalization may also be true, namely, that history and memory are becoming peculiarly joined: a genuine intermingling of cultures (exemplified above by the promiscuous presentation of cuisines) owing to the fact that changing values have caused the sacred to be profaned and the profane made sacred; to an increasing co-optation of regional identities; and to the perception widely shared by most folks that memory *is* history. Unless someone remembers "it," it might just as well not have happened. Conversely, history hinges upon memory: the necessarily selective, collective remembrance that suits a society. That's not merely the "common man's" view; it was the perspective of a sophisticated historian like Carl L. Becker sixty years ago.[93]

If the relationship between history and memory is fractured, it must be a compound fracture; and a compounded one as well. Taking Frisch's assertion on his own terms, I must wonder whether he really wants to include the word "contemporary." Hasn't the relationship between history and memory always been fractured: in 1840, in 1890, in 1930, or in 1970? The eighteen chapters that preceded this one have tried to suggest exactly that. Nostalgia, with its wistful memories, is essentially history without guilt. Heritage is something that suffuses us with pride rather than shame. Although written history can never be complete, memory must inevitably be much less so. History and memory are not merely fractured. They are frequently at odds.

Even so, despite all the fractures and ruptures, America's mythic past is also perceived in terms of socially sustaining continuities and connections. Contradictions between history and memory, or between conflicting interpretations of the past, nonetheless reveal dynamic patterns of persistence among the meta-myths and mega-histories that make inquiries concerning the past possible, important, and inescapable.

DEGREES OF DISTINCTIVENESS:

COMPARISONS

TOWARD THE CLOSE of his term as Pitt Professor of American History at Cambridge University in England (1943–44), J. Frank Dobie wrote a striking passage to his wife, Bertha, who had remained at home in Austin, Texas. The sentiments Dobie expressed would have been remarkable coming from any American at that time, but all the more so from this earnest Southwestern folklorist who, barely a generation earlier, had battled to have his countrymen believe that the region he loved possessed cultural qualities worthy of consideration. "I get belly tired of Texas bragging and nationalism fever," Dobie wrote from Cambridge. "What our people need is less satisfaction with themselves and more civilization that consists less of machinery. The time when I rated Custer's last stand painted on a wagon sheet as more important to the West than *Blue Boy* [by Gainsborough] is past. I still want to tell bear stories, but I think it is as important to know something about the Russian Bear as the California grizzly, and the Frogs of France are more important than the Frog of Calaveras County."[1]

This cowboy's cosmopolitanism resulted, in part, from a love of European literature that he had acquired as a college student early in the century; and in part from the internationalist enthusiasm that predictably peaked as World War II reached a crescendo. For almost three decades following the war, however, the comparative impulse that Dobie called for remained notably neglected. Indeed, an extraordinary degree of cultural parochialism continued to be the norm among most scholars as well as the lay public—a phenomenon that began to be known as "American exceptionalism" by the later 1970s.

A particular irony for our purposes is that many of the tendencies described in the preceding four chapters had their counterparts around the world, and those parallels need to be noted.[2] Ultimately, however, systematic comparisons are just as likely to turn up contrasts as similarities; and that, in fact, turns out to be the case in key respects. Consequently we shall proceed to notice, first, international aspects of the amnesia problem as well as the heritage and nostalgia trends; second, similarities around the world involving connections between nationalism and collective memory; third, some of the idiosyncrasies that seem associated with the dynamics of myth, memory, and history in developing nations; fourth, the peculiarities of arbitrary revisionism and artificial memory in totalitarian societies, most notably the Soviet Union; and finally some features of tradition in American culture that, taken together, appear to present a fairly distinctive configuration.

I

NOT ONLY are amnesia *and* an expanded concern for collective memory widespread developments internationally, they commonly occur in the very same cultures. In Germany ever since the later 1970s, for example, a growing desire to minimize the events of 1933–45, or at least to de-emphasize their uniqueness by placing them in "perspective," has been accompanied by the rise of enthusiastic interest in German history prior to the twentieth century, by heated debates over the nature and contents of two major history museums that are being planned, and by a "hunger for memory" that has prompted the historian Charles S. Maier to observe that "memory has become not just the portal to the past, but a subject of contemplation in its own right, to be analyzed as well as evoked."[3]

In France, where recondite history books written by scholars readily become bestsellers, where the sheer number and variety of popular-history magazines are astounding, and where historic preservation has been well supported at all levels since the 1970s, it turns out that a crisis of historical ignorance exists among French students ("uncovered" by an extensive survey taken in 1984) and that most older French men and women repressed their knowledge of just how extensive collaboration with the Nazis had been during World War II. That is why Marcel Ophuls's film *The Sorrow and the Pity* came as such a shock: it demythologized an appealing notion of how widespread heroic resistance to the Germans had been.[4]

In Argentina, which has a history of tumultuous political instability in tandem with a distinctively pluralistic population, "there can be no feeling for a past, for a heritage, for shared ideals, for a community of all Argentines." According to V. S. Naipaul, collective memory and public history there are "less an attempt to record and understand than a habit of reordering inconvenient facts; it is a process of forgetting."[5] Milan Kundera made a similar point about Czechoslovakia in his innovative novel *The Book of Laughter and Forgetting* (1979), though the situation that Kundera described was different from Argentina's in this crucial respect: Czech amnesia became a matter of state policy rather than the helter-skelter result of a present-minded, culturally disoriented populace.[6]

Whereas the repression of memory can be a matter of state policy in totalitarian regimes, critics on the left have been concerned, during the 1980s especially, to demonstrate that museums and historic sites have been used by dominant groups in "free" societies to rationalize and perpetuate their partisan vision of the nation's evolution. As Donald Horne puts it in his international survey of museums, "relics" have the capacity to convey authenticity and to legitimize rulers: "It really should not be new to anyone with a critical interest in modern industrial societies that monuments have a 'rhetorical' function—more likely than not to serve certain prevailing interests—and that these 'rhetorical' functions shift, as society shifts."[7]

Members of social and political elites have long been attracted as "tourists of the past, seeking justifications in history"; but the dramatic increase in tourism since the 1960s has democratized tradition on the one hand by making it much more accessible, yet has also made lucrative profits available to those who invest in the "heritage industry" and has helped to perpetuate appealing visions of the timeless past, of stable, evolutionary change, and of history with a minimum of conflict and a maximum amount of aesthetic and patriotic appeal. Those have been the predominant qualities of history popularized on television, of cultural heritage presented in theatrical performances, and of restoration villages around the world since the 1960s.[8]

Whether or not the so-called "heritage industry" in Great Britain is sensible and desirable has been a hotly contested subject in recent years. Few would deny that creation of the National Heritage Memorial Fund in 1980 resulted in the preservation of sites that might otherwise have been destroyed, and the presentation of exhibits that have been highly educational as well as visually attractive. The parliamentary act that created the fund did not attempt to define "heritage" (unlike Jimmy Carter's National Heritage Trust Task Force of 1979 in the United States), gave trustees of the Fund no precise mandate, and made no provision for regular government grants. Nonetheless its positive achievements range from saving Calke Abbey in Derbyshire—described as "a time capsule where nothing has ever been thrown away"—to a spectacular, eclectic exhibition called "Treasures for the Nation: Conserving Our Heritage" that appeared at the British Museum in 1988–89. It placed cheek by jowl a suit of field armor made in 1595 for Shakespeare's patron and a futuristic British-built automobile, "Bluebird," that in 1964 achieved a speed of 403.10 miles per hour.[9]

It is the blatant commercialization of the past that has caused so much controversy. The good news, if one hopes for a historically literate public, is that half of the 1,750 organizations listed by the Museums Association in Britain were founded between 1971 and 1986. The bad news from the perspective of purists and many policy makers, however, is that tourism has become Britain's fastest-growing major industry. By 1988 it was a $24-billion-a-year business, employing 1.4 million people and creating 45,000 new jobs each year. Heritage Projects, Ltd., one of the leading companies involved in Britain's thriving heritage industry, has created in York the Jorvik Viking Center, a historically precise re-creation of a tenth-century Viking village that attracts nearly 1 million visitors per year. They are moved in motorized "time cars" past scenes in which King Erik Bloodaxe and his bloody-minded chums roam the countryside with malice aforethought. Heritage Projects also has in the works a Chaucer Center at Canterbury that will celebrate the medieval poet's tales and another festive exhibit at Oxford that will laud the university's eight-hundred-year history.[10]

Critics feel hostile to these trends for varied reasons. "When museums become one of Britain's new growth industries," Robert Hewison asserts, "they are not signs of vitality but symbols of national decline." Hewison wishes the nation would invest in science and technology parks, not "theme parks of the past." Other critics worry that despite a marked increase in historic sites that pertain to working-class and everyday life, ordinary folks continue to visit the conventional elitist "shrines" while the more affluent and those of higher social status continue to ignore plebeian places of memory. Not only does the elite's sense of the past fail to become more inclusive, it is not even clear that the working-class vision of history becomes more expansive or integrated either.[11]

When Michel Foucault coined the phrase "popular memory" in 1974, it promptly became controversial in France and then elsewhere because of a lack of agreement about the meaning of the phrase, or even whether such a thing actually exists. The Musée Nationale des Arts et Traditions Populaires, located in the Bois de Boulogne, was founded in 1937–40 by Paul Rivet and Georges-Henri Rivière and remained the subject of heated discussion through various incarnations because of Rivière's role in the Popular Front and the intensely felt politics of culture in France throughout the later Third Republic. Similarly, the popular novelist Roger Martin du Gard became both more historical and more political (sympathetic to the left) starting in the 1930s because he could not "conceive a modern personality detached . . . from the society and history of its time." Serious writers who felt skeptical about the claims being made on behalf of popular memory, however, called attention to the anachronisms that they saw in such claims and emphasized what they referred to as "ambiguité de la mémoire."[12]

All that seems clear about popular memory is that it appears to be less interested in the major, manifest political events that have chronological specificity than in more patently socio-economic trends, modes of living (particularly pre-industrial and rural life), and on-going forms of entertainment such as old films, radio and television programs. Hence the immense appeal during the 1980s of the TV series called *Heimat* in West Germany, a series that stressed the local, domestic, and apolitical aspects of twentieth-century German history. Hence the finding that in small Irish villages such "great events" as the Fenian risings, the fall of Charles Parnell in 1891, and even the Easter Rising of 1916 pale in popular memory by comparison with upheavals related to the land: the great famine of the later 1840s and the nationwide farmers' rent strike of that decade.[13]

We cannot be too categorical about any of these generalizations, however, because motives as well as consequences are variable rather than consistent. The promotion of culture for touristic and commercial purposes unquestionably occurs. Thus the annual and elaborate promotion of carnival at Nice, France, in recent decades; or the pageants staged for Canada's Confederation Centennial in 1967; or the promotional brochures for the ninetieth anniversary of Sweden's Skansen in 1981 (the grand-daddy of all open-air museums).[14] Still other folkloric spectacles offer "invented traditions" with an unusual twist because they have developed as a means of creating or asserting local identity in the face of seasonal, mass foreign invasions by tourists.[15]

I I

THE OUTRIGHT invention of traditions, a concept that has not only become commonplace but is often misused, is more applicable and employed with relatively little awkwardness in developing nations compared with more established ones, as we shall see in the next section. "Traditions" may be fabricated from the top, which occurs in the case of Iraq, or have more spontaneous origins, as in the case of Israel, but the common ground is ideological necessity and the political manipulation of myth as an integral part of the state-building process. The relationship of collective memory to nationalism in older regimes tends to be less intensely political, or at least, less *overtly* political; and in the United States, as I shall insist in section V below, considerably less so.

Commenting upon the worst implications of unbridled individualism in the United States, Tocqueville felt that men had little need or regard for their fellow citizens because each one existed in and for himself: "He has not got a fatherland." With the passage of time that observation became less valid perhaps, yet it retained much of its truth in comparison with other cultures. Historians Marc Bloch and Lucien Febvre, for example, shared a profound French patriotism. They taught their students to "seek in France's soil and in the tangible evidence of France's monuments the keys to the riddles of historical interpretation." At the time of his death in 1956 Febvre was at work on a book that he called *Honor and Fatherland,* a history of patriotism, of fidelity to the nation as a collective state of mind. That is an exceedingly difficult enterprise.

Nothing comparable exists for the United States; but immediately following Febvre's death the manuscript of his book mysteriously disappeared.[16]

The political scientist Benedict Anderson has accepted as a given the well-established reality that states and peoples tend to adhere to sustaining myths and even distorted views of their own origins. He then makes a persuasive case that most modern nations are "imagined political communities," products of an invented past that makes the nation seem both older and more natural (or historically inevitable) than it actually is in fact. Anderson notes the necessity, in so many nationalist narratives, of a particular trope or device: the stupendous "awakening" from a historic period of dormancy. Modern nations may be differentiated from the great imagined communities that preceded them—the world religions and dynastic kingdoms—by "their secularity and their inherently limited stretch." Buried in the notion of each nation as a natural entity is what Anderson calls "a sense of fatality."

> Most people today feel they have as little choice in their nationality as in their parentage. It is just this secular fatality, in a plural world of nations, that makes History the necessary basis of the national narrative.[17]

Anderson has also called to our attention a paradoxical passage from Ernest Renan's 1882 essay, *Qu'est-ce qu'une nation?*: "Or, l'essence d'une nation est que tous les individus aient beaucoup de choses en commun et aussi que tous aient oublié bien des choses." (Now, the essence of a nation is that all its members have many things in common and also that they all have forgotten many things.) Sometimes the impulse to disremember seems a deliberate matter of government policy, exemplified by the Japanese use of germ warfare in Manchuria during the 1930s or Canada's unwillingness to admit many Jewish refugees from Europe between 1933 and 1945, lapses which became the subjects of best-selling books in Japan and Canada during the 1980s. The appetite for historical scandal can be voracious.[18]

At other times, and even more to the point, events are likely to be forgotten because they bore the wrong symbolic content, which was true of the Jewish mass suicide at Masada in the face of a Roman massacre, or aspects of American history that carried the potential for massive guilt (such as the forced migration and extermination of Native Americans), or else emphases that were incompatible with dominant social values (that the Civil War resulted, above all else, from the immorality and political strife caused by chattel slavery). We regard as the shrillest harpies those people whose homilies insist that we recall pieces of the past we are most eager to forget.[19]

Then there are events so central to a nation's history that they cannot be neglected even if a non-coercive government did not feel an obligation to make some sort of fuss about them. On this point the recurrent pattern of similarity from 1976 until 1989 is rather remarkable: mild indifference in the United States toward the bicentennial of Independence in 1976 and absolute boredom with the bicentennial of the Constitution in 1987. Much the same thing happened with the centennial of Canadian autonomy in 1967, the bicentennial of Australia's founding in 1987, and the bicentennial of the French Revolution in 1989. Eventually, with very little time to spare, each of these fêtes somehow got organized and made a respectable "showing"; but insiders can remember what a close call it was in each instance, while the lay public remembers precious little, which is the principal point.[20]

Be that as it may, most nations seem to have experienced a "great divide" which manages to resonate in popular historical thought. We do, however, require a typology to differentiate among the reasons why: (a) because the event remains highly controversial or else embarrassing (France in 1789, Germany's Third Reich); (b) because the state glorifies the event and regards all others as being merely precursors or natural consequences (Russia in 1917, China in 1949); and (c) because the event transformed the culture and even redefined its political arrangements (the American Civil War, Israeli Independence).[21]

I I I

THE ROLE of history, collective memory, and social identity in newly independent and developing nations is so diverse that one can find numerous similarities as well as divergences between them and the American experience. If one compares more recent cultural dynamics with those that occurred in the United States for about half a century after 1783, parallels abound. I also believe that the uses made of certain political and military myths bear notable resemblances, such as Masada in ancient Israel and the Alamo, or the Battle of Tel Hai (a massacre of Palestinian Jews by Arabs in 1920 that gave rise to the popular image of the "New Hebrew Man" in Zionist pioneering) and the struggles waged by Daniel Boone and others against Native Americans. Moreover, as Marc Bloch pointed out more than half a century ago, collective memory has long been used in the Western world to distort images of the past in order to suit present needs.[22] Therefore developing nations that do so in the contemporary world are not exactly committing an original sin.

Be that as it may, on balance I find myself somewhat more impressed by differences rather than similarities in the circumstances of tradition and collective memory. Let us begin with the seemingly simple (yet complex) problem of preserving or sprucing up historic sites. This costs a lot of money, obviously, yet countries such as the United States, Great Britain, France, and those in the Scandinavian region have decided that the investment is worthwhile even in a time of shrinking resources. Nations that are younger and have precarious economies would like to do much more in the way of historic preservation but find it very difficult because of military and political as well as economic constraints. Consequently casual looting and neglect ravage the temples and monuments of Angkor in Cambodia. Thailand struggles to restore the ruins of Sukhothai, its first royal capital, dating back to the thirteenth century. In China certain sites, such as the Forbidden City in Beijing, have become touristic showplaces while more ancient and interesting structures just a few miles away (a multi-roofed Buddhist pagoda whose origins date back to the fourth century) languish in the shadows of a thermal power plant whose coalyard blows perpetual black dust upon the pagoda. Only in 1980, as a result of international pressure, did the Greek government decide to take steps to save the Acropolis and its monuments from air pollution caused by industrial workshops, low-sulphur fuel used in nearby apartments, and vehicular emissions.[23]

In nations with ancient and deeply traditional cultures for which independence has been relatively recent (usually occurring in the wake of World War II), the omnipresence of tradition can be used by a skillful government or statesman to bolster the people's resolve or to legitimize a policy. More commonly, however, contending ethnic groups and political factions draw upon divergent traditions and memories in a manner that impedes progress and cohesiveness. That has surely been the case in India, where Hindus and Muslims have such varied views of Indian history, and in Israel, where nationalist-religious and nationalist-secular (Socialist Labor) groups commit themselves to quite different interpretations of the meaning of events such as the mass suicide at Masada, the futile rebellion led by Bar Kokhba against the Romans in A.D. 132–35, and the Tel Hai massacre that took place in the Galilee during 1920.[24]

Careful studies of such episodes and their meaning in the politics of culture show changes in the dominant imperatives of Israeli collective identity; reveal that conflicting texts and countertexts circulate simultaneously among schoolchildren as well as the adult population; and above all expose the extent to which myths can reinforce politically divisive tendencies within a society that is deeply split along ideological and religious-secular fault lines. Above all, what is revealed by the uses of these events that took place in Palestine, and by case studies of Jewish communities in Tunisia, is the remarkable way in which local events can be conceptualized to conform to paradigms of religious tradition or to the totally secular needs of a modern state struggling for existence. The net effect is a disjuncture between history and what passes for collective memory—a disjuncture as great if not greater than anything one can identify in the American experience. The dynamics of manipulation, moreover, involving groups that are devout and ones that are inflexibly agnostic, plus poles of meaning that range from biblical to modern history, transcend what is familiar to us from American cultural norms.[25]

Whereas the marketplace dictates how history texts are written, constantly rewritten, and selected for adoption within the United States, in newly independent nations that emerge from centuries of racist imperialism rather different criteria are mobilized, such as showing that black people who live in Zimbabwe (once Rhodesia) have been active participants in history rather than people who were merely acted upon. How best to narrate that tale, however, without mindlessly turning the story inside out, becomes contested terrain in which a new cadre of African historians seeks to strike a balance between national pride, racial anger, and sound scholarship. Once again, the impulses of radical revisionism exceed the norms of incremental revisionism to which we are accustomed in the United States.[26]

To illustrate the politics of collective memory in the Third World with one other example, let us turn to the fascinating case of Iraq, a multi-ethnic and multi-confessional culture that inherited a Museum of Arab Antiquities, a Museum of Costume and Folklore, and even a Museum of Western Art from its colonial past. Between 1962 and 1977 the Baathist regime established nine new museums, especially in provincial cities, in order to bolster its legitimacy by demonstrating Baathist populism as a worthy competitor with communism. The state emphasized popular culture and folklore, and it invented traditions shamelessly in an effort to provide a basis for national unity (among two variants of Islam as well as among Kurds) against the bitter enemy, Iran. The regime used history museums, old and new, as a way to get certain patriotic messages to the general public. By 1990 the president of Iraq himself headed an enterprise called the Project for Rewriting History, a project that involved not merely the politicization of museums but state-sponsored conferences and festivals, craft centers, films, photography exhibits, a revival of handicraft production, and a new passion for Iraqi folklore. The nation-state had taken total control of national memory. There is nothing remotely comparable in American history, either during the years that followed Independence or in more recent decades.[27]

I V

THE PROJECT for Rewriting History had a much larger and more consequential counterpart in the Soviet Union after the autumn of 1987, one that highlights quite dramatically some of the most fundamental differences between the character of collective memory in the free world and in totalitarian states. To appreciate that stunning contrast fully, it is necessary to begin with a look back before 1917 to czarist Russia.

For centuries the notion of Holy Russia had been a populist myth that was basically anti-statist. The notion underwent numerous transformations. During the sixteenth century, for example, a long-standing legend of the saintly princes was absorbed into a new myth of the godlike office of czar. From about 1500 until 1700 the very salvation of Russia depended upon the czar's orthodoxy and personal piety. So secular a figure as Peter the Great undercut that myth, but a new one gradually replaced it in which oppression inflicted upon the Russian people, even their misery, was evidence of "Holy Russia." Oppression sanctified the people who bore it so patiently and demonstrated that Russia had been chosen by God to suffer for a higher, Divine purpose. The spiritual ideal of Holy Russia had been an important concept by which the peasant masses expressed their collective personality against the centralized state by means of the one quality shared by all—orthodox faith. Curiously enough, many among the intelligentsia also sought salvation in the myth of Mother Russia—and that myth (or faith in the myth) persisted for many people beyond 1917.[28]

And then, for seven solid decades, control over collective memory in the Soviet Union became absolute, regulated relentlessly as a matter of ideological policy by the state and the Communist Party. Permissible margins for thinking "otherwise" were narrow indeed. An internationally recognized historian like Roy A. Medvedev, author of a critical book about the Stalin era called *Let History Judge,* received formal warnings in 1983 to stop his "political lampooning" or else face criminal charges. Medvedev responded with an eloquently fearless statement of his own—and then cooled into prudent quiescence.[29]

From the early months of 1987, however, Mikhail S. Gorbachev began to drop enigmatic hints that he might permit a far-reaching re-examination of Soviet history. In February, for instance, he asserted that "there should be no blank pages in history and literature. Otherwise it is not history or literature, but artificial constructions." For years such important Soviet figures as Leon Trotsky, Grigory Y. Zinoviev, Nikolai I. Bukharin (a Lenin loyalist and party theoretician), and Nikita S. Khrushchev had simply been ignored; but once Gorbachev started to propose a growing openness in dealing with the past, newspapers and magazines began very gingerly to test the limits of what could be discussed and what documents might now become accessible. Although a meeting of Soviet historians in April 1987 called for new candor about the nation's past, a backlash by pro-Stalin scholars in the establishment created a kind of six-month stalemate.[30]

Then, on November 2, 1987, Gorbachev gave the long-awaited speech in which he declared that Stalin had been guilty of "enormous and unforgivable crimes," praised Bukharin and Khrushchev, and explained that the U.S.S.R. could take control of its future only if it came to terms with the past. He explicitly linked the lessons of history to the desired success of political, economic, and social reforms that he had set in motion. Although some of his remarks seemed ambiguous—and left reeling writers still unsure of their ground—this speech was not only unprecedented in Soviet annals but a stunning example of collective memory quite literally functioning from the absolute top down—rather different, indeed, from the way it works in the United States.[31]

In terms of sheer scope the speech was a tour de force because it covered the main elements of Soviet history ever since 1917. Presented to an audience of five thousand government officials and foreign dignitaries in the Kremlin Palace of Congresses, it was also nationally televised (all two hours and forty-one minutes) and launched a week-long commemoration of the Bolshevik seizure of power in 1917. The address hedged its evaluations of certain episodes and individuals, thereby causing dissenters to express disappointment. In retrospect, however, it appears that Gorbachev felt some need to reassure conservative party members that he did not mean to threaten the Socialist system and its entire record. As he phrased it before the first hour of his lesson plan had ended, "If, at times, we scrutinize our history with a critical eye, we do so only because we want to obtain a better and fuller idea of the ways that lead to the future."[32]

Soviet historians, journalists, dramatists, broadcasters, and politicians understandably responded warily when the Western media asked for reactions. Kremlinologists all agreed that a pivotal event had occurred, but could not agree in response to the question: How pivotal? As evidence that intellectual confusion reigned at home, all secondary school examinations in history were cancelled in May 1988 until textbooks could be rewritten and published in accordance with Gorbachev's new guidelines. All history exams were supplanted by ungraded "oral discussion of current events." Memory had been effectively suspended. Anthony Lewis of the *New York Times* summed up the perspective of many Westerners once the whole process of revisionism had clearly been initiated: "To open the terrible closed pages of history is necessarily to open minds. Anyone who understands that official accounts of the past are open to question will be more inclined to accept questioning of today's policies."[33]

Between 1988 and 1990 a gradual series of ad hoc steps indicated that Gorbachev's invitation to revise the past would be achieved by increments rather than overnight. During the summer of 1988, for instance, Estonian newspapers published a secret protocol to the non-aggression pact of 1939 in which Stalin and Hitler agreed to spheres of influence that ultimately put the Baltic States under the control of the U.S.S.R. Official Soviet response to those publications was to modify only slightly its customary position that the documents were actually a fabrication by the West to discredit the "truth" that the Baltic States had joined the Soviet Union voluntarily. In April 1990, however, the Soviet academic establishment took a most extraordinary step by inviting fifty prominent Western Kremlinologists and historians to come to Moscow and participate in a four-day discussion whose purpose was to "dissect" and reassess the whole of Soviet history.[34]

In his Nobel Prize lecture, given in 1970, Aleksandr Solzhenitsyn declared that when a nation loses its memory, it loses its spiritual unity and integrity. After seventeen years, a situation that he so deplored had begun to be reversed—from the top down. That underscores a major difference between collective memory in the U.S.S.R. and the U.S.A. In free societies people forget and remember largely on their own, even though their memories may very well receive "assistance" from governmental as well as non-governmental sources; and a free press attempts to set the record straight when a high-level government official misspeaks. In unfree societies the constraints upon memory and amnesia are quite different. Even so, as Gorbachev enlarged his policy of "openness" to include the past, very strange things began to happen. In April 1988 the first issue of a new magazine called *Our Heritage* was published by a freshly established Soviet Fund for Culture, an officially sponsored organization. And a group called *Pamyat* (Memory) held meetings at which anti-Semitic slogans were shouted and other activities took place that were reminiscent of xenophobic nastiness in czarist times.[35] The more things change . . .

V

WHICH leads us, ultimately, to the question: What, then, if anything, is distinctive about the dynamics of tradition and the role of collective memory in American culture? The answer to that question, overall, is a matter of degree rather than one of absolutes, and at least four different categories must be noted: the role of government as a custodian of tradition; the extent to which historical issues are publicly contested; the need or desirability of reconciling tradition with a democratic ethos; and the never-ending dialectic between tradition and progress—values that wax and wane in ways that are interconnected more often than not.

Compared with most regimes elsewhere, the government of the United States is notably non-coercive about national memory, and it is moderately supportive, at best, of traditions (all sorts). Unlike most governments, for example, the United States has no ministry of culture; and legislation introduced in Congress in 1990 to create a cabinet-level department of culture received a tepid response, even from its own official supporters. This is clearly an idea whose time has not yet come.

We have just noted what a difference the Soviet regime makes in its manner of recording and disremembering the past. The same is true, in quite a different way, if we glance at the national control exercised by ministries of education in France, Japan, and Israel over the actual contents of history textbooks used in the schools.[36] For purposes of contrast among non-totalitarian societies, the case of France is highly illuminating. In 1914 the French government established the Caisse Nationale des Monuments Historiques et des Sites. Its American counterpart, the National Trust for Historic Preservation, came into being in 1949 as a non-governmental organization with no commitment of federal support. In 1958 the only line in the proposed national budget that was not cut by the French government was the line for the national folklore museum, the Musée des Arts et Traditions Populaires. During the 1960s it became a policy of the Gaullist government to preserve or revive regional traditions before they became extinct; and folk dancing in traditional costumes achieved increasing popularity as a consequence.[37]

Equally important—and once again it is a matter of degree—issues involving collective memory are not, ordinarily, hotly contested in the United States (occasional exceptions during the Reagan years to the contrary notwithstanding). The fierce public debate concerning historical revisionism in Germany during the mid-1980s provides a stunning contrast. In France ever since 1789, as many observers have noted, conflicting perceptions of the past, especially of the Revolution, have been a deeply divisive rather than a unifying force.[38]

In Czechoslovakia and Romania the "proper" interpretation of historical myths and national legends has been politically contested for centuries. Within Canada the province of Quebec repeatedly demonstrates a passionate (and divisive) commitment to the preservation of its *patrimoine.* And by the mid-1980s Afrikaners found themselves at odds with one another in ascribing "correct" meaning to mythic events in white South African history, such as the Voortrekkers' great migration of 1838 and the Battle of Blood River. The slogan of the dominant Nationalist Party, "Forward South Africa," has gradualist progressive connotations compared with never-say-die Afrikaners on the far right, whose motto is "On Trek to Our Own."[39]

How can this contrast with the United States best be understood? Partially, I believe, because the penchant for amnesia is greater here; but that too is a matter of degree and is a function of yet another phenomenon that we have now encountered repeatedly: namely, the American inclination to depoliticize the past in order to minimize memories (and causes) of conflict. That is how we healed the wounds of sectional animosity following the Civil War; and that is how we selectively remember only those aspects of heroes' lives that will render them acceptable to as many people as possible.[40]

A third degree of distinctiveness—and it too is only that, a matter of degree—seems to be contingent upon the need to reconcile tradition with democratic values, though not necessarily with the practice of democracy.* In Great Britain an enthusiasm for the rituals of monarchy

*On the day of Ronald Reagan's second inauguration (the one that turned out to be so cold that the parade had to be cancelled), ABC News took a half-page advertisement for

has, if anything, increased during the 1970s and 1980s. In Germany there are clear signs of nostalgia for empire, Reich, and Aryan supremacy among segments of the population. In Israel an exclusivist "chosen people" syndrome persists for politically comprehensible reasons. And even in France royalism remains an ideological counterpoint to republicanism even though one must acknowledge an on-going demand for democratization that runs from the Revolutionary era through the writings of Alfred Croiset to the public statuary of Jules Dalou, such as his *Fraternité*, which stands in front of city hall in the tenth arrondissement of Paris—a self-conscious attempt to visualize the political ethos of democracy.[41]

In the United States, however, as we have seen, successful monuments, historic places, and museums increasingly had to be compatible with democratic values and assumptions, whether the site be the Statue of Liberty, the Tomb of the Unknown Soldier, the Lincoln or the Jefferson Memorial.[42] Robert Penn Warren poignantly conceded how often we have fallen short of our ideals, yet he acknowledged that the very shortfall has provided a creative tension for commentators upon the American scene.

> At the same time that we have seized and occupied our continent, our poets have explored the crisis of the American spirit grappling with its destiny. They have faced, sometimes unconsciously, the tragic ambiguity of the fact that the spirit of the nation we had promised to create has often been the victim of our astounding objective success, and that, in our success, we have put at pawn the very essence of the nation we had promised to create—that essence being the concept of the free man, the responsible self.[43]

Finally, there has long been an all-too-casual assumption that progress, or at least the ideal of "Progress," has been an adversary or antithesis of tradition in the United States.[44] Although the two values have often been found in a dialogical relationship of tension, to be sure, there has also been a tradition of progress and a rationale for progress rooted in tradition that dates back to antebellum times at least. As the Chief Justice of Rhode Island put it in 1843: "Yes, let us sanctify the past, and let no hand . . . dare mar its venerable aspect. Change indeed must come, but then let it come by force of the necessary law of progress. So shall the present still ever build and improve on a patrimony formed by the deeds of heroic virtue, and the labors of exalted intellect."[45]

It has been argued compellingly that a combination of nostalgia and progress supplied the dual support system of the frontier myth in American culture. During the 1930s such writers as Lewis Mumford, Carl Sandburg, Stephen Vincent Benét, and Robert Sherwood shared a con-

---

its televised coverage. The lead-in declared, in bold type: CELEBRATE AN AMERICAN TRADITION. DEMOCRACY. (NYT, Jan 21, 1985, p. C26.)

ception of the national heritage that somehow emphasized the progressive aspects of traditional values and institutions. Robert Pinsky's extended historical poem *An Explanation of America* (1979) invokes Nostalgia and Progress as the most characteristic cultural motifs in the United States.[46]

At Disney World in Orlando this bi-form blend is deliberately highlighted in several ways. At the Hall of Presidents, for example, Disney's robotic Abraham Lincoln emerges from the past to make a speech that extends the dream of mastering by means of technology—*à la* Mark Twain's Connecticut Yankee and Henry Ford's achievement of changing the way people live, all the while preserving under glass the way they used to live. The cheery public relations volume that describes Walt Disney's EPCOT explains the criteria that were used in determining how to tell the basic story of America in twenty-nine minutes. What to include and what to omit from their fundamentally upbeat American Adventure?

> The negative aspects of our history are shown, then, but with one proviso: "If the event, no matter how tragic, has led to some improvement—a new burst of creativity, a better understanding of ourselves as partners in the American experience—we have included it."[47]

The most astute foreign observers of the American scene have a marvelous instinct for spotting the anomalies and inconsistencies that inevitably creep in when a culture wishes to cherish both tradition and progress. Take as an instance a single paragraph written by Umberto Eco in 1985:

> At Old Bethpage Village, on Long Island, they try to reconstruct an early nineteenth-century farm as it was; but "as it was" means with living animals just like those of the past, while it so happens that sheep, since those days, have undergone—thanks to clever breeding—an interesting evolution. In the past they had black noses with no wool on them; now their noses are white and covered with wool, so obviously the animals are worth more. And the eco-archeologists we're talking about are working to rebreed the line to achieve an "evolutionary retrogression." But the National Breeders' Association is protesting, loudly and firmly, against this insult to zoological and technical progress. A cause is in the making: the advocates of "ever forward" against those of "backward march."[48]

Within the United States, at least, a pattern is apparent that for innovations and "new traditions" to succeed it helps greatly to build them upon established traditions. The "agrarian myth" associated with Thomas Jefferson took hold so swiftly and endured because it already had roots in an eighteenth-century freehold concept of independent yeomen farmers that antedated Jefferson. The frontier myth enjoyed such widespread appeal at the turn of the present century because it drew upon a tradition, more than a century old, that linked westward expansion with an ideology of American uniqueness and mission. Horatio Alger and Charles Loring Brace were able to trade so successfully on the "country boy" legend in their stories because, we now know, the myth was already well established by the later nineteenth century.[49]

So it has been, so it is, so the pattern very likely shall continue. Americans will historicize the present in a somewhat facile, sometimes inadvertent way, and they will continue to depoliticize the past as a means of minimizing conflict. The party of hope and the party of memory will continue to jostle each other for position, just as they have since the early nineteenth century. Like the two large political parties, neither one is pure or monolithic. Devotees of memory are hopeful as well as wistful, and the advocates of hope do not abandon memory because they really cannot. In examining a nation so noted for mobility—physical and social mobility with their attendant manifestations of amnesia—it is worth recalling the words of the Ba'al Shem Tov, the charismatic founder of Hasidism: "Forgetfulness leads to exile, while remembrance is the secret of redemption."

Acknowledgments

I FIRST BEGAN to explore this path in 1977, and have been following it ever since—despite a few unfaithful detours. If the pursuit has been engaging, it has also been an extraordinary challenge. Ultimately it meant a marvelous itinerary for both personal and intellectual growth, as a quondam colonialist and political historian sought to comprehend nineteenth- and twentieth-century culture at a time when that particular subdiscipline was undergoing a critical malaise that gave way during the 1980s to creative renewal.

Institutions and individuals have helped enormously—many more than I can possibly mention here. Some contributed so much to this project, however, that it becomes a pleasure as well as a responsibility to express my appreciation. In 1980 the government of France created a new chair in American history and located it at the Ecole des Hautes Etudes en Sciences Sociales, based at the Maison de Science de l'Homme in Paris. As the first holder of that chair I explored many of the themes vital to this volume in a course taught jointly with David Brion Davis in 1980–81. Perhaps it was no more than serendipity, but the French Ministry of Culture had designated 1980 as *l'année du patrimoine.* That year as a visitor provided for me a kind of baptism by fire as a comparativist.

In January 1983 I was privileged to give the Paley Lectures in American Civilization at the Hebrew University of Jerusalem. I made a distillation from materials that appear in this book for my three lectures. I will long remember the hospitality extended to me by Emily and Sanford Budick, Yehoshua Arieli, Avihu Zakai, and Arthur Goren. One year later I presented a mini-course along similar lines at Nankai University in Tianjin, China. Among many gracious hosts there as well as in Beijing, Nanjing, Sujhou, and Shanghai, I recall with special fondness the warmth of Feng Cheng-bo, Zhang Zhilian, Qi Wen Ying, and Zhang Meng-bai. My five-week trip was made possible by the Committee on Scholarly Communication with the People's Republic of China.

A fellowship awarded in 1988–89 by the Spencer Foundation made it possible to finish the research and write a draft of half the book. I deeply appreciate the confidence shown by the late Lawrence M. Cremin and by Marion M. Faldet, who administers that Foundation in the least bureaucratic manner conceivable.

During the first half of 1990 I was blessed by the Smithsonian Institution with a Regents' Fellowship. The National Portrait Gallery, a museum of history and a component of the Smithsonian, served as my host, which meant that I enjoyed the collegial warmth of Director Alan Fern, historians Marc Pachter, Amy Henderson, Lillian B. Miller, James G. Barber, and Frederick Voss, along with co-operative and engaging curators like Ellen G. Miles, Wendy W. Reaves, and Robert G. Stewart. I also received every possible courtesy from the able staff of the library shared by the Portrait Gallery and the National Museum of American Art, especially Cecelia H. Chin and Martin R. Kalfatovic. Two curators at the N.M.A.A. came to my aid at key moments: Richard N. Murray in painting and sculpture and Lynda R. Hartigan in American folk art. All in all, my "extended family" at the Smithsonian, and especially my "nuclear family" at the Portrait Gallery, provided a wonderful blend of professional resource assistance and personal friendship. I could not have completed the book in its present form without them.

Closer to home, colleagues and students at Cornell University have tolerated this particular obsession for a long time now. Cornell permitted me sabbatical leaves in 1980–81 and 1988–89 that made much of the requisite reading and writing possible. The History Department's Return Jonathan Meigs Fund helped to defray various research-related expenses. Librarians too numerous to mention at Cornell's fine facilities performed countless essential services; and Robert P. Frankel, my research assistant in 1979–80, took precise notes in such prodigious quantity that I am still using them a decade later.

It is impossible to thank each helpful administrator, archivist, or librarian at every facility where I undertook research; but some of them went way beyond the call of duty in reacting to requests for material or in providing creative responses to my groping inquiries. I think of my former student D. Stephen Elliott, now Vice President and Chief Administration Officer at the Colonial Williamsburg Foundation, and Bland Blackford, Director of the Department of Archives and Records there; Steven K. Hamp, Chairman of the Collections Division at the Henry Ford Museum and Greenfield Village, along with Dr. John L. Wright, Director of Public Programs there, and Douglas A. Bakken, who was Director of the Ford Archives and Tannahill Library when I launched this enterprise; David W. Wright, Registrar of the Pierpont Morgan Library in New York; Joseph W. Ernst, former Director of the Rockefeller Archive Center in Pocantico Hills, New York, who permitted me to work in the family papers at Manhattan's Rockefeller Plaza even before the elegant facility had been set up at

Pocantico Hills in North Tarrytown; Thomas Rosenbaum, thoughtful Archivist at the Archive Center; Joseph T. Butler, Curator and Director of Collections at Sleepy Hollow Restorations (recently renamed Historic Hudson Valley) in Tarrytown; Frances S. Pollard, Senior Librarian at the Virginia Historical Society; Margaret Cook, Curator of Manuscripts and Rare Books at the Swem Library, College of William and Mary; David Moltkey-Hansen, Curator of the Southern Historical Collection at the University of North Carolina, Chapel Hill; Neda M. Westlake, Curator of Special Collections at the Van Pelt Library, University of Pennsylvania; Judith Austin at the Idaho State Historical Society; and in upstate New York, Ellen Fladger, Curator of Special Collections at the Schaffer Library, Union College; and last but hardly least, Amy Barnum, Librarian of the New York State Historical Association in Cooperstown.

I am especially obliged to a group of patient and precise typists who logged countless hours at their word processors with my handwritten drafts and many revisions. Principal among them is Jackie M. Hubble, aided by Dawn M. Drost, Tina Smyers, Kathleen O. Hershner, and Daphne Green (at the National Portrait Gallery). Once again Ann Adelman and Mel Rosenthal applied their superb skills and patience to preparation of the typescript for production; and Anne Eberle undertook the weighty task of making the index with her usual good cheer and masterful professionalism.

Then there are colleagues who gave me critical readings of particular chapters that coincided with their fields or periods of expertise: Paul R. Baker, Richard A. Baker, Sherman Cochran, John Fousek, Amy J. Kinsel, Walter LaFeber, Herman Lebovics, Dwight T. Pitcaithley, Richard Polenberg, Frederick L. Rath, Jr., Robert J. Smith, and Yael Zerubavel. There are also five friends who read it all and responded with constructive candor, occasional skepticism, and encouragement: Jane N. Garrett, my editor at Knopf and an enduring friend for thirty years; Dora G. Flash; Carol J. Greenhouse; James A. Hijiya; and R. Laurence Moore, who provides rigorous dissent when that is needed and probing questions from an angle of vision very different from my own.

Carol Kammen has also read every word critically, and she proofread most of them with me, too. She endured both my presence and my absence. I may never know which was more problematic; but my happiest memories of this project linger from visits that she and I made together to assorted museums, galleries, historic sites, and what the French like to call places of memory.

The book is dedicated to three remarkable individuals whose abiding friendship and professional support over many years have never ceased to please and surprise me: David Brion Davis, who listened to a jejune version of this project when we taught together in Paris in 1980–81; John Higham, whose work on national symbols, identities, and patterns of historical awareness has continually intrigued me;

and the late Walter Muir Whitehill of North Andover, Massachusetts, who was so generous when it mattered most years ago, and whose very life was lived according to the principle that places of memory are highly meaningful.

                                                              Michael Kammen

August 1990
Above Cayuga's Waters

Notes

List of Abbreviations Used in the Notes

AAS	American Antiquarian Society, Worcester, Mass.
AH	*American Heritage*
AHR	*American Historical Review*
ALUV	Alderman Library, University of Virginia, Charlottesville, Va.
APS	American Philosophical Society, Philadelphia, Pa.
AQ	*American Quarterly*
BLCU	Butler Library, Columbia University, New York, N.Y.
BLYU	Beinecke Library, American Literature Collection, Yale University, New Haven, Conn.
CMHS	*Collections* of the Massachusetts Historical Society
CSSH	*Comparative Studies in Society and History*
CUL	Cornell University Libraries, Ithaca, N.Y.
C.W.	Colonial Williamsburg
CWA	Colonial Williamsburg, Department of Archives and Records, Williamsburg, Va.
CWCC	Civil War Centennial Commission
DAB	*Dictionary of American Biography* (1928–)
EIHC	*Essex Institute Historical Collections* (Salem, Mass.)
FA	Ford Archives, Henry Ford Museum, Dearborn, Mich.
FDR	Franklin D. Roosevelt Library, Hyde Park, N.Y.
HEHL	Henry E. Huntington Library, San Marino, Calif.
HUA	Harvard University Archives, Pusey Library, Cambridge, Mass.
JAC	*Journal of American Culture*
JAH	*Journal of American History*
JDR	John D. Rockefeller, Jr.
JIH	*Journal of Interdisciplinary History*
JNH	*Journal of Negro History*
JPC	*Journal of Popular Culture*
JSAH	*Journal of the Society of Architectural Historians*
JSH	*Journal of Social History*
JSouthH	*Journal of Southern History*
MDLC	Manuscript Division, Library of Congress, Madison Building, Washington, D.C.

MHS	Massachusetts Historical Society
MinnHS	Minnesota Historical Society
MMWHC	*Montana: The Magazine of Western History and Culture*
NA	National Archives
NAR	*North American Review*
NAW	*Notable American Women, 1607–1950* (1971–80)
NEQ	*New England Quarterly*
NMAH	National Museum of American History, Smithsonian Institution, Washington, D.C.
NR	*The New Republic*
NYH	*New York History*
NYHS	New-York Historical Society, New York, N.Y.
NYPL	New York Public Library, New York, N.Y.
NYRB	*New York Review of Books*
NYSHA	New York State Historical Association, Cooperstown, N.Y.
NYT	*The New York Times*
PAACS	*Prospects: An Annual of American Cultural Studies*
PAH	*Perspectives in American History* (an annual published by Harvard University)
PH	*The Public Historian*
PMHB	*Pennsylvania Magazine of History and Biography*
RAC	Rockefeller Archive Center, Pocantico Hills, N.Y.
RAH	*Reviews in American History*
SAQ	*South Atlantic Quarterly*
SEP	*The Saturday Evening Post*
SHC	Southern Historical Collection, Wilson Library, Manuscripts Department, University of North Carolina, Chapel Hill, N.C.
SHR	Sleepy Hollow Restorations
SHSW	State Historical Society of Wisconsin
SLWM	Swem Library, College of William and Mary, Williamsburg, Va.
TMA	*The Magazine Antiques*
UCL	University of Chicago Library (Regenstein), Chicago, Ill.
VHS	Virginia Historical Society
VMHB	*Virginia Magazine of History and Biography*
WMQ	*William and Mary Quarterly*
WP	*Winterthur Portfolio*

Introduction

1. See João Ubaldo Ribeiro, *An Invincible Memory* (New York, 1989; first published in Portuguese in Rio de Janeiro, 1984); Charles S. Maier, *The Unmasterable Past: History, Holocaust, and German National Identity* (Cambridge, Mass., 1988); "Soviet Historians Told to Cite the Negative and the Positive," NYT, Mar. 24, 1987, p. A8; Henry Kamm, "Austria Opens a Flood of Wartime Memories," NYT, Jan. 22, 1988, p. A9.

2. Philippe Hoyau, "Heritage Year or the Society of Conservation," *Les Révoltes Logiques,* no. 12 (Paris, 1980), 70–77; Keith Tribe, "History and the Production of Memories," *Screen,* 17, no. 4 (1977–78), 21.

3. André Chastel, "La Notion de Patrimoine," in Pierre Nora, ed., *Les Lieux de Mémoire: La Nation* (Paris, 1986), II, 405–50.

4. See Robert Hewison, *The Heritage Industry: Britain in a Climate of Decline* (London, 1987); Michael Kammen, "History Is Our Heritage: The Past in Contemporary American Culture," in Paul Gagnon, ed., *Historical Literacy: The Case for History in American Education* (New York, 1989), 138–56.

5. See Eric Hobsbawm and Terence Ranger, eds., *The Invention of Tradition* (Cambridge, 1983); Richard Terdiman, "Deconstructing Memory: On Representing the Past," *Diacritics*, 15 (Winter 1985), 13–36; Maurice Agulhon, *Marianne into Battle: Republican Imagery and Symbolism in France, 1789–1880* (Cambridge, 1981); George L. Mosse, *The Nationalization of the Masses: Political Symbolism and Mass Movements in Germany from the Napoleonic Wars Through the Third Reich* (New York, 1975), esp. chs. 3–5.

6. Jaroslav Pelikan, *The Vindication of Tradition* (New Haven, 1984); Marina Warner, *Alone of All Her Sex: The Myth and Cult of the Virgin Mary* (New York, 1976); Yosef Hayim Yerushalmi, *Zakhor: Jewish History and Jewish Memory* (Seattle, 1982); Joanna Hubbs, *Mother Russia: The Feminine Myth in Russian Culture* (Bloomington, Ind., 1988).

7. Bernard Lewis, *History—Remembered, Recovered, Invented* (Princeton, 1975); Leonard Thompson, *The Political Mythology of Apartheid* (New Haven, 1985); Russel Ward, *The Australian Legend* (Melbourne, 1958, 1966); Carol Gluck, *Japan's Modern Myths: Ideology in the Late Meiji Period* (Princeton, 1985).

8. David Lowenthal, *The Past Is a Foreign Country* (Cambridge, 1985); Fred Davis, *Yearning for Yesterday: A Sociology of Nostalgia* (New York, 1979); Nina Tumarkin, *Lenin Lives! The Lenin Cult in Soviet Russia* (Cambridge, Mass., 1983); Robert G. Athearn, *The Mythic West in Twentieth-Century America* (Lawrence, Kans., 1986); Susan Porter Benson, et al., eds., *Presenting the Past: Essays on History and the Public* (Philadelphia, 1986); Michael Wallace, "Mickey Mouse History: Portraying the Past at Disney World," *Radical History Review*, no. 32 (March 1985), 33–57.

9. Edward Everett, "The Circumstances Favorable to the Progress of Literature in America," in *Orations and Speeches on Various Occasions* (Boston, 1879), I, 38–39. For twentieth-century assertions, see Russell E. Richey and Donald G. Jones, eds., *American Civil Religion* (New York, 1974), 39; Godfrey Hodgson, *America in Our Time* (Garden City, N.Y., 1976), 364. For a resounding affirmation of the value of tradition as a bulwark of cohesion, see *Continuity: A Journal of History*, nos. 4/5 (Spring/Fall 1982), a special issue entitled "Conservatism and History."

10. Pierre Bourdieu, *Reproduction: In Education, Society and Culture* (Beverly Hills, Calif., 1977), vi; Nathan Wachtel, "Memory and History: An Introduction," in *History and Anthropology*, 2 (1986), 207–24; Raphael Samuel, ed., *People's History and Socialist Theory* (London, 1981).

11. Richard Johnson and Graham Dawson, "Popular Memory: Theory, Politics, Method," in Johnson et al., eds., *Making Histories: Studies in History-Writing and Politics* (Minneapolis, 1982), 211; Eliot quoted in Stanley Edgar Hyman, *The Armed Vision: A Study in the Methods of Modern Literary Criticism* (rev. ed.: New York, 1955), 61–62.

12. Meyer Fortes, *The Dynamics of Clanship among the Tallensi* (London, 1967), xi.

13. Attention to the politics of culture has expanded noticeably in the past eight or nine years. See Alan Trachtenberg, *The Incorporation of America: Culture and Society in the Gilded Age* (New York, 1982), ch. 5, "The Politics of Culture"; David E. Whisnant, *All That Is Native & Fine: The Politics of Culture in an American Region* (Chapel Hill, N.C., 1983); Robbie Lieberman, *"My Song Is My Weapon": People's Songs, American Communism, and the Politics of Culture, 1930–1950* (Urbana, Ill., 1989); David D. Hall, "On Common Ground: The Coherence of American Puritan Studies," WMQ, 44 (1987), 229.

14. See Merle Curti, *The Roots of American Loyalty* (New York, 1946); and also Wilbur Zelinsky, *Nation into State: The Shifting Symbolic Foundations of American Nationalism* (Chapel Hill, N.C., 1988); David M. Potter, "The Historian's Use of National-

ism and Vice Versa," in Potter, *The South and the Sectional Conflict* (Baton Rouge, La., 1968), 34–83.

15. See John H. Schaar, "The Case for Patriotism," *American Review,* no. 17 (May 1973), 59–99; Charles DeBenedetti, *The Peace Reform in American History* (Bloomington, Ind., 1980); Charles DeBenedetti, ed., *Peace Heroes in Twentieth-Century America* (Bloomington, Ind., 1986).

16. David Montgomery, "Nationalism, American Patriotism and Class Consciousness among Immigrant Workers in the United States in the Epoch of World War I," in Dirk Hoerder, ed., *"Struggle a Hard Battle": Essays on Working-Class Immigrants* (DeKalb, Ill., 1986), 327–51; Wendell Rawls, "In America, Patriotism and Nationalism Are on Rise," NYT, Dec. 11, 1979, p. A20; R. W. Apple, Jr., "New Stirrings of Patriotism," NYT, Dec. 11, 1983, pp. 42–47; Morris Janowitz, *The Reconstruction of Patriotism: Education for Civic Consciousness* (Chicago, 1984).

17. Henry Nash Smith, *Virgin Land: The American West as Symbol and Myth* (2nd ed.: Cambridge, Mass., 1970), 34, 201, 215, 259–60.

18. Christopher Lasch, *The New Radicalism in America, 1889–1963: The Intellectual as a Social Type* (New York, 1965).

19. Quoted in Raymond Williams, *Culture and Society, 1780–1950* (New York, 1958), 11.

20. "Myth, Memory and History," in Moses Finley, *The Use and Abuse of History* (New York, 1975), 26–27.

21. Edward Shils, "Tradition," CSSH, 13 (1971), 126. See also Shils, *Tradition* (Chicago, 1981); Shils, "Tradition and the Generations: On the Difficulties of Transmission," *The American Scholar,* 53 (Winter 1983–84), 27–40; S. N. Eisenstadt, "Intellectuals and Tradition," *Daedalus,* 101 (Spring 1972), 1–19.

22. This has not been a particularly prominent theme in American scholarship; but see Lawrence J. Friedman, *Inventors of the Promised Land* (New York, 1975); Len Travers, "Hurrah for the Fourth: Patriotism, Politics, and Independence Day in Federalist Boston, 1783–1818," EIHC, 125 (1989), 129–61.

23. J. G. A. Pocock, *Politics, Language and Time: Essays on Political Thought and History* (New York, 1971), 80.

24. See Leonard W. Doob, *Patriotism and Nationalism: Their Psychological Foundations* (New Haven, 1964), 3–4.

25. See Gordon S. Wood, *The Creation of the American Republic, 1776–1789* (Chapel Hill, N.C., 1969); Joseph J. Ellis, *After the Revolution: Profiles of Early American Culture* (New York, 1979); H. Stuart Hughes, *Sophisticated Rebels: The Political Culture of European Dissent, 1968–1987* (Cambridge, Mass., 1988), 59.

26. "Patriotism and Nationalism in European History," in J. H. Huizinga, *Men and Ideas: History, the Middle Ages, the Renaissance* (New York, 1959), 97–155, the quotation at 99.

27. See Frederick Merk, *Manifest Destiny and Mission in American History* (New York, 1963); Richard Hofstadter, "Cuba, the Philippines, and Manifest Destiny," in *The Paranoid Style in American Politics and Other Essays* (New York, 1965), 145–87; James M. Mayo, *War Memorials as Political Landscape: The American Experience and Beyond* (New York, 1988), chs. 3 and 4.

28. Timothy L. Smith, "Religion and Ethnicity in America," AHR, 83 (1978), 1155–85, the quotation at 1169.

29. Herbert G. Gutman, *Work, Culture, and Society in Industrializing America: Essays in American Working-Class and Social History* (New York, 1976), esp. 3–78; Daniel T. Rodgers, "Tradition, Modernity, and the American Industrial Worker: Reflections and Critique," JIH, 7 (1977), 655–81, esp. 673.

30. See Morton Keller, *Affairs of State: Public Life in Late Nineteenth Century America* (Cambridge, Mass., 1977), 376; Joseph R. Gusfield, "The Sociological Reality of America: An Essay on Mass Culture," in Herbert J. Gans et al., eds., *On the Making of Americans: Essays in Honor of David Riesman* (Philadelphia, 1979), 61.

31. See Susan Prendergast Schoelwer, *Alamo Images: Changing Perceptions of a Texas Experience* (Dallas, 1985), esp. 102–03; Edward Tabor Linenthal, " 'A Reservoir of Spiritual Power': Patriotic Faith at the Alamo in the Twentieth Century," *Southwestern Historical Quarterly,* 91 (1988), 509–31.

32. See Johnson and Dawson, "Popular Memory: Theory, Practice, Method," 207; Alfred F. Young, "George Robert Twelves Hewes (1742–1840): A Boston Shoemaker and the Memory of the American Revolution," WMQ, 38 (1981), 561–623; Theodore Rosengarten, *All God's Dangers: The Life of Nate Shaw* (New York, 1974).

33. See the perceptive essay by John Bodnar, "Power and Memory in Oral History: Workers and Managers at Studebaker," JAH, 75 (1989), 1201–21; and Schoelwer, *Alamo Images,* plate 17.

34. Geoffrey Elton, *The Future of the Past* (Cambridge, 1968), 9–10; Meg Greenfield, "Chronic Political Amnesia," *Newsweek,* Sept. 22, 1980, p. 96.

35. See Patrick H. Hutton, "Collective Memory and Collective Mentalities: The Halbwachs-Ariès Connection," *Historical Reflections,* 15 (1988), 311–22; and a special issue of *The Psychohistory Review,* 14 (Spring 1986), devoted to the Wellfleet Conference on Historical Memory held in October 1985.

36. *Wallace Nutting's Biography* (Framingham, Mass., 1936), 78.

37. Thayer to Lodge, Jan. 17, 1921, Henry Cabot Lodge Papers, box 65, MHS.

38. John Zukowsky, "Monumental American Obelisks: Centennial Vistas," *Art Bulletin,* 58 (1976), 576.

39. Charles L. Griswold, "The Vietnam Veterans Memorial and the Washington Mall: Philosophical Thoughts on Political Iconography," *Critical Inquiry,* 12 (1986), 700, 708, 712.

40. Charles Reagan Wilson, *Baptized in Blood: The Religion of the Lost Cause, 1865–1920* (Athens, Ga., 1980); Gaines M. Foster, *Ghosts of the Confederacy: Defeat, the Lost Cause, and the Emergence of the New South, 1865 to 1913* (New York, 1987).

41. Ralph Barton Perry, *Puritanism and Democracy* (New York, 1944); Jan C. Dawson, *The Unusable Past: America's Puritan Tradition, 1830–1930* (Chico, Calif., 1984), esp. chs. 3–5.

42. Robert Penn Warren, *The Legacy of the Civil War: Meditations on the Centennial* (New York, 1961), 78; Daniel Joseph Singal, *The War Within: From Victorian to Modernist Thought in the South, 1919–1945* (Chapel Hill, N.C., 1982), 368.

43. See Jean V. Matthews, " 'Whig History': The New England Whigs and a Usable Past," NEQ, 51 (1978), 193–208.

44. Hayden White, "The Tasks of Intellectual History," *The Monist,* 53 (1969), 606.

45. For wonderfully vivid illustrations, see Gerald F. Linderman, *Embattled Courage: The Experience of Combat in the American Civil War* (New York, 1987), 267–70, and Françoise Zonabend, *The Enduring Memory: Time and History in a French Village* (Manchester, Engl., 1984), 200–01.

Chapter 1

1. See Harry Levin, "Society as Its Own Historian," in Levin, *Contexts of Criticism* (Cambridge, Mass., 1958), 171–89.

2. See Peter Burke, "Concepts of Continuity and Change in History," *The New Cambridge Modern History,* XIII (Cambridge, 1979), 6; Claude Lévi-Strauss, *Structural Anthropology* (New York, 1976), II, 268.

3. Quoted in Kenneth Lynn, *William Dean Howells: An American Life* (New York, 1971), 17.

4. See Archibald Kennedy, "Democracy and Literature," SAQ, 12 (1913), 97–108; Henry Seidel Canby, "Literature in a Democracy," *The Century,* 99 (January 1920), 396–401; Robert Penn Warren, *Democracy and Poetry* (Cambridge, Mass., 1975); Henry Nash Smith, *Democracy and the Novel: Popular Resistance to Classic American Writers* (New York, 1978).

5. See Vida D. Scudder, "Democracy and Society," *Atlantic*, 90 (September 1902), 348–54; Scudder, "Democracy and the Church," ibid. (October 1902), 521–27; Charles W. Eliot, "Democracy and Manners," *The Century*, 83 (December 1911), 173–78; John F. Kasson, *Amusing the Million: Coney Island at the Turn of the Century* (New York, 1978), 9.

6. Horace Kallen, *Culture and Democracy in the United States* (New York, 1924); for a contemporary variant of Kallen's point, see David A. Hollinger, "Two Cheers for the Melting Pot," *Democracy*, 2 (1982), 89–97.

7. Alexis de Tocqueville, *Democracy in America*, ed. J. P. Mayer (Garden City, N.Y., 1969), 487.

8. *Philadelphia Public Ledger*, Jan. 28, 1837, p. 2; ibid., June 26, 1837, p. 2; ibid., July 4, 1837, p. 2; *Richmond Enquirer*, May 7, 1839, p. 2.

9. Adams quoted in Clive Bush, *The Dream of Reason: American Consciousness and Cultural Achievement from Independence to the Civil War* (London, 1977), 19; John Zukowsky, "Monumental American Obelisks: Centennial Vistas," *Art Bulletin*, 58 (1976), 574–76. Kirk Savage, "The Self-Made Monument: George Washington and the Fight to Erect a National Memorial," WP, 22 (Winter 1987), 225–42, reveals a curious double standard. Republicanism seems to have been much less of a barrier to the erection of monuments at the state level than at the national level.

10. Nathaniel Hawthorne, *Mosses from an Old Manse* in *Complete Writings* (Boston, 1900), V, 197–99, 214–15, 219, 223, 227; Jaroslav Pelikan, *The Vindication of Tradition* (New Haven, 1984), 30, 40.

11. NYT, July 1, 1888, p. 16. When James Parton's biography of Andrew Jackson appeared late in 1859, reviewers praised its democratic emphasis. His opening chapters seemed "suited to our Western Hemisphere, where men are valued more for what they themselves are than what their grandfathers were—for making than for wearing an illustrious name." See Milton E. Flower, *James Parton: The Father of Modern Biography* (Durham, 1951), 58.

12. Michael G. Crowell, "John Russell Bartlett's *Dictionary of Americanisms*," AQ, 24 (1972), 228–42.

13. Paul R. Baker, *Richard Morris Hunt* (Cambridge, Mass., 1980), 152, 260, 263.

14. George C. Eggleston, *The First of the Hoosiers* (Philadelphia, 1903), 363; Jurgen Herbst, *The German Historical School in American Scholarship: A Study in the Transfer of Culture* (Ithaca, N.Y., 1965), 43, 115.

15. S. P. Langley, *Memoir of George Brown Goode, 1851–1896* (Washington, D.C., 1897), 23, 25; NYT, April 1, 1889, p. 2.

16. Eric F. Goldman, *John Bach McMaster: American Historian* (Philadelphia, 1943), 138, 155; J. B. McMaster, *History of the People of the United States* (New York, 1885), II, 51; Ernest Samuels, *Bernard Berenson: The Making of a Connoisseur* (Cambridge, Mass., 1979), 313, 325, 341.

17. George S. Hellman, *Lanes of Memory* (New York, 1927), 47. See also "The Value of Petitions," NYT, Aug. 12, 1885, p. 2.

18. Morton Keller, *Affairs of State: Public Life in Late Nineteenth Century America* (Cambridge, Mass., 1977), 478; Geoffrey Blodgett, "The Mugwump Reputation, 1870 to the Present," JAH, 66 (1980), 867–87.

19. William O. McDowell to Henry Baldwin, Feb. 15, 1893, and Baldwin to Edward H. Hazen, Jan. 15, 1902, Library Americana, box 3, NYPL Annex, N.Y. City; NYT, July 5, 1889, p. 8.

20. Richard Ruland, *The Rediscovery of American Literature: Premises of Critical Taste, 1900–1940* (Cambridge, Mass., 1967), ch. 1; Levin, "The Tradition of Tradition," in *Contexts of Criticism*, 55–66.

21. Joseph Hergesheimer, *From an Old House* (New York, 1925), 171.

22. Rhodes to Wendell, Nov. 15, 1920, in Robert Cruden, *James Ford Rhodes: The Man, the Historian, and His Work* (Cleveland, 1961), 182; Worthington C. Ford to Philip A. Bruce, Jan. 6, 1921, Bruce Papers (#2889), box 2, ALUV; Albert Bushnell Hart to Worthington C. Ford, Feb. 23, 1910, Ford Papers, box 7, NYPL.

23. Adams to Mark DeWolfe Howe, Dec. 29, 1929; to Henry Hazlitt, Jan. 6, 1930; to Miss McAfee, May 21, 1934, all in the James Truslow Adams Papers, box 11, BLCU.

24. Edward A. Purcell, Jr., *The Crisis of Democratic Theory: Scientific Naturalism & the Problem of Value* (Lexington, Ky., 1973); NYT, May 27, 1935, p. 15.

25. William Dean Howells, "The Modern American Mood," *Harper's Magazine,* 95 (July 1897), 204. See also William James, "The Social Value of the College Bred," in *Memories and Studies* (New York, 1911), 317.

26. Adams to Max Farrand, Jan. 2, 1916, Farrand Papers, HEHL.

27. Jameson to Farrand, May 18, 1932, ibid.

28. Jordan Schwarz, *The Speculator: Bernard M. Baruch in Washington, 1917–1965* (Chapel Hill, N.C., 1981), 112, 305.

29. Ruland, *Rediscovery of American Literature,* 61, 63, 66–70, 73; Jacob Zeitlin and Homer Woodbridge, comps., *Life and Letters of Stuart P. Sherman* (New York, 1929), esp. chs. 24–25.

30. Fred Lewis Pattee, "A Call for a History of American Literature," in *Tradition and Jazz* (New York, 1925), 247; Ruland, *Rediscovery of American Literature,* 190.

31. Charles A. Fenton, *Stephen Vincent Benét: The Life and Times of an American Man of Letters, 1898–1943* (New Haven, 1958), 277, 360–63, 372; Perry Miller, *Nature's Nation* (Cambridge, Mass., 1967), 220.

32. Charles F. Montgomery, "Francis P. Garvan," TMA, 121 (January 1982), 248; NYT, Apr. 18, 1937, sec. 11, p. 7; NYT, April 10, 1939, p. 19.

33. Robert E. Lane, *Political Ideology: Why the American Common Man Believes What He Does* (New York, 1962), esp. chs. 5–6 and pp. 408–09.

34. Hugh Trevor-Roper, "The Lost Moments of History," NYRB, Oct. 27, 1988, p. 67; William McNeill, "Make Mine Myth," NYT, Dec. 28, 1981, p. A19; McNeill, "The Care and Repair of Public Myth," *Foreign Affairs,* 61 (1982), 1–13.

35. Kent Ladd Steckmesser, *The Western Hero in History and Legend* (Norman, Okla., 1965), 5; Henry Nash Smith, *Virgin Land: The American West as Symbol and Myth* (Cambridge, Mass., 1970), 85–86.

36. Quoted in Paul Russell Cutright and Michael J. Brodhead, *Elliot Coues: Naturalist and Frontier Historian* (Urbana, Ill., 1981), 358.

37. See Alan Trachtenberg, *The Incorporation of America: Culture and Society in the Gilded Age* (New York, 1982), 22.

38. Claude Lévi-Strauss, "Overture to *Le Cru et le Cuit,*" in Jacques Ehrmann, ed., *Structuralism* (Garden City, N.Y., 1966), 54.

39. R. Richard Wohl, "The 'Country Boy' Myth and Its Place in American Urban Culture: The Nineteenth-Century Contribution," PAH, 3 (1969), 77–158; Guy B. Johnson, *John Henry: Tracking Down a Negro Legend* (Chapel Hill, N.C., 1929); Brett Williams, *John Henry: A Bio-Bibliography* (Westport, Conn., 1983).

40. Robert G. Athearn, *The Mythic West in Twentieth-Century America* (Lawrence, Kans., 1986), 257. See also Mason L. Weems, *The Life of Washington,* ed. Marcus Cunliffe (Cambridge, Mass., 1962); Brian W. Dippie, *Custer's Last Stand: The Anatomy of an American Myth* (Missoula, Mont., 1976).

41. Adams to Abbé De Mably, c. 1783, in Charles Francis Adams, ed., *The Works of John Adams* (Boston, 1851), V, 491–96; Madison to Edward Everett, Mar. 19, 1823, in Adrienne Koch, ed., *Notes of Debates in the Federal Convention of 1787 Reported by James Madison* (Athens, Ohio, 1966), xxii.

42. See George B. Forgie, *Patricide in the House Divided: A Psychological Interpretation of Lincoln and His Age* (New York, 1979), ch. 1; Ruth Miller Elson, *Guardians of Tradition: American Schoolbooks of the Nineteenth Century* (Lincoln, Nebr., 1964), 313. For the comparably conservative role of schoolbooks in Great Britain, see Valerie E. Chancellor, *History for Their Masters: Opinion in the English History Textbook, 1800–1914* (Bath, Engl., 1970).

43. Sydney George Fisher, *The True Benjamin Franklin* (Philadelphia, 1899), 6.

44. See Thomas L. Connelly, *The Marble Man: Robert E. Lee and His Image in American Society* (New York, 1977); Michael A. Lofaro, ed., *Davy Crockett: The Man, the*

Legend, the Legacy, 1786–1986 (Knoxville, Tenn., 1985); Wyn Wachhorst, *Thomas Alva Edison: An American Myth* (Cambridge, Mass., 1981).

45. Karal Ann Marling, *George Washington Slept Here: Colonial Revivals and American Culture, 1876–1986* (Cambridge, Mass., 1988), 145–46.

46. See Steckmesser, *Western Hero in History and Legend,* 123–24; Baker, *Richard M. Hunt,* 257, 263; Mary Carter Hunt to Lyon G. Tyler, July 17, 1931, Tyler Papers, group 1, box 21, SLWM; David Rankin Barbee to Tyler, Oct. 19, 1933, ibid., group 5, box 9.

47. William Greenleaf, *From These Beginnings: The Early Philanthropies of Henry and Edsel Ford, 1911–1936* (Detroit, 1964), 95–99; Marling, *George Washington Slept Here,* 285–86.

48. Patricia C. Cohen, *A Calculating People: The Spread of Numeracy in Early America* (Chicago, 1982), 150, 152, 154, 168; William Peirce Randel, *Edward Eggleston* (New York, 1946), 96; Arthur M. Schlesinger, "Edward Eggleston: Evolution of a Historian," in Schlesinger, *Nothing Stands Still* (Cambridge, Mass., 1969), 53; Peggy and Harold Samuels, *Frederic Remington: A Biography* (Garden City, N.Y., 1982), 342.

49. Mrs. Fred L. Liebman to John D. Rockefeller, Jr., Jan. 9, 1958, and Kenneth Schlesinger to same, Sept. 11, 1959, Rockefeller Papers, group 2, box 177, RAC; Marling, *George Washington Slept Here,* 315; Marling, *Wall-to-Wall America: A Cultural History of Post-Office Murals in the Great Depression* (Minneapolis, 1982), 106, 224.

50. Ron Powers, *White Town Drowsing* (Boston, 1986), 227.

51. Charles B. Hosmer, Jr., *Presence of the Past: A History of the Preservation Movement in the United States Before Williamsburg* (New York, 1965), 91, 141. In 1891 a Williamsburg antiquarian told the Association for the Preservation of Virginia Antiquities that "all the pretty, picturesque stories" make "history authentic." Quoted in James M. Lindgren, "The Gospel of Preservation in Virginia and New England: Historic Preservation and the Regeneration of Traditionalism" (unpubl. Ph.D. diss., College of William and Mary, 1984), 148–49.

52. W. G. Simms, *The Yemassee: A Romance of Carolina* (1835: New Haven, 1964), 22; Esther Forbes, "Problems of the Literary Craftsman: Historical Novels," *Saturday Review of Literature,* 32 (Apr. 23, 1949), 7–9; Robert Penn Warren, *Brother to Dragons: A Tale in Verse and Voices* (New York, 1953), xii.

53. Ernst Cassirer, *The Philosophy of Symbolic Forms.* Vol. II, *Mythical Thought* (New Haven, 1955), 5.

54. Marc Bloch, *Feudal Society* (Chicago, 1964), I, 92, 99, 102.

55. See John L. Greenway, *The Golden Horns: Mythic Imagination and the Nordic Past* (Athens, Ga., 1977); Michael Herzfeld, *Ours Once More: Folklore, Ideology, and the Making of Modern Greece* (Austin, Tex., 1982); Elton, *Future of the Past,* 9.

56. C. Vann Woodward, *The Strange Career of Jim Crow* (New York, 1955), viii.

57. Paul D. Erickson, "Daniel Webster's Myth of the Pilgrims," NEQ, 57 (1984), 44–64; Bruce Tucker, "The Reinterpretation of Puritan History in Provincial New England," ibid., 54 (1981), 481–98; H. R. Shurtleff, *The Log Cabin Myth: A Study of the Early Dwellings of the English Colonists in North America* (Cambridge, Mass., 1939), ch. 8.

58. Alan Trachtenberg, *The American Image: Photographs from the National Archives, 1860–1960* (New York, 1979), ix–xxxii ("Photographs as Symbolic History"); Neil Harris, "Iconography and Intellectual History: The Half-Tone Effect," in John Higham and Paul K. Conkin, eds., *New Directions in American Intellectual History* (Baltimore, 1979), 196–211; Ron Tyler, *The Image of America in Caricature & Cartoon* (Fort Worth, Tex., 1976).

59. J. H. Elliott, *The Old World and the New, 1492–1650* (Cambridge, 1970), 34–35; Robert Farris Thompson, *Flash of the Spirit: African and Afro-American Art and Philosophy* (New York, 1983), 197.

60. See Frances A. Yates, *The Art of Memory* (London, 1966); Albert B. Lord, *The Singer of Tales* (Cambridge, Mass., 1960); James W. Fernandez, "The Affirmation of Things Past: Alar Ayong and Bwiti as Movements of Protest in Central and Northern Gabon," in Ali A. Mazrui and Robert I. Rotberg, eds., *Protest and Power in Black Africa* (New York, 1970), 427–57.

61. See Sacvan Bercovitch, *The American Jeremiad* (Madison, Wis., 1978); Henry A. Hawken, ed., *Trumpets of Glory: Fourth of July Orations, 1786–1861* (Granby, Conn., 1976); Fred Somkin, *Unquiet Eagle: Memory and Desire in the Idea of American Freedom, 1815–1860* (Ithaca, N.Y., 1967).

62. Robert C. Winthrop, *Addresses and Speeches* (Boston, 1879), III, 81; Cephas and Eveline Warner Brainerd, eds., *The New England Society Orations* (New York, 1901), I, 354–70; Paul D. Erickson, *The Poetry of Events: Daniel Webster's Rhetoric of the Constitution and Union* (New York, 1986), 63–64.

63. Moses Finley, *The Use and Abuse of History* (New York, 1975), 25.

64. E. P. Thompson, "Patrician Society, Plebeian Culture," JSH, 7 (1974), 393; and see David Cannadine, "The Transformation of Civic Ritual in Modern Britain: The Colchester Oyster Feast," *Past and Present*, no. 94 (February 1982), 107–30.

65. H. W. Janson, *The Rise and Fall of the Public Monument* (New Orleans, [1976?]), 21, 39. See also Jacob Burckhardt, *The Civilization of the Renaissance in Italy* (New York, 1958), II, 505.

66. Francis Haskell, "The Manufacture of the Past in Nineteenth-Century Painting," *Past and Present*, 53 (November 1971), 109–20; Charles Dellheim, *The Face of the Past: The Preservation of the Medieval Inheritance in Victorian England* (Cambridge, 1982); James A. Schmiechen, "The Victorians, the Historians, and the Idea of Modernism," AHR, 93 (1988), 306, 309, 316.

67. Olive Anderson, "The Political Uses of History in Mid-Nineteenth-Century England," *Past and Present*, 36 (April 1967), 87–99, 105; H. T. Dickinson, "The Eighteenth Century Debate on the 'Glorious Revolution,' " *History*, 61 (1976), 28–45; Hugh Cunningham, "The Language of Patriotism, 1750–1914," *History Workshop: A Journal of Socialist Historians*, 12 (1981), 8–33.

68. Anderson, "Political Uses of History," 99–104.

69. See Paul Farmer, *France Reviews Its Revolutionary Origins: Social Politics and Historical Opinion in the Third Republic* (New York, 1944); Patrick H. Hutton, *The Cult of the Revolutionary Tradition: The Blanquists in French Politics, 1864–1893* (Berkeley, 1981); William R. Keylor, *Jacques Bainville and the Renaissance of Royalist History in Twentieth-Century France* (Baton Rouge, La., 1979).

70. Alexis de Tocqueville, *The State of Society in France Before the Revolution of 1789 and the Causes Which Led to That Event* (3rd ed.: London, 1888), 9.

71. H. Trevor Colbourn, *The Lamp of Experience: Whig History and the Intellectual Origins of the American Revolution* (Chapel Hill, N.C., 1965); Bernard Bailyn, *The Ideological Origins of the American Revolution* (Cambridge, Mass., 1967), esp. ch. 5; Michael Kammen, "The Meaning of Colonization in American Revolutionary Thought," *Journal of the History of Ideas*, 31 (1970), 337–58.

72. Tocqueville, *State of Society in France*, 11; Shirley M. Gruner, "Political Historiography in Restoration France," *History and Theory*, 8 (1969), 346–65.

73. Nathaniel Hawthorne, *Notes of Travel* (January 1858), in *The Writings of Nathaniel Hawthorne* (Boston, 1900), XXI, 140.

74. Eugen Weber quoted in Natalie Zemon Davis, "The Historian and Popular Culture," in Jacques Beauroy et al., eds., *The Wolf and the Lamb: Popular Culture in France from the Old Regime to the Twentieth Century* (Saratoga, Calif., 1977), 16; Ruth Behar, *Santa María del Monte: The Presence of the Past in a Spanish Village* (Princeton, 1985), ch. 15, the quotation at 275.

75. Behar, *Santa María del Monte*, esp. 267, 269, 276–77, 280–81.

76. As an example of each phenomenon drawn from a very substantial literature, see Robert H. Wiebe, *The Search for Order, 1877–1920* (New York, 1967), and Marling, *Cultural History of Post-Office Murals in the Great Depression*. For a shrewd exploration that integrates the two phenomena, see Barry Schwartz, "The Social Context of Commemoration: A Study in Collective Memory," *Social Forces*, 61 (1982), 374–402.

77. See Robert Darnton, "The High Enlightenment and the Low-Life of Literature in Pre-Revolutionary France," in Harold E. Pagliaro, ed., *Racism in the Eighteenth Century* (Cleveland, 1973), 92.

78. See Bloch, *Feudal Society,* I, 101.

79. Compare Charles C. Alexander, *Here the Country Lies: Nationalism and the Arts in Twentieth-Century America* (Bloomington, Ind., 1980), with W. J. Cash, *The Mind of the South* (New York, 1941); Henry D. Shapiro, *Appalachia on Our Mind: The Southern Mountains and Mountaineers in the American Consciousness, 1870–1920* (Chapel Hill, N.C., 1978); Edward K. Brown, *Willa Cather: A Critical Biography* (New York, 1953); and especially Paul Horgan, "Preface to an Unwritten Book," *Yale Review,* 65 (1976), 321–35.

80. James Sheehan, "What Is German History? Reflections on the Role of the *Nation* in German History and Historiography," *Journal of Modern History,* 53 (1981), 4.

81. See R. Richard Wohl and A. Theodore Brown, "The Usable Past: A Study of Historical Traditions in Kansas City," *Huntington Library Quarterly,* 23 (1960), 237–59; T. H. Breen, *Imagining the Past: East Hampton Histories* (Reading, Mass., 1989), 15, 38–39, 43, 61; Bernard S. Cohn, "The Pasts of an Indian Village," CSSH, 3 (1961), 241–49. Cohn observes that an appeal for action by the government of India, "based on what is thought to be a universal identification with a traditional or historic past, is meaningless or leads to antagonistic reactions of major parts of the population" (p. 249).

82. See Peter Novick, *That Noble Dream: The "Objectivity Question" and the American Historical Profession* (Cambridge, 1988); Erik H. Erikson, *Young Man Luther: A Study in Psychoanalysis and History* (New York, 1958), 37; James A. Sandos, "Junípero Serra's Canonization and the Historical Record," AHR, 93 (1988), 1253–69.

83. See Isaiah Berlin, *Vico and Herder: Two Studies in the History of Ideas* (New York, 1976), 58–59.

Chapter 2

1. Adams to Rush, Aug. 14, 1811, and Rush to Adams, Aug. 19, 1811, in John A. Schutz and Douglass Adair, eds., *The Spur of Fame: Dialogues of John Adams and Benjamin Rush, 1805–1813* (San Marino, Calif., 1966), 185–87.

2. *Notes of Travel,* March 27, 1856, in *Complete Writings of Nathaniel Hawthorne* (Boston, 1900), XX, 59.

3. See David D. Hall, *The Faithful Shepherd: A History of the New England Ministry in the Seventeenth Century* (Chapel Hill, N.C., 1972), 120, 124.

4. Ibid., 150; Sidney E. Mead, *The Lively Experiment: The Shaping of Christianity in America* (New York, 1963), 112; William G. McLoughlin, *Isaac Backus and the American Pietistic Tradition* (Boston, 1967), 2.

5. See Edward Wigglesworth, *The Authority of Tradition Considered. . . .* (Boston, 1778), 13; Carole Shammas, "English-Born and Creole Elites in Turn-of-the-Century Virginia," in Thad W. Tate and David L. Ammerman, eds., *The Chesapeake in the Seventeenth Century: Essays on Anglo-American Society* (Chapel Hill, N.C., 1979), 294.

6. Jack P. Greene, "Paine, America, and the 'Modernization' of Political Consciousness," *Political Science Quarterly,* 93 (1978), 77, 92; Philip S. Foner, ed., *The Complete Writings of Thomas Paine* (New York, 1945), I, 376.

7. Jefferson to Adams, Aug. 1, 1816, in Lester J. Cappon, ed., *The Adams-Jefferson Letters* (Chapel Hill, N.C., 1959), II, 485.

8. Emory Elliott, *Revolutionary Writers: Literature and Authority in the New Republic, 1725–1810* (New York, 1982), 65–66; Jacob E. Cooke, ed., *The Federalist* (Middletown, Conn., 1961), 88. See also James Madison to James Kirke Paulding, April 1831, in Adrienne Koch, ed., *The American Enlightenment: The Shaping of the American Experiment and a Free Society* (New York, 1965), 480.

9. See George B. Forgie, *Patricide in the House Divided: A Psychological Interpretation of Lincoln and His Age* (New York, 1979), 93–94; R. W. B. Lewis, *The American Adam: Innocence, Tragedy, and Tradition in the Nineteenth Century* (Chicago, 1955), 159; George Perkins Marsh, *The Goths in New-England* (Middlebury, Vt., 1843), 7.

10. Emerson, *Nature, Addresses, and Lectures,* ed. by Robert E. Spiller (Cambridge, Mass., 1979), 7, 87–89; Mark Van Doren, ed., *The Portable Emerson* (New York, 1946),

271–84, the quotations at 283–84. See also "Works and Days" in Emerson, *The Complete Works* (Boston, 1912), VII, 177.

11. Thoreau, *A Week on the Concord and Merrimack Rivers* (1849: New York, 1961), 158, 189–90; Kathryn Kish Sklar, *Catharine Beecher: A Study in American Domesticity* (New Haven, 1973), 256.

12. For Melville's *White-Jacket* (1850), see Sacvan Bercovitch, *The American Jeremiad* (Madison, Wis., 1978), 177; for the politics of culture in Thomas Hart Benton's rhetoric, see Henry Nash Smith, *Virgin Land: The American West as Symbol and Myth* (1950: Cambridge, Mass., 1970), 22–27, 37.

13. *Poetical Works of William Cullen Bryant* (New York, 1893), 121; Emerson, *Nature, Addresses, and Lectures*, 230, 244.

14. Lincoln, "Second Lecture on Discoveries and Inventions" [Feb. 11, 1859], and "Annual Message to Congress," Dec. 1, 1862, in Roy P. Basler, ed., *The Collected Works of Abraham Lincoln* (New Brunswick, N.J., 1953), III, 357, and V, 537.

15. Quoted in Thomas J. Wertenbaker, "What's Wrong with the United States?" *Scribner's Magazine*, 84 (October 1928), 433–40.

16. Washington Irving, *A Tour on the Prairies* (1835: New York, 1967), 36.

17. Thomas Cole, "Essay on American Scenery" (1835), in John McCoubrey, ed., *American Art, 1700–1960: Sources and Documents* (Englewood Cliffs, N.J., 1965), 108.

18. Quoted in Barbara Novak, *Nature and Culture: American Landscape and Painting, 1825–1875* (New York, 1980), 226.

19. Ruth Miller Elson, *Guardians of Tradition: American Schoolbooks of the Nineteenth Century* (Lincoln, Nebr., 1964), 37.

20. Alfred Runte, *National Parks: The American Experience* (Lincoln, Nebr., 1979), 21–22.

21. Roy Harvey Pearce, *Savagism and Civilization: A Study of the Indian and the American Mind* (Baltimore, 1965).

22. See Nancy C. Muller, *Paintings and Drawings at the Shelburne Museum* (Shelburne, Vt., 1976), 167 and fig. 419.

23. They are located, respectively, in the Yale University Art Gallery and in the Metropolitan Museum of Art in New York. See also John Neagle, *Henry Clay* (1843) in Michael Quick et al., *American Portraiture in the Grand Manner, 1720–1920* (Los Angeles, 1981), 145.

24. National Portrait Gallery, Washington, D.C., and the Metropolitan Museum of Art on loan from the New York Chamber of Commerce.

25. See Arthur A. Ekirch, Jr., *The Idea of Progress in America, 1815–1860* (New York, 1944); James A. Hijiya, *J. W. DeForest and the Rise of American Gentility* (Hanover, N.H., 1988), 39–40, 73–74.

26. Harriet Beecher Stowe, *Oldtown Folks* (Boston, 1859), iii; Henry T. Tuckerman, *America and Her Commentators* (New York, 1864), 421, 439. Nathaniel Hawthorne offered an overt corrective to the prevailing notion of progress being purely linear: "all human progress is in a circle." *The House of the Seven Gables* (1851: Boston, 1900), 378.

27. See Henry George, *Progress and Poverty* (New York, 1879); T. J. Jackson Lears, *No Place of Grace: Antimodernism and the Transformation of American Culture, 1880–1920* (New York, 1981); Richard N. Current, *Northernizing the South* (Athens, Ga., 1983), 85, 97, 103–05.

28. Ron Powers, *White Town Drowsing* (Boston, 1986), 66, 124. See also the fascinating and germane exchange of letters between William Roscoe Thayer and Henry Cabot Lodge, Jan. 17 and 19, 1921, and between James Bryce and Lodge, Feb. 7 and 23, 1921, Lodge Papers, box 65, MHS.

29. Smith, *Virgin Land*, 35, 38, 40; Merritt Roe Smith, *Harpers Ferry Armory and the New Technology: The Challenge of Change* (Ithaca, N.Y., 1977).

30. Paul G. Faler, *Mechanics and Manufacturers in the Early Industrial Revolution: Lynn, Massachusetts, 1780–1860* (Albany, 1981), 137.

31. See Leo Marx, "The Railroad-in-the-Landscape: An Iconological Reading of a Theme in American Art," PAACS, 10 (1985), 78–79.

32. Belknap to Ebenezer Hazard, Jan. 13, 1784, *Belknap Papers,* CMHS, ser. 5, vol. II, 294–95.

33. Edwin T. Martin, *Thomas Jefferson: Scientist* (New York, 1952), 19; Bancroft to Force, Mar. 21, 1836, Force Papers, MDLC; Tuckerman, *America and Her Commentators,* 429.

34. Adams to Col. Joseph Ward, June 6, 1809, and Aug. 31, 1809, Chicago Historical Society, Chicago, Ill.

35. Paul R. Baker, *Richard Morris Hunt* (Cambridge, Mass., 1980), 186; New York *Morning Herald,* June 21, 1839, p. 2.

36. *Richmond Enquirer,* July 14, 1837, p. 4; Anthony F. C. Wallace, *St. Clair: A Nineteenth-Century Coal Town's Experience with a Disaster-Prone Industry* (New York, 1987), 381–82; Charles Warren, "Fourth of July Myths," WMQ, 2 (1945), 258–72.

37. Francis Jennings, *The Invasion of America: Indians, Colonialism, and the Cant of Conquest* (Chapel Hill, N.C., 1975), Part 1, "Myths of the Marchlands"; David Montejano, *Anglos and Mexicans in the Making of Texas, 1836–1986* (Austin, Tex., 1987), 1.

38. Mead, *The Lively Experiment,* 75–76.

39. William R. Taylor, *Cavalier and Yankee: The Old South and American National Character* (New York, 1961); Larzer Ziff, *Literary Democracy: The Declaration of Cultural Independence in America, 1837–1861* (New York, 1981), esp. ch. 4.

40. Timothy L. Smith, "Protestant Schooling and American Nationality, 1800–1850," JAH, 53 (1967), 679–95, the quotation at 680.

41. J. F. C. Harrison, *The Second Coming: Popular Millenarianism, 1780–1850* (New Brunswick, N.J., 1979).

42. Quoted in Henry F. May, *The Enlightenment in America* (New York, 1976), 349; Perry Miller, *The Life of the Mind in America from the Revolution to the Civil War* (New York, 1965), 215.

43. See Elson, *Guardians of Tradition,* 5 and passim.

44. Smith, *Virgin Land,* 218–20.

45. E. L. Godkin, "The Constitution and Its Defects," NAR, 99 (July 1864), 137.

46. Editor's Table, "The American Mind," *Harper's,* 15 (October 1857), 692, 698.

47. McCoubrey, *American Art, 1700–1960,* 213.

48. Albert Barnes, *Practical Preaching* (1833), quoted in Miller, *Life of the Mind in America,* 68.

49. Deborah D. Waters, "Philadelphia's Boswell: John Fanning Watson," PMHB, 98 (1974), 12–14, 39–40.

50. Lewis Mumford, *The Highway and the City* (New York, 1963), 181–82; Constance Greiff, ed., *Lost America: From the Atlantic to the Mississippi* (Princeton, 1971), 3.

51. *Philadelphia Public Ledger,* Apr. 12, 1837, p. 2.

52. Susan Prendergast Schoelwer, *Alamo Images: Changing Perceptions of a Texas Experience* (Dallas, 1985), esp. ch. 4; Clara Driscoll, *In the Shadow of the Alamo* (New York, 1906).

53. William Paxton to John G. Riheldaffer, Nov. 1, 1849, Riheldaffer Papers, box 1, MinnHS; Charles B. Hosmer, Jr., *Presence of the Past: A History of the Preservation Movement in the United States before Williamsburg* (New York, 1965), 45, 157; C. F. Pisani, "The Tour of Prince Napoleon," AH, 8 (August 1957), 73–75; Grace King, *Mount Vernon on the Potomac* (New York, 1929), 10.

54. *Richmond Enquirer,* July 20, 1838, p. 2; Wilcomb E. Washburn, "Joseph Henry's Conception of the Purpose of the Smithsonian Institution," in Walter Muir Whitehill, ed., *A Cabinet of Curiosities: Five Episodes in the Evolution of American Museums* (Charlottesville, Va., 1967), 106–66.

55. *Philadelphia Public Ledger,* Jan. 25, 1837, p. 4. See also the *Richmond Enquirer,* Mar. 3, 1837, p. 3.

56. Thomas Addis Emmet, *Incidents of My Life* (New York, 1911), 216. For the sad story of how Aaron Burr's papers came to be destroyed, see ibid., p. 218.

57.   Hawthorne, *The Marble Faun* (1860), in *The Writings of Nathaniel Hawthorne* (Boston, 1900), IX, xxiv; Ernest Samuels, ed., *The Education of Henry Adams* (1918: Boston, 1973), 59.

58.   See Gerald Emanuel Stearn, ed., *Broken Image: Foreign Critiques of America* (New York, 1972), esp. 3–80; Peter Conrad, *Imagining America* (New York, 1980), chs. 1–4; Jacob Burckhardt, *Force and Freedom: Reflections on History* (New York, 1943), 85–86.

59.   Matilda Charlotte Frazer Houston, *Hesperos: or, Travels in the West* (London, 1850), 117.

60.   Michel Chevalier, *Society, Manners, and Politics in the United States: Letters on North America*, ed. John William Ward (1836: Ithaca, N.Y., 1961), 321, 406–07.

61.   Frederick von Raumer, *America and the American People* (New York, 1846), Author's Preface. For an interesting variation on this theme in a speech given by John Bright to a Trades Union meeting in 1863, see Samuels, ed., *Education of Henry Adams*, 189. Some enlightened Europeans perceived virtues in republican principles.

62.   See John Lukacs, "Obsolete Historians," *Harper's*, 261 (November 1980), 84; Smith, *Virgin Land*, 41.

63.   See Harry B. Henderson III, *Versions of the Past: The Historical Imagination in American Fiction* (New York, 1974), esp. 83–86 and passim; G. P. Gooch, *History and Historians in the Nineteenth Century* (2nd ed.: London, 1952), 267–68.

64.   Laurent Theis, "Guizot et les institutions de mémoire," in Pierre Nora, ed., *Les Lieux de Mémoire: La Nation* (Paris, 1986), II, 569–92; Charles Rearick, *Beyond the Enlightenment: Historians and Folklore in Nineteenth-Century France* (Bloomington, Ind., 1974); William R. Keylor, *Academy and Community: The Foundation of the French Historical Profession* (Cambridge, Mass., 1975).

65.   Nora, ed., *Les Lieux de Mémoire: La Nation*, II, 355–91; Jerre Mangione, *The Dream and the Deal: The Federal Writers' Project, 1935–1943* (Boston, 1972).

66.   Henry James, *A Little Tour in France* (New York, 1950), 96–97. In 1811 Archduke John established in Graz Austria's first provincial museum. See also Daniel J. Sherman, *Worthy Monuments: Art Museums and the Politics of Culture in Nineteenth-Century France* (Cambridge, Mass., 1989).

67.   Eugen Weber, *Peasants into Frenchmen: The Modernization of Rural France, 1870–1914* (Stanford, Calif., 1976), 57, 396, 428.

68.   Rearick, *Historians and Folklore in Nineteenth-Century France*, 28–29; Marina Warner, *Joan of Arc: The Image of Female Heroism* (New York, 1981); George Huppert, *The Idea of Perfect History: Historical Erudition and Historical Philosophy in Renaissance France* (Urbana, Ill., 1970), 205, 212.

69.   Mona Ozouf, "Les Galois à Clermont-Ferrand," *le débat*, no. 6 (November 1980), 93–103; Carl Schorske, *Fin-de-Siècle Vienna: Politics and Culture* (New York, 1980), xvii, 8.

70.   C. P. Snow, *The Masters* (New York, 1951), 349.

71.   Hugh Cunningham, "The Language of Patriotism, 1750–1914," *History Workshop: A Journal of Socialist Historians*, 12 (1981), 8–33, esp. 9; Rearick, *Historians and Folklore in Nineteenth-Century France*, 163, 170. See also Reuben A. Brower, "Seven Agamemnons," *Journal of the History of Ideas*, 8 (1947), 383–405.

72.   "Vereinigten Staaten" quoted in David Lowenthal, *The Past Is a Foreign Country* (Cambridge, 1985), 110.

73.   Washington Irving, *The Sketch Book of Geoffrey Crayon* in Irving, *Works* (New York, 1980), II, 16–17; Cooper, *Notions of the Americans Picked Up by a Travelling Bachelor* (1828: New York, 1963), II, 108; Robert A. Ferguson, *Law and Letters in American Culture* (Cambridge, Mass., 1984), 188–89.

74.   Rufus Choate, *Addresses and Orations* (3rd ed.: Boston, 1879), 482, 490; and see Waters, "John Fanning Watson," 27.

75.   For Boughton, see Christie's catalogue for March 11, 1988 *(American Watercolors, Drawings, Paintings. . . .),* p. 82, fig. 135; Henry Seidel Canby, "Literature in a Democracy," *The Century,* 99 (January 1920), 398.

76. Tuckerman, *America and Her Commentators,* 439; and see Lewis, *The American Adam,* 23.

Chapter 3

1. See Wesley Frank Craven, *The Legend of the Founding Fathers* (New York, 1956), chs. 2–3; Marcus Cunliffe, *Soldiers and Civilians: The Martial Spirit in America, 1775–1865* (Boston, 1968), ch. 10, "A Southern Military Tradition."

2. See John J. Waters, "Patrimony, Succession, and Social Stability: Guilford, Connecticut in the Eighteenth Century," PAH, 10 (1976), 147; Ronald P. Formisano, "Deferential Participant Politics: The Early Republic's Political Culture, 1789–1840," *American Political Science Review,* 68 (1974), 484.

3. Henry Nash Smith, *Virgin Land: The American West as Symbol and Myth* (1950: Cambridge, Mass., 1970), 76, 88; Maurice G. Baxter, *One and Inseparable: Daniel Webster and the Union* (Cambridge, Mass., 1984), 74.

4. Robert D. Arner, "Plymouth Rock Revisited: The Landing of the Pilgrim Fathers," JAC, 6 (1983), 25–35; Mark L. Sargent, "The Conservative Covenant: The Rise of the Mayflower Compact in American Myth," NEQ, 61 (1988), 233–43.

5. Sargent, "Conservative Covenant," 247–50; Jean V. Matthews, " 'Whig History': The New England Whigs and a Usable Past," NEQ, 51 (1978), 193.

6. Jan C. Dawson, *The Unusable Past: America's Puritan Tradition, 1830 to 1930* (Chico, Calif., 1984), 26.

7. See Michael Kammen, *A Season of Youth: The American Revolution and the Historical Imagination* (New York, 1978), 41–58.

8. Donald E. Pease, *Visionary Compacts: American Renaissance Writings in Cultural Context* (Madison, Wis., 1987), esp. 51–55, 68–76.

9. *Richmond Enquirer,* July 7, 1837, p. 2; ibid., July 11, 1837, p. 3; ibid., July 14, 1837, pp. 1, 4; ibid., July 18, 1837, p. 3.

10. *Richmond Enquirer,* July 13, 1838, p. 3; ibid., July 17, 1838, pp. 1, 2. See also Pease, *Visionary Compacts,* 112–14.

11. I am grateful to Professor Gail S. Rowe of the University of Northern Colorado for calling this to my attention.

12. William W. Austin, *Susanna, Jeanie, and the Old Folks at Home: The Songs of Stephen C. Foster from His Time to Ours* (New York, 1975), 105.

13. *Richmond Enquirer,* July 14, 1837, p. 3; ibid., July 17, 1838, p. 2.

14. See Peter Gay, *Style in History* (New York, 1974), 43.

15. Jefferson to Dr. James Mease, Sept. 26, 1825, in Andrew A. Lipscomb, ed., *The Writings of Thomas Jefferson* (Washington, D.C., 1903), XVI, 123. See also Anthony F. C. Wallace, *St. Clair: A Nineteenth-Century Coal Town's Experience with a Disaster-Prone Industry* (New York, 1987), 380–82.

16. *Philadelphia Public Ledger,* Jan. 26, 1837, p. 4; New York *Morning Herald,* Dec. 25, 1839, p. 2.

17. Paul R. Baker, *Richard Morris Hunt* (Cambridge, Mass., 1980), 172; Russell Lynes, *The Tastemakers* (New York, 1954), 47, 63.

18. David Levin, *History as Romantic Art: Bancroft, Prescott, Motley, and Parkman* (Stanford, Calif., 1959), 25, 56, 79, 94, 116, 127–28, 152–54, 164, 196, 229–30. John Adams also regarded historical writing and interpretation as, above all, a moral matter. See Kathryn Kish Sklar, "American Female Historians in Context, 1770–1930," *Feminist Studies,* 3 (1975), 176.

19. George H. Callcott, *History in the United States, 1800–1860* (Baltimore, 1970), 89, 93, 94, 96–97, 103; Frances FitzGerald, *America Revised: History Schoolbooks in the Twentieth Century* (Boston, 1970), 48–49, 75.

20. *Boston Daily Advertiser,* July 7, 1858, quoted in George B. Forgie, *Patricide in the House Divided: A Psychological Interpretation of Lincoln and His Age* (New York, 1979), 175.

21. *The Writings and Speeches of Daniel Webster* (Boston, 1903), I, 177–254; II, 67–84; XIII, 57–58; III, 277–93; XIII, 390–91; IV, 217–26.

22. Ibid., XIII, 463–97. See also Paul D. Erickson, *The Poetry of Events: Daniel Webster's Rhetoric of the Constitution and Union* (New York, 1986).

23. Job Durfee, "The Influence of Scientific Discovery and Invention on Social and Political Progress" (1843), in Clark S. Northup, ed., *Representative Phi Beta Kappa Orations* (New York, 1930), 75.

24. Susan Prendergast Schoelwer, *Alamo Images: Changing Perceptions of a Texas Experience* (Dallas, 1985), 32.

25. Tuckerman, "Holidays," NAR, 84 (1857), 363.

26. Squier's papers are now located at MDLC. Sketches of Squier, Barber, and William Bacon Stevens appear in the DAB.

27. Deborah D. Waters, "Philadelphia's Boswell: John Fanning Watson," PMHB, 98 (1974), 3–52, esp. 4, 11.

28. Ibid., esp. 4, 10, 11, 15.

29. Marjorie B. Cohn, *Francis Calley Gray and Art Collecting for America* (Cambridge, Mass., 1986), 1.

30. Josephine P. Driver, "Ben: Perley Poore of Indian Hill," EIHC, 89 (1953), 1–18.

31. Henry D. Shapiro, "Putting the Past Under Glass: Preservation and the Idea of History in the Mid-Nineteenth Century," PAACS, 10 (1985), 243–78, esp. 256–60, 267; Alexandra Oleson and Sanborn C. Brown, eds., *The Pursuit of Knowledge in the Early American Republic: American Scientific and Learned Societies from Colonial Times to the Civil War* (Baltimore, 1976), 21–32, 208–18.

32. Woolsey Rogers Hopkins, "Beginnings of the New England Society of New York," in Cephas and Eveline Warner Brainerd, eds., *The New England Society Orations . . . 1820–1885* (New York, 1901), I, 3, 7.

33. Winthrop's address is printed in ibid., I, 213–59. It is *very* long. For the news coverage, see New York *Morning Herald*, Dec. 25, 1839, p. 2.

34. Brainerd, *New England Society Orations*, I, 247–48. As a matter of note to historians, the phrasing of this speech is rather different in the contemporary newspaper account and in the volume published sixty-two years later. The substance remains unchanged, however.

35. See *Compilation of Works of Art and Other Objects in the United States Capitol* (Washington, D.C., 1965), 116–25. The Brooklyn Museum owns a smaller version of Weir's *Embarkation of the Pilgrims* that he painted in 1857.

36. Winthrop, *Oration Delivered before the City Council and Citizens of Boston, on the One Hundredth Anniversary of the Declaration of American Independence, July 4, 1876* (Boston, 1876), 19; Julian P. Boyd, "The Declaration of Independence: The Mystery of the Lost Original," PMHB, 100 (1976), 439, 441–43.

37. Philip Detweiler, "The Changing Reputation of the Declaration of Independence: The First Fifty Years," WMQ, 19 (1962), 572–74; Boyd, "Declaration of Independence," 466.

38. Carolyn Hoover Sung, "Peter Force: Washington Printer and Creator of the *American Archives*" (unpubl. Ph.D. diss., The George Washington University, 1985), ch. 4; John Spencer Bassett, *The Middle Group of American Historians* (New York, 1917), 247, 253–56, 267–70, 300. The partial subtitle of *American Archives* is: *consisting of a collection of authentick records, state papers, debates, and letters and other notices of publick affairs, the whole forming a documentary history of the origin and progress of the North American colonies; of the causes and accomplishment of the American Revolution. . . .*

39. Parton to Dawson, Sept. 20, 1858, quoted in Milton E. Flower, *James Parton: The Father of Modern Biography* (Durham, N.C., 1951), 50.

40. Adams to Rush, Aug. 23 and Dec. 4, 1805, in John A. Schutz and Douglass Adair, eds., *The Spur of Fame: Dialogues of John Adams and Benjamin Rush, 1805–1813* (San Marino, Calif., 1966), 33, 44.

41. Adams to Rush, July 23, 1806, ibid., 60–61.

42. George W. Kelley to Samuel P. Hildreth, Aug. 23, 1852, Hildreth Papers, Marietta College, Marietta, Ohio.

43. Sung, "Peter Force," ch. 6. Thomas J. Randolph sold Thomas Jefferson's papers to the federal government in 1848.

44. Mary C. Simms Oliphant et al., eds., *The Letters of William Gilmore Simms* (Columbia, S.C., 1952–56), I, xcii; IV, 563, 573, 575n.; V, 44–46; Morris Bishop, *A History of Cornell* (Ithaca, N.Y., 1962), 108, 175.

45. Graham H. Stuart, *The Department of State* (New York, 1949), 141–46; Gaillard Hunt, *The Department of State of the United States: Its History and Functions* (New Haven, 1914), 218, 222, 314–30.

46. James Russell Lowell, *Political Essays* (Boston, 1888), 306; Lyman Beecher, *The Memory of Our Fathers: A Sermon Delivered at Plymouth, on the Twenty-second of December, 1827* (Boston, 1828).

47. S. N. Eisenstadt, "Intellectuals and Tradition," *Daedalus: Journal of the American Academy of Arts and Sciences,* 101 (1972), 18.

48. See Kent Ladd Steckmesser, *The Western Hero in History and Legend* (Norman, Okla., 1965), 9.

49. Washington Irving, *A History of New York* (1809: New York, 1964), 115–16, 121, 351; W. G. Simms, *The Yemassee* (1835: New Haven, 1964), 404.

50. Nathaniel Hawthorne, *The House of the Seven Gables* (1851: Boston, 1900), 6, 19. See also Michael J. Colacurcio, *The Province of Piety: Moral History in Hawthorne's Early Tales* (Cambridge, Mass., 1984), esp. ch. 10, "The Death of the Past: History, Story, and the Use of Tradition."

51. Hawthorne, *House of the Seven Gables,* 124, 129, 176–78.

52. Ibid., 356. See also 118, 378.

53. Henry Seidel Canby, ed., *Favorite Poems of Henry Wadsworth Longfellow* (Garden City, N.Y., 1947), 149–50.

54. Ibid., 151.

55. Cecil B. Williams, *Henry Wadsworth Longfellow* (New York, 1964), 158–64.

56. Newton Arvin, *Longfellow: His Life and Work* (Boston, 1963), 154–80.

57. Ibid., 164.

58. Louise Hall Tharp, *Saint-Gaudens and the Gilded Era* (Boston, 1969), 46. He must have liked *The Courtship of Miles Standish* almost as much. In 1872 Saint-Gaudens returned two empty pie plates to a friend. On one he had painted a boy named John Alden, and on the other a girl named Priscilla (p. 49).

59. See Franz Stenzel, *James Madison Alden: Yankee Artist of the Pacific Coast, 1854–1860* (Fort Worth, Tex., 1975), plate C-36. Richard W. Cox, "American Illustrators and the Paul Revere Legend," JAC, 6 (1983), 85–93, notes that Revere had been quite neglected until Longfellow's poem appeared in 1863.

60. NYT, Sept. 30, 1888, p. 4.

61. Adams to Worthington C. Ford, March 9, 1909, Ford Papers, box 5, NYPL Annex.

62. Ibid.

63. *Philadelphia Public Ledger,* Jan. 7, 1837, p. 4; reprinted in ibid., May 11, 1837, p. 1.

64. Article from the New York *Gazette* reprinted in the *Richmond Enquirer,* April 25, 1837, p. 4.

65. *Richmond Enquirer,* Sept. 25, 1838, p. 4; James M. Lindgren, "The Gospel of Preservation in Virginia and New England: Historic Preservation and the Regeneration of Traditionalism" (unpubl. Ph.D. diss., The College of William and Mary, 1984), 182.

66. In 1987 the painting belonged to Judy Goffman Fine Art, 18 E. 77th Street, New York, NY 10021.

67. Morgan to Stone, June 10, 1844, Morgan Papers, NYHS.

68. Ibid.

69. *Compilation of Works of Art . . . in the United States Capitol,* 365.

70. Ibid., 290–92. See also Barry Schwartz, "The Social Context of Commemoration: A Study in Collective Memory," *Social Forces,* 61 (1982), 385.

71. Located in the Delaware Art Museum, Wilmington. For John W. DeForest's fascination during the 1840s and later with the Indians as a vanishing people, see James A. Hijiya, *J. W. DeForest and the Rise of American Gentility* (Hanover, N.H., 1988), 16–19, 140–41. He published a *History of the Indians of Connecticut* in 1851 and a narrative poem, "The Last of the Wampanoags," in 1901.

72. See Sidney Kaplan, *The Black Presence in the Era of the American Revolution, 1770–1800* (Washington, D.C., 1973).

73. See the charming but sad episode reported from Washington, D.C., in the *National Intelligencer* and reprinted in the *Philadelphia Public Ledger*, July 28, 1837, p. 1.

74. Robert J. Cottrol, "Heroism and the Origins of Afro-American History," NEQ, 51 (1978), 256–63.

75. See Sterling Stuckey, *Slave Culture: Nationalist Theory and the Foundations of Black America* (New York, 1987); William H. Wiggins, Jr., *O Freedom! Afro-American Emancipation Celebrations* (Knoxville, Tenn., 1987), ch. 2; Leon Litwack, "Trouble in Mind: The Bicentennial and the Afro-American Experience," JAH, 74 (1987), 321–22.

76. George M. Fredrickson, *The Inner Civil War: Northern Intellectuals and the Crisis of the Union* (New York, 1965), 149–50.

77. Quoted in Drew Gilpin Faust, *The Creation of Confederate Nationalism: Ideology and Identity in the Civil War South* (Baton Rouge, La., 1988), 27; and see Hijiya, *J. W. DeForest*, 54, 74–75.

78. Fredrickson, *Inner Civil War*, 144, 187; Kammen, *A Season of Youth*, 49–58.

79. Alexander Bullock, *The Relations of the Educated Man with American Nationality* (Boston, 1864), 4–5.

80. For a somewhat different but complementary emphasis, see Christopher Kent Wilson, "Winslow Homer's *The Veteran in a New Field*: A Study of the Harvest Metaphor and Popular Culture," *American Art Journal*, 17 (1985), 2–27.

Prolegomenon: Part Two

1. Ernest Samuels, ed., *The Education of Henry Adams* (Boston, 1973), 26, 232, 235, 312, 496–97. Raymond Williams regarded the years 1870–1914 as a distinctive period in the history of British public culture. See his *Culture and Society, 1780–1950* (New York, 1958), 296–97.

2. Russell Lynes, *The Tastemakers* (New York, 1954), 62; Thomas Wentworth Higginson, "Americanism in Literature," *Atlantic*, 25 (January 1870), 60.

3. William James, "The Moral Equivalent of War," quoted in George M. Fredrickson, *The Inner Civil War: Northern Intellectuals and the Crisis of the Union* (New York, 1965), 235.

4. Grafton is quoted in A. Dwight Culler, *The Victorian Mirror of History* (New Haven, 1985), 4.

5. It appears in TMA, 133 (January 1988), n.p.

6. Wendell to Sarah Barrett, June 6, 1905, in M. A. DeWolfe Howe, *Barrett Wendell and His Letters* (Boston, 1924), 170.

7. Peggy and Harold Samuels, *Frederic Remington: A Biography* (Garden City, N.Y., 1982), 134; Moncure D. Conway, *Autobiography: Memories and Experiences* (Boston, 1904), 2 vols. (a work begun in 1897); *Education of Henry Adams*, 43, 48.

8. Brian W. Dippie, *Custer's Last Stand: The Anatomy of an American Myth* (Missoula, Mont., 1976), 1; Charles B. Hosmer, Jr., *Presence of the Past: A History of the Preservation Movement in the United States before Williamsburg* (New York, 1965), 83–84, 90, 103.

9. Hosmer, *Presence of the Past*, 261, 342; H. C. Wood, "Memory," *Century Magazine*, 39 (1890), 776–79.

10. The Rev. Dr. Newell Dwight Hillis quoted in NYT, Jan. 1, 1900, p. 7.

11. See NYT, Nov. 4, 1889, p. 3; James is quoted in Edmund Wilson, *Patriotic Gore: Studies in the Literature of the American Civil War* (New York, 1962), 663; Robert Cruden, *James Ford Rhodes: The Man, the Historian, and His Work* (Cleveland, 1961), 46.

12. Edward L. Pierce, "Recollections as a Source of History," MHS *Proceedings*, ser. 2, X (1895–96), 473–90.

13. Robert Seager II, *Alfred Thayer Mahan: The Man and His Letters* (Annapolis, Md., 1977), 571; Adams to J. Franklin Jameson, April 1, 1910, Jameson Papers, box 45, MDLC.

14. See Daniel J. Boorstin, *Hidden History* (New York, 1987), 284; Barbara Novak, *Nature and Culture: American Landscape and Painting, 1825–1875* (New York, 1980), 177, 180.

15. Mark Twain, *Life on the Mississippi* (1883: New York, 1961), 316; see also Henry James, *The American Scene* (1907: New York, 1967), 19.

16. This was the view of historian Marc Bloch, whose argument is quoted and effectively mobilized by Ruth Behar in *Santa María del Monte: The Presence of the Past in a Spanish Village* (Princeton, 1986), 275.

17. For paintings that are remarkably similar to Johnson's in motif, see John George Brown, *To Decide the Question* (1897), in Natalie Spassky, comp., *American Paintings in the Metropolitan Museum of Art* (New York, 1985), II, 341, and Louis Moeller, *A Discussion* (1890s), in Doreen Bolger Burke, comp., ibid., III, 188–89. In both pictures three elderly, contemplative men sit and reminisce.

18. *Education of Henry Adams*, 382, 469, 470.

19. See William A. Coffin, "Kenyon Cox," *The Century*, 41 (January 1891), 333–37; Kenyon Cox, *The Classic Point of View* (New York, 1911).

20. See F. W. Dupee, *Henry James* (New York, 1951), 119.

21. Thomas Wakefield Goodspeed, *A History of the University of Chicago: The First Quarter-Century* (Chicago, 1916), 266.

22. Lois Marie Fink, "The Innovation of Tradition in Late Nineteenth Century American Art," *American Art Journal*, 10 (1978), 64.

23. Jan Vansina, "History in the Field," in D. G. Jongmans and P. C. W. Gutkind, eds., *Anthropologists in the Field* (Assen, The Netherlands, 1967), 107.

24. "First Inaugural Address—Final Text," Mar. 4, 1861, in Roy P. Basler, ed., *The Collected Works of Abraham Lincoln* (New Brunswick, N.J., 1953), IV, 266.

25. Ibid., 271.

26. *Federalist* number 14 in Jacob E. Cooke, ed., *The Federalist* (Middletown, Conn., 1961), 88.

27. *Federalist* number 51, in ibid., 349.

Chapter 4

1. NYT, Sept. 19, 1889, p. 4.

2. Peggy and Harold Samuels, *Frederic Remington: A Biography* (Garden City, N.Y., 1982), 11.

3. NYT, May 13, 1887, pp. 1, 4; NYT, May 15, 1887, p. 3.

4. For the curious circumstances responsible for a Union Memorial Day held at Charleston, South Carolina, in May 1865, see Lloyd Lewis, *Myths after Lincoln* (1929: New York, 1941), 304–05.

5. Ibid., 309–12. For the claim that Boalsburg, Pa., was the true birthplace of Memorial Day, and for descriptions of the "sacred ceremonies" associated with early phases of the occasion, see Conrad Cherry, ed., *God's New Israel: Religious Interpretations of American Destiny* (Englewood Cliffs, N.J., 1971), 1–4.

6. The picture is located in the Los Angeles County Museum of Art, Los Angeles, Calif.

7. NYT, May 30, 1888, p. 8; NYT, May 31, 1888, p. 8.

8. E. Merton Coulter, *The South During Reconstruction, 1865–1877* (Baton Rouge, La., 1947), 178; NYT, June 19, 1885, p. 1.

9. NYT, June 12, 1887, p. 1; NYT, Apr. 8, 1889, p. 1; Charles Reagan Wilson, *Baptized in Blood: The Religion of the Lost Cause, 1865–1920* (Athens, Ga., 1980), 28, 32.

10. Marcus Benjamin, "Patriotic Societies of the Civil War," *Munsey's Magazine*, 15 (June 1896), 324.

11. See NYT, Sept. 11, 1885, p. 2; NYT, Jan. 14, 1900, p. 9. See also the useful book by Wallace Evan Davies, *Patriotism on Parade: The Story of Veterans' and Hereditary Organizations in America, 1783–1900* (Cambridge, Mass., 1955), chs. 9–11.

12. NYT, July 2, 1888, p. 8; NYT, Oct. 20, 1889, p. 2; NYT, Nov. 26, 1889, p. 9.

13. NYT, July 5, 1887, pp. 3, 5.

14. NYT, July 5, 1888, p. 2.

15. NYT, Dec. 23, 1888, p. 16.

16. NYT, Aug. 20, 1885, p. 3.

17. NYT, June 20, 1887, p. 1; NYT, July 15, 1887, p. 2.

18. "The Confederate Veterans Re-Union at Nashville," *Scribner's Magazine*, 22 (September 1897), 394–95.

19. Davies, *Patriotism on Parade*, 352–53. See, for purposes of comparison, Robert W. Johannsen, *To the Halls of the Montezumas: The Mexican War in the American Imagination* (New York, 1985), esp. ch. 10.

20. See Paul H. Buck, *The Road to Reunion, 1865–1900* (Boston, 1937).

21. See reports from several New Orleans newspapers reprinted in NYT, Apr. 10, 1887, p. 6, and Apr. 24, 1887, p. 11.

22. NYT, Sept. 23, 1887, p. 1; NYT, Feb. 23, 1888, p. 5.

23. NYT, Aug. 1, 1889, p. 5; NYT, Sept. 21, 1889, p. 2.

24. NYT, Oct. 19, 1887, p. 3.

25. NYT, May 5, 1901, p. 3.

26. NYT, Aug. 1, 1889, p. 4.

27. NYT, Apr. 12, 1888, p. 8; NYT, Apr. 27, 1888, pp. 1, 2.

28. NYT, Nov. 29, 1902, p. 1; NYT, June 2, 1903, p. 8.

29. Edward Chase Kirkland, *Charles Francis Adams, Jr., 1835–1915* (Cambridge, Mass., 1965), 207; Thomas L. Connelly, *The Marble Man: Robert E. Lee and His Image in American Society* (New York, 1977), ch. 4, "Birth of a National Hero."

30. Michael Davis, *The Image of Lincoln in the South* (Knoxville, Tenn., 1971), 165–67.

31. Charles Rollinson Lamb to Tyler, July 3, 1908, and Tyler to Lamb, Sept. 2, 1908, Tyler Papers, group 5, box 3, SLWM.

32. Hayne to Margaret J. Preston, Dec. 15, 1871, in Rayburn S. Moore, ed., *A Man of Letters in the Nineteenth-Century South: Selected Letters of Paul Hamilton Hayne* (Baton Rouge, La., 1982), 93.

33. Hayne to Charles Gayarré, Jan. 27, 1885, in ibid., 239. For more of the same, see ibid., 240–41.

34. NYT, Aug. 4, 1889, p. 15.

35. A copy of the 1873 circular will be found in the William W. Corcoran Papers, vol. 20, fols. 286–89, MDLC.

36. Rollin G. Osterweis, *The Myth of the Lost Cause, 1865–1900* (Hamden, Conn., 1973), 9.

37. "Memory-fraught Richmond, the Soldier's Mecca," *Confederate Veteran*, 16 (April 1906), 175; Wilson, *Baptized in Blood*, 18; William B. Hesseltine and Larry Gara, eds., "The Historical Fraternity: Correspondence of Historians Grigsby, Henry, and Draper," VMHB, 61 (1953), 453.

38. Arthur Yager to Hart, Jan. 7, 1888, Hart Papers, box 19, HUA.

39. Henry E. Chambers, *A Higher History of the United States* (New Orleans, 1889), 414.

40. Brock served as corresponding secretary of the Virginia Historical Society (1875–93) and as secretary of the Southern Historical Society (1887–1914). His extensive collec-

tion of papers and correspondence (some 50,000 items) is located at the Henry E. Huntington Library in San Marino, California. His clients complained bitterly about his fees
for genealogical information.

41. J. William Jones to Johnston, June 14, 1899, Johnston Papers, box 1, ALUV.

42. All of Johnston's papers, including her manuscript autobiography and her short
essay on Lee, are located in the ALUV. See C. Ronald Cella, *Mary Johnston* (Boston,
1981); Lawrence G. Nelson, "Mary Johnston and the Historic Imagination" in
R. C. Simonini, Jr., ed., *Southern Writers: Appraisals in Our Time* (Charlottesville, Va.,
1961), 71–102.

43. Ellen Glasgow, *The Sheltered Life* (New York, 1932), 148, 156; and see 199, 208.
Glasgow's autobiography, *The Woman Within* (1954), is interesting although tantaliz-
ingly cryptic at times. See also C. Hugh Holman, "Ellen Glasgow and History: The
Battle-Ground," PAACS, 2 (1976), 385–98; Dorothy M. Scura, "Ellen Glasgow's Virginia,"
VMHB, 94 (1986), 40–59.

44. See Thomas Nelson Page, *In Ole Virginia* (New York, 1887); *Red Rock: A Chronicle of Reconstruction* (New York, 1898); and *The Old Dominion* (New York, 1908).

45. Wayne Mixon, "Joel Chandler Harris, the Yeoman Tradition, and the New South
Movement," *Georgia Historical Quarterly*, 61 (1977), 308–17.

46. Arlin Turner, "George W. Cable's Use of the Past," *Mississippi Quarterly*, 30
(1977), 512–16.

47. See Dan T. Carter, "From the Old South to the New: Another Look at the Theme
of Change and Continuity," in Walter J. Fraser, Jr., and Winfred B. Moore, Jr., eds., *From
the Old South to the New: Essays on the Transitional South* (Westport, Conn., 1981),
23–32.

48. Charles Washington Coleman, "Along the Lower James," *The Century*, 41 (January 1891), 333.

49. Owen Wister, "The Charleston Exposition," *The Century*, 64 (May 1902), 161–62;
James B. Townsend, "A Point Concerning the Charleston Exposition," ibid. (August
1902), 807.

50. Quoted in Arthur S. Link, *Wilson: The Road to the White House* (Princeton,
1947), 4.

51. Robert Dallek, *Democrat and Diplomat: The Life of William E. Dodd* (New York,
1968), 11, 17.

52. Thomas Hart Benton, *An Artist in America* (4th ed.: Columbia, Mo., 1983), 3–4.

53. NYT, May 31, 1887, p. 5; NYT, June 21, 1903, p. 9.

54. NYT, June 17, 1887, pp. 1, 4; NYT, June 18, 1887, p. 1.

55. John Hammond Moore, "William Cabell Bruce, Henry Cabot Lodge, and the
Distribution of Ability in the United States," VMHB, 86 (1978), 355–61. For an echo and
rebuttal to Lodge more than a generation later, see Dumas Malone, "The Geography of
American Achievement," *Atlantic*, 154 (December 1934), 669–79.

56. NYT, Jan. 27, 1903, p. 3; Connelly, *The Marble Man*, 115–22.

57. See Christopher D. Geist, "Historic Sites and Monuments as Icons," in Ray B.
Browne and Marshall Fishwick, eds., *Icons of America* (Bowling Green, Ohio, 1978),
57–66.

58. NYT, Feb. 6, 1902, p. 8.

59. Paul R. Baker, *Richard Morris Hunt* (Cambridge, Mass., 1980), 144–45, 300; NYT,
Oct. 30, 1889, p. 8; NYT, Oct. 31, 1889, pp. 1, 4.

60. John Zukowsky, "Monumental American Obelisks: Centennial Vistas," *Art Bulletin*, 58 (1976), 576–78; NYT, Oct. 20, 1887, p. 1; NYT, Oct. 22, 1887, p. 4.

61. NYT, Aug. 12, 1885, p. 5; NYT, Aug. 13, 1885, p. 3; NYT, Aug. 14, 1885, p. 4; NYT,
Aug. 28, 1889, p. 4.

62. NYT, Mar. 26, 1887, p. 4; NYT, Apr. 12, 1887, p. 1; NYT, Sept. 28, 1889, p. 8; NYT,
Oct. 4, 1889, p. 9; NYT, Oct. 5, 1889, p. 3.

63. Neil Harris, "The Battle for Grant's Tomb," AH, 36 (August 1985), 70–79; NYT,
Apr. 28, 1939, p. 27.

64. Connelly, *The Marble Man,* 97–98; Osterweis, *Myth of the Lost Cause,* 61; NYT, June 16, 1885, p. 2.

65. Stephen Davis, "Empty Eyes, Marble Hand: The Confederate Monument and the South," JPC, 16 (1982), 2–21; John Windberry, "Lest We Forget: The Confederate Monument in the Southern Townscape," *Southeastern Geographer,* 23 (1983), 107–21.

66. Davis, "The Confederate Monument and the South," 7, 13, 16; Gaines M. Foster, *Ghosts of the Confederacy: Defeat, The Lost Cause, and the Emergence of the New South* (New York, 1987), 128–32.

67. NYT, Sept. 9, 1889, p. 8.

68. NYT, July 6, 1889, p. 2.

69. Foster, *Ghosts of the Confederacy,* 116, 172; Wilson, *Baptized in Blood,* 26; and esp. NYT, Nov. 27, 1889, p. 1, the report of a passionate protest against plans by the Richmond School Board to demolish the mansion that Davis had lived in as President.

70. NYT, Mar. 6, 1887, p. 3; NYT, Apr. 10, 1887, p. 9; NYT, Dec. 16, 1889, p. 9.

71. NYT, Sept. 19, 1889, pp. 1, 4; NYT, Sept. 20, 1889, p. 2.

72. NYT, Aug. 11, 1988, p. A18; NYT, Sept. 16, 1988, p. A16; NYT, Nov. 2, 1988, p. A24.

73. George H. Putnam, *Memories of a Publisher, 1865–1915* (New York, 1915), 72; a copy of Jacobs's flyer is in the Worthington C. Ford Papers, NYPL Annex.

74. See the extended review of John D. Champlin's *Young Folks History of the War for the Union* that appeared in *The Century,* 23 (January 1882), 473; and E. S. Ellis to Lyon G. Tyler, Jan. 5, 1901, Tyler Papers, group 5, box 2, SLWM.

75. "School Histories of the Civil War," *Literary Digest,* 14 (1897), 755–56; Eric F. Goldman, *John Bach McMaster: American Historian* (Philadelphia, 1943), 80–81, 85.

76. Warner's book is reviewed and quoted in NYT, Aug. 4, 1889, p. 12. See also Albert B. Hart to James K. Hosmer, Feb. 9, 1907, Hosmer Papers, reserve file, MinnHS.

77. See Ruth Miller Elson, *Guardians of Tradition: American Schoolbooks of the Nineteenth Century* (Lincoln, Nebr., 1964), 177; Adams to J. Franklin Jameson, Apr. 30, 1890, Jameson Papers, box 46, MDLC.

78. NYT, Jan. 31, 1887, p. 8; NYT, Feb. 13, 1887, pp. 1, 2; NYT, Apr. 28, 1887, p. 5; and esp. ibid., p. 4.

79. Morton Keller, *Affairs of State: Public Life in Late Nineteenth Century America* (Cambridge, Mass., 1977), 544, 561; NYT, July 1, 1889, p. 4.

80. See the interesting accounts of Tammany Hall's carefully planned celebrations in 1887, and the positive responses by New Yorkers to a "long talk" by Governor Fitzhugh Lee of Virginia. NYT, June 26, 1887, p. 10; NYT, July 5, 1887, p. 8.

81. David W. Blight, " 'For Something Beyond the Battlefield': Frederick Douglass and the Struggle for the Memory of the Civil War," JAH, 75 (1989), 1156–78, the quotations at 1160–61.

82. NYT, Nov. 15, 1888, p. 4; Dennis P. Ryan, "The Crispus Attucks Monument Controversy of 1887," *Negro History Bulletin,* 40 (1977), 656–57.

83. In 1897 Booker T. Washington was the featured speaker at the dedication of the Robert Gould Shaw Monument on Beacon Street in Boston. Shaw rides solemnly on a spirited stallion, surrounded by earnestly marching blacks. See Louis R. Harlan, *Booker T. Washington: The Making of a Black Leader, 1856–1901* (New York, 1972), 236.

84. Eric Foner, *Reconstruction: America's Unfinished Revolution, 1863–1877* (New York, 1988), esp. 78–79; Leon F. Litwack, *Been in the Storm So Long: The Aftermath of Slavery* (New York, 1979).

85. William H. Wiggins, Jr., *O Freedom! Afro-American Emancipation Celebrations* (Knoxville, Tenn., 1987), xviii–xx.

86. NYT, June 19, 1885, p. 4 (a report from Scranton, Pa., where the principal speaker was John R. Lynch, a black former congressman from Mississippi); NYT, Aug. 7, 1885, p. 5 (a report from Rochester, N.Y.); and Blight, "Frederick Douglass and the Struggle for the Memory of the Civil War," 1175.

87. NYT, Nov. 21, 1887, p. 8; NYT, Nov. 25, 1887, p. 5.

88. R. R. Wright (president of the Georgia State Industrial College for Colored Youths, in Savannah) to Victor H. Paltsits, Feb. 16, 1907, Paltsits Papers, box 2, NYHS.

89. See John Hope Franklin, *George Washington Williams: A Biography* (Chicago, 1985), chs. 8–9.

90. NYT, Sept. 3, 1889, p. 5; NYT, Aug. 12, 1885, p. 3; Frank E. Vandiver, "Jefferson Davis—Leader Without Legend," JSH, 43 (1977), 3–18.

91. Roy F. Nichols, "United States versus Jefferson Davis, 1865–1869," AHR, 31 (1926), 266–84; Burton N. Harrison, "The Capture of Jefferson Davis," *The Century*, 27 (November 1883), 130–45; Zukowsky, "Monumental American Obelisks," 578. The Saratoga Battle Monument at Schuylerville, New York, begun in 1877 and completed in 1882, included bronze statues in three of its four niches (of Gates, Schuyler, and Morgan). The fourth niche was left deliberately vacant as a visual-moral lesson. It *would* have held a statue of Arnold had he not subsequently defected to the British side.

92. NYT, Apr. 7, 1887, p. 1; NYT, Apr. 17, 1887, p. 1; NYT, Apr. 24, 1887, p. 7; NYT, May 8, 1887, p. 1; NYT, July 1, 1887, p. 1; NYT, July 2, 1887, p. 4.

93. NYT, May 30, 1902, p. 1; NYT, May 26, 1888, p. 1; Foster, *Ghosts of the Confederacy*, 97–98, 136–37.

94. Wilson, *Baptized in Blood*, 18–19, 25; Davis, *Image of Lincoln in the South*, 141, 164–65.

95. NYT, May 31, 1908, p. 4 of the *Magazine* sec.; Charles Francis Adams, Jr., to J. Franklin Jameson, May 2, 1911, Jameson Papers, box 45, MDLC.

96. "A Memorial Tribute to Jefferson Davis, 1808–1908," Tyler Family Papers, group 1, box 24, SLWM; Enoch M. Banks, "A Semi-Centennial View of Secession," *Independent*, 70 (Feb. 9, 1911), 299–303; ibid. (Apr. 13, 1911), 806–07, and (Apr. 27, 1911), 900; Coulter, *The South During Reconstruction*, 176–77; Charles A. Fenton, *Stephen Vincent Benét: The Life and Times of an American Man of Letters, 1898–1943* (New Haven, 1958), 27.

97. Tyler to Charles Rollinson Lamb, Sept. 2, 1908, Tyler Papers, group 5, box 3, SLWM.

98. Ibid.

99. NYT, Feb. 26, 1888, p. 11; NYT, Nov. 2, 1888, p. 6; Davis, *Image of Lincoln in the South*, esp. chs. 4–5; Harold Holzer et al., *Changing the Lincoln Image* (Fort Wayne, Ind., 1985).

100. David Donald, "The Folklore Lincoln," in *Lincoln Reconsidered: Essays on the Civil War Era* (New York, 1956), 144–66, esp. 164–65.

101. See Lewis, *Myths After Lincoln;* Roy P. Basler, *The Lincoln Legend: A Study in Changing Conceptions* (Boston, 1935); NYT, Sept. 30, 1885, p. 4; NYT, Feb. 16, 1887, p. 2; NYT, Oct. 25, 1887, p. 3.

102. Quoted in Benjamin P. Thomas, *Portrait for Posterity: Lincoln and His Biographers* (New Brunswick, N.J., 1947), 60. In 1903 T.R. sent this message to the New York Republican Club: "All believers in the country should do everything in their power to keep alive the memory of Abraham Lincoln." Donald, *Lincoln Reconsidered*, 10–11.

103. Whitman to Horace Traubel, Oct. 27, 1888, in Traubel, *With Whitman in Camden* (New York, 1908), II, 543. See also Whitman, "Memories of President Lincoln" (written 1871–81 and 1888), in Louis Untermeyer, ed., *The Poetry and Prose of Walt Whitman* (New York, 1949), 319–27, and Wilson, *Patriotic Gore*, 785, where a letter from Oliver Wendell Holmes to Albert Beveridge is quoted: "Until I was middle-aged I never doubted that I was witnessing the growth of a myth [concerning Lincoln's greatness]."

104. NYT, Oct. 21, 1888, p. 19.

105. Donald, *Lincoln Reconsidered*, 10; G. P. Putnam's Sons to Andrew C. McLaughlin, April 5, 1905, McLaughlin Papers, box 1, UCL; Twain's letter to the editor, NYT, Jan. 13, 1907, p. 8.

106. Marcus Cunliffe, *The Doubled Images of Lincoln and Washington* (Gettysburg College, Pa., 1988), 9, 14, 25.

107. For the importance of Lincoln in American iconography of the late nineteenth century, see John Wilmerding, *Important Information Inside: The Art of John F. Peto and*

the Idea of Still-Life Painting in Nineteenth-Century America (Washington, D.C., 1983), 186, 189, 193–98, and the bronze statue of Lincoln standing (1878), by Truman Bartlett, located in the Louis A. Warren Lincoln Library and Museum, Fort Wayne, Ind.

108. NYT, Feb. 23, 1887, p. 4; NYT, Feb. 23, 1888, p. 2. See also NYT, Feb. 13, 1888, p. 1; NYT, Sept. 29, 1889, p. 11.

109. See Karal Ann Marling, *George Washington Slept Here: Colonial Revivals and American Culture, 1876–1986* (Cambridge, Mass., 1988), chs. 2–5; NYT, Aug. 4, 1889, p. 12.

110. J. A. C. Chandler to J. Franklin Jameson, June 7, 1907, Jameson Papers, box 99, MDLC. See also Pierre Sorlin, *The Film in History: Restaging the Past* (Totowa, N.J., 1980), 44.

111. Swanson in "Jamestown Day Last Monday," *Virginia Gazette*, May 18, 1907, quoted in James M. Lindgren, "The Gospel of Preservation in Virginia and New England: Historic Preservation and the Regeneration of Traditionalism" (unpubl. Ph.D. diss., The College of William and Mary, 1984), 154–55.

112. "A Bivouac of the Dead" (1903) in *The Collected Works of Ambrose Bierce* (New York, 1912), XI, 395–98, the quotation at 398. See also the shrewd analysis in Gerald F. Linderman, *Embattled Courage: The Experience of Combat in the American Civil War* (New York, 1987), 267–70.

Chapter 5

1. A. Lawrence Lowell, *Essays on Government* (Boston, 1889), 107.

2. Brooks Adams, "The Consolidation of the Colonies," *Atlantic*, 55 (March 1885), 307–08; J. R. Lowell, "Under the Old Elm," *The Complete Poetical Works of James Russell Lowell: Poems* (Boston, 1890), IV, 79–80.

3. Mark Twain, *Life on the Mississippi* (1883: New York, 1961), 15; Bernard DeVoto, *Mark Twain's America* (Boston, 1932), 195, 207.

4. R. W. B. Lewis, *Edith Wharton: A Biography* (New York, 1975), 143, 169, 313. The quotation is from a letter to Sara Norton, undated but presumably late nineteenth century.

5. Compare Adams, *History of the United States of America During the Administrations of Jefferson and Madison* (New York, 1891), IX, 224, with Thanet, "Folk-Lore in Arkansas," *Journal of American Folklore*, 5 (1892), 122.

6. Wilde, *A Woman of No Importance*, Act 1, quoted in Peter Conrad, *Imagining America* (New York, 1980), 67; Paul C. J. Bourget, *Outre-Mer: Impressions of America* (New York, 1895), 53; David A. Shannon, ed., *Beatrice Webb's American Diary, 1898* (Madison, Wis., 1963), 70–71.

7. Dec. 5, 1876, in James D. Richardson, comp., *Messages and Papers of the Presidents, 1789–1897* (Washington, D.C., 1897), VII, 399–400.

8. Paul A. Carter, *The Spiritual Crisis of the Gilded Age* (DeKalb, Ill., 1971), 164–75; Evarts, "Oration," July 4, 1876, in Henry Nash Smith, ed., *Popular Culture and Industrialism, 1865–1890* (New York, 1967), 3–18.

9. Milton E. Flower, *James Parton: The Father of Modern Biography* (Durham, N.C., 1951), 126, 129, 133, 168.

10. James D. McCabe, *The Illustrated History of the Centennial Exhibition* (Cincinnati, 1876), 723. See the painting by Montgomery Tiers, *Centennial Progress U.S.A. July 4, 1876* (painted at New York in 1875), reproduced in *Art News*, 76 (November 1977), 3.

11. *New-York Tribune Guide to the Exhibition* (New York, 1876), 707–08. See also Karal Ann Marling, *George Washington Slept Here: Colonial Revivals and American Culture, 1876–1986* (Cambridge, Mass., 1988), 40–42.

12. Edward H. Knight, "The First Century of the Republic, Introduction: Our Colonial Progress," *Harper's*, 49 (November 1874), 861–78; "Mechanical Progress," 50 (December 1874), 67–92.

13. Quoted in Charles B. Hosmer, Jr., *Presence of the Past: A History of the Preservation Movement in the United States before Williamsburg* (New York, 1965), 10.

14. NYT *Magazine*, Feb. 28, 1909, p. 7.

15. See, however, Robert W. Rydell, "The Fan Dance of Science: American World's Fairs in the Great Depression," *Isis*, 76 (1985), 525–42.

16. Winthrop, "Centennial Oration," in Winthrop, *Addresses and Speeches on Various Occasions* (Boston, 1879), III, 413.

17. Quoted in Brian W. Dippie, *Custer's Last Stand: The Anatomy of an American Myth* (Missoula, Mont., 1976), 13.

18. The literature is rich, but see especially Robert W. Rydell, *All the World's a Fair: Visions of Empire at American International Expositions, 1876–1916* (Chicago, 1984), ch. 1; Marling, *George Washington Slept Here*, ch. 2.

19. See Robert Post, ed., *1876: A Centennial Exhibition* (Washington, D.C., 1976).

20. See Dee Brown, *The Year of the Century: 1876* (New York, 1976).

21. "The Home of Washington," *Harper's Weekly*, 18 (March 1876), 223; Howells, "A Sennight of the Centennial," *Atlantic*, 38 (July 1876), 103; Howells, "The New Historical Romances," NAR, 171 (December 1900), 935–48.

22. Robert Swain Peabody quoted in Vincent J. Scully, Jr., *The Shingle Style and the Stick Style* (2nd ed.: New Haven, 1971), 44.

23. See Allen C. Beach, *The Centennial Celebrations of the State of New York* (Albany, 1879); Michael Kammen, *A Machine That Would Go of Itself: The Constitution in American Culture* (New York, 1986), ch. 5; Winthrop, *Addresses and Speeches on Various Occasions*, III, 79–133; IV, 104–08.

24. See Rydell, *Visions of Empire at American International Expositions, 1876–1916*; R. Reid Badger, *The Great American Fair: The World's Columbian Exposition and American Culture* (Chicago, 1979); "A New Reason for Going West," *The Century*, 70 (June 1905), 316.

25. Ernest Samuels, ed., *The Education of Henry Adams* (1918: Boston, 1973), 341; John Brinckerhoff Jackson, *American Space: The Centennial Years, 1865–1876* (New York, 1972), 235.

26. Extensively summarized and quoted in NYT, May 19, 1889, p. 11. See also Clarence W. Bowen, ed., *The History of the Centennial Celebration of the Inauguration of George Washington. . . .* (New York, 1892).

27. NYT, June 8, 1901, p. 1.

28. Natalie Spassky, *American Paintings in the Metropolitan Museum of Art* (New York and Princeton, 1985), II, 545–46.

29. NYT, Sept. 5, 1888, p. 8.

30. Jane W. Guthrie, "The Tercentennial of Henry Hudson," *Munsey's Magazine*, 30 (February 1904), 679.

31. Robert Meyer, Jr., *Festivals U.S.A.* (New York, 1950), 262–65; NYT, Aug. 14, 1887, p. 2. In 1897 the prominent Plymouth Church in Brooklyn combined its semi-centennial celebration with a tribute to Henry Ward Beecher, its long-time minister, though not exactly a saint.

32. NYT, Mar. 28, 1885, p. 1; NYT, Jan. 19, 1888, p. 4; NYT, Apr. 1, 1888, p. 12; NYT, Apr. 7, 1888, pp. 1, 8; NYT, Apr. 8, 1888, p. 2. When Chauncey Depew spoke at the Delmonico's banquet, he confessed that he was "not a son, a grandson, a brother-in-law, or a cousin of Ohio."

33. NYT, Apr. 8, 1888, p. 4; NYT, July 2, 1888, p. 5; NYT, July 4, 1888, p. 1.

34. NYT, Apr. 26, 1888, p. 1; NYT, Aug. 24, 1889, p. 1; NYT, Aug. 25, 1889, p. 8; NYT, Aug. 26, 1889, p. 5; NYT, Aug. 28, 1889, p. 2; NYT, Aug. 29, 1889, p. 4; NYT, Oct. 3, 1889, pp. 4, 9; NYT, Oct. 4, 1889, p. 1.

35. NYT, Sept. 4, 1888, p. 4; NYT, Apr. 24, 1889, p. 1.

36. NYT, Aug. 1, 1889, p. 3; Aug. 29, 1889, p. 2; NYT, Aug. 31, 1889, p. 4; NYT, Sept. 8, 1889, p. 16; NYT, Sept. 10, 1889, p. 1; NYT, Sept. 12, 1889, p. 4; NYT, Sept. 13, 1889, p. 1.

37. NYT, Oct. 24, 1889, p. 1; Douglas Story, "The City of a Great Tradition," *Munsey's Magazine,* 28 (October 1902), 1–9.

38. Edwin Erle Sparks, "The Centennial of Chicago," *Munsey's Magazine,* 30 (October 1903), 12–18; Anna Mathewson, "The Detroit Bicentennial Memorial," *The Century,* 60 (September 1900), 706–10.

39. Marks White Handly, "Tennessee and Its Centennial," *The Century,* 54 (May 1897), 92–97. The author may have been a bit unfair to Vermont. A cornerstone for the Bennington Battle Monument, made of rough-faced limestone, had been set in place on August 16, 1887, the 110th anniversary of victory by the Green Mountain Boys. Although the monument was actually completed in November 1889, it was not formally dedicated until August 19, 1891, in honor of Vermont's centennial.

40. Eliza Ruhamah Scidmore, "The Vancouver Centenary and the Discoverers of Pacific America," *The Century,* 47 (March 1894), 798–99.

41. NYT, Jan. 24, 1902, p. 1; Martha Anne Turner, *Clara Driscoll: An American Tradition* (Austin, Tex., 1979), 28; NYT, June 6, 1904, p. 2; NYT, Oct. 14, 1910, p. 7.

42. Theodore T. Munger, "The Centenary of Hawthorne," *The Century,* 68 (July 1904), 482–83; Robert S. Rantoul to Worthington C. Ford, Jan. 21, 1904, Ford Papers, NYPL Annex; Moncure Daniel Conway, *Autobiography: Memories and Experiences* (Boston, 1904), II, 442–43.

43. Cuyler Reynolds, *Historical Exhibit of New York State at Jamestown Exhibition, Norfolk, Va.* (Albany, 1907); Robert T. Taylor, "The Jamestown Tercentennial Exposition of 1907," VMHB, 65 (1957), 169–208; NYT *Magazine,* Dec. 16, 1906, p. 5; Thomas Nelson Page, "Jamestown: The Cradle of American Civilization," *The Century,* 74 (May 1907), 141–50.

44. See Charles M. Harvey, "American Progress Since Appomattox," *Munsey's Magazine,* 37 (April 1907), 82–85.

45. Elizabeth Walton Potter, "The Missionary and Immigrant Experience as Portrayed in Commemorative Works of Art," *Idaho Yesterdays,* 31 (1987), 96–97, 100.

46. See William B. Rhoads, "The Colonial Revival and American Nationalism," JSAH, 35 (1976), 239–54; Marling, *George Washington Slept Here,* esp. ch. 7.

47. Scully, *The Shingle Style and the Stick Style,* 4, 28, 37, 38–39. See also Harvey Green, "Popular Science and Political Thought Converge: Colonial Survival Becomes Colonial Revival, 1830–1910," JAC, 6 (1983), 3–24.

48. Walter Knight Sturges, "Arthur Little and the Colonial Revival," JSAH, 32 (1973), 147–64.

49. Samuel Adams Drake, *Our Colonial Homes* (Boston, 1894), 2. See *Wallace Nutting's Biography* (Framingham, Mass., 1936), 110: "The term Early American has been made to do duty for every conceivable period."

50. Oswald W. Seidensticker, "A Colonial Monastery," *The Century,* 23 (December 1881), 209–23; Noah Brooks, "An Old Town with a History," ibid., 24 (September 1882), 695–708; Richard Grant White, "Old New York and Its Houses," ibid., 26 (October 1883), 845–59.

51. The installments appeared in vols. 25 to 30 of *The Century* (1882–85). See also Charles C. Coffin, *Old Times in the Colonies* (New York, 1881).

52. Wilson to Ellen Louise Axson, Oct. 16, 1883, in Arthur S. Link, ed., *The Papers of Woodrow Wilson* (Princeton, 1967), II, 479; Lodge, "Colonialism in the United States," in *Studies in History* (Boston, 1885), 336.

53. "The Rage for Old Furniture," *Harper's Weekly,* Nov. 16, 1878, p. 718; Alan Axelrod, ed., *The Colonial Revival in America* (New York, 1985), 159–83, 217–40; NYT, June 22, 1885, p. 2.

54. NYT, Aug. 18, 1885, p. 5; NYT, May 17, 1885, p. 5; NYT, Apr. 24, 1889, p. 6; NYT, Apr. 28, 1889, p. 12; NYT, Oct. 27, 1889, p. 13.

55. See Irving W. Lyon, *The Colonial Furniture of New England* (Boston, 1891), the first comprehensive book on any aspect of American furniture; Samuel Adams Drake,

Our Colonial Homes (Boston, 1894); *Munsey's Magazine,* 20 (1899), for essays on various historic homes; NYT, Mar. 26, 1905, p. 4; Hosmer, *Presence of the Past,* 68.

56.   Charles H. Carpenter, Jr., "The Tradition of the Old: Colonial Revival Silver for the American Home," in Axelrod, ed., *Colonial Revival in America,* 146, 156–57.

57.   Rodris Roth, "The Colonial Revival and 'Centennial Furniture,' " *Art Quarterly,* 27 (1964), 57–81; Richard Guy Wilson, *The American Renaissance, 1876–1917* (New York, 1979), 215; Earl S. Pomeroy, *In Search of the Golden West: The Tourist in Western America* (New York, 1957), 162; Marling, *George Washington Slept Here,* 177, 179.

58.   *Wallace Nutting's Biography,* 107; Harold Sack and Max Wilk, *American Treasure Hunt* (New York, 1986), chs. 2–3; Elizabeth Stillinger, *The Antiquers* (New York, 1980), esp. ch. 16.

59.   See Charles C. Alexander, *Here the Country Lies: Nationalism and the Arts in Twentieth-Century America* (Bloomington, Ind., 1980), 59–61; Henry D. Shapiro, *Appalachia on Our Mind: The Southern Mountains and Mountaineers in the American Consciousness, 1870–1920* (Chapel Hill, N.C., 1978), 249; Daniel T. Rodgers, *The Work Ethic in Industrial America, 1850–1920* (Chicago, 1978), 78.

60.   Clifford K. Shipton, "The Museum of the American Antiquarian Society," in Walter M. Whitehill, ed., *A Cabinet of Curiosities: Five Episodes in the Evolution of American Museums* (Charlottesville, Va., 1967), 45; Richard Ellmann, *Oscar Wilde* (New York, 1988), 239–40.

61.   *American Renaissance, 1876–1917,* 171 and fig. 142. The painting is owned by the Union League Club in New York City.

62.   For a notably representative work by Henry, see *In the Old Stage Coach Days* (1907) in *Traditions: Babcock Galleries and American Art* (New York, 1989), fig. 16.

63.   *Howard Pyle's Book of the American Spirit* (New York, 1923); *American Renaissance, 1876–1917,* fig. 224.

64.   Donelson F. Hoopes, *Childe Hassam* (New York, 1979), is disappointingly thin; a typical statement by Hassam accompanies *The Church at Gloucester* in Doreen Bolger Burke, *American Paintings in the Metropolitan Museum of Art* (New York, 1980), III, 362–63.

65.   *Wallace Nutting's Biography,* 95.

66.   Ibid., 75–76. See also William L. Dulaney, "Wallace Nutting: Collector and Entrepreneur," WP, 13 (1979), 47–60.

67.   Joseph Everett Chandler, *The Colonial House* (New York, 1916); Virginia Robie, *The Quest of the Quaint* (Boston, 1916 and 1927).

68.   *Wallace Nutting's Biography,* 78–79. See also Peter J. Schmitt, *Back to Nature: The Arcadian Myth in Urban America* (New York, 1969).

69.   Constance Cary Harrison, "American Rural Festivals," *The Century,* 50 (July 1895), 323–33, the quotation at 331. Nevertheless, the author acknowledged that the oldest of these pageants had been "undertaken and carried out by the cultivated class of society" (p. 324).

70.   For Olmsted's vision, see Jackson, *American Space,* 218. For an intermediate view, quite literally a stage between the other two, see (fig. 5.5) Edmund C. Coates, *Washington's Headquarters at Newburgh* (1871). In this picture we are looking south on the Hudson toward Storm King Mountain from the northern end of Hasbrouck House.

71.   Annie Nathan Meyer, "What American Museums Are Doing for Native Art," *The Century,* 72 (September 1906), 922–43, the quotations at 930, 934.

72.   Neil Harris, "The Gilded Age Revisited: Boston and the Museum Movement," AQ, 14 (1962), 545–66; Helen L. Horowitz, *Culture and the City: Cultural Philanthropy in Chicago from the 1880s to 1917* (Lexington, Ky., 1976), chs. 2–5; Stillinger, *The Antiquers,* 159; Ernest Ingersoll, "The Making of a Museum" [the Smithsonian in Washington, D.C.], *The Century,* 29 (January 1885), 354–69.

73.   James I. Robertson, "Virginia Historical Society: The Energies of Some for the Enrichment of All," VMHB, 86 (1978), 131–45; Paul Finkelman, "Class and Culture in Late Nineteenth Century Chicago: The Founding of the Newberry Library," *American Studies,* 16 (1975), 5–22.

74. Stanley N. Katz, "The Institutional Mind: Independent Research Libraries, Learned Societies, and the Humanities in the United States," *Proceedings* of the AAS, 97 (1987), 288.

75. Charles Francis Adams, Jr., to J. Franklin Jameson, Apr. 19, 1910, and Jameson to Adams, Apr. 21, 1910, Jameson Papers, box 45, MDLC; "Third Annual Meeting of the American Folk-Lore Society," *Journal of American Folklore*, 5 (1892), 1.

76. Document in the Worthington C. Ford Papers, box 5, NYPL Annex. See also J. Franklin Jameson to Ford, June 24, 1908, ibid.

77. NYT, June 19, 1887, p. 9; NYT, Feb. 16, 1888, p. 1; NYT, Feb. 17, 1888, p. 2; NYT, Nov. 2, 1889, p. 9; NYT, Dec. 3, 1889, p. 1.

78. George S. Hellman, *Lanes of Memory* (New York, 1927), esp. 42.

79. *Grolier 75: A Biographical Retrospective to Celebrate the Seventy-Fifth Anniversary of the Grolier Club in New York* (New York, 1959), 18–20, 95–98; Hyatt H. Waggoner, ed., *Hawthorne's Last Notebook, 1835–1841* (College Station, Pa., 1978), 21.

80. T. J. Jackson Lears, *No Place of Grace: Antimodernism and the Transformation of American Culture, 1880–1920* (New York, 1981).

81. C. Vann Woodward, *The Burden of Southern History* (Baton Rouge, La., 1960; Vintage ed.), 138–39; *Education of Henry Adams,* 222–23.

82. Brian Fagan, *Elusive Treasure: The Story of Early Archaeologists in the Americas* (New York, 1977), chs. 12–15; Simon J. Bronner, *American Folklore Studies: An Intellectual History* (Lawrence, Kans., 1986).

83. Fiske to Abby Fiske, April 9, 1890, Fiske Papers, box 11, HEHL; same to same, Apr. 28, 1892, ibid., box 12.

84. Flower, *James Parton,* 190. Morse's papers, a rich but neglected resource for the cultural history of this period, are located in the MHS.

85. NYT, June 20, 1887, p. 3; NYT, Oct. 13, 1889, p. 19; R. L. O'Brien to Worthington C. Ford, Jan. 3, 1909, Ford Papers, box 5, NYPL Annex.

86. Paul Z. DuBois, *Paul Leicester Ford: An American Man of Letters, 1865–1902* (New York, 1977), esp. chs. 7–11. The Historical Printing Club, a bibliophile's "affair" with early Americana, was created in 1876 as a Ford family enterprise.

87. William F. McDonald, *Federal Relief Administration and the Arts* (Columbus, Ohio, 1969), 822; Frank Maloy Anderson to J. Franklin Jameson, Dec. 19, 1901, Jameson Papers, box 54, MDLC; Charles Francis Adams, Jr., to Jameson, Mar. 11, 1902, ibid., box 45.

88. Jameson to Worthington C. Ford, May 28, 1909, in Elizabeth Donnan and Leo F. Stock, eds., *An Historian's World: Selections from the Correspondence of John Franklin Jameson* (Philadelphia, 1956), 124. *Records of the Past,* a journal devoted to history, anthropology, and archaeology, appeared between 1902 and 1914 under the auspices of the Records of the Past Exploration Society, located in Washington, D.C.

89. Charles F. Adams, Jr., to Worthington C. Ford, May 24, 1909, Ford Papers, box 5, NYPL Annex.

90. Edward A. Purcell, Jr., *The Crisis of Democratic Theory: Scientific Naturalism and the Problem of Value* (Lexington, Ky., 1973), 75.

91. James M. Lindgren, " 'For the Sake of Our Future': The Association for the Preservation of Virginia Antiquities and the Regeneration of Traditionalism," VMHB, 97 (1989), 47–74; Dow is quoted in Hosmer, *Presence of the Past,* 213; Stillinger, *The Antiquers,* ch. 15.

92. Mary Bronson Hartt, "The Skansen Idea," *The Century,* 83 (April 1912), 916–20; Howard W. Marshall, "Folklife and the Rise of American Folk Museums," *Journal of American Folklore,* 90 (1977), 391–413.

93. NYT, Nov. 25, 1888, pp. 4, 6; NYT, May 27, 1889, p. 8.

Chapter 6

1. Markham, *Saratoga Monument. Historic Sculpture, Together with a Brief Reference to Some of the General and Elementary Principles Involved in a National Art.* . . . (n.p., 1886), unpaginated.

2. See Ernest Samuels, *Bernard Berenson: The Making of a Connoisseur* (Cambridge, Mass., 1979), 43, 313, 325, 341, 406–07.

3. "Tradition and Practice," in James Ballowe, ed., *George Santayana's America: Essays on Literature and Culture* (Urbana, 1967), 116; Merle Curti, "Dime Novels and the American Tradition," *Yale Review*, 26 (1937), 770.

4. Paul R. Baker, *Richard Morris Hunt* (Cambridge, Mass., 1980), 330–31, 372, 460; Kenyon Cox, *The Classic Point of View* (New York, 1911), 87.

5. William O. McDowell to Henry Baldwin, May 6, 1893, Library Americana, box 59, NYPL Annex.

6. Mark Twain, *The Innocents Abroad, or the New Pilgrims Progress* (1869: New York, 1966), 457.

7. William A. Coffin, "Souvenirs of a Veteran Collector," *The Century*, 53 (December 1896), 231–45; Aline B. Saarinen, *The Proud Possessors: The Lives, Times and Tastes of Some Adventurous American Art Collectors* (New York, 1958), 144–73, the quotation at 288–89.

8. Henry F. May, *The End of American Innocence: A Study of the First Years of Our Own Time, 1912–1917* (New York, 1959), xii, 30.

9. NYT, Jan. 1, 1901, p. 8.

10. See Richard J. Boyle, ed., *In This Academy: The Pennsylvania Academy of the Fine Arts, 1805–1976: A Special Bicentennial Exhibition* (Washington, D.C., 1976), 137–38; Lawrence W. Levine, *Highbrow/Lowbrow: The Emergence of Cultural Hierarchy in America* (Cambridge, Mass., 1988), 140–46.

11. Earl Pomeroy, *In Search of the Golden West: The Tourist in Western America* (New York, 1957), 32–36, 38–39, 44.

12. Ibid., 174; Percy MacKaye, "American Pageants and Their Promise," *Scribner's Magazine*, 46 (July 1909), 28–34.

13. These games will be found at the Margaret Woodbury Strong Museum in Rochester, N.Y.

14. NYT, Dec. 16, 1889, p. 6; "The Dearth of Antiques," *The Nation*, 89 (Aug. 26, 1909), 191–92; Harold Sack and Max Wilk, *American Treasure Hunt* (New York, 1986), 22–32.

15. Frederick Baekeland, "Collectors of American Painting, 1813 to 1913," *American Art Review*, 3 (1976), 120–66; Saarinen, *The Proud Possessors*, 25–91.

16. NYT, Mar. 22, 1887, p. 5; NYT, Mar. 23, 1887, p. 5; NYT, May 10, 1887, p. 4; NYT, May 12, 1887, p. 4; NYT, May 13, 1887, p. 4; Russell Lynes, *The Tastemakers* (New York, 1954), 197; Baekeland, "Collectors of American Painting," 149.

17. Located in the Metropolitan Museum of Art, the Corcoran Gallery of Art, and the Brooklyn Museum, respectively. See also Theodore E. Stebbins, Jr., *Close Observation: Selected Oil Sketches by Frederic E. Church* (Washington, D.C., 1978), 88–100.

18. The picture is located in the Oakland Museum, Oakland, Calif., and reproduced in Nancy Wall Moure, ed., *American Narrative Painting* (Los Angeles, 1974), 102.

19. TMA, 132 (October 1987), 725.

20. Mark Thistlethwaite, "Patronage Gone Awry: The 1883 Temple Competition of Historical Paintings," PMHB, 112 (1988), 545–78; Boyle, ed., *In This Academy*, 100.

21. For White, see Natalie Spassky, comp., *American Paintings in the Metropolitan Museum of Art* (New York, 1985), II, 74–75; Henry is quoted in Walter Knight Sturges, "Arthur Little and the Colonial Revival," JSAH, 32 (1973), 148.

22.   Sydney George Fisher, *Men, Women & Manners in Colonial Times* (Philadelphia, 1897), I, 9; Barr Ferree, "An 'American Style' of Architecture," *Architectural Record,* I (July 1891), 45.

23.   "Tradition in Architecture," *Scribner's Magazine,* 21 (June 1897), 787–88.

24.   John La Farge to Cass Gilbert, July 16, 1904, Cass Gilbert Papers, box 10, MinnHS; La Farge to Channing Seabury, July 16, 1904, ibid.

25.   Richard Guy Wilson, "Architecture and the Reinterpretation of the Past in the American Renaissance," WP, 18 (1983), 69–87, the quotation at 84; Baker, *Richard Morris Hunt,* esp. ch. 17; Herbert Small, *The Library of Congress: Its Architecture and Decoration* (New York, 1982).

26.   Cram, *My Life in Architecture* (Boston, 1936), 27, 30, 33; Michael D. Clark, "Ralph Adams Cram and the Americanization of the Middle Ages," *Journal of American Studies,* 23 (1989), 195–213; T. J. Jackson Lears, *No Place of Grace: Antimodernism and the Transformation of American Culture, 1880–1920* (New York, 1981), 204–08; Henry Adams, *Mont-Saint-Michel and Chartres* (1913: Garden City, N.Y., 1959).

27.   Bert James Loewenberg, *American History in American Thought: Christopher Columbus to Henry Adams* (New York, 1972), 370–77.

28.   See Henry C. Pitz, *Howard Pyle: Writer, Illustrator, Founder of the Brandywine School* (New York, 1975).

29.   *The Family Mark Twain* (New York, n.d.), 655, 682, 687, 692, 736.

30.   See James W. Gargano, "Mark Twain's Changing Perspectives on the Past," SAQ, 80 (1981), 454–65; Roger B. Salomon, *Twain and the Image of History* (New Haven, 1961).

31.   Charles Dellheim, *The Face of the Past: The Preservation of the Medieval Inheritance in Victorian England* (Cambridge, 1982); Adams, *Mont-Saint-Michel and Chartres,* 53; Raymond Williams, *Culture and Society, 1780–1950* (1958: New York, 1966), 82; Keith Thomas, *Religion and the Decline of Magic* (New York, 1971), 173.

32.   Baker, *Richard Morris Hunt,* 74–75, 112–13, 148–49, 204–08, 227; Hayne to Margaret J. Preston, Aug. 29, 1871, in Rayburn S. Moore, ed., *A Man of Letters in the Nineteenth-Century South: Selected Letters of Paul Hamilton Hayne* (Baton Rouge, La., 1982), 87; Milton E. Flower, *James Parton: The Father of Modern Biography* (Durham, N.C., 1951), 121, 177, 180.

33.   Julia Cartwright, *Jules Bastien-Lepage* (London, 1894), 50–53; Baker, *Richard Morris Hunt,* 286, 331–32.

34.   James, *A Little Tour in France* (1882: New York, 1950), 33.

35.   Kathleen A. Foster, *Edwin Austin Abbey* (New Haven, 1974).

36.   Edward Eggleston, "A Full-Length Portrait of the United States," *The Century,* 37 (March 1889), 790–91. See also Albert Matthews to Worthington C. Ford, Mar. 6, 1910, Ford Papers, box 7, NYPL Annex.

37.   Wendell to James K. Hosmer, July 7, 1892, Hosmer Papers, box 1, MinnHS; Mellen Chamberlain to Hosmer, Mar. 8, 1896, ibid.; Adams to Worthington C. Ford, Feb. 18, 1910, Ford Papers, box 7, NYPL Annex.

38.   The Secretaries for the Memorial . . . to Fiske, Sept. 9, 1900, Fiske Papers, box 13, HEHL. For context, see Stuart Anderson, *Race and Rapprochement: Anglo-Saxonism and Anglo-American Relations, 1895–1904* (Rutherford, N.J., 1981).

39.   Rhodes to Charles H. Firth, June 28, 1904, quoted in Robert Cruden, *James Ford Rhodes: The Man, the Historian, and His Work* (Cleveland, 1961), 104; George F. Parker, "History by Camera, with Examples of Photographic Records from the Exhibit to Be Made in the Louisiana Purchase Exposition of the Work of Sir Benjamin Stone," *The Century,* 68 (May 1904), 136–45.

40.   James Thorpe et al., *The Founding of the Henry E. Huntington Library and Art Gallery: Four Essays* (San Marino, Calif., 1969); *History of the William L. Clements Library, 1923–1973* (Ann Arbor, Mich., 1973).

41.   Matthews, "The American Language," *Munsey's Magazine,* 40 (December 1908), 346.

42. Ibid., 349.

43. "The Origin of Certain Americanisms," in Lodge, *The Democracy of the Constitution and Other Addresses and Essays* (New York, 1915), 246–73, the quotation at 270.

44. Hayne to Lanier, Jan. 19, 1875, in Moore, ed., *Selected Letters of Paul Hamilton Hayne,* 124.

45. R. W. B. Lewis, *Edith Wharton: A Biography* (New York, 1975), 29, 31, 86, 105–06. For the same pattern at large, see NYT, Mar. 22, 1887, p. 5; NYT, Mar. 23, 1887, p. 5.

46. James to Thomas Sergeant Perry, September 1867, quoted in Leon Edel, *Henry James, 1843–1870: The Untried Years* (Philadelphia, 1953), 264–65. In 1873 Henry and his brother William visited the Colosseum in Rome, which William described as "that damned blood-soaked soil." He then remarked of Italy in general that "the weight of the past here is fatal." Quoted in F. W. Dupee, *Henry James* (New York, 1951), 110.

47. Quoted in Harry Levin, *The Power of Blackness: Hawthorne, Poe, Melville* (New York, 1958), 244.

48. Henry James, *Hawthorne* (New York, 1879), 42–43; James, *The American Scene* (1907: New York, 1967), 53, 59.

49. James, *The American Scene,* 134–35, 145–46, 14.

50. Paul E. Cohen, "Barrett Wendell and the Harvard Literary Revival," NEQ, 52 (1979), 483–99; NYT, Oct. 13, 1889, p. 19.

51. "A Service to American Literature," *The Century,* 41 (January 1891), 475–76. In 1904 Paul Elmer More announced his intention to help create a truly American genre of literary criticism. As late as 1916, however, there was only one professor of American literature, so designated, in the entire United States. See Richard Ruland, *The Rediscovery of American Literature: Premises of Critical Taste, 1900–1940* (Cambridge, Mass., 1967), viii–ix.

52. Robert Seager II, *Alfred Thayer Mahan: The Man and His Letters* (Annapolis, Md., 1977), 209, 218; William Garrott Brown, "The Problem of the American Historian," *Atlantic,* 92 (November 1903), 649–61, the quotations at 659–60.

53. Fisher, *Men, Women & Manners in Colonial Times,* I, 8; "Edward Eggleston's Historical Papers," *The Century,* 30 (July 1885), 487.

54. Fiske to Edward Everett Hale, Apr. 16, 1879, Fiske Papers, box 8, HEHL. For a strangely contradictory memory of Fiske's feelings about American history early in the 1870s, see Hale, *Memories of a Hundred Years* (New York, 1902), II, 87. Discrepancies of this sort ought to serve as a powerful caution in using memoirs, Victorian or otherwise.

55. Morgan to Fiske, July 24, 1879, Fiske Papers, box 8, HEHL. See also Mellen Chamberlain to James K. Hosmer, Mar. 8, 1896, Hosmer Papers, box 1, MinnHS.

56. Frank L. McVey, "United States History in Secondary Schools," *The Century,* 52 (September 1896), 796–97; Carl Becker, "Frederick Jackson Turner," in *Everyman His Own Historian: Essays on History and Politics* (New York, 1935), 211.

57. See George J. Manson, "A Renaissance of Patriotism," *The Independent,* 52 (July 5, 1900), 1612–15.

58. William Dean Howells, "The Modern American Mood," *Harper's,* 95 (July 1897), 199.

59. Ibid., 200, 203, 204.

60. "American Temperament," *Scribner's Magazine,* 29 (May 1901), 505–06.

61. Lowell, "The Place of the Independent in Politics," *Political Essays* (Boston, 1888), 324; "Americanism in Song," NYT, Sept. 23, 1889, p. 4. See also NYT *Magazine,* Jan. 2, 1910, p. 10; Charles C. Alexander, *Here the Country Lies: Nationalism and the Arts in Twentieth-Century America* (Bloomington, Ind., 1980), 59–61.

62. See Michael Kammen, "Moses Coit Tyler: The First Professor of American History in the United States," in *Selvages and Biases: The Fabric of History in American Culture* (Ithaca, N.Y., 1987), 225, 227–28, 247, 251.

63. "Our Right to 'America,'" NYT, July 23, 1900, p. 8.

64. Ibid.

65. "Columbus's Day," *The Century,* 39 (January 1890), 479; Andrew C. McLaughlin to J. Franklin Jameson, Oct. 30, 1903, Jameson Papers, box 110, MDLC.

66. Dudley Gordon, *Charles F. Lummis: Crusader in Corduroy* (n.p., 1972), 151; and see Edwin R. Bingham, *Charles F. Lummis: Editor of the Southwest* (San Marino, Calif., 1955).

67. Leila Mechlin, "The Awakening of the West in Art," *The Century,* 81 (November 1910), 75–80.

68. George Wharton James, *In and Out of the Old Missions of California. . . .* (Boston, 1905), xv. See also H.H., "Father Junípero and His Work: A Sketch of the Foundations, Prosperity, and Ruin of the Franciscan Missions in California," *The Century,* 26 (May 1883), 3–18.

69. C. M. Burton to Waldo G. Leland, Dec. 27, 1904, Jameson Papers, box 113, MDLC; Burton to J. Franklin Jameson, Dec. 1, 1903, ibid.

70. Burton to Jameson, Feb. 19, 1906, and May 16, 1911, ibid.

71. Quoted in Brian Fagan, *Elusive Treasure: The Story of Early Archaeologists in the Americas* (New York, 1977), 225.

72. Ronald F. Lee, "The Antiquities Act of 1906" (U.S. Department of the Interior, National Park Service, typescript, 1970), 4–5.

73. Ibid., 9–13; A. Howard Clark, "What the United States Government Has Done for History," *Annual Report of the AHA for 1894* (Washington, D.C., 1895), 549.

74. Robert A. Trennert, Jr., "A Grand Failure: The Centennial Indian Exhibition of 1876," *Prologue,* 6 (1974), 118–29, esp. 126, 129.

75. Twain, *Innocents Abroad,* 24; Fagan, *Elusive Treasure,* 292.

76. Fagan, *Elusive Treasure,* 280–82.

77. Mark Twain, *Life on the Mississippi* (1883: New York, 1961), 329, 332, 335–36.

78. NYT, June 21, 1885, p. 10; NYT, Jan. 3, 1885, p. 3.

79. M. J. Galt, "Origin of the Association for the Preservation of Virginia Antiquities," *Yeare Booke of the A.P.V.A.* (1911–12), 46; Celara A. Smith to Victor H. Paltsits, Jan. 4, 1901, Paltsits Papers, box 2, NYHS (referring to the rare book collection of Edward A. Ayer of Chicago).

80. Peggy and Harold Samuels, *Frederic Remington: A Biography* (Garden City, N.Y., 1982), 60; Brian W. Dippie, *Custer's Last Stand: The Anatomy of an American Myth* (Missoula, Mont., 1976), 51, 54.

81. Michael Richman, *Daniel Chester French: An American Sculptor* (New York, 1976), 97.

82. John C. Ewers, "Cyrus E. Dallin: Master Sculptor of the Plains Indian," MMWHC, 18 (1968), 35–38.

83. Ibid., 39–43. At a time when equestrian statues enjoyed a great vogue, it should not be surprising that a stuffed horse achieved genuine popularity. One survivor of Custer's catastrophe in 1876 was a horse with the highly ironic name Comanche. He was pampered until his death in 1891, and then his stuffed remains were placed on display at the University of Kansas. (Dippie, *Custer's Last Stand,* 26.)

84. Pomeroy, *In Search of the Golden West,* 40–41; Lee Clark Mitchell, *Witnesses to a Vanishing America: The Nineteenth-Century Response* (Princeton, 1981), 170.

85. "Records of the Past and American Antiquities," *Records of the Past,* 1 (January 1902), 2.

86. Ibid., 3–4.

87. Lee, "Antiquities Act of 1906," esp. 21–24, 29, 68–69.

88. *U.S. Statutes at Large,* vol. 34, 59th Congress (1906), p. 225; Duane A. Smith, *Mesa Verde National Park: Shadows of the Centuries* (Lawrence, Kans., 1988), chs. 3–4.

89. NYT, Mar. 2, 1902, p. 6.

90. Fletcher and Hemenway appear in NAW, I, 630–31, and II, 179–81; Lee, "Antiquities Act of 1906," 15, 40. Less than a generation later, Mary Cabot Wheelwright of Boston established the Museum of Navaho Ceremonial Art in Santa Fe, New Mexico. See Walter Muir Whitehill, *Independent Historical Societies* (Boston, 1962), 407–14.

91.   Marshall B. Davidson, *The American Wing: A Guide* (New York, 1980), 9; Elizabeth Stillinger, *The Antiquers* (New York, 1980), 159–64.

92.   Henry Watson Kent is quoted in Stillinger, *The Antiquers*, 123 and 160. See also 132–33.

93.   Lynes, *The Tastemakers*, 160–61; Calvin Tomkins, *Merchants and Masterpieces: The Story of the Metropolitan Museum of Art* (New York, 1970), 100–01; William Walton, "American Paintings in the Metropolitan Museum," *Scribner's Magazine*, 42 (December 1907), 637–40; Kenyon Cox, "American Art and the Metropolitan Museum," *The Century*, 83 (December 1911), 204–13, the quotation at 207.

94.   Christian Brinton, "The Case for American Art," *The Century*, 77 (November 1908), 140; Leila Mechlin, "The Evans Collection in the National Gallery," ibid., 75 (December 1907), 316–18.

95.   Baekeland, "Collectors of American Painting," 159–60.

96.   NYT, Dec. 1, 1904, p. 8; Annie Nathan Meyer, "What American Museums Are Doing for Native Art," *The Century*, 72 (September 1906), 934; Brinton, "The Case for American Art," 139–42.

97.   Leila Mechlin, "The Awakening of the West in Art," *The Century*, 81 (November 1910), 80; John W. Alexander, "Is Our Art Distinctively American?," ibid., 87 (April 1914), 828.

98.   Herbert L. Satterlee, *J. Pierpont Morgan: An Intimate Portrait* (New York, 1940), 502, 517–18, 562–65; Bishop William Lawrence, "Memoir of J. P. Morgan," in John W. McCoubrey, ed., *American Art, 1700–1960: Sources and Documents* (Englewood Cliffs, N.J., 1965), 141. Morgan's son was less ambitious as a collector, but he continued to concentrate on European books from medieval times to the nineteenth century. See John Douglas Forbes, *J. P. Morgan, Jr., 1867–1943* (Charlottesville, Va., 1981), ch. 8.

99.   Florence Curtis Graybill and Victor Boesen, *Edward Sheriff Curtis: Visions of a Vanishing Race* (New York, 1976), 20–21, 54, 81.

100.   Perry Miller, ed., *Consciousness in Concord: The Text of Thoreau's Hitherto "Lost Journal" (1840–1841)* (Boston, 1958), 3, 6–7.

101.   J. Franklin Jameson to Franklin Delano Roosevelt, Jan. 29, 1908, Jameson Papers, box 125, MDLC; Abbey G. Baker, "The White House Collection of Presidential Ware," *The Century*, 76 (October 1908), 828–41.

102.   Brinton, "The Case for American Art," 141.

103.   NYT, Mar. 2, 1902, p. 6.

Chapter 7

1.   See Jean B. Quandt, "Religion and Social Thought: The Secularization of Postmillennialism," AQ, 25 (1973), 390–409; Daniel Walker Howe, "Victorian Culture in America," in Howe, ed., *Victorian America* (Philadelphia, 1976), 21. Vedder's painting is located in the Herbert F. Johnson Museum of Art, Cornell University, Ithaca, N.Y.

2.   Ernest Samuels, ed., *The Education of Henry Adams* (1918: Boston, 1973), 91.

3.   The writing desk is located at the NMAH. See Jefferson to Ellen W. Coolidge, Nov. 14, 1825, in Andrew A. Lipscomb, ed., *The Writings of Thomas Jefferson* (Washington, D.C., 1903), XVIII, 349–50.

4.   T. S. Eliot, *Notes Towards the Definition of Culture* (London, 1948), 15, 28.

5.   James M. Lindgren, "The Gospel of Preservation in Virginia and New England: Historic Preservation and the Regeneration of Traditionalism" (unpubl. Ph.D. diss., The College of William and Mary, 1984), 152.

6.   Paul Hamilton Hayne, "The Decline of Faith," *The Century*, 25 (January 1883), 458. The poem is misquoted and misused by Rolling G. Osterweis in *The Myth of the Lost Cause, 1865–1900* (Hamden, Conn., 1973), 47, where the word "soul" has been changed to "South."

7.   Charles Reagan Wilson, *Baptized in Blood: The Religion of the Lost Cause, 1865–1920* (Athens, Ga., 1980), delineates a distinctively Southern civil religion rooted in a blend of traditional Christian churches and Southern culture.

8.   Lawrence G. Nelson, "Mary Johnston and the Historic Imagination," in R. C. Simonini, Jr., ed., *Southern Writers: Appraisals in Our Time* (Charlottesville, Va., 1961), 74, 81, 99; Jack Temple Kirby, *Media-Made Dixie: The South in the American Imagination* (Baton Rouge, La., 1978), 4–8; Edward D. C. Campbell, Jr., *The Celluloid South: Hollywood and the Southern Myth* (Knoxville, Tenn., 1981), ch. 1.

9.   William Henry Hoyt, *The Mecklenburg Declaration of Independence* (New York, 1907); Richard N. Current, "An Imaginary Declaration of Independence, 1775–1975," in Current, *Arguing with Historians: Essays on the Historical and the Unhistorical* (Middletown, Conn., 1987), the quotation at 20.

10.   See Deborah L. Haines, "Scientific History as a Teaching Method: The Formative Years," JAH, 63 (1977), 892–912; Dorothy Ross, "Historical Consciousness in Nineteenth-Century America," AHR, 89 (1984), 924–28; Bert James Loewenberg, *American History in American Thought: Christopher Columbus to Henry Adams* (New York, 1972), chs. 18–20.

11.   *Charles Francis Adams, 1835–1915: An Autobiography* (Boston, 1916), 179; Edward Chase Kirkland, *Charles Francis Adams, Jr., 1835–1915: The Patrician at Bay* (Cambridge, Mass., 1965), 139–40; Robert L. Beisner, "Brooks Adams and Charles Francis Adams, Jr: Historians of Massachusetts," NEQ, 35 (1962), 48–70.

12.   Henry Adams, *The Degradation of the Democratic Dogma* (New York, 1919), 11; Henry Adams to Henry Osborn Taylor, Feb. 15, 1915, in Harold Dean Cater, ed., *Henry Adams and His Friends: A Collection of His Unpublished Letters* (Boston, 1947), 768–69.

13.   John W. Burrow, *A Liberal Descent: Victorian Historians and the English Past* (Cambridge, 1982), 234–35; John Clive, *Macaulay: The Shaping of the Historian* (New York, 1973), 45; Peter Gay, *Style in History* (New York, 1974), 144.

14.   Erich Heller, *The Disinherited Mind: Essays in Modern German Literature and Thought* (1952: London, 1975), 82 (see also 84 and 88); Jacob Burckhardt, *The Civilization of the Renaissance in Italy* (1885: New York, 1958), 427.

15.   David Levin, *History as Romantic Art: Bancroft, Prescott, Motley, and Parkman* (Stanford, Calif., 1959), 4–5.

16.   Milton E. Flower, *James Parton: The Father of Modern Biography* (Durham, N.C., 1951), 13–14, 99, 145. For Huxley, agnosticism, and British historians, see C. H. S. Fifoot, *Frederic William Maitland: A Life* (Cambridge, Mass., 1971), 179.

17.   William Peirce Randel, *Edward Eggleston* (New York, 1946), 14, 38, 42, 91, 93, 99, 144, 147, 154, 156, 166, 169.

18.   Hosmer's autobiography is with his papers at the MinnHS, box 1. The quotations are from pp. 19, 357. There is a memoir of his life, prepared by his family, in ibid., box 2. See also Hosmer, *The Last Leaf: Observations, During Seventy-Five Years, of Men and Events in America and Europe* (New York, 1912).

19.   Fiske's autobiography, which seems to have been written in 1884, is among his papers at the HEHL. Excerpts from "Autobiographical Notes, 1884," John Fiske, HM 18876. Reprinted by permission of the Huntington Library. On April 8, 1879, he wrote to Edward Everett Hale that he had never been "anything but a Christian," but then added that "there has been no time in my life when the study of history has not held the first place in my affections." Ibid., box 8. See also Milton Berman, *John Fiske: The Evolution of a Popularizer* (Cambridge, Mass., 1961).

20.   Robert M. Crunden, *The Mind and Art of Albert Jay Nock* (Chicago, 1964), 10–11, 14–15; Twain to Will Bowen, Aug. 31 [1876], in *Mark Twain's Letters to Will Bowen: "My First, & Oldest & Dearest Friend"* (Austin, Tex., 1941), 23–24.

21.   Michael Kammen, "Moses Coit Tyler: The First Professor of American History in the United States," in Kammen, *Selvages and Biases: The Fabric of History in American Culture* (Ithaca, N.Y., 1987), 225, 227–28, 251; Frances FitzGerald, *America Revised: History Schoolbooks in the Twentieth Century* (Boston, 1979), 61–62.

22.   See *Myself: The Autobiography of John R. Commons* (Madison, Wis., 1963), 44, 51, 53; Necah Stewart Furman, *Walter Prescott Webb: His Life and Impact* (Al-

buquerque, N.M., 1976), 19–21, 53; Burleigh Taylor Wilkins, *Carl Becker: A Biographical Study in American Intellectual History* (Cambridge, Mass., 1961), 9–11, 13, 17; *In and Out of the Ivory Tower: The Autobiography of William L. Langer* (New York, 1977), 32, 59, 81.

23. Marc Bloch, *Feudal Society* (1940: Chicago, 1961), I, 80. For persons and developments comparable to the United States in post–1870 Europe, see Karl J. Weintraub, *Visions of Culture* (Chicago, 1966); Hans A. Schmitt, ed., *Historians of Modern Europe* (Baton Rouge, 1971); Herman Ausubel et al., eds., *Some Modern Historians of Britain: Essays in Honor of R. L. Schuyler* (New York, 1951).

24. See William R. Hutchison, *The Modernist Impulse in American Protestantism* (Cambridge, Mass., 1976), esp. ch. 3; Ann Douglas, *The Feminization of American Culture* (New York, 1977), esp. chs. 4–5 and p. 182 for a pertinent quotation from the *Christian Examiner.*

25. Barbara MacDonald Powell, "The Most Celebrated Encampment: Valley Forge in American Culture, 1777–1983" (unpubl. Ph.D. diss., Cornell University, 1983), esp. chs. 3–4; Charles B. Hosmer, Jr., "The Broadening View of the Historical Preservation Movement," in Ian M. G. Quimby, ed., *Material Culture and the Study of American Life* (New York, 1978), 126.

26. W. Herbert Burk, *Making a Museum: The Confessions of a Curator* (n.p., 1926), 17, 21, 38, 49; Karal Ann Marling, *George Washington Slept Here: Colonial Revivals and American Culture, 1876–1986* (Cambridge, Mass., 1988), 32–37.

27. NYT, June 29, 1888, p. 8. After the death of architect Richard Morris Hunt in 1895, George W. Vanderbilt decided to place a stained-glass window honoring Hunt in the Church of All Souls at Biltmore Village. The subject of the window honoring Hunt, however, is the building of the Temple described in the Old Testament. The activities of design and construction were thereby legitimized as spiritually uplifting activities rather than the highly materialistic ones that they really were. Work and art had been Hunt's surrogates for religion; so there may be an element of poetic justice in his work being immortalized in the window of a church. See Paul R. Baker, *Richard Morris Hunt* (Cambridge, Mass., 1980), 454–55, 460.

28. "Religion as a Cultural System," in Clifford Geertz, *The Interpretation of Cultures* (New York, 1973), 89.

29. Letter from T. B. Richards of New York to the editor, NYT, Apr. 11, 1937, sec. 4, p. 9. Richards complained that "we are a nation of iconoclasts with no reverence for tradition or love for the beautiful if it is old."

30. NYT, Aug. 21, 1888, p. 5; NYT, May 27, 1888, p. 3; NYT, Mar. 5, 1889, p. 9; NYT, Aug. 24, 1889, p. 1; NYT, Sept. 6, 1889, p. 1.

31. NYT, Nov. 10, 1889, p. 3; NYT, Nov. 11, 1889, p. 1; NYT, Nov. 26, 1889, p. 8; NYT, Nov. 30, 1889, p. 1.

32. Lindgren, "The Gospel of Preservation in Virginia and New England," 93, 95, 399; Lyman P. Powell to Lyon G. Tyler, Mar. 1, 1894, Tyler Papers, group 5, box 1.

33. Lindgren, "The Gospel of Preservation in Virginia and New England," 76–77, 88, 185, 206, 366, 388–89; Wilson, *Baptized in Blood: The Religion of the Lost Cause,* 29–30.

34. Martin J. Wiener, *English Culture and the Decline of the Industrial Spirit, 1850–1980* (Cambridge, 1981), 45, 67.

35. Alfred T. Story, *American Shrines in England* (London, 1908); Tyler, *Glimpses of England: Social, Political, Literary* (New York, 1898), 219, 222.

36. Charles B. Hosmer, Jr., *Presence of the Past: A History of the Preservation Movement in the United States Before Williamsburg* (New York, 1965), 165, 173, 176, 179, 187, 262, 264, 265.

37. Harry Thurston Peck, "Famous American Shrines," *Munsey's Magazine,* 41 (April 1909), 3–17, the quotation at 4.

38. Ibid., 5. Compare to Surinder Mohan Bhardwaj, *Hindu Places of Pilgrimage in India* (Berkeley, 1973), chs. 6–11; Mary Lee Nolan and Sidney Nolan, *Christian Pilgrimage in Modern Western Europe* (Chapel Hill, N.C., 1989), esp. chs. 2–4.

39. See Howard N. Rabinowitz, "George Washington as Icon, 1865–1900," in Ray B. Browne and Marshall Fishwick, eds., *Icons of America* (Bowling Green, Ohio, 1978), 67–86.

40. "The Tomb of Washington/Mount Vernon and the Big Monument/How the Pilgrimage to Mount Vernon Is Made," NYT, June 20, 1885, p. 3; Richard J. Koke, comp., *American Landscape and Genre Paintings in the New-York Historical Society* (Boston, 1982), I, 285–93.

41. Marling, *George Washington Slept Here*, 26; for "Mary, the Mother of Washington" materials, see Lyon G. Tyler Papers, group 1, box 24, SLWM; Peter Karsten, *Patriot-Heroes in England and America: Political Symbolism and Changing Values Over Three Centuries* (Madison, Wis., 1978), 90.

42. Lloyd Lewis, *Myths after Lincoln* (1929: New York, 1941), 67–105; NYT, Nov. 1, 1889, p. 2.

43. NYT, May 2, 1887, p. 2; NYT, June 19, 1887, p. 1.

44. NYT, Oct. 20, 1889, p. 2; NYT, Nov. 26, 1889, p. 9.

45. NYT, Jan. 2, 1888, p. 8; NYT, Aug. 25, 1889, p. 4; NYT, Mar. 7, 1907, p. 8. For visual evidence of the flag's prominence and symbolic power, see Alan Trachtenberg, ed., *The American Image: Photographs from the National Archives, 1860–1960* (New York, 1979), 70, 109–11, and Michael Lesy, *Bearing Witness: A Photographic Chronicle of American Life, 1860–1945* (New York, 1982), 28–29, a marvelous late-nineteenth-century photograph of black children in a schoolyard at Hampton, Virginia, solemnly pledging allegiance to the flag, their right arms raised in front of them in a manner that we now associate with Fascists during the 1930s.

46. See Richard A. E. Brooks, "The Development of the Historical Mind," in Joseph E. Baker, ed., *The Reinterpretation of Victorian Literature* (Princeton, 1950), 130–52; Vilar, "Enseignement primaire et culture populaire en France sous la IIIe République," in Louis Bergeron, ed., *Niveaux de Culture et Groupes Sociaux* (Paris and The Hague, 1967), 267–76, the quotation at 274.

47. Temma Kaplan, *Anarchists of Andalusia, 1868–1903* (Princeton, 1977), 84–86; Nina Tumarkin, *Lenin Lives! The Lenin Cult in Soviet Russia* (Cambridge, Mass., 1983), 218–19.

48. NYT, Nov. 29, 1888, p. 2 NYT, Nov. 28, 1889, p. 8; NYT, Nov. 29, 1889, p. 3; NYT, Nov. 27, 1924, p. 18.

49. See W. Lloyd Warner, *The Living and the Dead: A Study of the Symbolic Life of Americans* (New Haven, 1959), 121, 126, 213, 215.

50. Ward McCallister, *Society As I Have Found It* (New York, 1890), 323–24; Laurence Veysey, "The Plural Organized Worlds of the Humanities," in Alexandra Oleson and John Voss, eds., *The Organization of Knowledge in Modern America, 1860–1920* (Baltimore, 1979), 51–92, esp. 52; Randel, *Edward Eggleston*, 199, 221; Joan Shelley Rubin, *Constance Rourke and American Culture* (Chapel Hill, N.C., 1980), 6–7.

51. John Foord, *The Life and Public Services of Andrew Haswell Green* (Garden City, N.Y., 1913), ch. 18; Stephen Jay Gould, *Time's Arrow, Time's Cycle: Myth and Metaphor in the Discovery of Geological Time* (Cambridge, Mass., 1987); Barbara Novak, *Nature and Culture: American Landscape and Painting, 1825–1875* (New York, 1980), 56, 144, 163, 198; Edwin T. Stanley, *Rambles in Wonderland* (New York, 1880).

52. Dorothy Ross, "The Liberal Tradition Revisited and the Republican Tradition Addressed," in John Higham and Paul K. Conkin, eds., *New Directions in American Intellectual History* (Baltimore, 1979), 125–27; Paul A. Carter, *The Spiritual Crisis of the Gilded Age* (DeKalb, Ill., 1971), esp. 18.

53. They appeared respectively as an editorial in *Harper's*, 72 (March 1886), 642, and an essay by Frederic Dan Huntington in *The Forum*, 1 (June 1886), 320.

54. Louise Hall Tharp, *Saint-Gaudens and the Gilded Era* (Boston, 1969), 184, 186, 209.

55. Barbara Miller Solomon, *Ancestors and Immigrants: A Changing New England Tradition* (1956: Chicago, 1972), 28–31; Brooks Adams, *The Emancipation of Massachu-*

setts: The Dream and the Reality, Introduction by Perry Miller (1887: Boston, 1962), xviii, xxxvii. See also Charles Francis Adams, Jr., *Three Episodes of Massachusetts History: The Settlement of Boston Bay; The Antinomian Controversy; A Study of Church and Town Government* (Boston, 1893), part 3, a history of Old Braintree and Quincy.

56. Jan C. Dawson, *The Unusable Past: America's Puritan Tradition, 1830 to 1930* (Chico, Calif., 1984), 109–12; Tharp, *Saint-Gaudens and the Gilded Era,* 211.

57. NYT, June 7, 1885, p. 9; NYT, June 17, 1885, p. 2.

58. NYT, June 7, 1885, p. 9. For another speech indicative of this intercity cultural competition, see "Puritan Principle and Puritan Pluck," in Charles Eliot Norton, ed., *Orations and Addresses of George William Curtis* (New York, 1894), I, 253–60: "In the game of persecution, as between New England and New York, the dishonors are easy. But when we have called the Puritan a sour-faced fanatic, have we done with him? . . . The root of Puritanism may have been gloomy bigotry, but the flower was liberty" (pp. 257–58).

59. NYT, Dec. 23, 1887, p. 3. For the contretemps caused in 1907 when Theodore Roosevelt dedicated a monument at Provincetown to the Pilgrims and repeatedly called them Puritans, and for the uncertainty among professional historians as to the significance of the episode, see J. Franklin Jameson to Albert Matthews, Oct. 22, 1907, in Elizabeth Donnan and Leo F. Stock, eds., *An Historian's World: Selections from the Correspondence of John Franklin Jameson* (Philadelphia, 1956), 110–11.

60. See Matthews, *The Term Pilgrim Fathers* (Cambridge, Mass., 1915), and the laudatory discussion of Lord in James K. Hosmer's manuscript autobiography, pp. 568–69, MinnHS.

61. Arthur Lord, "The Value of Tradition" [c. 1915], is a 36-page typescript owned by the Pilgrim Society and located in Pilgrim Hall at Plymouth. The material in this and the following paragraphs is based upon that address.

62. Ibid., 35–36.

63. Charles Dudley Warner, "The Pilgrim and the American of To-Day," an address given at the New England Society dinner held in Indianapolis on Dec. 21, 1892, in Warner, *Fashions in Literature and Other Literary and Social Essays & Addresses* (New York, 1902), 127; William DeWitt Hyde, "The Pilgrim Principle and the Pilgrim Heritage," *Forum,* 20 (December 1895), 488.

64. NYT, Aug. 2, 1889, pp. 1, 2; NYT, Dec. 22, 1889, p. 5.

65. NYT, Aug. 25, 1889, p. 4.

66. Henry F. May, *Protestant Churches and Industrial America* (New York, 1949), 129; NYT, May 15, 1887, p. 4; NYT, Sept. 23, 1889, p. 4; John Dewey, "The School as Social Center," *The Elementary School Journal,* 3 (1902), 84–85.

67. Wallace Evan Davies, *Patriotism on Parade: The Story of Veterans' and Hereditary Organizations in America, 1783–1900* (Cambridge, Mass., 1955), 231; Solomon, *Ancestors and Immigrants,* 53; Dawson, *The Unusable Past,* 48.

68. Rebecca Harding Davis, "In the Gray Cabins of New England," *The Century,* 49 (February 1895), 620–23; Matthews to Eggleston, Jan. 24, 1897, quoted in Randel, *Edward Eggleston,* 215–16. On December 23, 1889, when the New England Society of New York celebrated Forefathers' Day, the Rev. H. L. Wayland of Philadelphia gave the principal oration. He called it "Why the New-Englanders Are Unpopular," and explained that because they had always been both so self-righteous and successful, others simply envied them. NYT, Dec. 24, 1889, pp. 1–2.

69. Perry Miller, *Nature's Nation* (Cambridge, Mass., 1967), 208; Dawson, *The Unusable Past,* 64; NYT, Feb. 23, 1889, p. 3; NYT, Aug. 2, 1889, p. 4. On the more tranquil side, the New-England Society of Charleston, S.C., held annual Forefathers' Day banquets characterized by polite palaver. See NYT, Dec. 22, 1888, p. 2.

70. "The American Mind," *Harper's,* 15 (October 1857), 693; NYT, Dec. 22, 1888, p. 2; NYT, Dec. 19, 1889, p. 1; NYT, Dec. 22, 1889, p. 4; Roosevelt to Lummis, Aug. 5, 1907, in Dudley Gordon, *Charles F. Lummis: Crusader in Corduroy* (n.p., 1972), 20–21.

71. NYT, June 17, 1885, p. 2; James A. Hijiya, *J. W. DeForest and the Rise of American Gentility* (Hanover, N.H., 1988), 47; NYT, Dec. 23, 1888, p. 2; Society of Colonial Wars

dinner, Dec. 19, 1898, Charles P. Noyes Papers, box 2, MinnHS; Hart, "Some of the Big New Englanders Who Have Helped to Build Up the Great West," *Munsey's Magazine*, 38 (November 1907), 139–50, esp. 150; the same in Hart, *National Ideals Historically Traced* (New York, 1907), 46; Robert Cruden, *James Ford Rhodes: The Man, the Historian, and His Work* (Cleveland, 1961), 213.

72.   See George William Curtis, "The Puritan Principle: Liberty Under the Law," in Charles Eliot Norton, ed., *Orations and Addresses of George William Curtis* (New York, 1893), I, 246; Warner, "The Pilgrim and the American of To-Day," 118.

73.   Curtis, "Puritan Principle: Liberty Under the Law," 246–47; NYT, Dec. 23, 1887, pp. 1–2; NYT, Dec. 30, 1889, p. 8.

74.   Hoar to Lyon G. Tyler, Feb. 21, 1901, Tyler Papers, group 5, box 2, SLWM; Hoar to James W. Johnson (of Marion, S.C.), March 2, 1903, Hoar Papers, MHS.

75.   Richard E. Welch, Jr., *George Frisbie Hoar and the Half-Breed Republicans* (Cambridge, Mass., 1971), 315, 317, 332. For a comparison with Lodge, see "The Independent Spirit of the Puritans" (Dec. 22, 1884), and "The Puritans" (Dec. 22, 1887), in Lodge, *Speeches* (Boston, 1892), 1–10, 33–36.

76.   *The Education of Henry Adams*, 222.

77.   Rossiter's painting is located at the New-York Historical Society, New York City; Kathleen A. Foster, ed., *Edwin Austin Abbey (1852–1911): An Exhibition Organized by the Yale University Art Gallery* (New Haven, 1973), 24; Abbey's "Stony Ground" is located at the Brooklyn Museum; NYT, Nov. 1, 1889, p. 4; Opper's cartoons will be found in *Bill Nye's History of the United States* (Philadelphia, 1894).

78.   In one of the climactic chapters of *The House of the Seven Gables* (1851: Boston, 1900), 406–07, Hawthorne describes a portrait of the seventeenth-century Pyncheon progenitor that evokes an image similar to Schoonover's, or even to the Saint-Gaudens statue from the later 1880s.

79.   The Morse is located at the Charlestown branch of the Boston Public Library; the Corné is in the Diplomatic Reception Rooms of the State Department in Washington, D.C.; and for the *The Pilgrim*, see *American Art in the Newark Museum: Paintings, Drawings and Sculpture* (Newark, N.J., 1981), 408.

80.   Thomas W. Higginson, "Americanism in Literature," *Atlantic*, 25 (January 1870), 56–63; F. G. Ireland, "Puritanism and Manners," *Atlantic*, 43 (February 1879), 163.

81.   Theodore Clark Smith, "The Scientific Historian and Our Colonial Period," *Atlantic*, 98 (November 1906), 709–10; Robert Trent, ed., *Pilgrim Century Furniture: An Historical Survey* (New York, 1976).

82.   "Puritans and Witches" (editorial), *The Century*, 24 (July 1882), 460.

83.   John Murray, *Jerubbaal, or Tyranny's Grove Destroyed, and the Altar of Liberty Finished: A Discourse on America's Duty and Danger* (Newbury-Port, Mass., 1784), 62; NYT, July 4, 1837, p. 3; Webster, "The Dignity and Importance of History," Feb. 23, 1852, in *The Writings and Speeches of Daniel Webster* (Boston, 1903), XIII, 471, 489.

84.   Ralph Waldo Emerson, "Works and Days," *Society and Solitude* (1870), in Emerson, *The Complete Works* (Boston, 1912), VII, 177; Alexis de Tocqueville, *Democracy in America,* ed. J. P. Mayer (Garden City, N.Y., 1969), 508.

85.   NYT, June 25, 1885, p. 4; NYT, Dec. 25, 1887, p. 16; the Holmes quotation from Kenneth S. Lynn, *William Dean Howells: An American Life* (New York, 1971), 95.

86.   "The Point of View," *Scribner's Magazine*, 15 (February 1894), 262; "The Puritans," in Lodge, *Speeches* (Boston, 1892), 33.

87.   Solomon, *Ancestors and Immigrants*, 68, 112–13, 116.

88.   Concerning the rage for ancestor worship in Great Britain, ca. 1875–1915, see Martin J. Wiener, *English Culture and the Decline of the Industrial Spirit, 1850–1980* (Cambridge, 1981), 46, 69, 71; Anthony R. Wagner, *English Genealogy* (Oxford, 1972); and the satire of English ancestor worship in Gilbert and Sullivan's *Pirates of Penzance* (1878), Act II.

89.   Hoar to Mrs. John Bellows, Dec. 2, 1902, Hoar Papers, MHS; Hoar to Rockwood Hoar, Apr. 20, 1904, ibid.; Welch, *George F. Hoar*, 313–25, esp. 324.

90. Wilson, *Baptized in Blood,* 36; Haldvan Koht, *Education of an Historian* (New York, 1957), 189–90; Mary F. Goodwin to William G. Perry, May 29, 1931, CWA.

91. NYT, Dec. 7, 1889, p. 2; Solomon, *Ancestors and Immigrants,* 60; John C. Fitzpatrick to Worthington C. Ford, May 29, 1909, Ford Papers, box 5, NYPL Annex. See also F. A. Watkins to Clifford L. Hilton, Jan. 26, 1921, Minnesota Society of the Sons of the American Revolution Papers, box 1891–1923, MinnHS.

92. NYT, Nov. 1, 1885, p. 4; George J. Manson, "A Renaissance of Patriotism," *The Independent,* 52 (July 5, 1900), 1612–15; Minnie G. Cook to Lyon G. Tyler, June 5, 1913, Tyler Papers, group 5, box 3, SLWM.

93. See Davies, *Patriotism on Parade,* chs. 10–11, 13; Henry Baldwin to A. Howard Clark, Jan. 9, 1902, Library Americana, box 3, NYPL Annex; Lindgren, "The Gospel of Preservation in Virginia and New England," 250, 253.

94. Paul F. Boller, Jr., *Presidential Anecdotes* (New York, 1981), 226, 246; Sara A. Pryor to Lyon G. Tyler, April 1, 1892, Tyler Papers, group 5, box 1; Fitzhugh Lee (president of the Jefferson Memorial Road Association) to Edwin Warfield, Nov. 26, 1902, ibid., box 2; G. Washington Ball to Worthington C. Ford, May 19, 1894, Ford Papers, box 1, NYPL Annex; Mount Vernon Ladies Association, *Historical Sketch of Ann Pamela Cunningham: "The Southern Matron"* (Queens, N.Y., 1911), 48–49.

95. Robert M. Crunden, *Ministers of Reform: The Progressives' Achievement in American Civilization, 1889–1920* (New York, 1982), 3; Roosevelt to James J. Roche, Jan. 13, 1897, in *The Journal of the American-Irish Historical Society,* 1 (1898), 27–28.

96. NYT, Aug. 25, 1885, p. 5; Marcus Lee Hansen, *The Problem of the Third Generation Immigrant* (Rock Island, Ill., 1938), 11; *Historical Societies of the United States and Canada. A Handbook* (Indianapolis, 1936), 54.

97. Clyde A. Milner, "The Shared Memory of Montana Pioneers," MMWHC, 37 (1987), 2–13. For a similar episode involving the Arizona Pioneers Historical Society in 1884–85, see C. L. Sonnichsen, *The Ambidextrous Historian: Historical Writers and Writing in the American West* (Norman, Okla., 1981), 49–50.

98. NYT, July 4, 1888, p. 1, quoted in Powell, "The Most Celebrated Encampment," 105.

99. W. E. B. Du Bois, *Dusk of Dawn: An Essay Toward an Autobiography of a Race Concept* (New York, 1940), 115; Sylvia W. Razey to Du Bois, Feb. 13, 1940, in Herbert Aptheker, ed., *The Correspondence of W. E. B. Du Bois* (Amherst, Mass., 1973–78), II, 213.

100. Owen Wister, "The Evolution of the Cow Puncher," *Harper's Magazine,* 91 (September 1895), 604–14; Goldwin Smith to James K. Hosmer, Nov. 19, 1888, Hosmer Papers, box 1, MinnHS.

101. Shaler is quoted in Solomon, *Ancestors and Immigrants,* 93; D. O. S. Lowell, "The Quest of Ancestors," *Munsey's Magazine,* 34 (February 1906), 543–48; S. P. Langley, *Memoir of George Brown Goode, 1851–1896* (Washington, D.C., 1897), 4, 25–27.

102. Henry H. Goddard, *The Kallikak Family: A Study in the Heredity of Feeble-Mindedness* (New York, 1912); Daniel J. Boorstin, *The Americans: The Democratic Experience* (New York, 1973), 222; Henry D. Shapiro, *Appalachia on Our Mind: The Southern Mountains and Mountaineers in the American Consciousness, 1870–1920* (Chapel Hill, N.C., 1978), 79, 119, 218.

103. Louise Allan Mayo and Mary Lyons Mayo, "Some Colonial Dames," *Munsey's Magazine,* 16 (November 1896), 153–60. In 1895–96 *Munsey's* ran a lengthy series on "Prominent American Families," bearing a tone of family ancestor worship; Harvey Sutherland, "The American Westminster Abbey," ibid., 28 (March 1903), 831–42.

104. Dodd, "History and Patriotism," SAQ, 12 (1913), 109; Lincoln is quoted in George W. Pierson, *The Moving American* (New York, 1973), 96n.; *The Family Mark Twain* (New York, n.d.), 442.

105. See NYT, Mar. 20, 1887, p. 6; Florida Pier, "The Power of Ancestors," *The Century,* 71 (January 1906), 445–47; Edward Chase Kirkland, *Charles Francis Adams, Jr., 1835–1915: The Patrician at Bay* (Cambridge, Mass., 1965), 213–14.

106. Johan Huizinga, *America: A Dutch Historian's Vision from Afar and Near* (New York, 1972), 193. For contemporary evidence that supports Huizinga's judgment, see

Gamaliel Bradford to Lyon G. Tyler, Jan. 5, 1922, Tyler Papers, group 1, box 20, SLWM; Samuel Herrick to Tyler, June 24, 1930 (writing on behalf of the General Court of the Order of the Founders and Patriots of America), ibid., box 24.

107.   See Theodore Zeldin, *France, 1848–1945: Ambition and Love* (1973: Oxford, 1979), 66, 89, 146; Eric Hobsbawm and Terence Ranger, eds., *The Invention of Tradition* (Cambridge, 1983), 291–96.

108.   Georges Duby, *The Three Orders: Feudal Society Imagined* (Chicago, 1980), 6–8; Donald R. Kelley, *Foundations of Modern Historical Scholarship: Language, Law, and History in the French Renaissance* (New York, 1970), 145.

109.   Claude Lévi-Strauss, *The Savage Mind* (London, 1966), 238, 241; John L. Greenway, *The Golden Horns: Mythic Imagination and the Nordic Past* (Athens, Ga., 1977), 50–51.

110.   Meyer Fortes, "An Introductory Commentary" in William H. Newell, ed., *Ancestors* (The Hague, 1976), 2–3. For instructive examples, see P. Steven Sangren, *History and Magical Power in a Chinese Community* (Stanford, Calif., 1988); Emily M. Ahern, *The Cult of the Dead in a Chinese Village* (Stanford, Calif., 1973); Roger L. Janelli and Dawnhee Yim Janelli, *Ancestor Worship and Korean Society* (Stanford, Calif., 1982).

111.   For purposes of contrast with the United States, see Robert J. Smith, *Ancestor Worship in Contemporary Japan* (Stanford, Calif., 1974); Frances FitzGerald, *Fire in the Lake: The Vietnamese and the Americans in Vietnam* (New York, 1972), 303, 572–73.

112.   See James W. Fernandez, "The Affirmation of Things Past: Alar Ayong and Bwiti as Movements of Protest in Central and Northern Gabon," in Robert I. Rotberg and Ali Mazrui, eds., *Protest and Power in Black Africa* (New York, 1970), 427–57, esp. 440–41.

113.   For condescending American interest in the ancestral practices of others, see Carl Holliday, "The Japanese Feast of the Departed," *Overland Monthly* [*Outwest Magazine*], 91 (November 1933), 157.

114.   Nelson, "Mary Johnston," 74; Howells, "An Earlier American," NAR, 172 (June 1901), 934–44, the quotation at 943. This was actually an essay review about a journalist, William James Stillman, who was "of a New England stock, in which the inherited Puritanism was condensed and intensified by the narrowness of a minute sect."

115.   Christie's catalogue, May 26, 1988, p. 4. For a wonderfully parodic photograph by Jennie Hatch (c. 1915–18), titled "Three Generations," see Marilyn F. Motz, "Visual Autobiography: Photograph Albums of Turn-of-the-Century Midwestern Women," AQ, 41 (1989), 82.

116.   Grafly's *Aeneas* is located in the Philadelphia Academy of the Fine Arts. For an illustration and descriptive text, see *Philadelphia: Three Centuries of American Art* (Philadelphia, 1976), 440 and fig. 376. This motif also has sources in Christian art as well as classical literature. There is a Byzantine icon from Crete called *St. Anne Enthroned with the Virgin and Child,* painted with tempera on wood during the 1430s. Three generations of the holy family are seated on a green marble throne: The Christ child is on Mary's lap, and she in turn sits on the lap of her mother, Anne. Each figure is proportionately larger according to age. The icon originated in the Church of St. Nicholas Molos on the island of Zakynthos. It was exhibited during the spring of 1989 at the Kimbell Art Museum in Fort Worth, Texas.

117.   See Alan Axelrod, ed., *The Colonial Revival in America* (New York, 1985), 247–48; David P. Handlin, *The American Home: Architecture and Society, 1815–1915* (Boston, 1979), 412–13; Marling, *George Washington Slept Here,* 170, 175.

118.   Hoar to Rockwood Hoar, Apr. 20, 1904, Hoar Papers, MHS. The importance of transmitting tradition "from man to man, and from generation to generation" appears in George Santayana, "Tradition and Practice" (1904), in James Ballowe, ed., *George Santayana's America: Essays on Literature and Culture* (Urbana, Ill., 1967), 110.

119.   See Geoffrey West, "Joseph Hergesheimer," VQR, 8 (1932), 95–108.

Chapter 8

1.　James Russell Lowell, "The Place of the Independent in Politics" (1888), in *Complete Works of James Russell Lowell: Literary and Political Addresses* (Boston, 1910), VI, 219.

2.　Ibid., 205.

3.　Rowland T. Berthoff, *British Immigrants in Industrial America, 1790–1950* (Cambridge, Mass., 1953), 162, 165, and chs. 10–11 generally; NYT, May 31, 1887, p. 8.

4.　NYT, June 1, 1885, p. 8; NYT, June 21, 1885, p. 4.

5.　Michael R. Weisser, *A Brotherhood of Memory: Jewish Landsmanshaftn in the New World* (New York, 1985); Marcus Ravage is quoted in Irving Howe, *World of Our Fathers* (New York, 1976), 76. See also 59, 70, 71, 74, 105, 106, and 116 for the pressures that American life placed upon the survival of Old World customs.

6.　See Donald C. Bellomy, "Two Generations: Modernists and Progressives, 1870–1920," PAH, n.s., 3 (1986), 298.

7.　David Montgomery, "Nationalism, American Patriotism and Class Consciousness among Immigrant Workers in the United States in the Epoch of World War I," in Dirk Hoerder, ed., *"Struggle a Hard Battle": Essays on Working-Class Immigrants* (DeKalb, Ill., 1986), 335.

8.　Ibid., 336. See generally Edward George Hartmann, *The Movement to Americanize the Immigrant* (New York, 1948).

9.　Quoted in Mona Harrington, "Loyalties: Dual and Divided," in Stephan Thernstrom, ed., *Harvard Encyclopedia of American Ethnic Groups* (Cambridge, Mass., 1980), 678.

10.　Ibid.; Louis L. Gerson, *The Hyphenate in Recent American Politics and Diplomacy* (Lawrence, Kans., 1964); Maldwyn A. Jones, *The Old World Ties of American Ethnic Groups* (London, 1976).

11.　For general context, see Herbert G. Gutman, *Work, Culture, and Society in Industrializing America: Essays in American Working-Class and Social History* (New York, 1976), 3–78; John Higham, *Send These to Me: Jews and Other Immigrants in Urban America* (New York, 1975), esp. chs. 2, 5.

12.　NYT, Sept. 17, 1888, p. 4; NYT, Sept. 16, 1889, p. 1.

13.　NYT, Aug. 18, 1889, p. 15; NYT, Sept. 8, 1889, p. 16.

14.　NYT, Oct. 20, 1889, p. 17; NYT, Oct. 31, 1889, p. 4.

15.　Marcus Lee Hansen, *The Problem of the Third Generation Immigrant* (Rock Island, Ill., 1938), 12. In addition to figure 8.1, see the fine photograph by Eve Arnold, *In America* (New York, 1983), p. 44, "Feast of San Gennaro/New York City."

16.　Daniel T. Rodgers, "Tradition, Modernity, and the American Industrial Worker: Reflections and Critique," JIH, 7 (1977), 655–81, esp. 666–67, 673.

17.　NYT, Jan. 9, 1888, p. 3. For the on-going persistence of this pressure, see George Creel, "The Hopes of the Hyphenated," *The Century*, 91 (January 1916), 350–63.

18.　Quoted in Gutman, *Work, Culture, and Society in Industrializing America*, 69. See also Philip Gleason, "The Melting-Pot: Symbol of Fusion or Confusion?" AQ, 16 (1964), 26.

19.　See Cahan, *The Rise of David Levinsky* (1917: New York, 1960), Introduction by John Higham; A. Scott Berg, *Goldwyn: A Biography* (New York, 1989), esp. chs. 1–3.

20.　"Reports of Leon Hühner, Curator," *Publications of the American Jewish Historical Society*, 22 (1914), xxxv.

21.　NYT, Nov. 3, 1889, p. 3.

22.　Quoted in Richard Polenberg, *Fighting Faiths: The Abrams Case, the Supreme Court, and Free Speech* (New York, 1987), 118.

23.　See the invaluable essay by Philip Gleason, "American Identity and Americanization," in Thernstrom, ed., *Harvard Encyclopedia of American Ethnic Groups*, 38.

24. Brander Matthews, "The American of the Future," *The Century,* 74 (July 1907), 477.

25. Herbert N. Casson, "The Americans in America," *Munsey's Magazine,* 36 (January 1907), 432–36, the quotation at 436.

26. George Lincoln Burr, "Henry Charles Lea,"_Publications of the American Jewish Historical Society,* 19 (1910), 181.

27. Kallen's major publications are conveniently summarized and placed in their proper cultural context in Gleason, "American Identity and Americanization," 43.

28. Ibid., 44.

29. Paul B. Worthman, "Working Class Mobility in Birmingham, Alabama, 1880–1914," in Tamara K. Hareven, ed., *Anonymous Americans: Explorations in Nineteenth-Century Social History* (Englewood Cliffs, N.J., 1971), 172–213; Herbert G. Gutman, *Power & Culture: Essays on the American Working Class* (New York, 1987), ch. 12. See also Hjalmar R. Holand to J. Franklin Jameson, Apr. 8, 1909, Jameson Papers, box 94, MDLC: "The great bulk of the Norwegians of America live in the Middle Northwest, where they, as a rule, have been the pioneers in the settlement of the country. Very little has been done to preserve the memory of these sturdy pioneers."

30. Eggleston to Baldwin, Nov. 25, 1892, Library Americana, box 60, NYPL Annex.

31. Constance Fenimore Woolson, *Mentone, Cairo, and Corfu* (New York, 1896), 278.

32. NYT, May 3, 1903, p. 3, from Reginald H. Williams. For a subsequent example of realism and moderation, see Creel, "The Hopes of the Hyphenated," 350–63.

33. See NYT, Mar. 17, 1888, p. 8.

34. Peggy and Harold Samuels, *Frederic Remington: A Biography* (Garden City, N.Y., 1982), 195; Morton Keller, *Affairs of State: Public Life in Late Nineteenth Century America* (Cambridge, Mass., 1977), 441–42.

35. H. Addington Bruce, *The Romance of American Expansion* (New York, 1909), xii; William O. McDowell to Henry Baldwin, Feb. 8, 1893, Library Americana, box 59, NYPL Annex.

36. Quoted in George M. Fredrickson, *The Black Image in the White Mind: The Debate on Afro-American Character and Destiny, 1817–1914* (New York, 1971), 305; Elizabeth Stillinger, *The Antiquers* (New York, 1980), 205.

37. Lowell, "The Place of the Independent in Politics," 205.

38. Henry T. Tuckerman, *America and Her Commentators: With A Critical Sketch of Travel in the United States* (New York, 1864), 439–40; Lowell, "Democracy" (1884), in *Complete Works of Lowell,* VI, 22.

39. NYT, May 15, 1887, p. 4. For a fine contextual discussion of steady shifts in the values of the established elite, see Frederic Cople Jaher, "The Boston Brahmins in the Age of Industrial Capitalism," in Jaher, ed., *The Age of Industrialism in America: Essays in Social Structure and Cultural Values* (New York, 1968), 188–243.

40. Geoffrey Blodgett, "The Mugwump Reputation, 1870 to the Present," JAH, 66 (1980), 867–87; John G. Sproat, *"The Best Men": Liberal Reformers in the Gilded Age* (New York, 1968).

41. Barbara Miller Solomon, *Ancestors and Immigrants: A Changing New England Tradition* (1956: Chicago, 1972), 87; James, *The American Scene* (1907: New York, 1967), 265–72.

42. John Spencer Clark, *The Life and Letters of John Fiske* (Boston, 1917), II, 26.

43. NYT, Mar. 14, 1888, p. 8; NYT, Mar. 21, 1888, p. 5.

44. NYT, May 5, 1888, p. 1; NYT, May 6, 1888, p. 4.

45. NYT, June 23, 1902, p. 8.

46. NYT, Oct. 16, 1887, p. 11; NYT, July 5, 1889, p. 3.

47. NYT, May 20, 1889, p. 2. See also Hartmut Keil, ed., *German Workers' Culture in the United States, 1850–1920* (Washington, D.C., 1988).

48. Susan Prendergast Schoelwer, *Alamo Images: Changing Perceptions of a Texas Experience* (Dallas, 1985), ix, 43–50, 56–58; Martha Anne Turner, *Clara Driscoll: An American Tradition* (Austin, Tex., 1979), 18.

49. Schoelwer, *Alamo Images,* 24, 39, 43, 47–48.

50. Turner, *Clara Driscoll,* 17–29; and Driscoll's romantic historical tales, *In the Shadow of the Alamo* (New York, 1906).

51. Jack C. Butterfield, *Clara Driscoll Rescued the Alamo* (pamphlet: n.p., n.d.).

52. Schoelwer, *Alamo Images,* 48–59; Kenneth B. Ragsdale, *The Year America Discovered Texas: Centennial '36* (College Station, Tex., 1987), 156–57, 171, 174.

53. NYT, Apr. 19, 1903, p. 8.

54. Oscar J. Falnes, "New England Interest in Scandinavian Culture and the Norsemen," NEQ, 10 (1937), 211–42; Joseph Story Fay to John Fiske, Nov. 11, 1879, Fiske Papers, box 8, HEHL; Marie A. Brown, *The Icelandic Discoverers of America; or, Honor to Whom Honor Is Due* (Boston, 1888); "Eben Norton Horsford" (1818–93) in DAB.

55. Edmund B. Delabarre, "The Runic Rock on No Man's Land, Massachusetts," NEQ, 8 (1935), 365–77; and see Edward F. Gray, *Leif Eriksson, Discoverer of America, A.D. 1003* (New York, 1930), the work of a true believer. Delabarre believed the runic inscription was cut by Walton Ricketson (1839–1923) of New Bedford, Mass.

56. Hjalmar R. Holand to J. Franklin Jameson, Apr. 8, 1909, Jameson Papers, box 94, MDLC; Erik Wahlgren, *The Kensington Stone: A Mystery Solved* (Madison, Wis., 1958); R. A. Skelton et al., comps., *The Vinland Map and the Tartar Relation* (New Haven, 1965).

57. NYT, Jan. 21, 1889, p. 5; NYT, Oct. 22, 1889, p. 9; NYT, Oct. 28, 1889, p. 9; NYT, Nov. 3, 1889, p. 4.

58. James Thorpe, "The Founder and His Library," in *The Founding of the Henry E. Huntington Library and Art Gallery: Four Essays* (San Marino, Calif., 1969), 298; Storrs, *The Early American Spirit, and the Genius of It* (New York, 1875), 69.

59. NYT, Oct. 24, 1889, p. 2; Arthur M. Schlesinger, Jr., *The Age of Roosevelt: The Politics of Upheaval* (Boston, 1960), 425; NYT, May 30, 1939, p. 16.

60. Brander Matthews, "The American of the Future," *The Century,* 74 (July 1907), 474–80, the quotations at 476 and 477. See also Lawrence J. Oliver, "Theodore Roosevelt, Brander Matthews, and the Campaign for Literary Americanism," AQ, 41 (1989), 93–111.

61. Charles B. Hosmer, Jr., *Presence of the Past: A History of the Preservation Movement in the United States before Williamsburg* (New York, 1965), 104–06, 138–39, 148–49; Karal Ann Marling, *George Washington Slept Here: Colonial Revivals and American Culture, 1876–1986* (Cambridge, Mass., 1988), 162–64.

62. Solomon, *Ancestors and Immigrants,* 84–85; NYT, June 29, 1889, p. 2; NYT, Nov. 25, 1887, p. 5; Montgomery, "Nationalism, American Patriotism and Class Consciousness among Immigrant Workers," 343.

63. Goldwin Smith to James K. Hosmer, Nov. 19, 1888, Hosmer Papers, box 1, MinnHS; Marling, *George Washington Slept Here,* 202, 205; George Bird Grinnell, *Beyond the Old Frontier: Adventures of Indian Fighters, Hunters, and Fur Traders* (New York, 1913), vii; NYT, Feb. 18, 1935, p. 10.

64. NYT, Jan. 3, 1900, p. 3.

65. Rolla M. Tryon, *The Social Sciences as School Subjects* (New York, 1935), 131, 177; Theodore R. Sizer, *Secondary Schools at the Turn of the Century* (New Haven, 1964), 126; *The Study of History in Schools: Report to the American Historical Association* (New York, 1899), 18–26.

66. Solomon, *Ancestors and Immigrants,* 85–86.

67. NYT, Mar. 2, 1889, p. 3; NYT, Mar. 4, 1889, p. 3; Frank L. McVey, "United States History in Secondary Schools," *The Century,* 52 (September 1896), 797.

68. These developments occurred between 1894 and 1898. See William Peirce Randel, *Edward Eggleston* (New York, 1946), 207, 209, 222.

69. Letter from Reginald H. Williams, NYT, May 3, 1903, p. 3. See also NYT, Dec. 17, 1902, p. 16.

70. "A Great Day," *Harper's Weekly,* Dec. 8, 1883, 778; NYT, Dec. 12, 1889, p. 9; Marling, *George Washington Slept Here,* 153.

71. Edward Hagaman Hall, comp., *The Hudson-Fulton Celebration, 1909* (Albany, 1910), I, 7–8. According to one authority, hyphenated Americanism, with the connotation

of inevitably divided loyalties, did not become a pejorative term until around 1915. See Gleason, "American Identity and Americanization," 40.

72.   NYT, Jan. 2, 1910, p. 9.

73.   *Salem News,* Aug. 25, 1907, quoted in Anne Farnam, "George Francis Dow: A Career of Bringing the 'picturesque traditions of sleeping generations' to Life in the Early Twentieth Century," EIHC, 121 (1985), 82. For Dow, see also Elizabeth Stillinger, *The Antiquers* (New York, 1980), 149–54.

74.   Laurence R. Veysey, *The Emergence of the American University* (Chicago, 1965), 172; NYT, Dec. 8, 1907, p. 16.

75.   H. Morse Stephens to Andrew Dickson White, May 11, 1897, White Papers, box 80, CUL; Michael Kammen, "Richard Watson Gilder and the New York Tenement House Commission of 1894," *Bulletin* of the NYPL, 66 (1962), 366–67.

76.   Edward A. Purcell, Jr., *The Crisis of Democratic Theory: Scientific Naturalism & the Problem of Value* (Lexington, Ky., 1973), 32; Fred H. Matthews, *Quest for an American Sociology: Robert E. Park and the Chicago School* (Montreal, 1977).

77.   See T. J. Jackson Lears, *No Place of Grace: Antimodernism and the Transformation of American Culture, 1880–1920* (New York, 1981); John Higham, *Strangers in the Land: Patterns of American Nativism, 1860–1925* (2nd ed.: New Brunswick, N.J., 1988), esp. chs. 3–5.

78.   NYT, Mar. 20, 1887, p. 6; S. P. Langley, *Memoir of George Brown Goode, 1851–1896* (Washington, D.C., 1897), 25–27.

79.   Wallace Evan Davies, *Patriotism on Parade: The Story of Veterans' and Hereditary Organizations in America, 1783–1900* (Cambridge, Mass., 1955), 60–63, 67–69, 85–86, 283.

80.   Ibid., 70–71, 138.

81.   Keith Thomas, "History and Anthropology," *Past & Present,* no. 24 (April 1963), 13–14.

82.   "A Republican Aristocracy," *Scribner's Magazine,* 35 (February 1904), 124.

83.   *Frank Leslie's Illustrated Newspaper,* Mar. 11, 1876, pp. 8–9, 12–13.

84.   Baldwin to Col. A. S. Hubbard, Feb. 18, 1902, Baldwin Papers, box 3, NYPL Annex.

85.   Baldwin's circular letter, Jan. 9, 1891, Library Americana, box 59, NYPL Annex; Baldwin to G. Brown Goode, Oct. 20, 1891, ibid., box 60.

86.   Joseph Reynolds to Baldwin, Feb. 6, 1892, Library Americana, box 60, NYPL Annex; A. F. Spear to Baldwin, Feb. 16, 1892, ibid.

87.   McDowell to Baldwin, June 29, 1892, July 5, 1892, Library Americana, box 60, NYPL Annex; McDowell letterheads in ibid., box 59; Baldwin to McDowell, Jan. 16, 1902, ibid., box 3.

88.   Edward S. Deemer to Baldwin, Nov. 23, 1895, ibid., box 2; Baldwin to John L. Cadwalader, May 22, 1901, ibid., box 3; Baldwin to J. C. Pumpelly, Jan. 14, 1902, ibid.

89.   Baldwin to the Trustees of the Library Americana, Apr. 1, 1902, ibid. (Mailed on May 22, 1901, to McDowell.)

90.   See the Foreign Press Committee to Lyon G. Tyler, Jan. 28, 1914, Tyler Family Papers, group 1, box 21, SLWM. "We are gratified to note that your views on the subject of a literacy test for immigrants are so sound and entirely in accord with the best traditions of our country."

Chapter 9

1.   Lowell, "The Place of the Independent in Politics" (1888), in *The Complete Works of James Russell Lowell: Literary and Political Addresses* (Boston, 1910), VI, 201–02.

2.   David Glassberg, "History and the Public: Legacies of the Progressive Era," JAH, 73 (1987), 979–80.

3. Neil Harris, "Iconography and Intellectual History: The Half-Tone Effect," in John Higham and Paul K. Conkin, eds., *New Directions in American Intellectual History* (Baltimore, 1979), 196–211, esp. 199.

4. J. Collins Warren to Worthington C. Ford, March 15, 1910, Ford Papers, box 7, NYPL Annex.

5. NYT, May 31, 1888, pp. 1–2; NYT, May 6, 1900, p. 16.

6. NYT, July 5, 1889, p. 8.

7. Lawrence W. Levine, "Progress and Nostalgia: The Self Image of the Nineteen Twenties," in M. Bradbury and D. Palmer, eds., *The American Novel and the 1920s* (London, 1970), 46; James T. Adams to Mark A. Howe, July 3, 1936, Adams Papers, box 11, BLCU.

8. NYT, July 4, 1935, p. 1; NYT, June 28, 1936, sec. 10, p. 6.

9. James Lane Allen, "The National Spirit of Thanksgiving," *Munsey's Magazine*, 46 (November 1911), 158–63.

10. Ibid., 164–65.

11. Ibid., 165–67.

12. Michael Kammen, *A Machine That Would Go of Itself: The Constitution in American Culture* (New York, 1986), 220–23, 278, 284, 348–49, esp. 385; Kammen, "Let There Be a Constitution Day!" *Newsday*, July 5, 1987, Ideas Section, p. 3.

13. Susan Prendergast Schoelwer, *Alamo Images: Changing Perceptions of a Texas Experience* (Dallas, 1985), 82–83, 102; Brian W. Dippie, *Custer's Last Stand: The Anatomy of an American Myth* (Missoula, Mont., 1976), esp. 30.

14. Dos Passos, *Adventures of a Young Man* (New York, 1938), 6–8.

15. James Hoopes, *Van Wyck Brooks: In Search of American Culture* (Amherst, 1977), 59–69; Macy, *The Spirit of American Literature* (1908: Garden City, N.Y., 1913), 4–6, 9; James J. Martine, *Fred Lewis Pattee & American Literature* (University Park, Pa., 1973), 65.

16. Charles C. Alexander, *Here the Country Lies: Nationalism and the Arts in Twentieth-Century America* (Bloomington, Ind., 1980), 58, 68, 128–29.

17. Elizabeth Stillinger, *The Antiquers* (New York, 1980), 104–05, 233–39; Rhodes to Mrs. C. H. Toy, March 31, 1912, in Robert Cruden, *James Ford Rhodes: The Man, the Historian, and His Work* (Cleveland, 1961), 139.

18. William E. Dodd, "History and Patriotism," SAQ, 12 (1913), 117.

19. E. W. Fielder to Claude Van Tyne, Dec. 13, 1910, to which Van Tyne added comments and sent it along to McLaughlin, McLaughlin Papers, box 1, UCL; McLaughlin to D. Appleton and Co., Dec. 23, 1910, ibid.

20. See Charles B. Hosmer, Jr., *Presence of the Past: A History of the Preservation Movement in the United States before Williamsburg* (New York, 1965); Hosmer, *Preservation Comes of Age, from Williamsburg to the National Trust, 1926–1949* (Charlottesville, Va., 1981), 2 vols.

21. A copy of the AHA proposal is located in the Worthington C. Ford Papers, box 6, NYPL Annex; Wharton, *French Ways and Their Meaning* (New York, 1919), 37–38.

22. Lewis Mumford, *The Highway and the City* (New York, 1963), 176–214.

23. Edward M. Riley, "The Independence Hall Group," in *Historic Philadelphia, from the Founding until the Early Nineteenth Century* (*Transactions* of the APS, 43 [March 1953], 7–42).

24. Roger Butterfield, "Henry Ford, the Wayside Inn, and the Problem of 'History is Bunk,'" *Proceedings* of the MHS, 77 (1965), 53–66.

25. NYT, May 10, 1889, p. 4; Hosmer, *Presence of the Past*, 55; Hosmer, *Preservation Comes of Age*, 66–67, 478–93.

26. James M. Lindgren, "'For the Sake of Our Future': The Association for the Preservation of Virginia Antiquities and the Regeneration of Traditionalism," VMHB, 97 (1989), 47–74.

27. Hosmer, *Presence of the Past*, 106–07; Paul R. Baker, *Stanny: The Gilded Life of Stanford White* (New York, 1989), 39–40; George Sheldon, *A Guide to the Museum of the Pocumtuck Valley Memorial Association* (2nd ed.: Deerfield, Mass., 1920).

28. NYT, Mar. 13, 1888, p. 8; NYT, Jan. 3, 1889, p. 4; NYT, Aug. 29, 1889, p. 4; William Butler, "Another City Upon a Hill: Litchfield, Connecticut, and the Colonial Revival," in Alan Axelrod, ed., *The Colonial Revival in America* (New York, 1985), 23.

29. George Parsons Lathrop, "An American Lordship," *The Century,* 31 (December 1885), 217–28; John Williamson Palmer, "Old Maryland Homes and Ways," *The Century,* 49 (December 1894), 244–61; Palmer, "Old Georgetown—A Social Panorama," *The Century,* 53 (April 1897), 803–20. See also Edwin Whitefield, *Homes of Our Forefathers in Massachusetts* (Boston, 1880); Whitefield, *Homes of Our Forefathers in Maine, New Hampshire and Vermont* (Reading, Mass., 1886); Norman M. Isham, *Early Connecticut Houses: An Historical and Architectural Study* (Providence, R.I., 1900); Marion Harland, *Colonial Homesteads and Their Stories* (New York, 1912).

30. Walter Sargent, "The Passing of the Old Red Schoolhouse," *New England Magazine,* n.s., 23 (December 1900), 422. See also Alan S. Wheelock, "The Burden of the Past," EIHC, 110 (1974), 86–110, esp. 102.

31. John Foord, *The Life and Public Services of Andrew Haswell Green* (Garden City, N.Y., 1913), 213; F. W. Dupee, *Henry James* (New York, 1951), 276; Burton R. Pollin, "Theodore Roosevelt to the Rescue of the Poe Cottage," *Mississippi Quarterly,* 34 (1980–81), 51–59, the quotation at 54.

32. Martha Anne Turner, *Clara Driscoll: An American Tradition* (Austin, Tex., 1979), 17, 20, 23, 25–29.

33. NYT, Oct. 17, 1885, p. 6; "Background," *Exploration* (1970), 8–9 (a publication of what is now called the School of American Research).

34. Lee Clark Mitchell, *Witnesses to a Vanishing America: The Nineteenth-Century Response* (Princeton, 1981), 88–89; George Wharton James, *In and Out of the Old Missions of California: An Historical and Pictorial Account of the Franciscan Missions* (Boston, 1905).

35. Dudley Gordon, *Charles F. Lummis: Crusader in Corduroy* (n.p., 1972), 118–19, 223; Mitchell, *Witnesses to a Vanishing America,* 90; Sarah Comstock, "As the Padres Built," *Munsey's Magazine,* 30 (November 1903), 260–63.

36. NYT, Oct. 2, 1889, p. 9; NYT, Dec. 15, 1889, p. 16.

37. Martin J. Wiener, *English Culture and the Decline of the Industrial Spirit, 1850–1980* (Cambridge, 1981), 67, 69; Hosmer, *Presence of the Past,* 255, 302.

38. James Lees-Milne, *Ancestral Voices* (London, 1975).

39. Ronald F. Lee, *The Origin and Evolution of the National Military Park Idea* (Washington, D.C., 1973), 7, 13.

40. Hosmer, *Presence of the Past,* 120–22, 166, 169, 301–02; editorial, "A New Reason for Going West," *The Century,* 70 (June 1905), 316.

41. Appleton to Mrs. Martin Littleton, Nov. 4, 1912, quoted in Hosmer, *Presence of the Past,* 167.

42. NYT, Dec. 8, 1889, p. 13.

43. See Samuel P. Hays, *Conservation and the Gospel of Efficiency: The Progressive Conservation Movement, 1890–1920* (2nd ed.: New York, 1969); John F. Reiger, *American Sportsmen and the Origins of Conservation* (New York, 1975), who pushes the period of genesis back two decades to the 1870s, esp. chs. 5–6; Alfred Runte, *National Parks: The American Experience* (Lincoln, Nebr., 1979), 11. See also Roderick Nash, "The American Invention of National Parks," AQ, 22 (1970), 726–35.

44. See Sarah Burns, *Pastoral Inventions: Rural Life in Nineteenth-Century American Art and Culture* (Philadelphia, 1989), part 3, "The Anxieties of Nostalgia"; Peter J. Schmitt, *Back to Nature: The Arcadian Myth in Urban America* (New York, 1969).

45. See the admirable essay by Phyllis Keller in NAW, II, 179–81; the autobiography of James K. Hosmer (typescript), 4, 253–57, 261, Hosmer Papers, MinnHS; Edwin D. Mead, *The Old South Work* (Boston, 1892).

46. Karal Ann Marling, *George Washington Slept Here: Colonial Revivals and American Culture, 1876–1986* (Cambridge, Mass., 1988), 44. Caroline Emmerton of Salem supplies an interesting case in point. In 1907 she purchased the House of the Seven

Gables, founded a House Association, and ultimately used the restored House as a philanthropic center, a settlement house.

47. Irving, *Knickerbocker's History of New York* (1809: New York, 1964), 42; Franklin, "Remarks Concerning the Savages of North America" (1784), in Adrienne Koch, ed., *The American Enlightenment: The Shaping of the American Experiment and a Free Society* (New York, 1965), 138.

48. Jean Strouse, *Alice James: A Biography* (New York, 1982), xix, 27, 44, 173, 174; Anna Bowman Dodd, *In the Palaces of the Sultan* (New York, 1903), 95–96; Mrs. R. A. (Sara) Pryor, *My Day: Reminiscences of a Long Life* (New York, 1909), 425.

49. NYT, July 8, 1900, p. 13. See also NYT, Nov. 4, 1888, p. 11.

50. Mrs. Hester Dorsey Richardson to J. Franklin Jameson, Feb. 20, 1907, Jameson Papers, box 99, MDLC. Jameson's discouraging response is dated Feb. 23.

51. NYT, July 17, 1888, p. 5; NYT, May 10, 1889, p. 5; NYT, Sept. 8, 1889, p. 9; NYT, Sept. 22, 1889, p. 13.

52. NAW, II, 15–17.

53. George and Mary Roberts, *Triumph on Fairmount: Fiske Kimball and the Philadelphia Museum of Art* (Philadelphia, 1959), 32, 35, 41, 45, 49.

54. NAW, III, 185–87; ibid., 20–22.

55. Susan Elizabeth Lyman, *Lady Historian: Martha J. Lamb* (Northampton, Mass., 1969), the quotation at 44.

56. Alice Foster Perkins Hooper to Solon J. Buck, July 3, 1926, Buck Papers, MinnHS; Ray Allen Billington, ed., *"Dear Lady": The Letters of Frederick Jackson Turner and Alice Forbes Perkins Hooper, 1910–1932* (San Marino, Calif., 1970).

57. Violet Oakley, "The Vision of William Penn: Mural Paintings in the Capitol of Pennsylvania," *Pennsylvania History*, 20 (1953), 317–38; Harrison S. Morris, "A New Motive in Decoration: Miss Violet Oakley's Paintings for a Private House," *The Century*, 81 (March 1911), 736–38; B. H. Friedman, *Gertrude Vanderbilt Whitney* (Garden City, N.Y., 1978).

58. *Wallace Nutting's Biography* (Framingham, Mass., 1936), 106. See Barbara J. Howe, "Women in Historic Preservation: The Legacy of Ann Pamela Cunningham," PH, 12 (1990), 31–61, esp. 35–40.

59. Elizabeth Stillinger, *The Antiquers* (New York, 1980), esp. 133–41, 204–14, 222–54.

60. See David W. Marcell, *Progress and Pragmatism: James, Dewey, Beard and the American Idea of Progress* (Westport, Conn., 1974); Bernard Lee Allen, "John Dewey's Views on History, 1859–1952" (unpubl. Ph.D. diss., Univ. of West Virginia, 1971).

61. Wilson, *The New Freedom* (1913: Garden City, N.Y., 1921), 44; Richard Slotkin, "Nostalgia and Progress: Theodore Roosevelt's Myth of the Frontier," AQ, 33 (1981), 608–37.

62. Daniel T. Rodgers, "Socializing Middle-Class Children: Institutions, Fables, and Work Values in Nineteenth-Century America," JSH, 13 (1980), 363; David Glassberg, "Restoring a 'Forgotten Childhood': American Play and the Progressive Era's Elizabethan Past," AQ, 32 (1980), 351–68.

63. NYT, Mar. 25, 1888, p. 10; NYT, Apr. 1, 1888, p. 10; Howells, "The Modern American Mood," *Harper's Magazine*, 95 (July 1897), 204; Robert G. Athearn, *The Mythic West in Twentieth-Century America* (Lawrence, Kans., 1986), 196–98; Hosmer, *Presence of the Past*, ch. 13.

64. Walter Lippmann, *Drift and Mastery: An Attempt to Diagnose the Current Unrest* (New York, 1914), 265, and see 266–67.

65. Louis Howland, "Provincial or National?" *Scribner's Magazine*, 43 (April 1908), 453. See also Richard Hofstadter, *Anti-intellectualism in American Life* (New York, 1963), 238–41, esp. 241.

66. Compare Robert M. Crunden, *Ministers of Reform: The Progressive's Achievement in American Civilization, 1889–1920* (New York, 1982), with Russell Lynes, *The Tastemakers* (New York, 1954), 222.

67. Morse to Lodge, Jan. 23, 1921, Lodge Papers, box 65, MHS.

68. John Dewey, "Americanism and Localism," *The Dial*, 68 (June 1920), 687.

69. Ibid., 684–85.

70. Graham Daves to Henry Baldwin, July 13, 1894, Library Americana, box 2, NYPL Annex. See also David J. Russo, *Keepers of Our Past: Local Historical Writing in the United States, 1820s–1930s* (Westport, Conn., 1988), 79–86.

71. Scott, *Sir Tristrem. A Metrical Romance of the Thirteenth Century* (Edinburgh, 1804), xxvi.

72. Constance Rourke, *American Humor: A Study of the National Character* (New York, 1931), 227; Henry D. Shapiro, *Appalachia on Our Mind: The Southern Mountains and Mountaineers in the American Consciousness, 1870–1920* (Chapel Hill, N.C., 1978), 15; Vincent J. Scully, Jr., *The Shingle Style and the Stick Style: Architectural Theory and Design from Downing to the Origins of Wright* (2nd ed.: New Haven, 1971), 47, quoting an editorial from *American Architect.*

73. Edward C. Kirkland, *Charles Francis Adams, Jr., 1835–1915: The Patrician at Bay* (Cambridge, Mass., 1965), 204–05; John Fiske to Rufus A. Grider, Feb. 21, 1896, Fiske Papers, box 13, HEHL; Howland, "Provincial or National?" 450–52.

74. NYT, Apr. 14, 1889, p. 20; J. William Jones to Lyon G. Tyler, May 31, 1898, Tyler Papers, group 1, box 24, SLWM; William E. Dodd, "The Status of History in Southern Education," *The Nation*, 75 (Aug. 7, 1902), 109–11; Dodd, "Some Difficulties of the History Teacher in the South," SAQ, 3 (1904), 117–22.

75. NYT, May 27, 1888, p. 10; Charles Francis Adams, Jr., *Historians and Historical Societies* (Cambridge, Mass., 1899); Salmon file in the J. Franklin Jameson Papers, box 94, MDLC.

76. Miss Idress Head to J. Franklin Jameson, Jan. 2, 1912 [1913], and Jameson to Head, Jan. 11, 1913, Jameson Papers, box 113, MDLC; Frank L. Riley (for the Mississippi Historical Society), to Jameson, Dec. 20, 1907, ibid., box 113; Milo M. Quaife (for the State Historical Society of Wisconsin) to Victor H. Paltsits, Feb. 5, 1917, Paltsits Papers, NYHS.

77. Elisabeth W. Potter, "The Missionary and Immigrant Experience as Portrayed in Commemorative Works of Art," *Idaho Yesterdays*, 31 (1987), 101.

78. Athearn, *The Mythic West in Twentieth-Century America*, 70, 240, 242–43; Earl S. Pomeroy, *In Search of the Golden West: The Tourist in Western America* (New York, 1957), 41–42.

79. Cosmos Club Papers, box 90, K. Ross Toole Archives, Mansfield Library, University of Montana, Missoula.

80. Athearn, *The Mythic West in Twentieth-Century America*, 50; Gordon, *Charles F. Lummis*, ch. 19.

81. Howland, "Provincial or National?" 450–55, the quotation at 453.

82. Ibid., 455.

83. NYT, Apr. 7, 1901, p. 26; Joseph G. Rosa and Robin May, *Buffalo Bill and His Wild West: A Pictorial Biography* (Lawrence, Kans., 1989); Lewis O. Saum, " 'Astonishing the Natives': Bringing the Wild West to Los Angeles," MMWHC, 38 (1988), 2–13.

84. Athearn, *The Mythic West in Twentieth-Century America*, 11–15; G. Edward White, *The Eastern Establishment and the Western Experience: The West of Frederic Remington, Theodore Roosevelt, and Owen Wister* (New Haven, 1968), 137–44, the quotation at 138.

85. Arthur Chapman, "The New West and the Old Fiction," *The Independent*, 54 (Jan. 9, 1902), 98–100.

86. Pomeroy, *In Search of the Golden West*, 97, 177; Charles M. Harvey, "Kit Carson, Last of the Trail-Makers: Apropos of the Denver Memorial," *The Century*, 80 (October 1910), 871–76, the quotation at 876; Richard Slotkin, "Nostalgia and Progress: Theodore Roosevelt's Myth of the Frontier," AQ, 33 (1981), 608–37.

87. Gordon, *Charles F. Lummis*, 119, 133, 153–54; Athearn, *The Mythic West in Twentieth-Century America*, 141–43, 166; Drake Hokanson, *The Lincoln Highway: Main Street Across America* (Iowa City, 1988), Part I.

88. Marling, *George Washington Slept Here*, 213; William Bayard Hale, "The Old National Road," *The Century*, 83 (December 1911), 163–72, a reminiscence of the 1830s and '40s; Ralph D. Paine, "Discovering America by Motor," *Scribner's Magazine*, 53 (February 1913), 137–48; Louise Closser Hale, "We Discover New England: The Chronicle of Two Happy Motorists," *The Century*, 90 (1915), a four-part series.

89. Pomeroy, *In Search of the Golden West*, 17, 163–64; E. K. Brown and Leon Edel, *Willa Cather: A Critical Biography* (New York, 1953), 171.

90. Henry James, *The American Scene* (1904: New York, 1967), 244; Arthur Farwell, "Community Music-Drama," *Craftsman*, 26 (July 1914), 422.

91. See Paul Boyer, *Urban Masses and Moral Order in America, 1820–1920* (Cambridge, Mass., 1978), 256–60; Alexander, *Here the Country Lies: Nationalism and the Arts in Twentieth-Century America*, 60, 63–66; Marling, *George Washington Slept Here*, 196–201; David Glassberg, "Public Ritual and Cultural Hierarchy: Philadelphia's Civic Celebrations at the Turn of the Twentieth Century," PMHB, 107 (1983), 421–48; and Glassberg, "American Play and the Progressive Era's Elizabethan Past," 351–68.

92. NYT, Feb. 19, 1889, p. 8; NYT, Mar. 24, 1889, p. 1; NYT, Apr. 21, 1889, p. 16.

93. NYT, May 1, 1889, pp. 10–11; NYT, Apr. 29, 1889, p. 4.

94. NYT, Sept. 16, 1889, p. 4; NYT, Nov. 22, 1889, p. 2; Neil Harris, "The Battle for Grant's Tomb," AH, 36 (August 1985), 78–79.

95. Du Bois to S. L. Smith, May 10, 1932, in Herbert Aptheker, ed., *The Correspondence of W. E. B. Du Bois* (Amherst, Mass., 1973), I, 457–58. In conjunction with the bicentennial of Washington's birth (1932), Du Bois prepared another pageant on George Washington and the Negro.

96. Barr Ferree, "Elements of a Successful Parade," *The Century*, 60 (July 1900), 457–64.

97. Mary Fanton Roberts, "The Value of Outdoor Plays to America: Through the Pageant Shall We Develop a Drama of Democracy?" *The Craftsman*, 16 (August 1909), 491–506; Percy MacKaye, "The New Fourth of July," *The Century*, 80 (July 1910), 394–96.

98. MacKaye, "New Fourth of July," 394.

99. For an account of the Philadelphia pageant, see NYT, Oct. 10, 1908, p. 9; Oberholtzer, "Historical Pageants in England and America," *The Century*, 80 (July 1910), 416–27.

100. Oberholtzer, "Historical Pageants in England and America," 422; Boyer, *Urban Masses and Moral Order*, 258.

101. James K. Hosmer, MS autobiography, pp. 478–79, Hosmer Papers, MinnHS; David Glassberg, "History and the Public: Legacies of the Progressive Era," JAH, 73 (1987), 970; Hosmer, *Preservation Comes of Age*, I, 400.

102. Glassberg, "Public Ritual and Cultural Hierarchy," 446–47. For a highly comparable situation in England, see Elizabeth Hammerton and David Cannadine, "Conflict and Consensus on a Ceremonial Occasion: The Diamond Jubilee in Cambridge in 1897," *Historical Journal*, 24 (1981), 111–46.

103. See the speech given by Joseph Hodges Choate in New York on St. Patrick's Day in 1893, in Edward S. Martin, *The Life of Joseph Hodges Choate* (New York, 1920), I, 440–41; Stillman H. Bingham to Charles W. Eddy, Apr. 3, 1916, papers of the Minnesota Society of the Sons of the American Revolution, box 1, MinnHS.

104. William L. Langer, *In and Out of the Ivory Tower: Autobiography* (New York, 1977), 17; "My Path to History," in Johan Huizinga, *Dutch Civilization in the Seventeenth Century and Other Essays* (London, 1968), 246. See also G. M. Trevelyan, "Autobiography of an Historian," in *An Autobiography & Other Essays* (London, 1949), 3–4.

105. See Jacob Burckhardt, *The Civilization of the Renaissance in Italy* (1860: New York, 1958), II, 401; Edward Muir, *Civic Ritual in Renaissance Venice* (Princeton, 1981); Alan Dundes and Alessandro Falassi, *La Terra in Piazza: An Interpretation of the Palio of Siena* (Berkeley, 1975); David M. Bergeron, *English Civic Pageantry, 1558–1642* (Columbia, S.C., 1971); Albert Mackie, *Scottish Pageantry* (London, 1967).

106. Glassberg, "History and the Public: Legacies of the Progressive Era," 970–71; John W. Burrow, *A Liberal Descent: Victorian Historians and the English Past* (Cambridge, 1982), 249.

107. See Roberto DaMatta, *Exploraçoes: Ensaios de Sociologia Interpretativa* (Rio de Janeiro, 1986), 74–87; William H. Beezley, *Judas at the Jockey Club and Other Episodes of Porfirian Mexico* (Lincoln, Nebr., 1987); Pierre Bourdieu and J. C. Passeron, *Reproduction: In Education, Society and Culture* (Beverly Hills, Calif., 1977), book 2, "Keeping Order"; Charles Zika, "Hosts, Processions and Pilgrimages: Controlling the Sacred in Fifteenth-Century Germany," *Past & Present*, no. 118 (February 1988), 25–64; Claude Gaignebet, *Art Profane et Religion Populaire au Moyen Age* (Paris, 1985).

108. For an excellent illustration, see the centennial exercises held during a four-day span, October 18–21, 1881, to dedicate the Yorktown Monument to the Alliance and Victory (at Yorktown, Virginia), a joint project of the federal government and the private sector. Paul R. Baker, *Richard Morris Hunt* (Cambridge, Mass., 1980), 302. See also Samuel Kinser, *Carnival, American Style: Mardi Gras at New Orleans and Mobile* (Chicago, 1990); W. Lloyd Warner, *The Living and the Dead: A Study of the Symbolic Life of Americans* (New Haven, 1959), ch. 6.

109. See NYT, June 30, 1889, p. 6; A. Dwight Culler, *The Victorian Mirror of History* (New Haven, 1986); Paul A. Carter, *The Spiritual Crisis of the Gilded Age* (DeKalb, Ill., 1971); T. J. Jackson Lears, *No Place of Grace: Antimodernism and the Transformation of American Culture, 1880–1920* (New York, 1981).

110. James, *The American Scene,* 169.

Coda to Part Two

1. See Freeman, *Some Impressions of the United States* (New York, 1883); Muirhead, *The Land of Contrasts: A Briton's View of His American Kin* (Boston, 1898); Bourget, *Outre-Mer: Impressions of America* (New York, 1895).

2. Edith Wharton, *A Motor-Flight Through France* (New York, 1908), 5, 11; Wharton, *French Ways and Their Meaning* (New York, 1919), 32.

3. Henry James, *A Little Tour in France* (1885: New York, 1950), 80.

4. Jacob Burckhardt, *Force and Freedom: Reflections on History* (New York, 1943), 85–86.

5. See Karl J. Weintraub, *Visions of Culture* (Chicago, 1966), 117, 135.

6. See esp. Robert Colls and Philip Dodd, eds., *Englishness: Politics and Culture, 1880–1920* (London, 1986), 1–61; John Clive, "The Use of the Past in Victorian England," *Salmagundi,* nos. 68–69 (Fall–Winter 1985–86), 48–65; Maurice Agulhon, *Marianne into Battle: Republican Imagery and Symbolism in France, 1789–1880* (Cambridge, 1981), 12.

7. Jan Romein, *The Watershed of Two Eras: Europe in 1900* (Middletown, Conn., 1978), ch. 31 and p. 529; Eugen Weber, *France: Fin de Siècle* (Cambridge, Mass., 1986), 2.

8. William R. Keylor, *Academy and Community: The Foundation of the French Historical Profession* (Cambridge, Mass., 1975), 58–59; Robert Colls, "Englishness and the Political Culture," in Colls and Dodd, eds., *Englishness: Politics and Culture, 1880–1920,* 29–54. This had by then become a familiar issue in British politics. See Isaac Kramnick, "Augustan Politics and English Historiography: The Debate on the English Past, 1730–35," *History & Theory,* 6 (1967), 33–56.

9. Eric Hobsbawm and Terence Ranger, eds., *The Invention of Tradition* (Cambridge, 1983), 160; Alfred Cobban, *A History of Modern France,* III: *France of the Republics, 1871–1962* (Harmondsworth, Middlesex, 1965), 78; William R. Hutchison, *The Modernist Impulse in American Protestantism* (Cambridge, Mass., 1976), esp. chs. 4–6.

10. Keylor, *Academy and Community,* 19, 41, 91–92, 99–100; Pieter Geyl, *Napoleon: For and Against* (New Haven, 1949), 351; Régine Pernoud, *Joan of Arc, by Herself and Her Witnesses* (London, 1964), ch. 9, "Rehabilitation"; Sanford Elwitt, "Social Reform and

Social Order in Late Nineteenth-Century France: The Musée Sociale and Its Friends," *French Historical Studies,* 11 (1980), 431–51.

11.   Eugen Weber, *Peasants into Frenchmen: The Modernization of Rural France, 1870–1914* (Stanford, Calif., 1976), 165, 225–26; Daniel J. Boorstin, *The Americans: The Democratic Experience* (New York, 1973), 131–35.

12.   Alun Hawkins, "The Discovery of Rural England," in Colls and Dodd, eds., *Englishness: Politics and Culture, 1880–1920,* 62–88.

13.   Sarah Burns, *Pastoral Inventions: Rural Life in Nineteenth-Century American Art and Culture* (Philadelphia, 1989), part three, "The Anxieties of Nostalgia"; *Wallace Nutting's Biography* (Framingham, Mass., 1936), 84, 125.

14.   Martin J. Wiener, *English Culture and the Decline of the Industrial Spirit, 1850–1980* (Cambridge, 1981), 65–66; Francis Haskell, "The Manufacture of the Past in Nineteenth-Century Painting," *Past & Present,* 53 (November 1971), 109–20; Roy Strong, *Recreating the Past* (London, 1978), esp. 13–46; Ernest Samuels, *Bernard Berenson: The Making of a Connoisseur* (Cambridge, Mass., 1979), 86, 101.

15.   Kenneth Hudson, *Museums of Influence* (Cambridge, 1987), esp. chs. 2–6; D. K. Van Keuren, "Museums and Ideology: Augustus Pitt-Rivers, Anthropology Museums and Social Change in Later Victorian Britain," *Victorian Studies,* 28 (1984), 171–89; William H. Tolman, "European Museums of Security," *The Century,* 72 (June 1906), 307–14.

16.   Charles Rearick, *Beyond the Enlightenment: Historians and Folklore in Nineteenth Century France* (Bloomington, Ind., 1974); Michael Herzfeld, *Ours Once More: Folklore, Ideology, and the Making of Modern Greece* (Austin, Tex., 1982); John I. Kolehmainen, *Epic of the North: The Story of Finland's Kalevala* (New York, 1973); Vic Gammon, "Folk Song Collecting in Sussex and Surrey, 1843–1914," *History Workshop: A Journal of Socialist Historians,* no. 10 (Autumn 1980), 61–89; Simon J. Bronner, *American Folklore Studies: An Intellectual History* (Lawrence, Kans., 1986), 57–74.

17.   Information from the Bishop Museum in Honolulu, which has a portrait of the king made by William Cogswell in 1878.

18.   See Sigurd Aa. Aarnes, "Myths and Heroes in Nineteenth-Century Nation Building in Norway," in J. C. Eade, ed., *Romantic Nationalism in Europe* (Australian National University, 1983), 101–14; Donald R. Kelley, *Foundations of Modern Historical Scholarship: Language, Law, and History in the French Renaissance* (New York, 1970), 225; John L. Greenway, *The Golden Horns: Mythic Imagination and the Nordic Past* (Athens, Ga., 1977), 67.

19.   See George L. Mosse, *The Nationalization of the Masses: Political Symbolism and Mass Movements in Germany from the Napoleonic Wars Through the Third Reich* (1975: New York, 1977), 2; Agulhon, *Marianne into Battle,* 12.

20.   Dodd, "Englishness and the National Culture," in Colls and Dodd, eds., *Englishness: Politics and Culture, 1880–1920,* 1, 22; David Cannadine, "The Context, Performance and Meaning of Ritual: The British Monarchy and the 'Invention of Tradition,' c. 1820–1977," in Hobsbawm and Ranger, eds., *Invention of Tradition,* 108.

21.   Michael Edwardes, *High Noon of Empire: India Under Curzon* (London, 1965), 97, 152, 157.

22.   John Hutchinson, *The Dynamics of Cultural Nationalism: The Gaelic Revival and the Creation of the Irish Nation State* (London, 1987), esp. chs. 4–5; Martin Williams, "Ancient Mythology and Revolutionary Ideology in Ireland, 1878–1916," *Historical Journal,* 26 (1983), 307–28, esp. 323. For James Joyce on Irish traditions, see Richard Ellmann, *James Joyce* (New York, 1959), 254.

23.   Joanna Hubbs, *Mother Russia: The Feminine Myth in Russian Culture* (Bloomington, Ind., 1988); Michael Cherniavsky, *Tsar and People: Studies in Russian Myths* (New Haven, 1961).

24.   Karl Mannheim, *Essays on Sociology and Social Psychology* (London, 1953), 99, and see 74–164 generally.

25.   Victor S. Mamatey, "The Battle of the White Mountain as Myth in Czech History," *East European Quarterly,* 15 (1981), 335–45; Keylor, *Academy and Community,* 93

(where the quotation from Lavisse appears), 97–98, 147. See also Quentin Skinner, "History and Ideology in the English Revolution," *Historical Journal,* 8 (1965), 151–78.

26. Weber, *Peasants into Frenchmen,* 111, 114.

27. Mosse, *Nationalization of the Masses,* 73; Harry C. Payne, "The Ritual Question and Modernizing Society, 1800–1945—A Schema for a History," *Historical Reflections,* 11 (1984), 403–32; Charles Rearick, "Festivals and Politics: The Michelet Centennial of 1898," in Walter Laqueur and George L. Mosse, eds., *Historians in Politics* (London, 1974), 59–78.

28. Valerie E. Chancellor, *History for Their Masters: Opinion in the English History Textbook, 1800–1914* (Bath, Engl., 1970), esp. 139, 141; Keylor, *Academy and Community,* 23; Ben Eklof, *Russian Peasant Schools: Officialdom, Village Culture, and Popular Pedagogy, 1861–1914* (Berkeley, 1986).

29. Ruth Miller Elson, *Guardians of Tradition: American Schoolbooks of the Nineteenth Century* (Lincoln, Nebr., 1964); Michael W. Apple, "The Culture and Commerce of the Textbook," *Journal of Curriculum Studies,* 17 (1985), 147–62.

30. Joseph Fiévée, quoted in Stanley Mellon, *The Political Uses of History: A Study of Historians in the French Restoration* (Stanford, Calif., 1958), 149. See also Eade, *Romantic Nationalism in Europe;* Mamatey, "Battle of the White Mountain as Myth in Czech History," 335–45; Stephen Fischer-Galati, "Myths in Romanian History," *East European Quarterly,* 15 (1981), 327–34; David G. Roskies, *Against the Apocalypse: Responses to Catastrophe in Modern Jewish Culture* (Cambridge, Mass., 1984), chs. 7–9.

31. George L. Mosse, *Masses and Man: Nationalist and Fascist Perceptions of Reality* (New York, 1980), esp. 52–68, 104–18; Mosse, *Nationalization of the Masses,* 61–62, 66, 69, 92; Stephen Wilson, "A View of the Past: Action Française Historiography and Its Socio-Political Function," *Historical Journal,* 19 (1976), 135–61, esp. 148; Dodd, "Englishness and the National Culture," in Colls and Dodd, eds., *Englishness: Politics and Culture, 1880–1920,* 10–11.

32. Isabel V. Hull, "Prussian Dynastic Ritual and the End of Monarchy," in Carole Fink, Isabel V. Hull, and MacGregor Knox, eds., *German Nationalism and the European Response* (Norman, Okla., 1985), 13–42; Mosse, *Nationalization of the Masses,* chs. 1 and 7.

33. James J. Sheehan, "What Is German History? Reflections on the Role of the *Nation* in German History and Historiography," *Journal of Modern History,* 53 (1981), 4, 22; Mosse, *Nationalization of the Masses,* 32, 50–51, 60–61, 65–66, 68–70.

34. See Paul Farmer, *France Reviews Its Revolutionary Origins: Social Politics and Historical Opinion in the Third Republic* (New York, 1944); Geyl, *Napoleon: For and Against,* 133–35, 254–55; Pieter Geyl, *Encounters in History* (London, 1961), 172–73.

35. Louis R. Gottschalk, "The French Revolution: Conspiracy or Circumstance?" in *Persecution and Liberty: Essays in Honor of George Lincoln Burr* (New York, 1931), 445–72, esp. 454; Patrick H. Hutton, *The Cult of the Revolutionary Tradition: The Blanquists in French Politics, 1864–1893* (Berkeley, 1981); Wilson, "Action Française Historiography and Its Socio-Political Function," 135–61.

36. Edmund Wilson, *Patriotic Gore: Studies in the Literature of the American Civil War* (New York, 1962); Daniel Aaron, *The Unwritten War: American Writers and the Civil War* (New York, 1973); Edouard-René L. Laboulaye, *The United States and France* (Boston, 1862), 13. This book, which supported the Union cause, was also published in Paris in August 1862.

37. Mlle Valentine B. Puthod to John Fiske, Dec. 5, 1899, Fiske Papers, box 13, HEHL; Marcia Pointon, "Voisins et Alliés: French and British at the International Exhibition of 1855" (unpubl. lecture at Cornell University, Apr. 14, 1980, which emphasized the French fascination with British national character as manifest in British art).

38. Arthur F. Wright, "Values, Roles, and Personalities," in Wright and Denis Twitchett, eds., *Confucian Personalities* (Stanford, Calif., 1962), 8–9; E. A. Kracke, Jr., "Sung Society: Change Within Tradition," *Far Eastern Quarterly,* 14 (1954–55), 479–88.

39. Robert J. Smith, *Japanese Society: Tradition, Self and the Social Order* (Cambridge, 1983), ch. 1, "The Creation of Tradition," the quotation at p. 9.

40. Ibid., 14–16, 31 (where the quotation appears); Carol Gluck, *Japan's Modern Myths: Ideology in the Late Meiji Period* (Princeton, 1985), chs. 2–3. See also Mosse, *Nationalization of the Masses*, 2, 4, 6, 16, 51, 75, 77–80; Hutchinson, *Dynamics of Cultural Nationalism*, 116.

41. Smith, *Japanese Society*, 16, 32; Robert H. Wiebe, *The Segmented Society: An Introduction to the Meaning of America* (New York, 1975), ch. 2.

42. Gluck, *Japan's Modern Myths*, ch. 5; Mosse, *Nationalization of the Masses*, chs. 2–4; Leonard Thompson, *The Political Mythology of Apartheid* (New Haven, 1985), chs. 5–6.

43. See Nina Tumarkin, *Lenin Lives! The Lenin Cult in Soviet Russia* (Cambridge, Mass., 1983); A. Howard Clark, "What the United States Government Has Done for History," *Annual Report of the AHA for 1894* (Washington, D.C., 1895), 549–61; William B. Hesseltine and Donald R. McNeil, eds., *In Support of Clio: Essays in Memory of Herbert A. Kellar* (Madison, Wis., 1958), 9.

44. George T. Blakey, *Historians on the Homefront: American Propagandists for the Great War* (Lexington, Ky., 1970); Alfred Haworth Jones, *Roosevelt's Image Brokers: Poets, Playwrights, and the Use of the Lincoln Symbol* (Port Washington, N.Y., 1974).

45. See Thompson, *Political Mythology of Apartheid*, chs. 2–4; George M. Fredrickson, *White Supremacy: A Comparative Study in American and South African History* (New York, 1981), esp. chs. 3, 4, and 6; C. Vann Woodward, *The Strange Career of Jim Crow* (3rd ed.: New York, 1974).

46. See Jean Starobinski, "The Idea of Nostalgia," *Diogenes*, no. 54 (1966), 81–103.

47. In addition to the works already cited, see Richard Drake, *Byzantium for Rome: The Politics of Nostalgia in Umbertian Italy, 1878–1900* (Chapel Hill, N.C., 1980); Russel Ward, *The Australian Legend* (Melbourne, 1958; 1966), ch. 8.

48. Agulhon, *Marianne into Battle*, 101, 132.

49. Horst W. Janson, *The Rise and Fall of the Public Monument* (New Orleans, 1976), 2, 5, 21; Mosse, *Nationalization of the Masses*, 36.

50. Visible and invisible legacies do actually converge. See Wilbur Zelinsky, *Nation into State: The Shifting Symbolic Foundations of American Nationalism* (Chapel Hill, N.C., 1988); Kent Ladd Steckmesser, *The Western Hero in History and Legend* (Norman, Okla., 1965); Michael A. Lofaro, ed., *Davy Crockett: The Man, the Legend, the Legacy, 1786–1986* (Knoxville, Tenn., 1985).

51. See R. Richard Wohl and A. Theodore Brown, "The Usable Past: A Study of Historical Traditions in Kansas City," *Huntington Library Quarterly*, 23 (1960), 237–59; Bernard S. Cohn, "The Pasts of an Indian Village," CSSH, 3 (1961), 241–49; Mamatey, "Battle of the White Mountain as Myth in Czech History."

52. Weber, *Peasants into Frenchmen*, 130.

53. See Theodore Rosengarten, *All God's Dangers: The Life of Nate Shaw* (New York, 1974), 3, 15, 548; John Bodnar, "Power and Memory in Oral History: Workers and Managers at Studebaker," JAH, 75 (1989), 1201–21; Linda Shopes, "Oral History and Community Involvement: The Baltimore Neighborhood Heritage Project," in Susan Porter Benson et al., eds., *Presenting the Past: Essays on History and the Public* (Philadelphia, 1986), 249–63.

Prolegomenon: Part Three

1. Some of the complexity in this situation is conveyed by Miles Orvell, *The Real Thing: Imitation and Authenticity in American Culture, 1880–1940* (Chapel Hill, N.C., 1989); and Stephen Kern, *The Culture of Time and Space, 1880–1918* (Cambridge, Mass., 1983). See also Edward Engelberg, " 'Space, Time, and History': Towards the Discrimination of Modernisms," *Modernist Studies: Literature & Culture, 1920–1940*, I (1974), 7–25.

2. David Glassberg, "History and the Public: Legacies of the Progressive Era," JAH, 73 (1987), 970; Alfred Kazin, *On Native Grounds* (New York, 1942), 314; Coolidge is quoted in Karal Ann Marling, *George Washington Slept Here: Colonial Revivals and American Culture, 1876–1986* (Cambridge, Mass., 1988), 270–71, and 220, 371.

3. Harvey Green, *Fit for America: Health, Fitness, Sport, and American Society* (New York, 1986), 314. For general context, see Lawrence W. Levine, "Progress and Nostalgia: The Self Image of the Nineteen Twenties," in Malcolm Bradbury and David Palmer, eds., *The American Novel and the 1920s* (London, 1970), 37–56.

4. Account of a dinner given at the Nicollet House, Jan. 29, 1904, Hosmer Papers, box 1, MinnHS.

5. William E. Dodd, "History and Patriotism," SAQ, 12 (1913), 109–21, esp. 110, 116. For a very similar view expressed by a historian who was younger than Hosmer but older than Dodd, see Dixon Ryan Fox, *Herbert Levi Osgood: An American Scholar* (New York, 1924), 64–65.

6. John Dewey, *Human Nature and Conduct: An Introduction to Social Psychology* (New York, 1922), 9–10; James Truslow Adams, "History and the Lower Criticism," *Atlantic*, 132 (September 1923), 316.

7. Karal Ann Marling, *Tom Benton and His Drawings: A Biographical Essay and a Collection of His Sketches* (Columbia, Mo., 1985), ch. 9; Thomas Hart Benton, *An Artist in America* (4th ed.: Columbia, Mo., 1983), 49, 380–81.

8. Henry Seidel Canby, "Literature in a Democracy," *The Century*, 99 (January 1920), 398.

9. Richard Ruland, *The Rediscovery of American Literature: Premises of Critical Taste, 1900–1940* (Cambridge, Mass., 1967), 57; Jacob Zeitlin and Homer Woodbridge, eds., *Life and Letters of Stuart P. Sherman* (New York, 1929), 476, 489, 507–08.

10. Zeitlin and Woodbridge, *Life and Letters of Sherman*, 484–85, 498. For the development of these issues half a century later, in terms that Sherman would (I believe) have approved, see Robert Penn Warren, *Democracy and Poetry* (Cambridge, Mass., 1975); and Henry Nash Smith, *Democracy and the Novel: Popular Resistance to Classic American Writers* (New York, 1978).

11. Stuart P. Sherman, *The Emotional Discovery of America and Other Essays* (New York, 1932), 9, 31. For a proleptic anticipation of Sherman's direction, see *The Genius of America: Studies in Behalf of the Younger Generation* (New York, 1923), esp. chs. 2 and 6: "What Is a Puritan?" and "Education by the People"; Zeitlin and Woodbridge, *Life and Letters of Sherman*, 689–90.

12. Waldo Frank, *The Re-discovery of America* (1929: New York, 1940), 221–22. See also Joseph Stella, "Discovery of America: Autobiographical Notes," *Art News*, 59 (November 1960), 41–42, 64–67.

13. Ernest Boyd, "When Americans Discover America and Accept the Painful Facts of Existence," *The Century*, 113 (December 1926), 230–36, esp. 233.

14. Faith Baldwin Cuthrell to James Boyd, July 2, 1925, Boyd Papers, box 3, SHC.

15. Dickran Tashjian, *William Carlos Williams and the American Scene, 1920–1940* (New York, 1978); Constance D. Rourke (mother of the author) to Linda Butler [Feb. 15, 1930], Butler Papers, box 1, BLYU; Stanley Edgar Hyman, *The Armed Vision: A Study in the Methods of Modern Literary Criticism* (rev. ed.: New York, 1955), 119.

16. Ruth Suckow, "The Folk Idea in American Life," *Scribner's Magazine*, 88 (September 1930), 245; William B. Rhoads, "Roadside Colonial: Early American Design for the Automobile Age, 1900–1940," WP, 21 (1986), 147; Geoffrey C. Upward, *A Home for Our Heritage: The Building and Growth of Greenfield Village and Henry Ford Museum, 1929–1979* (Dearborn, Mich., 1979), 11.

17. George T. Blakey, *Historians on the Homefront: American Propagandists for the Great War* (Lexington, Ky., 1970); Matthew Page Andrews to Lyon G. Tyler, July 12, 1918, Tyler Papers, group 5, box 4, SLWM.

18. Brander Matthews, "The Centenary of a Question," *Scribner's Magazine*, 67 (January 1920), 41–46; Adams to Henry Hazlitt, Jan. 6, 1930, Adams Papers, BLCU.

19. Sherman, *The Emotional Discovery of America,* 33; John Tebbel, *George Horace Lorimer and the Saturday Evening Post* (Garden City, N.Y., 1948), 136. See also Ernest Samuels, ed., *The Education of Henry Adams* (1918: Boston, 1973), 469–70.

20. H. J. Eckenrode to Philip A. Bruce, Mar. 22 and Apr. 11, 1927, Bruce Papers, box 2, ALUV; Rhoads, "Roadside Colonial," 133–52; Earl S. Pomeroy, *In Search of the Golden West: The Tourist in Western America* (New York, 1957), 150–51, 154. On November 18, 1932, Chorley gave the after-dinner speech at Williamsburg to members of the American Association of State Highway Officials. They met at Williamsburg again in October 1939. See Kenneth Chorley Papers, scrapbook no. 3, RAC. Chorley also developed a conveniently cordial relationship with the Virginia State Highway Commissioner, and one result was construction of a by-pass around the town, a common procedure today but not at that time.

21. Rhoads, "Roadside Colonial," 139; Susan Croce Kelly and Quinta Scott, *Route 66: The Highway and Its People* (Norman, Okla., 1988), chs. 3–4.

22. Paul Russell, *Abroad: British Literary Traveling Between the Wars* (New York, 1980), 210.

23. See Arthur C. Parker, *A Manual for History Museums* (New York, 1935); Richard F. Bach, "Museums and the Factory: Making the Galleries Work for the Art Trades," *Scribner's Magazine,* 71 (June 1922), 763–68; see also NYT, May 26, 1935, sec. 10, p. 7.

24. Albert J. Beveridge to Henry Cabot Lodge, Feb. 15, 1919, Lodge Papers, box 52, MHS; Marling, *George Washington Slept Here,* 292, 296; Dos Passos, *The Ground We Stand On: Some Examples from the History of a Political Creed* (New York, 1941), 365.

25. See Joan Shelley Rubin, *Constance Rourke and American Culture* (Chapel Hill, N.C., 1980), xi. Utterances by George Santayana and H. L. Mencken during the early 1920s are supportive of Rubin's phasing.

26. In addition to the cumulative evidence in the next four chapters, see Amy Lowell, "Is There a National Spirit in 'The New Poetry' of America?" *The Craftsman,* 30 (1916), reprinted in Barry Sanders, ed., *The Craftsman: An Anthology* (Santa Barbara, Calif., 1978), 316–25; and Fred Lewis Pattee, "Call for a Literary Historian," *American Mercury,* 2 (June 1924), 134–40.

27. NYT, Mar. 5, 1939, World's Fair Supplement, p. 7.

28. Brooks, "Letters and Leadership" (1918) in Brooks, *Three Essays on America* (New York, 1934), 118–19, 124–25; James Hoopes, *Van Wyck Brooks: In Search of American Culture* (Amherst, Mass., 1977), 143. The astute comparisons of successive *Mark Twain* editions were made by Hyman, *The Armed Vision,* 103–05.

29. Aaron Copland and Vivian Perlis, *Copland: 1900 Through 1942* (New York, 1984), 16, 28–29, 55.

30. Ellen Glasgow, *The Sheltered Life* (New York, 1932), 295. See also Glasgow's autobiography, *The Woman Within* (New York, 1954), 222–23.

Chapter 10

1. Rossiter Howard, "Changing Ideals of the Art Museum," *Scribner's Magazine,* 71 (January 1922), 125–26.

2. Ibid., 127–28.

3. "Americana," *The Americana Collector: A Monthly Magazine for Americana-Lore and Bibliography,* published by Charles F. Heartman and edited by Malcolm Vaughan, I (October 1925), 3. *The Americana Collector* began to appear in 1942, published in New York City by the Collectors Publishing Company, Inc.

4. Calvin Tomkins, *Merchants and Masterpieces: The Story of the Metropolitan Museum of Art* (New York, 1970), 256–61.

5. Wilmarth Sheldon Lewis, *One Man's Education* (New York, 1967), esp. chs. 13–14; Israel Shenker, "Can He Be the Real Walpole or Is He Wilmarth Lewis?" *Smithsonian Magazine,* 10 (May 1979), 102–08.

6. Josephine Young Case and Everett Needham Case, *Owen D. Young and American Enterprise: A Biography* (Boston, 1982), 401–15, 750. For another collector who "stuck" with European objects, perhaps in deference to his father's taste, see John Douglas Forbes, *J. P. Morgan, Jr., 1867–1943* (Charlottesville, Va., 1981), ch. 8. The younger Morgan bought mainly books.

7. Elizabeth Shackleton, "The Flood Tide of Antiques in Europe," SEP, 196 (Oct. 6, 1923), 137, 141–43; Shackleton, "Fads and Fancies of Collectors," ibid., 197 (Aug. 9, 1924), 9, 125–26; Edwin Lefèvre, "Antiques from Abroad," ibid., 201 (Dec. 29, 1928), 40–41, 78, 80–82, with subsequent installments during the early winter of 1929.

8. [Ruth Dyer Wells], *The Wells Family: Founders of the American Optical Company and Old Sturbridge Village* (Southbridge, Mass., 1979), viii–x, 2, 7.

9. Louise Kosches Iscoe, *Ima Hogg, First Lady of Texas: Reminiscences and Recollections of Family and Friends* (n.p., 1976); David B. Warren, "Ima Hogg, Collector," TMA, 121 (January 1982), 228–43.

10. Stokes to Edward S. Wilde, Apr. 8, 1913, Stokes Papers, letterbook 9, NYHS; Hyde to W. R. Castle, Jr., Dec. 1, 1917, Hyde Papers, Houghton Library, Harvard University.

11. Charles A. Fenton, *Stephen Vincent Benét: The Life and Times of an American Man of Letters, 1898–1943* (New Haven, 1958), 180–94; Joan Shelley Rubin, *Constance Rourke and American Culture* (Chapel Hill, N.C., 1980), 35.

12. NYT editorial quoted in Russell Lynes, *Good Old Modern: An Intimate Portrait of the Museum of Modern Art* (New York, 1973), 54; Robert S. Lynd to A. M. Schlesinger, Feb. 21, 1930, Schlesinger Papers, box 5, HUA.

13. Abram Lerner, "Development of a Collector: Joseph Hirshhorn," *American Art Review*, 2 (1975), 79–94; "A Modernist at Home with Antiques," NYT, July 6, 1978, pp. C1, 8.

14. Frances Weitzenhoffer, "Louisine Havemeyer and Electra Havemeyer Webb," TMA, 133 (February 1988), 430–37.

15. See William B. Rhoads, "Roadside Colonial: Early American Design for the Automobile Age, 1900–1940," WP, 21 (1986), 137; William Greenleaf, *From These Beginnings: The Early Philanthropies of Henry and Edsel Ford, 1911–1936* (Detroit, 1964), ch. 5.

16. *Grolier 75: A Biographical Retrospective to Celebrate the Seventy-fifth Anniversary of the Grolier Club in New York* (New York, 1959); John E. Pomfret, *The Henry E. Huntington Library and Art Gallery from Its Beginnings to 1969* (San Marino, Calif., 1969), chs. 1–2; Carl L. Cannon, *American Book Collectors and Collecting from Colonial Times to the Present* (New York, 1941), 310–11.

17. Adams to McGregor, Dec. 4, 1931, Aug. 16, 1934, and Dec. 23, 1935, in McGregor Papers, ALUV; *University of Virginia News Letter*, 39 (July 15, 1963), p. 1.

18. John Parker, *James Ford Bell and His Books* (pamphlet, n.p., n.d.).

19. Hubert Howe Bancroft, *Retrospection: Political and Personal* (New York, 1912); John W. Caughey, "Hubert Howe Bancroft, Historian of Western America," AHR, 50 (1945), 461–70; Archibald Hanna, "Western Americana Collectors and Collections," *Western Historical Quarterly*, 2 (1971), 401–03.

20. Hanna, "Western Americana Collectors," 403.

21. *The Celebrated Collection of Americana Formed by the Late Thomas Winthrop Streeter. . . .* (New York, [1966]); James J. Heslin, "Thomas Winthrop Streeter," NYHS *Quarterly*, 49 (1965), 387–89; NYT, Apr. 4, 1937, sec. 7, p. 27.

22. See Henry Watson Kent, *What I Am Pleased to Call My Education* (New York, 1949); Elizabeth Stillinger, *The Antiquers* (New York, 1980), parts 2 and 3.

23. Wendy Kaplan, "R. T. H. Halsey: An Ideology of Collecting American Decorative Arts," WP, 17 (1982), 43–45.

24. Ibid., 49–50; Halsey and Elizabeth Tower, *The Homes of Our Ancestors* (Garden City, N.Y., 1925), xxii.

25. John A. H. Sweeney, *Henry Francis du Pont* (Winterthur, Del., 1980), unpaginated pamphlet.

26. John A. H. Sweeney, "Recollecting a Collector," and James Morton Smith and Charles F. Hummel, "The Henry Francis du Pont Winterthur Museum," in TMA, 113 (June 1978), 1266–1306.

27. Aline B. Saarinen, *The Proud Possessors: The Lives, Times and Tastes of Some Adventurous American Art Collectors* (New York, 1958), 287–306; Walter Karp, "Electra Webb and Her American Past," AH, 33 (April 1982), 16–29.

28. Saarinen, "Electra Havemeyer Webb," 292; Cynthia Nadelman, "The Shocking Blue Hair of Elie Nadelman," AH, 40 (March 1989), 80–91; Jean Lipman and Alice Winchester, *The Flowering of American Folk Art, 1776–1876* (New York, 1974), esp. 8–14.

29. Cleota Reed, *Henry Chapman Mercer and the Moravian Pottery and Tile Works* (Philadelphia, 1987).

30. "An Open Letter to John D. Rockefeller, Jr.," *The Americana Collector,* 2 (June 1926), 323–25; *Selected Works of Stephen Vincent Benét* (New York, 1942), I, 367–68. See also Esther Singleton, "Patriotism on Chintz & China," SEP, 198 (Mar. 27, 1926), 24, 143, 145, 149; *Outward Signs of Inner Beliefs: Symbols of American Patriotism* (exhibit catalogue) (Cooperstown, N.Y., 1975).

31. Elizabeth Shackleton, "The Passion for the Primitive," SEP, 198 (Aug. 22, 1925), 68, 70; Joseph Hergesheimer, "Of Ultimate Antiques," SEP, 201 (Dec. 22, 1928), 8–9, 69–70, 72–73. See also Hergesheimer, *From an Old House* (New York, 1926); William L. Langer, *In and Out of the Ivory Tower* (New York, 1977), 129.

32. Virginia Robie, *The Quest of the Quaint* (1916 and rev. ed.: Boston, 1927); Caroline Camp, "The Antique Habit," *Scribner's Magazine,* 78 (July 1925), 91–96; Eleanor Butler Roosevelt, "Furniture-Hunting in New England," ibid., 83 (April 1928), 429–32; anon., "The Criminal Confessions of a Collector," SEP, 196 (Apr. 19, 1924), 24, 197; anon., "The Junk Snupper," ibid., 25, 150, 153.

33. John Tebbel, *George Horace Lorimer and the Saturday Evening Post* (Garden City, N.Y., 1948), 277–85, 288; Kenneth L. Roberts, ed., *Antiquamania: The Collected Papers of Professor Milton Kilgallen* (Garden City, N.Y., 1928).

34. John T. Winterich, *The Grolier Club, 1884–1967: An Informal History* (New York, 1967); *Catalogue of an Exhibition of Historical and Literary Americana, from the Collections of Thomas W. Streeter and C. Waller Barrett . . . Grolier Club, September 1959* (New York, 1960).

35. *The Walpole Society Note Book* (n.p., 1932); *The Walpole Society Note Book* (n.p., 1942); *The Walpole Society Note Book* (n.p., 1954); Stillinger, *The Antiquers,* 165–70.

36. M. L. Blumenthal, "Antiqueering," SEP, 196 (Feb. 16, 1924), 19; Esther Singleton, "Going, Going, Gone! Price Wise and Otherwise," SEP, 198 (May 22, 1926), 20–21, 82, 84, 86; Hergesheimer, "Of Ultimate Antiques," 8, 70; Richard H. Rush, *Antiques as an Investment* (New York, 1968).

37. Blumenthal, "Antiqueering," 18–19, 135, 137, 138, 141, 142; Philip Meredith Allen, "Furnished in Antiques," SEP, 198 (Nov. 14, 1925), 34–35, 86, 88, 90, 93, 94, 96; C. R. Clifford, "New Trails to Old Things for the Collector of Americana," SEP, 198 (Sept. 26, 1925), 44, 46, 99, 100; Esther Singleton, "American Antiques: Good and Bad," SEP, 198 (Jan. 9, 1926), 30–31, 177.

38. George Sheldon, "Note to Visitors," in *Catalogue of the Collection of Relics in Memorial Hall* (1908: Deerfield, Mass., 1920), n.p.; NYT, Jan. 13, 1889, p. 14; NYT, June 21, 1887, p. 4; "Relics of Lee's Surrender," *The Century,* 55 (February 1898), 637.

39. NYT, Apr. 17, 1887, p. 6; Susan Prendergast Schoelwer, "Curious Relics and Quaint Scenes: The Colonial Revival at Chicago's Great Fair," in Alan Axelrod, ed., *The Colonial Revival in America* (New York, 1985), 197–98, 212; Charles F. Montgomery, "Classics and Collectibles: American Antiques as History and Art," *Art News,* 76 (November 1977), 126–36, esp. 126–27.

40. *Wallace Nutting's Biography* (Framingham, Mass., 1936), 99, 109; William L. Dulaney, "Wallace Nutting: Collector and Entrepreneur," WP, 13 (1979), 47–60; Myers to Halsey, Dec. 5, 1924, archives of the American Wing, Metropolitan Museum of Art (Department of American Decorative Arts).

41. "The Criminal Confessions of a Collector," SEP, 196 (Apr. 19, 1924), 24, 197; Elizabeth Shackleton, "The Passion for the Primitive," SEP, 198 (Aug. 22, 1925), 70; "Rare Antiques in a New York Exhibition," NYT, Oct. 4, 1936, sec. 6, p. 16.

42. Charles B. Hosmer, Jr., *Presence of the Past: A History of the Preservation Movement in the United States before Williamsburg* (New York, 1965), 179, 189, 209–10, 227, 234–35, 271; George and Mary Roberts, *Triumph on Fairmount: Fiske Kimball and the Philadelphia Museum of Art* (Philadelphia, 1959), 74–75. The last quotation appears in Hosmer, *Presence of the Past,* 284. See also Eve M. Kahn, "Still Mysterious Architect Gets Her Due" [Alice Washburn], NYT, Mar. 1, 1990, p. C10.

43. Hosmer, *Presence of the Past,* 113, 116, 119–20; Saarinen, *The Proud Possessors,* "Americana: Electra Havemeyer Webb," 297; Hosmer, *Preservation Comes of Age: From Williamsburg to the National Trust, 1926–1949* (Charlottesville, Va., 1981), 377, 515.

44. Kenyon Cox, "The American School of Painting," *Scribner's Magazine,* 50 (December 1911), 765–68; Benton is quoted in Oliver W. Larkin, *Art and Life in America* (New York, 1957), 416.

45. Marjorie Phillips, *Duncan Phillips and His Collection* (Boston, 1970), 98–99, 118–19; John Russell, "In Washington, Rich Legacies of Two Collections," NYT, Aug. 3, 1986, sec. 2, p. 1.

46. Harold Sack and Max Wilk, *American Treasure Hunt* (New York, 1987), 262; Philip Meredith Allen, "Anecdotes and Antidotes on Antiques," SEP, 198 (June 12, 1926), 38, 40; Laurie Lisle, *Portrait of an Artist: A Biography of Georgia O'Keeffe* (New York, 1981), 348.

47. Susan Fillin-Yeh, *Charles Sheeler: American Interiors* (New Haven, 1987), 23, 48.

48. Ibid., 10, 13.

49. Ibid., 15, 56; Constance Rourke, *Charles Sheeler: Artist in the American Tradition* (New York, 1938); *Charles Sheeler: Retrospective Exhibition, Allentown Art Museum,* exhibition catalogue, Nov. 17–Dec. 31, 1961 (Allentown, Pa., 1961).

50. Fillin-Yeh, *Charles Sheeler,* 67; Joan Shelley Rubin, "A Convergence of Vision: Constance Rourke, Charles Sheeler, and American Art," AQ, 42 (1990), 191–222; Axelrod, *Colonial Revival,* 259.

51. Betsy James Wyeth, ed., *The Wyeths: The Letters of N. C. Wyeth, 1901–1945* (Boston, 1971); Wyeth's *Thanksgiving Day* (1921) in Parke-Bernet catalogue #4408 (July 10, 1980), fig. 88; Rockwell's "The Kiss" on SEP, July 25, 1931.

52. *Howard Chandler Christy: Artist/Illustrator of Style,* exhibition catalogue, Sept. 25–Nov. 6, 1977 (Allentown, Pa., 1977).

53. Gilbert C. Fite, *Mount Rushmore* (Norman, Okla., 1952), 46, 58, 182, 205.

54. Ibid., 33–43.

55. Wilson and Wilson to Moore, Dec. 9, 1923; C. Bascom Slemp to Moore, Dec. 18, 1923; Bland to Moore, Jan. 8, 1924; George C. Perry to Moore, Jan. 11, 1924; all in the Lee Chapel Papers (#2373), ALUV. See also the papers of Ann Norvell Otey Scott, Washington and Lee University Library, Special Collections, Lexington, Va. Mrs. Scott served as president of the Virginia Division of the U.D.C.

56. Keyes to Mrs. Maurice Moore, Jan. 14, 1924, Lee Chapel Papers, ALUV; Bruce to Moore, Jan. 15, 1924, ibid.

57. J. Taylor Ellyson to Henry Lewis Smith, Nov. 14, 1922, and Leonora Rogers Schuyler to Mrs. Thomas S. Burwell, Aug. 22, 1922, Ann Norvell Otey Scott Papers, Washington and Lee; Resolutions Adopted at Convention of Virginia Division, U.D.C., Oct. 11, 1922, ibid.; J. Field Wardlaw to Mary Moore, Jan. 24, 1924, Lee Chapel Papers, ALUV.

58. Michael Richman, *Daniel Chester French: An American Sculptor* (New York, 1976), 121–29, 171–86.

59. Wendell to Lodge, Apr. 5, 1912, Lodge Papers, box 108, MHS; George E. Mowry, "The Uses of History by Recent Presidents," JAH, 53 (1966), 14–15; Fite, *Mount Rushmore,* 100.

60. Roy P. Basler, *The Lincoln Legend: A Study in Changing Conceptions* (Boston, 1935); Benjamin P. Thomas, *Portrait for Posterity: Lincoln and His Biographers* (New Brunswick, N.J., 1947), ch. 8.

61. Dixon Ryan Fox to J. Franklin Jameson, Dec. 21, 1921, Jameson Papers, box 85, MDLC; Karal Ann Marling, "Of Cherry Trees and Ladies' Teas: Grant Wood Looks at Colonial America," in Axelrod, *Colonial Revival in America*, 294–319; joint program of the S.R. and S.A.R., Feb. 22, 1933, in Lyon G. Tyler Papers, group 1, box 24, SLWM.

62. "Americana," *American Mercury*, I (April 1924), 429; Rourke is quoted in Rubin, *Constance Rourke*, 157.

63. NYT, July 3, 1887, p. 11.

64. Wilson, "Talking United States" (July 15, 1936), in Wilson, *The Shores of Light: A Literary Chronicle of the Twenties and Thirties* (New York, 1952), 630–39.

65. Fenton, *Stephen Vincent Benét*, 101, 126–28, 154–55; John P. Diggins, "Visions of Chaos and Visions of Order: Dos Passos as Historian," *American Literature*, 46 (1974), 329–46.

66. Richard Ruland, *The Rediscovery of American Literature: Premises of Critical Taste, 1900–1940* (Cambridge, Mass., 1967), 221, 223, 276; Carl Van Doren to Frederic Bancroft, May 24, 1914, Bancroft Papers, BLCU; F. O. Matthiessen, *From the Heart of Europe* (New York, 1948), 73–74; James Hoopes, *Van Wyck Brooks: In Search of American Culture* (Amherst, Mass., 1977), 152, 205, 247.

67. Kermit Vanderbilt, *American Literature and the Academy: The Roots, Growth, and Maturity of a Profession* (Philadelphia, 1986), which concentrates on the period 1913–48; Mumford, "American Condescension," *Scribner's Magazine*, 87 (May 1930), 523; Joan Shelley Rubin, "Constance Rourke in Context: The Uses of Myth," AQ, 28 (1976), 585.

68. White to Adams, Mar. 28 and Apr. 3, 1936, Adams Papers, BLCU.

69. Carl Becker, *Everyman His Own Historian: Essays on History and Politics* (New York, 1935), 224–25; Matthew Josephson, *Life among the Surrealists: A Memoir* (New York, 1962), 357. See also Marsden Hartley's unpublished autobiographical memoir, "Somehow a Past," p. 108, in the Hartley Papers, BLYU.

70. George McLean Harper, "Seeing Americans First: What Recent Biographies Reveal," *Scribner's Magazine*, 86 (December 1929), 649–55.

71. Booth Tarkington, "America and Culture," SEP (Mar. 2, 1929), 25, 120.

72. Northern Pacific Railway Co., Villard Excursion file 1883 (microfilm M258), MinnHS.

73. "History for the Tourist," NYT, Apr. 26, 1936, sec. 9, p. 3.

74. Fitzhugh Lee to Edwin Warfield, Nov. 26, 1902, Lyon G. Tyler Papers, group 5, box 2, SLWM; NYT, May 28, 1939, sec. 4, p. 8; Ron Powers, *White Town Drowsing* (Boston, 1986), 225.

75. SEP, 202 (July 13, 1929), cover; NYT, June 9, 1935, sec. 1, p. 10.

76. Fenton, *Stephen Vincent Benét*, 8, 20; Benton, *An Artist in America* (4th ed.: Columbia, Mo., 1983), 381; Ben Maddow, *Edward Weston: Fifty Years* (Millerton, N.Y., 1973), 222–23; Wood to Dos Passos, May 31, 1939, Dos Passos Papers, box 5, ALUV.

77. Lawrence, *Mornings in Mexico* (1927), quoted in Paul Fussell, *Abroad: British Literary Traveling Between the Wars* (New York, 1980), 161.

78. See Lawrence W. Levine, *Highbrow/Lowbrow: The Emergence of Cultural Hierarchy in America* (Cambridge, Mass., 1988), esp. ch. 3; Howard, "Changing Ideals of the Art Museum," 127–28.

79. Phillips, *Duncan Phillips and His Collection*, 304; *Wallace Nutting's Autobiography*, 124–25; Rhoads, "Roadside Colonial," 147–48, n. 38; Dulaney, "Wallace Nutting," 54, 58.

80. Dana S. Creel to John C. Traphagen, Sept. 28, 1955, SHR Archives, box 17, RAC; memorandum from Creel, Oct. 31, 1955, ibid.

81. Edwin Wolf 2nd and John F. Fleming, *Rosenbach: A Biography* (Cleveland, 1960), 259–61.

82. Fenton, *Stephen Vincent Benét*, 212–15, 219–20, 227, 363–65.

83. Robert J. Thompson, ed., *"Adequate Brevity": A Collation and Co-Ordination of the Mental Processes and Reactions of Calvin Coolidge, as Expressed in His Addresses and Messages* (Chicago, 1924), 46.

Chapter 11

1. Reynold M. Wik, *Henry Ford and Grass-roots America* (Ann Arbor, Mich., 1973), 210.

2. William L. Dulaney, "Wallace Nutting: Collector and Entrepreneur," WP, 13 (1979), 53.

3. Elinor Des Verney Sinnette, *Arthur Alfonso Schomburg: Black Bibliophile and Collector* (Detroit, 1989), 98–102; John A. H. Sweeney, *Henry Francis du Pont, 1880–1969* (n.p., 1980), pamphlet without pagination.

4. Charles F. Montgomery, "Francis P. Garvan," TMA, 121 (January 1982), 244–49. In March 1974 the New York State Historical Association sponsored a series of five lectures entitled "Great Collectors and Their Collections." The subjects included Henry Ford, Henry Francis du Pont, Henry Chapman Mercer, Francis P. Garvan, and Margaret Woodbury Strong. The lectures were not published.

5. John R. Lane, "Maxim Karolik, Benefactor to the Museum of Fine Arts, Boston," *American Art Review*, 2 (1975), 103–13.

6. Alice Winchester, "Maxim Karolik and His Collections," *Art in America*, 45 (1957), 34–39, 70; Edwin J. Hipkiss, *Eighteenth-Century American Arts: The M. and M. Karolik Collection. . . .* (Cambridge, Mass., 1941).

7. Harold Sack and Max Wilk, *American Treasure Hunt* (New York, 1987), 153; Lane, "Maxim Karolik," 107, 110.

8. Karolik, "The American Way: A Conversation Piece," *Atlantic*, 170 (October 1942), 101–04.

9. Ibid., 104–05.

10. Lane, "Maxim Karolik," 106, 110; Winchester, "Maxim Karolik and His Collections," 40.

11. Dianne H. Pilgrim, "Inherited From the Past: The American Period Room," *American Art Journal*, 10 (1978), 7–8; Melinda Young Frye, "The Beginnings of the Period Room in American Museums: Charles P. Wilcomb's Colonial Kitchens, 1896, 1906, 1910," in Alan Axelrod, ed., *The Colonial Revival in America* (New York, 1985), 217–40.

12. Pilgrim, "The American Period Room," 28; Lockwood, "The New Section of Early American Rooms," *The Brooklyn Museum Quarterly*, 17 (January 1930), 1.

13. Pilgrim, "The American Period Room," 5–6, 13; Fay Campbell Kaynor, "Thomas Tileston Waterman: Student of American Colonial Architecture," WP, 20 (1985), 123–24.

14. Pilgrim, "The American Period Room," 12–13; George and Mary Roberts, *Triumph on Fairmount: Fiske Kimball and the Philadelphia Museum of Art* (Philadelphia, 1959), 53, 66–68, 76, 165, 167.

15. Aline B. Saarinen, *The Proud Possessors: The Lives, Times and Tastes of Some Adventurous American Art Collectors* (New York, 1958), 307–25.

16. David Randolph Milsten, *Thomas Gilcrease* (San Antonio, Tex., 1969), esp. book 6. Gilcrease died in 1962.

17. Marshall Davidson, "Those American Things," *Metropolitan Museum Journal*, 3 (1970), 227–28; Davidson, *The American Wing: A Guide* (New York, 1980), 9–10.

18. Davidson, "Those American Things," 229–31; James A. Hijiya, "Four Ways of Looking at a Philanthropist: A Study of Robert Weeks de Forest," *Proceedings of the APS*, 124 (December 1980), 409–10, 416–17.

19. Quoted in Davidson, "Those American Things," 231–32. James Hijiya has observed that de Forest associated democracy with face-to-face relationships in simpler

times. Therefore de Forest, who felt strongly about republican simplicity, believed that colonial America had been democratic in basic ways.

20. Davidson, "Art of Our Ancestors," TMA, 50 (October 1946), 238; Mumford, "American Interiors," NR, 41 (Dec. 31, 1924), 139–40.

21. Mumford, "American Interiors," 140. Reprinted by permission of Gina Maccoby Literary Agency for the Estate of Lewis Mumford.

22. Joseph Downs, "The History of the American Wing," TMA, 50 (October 1946), 234–37, the quotation at 235.

23. Ibid., 235.

24. Charles B. Hosmer, Jr., *Presence of the Past: A History of the Preservation Movement in the United States Before Williamsburg* (New York, 1965), 233; NYT, Apr. 9, 1935, p. 23; NYT, Oct. 4, 1936, sec. 6, p. 16.

25. Quoted in Downs, "History of the American Wing," 233.

26. See Wendy Kaplan, "R. T. H. Halsey: An Ideology of Collecting American Decorative Arts," WP, 17 (1982), 51–53; Davidson, "Art of Our Ancestors," 238–39.

27. Rockefeller to Ford, May 26, 1930, FA; Ford interview with S. J. Woolf, NYT, Jan. 12, 1936, sec. 7, p. 1.

28. The first is quoted in William Greenleaf, *From These Beginnings: The Early Philanthropies of Henry and Edsel Ford, 1911–1936* (Detroit, 1964), 96; the second in Geoffrey C. Upward, *A Home for Our Heritage: The Building and Growth of Greenfield Village and Henry Ford Museum, 1929–1979* (Dearborn, Mich., 1979), 154.

29. Woolf, NYT, Jan. 12, 1936, sec. 7, p. 20.

30. Keith Sward, *The Legend of Henry Ford* (New York, 1948), 261; Upward, *A Home for Our Heritage*, 2, 8, 11.

31. Upward, *A Home for Our Heritage*, 4, 18.

32. Roger Butterfield, "Henry Ford, the Wayside Inn, and the Problem of 'History Is Bunk,'" *Proceedings* of the MHS, 77 (1965), 58–60.

33. Ibid., 60–61; Ford, *Today and Tomorrow* (Garden City, N.Y., 1926), 224–28.

34. Upward, *A Home for Our Heritage*, 15; Butterfield, "Henry Ford, the Wayside Inn," 64–66.

35. Karal Ann Marling, *George Washington Slept Here: Colonial Revivals and American Culture, 1876–1986* (Cambridge, Mass., 1988), 283–88.

36. Upward, *A Home for Our Heritage*, 78, 94; James S. Wamsley, *American Ingenuity: Henry Ford Museum and Greenfield Village* (New York, 1985).

37. Quoted in John L. Wright et al., "Report of the Curriculum Committee, 1981," unpublished report of the Edison Institute, Henry Ford Museum and Greenfield Village, FA.

38. Upward, *A Home for Our Heritage*, 128, 136.

39. Ibid., 76, 78.

40. Ibid., 75; Wik, *Ford and Grass-roots America*, 206–09; Ruth Kedzie Wood, "Henry Ford's Greatest Gift to the American People," *The Mentor*, 17, no. 5 (June 1929), 5, 10.

41. Wood, "Ford's Greatest Gift to the American People," 9.

42. Rockefeller to Ford, Nov. 4, 1929, FA.

43. Same to same, May 26, 1930, ibid.

44. Campsall to Edsel B. Ford, May 23, 1930, ibid.

45. Goodwin to Henry Ford, May 8, 1929, and Dec. 3, 1929, CWA, Henry Ford file; Goodwin to Frank Campsall, Jan. 9, 1930, ibid.

46. Henry Ford to Rockefeller, Apr. 2, 1930, FA; Rockefeller to Ford, Apr. 9, 1930, ibid.; Chorley to Henry Ford, Feb. 5, 1935, ibid.; Rockefeller to Edsel Ford, Feb. 7, 1935, ibid.; Edsel Ford to Rockefeller, Feb. 14, 1935, ibid.

47. Rockefeller to Edsel Ford, Sept. 7, 1929, FA; Edsel Ford to Rockefeller, Sept. 20, 1929, ibid.; Rockefeller to E. Ford, Oct. 2, 1929, ibid.

48. *Richmond Enquirer*, July 18, 1837, p. 4.

49. "A Visit to Williamsburg, Va., in 1887: Extracts from letters written to her sisters by Mrs. Daniel Coit Gilman," unpublished account sent by Miss Elizabeth Gilman (her

daughter) to JDR, July 4, 1934, ts. located in JDR Papers, ser. II (cultural), box 163, RAC.

50.   Quoted in an unpublished history of C.W. written in the 1950s by Thomas J. Wertenbaker, ch. 8, p. 8, typescript in CWA.

51.   Cabell Phillips, "The Town That Stopped the Clock," AH, 11 (February 1960), 23, 81. For a refreshing sense of *déjà vu,* because these emotional struggles seem to occur in cycles, see Richard Crane to JDR, June 8, 1933, JDR Papers, ser. II (cultural), box 163.

52.   Goodwin to Ford, June 13, 1924, FA (there is also a copy in CWA); *Baltimore Sun,* Nov. 4, 1924; this and other clippings will be found in the Goodwin records, CWA.

53.   Goodwin to William Mitchell, Apr. 15, 1926, Goodwin records, CWA; Alvin Moscow, *The Rockefeller Inheritance* (Garden City, N.Y., 1977), 103–04.

54.   See Charles B. Hosmer, Jr., *Preservation Comes of Age: From Williamsburg to the National Trust, 1926–1949* (Charlottesville, Va., 1981), I, 11–73; Raymond B. Fosdick, *John D. Rockefeller, Jr.: A Portrait* (New York, 1956), 272–301; Carlisle H. Humelsine, *Fifty Years of Colonial Williamsburg,* pamphlet reprinted from TMA (December 1976).

55.   Rockefeller to Goodwin, Nov. 29, 1926, JDR Papers, ser. II (cultural), box 163, RAC.

56.   Memorandum from Goodwin to Col. Arthur Woods, Oct. 11, 1930, Goodwin records, CWA.

57.   See, e.g., the extensive Visitor Analysis Study made under the direction of Raymond Franzen in 1960 by Child & Waters, Inc., of New York, for C.W., located in the Office of the Secretary, C.W. Foundation. I am indebted to D. Stephen Elliott, Vice President of Colonial Williamsburg, for making this study available to me.

58.   Memorandum from Goodwin to Colonel Arthur Woods, Oct. 11, 1930, Goodwin records, CWA.

59.   Minutes of a meeting of the C.W. Committee on Purchase of Antiques and Historical Objects, held in New York City on Oct. 16, 1928, Goodwin records, CWA; du Pont to Susan Higginson Nash, Nov. 20, 1934, general correspondence, CWA.

60.   Goodwin to Charles O. Heydt, Apr. 23, 1929, JDR Papers, ser. II (cultural), box 163, RAC; JDR to John S. Charles, Oct. 18, 1928, ibid.

61.   Chorley's speech of Oct. 22, 1934, is in the Chorley "scrapbooks," arranged chronologically, RAC.

62.   C. G. Milham to JDR, May 16 and Nov. 18, 1935, JDR Papers, ser. II (cultural), box 190; Chorley to JDR, May 18, 1935, ibid.

63.   Fosdick to JDR, Dec. 14, 1935, ibid.

64.   JDR to C. G. Milham, Feb. 21, 1936, ibid.

65.   William G. Perry to Col. Arthur Woods, Jan. 3, 1931, Furnishings-General, CWA; Chorley speech, Oct. 21, 1932, the Chorley "scrapbooks," #3, RAC.

66.   Chorley, Rotary Club address, Oct. 22, 1934, ibid.; Chorley, address to the C.W. hostesses, Dec. 13, 1934, ibid.; Sarah M. Wertenbaker to JDR, Sept. 7, 1935, JDR Papers, ser. II (cultural), box 163, RAC.

67.   Charles O. Heydt to E. L. Ballard, Apr. 16, 1932, JDR Papers, ser. II (cultural), box 163; JDR to Chorley, Aug. 7, 1933, ibid.; Stephen Birmingham, *The Late John Marquand: A Biography* (Philadelphia, 1972), 102.

68.   Chorley to JDR III, Apr. 9, 1934, CWA; official attendance figures courtesy of the Secretary to the C.W. Foundation.

69.   Moscow, *The Rockefeller Inheritance,* 119–20; NYT, May 7, 1936, p. 9; Chorley's address to the hostesses, Dec. 13, 1934, Chorley "scrapbooks" #3, RAC.

70.   W. A. R. Goodwin to Col. Arthur Woods and Charles Heydt, Nov. 23, 1928, "Restoration" folder, CWA; Chorley's speeches to the Society of Colonial Wars, Feb. 25, 1935, and to the Current Events Club, Mar. 4, 1935, Chorley "scrapbooks," RAC. For a note on "Negro properties" purchased 1927–29, see "Restoration—Its Conception," dated January 1929, CWA; JDR to Chorley, Aug. 16, 1938, and Chorley to JDR, Dec. 3, 1938, JDR Papers, ser. II (cultural), box 177, folder marked Negro Education Project, 1938–42, RAC; memorandum from Jackson Davis to JDR, June 26, 1940, ibid.; "Patterson brickyard," two-page memorandum, general correspondence, CWA.

71. Chorley to JDR, Sept. 4, 1942; JDR to Chorley, Sept. 18, 1942, and Jan. 6, 1943, JDR Papers, ser. II (cultural), box 169, RAC; A. E. Kendrew to JDR, Jan. 4, 1943, ibid., box 170, folder 63; JDR to Chorley, May 5, 1943, ibid.

72. NYT, Nov. 1, 1936, p. 7; NYT, Apr. 4, 1937, sec. 2, p. 4; NYT, May 16, 1937, sec. 9, p. 2 (Rotogravure Section).

73. Chorley to JDR, Sept. 30, 1936, CWA; Sidney N. Shurcliff to B. W. Norton, Mar. 16, 1936, CWA; Chorley to Stettinius, Apr. 7, 1941, JDR Papers, ser. II (cultural), box 170, RAC.

74. Chorley to JDR, Nov. 28, 1940, ibid., box 169.

75. See the Chorley "scrapbooks," 1941–48, RAC.

76. See Elisabeth Donaghy Garrett, *The Arts of Independence: The DAR Museum Collection* (Washington, D.C., 1985), 15–16; Debra A. Hashim, "American Silver at the D.A.R. Museum," TMA, 117 (March 1980), 634–41.

77. Peter J. Schmitt, *Back to Nature: The Arcadian Myth in Urban America* (New York, 1969), 164; Donald C. Stewart, "Yellowstone's Madison Museum," MMWHC, 25 (1975), 60–66, built in 1928 with funds from the Laura Spelman Rockefeller Foundation; Marling, *George Washington Slept Here: Colonial Revivals and American Culture, 1876–1986*, 348.

78. Michael Kammen, "Heritage, Memory, and Hudson Valley Traditions," in Kammen, *Selvages & Biases: The Fabric of History in American Culture* (Ithaca, N.Y., 1987), 318–21; Fosdick, *John D. Rockefeller, Jr.,* 350–51.

79. A. E. Kendrew to Hugh Grant Rowell, June 7, 1944, JDR Papers, ser. II (cultural), box 170, RAC; Nancy Newhall, *A Contribution to the Heritage of Every American: The Conservation Activities of John D. Rockefeller, Jr.* (New York, 1957), 31–43.

80. Kendrew to Rowell, June 7, 1944, JDR Papers, ser. II (cultural), box 170, RAC.

81. Ruth Scott Miller, "Our Early American Builders," SEP, 197 (Sept. 20, 1924), 16, 62, 67. On Nov. 7, 1923, John Drinkwater wrote to Mrs. Maurice Moore of Lynchburg, Va., that historical buildings in America "are at present relatively rare," and consequently ought to be saved. Lee Chapel Papers (#2373), ALUV.

82. Hosmer, *Presence of the Past,* 255; TMA, 116 (October 1979), an entire issue devoted to Old Sturbridge Village; letter from Virginia S. Dugan of Mystic Seaport, Inc., to the author, March 9, 1979; NYT, July 30, 1989, p. 48.

83. Isaac Newton Phelps Stokes, *Random Recollections of a Happy Life* (New York, 1941), 136; Charlotte N. Cutts to I. N. P. Stokes, Aug. 8 and 18, 1923, Misc. Mss., NYHS; Cynthia H. Barton, *A New Eden: Clara Endicott Sears, Founder of Fruitlands Museums* (Harvard, Mass., 1988), 27-page pamphlet; James M. Lindgren, "The Gospel of Preservation in Virginia and New England: Historic Preservation and the Regeneration of Traditionalism" (unpubl. Ph.D. diss., The College of William and Mary, 1984), 394.

84. Hosmer, *Preservation Comes of Age: From Williamsburg to the National Trust, 1926–1949,* I, 240–42; William B. Hesseltine and Donald R. McNeil, eds., *In Support of Clio: Essays in Memory of Herbert A. Kellar* (Madison, Wis., 1958), 204–06; Charles B. Hosmer, Jr., "The Colonial Revival in the Public Eye: Williamsburg and Early Garden Restoration," in Axelrod, *Colonial Revival in America,* 65; NYT, Apr. 23, 1939, sec. 11, p. 2.

85. NYT, Mar. 1, 1936, sec. 7, p. 13; NYT, June 6, 1937, sec. 6, p. 9; NYT, Sept. 12, 1937, sec. 1, p. 32; NYT, Sept. 30, 1937, p. 25. For the dedication of the Oregon Trail Museum in the Scott's Bluff National Monument, see NYT, Jan. 17, 1937, sec. 11, p. 11.

86. Vestal Thomas Grigg to Douglas Southall Freeman, Sept. 12, 1940, Freeman Papers, box 10, ALUV; oral interview with Riley, made in 1972, tape at RAC.

87. Barton, *A New Eden,* 21–23; *The Wells Family: Founders of the American Optical Company and Old Sturbridge Village* (Southbridge, Mass., 1979), 2; *The Carriage Collection: The Museums at Stony Brook* (Stony Brook, N.Y., 1986), 13. See also Charles B. Hosmer, "The Broadening View of the Historical Preservation Movement," in Ian M. G. Quimby, ed., *Material Culture and the Study of American Life* (New York, 1978), 123, for a remarkable statement in support of saving Harewood, a country home near Charlestown, W. Va.

88. Greenleaf, *The Early Philanthropies of Henry and Edsel Ford*, ch. 5; interview with Riley (1972), tape at RAC.

89. Chorley speech, Dec. 13, 1934, Chorley "scrapbooks," RAC.

90. Ibid.; Chorley to JDR, Nov. 28, 1940, JDR Papers, ser. II (cultural), box 169, RAC (esp. p. 3 of this memorandum).

Chapter 12

1. Charles A. Fenton, *Stephen Vincent Benét: The Life and Times of an American Man of Letters, 1898–1943* (New Haven, 1958), 341–42.

2. Charles B. Hosmer, Jr., *Preservation Comes of Age: From Williamsburg to the National Trust, 1926–1949* (Charlottesville, Va., 1981), I, 393; Solon J. Buck to James A. Barnes, Sept. 13, 1933, Buck Papers, box 13, MinnHS.

3. Stanley Edgar Hyman, *The Armed Vision: A Study in the Methods of Modern Literary Criticism* (rev. ed.: New York, 1955), 77; Dixon Ryan Fox, ed., *Sources of Culture in the Middle West: Backgrounds versus Frontier* (New York, 1934).

4. Fox to Hendricks, Jan. 29, 1937, Fox Papers, Union College Library, Schenectady, N.Y. There is also extensive correspondence between Fox and Hendricks in the Fox Papers, box 6, folder H, NYSHA.

5. Gamaliel Bradford to Lyon G. Tyler, Jan. 5, 1922, Tyler Family Papers, group 1, box 20, SLWM. See also Worthington C. Ford to Tyler, Dec. 29, 1921, and Jan. 16, 1922, ibid., group 5, box 4.

6. Lyon G. Tyler to Gamaliel Bradford, Mar. 7, 1923, ibid., box 4. See also NYT, Jan. 3, 1937, Book Review section, pp. 6, 20.

7. Worthington C. Ford to Philip A. Bruce, Mar. 27, 1924, Bruce Papers, box 2, ALUV. See also Howard Mumford Jones, "The Southern Legend," *Scribner's Magazine*, 85 (May 1929), 538–42.

8. Bradford to Lyon G. Tyler, Oct. 15, 1927, Tyler Family Papers, group 1, box 20, SLWM. For statements deeply offensive to Southerners, see W. DeLoss Love, *The Fast and Thanksgiving Days of New England* (Boston, 1895), 398.

9. Schlesinger to Nevins, Feb. 14, 1928, Nevins Papers (professional), BLCU; Ford to Lyon G. Tyler, July 7, 1924, Tyler Papers, group 5, box 4, SLWM. To Ford, the book was "exactly what was needed to counteract the absurd worship of everything that is of New England and this closing the eyes to incidents in the career of our 'heroes' that are even more illuminative on their character than their so-called patriotism."

10. Benjamin P. Thomas, *Portrait for Posterity: Lincoln and His Biographers* (New Brunswick, N.J., 1947), 3–4; Tyler to Albert B. Hart, Jan. 4, 1932, Tyler Papers, group 5, box 7, SLWM; Dodd to Tyler, Oct. 21, 1920, ibid., Family group 1, box 20, SLWM; Tyler to Dodd, Nov. 4, 1920, ibid., group 5, box 4.

11. Eric F. Goldman, *John Bach McMaster: American Historian* (Philadelphia, 1943), 79.

12. See Ludwig Lewisohn, *Expression in America* [*The Story of American Literature*] (New York, 1932); James P. Hendrix, Jr., "From Romance to Scholarship: Southern History at the Take-Off Point," *Mississippi Quarterly*, 30 (1977), 196–97; Potter, "Interpreting American History," in John A. Garraty, ed., *Interpreting American History: Conversations with Historians* (New York, 1970), II, 321.

13. Miss Mildred Rutherford to Hart, Jan. 29, 1917, Hart Papers, box 22, HUA. See also E. C. Glass (Superintendent of Schools, Lynchburg, Va.) to Lyon G. Tyler, Apr. 29, 1922, Tyler Papers, group 1, box 21, SLWM.

14. Hart to Tyler, June 27, 1928, Tyler Papers, group 5, box 5, SLWM. Hart had written Tyler a long and similar letter on Jan. 13, 1922. Lincoln, he remarked, "was the conspicuous statesman who understood the character and ways of the South. Had he lived, he would have proposed, and without doubt would have put over a much milder plan of reconstruction. . . . Why don't you close the books of your ancestors, and start out on the basis that they made their mistakes, as we are making our mistakes, which our grandchildren will correct." (Ibid., group 5, box 4.)

15. Henry T. McDonald to Tyler, Feb. 13, 1934, Tyler Papers, group 5, box 9, SLWM. See also William E. Dodd to Tyler, Mar. 12, 1931, ibid., box 6. For Tyler's often reiterated response to Dodd, see his letter of Nov. 4, 1920, ibid., group 1, box 20.

16. J. G. de Roulhac Hamilton, "The Many-Sired Lincoln," *American Mercury*, 5 (June 1925), 129–35; David Rankin Barbee to Lyon G. Tyler, June 18, 1932, Tyler Papers, group 5, box 7, SLWM. See also Barbee to Tyler, July 7, 1930, ibid., group 1, box 20.

17. G. D. Eaton to G. S. H. Holland, Apr. 26, 1928, Tyler Papers, group 1, box 21, SLWM.

18. A. S. Salley, Jr., to Lyon G. Tyler, Jan. 4, 1929, ibid. group 5, box 5, SLWM; Tyler to *Richmond Times-Dispatch*, n.d., ibid.; Rev. Joseph B. Lutz to Tyler, July 25, 1932, ibid., group 1, box 22; E. F. G. Harper to Tyler, Sept. 22, 1930, ibid., group 5, box 6.

19. The *Confederate Veteran* was published in Nashville; *Confederate Veteran* to Lyon G. Tyler, Sept. 5, 1917, Tyler Papers, group 1, box 22, SLWM; Raymond S. Tompkins, "Confederate Daughters Stand Guard," *Scribner's Magazine*, 92 (July 1932), 34–36.

20. Susie B. Harrison to Lyon G. Tyler, June 22, 1929, Tyler Papers, group 5, box 5, SLWM.

21. Arthur S. Link, *Wilson: The Road to the White House* (Princeton, 1947), 1–4, 388.

22. Landon C. Bell to Tyler, Sept. 20, 1929, Tyler Papers, group 1, box 20, SLWM; A. S. Salley, Jr., to Tyler, Oct. 21, 1929, ibid., box 23; David Rankin Barbee to Tyler, July 15 and 27, 1930, ibid., boxes 20 and 6; Gordon Hurlbutt to Tyler, Apr. 2, 1934, ibid., group 1, box 21.

23. Mary D. Carter to Tyler, Mar. 26, 1930, and Mar. 20, 1934, Tyler Papers, group 5, box 6, and group 1, box 20; M. C. McConkey to Carter, Dec. 30, 1931, ibid., group 5, box 7; Matthew Page Andrews to Tyler, June 30, 1932, ibid. Tyler received equally judicious letters from William Cabell Bruce, Nov. 9, 1928, and F. I. Herriott, Dec. 5, 1930, ibid., group 1, box 20, and group 5, box 6.

24. William Hodges Mann to Tyler, July 9, 1910, Tyler Papers, group 5, box 3, SLWM; Dandridge Spotswood to Tyler, Sept. 6, 1932, ibid., group 1, box 23.

25. Philip G. Auchampaugh to Tyler, May 13, 1931, Tyler Papers, group 5, box 6; Robert M. Hughes to Tyler, May 27, 1931, ibid.; G. S. P. Holland to Committee on School Books (State Senate, Richmond), Feb. 19, 1932, ibid., group 5, box 7; Arthur H. Jennings to Tyler, Mar. 5, 1932, ibid.

26. C. Vernon Eddy (of the Winchester, Va., Historical Society) to Tyler, July 20, 1932, Tyler Papers, group 1, box 21; Mrs. J. M. Hightower (Pine Bluff) to Tyler, Aug. 29, 1932, ibid.; Dandridge Spotswood to Tyler, Sept. 6, 1932, ibid., group 1, box 23; Mrs. John C. Abernathy (Chicago) to Tyler, Sept. 19, 1932, ibid., group 1, box 20. President Henry T. McDonald of Storer College in Harpers Ferry, who taught history and political science, largely agreed but expressed polite dissent from Tyler's orthodox states' rights position (June 18, 1934, ibid., group 1, box 22).

27. Abernethy to Tyler, Sept. 19, 1932, Tyler Papers, group 1, box 20; Rowland, *The "Dictionary of American Biography"; A Partisan, Sectional, Political Publication: A Protest* (Jackson, Miss., 1931).

28. Richard N. Current, *Northernizing the South* (Athens, Ga., 1983), 14. For Southern ambivalence about progress, see 85, 97, 103–05.

29. Lodge to Adams, Sept. 19, 1919, Lodge Papers, box 52, MHS; Adams, *The Emancipation of Massachusetts* (Boston, 1887; 2nd ed. 1919).

30. Bernard DeVoto, "New England: There She Stands," *Harper's* (March 1932), in DeVoto, *Forays and Rebuttals* (Boston, 1936), 158. For DeVoto's ambivalent (virtually tortured) relationship with New England culture, see Wallace Stegner, *The Uneasy Chair: A Biography of Bernard DeVoto* (Garden City, N.Y., 1974), 78–106.

31. George P. Blow to Lyon G. Tyler, May 26, 1920, Tyler Papers, group 5, box 4, SLWM; Philip A. Bruce to Tyler, Aug. 24, 1925, ibid.

32. George O. Trevelyan to Lodge, Jan. 28, 1921, Lodge Papers, box 65, MHS; Lodge to Trevelyan, Feb. 14, 1921, ibid.; Frederick W. Bittinger, *The Story of the Pilgrim Tercentenary Celebration* (Plymouth, 1923), esp. 89–91.

33. Samuel McChord Crothers, "The Pilgrims and Their Contemporaries," *The Century*, 100 (May 1920), 1–11.

34. See the speech given at Jacksonville, Florida, by Governor Aycock of North Carolina in 1903, in R. D. W. Connor and Clarence Poe, eds., *The Life and Speeches of Charles Brantley Aycock* (New York, 1912), 130–31, 156, 280–81; Thomas J. Wertenbaker to Lyon G. Tyler, Mar. 24, 1914, Tyler Papers, group 5, box 4, SLWM; Darrett B. Rutman, "Philip Alexander Bruce: A Divided Mind of the South," VMHB, 68 (1960), 387–407.

35. Bruce to Tyler, Aug. 12, 1920, Tyler Papers, group 5, box 4, SLWM.

36. Tyler to Bruce, Mar. 16, 1922, Tyler Papers, group 1, box 20; Tyler to Southern Publishing Co. (Dallas), Apr. 3, 1922, ibid., group 5, box 4; Tyler to Harris Hart, Mar. 28, 1923, ibid., group 1, box 21.

37. Bruce to Tyler, July 26, Aug. 10, and Sept. 4, 1925, Tyler Papers, group 5, box 4.

38. David Rankin Barbee to Tyler, July 19, 1933, Tyler Papers, group 5, box 8; William W. Brewton to Tyler, Oct. 28, 1932, ibid.; anon. letter to the editor of the *Richmond Times-Dispatch*, Feb. 23, 1932, clipping in ibid., box 7.

39. George M. Beltzhoover, Jr., to Tyler, Mar. 7, 1925, Tyler Papers, group 5, box 4.

40. NYT, Nov. 23, 1887, p. 2.

41. NYT, Nov. 25, 1971, p. 37; William B. Browne to Tyler, Nov. 20, 1931, Tyler Papers, group 5, box 7, SLWM.

42. NYT, Mar. 29, 1936, sec. 10, p. 1; NYT, Dec. 6, 1936, p. E8; NYT *Sunday Magazine*, Feb. 14, 1937, p. 9; NYT, Sept. 23, 1937, p. 26; Freeman to Glasgow, Feb. 11, 1938, Freeman Papers, box 30, MDLC. For a very strong sense of Southern pride in 1942, see the Freeman Papers, box 43, the folder of correspondence pertaining to Freeman's multi-volume work *Lee's Lieutenants*.

43. Felix Frankfurter, *Mr. Justice Holmes and the Supreme Court* (Cambridge, Mass., 1961), 2. See also Norman Foerster, ed., *Humanism and America* (New York, 1930), xiii.

44. Alan Axelrod, ed., *The Colonial Revival in America* (New York, 1985), 20–21, 23, 47–48, 51.

45. Paltsits to William F. Brewster, Jan. 4, 1921, Paltsits Papers, NYHS; Richard W. Westwood (editor of *Nature*) to Lyon G. Tyler, Sept. 20, 1928, Tyler Papers, group 5, box 5, SLWM; Jordan to Tyler, Oct. 15, 1928, ibid.

46. L. Lamprey to Tyler, Oct. 25, 1928, Tyler Papers, group 5, box 5, SLWM; Samuel Stoney quoted in Hosmer, *Preservation Comes of Age*, I, 273.

47. See Frederick J. Hoffman, "Philistine and Puritan in the 1920s: An Example of the Misuse of the American Past," AQ, 1 (1949), 247–63; Jan C. Dawson, *The Unusable Past: America's Puritan Tradition, 1830 to 1930* (Chico, Calif., 1984), chs. 7 and 10.

48. Arthur Train, "Puritan's Progress," SEP, 201 (May 25, 1929), 12–13, 197–98, 200–02; Train, "The Puritan Shadow," *Scribner's Magazine*, 88 (September 1930), 314–26.

49. Elizabeth Stillinger, *The Antiquers* (New York, 1980), 140–41; Daniel Bell, *The Social Sciences Since the Second World War* (New Brunswick, N.J., 1982), 39; Morison to Adams, Nov. 25, 1929, Adams Papers, BLCU.

50. Brooks, *Three Essays on America* (1934: New York, 1970); Claire Sprague, ed., *Van Wyck Brooks: The Early Years. A Selection from His Works, 1908–1921* (New York, 1968), 112; Richard H. Pells, *Radical Visions and American Dreams: Culture and Social Thought in the Depression Years* (New York, 1973), 315.

51. See Henry F. May, *The End of American Innocence: A Study of the First Years of Our Own Time, 1912–1917* (New York, 1959), 214–15; Charles A. Beard, "On Puritans," NR, 25 (Dec. 1, 1920), 15–17.

52. See Richard Ruland, *The Rediscovery of American Literature: Premises of Critical Taste, 1900–1940* (Cambridge, Mass., 1967), 159–61.

53. Stuart P. Sherman, "What Is a Puritan?" *Atlantic*, 128 (September 1921), 345–48, repr. in Sherman, *The Genius of America: Studies in Behalf of the Younger Generation* (New York, 1923), 33–75.

54. V. F. Calverton, "The Puritan Myth," *Scribner's Magazine*, 89 (March 1931), 251–57, the quotation at 255.

55. NYT, Apr. 15, 1935, p. 15; R. L. Duffus, "In Kansas the Old Traditions Echo," NYT, July 5, 1936, sec. 7, p. 5.

56. NYT, Oct. 10, 1936, p. 15; NYT, Nov. 12, 1936, p. 29.

57. Gail Levin, *Edward Hopper: The Art and the Artist* (New York, 1980), plate 231.

58. James L. Ford, "Early Memories of New England," *Scribner's Magazine*, 71 (April 1922), 491–96; Claude M. Fuess, "What Is a Yankee?" *Yankee Magazine*, 1 (December 1935), 14–17. For the genesis of *The New England Quarterly*, see the interesting letter from Samuel Eliot Morison to J. Franklin Jameson, Dec. 21, 1925, Jameson Papers, box 114, MDLC. "We believe that New England has a cultural unity, which put forth its fairest flowers in the time of Emerson, but which has not yet spent its force; and although we have no intention to exclude articles on political or economic history, we wish to make the review primarily an organ of kulturgeschichte."

59. Alice Hooper to Solon J. Buck, July 3, 1926, and May 25, 1927, Buck Papers, box 11, MinnHS.

60. Michael Kammen, "Business Leadership and the American Heritage," *Cornell Enterprise* (Fall 1986), 18–27.

61. Howard R. Driggs, *Covered-Wagon Centennial and Ox-Team Days* (Yonkers, N.Y., 1932), 51–52.

62. A. Edward Newton, "Westward," *Atlantic*, 149 (May 1932), 527–37, the quotation at 533–34; Laurence Stallings to James Boyd (from Beverly Hills), Nov. 19, 1927, Boyd Papers, box 3, SHC. See also Geoffrey West, "Joseph Hergesheimer," *Virginia Quarterly Review*, 8 (1932), 99.

63. Dudley Gordon, *Charles F. Lummis: Crusader in Corduroy* (Los Angeles, 1972), 223, 225–27, 233.

64. Robert W. Rydell, *All the World's a Fair: Visions of Empire at American International Expositions, 1876–1916* (Chicago, 1984), 209; Eugen Neuhaus, *The San Diego Garden Fair* (San Francisco, 1916), xii–xiii. See also "California's Contribution to a National Architecture: Its Significance and Beauty as Shown in the Work of Greene and Greene, Architects" [c. 1914], in Barry Sanders, ed., *The Craftsman: An Anthology* (Santa Barbara, Calif., 1978), 251–63.

65. NYT, May 19, 1935, sec. 9, pt. 2, pp. 1–2; NYT, Dec. 3, 1936, p. 7.

66. Kenneth B. Ragsdale, *Centennial '36: The Year America Discovered Texas* (College Station, Tex., 1987), xvii, 45, 55.

67. Peggy and Harold Samuels, *Frederic Remington: A Biography* (Garden City, N.Y., 1982), 155, 204, 322, 394.

68. Dorys Crow Grover, "W. H. D. Koerner and Emerson Hough: A Western Collaboration," MMWHC, 29 (1979), 2–15. For Western murals commissioned in 1910 for the Indian Room of the Doheny home in Los Angeles and completed in 1926, see *Christie's Catalogue*, Feb. 3 and 4, 1988, p. 85.

69. R. P. Crawford, "Discovering a Real American Art," *Scribner's Magazine*, 73 (March 1923), 380–84. The Quivira Society Publications, devoted to the history of the Spanish borderlands, began to appear in 1929 and continued until 1958.

70. Thomas Welles, "The Pony Express Museum," *Overland*, 2nd ser., 91 (March 1933), 44–45, 47.

71. C. B. Galbreath, "Ezra Meeker: Ohio's Illustrious Pioneer," *Ohio Archaeological and Historical Publications*, 36 (January 1927), 2–35.

72. Driggs, *Covered-Wagon Centennial and Ox-Team Days*, 2–3, 5; Galbreath, "Ezra Meeker," 38–43.

73. Driggs, *Covered-Wagon Centennial and Ox-Team Days*, 10, 13–14. For a superb portrait of Meeker that is privately owned, see *Howard Chandler Christy: Artist/Illustrator of Style, Sept. 25 through Nov. 6, 1977* (Allentown Art Museum catalogue, 1977), no. 35. For a portrait that probably was inspired by Meeker, see George Bellows, *The Old Pioneer* (1919), in *American Paintings V, 1988: Berry Hill Galleries, Inc.* (New York, 1988), 174–75.

74. John Tebbel, *George Horace Lorimer and the Saturday Evening Post* (Garden City, N.Y., 1948), 112; Driggs, *Covered-Wagon Centennial and Ox-Team Days,* 19.

75. Driggs, *Covered-Wagon Centennial and Ox-Team Days,* 23, 27–28; NYT, Mar. 30, 1930, sec. 9, p. 9; Arthur Chapman, *The Covered Wagon Centennial,* a small booklet that first appeared in the New York *Herald Tribune Sunday Magazine,* Apr. 6, 1930; NYT, Apr. 6, 1930, sec. 5, p. 12; NYT, Apr. 10, 1930, p. 26; NYT, July 4, 1930, p. 12.

76. Driggs, *Covered-Wagon Centennial and Ox-Team Days,* 101–04; NYT, Dec. 30, 1930, pp. 13, 20; NYT, Jan. 4, 1931, sec. 8, p. 16; NYT, Jan. 9, 1931, p. 20. For the same anti-Eastern resentment coupled with passionate advocacy of Southwestern culture, at about the same time, see J. Frank Dobie, *Some Part of Myself* (Boston, 1967), 237.

77. Robert G. Athearn, *The Mythic West in Twentieth-Century America* (Lawrence, Kans., 1986), 65, 136, 139–40, 152–53, 156, 166; Earl S. Pomeroy, *In Search of the Golden West: The Tourist in Western America* (New York, 1957), 175.

78. Marie MacDonald, " 'Kid' Foss and the Birth of Rodeo," MMWHC, 21 (1971), 56–63; Robert Meyer, Jr., *Festivals U.S.A.* (New York, 1950), 271–72; NYT, Sept. 1, 1935, sec. 10, p. 1.

79. Elisabeth Walton Potter, "The Missionary and Immigrant Experience as Portrayed in Commemorative Works of Art," *Idaho Yesterdays,* 31 (1987), 106–07, 109, 111. The Astoria Column, erected and dedicated in 1926 on Coxcomb Hill in Astoria, Oregon, commémorates historical events that took place on the lower Columbia River, beginning with Robert Gray's "discovery" of the Columbia in 1792 through the coming of the railroad. The Great Northern Railroad sponsored the monument as part of its historical expedition to the Pacific in 1926.

80. Manuscript MS-Z, folder 426, Idaho Historical Society, Library and Archives, Boise.

81. Based on a chronology found in the Stevensville Historical Society Papers, located in the K. Ross Toole Archives (Manuscript Collections) at the Mansfield Library, University of Montana, Missoula. See George M. Lubick, "A Murmuring of Voices: Historic Preservation and the Search for Montana's Past," in Rex C. Myers and Harry W. Fritz, eds., *Montana and the West: Essays in Honor of K. Ross Toole* (Boulder, Colo., 1984), 167–88.

82. Bernard DeVoto, "The Anxious West," *Harper's Magazine,* 193 (December 1946), 481–91, the quotations at 484, 485. For evidence of just the sort of thing that DeVoto had in mind, see MacDonald, " 'Kid' Foss and the Birth of Rodeo," 62.

83. Allen Tate, "A Southern Mode of the Imagination," in Joseph J. Kwiat and Mary C. Turpie, eds., *Studies in American Culture: Dominant Ideas and Images* (Minneapolis, 1960), 99; Tate, *Memoirs and Opinions, 1926–1974* (Chicago, 1975), 5–8; Michael O'Brien, *The Idea of the American South, 1920–1941* (Baltimore, 1979), 139, 152; Tate, "Regionalism and Sectionalism," NR, 69 (Nov. 23, 1931), 158–61.

84. Daniel Joseph Singal, *The War Within: From Victorian to Modernist Thought in the South, 1919–1945* (Chapel Hill, N.C., 1982), 249; Tate to John Gould Fletcher, Dec. 3, 1930, quoted in O'Brien, *The Idea of the American South,* 148–49.

85. Browne to Tyler, Mar. 12, 1932, Tyler Papers, group 5, box 7, SLWM. For more of this engaging correspondence, see Browne to Tyler, Oct. 8, 21, and 30, 1930, Nov. 10 and 20, 1930, Dec. 10, 1930, Aug. 3, 1931, Oct. 31, 1931, Nov. 3 and 12, 1931, Jan. 28, 1932, and Mar. 28, 1932, all in ibid., boxes 6 and 7.

86. See NYT, Dec. 2, 1889, p. 2; Charles Francis Adams, Jr., to J. Franklin Jameson, Jan. 6, 1903, Jameson Papers, box 45, MDLC; George Clinton Batcheller to Lyon G. Tyler, Dec. 5, 1906, Tyler Papers, group 2, box 15, SLWM; Allmond Blow's speech at the dedication of a statue to Captain John Smith at Jamestown in 1909, quoted in James M. Lindgren, "The Gospel of Preservation in Virginia and New England: Historic Preservation and the Regeneration of Traditionalism" (unpubl. Ph.D. diss.; The College of William and Mary, 1984), 180; N. O. Nelson to James K. Hosmer, Dec. 20, 1912, Hosmer Papers, box 1, MinnHS.

87. John Erskine, "Culture: An Interplay of Life and Ideas," *The Century,* 116 (May 1928), 83–88; a copy of the 1928 U.D.C. resolution will be found in the Tyler Family

Papers, group 1, box 24, SLWM; Hosmer, *Preservation Comes of Age from Williamsburg to the National Trust,* I, 190–92, 194, 196; II, 473, 907; Mrs. H. L. Rust, Sr., to Lyon G. Tyler, Nov. 29, 1930, Tyler Family Papers, group 1, box 26, SLWM. See also Dumas Malone, "A Challenge to Patriots," *Virginia Quarterly Review,* 4 (1928), 481–92, and Joseph Hergesheimer, *Swords & Roses* (New York, 1929), esp. 67–97.

88.   Ford to Tyler, Oct. 29, 1921, Tyler Papers, group 1, box 21, SLWM; AAS *Proceedings,* 40 (1931), 17–26; Alex McBee to Tyler, Dec. 8, 1931, Tyler Papers, group 5, box 7, SLWM; Adams to Tyler, Oct. 9, 1933, ibid., group 5, box 9. See also Stephen L. Gilchrist (director of the Henry B. Joy Historical Research, located in Detroit) to Tyler, Nov. 24, 1931, ibid., group 1, box 21.

89.   Perkins to Boyd, Jan. 19 and Oct. 25, 1924, Boyd Papers, box 3, SHC; Boyd, "The N. Carolinian" (June 1925), ibid.

90.   NYT, Mar. 4, 1937, sec. 11, p. 3; Ford to Adams, Aug. 3, 1937, Adams Papers, BLCU; Brooks to Adams, Mar. 31, 1941, ibid.

Chapter 13

1.   See Raymond Williams, *Keywords: A Vocabulary of Culture and Society* (New York, 1976), 79; Kenneth Hudson, *Museums of Influence* (Cambridge, 1987), 120–25; John W. Burrow, *A Liberal Descent: Victorian Historians and the English Past* (Cambridge, 1982), 211.

2.   Phyllis Franklin, "English Studies in America: Reflections on the Development of a Discipline," AQ, 30 (1978), 22; Lawrence W. Levine, *Highbrow/Lowbrow: The Emergence of Cultural Hierarchy in America* (Cambridge, Mass., 1988), ch. 3.

3.   Gene Wise strangely contended that for a full generation starting in the 1930s a consensus existed as to what American culture was and how to study it. In this chapter I take the opposite position. See Wise, "Some Elementary Axioms for an American Culture Studies," PAACS, 4 (1979), 518.

4.   See Langdon Mitchell, *Understanding America* (New York, 1927), esp. 34–42, 74–109, 156–58, 221–29; Jerre Mangione, *The Dream and the Deal: The Federal Writers' Project, 1935–1943* (New York, 1972), 49; Thomas L. Hartshorne, *The Distorted Image: Changing Conceptions of the American Character Since Turner* (Cleveland, 1968).

5.   Roland B. Dixon, "The Building of Cultures," *Scribner's Magazine,* 82 (September 1927), 347–53, the quotation at 349.

6.   John Erskine, "Culture: An Interplay of Life and Ideas," *The Century,* 116 (May 1928), 85–86; Booth Tarkington, "America and Culture," SEP, 201 (Mar. 2, 1929), 25, 120; Robert Briffault, "What's Wrong with American Culture?" *Scribner's Magazine,* 98 (October 1935), 208–09.

7.   Lothrop Stoddard, "Lo, The Poor American," SEP, 195 (Jan. 6, 1923), 9, 58, 61.

8.   Bernard DeVoto, "The Well-Informed, 1920–1930" (1931), in his *Forays and Rebuttals* (Boston, 1936), 221–39; Wolfe to Boyd, Apr. 17, 1930, Boyd Papers, box 3, SHC.

9.   Allan Nevins, *James Truslow Adams: Historian of the American Dream* (Urbana, Ill., 1968), 71–72; Charles C. Alexander, *Here the Country Lies: Nationalism and the Arts in Twentieth-Century America* (Bloomington, Ind., 1980), 193; Esther Forbes, "Historical Novels," *Saturday Review of Literature,* 32 (Apr. 23, 1949), 9.

10.   See Charles A. Fenton, *Stephen Vincent Benét: The Life and Times of an American Man of Letters, 1898–1943* (New Haven, 1958), 187, 189, 215; Aaron Copland and Vivian Perlis, *Copland: 1900 Through 1942* (New York, 1984), 248–51.

11.   See Alexander, *Here the Country Lies,* 91; Charles Messer Stowe, "Milestones," TMA, 41 (January 1942), 22–23.

12.   Joan Shelley Rubin, *Constance Rourke and American Culture* (Chapel Hill, N.C., 1980), 57–58, 91, 118, 167, 169, 180, 183. For evidence that Rourke disdained mass culture ("the almost unnoticed cheapening in attitude, subject, and style on the part of the new vastly popular magazines"), see her letter to Brooks, Sept. 15, 1940, Brooks Papers, Rourke folder, Van Pelt Library, University of Pennsylvania.

13. Rourke to Brooks, Oct. 12, 1939, Brooks Papers, Rourke folder, Van Pelt Library, University of Pennsylvania. For a fine succinct comparison of the two, see Stanley Edgar Hyman, *The Armed Vision: A Study in the Methods of Modern Literary Criticism* (rev. ed.: New York, 1955), 130–31.

14. Rubin, *Rourke and American Culture,* 42–43, 48–50, 53–54, 59–60, 74–77; Constance Rourke, *The Roots of American Culture* (New York, 1942), 24; Rourke, *American Humor: A Study of the National Character* (New York, 1931), 220, 274.

15. Rubin, *Rourke and American Culture,* 122.

16. Rourke, *American Humor,* 287.

17. See David Levering Lewis, *When Harlem Was in Vogue* (New York, 1981), esp. 193–96.

18. Ibid., 246; Martin Bauml Duberman, *Paul Robeson* (New York, 1988), 170.

19. Robert E. Hemenway, *Zora Neale Hurston: A Literary Biography* (Urbana, Ill., 1977), 21, 62–63, 81, 88–101, 163–64, 206–14; Rubin, *Rourke and American Culture,* 68; E. Burchenal to Solon J. Buck, Feb. 20, 1932, Buck Papers, MinnHS.

20. R. W. B. Lewis, *Edith Wharton: A Biography* (New York, 1975), 392, 432; Richard Ruland, *The Rediscovery of American Literature: Premises of Critical Taste, 1900–1940* (Cambridge, Mass., 1967), 256.

21. Robert Redfield, *The Little Community,* and *Peasant Society and Culture* (Chicago, 1962), ch. 3 of *Peasant Society,* "The Social Organization of Tradition," esp. 41–43.

22. Brooks is quoted in Helen Howe, *The Gentle Americans, 1864–1960: Biography of a Breed* (New York, 1965), xv; Downs, "The History of the American Wing," TMA, 50 (October 1946), 235.

23. NYT, Aug. 25, 1889, p. 5; T. J. Jackson Lears, *No Place of Grace: Antimodernism and the Transformation of American Culture, 1880–1920* (New York, 1981), 206.

24. See Harold E. Stearns, ed., *Civilization in the United States: An Inquiry by Thirty Americans* (New York, 1922); *The Nation,* 127 (Oct. 3, 1928), pp. 311–12.

25. Thomas L. Cripps, *Slow Fade to Black: The Negro in American Film, 1900–1942* (New York, 1977), 26–32; Eric Foner, *Reconstruction: America's Unfinished Revolution, 1863–1877* (New York, 1988), xix–xxvii.

26. Mary Johnston, "The Character of Lee," Aug. 22, 1932, unpublished typescript, Johnston Papers, ALUV.

27. Herbert Croly, "The Paradox of Lincoln," NR, 21 (Feb. 18, 1920), 350–53, the quotation at 352.

28. NYT, Apr. 14, 1935, sec. 4, p. 6; NYT, Sept. 5, 1935, p. 17; NYT, Sept. 6, 1937, p. 17; NYT, Sept. 8, 1937, p. 13; NYT, Sept. 9, 1937, p. 48; NYT, Sept. 10, 1937, p. 1.

29. Amy J. Kinsel, " 'From These Honored Dead': Gettysburg in American Culture" (unpubl. Ph.D. dissertation, Cornell University, 1992).

30. NYT, May 23, 1937, sec. 2, p. 10; NYT, Apr. 30, 1939, sec. 12, p. 3.

31. NYT, Sept. 18, 1937, p. 20.

32. Bloom to Markham, Aug. 5, 1931, and Markham to Bloom, Sept. 1 and Dec. 15, 1931, Bloom Papers (Addenda), box 52, NYPL.

33. Masters, "Histories of the American Mind," *American Mercury,* 35 (July 1935), 343; Masters to Brooks, Dec. 28, 1944, Brooks Papers, Masters folder, Van Pelt Library, University of Pennsylvania.

34. Brooks, "Toward a National Culture," *Seven Arts,* I (March 1917), 540–44, reprinted in Claire Sprague, ed., *Van Wyck Brooks: The Early Years. A Selection from His Works, 1908–1921* (New York, 1968), 191.

35. Quoted in Hyman, *The Armed Vision,* 104.

36. A. Edward Newton, "Westward," *Atlantic,* 149 (May 1932), 534; Fred Lewis Pattee, "A Call for a History of American Literature" (1924), in Pattee, *Tradition and Jazz* (New York, 1925), 236, 255.

37. Pound, "The Jefferson-Adams Letters as a Shrine and a Monument," in Noel Stock, ed., *Impact: Essays on Ignorance and the Decline of American Civilization* (Chicago, 1960), 168, 179; Pound, "National Culture: A Manifesto," in ibid., 3.

38. Pound, "National Culture: A Manifesto," 4–11, the long quotation at 6; David Grimsted, "Books and Culture: Canned, Canonized, and Neglected," *Proceedings* of the AAS, 94 (1985), 307.

39. Arthur H. Brook to Dixon Ryan Fox, Nov. 26, 1928, Fox Papers, box 8, NYSHA; Robert Lee Bullard to Fox, Nov. 29, 1933, ibid., box 5; Joy Elmer Morgan, "A National Culture—By-product or Objective of National Planning?" in Tracy F. Tyler, ed., *Radio as a Cultural Agency* (Washington, D.C., 1934), 26–31.

40. A. M. Schlesinger, "An Editor's Second Thoughts," in William E. Lingelbach, ed., *Approaches to American Social History* (New York, 1937), 97; Richard H. Pells, *Radical Visions and American Dreams: Culture and Social Thought in the Depression Years* (New York, 1973), 253.

41. Perkins to Boyd, Jan. 6 and Mar. 14, 1927, Boyd Papers, box 3, SHC.

42. Copland and Perlis, *Copland: 1900 Through 1942*, 302, 304.

43. Henry Chapman Mercer to W. H. Graves, Nov. 14, 1925, in Cleota Reed, *Henry Chapman Mercer and the Moravian Pottery and Tile Works* (Philadelphia, 1987), 237; David P. Peeler, *Hope Among Us Yet: Social Criticism and Social Solace in Depression America* (Athens, Ga., 1987), 98, 100.

44. Worthington C. Ford to Philip A. Bruce, Mar. 27, 1924, Bruce Papers, ALUV; Theodore C. Blegen, *Grass Roots History* (Minneapolis, 1947), 172.

45. Cedric Larson, "The Rising Tide of Genealogical Publications in America," *The Colophon*, n.s., 3 (Winter 1938), 100–12, the quotations on 111.

46. A. V. Huff, Jr., "The Democratization of Art: Memorializing the Confederate Dead in South Carolina, 1866–1914," in David Moltke-Hansen, ed., *Art in the Lives of South Carolinians* (Charleston, S.C., 1978), book 1; NYT, Mar. 3, 1935, sec. 6, p. 6; NYT, June 3, 1937, p. 10.

47. "Historic Document Made 'Easy to Read,' " NYT, Feb. 13, 1936, p. 24.

48. Oliver J. Sands to Douglas S. Freeman, June 20, 1921, Virginia Historical Pageant Association Papers (collection #5220), box 18, ALUV; W. B. Cridlin to Freeman, Oct. 28, 1921, ibid.

49. See pp. 277–281 of chapter nine above, and David Glassberg, *American Historical Pageantry: The Uses of Tradition in the Early Twentieth Century* (Chapel Hill, N.C., 1990), chs. 1–6.

50. See Richard Connell, "Mr. Pottle and Pageantry," SEP, 194 (Jan. 14, 1922), 10–11, 34, 36, 39; A. J. F. Van Laer to Victor H. Paltsits, Aug. 3, 1927, Paltsits Papers, NYHS.

51. Brian W. Dippie, *Custer's Last Stand: The Anatomy of an American Myth* (Missoula, Mont., 1976), 92–93; NYT, July 14, 1935, sec. 10, p. 11; NYT, Aug. 17, 1935, p. 17; NYT, May 17, 1936, sec. 8, p. 5; NYT, Sept. 19, 1937, sec. 1, p. 42, and sec. 2, p. 2; NYT, Sept. 13, 1937, p. 23.

52. Edward Ingle to Lyon G. Tyler, Jan. 17, 1922, Tyler Papers, group 1, box 22, SLWM; Howard R. Driggs, *Covered-Wagon Centennial (1830–1930)*, (Yonkers, N.Y., 1932), 44, 71–72; NYT, June 28, 1936, sec. 10, p. 14; Northwest Territory Celebration Commission Papers, B16 N879, MinnHS.

53. Michael Kammen, "Business Leadership and the American Heritage," *Cornell Enterprise*, 3 (1986), 21–26; Earl S. Pomeroy, *In Search of the Golden West: The Tourist in Western America* (New York, 1957), 175, 178, 180–81.

54. D. H. Burnham to Solon J. Buck, Feb. 3, 1931, Buck Papers (B922), box 13, MinnHS; Robert W. Rydell, "The Fan Dance of Science: American World's Fairs in the Great Depression," *Isis*, 76 (1985), 525–42; NYT, May 1, 1939, p. 8.

55. Goodwin to Rockefeller, Mar. 3, 1934, Goodwin Papers (Restoration—Its Conception), CWA.

56. NYT, May 5, 1935, sec. 2, p. 2; Vincent S. Kenny, *Paul Green* (New York, 1971), part I and chs. 6–9; Charles B. Hosmer, Jr., *Preservation Comes of Age: From Williamsburg to the National Trust, 1926–1949* (Charlottesville, Va., 1981), I, 290, 309, 933.

57. NYT, Jan. 20, 1935, sec. 2, p. 6; NYT, Jan. 26, 1935, p. 12; NYT, Sept. 5, 1937, sec. 1, p. 2, NYT, May 24, 1939, p. 28.

58. NYT, June 28, 1936, sec. 10, p. 14; NYT, Sept. 12, 1937, sec. 12, p. 4.

59. E. L. Austin and Odell Hauser, *The Sesqui-Centennial International Exposition* (Philadelphia, 1929), 241; NYT, Sept. 16, 1937, p. 16.

60. Du Bois, "The Black Man Brings His Gifts," *The Survey,* 53 (Mar. 1, 1925), 655–57, 710, reprinted in Herbert Aptheker, ed., *Creative Writings by W. E. B. Du Bois* (White Plains, N.Y., 1985), the quotation at 143.

61. See Simon J. Bronner, *American Folklore Studies: An Intellectual History* (Lawrence, Kans., 1986), esp. 57–66; Edward Eggleston, "Folk-Speech in America," *The Century,* 48 (October 1894), 867–75; Henry Melvin Belden, "The Study of Folk-Song in America," *Modern Philology,* 2 (1905), 573–79.

62. A "summary" of the founding of the V.F.S. appears in the Douglas Southall Freeman Papers (#5220), box 7, ALUV; "George Francis Dow" (necrology) in *Proceedings* of the AAS, 46 (1936), 124–25.

63. Rubin, *Constance Rourke and American Culture,* 18, 27; NYT, Mar. 24, 1941, p. 17.

64. Necah Stewart Furman, *Walter Prescott Webb: His Life and Impact* (Albuquerque, N.M., 1976), 85–86; Hemenway, *Zora Neale Hurston,* 85; John A. Jakle, *The Tourist: Travel in Twentieth-Century North America* (Lincoln, Nebr., 1985), 34.

65. Cahill to Rockefeller, Mar. 9 [1935], Abby Aldrich Rockefeller Papers, box 9, RAC; Warren Susman, ed., *Culture and Commitment, 1929–1945* (New York, 1973), 20–21.

66. Ruth Suckow, "The Folk Idea in American Life," *Scribner's Magazine,* 88 (September 1930), 245–55; NAW: *The Modern Period* (Cambridge, Mass., 1980), 666–67.

67. Fenton, *Stephen Vincent Benét,* 169, 189, 351.

68. Rourke, "Traditions for Young People," *The Nation,* 145 (Nov. 20, 1937), 562–64.

69. Henry D. Shapiro, *Appalachia on Our Mind: The Southern Mountains and Mountaineers in the American Consciousness, 1870–1920* (Chapel Hill, N.C., 1978), 199–200, 219–20, 247; Rollin Lynde Hartt, "The Mountaineers: Our Own Lost Tribes," *The Century,* 95 (January 1918), 395–404; Corsey C. Buchanan to Paul Green, Dec. 15, 1931, Green Papers (coll. #3693), folder 166, SHC.

70. Lon Tinkle, *An American Original: The Life of J. Frank Dobie* (Boston, 1978), 102, 107–08, 111; Furman, *Walter Prescott Webb,* 87, 99–100; DeVoto, *Mark Twain's America* (Boston, 1932), xi–xii, 40–41, 77; Michael O'Brien, *The Idea of the American South, 1920–1941* (Baltimore, 1979), 181.

71. Hemenway, *Zora Neale Hurston,* 100–01, 204–05, 328, 331.

72. Edmund Wilson, "American Ballads and Their Collectors," NR, 47 (June 30, 1926), 168; Anne Warner, ed., *Traditional American Folk Songs from the Anne and Frank Warner Collection* (Syracuse, N.Y., 1984).

73. John P. McConnell (president of Virginia State Teachers College) to John Powell, Aug. 19, 1931, John Powell Papers (#7284), box 5a, Manuscripts Division, Special Collections, ALUV; Walter Howe to Powell, Aug. 26, 1931, ibid.; A. R. Rogers to Powell, Sept. 8, 1931, ibid.; R. Dean Shure to Powell, Sept. 17, 1931, ibid. Shure offered his Washington cantata for the 1932 festival, the bicentennial year of George Washington's birth, because "the scenes are nearly all laid in your state. Kindly observe the very opening sentence for tenor soloist which runs 'Virginia, thy sacred earth,' etc."

74. Powell to Eleanor Roosevelt, Jan. 17, 1934, John Powell Papers (#7284), box 5a, ALUV.

75. Powell to Roosevelt, Mar. 3 and Apr. 9, 1934, ibid. Also Powell, "The Value of Our Musical Tradition," *Magazine of Art,* 30 (May 1937), 293.

76. For sharp differences of opinion concerning Powell's integrity and authenticity, compare L. Moody Simms, Jr., "Folk Music in America: John Powell and the 'National Musical Idiom,' " JPC, 7 (1973), 510–17, with David E. Whisnant, *All That Is Native & Fine: The Politics of Culture in an American Region* (Chapel Hill, N.C., 1983), 186–248.

77. Mrs. John P. Buchanan to Paul Green, July 27, 1934, Paul E. Green Papers (#3693), folder 282, SHC, Library of the University of North Carolina at Chapel Hill; Aaron Copland and Vivian Perlis, *Copland: 1900 Through 1942* (New York, 1984), 86, 226–27, 279, 282, 291.

78. Wright to Arthur M. Schlesinger, Sr., Oct. 1, 1925, Schlesinger Papers, box 3, HUA; S. C. Wolcott to Lyon G. Tyler, Jan. 11, 1934, Tyler Family Papers, group 5, box 9, SLWM; NYT, Apr. 12, 1936, sec. 7, p. 16; NYT *Sunday Magazine,* Nov. 8, 1936, p. 16.

79. NYT, Apr. 16 and 27, 1935, pp. 19 and 20; Wanda M. Corn, "The Return of the Native: The Development of Interest in American Primitive Painting" (unpubl. M.A. thesis, New York University, 1965), 11–13, 18–19, 22; Lincoln Kirstein, *Elie Nadelman* (New York, 1973); Avis Berman, "The Force Behind the Whitney" [Juliana Force], AH, 40 (September 1989), 107–09.

80. Holger Cahill, "American Folk Art," *American Mercury,* 24 (September 1931), 46; Cahill, *American Folk Art: The Art of the Common Man in America, 1750–1900* (New York, 1932).

81. Obituary of Halpert in NYT, Oct. 7, 1970, p. 46; Avis Berman, "Pioneers in American Museums: Edith Halpert," *Museum News,* 54 (November–December 1975), 34–37, 61–64; Corn, "The Return of the Native: Interest in American Primitive Painting," 23, 25–26.

82. Walter Karp, "Electra Webb and Her American Past," AH, 33 (April 1982), 16–29, the quotation at 19.

83. Beatrix Rumford, "Uncommon Art of the Common People," in Ian M. G. Quimby and Scott T. Swank, eds., *Perspectives on American Folk Art* (New York, 1980), 25–27, 35–37, 39, 42–43; Aline B. Saarinen, *The Proud Possessors: The lives, times and tastes of some adventurous American art collectors* (New York, 1958), 363.

84. See especially the essays by Francis E. Mineka and Louis C. Jones in Warren S. Walker, ed., *Whatever Makes Papa Laugh: A Folklore Sheaf Honoring Harold W. Thompson* (Cooperstown, N.Y., 1958), 1–8, 17–28.

85. Louis C. Jones, "HWT: NYSCT: BBB: NYFS," in ibid., 8–9, 21; "What Is American Folk Art? A Symposium," TMA, 57 (May 1950), 355–62.

86. Mrs. John P. Buchanan to Paul Green, July 27, 1934, Green Papers, folder 282, SHC; NYT, Apr. 21, 1935, sec. 9, p. 1; NYT, July 28, 1935, sec. 11, pp. 2, 3; Constance Rourke, "The National Folk Festival," *Modern Literature,* 4 (Mar. 1–14, 1936), 1, 3.

87. Elizabeth Burchenal to Solon J. Buck, Feb. 20, 1932, Buck Papers (B922), box 14, MinnHS; Jane De Hart Mathews, "Arts and the People: The New Deal Quest for a Cultural Democracy," JAH, 62 (1975), 324; Blegen, *Grass Roots History,* 11; Carlton C. Qualey to J. M. Nolte, Apr. 30, 1949, Minnesota Territory Centennial Papers (P336), box 8, MinnHS.

88. Malcolm Cowley, *Exiles' Return: A Narrative of Ideas* (New York, 1934), 107; Matthew Josephson, *Life among the Surrealists: A Memoir* (New York, 1962), 354–59; James Korges, *Erskine Caldwell* (Minneapolis, 1969), 8, 14.

89. Fenton, *Stephen Vincent Benét,* 27, 286, 292–95, 334, 337; NYT, May 14, 1939, sec. 11, p. 1.

90. Percy MacKaye, *The Playhouse and the Play, and Other Addresses Concerning the Theatre and Democracy in America* (New York, 1909); MacKaye, *Tall Tales of the Kentucky Mountains* (New York, 1926); MacKaye, *Yankee Fantasies: Five One-Act Plays* (New York, 1912).

91. James Boyd to Green, July 26, 1938, Green Papers, folder 431, SHC; Cecilia R. Berry to Green, Dec. 29, 1938, ibid.; Howard Bailey to Green, Jan. 17, 1939, ibid., folder 471; Maude McFie Bloom to Green, June 20, 1940, ibid., folder 513.

92. Karal Ann Marling, *Wall-to-Wall America: A Cultural History of Post-Office Murals in the Great Depression* (Minneapolis, 1982), 93; Matthew Baigell, *Thomas Hart Benton* (New York, 1973), 139–47.

93. Hyman, *The Armed Vision: A Study in the Methods of Modern Literary Criticism,* 130–31.

94. See Theodore Rosengarten, "Stepping Over Cockleburs: Conversations with Ned Cobb," in Marc Pachter, ed., *Telling Lives: The Biographer's Art* (Washington, D.C., 1979), 105–31.

95. Hilton Kramer, "The New Discovery of America," NYT *Book Review,* Jan. 20, 1974, p. 4.

96. Botkin to Paul Green, Apr. 11, 1938, Green Papers, folder 431, SHC; Ford to Adams, May 7, 1938, Adams Papers, BLCU.

97. Edith Wharton, *French Ways and Their Meaning* (New York, 1919), 49–50; H. B. Ayers to Hon. Clifford Hilton, July 10, 1921, Minn. Society of the S.A.R. Papers, box 1891–1923, MinnHS; Harry P. Stanford to Ralph Budd, July 12, 1926, Budd Papers (#11620), MinnHS; James Ford Rhodes to Albert B. Hart, Jan. 12, 1926, Hart Papers, box 22, HUA; NYT, Apr. 9, 1937, p. 23.

98. Willa Cather, "Nebraska: The End of the First Cycle," in Ernest Gruening, ed., *These United States: A Symposium* (New York, 1924), 147.

99. M. E. Ravage, "The Loyalty of the Foreign Born," *The Century*, 94 (June 1917), 201–09, the quotations at 202. See also Mona Harrington's invaluable essay, "Loyalties: Dual and Divided," in Stephan Thernstrom, ed., *Harvard Encyclopedia of American Ethnic Groups* (Cambridge, Mass., 1980), 679.

100. See Geoffrey Gorer, *The American People: A Study in National Character* (New York, 1948); David M. Potter, *Freedom and Its Limitations in American Life* (Stanford, Calif., 1976), 44; and for a wry view of all this, Don Marquis, "O'Meara, the 'Mayflower'—and Mrs. MacLirr," *Scribner's Magazine*, 83 (January 1928), 33–41.

101. J. Franklin Jameson to Amandus Johnson, Jan. 8, 1925, Jameson Papers, box 99, MDLC; Marcus Lee Hansen, *The Problem of the Third Generation Immigrant* (Rock Island, Ill., 1938), 12; NYT, Apr. 4, 1937, sec. 1, p. 22; NYT, Sept. 24, 1937, p. 16.

102. D. G. Ristad, "The Norwegian-American Historical Association," *Studies and Records*, I (1926), 148–49; Theodore C. Blegen to J. Franklin Jameson, May 14, 1927, Jameson Papers, box 116, MDLC; Carlton C. Qualey to Dixon Ryan Fox, Fox Papers, box 5, NYSHA.

103. Twain, *Life on the Mississippi* (1883: New York, 1961), 170; W. C. Miller to Fellow Members of the Huguenot Society, Oct. 20, 1926, Tyler Family Papers, group 1, box 24, SLWM.

104. Frank Monaghan, *French Travellers in the United States, 1765–1932: A Bibliography* (New York, 1933); Monaghan, *Franco-American Research and Friendship* (New York, 1935), a seven-page pamphlet; NYT, Aug. 25, 1935, sec. 4, p. 12. See also Willa Cather's popular novel set in seventeenth-century Quebec, *Shadows on the Rock* (1931).

105. George L. Scherger (for *The Progressive*) to Arthur M. Schlesinger, May 13, 1927, Schlesinger Papers, HUA; NYT, May 31, 1939, p. 2.

106. Isidore S. Meyer, "Lee Max Friedman," *American Jewish Historical Quarterly*, 47 (1958), 211–15; Frank L. Kozol, "Lee M. Friedman: A Biographical Profile," ibid., 56 (1967), 261–67.

107. Obituary of Feinstone, NYT, Oct. 19, 1980, p. 44; Feinstone, *Ten Days That Changed the World (George Washington's Finest Hour)* (Syracuse, N.Y., 1971), and *Two Revolutions: The Liberty Bell vs. the Black Wagon* (Syracuse, N.Y., 1969), both reprinted from the *Congressional Record*.

108. NYT, Oct. 26, 1936, p. 38; NYT, May 31, 1937, p. 10; NYT, May 31, 1939, p. 3. On May 21, 1939, Senate Majority Leader Alben W. Barkley called Haym Salomon the "forgotten man" of the American Revolution. Barkley praised the Jewish financier following a dinner of the Patriotic Foundation of Chicago, which was erecting a monument to Salomon, George Washington, and Robert Morris. (NYT, May 22, 1939, p. 9.)

109. NYT, Apr. 21, 1935, sec. 2, p. 1; NYT, Sept. 5, 1937, sec. 4, p. 9; NYT, Sept. 12, 1937, sec. 4, p. 8; NYT, Feb. 17, 1935, sec. 1, p. 7; NYT, Aug. 24, 1935, p. 16.

110. NYT, June 6, 1937, sec. 10, p. 2; NYT, Apr. 9, 1939, sec. 11, p. 1.

111. John Hope Franklin, *George Washington Williams: A Biography* (Chicago, 1985); Rayford W. Logan, "Carter G. Woodson: Mirror and Molder of His Time, 1875–1950," JNH, 58 (1973), 8; John Hope Franklin, ed., *Reminiscences of an Active Life: The Autobiography of John Roy Lynch* (Chicago, 1970), esp. xxxii–xxxvii.

112. Ernestine Rose to Du Bois, Mar. 25, 1924, in Herbert Aptheker, ed., *The Correspondence of W. E. B. Du Bois* (Amherst, Mass., 1973), I, 285. In 1926 Du Bois successfully pleaded with Governor Pinchot of Pennsylvania to include black history in the Sesquicentennial Exhibition being planned for Philadelphia later that year. Ibid., 336–37.

113. Schomburg, "The Negro Digs Up His Past," in Alain Locke, ed., *The New Negro: An Interpretation* (New York, 1925), 231–37. The next essay is by Arthur Huff Fauset, "American Negro Folk Literature."

114. Elinor Des Verney Sinnette, *Arthur Alfonso Schomburg: Black Bibliophile and Collector* (Detroit, 1989), 131–48; "Arthur Alonzo [sic] Schomburg," JNH, 23 (1938), 403–04.

115. Logan, "Carter G. Woodson," 1–17; DAB, Supp. IV. For Woodson's various projects and perpetual quest for financial support, see Woodson to J. Franklin Jameson, May 15, 1916, Jameson Papers, box 55, MDLC; Jameson to Woodson, May 17, 1916, ibid.; Woodson to Jameson, May 18 and Oct. 26, 1916, and Jameson to Woodson, June 24, 1916, ibid.,; Jameson to Woodson, Apr. 26, 1927, ibid., box 136; Jameson to JDR, Apr. 1, 1930, ibid., box 125; Woodson to Evarts B. Greene, Sept. 25, 1928, and May 11, 1929, Greene Papers, BLCU; Jameson to JDR, Apr. 30, 1935, Jameson Papers, box 115, MDLC.

116. Rayford W. Logan to W. E. B. Du Bois, Apr. 29, 1950, Aptheker, ed., *Correspondence of Du Bois,* III, 282–84. Written in response to an inquiry from Du Bois, who had not been on friendly terms with Woodson for decades.

117. Quoted in August Meier and Elliott Rudwick, *Black History and the Historical Profession, 1915–1980* (Urbana, Ill., 1986), 9; Woodson, "Negro History Week," JNH, 11 (1926), 239.

118. Arnold Rampersad, *The Life of Langston Hughes, 1902–1941: I, Too, Sing America* (New York, 1986), 134, 140, 144, 149, 157, 163–64, 183, the quotation at 173; Arna Bontemps, *Black Thunder* (New York, 1935); Bontemps, "Buried Treasures of Negro Art," manuscript of an article submitted to the *Negro Digest,* Bontemps Papers, Arents Rare Book Library, Syracuse University; NYT, Sept. 8, 1937, p. 13.

119. Lewis, *When Harlem Was in Vogue,* 98, 114, 136, 176–77, 179, 180–85, 195; Rampersad, *Langston Hughes,* I, 109; NYT, Oct. 20, 1935, sec. 10, p. 1.

120. Daniel Joseph Singal, *The War Within: From Victorian to Modernist Thought in the South, 1919–1945* (Chapel Hill, N.C., 1982), 317–20, 323; Geoffrey C. Upward, *A Home for Our Heritage: The Building and Growth of Greenfield Village, 1929–1979* (Dearborn, Mich., 1979), 100, 112; Rourke, *Roots of American Culture,* 262–74.

Chapter 14

1. NYT, July 23, 1888, p. 4; NYT, May 15, 1889, p. 5; NYT, July 26, 1889, p. 4; NYT, Aug. 20, 1889, pp. 4, 8; NYT, Aug. 21, 1889, p. 4; NYT, Oct. 8, 1889, p. 2; NYT, Oct. 9, 1889, p. 4; NYT, Oct. 17, 1889, p. 8; NYT, Oct. 18, 1889, p. 8.

2. C. A. Browne, "A National Museum of Agriculture: The Story of a Lost Endeavor," *Agricultural History,* 13 (1939), 137–48; J. Franklin Jameson to Worthington C. Ford, Feb. 24, 1909, Ford Papers, box 5, NYPL Annex; Julian P. Boyd, "A Modest Proposal to Meet an Urgent Need," AHR, 70 (1965), 333–41.

3. Frances Carpenter, ed., *Carp's Washington* (New York, 1960), 298; Margaret Leech, *In the Days of McKinley* (New York, 1959), 471; Michael Zuckerman, "Fiction and Fission: Twentieth-Century Writing on the Founding Fathers," in *Religion, Ideology, and Nationalism in Europe and America: Essays Presented in Honor of Yehoshua Arieli* (Jerusalem, 1986), 232.

4. NYT, Jan. 30, 1887, p. 6; Albert B. Hart to Worthington C. Ford, Feb. 16, 1893, Ford Papers, box 1, NYPL Annex; John A. DeNovo, "The Enigmatic Alvey A. Adee and American Foreign Relations, 1870–1924," *Prologue,* 7 (1975), 69–80.

5. Clarence W. Bowen to Worthington C. Ford, Oct. 29, 1889, Ford Papers, box 1, NYPL Annex; William F. Poole to Ford, Nov. 15, 1889, ibid.; J. Franklin Jameson to Theodore Roosevelt, Dec. 12, 1907, Jameson Papers, box 125, MDLC; Donald R. McCoy, *The National Archives: America's Ministry of Documents, 1934–1968* (Chapel Hill, N.C., 1978), ch. 1.

6. J. Franklin Jameson to Worthington C. Ford, Jan. 7, 1909, Ford Papers, box 5, NYPL Annex; William MacDonald to Ford, Mar. 18, 1909, ibid.; Ford to Jameson, Sept. 28, 1912, Jameson Papers, box 84, MDLC.

7. Public Resolution No. 42, 66th Congress, copy in the Henry Cabot Lodge Papers, box 65, MHS; Merrill D. Peterson, *The Jefferson Image in the American Mind* (New York, 1960), 350, 434, 439; Stephen W. Stathis and Barbara L. Schwemle, "Commemorative Legislation," 18-page report prepared for the Congressional Research Service, Mar. 30, 1990 (no. 90–183 GOV).

8. Meeker, address at Old Fort Hall near Pocatello on July 27, 1921, *Covered-Wagon Centennial and Ox-Team Days: Oregon Trail Memorial Edition* (Yonkers, N.Y., 1932), 282–83; W.M.B. to E. M. Hawes, Sept. 21, 1937, Northwest Territory Celebration Commission of Minnesota Papers (BI6 N879), MinnHS.

9. J. Franklin Jameson to Charles Francis Adams, Jr., Aug. 19, 1914, Jameson Papers, box 45, MDLC; Stephen Vaughn, *Holding Fast the Inner Lines: Democracy, Nationalism, and the Committee on Public Information* (Chapel Hill, N.C., 1980); Lester J. Cappon, "Waldo Gifford Leland, 1879–1966," *American Archivist,* 30 (1967), 125–28; Carl Becker, "Money for the Historians," NR, 46 (Apr. 14, 1926), p. 227; Michael Kammen, ed., *"What Is the Good of History?" Selected Letters of Carl L. Becker, 1900–1945* (Ithaca, N.Y., 1973), 72–74, 77.

10. See George E. Mowry, "The Uses of History by Recent Presidents," JAH, 53 (1966), 5–18; John F. McClymer, "The Federal Government and the Americanization Movement, 1915–1924," *Prologue,* 10 (1978), 23–41.

11. Richard Slotkin, "Nostalgia and Progress: Theodore Roosevelt's Myth of the Frontier," AQ, 33 (1981), 608–37; Wilson is quoted in Langdon Mitchell, *Understanding America* (New York, 1927), 193–94.

12. Robert K. Murray, "Harding on History," JAH, 53 (1967), 783.

13. Straus to Coolidge, June 9, 1925, Oscar S. Straus Papers, box 15, MDLC; Coolidge to Straus, June 12, 1925, ibid. See also Naomi W. Cohen, *A Dual Heritage: The Public Career of Oscar S. Straus* (Philadelphia, 1969).

14. Quoted in Gilbert C. Fite, *Mount Rushmore* (Norman, Okla., 1952), 75.

15. Alan Havig, "Presidential Images, History, and Homage: Memorializing Theodore Roosevelt, 1919–1967," AQ, 30 (1978), 514–32.

16. Paul F. Boller, Jr., *Presidential Anecdotes* (New York, 1981), 259. See also Torbjorn Sirevag, "Franklin D. Roosevelt and the Use of History," *Americana Norwegica,* 2 (1968), 299–342.

17. Arthur M. Schlesinger, Jr., *The Age of Roosevelt: The Politics of Upheaval* (Boston, 1960), 425; Alfred Haworth Jones, *Roosevelt's Image Brokers: Poets, Playwrights, and the Use of the Lincoln Symbol* (Port Washington, N.Y., 1974), 66; NYT, Apr. 26, 1935, p. 21.

18. Jones, *Roosevelt's Image Brokers,* 66; NYT, Nov. 22, 1936, p. E2.

19. Peter Karsten, *Patriot-Heroes in England and America: Political Symbolism and Changing Values over Three Centuries* (Madison, Wis., 1978), 105; NYT, Feb. 12, 1935, p. 10; NYT, Feb. 13, 1935, p. 23.

20. Samuel I. Rosenman, ed., *The Public Papers and Addresses of Franklin D. Roosevelt,* V (New York, 1938), 222; Jones, *Roosevelt's Image Brokers,* chs. 5–8.

21. Bessie Forbes Taylor Robinson to R. Walton Moore, Nov. 16, 1933, Moore Papers, box 7, Roosevelt Library, Hyde Park, N.Y.; Moore to Roosevelt, Jan. 23, 1936, ibid., box 10.

22. A typescript of Bloom's Edenton speech, Apr. 28, 1932, is located in the Jessica Smith Papers, North Carolina State Archives, Raleigh; "The Heritage of Americanism" (Apr. 28, 1938), in Bloom, *Our Heritage: George Washington and the Establishment of the American Union* (New York, 1944), 336–38. Pages 3–54 of this volume comprise a biographical sketch of Bloom's "Public Service" written by Ira E. Bennett.

23. Quoted in Fite, *Mount Rushmore,* 228.

24. NYT, May 6, 1937, p. 1; NYT, May 7, 1937, p. 24; and for subsequent errors on this subject discussed in the *Times,* see NYT, May 11, 1937, p. 24.

25. W. Lloyd Warner, *The Living and the Dead: A Study of the Symbolic Life of Americans* (New Haven, 1959), 107–225; David Glassberg, "History and the Public: Legacies of the Progressive Era," JAH, 73 (1987), 974.

26. See Michael Kammen, "The Revival of States' Rights in American Political Culture, ca. 1918–1938: Reflections on the Ambiguities of Ideological Constitutionalism," in Kammen, *Sovereignty and Liberty: Constitutional Discourse in American Culture* (Madison, Wis., 1988), 157–88.

27. Sullivan to Sol Bloom, Jan. 29, 1934, Bloom Papers, folder 50, NYPL; J. Franklin Jameson to Bloom, Jan. 24, 1934, ibid.

28. The press release, copies of several speeches about Taylor, and correspondence among the principals involved will all be found in the R. Walton Moore Papers, box 19 (Zachary Taylor folder), Franklin D. Roosevelt Library, Hyde Park, N.Y.

29. Assorted documentation will be found in ibid., box 7 (Fredericksburg Battlefield Park folder).

30. Branch Spalding to Arno Cammerer, Aug. 4, 1937, ibid.; Moore to Grosvenor, Nov. 20, 1937, ibid.; Ronald F. Lee to Arno Cammerer, Mar. 29, 1939, ibid.

31. Park W. T. Loy to Governor Herbert Lehman of New York, Aug. 27, 1937, Dixon Ryan Fox Papers, box 2, NYSHA; Michael Kammen, *A Machine That Would Go of Itself: The Constitution in American Culture* (New York, 1986), ch. 10.

32. E. M. Hawes to Theodore C. Blegen, Dec. 14, 1937, Northwest Territory Celebration Commission of Minnesota Papers, MinnHS.

33. E. M. Hawes to Blegen, Oct. 15, 1936, ibid.; printed materials located in the same collection.

34. Hawes to Blegen, April 18, 1935, with an attached three-page prospectus of the anniversary observance, in ibid.; Hawes to James C. Kelley, May 14, 1938, ibid.

35. "Freedom on the March," a pageant in eight episodes, by O. K. Reames, director of pageantry, in ibid. See also NYT, Sept. 5, 1937, sec. 2, p. 3.

36. NYT, Apr. 25, 1937, sec. 2, p. 2.

37. NYT, Apr. 22, 1937, p. 22; NYT, May 25, 1939, p. 21; Fite, *Mount Rushmore,* 161.

38. Howard Mumford Jones, "Amidst the Encircling Gloom," *Scribner's Magazine,* 87 (April 1930), 405–11.

39. William Michael Ferraro, "The National Anthem Act of 1931: The Emergence of a Legal Symbol" (unpubl. honors thesis, Georgetown University, 1982). In 1931 Charles Demuth painted . . . *And the Home of the Brave* (located at the Art Institute of Chicago), depicting a water tower above a factory and a street light—sardonic treatment of the new national anthem in grim times.

40. For a 1937 controversy over whether the national anthem should be "quietly listened to instead of sung," see NYT, Sept. 27, 1937, p. 20; and for residual resentment that "The Star-Spangled Banner" had been designated by Congress in 1931, see NYT, Apr. 23, 1939, sec. 4, p. 8.

41. Quoted in Barry Mackintosh, "The National Park Service Moves into Historical Interpretation," PH, 9 (1987), 54. See also Roosevelt to George White et al., Apr. 20, 1935, Gutzon Borglum Papers, box 11, MDLC.

42. Harlan D. Unrau and G. Frank Williss, "To Preserve the Nation's Past: The Growth of Historic Preservation in the National Park Service during the 1930s," PH, 9 (1987), 33–34, 37, 44; Jane De Hart Mathews, "Arts and the People: The New Deal Quest for a Cultural Democracy," JAH, 62 (1975), 324.

43. Jerre Mangione, *The Dream and the Deal: The Federal Writers' Project, 1935–1943* (Boston, 1972), 244, 247–48, 252.

44. NYT, Dec. 8, 1935, sec. 2, p. 3; NYT, Feb. 4, 1936, p. 23; NYT, Feb. 28, 1937, sec. 12, p. 6; NYT, Mar. 27, 1937, p. 9. In 1937 Franklin D. Roosevelt decided to give his papers and extensive collections to the United States. After prolonged controversy, Congress passed a law in 1939 accepting the gift on F.D.R.'s terms. The Roosevelt Library at Hyde Park was dedicated on June 30, 1941. Donald R. McCoy, "The Beginnings of the Franklin D. Roosevelt Library," *Prologue,* 7 (1975), 137–50.

45. David Gebhard, "The American Colonial Revival in the 1930s," WP, 22 (1987), 109–48.

46. Ibid., 127, 134–35.

47. Ibid., 114, 116, 141–42.

48. Karal Ann Marling, *Wall-to-Wall America: A Cultural History of Post-Office Murals in the Great Depression* (Minneapolis, 1982).

49. Mangione, *The Dream and the Deal*, 365, 371; Mathews, "The New Deal Quest for a Cultural Democracy," 325.

50. Claude G. Bowers to Mary D. Carter, Nov. 20, 1932, Lyon G. Tyler Papers, group 5, box 8, SLWM.

51. Peterson, *Jefferson Image in the American Mind*, ch. 7; Hilbert F. Day to Arthur M. Schlesinger, Apr. 2, 1931, Schlesinger Papers, box 6, HUA; Mark A. DeWolfe Howe to James Truslow Adams, Feb. 11, 1936, Adams Papers, BLCU.

52. Mathews, "The New Deal Quest for a Cultural Democracy," 334; V. F. Calverton, "The American Revolutionary Tradition," *Scribner's Magazine*, 95 (May 1934), 352–57.

53. See Bloom, *Our Heritage: George Washington and the Establishment of the American Union*, 15, 511–12 (an appendix that reprints Beck's speech in the House, June 11, 1934); NYT, Nov. 6, 1936, p. 6.

54. See Charles C. Alexander, *Here the Country Lies: Nationalism and the Arts in Twentieth-Century America* (Bloomington, 1980), 182–83; Ann Banks, ed., *First-Person America* (New York, 1980), xix.

55. Lewis Mumford, "Writers' Project," NR, 82 (Oct. 20, 1937), 306–07.

56. Hal Rothman, *Preserving Different Pasts: The American National Monuments* (Urbana, Ill., 1989), 188–89; Unrau and Williss, "The Growth of Historic Preservation in the National Park Service During the 1930s," 22, 47.

57. Alfred Runte, *National Parks: The American Experience* (Lincoln, Nebr., 1979), 106.

58. Rothman, *Preserving Different Pasts: The American National Monuments*, 133–37, 144.

59. Runte, *National Parks: The American Experience*, 111; Rothman, *Preserving Different Pasts: The American National Monuments*, 163, 173, 200; Barry Mackintosh, "The National Park Service Moves into Historical Interpretation," PH, 9 (1987), 55. Those responsible for planning the George Washington Bicentennial declared that "we intend to make the event largely educational, in an effort to impress the story of Washington's life and achievements upon our foreign-born population." See John A. Stewart to JDR, Mar. 14, 1927, JDR Papers, ser. II (cultural), RAC.

60. Chatelain to Solon J. Buck, Aug. 13 and Nov. 2, 1931, Buck Papers, box 13, MinnHS; Edwin C. Bearss, "The National Park Service and Its History Program: 1864–1986," PH, 9 (1987), 10–11; Mackintosh, "The National Park Service Moves into Historical Interpretation," ibid., 51.

61. Donald C. Swain, *Wilderness Defender: Horace M. Albright and Conservation* (Chicago, 1970), 199–200. See also Horace M. Albright as told to Robert Cahn, *The Birth of the National Park Service: The Founding Years, 1913–33* (Salt Lake City, 1985), 234–61.

62. Swain, *Horace M. Albright and Conservation*, 227–28; Albright and Cahn, *Birth of the National Park Service*, 293–97.

63. Ronald F. Lee, *The Origin and Evolution of the National Military Park Idea* (Washington, D.C., 1973), 52; Rothman, *Preserving Different Pasts: The American National Monuments*, 165–66, 171, 187–88, 196–99.

64. Charles B. Hosmer, Jr., *Preservation Comes of Age, from Williamsburg to the National Trust, 1926–1949* (Charlottesville, Va., 1981), 395; Unrau and Williss, "The Growth of Historic Preservation in the National Park Service during the 1930s," 24, 28; Rothman, *Preserving Different Pasts: The American National Monuments*, 170. A copy of the poster has been preserved at the National Archives, Washington, D.C.

65. Unrau and Williss, "The Growth of Historic Preservation in the National Park Service during the 1930s," 49; Hosmer, *Preservation Comes of Age*, ch. 7; Mrs. Edward

Bartlett Lee to Dixon Ryan Fox, n.d., Fox Papers, box 2, NYSHA; Fox to Lee, May 21, 1942, ibid.

66. Ronald F. Lee to Guy Stanton Ford, Dec. 10, 1937, Ford Papers, folder #110, University of Minnesota Archives; Ford to Harold Ickes, Jan. 6, 1938, ibid.

67. Hosmer, *Preservation Comes of Age*, ch. 8; Rothman, *Preserving Different Pasts: The American National Monuments*, 159. For a critical view (by an "insider") of the Park Service's complicity in questionable preservation enterprises, see Dwight T. Pitcaithley, "Pious Frauds: Federal Reconstruction Efforts during the 1930s" (unpubl. paper presented at the April 1989 annual meeting of the Organization of American Historians, St. Louis, Mo.).

68. *U.S. Statutes at Large*, 74th Congress (1935–36), vol. 49, *Public Laws*, 665–68.

69. NYT, Aug. 11, 1935, sec. 2, p. 4; NYT, Apr. 19, 1936, sec. 10, p. 1; Unrau and Williss, "The Growth of Historic Preservation in the National Park Service During the 1930s," 34; John Bodnar, "Symbols and Servants: Immigrant America and the Limits of Public History," JAH, 73 (1986), 148; Hosmer, *Preservation Comes of Age*, 595–600.

70. Albright to Rockefeller, May 3, 1934, and Rockefeller to Albright, May 10, 1934, JDR Papers, ser. II (cultural), box 170, RAC; Albright to JDR, Feb. 4, 1939, ibid., box 42; Unrau and Williss, "The Growth of Historic Preservation in the National Park Service During the 1930s," 32; Mackintosh, "The National Park Service Moves into Historical Interpretation," 57–61.

71. The A.P.V.A. press release, dated Sept. 20, 1940, will be found in the Douglas Southall Freeman Papers, box 1, ALUV.

72. Ibid. See also Franklin D. Roosevelt to George White et al., Apr. 20, 1935, Gutzon Borglum Papers, box 11, MDLC.

73. William F. McDonald, *Federal Relief Administration and the Arts* (Columbus, Ohio, 1969), 767–68.

74. Jerrold Hirsch, "Cultural Pluralism and Applied Folklore: The New Deal Precedent," in Bert Feintuch, ed., *The Conservation of Culture: Folklorists and the Public Sector* (Lexington, Ky., 1988), 62; Zioncheck quoted in Fite, *Mount Rushmore*, 167.

75. Mathews, "The New Deal Quest for a Cultural Democracy," 328, 339.

76. Wallace, "Visiting the Past: History Museums in the United States," in Susan Porter Benson et al., eds., *Presenting the Past: Essays on History and the Public* (Philadelphia, 1986), 149.

77. Benjamin A. Botkin, "WPA and Folklore Research: 'Bread and Song,' " in Feintuch, ed., *The Conservation of Culture: Folklorists and the Public Sector*, 258–63.

78. NYT, Feb. 9, 1936, sec. 11, p. 1.

79. Compare Mangione, *The Dream and the Deal: The Federal Writers' Project*, 50, with Ronald W. Taber, "Vardis Fisher and the 'Idaho Guide,' " in Richard W. Etulain and Bert W. Marley, eds., *The Idaho Heritage: A Collection of Historical Essays* (Pocatello, Idaho, 1974), 143–50, esp. 147. See also Norman R. Yetman, "The Background of the Slave Narrative Collection," AQ, 19 (1967), 534–53.

80. Mangione, *The Dream and the Deal: The Federal Writers' Project*, 351–53, the Cantwell quotation from NR on 353.

81. Marling, *Wall-to-Wall America: A Cultural History of Post-Office Murals in the Great Depression*; Richard D. McKinzie, *The New Deal for Artists* (Princeton, 1973); Francis V. O'Connor, ed., *Art for the Millions: Essays from the 1930s by Artists and Administrators of the WPA Federal Art Project* (Greenwich, Conn., 1973), 20.

82. Obituary of Cahill in the *Berkshire Eagle*, July 8, 1960; NYT, Sept. 20, 1936, sec. 7, p. 10; Eugene W. Metcalf, Jr., and Claudine Weatherford, "Modernism, Edith Halpert, Holger Cahill, and the Fine Art Meaning of American Folk Art," in Jane S. Becker and Barbara Franco, eds., *Folk Roots, New Roots: Folklore in American Life* (Lexington, Mass., 1988), 156–65.

83. Beatrix T. Rumford, "Uncommon Art of the Common People: A Review of Trends in the Collecting and Exhibiting of American Folk Art," in Ian M. G. Quimby and Scott T. Swank, eds., *Perspectives on American Folk Art* (New York, 1980), 23–27, 30, 35–36, 40–41.

84. B. W. Norton to Douglas Southall Freeman, Jan. 30, 1937, Freeman Papers, box 19, ALUV.

85. NYT, Jan. 28, 1982, p. C17.

86. See *U.S. Statutes at Large,* vol. 48, *Public Laws,* 73rd Congress (1933–34), 1122–24; NYT, Apr. 18, 1937, sec. 4, p. 12.

87. See Monty Noam Penkower, *The Federal Writers' Project: A Study in Government Patronage of the Arts* (Urbana, Ill., 1977), ch. 10, "The Loss of Control." And for the view that the private sector (rather than government) should "foot the bill," expressed in a highly popular 1939 Capra film, see Charles J. Maland, *American Visions: The Films of Chaplin, Ford, Capra, and Welles, 1936–1941* (New York, 1977), 263.

88. NYT, Apr. 16, 1935, p. 22.

89. Hervey Allen, *Action at Aquila* (New York, 1938), the quotation at p. 123. See also Stuart E. Knee, *Hervey Allen (1889–1949): A Literary Historian in America* (Lewiston, N.Y., 1988), 352–63.

90. NYT, May 29, 1939, pp. 1, 5; NYT, May 31, 1939, pp. 3, 4. For the post–World War I roots of American pacifism, see Glenn Frank, "Patriotism and Pacifism: An Attempt to Be Honest about the Church and the War," *The Century,* 108 (July 1924), 421–25.

91. NYT, May 14, 1939, sec. 4, p. 8; Maland, *American Visions: The Films of Chaplin, Ford, Capra, and Welles, 1936–1941,* 253–68.

92. John Dos Passos, *The Ground We Stand On: Some Examples from the History of a Political Creed* (New York, 1941), 3, 20.

93. Maurice Matloff, "The Nature and Scope of Military History," in Russell F. Weigley, ed., *New Dimensions in Military History: An Anthology* (San Rafael, Calif., 1975), 403.

94. Rothman, *Preserving Different Pasts: The American National Monuments,* ch. 11.

Chapter 15

1. See Peter Burke, "History as Social Memory," in Thomas Butler, ed., *Memory: History, Culture and the Mind* (Oxford, 1989), 103–04. See also Ernst Cassirer, *The Myth of the State* (New Haven, 1946), 3–49; Mircea Eliade, *The Myth of the Eternal Return* (New York, 1954), 34–48; and Bruce Kuklick, "Myth and Symbol in American Studies," AQ, 24 (1972), 435–50.

2. Wilson to Dos Passos, Feb. 12, 1937, Dos Passos Papers, box 5, ALUV; Cowley quoted in James Hoopes, *Van Wyck Brooks: In Search of American Culture* (Amherst, Mass., 1977), 205. Brooks himself described the purpose of his series as "reviving the special kind of memory that fertilizes the living mind and gives it the sense of a base on which to build."

3. Elizabeth Donaghy Garrett, *The Arts of Independence: The DAR Museum Collection* (Washington, D.C., 1985), 12. See also W. Lloyd Warner, *The Living and the Dead: A Study of the Symbolic Life of Americans* (New Haven, 1959), 119, 124; Lindsey Blayney, "American Ideals and Traditions," NAR, 215 (May 1922), 577–89.

4. Speech by Charles Phelps Noyes, May 27, 1899, Noyes Papers (N953), box 2, MinnHS. See also Wayne Mixon, "Joel Chandler Harris, the Yeoman Tradition, and the New South Movement," *Georgia Historical Quarterly,* 61 (1977), 308–17; Arlin Turner, "George W. Cable's Use of the Past," *Mississippi Quarterly,* 30 (1977), 512–15.

5. See Richard Slotkin, "Nostalgia and Progress: Theodore Roosevelt's Myth of the Frontier," AQ, 33 (1981), 608–37, esp. 609–10.

6. Lodge, "An American Myth," in Lodge, *The Democracy of the Constitution* (New York, 1915), 208–11. Lodge attacked James Parton and John C. Hamilton, in particular, for relying upon "hearsay and wandering traditions."

7. James Harvey Robinson, "What Is National Spirit?" *The Century,* 93 (November 1916), 59, 63–64. For a healthy corrective to Robinson's erroneous history, see Johan Huizinga, "Patriotism and Nationalism in European History," in Huizinga, *Men and Ideas: History, the Middle Ages, the Renaissance* (New York, 1959), 97–155.

8. Henry Seidel Canby, "Educating by Tradition," *The Century*, 98 (August 1919), 521–28. For evidence that supports Canby's contention, see Katharine Ford to Arthur M. Schlesinger, Jan. 18, 1929, Schlesinger Papers, box 4, HUA.

9. Bethany Andreasen, "Treason or Truth: The New York City Textbook Controversy, 1920–1923," NYH, 66 (1985), 397–419; Jordan Schwartz, *The Speculator: Bernard M. Baruch in Washington, 1917–1965* (Chapel Hill, N.C., 1981), 249–50.

10. James Sullivan to Albert Bushnell Hart, n.d. [1922], Hart Papers, box 4, HUA; A. C. Olney to Marshall Stimson, April 18, 1922, ibid.; anon., *An Analysis of the Emphasis Upon War in Our Elementary School Histories* (18-page pamphlet: Chicago, 1923).

11. James Truslow Adams, "History and the Lower Criticism," *Atlantic*, 132 (September 1923), 308–17, the quotation at 315. By 1926 the principal issue had shifted to patriotic indoctrination. See NR, 47 (June 23, 1926), 129; Allan Nevins to Adams, Dec. 16, 1929, Adams Papers, BLCU (regarding Adams's anglophilia).

12. Lois B. Merk, "Boston's Historic Public School Crisis," NEQ, 31 (1958), 172–99; NYT, Jan. 6, 1900, p. 6; Claude H. Van Tyne to Andrew C. McLaughlin, Oct. 11, 1910, McLaughlin Papers, box 1, UCL; McLaughlin to Van Tyne, Oct. 7 and 13, 1910, ibid.; McLaughlin to D. Appleton & Co., May 8, 1911, ibid.

13. Rudolf A. Clemen to Schlesinger, April 18, 1927, Schlesinger Papers, box 3, HUA; Charles H. Smyth to Schlesinger, Dec. 1927, ibid.; Lawrence L. Winship to Schlesinger, Oct. 25, 1927, ibid.; Claude H. Van Tyne to Schlesinger, Nov. 8 [1927?], ibid.

14. See Alfred T. Story, *American Shrines in England* (London, 1908); Anne Hollingsworth Wharton, "A Patriotic Pilgrimage," *Scribner's Magazine*, 55 (June 1914), 774–85; John A. Stewart to JDR, Jr., Jan. 15, 1924, JDR Papers, ser. II (cultural), box 8, RAC.

15. John A. Stewart to W. S. Richardson, Dec. 14, 1918, JDR Papers, ser. II (cultural), box 8, RAC.

16. Ibid.; Helen Gilman Brown to Abby Aldrich Rockefeller, Jan. 29, 1924, ibid.

17. For the popularity of pilgrimages during the first half of the nineteenth century, see Wesley Frank Craven, *The Legend of the Founding Fathers* (New York, 1955), 110–11.

18. Gilbert C. Fite, *Mount Rushmore* (Norman, Okla., 1952), 106, 171, 211; NYT, Feb. 21, 1937, sec. 11, p. 1; NYT, May 31, 1939, p. 19.

19. William Mann Irvine to Max Farrand, Sept. 21, 1925, Farrand Papers, HEHL; LeRoy Hodges to O. K. Brown, Sept. 8, 1927, JDR Papers, ser. II (cultural), box 190, RAC; H. R. McIlwaine to W. A. R. Goodwin, Feb. 5, 1930, Lyon G. Tyler Papers, group 1, box 26, SLWM; NYT, Oct. 13, 1935, sec. 2, p. 13; NYT, May 2, 1937, sec. 6, p. 4.

20. NYT, Feb. 29, 1924, p. 14; NYT, Apr. 6, 1924, sec. 4, p. 7.

21. JDR to Goodwin, July 16, 1928, JDR Papers, CWA; Goodwin to James H. Dillard, Apr. 20, 1926, C. W. Restoration files, CWA; Goodwin to Robert M. Hughes, Jan. 27, 1928, ibid.; Goodwin to Ford, May 8, 1929, Goodwin Papers (Conception of Restoration), CWA. In 1931, when Verne Chatelain referred to "certain 'shrines' " over which the National Government has control," he used single quotes. See Chatelain to Solon J. Buck, Mar. 26, 1931, Buck Papers, box 13, MinnHS.

22. Charles B. Hosmer, Jr., *Preservation Comes of Age, from Williamsburg to the National Trust, 1926–1949* (Charlottesville, Va., 1981), 308–11; NYT, Aug. 16, 1936, p. 1.

23. Albert Bushnell Hart to Ross H. Currier, Jan. 3, 1933, Hart Papers, box 24, HUA; NYT, Apr. 29, 1935, p. 4; NYT, July 5, 1935, p. 15; NYT, Oct. 27, 1935, sec. 1, p. 38; NYT, Apr. 16, 1939, sec. 11, p. 1.

24. John Drinkwater to Mrs. Maurice Moore, Nov. 7, 1923, Lee Chapel Papers, box A, ALUV; J. Prescott Carter to Moore, Dec. 30, 1923, ibid.; Mary de C. M. Moore, "Clad with the Beauty of Holiness," typescript of essay for the *Lynchburg News*, Jan. 17, 1924, ibid. See also Karal Ann Marling, *George Washington Slept Here: Colonial Revivals and American Culture, 1876–1986* (Cambridge, Mass., 1988), 310.

25. E. Lee Trinkle to chairman of the Jefferson Foundation, April 6, 1923, Freeman Papers, box 10, ALUV; Mrs. E. D. Hotchkiss to Douglas S. Freeman, June 25, 1923, ibid.

26. John A. Stewart to J. Franklin Jameson, April 2, 1924, Jameson Papers, box 134, MDLC; minutes of the Sulgrave board meeting and resolution, Jan. 16, 1924, in ibid.

27. An organizational letter for the Friends of Lafayette appears in the Victor H. Paltsits Papers, NYHS; P. E. Byrne, "The Custer Myth," *North Dakota Historical Quarterly*, 6 (1932), 187–200; Michael A. Lofaro, ed., *Davy Crockett: The Man, the Legend, the Legacy, 1786–1986* (Knoxville, Tenn., 1985), ch. 6.

28. Masters, *Lincoln the Man* (New York, 1931); Lois Hartley, "Edgar Lee Masters—Biographer and Historian," *Journal of the Illinois State Historical Society*, 54 (1961), 56–83; NYT, Oct. 13, 1935, p. 39. See also Harold Brackman, " 'Biography Yanked Down Out of Olympus': Beard, Woodward, and Debunking Biography," *Pacific Historical Review*, 52 (1983), 403–27.

29. Gilbert C. Fite, *Mount Rushmore* (Norman, Okla., 1952), 16–17, 22, 25–26, 46–47, 58.

30. Ibid., 205, 100–01.

31. Ibid., 102–06.

32. Rex Alan Smith, *The Carving of Mount Rushmore* (New York, 1985), 278–83.

33. Gerald W. Johnson, "Sophocles in Georgia," *The Century*, 112 (September 1926), 565–71; Fite, *Mount Rushmore*, 33–34, 42.

34. NYT, Apr. 9, 1939, sec. 4, p. 7.

35. Hosmer, *Preservation Comes of Age, from Williamsburg to the National Trust*, 184; Stephen Davis, "Southern Writers and the Image of Johnny Reb: Reflections of Regional Change Since Appomattox," in Walter J. Fraser and Winfred B. Moore, Jr., eds., *From the Old South to the New: Essays on the Transitional South* (Westport, Conn., 1978), 138; Bertram Wyatt-Brown, *Southern Honor: Ethics and Behavior in the Old South* (New York, 1982), ix.

36. W. A. R. Goodwin's scrapbook of newspaper clippings, vol. IIa, CWA; NYT, May 13, 1935, p. 5; and see Morris Schaff to Mary D. Carter, July 27, 1924, Lyon G. Tyler Papers, group 5, box 4, SLWM; Albert Bushnell Hart to Tyler, Dec. 31, 1931, ibid., box 7.

37. Tom Ferril's "Westering" (1934) is quoted in Robert G. Athearn, *The Mythic West in Twentieth-Century America* (Lawrence, Kans., 1986), 176; and see 272 along with Lon Tinkle, *An American Original: The Life of J. Frank Dobie* (Boston, 1978), 119–20, 127, 153, 168.

38. Carey McWilliams, "Myths of the West," NAR, 232 (November 1931), 425–26.

39. Bernard DeVoto, "Footnote on the West," *Harper's*, 155 (November 1927), 717.

40. DeVoto, "The West: A Plundered Province," *Harper's*, 169 (August 1934), 356, 363; DeVoto, "The Anxious West," *Harper's*, 193 (December 1946), 481–91.

41. Albert Jay Nock, "Return of the Patriots," *Virginia Quarterly Review*, 8 (1932), 165. See also Ralph Barton Perry, "Uncle Sam and the Statue of Liberty," *The Century*, 107 (February 1924), 608–14.

42. William F. Brewster to Victor H. Paltsits, Dec. 23, 1920, Paltsits Papers, NYHS; Paltsits to Brewster, Jan. 4, 1921, ibid.; Craven, *Legend of the Founding Fathers*, 179.

43. Elizabeth Frazer, "1776–1926 at the Sesqui-Centennial," SEP, 199 (Sept. 11, 1926), 50, 52, 65–66.

44. Material pertaining to the Henry bicentennial is in the R. Walton Moore Papers, box 15, Franklin D. Roosevelt Library, Hyde Park, N.Y.

45. NYT, May 21, 1937, pp. 1, 3; NYT, Apr. 16, 1939, sec. 11, pp. 1, 10.

46. See Minnie G. Cook to Lyon G. Tyler, June 5, 1913, Tyler Papers, group 5, box 3, SLWM; Adams, "History and the Lower Criticism," 309, 315; John V. Bouvier to Sol Bloom, May 11, 1934, Bloom Papers, folder 50, NYPL; Hosmer, *Preservation Comes of Age, from Williamsburg to the National Trust*, 126.

47. Saving the Hamilton Grange in 1924 is documented by correspondence between Louise Lee Schuyler (his descendant) and Dr. George Kunz, located in the Pierpont

Morgan Library, New York City; Bruce is quoted in Darrett B. Rutman, "Philip Alexander Bruce: A Divided Mind of the South," VMHB, 68 (1960), 406–07.

48. Chauncey Brewster Tinker, "On the Importance of Being Indifferent to One's Ancestors," *Atlantic*, 135 (February 1925), 208–15; Joan Shelley Rubin, *Constance Rourke and American Culture* (Chapel Hill, N.C., 1980), 191. See also Perry, "Uncle Sam and the Statue of Liberty," 609.

49. Letter from Gwathmey to the author, Dec. 15, 1981. For culturally related works of art, see Philip Evergood, *My Forebears Were Pioneers* (1940), in the University of Georgia Museum of Art, Athens, and Jacob Lawrence, *Tombstones* (1942), in the Whitney Museum of American Art. In the gouache on paper by Lawrence, a black child has discarded a white doll.

50. William M. Ferraro, "The National Anthem Act of 1931: The Emergence of a Legal Symbol" (unpubl. honors thesis, Georgetown University, 1982), 16–17, 30; James A. Moss to J. Franklin Jameson, Sept. 2, 1924, Jameson Papers, box 133, MDLC; Moss to Arthur M. Schlesinger, Oct. 19, 1928, Schlesinger Papers, box 4, HUA.

51. John Maas, "Architecture and Americanism, or Pastiches of Independence Hall," *Historic Preservation*, 22 (April 1970), 17–25.

52. Caroline E. MacGill, "American Mythology," *Scribner's Magazine*, 77 (March 1925), 242–45; and see Elmer S. Hader, "A Gallery of American Myths," *The Century*, 107 (April 1924), n.p.

53. Chester T. Crowell, "New Myths about Uncle Sam," SEP, 200 (July 9, 1927), 27, 123; editorial, "Materialism in America," SEP, 199 (Aug. 21, 1926), 24; John Erskine, "The Centurion," *The Century*, 113 (February 1927), 501–06; Gilbert Seldes, "A Super-American Credo," SEP, 201 (July 21, 1928), 23, 45–46.

54. George T. Blakey, *Historians on the Homefront: American Propagandists for the Great War* (Lexington, Ky., 1970); Adams, "History and the Lower Criticism," 315; Glenn Frank, "Americanism, Selective or Sentimental: Must the Patriot Surrender His Right of Criticism?" *The Century*, 109 (November 1924), 137; F. L. Pattee, "A Call for a Literary Historian," *American Mercury*, 2 (June 1924), 134–40, reprinted in Pattee, *Tradition and Jazz* (New York, 1925), 231–55.

55. A lengthy editorial clipped from *Good Housekeeping* (February 1930) is in the Lyon G. Tyler Papers, group 5, box 6, SLWM; André Maurois, "The Myth of Myth," *Virginia Quarterly Review*, 8 (January 1932), 90–94; Karal Ann Marling, "A Note on New Deal Iconography: Futurology and the Historical Myth," PAACS, 4 (1979), 421–40, esp. 427–28.

56. Beard suggested to a friend that "about a half a dozen of us . . . get together for the next ten years and reconstruct the Encyclopedia of Mythology known as American history." Quoted in Robert Dallek, *Democrat and Diplomat: The Life of William E. Dodd* (New York, 1968), 147. See also William Carlos Williams, *In the American Grain* (1925: New York, 1956); DeVoto to Catherine Drinker Bowen, n.d. [1930s], in Wallace Stegner, ed., *The Letters of Bernard DeVoto* (Garden City, N.Y., 1975), 285–86; an interesting statement by Holland (1934) appears in Hosmer, *Preservation Comes of Age, from Williamsburg to the National Trust*, 447.

57. Sandburg's Introduction to Lloyd Lewis, *Myths After Lincoln* (2nd ed.: New York, 1941), vii; Hamlin to Dos Passos, Nov. 20, 1944, Dos Passos Papers, box 2, ALUV. See also Melville Herskovits, *The Myth of the Negro Past* (New York, 1941). For examples of the older view (c. 1840 to 1920) that the United States lacked myths and legends, see Charles C. Alexander, *Here the Country Lies: Nationalism and the Arts in Twentieth-Century America* (Bloomington, Ind., 1980), 7, 76.

58. Thomas Daniel Young, "Allen Tate's Double Focus: The Past in the Present," *Mississippi Quarterly*, 30 (1977), 517–25; Marling, *George Washington Slept Here: Colonial Revivals and American Culture, 1876–1986*, 317–19, 335–37, 360–61; Darrell Garwood, *Artist in Iowa: A Life of Grant Wood* (New York, 1944), 227; Cecile Whiting, "American Heroes and Invading Barbarians: The Regionalist Response to Fascism," PAACS, 13 (1988), 296, 301–02, 307–08.

59. Charles A. Fenton, *Stephen Vincent Benét: The Life and Times of an American Man of Letters, 1898–1943* (New Haven, 1958), 275–76, 282–83, 295, 351; Benét, "The Lost Cause in Literature," *Saturday Review of Literature*, 21 (Nov. 25, 1939), 6; *Selected Works of Stephen Vincent Benét*, I, *Poetry* (New York, 1942), 471–87.

60. Rubin, *Constance Rourke and American Culture*, 46, 55, 58–59, 89, 100, 105, 117, 120, 125, 133; Rourke, *American Humor: A Study of the National Character* (New York, 1931).

61. David S. Muzzey to Adams, Sept. 22, 1931, Adams Papers, BLCU; Robert Underwood Johnson to Adams, Aug. 20, 1932, ibid.

62. Ellen Glasgow, *A Certain Measure* (New York, 1943), 27, 170, 237–38; Glasgow, *The Woman Within* (New York, 1954); Stark Young, "Memories of the Deep South," NR, 72 (Aug. 17, 1932), 18–19.

63. See Mark P. Leone, *Roots of Modern Mormonism* (Cambridge, Mass., 1979), 205; Hurston to Du Bois, June 11, 1945, in Herbert Aptheker, ed., *The Correspondence of W. E. B. Du Bois* (Amherst, Mass., 1973–78), III, 41–42.

64. Lawrence M. Larsen to Guy Stanton Ford, Nov. 12, 1935, Ford Papers, folder 39, University of Minnesota Archives, Minneapolis; Barry Mackintosh, "The National Park Service Moves into Historical Interpretation," PH, 9 (1987), 57–59.

65. NYT, Dec. 18, 1936, p. 8; NYT *Sunday Magazine*, Jan. 17, 1937, p. 21; NYT, Mar. 6, 1937, p. 16; NYT, Mar. 12, 1937, p. 22; NYT, Apr. 5, 1937, p. 21.

66. Stuart E. Knee, *Hervey Allen, 1889–1949: A Literary Historian in America* (Lewiston, N.Y., 1988), 352–63; Ann Douglas, "*Studs Lonigan* and the Failure of History in Mass Society: A Study of Claustrophobia," AQ, 29 (1977), 487–505; W. W. Livengood to Carl Carmer, Nov. 22, 1938, Carmer Papers, box 7, NYSHA.

67. Richard H. Pells, *Radical Visions and American Dreams: Culture and Social Thought in the Depression Years* (New York, 1973), 328. For a complementary perspective, see Melvyn Dubofsky, "Not So 'Turbulent Years': Another Look at the American 1930's," *Amerikastudien*, 24 (1979), 5–20, which provides a parallel explanation for the working class.

68. G. M. Harper, "Seeing Americans First," *Scribner's Magazine*, 86 (December 1929), 650; Matthew Josephson, *Life among the Surrealists: A Memoir* (New York, 1962), 355–57, 366.

69. Ruth Suckow, "The Folk Idea in American Life," *Scribner's Magazine*, 88 (September 1930), 254; James A. Hijiya, "Four Ways of Looking at a Philanthropist: A Study of Robert Weeks de Forest," *Proceedings of the APS*, 124 (1980), 416; Ellen Glasgow, *A Sheltered Life* (New York, 1932), 233.

70. "Informal Extemporaneous Remarks at a Religious Service in Rockport, Arkansas, June 10, 1936," in Samuel I. Rosenman, ed., *The Public Papers and Addresses of Franklin D. Roosevelt*, V (New York, 1938), 194.

71. See Alfred Kazin, *On Native Grounds* (New York, 1942), 247; Masters, *The Sangamon* (New York, 1942), 116; Joan Richardson, *Wallace Stevens: The Later Years, 1923–1955* (New York, 1988), 290, 402.

72. Nick Salvatore, *Eugene V. Debs: Citizen and Socialist* (Urbana, Ill., 1982), 3; Henry Watson Kent to James Truslow Adams, Sept. 24, 1942, Adams Papers, BLCU. For a comparative perspective on the personal role of historical memory, see Carlo Ginzburg, *The Cheese and the Worms: The Cosmos of a Seventeenth-Century Miller* (New York, 1982), 87; and John Buchan, *Memory Hold-the-Door* (London, 1940), esp. ch. 11.

73. Ronald Steel, *Walter Lippmann and the American Century* (Boston, 1980), 66; Becker to Henry Johnson [Dec. 1922] in Michael Kammen, ed., "*What Is the Good of History?*", *Selected Letters of Carl L. Becker, 1900–1945* (Ithaca, N.Y., 1973), 86. For an elaboration of this idea, see Becker, *Everyman His Own Historian: Essays on History and Politics* (1935: Chicago, 1966), 234–35, 248.

74. Ernest Boyd, "When Americans Discover America," *The Century*, 113 (December 1926), 233; *Covered-Wagon Centennial and Ox-Team Days* (Yonkers, N.Y., 1932), 30;

Erskine, "Centurion," *The Century* (February 1927), 502–03; DeVoto, "The Anxious West," 485.

75. Ann Banks, *First-Person America* (New York, 1980), 67; Studs Terkel, *Hard Times: An Oral History of the Great Depression* (1970: New York, 1986), 107–08, 111, 150, 170, 529–30, the quotation at 75.

76. "I Am the People, the Mob," in Carl Sandburg, *Complete Poems* (New York, 1950), 71.

77. Chorley used these phrases in talks to the Society of Colonial Wars, the Current Events Club, and the Daughters of Founders and Patriots of America, all in 1935. Chorley scrapbooks, Chorley Papers, RAC; Alfred Kazin, "What Have the 30's Done to Our Literature?", *New York Herald Tribune Books,* Dec. 31, 1939, p. 1; Bloom's speeches are located in the papers of the Constitution Sesquicentennial Commission, box 14, record group 148, NA.

78. John B. Gordon to Albert B. Hart, Nov. 6, 1930, Hart Papers, box 24, HUA; NYT, May 31, 1937, pp. 1–2, the quotation from p. 2.

79. T. J. Jackson Lears, "Packaging the Folk," in Jane S. Becker and Barbara Franco, eds., *Folk Roots, New Roots: Folklore in American Life* (Lexington, Mass., 1988), 124; Archibald MacLeish, "The Tradition of the People," *New Masses,* 20 (Aug. 11, 1936), 25–27; Pells, *Radical Visions and American Dreams,* 312, 314–16.

80. Forbes to R. N. Lincott, July 24, 1940, Forbes Papers, Houghton Library, Harvard University; Samuel H. Brockunier to John Dos Passos [re: Roger Williams], Dec. 19, 1939, Dos Passos Papers, ALUV; Van Wyck Brooks to James Truslow Adams [re: Paine], Aug. 26, 1940, Adams Papers, BLCU.

81. See Albert B. Hart to Henry E. Scott, Dec. 13, 1924, Hart Papers, box 24, HUA; Institute of American Genealogy to Lyon G. Tyler, Dec. 17, 1929, Tyler Papers, group 1, box 24, SLWM; circular announcement to members of the Institute, 1932, Tyler papers, group 2, LGT History. For W. E. B. Du Bois's preparation of his genealogy (in order to join the Descendants of the American Revolution), see Sylvia Wilcox Razey to Du Bois, Feb. 13, 1940, in Aptheker, ed., *Correspondence of W. E. B. Du Bois,* II, 213.

82. Mary Clearman Blew, "Myths, History, and the Precarious Margin of Fiction," MMWHC, 34 (1984), 2–9; F. Allan Morgan, "Memories: Life in the U.S., Photographic," *Scribner's Magazine,* 104 (August 1938); E. M. Hawes to Theodore C. Blegen, Oct. 15, 1936, Northwest Territory Commission Papers, MinnHS; Arthur J. Larsen, "The Community's Roots in the Past" (c. 1941), for the Rice County Historical Society in the Minnesota Territory Centennial Records, box 296, MinnHS.

83. E. M. Hawes to Borglum, Oct. 17 and 26, 1936, Borglum Papers, box 111, MDLC; Borglum to Hawes, Nov. 8, 1936, ibid.; seven-page typed "Memorandum as to the Memorial" [written by Hawes ?] in ibid. A storm of criticism arose in 1937 when the design for the Jefferson Memorial in Washington, D.C., was announced. The main objection was epitomized by this query: "Can imitation of Imperial Rome in a democratic country at our point of cultural development procure for us the admiration of the world?" NYT, Apr. 25, 1937, sec. 10, p. 9.

84. Michele H. Bogart, *Public Sculpture and the Civic Ideal in New York City, 1890–1930* (Chicago, 1989); letter to the author from John W. Smith, archivist at the Art Institute of Chicago, Nov. 1, 1988, enclosing a descriptive list of the Ferguson Monument Fund Commission.

85. Bogart, *Public Sculpture and the Civic Ideal,* 271; James M. Mayo, *War Memorials as Political Landscape: The American Experience and Beyond* (New York, 1988), 5; Fite, *Mount Rushmore,* 108, 122, 131, 210.

86. Christopher B. Coleman to Solon J. Buck, Aug. 23, 1933, Buck Papers, box 13, MinnHS; a copy of the program for Sept. 3, 1933, is attached in ibid.

87. NYT, Mar. 21, 1935, p. 15; NYT, May 5, 1935, p. 7; NYT, Oct. 27, 1935, sec 10, p. 2.

88. Anne Farnam, "George Francis Dow: A Career of Bringing the 'picturesque traditions of sleeping generations' to Life in the Early Twentieth Century," EIHC, 121

(1985), 78; Warren James Belasco, *Americans on the Road: From Autocamp to Motel, 1910–1945* (Cambridge, Mass., 1979).

89. NYT, Apr. 9, 1939, sec. 3, p. 5; NYT, Apr. 16, 1939, sec. 1, p. 16; NYT, Apr. 19, 1939, p. 17; NYT, Apr. 21, 1939, p. 19; NYT, Apr. 23, 1939, sec. 9, p. 3 (Rotogravure Picture Section).

90. NYT, Apr. 18, 1939, p. 25; NYT, Apr. 20, 1939, p. 17; NYT, Apr. 22, 1939, p. 3; NYT Apr. 23, 1939, sec. 1, p. 35; NYT, Apr. 24, 1939, p. 3; NYT, Apr. 25, 1939, p. 3; NYT, May 7, 1939, sec. 1, p. 42.

91. NYT, Apr. 17, 1939, p. 16; NYT, Apr. 28, 1939, p. 24.

92. NYT, May 6, 1889, p. 8; Henry James, *A Little Tour of France* (New York, 1950), 48, where James observes that "regret, as well as memory, has its visions; especially when, like memory, it is assisted by photographs."

93. American Patriotic League to Guy Stanton Ford, Dec. 27, 1923, Ford Papers, University of Minnesota Archives, Minneapolis; Wilmarth S. Lewis to Archibald MacLeish, June 3, 1942, carbon in the Max Farrand Papers, HEHL; Nelson A. Rockefeller to Kenneth Chorley, Feb. 28, 1940, along with an attached memo dated Feb. 28, 1940, JDR Papers, ser. II (Cultural), box 169, RAC.

94. Charles J. Maland, *American Visions: The Films of Chaplin, Ford, Capra, and Welles, 1936–1941* (New York, 1971); Edward Countryman, "John Ford's *Drums Along the Mohawk:* The Making of an American Myth," in Susan Porter Benson et al., eds., *Presenting the Past: Essays on History and the Public* (Philadelphia, 1986), 87–102; Edward D. C. Campbell, Jr., "Gone With the Wind: Film as Myth and Message," in Fraser and Moore, eds., *From the Old South to the New,* 143–51, the quotation at 148.

95. John Steinbeck, *The Grapes of Wrath* (1939: New York, 1958), 95–96.

96. See Marling, *George Washington Slept Here,* 366, 435 n. 8; Philip Gleason, "World War II and the Development of American Studies," AQ, 36 (1984), 348–49.

97. NYT, Apr. 2, 1939, sec. 3, p. 3; *Life in America: A Special Loan Exhibition of Paintings Held during the Period of the New York World's Fair* (New York, 1939); Calvin Tomkins, *Merchants and Masterpieces: The Story of the Metropolitan Museum of Art* (New York, 1970), 243, 272, 277.

98. See NYT, Apr. 29, 1937, p. 18; NYT, Sept. 15, 1937, p. 25; George W. Cook to W. E. B. Du Bois, July 22, 1938, in Aptheker, ed., *Correspondence of W. E. B. Du Bois,* II, 169–70; Paul Green to James Boyd, July 30, 1938, Boyd Papers, box 4, SHC.

99. Thompson to Adams, five-page telegram [1939], Adams Papers, BLCU.

100. Keller to James Truslow Adams, Nov. 26 and Dec. 5, 1940, ibid.

101. Flexner to Forbes, April 12, 1940, Forbes Papers, private collection, Worcester, Mass.

102. Boyd to Robert F. Sherwood, Oct. 2, 1940, Boyd Papers, box 4, SHC; Boyd to Walter Lippmann, Feb. 17, 1941, ibid.; Augustin G. Rudd to Francis Biddle, April 28, 1941, ibid.; John A. Lapp to Boyd, May 3, 1941, ibid.; Saroyan to Boyd, Feb. 23, 1941, ibid.

103. See James Boyd, ed., *The Free Company Presents. . . . A Collection of Plays about the Meaning of America* (New York, 1941); Sidney Kingsley, *The Patriots* (New York, 1943); Esther Forbes, untitled five-page typescript, April 1944, Forbes Papers (616) 5, Houghton Library, Harvard University; Forbes to Mr. Ticknor, July 1, 1941, ibid.

104. See Lawrence J. Friedman, *Inventors of the Promised Land* (New York, 1975), ch. 2; Merrill D. Peterson, *The Jefferson Image in the American Mind* (New York, 1960), Book 2, ch. 7; Charles J. Nolan, *Aaron Burr and the American Literary Imagination* (Westport, Conn., 1980), 105; Nathan Schachner, *Aaron Burr* (New York, 1937); David R. Johnson, "Benedict Arnold: The Traitor as Hero in American Literature" (unpubl. Ph. D. diss., Pennsylvania State University, 1975); Marling, "A Note on New Deal Iconography," 425–26; Michael H. Frisch, "The Memory of History," in Benson et al., eds., *Presenting the Past: Essays on History and the Public,* 12, and see also 145, 151.

105. Jo H. Chamberlin, "Santa Fe Fiesta," *Scribner's Magazine,* 102 (September 1937), 84–87.

106. Kazin, *On Native Grounds: An Interpretation of Modern American Prose Literature*, 490.

107. Ibid., ix.

108. See Helen A. Harrison, ed., *Dawn of a New Day: The New York World's Fair, 1939/40* (New York, 1980); Warren Susman, "The People's Fair: Cultural Contradictions of a Consumer Society," in Susman, *Culture as History: The Transformation of American Society in the Twentieth Century* (New York, 1984), 211–29.

Coda to Part Three

1. Lewis Mumford, "American Condescension and European Superiority," *Scribner's Magazine*, 87 (May 1930), 523, 525. These and the quotations that follow are reprinted by permission of Gina Maccoby Literary Agency for the Estate of Lewis Mumford.

2. Ibid., 523.

3. V. F. Calverton, "The American Revolutionary Tradition," *Scribner's Magazine*, 95 (May 1934), 356–57.

4. Joan Shelley Rubin, "Constance Rourke in Context: The Uses of Myth," AQ, 28 (1976), 578–82; Auden quoted in Edmund Wilson, *Patriotic Gore: Studies in the Literature of the American Civil War* (New York, 1962), 491.

5. Robinson's Introduction to M. E. Ravage, "The Loyalty of the Foreign Born: An Interpretation," *The Century*, 94 (June 1917), 201–02.

6. Robert Anthony Orsi, *The Madonna of 115th Street: Faith and Community in Italian Harlem, 1880–1950* (New Haven, 1985), 168–71; Mumford, "American Condescension and European Superiority," 522.

7. Richard H. Pells, *Radical Visions and American Dreams: Culture and Social Thought in the Depression Years* (New York, 1973), 66; Dodd to Andrew C. McLaughlin, Dec. 6, 1935, McLaughlin Papers, box 2, UCL. See also Worthington C. Ford to James Truslow Adams, Nov. 5, 1935, Adams Papers, BLCU; NYT, Apr. 11, 1939, p. 16.

8. See Michael Cherniavsky, *Tsar and People: Studies in Russian Myths* (New Haven, 1961); Joanna Hubbs, *Mother Russia: The Feminine Myth in Russian Culture* (Bloomington, Ind., 1988), ch. 6.

9. George L. Mosse, *The Nationalization of the Masses: Political Symbolism and Mass Movements in Germany from the Napoleonic Wars through the Third Reich* (New York, 1975), 96, 204–06.

10. Kenneth Hudson, *Museums of Influence* (Cambridge, 1987), 154, 167.

11. Anne Walthall, "Japanese *Gimin*: Peasant Martyrs in Popular Memory," AHR, 91 (1986), 1076–1102; Paul Avrich, *The Haymarket Tragedy* (Princeton, 1984).

12. Carol Gluck, *Japan's Modern Myths: Ideology in the Late Meiji Period* (Princeton, 1985), 143, 145–46; Mumford, "American Condescension and European Superiority," 525.

13. See Lawrence W. Levine, "American Culture and the Great Depression," *The Yale Review*, 74 (1985), 196–223.

14. See Alfred Kazin, *On Native Grounds: An Interpretation of Modern American Prose Literature* (New York, 1942), ch. 16, "America! America!" which remains one of the most astute discussions of American cultural impulses during the 1930s. I am also indebted to perceptive comments made by Alan Brinkley at a session titled "Memory of Things Past and National Identity: America and Europe in the Interwar Years" that took place at the annual convention of the American Studies Association, Nov. 4, 1989, in Toronto, Canada.

15. Paul Fussell, *Abroad: British Literary Traveling Between the Wars* (New York, 1980), 127; Peter Conrad, *Imagining America* (New York, 1980), esp. chs. 6–9.

16. Alun Hawkins, "The Discovery of Rural England," in Robert Colls and Philip Dodd, eds., *Englishness: Politics and Culture, 1880–1920* (London, 1986), 62–88; Peter J. Schmitt, *Back to Nature: The Arcadian Myth in Urban America* (New York, 1969).

17. Valerie E. Chancellor, *History of Their Masters: Opinion in the English History Textbook, 1800–1914* (Bath, Engl., 1970); Theodore R. Sizer, *Secondary Schools at the Turn of the Century* (New Haven, 1964).

18. Robert Wohl, *The Generation of 1914* (Cambridge, Mass., 1979), 89; Martin J. Wiener, *English Culture and the Decline of the Industrial Spirit, 1850–1980* (Cambridge, 1981), 73.

19. Michael O'Brien, *The Idea of the American South, 1920–1941* (Baltimore, 1979), 201; Paul Fussell, *The Great War and Modern Memory* (New York, 1975), 258–59.

20. Janet Hobhouse, *Everybody Who Was Anybody: A Biography of Gertrude Stein* (London, 1975), 207–08.

21. Carlton J. H. Hayes, *France: A Nation of Patriots* (New York, 1930); William R. Keylor, *Jacques Bainville and the Renaissance of Royalist History in 20th-Century France* (Baton Rouge, La., 1979).

22. Sir Edward Spears, *Assignment to Catastrophe: The Fall of France, June 1940* (New York, 1955), II, 84–87.

23. I am indebted to Professor Herman Lebovics of the State University of New York at Stony Brook for sharing with me his work-in-progress on this subject.

24. See Simon Schama, *Two Rothschilds and the Land of Israel* (New York, 1978).

25. Hudson, *Museums of Influence,* 115; Geoffrey C. Upward, *A Home for Our Heritage: The Building and Growth of Greenfield Village and Henry Ford Museum, 1929–1979* (Dearborn, Mich., 1979).

26. Nina Tumarkin, *Lenin Lives! The Lenin Cult in Soviet Russia* (Cambridge, Mass., 1983), esp. 236, 262; Karal Ann Marling, *George Washington Slept Here: Colonial Revivals and American Culture, 1876–1986* (Cambridge, Mass., 1988), ch. 11.

27. Russel Ward, *The Australian Legend* (1958: Melbourne, 1966); Kent Ladd Steckmesser, *The Western Hero in History and Legend* (Norman, Okla., 1965); Ray Allen Billington, *Frederick Jackson Turner: Historian, Scholar, Teacher* (New York, 1973), ch. 8.

28. C. J. Taylor, "Some Early Problems of the Historic Sites and Monuments Board of Canada," *Canadian Historical Review,* 64 (1983), 3–4, 24.

29. Ibid., 3–4, 22–23.

30. Ibid., 5 and passim; J. Clarence Webster to Victor H. Paltsits, June 5, 1934, Paltsits Papers, NYHS.

31. Robin W. Winks, *The Relevance of Canadian History: U.S. and Imperial Perspectives* (Toronto, 1979), 18.

32. Wilbur Zelinsky, "A Sidelong Glance at Canadian Nationalism and Its Symbols," *North American Culture,* 4 (1988), 2–6.

33. Ibid., 7, 9–11; Melville Watkins, "Technology and Nationalism," in Peter Russell, ed., *Nationalism in Canada* (Toronto, 1966), 295; George Tomkins, "National Consciousness, the Curriculum, and Canadian Studies," in Geoffrey Milburn and John Herbert, eds., *National Consciousness and the Curriculum: The Canadian Case* (Toronto, 1974), 15–129, esp. 21.

34. See George M. Fredrickson, *White Supremacy: A Comparative Study in American and South African History* (New York, 1981); C. Vann Woodward, *American Counterpoint: Slavery and Racism in the North-South Dialogue* (Boston, 1976).

35. Leonard Thompson, *The Political Mythology of Apartheid* (New Haven, 1985), esp. 39, 183–84.

36. See Howard R. Driggs, *Covered-Wagon Centennial and Ox-Team Days: Oregon Trail Memorial Edition* (Yonkers, N.Y., 1932).

37. "The Spirit of the Netherlands," in J. H. Huizinga, *Dutch Civilisation in the Seventeenth Century and Other Essays* (New York, 1968), 115.

38. Huizinga, *In the Shadow of Tomorrow* (New York, 1936), 216; George L. Mosse, *Masses and Man: Nationalist and Fascist Perceptions of Reality* (New York, 1980), 52–68, 104–18.

39. Jacques Maritain, *Christianity and Democracy* (New York, 1944), 12, 15.

40. Ralph Barton Perry, *Puritanism and Democracy* (New York, 1944), 630–31. Perry surely had read A. S. P. Woodhouse, *Puritanism and Liberty* (London, 1938), which argued that Puritanism had helped to beget both liberty and democracy.

41. Perry, *Puritanism and Democracy*, 631. See also Ben Halpern, " 'Myth' and 'Ideology' in Modern Usage," *History and Theory*, 1 (1961), 129–49.

42. Sidney Harmon to James Boyd, Mar. 24, 1941, Boyd Papers, box 4, SHC.

43. Pierre Sorlin, *The Film in History: Restaging the Past* (Totowa, N.J., 1980); John F. Kasson, "The Invention of the Past: Technology, History, and Nostalgia," in Charles Strain and Steven Goldberg, eds., *Technological Change and the Transformation of America* (Carbondale, Ill., 1987), 37–52; George Lipsitz, *Time Passages: Collective Memory and American Popular Culture* (Minneapolis, 1990), chs. 3, 4, 7, 8.

Prolegomenon: Part Four

1. Aaron Copland and Vivian Perlis, *Copland: 1900 Through 1942* (New York, 1984), 341–48. For other examples, see Robert Penn Warren, *All the King's Men* (New York, 1945), esp. the final page; Robert Coles, *Erik H. Erikson: The Growth of His Work* (Boston, 1970), 103.

2. John A. Krout to Fellows of the Society of American Historians, Apr. 10, 1943, Douglas Southall Freeman Papers, ALUV; Dixon Ryan Fox to Edward W. Stitts, Jr., Apr. 4, 1944, Fox Papers, Union College Library, Schenectady, N.Y.; Beard to Merle Curti, Sept. 28, 1944, quoted in Ellen Nore, *Charles Beard: An Intellectual Biography* (Carbondale, Ill., 1983), 200; Henry G. Leach to Adams, Apr. 4, 1945, Adams Papers, BLCU.

3. See Philip Gleason, "Americans All: World War II and the Shaping of American Identity," *Review of Politics*, 43 (1981), 483–518; Margaret W. Caffrey, *Ruth Benedict: Stranger in This Land* (Austin, Tex., 1989), ch. 9; Thomas Hart Benton, *An Artist in America* (4th ed.: Columbia, Mo., 1983), 326.

4. Frankfurter, "The Permanence of Jefferson," in *The Thomas Jefferson Bicentennial* (Washington, D.C., 1943), 3; John A. Krout to Fellows of the S.A.H., Apr. 10, 1943, Freeman Papers, ALUV.

5. Quoted in David Cannadine, "The Context, Performance and Meaning of Ritual: The British Monarchy and the 'Invention of Tradition,' c. 1820–1977," in Eric Hobsbawm and Terence Ranger, eds., *The Invention of Tradition* (Cambridge, 1983), 157.

6. Robert G. Hartje, *Bicentennial U.S.A.: Pathways to Celebration* (Nashville, Tenn., 1973), 64, 75–77, 80, 87, 89, 92, 138, 140–41. The papers of Virginia's 350th Anniversary Commission for the years 1954–57 are located in the VHS.

7. Czeslaw Milosz, "A Legend," in Milosz, *The Collected Poems, 1931–1987* (New York, 1988), 102–04.

8. Howard W. Marshall, "Folklife and the Rise of American Folk Museums," *Journal of American Folklore*, 90 (1977), 391–413; Richard Bardolph, "Preserving Our Heritage," *North Carolina Historical Review*, 58 (1981), 139–45.

9. Charles Beard, *The Republic: Conversation on Fundamentals* (New York, 1943), 81.

10. See Charles Royster, *A Revolutionary People at War: The Continental Army and American Character, 1775–1783* (Chapel Hill, N.C., 1979), 61; Douglas Southall Freeman, *The South to Posterity* (New York, 1939), 4; Jean Starobinski, "The Idea of Nostalgia," *Diogenes*, no. 54 (1966), 81–103.

11. The paintings by Gorky are located in the Los Angeles County Museum of Art. And see Karal Ann Marling, *Wall-to-Wall America: A Cultural History of Post-Office Murals in the Great Depression* (Minneapolis, 1982), 220.

12. NYT, Apr. 2, 1939, sec. 4, p. 8.

13. See H. Stuart Hughes, *The Obstructed Path* (New York, 1968), 131; L. P. Hartley, *The Go-Between* (London, 1953), xvi.

14. Robert Jay Lifton, "Protean Man," in Lifton, *History and Human Survival* (New York, 1971), 311–31, esp. 318–19. See also Lifton, *The Broken Connection: On Death and*

the Continuity of Life (New York, 1979); Geoffrey Barraclough, *History in a Changing World* (Norman, Okla., 1956), 9, 135.

15.   See George Lipsitz, *Time Passages: Collective Memory and American Popular Culture* (Minneapolis, 1990), esp. 70, 89; Fred Davis, *Yearning for Yesterday: A Sociology of Nostalgia* (New York, 1977); Arthur P. Dudden, "Nostalgia and the American," *Journal of the History of Ideas,* 22 (1961), 515–30.

16.   Maurice R. Stein, *The Eclipse of Community: An Interpretation of American Studies* (1960: Princeton, 1972), 397–98.

17.   Kenneth Keniston, *The Uncommitted: Alienated Youth in American Society* (New York, 1965), 105–07, 180–83.

· 18.   See Michael Wallace, "Mickey Mouse History: Portraying the Past at Disney World," in Warren Leon and Roy Rosenzweig, eds., *History Museums in the United States: A Critical Assessment* (Urbana, Ill., 1989), 158–80.

Chapter 16

1.   Charles B. Hosmer, Jr., *Preservation Comes of Age, from Williamsburg to the National Trust, 1926–1949* (Charlottesville, Va., 1981), 298, 308, 349, 415, 424, 651, 783, 818, 833, 859, 1048, 1062; Samuel F. Bemis to Van Wyck Brooks, June 12, 1953, Brooks Papers, Van Pelt Library, University of Pennsylvania; Robert Hartje, *Bicentennial U.S.A.: Pathways to Celebration* (Nashville, Tenn., 1973), 59. In 1949 Malcolm Forbes launched an unsuccessful magazine titled *Nation's Heritage.*

2.   Mr. and Mrs. Thomas Armstrong to JDR, July 26, 1952, JDR Papers, ser. II (cultural), box 176, RAC; Carl A. Terry to JDR, Apr. 16, 1953, ibid.; Mrs. Carl Frode to JDR, Jan. 19, 1960, ibid., box 177. Boxes 176 and 177 in this collection are filled with fan letters sent from all over the United States by appreciative visitors for whom an enhanced sense of heritage was the basic shared experience.

3.   Roy Rosenzweig, *"American Heritage* and Popular History in the United States," in Susan Porter Benson et al., eds., *Presenting the Past: Essays on History and the Public* (Philadelphia, 1986), 27; William H. Latham to JDR III, Apr. 28, 1958, JDR Papers, ser. II (cultural), box 177, RAC; Miriam R. LeVin to JDR, Nov. 1952, ibid., box 176; Myron Hechler to JDR, Aug. 20, 1953, ibid.; John Cabitor to JDR, June 18, 1958, ibid., box 177.

4.   Chorley speech at the Shelburne Museum in Vermont, May 20, 1957, Chorley scrapbooks, RAC; Mrs. J. F. Bennett to JDR, July 2, 1958, JDR Papers, ser. II (cultural), box 177, RAC; V. T. H. Bien to JDR, Aug. 7, 1958, ibid.

5.   Mrs. James de Fremery to JDR, May 28, 1951, JDR Papers, ser. II (cultural), box 176; Mrs. Robert John to JDR, Aug. 25, 1952, ibid.; Walter L. Huber to Horace M. Albright, Nov. 13, 1957, ibid.

6.   Edward P. Alexander, "Historical Restorations," in William B. Hesseltine and Donald R. McNeil, eds., *In Support of Clio: Essays in Memory of Herbert A. Kellar* (Madison, Wis., 1958), 199. See also Alfred Runte, *National Parks: The American Experience* (Lincoln, Nebr., 1979), 158, 170, 173–74; Susan Croce Kelly, *Route 66: The Highway and Its People* (Norman, Okla., 1988).

7.   John Dos Passos to Allan Nevins, Oct. 8, 1955, Nevins Papers (professional), BLCU; Geoffrey C. Ward (editor of *American Heritage*) to the author, Oct. 30 and Dec. 20, 1981.

8.   Edward O. Dorman to Victor H. Paltsits, Oct. 1, 1907, Paltsits Papers, box 2, NYHS. For other efforts at popularizing American history at that time, see Charles W. Burrows to Paltsits, Feb. 17, 1905, ibid.; Lyman Horace Weeks (of the Society Americana in Boston) to J. Franklin Jameson, Apr. 3, 1908, Jameson Papers, box 129, MDLC.

9.   Frederic Melcher *(Publisher's Weekly)* to Arthur M. Schlesinger, Dec. 23, 1927, Schlesinger Papers, HUA; Max Farrand to J. Franklin Jameson, June 5, 1922, Jameson Papers, box 115, MDLC; Jameson to Farrand, June 9, 1922, ibid.; Frank Allaben to Guy Stanton Ford, Aug. 5, 1922, ibid., box 84; B. E. Steel to Lyon G. Tyler, Feb. 11, 1926, Tyler Papers, group 1, box 23, SLWM; John F. Benyon to Tyler, Apr. 26, 1929, ibid., group 1, box 20; W. A. R. Goodwin to Tyler, Feb. 3, 1930, ibid., group 1, box 26.

10.   Nevins to James T. Adams, Sept. 20, 1938, Feb. 6 and Apr. 16, 1939, Adams Papers, BLCU; Pringle to Adams, June 17, 1941, ibid.; John A. Krout (secretary of the S.A.H.) to Fellows of the Society of American Historians, Apr. 10, 1943, Freeman Papers, S.A.H. folder, ALUV.

11.   Nevins to Merle Curti, Mar. 7 and Apr. 4, 1947, Curti Papers, box 27, SHSW; Guy Stanton Ford to George Creel, Dec. 5, 1951, Ford Papers, folder no. 50, University of Minnesota Archives, Minneapolis; Frank B. Hubachek to Harold Dean Cater, Aug. 23, 1951, MinnHS archives (30.C.14.8F), MinnHS.

12.   James F. Simon, *Independent Journey: The Life of William O. Douglas* (New York, 1980; Penguin ed., 1981), 229; for paintings by Molly Luce, see Christie's catalogue of the Congoleum Corporate Collection sale, Jan. 27, 1987, 47–55; Russell Lynes, *The Tastemakers* (New York, 1954), 306; A. E. Kendrew to JDR, n.d., JDR Papers, ser. II (cultural), box 163, RAC; A. D. Whiteside to JDR, June 23, 1947, ibid.

13.   Matthew Lahti to Arthur J. Larsen, Mar. 17, 1947, Minnesota Territorial Centennial, St. Paul Papers (BX7), MinnHS; Nils G. Sahlin to Alford Roos, Aug. 4, 1949, ibid. (P336); Hartje, *Bicentennial U.S.A.,* 144–45.

14.   Martin Behrman to Lyon G. Tyler, Dec. 10, 1913, Tyler Papers, group 5, box 3, SLWM; Robert Moore to John C. Fitzpatrick, Oct. 13, 1936, Fitzpatrick Papers, box 16, MDLC.

15.   Robert Glasgow to Max Farrand, Sept. 9, 1921, Farrand Papers, HEHL; Nathaniel W. Stephenson to Albert B. Hart, Dec. 23, 1922, Hart Papers, box 24, HUA; Dixon Ryan Fox to W. Howard Pillsbury, Nov. 10, 1938, Fox Papers, Schaffer Library, Union College, Schenectady, N.Y.; Fox to Dorothy Burne Goebel, Mar. 20, 1942, ibid.

16.   Geoffrey C. Upward, *A Home for Our Heritage: The Building and Growth of Greenfield Village and Henry Ford Museum, 1929–1979* (Dearborn, 1979), 139; Green to Nevins, Aug. 6, 1954, Nevins Papers (professional), BLCU; Eric Foner, "The Televised Past," *The Nation,* June 16, 1979, 724–25.

17.   Arthur H. Brook to Arthur M. Schlesinger, Nov. 26, 1928, Schlesinger Papers, box 4, HUA; Tracy W. McGregor to Randolph G. Adams, Mar. 22, 1935, McGregor Papers, ALUV; Raymond K. Meixsell to Dixon Ryan Fox, Sept. 1, 1938, Fox Papers, Schaffer Library, Union College, Schenectady, N.Y. In 1940 a president of the A.H.A (Max Farrand) urged that history be popularized by means of radio and film. The A.H.A. briefly sponsored a radio program titled "The Story Behind the Headlines." See Herman Ausubel, *Historians and Their Craft: A Study of the Presidential Addresses of the American Historical Association, 1884–1945* (New York, 1950), 107–08.

18.   Daniel J. Boorstin to Mark DeWolfe Howe, Aug. 22, 1961 (with statement of scope and purpose attached), Howe Papers, box 1, Harvard University Law Library; Virginius Dabney (for the U.S. Bicentennial Society) to Irving Brant, Nov. 5, 1975, Brant Papers, box 5, MDLC; Edmund S. Morgan, "Popular History," *Huntington Spectator* (a newsletter) (Winter 1983).

19.   The Fund for the Republic Archives, boxes 55 and 56, Seeley G. Mudd Manuscript Library, Princeton University.

20.   Wilson to Dos Passos, Nov. 27, 1951, in Edmund Wilson, *Letters on Literature and Politics, 1912–1972,* ed. Elena Wilson (New York, 1977), 504; MacLeish to Dos Passos [n.d., 1951?], Dos Passos Papers, box 3, Manuscripts Division, Special Collections, ALUV, reprinted by permission of the Estate of Archibald MacLeish and of Elizabeth Dos Passos; Richard Chase, "Our Country and Our Culture," *Partisan Review,* 19 (1952), 567–68. For the persistence of Wilson's distressed and gloomy perspective, see Lewis Mumford to Waldo Frank, July 30, 1960, Frank Papers, box 85, Van Pelt Library, University of Pennsylvania.

21.   Van Doren to Trilling, Aug. 10, 1950, Trilling Papers, BLCU (reprinted by permission of Diana Trilling); Trilling to Van Doren, Aug. 30, 1950, Van Doren Papers, BLCU. The book at issue was Howe's *Sherwood Anderson* (New York, 1951).

22.   Dan G. Hoffman, "Sandburg and 'The People': His Literary Populism Reappraised," *Antioch Review,* 10 (1950), 265–78; R. W. B. Lewis, "Warren's Long Visit to

American Literature," *Yale Review,* 70 (1981), 568–91, esp. 570–71; Esther Forbes to Austin Olney [n.d., 1954?], Forbes Papers, private collection.

23. See *Gwathmey: Works from 1941–1983,* an exhibition at the Guild Hall Museum, 1984 (East Hampton, N.Y., 1984); Gwathmey, *Across the Tracks* (1946), in Christie's sale catalogue for Dec. 1, 1989, no. 288; NYT, Aug. 5, 1981, p. C19; Anna Kisselgoff, "Erick Hawkins," *Harvard Magazine* (May–June 1980), 47.

24. Edward Tabor Linenthal, " 'A Reservoir of Spiritual Power': Patriotic Faith at the Alamo in the Twentieth Century," *Southwestern Historical Quarterly,* 91 (1988), 515; C. R. Chandler, "World War II as Southern Entertainment: The Confederate Air Force and Warfare Re-enactment Ritual," in Ray B. Browne, ed., *Rituals and Ceremonies in Popular Culture* (Bowling Green, Ohio, 1980), 258–69.

25. Corning B. Gibbs to JDR, Oct. 14, 1950, JDR Papers, ser. II (cultural), box 176, RAC; Bess Stenbuck to JDR, Nov. 2, 1953, ibid.; Henry R. Howell to JDR, Feb. 24, 1958, ibid., box 177; Olga Lewek to JDR, July 11, 1958, ibid.

26. Paul W. Platter to JDR, Feb. 28, 1953, ibid., box 176; Laurens M. Hamilton to JDR, Feb. 2, 1959, ibid., box 177. See also dozens of similar letters in boxes 176 and 177, and Helen J. Campbell, *Diary of a Williamsburg Hostess* (New York, 1946), 5, 12, 52, 77, 89.

27. Hosmer, *Preservation Comes of Age,* 772, 774, 777; Hugh Grant Rowell to Howard Gould, Oct. 17, 1946, Sleepy Hollow Restoration Archives, box 6, RAC. See also Kenneth A. Erickson, "Ceremonial Landscapes of the American West," *Landscape,* 22, (1977), 39–47.

28. Minette B. Lange to JDR [c. Oct. 1, 1950], JDR Papers, ser. II (cultural), box 176, RAC; Larkin Hoyt to JDR, Feb. 20, 1959, ibid., box 177; Grace D. Cooper to JDR, June 25, 1959, ibid. See also Mrs. George J. Schorr to JDR, July 24, 1959, ibid.; anon. postal card to JDR, Sept. 8, 1951, ibid., box 176; Mrs. Hugh Ely Pankey to JDR, May 9, 1953, ibid.

29. Harold O. Voorhis to Alice M. Runyon, Nov. 6, 1947, SHR Archives, box 6, RAC; Voorhis to Thomas M. Debevoise, May 3, 1948, ibid.; Elliot Baldwin Hunt to Hugh Grant Rowell, Nov. 17, 1949, ibid., box 2.

30. Marquand to Forbes, June 29, 1953, Forbes Papers, Houghton Library, Harvard University; Forbes to Marquand [n.d., 1953], ibid. For the feud between Plymouth and Provincetown concerning the true site of the Pilgrims' first landfall, see NYT, Apr. 28, 1935, sec. 2, p. 1.

31. Earl S. Pomeroy, *In Search of the Golden West: The Tourist in Western America* (New York, 1957), 213; A. B. Guthrie, *The Big Sky* (New York, 1947), 258.

32. Guthrie, *The Big Sky,* 194, 212.

33. Leona Lampi, "Red Lodge: From a Frenetic Past of Crows, Coal and Boom and Bust Emerges a Unique Festival of Diverse Nationality Groups," MMWHC, 11 (1961), 20–31.

34. The papers of Virginia's 350th Anniversary Commission for the years 1954–57 are located in the VHS; Hartje, *Bicentennial U.S.A.,* 136–46.

35. NYT, Apr. 9, 1939, sec. 1, p. 2; *Virginia Gazette,* Feb. 7, 1947, special issue urging a restoration of St. George's in Bermuda.

36. All of the pertinent documents are located in the JDR Papers, ser. II (cultural), box 1, RAC, including Clark to JDR, Jan. 21, 1944; JDR to Hugh Grant Rowell, Feb. 1, 1944; JDR to Dewey, Feb. 11 and 21, and Mar. 8, 1944; Dewey to JDR, Mar. 10, 1944.

37. Report of the Temporary Visiting Committee to Sleepy Hollow Restorations, Inc., Oct. 17, 1952, SHR Archives, RAC; Cater's appointment is described in a press release dated Apr. 25, 1955, ibid., box 6; special events are described in a press release dated Oct. 1, 1956, ibid.; Henk Nieuwenhuize to Mr. Jansen, Apr. 10, 1957, ibid., box 7; Nieuwenhuize to Cater, Mar. 30, 1957; Gilbert Field to Cater, Mar. 15, 1957, ibid.; Edward P. Alexander to Cater, Nov. 11, 1957, ibid., box 7.

38. The survey and all responses are located in ibid., box 17.

39. Thomas G. McCaskey to Joseph Chamberlin, Oct. 16, 1957, ibid., box 7.

40. Arthur Goodfriend to JDR III, Mar. 9, 1954, JDR Papers, ser. II (cultural), box 183, RAC; Kenneth Chorley to JDR III, Apr. 1, 1954, ibid.

41. Goodfriend to JDR III, Mar. 9, 1954, ibid.

42. Minnie Kelter Goldberg to JDR, Nov. 3, 1947, ibid., box 163; Goldberg to Mrs. I. L. Jones, Dec. 1, 1947, ibid.; Kenneth Chorley to JDR, Nov. 18, 1959, ibid.

43. George E. Cohron to Allston Boyer, Mar. 6, 1950, ibid.; James E. Hudson, "Observations on Williamsburg Visit," Nov. 26, 1951, ibid., box 170.

44. JDR to Chorley, Mar. 11, 1948, Chorley Papers, box 2, RAC; Chorley to JDR, Feb. 15, 1952, JDR Papers, ser. II (cultural), box 170, RAC; JDR to Chorley, Feb. 18, 1952, ibid.; JDR III to Chorley, Feb. 10, 1950, ibid.

45. Mrs. Joseph Amore to JDR, Jan. 18, 1958, JDR Papers, ser. II (cultural), box 177, RAC; Wanda Anderson to JDR, June 28, 1959, ibid.

46. David F. Chapman to JDR, Dec. 5, 1949, ibid., box 176; anon. to JDR [Mar. 15, 1953], ibid.; S. G. Nicholas to JDR, Mar. 18, 1960, ibid., box 177.

47. Nelson Rockefeller to Kenneth Chorley, Apr. 2, 1941, box 170; Chorley to Edward R. Stettinius, Apr. 7, 1941, ibid.; Maisie and Bernard Condon to JDR, June 29, 1953, ibid., box 176; James A. Gray, Jr., to JDR, May 30, 1950, ibid.

48. Ralph E. Carpenter, Jr., to Chorley, June 5, 1957, Chorley Papers, box 10, RAC; Chorley, *The Shelburne Museum* (May 20, 1957), a pamphlet in ibid.; remarks by Kenneth Chorley at Wentworth-by-the-Sea, July 22, 1965, in ibid.

49. Agee to Rev. James H. Flye, Jan. [24 ?], 1955, in *Letters of James Agee to Father Flye* (New York, 1962), 222.

50. Chorley to Frank Campsall, June 6, 1944, Chorley Papers, CWA.

51. Upward, *A Home for Our Heritage,* chs. 5–6; Jerome I. Smith, *Robert Hudson Tannahill Research Library* (Dearborn, 1974); Geraldine Strozier, "Henry Ford," *Detroit Free Press,* Dec. 4, 1977, p. 1 of the Women's section.

52. *The Herald,* 6 (Summer 1977), a special issue devoted to "Crossing Over to New Eras" published in Dearborn; unpublished extract from the Ford Museum's Strategic Plan, 1987–89; John L. Wright et al., Report of the Curriculum Committee: The Edison Institute, Henry Ford Museum and Greenfield Village (unpubl. 100-page report, 1981).

53. [Ruth Dyer Wells], *The Wells Family: Founders of the American Optical Company and Old Sturbridge Village* (Southbridge, Mass., 1979), 207–11, 221–30; Robert A. Gross, "Living Farm History, Slightly Revisionist," NYT, April 8, 1973, sec. 10, pp. 4, 17. I am indebted to Ruth Dyer Wells for sending me an unpublished chronology of events in the history of Old Sturbridge Village (covering 1936–73).

54. See Warren Leon and Roy Rosenzweig, eds., *History Museums in the United States: A Critical Assessment* (Urbana, Ill., 1989), esp. chs. 1–5.

55. Letter to the author from John S. Williams, Aug. 6, 1979, with a descriptive enclosure, brochure, and brief history of the Museum. Visit to the Museum by the author on July 27, 1979.

56. Personal visit by the author on Apr. 5, 1986; NYT, Oct. 16, 1972, p. 73; *The Voorlezer's House: An Illustrated Guide* (Richmondtown pamphlet, 1985).

57. Roger Holmes and Paul Bailey, *Fabulous Farmer: The Story of Walter Knott and His Berry Farm* (Los Angeles, 1956), 13–14, 145–46.

58. Ibid., 149; Pomeroy, *In Search of the Golden West,* 193.

59. Richard Schickel, *The Disney Version: The Life, Times, Art and Commerce of Walt Disney* (New York, 1985), ch. 10; Richard V. Francaviglia, "After Walt Disney: The Role of Historic Image-Building in the Preservation and Revitalization of Main Street U.S.A.," paper presented at the annual meeting of the Organization of American Historians, Apr. 8, 1989, St. Louis, Mo. See also Umberto Eco, *Travels in Hyper-Reality: Essays* (San Diego, 1986), 3–58, esp. 4–6, 8–11.

60. Donald R. Friary, "The Noncollectors: Henry and Helen Flynt at Historic Deerfield," TMA, 121 (January 1982), 250–57.

61. Remsen D. Bird to Henry Flynt, June 26, 1957, copy in the JDR Papers, ser. II (cultural), box 163, RAC; David E. Finley, *History of the National Trust for Historic Preservation, 1947–1963* (Washington, D.C., 1965), 14–15.

62. In addition to Finley's short book just cited, see Elizabeth D. Mulloy, *The History of the National Trust for Historic Preservation, 1963–1973* (Washington, D.C., 1976).

63. Guy Stanton Ford to Harry A. Bullis, Dec. 12, 1949, Ford Papers, folder no. 107, University of Minnesota Archives. For an important example of the residual strength of that private sector emphasis on the part of Virginius Dabney, an influential newspaper editor in Richmond, see Francis L. Berkeley, Jr., to Earl G. Swem, Oct. 4, 1955, in Virginia's 350th Anniversary Commission Papers (MSS4 V8 b), VHS.

64. U. S. Grant III, *The Formation of the National Council for Historic Sites and Buildings* (pamphlet: Washington, D.C., n.d.), p. 2, in ibid.

65. Frederick L. Rath, Jr., "The National Trust, 1947–1955: A Summary [unpub.] Report" (May 19, 1956), in Ford Papers, folder no. 112, University of Minnesota Archives.

66. Ibid.

67. "Preservation Week: 'The People's Choice,' " *Preservation News* (February 1988), p. 6; National Trust for Historic Preservation, unpublished "Planning Report on Its Goals" (June 10, 1957), Appendix to Section I: "Policy," Guy Stanton Ford Papers, folder 112, University of Minnesota Archives; letter to new members from President J. Jackson Walter, Aug. 16, 1986.

68. *The Georgia Historical Quarterly,* 63 (Spring 1979), a special issue devoted to "Historic Preservation in Georgia," esp. Jann Haynes Gilmore, "Georgia's Historic Preservation Beginning: The Georgia Historical Commission (1951–1973)," 9–21; NYT, May 15, 1978, p. B5; materials pertaining to historic preservation efforts in Utah are located in the papers of the Matthias Farnsworth Chapter, Utah State Society, Daughters of American Colonists, in the Marriott Library, University of Utah; Merle Wells, "Early Idaho Historic Preservation," unpublished paper (Sept. 16, 1988); brochure of the Preservation League of New York State, 1987.

69. Edmund Drago and Ralph Melnick, "The Old Slave Mart Museum, Charleston, S.C.: Rediscovering the Past," *Civil War History,* 27 (1981), 138–54.

70. Harold Dean Cater to Mrs. Copeland, Feb. 28, 1958, SHR Archives, box 7, RAC; Kenneth Chorley to Vanderbilt Webb et al., Feb. 25, 1955, Chorley Papers, box 1, RAC; Chorley to Meyner, Mar. 11, 1957, ibid.

71. Ada Louise Huxtable, "Experts on Preservation End 4-Day Meeting at Williamsburg," NYT, Sept. 12, 1963, p. 37.

72. Ibid. For the most eloquent and on-going critique of preservation activities in the United States, see Peirce F. Lewis, "The Future of the Past: Our Clouded Vision of Historic Preservation," *Pioneer America,* 7 (1975), 1–20; Lewis, "Defining a Sense of Place," *The Southern Quarterly,* 17 (1979), 24–46.

73. NYT, Nov. 8, 1971, p. 54; Idaho Historic Preservation Council to Redwood City Council, July 18, 1972, Idaho Historic Preservation Council Papers (MS 2/444), Idaho Historical Society, Boise; NYT, Mar. 5, 1978, p. 51; NYT, Sept. 20, 1980, p. 23; NYT, Nov. 2, 1980, sec. 1, p. 45; NYT, Sept. 20, 1981, p. 56; NYT, Mar. 21, 1982, p. 39. For an invaluable overview, see Nathan Weinberg, *Preservation in American Towns and Cities* (Boulder, Colo., 1979).

74. NYT, Feb. 15, 1976, p. 24; Ada Louise Huxtable, "Budget Cutters Are Undermining Historic Buildings," NYT, Apr. 4, 1976, p. D29; NYT, Apr. 11, 1981, p. 22.

75. Jerold S. Kayden, "Penn Central: Ten Years after 'High Noon,' " *Preservation News* (October 1988), p. 5; NYT, July 2, 1978, p. E5.

76. "Preservation and Higher Education," a *Preservation News Supplement* (October 1977), p. 1; NYT, Nov. 19, 1978, p. 85; Steven V. Roberts, "A Small Mill Town Salvages Pieces of America's Past," NYT, Jan. 4, 1979, p. C6; NYT, May 5, 1980, p. B2; NYT, Oct. 12, 1984, p. B1; NYT, Jan. 19, 1986, p. 38.

77. Tamara Hareven, "The Search for Generational Memory," *Daedalus,* 107 (1978), 147; *Preservation News* (October 1982), p. 8; Sara Chase, "My Fling With Fame," *Historic Preservation,* 40 (January 1988), 57–59; NYT, Aug. 25, 1988, p. C10.

78. See John Maass, "Architecture and Americanism, or Pastiches of Independence Hall," *Historic Preservation,* 22 (April 1970), 17–25.

79. Ainslie, ". . . A National Memory," *Preservation News* (March 1982), p. 5.

80. Barbara Gamarekian, "Preservation Fights to Preserve Itself," NYT, Oct. 11, 1985, p. A22. For an excellent analysis of the preservation movement as a window on American capitalism, see Michael Wallace, "Reflections on the History of Historic Preservation," in Benson et al., eds., *Presenting the Past: Essays on History and the Public,* 165–99.

81. The documentation for this project is located in the Fund for the Republic Papers, box 113 (Hall of Our History), Mudd Library, Princeton University. One of the most detailed schematizations is a two-page memorandum from Montgomery S. Bradley to Mr. Freeman, Sept. 25, 1953.

82. Ibid.

83. Ibid. Hand's essay appeared on Aug. 9, 1953.

84. Rev. W. Herbert Burk, *Making a Museum: The Confessions of a Curator* (Valley Forge, Pa., 1926), 54–55.

85. See Aline B. Saarinen, *The Proud Possessors: The Lives, Times and Tastes of Some Adventurous American Art Collectors* (New York, 1958), 287–325; John A. H. Sweeney, *Henry Francis du Pont* (Winterthur, Del., 1980); Walter Karp, "Electra Webb and Her American Past," AH, 33 (April 1982), 16–29.

86. Donald R. Friary, "The Noncollectors: Helen and Henry Flynt at Historic Deerfield," TMA, 121 (January 1982), 250–57; Abbot Lowell Cummings, ed., "Restoration Villages," a special issue of *Art in America,* 43 (May 1955); John Parker, *James Ford Bell and His Books* (pamphlet: n.p., n.d.); Edwin Wolf, 2nd, *Rosenbach: A Biography* (Cleveland, 1960), 217, 257.

87. *The Abby Aldrich Rockefeller Folk Art Collection: An Address by Mitchell A. Wilder . . . on the Occasion of the Opening of the Collection, Mar. 15, 1957* (pamphlet: n.p., 1957); Kenneth Chorley to JDR, Mar. 21, 1957, JDR Papers, ser. II (cultural), box 174, RAC; David B. Warren, "Ima Hogg, Collector," TMA, 121 (January 1982), 228–43.

88. Alice Winchester to the author, July 6, 1981; Wanda M. Corn, "The Return of the Native: The Development of Interest in American Primitive Painting" (unpubl. M.A. thesis, New York University, 1965), 38–40.

89. Meryl Secrest, "Pokety: Americana, Art and Peace of Mind," *The Washington Post,* June 1, 1969, p. E1; obituary of Walter P. Chrysler, Jr., NYT, Sept. 10, 1988, p. B10; *Washington Evening Star,* June 13, 1969, p. E4.

90. James T. Flexner, "The Cult of the Primitives," AH, 6 (February 1955), 38–47; Louis C. Jones, "The Folk Art Collection," *Art in America,* 38 (1950), 109–28; "What Is American Folk Art? A Symposium," TMA, 57 (May 1950), 355–62; Jane S. Becker and Barbara Franco, eds., *Folk Roots, New Roots: Folklore in American Life* (Lexington, Mass., 1988), 141–93.

91. "Remarks by Mr. Wilder" (Mar. 15, 1957), pp. 3 and 5 of a typescript supplied to the author by Beatrix T. Rumford, Vice President (Museums) at C.W. See also Bruce R. Buckley, "New Beginnings and Old Ends: Museums, Folklife, and the Cooperstown Experiment," *Folklore Historian,* 1 (1984), 24–31.

92. *The Museums at Stony Brook: Highlights of the Collection* (Stony Brook, N.Y., 1982); *The Carriage Collection* (Stony Brook, N.Y., 1986); David Cassedy and Gail Shrott, *William Sidney Mount: Works in the Collection of the Museums at Stony Brook* (Stony Brook, N.Y., 1983); "History of the Museums at Stony Brook," in *The Carriage Museum* (Stony Brook, N.Y., 1987), 19–37.

93. Peter J. Gomes, "Henry Hornblower II," *Proceedings* of the MHS, 97 (1985), 157–60; NYT, Oct. 23, 1985, p. B6.

94. Charles F. Montgomery, "Francis P. Garvan," TMA, 121 (January 1982), 244–49; John B. Hench, "Pierce Welch Gaines," *Proceedings* of the AAS, 87 (October 1977), 257–59; Michael Walsh, "Adventures in Americana," in George Allen et al., *Four Talks for Bibliophiles* (Philadelphia, 1958), 83–85; *Americana—Beginnings. A Selection from the Library of Thomas W. Streeter . . . May 3, 1951* (Morristown, N.J., 1952).

95. Rita Reif, "In Pursuit of Pewter Tankards and Teapots," NYT, Apr. 5, 1981, sec. 2, p. 29; Rita Reif, "Masters of Early American Furniture," NYT, Oct. 12, 1986, p. H35; *The Washington Post,* June 7, 1989, p. C1.

96. Abram Lerner, "Development of a Collector: Joseph Hirshhorn," *American Art Review*, 2 (1975), 79–94; Saarinen, *The Proud Possessors*, 269–86.

Chapter 17

1. Harlan D. Unrau and G. Frank Williss, "To Preserve the Nation's Past: The Growth of Historic Preservation in the National Park Service During the 1930s," PH, 9 (1987), 40–41.

2. Warren I. Susman, *Culture as History: The Transformation of American Society in the Twentieth Century* (New York, 1984), 256. See also Walter Rundell, Jr., "Uncle Sam the Historian: Federal Historical Activities," *The Historian*, 33 (1970), 1–20.

3. William E. Leuchtenburg, *In the Shadow of FDR: From Harry Truman to Ronald Reagan* (Ithaca, N.Y., 1983), 32; Ernest R. May, *"Lessons of the Past": The Use and Misuse of History in American Foreign Policy* (New York, 1973). See also Charles A. Miller, *The Supreme Court and the Uses of History* (Cambridge, Mass., 1969).

4. George E. Mowry, "The Uses of History by Recent Presidents," JAH, 53 (1966), 1–18; Arthur M. Schlesinger, Jr., "The Historian and History," *Foreign Affairs*, 41 (1963), 491–97.

5. For theoretical context and background, see Samuel H. Beer, "Federalism, Nationalism, and Democracy in America," *American Political Science Review*, 72 (1978), 9–21; Paul Horgan, "Preface to an Unwritten Book," *Yale Review*, 65 (1976), 321–35.

6. See Allen Weinstein, "The Symbolism of Subversion: Notes on Some Cold War Icons," *Journal of American Studies*, 6 (1972), 165–79; "A Report to the National Security Council by the Executive Secretary (James S. Lay, Jr.), Apr. 14, 1950, approved by President Truman on Apr. 12, 1950 (known as NSC 68), in *Foreign Relations of the United States*, I (1950), 235–93.

7. Calvin Tomkins, *Merchants and Masterpieces: The Story of the Metropolitan Museum of Art* (New York, 1970), 291.

8. Roy Rosenzweig, "Marketing the Past: *American Heritage* and Popular History in the United States," in Susan Porter Benson et al., eds., *Presenting the Past: Essays on History and the Public* (Philadelphia, 1986), 25, 364; Guthrie, *The Way West* (New York, 1950), 307, 340; Perry Miller, "Europe's Faith in American Fiction," in Miller, *The Responsibility of Mind in a Civilization of Machines* (Amherst, Mass., 1979), 132–33.

9. Russell Weigley, ed., *New Dimensions in Military History: An Anthology* (San Rafael, Calif., 1975), 7, 20; John Hellmann, *American Myth and the Legacy of Vietnam* (New York, 1986), 44–45.

10. This and the paragraphs that follow are based upon the American Heritage Foundation Papers, National Archives Gift Collection, Record Group 200, Washington, D.C., and the Thomas D'Arcy Brophy Papers located in the Wisconsin State Historical Society, Madison.

11. In addition to the two large collections cited in note 10, I am indebted to James Gregory Bradsher, "Taking America's Heritage to the People: The Freedom Train Story," *Prologue*, 17 (1985), 229–46, and John Fousek, "The Freedom Train, 1947–1949" (unpubl. graduate seminar paper, Cornell University, 1986).

12. Nina Tumarkin, *Lenin Lives! The Lenin Cult in Soviet Russia* (Cambridge, Mass., 1983), 68.

13. Chorley to JDR III, Apr. 7, 1948, Chorley Papers, box 1, RAC. In this same letter Chorley mistakenly referred to Brophy as president of the Hermitage Foundation.

14. JDR to Henry Ford, July 26 and Oct. 10, 1941, and Ford to JDR, Oct. 7, 1941, FA.

15. Memorandum from Chorley to JDR, 1941, Chorley Papers, box 1, RAC; JDR III to Paley, July 17, 1942, JDR Papers, ser. II (cultural), box 172, RAC; Paley to JDR III, July 31, 1942, ibid.; Abby Aldrich Rockefeller to Mrs. Alice Griswold, Apr. 30, 1943, AAR Papers, box 9, RAC.

16. JDR III to JDR, Aug. 31 and Nov. 22, 1949, JDR Papers, ser. II (cultural), box 182, RAC; confidential memorandum written by JDR III, Mar. 28, 1951, ibid.

17. "Explicit Statement of Purposes of Trip," undated memorandum by JDR III, ibid.; JDR III to John J. McCloy (U.S. High Commissioner for Germany), June 2, 1950, ibid.

18. John C. Goodbody to JDR III, Oct. 30, 1950, ibid.; Kershaw Burbank to JDR III, Nov. 6, 1950, ibid.

19. Ibid.; untitled confidential memorandum by JDR III, Mar. 28, 1951, ibid.; JDR to McCloy, June 2, 1950, ibid.

20. The undated eight-point program is located in ibid.; Chorley to JDR and JDR III, Feb. 19, 1951, ibid., box 184.

21. JDR III to James E. Webb (Acting Secretary of State), Apr. 12, 1950, ibid., box 183; Webb to JDR III, May 22, 1950, ibid.

22. NYT, May 30, 1983, p. 38; NYT, Jan. 10, 1984, pp. A1 and 6.

23. Much of the documentation for these conferences and visits will be found in the JDR Papers, ser. II (cultural), boxes 182–84. See esp. Allen Matthews to Kershaw Burbank, Feb. 19, 1951, ibid., box 182. Matthews was the producer of *The Common Glory,* an outdoor historical drama sponsored by the Jamestown Corporation. For context concerning the conference of exiled leaders, see Piotr Wandycz, *The United States and Poland* (Cambridge, Mass., 1980), 351.

24. JDR to JDR III, Nov. 30, 1949, and June 16, 1952, JDR Papers, ser. II (cultural), box 182; JDR III to JDR, Nov. 19, 1952, ibid.; JDR III to Chorley, Jan. 12, 1955, ibid.; Chorley's memorandum to Laurence S. Rockefeller, Apr. 27, 1964, illuminates the basic attitudes of JDR, Jr., toward C.W.

25. Statement from the Board of C.W. to JDR III, Dec. 6–7, 1954, ibid., box 182.

26. Confidential memorandum written by JDR III, Mar. 28, 1951, ibid.; Dr. Victor Davis Miller to JDR, Oct. 30, 1950, ibid., box 176.

27. NYT, Oct. 19, 1950, pp. 13, 15; NYT, Oct. 23, 1950, p. 22; Kershaw Burbank to JDR III, Nov. 6, 1950, JDR Papers, ser. II (cultural), box 182; Chorley to Mr. and Mrs. JDR, Feb. 20, 1956, ibid., box 166.

28. Kenneth Chorley to Janet Warfield, June 27, 1956, JDR Papers, ser. II (cultural), box 163.

29. See, however, Michael Kammen, *A Season of Youth: The American Revolution and the Historical Imagination* (New York, 1978), and Kammen, *A Machine That Would Go of Itself: The Constitution in American Culture* (New York, 1986).

30. Copies of the Commission's Interim Report (June 15, 1956) and Eisenhower's Proclamation will be found in the papers of the Abraham Lincoln Sesquicentennial Commission, box 38, MDLC.

31. See ibid. for folders pertaining to the Illinois and Indiana commissions and the Lincoln Group of Washington. Box 37 contains the Sesquicentennial Commission's general correspondence.

32. The typescript of Brandt's address will be found in ibid., box 38.

33. Some useful background may be found in Robert G. Hartje, *Bicentennial U.S.A.: Pathways to Celebration* (Nashville, Tenn., 1973), ch. 4.

34. William H. Stauffer to U. S. Grant III, Jan. 12, 1958, CWCC Papers, box 8, NA.

35. *The Washington Post,* Apr. 9, 1958, p. A13. Other familiar names surfaced during the Centennial. Robert E. Lee IV served as national advertising manager of the *San Francisco Chronicle* and assisted the Centennial Commission's Television and Radio Committee. Lyon G. Tyler, Jr., served as assistant director of the Virginia Civil War Commission.

36. Milton Rubincam, "Major General U. S. Grant, 3rd, 1881–1968," in *Records of the Columbia Historical Society, 1966–1968* (Washington, D.C., 1969), 369–408; *The National Cyclopedia of American Biography,* 54 (Clifton, N.J., 1973), 401–02; NYT, Aug. 30, 1968, p. 33.

37. *The Washington Post,* June 20, 1959, p. A12; Joseph S. Clark to Clinton Anderson, Aug. 11, 1959, and Anderson to Clark, Aug. 15, 1959, Clinton P. Anderson Papers (Special Committees series), box 874, MDLC. I am indebted to Richard A. Baker, Historian of the U.S. Senate, for copies of these and other documents in the Anderson Papers.

38.   Grant to Francis A. Lord, Mar. 23, 1960, CWCC Papers, box 96, NA; Grant to Karl S. Betts, Aug. 28, 1960, ibid.; Grant to Frank C. Bollinger, Sept. 25, 1961, ibid.

39.   The Commission's two-page press release about Betts, dated for release on Apr. 6, 1958, in ibid., box 94. See Hartje, *Bicentennial U.S.A.*, 69; and John L. Blount to U.S. Grant III, Feb. 6, 1958, CWCC Papers, box 96, NA. Blount wrote on behalf of the Century Mark Association of America, an African-American group based in Seattle that planned to celebrate the centennial of emancipation.

40.   Betts to Conrad L. Wirth, Oct. 31, 1957, CWCC Papers, box 100, NA.

41.   A copy of the brochure and material from *Printer's Ink,* Apr. 28, 1960, can be found in ibid., box 8; H. W. Pearson (Pearson Sales Company, Advertising Specialties) to Karl S. Betts, Nov. 14, 1960, ibid.; William J. Dopkowski (Animated Displays Company) to Karl S. Betts, Mar. 23, 1961, ibid., box 28.

42.   A copy of the service bulletin (April–May 1960) is located in ibid., box 8.

43.   A copy of the speech is located in ibid., box 96. In July 1961 Congressman Emanuel Cellar, chairman of the House Judiciary Committee, criticized Grant sharply for his carelessness in permitting commercialization by private firms. See Cellar to Grant, July 6, 1961, and Grant's reply, July 20, 1961, in ibid., box 22.

44.   A copy of Nevins's statement is located in ibid., box 97.

45.   Documents and programs that illustrate these points are located in ibid., boxes 54, 94, and 97.

46.   For Centennial Night in Kansas City, St. Louis, and Wilmington, see ibid., box 30.

47.   Ylavaune Howard to James I. Robertson, July 31 and Nov. 8, 1962, ibid., box 55 (Mrs. Howard of Massillon, Ohio, was president of the Daughters of Union Veterans); Hartje, *Bicentennial U.S.A.*, 80–81; Catton is quoted in the *Richmond News Leader,* May 2, 1961, p. 10.

48.   I am indebted to Dr. Richard A. Baker, Historian of the U.S. Senate, for providing me with a copy of the unpublished transcript of Proceedings, Aug. 30, 1961, from the papers of Senator Clinton Anderson. There was an amusing moment at the outset when confusion emerged over the written call to the meeting: a "personnel problem" or a "personal problem"?

49.   Robertson refused the position when first asked. "Upon reflection, however, I reasoned that if a Southerner did not move into the hierarchy of the Commission, it would not only jeopardize future action but alienate our Southern commissions as well." Robertson to T. R. Hay, Feb. 21, 1962, CWCC Papers, box 100, NA.

50.   *The Washington Post,* Oct. 17, 1961, p. B10; Nevins's "Speech of Welcome" to the State and National Commission delegates, Washington, D.C., Jan. 31, 1962, CWCC Papers, box 69, NA.

51.   Nevins to James Robertson, Feb. 17, 1962, CWCC Papers, box 97, NA; A. B. Moore to Allan Nevins, Mar. 21, 1962, Nevins Papers, box 88, BLCU.

52.   Nevins to Stevenson, Aug. 24, 1962, CWCC Papers, box 97, NA; James I. Robertson, Jr., to the author, Oct. 26, 1981.

53.   "At the Lincoln Memorial," Archibald MacLeish, *New & Collected Poems, 1917– 1976* (Boston, 1976), 432–35.

54.   Robertson to Nevins, June 18, 1963, CWCC Papers, box 97, NA.

55.   Nevins to Edmund C. Gass, Apr. 25, 1966, ibid., box 101. For similar issues and problems when John Y. Simon attempted his assessment of the Centennial, see Simon to Gass, Aug. 23, 1965, and Gass to Simon, Sept. 10, 1965, ibid., box 96.

56.   Grant to Betts, Mar. 4, 1961, ibid., box 96; Edmund C. Gass to John Y. Simon, Sept. 2, 1965, ibid.

57.   Hartje, *Bicentennial U.S.A.*, 74, 77, 88; Betts to Grant, July 5, 1961, CWCC Papers, box 96, NA; Betts to Charles T. Moses, Feb. 16, 1960, ibid., box 90.

58.   Press release by the Virginia Civil War Commission, May 8, 1959, CWCC Papers, box 90, NA; James J. Geary to James I. Robertson, Mar. 4, 1964, and Robertson to Geary, Mar. 9, 1964, ibid., box 91. Robertson assured Geary that "the thing we are most desirous of preventing in 1965 is a series of commemorations that will ostensibly conflict or

compete with one another. . . . My concern is that an historical or commemorative fight might break out between Appomattox and Durham Station. This I think we should prevent at all costs."

59.   A copy of the program for Apr. 9, 1965, is located in ibid., box 91.

60.   Hartje, *Bicentennial U.S.A.*, 84; "Program of the Kentucky Civil War Centennial, 1961–1965," CWCC Papers, box 76, NA.

61.   A description of events arranged for Fort Sumter in April 1961 by the South Carolina Confederate Centennial Commission and the Greater Charleston Chamber of Commerce is located in CWCC Papers, box 100, NA; U. S. Grant III to Mrs. George Northrup Foote (of Batavia, N.Y.), Feb. 12, 1961, ibid., box 96; Ray Ward (of Towanda, Pa.) to Centennial Commission, Apr. 22, 1963, ibid., box 54.

62.   Grant to Betts, Oct. 9, 1960, ibid., box 96; William L. Shaw to Centennial Commission, Mar. 29, 1963, ibid., box 30.

63.   Grant to Frank T. Bow, May 22, 1961, ibid., box 96; *Richmond News Leader*, May 2, 1961, p. 10; Hartje, *Bicentennial U.S.A.*, 87–89.

64.   Nevins to James I. Robertson, June 1, 1962, CWCC Papers, box 97, NA; Robertson to Nevins, July 10 and Aug. 22, 1962, ibid.; Gass to John Simon, Sept. 10, 1965, ibid., box 96.

65.   Robert Penn Warren, *The Legacy of the Civil War* (Cambridge, Mass., 1961), 3, 59, 60.

66.   Wilson to Dos Passos, May 30, 1962, Dos Passos Papers, box 5, ALUV. Used with the permission of Edmund Wilson's Estate, copyright © 1990 by Helen Miranda Wilson.

67.   Kenneth Stuart to R. C. Brown, Nov. 25, 1960, CWCC Papers, box 8, NA.

68.   Paley to Betts, Feb. 25, 1960, ibid., box 98; Mort R. Lewis to Betts, June 16, 1960, ibid.

69.   James I. Robertson to Nevins, Aug. 1 and 9, 1963, ibid., box 97; Nevins to Robertson [August 1963], and Aug. 7, 1963, ibid.

70.   Robertson to Nevins, Feb. 11 and 12, 1963, ibid.; Robertson to Wiley, Oct. 22, 1963, ibid., box 99.

71.   Robertson to Nevins, Jan. 11, 1963, ibid., box 97. The Civil War Centennial Commission had a standing committee with the curious title of Criteria and Recognition whose duties were to "adopt standards for the selection of Civil War women for recognition and also select those women from the nominees."

72.   Robertson to Schwengel, Nov. 16, 1962, ibid., box 99; Mrs. L. M. Bashinsky (Chairman of the Jefferson Davis Hall of Fame Committee) to U. S. Grant III, Apr. 13, 1960, ibid., box 55.

73.   O'Mahoney's resolution is located in ibid., box 100; literature produced by patriotic societies in box 54.

74.   A detailed calendar of pilgrimages and related events is located in ibid., box 30; Thomas L. Blake to Karl S. Betts, Jan. 4, 1960, ibid., box 29; copy of the *Guide* in ibid., box 28, see p. 8.

75.   Clifford Dowdey, "The Case for the Confederacy," in Louis D. Rubin, Jr., and James J. Kilpatrick, eds., *The Lasting South: Fourteen Southerners Look at Their Home* (Chicago, 1957), 34; documents pertaining to the Confederate High Command, including a "short history" of it, are located in CWCC Papers, box 54, NA.

76.   The text of Wirth's presentation will be found in CWCC Papers, box 11, NA.

77.   See Martin Anderson, *The Federal Bulldozer: A Critical Analysis of Urban Renewal, 1949–1962* (Cambridge, Mass., 1964); Lewis Mumford, *The Highway and the City* (New York, 1963). For an especially balanced and shrewd analysis, see Kevin Lynch, *What Time Is This Place?* (Cambridge, Mass., 1972), ch. 2, "The Presence of the Past."

78.   See Robert E. Stipe and Antoinette J. Lee, eds., *The American Mosaic: Preserving a Nation's Heritage* (Washington, D.C., 1987); Conrad L. Wirth, *Parks, Politics, and the People* (Norman, Okla., 1980); Theodore R. Johnson, "The Memorialization of Woodrow Wilson" (unpubl. Ph.D. diss., The George Washington University, 1979).

79.   Robert G. Athearn, *The Mythic West in Twentieth-Century America* (Lawrence, Kans., 1986), 215; Ronald F. Lee, *United States: Historical and Archaeological Monu-*

ments (Mexico City, 1951); Edwin C. Bearss, "The National Park Service and Its History Program: 1864–1986—An Overview," PH, 9 (1987), 15; Hal Rothman, *Preserving Different Pasts: The American National Monuments* (Urbana, Ill., 1989), xvi–xvii.

80. Brian W. Dippie, *Custer's Last Stand: The Anatomy of an American Myth* (Missoula, Mont., 1976), 25; Constance M. Greiff, *Independence: The Creation of a National Park* (Philadelphia, 1987), esp. chs. 3–4, 6–7; William E. Lingelbach, "Philadelphia and the Conservation of the National Heritage," *Pennsylvania History*, 20 (1953), 339–56.

81. Malcolm Freiberg, "From Family to Nation: The Old House Becomes a National Historic Site," MHS *Proceedings*, 98 (1986), 60–77; Dwight T. Pitcaithley, "Longfellow National Historic Site: A Preservation History," paper presented to the Organization of American Historians, New York City, April 1986.

82. Barbara Blumberg, *Celebrating the Immigrant: An Administrative History of the Statue of Liberty National Monument, 1952–1982* (Boston, 1985); John Bodnar, "Symbols and Servants: Immigrant America and the Limits of Public History," JAH, 73 (1986), 137–51; NYT, Nov. 26, 1978, p. 56.

83. Lester J. Cappon, "Why Presidential Libraries?" *Yale Review*, 68 (1978), 11–34; NYT, Oct. 21, 1979, p. 30; NYT, Oct. 22, 1979, p. A16; NYT, Nov. 11, 1979, p. 50; NYT, Apr. 29, 1979, p. E19; NYT, Aug. 27, 1984, p. A18.

84. See, however, Leuchtenburg, *In the Shadow of FDR*, 57, 59; Arthur M. Schlesinger, Jr., to Richard Hofstadter, Dec. 11, 1967, Hofstadter Papers, BLCU; Arthur M. Schlesinger, Jr., *The Imperial Presidency* (Boston, 1973), x.

85. Jay David, ed., *The Kennedy Reader* (Indianapolis, 1967), 8; John F. Kennedy to Dos Passos, Sept. 14, 1961, Dos Passos Papers, box 2, ALUV; Schlesinger to Merle Curti, May 1, 1962, Curti Papers, box 36, SHSW.

86. John Greenya, "The Quiet Power of Gordon Gray," *Historic Preservation*, 35 (September 1983), 26–29; Oscar S. Gray, "The Response of Federal Legislation to Historic Preservation," *Law and Contemporary Problems*, 36 (1971), 312–28; Jacob H. Morrison, *Historic Preservation Law* (1957: Washington, D.C., 1965).

87. Michael Wallace, "Reflections on the History of Historic Preservation," in Benson et al., eds., *Presenting the Past: Essays on History and the Public*, 185; Edmund Drago and Ralph Melnick, "The Old Slave Mart Museum, Charleston, S.C.: Rediscovering the Past," *Civil War History*, 27 (1981), 140.

88. Public Law 89-674 (Oct. 15, 1966), in *U.S. Statutes at Large*, vol. 80, 89th Congress (1966), p. 953; Fred Schwengel to the author, Feb. 3, 1982, and interviews with Schwengel in March 1982 while Schwengel served as president of the U.S. Capitol Historical Society.

89. Bearss, "The National Park Service and Its History Program," 17; AHA *Newsletter* (April 1978), p. 2; NYT, Apr. 6, 1986, p. 43; Lloyd Falgoust (U.S. Department of Education) to LaVerne D. Knezek (Texas Christian University), Sept. 29, 1981, announcing abolition of the Ethnic Heritage Studies Program. See Louis Morton, "The Historian and the Federal Government: A Proposal for a Government-wide Historical Office," *Prologue*, 3 (1971), 3–14.

90. Dippie, *Custer's Last Stand*, 47; Frederick L. Rath, Jr., "A Case Study of the Operations of Eastern National Park & Monument Association in Support of National Parks: A Site Specific Example of Public-Private Partnership," unpublished paper (Apr. 9, 1986); Jerry L. Rogers, "The National Register of Historic Places: A Personal Perspective on the First Twenty Years," PH, 9 (1987), 96.

91. Martin Filler, "A Clash of Tastes at the White House," NYT *Magazine*, Nov. 2, 1980, pp. 82–84, 86, 89, 108; Barbara Gamarekian, "A Curator's Philosophy," NYT, Nov. 10, 1982, p. B6.

92. Walter Rundell, Jr., *In Pursuit of American History* (Norman, Okla., 1970), vii; NYT, Dec. 6, 1979, p. A30; NYT, Dec. 17, 1979, p. A26; NYT *Magazine*, Dec. 2, 1973, pp. 96–97; OAH *Newsletter* (November 1983); *The Washington Post*, Dec. 18, 1989, p. D7.

93. Marion Clawson, "Living Historical Farms: A Proposal for Action," *Agricultural History*, 39 (1965), 110–11; NYT, June 24, 1981, p. A14; NYT, Dec. 10, 1981, p. B3; NYT,

Dec. 26, 1981, p. A14; NYT, Jan. 31, 1982, p. 32; Public Law 372 (Aug. 11, 1955), in *U.S. Statutes at Large*, vol. 69, 84th Congress (1955), p. 694.

94. Richard Polenberg, *One Nation Divisible: Class, Race, and Ethnicity in the United States Since 1938* (New York, 1980), 244, 246, 248. Needless to say, such interest was not unprecedented. Scandinavian-Americans, for example, celebrated a variety of centennials with considerable enthusiasm between 1938 and 1948 when Swedish-Americans promoted their Pioneer Centennial. For documentation, see the Minnesota Territory Centennial Papers (P336), box 13, MinnHS.

95. *U.S. Statutes at Large*, vol. 86, 92nd Congress (1972), pp. 346–48 (Sec. 504, Title IX, amending the Elementary and Secondary Education Act of 1965); NYT, Jan. 28, 1974, p. 11.

96. See Howard W. Marshall, "Folklife and the Rise of American Folk Museums," *Journal of American Folklore*, 90 (1977), 391–413; Angus K. Gillespie and Tom Ayres, "Folklore in the Pine Barrens: The Pinelands Cultural Society," *New Jersey History*, 97 (1979), 221–43; Jerrold Hirsch, "Folklore in the Making: B. A. Botkin," *Journal of American Folklore*, 100 (1987), 3–38.

97. Archie Green, "A Keynote: Stitching Patchwork in Public," in Burt Feintuch, ed., *The Conservation of Culture: Folklorists and the Public Sector* (Lexington, Ky., 1988), 20; Public Law 94-201 (Jan. 2, 1976), in *U.S. Statutes at Large*, vol. 89, 94th Congress (1976), pp. 1129–33.

98. Ibid., p. 1129.

99. Barry Mackintosh, *The National Historic Preservation Act and the National Park Service: A History* (Washington, D.C., 1986), 66–72.

Chapter 18

1. Gerald Clarke, "The Meaning of Nostalgia," *Time*, May 3, 1971, p. 77; "Exploring America's Past," *Newsweek*, July 9, 1973, pp. 50–56; Martin E. Marty, "Looking Backward into the Future," NYT, Feb. 6, 1975, p. 33.

2. Fred Davis, *Yearning for Yesterday: A Sociology of Nostalgia* (New York, 1979); "American Anxiety on the Rise," *Human Ecology Forum*, 10 (Fall 1979), 19; Tom Wicker, "The Hunters in the Woods," NYT, Nov. 26, 1972, p. E9; David Glassberg, "History and the Public: Legacies of the Progressive Era," JAH, 73 (1987), 979–80.

3. MacLeish to Dos Passos, Mar. 29, [1967 ?], and undated, Dos Passos Papers, box 3, ALUV.

4. Wallace Stegner, *The Sound of Mountain Water* (Garden City, N.Y., 1969), 192. See also Arthur P. Dudden, "Nostalgia and the American," *Journal of the History of Ideas*, 22 (1961), 515–30; Richard Mervin Weaver, *The Southern Tradition at Bay: A History of Postbellum Thought* (New Rochelle, N.Y., 1968).

5. Walter Muir Whitehill, "History in the Country," NYH, 43 (1962), 319–35; John T. Schlebecker, *Living Historical Farms: A Walk into the Past* (Washington, D.C., 1968), 5, 8; Stuart Bolger, *Genesee Country Museum: Scenes of Town & Country in the Nineteenth Century* (Rochester, N.Y., 1985); Jerry Klein, "Grant's Galena: An Illinois Town That Time Forgot," NYT, Nov. 26, 1978, sec. 10, p. 1.

6. Tamara K. Hareven and Randolph Langenbach, "Living Places, Work Places and Historical Identity," in David Lowenthal and Marcus Binney, eds., *Our Past Before Us: Why Do We Save It?* (London, 1981), 115–16.

7. David B. Warren, *Bayou Bend* (Houston, 1975), viii; Robert E. Spiller, ed., *The Van Wyck Brooks–Lewis Mumford Letters: The Record of a Literary Friendship* (New York, 1970), 2; Malcolm Forbes, *More Than I Dreamed* (New York, 1989), 208, 210.

8. See Robert Hewison, *The Heritage Industry: Britain in a Climate of Decline* (London, 1987), and *British Heritage*, a popular magazine that began publication in 1979. Scotland offers the [Robert] Burns Heritage Trail (Alloway to Dumfries); Linlithgow

Heritage Trail; and Dunfermline Heritage, which includes the burial place of Robert the Bruce and the birthplace of Andrew Carnegie. Examples in Canada include Heritage Park in Calgary, and Heritage Collection at the Whyte Museum of the Canadian Rockies in Banff, both located in Alberta. See also Siegfried Lenz, *The Heritage: The History of a Detestable Word* (New York, 1981), a German novel whose original title (1978) literally translated as *The Homeland Museum.* The book's principal theme is the huge chasm between Germany's perception of past and present, a gap caused by the Nazis' warped use of the concepts of "homeland," heritage, and history to legitimize nationalistic xenophobia and the doctrine of racial purity.

9. See *Preservation News* (September 1986), pp. 7, 11; proclamation issued by Governor Cuomo on Dec. 18, 1987.

10. The Cunneen-Hackett Cultural Center in Poughkeepsie, N.Y., is described as a "Center for Our Nineteenth-Century Heritage at Work in Today's Community." A *Guide to Mendocino County Heritage Attractions* in Northern California is structure-oriented; and brochures published by the Preservation Society of Newport County, R.I., have reiterated a "heritage" emphasis ever since 1970.

11. *Los Angeles Times,* Dec. 23, 1976, p. 6.

12. Ibid., p. 4.

13. The annual Penn School Heritage Celebration started in 1981 on St. Helena Island, S.C., and responds to the question: What Is the Gullah Culture? In 1989 several institutions located in the Southern Tier sponsored a conference and exhibit titled "A Heritage Uncovered: The Black Experience in New York State."

14. NYT, Nov. 8, 1987, p. 62.

15. In 1963 the D.A.R. designated "American Heritage" programs as its foremost educational priority. *The Black Powder Report* is a Western magazine devoted to "Preserving the American Heritage Through Black Powder Shooting."

16. NYT, Sept. 8, 1985, p. A78.

17. See Carl Becker, *Everyman His Own Historian: Essays on History and Politics* (New York, 1935), pp. 247–48.

18. *Smithsonian* (December 1985), p. 143. The D.C. Committee to Promote Washington offers a D.C. Heritage Packet; and Heritage Trails offers nine tours of Connecticut that range from a Colonial Candlelight Dinner in Farmington to Hartford in One Hour.

19. *Preserving Our Heritage Through "Living History"* (Green Bay, Wis., n.d.).

20. Michael Wallace, "Reflections on the History of Historic Preservation," in Susan Porter Benson et al., eds., *Presenting the Past: Essays on History and the Public* (Philadelphia, 1986), 177. Early in the 1980s the National Trust and Christie's auction house jointly established a Gifts of Heritage program in order to raise money for historic preservation. "The tax advantages of making such a gift may be significant."

21. A flossy magazine titled *Alabama Heritage* invites the reader to "take an Alabama Odyssey." In 1988, the Theatre Department at the University of Idaho presented "Idaho Heritage," a musical dramatization of Idaho history that toured the state in order to inaugurate its centennial celebration. The Gene Autry Western Heritage Museum in Los Angeles is devoted to portraying the American West "and the development of our current fictional image of the West." Early in the 1980s the American Peoples' Heritage Center, located in Minneapolis, changed its name to the Citizen Heritage Center, a non-profit organization devoted to "the democratic tradition in America."

22. NYT, Dec. 20, 1975, p. 26. See the 1987 prospectus for the Minnetrista Cultural Center in Muncie, Indiana: "Preserving the Heritage of East Central Indiana." The Center opened late in 1988.

23. Claudia J. Hoone, "Planning for Local Heritage Projects," *Hoosier Heritage,* 3 (March 1986); Joan R. Challinor and Wilcomb E. Washburn, "Five Ways We Can Hail Columbus," *The Washington Post,* Oct. 11, 1987, p. H5. See also "The National Park Service and Historic Preservation," a special issue of PH, 9 (1987); Betty Shaw, "Interpreting Our Outdoor Heritage," *Museum News,* 44 (June 1966), 24–28.

24. Bemis to Brooks, June 12, 1953, Brooks Papers, Van Pelt Library (Rare Book Collection), University of Pennsylvania, Philadelphia. See also Perry Miller, *Errand into the Wilderness* (Cambridge, Mass., 1956), viii–ix.

25. Countee Cullen, *On These I Stand* (New York, 1947), 24–28. It may be instructive, though not entirely attractive, to contemplate a letter that Herbert Hoover wrote in 1912: "In these days of stifling struggle our people need something to bring back to them the heritage, not only of the combat of immediate fathers in the upbuilding of the West, but also to bring to the people that they have a heritage of race." Quoted in Robert W. Rydell, *All the World's a Fair: Visions of Empire at American International Expositions, 1876–1916* (Chicago, 1984), 208.

26. See Herbert G. Gutman, "Historical Consciousness in Contemporary America," in Ira Berlin, ed., *Power & Culture: Essays on the American Working Class* (New York, 1987), 395–412; Henry F. May, *Coming to Terms: A Study in Memory and History* (Berkeley, 1987), esp. xi, 146; William Maxwell, *Ancestors* (New York, 1971). See also Ralph Ellison, *Invisible Man* (New York, 1952: Signet Books edition), 264, 268, 439; Wynton Marsalis, "Why We Must Preserve Our Jazz Heritage," *Ebony* (February 1986), 131.

27. *U.S.A. Weekend, Ithaca Journal,* May 23, 1986; and a personal visit by the author in July 1986.

28. See T. H. Breen, *Imagining the Past: East Hampton Histories* (Reading, Mass., 1989), esp. 292–95; Ron Powers, *White Town Drowsing* (Boston, 1986), esp. 19, 69, 108, 111, 206, 257, 267, 271–72, 274, 277, 287. For the failure of a Mark Twain Heritage Theme Park to develop, as planned, near Hannibal, Mo., see 115, 128–37.

29. See Merritt Roe Smith, *Harpers Ferry Armory and the New Technology: The Challenge of Change* (Ithaca, N.Y., 1977); Richard N. Current, *Northernizing the South* (Athens, Ga., 1983), 85, 97, 103–05; Neil Harris, "Cultural Institutions and American Modernization," *The Journal of Library History,* 16 (1981), 43; and T. J. Jackson Lears, *No Place of Grace: Antimodernism and the Transformation of American Culture, 1880–1920* (New York, 1981).

30. "Editor's Notebook," *Preservation News* (March 1982), p. 5.

31. Letter to the author from James C. Massey (executive director of HHAA), Mar. 20, 1979, with enclosures; NYT, Apr. 4, 1981, p. 27; Bob Summer, "The 'White Castle of Louisiana' Is Opened to the Public," NYT, Apr. 12, 1981, sec. 10, p. 23; Michael deCourcy Hinds, "2 Hardy Survivors amid Urban Growth," NYT, May 21, 1981, p. C1; Clyde Haberman, "Panel Creates Historical District on East Side Near Central Park," NYT, May 20, 1981, pp. A1 and B3; Paul Goldberger, "Preservation Victory," NYT, May 21, 1981, pp. B1 and B6.

32. Rouse appeared on the cover of *Time* on Aug. 24, 1981. Other stories about him and his diverse projects appear in *Builder* (November 1984), 74–81; *Engineering News-Record* (Feb. 14, 1985); and *The Washington Post,* Mar. 24, 1988, p. C1.

33. Records of the Stevensville Historical Society are located in the Ross Toole Archives, University of Montana Library, Missoula.

34. Records of the Society of Mayflower Descendants, Idaho, are located in the Idaho Historical Society, MS-2 (fol. 195), Boise.

35. George C. Neumann (Durham, Conn.) to the author, Dec. 10, 1979.

36. Robert G. Hartje, *Bicentennial U.S.A.: Pathways to Celebration* (Nashville, Tenn., 1973), 76; Frank E. Everett, Jr., *Brierfield: Plantation Home of Jefferson Davis* (Oxford, Miss., 1980); NYT, Nov. 24, 1980, p. A20; NYT, June 9, 1983, p. B10.

37. NYT, Dec. 21, 1978, p. C19; NYT, Aug. 5, 1984, p. H23. See also Hart M. Nelson, "The Democratization of the Antique: Meanings of Antiques and Dealers' Perceptions of Customers," *Sociological Review,* 18 (1970), 407–19.

38. NYT *Sunday Magazine,* Apr. 16, 1978; Quoted in Wendy Cooper, "In Praise of America, 1650–1830," TMA, 117 (March 1980), 603.

39. Allison M. Eckardt (of TMA) to the author, Mar. 26, 1980; Paulette Tavormina (of Sotheby Parke Bernet) to the author, Apr. 9, 1980; "Going . . . Going . . . Gone! The

Auction Business Is Booming as More and More Americans Catch Art-Collecting Fever," *Time,* Dec. 31, 1979, pp. 46–57. See also Richard Hislop, ed., *Auction Prices of American Artists at Auction Sales, 1970–1978* (Surrey, Engl., 1979); Wesley Towner and Stephen Varble, *The Elegant Auctioneers* (New York, 1970), a history of Sotheby Parke Bernet.

40. NYT, Oct. 28, 1972, p. 21; NYT, Jan. 29, 1978, p. D27; NYT, Jan. 25, 1979, p. C1; NYT, May 25, 1980, p. A1; NYT, July 18, 1980, p. C23; NYT, July 24, 1981, p. C19; NYT, Jan. 15, 1981, pp. C1 and C6; NYT, Jan. 13, 1983, p. C8.

41. NYT, Apr. 23, 1978, p. D26; "An Everything-Else Boom," *Newsweek,* Apr. 24, 1978, pp. 86–88; NYT, May 7, 1980, p. C20; NYT, Aug. 1, 1980, p. A22; NYT, Feb. 9, 1984, p. C7; "Black Heritage Preserved in Collectibles," *USA Weekend,* June 2, 1989, p. 18; *The Washington Post,* Feb. 6, 1990, p. C5.

42. Victor Greene, "E. Pinkowski, Lay Collector: A Neglected Historical Resource," *Journal of American Ethnic History,* 8 (1988), 10–20; Sylvia O'Neill Dorn, *The How to Collect Anything Book: Treasure to Trivia* (Garden City, N.Y., 1976); Jean and Jim Young, *Great Trash: New Trends in Antiquing, Auctions, Bargaining and Bartering, Buying for Resale, Collectibles, Garage Sales, Flea Markets, House Sales, Folk Art, Careers in Collecting and Raising Cash* (New York, 1979).

43. See Frederick Baekeland, "The Art Collector: Clues to a Character Profile," NYT, Sept. 16, 1984, sec. 2, p. 1; Aline B. Saarinen, *The Proud Possessors: The Lives, Times and Tastes of Some Adventurous American Art Collectors* (New York, 1958); Jean Lipman, comp., *The Collector in America* (New York, 1970); Michael deCourcy Hinds, "One Man's Historic Village," NYT, July 10, 1980, pp. C1 and C10.

44. D. Stephen Elliott (Vice President, Colonial Williamsburg Foundation) to the author, Mar. 20, 1980; Nancy D. Kolb (Historic Site Administrator, Pennsbury Manor) to the author, Apr. 8, 1980; NYT, Apr. 7, 1973, p. 36; NYT, Jan. 19, 1974, p. 28.

45. Rita Reif, "A Rare Assemblage of Folk Carvings on the Block," NYT, Apr. 20, 1980, p. D32; Jean Lipman and Alice Winchester, *The Flowering of American Folk Art, 1776–1876* (New York, 1974).

46. Betsy Brayer, *Margaret Woodbury Strong and the Origin of the Strong Museum* (Rochester, N.Y., 1982); Barbara Moynehan, "The Legacy of Margaret Woodbury Strong," *Americana* (September–October 1982), 82–86; Krystyna Poray Goddu, "The Margaret Woodbury Strong Museum: A Collector's Dream Comes to Life," *Collector Editions* (Fall 1982), 54–56.

47. Rita Reif, "Americana: From Auction to Museum," NYT, Sept. 12, 1982, p. H34; Reif, "What the Collector Can Learn from Period Rooms," NYT, Apr. 6, 1980, p. D32; Reif, "Antiques: Silver by Area," NYT, Feb. 23, 1974, p. C28.

48. See the *Cape Cod Times,* 1980 Summer Preview, p. C3; NYT, Nov. 6, 1983, p. 17; NYT, Sept. 4, 1988, p. A28; *Los Angeles Times,* Mar. 13, 1989, pt. 6, p. 1.

49. NYT, May 19, 1980, p. C15; NYT, June 9, 1985, p. H28; NYT, June 16, 1985, p. H15. For a biographical sketch of Lila Acheson Wallace (co-chairman of *Reader's Digest*) and her historically oriented philanthropies, see NYT, May 9, 1984, p. A1. See also Larry Lankton, "Something Old, Something New: The Reexhibition of the Henry Ford Museum's Hall of Technology," in *Technology and Culture,* 21 (1980), 594–613, and John M. Staudenmaier, "The Giant Wakens: Revising Henry Ford's History Book," ibid., 29 (1988), 118–24.

50. NYT, July 27, 1985, p. A36; NYT, Jan. 21, 1985, p. A14; NYT, Oct. 6, 1988, p. A18; Michael Berenbaum, "The Creation of the U.S. Holocaust Museum," paper presented at the annual meeting of the Organization of American Historians, Apr. 23, 1990, Washington, D.C.

51. Janet R. MacFarlane, "The Farmers' Museum in Cooperstown, New York," TMA, 50 (September 1946), 161–63; Linda Charlton, "Colonial Life-Style Recreated at Farm Near Capital," NYT, Mar. 18, 1974, p. 31; NYT, Sept. 4, 1983, p. 50; Nancy Kriplen, "A Village Prepares for Christmas 1836," NYT, Nov. 30, 1980, sec. 10, pp. 1, 12–13; Ira Henry Freeman, "New Jersey's Historic Waterloo Village Turns Back the Clock," NYT, sec. 10, p. 7; Darwin P. Kelsey, "Outdoor Museums and Historical Agriculture," *Agricultural*

History, 46 (1972), 105–27. Americana Village, near Hamilton, N.Y., has been in gestation since 1978. The Western Reserve Historical Society (based in Cleveland) runs the Hale Farm and Village in the Cuyahoga Valley National Recreation Area.

52. NYT, Dec. 2, 1984, p. 68; John A. Herbst, *A Slice of the Earth* (n.p., n.d., pamphlet). See also Caroline Gibbs, "The National Museum of Labour History," *History Workshop,* no. 10 (Autumn 1980), 191–93, and Mike Wallace, "Industrial Museums and the History of Deindustrialization," PH, 9 (1987), 9–19.

53. NYT, Aug. 5, 1983, p. A6; *Ithaca Journal,* Dec. 27, 1983, p. 15. For the North Carolina Transportation Museum, located at Spencer, N.C., site of one of the largest and busiest railroad workshops in the United States, see NYT, Jan. 20, 1985, sec. 10, p. 20.

54. NYT, June 20, 1982, p. 34; NYT, June 3, 1985, p. B4; NYT, Sept. 8, 1985, p. 56.

55. NYT, Dec. 21, 1984, p. A29; NYT, Jan. 20, 1985, p. A16; NYT, May 23, 1985, p. D27; NYT, July 3, 1989, p. 23; NYT, Apr. 14, 1990, p. 7. See also Gaile McGregor, "The Technomyth in Transition: Reading American Popular Culture," *Journal of American Studies,* 21 (1987), 387–409.

56. Most of this information is taken from the museums' brochures, but see *Cape Cod Times,* June 25, 1980, p. 37, for a feature about Thacher; and John Lukacs, "Obsolete Historians," *Harper's,* 261 (November 1980), 80.

57. NYT, Jan. 31, 1985, p. C7; *Ithaca Journal,* Nov. 12, 1983, p. 19; NYT, Dec. 28, 1988, p. A14.

58. NYT, Apr. 13, 1988, p. B4; *The Washington Post,* Jan. 27, 1990, p. C9; Barbara Blumberg, *Celebrating the Immigrant: An Administrative History of the Statue of Liberty National Monument, 1952–1982* (Boston, 1985); Arnold Berke, "Tenement Museum to Showcase Immigrant Life," *Preservation News* (September 1989), p. 3; and see John Bodnar, "Symbols and Servants: Immigrant America and the Limits of Public History," JAH, 73 (1986), 137–51.

59. See Barbara L. Kellerman, "Even in a Museum Depicting His History, the Indian Is Cheated," NYT, Nov. 27, 1980, p. A27; Wayne King, "Alamo Under Siege: Defenders Standing Firm Against Illinois History Buff," NYT, Apr. 12, 1984, p. A16.

60. Debora Wiley, "Museum, College Battle Over Title to Artifacts," *Des Moines Sunday Register,* Aug. 16, 1989; Peter Swords, "Taxing Museums," NYT, Apr. 2, 1983, p. 19; Olivia Buehl, "Museums and the Art of Retail," *Allegheny Airlines Flighttime* (April 1979), 9–11.

61. Wilcomb Washburn, "Are Museums Necessary?" *Museum News,* 47 (October 1968), 9–10; Washburn, "Collecting Information, Not Objects," ibid., 62 (February 1984), 5–15; Michael Wallace, "Mickey Mouse History: Portraying the Past at Disney World," *Radical History Review,* no. 32 (March 1985), 33–57; Andrea Stulman Dennett, "A Postmodern Look at EPCOT's American Adventure," JAC, 12 (1989), 47–53.

62. Compare Richard R. Beard, *Walt Disney's EPCOT: Creating the New World of Tomorrow* (New York, 1982) with Wallace, "Mickey Mouse History," 50–57, and Richard Schickel, *The Disney Version: The Life, Times, Art and Commerce of Walt Disney* (2nd ed.: New York, 1985), 157, 208, 211, 213, 301–02, 322, 334–35, 361, 367.

63. Chorley to Mrs. JDR, Nov. 21, 1960, and Dec. 26, 1961, Chorley Papers (personal), box 1, RAC.

64. Earl Pomeroy, *In Search of the Golden West: The Tourist in Western America* (New York, 1957), 218; Reynold M. Wik, *Henry Ford and Grass-roots America* (Ann Arbor, Mich., 1973), 57; J. Warren McClure to Chorley, Dec. 18, 1956, Chorley Papers (personal), box 10, RAC; memorandum from Harold Dean Cater to Mrs. C. Thornton (the hostess in charge of distributing literature at Sleepy Hollow Restorations), Aug. 21, 1956, SHR Archives, box 7, RAC.

65. Burton I. Woolf (Director, Metropolitan Cultural Alliance, based in Boston) to the author, June 3, 1980, with statistical tables enclosed for 1974–80; Robert N. Sieber (Director, Pa. Farm Museum) to the author, June 25, 1980, with data covering 1960–80; Albert C. Cook (Director, Sandwich Glass Museum) to the author, June 30, 1980, with data covering 1968–79; Lewis C. Price et al., *Museum Program Survey, 1979* (Washington, D.C., 1981).

66. In addition to "Boardom," a monthly report distributed to NYSHA trustees throughout the 1980s, I am deeply grateful to Wilbur Zelinsky, Professor Emeritus of Geography at Pennsylvania State University, who sent me thoughtful letters with statistical compilations on Apr. 6, 1983, and Dec. 4, 1989.

67. See James A. Hijiya, "Roots: Family and Ethnicity in the 1970s," AQ, 30 (1978), 548–56.

68. Van Wyck Brooks, *Days of the Phoenix: The Nineteen Twenties I Remember* (New York, 1951), 2–3.

69. Tom Buckley, "Curiosity about Roots of the Family Tree Is Growing," NYT, May 3, 1974, pp. 35, 48. See also William Maxwell, *Ancestors* (New York, 1971); Dudley Randall, "Ancestors," in Randall, ed., *The Black Poets: A New Anthology* (New York, 1971), 148, 166–67; James T. Wooten, *Dasher: The Roots and Rising of Jimmy Carter* (New York, 1978), 62.

70. Paul D. Zimmerman, "In Search of a Heritage," *Newsweek* (Sept. 27, 1976), 94–96; NYT, Feb. 15, 1979, p. C15; Fred Ferretti, "Traces of Their Female Ancestry," NYT, Apr. 26, 1980, p. 20; NYT, Jan. 25, 1981, p. 45; Isabel Wilkerson, "Setting Out to Dig Up a Buried Heritage," NYT, Mar. 6, 1990, p. A16.

71. Gary B. and Elizabeth Shown Mills, "*Roots* and the New 'Faction,'" VMHB, 89 (1981), 3–26; Willard R. Espy, *Oysterville: Roads to Grandpa's Village* (New York, 1977); Dorothy Gallagher, *Hannah's Daughters: Six Generations of an American Family* (New York, 1976); Nicholas P. Hardeman, *Wilderness Calling: The Hardeman Family in the American Westward Movement, 1750–1900* (Knoxville, Tenn., 1977).

72. See Peirce Lewis, "Defining a Sense of Place," *Southern Quarterly*, 17 (Spring–Summer 1979), 24–46; Tamara K. Hareven, "The Search for Generational Memory: Tribal Rites in Industrial Society," *Daedalus*, 107 (1978), 139.

73. Wilkerson, "Setting Out to Dig Up a Buried Heritage," NYT, Mar. 6, 1990, p. A16.

74. The three-part Gannett series appeared in the *Ithaca Journal* on Feb. 15, 16, and 17, 1979. See also Seth S. King, "Seeking Family History on a Visit to the National Archives," NYT, June 7, 1981, sec. 10, p. 3.

75. Richard F. Shepard, "U.S. Jewish Landmarks, Big and Small," NYT, Apr. 20, 1980, sec. 10, p. 5; Douglas C. McGill, "A Boom in Sales of Judaica," NYT, July 10, 1984, p. C13; NYT, Oct. 4, 1979, p. B14; NYT, Dec. 12, 1980, p. B7.

76. In 1939 Henry Adams II (1875–1951) remarked that "family history is my only amusement." Three years later, referring to the Adams homesite in Braintree, he lamented that "the younger generation look on the place as a curio heap. . . . They never visit it and never do any work in connection with it." Quoted in Malcolm Freiberg, "From Family to Nation: The Old House Becomes a National Historic Site," MHS *Proceedings*, 98 (1986), 67.

77. NYT, May 4, 1980, p. 76; NYT, July 27, 1981, p. A13; NYT, Sept. 15, 1986, p. B1.

78. For family history exemplified in the decorative arts, see the Haskins family quilt (c. 1870) at the Shelburne Museum in Vermont. It was made of pieced, embroidered, and appliquéd cotton by Mrs. Samuel Glover Haskins of Granville, Vermont.

79. Robert M. Taylor, Jr., "Summoning the Wandering Tribes: Genealogy and Family Reunions in American History," JSH, 16 (1982), 21–37; Susan Chira, "Family That Grew with the U.S. Holds Reunion," NYT, Aug. 15, 1983, p. B2. For comparable activity in Great Britain, however, see Stan Newens, "Family History Societies," *History Workshop*, no. 11 (1981), 154–59.

80. Dorothy Spruill Redford with Michael D'Orso, *Somerset Homecoming: Recovering a Lost Heritage* (New York, 1988); NYT, Aug. 31, 1986, pp. 1, 26. For the 1989 reunion of 1,400 black and white members of the Hairston family at High Point, N.C., see NYT, Sept. 10, 1989, p. 26; and see Lisa W. Foderaro, "Digging for Key to Freed Slaves' Lives," NYT, Oct. 11, 1988, p. B2.

81. For purposes of context, the most useful works are Merle Curti, *The Roots of American Loyalty* (New York, 1946), and Wilbur Zelinsky, *Nation Into State: The Shifting Symbolic Foundations of American Nationalism* (Chapel Hill, N.C., 1988).

82. Matthew Page Andrews to J. Franklin Jameson, Apr. 11, 1918, and Mar. 17, 1923, Jameson Papers, box 55, MDLC; "H.F." (for the American Patriotic League) to Guy Stanton Ford, Dec. 27, 1923, Ford Papers, folder no. 89, University of Minnesota Archives.

83. Dixon Ryan Fox, "The American Faith—Reaffirmation," unpublished typescript, c. 1940, Fox Papers, Schaffer Library, Union College, Schenectady, N.Y.; Frederick L. Rath, Jr., "Musings on the Contemporary Scene—A Confession of Faith," unpublished typescript, Spring 1941, by courtesy of F. L. Rath, Jr. See also Richard M. Ketchum, *The Borrowed Years, 1938–1941: America on the Way to War* (New York, 1989), esp. 659–796.

84. See Lary May, ed., *Recasting America: Culture and Politics in the Age of Cold War* (Chicago, 1989), esp. 1–16, 19–37, 195–220, 285–301; Donald J. Mrozek, "The Cult and Ritual of Toughness in Cold War America," in Ray B. Browne, ed., *Rituals and Ceremonies in Popular Culture* (Bowling Green, Ohio, 1980), 178–91.

85. Minneapolis Chapter, Sons of the American Revolution, board meeting of Apr. 18, 1956, S.A.R. Papers, folder for chapter papers 1955–58, MinnHS.

86. Virginia 350th Anniversary Papers, executive committee minutes for July 11, 1956, VHS (MSS 4 V8 b); minutes of the board of directors, The Naturalized Citizens of America, July 30, 1956, ibid.

87. NYT, June 5, 1980, p. B3; Susan Prendergast Schoelwer, *Alamo Images: Changing Perceptions of a Texas Experience* (Dallas, 1985), 167–68. For precedents in French history, see Norma Evenson, *Paris: A Century of Change, 1878–1978* (New Haven, 1979), 9.

88. Brian W. Dippie, *Custer's Last Stand: The Anatomy of an American Myth* (Missoula, Mont., 1976), 139.

89. Schoelwer, *Alamo Images,* 16–17. For an amazingly comparable "scenario," see Karal Ann Marling and John Wetenhall, *Iwo Jima: Monuments, Memories, and the American Hero* (Cambridge, Mass., 1991).

90. John H. Schaar, "The Case for Patriotism," *American Review,* no. 17 (May 1973), 59–99, esp. 62, 72, 77.

91. Ibid., 84, 87, 89, 94. Cf. Samuel P. Huntington, *American Politics: The Promise of Disharmony* (Cambridge, Mass., 1981); John J. Pullen, *Patriotism in America: A Study of Changing Devotions, 1770–1970* (New York, 1971).

92. See Raphael Samuel, ed., *Patriotism: The Making and Unmaking of British National Identity* (London, 1988), 3 vols.

93. Thornton Wilder, "Toward an American Language," *Atlantic,* 190 (July 1952), 31. See also Wilder, "The American Loneliness," ibid. (August 1952), 65–69.

94. I am indebted to an excellent paper by David McCarthy, "Tom Wesselmann and the Americanization of the Nude, 1957–1965," presented at the National Museum of American Art in Washington, D.C., on Jan. 26, 1990.

95. For anecdotes suggesting that George Washington was savvy about sex, see Paul F. Boller, Jr., *Presidential Anecdotes* (New York, 1981), 17.

96. Robin Brantley, "Kenneth Koch Stages Two Plays," NYT, Jan. 12, 1979, p. C7; Kenneth Koch, *George Washington Crossing the Delaware* (New York, 1967).

97. Wendell Rawls, Jr., "In America, Patriotism and Nationalism Are on Rise," NYT, Dec. 11, 1979, p. A20.

98. R. W. Apple, Jr., "New Stirrings of Patriotism," NYT *Magazine,* Dec. 11, 1983, pp. 43–47, 89–96, 128–33; Charles Fried, "Liberals and Love," NR, Dec. 24, 1984, pp. 40–42.

99. See NYT, June 22, 1989, pp. A1, B8; R. Drummond Ayres, Jr., "Keepers of the Flame of 1776 Stoke the Fire," NYT, Oct. 16, 1989, p. A14.

100. Jean-Louis Beaucarnot, "A la recherche de vos ancêtres," *Histoire Magazine,* no. 13 (February 1981), 98–101; George Gibian, "Icons, Not Sickles, on the Soviet Literary Scene," *Christian Science Monitor,* Sept. 28, 1979, p. 24; Gibian, "Reviving Russian Nationalism," *The New Leader,* Nov. 19, 1979, pp. 13–14.

101. George Gibian to the author, Oct. 19, 1979, and May 21, 1980.

102. Alvin Shuster, "Last Trip for Famed British Train," NYT, May 2, 1972, p. 4.

103. Ira Henry Freeman, "In Europe, the Place to Discover America Is the Museum at Claverton Manor," NYT, Feb. 4, 1979, sec. 10, pp. 14–15.

Chapter 19

1. Larry McMurtry, *Cadillac Jack: A Novel* (New York, 1982); Lucinda Hilbrink, "Transplanting Roots: In a Restless Age, a Grandfather's Gift Provides a Sense of Permanence," *The Washington Post* "Home" section, Jan. 25, 1990, pp. 9–10.

2. W. D. Wetherell, *Souvenirs* (New York, 1981), 4, 23, 53–54, 105, 119–20, 141, 164–65, 175, 191. Two novels by Walker Percy share a protagonist named Will Barrett. In *The Last Gentleman* (1966) he is afflicted with amnesia; in *The Second Coming* (1980), he suffers from acute attacks of memory that recall a painful past.

3. John Mebane, *The Poor Man's Guide to Trivia Collecting* (Garden City, N.Y., 1975), 2; Ray Anello, "The Old Neighborhood," NYT, Feb. 11, 1978, p. A21; Meg Greenfield, "How to Think about the '60s," *Newsweek*, Apr. 10, 1978, p. 108; Anthony Brandt, "A Short Natural History of Nostalgia," *Atlantic*, 242 (December 1978), 58–63; Christopher Lasch, "The Politics of Nostalgia," *Harper's*, 269 (November 1984), 65–70; Marilynne Robinson, "Writers and the Nostalgic Fallacy," NYT *Book Review*, Oct. 13, 1985, pp. 1, 34–35.

4. Sven Birkerts, "The Nostalgia Disease," *Tikkun*, 4 (March 1989), 20–22, 117–18; Georgia Dullea, "Sick of the 60's, 3 Men of the 80's Try to Give Nostalgia a Bad Name," NYT, Apr. 30, 1989, p. 50; Peggy Andersen, "Nostalgia Stinks," *Ithaca Journal*, Apr. 21, 1989, p. 12A.

5. Richard M. Weaver, *Visions of Order: The Cultural Crisis of Our Time* (Baton Rouge, La., 1964), 40; Dullea, "Sick of the 60's," NYT, Apr. 30, 1989, p. 50.

6. William H. McNeill, "The Care and Repair of Public Myth," *Foreign Affairs*, 61 (Fall 1982), 1–13; John Hellmann, *American Myth and the Legacy of Vietnam* (New York, 1986); the Popular Culture Association devoted a session to "The Vietnam War and Modern Memory" at its annual meeting held at St. Louis in April 1989. For scholars writing in the 1960s and 1970s with a less positive view of myths than McNeill, see George B. Tindall, "Mythology: A New Frontier in Southern History," in Frank E. Vandiver, ed., *The Idea of the South: Pursuit of a Central Theme* (Chicago, 1964), 1–15; Patrick Gerster and Nicholas Chords, "The Northern Origins of Southern Mythology," JSouthH, 43 (1977), 567–82.

7. Richard Bardolph, "Preserving Our Heritage," *North Carolina Historical Review*, 58 (1981), 139–45; Meg Greenfield, "Chronic Political Amnesia," *Newsweek*, Sept. 22, 1980, p. 96.

8. The philosopher Susanne K. Langer commented that "Memory is the great organizer of consciousness," and that "Actual experience is a welter of sights, sounds, feelings, physical strains, expectations, and minute, undeveloped reactions. Memory . . . simplifies and composes our perceptions"—*Feeling and Form* (London, 1953), 263. In 1982 a prominent humanist and university administrator told the annual meeting of the National Trust (in Louisville) that educators and preservationists belonged to the same union: the amalgamated union of memory workers. (Professor Roderick French of The George Washington University.)

9. Herblock, "Ronald Reagan: The Amnesia Years," *The Washington Post*, Feb. 18, 1990, p. B6.

10. Karal Ann Marling and John Wetenhall, *Iwo Jima: Monuments, Memories and the American Hero* (Cambridge, Mass., 1991), ch. 9, "It Didn't Really Happen That Way."

11. Ibid., ch. 10, "The Business of Remembering." For a story about the Japanese-made models, see "Japs Are Profiting from a Loss," *Washington Daily News*, July 8, 1959.

12. Harold Sack and Max Wilk, *American Treasure Hunt* (Boston, 1986), 186. For diverse examples of historical amnesia, indifference, and ignorance by radicals, politicians, and the general public, see David S. Broder, *Changing the Guard: Power and*

Leadership in America (New York, 1980), 139; NYT, Mar. 21, 1982, p. 41; Meg Greenfield, "How We Shred the Past," *The Washington Post,* Sept. 29, 1987, p. A19.

13. Francis L. Loewenheim, "Reaganscribing History," NYT, Mar. 23, 1981, p. A17. See also Michael Rogin, " 'Make My Day!': Spectacle as Amnesia in Imperial Politics," *Representations,* 29 (1990), 99–123.

14. NYT, Dec. 23, 1981, p. A12; Charles Mohr, "Reagan Seems Confused on Vietnam's History," NYT, Feb. 19, 1982, p. A8; James David Barber, "The Oval Office Aesop," NYT, Nov. 7, 1982, p. E17; letter from Robert J. Goldstein, NYT, May 27, 1985, p. 18. For a defense of Reagan's historical statements, see the letters in NYT, Jan. 2, 1984, p. 22.

15. Clinton Rossiter, *Conservatism in America: The Thankless Persuasion* (2nd ed.: New York, 1962), 44–45; NYT, Apr. 11, 1981, p. 22; *Ithaca Journal,* Feb. 4, 1982, p. 18. Within eleven months of taking office the Reagan administration decided to stop lending microfilmed Census Bureau records to the nation's libraries, where people had been using them to trace their family histories. The cut was designed to eliminate seventeen jobs and save $250,000 in the federal budget.

16. NYT, Jan. 4, 1982, p. A19; NYT, Jan. 22, 1982, p. A16; *Ithaca Journal,* Mar. 11, 1982, p. 22; NYT, Mar. 8, 1982, p. A18; NYT, Mar. 16, 1982, p. A20; Amity Shlaes, "Why the Archives Are in Tatters," NR, 187 (Sept. 20, 1982), 16–19. See also Warren I. Cohen, "At the State Dept., Historygate," NYT, May 8, 1990, p. A29.

17. Garry Wills, *Reagan's America: Innocents at Home* (Garden City, N.Y., 1987), 371. For a similar mood at a totally different socio-political level, see Jim Wayne Miller, "Nostalgia for the Future," *Kentucky Review,* 8 (Summer 1988), 18–39, concerning the future in Appalachian Kentucky.

18. NYT, Jan. 12, 1989, p. A1; the full text of his address appears in ibid., p. 8. See also Michael Wallace, "Ronald Reagan and the Politics of History," *Tikkun,* 2 (Winter 1987), 13–18, 127–31.

19. The Bitburg quotation in ibid., 14; Ramberg's *Vertical Amnesia* (1980), acrylic on masonite, is located at Madison Art Center, Madison, Wis.

20. Anthony Lewis, "Which Side Are We On?" NYT, May 31, 1982, p. A13; Arthur Holmberg, "Carlos Fuentes Turns to Theater," NYT, June 6, 1982, sec. 2, p. 1.

21. Harry W. Haines, " 'What Kind of War?' An Analysis of the Vietnam Veterans Memorial," *Critical Studies in Mass Communication,* 3 (1986), 1–20; Fox Butterfield, "The New Viet Nam Scholarship," NYT *Magazine,* Feb. 13, 1983, pp. 26–32; Charles L. Griswold, "The Vietnam Veterans Memorial and the Washington Mall: Philosophical Thoughts on Political Iconography," *Critical Inquiry,* 12 (1986), 688–719; Karal Ann Marling and Robert Silberman, "The Statue Near the Wall: The Vietnam Veterans Memorial and the Art of Remembering," *Smithsonian Studies in American Art,* 1 (Spring 1987), 4–29.

22. George C. Herring, "Vietnam Remembered," JAH, 73 (1986), 152–64; Karal Ann Marling and John Wetenhall, "The Sexual Politics of Memory: The Vietnam Women's Memorial Project and 'The Wall,' " PAACS, 14 (1989), 341–72; Varick A. Chittenden, " 'These Aren't Just My Scenes': Shared Memories in a Vietnam Veteran's Art," *Journal of American Folklore,* 102 (1989), 412–23; Michael H. Frisch, "The Memory of History," in Susan Porter Benson, et al., eds., *Presenting the Past: Essays on History and the Public* (Philadelphia, 1986), 8–9.

23. Vincent Gordon Harding, "Beyond Amnesia: Martin Luther King, Jr., and the Future of America," and Nathan Irvin Huggins, "Martin Luther King, Jr.: Charisma and Leadership," JAH, 74 (1987), 468–81. See also Timothy Egan, "Old West's Centennial Effort: Hail Indians (and Custer, Too)," NYT, Dec. 31, 1988, p. A1; and Michael A. Lofaro, "The Hidden 'Hero' of the Nashville Crockett Almanacs," in Lofaro, ed., *Davy Crockett: The Man, the Legend, the Legacy, 1786–1986* (Knoxville, Tenn., 1985), 47.

24. See diverse essays in Benson, et al., eds., *Presenting the Past: Essays on History and the Public,* 12, 21, 37–38, 111, 145, 151; Michael Wallace, "Mickey Mouse History: Portraying the Past at Disney World," in Warren Leon and Roy Rosenzweig, eds., *History Museums in the United States: A Critical Assessment* (Urbana, Ill., 1989), 173; NYT, Mar. 28, 1990, p. A18.

25. Charles Francis Adams to J. Franklin Jameson, June 13, 1900, with printed enclosure, Jameson Papers, box 45, MDLC.

26. Considerable correspondence, memoranda, and responses to a joint "formulation" (proposed statement) dating from 1922–23 will be found in the Arthur M. Schlesinger Papers, HUA. See also Henry Johnson, *The Other Side of Main Street: A History Teacher from Sauk Center* (New York, 1943), 233, for a bizarre but obscure aspect of this investigation.

27. Bethany J. Andreasen, "Reconstructing the Social Order: The American Historical Association Commission on the Social Studies" (unpubl. Ph.D. diss., Cornell University, 1987).

28. Fox to Mrs. Arthur Hays Sulzberger, July 6, 1942, and Mrs. Sulzberger to Fox, July 17, 1942, Fox Papers, Schaffer Library, Union College, Schenectady, N.Y.; Fox to Nevins, May 12, 1943, ibid.; Fox to Max Savelle, Aug. 7, 1944, ibid.

29. Erling M. Hunt, "The *New York Times* 'Test' on American History," *Social Education*, 7 (May 1943), 195–200, 240; Belmont Farley (Director of Public Relations for the National Education Association) to the editors of various newspapers, May 7, 1943, copy in the Douglas S. Freeman Papers, box 8, ALUV.

30. A. L. Rowse to Colgate W. Darden, Jr., Mar. 8, 1951, Thomas Perkins Abernethy Papers, box 1, ALUV; R. Richard Wohl, "Intellectual History: An Historian's View," *The Historian*, 16 (1953), 72; NYT, Nov. 30, 1975, p. 45.

31. The *New York Times* provided extensive coverage of the survey on May 2, 3, and 4, 1976. See esp. "Test Finds Knowledge of American History Limited," NYT, May 2, 1976, pp. A1, 65 and 66; "The Students in 1943 vs. the Students Now," ibid., p. 65; "Instruction of History Displays Shift Away from Factual Content to 'Concepts,'" NYT, May 3, 1976, p. 43.

32. "History in the Public Schools: A Position Paper," *Carolina Comments*, 26 (1978), 43–47.

33. Quotations are from *The New Yorker*, Mar. 5, 1979, pp. 59–60, 76; ibid., Mar. 12, 1979, pp. 77–78. The final version is FitzGerald, *America Revised: History Schoolbooks in the Twentieth Century* (Boston, 1979).

34. Theodore Shabad, "Americans Get a Failing Grade on Geography," NYT, May 27, 1982, p. A7; Nick Thimmesch, "Back to Basics in Teaching History," *The Washington Post*, Jan. 8, 1983, p. A19; "History as Mush" (editorial), NYT, June 6, 1983, p. A16.

35. Diane Ravitch, "Decline and Fall of Teaching History," NYT *Magazine*, Nov. 17, 1985, pp. 50, 52, 54, 56, 101, 117; Ravitch and Chester E. Finn, *What Do Our Seventeen-Year Olds Know? A Report on the First National Assessment of History and Literature* (New York, 1987); Lynne V. Cheney, *American Memory: A Report on the Humanities in the Nation's Public Schools* (Washington, D.C., 1988); Kenneth Jackson and the Bradley Commission on History in Schools, *Building a History Curriculum: Guidelines for Teaching History in Schools* (n.p., 1988); Paul Gagnon, ed., *Historical Literacy: The Case for History in American Education* (New York, 1989).

36. Michael Knight, "Lawrence, Mass., Reliving 1912 Strike," NYT, Apr. 27, 1980, p. 26; Marvin Ciporen, "Labor's Use of History," PH, 2 (1980), 66–69.

37. Paul Cowan, "Whose America Is This?" *The Village Voice*, Apr. 2, 1979, pp. 1, 11–17; Herbert G. Gutman, *Power & Culture: Essays on the American Working Class* (New York, 1987), esp. ch. 12; NYT, Nov. 15, 1981, p. 40.

38. See Stephen William Foster, *The Past Is Another Country: Representation, Historical Consciousness and Resistance in the Blue Ridge* (Berkeley, 1988); George W. McDaniel, *Hearth & Home: Preserving a People's Culture* (Philadelphia, 1982); Theodore Rosengarten, *All God's Dangers: The Life of Nate Shaw* (New York, 1974); Elizabeth Kolbert, "Memories Wanted for History of Ellis Island," NYT, Nov. 24, 1985, p. 51; Lucy S. Dawidowicz, *The Holocaust and the Historians* (Cambridge, Mass., 1981); Lawrence L. Langer, *The Holocaust and the Literary Imagination* (New Haven, 1975).

39. NYT, Feb. 15, 1981, p. 64; Douglas E. Kneeland, "Muskets and Tomahawks: An Escape into the Past," NYT, May 15, 1981, p. A14. See *The Buckskin Report*, an annual newsletter that is mailed to enthusiasts of the mountain men and their lifestyle; John

Stromnes, "Rendezvous Is a Natural for Trappers," University of Montana *Missoulian,* Mar. 1, 1987. The rendezvous revival began in 1982.

40.   Joan Didion, *The White Album* (New York, 1979), 99; Carol J. Greenhouse, *Praying for Justice: Faith, Order, and Community in an American Town* (Ithaca, N.Y., 1986), ch. 2.

41.   NYT, July 4, 1973, p. 44; NYT, Oct. 11, 1981, p. 22; *Philadelphia Inquirer,* July 6, 1980, p. G1; NYT, Nov. 5, 1983, p. C3; NYT, Nov. 25, 1983, p. A31. See Stephen W. Stathis and Barbara L. Schwemle, "Commemorative Legislation," 18-page report prepared by the Congressional Research Service, no. 90–183 (Washington, D.C., 1990).

42.   *Ithaca Journal,* Dec. 26, 1981, p. 13; NYT, Feb. 25, 1988, p. C8; Michael Griffith and Chet Orloff, "Historical Societies and Legal History," *California Western Law Review,* 24 (1987–88), 357–60; NYT, July 13, 1980, p. 32; *Boston Herald Traveler,* Apr. 5, 1970, p. 43; Peter Applebome, "Remarkably, Din of Civil War Is Growing Louder," NYT, Apr. 22, 1990, p. 22.

43.   See Lon Tinkle, *An American Original: The Life of J. Frank Dobie* (Boston, 1978), 190; Lary May, ed., *Recasting America: Culture and Politics in the Age of Cold War* (Chicago, 1989), 201, 206; Donald L. Miller, *Lewis Mumford: A Life* (New York, 1989), chs. 10, 25, 27, and esp. p. 173.

44.   See Charles Haines, "The Making of Victorian America: Henry Ford Museum's 'Mass-Produced Elegance,' " *Technology and Culture,* 25 (1984), 832–38; Charles K. Hyde, " 'Streamlining America': An Exhibit at the Henry Ford Museum, Dearborn, Michigan," ibid., 29 (1988), 125–29; John M. Staudenmaier, "The Automobile in American Life," PH, 10 (1988), 89–92.

45.   Robert Jewett and John Shelton Lawrence, *The American Monomyth* (Garden City, N.Y., 1977); Robert G. Athearn, *The Mythic West in Twentieth-Century America* (Lawrence, Kans., 1986), 183; Jack Temple Kirby, *Media-Made Dixie: The South in the American Imagination* (Baton Rouge, La., 1978); Edward D. C. Campbell, *The Celluloid South: Hollywood and the Southern Myth* (Knoxville, Tenn., 1981), esp. ch. 1.

46.   Hellmann, *American Myth and the Legacy of Vietnam,* 220. See pp. 167–69 for a fine discussion of important novels concerning Vietnam and national mythology, works of fiction that portray "an irresolvable tension between the memory of Vietnam and the memory of the previous mythic American landscape."

47.   Susan G. Davis, " 'Set Your Mood to Patriotic': History as Televised Special Event," *Radical History Review,* no. 42 (1988), 122–43, esp. 128, 140. See also Roberta Brandes Gratz and Eric Fettmann, "The Selling of Miss Liberty," *The Nation,* 241 (Nov. 9, 1985), 465–76; Gratz and Fettmann, "The Battle for Ellis Island," ibid. (Nov. 30, 1985), 579–82; Martin Gottlieb, "Marketing of Statue Is Changing Fund-Raising," NYT, June 15, 1986, p. 29.

48.   Information derived from a 67-page booklet, *David L. Wolper: A Retrospective,* prepared when the University of Southern California School of Performing Arts presented its first Distinguished Alumni Award to Wolper on Nov. 18, 1979, in Beverly Hills; also extensive biographical information provided by Auriel K. Sanderson (Vice President, Wolper Productions, Inc.) to the author, Feb. 12, 1990.

49.   Typed 53-page transcript of an interview with David L. Wolper and Elton H. Rule (President, ABC), Feb. 20, 1985, made at the American Film Institute with Jean Firstenberg as moderator (p. 21).

50.   Ibid., pp. 36, 51.

51.   Ibid., pp. 12–13.

52.   For comparisons with the situation in Great Britain, see Colin McArthur, *Television and History* (London, 1978: BFI Television Monograph no. 8), 60-page booklet.

53.   Richard B. Harwell, "The Confederate Heritage," in Louis D. Rubin and James J. Kilpatrick, eds., *The Lasting South: Fourteen Southerners Look at Their Home* (Chicago, 1957), 23. See also Stephen A. Smith, "The Old South Myth as a Contemporary Southern Commodity," JPC, 16 (1982), 22–29.

54.   Daniels is quoted in Michael Wallace, "Reflections on the History of Historic Preservation," in Benson et al., eds., *Presenting the Past: Essays on History and the Public,*

176; Stephen Spender, *Love-Hate Relations: A Study of Anglo-American Sensibilities* (London, 1974), 121.

55. Terry Murphy and others, "Rediscover the USA: An Event of Historic Proportions," *USA Weekend,* Mar. 27–29, 1987, p. 8.

56. Ibid., pp. 9–13. See also John A. Jakle, *The Tourist: Travel in Twentieth-Century North America* (Lincoln, Nebr., 1985).

57. Michael Kiefer, "Hitting the Road for History," *USA Weekend,* June 2–4, 1989, p. 15.

58. Rath, "Historic Preservation: The Challenge and a Plan," address given in Cooperstown, N.Y., September 1955, p. 7, typescript in the Guy Stanton Ford Papers, fol. 112, University of Minnesota Archives, Minneapolis; PASSPORT fact sheet issued by the Eastern National Park & Monument Association, Apr. 3, 1986.

59. See the full-page ad by the North Carolina Travel Department, featuring the smiling warmth of a Seagrove folk potter at ease in front of his kiln ("For two hundred years and more. . . .") in NYT *Magazine,* Jan. 13, 1985, p. 61; and by Maryland Tourism, featuring the smiling warmth of a Chesapeake Bay fisherman holding a huge basket of fresh crabs, in *Americana* (March 1985), p. 15.

60. Every need and effort at preservation did not meet with success, however. See Robert Suro, "Plantations Slip into Texas History," NYT, Feb. 27, 1990, p. A18. For criticism of historic preservation activists on the grounds that they are either aesthetic antiquarians with ahistorical concerns or else cultural elitists, see J. Meredith Neil, "Is There a Historian in the House? The Curious Case of Historic Preservation," PH, 2 (1980), 30–38; Richard Handler, "Heritage and Hegemony: Recent Works on Historic Preservation and Interpretation," *Anthropological Quarterly,* 60 (1987), 137–41, an essay review.

61. Jack L. Helm of the Jack Daniel Distillery to the author, July 11, 1989, with numerous enclosures. See also David W. Dunlap, "25 Years of Landmarks Preservation," NYT, Apr. 29, 1990, p. 32.

62. See Randolph Langenbach, "An Epic in Urban Design," *Harvard Alumni Bulletin,* Apr. 13, 1968, pp. 19–28; the Idaho Historic Preservation Council, document for June–July 1972, MS2, fol. 444, Idaho Historical Society, Boise; NYT, July 16, 1989, p. 37. In June 1990 construction began on sixteen plazas that will provide rest stops along the New York State Thruway. Each one will be built in the rustic Adirondack camp style that became popular at the turn of the century. According to the New York City architectural firm that won the contract, "the period of architecture makes you smile and brings up images of holidays and vacations." NYT, Apr. 5, 1990, p. C3.

63. NYT, Aug. 5, 1968, p. C41; John Updike, *Three Texts from Early Ipswich: A Pageant* (Ipswich, Mass., 1968); John D. Dorst, *The Written Suburb: An American Site, An Ethnographic Dilemma* (Philadelphia, 1989), esp. chs. 2 and 4.

64. William E. Geist, "In Litchfield, Hue and Cry for 'Tradition,' " NYT, Dec. 3, 1982, p. B1.

65. Rita Reif, "Fallout from the $1 Million Tea Table," NYT, Feb. 9, 1986, sec. 2, p. 37; Reif, "Colonial American Desk Is Sold for $12.1 Million," NYT, June 4, 1989, p. 36; Jim Kemp, "Cloning Antiques: Museum Reproductions," NYT, Feb. 26, 1981, p. C1.

66. NYT, Nov. 11, 1980, p. 1; NYT, Nov. 17, 1989, p. C13.

67. *The Houston Post,* Feb. 4, 1990, p. A1. See also Barbara Gamarekian, "A Bully New White House," NYT, Apr. 27, 1989, p. C12.

68. AH, 40 (April 1989), p. 70.

69. See Howard Wight Marshall, "Folklife and the Rise of American Folk Museums," *Journal of American Folklore,* 90 (1977), 391–413; Gloria Levitas, "Living History in Iowa," NYT, July 17, 1983, sec. 10, p. 19.

70. John Jacob Niles obituary, NYT, Mar. 3, 1980, p. D11; Tinkle, *Life of J. Frank Dobie,* 156–57.

71. Samuel L. M. Barlow to Carl Carmer, Mar. 23, 1948, Carmer Papers, box 7, NYSHA; Earle W. Newton to Carmer, Mar. 1, 1955, ibid.; Carmer to Mary Ellen Buell, Jan. 28, 1962, ibid.

72. A price list and appraisal sheet for some of Mrs. Rockefeller's folk art will be found in JDR Papers, ser. II (cultural), box 174, RAC; Rita Reif, "A Goldmine of American Folk Art," NYT, Nov. 8, 1981, p. D30.

73. Dudley Clendinen, "Faces of America Hang in the Houses of Three Collectors," NYT, Feb. 18, 1982, p. C1; Rita Reif, "Stuart Feld Brings Zest to Americana," NYT, Jan. 10, 1988, p. H36; Ann Barry, "Jacquard Coverlets Weave a Spell," NYT, Feb. 28, 1988, p. H37.

74. Stuart P. Feld, "The Tradition of the Primitive—Denied," TMA, 83 (January 1963), 99–101.

75. Keith Graham, "Appalachia's Unlikely Hero," *Historic Preservation,* 41 (July 1989), 38–42.

76. Linda Blanken, "Foxfire: Folklore and Oral History Light Up a Curriculum," *Humanities,* 1, no. 6 (December 1980), 9–10. For an illuminating study of historical change and discontinuity as perceived from within by the people of Appalachia, see Foster, *The Past Is Another Country: Representation, Historical Consciousness and Resistance in the Blue Ridge.*

77. Ormond H. Loomis, ed., *Cultural Conservation: The Protection of Cultural Heritage in the United States* (Washington, D.C., 1983); Chris Warner, "Lee Adler Finds a Way," *Historic Preservation,* 40 (May 1988), 64–66. In a striking contrast, the Mormons (Church of Jesus Christ of Latter Day Saints) battled for years with the Utah Heritage Foundation, a preservationist organization, because the Mormons decided to tear down historic structures with moderate rent apartments in Salt Lake City in order to expand their church headquarters, already housed in a skyscraper. NYT, Nov. 30, 1980, p. 26.

78. Du Bois to board of directors of the NAACP, Nov. 5, 1956, in Herbert Aptheker, ed., *The Correspondence of W. E. B. Du Bois* (Amherst, Mass., 1978), III, 405–06.

79. Minutes of the Executive Committee, July 17, 1957, Virginia 350th Anniversary Commission Papers (MSS 4 V8 b), VHS; Charles H. Wesley, "Creating and Maintaining an Historical Tradition," *Journal of Negro History,* 49 (1964), 13–33; Ralph Ellison, *Invisible Man* (New York, 1952), 264, 268, 439.

80. Kenneth Hudson, *Museums of Influence* (Cambridge, 1987), 179–81; William E. Schmidt, "Denver Museum Preserving Records of Black Pioneers in West," NYT, July 28, 1983, p. A12.

81. Marie Tyler-McGraw and Gregg D. Kimball, *In Bondage and Freedom: Antebellum Black Life in Richmond, Virginia* (Richmond, Va., 1988); "A More Honest History Lesson," *Time,* 134 (July 31, 1989), p. 52.

82. Patricia Leigh Brown, "Restoring a Past Some Would Bury," NYT, Sept. 12, 1988, p. A10. For a candid account of the problems encountered when middle-class whites attempt to reconstruct the physical lives of nineteenth- and early-twentieth-century blacks in the upper South, see George W. McDaniel, *Hearth & Home: Preserving a People's Culture* (Philadelphia, 1982), esp. 26–27.

83. Brown, "Restoring a Past," NYT, Sept. 12, 1988, p. A10; NYT, Jan. 18, 1981, p. 15; "Mississippi Will Restore Black's House," *Preservation News* (May 1989), p. 1.

84. Agis Salpukas, "New U.S. History Textbooks Putting Stress on Minorities Contribution to Building Nation," NYT, Apr. 28, 1974, p. 55; Barbara Gamarekian, "Smithsonian Recognizes Influence Beyond White," NYT, June 17, 1989, p. B6; "Discovering the Truth about Columbus," *Utne Reader* (March 1990), pp. 24–25.

85. Harold Faber, "New York Returning Wampum Belts to Onondagas," NYT, Aug. 13, 1989, p. 39; NYT, Apr. 23, 1990, p. A16.

86. NYT, Jan. 5, 1990, p. A17. See also Richard Severo, "Archaeological Conservancy Guarding Buried Treasures of America's Heritage," NYT, June 27, 1982, p. A22; Douglas H. Ubelaker and Lauryn Guttenplan Grant, "Human Skeletal Remains: Preservation or Reburial?" *Yearbook of Physical Anthropology,* 32 (1989), 249–87.

87. John Williams Corrington, "Reunion," in Corrington, ed., *Southern Writing in the Sixties: Fiction* (Baton Rouge, La., 1966), 184. See also Lewis P. Simpson, *The Dispossessed Garden: Pastoral and History in Southern Literature* (Athens, Ga., 1975), 89.

88. Didi Barrett, "Commentary: On Memories and Memory Art," in *A Time to Reap: Late Blooming Folk Artists* (South Orange, N.J., 1985), the catalogue of an exhibit co-sponsored by Seton Hall University and the Museum of American Folk Art; NYT, Mar. 22, 1990, p. C13. Eiko and Koma are choreographers and performing dancers who left Japan for New York in 1974. On Apr. 3, 1990, they presented the premiere of a new work titled *Memory*. NYT, Apr. 5, 1990, p. C20.

89. Memorandum from Al Silverman to Ed Fitzgerald et al., Oct. 25, 1976, Book-of-the-Month Club files; Richard R. Beard, *Walt Disney's EPCOT: Creating the New World of Tomorrow* (New York, 1982), 139.

90. See James Combs, "Celebrations: Rituals of Popular Veneration," JPC, 22 (1989), 71–77.

91. Smith, "The Old South Myth as a Contemporary Southern Commodity," 22–29; Ronald Smothers, "South, in One Volume: Myths and Moon Pies," NYT, May 23, 1989, p. A16.

92. Michael H. Frisch, "The Memory of History," in Benson et al., eds., *Presenting the Past: Essays on History and the Public*, 6.

93. Carl L. Becker, *Everyman His Own Historian: Essays on History and Politics* (New York, 1935), 248–49; T. H. Breen, *Imagining the Past: East Hampton Histories* (Reading, Mass., 1989), 66–67.

Coda to Part Four

1. Lon Tinkle, *An American Original: A Biography of J. Frank Dobie* (Boston, 1978), 190.

2. For some of the most useful work that is theoretical and risks comparative generalizations, see Nathan Wachtel, "Memory and History: An Introduction" to a special issue of *History and Anthropology*, 2 (1986), 207–24; Raphael Semmes, ed., *People's History and Socialist Theory* (London, 1981); Richard Johnson et al., eds., *Making Histories: Studies in History-Writing and Politics* (Minneapolis, 1982), esp. ch. 6, "Popular Memory: Theory, Politics, Method"; Maurice Halbwachs, *The Collective Memory* (Paris, 1950; New York, 1980); Patrick H. Hutton, "Collective Memory and Collective Mentalities: The Halbwachs-Ariès Connection," *Historical Reflections*, 15 (1988), 311–22.

3. Ellen Lentz, "Prussia Rediscovered in West German Display," NYT, Aug. 24, 1981, p. C14; NYT, Mar. 2, 1986, p. A3; Geoff Eley, "Nazism, Politics and the Image of the Past: Thoughts on the West German *Historikerstreit*, 1986–1987," *Past & Present*, no. 121 (1988), 171–208; Charles S. Maier, *The Unmasterable Past: History, Holocaust, and German National Identity* (Cambridge, Mass., 1988), 149.

4. E. J. Dionne, Jr., "To the Battles of France, Add That Over History," NYT, Apr. 24, 1984, p. A2; Keith Tribe, "History and the Production of Memories," *Screen*, 18 (Winter 1977–78), 21. For contemporary confusion among French and German schoolchildren about their national histories, see Keith Robbins, "National Indentity and History: Past, Present and Future," *History*, 75 (1990), 378.

5. V. S. Naipaul, *The Return of Eva Perón; With the Killings in Trinidad* (New York, 1980), 151, 166.

6. Kundera's book opens with the unforgettable story of a Czech politician who fell from favor being removed from a famous photograph by the Communist regime and henceforth from Czech history books. For a notably similar episode in which Lyndon B. Johnson had a governor of Texas "effaced" from a photograph with Franklin D. Roosevelt, see William E. Leuchtenberg, *In the Shadow of FDR: From Harry Truman to Ronald Reagan* (Ithaca, N.Y., 1983), 126.

7. Donald Horne, *The Great Museum: The Re-Presentation of History* (London, 1984), 251; Richard Johnson and Graham Dawson, "Popular Memory: Theory, Politics, Method," in Johnson et al., eds., *Making Histories: Studies in History-Writing and Poli-*

tics, 205–52; Michael Wallace, "Visiting the Past: History Museums in the United States," *Radical History Review,* no. 25 (1981), 63–96.

8.   Horne, *The Great Museum,* 95; Anthony J. Hall, "A Consideration of 'The New-comers . . . Inhabiting a New Land,' " *Canadian Historical Review,* 62 (1981), 252–57; Jennifer Dunning, "Dance: Zairians Relate Stories of Their Heritage," NYT, Oct. 11, 1981, p. 70; Buck Jenkins, "The Old Town in Aarhus," *Scanorama* (July–August 1981), 59–62. The BBC television series "Heritage" concentrated upon English pageantry.

9.   John Russell, "Britain's Heritage, a Rich Attic on View," NYT, Feb. 15, 1989, p. C15.

10.   Steve Lohr, "British Find the Past Enriching," NYT, Mar. 29, 1988, pp. D1, 20; Robert Hewison, *The Heritage Industry: Britain in a Climate of Decline* (London, 1987), 24.

11.   Hewison, *The Heritage Industry,* 24; Patrick Wright, *On Living in an Old Country: The National Past in Contemporary Britain* (London, 1985).

12.   Johnson, *Making Histories: Studies in History-Writing and Politics,* 218; Herman Lebovics, "Whose *Patrimoine?* The Politics of French Folklore from Popular Front to Vichy," paper prepared for a conference on Public Memory and Collective Identity held at Rutgers University on Mar. 16–17, 1990; David L. Schalk, *Roger Martin du Gard: The Novelist and History* (Ithaca, N.Y., 1967); Louis Chevalier, *Histoire anachronique des Français* (Paris, 1974).

13.   See Françoise Zonabend, *The Enduring Memory: Time and History in a French Village* (Manchester, Engl., 1984), 2–3, 196–98; Anton Kaes, *From Hitler to Heimat: The Return of History as Film* (Cambridge, Mass., 1989); Henry Glassie, *Passing the Time in Ballymenone: Culture and History of an Ulster Community* (Philadelphia, 1982), part nine; Paul Connerton, *How Societies Remember* (Cambridge, 1989), 20–21.

14.   Annie Sidro, *Le Carnaval de Nice et ses Fous* (Nice, 1979); Robert G. Hartje, *Bicentennial USA: Pathways to Celebration* (Nashville, Tenn., 1973), 44–45, 47–49, 54; Theodore R. Johnson, "The Memorialization of Woodrow Wilson" (unpubl. Ph.D. diss., The George Washington University, 1979), 110–11.

15.   Regina Bendix, "Tourism and Cultural Displays: Inventing Traditions for Whom?" *Journal of American Folklore,* 102 (1989), 131–46; Dean MacCannell, *The Tourist: A New Theory of the Leisure Class* (1976: New York, 1989), esp. ch. 5.

16.   Alexis de Tocqueville, *Democracy in America,* ed. by J. P. Mayer (Garden City, N.Y., 1969), 692; H. Stuart Hughes, *The Obstructed Path: French Social Thought in the Years of Desperation, 1930–1960* (New York, 1968), 20, 31; Fernand Braudel, "Personal Testimony," *Journal of Modern History,* 44 (1972), 466–67.

17.   Benedict Anderson, *Imagined Communities: Reflections on the Origin and Spread of Nationalism* (London, 1983); Anderson, "Narrating the Nation," *Times Literary Supplement,* June 13, 1986, p. 659.

18.   Henry Scott Stokes, "Japan Looks at Grisly Side of Its Past," NYT, July 13, 1982, p. A3; Michael T. Kaufman, "Canada Admitted Few Refugee Jews," NYT, Jan. 2, 1983, p. 12; Irving Abella and Harold Troper, *None Is Too Many: Canada and the Jews of Europe, 1933–1948* (Toronto, 1982).

19.   See Barry Schwartz, Yael Zerubavel, and Bernice M. Barnett, "The Recovery of Masada: A Study in Collective Memory," *The Sociological Quarterly,* 27 (1986), 147–64; "Memory and American History," a special issue of JAH, 75 (March 1989), 1117–1280, edited by David Thelen.

20.   See Michael Zuckerman, "The Irrelevant Revolution: 1776 and Since," AQ, 30 (1978), 224–42; Hartje, *Bicentennial USA,* ch. 3, "A Concert of People: The Canadian Centennial of Confederation"; Wilbur Zelinsky, "A Sidelong Glance at Canadian Nationalism and Its Symbols," *North American Culture,* 4 (1988), 3–27; Barbara Crossette, "In Australia, Bicentennial with a Yawn," NYT, Aug. 3, 1986, p. A5; James M. Markham, "For Lovers of Turmoil, Here Comes 1789 Again," NYT, Sept. 15, 1988, p. A4.

21.   The potential literature is vast, but see Harold T. Parker, *The Cult of Antiquity and the French Revolutionaries: A Study in the Development of the Revolutionary Spirit*

(Chicago, 1937); Eugen Weber, *Peasants into Frenchmen: The Modernization of Rural France, 1870–1914* (Stanford, Calif., 1976), 109; Jonathan Spence, *The Gate of Heavenly Peace: The Chinese and Their Revolution, 1895–1980* (New York, 1981); Edmund Wilson, *Patriotic Gore: Studies in the Literature of the American Civil War* (New York, 1962).

22. See Hughes, *The Obstructed Path: French Social Thought in the Years of Desperation*, 43.

23. NYT, Apr. 14, 1980, p. A3; NYT, Apr. 15, 1980, p. A2; NYT, Apr. 16, 1980, p. A3; NYT, Sept. 7, 1980, p. A11; NYT, Apr. 23, 1990, p. A4. See also "Confrontation Over Conservation," *The Jerusalem Post,* Jan. 10, 1983, p. 5.

24. Lloyd I. Rudolph and Susanne Hoeber Rudolph, *The Modernity of Tradition: Political Development in India* (Chicago, 1967); J. L. Talmon, "Reflections of an Historian in Jerusalem," *Encounter,* 46 (May 1976), 82–90; Yael Zerubavel, "The Politics of Interpretation: Tel Hai in Israeli Collective Memory," paper prepared for a conference on Public Memory and Collective Identity held at Rutgers University on Mar. 16–17, 1990.

25. Zerubavel, "Tel Hai in Israeli Collective Memory," 1–2, 41; Lucette Valensi, "From Sacred History to Historical Memory and Back: The Jewish Past," *History and Anthropology,* 2 (October 1986), 283–305.

26. Joseph Lelyveld, "In Zimbabwe, Blacks Make History Anew," NYT, Oct. 17, 1982, p. A11. See also "Hindus Seek to Revise Role in India's History," NYT, May 24, 1982, p. A10.

27. Compare Eric Davis, "The Making of Museums in the Contemporary Middle East," paper prepared for a conference on Public Memory and Collective Identity held at Rutgers University on Mar. 16–17, 1990, with Wilbur Zelinsky, *Nation into State: The Shifting Symbolic Foundations of American Nationalism* (Chapel Hill, N.C., 1988). For the subtle and casual implications of President Bush's call for "preserving America's heritage" in his 1990 budget message to Congress, see William H. Honan, "The Endowment That Has Stayed Out of Trouble," NYT, Apr. 16, 1990, p. C13.

28. See the fascinating book by Michael Cherniavsky, *Tsar and People: Studies in Russian Myths* (New Haven, 1961), esp. 44, 52, 71, 102, 202, 227, 231; George Gibian, "Beneath Communism, There Is Russia," *Wall Street Journal,* Mar. 4, 1988, p. 28.

29. Anthony Austin, "Stalin Museum in Soviet Guards Shreds of His Reputation," NYT, Dec. 16, 1979, p. 26; John F. Burns, "Medvedev, a Dissident Historian, Is Given Formal Warning in Soviet," NYT, Jan. 20, 1983, p. A14; "Gorbachev Hands Over Katyn Papers," NYT, Apr. 14, 1990, p. 5.

30. Philip Taubman, "Soviet Partly Lifts Veil on Its Past, Exciting Many but Irking Others," NYT, Oct. 26, 1987, p. A1; Dev Murarka, "A New Revolution in Consciousness," *The Nation,* 245 (Oct. 31, 1987), 486–90.

31. NYT, Nov. 3, 1987, pp. A1 and A11, with several analytical features on A10 and major sections of the text printed on pp. A11–A13.

32. NYT, Nov. 3, 1987, pp. A10 and A11.

33. Richard Bernstein, "Scholars Say Gorbachev Fell Short on Objectivity," NYT, Nov. 4, 1987, p. A4; Philip Taubman, "Soviet Historians Greet the Openness, Warily," NYT, Nov. 5, 1987, p. A6; Esther B. Fein, "Soviet Pupils Spared Exams While History Is Rewritten," NYT, May 31, 1988, p. A1; Anthony Lewis, "When Memory Comes," NYT, June 19, 1988, p. E27; Daniel Singer, "On Recapturing the Soviet Past," *The Nation,* 245 (Dec. 12, 1987), pp. 716–18.

34. Celestine Bohlen, "Tricks of Official Memory in the Baltic Republics," NYT, Oct. 30, 1988, p. E3; Craig R. Whitney, "Western Historians Join Russians to Dissect Past," NYT, Apr. 7, 1990, p. 7.

35. Gibian, "Beneath Communism, There Is Russia," *Wall Street Journal,* Mar. 4, 1988, p. 28.

36. See Jacques Dupâquier and Marcel Lachiver, *Les Temps Modernes* (Paris, 1971); Denis François et al., *L'Epoque Contemporaine* (Paris, 1971); James Reston, Jr., "How Japan Teaches Its Own History," NYT *Magazine,* Oct. 27, 1985, pp. 52ff.; G. Cameron Hurst, "Weaving the Emperor's New Clothes: The Japanese Textbook 'Revision' Contro-

versy," UFSI *Reports,* 1982, no. 46; Hurst, "Cultural Nationalism in Contemporary Korea," UFSI *Reports*, 1985, no. 33.

37. See Felix Gilbert, *History: Choice and Commitment* (Cambridge, Mass., 1977), 448, 450–51; Charles Rearick, *Beyond the Enlightenment: Historians and Folklore in Nineteenth-Century France* (Bloomington, Ind., 1974), 162–63; Robert R. Bowie, ed., *In Search of France* (Cambridge, Mass., 1963), 197–98; Alfred Cobban, *A History of Modern France,* III, *France of the Republics, 1871–1962* (Harmondsworth, Middlesex, 1965), 243.

38. Maier, *The Unmasterable Past: History, Holocaust, and German National Identity,* passim; Eric Hobsbawm and Terence Ranger, eds., *The Invention of Tradition* (Cambridge, 1983), 272; Richard Eder, "A Reporter's Notebook: Liberté, Egalité et le Déluge," NYT, July 15, 1980, p. A2. Cf. the consensual response to the American Revolution described in Kammen, *A Season of Youth: The American Revolution and the Historical Imagination* (New York, 1978).

39. Stephen Fischer-Galati, "Myths in Romanian History," *East European Quarterly,* 15 (1981), 327–34; Victor S. Mamatey, "The Battle of the White Mountain as Myth in Czech History," *East European Quarterly,* 15 (1981), 335–45; Richard Handler, "On Having a Culture: Nationalism and the Preservation of Quebec's Patrimoine," *History of Anthropology,* 3 (1985), 192–217; John D. Battersby, "Afrikaners Feud Over Past, and Path to the Future," NYT, Aug. 30, 1988, p. A4.

40. In addition to various illustrations already cited, see the extraordinary example involving the U.S.S. *Intrepid* as a naval museum, described by Michael Wallace, "The Politics of Public History," in Jo Blatti, ed., *Past Meets Present: Essays about Historic Interpretation and Public Audiences* (Washington, D.C., 1987), 48; and for the depoliticization of the Vietnam War see Michael Frisch, *A Shared Memory: Essays on the Craft and Meaning of Oral and Public History* (Albany, 1990), 162.

41. David Cannadine, "The Context, Performance and Meaning of Ritual: The British Monarchy and the 'Invention of Tradition,' c. 1820–1977," in Hobsbawm and Ranger, eds., *Invention of Tradition,* 101–64; Parker, *The Cult of Antiquity and the French Revolutionaries,* ch. 12, "The Cult Goes Democratic"; Alfred Croiset, *Enseignement et démocratie* (Paris, n.d.), and Croiset, *L'Education de la démocratie* (Paris, 1907).

42. Marvin Trachtenberg, *The Statue of Liberty* (New York, 1976); Conrad L. Wirth, *Parks, Politics, and the People* (Norman, Okla., 1980). See for comparisons James E. Young, "The Biography of a Memorial Icon: Nathan Rapoport's Warsaw Ghetto Monument," *Representations,* no. 26 (Spring 1989), 69–106.

43. Robert Penn Warren, *Democracy and Poetry* (Cambridge, Mass., 1975), 31. See Emilia Viotti da Costa, *The Brazilian Empire: Myths and Histories* (Chicago, 1985), ch. 9, "The Myth of Racial Democracy: A Legacy of the Empire."

44. See Peter L. Berger's review of Edward Shils's *Tradition* (1981), in NYT *Book Review,* Feb. 14, 1982, pp. 9, 26, and Mark Lilla's review of Hobsbawm and Ranger, eds., *The Invention of Tradition* (1983) in NR, 190 (Feb. 20, 1984), 35–39.

45. Job Durfee, "The Influence of Scientific Discovery and Invention on Social and Political Progress" (1843), in Clark S. Northup, ed., *Representative Phi Beta Kappa Orations* (New York, 1930), 75. For subsequent statements in the century that followed, see William Maxwell Evarts, "Oration" (1876), in Henry Nash Smith, ed., *Popular Culture and Industrialism, 1865–1890* (New York, 1967), 14; Stuart Pratt Sherman, "The Emotional Discovery of America," in Sherman, *The Emotional Discovery of America and Other Essays* (New York, 1932); 29.

46. Richard Slotkin, "Nostalgia and Progress: Theodore Roosevelt's Myth of the Frontier," AQ, 33 (1981), 636; Donald L. Miller, *Lewis Mumford: A Life* (New York, 1989), 251; Alfred H. Jones, *Roosevelt's Image Brokers: Poets, Playwrights, and the Use of the Lincoln Symbol* (Port Washington, N.Y., 1974), 4; Robert Pinsky, *An Explanation of America* (Princeton, 1979), 54; Theodore Rosengarten, *All God's Dangers: The Life of Nate Shaw* (New York, 1974), 551.

47. John F. Kasson, "The Invention of the Past: Technology, History, and Nostalgia," in Charles Strain and Steven Goldberg, eds., *Technological Change and the Transforma-*

tion of America (Carbondale, Ill., 1987), 49–50; Richard Beard, *Walt Disney's EPCOT Center: Creating a World of Tomorrow* (New York, 1982), 139.

48. "The Fortress of Solitude," in Umberto Eco, *Travels in Hyperreality: Essays* (New York, 1986), 11. See also Robert P. Frankel, Jr., "British Observers of America, 1890–1950" (unpubl. Ph.D. diss., Harvard University, 1989); W. Warren Wagar, *Good Tidings: The Belief in Progress from Darwin to Marcuse* (Bloomington, Ind., 1972); Jonathan Raban, *Old Glory: An American Voyage* (New York, 1981), 61.

49. See Richard Bridgman, "Jefferson's Farmer Before Jefferson," AQ, 14 (1962), 567–77; Henry Nash Smith, *Virgin Land: The American West as Symbol and Myth* (Cambridge, Mass., 1950), book three; Slotkin, "Nostalgia and Progress: Theodore Roosevelt's Myth of the Frontier," 608–09; R. Richard Wohl, "The 'Country Boy' Myth and Its Place in American Urban Culture: The Nineteenth-Century Contribution," PAH, 3 (1969), 77–158. For a more generalized and theoretical perspective, see Paul Oskar Kristeller, " 'Creativity' and 'Tradition,' " *Journal of the History of Ideas,* 44 (1983), 105–13.

Index

Abbey, Edwin Austin, 172, 207, 213
Abernethy, Thomas Perkins, 383
Abrams v. *United States,* 234
Action Française, 292, 520
Adams, Brooks, 23, 133, 206–7, 384
Adams, Cassily, 186
Adams, Charles Francis, Jr., 31 and
   illus., 84–5, 96, 109, 145, 174, 196,
   221, 663
Adams, Henry, 18, *illus.* 30, 31, 56, 93,
   95, 97, 139, 158, 170, 172, 194,
   196–7
Adams, Herbert Baxter, 20, 121, 171
Adams, James Truslow, 22–3, 29, 301,
   304, 336, 378, 389, 405, 410, 485,
   498, 499
Adams, John, 27, 40, 49, 66, 75, 76–7,
   156
Adams, John Quincy, 19, 64, 75
advertising, 300 and *n.*
   Civil War Centennial publicity, 593–6,
      606, 607
   Freedom Train publicity, 576, 578–9,
      580–1
   for museums, 640
   and tourism, 674–5
aesthetic, American
   19th century, 188–92
   20th century, 12, 307, 324–7, 334–5
African-Americans
   Colonial Williamsburg and, 368, 552–3,
      684
   commemorative occasions and
      pageants, 101, 122–3, *illus.* 124, 278;
      see also Emancipation Proclamation:
      celebrations of

culture ignored: 19th century, 63, 87,
   131 *n.*; 20th century, 248, 425–6,
   524, 683, 684–5
   folk culture, 408, 413–14, 426, 428–9,
      442, 632
   Harlem Renaissance, 413–14, 442
   historical consciousness: 19th century,
      121–5, *illus.* 123–4; 20th century,
      440–3, 643, 644
   museums, 638, 683–4
   pageants and ceremonies, 425, 683
   portrayed in art, 87, 113
   traditions and culture: 19th century,
      124–5, 144; 20th century, 440–3,
      624, 644
   see also racism and race relations;
      slavery
Agee, James, 435, 554–5
agrarianism, American, 6, 47, 93, 135,
   703–4
Agrarians ("Fugitives"), 22, 404, 519
agriculture
   historical farms, 615–16, 619, 635–6,
      679
   national museum of, 445
Alamo battle site, San Antonio, 9, 53,
   107, 240–2, 262, 487, 546–7, 647
Alaska-Yukon-Pacific Exposition (Seattle,
   1909), 139
Albright, Horace M., 466 and *illus.,*
   467–8, 470, 472
Alden, James Madison, 84
Alfred the Great, King, 174
Alger, Horatio, 27
Allen, Hervey, 434, 478, 501, 544
Allen, Richard, 124

Alsberg, Henry G., 475
America First movement, 5
Americana, collecting of, 12, 258, 311–23
  associations (objects valued for), 157,
    200, 324–5
  attitudes toward, compared with
    European, 166, 168, 188–92, 311–12
  in Britain, 653–4
  commercialization, 631–2
  democratization of, 317, 567–8, 632–4,
    679, 691
  Hudson-Fulton Loan Exhibition (1909),
    149, *illus.* 150, 188–9, 278, 318, 348
  motivations for, 322–4
  by museums, 188–92, 306, 313, 318,
    325, 342–74; *see also* museums
  networks and organizations, 258, 311,
    323 and *n.*, 411, 631
  prices, 156–7, 168, 461, 632
  20th century, 313, 461, 631–4
  see also American aesthetic; antiques;
    art(s), American; collections,
    individual; collectors and collecting;
    decorative arts; folk art(s)
Americana Collector, The (periodical),
  311
American aesthetic
  19th century, 188–92
  20th century, 12, 307, 324–7, 334–5
American Antiques and Crafts Society,
  631
American Folklife Preservation Act
  (1976), 429 *n.*, 617
American Folklore Society, 156,
  268
American Heritage Foundation, and
  Freedom Train, 576, 577, 579
American Heritage magazine, 538, 539,
  540, 541, 573, 627, 679
  circulation, 540 *n.*
American Historical Association, 74, 159,
  198, 259, 273, 446, 541, 663
  Committee of Seven on the Study of
    History in Schools, 248
Americanism, *see* exceptionalism,
  American
American Jewish Historical Society, 233,
  438
American language, *see* language,
  American
American Military Institute, 478
American Museum, Bath, England,
  653–4
American Museum of Immigration, New
  York, 7, 11, 638

American People's Historical Society,
  Burlington, Vt., 630–1
American Revolution
  African-American participation, 87
  documents of, 316, 349, 446 *n.*
  and French, contrasted, 35–6, 291–2,
    463
  heritage and tradition of, 463, 630
  mythicization of, 27, 65
  warped perceptions of (19th century),
    40, 89
American Scenic and Historic
  Preservation Society, 205–6, 262, 326
American's Creed, The, 304
American Women's Heritage Society,
  Philadelphia, 624
amnesia, collective, 9, 12, 503–4, 527,
    532, 535, 563, 572, 626, 658
  and desire for reconciliation, 13, 106
  of immigrants, 232, 236
  international, 690–3; and U.S.,
    compared, 701
  in pageantry, 280
  politically motivated, 658–63, 663 *n.*,
    690–3 *passim*
  and uncomfortable social reality, 50,
    101, 518, 639, 662–3, 694, 695
  see also memory, selective
Anacostia (D.C.) Museum, 683
anarchy and anarchists, 234
ancestor worship, 215–23, 236, 493,
    494–5, *illus.* 496
  in Germany and U.S., contrasted, 291
  racism in, 220
  resistance to, 221–2, 235
  in traditional societies, 222, 223 and
    illus., *illus.* 224
  in West (U.S.), 274
  see also hero worship
ancestral organizations, 218, 232, *illus.*
    333, 417
  family associations, 421
Anderson, Florence Bennett, 429
Anderson, Marian, 24
Anderson, Sherwood, 424, 511
Anglo-Saxon supremacy, tradition of, 220,
    236, 242
anniversaries, historic, *see* Bicentennial
    of Independence; Centennial of
    Independence; Civil War
    Centennial; commemorative days
    and celebrations; Constitutional
    Convention, 50th anniversary;
    Fourth of July; holidays, national;
    Sesquicentennial of Independence

Anshutz, Thomas, 225
Anthony, Susan B., 267
anti-communism, 544, 546–7, 573, 574, 579, 582, 587, 647; *see also* Cold War
Antietam battlefield (Md.), 120, 264, 425, 457
anti-modernism, 157, 248, 322
antiquarians and antiquarianism, American
  antebellum, 63, 71–5
  attitudes toward, 157–8
  and myth and tradition, 30–1
  see also collectors and collecting; historical societies; *and individual antiquarians by name*
antiques
  American aesthetic and, 326
  American collectors (20th century), 258, 312–24 *passim*, 569, 631–3; *see also* collectors and collecting
  colonial revival and rage for, 148–9
  commercial aspects, 148–9
  European *vs.* American objects valued, 168
  as investment, 324
  museums and, 318, 348–51 *passim*, 356, 364
  prices, 632, 677–8
  see also Americana, collecting of; furniture (antiques); silver (antique)
antiques fairs and shows, 250, 351, 633
Antiquities Act (U.S., 1906), 187, 259, 470, 479, 611
antiquities and ruins, American, *see* archaeology, American; ethnography, American; historic sites; preservation, historic
Appalachia, 221, 428
Appleton, William Sumner, 10, 264–5, 347, 371
Appomattox, Va., 108, 472 and *illus.*
  centennial (1965), 603, *illus.* 604
Archaeological Institute of America, 184, 262, 347
Archaeological Resources Protection Act (U.S., 1979), 611
archaeology, American, 184, 188, 262, 348, 684
architecture, American
  colonial revival, 146–7, 169–70, 261, 305, 325 *n.*, 387, 461–2
  historical architects, training of, 370
  Historic American Buildings Survey, 468, 469, 474, 614

  medieval revival, 170–1
  national style, 415
  past styles favored (Hunt), 164–5
  Renaissance influences, 170, 172
  20th century, 268
  Western U.S., 167, 182; mission style, 394, 396
  see also preservation, historic
architecture, British, 34, 172
archives, *see* National Archives (U.S.); records, public
Arensberg, Walter, *et ux.*, 327
Armory Show (New York, 1913), 271
Arneson, Robert, *illus.* 651, 652
Arnold, Benedict, 125, 511
Arnold, Matthew, 283
art(s), American
  acceptance of (early 20th century), 188–92, 306–7
  American aesthetic and, 326
  collectors of, 168–9; *see also* collecting and collectors
  depoliticized, 511
  folk elements in, 430–1, 434; *see also* folk art(s), American
  government and, 462, 464; *see also* government, cultural role of
  historical authenticity of, 28
  intergenerational continuity as theme in, 224–7 and *illus.*
  memory depicted in, 93–5 and *illus.*
  Old West in, 182, 395–6, 401
  Pilgrims and Puritans in, 206, 207–8, 213, *illus.* 214–15, 391, *illus.* 392
  post–World War II, 545–6
  prices, 157, 168, 461, 632
  see also architecture, American; collectors and collecting; dance, American; decorative arts, American; folk art(s), American; music, American; painting(s), American; photography; sculpture, American
Arthur, Chester A., 129, *illus.* 130
Art Institute of Chicago, 154, 170, 189, 190
Art Institute of Indianapolis, 154
Association for the Preservation of the Missions, 262–3
Association for the Preservation of Virginia Antiquities (A.P.V.A.), 130, 185, 195, 260, 331, 473
Association for the Study of Negro Life and History, 441
associations, *see* Americana, collecting of: networks and organizations; folklore,

associations (*continued*)
  American: societies; historical
    societies; preservation, historic:
    organizations for
Atkinson, Edward, 106
Attucks, Crispus, 87, 122
Auden, Wystan Hugh, 515
Audubon Museum, Henderson, Ky.,
    458
Australia, role of tradition, 521
authenticity, historical
  American obsession with, 18, 28–9,
    299, 345, 351, 482
  in fiction, 28, 29
  of reconstructions and reproductions,
    305, 342, 373 and *n.*, 626
  in television docudramas, 671
automobile(s), 97
  democratizes travel, 304, 506, 539–40
  see also highways; tourism and travel
Aztecs, 32

B

Babbitt, Irving, 22, 24
Bach, Richard F., 306
Bainville, Jacques, 520
Balch, Col. George T., 245
Baldwin, Henry, 236–7, 250 and *n.*,
    251–3
Baltimore, Md., 142–3, 162, 166, 201
Bancroft, George, 10, 34, 49, 70, 135,
    197
Bancroft, Hubert Howe, 317
Barber, John Warner, 71–2
Bartlett, John Russell, 19
Baruch, Bernard, 23
Bastien-Lepage, Jules, 172, *illus.* 173
Batcheller, George Clinton, 109, 192 *n.*
battle monuments and battlefields, 11,
    456–7
  of Civil War, 119–20; as sacred sites,
    202; *see also specific sites*
  democratization of, 422
  National Park Service and, 467–8, 609,
    610–11
  private *vs.* government funding of
    preservation, 55, 119–20, 263–4
  threatened by commercial
    development, 609–11, 674
  see also Alamo; Antietam; Bunker Hill;
    Chickamauga; Custer Battlefield;
    Gettysburg; historic sites; Manassas;
    national military parks; Saratoga;
    Shiloh; Yorktown
battle re-enactments, 142, 425, 456, 533,
    547, 628
  for Civil War Centennial, 605, 606 and
    illus., 609
Bayou Bend museum, Houston, 313,
    illus. 314, 566
Beard, Charles A., 248, 446, 498, *illus.*
    499, 531, 533
Beauregard, Gen. Pierre G. T., 126
Bebie, Hans Heinrich, 169
Becker, Carl L., 179, 199, 336, 503, 531,
    541, 688
Beecher, Catharine, 43
Beecher, Lyman, 79
Belknap, Jeremy, 48, 373
Bell, James Ford, 317, 566
Bellow, Saul, 686
Benedict, Ruth F., 389, 414, 515, 531
Benét, Stephen Vincent, 24, 313, 322,
    334, 339, 341, 375, 410, 427, 434,
    498–9, *illus.* 500, 511, 702
Benton, Thomas Hart, 57, 114, 186, 301,
    339, 376, 410–11, 434, 668
Berenson, Bernard, 21, 164, 268
Betts, Karl S., *illus.* 593, 594, 598–9
Bibliographical Society of America, 156
Bicentennial of Independence (1975–76),
    572
  apathy about, 588–9, 695
Biddle, E. G., 85
Bierce, Ambrose, 131
Bill of Rights (U.S.), 257, 510, 666
  Bicentennial, 588
  exhibited, 574, 576, *illus.* 580
Billy the Kid (William H. Bonney), 397
biography, American, 28, 120, 159–60,
    337, 588
  biased versions, 378–9
Bixby, William K., 316
black Americans, *see* African-Americans
Black American West Museum, Denver,
    683
Black History Month, 630; *see also* Negro
    History Week
Bloch, Marc, 30–1, 37, 199, 693, 695
Bloom, Sol, 452–3, 456, 464, 503–4, 592
Boas, Franz, 414–15, 426
Bok, Edward, 149
Bolles, Eugene, 189
Bontemps, Arna, 414, 442
books, collecting, 156, 243, 312, 313,
    316–18, 440, 566, 569, 632; *see also*
    libraries; manuscripts

Boone, Daniel, 26, 80, 86–7, 489, 695

Borglum, Gutzon, 329, 449, 489 and
    illus., 490–1, 505, 509

Boston, 143, 186, 201, 245; *see also*
    Museum of Fine Arts, Boston; Old
    South Meeting House; Patriots' Day

Boston Public Library, 150, 170

Botkin, Benjamin A., 435–6

Botsford Tavern, Detroit, 354, 355

Boughton, George Henry, 61

Bourget, Paul, 283

Bourke-White, Margaret, 434

Bourne, Randolph, 416

Boyd, Ernest, 303, 503

Boyd, James, 303, 405–6, 410, 420,
    510–11

Bradford, Gamaliel, 337, 377, 378

Bradford, William, 64, 160, 196

Brawley, Benjamin, 414

Breckinridge, William C. P., 107, 210,
    211

bridges, 339, 505, 506

Britain, *see* Great Britain

Brock, Robert Alonzo, 112, 727–8

Brooklyn (N.Y.) Museum, 346–7

Brooks, Phillips, 239

Brooks, Van Wyck, 410, *illus.* 412, 416,
    607
    on history, 257, 306
    on New England culture and attitudes,
        389, 406
    and Rourke, 411–12, 499
    views and opinions, 257, 309, 335, 415,
        418–19, 482, 499 *n.*, 503, 641

Brophy, Thomas D'Arcy, 576, 580

Brown, William Garrott, 178, 179

Brown, William Wells, 87

Brownson, Orestes A., 42

Bruce, John E., 125

Bruce, Philip A., 330–1, 385–6, 495

Bruce, William Cabell, 115, 337

Bryan, William Jennings, 109

Bryant, William Cullen, 43, 44, 60

Bryce, James, Viscount Bryce, 121, 173

Budd, Ralph, 393

Bunker Hill (Mass.) battle monument, 19,
    55, 71

Bunyan, Paul (legendary figure), 426, 526

Burckhardt, Jacob, 10, 197, 284

Burk, W. Herbert, 200

Burke, Edmund, 6

Burnside, Gen. Ambrose E., 129, *illus.*
    130

Burr, Aaron, 511, 644

Burton, Clarence A., 183–4

Burwell, Mary Travis, *illus.* 127

Bush, George, 652

Butler, Nicholas Murray, 246, 388

C

Cable, George Washington, 113

Cahan, Abraham, 233

Cahill, Holger, 320–1, 326, 327, 426, 431,
    433, 476

Caldwell, Erskine, 433–4

Calhoun, John C., 106, 117

California
    cultural preservation and museums,
        181–2, 274, 396–7
    interest in past, 394
    missions, preservation and restoration
        of, 183, 262–3, 394
    see also Los Angeles; San Diego; San
        Francisco

California Landmarks Club, 263

Calverton, V. F., 390–1, 463, 515

Calvin, John, 41

Calvinism, 65, 210, 212, 271

Canada
    apathy about national
        commemorations, 695
    role of tradition, 521–4, 701

Canby, Henry Seidel, 484

Capitol building (Washington, D.C.),
    Rotunda, paintings, 75–6, 86–7, 213

Carey, Mathew, 235

Carmer, Carl, 434, 680

Carmiencke, Johann H., 46

Carnegie, Andrew, 239

Carnegie Institution, Washington, D.C.,
    156, 267, 439, 440

Carson, Kit, 26, 276

Carter, Amon, 566

Carter, Elliott, 431

Carter, Jimmy, 617, 630

Carter, Mary D., 382

Carver, George Washington, 442–3

Casa Amesti, Monterey, Calif., 558, 559

Cass, Lewis, 76

Cassirer, Ernst, 30

Castillo de San Marco, St. Augustine,
    Fla., 468 and *illus.*

Cater, Harold Dean, 340, 550

Cather, Willa, 276, 334, 420, 436, 502

Catlin, George, 83, 86

Catton, Bruce, 540, 544, 597, 605, *illus.*
    671, 679

Causici, Enrico, 87
CCC (Civilian Conservation Corps), 458,
     469, 474
cemeteries, 274, 500
Centennial of Independence (1876), 134,
     272
   Exposition, Philadelphia, 135–6, 137–8,
     169, 185
Centennial of U.S. (New York, 1889), 445
Central Park, New York, 19–20
Century of Progress Exposition (Chicago,
     1933), 305, 424, 461
Cerf, Bennett, 420
Chalmette Battle Monument (La.), 11, 19
Chambers, Henry E., 112
change, social and cultural
   European and American (18th–19th
     centuries), contrasted, 37
   in literature, 334–5
   Lowell and, 228
   1960s, 618–19
   post–World War II, 534, 537, 538, 539,
     545
   Progressives and, 269–70
   resistance to, 59–60, 237–8, 248;
     collective amnesia as, 50, 101, 518,
     639, 662–3, 694, 695; nostalgia as,
     294–5, 653
   in South, post-Civil War, 113–14
   tradition(s) and, 7, 10–11, 408
Channing, Edward, 217
Chapin, Samuel, 206
Chapman, John G., 75
Chappel, William P., *illus.* 67
Charleston, S.C., 114, 117, 201
   Cypress Gardens Plantation, 560
   Middleburg Plantation, 684
   Old Slave Market museum, 560
Chase, Richard, 544–5
Chatelain, Verne E., 465
chauvinism, *see* patriotism
Chevalier, Michel, 56–7
Chicago
   centennial (1903), 143
   Century of Progress International
     Exhibition (World's Fair, 1933), 305,
     424, 461
   monuments, endowment of, 154
   World's Columbian Exhibition (1893),
     139, 170, 186, 246, 325 and *n.*, 496,
     533
   see also Art Institute of Chicago;
     Newberry Library
Chickamauga (Tenn.) Battlefield, 107,
     119, 264

Child, Francis, 407
Chilton, Mary, 209
China, tradition in, 293, 696
Choate, Rufus, 56, 60, 87
Chorley, Kenneth, 358, 365, 366, 368–70,
     373 and *n.*, 374, 503, 539, 554, 555,
     560, 580, 583, 587 and *n.*, 762
Christy, Howard Chandler, 86, 213, *illus.*
     214, 328–9 and *n.*
Chrysler, Walter, 567
Church, Frederic E., 168
churches
   anniversaries, 201
   growth of (20th century), 502
cities in U.S.
   commemorative celebrations (late 19th
     century), 137–43 *passim; see also*
     commemorative days and
     celebrations
   data collected on, 248
   historic urban districts, 372, 534, 561,
     564, 675–6, 682; urban renewal and,
     610, 614, 629
   see also specific cities
civil religion, 66, 68, 537
   in France, 204
   history and tradition as, 194–206
   in Japan, 293–4
   and orthodox religion, 204–6, 741
   and patriotism, 192, 204–5
   and post-Civil War reconciliation,
     107
   secularized (20th century), 678
   "shrines" of, 201–4, 259, 486–8, 532,
     547–8, 589, 590, 608–9, 687
Civil War (U.S.), 88–90, 101–7, 109–31
   false patriotism and, 301
   politicization of its history, 121
   post-war bitterness and resentment,
     110–15
   post-war reconciliation, 103, 106–9,
     114–15, 126, 257, 404–5, 406 *n.*, 416,
     417, 491, 701
   veterans, 103–6, 111–14, 201–2, 591;
     Blue-Gray reunions, 105, 106–7,
     417–18, 457
   writings and textbooks on, 120–1,
     382–3, 485
   see also Confederacy
Civil War (U.S.), monuments and
     commemorations, 71, 102–6, 110–11,
     115–18, 456
   Borglum's, 329, 491
   Centennial, *see* Civil War Centennial
     (1960s)

displays of war relics and memorabilia, 118–19, *illus.* 120
Garfield memorial, 102
Golden Jubilee (1911–15), 416
in North, 116–17
in Richmond (proposed), 108, 110, 111, 167 *n.*
in South, 117–18, 126, 416, 591
see also under battle sites and individuals honored
Civil War Centennial (1960s), 532, 538, 540, 572, 588, 590–610
   Commission, 592–607, 609, 806; racial issues, 592, 594, 597, 598, 601–2
   publicity and commercial aspects, 588, 593–6, *illus.* 596, 606, 607
Clark, Tom C., 574, 575, *illus.* 577, 579
Clark, Walter Van Tilburg, 511
Clark, William Andrews, 174
classes, social
   and anti-modernism, 248
   and ethnicity, 228, 236
   conflict among (pageants obscure), 280
   see also elites; working class, American
classical cultural models, 33, 68, 167 and *n.*, 170, 190, 225, 226, 747
Clayton, Henry DeLamar, Jr., 234
Clearwater, Alphonso, 269, 389
Clemens, Samuel, *see* Twain, Mark
Clements, William L., 174, 316
clergy (historians as), 199–200
Cleveland, Grover, 102, 115, 126
Cloisters, New York, 311
Clough, Arthur Hugh, 197
Coates, Edmund C., *illus.* 155
Cochin, Auguste, 292
Cody, William Frederick ("Buffalo Bill"), 27, 269, 275, 400 *n.*
Coe, William R., 317
Cold War, 5, 367, 544, 572–3, 592; *see also* anti-communism
Cole, Thomas, 43, 69
Coleman, Cynthia, 195
Coleridge, Samuel Taylor, 202
collections, individual
   Bancroft, 317
   Bell, 317, 566
   Bixby, 316
   Bolles, 189
   Carter (A.), 566
   Chrysler, 567
   Clearwater, 269, 389
   Clements, 316–17
   Coe, 317
   Deering, 569

Du Pont, 319–20, 343, 566
   Feinstone, 439
   Ford, 352 and *n.*, 353–8 *passim*
   Gaines, 569
   Garbisch, 567
   Garvan, 24, 343, 569
   Gilcrease, 347–8
   Gray, 73
   Halsey, 318
   Hirshhorn, 313–14, 569–70
   Huntington, 316
   Jenckes, 569
   Karolik, 344–6
   Lipman, 680–1
   Lummis, 181
   Lyon, 396–7
   McGregor, 317
   Melville, 568
   Mercer, 321–2, 421
   Morgan, 190, 343
   Phillips, 326, 340, 343
   Poore, 73
   Rockefeller (A.), 268, 321, 426–7, 431–2, 566, 680
   Sang, 591
   Schomburg, 343, 440
   Simms, 78
   Sparks, 78
   Stokes, 343
   Streeter, 317–18, 569
   Wakeman, 157
   Walters, 166
   Webb (E.H.), 320, 566
   Williams (J.), 556
   Young, 312
   see also collectors and collecting
collectors and collecting
   (19th century), 73, 154–61 *passim*
   (20th century), 154–61 *passim*, 174, 190–2, 311–23, 461, 568–70, 631–4, 679
   of Americana, *see* Americana, collecting of
   of art, 168–9; *see also* art(s), American
   benefactors, motives and role of, 157–8, 565–6
   of folk art, *see* folk art(s), American
   organizations and networks, 258, 311, 323 and *n.*, 566, 623
   women, 166, 269; *see also individual collectors*
   see also antiquarians, American; antiques; decorative arts in U.S.; folklore; furniture; painting(s), American; silver; *and individual collectors*

College of William and Mary,
    Williamsburg, Va., 109, 126, 358,
    359, 382, 542
Collier, John, Jr., 421
Collins, Robertson E., 628
Colonial Dames of America, 148, 218,
    244, 332, 343, 351, 366, 437
colonialism, American, 238
Colonial National Monument (Va.), 450
    and *n.*, 451
Colonial Order of the Acorn, 218
colonial revival, 6, 146–52
    architecture, 146–7, 169–70, 261, 305,
        325 *n.*, 387, 461–2
    in Britain, 286
    women and, 266
Colonial Williamsburg (Va.), 359–70,
    581–7
    attendance figures, 367, 551–2, 640
    authenticity of, 28, 362, 369
    ceremonial and state visits, 583–4,
        illus. 584–6
    Goodwin and, 200, 359–66
    influence on other institutions, 370,
        550, 554
    and patriotism, 580–7
    preservation policies, 367, 369
    race relations, 368, 552–3, 684
    as "shrine," 487, 492
    Southern attitudes toward, 491–2
    visitor comments and responses, 364,
        368–9, 547, 552, 553–4
    see also Chorley, Kenneth
Columbian Exposition (Chicago, 1893),
    139, 170, 186, 246, 325 and *n.*, 496,
    533
Columbus, Christopher, 439
    quincentennial (1992), 627, 685
Columbus Day, 181, 242, 243 and *n.*
Commager, Henry Steele, 540, 607
commemorative days and celebrations
    (19th century), 134–45, 162
    (early 20th century), 162, 255
    (mid-20th century), 542–3, 587–610
    apathy about, 49, 494, 588–9, 695
    Canadian, 523
    educational mission, 137
    of immigrant groups, 437–40; *see also*
        under specific ethnic groups
    local, 140–5, 162; *see also by locale*
    nostalgia of, 237–8
    religious aspect, 201, 205; *see also* civil
        religion
    in West (20th century), 144–5, 274,
        394–5, 398 and *n.*, 399, 401

    see also African-Americans:
        commemorative occasions of; Civil
        War (U.S.), monuments and
        commemorations; expositions;
        holidays, national; pageants and
        pageantry
commercialization of culture and the
    past, 343, 535–6, 628, 655, 672–8
    and antiques, 148–9
    in Britain, 691–2
    in literature, 334–5
    media and, 536, 543–4, 669–72
    and museum policy, 306; at Colonial
        Williamsburg, 365
    and pageants, 423
    resistance to, 398
    for tourism, 10, 13, 276 *n.*, 402–3,
        439–40, 465, 534, 537, 673–4, 693
    in West, 270, 401, 402–3, 549, 676,
        illus. 677
    see also advertising; Civil War
        Centennial: publicity and
        commercial aspects
Commons, John R., 199
communism in U.S.
    (1930s), 463, 464, 475, 515
    fear of, 237, 657
    see also anti-communism; Cold War
Comte, Auguste, 196
Confederacy
    documents of, 114
    Lost Cause tradition, 11, 101, *illus.*
        108, 113, 126, 195, 217, 275, 491,
        609
    monuments, *see* Civil War (U.S.),
        monuments and commemorations
    reunions of veterans, 105, 111, 114,
        201–2; Blue-Gray, 106–9, 417–18,
        457
Confederate Museum, Richmond, Va.,
    381
Conger, Clement E., 615
consensus (social) *vs.* diversity, *see*
    pluralism, cultural
conservation movement and policy, 263,
    265–6
    National Park Service and, 465–73
        passim
    states and, 469
    see also parks, national
conservatism and conservatives
    and immigrants, 244–8, 250
    and myth, 17, 30
    and Puritanism, 212
    reverence for history, 660

and tradition, 289, 409
see also right (political)
Constitution (U.S.)
  anniversaries of: (1887), centennial,
    445; (1937), sesquicentennial, 423,
    457, 543; (1947), 160th, 576; (1987),
    bicentennial, 588, 695
  displayed, 487, 577
  preservation and storage, 75
  Thirteenth Amendment, 123
  see also Bill of Rights (U.S.)
Constitutional Convention, 50th
  anniversary (1837), 49
Constitution Day, 257
Continental Congress, its papers, 75
Conway, Moncure D., 95, 145
Coolidge, Calvin, 341, 388, 423, 444,
  448–9, 490
Coolidge, Grace, 300
Coolidge, Mrs. Thomas Jefferson, Jr.,
  268
Cooper, James Fenimore, 18, 27, 37,
  60–1, 82
Copland, Aaron, 309, 411, 420–1, 430–1,
  531
Copp Collection of Colonial Costumes,
  Washington, D.C., 205
Corcoran Gallery of Art, Washington,
  D.C., 93, 170, 189
Corné, Felix Michel, 213
Cornell University (Ithaca, N.Y.), Sparks
  collection, 78
Coues, Elliot, 26
"country boy" myth, 26–7, 704
Covered Wagon Days, 398, 423
cowboy culture and lore, 220, 258, 275,
  276, 431, 492
  rodeos, 401, 423
Cowley, Malcolm, 389, 433, 482
Cox, Kenyon, 98 and *illus.*, 99 and *illus.*,
  165, 189, 326
Cram, Ralph Adams, 149, 170
Craven, Thomas, 416
Crockett, Davy, 28, 241, 489, 647, 680
Croly, Herbert, 270, 416–17
Cropsey, Jasper F., 153, *illus.* 154–5
Cullen, Countee, 414, 627
cultural geography, 243
cultural imperialism, 238
cultural pluralism, *see* pluralism, cultural
cultural relativism, 515, 531
cultural transmission, 224–7
culture, *see* folk culture, American; high
  culture; pluralism, cultural; politics
  of culture; popular culture

Cunliffe, Marcus, 129
Cunningham, Ann Pamela, 260
Curry, John Steuart, 376, 434
Curtis, Edward S., 191
Curtis, George William, 208, 212
Curzon, George Nathaniel, Baron,
  288
Cushing, Frank, 188
Custer, Gen. George A., last stand of
  (1876), 9, 138, 257, 275, 489, 647,
  739
  iconography, 186
  pageants, 423, 425
Custer Battlefield National Monument
  (Mont.), 611 and *illus.*
Czechoslovakia
  collective memory and amnesia in,
    690–1, 701
  myth and tradition in, 289

D

Dallin, Cyrus E., 186–7, 395
dance, American, 545
D.A.R. (Daughters of the American
  Revolution), 218, 219, 220, 244, 259,
  332, 401, 425
  Museum, Washington, D.C., 370
Darling, J. N. ("Ding"), 400 and *n.*
Darwinism, 194, 285
Daughters of the American Colonists,
  illus. 333
Daughters of the Republic of Texas,
  240–1, 262, 647
Davenport, John, 142
Davis, Jefferson, 103, 119, 125–6, 131 *n.,*
  381, 383, 630
Davis, Stuart, 306–7, *illus.* 308
Dawson, Henry B., 76, 80
Debs, Eugene V., 502–3
debunking, 463, 481, 488, 497, 498, 519
decentralization of culture and tradition,
  12, 14, 317
  later 20th century, 572, 588
Declaration of Independence
  in "accessible English," 422
  displayed, 487, 577
  preservation and storage, 75
  replicas, 76
Decoration Day, *see* Memorial Day
decorative arts in U.S.
  antiques, *see* antiques
  collecting (20th century), 318–21, 408,
    615

decorative arts in U.S. (*continued*)
  courses in, 343
  museums and, 348–58 *passim,* 370
  prices, 461
  see also Americana, collecting of; folk
    art(s), American; Hudson-Fulton
    Loan Exhibition (1909)
Deerfield, Mass.
  restoration in, 261, 557, 566
  see also Historic Deerfield, Inc. (Mass.)
Deering, Frank C., 569
Defenders' Day (Baltimore), 162
De Forest, John William, 212
De Forest, Robert Weeks, 342, 348–9,
  502
Deland, Margaret, 150
Delano, Jack, 421
democracy
  in Europe, World War II and, 525–6
  in France, 292
democracy in U.S.
  and ancestors (attitudes toward), 216
  attitudes toward, 18, 20–4, 179–80;
    excess feared, 6, 20–1, 22–3, 239
  elite as leaders of, 19
  and ethnicity, 236, 238
  and humanism, 22
  and literature, 20–1, 32, 420
  and pageants, 167, 279, 280–1
  perceived as threatened, 250, 504, 510,
    531–2
  Puritans and, 390
  and Southern sectionalism, 404
  and tradition, 19, 21–2, 24, 292, 407,
    408, 435, 701–2; *see also*
    democratization of culture and
    tradition
  vogue for (1880s), 239
  see also equality, social; pluralism,
    cultural
democratization of culture, 12, 13, 23,
    300–2, 343, 346, 407, 412, 419–43
    passim, 464, 493, 504–5, 588, 655,
    679–85
  in Britain, 19
  and collectors of Americana, 317,
    567–8, 632–4, 679, 691
  of education, 422
  of genealogy, 421
  "heritage syndrome" and, 628
  in museums, 20, 156, 163, 306, 310,
    340, 353, 356, 509
  of national parks and historic sites, 465,
    471
  of photography, 421

resistance to, 473
  of travel, 304, 340, 420, 506, 539–40
  of war and battle monuments,
    422
Demuth, Charles, 306, *illus.* 307
Depew, Chauncey M., 108, 129, 255
depoliticizing traditions and myths, 13,
    448–55, 511–12, 662–3, 701, 704
Depression (economic), 367, 410, 502,
    503
Detroit Institute of Art, 190
DeVoto, Bernard, 133, 384, 402–3, 413,
    428, 493, 498
Dewey, John, 210, 271–2, 301, 516
De Zavala, Adina, 240–2
Dictionary of American Biography,
    159–60, 383
discovery of America, 242–3
Disney, Walt, 534, 535 and *illus.*
Disneyland, Anaheim, Calif., 534, 535,
    557, 639, 662–3
  see also EPCOT Center
dissent and dissenters in U.S.,
  omitted from histories and museums,
    248, 639
  and patriotism, 645, 647, 648, 649,
    illus. 650
  vs. Vietnam War, 5, 585, 645
  see also anarchy and anarchists
distinctiveness, American, *see*
    exceptionalism, American
diversity *vs.* unity, *see* pluralism, cultural
Dixon, Thomas, 195–6
Dobie, (James) Frank, 428, 668, 680, 689
documents, public, *see* records, public
Dodd, Anna Bowman, 267
Dodd, William E., 114, 221, 248, 258,
    301, 378–9, 406 *n.,* 516
Dooley, Mr. (Finley Peter Dunne), 210
Dos Passos, John, 257, 306, 334–5, *illus.*
    335, 479
Douglas, William O., 542
Douglass, Frederick, 87, 121–2, 124
Dow, George Francis, 160, *illus.* 161,
    162, 247, 258, 346, 426, 506
Downs, Joseph, 350, 415
Drake, Samuel Adams, 146–7
Driscoll, Clara, 240–2, 262
Du Bois, William Edward Burghardt,
    220, 278, 414, 425–6, 440
Dunne, Finley Peter, 210
Dunsmore, John Ward, 203
Du Pont, Henry Francis, 10, 319–20,
    343, 566, 633; *see also* Winterthur
    Museum, Wilmington, Del.

Durand, Asher B., 45–6, *illus.* 46, 52, 157

Dwight, Timothy, 42, 181

E

Earle, Alice Morse, 80, 148

Early, Gen. Jubal A., 111

Eastman, George, 96

Edison, Thomas A., 353, 355 and *n*.

Eco, Umberto, 703

education
  Civil War Centennial and, 603–4, 607–8
  democratized, 422
  and immigrant population, 244–8, 349
  media and, 543–4
  as role of museums and other cultural institutions, 132, 247, 305, 310, 316, 340, 349, 356, 373, 398, 509, 555, 556; national parks, 465, 466–7
  as tradition-bound, 484
  travel as, 340, 393, 403 and *n*., 423
  see also history, teaching of; textbooks, in history

Eggleston, Edward, 20 and *illus.*, 28, 80, 128, 147, 173–4, 178, 197–8, 205, 211, 246 and *n*., 248, 410

Eisenhower, Dwight D., 592, 610, 613, 663

Eisenstadt, S. N., 79–80

Eliade, Mircea, 26

Eliot, Charles W., 21, 136, 239

Eliot, John, 213

Eliot, Thomas Stearns, 5, 14, 195, 414

elites
  and civil religion, 205
  and conservation policy and activities, 265–6
  and immigrants, 237–9
  as leaders: of American democracy, 19; in the arts, 24, 164, 192; of cultural institutions, 24, 156, 318–19
  and lineage and patriotic societies, 218, 646–7
  and museum collections and policy, 350
  and travel and tourism, 306
  see also collectors and collecting; high culture; intellectuals

Ellyson, Lora, 195

Emancipation Proclamation, 577
  celebrations of, 123, 124, *illus.* 125, 257, 278, 599, *illus.* 600–1

Emerson, Ralph Waldo, 43, 44–5, 145, 216

England, *see* Great Britain

Enlightenment, American, 65

environmentalists, *see* conservation movement and policy

Environmental Protection Act (U.S., 1969), 614

EPCOT Center, Orlando, Fla., 534, 639, 663, 687, 703

equality, social
  concerns and fears about, 228, 238
  see also democracy

Ericsson, John, 47, 505

Eriksson, Leif
  commemoration day, 243 *n*., 437
  statues of, 242 and *n*.

Erskine, John, 497

Essex Institute, Salem, Mass., 160, 247, 258, 346, 426

esthetic, American, *see* aesthetic, American

ethnic groups
  conflicting memories of, 38
  contest for recognition among, 240
  cuisine of, interest in, 687
  education and, 244–8, 349
  federal cultural policy and, 230–1, 616
  and folk culture, 435–40
  and genealogy, 643–4
  pageants and rituals, 277–8, 425
  and selection of traditions to retain, 13
  their uses of the past, 10
  xenophobia and, 228, 232, 236–40, 252–3, 436
  see also African-Americans; immigrants to U.S.; Native Americans; naturalized Americans; *and under nationalities of origin*

Ethnic Heritage Studies Act (U.S., 1972), 616

ethnicity
  and class, 228, 236
  and cultural pluralism, 235–6, 243
  and folk culture, 408
  in literature, 483
  and pageantry, 279, 281
  and religious affiliation, 8
  study of, 616
  in West, 549
  see also "folk," the

ethnography, American, 72, 86, 87, 185–7 *passim*, 415

European culture
  American attitudes toward, 41–2, 73,
    134, 163–8 *passim*, 175, 326, 408,
    510
  its art preferred to American, 154,
    166, 168, 189, 318
  its history preferred to American, 178
    and *n*.
  role of tradition in, 284–90
  see also France; Germany; Great
    Britain; Spain
Europe and U.S., compared
  American disadvantage, efforts to
    reverse, 336, 338
  attitudes toward: folk and national
    culture, 407; past, 56–60 *passim*;
    ruins, 53–4
  cultural role of tradition (20th
    century), 284–90, 652
  cultural trends (19th century), 34–7
  differences emphasized, 164, 165, 510,
    515
  folktales, 426
  pageantry (civic), 281
  relative value of art from, 154, 165,
    166, 168, 188–92, 311–12, 318, 326
  social dynamics of myth and tradition,
    516–17, 518–20
Evacuation Day, 162, 281
evangelicalism, 50, 93, 200, 667
Evans, Luther, 473
Evans, Rudulph, *illus.* 463
Evans, Walker, 421, 435
Evans, William T., 189
Evarts, William Maxwell, 135
Everett, Edward, 4, 33, 80, 259
evolution, 194
exceptionalism, American, 18, 290–4,
    303–4, 310, 408, 409, 510, 513–18,
    653, 689, 700–4
  in art(s), 190
  in civil religion, 202, 205
  and cultural pluralism, 243
  linguistic aspect, 174, 175, 334,
    648–9
  in literature, 37, 175, 177, 258, 416
  myth(s) and, 26, 27–8, 515
expositions, 132, 138–9
  and economic conditions, 502
  technology celebrated, 514
  world's fairs, 424, 458
  see also Centennial of American
    Independence (1876): Exposition,
    Philadelphia; Chicago: Century of
    Progress International Exhibition . . .
    (1933); Columbian Exposition

(Chicago, 1893); New York City:
    World's Fair (1939);
    Panama-California Exposition
    (1915–16); Southern States
    Pan-American Exposition . . . (1914)

F

family traditions
  19th century, 63, 81
  20th century, 218, 227, 421, 504–5,
    644–5
  intergenerational continuity, 244–7
    and *illus.*
  reunions, 216 and *illus.*, 644
  see also ancestor worship; genealogy
farm museums, 615–16, 619, 635–6, 679;
    see also village museums
Farrell, James T., 501
Faulkner, William, 272, 306, 495
Fauset, Arthur Huff, 414
Fauset, Jesse, 414
Febvre, Lucien, 693–4
Federal Art Project, 431, 476
Federal Hall Memorial Historical Site,
    New York, 472
Federalist Papers, Number 14, 42
Federalists, 22
Federal Theatre Project, 423, 460,
    476–7, 509
Federal Writers Project, 457, 460–1, 462,
    464, 474–6, 503
Feinstone, Saul, 438–9
Feld, Stuart P., 681
Ferguson, Benjamin, 154
Fern, Fanny (Sara Willis Parton), 135
Fetterman, Capt. William Judd, 257
fiction, historical
  authenticity of, 28, 29
  19th century, 80–4 *passim;* dime
    novels, 63, 164; in South, post–Civil
    War, 112–13, 195–6
  20th century, 334–5, 420, 491, 573,
    607
Field, Cyrus W., 47
Field, Erastus Salisbury, 129, *illus.* 130
Field, Hamilton Easter, 431
films, *see* motion pictures
Filson, John, 26
Finley, Moses, 6–7, 33
Fish, Hamilton, 78
Fisher, Alvin T., 87
Fisher, Sydney George, 169–70, 178

Fiske, John, 157, 158, 174, 178–9, 198–9, 239, 266

flag, American
  exclusivity of, 239, 240
  satiric artistic use of, 649, *illus.* 650
  worship of, 204, 495–6; and Canadian attitudes to flag, 523 and *illus.*

Flanagan, Hallie, 420, 460

Fletcher, Alice Cunningham, 188

Flexner, James T., 510

Flint, Timothy, 80

Flynt, Henry N., 557, 566, 622

Fogg Art Museum, Cambridge, Mass., 73

Folger, Henry Clay, 174

"folk," the (mythic theme), 518

folk art(s), American
  collecting (20th century), 149, 320–1, 327, 431–2, 567–8, 633–4, 679–82
  commercialism and, 428
  and "fine" art(s), 464
  prices, 633, 680
  Rockefeller (A.) collection, 268, 321, 426–7, 431–2

folk culture, American, 307, 426–35
  African-American, 408, 413–14, 426, 428–9, 442, 632
  attitudes toward, contrasted with European, 407
  courses in, 432
  definition, 408
  vs. national culture, 407–43
  post–World War II, 533, 679–82
  regionalism in, 428, 434–5
  Rourke and, 411–13, 426, 427–8, 432, 435, 443
  WPA and, 427, 431, 460–1, 474–5, 476–7
  see also folk art(s), American; folklife, American

folklife, American, 616–17; *see also* folk culture, American

folklore, American
  African-American, 426, 428–9
  archives, 680
  collecting, 268, 287, 680–2
  courses in, 432
  cowboy songs, 258
  festivals, 432, 435
  and pageantry, 279
  societies, 156, 426, 432–3
  and traditional "literature," 411
  WPA and, *see* Federal Writers Project

Folklore Institute of America, 432

Forbes, Esther, 29, 410, *illus.* 411, 428, 504, 511, 545, 548

Forbes, Malcolm, 620

Force, Peter, 49, 76, 77, 78

Ford, Clara, 315 and *illus.*

Ford, Edsel, 357 and *illus.*, 358

Ford, Gerald R., 662

Ford, Henry, 28, 244, 260, 300, 304, *illus.* 305, 315 and *illus.*, 341, 342, 351–8, *illus.* 352, *illus.* 357, 442, 500; *see also* Henry Ford Museum & Greenfield Village, Dearborn, Mich.

Ford, Paul Leicester, 80, 159, 203

Ford, Worthington Chauncey, 31, 159, 377, 378, 405, 406, 436, 771

Ford administration, and historic preservation, 562

Ford Museum, Dearborn, Mich., *see* Henry Ford Museum & Greenfield Village, Dearborn, Mich.

Forefathers' Day, 63–4, 208, 211

foreigners in U.S., *see* ethnic groups; immigrants to U.S.; naturalized Americans

foreign observers in U.S.
  on American cultural anomalies, 703
  on American exceptionalism, 518
  on lack of memory and indifference to past, 56–60, 134, 532
  late 19th century, 139–40

foreign relations (U.S.)
  19th century, 8
  Cold War, 5, 544, 572–3, 592
  1970s–80s, 652

foreign travelers, American (20th century), 237, 313, 338, 516–17

Forsyth, John, 76

Fort Kearney massacre (1866), 257

Fort McHenry, Baltimore, 142, *illus.* 460, 468

Fort Owen (Mont.), 402, 629

Foster, Stephen Collins, 66

Foucault, Michel, 692

Founding Fathers (U.S.), adulation of, 19, 27, 62; *see also under individuals*

Fourth of July, 66, *illus.* 67, 68, *illus.* 69, 161, *illus.* 646
  celebrations, 104–5, 255–6, 279, 358
  and civil religion, 205
  public apathy about, 49
  rural-urban differences, 255–6

Fox, Dixon Ryan, 376 and *illus.*, 663

Foxfire collections, 681–2

France
  American cultural Francophiles and Francophobes, 172
  attitudes contrasted with American: on history and public policy, 35–6, 700–1; on past and tradition, 57–60,

France (*continued*)
  285–6, 287, 288, 289, 519–20, 652,
    702
  civil religion in, 204
  collective memory and amnesia in,
    3–4, 690, 701
  cultural politics in, 290, 291–2, 520,
    692
  history-teaching methods and texts,
    248, 289, 290
  patriotism, 693–4
  popular memory in, 692
  see also French Revolution
Frank, Waldo, 303, 416, 428
Frankfurter, Felix, 532
Franklin, Benjamin, 28, 53, 266
Frazer, Sir James, 414
Freedom Train (1947–49), 119, 573–81,
    illus. 574–5, *illus.* 577–8, *illus.* 580
  commercial aspects, 580–1
freed slaves, 121
Freeman, Douglas Southall, 387, 454,
    541
Freeman, Edward A., 283, 407
Freeman, Frederick, 74
French, Alice, 134
French, Daniel Chester, 93, *illus.* 94,
    186, 213, 331
French-Americans, 436, 437–8
French Revolution
  and American Civil War, compared,
    292
  and American Revolution, contrasted,
    35–6, 291–2, 463
  bicentennial (1989), 695
Friedman, Lee Max, 438
frontier (myth) in U.S., 396, 401, 402–3,
    483–4, 493, 573, 704
  religious tradition, 502
  see also pioneers; Western U.S.
Frontier Days/Week, 401, 402–3
Froude, James Anthony, 197
Fuentes, Carlos, 662
"Fugitives" (Agrarians), 22, 404, 519
funding, governmental, 55, 571, 610
  of battlefield sites, 119–20; *see also*
    National Park Service
  for commemorative celebrations, 144,
    384, 447, 494, 602, 615
  cooperation with private sponsors, *see*
    under funding, private
  for monuments, 445
  for museums, 445, 570
  for preservation activities, 263–5,
    445–7, 460, 467–73, 562, 563, 660–1

  resistance to, 473, 474, 477
  see also government, cultural role of
funding, private
  of commemoration, 11, 13, 55, 444,
    445
  cooperation with government
    sponsorship, 444, 455–8, 587 and *n.*,
    609, 610, 612–13, 615–16, 629, 674;
    national parks and historic sites, 465,
    472–3
  of Freedom Train, 573–81 *passim*
  of preservation activities, 263–4; *see*
    also preservation, historic

G

Gaines, Pierce Welch, 569
games, historical, 167–8; *see also* battle
    re-enactments
G.A.R., *see* Grand Army of the Republic
Garbisch, Bernice and Edgar, 567
Gardiner's Island, N.Y., 261
Gardner, Isabella Stewart, 168, 267–8
Garfield, James, 102
Garland, Hamlin, 410
Garrison, William Lloyd, 87
Garvan, Francis P., 24, 258, 343, 569
Gayarré, Charles, 195
Gegoux, Theodore, 401
genealogy, 112, 217, 218, 220–1, 222,
    249–50, 421, 473, 483, 504, 630, 641,
    642, 643–4, 816
German-Americans, 219, 232, 240, 277,
    278, 438
  domestic arts, 350
Germany
  collective memory and amnesia in, 3,
    690, 701
  cultural politics in, 291, 516, 517
  National Museum, Nuremberg, 520
  nostalgia in, 702
Gettysburg (Penna.) battle site
  Civil War Heritage Days, 628
  monuments, 115, 416, 417
  preservation, 264, 468
  reunion, 457
Gifford, Sanford Robinson, 168
Gilbert, Cass, 170
Gilcrease, Thomas, 347–8
Gilcrease Museum of American History
    and Art, Tulsa, Okla., 348, 566
Glackens, William James, *illus.* 229
Glasgow, Ellen, 112–13, 304, 309, 491,
    500, 502

Godkin, Edwin Lawrence, 51
Goethe, Johann Wolfgang von, 57, 60
Goldwyn, Samuel, 233
Goode, George Brown, 20, 249, 251
Goodrich, Samuel, 70
Goodwin, W. A. R., 200, 358, 359–66, *illus.* 360–1, 424, 455
Gorbachev, Mikhail S., 698–700
Gordon, Jan and Cora, 426
Gorky, Arshile, 533
government, cultural role of
  conflicts and turf wars, 444, 457–8
  cooperation with private sector, 444, 455–8, 587 and *n.*, 609, 610, 612–13, 615–16, 629, 674; Freedom Train, 573–81 *passim;* national parks and historic sites, 465, 472–3
  as custodian of memory and tradition, 12, 14, 41, 78; federal, 55, 184–5, 294, 443, 444–80, 570, 571–2, 610–17
  documents preservation, 75–8, 445–7; *see also* Library of Congress
  in France, 57–8
  in funding commemoration and preservation, *see* funding, governmental
  historical murals in government buildings, 462, 464, 498, 533
  and immigrants, 230–1
  in preservation activities, 184–7 *passim,* 263–5, 445–7, 460, 467–73, 558–64 *passim,* 660–1
  state governments, *see* states, cultural role of
  and tourism and travel, 338
  see also National Park Service
Grady, Henry, 112
Graff, Everett D., 317
Grafly, Charles, 225, *illus.* 226
Grafton, Richard, 93–4
Grand Army of the Republic (G.A.R.), 103–5 *passim,* 115, 116, 120–1, 204, 416
Grand Canyon, 167, 265, 371
Grant, Madison, 236
Grant, Ulysses S., 108, 109, 122, 129, *illus.* 130, 135, 590
  his tomb (New York), 104, 116, 117, 278
Grant, Ulysses S., III, 417, 592–6 *passim, illus.* 593, 602, 605
Gray, Francis Calley, 73
Great Britain
  American cultural Anglophilia and Anglophobia, 172–5, 304, 484–6

  architecture, 34, 172
  "heritage industry," 691–2
  history-teaching, 248, 519
  national memory and myth, as obsession, 286, 288
  nostalgia in, 33, 202; rural, 519
  pageantry (civic), and U.S., contrasted, 281
  popular memory in, 9
  preservation movement, 263
  sense of history in, 34–5
  in textbooks on U.S. history, 404–6
  tradition in, 19, 286, 288, 653, 701–2
Great Depression, 367, 410, 502, 503
Greece
  folklore collecting, 287
  preservation activity, 696
Green, Andrew Haswell, 71, 262
Green, Paul, 420, 424, 434, 511, 543, 667
Greenfield Village, *see* Henry Ford Museum & Greenfield Village, Dearborn, Mich.
Greenough, Horatio, 86
Griffith, D. W., 196
Grolier Club, 323
Guizot, François, 57, *illus.* 58
Guthrie, A. B., 549, 573
Gwathmey, Robert, 495, *illus.* 496, 545

H

Haley, Alex, *illus.* 642
  Roots, 641–5, 668, 669, 672
Hall, Edward Hagaman, 246–7
Hall of Our History, Inc. (Ga.), 564–5
Halpert, Edith, 320, 326–7, 431–2
Halsey, Richard Townley Haines, 238, 269, 318–19, 349
Hamilton, Alexander, 21, 462–3, 495, 588–9
Hamlin, Talbot, 498
Hammond, John Hays, Jr., 321–2 *n.*
Hancock, John, 116
Hansen, Marcus Lee, 232
Harding, Warren G., 332, 448, *illus.* 466
Harlem Renaissance, 413–14, 442
Harris, Joel Chandler, 113, 483
Harrison, Benjamin, 142, 281
Hart, Albert Bushnell, 22, 112, 160, 212, 379–80, 405, 771 *n.*14
Harte, Bret, 273, 275
Hartz, Louis, 35
Harvard, John, 213
Haskins, Charles Homer, 248

Hassam, Childe, 150, 325, 328, 416
Havemeyer, Electra, *see* Webb, Electra Havemeyer
Havemeyer, Louisine, 166, 315
Hawaii, tradition in, 287
Hawkins, Erick, 545–6
Hawthorne, Nathaniel, 19, 29, 36, 40, 61, 81–2, 145
(mentioned), 37, 48, 56, 66, 302
Hayden, Charles, 154
Hayes, Rutherford B., 129, *illus.* 130
Hayne, Paul Hamilton, 110–11, 172, 175, 195
Healy, George P. A., *illus.* 58, *illus.* 82
Hearst, William Randolph, 263, 464, 633
Heckewelder, John, 83
Hegel, Georg Wilhelm Friedrich, 57
Hellman, George S., 157
Hemenway, Mary, 179, 188, 198, 266
Hemingway, Ernest, 420
Henri, Robert, 271
Henry, Edward Lamson, 150, 169
Henry, John (legendary figure), 27, 442
Henry, William Wirt, 195
Henry Ford Museum & Greenfield Village, Dearborn, Mich., 48, 201, 304, 355–8, 555, 640
Herblock, 658, *illus.* 659
Herder, Johann Gottfried von, 38, 413
Hergesheimer, Joseph, 22, 227, 322, 323, 324
heritage
  Canadian movement, 522
  commercial aspects, 628
  and history, 626–8
  preoccupation with concept, 4, 12, 532–3; "heritage industry" (Britain), 691–2; "heritage syndrome," 538–46, 572, 621–8
  and progressivism, 702–3
Heritage Hill State Park, Green Bay, Wis., 621–2, 626
Herman, Augustine, 232
Hermitage, The (Tenn.), 265
heroes
  collecting objects associated with, 157, 200, 324–5
  of ethnic groups, 439
  individual *vs.* collective, 505, 522
  monuments to, 33, 488–9, 505; *see also* monuments, commemorative and historical
  myth-making and, 27
  see also myth(s) in American culture; *and individuals*

hero worship, 19, 27, 417–18, 486–7, 497, 498
  African-American, 122
  and civil religion, 205
  after Civil War, 110–11, 125–6
  1970s–80s, 620
  see also ancestor worship
Hertle, Louis, 343
Hewitt, Abram, 106, 239
Heye, George Gustave, 638
Higginson, Francis, 217
Higginson, Thomas Wentworth, 84, 145, 213
high culture, 24
  and civil religion, 205
  declining visitation to sites of, 687
  decorative arts (collecting) as, 318–20
  democratization of, 306, 340, 341, 398, 464
  and folk culture, 149, 411–15 *passim*, 680–1
  museums and, 350
  shrines and "sacred" places of, 202
  see also art(s), American; elites; museums
highways, 276 and *n.*, 338–9, 395, 397–8, 400, 505, 506
  construction threatens historic sites, 610
Hirshhorn, Joseph, 313–14, 327, 569–70
Hirshhorn Gallery, Washington, D.C., 570
Hirst, Claude Raguet, 94
Hispanic-Americans
  culture and traditions, 439, 524
  in textbooks, 685
Historical and Genealogical Society of New England, 184
historical periodicals, 538–42 *passim*
historical scholarship
  African-American, 125
  and African history, 697
  and oral tradition, 96
  popular *vs.* academic, 627
  professionalization of, 38
  see also historical writing
historical societies
  local and state, 272–3
  19th century, 74–5
  20th century, 332, 485, 540–1, 630–1
  see also Americana, collecting of: networks and organizations; antiquarians, American; Essex Institute, Salem, Mass.; lineage societies; National Trust for Historic

Preservation; preservation, historic:
organizations for; *and specific
societies*
historical writing
Adams (H.) and, 196–7
democracy and, 20
Herder on, 413
19th century, 62, 69–70, 72, 75, 76–7,
158, 160, 178–9
professionalization of, 196, 485
20th century, 336–7, 541
see also biography, American;
textbooks, in history
Historic American Buildings Survey, 468,
469, 474, 614
Historic Deerfield, Inc. (Mass.), 557, 566,
622, 640
historic markers and signs, 276, 305, 388,
393, 401–2, 437, 447, 505
historic preservation, *see* preservation,
historic
historic sites
attendance figures, 539–40, 620,
639–41
in Europe and U.S., 517, 695–6
government support for, 184–5, 263–5,
445–7, 455, 467–73, 558–60, 610–17,
661
indifference to and neglect, 52–4, 259
mid-20th century, 557–64, 610–17
as museums, *see* village museums
National Register of Historic Places,
570
National Survey of Historic Sites and
Buildings, 468, 469, 474, 614
National Trust and, 558–60, 563–4
number of, 439, 559
"pilgrimages" to, 201–4, 259, 486–8,
532, 547–8, 589, 590, 608–9, 687
in South, importance of, 201–2
theatrical appeal of, 424
threatened by commercial
development, 609–11, 674; *see also*
urban districts, historic: urban
renewal and
see also battle monuments and
battlefields; preservation, historic;
restoration, historic
Historic Sites Act (U.S., 1935), 460, 468,
470–1
Historic Sites Commission (U.S.), 259
Historic Sites Survey (National Park
Service), 468, 469, 474, 614
history
and art, 206

ignorance of and indifference to, 12,
41, 49–56, 133, 136, 185, 284, 301,
448, 503, 655, 657, 663–5, 666
interest in and reverence for, 257,
449–55, 462, 531–2, 534, 666–7
and memory, *see* history and memory
and myth, 17, 30, 31, 481, 484, 485,
498
as surrogate for religion, 70
as vocation, and theology, 197–9
see also authenticity, historical
history, local, 272; *see also* local
traditions and memories; regionalism
history, military (courses in), 573
history, teaching of (in colleges and
universities), 23–4, 509
history, teaching of (in primary and
secondary schools)
in Britain and U.S., 519
in Canada, 524
and immigrant population, 245–8
late 20th century, 663–5
place of, in curriculum, 21, 51, 245–6,
251, 268, 531
in South, 112
see also textbooks
history, teaching of (public)
lectures, 158, 198–9, 205, 245, 398, 453
radio as medium, 419, 543, 630
sermons, 200
travel as, 340, 393, 403 and *n.*, 423
history and memory, 503, 687–8
contrasted or conflicted, 9–10, 696
in developing nations, 695–7
and "heritage," 626
and myth, 31
history and tradition, *see* tradition and
history
Hoar, George Frisbie, 184, 212, 226
hoaxes, historical, 243, 287, 500–1
Hodgenville (Ky.), Lincoln birthplace,
109, 129, 202, 452, 589
Hogg, Ima, 269, 312–13, *illus.* 314, 566,
567, 620
holidays, national, 255–7
and civil religion, 205
see also Columbus Day; Fourth of July;
"Juneteenth" celebration; Labor
Day; Lincoln, A.: birthday; Memorial
Day; Thanksgiving Day; Veterans'
Day; Washington, G.: birthday
Holland, Josiah G., 378
Holland, Leicester B., 498
Holmes, Oliver Wendell, Jr., 387
Holmes, Oliver Wendell, Sr., 216

Homer, Winslow, 89 and *illus., illus.* 124
Hooper, Alice Foster Perkins, 268
Hoover, Herbert, 137, 444, 459, 613
Hoover, J. Edgar, 579
Hopkins, Mark, 391
Hopkinson, Joseph, 181
Hornblower, Henry, II, 568–9
Hosmer, James K., 160, 198, 266, 300, 339
Hough, Emerson, 275, 396, 492
house museums, 258, 326, 340, 346–7, 402, 431, 438, 560
  Bayou Bend, Houston, 312, 566, 620
  Casa Amesti, Monterey, 558, 559
  see also farm museums; village museums
Houston, Sam, 9, 145
Howe, Henry, 72
Howe, Irving, 545
Howe, Julia Ward, 145
Howells, William Dean, 23, 138, 179–80, 224, 270
Hudson-Fulton celebration (New York, 1909), 246–7, 522
  Loan Exhibition, Metropolitan Museum, 149 and *illus.,* 188–9, 278, 318, 348
Hughes, Langston, 414, 442
Huizinga, Johan H., 8, 221–2, 281, 525
Humboldt, Alexander von, 57
humor, American, 413, 420 *n.,* 428
Hunt, Richard Morris, 19–20, 116, 164–5, 170, 172, 742
Huntington, Arbella, 168, 315
Huntington, Daniel, 47
Huntington, Henry E., 168, 174, 243, 315, 316
Hurston, Zora Neale, 339, 408, 414 and *illus.,* 415, 426, 428–9, 500
Hutchinson, Ellen M., 177
Hutchinson, Thomas, 174
Hyman, Stanley Edgar, 435

I

Ickes, Harold, 24, 461
idealism, American, 301, 303, 532
immigrants to U.S., 228–53
  assimilation of, 52, 229, 234–6, 243, 244, 247–8, 290–1, 515–16
  associations of, 219, 230, 231
  educated for citizenship, 244–8, 290–1
  expectations of, 26
  and folk culture, 435–40
  and industrialization, 8, 666
  memories disclosed, 666
  patriotism, 244–5
  philanthropic efforts for, 250
  relationship to traditions of origin, 228–36 *passim, illus.* 229, 244, 247–8, 290–1, 436, 516
  and traditionalism, 8, 41
  see also ethnic groups; naturalized Americans
immigration to U.S.
  museums of, 7, 11, 638
  restriction of, 252–3
imperialism, cultural, 238
independence (American), anniversaries of, *see* Bicentennial of Independence (1975–76); Centennial of American Independence (1876); Sesquicentennial of Independence (1926)
Independence Day, *see* Fourth of July
Independence Hall, Philadelphia, 53, 201, 259, 355, 496–7
Index of American Design, 433, 476
Indians of North America, *see* Native Americans
industrialism, resistance to, 305–6
  and nostalgia, 152
intellectuals, cultural role(s) of
  and American myths, 497–501 *passim*
  and Civil War Centennial, 606–7
  and folk culture, 427
  and nationalism, 416, 443
  19th century, 80–4, 147
  as travelers abroad, 516–17
  see also antiquarians and antiquarianism, American; literature, American; fiction, historical
intergenerational continuity, 224–7 and *illus.,* 253, 289
  and conservation movement, 266
  immigrant groups and, 232–3
  see also ancestor worship; family traditions
intermountain West
  historical awareness and organizations, 273–4, 401–2
  rodeos, 401, 423
  see also Western U.S.
International Commission on Folk Arts, 432–3
inventions, *see* technological innovation

Iran-Contra affair, 658, 660
Ireland, Gaelic revival, 288–9
Irving, Washington, 44, 80, 181, 266
Israel: tradition, myth and identity, 3, 693, 696–7, 702
Italy, cultural heritage, 286
Ives, Charles, 258, 271
Iwo Jima flag raising, 658–9

J

Jackson, Andrew, 11, 19, 68, 265, *illus.* 451, 464
Jackson, Mahalia, 599, *illus.* 601
Jackson, Thomas J. ("Stonewall"), 111, 456, 491, 608
James, Alice, 267
James, George Wharton, 262
James, Henry, 58–9, 60, 93, 100, 172, 176–7, 284
    mentioned, 95, 158, 239, 262, 277
James, Marquis, 540
Jameson, John Franklin, 23, 31, 159–60
Jamestown, Va., 201, 260, 450, 466–7, 473, 486, 542, 679
    Tercentenary Exposition (1907), 130, 145, 267, 496
    350th anniversary Festival (1957), 549, 646–7, 682
Japan
    cultural role of tradition, 293–4
    politicized myth and memory, 517–18
Jay, John, 68
Jefferson, Thomas, 6, 19, 21, 42, 75, 77, 194–5, 218, 259, 462, 511, 588; *see also* Monticello (Va.)
Jefferson Memorial, Washington, D.C., 24, 449–50, *illus.* 463, 792
Jefferson National Expansion Memorial, St. Louis, 571
Jenckes, George and Marian, 569
Jewish-Americans, 233–4, 438–9
    Colonial Williamsburg and, 552
    fraternal organizations, 230, 231, 233
    and genealogy, 643–4
Jim Crow laws, 31, 592
Joan of Arc, 59, *illus.* 173, 285
Johnson, Eastman, 96, 97 and *illus.*
Johnson, Edward A., 124
Johnson, Guy Benton, 442
Johnson, James Weldon, 414
Johnson, Lyndon B., 570, 585, *illus.* 586
    presidential library, 613

Johnston, Gen. Albert Sidney, 126
Johnston, Mary, 112, 195, 224, 416
Jonathan, Brother, 59
Jones, Absalom, 124
Jones, E. Alfred, 148
Jones, John Paul, 115
Jonkonnu (*or* Jonkeroo) celebration, *illus.* 124
Jordan, David Starr, 388
Josephson, Matthew, 336–7, 501–2
"Juneteenth" celebration, 122–3

K

Kallen, Horace, 18, 235–6, 409
Karolik, Martha Codman, 344
Karolik, Maxim, 342, 344–6, 566
Kaufman, George M. and Linda H., 569
Kazin, Alfred, 512–13
Keller, Helen, 510
Keller, Morton, 131 *n.*
Kennedy, Jacqueline Bouvier, *see* Onassis, Jacqueline Kennedy
Kennedy, John F., presidential library, 613
Kennedy administration, and culture, 610
Kensington Rune Stone, 243, 500
Kent, Henry Watson, 323, 349
Kent, James, 51
Keyes, Frances Parkinson, 331
Kimball, Fiske, 268, 325, 347
King, Martin Luther, Jr., 600, 662
Knott's Berry Farm, Buena Park, Calif., 557, 563
Koch, Kenneth, 650, *illus.* 651
Koerner, W. H. D., 396
Korean War Veterans Memorial, Washington, D.C. (proposed), 11
Kramer, Hilton, 435
Krimmel, John Lewis, *illus.* 67
Kundera, Milan, 690–1

L

Labor Day, 257
Lacey, John F., 187
La Farge, John, 97, 170
Lamb, Martha J., 80, 268
landmarks (historic), identification and preservation of, *see* historic sites; preservation, historic

Langdell, Christopher C., 160
Langer, William L., 199, 281
language, American
  colloquial, 19, 419
  dialect and folk idiom, 334
  as distinct from English, 174, 175,
    648–9
  Mencken and, 22, 334
Lanier, Sidney, 175, 195
law and tradition, 51
Lawrence, David Herbert, 339–40
Lay, Oliver, *illus.* 77
lectures and lecture tours, on history,
  158, 198–9, 205, 245, 398, 453
Lee, Gen. Robert E., 9, 108 and *illus.*,
  386
  birthplace (Stratford Hall, Va.), 405,
    487
  and Lincoln, 380–1, 385
  Memorial Chapel, Washington and Lee
    University,109,117,329–31,*illus.* 330
  monuments and memorials, 109, 110,
    111, 115, 117, *illus.* 118, 405, 416
Lee, Ronald F., *illus.* 470
left (political)
  on American Revolutionary tradition,
    463
  on past and memory, 5, 464
legal study, case method, 160
Leland, Waldo G., 213 *n.*
L'Enfant, Pierre Charles, 115
Leslie, Frank, 72
Lévi-Strauss, Claude, 17, 26, 222
Lewis & Clark Expedition (1804–06), 26
  Centennial (Portland, Ore., 1905), 139
  Trail, 400
Libbey, Edward Drummond, 343
liberalism, American, 6; *see also* left
  (political)
libraries, 439
  Burton, Detroit, 183–4
  Newberry, Chicago, 156, 317, 569
  presidential, 612 and *illus.*, 613
  Tannahill, Dearborn, Mich., 555
  see also Library of Congress,
    Washington, D.C.
*Library of American Literature, A: From
  the Earliest Settlements to the
  Present Time* (1889), 20
Library of Congress, Washington, D.C.
  archival role, 75, 77, 438, 487
  and folk culture, 429 and *n.*, 617, 680
Lifton, Robert Jay, 533–4
Lincoln, Abraham, 21, 43, 99–100, 262
  biographies, 309, 378, 417, 489, 509

birthday holiday and celebrations, 109,
  129, 280, 332, 588, 589–90
blacks and, 122, *illus.* 123; *see also*
  Emancipation Proclamation
buildings and associations, 29, 109,
  129, 202, 332, 452, 589
collecting of Lincolniana, 128, 157, 204
depoliticized memory of, 511
drama and music about, 294, 448, 452,
  509, 521
iconography, 416; *see also the subentry*
  monuments and memorials
monuments and memorials, 110, 116,
  126–7, 202, 487; *see also* Lincoln
  Memorial, Washington, D.C.
"mystic chords of memory," 33, 100,
  101, 102, 130, 332, 590
mythology and idealization of, 128–9,
  204, 218, 416–17, 509
politicization of his memory, 129, 264
Roosevelt (F.D.) and, 294, 448, 452,
  521
Southern attitudes and feelings on,
  110, 126–7, 379–81, 405, 771
and Washington, pairing of, 129, 130
  and *illus.*, 131 *n.*, 202–3
Lincoln Memorial, Washington, D.C., 24,
  331–2, 589
Lindbergh, Charles A., 494
Lindsay, Vachel, 387
lineage societies, 218, 332, *illus.* 333, 417
  family associations, 421
  see also specific societies
Lipman, Jean and Howard, 680–1
Lippmann, Walter, 270, 503
Litchfield, Conn., 261, 387, 676–7
literature, American
  American aesthetic and, 194, 334–5
  anthologies, 158–9, 177, 460–1
  attitudes toward past in (20th century),
    544–5
  vs. communism, 573
  courses in, 335
  democracy and, 20–1, 302, 420
  dialect and folk idiom in, 334, 411,
    434, 483, 680
  distinctiveness of, 37, 175, 177, 257–8,
    416
  national, 418, 419
  regionalism in, 337, 376, 408
  Southern (19th century), 112–13
  see also biography, American; fiction,
    historical; folklore, American;
    historical writing
Little, Arthur, 146

Livingston, Edward, 76
local traditions and memories
  commemorative days and celebrations,
    140–5, 375, 437–9, 494, 603–4, 609
  conflicting, 296
  development of, in U.S., 37–8
  and Fourth of July, 66
  growing importance of (20th century),
    271–7, 505
  museums (20th century), 372–3
  1960s–70s, 621–4
  patronage of, 181–4
  post–World War II, 548–9
  stronger than national, 37, 140–1, 522,
    572
  see also pageants and pageantry;
    regionalism; *and specific locales*
Locke, Alain, 414, 440
Lockwood, Luke Vincent, 346
Lodge, Henry Cabot, 28, 115, 147, 150,
  175, 179, 211, 217, 332, 384, 484
log cabin myth, 32
Longfellow, Henry Wadsworth, 82–4,
  illus. 82, 85, 115, 260
Lomax, John A., 258, 429
Lord, Arthur, 208–9
Lorimer, George Horace, 323
Loring, William C., *illus.* 152
Los Angeles, 181, 182, 274
  Heritage Square, 622–3
Lossing, Benson, 203
Lost Cause tradition (of South), 11, 101,
  illus. 108, 113, 126, 195, 217, 275,
  491, 609
Louisiana Purchase Exposition (St. Louis,
  1904), 139, 174, 186
Lowell, A. Lawrence, 133, 393
Lowell, James Russell, 78–9, 133, 180,
  228, 238, 254, 295
Loyalists, 35, 50, 174
Luce, Henry, 24
Lummis, Charles F., 181–2, *illus.* 183,
  211, 262–3, 274, 276, 394
Lynch, John R., 440
Lyon, W. Parker, 396–7

M

Macaulay, Thomas Babington, 197
MacBeth, William, 168
MacKaye, Percy, 167, 279, 410, 434
MacLeish, Archibald, 504, 511, 544, 599,
  600, 619

MacMonnies, Frederick, 276
Macy, John, 257
Madison, James, 19, 27, 42, 55, 100, 259
Mahan, Alfred Thayer, 96, 178
Malinowski, Bronislaw, 17
Manassas (Va.) battlefield, 120, 491, 674
  battle re-enactment, *illus.* 606
manifest destiny, 303
Manoogian, Richard, 569
manuscripts
  collecting, 156, 157, 191, 312, 316,
    317, 632
  government's role in collecting and
    preserving, 446
Maritain, Jacques, 525–6
Markham, Edwin, 418
Marquand, John P., 548
Marsh, George Perkins, 42
Marshall, John, 65, 587
Martin, Elmer and Joanne, 638
Mason, Otis, 156
Massachusetts Historical Society, 122,
  156, 373
Massachusetts Tercentenary (1930), 455
Masters, Edgar Lee, 418, 489, 502
Mather, Cotton, 65, 196
Mather, Stephen T., 454, 465, *illus.* 466
Matthews, Albert, 31, 208
Matthews, Brander, 174–5, 211, 234–5,
  244, 304
Matthiessen, F. O., 335–6, 413
May, Henry F., 166
May Day, 33, 255
Mayflower Compact, 64, 209, 630
McCarthy, Joseph, 5
McClellan, Gen. George, 116
McConkey, James, 686
McDowell, William O., 250, 251–2
McGregor, Tracy W., 316–17
McGuffey, William Holmes, 80
McKay, Claude, 414
McKim, Charles, 170
McKim, Mead & White (firm), architects,
  170, 261
McKinley, William, 107, 139
McLaughlin, Andrew C., 258–9
McMaster, John Bach, 21, 379
McMillan, Loring, 556
McMurtry, Larry, 656
McNeill, William H., 25, 657
Mecklenburg (N.C.) Declaration of
  Independence, 196, 423
media
  and commercialization of tradition and
    memory, 536, 543–4, 669–72

media (*continued*)
  cultural function, 527, 667–9
  see also motion pictures; press; radio;
    television
medieval revival, 170–2
Meeker, Ezra, 397–9, *illus.* 399, 447
melting pot, U.S. as, 8, 52, 229, 234–6,
    243, 244, 247–8, 290–1, 515–16
Melville, Herman, 18, 43, 158, 176
Melville, Ward and Dorothy, 568
Memorial Day, 103, 162, 255, 478, 504
memory, civic, 9, 132
  and popular memory, 10, 11
memory, failure of, *see* amnesia,
    collective
memory, manipulation of, 3–4, 5, 9, 10,
    293–4
  political, 4–5, 464, 503, 517–18, 520–7
    passim, 534, 677–8, 696–7
memory, popular, 93–5, 692–3
  accuracy and durability of, 9
  and civic memory, 9, 10, 11
  commercialization of, 685–8, *illus.* 686;
    see also commercialization of culture
    and the past
  mistrust of, 96
  in pre-modern societies, 32
memory, selective, 4, 10, 12, 13, 31, 61,
    309, 535, 655, 658–63
  and African-American history and
    culture, 121
  heritage as, 625
  and nostalgia, 626
  and patriotism, 5
  and (uncomfortable) social realities,
    518, 658–63 *passim*, 695, 701
  see also amnesia, collective
memory and history, *see* history and
    memory
memory and myth, 17, 258, 481, 502–4
memory and tradition, 514
Mencken, Henry Louis, 22, 74, 390,
    408
Mercer, Henry Chapman, 321–2, 327,
    421
Merritt, Susan, *illus.* 69
Mesa Verde National Park (Colo.), 188,
    264 and *illus.*, 265
Metropolitan Museum of Art, New York,
    166, 268, 269, 345 *n.*, 347, 509, 573
  American Wing, 189, 311, 318, 349–51,
    502, 635
  Hudson-Fulton Loan Exhibition of
    Americana (1909), 149 and *illus.*,
    188–9, 278, 318, 348

Mexican-Americans: Tejanos and the
    Alamo, 240–2
Michelet, Jules, 34
military veterans, *see* veterans
Military Order of America (proposed),
    105
Mill, John Stuart, 196
millennialism, 206
Miller, Arthur, 572
Miller, Perry, 573
Millet, Francis David, 150
Milosz, Czeslaw, 532
MISSION 66 program, 540, 609, 610–11
Mitchell, Arthur W., 442
Mitchell, S. Weir, 80, 150, *illus.* 151
mobility, physical and social, 51, 106
modernism, 12, 14, 271, 299, 300, 327,
    537; *see also* anti-modernism;
    progress, tradition of
Montejano, David, 50
Montesquieu, Charles de Secondat,
    Baron de la Brède et de, 68
Monticello (Va.), 54, 202, 264, 325, 452,
    486, 488, 684
monuments, commemorative and
    historical
  Canadian, 523–4
  in Chicago, endowment for, 154
  of Civil War, *see* Civil War,
    monuments and commemorations
  classical models for, 167 *n.*
  democratization of, 422
  by immigrant groups, 437–9
  individual *vs.* collective, 55, 505
  Markham on, 163–4
  national, run by Park Service, 469
  and nostalgia, 295
  popularity of (19th century), 69, 71
  role in forming memory, 33, 115
  in Washington, lack of inscriptions, 140
  in West, 395 and *n.*
  see also battle monuments and
    battlefields; government: as
    custodian of memory and tradition
Moore, Mary (Mrs. Maurice), 329–31
Moore, R. Walton, 452, 456
Moore, Tom, 230
More, Paul Elmer, 22, 24, 738
Morgan, John Pierpont, 21, 157, 168,
    190, 191 and *illus.*
Morgan, John Pierpont, Jr., 152, 343
Morgan, Lewis Henry, 86, 179
Morison, Samuel Eliot, 388, 389, 393
Mormons, 141, 395, 500, 820
  genealogy, 641 and *n.*

Morris, Edmund, 661
Morris, William, 202
Morristown (N.J.) National Historical
    Park, 468, *illus.* 469
Morse, John T., 158, 178 *n.*, 271
Morse, Samuel F. B., 213
Morton, Levi P., 235
motion pictures, 4, 29, 196, 406, 421,
    434, 435 *n.*, 668–9, 690
  and commercialization of history,
    543
  on history, educational, 508
  Old West in, 396, 398
  patriotism and, 479, 647
  Puritans depicted in, 391 *n.*
Motley, John Lothrop, 70
Mott, Jordan L., 47
Mount, William Sidney, 568
Mount Rushmore National Monument
    (S.D.), 329, 449 and *illus.*, 453–4 and
    illus., 473, 486, *illus.* 487, 489–90,
    509
Mount Vernon (Va.), *illus.* 54
  as "pilgrimage" site, 201, 202, 230, 488
  preservation, 54, 138, 260
Mugwumps, 239
Muir, John, 210, 265, 270
Muirhead, James Fullarton, 283
Mumford, Lewis, 428, 464
  on tradition(s), 336, 349–50, 515, 516,
    620, 668, 702–3
  views and opinions, 308, 413, 416, 498,
    518
Munsell, Joel, 72
Museum of American Folk Art, New
    York, 680
Museum of the City of New York, 372–3
Museum of Fine Arts, Boston, 148, 154,
    166, 186, 344–7 *passim*
Museum of Modern Art, New York, 313,
    432
Museum of Our National Heritage,
    Lexington, Mass., 621
museums
  of African-American culture, 638,
    683–4
  and Americana, 188–92, 306, 313, 318,
    325, 372–4
  attendance figures, 551, 620, 639–41
  of Civil War memorabilia, 119
  controversy and conflict about, 638–9
  costumed guides, 161, 247, 346, 362,
    517, 551, 569
  democratization of, 20, 156, 163, 306,
    310, 340, 353, 356, 509

educational role, 247, 305, 310, 316,
    340, 349, 356, 373, 398, 509, 555,
    556; in Europe, 286
  in Europe (20th century), 286–7; and
    U.S., contrasted, 517
  farms, 615–16, 619, 635–6, 679
  founding of, 154–61 *passim*, 166,
    634–41 *passim*
  in France, 58–9
  government funding and support for,
    see government, cultural role of
  impact on American taste, 192
  number of, 635
  open-air, 161, 321–2, 326, 346; *see also*
    village museums
  patriotic aspect, 520
  period rooms, 160, *illus.* 162, 247, 346,
    347
  specialized (late 20th century), 635–7
  in Third World, 697
  20th century, 342–74, 634–41
  see also house museums; village
    museums; *and specific museums*
museum villages, *see* village museums
music, American, 149, 258, 325, 430–1,
    591, 599
  and European, popularity contrasted, 167
  folk, 411, 426, 428, 429–30; cowboy
    songs, 258
  folk operas, 429, 442
Muzzey, David S., 199, 382, 485
Myers, Louis Guerineau, 325, 364
"mystic chords of memory" (Lincoln), 33,
    100, 101, 102, 109, 130, 332, 590
Mystic (Conn.) Seaport Museum, 372,
    631, 636
myth and memory, 12, 17–18, 62, 258,
    481, 502–4
myth(s) in American culture, 25–8, 84,
    254, 295, 481–514, 657–8
  collective acceptance of, 4, 481, 532
  depoliticized, 511–12, 662–3, 701, 704
  as distinctive (unique), 26, 27–8, 515
  and history, 17, 30, 31, 481, 484, 485,
    498
  manipulation of, 481, 499–500; *see also*
    memory, manipulation of
  new ones created, 288; in Japan and
    Germany, 294; *see also* tradition:
    invented
  and Old West, 27, 275–6, 401, 492–3
  suspicion of and resistance to, 481,
    497–8, 501; *see also* debunking
  and tradition, defined and contrasted,
    25

N

Nadelman, Elie, *et ux.*, 320–1, 327, 431, 680
Naipaul, V. S., 690
name, national (U.S.), 181, 243
Napoleon I, Emperor of the French, 33, 36, 285
Napoleon III (Louis Napoleon), Emperor of the French, 58
Nast, Condé, 540
Nast, Thomas, 108, 131 *n.*
Nathan, Adele, 608
National Archives (U.S.), 446, 477, 661
  and Freedom Train, 574, 575, 577
National Council of Patriotic Organizations, 251
National Gallery of Art, Washington, D.C., 189, 569
National Heritage Fellowships, 625
National Heritage Trust Force, 617, 691
National Historical Publications Commission, 615
National Historical Society (three different organizations), 438, 540, 630
National Historic Preservation Act (U.S., 1966), 570, 613–14
nationalism, cultural, 132, 163–93, 415–20, 460–1
  British and American, 519
  Canadian and American, 523–4
  definition, 408
  diversity within, 271, 275, 518, 533; *see also* pluralism, cultural
  early 20th century, 271, 277
  efforts to define national identity, 518
  vs. folk culture, 407–43
  vs. Old World traditions, 163–75, 277
  and patriotism, 204, 308, 648
  vs. regionalism, 141, 276, 408–9, 461, 477, 547, 572
national military parks, 264
National Museum Act (U.S., 1966), 570, 613, 614
National Museum of American History, Washington, D.C., 48, 200
National Naval Historical Society, 156
national parks, *see* parks, national
National Park Service, 454, 456, 465–73
  educational role, 371, 466–7, 469, 471, 603
  and National Trust, 558
  policies, 326, 465–70, 561
  preservation role, 467–73, 609, 610–12, 615

National Register of Historic Places, 570
National Society of Colonial Dames, *see* Colonial Dames of America
national song, 180, 415; *see also* "Star-Spangled Banner"
National Survey of Historic Sites and Buildings, 468, 469, 474, 614
National Trust (British), 263
National Trust for Historic Preservation (U.S.), 263, 521, 537, 558–60, 561, 562, 563–4, 621, 626, 628–9, 661, 674, 701
Native Americans
  art and artifacts, collected, 185, 347–8
  history and traditions, others' relationship to, 62, 63, 85–7, 175, 184–5, 187, 188, 248, 276, 442, 685
  iconography, *see* Native Americans, portrayed in art
  ignored at Centennial Exposition (1876), 138, 185
  in literature, *see* Native Americans, portrayed in literature
  museum, 638
  psalters and Bibles printed for, 157
  relations with white people, *see* Native Americans, relations with white people
  women's roles, 266
  see also archaeology, American; ethnography, American
Native Americans, portrayed in art
  Capitol Rotunda reliefs, 86–7
  Catlin, 83
  Curtis's photographs, 191
  Durand, 46 and *illus.*
  19th century, 86–7, *illus.* 88, 186–7
  Remington, 28
  Russell, 225 and *illus.*
  20th century, 396, 505
Native Americans, portrayed in literature
  Cooper, 27
  in history texts, 258–9
  Longfellow, 83
  19th century, 28, 85–7
  Simms, 29
Native Americans, relations with white people, 396, 442 *n.*
  in fiction, 27, 29
  Pilgrims and Puritans, 210
  public amnesia about, 50, 525, 695
nativism, 250–3, 318
  and education of immigrants, 244–8
  and social class, 248

naturalized Americans
and folk culture, 435–40
organizations of, 219
traditions preserved and celebrated, 542
xenophobia and, 228, 232, 236–40, 252–3, 436
see also ethnic groups; immigrants to U.S.
nature, tradition of, 44–5, 63, 153
Negroes, *see* African-Americans
Negro History Week, 10, 441, 442, 630
Negro Society for Historical Research, New York, 125, 440
Nell, William C., 87
Netherlands, tradition in culture, 525
Neumann, George C., 612
Nevins, Allan, 540–1, 543, 663
on Civil War Centennial Commission, 596–7, *illus.* 597, 599–608 *passim*
Newberry, Walter L., 156
Newberry Library, Chicago, 156, 317, 569
Newburyport, Mass., 136, 142, 563
New Deal, 444, 458, 469, 473, 474–7; *see also* CCC; WPA
New England
and Civil War Centennial, 604
historical associations in other regions, 74–5
and immigrant groups, 436
importance of tradition in, 143, 384, 387
internal criticism of, 384
nostalgia about, 392, 548
Puritans and, 211, 212, 214, 388–92, 744
resentment of, 377–9, 384–6, 388–92, 493, 744, 771
South and, 115, 211, 214, 377–9, 384, 493, 549
visitors' impressions of, 210–11
and (the) West, 274–5, 393–4
New England Society of New York, 74, 208, 217
Newman, John Henry, 19
New Orleans, battle of (1815)
battlefield site, 11
celebration (1837) of victory, 68
New York City
architecture (19th century), 147
Central Park, 19–20
Civil War monuments, 116
education of immigrants in, 245, 246
World's Fair (1939), 424, 458, 507, 510, 513–14, 533

see also Cloisters; Federal Hall Memorial Historical Site; Metropolitan Museum of Art; Museum of American Folk Art; Museum of the City of New York; Museum of Modern Art
New York Southern Society, 109, 217, 456
New York State Museum, Albany, 166
Niles, John Jacob, 680
Nixon, Richard M., 613, 614, 661
Nock, Albert Jay, 199, 493
Norse explorers, 242–3 and *nn*.
North Point (Md.), battle of (1814), 142
Northwest Territory
centennial (1887), 141–2
sesquicentennial (1938), 375, 423, 438, 478, 505
Norton, Charles Eliot, 133
nostalgia, 12
and architecture, 461
British, 33, 202, 519
and collecting Americana, 316, 322
and collective memory, 4
commercial exploitation of, 152; *see also* commercialization of culture and the past
and conservation movement, 266
and cultural "shrines," 201–4
as escapist, 294–5
and familial continuity, 225
and idealized past, 238, 410
and New England, 392, 548
1960s, 618, 657
1970s–80s, 533, 618, 656–7, 688
and "Old West," 275–6
and pageants, 277, 278–9
post–World War II, 532–6
and preservation movement, 262
and progress, 47, 356, 702–3
and Progressives, 270, 271
rural, 152–3, 266, 286, 519, 619
and selective memory, 626
and technology (resistance to), 47
temporal *vs.* geographical meanings, 533
uses of, 295
novels, *see* fiction, historical; literature, American
Nugent, Richard Bruce, 414
Nutting, Wallace, 10, 149, 151, 152 and *illus.*, 199, 225–6, 258, 286, 325, 340, 343

O

Oakley, Violet, 268–9
Odum, Howard W., 442
Old Deerfield (Mass.), 557, 566; *see also*
    Historic Deerfield, Inc. (Mass.)
Old Salem (N.C.), 554
Old South Meeting House (Boston),
    preservation of, 198, 244, 261, 266
Old Sturbridge Village, Southbridge,
    Mass., 312, 345 *n*., 371, 373, 556
Olmsted, Frederick Law, 153
Onassis, Jacqueline Kennedy, 613,
    659–60
Ophuls, Marcel, 4
Opper, Frederick Burr, 213
oral tradition and history, 134, 429
    discounted, 48
    reliability of, 96, 209
oratory, public
    commemorative orations, 69, 70–1; for
        Emancipation Day, 123–4
    discounted historically, 49
    lectures and lecture tours, on history,
        158, 198–9, 205, 245, 398, 453
    and memory, 32–3, 137
    see also Fourth of July: speeches; Hoar,
        G. F.; sermons; Webster, D.
Oregon Trail, 397–9, 398 *n*., 471
    Centennial (1930), 393, *illus.* 400, 503,
        525
    memorial, 447
    pageant, 423
outdoor museums, *see* farm museums;
    village museums
Ovington, Mary White, 414
Owsley, Frank, 428

P

Page, Thomas Nelson, 113, 201
pageants and pageantry, 167, 267,
    277–81, 422–5, 457, 458, 489, 494,
    506–7, 512, 532
    European antecedents, 279–80, 281
    religious component, 205
    see also battle re-enactments
Paine, Tom, 42, 504
painting(s), American
    in Capitol Rotunda, 75–6, 86–7, 213
    collecting (20th century), 313; *see also*
        Americana, collecting of
    early 20th century, 149–50, 189–90

European subjects and influences,
    168–9
historical murals (20th century), 462,
    464, 476, 498, 533
landscapes, 63, 153, *illus.* 154–5, 189
Native Americans portrayed in, *see*
    Native Americans, portrayed in art
19th century, 97–8, *illus.* 97–9, 153,
    illus. 154–5, 168–9
    prices, 160
    progress as theme in, 45–7, *illus.* 46
    regionalism in, 307, 408, 434–5; *see
        also by region*
Palfrey, John Gorham, 197
Palmer, Fanny, 84
Paltsits, Victor Hugo, 388
Panama-California Exposition (San Diego,
    1915–16), 139, 394–5
Panama Canal, 139
Pan-American Exposition (Buffalo, N.Y.,
    1901), 139
parades, *see* pageants
Paris Salon (1899), 186
Parkhurst, Charles H., 233
Parkman, Francis, 70, 186
parks, national, 45, 265–6, 465–73, 479,
    611–12, 615, 674
    and Canada's, compared, 522
    educational role, 465, 466–7
    historical, 468
    Mesa Verde, 188, 264 and *illus.*, 265
    MISSION 66 program, 540, 609, 610–11
    patriotic role, 646
    Yellowstone, 265, *illus.* 466
    Yosemite, 265, 371
    see also national military parks
Parley, Peter (Samuel Goodrich), 70
Parrington, Vernon L., 24, 336
Parsons, Elsie Clews, 268
Parton, James, 76, 135, 158, 172, 197
Parton, Sara Willis, 135
past
    aesthetic aspect, 10
    attitudes toward (early 20th century),
        164–5
    commercialization of, *see*
        commercialization of culture and the
        past
    ignorance of and indifference to: 19th
        century, 41, 48–56, 133, 136; 20th
        century, 534, 677–8, 696–7; foreign
        observers on, 56–60
    manipulation and reconstruction of,
        3–4, 5, 10; politicization (20th
        century), 448–51, 511; *see also*

traditions: politically motivated manipulation
-present relationship, 5, 40, 136, 279, 280, 282, 353
repudiation of, in early America, 41–3
pastoral nostalgia, 152–3, 266, 286, 519, 619
in Britain, 286
patriotic societies, 218, 267, 332, 588, 646–7
conflicts, 249, 250–2, 253
patriotism
in Britain, 59
in France, and history-teaching, 289
in Japan, as civil religion, 293–4
patriotism, American, 8
and Americanism, 5
in (the) arts, 546
and biography, 337
and Borglum's Mount Rushmore, 329, 449
and capitalism, 573
and civil religion, 192, 204–5
and collectors of Americana, 321, 344, 345
Colonial Williamsburg and, 580–7
commercial aspects, 395; *see also* commercialization of culture and the past; Freedom Train
diversity of, 7–8
ignorance and, 301
and myth, 484
and nationalism, 308, 648
and national memory, contrasted, 13
1960s–80s, 620, 645–52
and pageantry, 279–80
and populism, 464, 465
post–World War II, 546–55
and preservation organizations, 260
renaissance of late 19th century, 179–80
20th century, 5, 12, 307–8, 332–3, 459–64, 481
veterans' groups and, 103–4
women and, 267
World War II and, 479, 510–11, *illus.* 512
and xenophobia, 239–40, 436
see also ancestor worship; flag, American; Freedom Train
Patriots' Day (Mass.), 162
Pattee, Fred Lewis, 257–8, 498
Pattie, James Ohio, 80
Paullin, Charles O., 160
Peabody Museum, Cambridge, Mass., 185

peace
movements: Vietnam War, 585, 645; World War II, 478
as theme of Centennial Exposition, Philadelphia, 137–8
Peale, Charles Willson, *illus.* 65
Penfield, Edward, *illus.* 182
Penn, William, 72, 86, 150, 235
Pennsylvania Academy of Fine Arts, Philadelphia, 169
Perry, Enoch Wood, 94, *illus.* 95
Perry, Ralph Barton, 390 and *n.*, 526
Philadelphia
Belmont mansion, 624
centennial of Constitution (1887), 445
Centennial Exposition (1876), 135–6, 137–8, 169, 185
historic preservation in, 29, 53, 259
Independence Historical Park, 611
Saint-Gaudens' *Pilgrim,* 207–8
Sesquicentennial of Independence (1926), 425, 447, 494
see also Independence Hall; Pennsylvania Academy of Fine Art; Ross (Betsy) House
Philadelphia Museum of Art, 323, 347
philanthropists, American, 154, 156, 157–8; *see also individuals*
Philipse Castle, Tarrytown, N.Y., 340, 371, 550
Phillips, Duncan, 326, 327 *n.*, 340
Phillips, John M., 343
photography, 96, 254, 339, 507–8
and authenticity (historical), 31
documentary, 421, 434, 507–8
Nutting's, 151–2
Pidgeon, William, 184
pilgrimages, historical, *see* "shrines" and pilgrimages, historical
Pilgrim Monument, Plymouth, Mass., 107, 210, 211
Pilgrims, 208–11, 213 and *n.*, 214–15
anniversaries of landing at Plymouth, *see under* Plymouth, Mass.
commemorations of, 74; *see also* Pilgrim Tercentenary (1920–21)
Forefathers' Day celebrations, 63–4, 208, 211
iconography, 207–8, 213
Mayflower Compact, 64, 209, 630
myths about, 32, 64, 385
and Puritans, 64, 207–15 *passim,* 387–8
Pilgrim Tercentenary (1920–21), 186, 384–5, 387, 493–4

Pioneer Day(s), 141, 274, 399–400, 401,
    402, 423, 425
Pioneer Memorial, Denver, 276
pioneers
    celebration of, 423, 504
    descendants of, memoirs and
        organizations, 219, 220 and *n*.
    see also frontier myth in U.S.
Pioneer Village, Salem, Mass., 372, 455
Pittsburgh Survey (1909), 248
Plumb, Preston B., 184–5
pluralism, cultural, 4–5, 8, 13, 18, 38, 101
    and assimilation, 52, 235–6, 243
    vs. cultural homogenization, 408–9,
        427
    and indifference to past, 41, 50
    and memory, 687–8
    and national identity, 271, 275, 518,
        533
    resistance to, 409
    see also ethnic groups; immigrants to
        U.S.; local traditions and memories;
        regionalism
Plymouth, Mass.
    anniversaries of Pilgrim landing:
        200th (1820), 64; 250th, 33; 300th
        (1921), 384–5, 387, 447
    Massasoit statue (Dallin), 186–7
    Pilgrim monument, 107, 210, 211
    Plimoth Plantation, 370, 568–9, 640
    Plymouth Rock, 64, 209, 678
Pocahontas, 75, 85–6
Pocock, J. G. A., 7
Poe, Edgar Allan, 262
politics of culture, 5, 13, 14, 287, 289–92
    in China and Japan, 293–4, 517–18,
        696
    and discovery of America, 243
    international, 293–4, 690–3 *passim*
    politicization of memory, 4–5, 464,
        503, 517–18, 520–7 *passim*, 534,
        677–8, 696–7
    politicization of past, 448–51, 511
Pony Express, 397 and *n*., 471
Poore, Ben: Perley, 73 and *illus*., 74
Pope, Alexander, *illus*. 120
popular culture
    in democracy, 18
    elite and, 291, 525
    and high culture, distinction blurred
        by democratization, 205, 306, 340,
        341, 398, 464
    literary, 63, 164, 341, 492
    museums and, 350–1, 356
    myth(s) and, 482

shrines and "sacred" places of, 202
    in West, 398
    see also folk culture; memory, popular;
        pageants
popular memory, *see* memory, popular
popular sovereignty, 19
populism, 20, 238, 443, 470, 504, 616
    and Federal Writers Project
        guidebooks, 474
    and folk culture, 408, 412, 420
    in France, 520
    and patriotism, 464, 465
Potter, David, 379
Pound, Ezra, 408, 413, 419
Powell, John, 429–30
Powell, William H., 75
Powers, Hiram, 87, *illus*. 88
pre-Columbian history, 175
Prescott, William Hickling, 70
preservation, historical
    and American aesthetic, 325
    authenticity issue, 29
    in Britain (19th century), 34
    of California missions, 183, 262–3, 394
    Canadian government and, 522
    conflicts in movement, 561
    developers cooperate with, 629, 674
    economic impact of, 554, 559
    educational role, 244, 554
    government's role, 184–5, 263–5,
        445–7, 460, 467–73, 558–64 *passim*,
        660–1
    and "heritage," 622–8 *passim*
    indifference to history and, 52–5
    mid-20th century, 557–64, 628–31
    vs. museum villages, 200–1
    National Park Service and, 467–70
    National Register of Historic Places,
        570
    organizations for, 201, 260–6 *passim*,
        562, 628–31; *see also* historical
        societies
    Progressivism and, 270
    ruins neglected (19th century), 53–4,
        184, 187
    women in, 240–2, 260, 265, 266–9
        passim
    see also historic sites; restoration,
        historic
Preservation Week, 559–60
Presidential Libraries Act (U.S., 1955),
    612
press (19th century), illustrations in, 31
press (20th century), and Freedom Train,
    576, 578–9

Pringle, Henry, 540–1
private funding, *see* funding, private
progress, tradition of, 6, 14, 45–7, 52, 60,
  136–7, 142, 268
  in American West, 273
  museums and, 306
  and nostalgia, 47, 356, 702–3
  resistance, ambivalence or hostility to,
    47–8, 539
  and tradition, 139, 513–14, 702
  see also modernism
Progressives and progressivism, 255, 265,
  269–71, 423, 703
property rights, *vs.* heritage
  preservation, 120, 627
publicity, *see* advertising
public records, *see* records, public
publishers
  and Civil War material, 120
  and multi-volume history series,
    158–60, 544
  and Old West material, 395–6
"Publius" (James Madison), 100
Puritans and Puritanism, 11, 64–5, 195,
  206–7, 211–14, 302, 379 *n.*, 388–91
  and Cavaliers, 385 *n.*, 405, 409
  and democracy, 526
  iconography, 206, 207, 213, *illus.* 214.
    illus. 215, 391, *illus.* 392
  in literature, 213, 391 *n.*
  myths about, 32
  and New England, 41, 211, 212, 214,
    388–92, 744
  and Pilgrims, 64, 207–15 *passim,*
    387–8
Puvis de Chavannes, Pierre, *illus.*
  287
Pyle, Howard, 150, 171

Q

Queens County Farm Museum, 636

R

race and tradition, 13
racism and race relations, 24
  in ancestor worship, 220
  Civil War Centennial Commission and,
    592, 594, 597, 598, 601–2
  at Colonial Williamsburg, 368, 552–3,
    684
  Freedom Train and, 578
  19th century, 122, 196
  Roots phenomenon and, 642
  in South Africa, 524–5
  see also Jim Crow laws; Native
    Americans, relations with white
    people
radio broadcasts
  educational, 465, 555
  folk music, 430
  historical, 419, 543, 630
  patriotic, 510–11, 578, 579
railroads
  nostalgia about, 48, 148
  social mobility enabled by, 106
  and tourism and historical education,
    276, 338, 393, 423, 437
  see also Freedom Train
Randolph, Vance, 429
Ransom, John Crow, 376
rare books, collecting, 243, 312, 316–18,
  566, 569, 632; *see also* libraries
Raumer, Frederick von, 57
Rawson, Marion Nicholl, 429
Reagan, Ronald, 12, 579, 583, 652, 655,
  658–61, *illus.* 659
Reagan administration, and historic
  preservation, 562, 563, 614, 660–1,
  816
Reconstruction era (U.S.), 71, 110, 134,
  196, 416, 417, 440, 771
reconstruction of buildings and historic
  sites, *see* restoration, historic
records, private
  failure to retain, in early republic,
    48–9, 76–7
  Madison's papers, 55
records, public
  of American Revolution, 439, 446 *n.*
  of Confederacy, 114
  displayed on Freedom Train, 573–81
    and *illus.*
  European documents on American
    history, transcribed, 437–8
  national archive, 77; *see also* National
    Archives (U.S.)
  preservation: 19th century, 55–6, 75–8;
    20th century, 183–4, 445–7, 473,
    479, 571
  presidential papers, collected, 159,
    612–13
  publication of, 544
Records of the Past (periodical), 187

Redfield, Robert, 415
regionalism, 12, 271–7, 375–406
  in art, 307, 408, 434–5; *see also by
    region*
  Civil War and, 88, 121
  and colonial revival, 461
  Colonial Williamsburg and, 364–5, 366
  and folk culture, 428, 434–5
  in literature, 337, 376, 408
  or nationalism, 276, 408–9, 461, 477,
    548, 572
  pride of place and, 181–4
  rivalries and conflicts, 14, 50, 163,
    210–11, 376–87, 399, 457–8, 477, 548
  and selection of traditions to retain, 13
  Southern (20th century), 403–6
  see also local traditions and memories
religious traditions and affiliations
  American sects and denominations,
    and tradition, 41–2
  and ethnic identity, 8
  evangelicalism, 50, 93, 667
  history and tradition as surrogate for,
    194–206
  science and, 194, 196
  spiritual crisis (late 19th century),
    194–7 *passim;* of historians, 199
  20th century, 502
  see also civil religion; clergy;
    Mormons; Puritans; sermons
Remington, Frederic, 28, 94, 186, 220,
    237, 395–6
Remington, S. Pierre, 102
republicanism, 19
Republican party, and politicization of
    Lincoln's memory, 129, 294
research, historical, *see* historical
    scholarship
restoration, historic, 259–66 *passim*
  American aesthetic and, 326
  of California missions, 183, 262–3, 394
  educational role, 244, 340, 554
  later 20th century, 678, 679
  National Park Service and, 467–73
  in Philadelphia, 259
  of questionable value or authority, 342,
    561
  ruins neglected (19th century), 53–4,
    184, 187
  in Texas, 313; *see also* Alamo battle
    site, San Antonio
  see also authenticity, historical: of
    reconstruction and reproductions;
    Colonial Williamsburg (Va.); historic
    sites; preservation, historic

Revere, Paul, 84, 186, 218, 244, 370, 504
Revolution, American, *see* American
    Revolution
revolutionary tradition (U.S.), 515
rhetoric, *see* oratory, public; sermons
Rhodes, James Ford, 22, 95–6, 174, 258,
    440
Richards, William Trost, 54 and *illus.*,
    168
Richardson, James D., 159
Richmond, Va.
  bicentennial (1937), 387, 425
  Civil War Centennial in, *illus.* 605
  Confederate museum, 119
  Emancipation Day decorations, *illus.*
    125
  memorials proposed, to: Confederate
    soldiers, 167 *n.*; Davis (J.), 126;
    Grant, 108; Lee, 111, 117; Lincoln,
    110
  see also Valentine Museum
Richmondtown Resoration (N.Y.), 556–7
right (political)
  on past and memory, 5
  see also conservatism
Riley, Edward M., 373
Rising Sun Inn (Letitia Penn House),
    Philadelphia, 53
Rivers, Larry, 649, 650
Rivière, Georges-Henri, 520, 692
roads, *see* highways
roadside markers, *see* historic markers
    and signs
Robertson, James I., 599, 600–1, 607–8
Robinson, James Harvey, 248, 484, 516
Rockefeller, Abby Aldrich, 269, 315, 327
  folk art collection, 268, 321, 426–7,
    431–2, 566, 680
Rockefeller, John D., Jr., 28, 311, 315,
    342, 356–7, *illus.* 361–2, 370–1, 437,
    550
  and Colonial Williamsburg, 358–70,
    373 *n.*
Rockefeller, John D., III, 580–7
Rockwell, Norman, 328
Roman, Charles Victor, 440
Roman Catholic Church
  and ancestor worship, 222
  anniversaries of local parishes and
    dioceses, 201, 232
  in Southwestern U.S., 195
Roosevelt, Eleanor, 429–30
Roosevelt, Franklin D., 192, 294, 417,
    448, 450–2, *illus.* 450, *illus.* 453,
    464, 479, 502, 571

birthday centennial, 616
and Lincoln, 294, 448, 452, 521
presidential library, 612 and *illus.*
Roosevelt, Theodore, 128, 191, 262, 275,
276, 396, 446, 448, 449–50, 483–4
on ancestor awareness and heritage,
218–19
on Puritans, 211
Root, Elihu, 349
Roots (Haley), 641–5, 668, 669, 672
Roseland, Harry, *illus.* 123
Rosenbach, Abraham S. Wolf, 341
Ross (Betsy) House, Philadelphia, 29,
192 *n.*, 501
Ross, Edward, 235 *n.*
Rossiter, Thomas P., 213
Rothschild, Edmond de, 520
Rourke, Constance, 205, 313, 411–13,
illus. 412, 414–15, 420 *n.*, 443
and folk arts and folklore, 339, 411–15
passim, 426, 427–8, 435
on myth(s), 499–500, 515
on tradition(s), 24, 39, 303, 333–4, 336,
413
Rouse, James W., 629
Rousseau, Jean-Jacques, 290
rural and pastoral life
American aesthetic and, 326
nostalgia for, 152–3, 266, 286, 519,
619; in Britain, 286
see also "country boy" myth
Rush, Benjamin, 40, 76
Rushmore, Mount, *see* Mount Rushmore
National Memorial (S.D.)
Russell, Charles M., 225 and *illus.*
Rutherford, Mildred Lewis, 126
Ryder, Albert Pinkham, 168

S

sabbatarianism, 68
Sack, Harold, 660
Sack, Israel, 326, 354 *n.*
Sage, Margaret Olivia (Mrs. Russell), 189,
348–9
Saint-Gaudens, Augustus, 84, 116, 167,
206, 207 and *illus.,* 208
Salem, Mass., 145
Maritime National Historic Site, 471
and *illus.*
Pioneer Village, 372, 455
Ward House, 258, 346
see also Essex Institute
Salley, Alexander S., 31

Salmon, Lucy M., 248, 273
Sample, Paul, 391, *illus.* 392, 501
Sandburg, Carl, 309, 413, 417, 420, 426,
477, 498, 503, 509 and *illus.,* 545,
589, 702
San Diego, Calif.
Panama-California Exposition
(1915–16), 139, 394–5
preservation, 263
San Francisco, exposition (1915), 139
Sang, Philip D., 591
San Jacinto, battle of (1836), 9, 145
battle flag restored, 678
Santa Fe, N.M., 262, 396, 511–12
Santayana, George, 164
Saratoga Battle Monument, Schuylerville,
N.Y., 163, 730
Sargent, John Singer, *illus.* 151
Saroyan, William, 511
Sawyer, Joseph Dillaway, 387
Scandinavian-Americans, 231, 436–7,
808; *see also* Swedish-Americans
Schlesinger, Arthur M., 378, 485–6
Schlesinger, Arthur M., Jr., 613
scholarship, historical, *see* historical
scholarship
Schomburg, Arthur A., 125, 343, 440–1
Schoolcraft, Henry Rowe, 83, 86
schools, history teaching in, *see* history,
teaching of (in primary and
secondary schools); textbooks, in
history
Schoonover, Frank E., *illus.* 215
Schurman, Joseph Gould, 198
Schurz, Carl, 235, 438
Schussele, Christian, 47
Scott, Sir Walter, 57, 171, 272
sculpture, American
civic (20th century), 329, 505
collecting, 569, 615
as monuments, *see* monuments,
commemorative and historical
see also Borglum, G.; French, D. C.;
Saint-Gaudens, A.
Seattle, Chief, 442 *n.*
sectionalism, *see* regionalism
See America First, 276, 338
selective memory, *see* memory, selective
sermons, historical content of, 32, 200,
245
Sesquicentennial of Independence
(Philadelphia, 1926), 425, 447, 494
Seward, William H., 100
Shaker Museum, Old Chatham, N.Y.,
556

Shakespeare, William, 11, 41
Sheeler, Charles, 327–8
Shelburne (Vt.) Museum, 320 and *n*.,
    554, 566, 640
Sheldon, George W., 189, 324
Sherman, Stuart Pratt, 23–4, 302–3, 335,
    390, 416
Sherman, Gen. William Tecumseh, 108,
    115, 125
Shiloh (Tenn.), battle of, 126
    battlefield, 264
"shrines" and pilgrimages, historical,
    201–4, 259, 486–8, 532, 547–8, 589,
    590, 608–9, 687
Sierra Club, 263, 265
signs (roadside), *see* historic markers and
    signs
silver (antique)
    collections, 192, 269, 323, 389
    colonial revival and, 148
    exhibition at Boston (1906), 148
Simms, William Gilmore, 29, 78, 80–1,
    181
sites, historic, *see* historic sites
Skinner, Constance Lindsay, 413, 434
slavery
    Carter's Grove (Va.), slave cabins,
        684
    criticism of, 75
    outlawed by Thirteenth Amendment,
        123
    reunion of slave descendants, 644
    see also Emancipation Proclamation;
        freed slaves
Sleeper, Henry Davis, 319, 320
Sleepy Hollow Restorations, 340–1, 371,
    548, 550–1; *see also* Philipse Castle;
    Sunnyside, Tarrytown, N.Y.
Smith, Charlotte, 267
Smith, Henry Nash, 6
Smith, Sidney, 43
Smith, Timothy L., 8
Smithsonian Institution, Washington,
    D.C., 189, 200, 445, 635, 673
    Indian culture, exhibits and collections,
        138, 185, 685
    see also Hirshhorn Gallery,
        Washington, D.C.; National Museum
        of American History, Washington,
        D.C.
social change, *see* change, social and
    cultural
social history, 244, 420
    Federal Writers Project guides as,
        475–6

socialism, 104
    fear of, 237, 248
    see also communism in U.S.
societies, *see* Americana, collecting of:
    networks and organizations;
    historical societies; lineage societies;
    patriotic societies; preservation,
    historic: organizations; *and under*
    regions, e.g., Western U.S.
Society of American Historians, 341
Society of the Army and Navy of the
    Confederate States, 211
Society of Art Collectors: "Comparative
    Exhibition of Native and Foreign
    Art, The," 189
Society of the Cincinnati, 218
Society of Mayflower Descendants, 218
Society for the Preservation of New
    England Antiquities (S.P.N.E.A.),
    261, 556
Society of Western Artists, 182
Soldiers' and Sailors' Monument,
    Brooklyn, N.Y., 116
Solzhenitsyn, Aleksandr, 700
song, national, 180, 415; *see also*
    "Star-Spangled Banner"
Sons of the American Revolution, 218,
    219, 220, 239, 249, 252, 332, 486,
    646
    political/social positions of, 21
Sons of Veterans, 103, 104
South (U.S.)
    ancestor obsession and filiopiety in,
        112, 217–18
    bitterness over Civil War, 110–15,
        404–5, 491
    change and continuity after Civil War,
        113–14
    and Civil War Centennial, 591, 598,
        602–4, 609
    culture and tradition (20th century),
        403–6
    historical consciousness in, 121, 384–7,
        403–6
    and Lincoln, 110, 126–7, 397–8, 405,
        771
    Lost Cause tradition, 11, 101, *illus.*
        108, 113, 126, 217, 275, 491, 609
    and New England, 115, 211, 214,
        377–9, 384, 493, 549
    reconciliation after Civil War, 103,
        106–9, 114–15, 126, 257, 404–5,
        416
    religious faith and values, 194, 195
    see also Civil War; Confederacy

South Africa
  memory and interpretation of
    tradition, 701
  political mythology, 294, 524–5
Southern Agrarians ("Fugitives"), 22,
  404, 519
Southern Historical Society, 111
Southern States Pan-American Exposition
  (New Orleans, 1914), 542–3
Southwest, American
  "discovery" of (20th century), 276
  ignorance of its history, 50, 182
  Lummis and, 181–2
  museums of its art and culture, 182,
    274, 276, 396
  preservation activities and
    organizations, 262, 348
  see also Santa Fe, N.M.; Western U.S.
Southwest Museum of Art, History and
  Science, Los Angeles, 182, 274, 276
sovereignty, popular, 19
Soviet Union, 516–17
  civil religion in, 205
  collective memory in, 3
  "Holy Russia" ideal, 698
  nostalgia for Old Russia, 653
  politicization of memory and tradition,
    520–1, 697–700
  traditions and myth in, 289
Spain
  civil religion in, 204–5
  national culture develops, 36–7
Sparks, Jared, 49, 78 and *illus.*, 197
speeches, *see* oratory, public
Springer, Frank, 396
Squier, Ephraim G., 72
Standish, Miles, 209
"Star-Spangled Banner," 142–3, 180, 459,
  illus. 460, 577
states, cultural role of
  conservation policies, 469
  and folk arts, 433
  funding monuments, preservation, and
    commemorative events, 445, 447
  historical parks, 468, 469
  preservation activities, 265, 560
  state historians, 421
statues, *see* battle monuments and
  battlefields; monuments,
  commemorative and historical;
  sculpture, American
Stearns, Harold, 416
Stedman, Edmund Clarence, 177
Stegner, Wallace, 619
Stein, Gertrude, 519

Steinbeck, John, 508
Stevens, Wallace, 52, 502
Stickley, Gustave, 149
Stieglitz, Alfred, 326, 408
Stokes, Isaac Newton Phelps, 191–2, 313,
  343
Stone, Sir Benjamin, 174
Stone, William Leete, 86
Stone Mountain (Ga.), 329, 491
Storrs, Richard S., 211, 243
Stowe, Harriet Beecher, 47
Streeter, Thomas Winthrop, 317–18,
  569
Strong, Margaret Woodbury, 633
success, myth of, 8–9
Suckow, Ruth, 427, 435
Sulgrave Institution (Britain), 486, 488
Sully, Thomas, *illus.* 78
Sumner, Charles, 84, 157
Sunnyside, Tarrytown, N.Y., 340, 371,
  547, 548, 550, 551
Sutter's Fort (Calif.), 263
Swedish-Americans, 7, 231, 437, 457,
  505, 542

T

Taine, Hippolyte, 292
Tannahill, Robert H., 190, 555
Tarkington, Booth, 304, 338, 409
Tate, Allen, 376, 403–4, 404 *n*.
Taylor, Francis H., 509
Taylor, Henry F., 226, 227 and *illus.*
Taylor, Henry Osborn, 311
Taylor, Zachary, 68, 455
teaching history, *see* history, teaching of
technological innovation
  celebrated, 136; in art, 46–7; at
    expositions, 514
  and historical authenticity, 32
  in printing, 540
  resistance to, and nostalgia, 47
  and sense of past, 254, 507, 668
  steamboat, 386
  telephone, electric light, typewriter
    (1876), 138, 139
  see also automobile(s); media;
    photography; railroads
television
  and Civil War Centennial, 607
  and commercialization of history, 543,
    669–72
  educational uses, 555, 563

television (*continued*)
  historical docudramas, 534, 641,
    669–72; *Roots* phenomenon, 641–5
    passim, 668, 669, 672
Ten Eyck, James, 269
Tennessee centennial (1897), 143–4
Terkel, Studs, 503
Texas
  centennial (1936), 242, 395 and *n.,*
    506, 680
  independence and annexation, 50
  see also Alamo
textbooks, in history (19th century)
  African-Americans in, 124
  chauvinism in, 45
  Civil War in, 121
  decentralized control of, 290
  morality stressed in, 70
  Native Americans in, 258–9
textbooks, in history (20th century), 272,
    301, 378, 382–3, 385 *n.,* 422, 484–6,
    505, 663 *n.,* 664–5
  in Africa, 697
  in Canada, 524
  in Europe, 289, 290, 519
  minorities in, 685
Thanet, Octave (Alice French), 134
Thanksgiving Day, 64, 205, 210, 256–7,
    386
  iconography, 207
Thierry, Augustin, 59
Thomas, Keith, 249–50
Thompson, Alfred Wordsworth, 140
Thompson, Dorothy, 510
Thompson, Harold W., 432, *illus.* 433
Thompson, Virgil, 545
Thompson, William Hale, 485–6
Thoreau, Henry David, 43, 66, 191
Thurman, Wallace, 414
time, historical and mythical, 206
  and culture, 97
  and history, 5
  see also past: -present relationship
Tinker, Chauncey Brewster, 495
Tocqueville, Alexis de, 18, 35–6, 216,
    693
Tojetti, Domenico, 169
Tomlinson, Everett T., 80
Toombs, Robert, 125
totalitarianism, 481, 532, 586
tourism and travel (domestic)
  Civil War Centennial and, 596, 604
  commercialization of past for, 10, 13,
    276 *n.,* 402–3, 439–40, 534, 537,
    673–4, 693

democratization of, 304, 340, 506,
    539–40
early 20th century, 276, 304–5,
    338–40, 506; British, 305–6
economic importance of, 369, 559,
    673–4
as educational, 340, 393, 403 and *n.,*
    423
Indian culture used to promote, 187
and museums and historic sites, 639–41
and national parks, 465–6, 610–11
National Trust and, 559
1960s, 618
and Washington's birthday, 71
see also highways; historic markers and
    signs; railroads; See America First;
    village museums
tradition, 4–7, 28, 33, 40
  in Britain, 19, 286, 288, 653, 701–2
  commercialization of, *see*
    commercialization of culture and the
    past
  cultural role of, 4, 5, 6, 7, 11, 13, 19,
    164–6; in China and Japan, 293–4
  decentralization of, 12, 14, 572, 588
  defined, 7, 25
  and democracy, 24, 39, 292, 407, 408,
    435, 701–2; *see also* democratization
    of culture and tradition
  folk *vs.* national, 407–43
  government as custodian of, 12, 14, 41,
    55, 78, 184–5, 294, 444–80, 570,
    571–2, 610–17
  and history, *see* tradition and history
  invented, 4, 7, 30, 37, 99, 181, 287–8,
    703; abroad, 517, 693–5
  lack of, 9, 56, 90–1, 309, 499–500, 515,
    532; *see also* amnesia, collective
    and memory, 514
  and myth, defined and contrasted, 25
  pessimism about (20th century), 270
  and progress, 139, 513–14, 702
  and race, 13
  repudiated, in early America, 41–3,
    48–52, 56–61
  steadying influence of (Thayer), 10
  see also traditions
traditionalism (20th century), 271,
    299–309 *passim,* 327
tradition and history, 17
  in conflict, 677
  distinguished (Twain), 171
  intermingled, 258
  in South and elsewhere, contrasted,
    383 and *n.*

traditions
  definitions, 6–7
  elite commitment to, 318–19
  European and American attitudes,
    contrasted, 56–60, 164–5
  heterogeneity of (20th century), 270
  invented, *see* tradition: invented
  local, *see* local traditions and memories
    and pageantry, 279
  politically motivated manipulation of,
    4–5, 464, 503, 517–18, 520–7 *passim,*
    534, 677–8, 696–7
  selection and prioritizing of, 13
Train, Arthur, 388–9
trains, *see* Freedom Train; railroads
Trans-Mississippi Exposition (Omaha,
  1898), 139
transportation, *see* automobile(s);
  railroads; tourism and travel
travel, democratization of, 304, 506,
  539–40
travel, domestic, *see* highways; railroads;
  tourism and travel
travel, foreign (by Americans), 237, 313,
  338, 516–17
Trilling, Lionel, 545
Truman, Harry S., 571, 572
  and Freedom Train, 574, *illus.* 577,
    578, 579
  presidential library, 613
Trumbull, John, 53, 75–6
Tuckerman, Henry T., 47, 61, 71, 80
Turner, Frederick Jackson, 179, 268, 376,
  379 and *n.,* 492
Twain, Mark, 29, 53, 90, 96, 129, 133,
  165, 171, 185, 221, 302
Tweed, William Marcy ("Boss"), 138
Tyler, Lyon G., 110, 126, 127 and *illus.,*
  378 and *n.,* 379, 380 and *n.,* 381–3,
  385–6, 388, 404, 405, 540
Tyler, Moses Coit, 180–1, 199, 202

U

Uncle Sam, 59
uniqueness, American, *see*
  exceptionalism, American
United Confederate Veterans, 105,
  201–2, 272, 381
United Daughters of the Confederacy
  (U.D.C.), 126, 329, 331, 380, 381,
  405
United States History Association, 540
unity *vs.* diversity, *see* pluralism, cultural

Upham, Charles Wentworth, 64, 197
urban districts, historic, 372
  restoration of, 534, 561, 564, 575–6,
    682
  urban renewal and, 610, 614, 629
USSR, *see* Soviet Union

V

Valentine, Edward, 117, *illus.* 118, 169
Valentine Museum, Richmond, Va., 684
Valley Forge, Penna., 95, 220, 486
  National Historic Park, 612
  Washington Memorial Chapel, 200,
    203–4
Vance, William L., 54 *n.*
Vancouver, George, 144
Vanderbilt family, 157, 190
Vanderlyn, John, 75
Van Doren, Carl, 336
Van Doren, Mark, 545
Van Tyne, Claude H., 258–9
Van Vechten, Carl, *illus.* 414, 442
Vedder, Elihu, 103, 194
vernacular culture, *see* folk culture,
  American; folklife, American
Vespucci, Amerigo, 243
veterans
  of Civil War, 103–6, 111, 114, 201–2;
    Blue-Gray reunions, 105, 106–7,
    417–18, 457; descendant groups, 591
  groups integrate activities, 103, 105
  Jewish, 439
Veterans' Day, 162
Vico, Giovanni, 39
Vietnam Veterans Memorial,
  Washington, D.C., 11, 662
Vietnam War, 647, 652
  mythology about, 657, 662
  protests against, 5, 585, 645
Vilar, Pierre, 204
village improvement societies, 238
village museums, 321–2, 354–5, 371–2,
  537, 551–6, 568–9, 619
  attendance figures, 551
  depoliticized, 511
  see also Colonial Williamsburg (Va.);
    Historic Deerfield, Inc. (Mass.);
    Monticello (Va.); Mount Vernon
    (Va.); Mystic (Conn.) Seaport
    Museum; Old Sturbridge Village,
    Southbridge, Mass.; Shelburne (Vt.)
    Museum

Vinland Map, 243
Virgil: *Aeneid,* in art, 225, *illus.* 226, 747
Volney, Constantin, Comte de, 53
Vroman, Adam Clark, 262–3

W

Wadsworth Atheneum, Hartford, Conn.,
    148, 152, 343, 634
Wagner, Henry Raup, 317
Wakefield (Va.), Washington birthplace,
    371, 467, 472, 500–1
Wakeman, Stephen H., 157, 191
Wallace, Lew, 167
Walpole Society, 258, 323
Walters, Henry, 166
Walters, William T., 166
war(s)
    and American memory, 13
    and cultural institutions, 478
    monuments, *see* battle monuments and
        battlefields; veterans; *and specific
        wars*
Ward, John Quincy Adams, 208, 210
Ward House, Salem, Mass., 258, 346
Warner, Charles Dudley, 120
Warner, W. Lloyd, 142
Warren, Robert Penn, 11, 29, 306, 545,
    606, 702
Washington, Booker T., 442
Washington, George
    birthday, 71, 106, 109, 129, *illus.* 182,
        375, 417–18, 447, 455, 464, 488, 521,
        588
    birthplace (Wakefield, Va.), 260, 371,
        467, 472, 500–1
    headquarters, 200, 371, 468, *illus.* 469;
        in art, 153, *illus.* 154–5; *see also*
        Valley Forge, Penna.
    honor and adulation of, 66, 130, 202–4,
        218, 486
    inauguration, anniversaries, 139, 277,
        424, 506–7, *illus.* 507, 513
    and Lincoln, pairing of, 129, 130 and
        illus., 131 *n*., 202–3
    presidential mansion (Philadelphia),
        destroyed, 53
    "relics" of, collecting, 200, 203, 507
    visit to Boston (1789), centennial, 143
    see also Mount Vernon (Va.)
Washington, George, biographies and
    fables
    Ford, 203

Lodge, 28
Sparks, 49
Weems, 27, 159, 203
Wilson, 150, 203
Washington, George, iconography and
    monuments, *illus.* 130, 154–5, 455,
    649–50, *illus.* 650–1, 652
    ancestral home in England, 486
    Dunsmore's depictions, 203
    Mount Rushmore bust, 486, *illus.* 487
    see also Valley Forge (Penna.):
        Washington Memorial Chapel;
        Washington Monument, Washington,
        D.C.
Washington, Mary Ball, 203, 405 *n*.
    Association, 218
    burial site, *illus.* 203
    home, 260, 547, *illus.* 548
Washington, D.C., monuments, *see*
    Jefferson Memorial; Korean War
    Veterans Memorial; Lincoln
    Memorial; Vietnam Veterans
    Memorial
Washington and Lee University,
    Lexington, Va., 109
    Lee Memorial Chapel, 109, 117,
        329–31, *illus.* 330, 488
Washington Association, 200
Washington Monument, Washington,
    D.C., 11, 203, 647
Waterman, Thomas Tileston, 324
Watson, John Fanning, 52–3, 72
Watt, James, 614
Wayside Inn, Sudbury, Mass., 84, 244,
    260, 300, 354, 355
Webb, Beatrice, 134
Webb, Electra Havemeyer, 166, 269,
    315, 320, *illus.* 321, 432, 566, 633,
    680
Webb, Walter Prescott, 199, 426, 428
Weber, Eugen, 59, 285, 289, 296
Webster, Daniel, 33, 63, 64, 70–1, 216,
    393, 493–4
Weems, Mason Locke ("Parson"), 27,
    28, 65 and *illus.*, 80, 82, 159, 203
Weir, Julian Alden, 47, 326
Weir, Robert W., 75, 213
Wells family (Southbridge, Mass.), 312,
    371–2
Wendell, Barrett, 94, 174, 332
Wesselmann, Tom, 649, *illus.* 650
Western U.S., 393–403
    African-American history in, 683–4
    in art, 182, 395–6, 401; *see also*
        Remington, F.

collecting Americana from, 317;
museums, 182, 274, 396, 809
commemorative days and celebrations,
144–5, 274, 394–5, 398 and *n.*, 401
commercialization of, 270, 401, 402–3,
549, 676, *illus.* 677
cowboy mythology and lore, 258, 276,
492
Easterners and, 274–5, 393–4, 400
ethnic diversity, 549
and European cultural models, 167
folk culture, 428
frontier myth, 396, 401, 402–3, 483–4,
493, 573, 704
historical and preservation societies,
398–403 *passim*
indifference to past in, 51, 394
Old West nostalgia, 395–7, 400–1, 483;
see also myth(s) in American culture:
and Old West
post–World War II, 548–9
rodeos, 401, 423
Wild West stereotypes and myths, 27,
275–6, 401, 492–3
see also intermountain West;
Southwest, American
Weston, Edward, 339
Wetherell, W. D., 656
Wharton, Anne Hollingsworth, 146
Wharton, Edith, 133–4, 175–6, 276,
383–4, 415, 436
Wheeler, Gen. Joseph, 105
White, Edwin, 169
White, Walter, 414
White, William Allen, 336
White House, Washington, D.C.
historical collections in, 192
redecorated, 613 and *n.*, 659–60
White Top Folk Festival (Va.),
429–30
Whitman, Marcus and Narcissa, 145
Whitman, Walt, 43, 128, 140, 309
Whitney, Gertrude Vanderbilt, 269
Whittier, John Greenleaf, 212, 261
Wigginton, Eliot, 681
Wilde, Oscar, 134, 149, 283
Wilder, Thornton, 420–1, 648–9
Willard, Emma, 70
Williams, George Washington, 440
Williams, John S., 556
Williams, Roger, 439, 504
Williams, William Carlos, 303, 306, 328,
498
Williamsburg, Va., 358–9
preservation and restoration, 260

see also College of William and Mary;
Colonial Williamsburg
Williamsburg (Va.) Antiques Forum, 566,
illus. 567, 633
Williamsburg (Va.) Inn, 358, 368
Williamson, William, 453–4
Wilson, Edmund, 334, 429, 544, 606–7
Wilson, James, 51
Wilson, Woodrow, 114, 147, 150, 203,
230–1, 269–70, 381, 447, 448, 483–4,
587–8
Winchester, Alice, 566
Winterthur Museum, Wilmington, Del.,
313, 319, 343, 347, 351, 566
Winthrop, John, 64, 88, 160
Winthrop, Robert C., 33, 74–5, 80, 137
Wirt, William, 65 and *illus.*
Wirth, Conrad L., 609–10
Wister, Owen, 220, 275, 400–1
Wolper, David L., 669–72, *illus.* 670–1
women and tradition in U.S., 188, 266–9
blamed for historical misconceptions,
269, 389, 608, 673
and Civil War Centennial, 608, 806
as collectors, 166, 269; *see also*
individual collectors
Driscoll vs. *De Zavala*, over Alamo,
240–2
feminists and feminism, 138, 249,
267
and folklore, 428–9; *see also* Rourke,
Constance
memories and experience of, omitted
from collective memory, 503
in Tennessee, 265
in textbooks, 685
in Virginia, 260
Women's Hall of Fame, Seneca Falls,
N.Y., 631
Wood, Grant, 332, 339, 376, 434, 498
Woodson, Carter G., 10, 440, 441–2,
illus. 441
Woodville, Richard Caton, 79 and *illus.*
Woolson, Constance Fenimore, 237
working class, American
and democracy, 24
labor strike (1912) re-enacted, 65–6
memories and associations, 619
national culture of, 420
and nativism, 248
repress difficult memories, 503
social history of, 8
World's Columbian Exposition (Chicago,
1893), 139, 170, 186, 246, 325 and
n., 496, 533

World War I
  and government's role in memory and
    preservation, 447
  immigrant groups and, 230
World War II (cultural impact of), 478,
    479, 525, 526–7, 531–2, 571
  and patriotism, 479, 510–11, *illus.* 512
  propaganda, 512–13, *illus.* 513
WPA (Works Progress Administration)
  cultural works, 395 *n.*, 457, 458,
    460–1, 462, 477, 478, 479
  and folk art(s), 427, 431, 460–1, 474–5,
    476–7
  see also Federal Art Project; Federal
    Theatre Project; Federal Writers
    Project
Wright, Frank Lloyd, 271, 408, 415
Wright, Richard, 461
Wright, Richardson, 431
Wright, Wilbur, 487
writers, American, *see* biography,
    American; historical writing;
    literature, American
Wyeth, Andrew, 546 and *illus.*
Wyeth, Newell Convers, 328

X

xenophobia, 409
  and immigrants, 228, 232, 236–40,
    252–3, 436

Y

Yellowstone National Park (Wyo.), 265,
    illus. 466
Yorktown (Va.), battle of
  anniversary celebrations, 130, 137, 375,
    429, *illus.* 450, 455
  monument, 55, 450, 467
Yosemite National Park (Calif.), 265, 371
Young, Owen D., 312
Young, Stark, 500, 668
Young America movement, 43

Z

Zangwill, Israel, 234
Zavala, Lorenzo de, 241

Permissions Acknowledgments

*Grateful acknowledgment is made to the
following for permission to reprint previously published
material:*

The Ecco Press, Penguin Books Ltd., and Czeslaw Milosz: Excerpt from "A Legend," from *Czeslaw Milosz: The Collected Poems, 1931–1987,* translated by Czeslaw Milosz and Robert Hass. Copyright © 1988 by Czeslaw Milosz Royalties, Inc. First published by The Ecco Press in 1988. Rights outside the U.S. and Canada administered by Penguin Books Ltd. Reprinted by permission of The Ecco Press, Penguin Books Ltd., and Czeslaw Milosz.

Farrar, Straus & Giroux, Inc.: Excerpt from a letter from Edmund Wilson to John Dos Passos, May 30, 1962. Copyright © 1990 by Helen Miranda Wilson. Reprinted by permission of the Estate of Edmund Wilson and Farrar, Straus & Giroux, Inc.

GRM Associates, Inc.: Excerpt from "Heritage," from *On These I Stand* by Countee Cullen (Harper & Brothers, New York, 1947). Copyright 1925 by Harper & Brothers. Copyright renewed 1953 by Ida M. Cullen. Reprinted by permission of GRM Associates, Inc., Agents for the Estate of Ida M. Cullen.

Harcourt Brace Jovanovich, Inc.: Excerpt from "I Am the People, the Mob," from *Chicago Poems* by Carl Sandburg. Copyright 1916 by Holt, Rinehart and Winston, Inc. Copyright renewed 1944 by Carl Sandburg. Reprinted by permission of Harcourt Brace Jovanovich, Inc.

Harcourt Brace Jovanovich, Inc. and *Faber and Faber Limited:* Excerpt from "East Coker," from *Four Quartets* by T. S. Eliot. Copyright 1943 by T. S. Eliot. Copyright renewed 1971 by Esme Valerie Eliot. Rights outside U.S. in *Collected Poems, 1909–1962* administered by Faber and Faber Limited. Reprinted by permission of Harcourt Brace Jovanovich, Inc. and Faber and Faber Limited.

Houghton Mifflin Company: Excerpts from "At the Lincoln Memorial," from *New and Collected Poems: 1917–1982* by Archibald MacLeish. Copyright © 1985 by the Estate of Archibald MacLeish. Reprinted by permission.

Alfred A. Knopf, Inc. and *Harold Ober Associates, Inc.:* "History," from *The Panther and the Lash* by Langston Hughes. Copyright © 1967 by Arna Bontemps and George Houston Bass. Reprinted by permission of Alfred A. Knopf, Inc. and Harold Ober Associates, Inc.

Additional acknowledgments are incorporated in the Notes section beginning on page 709.